Managing Financial Institutions

An Asset/Liability Approach

THIRD EDITION

Managing Financial Institutions
An Asset/Liability Approach

THIRD EDITION

MONA J. GARDNER
Illinois Wesleyan University

DIXIE L. MILLS
Illinois State University

The Dryden Press
Harcourt Brace College Publishers

Fort Worth   Philadelphia   San Diego   New York   Orlando   Austin   San Antonio
Toronto   Montreal   London   Sydney   Tokyo

Publisher	Elizabeth Widdicombe
Director of Editing, Design, & Production	Diane Southworth
Acquisitions Editor	Rick Hammonds
Developmental Editor	Carla Houx
Project Editor	Doug Smith
Art Director	Beverly Baker
Production Manager	Marilyn Williams
Marketing Manager	Diana Farrell
Copy Editor	Donna Regen
Indexer	Leoni McVey
Compositor	GTS Graphics, Inc.
Text Type	Times Roman
Cover Images	Super Stock, Inc.

Address for Editorial Correspondence
The Dryden Press, 301 Commerce Street, Suite 3700, Fort Worth, TX 76102

Address for Orders
The Dryden Press, 6277 Sea Harbor Drive, Orlando, FL 32887
1-800-782-4479, or 1-800-433-0001 (in Florida)

ISBN: 0-03-098079–8

Library of Congress Catalog Card Number: 93-71151

Printed in the United States of America

7 8 9 0 1 2   039   9 8 7 6 5

The Dryden Press
Harcourt Brace College Publishers

To our students—
past, present, and future.

THE DRYDEN PRESS SERIES IN FINANCE

Amling and Droms
Investment Fundamentals

Berry and Young
*Managing Investments: A Case
    Approach*

Bertisch
Personal Finance

Boyet
*Security Analysis for Investment
    Decisions: Text and Software*

Brigham
Fundamentals of Financial Management
Sixth Edition

Brigham, Aberwald, and Gapenski
Finance with Lotus 1-2-3
Second Edition

Brigham and Gapenski
*Cases in Financial Management:
    Directed, Non-Directed, and by
    Request*

Brigham and Gapenski
*Cases in Financial Management:
    Module A*
Second Edition

Brigham and Gapenski
*Cases in Financial Management:
    Module B*
Second Edition

Brigham and Gapenski
*Cases in Financial Management:
    Module C*
Second Edition

Brigham and Gapenski
*Financial Management: Theory and
    Practice*
Seventh Edition

Brigham and Gapenski
Intermediate Financial Management
Fourth Edition

Chance
An Introduction to Options and Futures
Second Edition

Clauretie and Webb
*The Theory and Practice of Real Estate
    Finance*

Cooley
*Advances in Business Financial
    Management: A Collection of
    Readings*

Cooley
Business Financial Management
Third Edition

Curran
Principles of Corporate Finance

Dickerson, Campsey, and Brigham
Introduction to Financial Management
Fourth Edition

Evans
*International Finance: A Markets
    Approach*

Fama and Miller
The Theory of Finance

Gardner and Mills
*Managing Financial Institutions: An
    Asset/Liability Approach*
Third Edition

Gitman and Joehnk
Personal Financial Planning
Sixth Edition

Greenbaum and Thakor
Contemporary Financial Intermediation

Harrington and Eades
*Case Studies in Financial Decision
    Making*
Third Edition

Hayes and Meerschwam
*Financial Institutions: Contemporary
    Cases in the Financial Services
    Industry*

Johnson
*Issues and Readings in Managerial
    Finance*
Third Edition

Kidwell, Peterson, and Blackwell
*Financial Institutions, Markets, and
    Money*
Fifth Edition

Koch
Bank Management
Second Edition

Kohn
Money, Banking, and Financial Markets
Second Edition

Lee and Finnerty
*Corporate Finance: Theory, Method,
    and Application*

Maisel
Real Estate Finance
Second Edition

Martin, Cox, and MacMinn
*The Theory of Finance: Evidence and
    Applications*

Mayo
Finance: An Introduction
Fourth Edition

Mayo
Investments: An Introduction
Fourth Edition

Pettijohn
PROFIT+

Reilly
*Investment Analysis and Portfolio
    Management*
Fourth Edition

Reilly
Investments
Third Edition

Sears and Trennepohl
Investment Management

Seitz
*Capital Budgeting and Long-Term
    Financial Decisions*

Siegel and Siegel
Futures Markets

Smith and Spudeck
*Interest Rates: Principles and
    Applications*

Stickney
*Financial Statement Analysis: A
    Strategic Perspective*
Second Edition

Turnbull
Option Valuation

Weston and Brigham
Essentials of Managerial Finance
Tenth Edition

Weston and Copeland
Managerial Finance
Ninth Edition

Wood and Wood
Financial Markets

**The Harcourt Brace College Outline
    Series**

Baker
Financial Management

CONTENTS IN BRIEF

CONTENTS

PREFACE

When we began to write the first edition of this book in 1984, it was abundantly clear that following many decades of regulatory policy and management practice influenced by the Great Depression and World War II, the financial system was in the midst of dramatic change. But little did we realize then that the pace of financial and regulatory evolution would continue virtually unabated well into the text's third edition. (Definitely) older and (we hope) somewhat wiser now, we are more willing to predict that recent events we have attempted to incorporate thoroughly and comprehensively into this edition are another important, but by no means definitive, stage in the development of financial institutions management.

As with the second edition, our major task has been to consider the implications of important new financial legislation—in this instance, the Federal Deposit Insurance Corporation Improvement Act of 1991 (FDICIA) and subsequent new rules and regulations. At first believed by many observers to bring about relatively minor changes compared to its predecessor, the Financial Institutions Reform, Recovery, and Enforcement Act of 1989 (FIRREA), FDICIA has quickly proved to affect virtually every aspect of financial institutions management covered in this text. And, as we complete the third edition, many experts predict yet other major legislation on the horizon, destined once again to change the financial landscape. We continue to believe our opening comment in the preface to the first edition, "Perhaps the only task more challenging than managing financial institutions today is writing for students who will manage them tomorrow."

For a book of this length, it would be impossible to list all the changes since the last edition. Among the most important, however, are coverage of:

■ recently revised capital adequacy standards for financial institutions

■ plans for the introduction of risk-adjusted risk deposit insurance
■ new rules for market value accounting
■ developments in the European Community, particularly progress toward implementing the Maastricht Treaty
■ FDICIA provisions and implications
■ international issues affecting financial management
■ the growing influence of new technology

Sections on managed futures, swaptions, and option-adjusted spreads reflect our commitment to incorporate ever more-sophisticated risk-management tools where possible and appropriate.

Some chapters have been specifically structured in response to user needs and suggestions.

■ Chapter 10 stresses the dynamic nature of the futures markets and gives the student a sense of the amazing range of new products that have appeared.
■ Chapter 11, which previously covered interest rate options and stock index futures and options, now also contains introductory material on swaps.
■ The detailed examples of swaps as supplements to GAP management continue in Chapter 19.
■ Chapter 24, on insurance, has been considerably revised, with the very capable help of Professor Julie Cagle of Xavier University. Previous information has been updated and the analytical content of the chapter has been strengthened.
■ Chapter 25 emphasizes the growing importance of pension and mutual funds.

All 27 chapters, including figures and tables, have been carefully updated to incorporate new research and political and economic events, as well as technological and financial innovations.

Throughout, we have maintained the relatively large number of end-of-chapter questions and problems and the level of analytical sophistication required to answer some of them, especially those best approached by using spreadsheet analysis. Finally, we believe both students and instructors will benefit from use of two colors in this edition. In particular, tables and figures should be much easier to interpret.

Still, we have continued to preserve the original focus of the first edition: an asset/liability management theme crossing industry lines. Despite the acknowledged importance of commercial banks, we believe there continues to be a need for a focused text covering more than commercial banking. The early parts of the book provide a theoretical framework that transcends the changes in the institutional environment we now routinely expect. At the same time, we hope to give students a sense of the dynamic nature of financial markets and institutions and of the challenges faced by those who choose a career in institutions management. Also as in other editions, latter portions of the book cover specific management problems in specific types of institutions. The book continues to be written for upper-level undergraduate and master's students, and all readers will benefit considerably from an introductory course in corporate finance. In many cases, introductory material in typical courses on money and banking or money and capital markets is also useful, although not essential.

ORGANIZATION AND USE OF THE BOOK

The book is divided into five parts. The first (Chapters 1–5) explores the domestic and international regulatory and market environment in which asset/liability management is conducted. The second (Chapters 6–11) develops theories of interest rate determination, interest rate risk, and interest rate and exchange rate risk management. The third part (Chapters 12–17) investigates separate issues in the management of assets and liabilities at depository institutions. Part IV (Chapters 18–22) looks at integrated asset/liability management strategies in depositories. Finally, Part V (Chapters 23–27) covers asset/liability management in nondepositories. A more detailed discussion of each part of the book is included at the end of Chapter 1.

POSSIBLE COURSE OUTLINES

Faculty colleagues using both previous editions of the book have found many ways to do so. At most schools, students have completed an introductory course in financial management and an introductory course in money and banking or financial markets. Without the money and banking or markets prerequisite, instructors often place more emphasis on Chapters 1–7. Many instructors also supplement the text material with simulations, cases, readings from the professional and academic literature (many are suggested at the end of each chapter), and exercises using Lotus 1-2-3 or a comparable spreadsheet program.

The book has an additional benefit in its proven flexibility, facilitating the use of a variety of alternative syllabi for instructors. Faculty users on both quarter and semester systems have suggested the following outlines:

1. **Two-quarter sequence for undergraduates:**
First quarter—*Introduction to Financial Markets and Institutions*
Chapters 1–11 Financial markets, interest rates, interest rate risk
Chapters 12, 23–27 Introductory material on financial institutions
Second quarter—*Management of Financial Institutions*
Chapters 13–22 Financial institution management techniques
Selected reference to other chapters
Spreadsheet exercises, cases or simulations

2. **One-quarter course for undergraduates:**
Introductory Course in Institutions
Chapters 1–8 Financial markets, interest rates
Chapters 12–17 Depository institutions: techniques for asset and liability management
Chapters 23–27 Management of nondepositories
Some complex analytical material is omitted.

3. **One-semester courses for undergraduates:**
A. *Management of Financial Institutions:*
Chapters 1–7 Financial markets and interest rates—review (2–3 weeks)
Chapters 8–11 Interest rate risk management—duration, futures and options (2–3 weeks)
Chapters 12–22 Depository institutions management (7–8 weeks)
Chapters 23–27 Selected topics in management of nondepositories and diversified financial services firms (2–3 weeks)
Cases and spreadsheet exercises
B. *Management of Depository Institutions:*
Chapters 1—7 Financial markets and interest rates—review (2–3 weeks)

Chapters 8–11 Interest rate risk management: duration and futures (2–3 weeks)

Chapters 12–22 Depository institution management (10 weeks)

Simulations, cases, and/or spreadsheet exercises

4. **MBA or MS elective course:**
Chapters 1–27 (entire book)
Simulations and/or cases, research assignments
Journal articles (suggested in footnotes and end-of-chapter reference lists)

SPECIAL FEATURES

We believe the book has several features that continue to distinguish it from others currently available. First, the consistent framework of asset/liability management encourages students to integrate material throughout the course, rather than to view topics as fragmented pieces of information. Second, combining the treatment of all depositories in Parts III and IV assists students in understanding the massive changes that have occurred in the financial system in the last decades, while at the same time grasping the differences that remain among the most numerous institutions. We believe this approach has taken on added importance, considering the changes in laws and regulations in the last several years.

The thorough coverage of interest rates and tools for managing interest rate risk in the early part of the book provides a good foundation for appreciating the specific management problems discussed later. For example, many users find it most helpful to be able to cover GAP management supplemented by futures and other hedging tools in Chapter 19 without interrupting the discussion with introductory material. We continue to believe that the text's coverage of GAP management, duration, and other strategies for integrated financial management is comprehensive and clear.

As in the first and second editions, given the dynamic nature of the material, we have put special effort into identifying issues for which significant change is possible in the next several years, such as an overhaul of the regulatory structure, and the potential entry of commercial banks into insurance and securities underwriting on a large scale. Our approach is to outline clearly as many facets of these issues as possible, so that students understand the nature and history of current controversies. When change occurs, instructors should have a relatively smooth time incorporating the specific course of action taken by regulators or by Congress.

Users have told us that their students find the book interesting and well-organized. The opening quotations and vignettes, almost all of which have been completely revised with each edition, often inject a humorous note to catch students' attention. In addition, we have tried throughout to provide useful and interesting examples of the application of many management tools. Students have enjoyed using spreadsheets to solve designated end-of-chapter problems in both of the previous editions. As noted earlier, we have tried to attain a relatively challenging level for many of these problems.

ANCILLARY MATERIALS

The text is accompanied by an Instructor's Manual (IM) with complete answers to end-of-chapter questions and problems. The IM also contains additional references, teaching suggestions, and some tables and figures suitable for transparencies. In many chapters, problems requiring complex or repetitive calculations are designated in the margin as "diskette" problems by this symbol: ◘ . A solution diskette using Lotus 1-2-3 or compatible spreadsheets is available to adopters of the text. Many of these problems have been classroom-tested. The text also contains cases for which solutions are provided in the IM. The test bank has been completely revised with new multiple choice questions, essays, and problems.

ACKNOWLEDGEMENTS

This edition has benefited immeasurably from the comments of both users of the first two editions and reviewers of the revised manuscript. Although we know we have not succeeded in completely satisfying them in this edition, we have considered every suggestion seriously and carefully. We extend special appreciation to the following people:

Sheldon Balbirer, University of North Carolina–Greensboro

Tony Cherin, San Diego State University

Elizabeth Cooperman, University of Baltimore
David Durst, University of Akron
James R. Gale, Michigan Technological University
Sylvia Hudgins, Old Dominion University
Pamela Lowry, Illinois Wesleyan University
Jeff Moore, Texas Christian University
Phillip R. Perry, State University of New York–Buffalo
Todd M. Shank, University of Portland

Users or readers who provided complete or partial reviews of the first two editions and made suggestions that continue to shape the text in important ways include:

Bruce Bagamery, Central Washington University
Elijah Brewer, III, Federal Reserve Bank of Chicago
M. Cary Collins, University of Tennessee
Gary Dokes, San Diego State University
David Ely, San Diego State University
Harvey Faram, Northern Arizona University
Deborah Ford, University of Baltimore
Phil Glasgo, Xavier University
George Hachey, Bentley College
John H. Hand, Auburn University
Jack Hayden, Eastern Montana University
Muhamad Husan, Kent State University
Jerry Johnson, University of South Dakota
Keith Johnson, University of Connecticut
Han Bin Kang, Illinois State University
Dan Kaufman, Wright State University
Gary Koppenhaver, Iowa State University
William Kracaw, Pennsylvania State University
Rick Le Compte, Wichita State University
C. F. Lee, Rutgers University
John Lewis, Stephen F. Austin University
Robert L. Mills, Jr., Western Southern Life Insurance
Theresa Morgan, Illinois State University
Louis Mougoue, Loyola University–New Orleans
Prasad Nanisetty, Indiana University
Joe Newman, Northern Illinois University
James Nielsen, Oregon State University
Carl Nielson, Wichita State University
Nanda Rangan, Southern Illinois University
Alan Reichert, Cleveland State University
John Rozycki, Pennsylvania State University
William Sartoris, Indiana University

William Scott, Illinois State University
Michael Seeborg, Illinois Wesleyan University
Alan Severns, University of Detroit
John Simms, University of North Carolina–Greensboro
Mike Spivey, Clemson University
Roger Stover, Iowa State University
Maurice Tse, Michigan State University
Ronald Watson, Custodial Trust Company
Walter Woerheide, Rochester Institute of Technology
Harold Wolfe, University of Texas–Austin

Students who were particularly helpful in the development of various editions include Bala Balakumar, Rhonda Jenkins, Kristen McGavin Anthony (now of Allstate Insurance Company), Sergio Murer (now of Prudential Mortgage), Diane M. Hustad (now of Del E. Webb Corporation), Thomas Smith (now of Continental Illinois National Bank), Kevin Stoelting (now of United Parcel Service), Michael J. Wright (now of Arthur Andersen and Company), Michelle Woodham and Lisa Wurm. We also appreciate the moral support we have received from Dean Robert Jefferson at Illinois State University and from colleagues at Illinois Wesleyan University.

Finally, we thank the staff at The Dryden Press. We are particularly grateful to Carla Houx, our developmental editor, who took a real interest in the project and its successful completion. Thanks are also due to Doug Smith, project editor; Donna Regen, copy editor; Janet Willen, proofreader; and Leoni McVey, who updated the index. The book continues to benefit from the previous work of Liz Widdicombe, Ann Heath, Betsy Webster, Dan Coran, Karen Vertovec, Karen Shaw, Jeanne Calabrese, Wendy Kemp, Judy Lary, Alan Wendt, and Karen Schenkenfelder, who held various editorial assignments for the first two editions. The inevitable errors, however regrettable, are our own.

Mona J. Gardner
Dixie L. Mills
Bloomington, Illinois

July 1993

PART ONE

THE
ENVIRONMENT
OF
ASSET/LIABILITY
MANAGEMENT

Are banks obsolete?
Title of *Business Week* article (1987)

Commercial banks are not obsolete—
and the federal government should stop trying to make them so.
Bert Ely,
Banking Analyst and Consultant (1992)

———————————

Facing extinction? Or simply evolving? As suggested by the conflict in the opening quotations, observers of financial institutions are wrestling with these questions today. But those who know Fleet Financial Group would surely argue that banks are *not* approaching obsolescence. Fleet, headquartered in Providence, Rhode Island, is a prime example of a contemporary American financial institution. It makes real estate and consumer loans, lends to established firms, provides venture capital to start new companies, offers data-processing services, operates a discount brokerage unit, underwrites municipal bonds, and manages mutual funds. In November 1988, Fleet was added to the S&P 500 Stock Price Index, joining the ranks of major national corporations. In 1991, Fleet again made headlines when it teamed with controversial leveraged-buyout specialist KKR to acquire the failed Bank of New England (BNE) from federal regulators who had taken over BNE earlier that year.

Actually, Fleet was founded in 1791, the year the Bill of Rights was ratified and 5 years before George Washington gave his farewell address as President of the United States. It was called Providence Bank, and as times and the country changed, it became the Industrial National Bank. In 1982, the firm paid a consultant $1 million to recommend a name to match its new image. In January 1988, Fleet merged with Norstar Bancorp of Albany, New York, intending to become a strong competitor on a national level. At the end of 1991, most of its earnings came from financial activities outside traditional banking.

During this process of change, Fleet encountered difficulties its founders could never have anticipated. For example, until the last decade, the merger of a Rhode Island bank and a New York bank would have been prohibited. Ironically, because of the patchwork of new state laws on interstate banking, the merged firm was forced to divest itself of holdings in neighboring Connecticut. Juggling the new product mix has not been smooth either; Fleet's discount brokerage unit was adversely affected by the stock market "crash" of 1987. Fleet also ventured into Latin American lending and later faced almost $30 million in bad debts as a result. Finding the right employees to serve the diverse clientele the firm seeks in the 1990s has not been easy. Commercial real estate losses have been heavy, and the firm has tangled with regulators

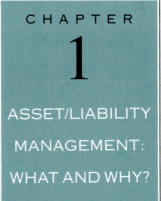

CHAPTER

1

ASSET/LIABILITY

MANAGEMENT:

WHAT AND WHY?

about its financial reporting practices. Still, the firm entered the 1990s as the largest bank in its region, with an optimistic future.[1]

Although not all financial institutions have adopted such aggressive strategies, all have faced similar challenges and opportunities in recent years. Some, like Fleet, have been profitable for the most part; others, like BNE, have faltered or failed. Their success or failure is often traced to how well their managers understand the new financial environment and whether they respond by adapting financial management techniques. This book addresses financial management in financial institutions in the 1990s.

---

[1] Fleet/Norstar Financial Group, *Annual Report,* various years; John W. Milligan, "KKR, Member FDIC," *Institutional Investor,* June 1991, 59–60; Ron Suskind, "Fleet/Norstar, Not Loved By All, Gets the Job Done," *The Wall Street Journal,* March 25, 1992, B4; Geoffrey Smith, "Fleet's Ship Comes In," *Business Week,* November 9, 1992, 104.

CHANGING TIMES FOR FINANCIAL INSTITUTIONS

Many people think of financial institutions as "money specialists," as opposed to specialists in consumer or industrial products such as soap or machinery. Until recently, people paid little attention to the fact that financial institutions have their own financial management problems. Instead, the common belief was that financial institutions exist to solve the financial management problems of others—not a surprising thought because most individuals have relationships with several financial institutions, beginning at an early age. A typical consumer might have a checking account at a local bank; a credit card issued by a bank headquartered in another state; a home mortgage from an area savings and loan association; an automobile loan from the credit union at work; a life insurance policy from an insurer with offices in 50 states; automobile and homeowner's insurance from a different firm; savings for retirement entrusted to a mutual fund; and an account with the regional office of a national brokerage company.

LOOKING BACK FOR A VIEW FROM THE 1930s

So many financial institutions operate today in the United States, and people have grown so accustomed to them, that their existence, functions, and continued operations are often taken for granted. This was not always the case. In the early 1930s, such widespread concern emerged about the safety and soundness of financial institutions that state and federal legislatures enacted laws to assure the public that the businesses to which its funds were entrusted were, in fact, viable.

By law, the activities of most financial institutions were limited so that, for several decades, their financial management was not a terribly complex process. Managers engaged in specific activities that were legally permissible, charging prices whose maximums were legally mandated, and incurring costs that were legally determined. Regulators set prices and costs such that financial institutions were usually profitable and relatively few failed.

A DIFFERENT VIEW FROM THE 1970s AND 1980s

As time passed and memories of the 1930s faded, the perceived need for regulation of financial institutions diminished. Also, as interest rates rose in the 1970s, depositors became dissatisfied with the low rates paid by financial institutions and withdrew their funds in search of higher returns elsewhere. Many financial institutions were unable to respond because the rates they could offer were limited by laws of the 1930s.

Congress and government regulators responded to these developments, and beginning in 1978, many restrictions on financial institutions were loosened or removed. This period of deregulation coincided with, and was encouraged by, rapid developments in technology and innovation in the products that financial institutions offer. Although virtually all financial institutions are still regulated, regulations are less restrictive than in previous decades.

During deregulation, the U.S. economy experienced significant changes, such as population migration to the South and West and a decline in the fortunes of basic manufacturing, agricultural, and energy-related industries. These fundamental changes resulted in the movement of money from one region to another and from some industries to others. Because financial institutions are "money specialists," they were definitely affected. As a result of these combined forces, the complexity of managing a financial institution increased dramatically.

A VIEW INTO THE 1990s

By 1990, it was clear that changes in the economic and financial system would continue and that further adaptations in the regulatory environment were necessary as a result. The globalization of financial markets, reflected in unprecedented competition from Japanese and European financial institutions, forced Congress and U.S. regulators to recognize the need for international policy coordination. Management excess and abuse, as illustrated by the thrift crisis, left no doubt that customers and taxpayers must be protected from unacceptable risks by new approaches to regulation and supervision. Widespread access to computers and increasingly sophisticated information technology caused some experts to pose questions similar to the quotations at the beginning of this chapter: Are banks or other types of financial institutions facing extinction? Do customers still need traditional intermediaries to obtain the financial services they desire? If financial intermediaries continue to exist, are some institutions special—that is, do they serve a unique economic role and thus require unique regulatory treatment? Financial institutions' managers must address these complex issues during this decade.

CHANGE ISN'T EASY

Evidence suggests that the public may not be altogether comfortable with or accustomed to the new financial environment.[2] Few industries in financial difficulty reap the media attention accorded financial institutions, and indeed, few businesses seem as fragile. The reaction of the public, President Bush, the press, regulators, and Congress to the savings and loan crisis of 1989 provides a striking example of this fragility. Headlines such as "The Thrift Crisis: Now It's Bigger Than Texas," "Callers Want S&L Cheats Punished," and "Federal Rescue Efforts for Failed Thrifts Are a Crisis in Themselves" were common for many months.[3] In the 1980s, in part inspired by liberalized federal regulations, savings and loan regulators in several states (including California and Florida) enacted even more permissive policies for state-chartered institutions. Some owners and managers engaged in high-risk and even fraudulent energy- and real estate-related lending, funding those loans with insured deposits. Disastrous results followed the collapse of oil prices, and in 1989, federal deposit insurers faced obligations far exceeding their resources. The solution devised by the President, Congress, and regulators required a significant bailout of the deposit insurance system with

taxpayers' money. With effects extending into the 1990s, the bailout, followed by a wave of commercial bank failures, prompted headlines such as "How Deep Is the Hole?"[4]

The impact of this crisis was felt in other financial institutions throughout the United States and even extended to the foreign exchange markets. This series of events, and similar ones—such as the collapse of a private deposit insurance system in Rhode Island in 1991 and the failure of many of the largest banks in Texas and New England—further emphasizes the importance of financial management in financial institutions as a topic of study. It is appropriate to begin that study with some basic definitions.

FINANCIAL VERSUS REAL ASSETS

Assets include a broad range of both tangible and intangible things that provide their owners with expected future benefits. An individual's education, good health, and favorable reputation provide future benefits, as do a home, an automobile, and a savings account. A business expects future benefits in the form of cash from the sale of its products and services, as well as from owning a recognizable trademark or slogan (Just Do It—Nike) or having a patent on a production process.

Because so many things are assets, it is convenient to divide them into two major subsets: **real** and **financial assets.** Real assets are those expected to provide benefits based on their fundamental qualities. A person's home provides benefits commensurate with the quality of its construction, its location, and its size. A corporation's main computer provides benefits based on its speed, the size of its memory, the ease of its use, and the frequency with which it needs repair.

In contrast, financial assets are those expected to provide benefits based solely on another party's performance—that is, they are claims against others for

---

[2] Lucinda Harper and Ellen E. Schultz, "Public Is Edgy About Banks and Insurers," *The Wall Street Journal,* September 27, 1991, C1, C13.

[3] Frederic A. Miller, Teresa Carson, and Catherine Yang, "The Thrift Crisis: Now It's Bigger Than Texas," *Business Week,* May 2, 1988, 112–113; Paulette Thomas and Paul Duke, Jr., "Federal Rescue Efforts for Failed Thrifts Are a Crisis in Themselves," *The Wall Street Journal,* January 13, 1989, A1, A10; and Denise Kalette, "Callers Want S&L Cheats Punished," *USA Today,* February 15, 1989, 1.

[4] See Brumbaugh 1988; Bush and Morrall 1989. (References are listed in full at the end of this chapter.) Dean Foust et al. "How Deep Is the Hole?" *Business Week,* December 9, 1991, 30–32; Lawrence Ingrassia, "Banking Crisis in Rhode Island Nears Its Close," *The Wall Street Journal,* June 29, 1992, A2.

future benefits. A bank savings account will provide future benefits only if the bank continues to operate and to pay interest on the account; the account holder depends on the bank's performance for any benefits from the financial asset. It follows from this concept of financial assets that one party's financial asset is another party's **financial liability**—that is, the latter has an obligation (often a legal one) to provide future benefits to the owner of the financial asset.

FINANCIAL INSTITUTIONS VERSUS NONFINANCIAL FIRMS

Most business firms—steel makers, automobile manufacturers, restaurants, and department stores—exist to acquire and use real assets in a way that makes the value of future benefits received greater than the cost of obtaining them. Cash to acquire assets may come from lenders or creditors, who have a legal expectation of repayment from the firm's use of real assets. Cash may also come from those who take an ownership (or equity) interest in the firm, hoping for (but with no legal promise of) a share in the excess of asset benefits over costs. Regardless of the sources of its funds, however, the firm has issued obligations that become the financial assets of others. Funds generated by issuing financial obligations are then used to acquire real assets.

Like other businesses, financial institutions exist to acquire and use assets so that the value of their benefits exceeds their costs. The key difference between financial institutions and other firms is that most of the assets financial institutions hold are financial assets. Financial institutions use funds from their own creditors and owners to acquire financial claims against others. They may lend funds to individuals, businesses, and governments, or they may purchase ownership shares in other businesses. The future benefits that financial institutions expect to receive thus depend on the performance of the parties whose financial liabilities they purchase. The main distinction between financial institutions and other firms is not so much in how they raise funds, because all businesses issue financial liabilities to do so, but in what they do with these funds.

FINANCIAL INSTITUTIONS: WHAT ARE THEY?

Although all financial institutions share operating characteristics and economic functions, they vary in the products they offer and the financial assets in which they specialize. The chapters to follow explore those similarities and differences in detail. First, however, it is useful to consider Table 1.1, which introduces the specific institutions that are the focus of this textbook.

DEPOSITORY INSTITUTIONS

Depository institutions control the largest proportion of assets. This category includes commercial banks, savings banks, savings and loan associations, and credit unions; they are grouped together because of their traditional emphasis on deposits, their primary financial liabilities.

At year-end 1991, **commercial banks** held financial assets in excess of $3,000 billion (over $3 trillion). They have long served the corporate community as a main source of short- and intermediate-term loans and for years, by regulatory restriction, were the only depositories allowed to offer checking accounts payable on demand. The Fleet Financial Group's activities indicate that such a description is hardly adequate in the current era. Banks are expanding their services and markets rapidly, and many offer a diversified set of products. They also have recently encountered considerable competition in their traditional areas of specialization, as is apparent from the decline in banks' share of total institutional assets. Within the banking industry, increasingly aggressive competition has arisen between domestic and foreign institutions.

Depositories broadly classified as **thrift institutions** include **savings and loan associations (S&Ls)** and **savings banks** because of their traditional reliance on savings deposits as sources of funds, although they are now able to offer checkable deposits. Table 1.1 indicates that thrifts' share of total financial assets peaked in the 1970s and then declined after 1980. S&Ls, the largest of the thrifts by total asset size, have expanded beyond their traditional role as suppliers of mortgage loans since economic changes and Congressional action gave them the power to do so. This expansion has met with mixed success, as is discussed

TABLE 1.1	**Percentage Distribution of Financial Assets of Financial Institutions**

An increasingly competitive financial environment is evident. The percentage of total financial assets held by commercial banks and life insurers has declined significantly over the past four decades. The total share held by thrift institutions (S&Ls and savings banks) peaked in the mid-1970s, then fell sharply. Private pension funds have enjoyed considerable growth, and investment companies' and finance companies' shares of financial assets has increased markedly since 1980.

	Year								
Institution	**1950**	**1955**	**1960**	**1965**	**1970**	**1975**	**1980**	**1985**	**1990**
Commercial banks	56.88%	49.80%	41.88%	38.21%	40.38%	41.39%	38.57%	35.26%	33.11%
Savings and loan associations	5.69	8.91	11.62	14.24	13.51	15.56	16.19	15.67	10.86
Savings banks	7.54	7.40	6.60	6.61	6.19	5.66	4.46	3.21	2.61
Credit unions	0.34	0.64	1.02	1.23	1.40	1.72	1.80	1.99	2.15
Finance companies	3.13	4.33	4.49	5.00	5.00	4.63	5.27	5.75	7.73
Life insurers	21.55	21.37	19.44	17.24	15.67	13.07	12.08	11.79	13.54
Property/liability insurers	NA	NA	4.89	4.08	3.89	3.61	4.54	4.27	5.08
Private pension funds	2.39	4.33	6.19	8.32	8.74	10.51	12.22	12.45	11.52
Investment companies	1.11	1.84	2.76	3.93	3.96	2.84	3.68	7.29	10.80
Securities firms	1.36	1.39	1.09	1.16	1.27	1.00	1.19	2.31	2.60
Total percent	100.00	100.00	100.00	100.00	100.00	100.00	100.00	100.00	100.00
Total assets (billions)	$296.94	$423.10	$615.10	$894.64	$1,281.73	$2,140.30	$3,842.20	$6,752.60	$10,095.80

NA = Not Available

Sources: U.S. League of Savings and Loans, *Savings and Loan Fact Book,* 1979, 1980. Board of Governors of the Federal Reserve System, *Flow of Funds, 1964–1987; Financial Assets and Liabilities,* First Quarter, 1992.

in later chapters. Savings banks resemble S&Ls, but they have a more diversified asset base than S&Ls. Analysts observe that alliances have emerged among small commercial banks and institutions traditionally classified as thrifts. These developments may eventually result in a new category of depositories emphasizing **community banking** and the disappearance of the thrift category.

Credit unions (CUs) are distinguished by the fact that their services are available only to members, who must share some "common bond" representing the basis for forming the union. Another important difference between CUs and other financial institutions is that they are not-for-profit organizations and therefore exempt from taxation. Thus, their managerial objectives and resulting strategies may have a focus somewhat different from those of other depositories. CUs' tax-exempt status is controversial among their competitors.

FINANCE COMPANIES

Similar to depositories in the financial assets they hold are **finance companies,** which specialize in loans to businesses and consumers. Their financial liabilities are quite different from those of depositories, however, because they acquire most of their funds by selling commercial paper and bonds or by borrowing from their rivals, commercial banks.

CONTRACTUAL INTERMEDIARIES

A third category of institutions consists of **insurance companies** (both life insurers and property/liability insurers) and **pension funds,** which are considered **contractual savings institutions** because of the formal agreements with policyholders or pensioners who entrust their funds to these firms. The insurance industry has sold risk protection to the public for hundreds of years. Life insurers, because their commitments to customers are long term, have traditionally held an asset portfolio structure quite different from the property/liability insurers, who offer shorter-term policies such as automobile and home coverage.

Pension funds generally are designed to collect funds from employers and sometimes employees and to repay those funds, along with investment returns, after employees have retired or become disabled. The most widely known retirement fund is the Social Security program, but there are many other public and private funds. Table 1.1 includes only the assets of private pension funds.

INVESTMENT COMPANIES

Investment companies provide a means through which small savers can pool funds to invest in a variety of financial instruments. The resulting economies of scale offer investors the benefits of professional portfolio management, reduced transactions costs, and the lower risk exposure of a large diversified portfolio. The best known and largest type of investment company is the **mutual fund.** In the early 1980s, **money market mutual funds** dominated the industry. The easy access to funds, along with the market rate of return they offer to investors, allowed them to achieve an enviable rate of growth. By the 1990s, stock and bond funds had increased in popularity, despite rather pronounced swings in the financial markets during that period. The lowest short-term interest rates in 50 years caused investors to flee money market funds in pursuit of higher returns.

SECURITIES FIRMS

Securities firms assist customers with purchasing and selling stocks, bonds, and other financial assets. The industry is often subdivided according to two major activities, investment banking and brokerage. **Investment bankers** assist in the creation and issuance of new securities, and **brokers** assist in the transfer of ownership of previously issued securities. Both **full-service brokers** and **discount brokers** exist. Full-service brokers advise clients in addition to arranging securities purchases and sales; discount brokers execute trades but give no advice. Many securities firms engage in both investment banking and brokerage.

BALANCE SHEETS REVEAL INDUSTRY DIFFERENCES

Differences in financial industries are reflected in their asset and liability structures. Although comparisons are made in greater detail in later chapters, Figure 1.1 identifies major distinctions among three types of firms—commercial banks, life insurance companies, and mutual funds.

The assets of the three industries as of year-end 1991 are shown in the upper panel. Well over half the assets of commercial banks are loans to individuals and businesses. Of the three institutions, banks alone hold a significant quantity of cash. Insurance companies also make loans, but half their assets are invested in corporate securities, which banks are not permitted to hold to as large an extent. The mutual fund industry had more than one-third of its assets invested in short-term securities, with the remainder in bonds and stocks.

Differences are also evident in the liability structures of the three institutions, shown in the lower panel of Figure 1.1. Deposits constitute a large majority of the funds of commercial banks. In contrast, obligations to policyholders are the major liabilities of life insurers. Mutual funds are quite different, because they have virtually no debt obligations and derive all their funds from shareholders' investment. The shareholders of banks and insurers, however, provide only a small proportion of funds.

FINANCIAL INSTITUTIONS AND THE TRANSFER OF FUNDS

The term **primary securities** refers to direct financial claims against individuals, governments, and nonfinancial firms. **Secondary securities** are the financial liabilities of financial institutions—that is, the claims against them. For example, in Figure 1.1 on page 10, the asset holdings of banks, insurers, and mutual funds are primary securities—direct claims by these institutions against other parties. The institutions' liabilities—deposits, policyholder obligations, and mutual fund shares—are secondary securities or claims against financial institutions.[5]

FIGURE 1.1   **Assets and Liabilities of Selected Financial Institutions**

Commercial banks' asset portfolios are dominated by loans, and their liabilities by deposits. In contrast, life insurers invest heavily in government and corporate securities, whereas their major liabilities are obligations to policyholders. Mutual funds also invest in corporate and government securities, but the major claims against them are from their own shareholders.

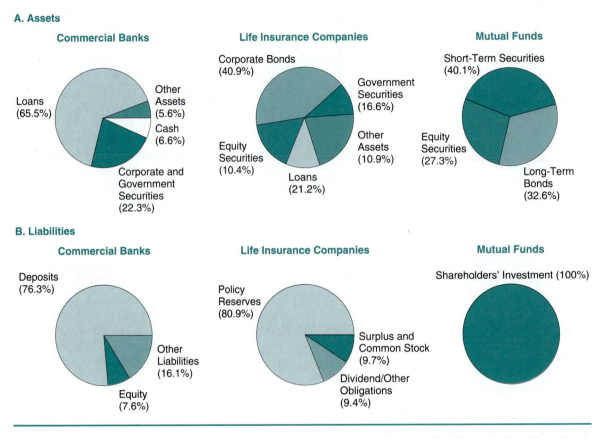

A. Assets

Commercial Banks **Life Insurance Companies** **Mutual Funds**

Loans (65.5%) Other Assets (5.6%) Cash (6.6%) Corporate and Government Securities (22.3%)

Corporate Bonds (40.9%) Government Securities (16.6%) Other Assets (10.9%) Loans (21.2%) Equity Securities (10.4%)

Short-Term Securities (40.1%) Equity Securities (27.3%) Long-Term Bonds (32.6%)

B. Liabilities

Commercial Banks **Life Insurance Companies** **Mutual Funds**

Deposits (76.3%) Other Liabilities (16.1%) Equity (7.6%)

Policy Reserves (80.9%) Surplus and Common Stock (9.7%) Dividend/Other Obligations (9.4%)

Shareholders' Investment (100%)

Source: Prepared by the authors with data from Board of Governors of the Federal Reserve System, *Federal Reserve Bulletin; Flow of Funds, First Quarter 1992;* Investment Company Institute, *1992 Mutual Fund Fact Book.*

Figure 1.2 illustrates the general difference between financial and nonfinancial firms and the origin of primary and secondary securities. Investors buy financial assets, either primary or secondary securities, because they have cash not needed for the immediate purchase of consumption goods or real assets. Rather than storing excess cash in a piggy bank, most investors wish to earn interest by purchasing a financial

---

[5]Unfortunately, like most fields, finance sometimes uses confusing terminology. Readers should be careful not to confuse the use of the words "primary" and "secondary" in this discussion with their use in other contexts. For example, students who have previously studied corporate finance or investments may have encountered the terms *primary* and *secondary markets;* primary markets are defined as those for the original issuance of securities, and secondary markets are for securities resale. In the context of this chapter, "primary" and "secondary" are used to distinguish between *issuers* of securities and not to differentiate between changes in securities ownership.

FIGURE 1.2	**Intermediation and Direct Investment**

Direct investment occurs when lenders supply funds to the ultimate demanders, with the assistance of brokers or investment bankers. Indirect investment is the supply of funds to financial institutions, which issue secondary securities in return. Intermediation occurs when institutions transform secondary securities into primary securities through their own direct investment.

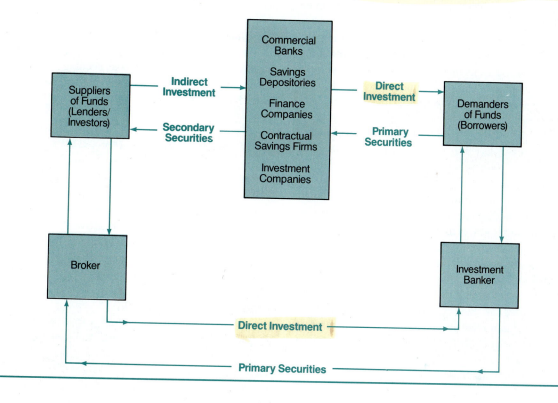

asset.[6] For every financial asset, there is an offsetting financial liability issued by a party who needs more cash and who is willing to pay interest to obtain it. Financial assets and liabilities are the means through which excess funds are transferred in the economic system at rates of return (or costs) anticipated in advance by the lender (or borrower).

As time passes, the actual rate of return a lender earns may differ from initial expectations. In other words, owning financial assets involves risk, where

risk is defined as potential variation in expected returns to the investor. If investors anticipate that the returns on an investment will vary, they will not lend unless the *expected* return is high enough to compensate for the risk.

DIRECT VERSUS INDIRECT INVESTMENT

Funds transfers can occur directly between parties, as when an individual lends to a friend or purchases stock in a large nonfinancial corporation. In these cases, the lender/investor has a claim on the friend or on the corporation; that is, the investor is engaged in **direct investment.** Direct investment results in the creation of a primary security.

[6]In practice, returns on financial assets take other forms besides interest payments, such as dividend payments and the appreciation or decline in the price of the asset. In this context, "interest" is used generically to refer to rewards investors expect for deferring consumption.

The transfer of funds from one party to another can also occur with the assistance of a financial institution, taking one of two forms. One form occurs when an investor with excess funds purchases a secondary security, such as a life insurance policy or a savings account, allowing the financial institution to determine the ultimate recipient of the funds. For instance, a life insurer may invest the premium payments of its policyholders in corporate bonds, or a CU may invest the savings of some of its members in home-improvement loans to other members. The policyholder or the saver is engaged in **indirect investment;** his or her claim is on the financial institution, while the institution holds a direct claim on the corporation or the homeowner. The institution has thus transformed a secondary security into a primary security. This transformation is called **intermediation.**

Not all funds transfers involving financial institutions occur through intermediation. Sometimes an institution arranges or assists in the transfer of funds between parties, without issuing its own financial liabilities in the process. When a financial institution acts in this more limited capacity, it is acting as a broker. This role is illustrated in the lower portion of Figure 1.2. As noted earlier, securities brokers and investment bankers seldom issue secondary securities themselves but rather assist in the transfer of funds from suppliers to demanders. Many financial institutions act as both intermediaries and brokers from time to time.

WHY INTERMEDIARIES? REDUCED TRANSACTIONS AND INFORMATION COSTS

In creating indirect investment possibilities through intermediation, or in acting as brokers, financial institutions provide important benefits that are unavailable with direct investment. Most of these benefits can be categorized as reductions in the costs of transactions, information, or both.[7] Because the return expected from a financial asset is reduced by the costs of acquiring the asset, a demand for an institution's services will

exist if the costs are less than those incurred through direct investment. Conversely, institutions issuing financial liabilities want to minimize their noninterest transactions costs. Most costs reduced by intermediation or brokerage fall into five categories.

SEARCH COSTS

Financial institutions provide ways to identify those with excess funds and those needing funds, making it unnecessary for individual lenders and borrowers to find one another.

PORTFOLIO SELECTION COSTS

Lenders may wish to invest in financial assets in different dollar amounts, with different maturities, or with a different risk level from the financial liabilities borrowers wish to issue. Financial institutions issue secondary securities in forms attractive to lenders, and then repackage the funds they obtain in forms attractive to borrowers.

MONITORING COSTS

When two parties agree to a transfer of funds, whether through direct or indirect investment, the arrangement is usually formalized by a **financial contract.** Typical contracts specify the terms of a funds transfer—for example, its maturity and the interest rate at which it will occur—and outline provisions to protect both borrower and lender, such as the lender's recourse in case the borrower absconds with the funds.

Finance theorists have noted that financial contracts are often characterized by **asymmetric information;** that is, the contracting parties are not equally and fully informed about each other. In particular, borrowers often know more about their own financial situations and their abilities to honor contracts than do lenders. Information asymmetry in turn gives rise to **monitoring costs**—expenses incurred by lenders to gather information on an ongoing basis, allowing intervention if a borrower's financial condition changes.

Financial institutions provide economies of scale in monitoring by employing appraisers, financial analysts, and other specialists to investigate a large number of claims on a full-time basis. For this reason, many lenders' monitoring costs will be lower if they

---

[7] Parts of the following discussion are based on the analyses of Benston and Smith 1976; Diamond 1984; Berlin 1987; Williamson 1987; Haubrich 1989; Gorton and Pennacchi 1990; O'Hara 1990; and Seward 1990.

invest through financial intermediaries instead of purchasing primary securities. In recent years, some experts have concluded that the reduction of monitoring costs is the most important reason for the existence of financial intermediaries.

RISK MANAGEMENT COSTS

Many investors want a variety of financial assets to reduce the risk of holding a single claim against a party who may fail to meet its obligations. The investor can avoid that risk by holding secondary securities because the financial institution holds a diversified portfolio. Although the investor must still monitor the financial institution, its diversified portfolio reduces the probability that the institution will fail because all its investments fail simultaneously. Also, some secondary securities, such as those issued by depositories, offer low risk exposure because they are insured against the institution's failure.

LIQUIDITY COSTS

If lenders holding primary securities unexpectedly need cash, they may find it difficult or impossible to obtain without incurring substantial expense. The borrower may have used the funds for a purpose that cannot easily be liquidated on short notice. By investing in secondary securities, investors obtain financial assets, such as demand deposits, that they can convert to cash almost instantaneously at little more than the cost of writing a check.

ASSET/LIABILITY MANAGEMENT: WHAT IS IT?

Organizing and running a business whose primary function is reducing the transactions and information costs of others is itself a costly endeavor. By far the largest expenses to institutions are the interest costs resulting from their liabilities. There are also noninterest costs of intermediation and brokerage, such as the need to pay managers and other personnel and to maintain places of business. Like other firms, institutions can operate only if they can perform their functions as profitably as or more profitably than their competitors.

Given the variety of financial institutions shown in Table 1.1, the competition faced by a single institution is often substantial. Success therefore requires careful attention to the financial implications of intermediation and brokerage.

MANAGING THE SPREAD

Because financial institutions interact in the financial markets by issuing financial liabilities and purchasing financial assets, one critical element of the financial management of financial institutions is managing the **spread,** the dollar difference between the interest earned on assets and the interest cost of liabilities. This spread, expressed as a percentage of total assets, is called the **net interest margin (NIM):**[8]

$$\text{NIM} = \frac{\text{Interest on Assets} - \text{Interest Cost of Liabilities}}{\text{Total Assets}} \qquad [1.1]$$

If the NIM is high enough, the institution may use it to offset the noninterest costs of the intermediation and brokerage services it provides. Most institutions charge fees for these services, but unless the fees are competitive, investors may find it more economical to switch to another institution or to engage in direct investment. When the spread is negative for an extended period of time and interest costs actually exceed interest earned on assets, few institutions can make up the difference with other sources of income, and many have failed as a result.

ASSET/LIABILITY MANAGEMENT DEFINED

Added to the importance of managing the size of the NIM is the problem of managing its riskiness. Both aspects of the NIM must be considered to achieve successful financial performance. **Asset/liability management** is the management of the net interest margin

---

[8] Some sources, including banking industry publications, use earning assets in the denominator of the NIM equation. Earning assets are total assets minus those, such as buildings and equipment, on which no explicit return is generated. It is common for definitions of financial ratios to vary among users.

to ensure that its level and riskiness are compatible with the risk/return objectives of the institution.[9]

Asset/liability management is more than just managing individual asset and liability categories well. It is an integrated approach to financial management, requiring simultaneous decisions about the types and amounts of financial assets and liabilities the institution holds, or the asset/liability mix and volume. In addition, asset/liability management requires an understanding of a broad range of financial markets in which institutions operate. Among the most significant financial market issues are how interest rates are determined, why they change over time, and what impact those changes have on the NIM and the value of an institution's assets and liabilities.

ASSET/LIABILITY MANAGEMENT: WHO SETS OBJECTIVES?

Because asset/liability management involves managing the NIM in accordance with the institution's objectives, managers cannot carry it out unless they clearly understand what those objectives are and who sets them. For financial institutions, identification of objectives is somewhat more complex than for other businesses. To understand this complexity, it is helpful to have a brief outline of theories on the setting of managerial objectives. These theories have arisen from the study of financial management of nonfinancial firms.

A NORMATIVE APPROACH

In nonfinancial firms operating in competitive product markets, it is often argued that the firm's owners should set managerial objectives. Owners, unlike creditors, provide the initial funds to operate the business and therefore are entitled to any benefits resulting from superior operations.

Under this **classical theory,** managers are directed to ignore their personal risk/return preferences in making the firm's investment decisions. Instead, they should concentrate on maximizing expected benefits to owners, consistent with the risk owners are willing to bear. Managers who allow nonowner-determined objectives to influence their decisions will presumably be removed by unhappy owners. Also, financing decisions, such as whether to borrow or not, are regarded as much less important than decisions involving investment in real assets.

The classical theory of the firm focuses on how managers *should* act, and thus it is considered a **normative theory** of decision making.[10] Under this approach, the criterion for managerial decision making is clear: If a decision provides net benefits to owners, it should be made; otherwise, it should not. The classical theory leaves no doubt that the institution's owners are the ones to set objectives for asset/liability management.

A POSITIVE APPROACH

Positive theories of managerial behavior focus on explaining how decisions *are* made by business managers rather than on prescribing how they *should* be made. When owners and managers are the same people, the way managers should behave with respect to owners will be the same as the way they do behave. But if owners and managers are different, it is possible that managers' risk/return preferences will differ from those of owners. Under these circumstances, what do managers do? Positive theories of managerial objectives attempt to explain the behavior of managers arising from the separation of ownership and control.

Agency theory, a positive view of managerial decision making, suggests that managers are no different from other individuals and, if left unmonitored, will pursue their personal risk/return preferences. Thus, owners may incur costs in making sure that *their* preferences are recognized. Agency theory examines the relationships between nonowner-managers

---

[9] Some authors have defined asset/liability management as the attempt to *stabilize* net interest margin with no expected variation—that is, as the attempt to minimize risk. See O'Brian, Sollenberger, and Olson, 1982.

As Deshmukh, Greenbaum, and Kanatas (1983) noted, however, such an objective is appropriate only for institutions choosing to perform brokerage, rather than intermediation, functions. The intermediation function, by definition, implies that the institution assumes some risk.

---

[10] The classical theory of managerial objectives is developed in Fisher 1930. Extensions of Fisher's work are provided in Hirschleifer 1958 and in Hirschleifer 1965.

(agents) and owners (principals) and the contracts arising as a result. (These agent/principal agreements are yet another form of financial contracting from which associated monitoring costs arise.) At one extreme, an agent/principal contract could be structured so that every action of the agent would be prescribed and closely monitored, leaving the manager no discretion. Such a contract would be very costly for the principal to enforce. At the other extreme, the owner could take a "hands off" approach, leaving all matters to the manager's judgment. Although monitoring costs would be nil under such a contract, the potential losses to owners could be considerable if managers pursued their own interests exclusively. Normally, therefore, terms of agent/principal contracts will fall between the extremes. Any reductions in benefits to owners stemming from contracts governing the separation of ownership and control are known as **agency costs.**[11]

In practice, agency costs can take many different forms, such as the legal expenses of drawing up contracts to limit managers' salaries and expense accounts or the resources managers spend on annual reports convincing owners that owners' wishes are being considered, both examples of explicit monitoring costs. Agency costs arising from managers' unmonitored actions—such as potential benefits lost when a manager lends to a friend's business at a rate lower than might be strictly justified by the risk of the loan—may be more difficult to measure. A special type of agency cost that may be incurred when managers are not closely monitored is **managerial expense preference,** the tendency for some managers to enhance the benefits they receive from the institution by hiring larger staffs than necessary, furnishing offices lavishly, or enjoying large travel and expense accounts.[12] All types of agency costs reduce owners' welfare and would not be incurred if owners and managers were the same people.

Many experts argue that the agency relationship is so important today that a discussion of managerial objectives is realistic only if it includes agent/principal

contracts. Thus, attention must be focused on ways to minimize agency costs. Under this positive theory, the criterion managers use in decision making is whether they receive net benefits from an action. If they do, they will undertake the action; otherwise, they will not. Owners must therefore structure contracts with costs that are lower than the costs of letting managers operate unchecked. Agency theory implies that managers set asset/liability objectives and that owners protect their interest by setting appropriate constraints.

MANAGERIAL OBJECTIVES IN FINANCIAL INSTITUTIONS

Although the classical theory has been applied to managerial decision making in financial institutions, one can argue that it is inadequate on both theoretical and empirical grounds.[13]

CUSTOMER NEEDS AFFECT OBJECTIVES. Because financial institutions provide liquidity to customers when issuing secondary securities such as demand deposits, the problems of financial institutions differ from those of nonfinancial firms, which need not honor financial liabilities on demand. Therefore, the need to provide customers with the benefits of intermediation must be considered in establishing managerial objectives for financial institutions. In addition, asset and liability decisions must be made simultaneously in financial institutions, even though joint consideration of investment and financing decisions is not necessary according to the classical theory of nonfinancial firms.[14]

OWNERSHIP STRUCTURE AFFECTS OBJECTIVES. The ownership structure of many financial institutions is also different from that of nonfinancial firms. Instead of being owned by stockholders (persons who have risked funds to start a business and who are entitled to residual profits if the firm operates exceptionally well), many financial institutions are mutually owned. The **mutual form of organization** is particularly prevalent among insurance companies, savings banks, and S&Ls.

---

[11] Formal development of agency theory is attributed to Jensen and Meckling 1976. Jensen and Meckling, however, were not the first to recognize that the classical theory of firm behavior may not be adequate when owners and managers are different.

[12] The theory of managerial expense preference was developed by Williamson 1963.

---

[13] An example is Towey 1974.

[14] See Sealey 1983.

The implications of mutual ownership are explored in detail in Chapter 4, but for now it is enough to recognize that so-called owners of mutual institutions are not owners in the classical sense, because they are not entitled to personal claims on the institution's residual profits. Therefore, the classical theory—based on the idea that those who risk funds are entitled to establish the objectives of the enterprise—may not be directly relevant.

SOME EVIDENCE FROM RESEARCH. In stockholder-owned institutions, empirical evidence suggests that unmonitored managers *do*—whether or not they *should*—act to maximize their own rather than owners' welfare.[15] Thus, agency costs arise. Researchers have noted, however, that there may be built-in "brakes" on managements' behavior in stockholder-owned firms that help to reduce these costs. These limitations arise both from the monitoring actions that current stockholders themselves may take and from the discipline imposed on managers by external financial market participants. For example, contracts may specify that managers will be compensated in part through stock options, thus ensuring that their interests and those of current owners will be at least partially compatible. Further, stockholders, through the voting control they exercise, can oust managers they believe are too self-interested. Finally, for stockholder-owned firms, there is a **market for corporate control:** Outsiders who believe that an institution is not well served by current management may bid for the firm's stock and hire new managers to control the assets.[16]

In mutual firms, however, experts have noted that some of these mechanisms to reduce agency costs do not exist. For example, there is no market for corporate control of a mutual firm, nor can managers' compensation contracts be structured to include stock options. Thus, some researchers have argued that managers' tendencies to pursue their own goals are even stronger in mutually owned rather than stockholder-owned firms. Recent empirical evidence on this question is mixed.[17]

REGULATION AFFECTS OBJECTIVES. Furthermore, even if owners and managers of financial institutions were the same persons, agency relationships would still exist for these owner/managers. They would arise from another agent/principal relationship: the one that exists between financial institutions and governments. This agency relationship is quite strong for some financial firms, such as commercial banks, which for many years have been expected to assist in carrying out the federal government's fiscal and monetary policies.[18]

The agency relationship with government exists for virtually all financial institutions, because most are involved in carrying out public policies such as the distribution of credit to disadvantaged borrowers. And because governments provide insurance for many financial institutions, they regularly employ monitor-examiners to ensure that managerial decisions do not unduly strain government insurance funds. In some instances, government agencies may actually remove managers from their positions if they are performing their roles improperly.[19] Although the S&L crisis of the 1980s revealed the inadequacy of the financial contracts that existed between regulators and some thrift managers, there is little doubt that the agent/principal relationship between regulators and managers will continue to exist. For example, some observers in the early 1990s argued that bank managers were too sensitive to the views of regulators when they denied some loan applications that might have been approved in earlier periods. Critics accused banks of creating a credit crunch, worsening the effects of a weakened economy. It is unlikely, therefore, that the managers of any financial institution will, or can, pursue asset/lia-

[15] See Edwards 1977; Hannan and Mavinga 1980.

[16] See Mester 1989. Empirical research on large banks and thrifts suggests that the higher management's total compensation, the better their firm's performance, and that managers' risk-taking behavior is positively related to the value of their holdings of the firm's stock. See Cole and Mehran 1991; Mullins 1991; and Allen and Cebenoyan 1991.

[17] See Mester 1993; Cebenoyan, et al. 1993; Akella and Greenbaum 1988; and Verbrugge and Jahera 1981. Early research is reviewed in Woerheide 1984.

[18] For a discussion of the origin of the agency relationship between governments and commercial banks, see Shull 1984.

[19] For example, the Federal Deposit Insurance Corporation exercised this power in its handling of the near-failure of Continental Illinois National Bank in 1984.

bility management solely for the benefit of the institution's owners.

A BALANCING ACT

How, then, are asset/liability management objectives set? The perspective used in this book is one suggested in a model recognizing that owners, regulators, and managers themselves all influence managerial behavior. The model was developed specifically for banking firms, but its insight holds for other financial institutions. As the author expresses it:[20]

The banking firm is a complex organization. As a financial intermediary, it performs both a brokerage and a risk transformation function. As a business, it must yield a return to its owners. As a regulated enterprise, it must operate within the bounds specified by the supervisory agencies.

In most institutions, an individual manager or a management team is responsible for balancing the risk/return preferences of all parties. Most managers may personally wish to maximize the NIM because their salaries and expense accounts depend on funds remaining after interest obligations are paid. However, they also recognize that institutions must provide liquidity to customers, a requirement that may prohibit a risky plan to maximize the spread. Owners whose risk/return preferences differ from those of managers may further restrict managers' actions by imposing constraints such as salary or expense limitations or by structuring incentive plans, such as stock options, that reward managers for minimizing noninterest costs.

Finally, public policy conveyed by government regulation also influences managers, and the ultimate NIM targets differ from those in the absence of an institution/government relationship. Thus, from a manager's point of view, the objective of asset/liability management is to maximize the NIM, subject to the constraints imposed by owners, regulators, and the intermediation function. These constraints result in the pursuit of a NIM target and a risk level that differ from the specific preferences of any single individual or group but that consider all parties.

SUMMARY

Financial institutions are a unique set of business firms whose assets and liabilities, regulatory restrictions, and economic functions establish them as an important subject of study. The vast quantity of assets controlled by institutions, the changes introduced by deregulation in the 1970s and 1980s, and the challenges posed by globalization of financial markets and information technology have sparked a growing interest in asset/liability management techniques.

Firms classified as financial institutions hold portfolios primarily composed of financial assets, in contrast to the real asset holdings of nonfinancial firms. Institutions are designed to offer intermediary or brokerage services to assist savers in the allocation of their funds. The services provided by financial institutions reduce transactions and information costs, including search, portfolio selection, monitoring, risk management, and liquidity costs to investors.

As in any other business, a key to successful management of a financial institution is earning a return on assets that exceeds the cost to the firm of acquiring those assets, including their financing costs. Because financial assets dominate the balance sheets of financial institutions, the difference between returns and costs can be measured by the NIM, the focus of asset/liability management. Targets for the size of the NIM also involve consideration of its riskiness, or potential variability. The chapters to follow examine management of the NIM to ensure that its level and riskiness are compatible with the institution's risk/return objectives. This is the operational definition of asset/liability management throughout the text.

Asset/liability objectives set by institutions must be responsive to the risk/return preferences of four important audiences: owners, regulators, customers, and managers themselves. In recent years, agency theory has provided useful insights into the costs associated with management of complex organizations such as intermediaries and the financial contracts arising as a result. Proper management of a financial institution

---

[20] See O'Hara 1983. Crouhy and Galai 1991 also examined this issue.

means making simultaneous decisions about asset choices and sources of funds while balancing the frequently disparate needs and preferences of those four groups.

PLAN OF THE BOOK

Part One of the book encompasses Chapters 1 through 5. The four chapters following this one examine the environment of asset/liability management. Chapter 2 profiles the regulatory environment, Chapter 3 highlights the Federal Reserve System and global regulatory concerns, and Chapter 4 provides more details on how the ownership structure of financial institutions affects asset/liability management. Chapter 5 introduces specific assets and liabilities important to virtually all institutions and illustrates how to calculate effective rates of return on these instruments.

Part Two is concerned with interest rates—how they are determined in the markets, how they affect the risks to which an institution is exposed, and how to manage those risks. Chapters 6 and 7 explain the main theories of the general level and term structure of interest rates and examine ways these theories are incorporated into asset/liability management. Chapter 8 introduces the concept and measurement of "interest rate risk." Chapters 9 through 11 develop the theory and application of several major tools for managing interest rate risk, including duration, financial futures, options, and swaps. Each plays a part in the overall asset/liability management of financial institutions.

The third part of the book is about the management of assets and liabilities in depository institutions. Chapter 12 introduces, compares, and contrasts different depository institutions. Chapter 13 is concerned with liquidity and securities portfolio management in depositories, and Chapters 14 and 15 are about these institutions' lending decisions. Liability management and capital management policies are the subjects of Chapters 16 and 17.

Part Four begins with Chapters 18 and 19, integrating materials from the preceding chapters into overall asset/liability management strategies for depositories. Chapters 20 and 21 discuss the role of noninterest income and noninterest expense in asset/liability management and cover such topics as capital investment decisions and the management of fee-based services. Finally, Chapter 22 provides techniques for evaluating the effectiveness of asset/liability management in depositories.

Part Five discusses asset/liability management in nondepository institutions, beginning with Chapter 23 on finance companies. Insurance companies are the subject of Chapter 24, whereas Chapters 25 and 26 discuss financial management in pension funds, investment companies, and securities firms. The book ends with Chapter 27 on diversified financial services companies.

QUESTIONS

1. Trace the changes in the financial and regulatory environment that have made financial institution management more challenging in the 1990s than it was before 1980.

2. Find one or more articles on the failure of BCCI (the Bank of Commerce and Credit International) in 1991. How did this incident highlight the increased globalization of financial markets and the importance of international policy coordination?

3. Find a newspaper or magazine article on a bank or savings institution that has failed in your state in the past five years. To what was the failure attributed (for example, economic conditions, poor management, or fraud)? Do you think different state or federal regulations could have prevented the failure? Why or why not?

4. How do real assets and financial assets differ? How does asset composition in most business firms differ from that in financial institutions?

5. Use your personal checking or savings account as an example to explain the relationship between financial assets and financial liabilities.

6. What financial and operating characteristics have traditionally distinguished banks and S&Ls? Provide two examples of the ways recent regulatory or economic changes have made them more similar. Do you think small banks have more in common with thrifts than they do with large banks? Why or why not?

7. Relying on your knowledge of financial management concepts, explain how the tax-exempt status of credit unions might affect their asset/liability management.

8. Why are insurance companies and pension funds called contractual savings institutions? Given the differences between the obligations of life insurers and pension funds and those of property/liability insurers, what types of investments would you expect each to hold?

9. What is the distinction between primary and secondary securities? If you want to own primary securities, what types of financial institutions should you contact? Contrast the concept of primary and secondary markets with that of primary and secondary securities.

10. How do services provided by securities firms differ from those offered by investment companies? Compare and contrast direct and indirect investment, and explain which industry is more closely associated with each type of investment.

11. Define risk. Why does owning financial assets involve risk?

12. Financial agreements typically require financial contracts characterized by information asymmetry. What is information asymmetry? How might an agreement such as an automobile or mortgage loan involve asymmetric information? How does asymmetric information affect the risk position of the investor (lender)?

13. Suppose you have a choice between buying corporate bonds or investing $10,000 in a mutual fund. Explain how choosing the mutual fund would affect your liquidity and portfolio selection costs.

14. Suppose you inherit $75,000. If you choose not to invest through a financial intermediary, how will your monitoring and risk management costs be affected? Provide an example of each type of cost.

15. How might the same institution act sometimes as a broker and other times as an intermediary? What is the difference between the two functions?

16. What is the net interest margin? The spread? What is the role of the NIM in asset/liability management?

17. What is the classical theory of firm behavior? Is it a normative or positive theory? How does the separation of ownership and management complicate this theory of the firm?

18. Explain the role of monitoring costs in the agent/principal view of the firm. Give an example of a monitoring cost that might exist in a large commercial bank. What is the trade-off between monitoring costs incurred by owners and the degree of discretion allowed to managers?

19. Give an example of an agency cost owners incur as a result of not monitoring managers closely. What is managerial expense preference behavior? How does this form of behavior affect agency costs?

20. Explain how the stockholder form of ownership may allow owners, even in a large firm, to exert control over managerial behavior without incurring high agency costs. Are any similar controls available for mutual firms? Why or why not?

21. In addition to owners, what important groups influence the asset/liability management objectives pursued by financial institutions? Give an example of a situation in which the objectives of regulators and those of owners might conflict. How do managers set asset/liability objectives?

22. Find an article on a financial institution that is doing well financially and one on an institution that is doing poorly or has failed. What seem to be the causes of the differences in performance?

SELECTED REFERENCES

Akella, Srinivas R., and Stuart I. Greenbaum. "Savings and Loan Ownership Structure and Expense-Preference." *Journal of Banking and Finance* 12 (September 1988): 419–437.

Allen, Linda, and A. Sinan Cebenoyan. "Bank Acquisitions and Ownership Structure: Theory and Evidence." *Journal of Banking and Finance* 15 (1991): 425–448.

Benston, George J., and Clifford W. Smith, Jr. "A Transactions Cost Approach to the Theory of Financial Intermediation." *Journal of Finance* 31 (May 1976): 215–231.

Berlin, Mitchell. "Bank Loans and Marketable Securities: How Do Financial Contracts Control Borrowing Firms?" *Business Review* (Federal Reserve Bank of Philadelphia) (July/August 1987): 9–18.

Brumbaugh, R. Dan, Jr. *Thrifts Under Siege.* Cambridge, MA: Ballinger Publishing Company, 1988.

Bush, Vanessa, and Katherine Morrall. "The Law: The Business Reviews a New Script." *Savings Institutions* 110 (October 1989): 30–35.

Cebenoyan, A. Sinan, Elizabeth S. Cooperman, Charles A. Register, and Sylvia C. Hudgins. "The Relative Efficiency of Stock versus Mutual S&Ls: A Stochastic Cost Frontier Approach." *Journal of Financial Services Research* 7, forthcoming 1993.

Cole, Rebel A., and Hamid Mehran. "Executive Compensation and Corporate Performance: Evidence from Thrift Institutions." *Proceedings of a Conference on Bank Structure and Competition.* Chicago: Federal Reserve Bank of Chicago, 1991: 227–247.

Crouhy, Michel, and Dan Galai. "A Contingent Claim Analysis of a Regulated Depository Institution." *Journal of Banking and Finance* 15 (1991): 73–90.

Deshmukh, Sudhakar D., Stuart I. Greenbaum, and George Kanatas. "Interest Rate Uncertainty and the Financial Intermediary's Choice of Exposure." *Journal of Finance* 38 (March 1983): 141–147.

Diamond, Douglas W. "Financial Intermediation and Delegated Monitoring." *Review of Economic Studies* 51 (July 1984): 393–414.

Edwards, Franklin R. "Managerial Objectives in Regulated Industries: Expense-Preference Behavior in Banking." *Journal of Political Economy* 85 (February 1977): 147–162.

Fama, Eugene F. "What's Different About Banks?" *Journal of Monetary Economics* 15 (1985): 29–39.

Fisher, Irving. *The Theory of Interest.* New York: Macmillan, 1930.

Gorton, Gary, and George Pennacchi. "Financial Intermediaries and Liquidity Creation." *Journal of Finance* 45 (March 1990): 49–71.

Hannan, Timothy H., and Ferdinand Mavinga. "Expense Preference and Managerial Control: The Case of the Banking Firm." *The Bell Journal of Economics* 11 (Autumn 1980): 671–682.

Haubrich, Joseph G. "Financial Intermediation: Delegated Monitoring and Long-Term Relationships." *Journal of Banking and Finance* 13 (March 1989): 9–20.

Hirschleifer, Jack. "On the Theory of Optimal Investment Decision." *Journal of Political Economy* 67 (August 1958): 329–352.

———. "Investment Decision Under Uncertainty: Choice Theoretic Approaches." *Quarterly Journal of Economics* 79 (November 1965): 509–536.

Jensen, Michael C., and William H. Meckling. "Theory of the Firm: Managerial Behavior, Agency Costs, and Ownership Structure." *Journal of Financial Economics* 3 (1976): 305–360.

Mester, Loretta J. "Owners versus Managers: Who Controls the Bank?" *Business Review* (Federal Reserve Bank of Philadelphia) (May/June 1989): 13–22.

———. "Efficiency in the Savings and Loan Industry." *Journal of Banking and Finance* 17 (April 1993).

Mullins, Helena M. "The Management Reward Structure and Risk-Taking Behavior of U.S. Commercial Banks."

Proceedings of a Conference on Bank Structure and Competition. Chicago: Federal Reserve Bank of Chicago, 1991: 248–272.

O'Brian, J. A., Harold M. Sollenberger, and Ronald Olson. *Asset/Liability Management: A Model for Credit Unions.* Richmond, VA: Robert F. Dame, 1982.

O'Hara, Maureen. "Financial Contracts and International Lending." *Journal of Banking and Finance* 14 (1990): 11–31.

———. "A Dynamic Theory of the Banking Firm." *Journal of Finance* 38 (March 1983): 127–140.

Santomero, Anthony M. "Modeling the Banking Firm: A Survey." *Journal of Money, Credit, and Banking* 16 (November 1984, Part 2): 526–616.

Sealey, C. W. "Valuation, Capital Structure, and Shareholder Unanimity for Depository Financial Intermediaries." *Journal of Finance* 38 (June 1983): 857–871.

Seward, James K. "Corporate Financial Policy and the Theory of Financial Intermediation." *Journal of Finance* 45 (June 1990): 351–377.

Shull, Bernard. "The Separation of Banking and Commerce: An Historical Perspective." *Proceedings of a Conference on Bank Structure and Competition.* Chicago: Federal Reserve Bank of Chicago, 1984: 63–78.

Towey, Richard E. "Money Creation and the Theory of the Banking Firm." *Journal of Finance* 29 (March 1974): 57–72.

Verbrugge, James A., and John S. Jahera, Jr. "Expense-Preference Behavior in the Savings and Loan Industry." *Journal of Money, Credit, and Banking* 13 (November 1981): 465–476.

Williamson, Oliver. "Managerial Discretion and Business Behavior." *American Economic Review* 53 (December 1963): 1032–1067.

Williamson, Stephen D. "Recent Developments in Modeling Financial Intermediation." *Quarterly Review* (Federal Reserve Bank of Minneapolis) 11 (Summer 1987): 19–29.

Woerheide, Walter J. *The Savings and Loan Industry: Current Problems and Possible Solutions.* Westport, CT: Quorum Books, 1984.

In Russia they are trying to move away from this kind of regulation,
and instead we're going toward it.
John G. Medlin, Jr.,
CEO, Wachovia Corporation (1992)

————————————————

Financial institutions, whose operations are traditionally regulated
very closely by federal and state agencies, know they may face stiff
penalties if they fail to follow the rules established by legislators and
regulators. In the early 1990s, however, a federal savings bank turned
the tables on its overseer when it sued the U.S. government for breach
of contract and won its case in U.S. Claims Court. The thrift, Glendale
Federal, asserted that Congress, in major legislation passed in 1989, had
violated agreements made earlier with Glendale.

The controversy can be traced to the early 1980s, when many
thrifts were encountering severe financial difficulties. At that time, federal regulators offered favorable treatment to healthy savings institutions
willing to acquire other, troubled depositories; the acquisitions saved the
deposit insurance fund the cost of closing down the failing thrifts. Glendale, after acquiring a failing savings institution in Florida in 1981,
entered into one of these special agreements. But in 1989, Congress disallowed those provisions, placing many thrifts in jeopardy. Glendale
sued, and the federal court agreed with its arguments that the U.S. government had breached a contract. The court decision added a new
dimension to the very complex relationships that exist between financial
institutions and their regulators.[1]

Financial institutions in general, and depository institutions in particular, are among the most closely regulated firms in the United States.
Over the years, limitations have been imposed on the way they raise
funds, on the costs that can be incurred in doing so, on asset choices,
on product and geographical diversification, and more. Although the initial justification for these regulations was to protect the safety and
soundness of the economic system, subsequent modifications are not

C H A P T E R

2

REGULATION,

TECHNOLOGY,

AND FINANCIAL

INNOVATION

————————————————

[1] Glendale's legal victory did not translate automatically into a financial victory. However, as
this book went to press, Glendale's closure by regulators was delayed after the sale of new
stock brought its capital closer to minimum requirements. If closed, Glendale would become
the biggest of the many thrift institution failures since the mid-1980s. See Sam Zuckerman,
"Glenfed Shows Private Capital Is Alternative to Intervention," *American Banker,* August 23,
1993, 1, 5; "Claims Court Rules for Thrift Firms," *BNA's Banking Report,* August 3, 1992,
183; Paulette Thomas, "Judge Rules Against U.S. Government on S&L Rule Change Involving Glenfed," *The Wall Street Journal,* July 27, 1992, A3; Amy Barrett, "Glenfed Hangs on
to a Lifeline," *Business Week,* October 19, 1992, 99.

necessarily aimed at that goal. In fact, regulations and motivations for them reflect an evolutionary process that responds to innovations in the financial markets and to new asset/liability management techniques.

The suit by Glendale Federal exemplifies the debate over how much regulation is required, whose interests are served by regulations, and whether the rules should be changed. The pages that follow explore the traditional regulatory structure and recent developments. A discussion such as this is never complete, because more changes are always on the horizon, many as this book was written. The possibility of continued change means that managers can never take a given set of rules and regulations for granted and that developing strategies in a fluid environment can be frustrating. To conduct successful asset/liability management, financial managers must understand not only existing regulations but also the regulatory process.

THE REGULATORY DIALECTIC: A CONCEPTUAL FRAMEWORK FOR REGULATION, INNOVATION, AND REFORM

A simple list of regulations and regulatory agencies governing financial institutions in the United States cannot capture the impact of restrictions on managerial decisions. The relationship between regulators and regulated institutions is complex, and it is best described as interactive. Only through an exploration of the interaction can historical developments and potential changes be viewed in proper perspective.

The word **dialectic** refers to change occurring through a process of action and reaction by opposing forces. In his classic presentation, the philosopher Hegel described the dialectic process as: 1) an initial set of arguments or rules (the **thesis**); 2) a conflicting set of arguments or responses (the **antithesis**); and 3) a change or modification (the **synthesis**) resulting from an exchange or interaction between the opposing forces. The idea that regulation of financial institutions is a dialectic—one of cyclical interaction between opposing political and economic forces—was introduced by Professor Edward Kane in the late 1970s.[2] Kane's **regulatory dialectic** has since been widely adopted as an insightful characterization of regulatory developments.

THE THESIS: FINANCIAL INSTITUTION REGULATIONS

Relationships between financial institutions and government regulators precede even the National Currency and Banking Acts of 1863 and 1864, but the Federal Reserve Act of 1913 set the stage for comprehensive regulation of the banking system. Table 2.1 provides a chronological summary of major federal legislation affecting financial institutions.

Legislators and government agencies usually provide a justification for regulations when they are introduced, but experts believe that unannounced motivations often influence the regulators' decisions. Although financial institution regulations have eventually served other purposes, from the 1930s to 1980 their stated intent was to maintain stability in the nation's financial system.

THE 1930s: SAFETY AND SOUNDNESS. The core of modern financial regulation was drafted in the aftermath of the financial crisis of the 1930s. Laws and regulations centered on prohibiting excessive competition among financial institutions, which legislators viewed as a source of unacceptable risk.

The **Banking Act of 1933,** widely known as the **Glass-Steagall Act (G-S),** is the cornerstone of restrictions applied to the commercial banking industry. Created by this act were ceilings on deposit interest rates, thereafter known by Federal Reserve **Regulation Q (Reg Q),** which enforced them. G-S also attempted to separate the commercial banking and securities industries, and it reinforced geographic restrictions on bank branching outlined in the **McFadden-Pepper Act of 1927.**

Additional regulation focused on thrift institutions in the **Federal Home Loan Bank Act of 1932** and the **National Housing Act of 1934.** Attention turned to credit unions in the **National Credit Union Act of 1934.** Later, geographic and product restrictions on commercial banks were extended further by the **Bank Holding Company (BHC) Act of 1956** and by its **1970 Amendments. Bank holding companies** (discussed in Chapter 4) are corporations that hold voting control over one or more commercial banks. Through these laws, the operations of depository institutions, and particularly commercial banks, were separated from other sectors of the financial markets.

Regulations restricting nondepository institutions were already in place in the 1930s, and additional ones were added then and in the decades to follow. Of particular importance were the **Securities Act of 1933** and the **Securities Exchange Act of 1934,** placing federal restrictions on brokers and investment bankers. These laws were followed by the **Investment Company Act of 1940,** bringing the practices of investment companies under federal control. For other firms, such as insurers and finance companies, regulations were and still are concentrated at the state level. Table 2.1 includes these and other acts mentioned later in the chapter; together, they are the thesis of the dialectic.

---

[2]The concept of the regulatory dialectic was introduced in Kane 1977 and further developed in Kane 1981, Kane 1986, and Kane 1989a. (References are listed in full at the end of this chapter.)

TABLE 2.1   Major Financial Legislation before 1980

Many of the most influential laws affecting financial institutions before 1980 were passed in the aftermath of the Great Depression. These laws and others that followed emphasized protecting customers and preserving stability in the financial system. These laws are the thesis of the regulatory dialectic before 1980.

Date	Law	Key Provisions
1863	National Currency Act	Established Office of the Comptroller of the Currency; authorized national bank notes; limited asset choices of banks issuing national bank notes; established a system of reserve requirements
1864	National Banking Act	Authorized the granting of federal bank charters; origin of dual banking system attributed to this and the 1863 law
1913	Federal Reserve Act	Established system of Federal Reserve Banks to serve as a lender of last resort to commercial banks, promote an elastic money supply, provide a nationwide payments system and closer supervision of banks
1919	Edge Act	Permitted banks to establish subsidiaries outside their home territory for the purpose of conducting international banking
1927	McFadden-Pepper Act	Permitted national banks to branch if state banks in the same state could; left interstate branching decisions to the states
1932	Federal Home Loan Bank Act	Established Federal Home Loan Bank System to serve as a lender of last resort to S&Ls
1933	Banking Act of 1933 (Glass-Steagall Act)	Prohibited the payment of interest on demand deposits; mandated ceilings on deposit interest rates; separated Federal Reserve System member banks from the securities industry; established the Federal Deposit Insurance Corporation; further restricted asset choices of national banks
1933	Home Owners' Loan Act	Authorized the granting of federal charters for S&Ls, under the supervision of the Federal Home Loan Bank Board
1933	Securities Act of 1933	Required registration of new securities and disclosure of truthful financial information on issuers
1934	Securities Exchange Act	Established the Securities and Exchange Commission
1934	National Housing Act	Established the Federal Savings and Loan Insurance Corporation
1934	National Credit Union Act	Established a federal credit union regulator that later became the National Credit Union Administration; authorized the granting of federal charters for credit unions
1935	Banking Act of 1935	Strengthened the power and autonomy of the Federal Reserve Board; gave Comptroller more discretion in the granting of national bank charters

THE 1960s AND BEYOND: OTHER INTENTIONS? In the years after the Great Depression, the economic environment changed but regulations did not. For many financial institutions, limitations remained on starting new firms, entering distant markets, and developing new products, to name a few. Kane argues that eventually the implicit thrust of regulations was to limit competition—*not* for safety reasons but to benefit selected market participants, such as small or weak institutions, that would suffer in a more competitive environment. Recently, Kane suggested another more controversial intention: that regulators and legislators may delay revelations of serious and costly problems in the institutions they regulate. Kane argues that by attempting to hide defects in existing regulations, they are reducing the possibility of being embarrassed or even removed from office.

THE ANTITHESIS: REGULATORY AVOIDANCE

The relationship between regulators and the regulated has been described as a cat-and-mouse game. According to Kane, the existence of operating rules that benefit a protected class provides a strong incentive for other regulated institutions to find loopholes.

TABLE 2.1 *CONTINUED*

Date	Law	Key Provisions
1940	Investment Company Act	Required disclosure of financial statements and investment objectives by investment companies; specified shareholder rights
1940	Investment Advisers Act	Required individuals or firms selling investment advice to register with the Securities and Exchange Commission
1945	McCarran-Ferguson Act	Established the right of the federal government to regulate insurance companies if states fail to do so adequately; exempted insurers from certain antitrust laws
1956	Bank Holding Company Act and Douglas Amendment to the Act	Gave the Federal Reserve System control over the formation, expansion, and supervision of multibank holding companies; identified factors to be used in evaluating bank holding company acquisitions; prohibited multibank holding companies from acquiring out-of-state banks
1966	Interest Rate Adjustment Act	Extended Regulation Q ceilings to thrifts
1968	Consumer Credit Protection Act (Truth-in-Lending)	Required disclosure of lending terms to consumers
1970	Amendments to Bank Holding Company Act	Extended Federal Reserve authority over one-bank holding companies; limited holding company acquisitions to businesses "closely related" to banking
1970	Amendments to Federal Credit Union Act	Established National Credit Union Share Insurance Fund
1970	Securities Investor Protection Act	Established the Securities Investor Protection Corporation to promote investor confidence in the securities industry
1974	Equal Credit Opportunity Act	Prohibited discrimination in the granting of credit
1974	Employee Retirement Income Security Act	Imposed fiduciary responsibility on pension fund managers; provided for vesting of benefits and full funding of pension funds; established the Pension Benefit Guaranty Corporation
1975	Securities Acts Amendments	Mandated the development of a national securities market
1977	Community Reinvestment Act	Required depository institutions to consider the needs of all economic groups in their communities when granting credit
1978	International Banking Act	Imposed insurance premiums and branching restrictions on foreign banks operating in the United States

The desire to compete may eventually make regulatory avoidance an end unto itself to which institutions devote energy and resources rather than simply a means to more competitive freedom. One of management's goals becomes circumvention of restrictions in an effort to capture a portion of a market otherwise denied. Regulators look unfavorably on this "avoidance" behavior, and if institutions are too successful in circumventing the rules, regulations will be revised. The revisions inspire further avoidance efforts, and the cycle begins anew.

FINANCIAL INNOVATION. Regulatory avoidance is often more than just psychological warfare between the regulated and the regulator. Regulated firms incur costs—called **regulatory taxes** by economists—as a result of operating restrictions that prevent them from conducting business in a profit-maximizing fashion.

Managers' logical desire to reduce these taxes creates fertile ground for the birth of **financial innovations**— new financial products and processes that improve the economic efficiency with which financial transactions are conducted, either by serving customers' needs in new unregulated ways or by lowering costs.

The process of financial innovation has been studied extensively in recent years.[3] Many of the financial products and asset/liability management tools discussed in later chapters (such as negotiable certificates of deposit, zero-coupon securities, and financial futures) were financial innovations at the time they were introduced and have now become a permanent

---

[3] Thought-provoking discussions of financial innovation are found in Flood 1992; Finnerty 1988; Miller 1986; Van Horne 1985; and Silber 1983. The Miller article is the source for the definition of a "successful, significant" innovation.

part of the landscape, even after some or all of the motivations leading to their origin have disappeared. Experts term these products and techniques "successful, significant" innovations; both institutions and customers have found uses for them that were unintended at the time of their introduction. Other innovations arise in a climate of regulatory avoidance and wither after only a short period; they have temporary and limited economic significance. Whether successful or not, financial innovations add to the challenges both regulators and managers face.

THE ANTITHESIS ILLUSTRATED. Good examples of the cat-and-mouse game and financial innovation are institutions' activities to avoid restrictions on sources of and interest rates paid on deposits. In the 1960s, large commercial banks developed new kinds of deposits and tapped foreign markets to avoid Reg Q ceilings on domestic deposit interest rates. As regulators observed the success of institutions at raising funds through these unconventional methods, they changed regulations to again limit institutions' ability to compete. Large banks responded to each regulatory adjustment by introducing a substitute sufficiently different to avoid the new rules. In playing this game, regulator and regulated alike expended considerable resources, but several successful financial innovations that arose from these efforts, such as Eurodollar deposits and negotiable certificates of deposit (CDs), are widely used today.[4]

A less economically efficient example of regulatory avoidance is found in the decisions by banks and thrifts to offer noninterest incentives to attract deposits. By the late 1970s, many depositories were offering small appliances, dishes, luggage, or other rewards to customers who deposited funds. Because Reg Q prevented institutions from offering competitive rates, they offered customers tangible assets. This strategy diminished after the **Depository Institutions Deregulation and Monetary Control Act (DIDMCA) of 1980** ended deposit interest rate ceilings. That law, discussed in more detail later, freed institutions to offer customers a competitive interest rate on deposits.

FURTHER CATALYSTS FOR FINANCIAL INNOVATION: TECHNOLOGY AND ECONOMIC CONDITIONS

Additional incentives drive the antithesis of the regulatory dialectic. As institutions search for financial innovations that do not violate existing regulations, changes in technology and the economy enhance opportunities for institutions to innovate and cause customers to demand new products. For example, along with the efforts of regulated institutions, catalysts for change included the "computer revolution" and increased volatility in inflation and interest rates.[5]

Table 2.2 identifies several major "successful, significant" innovations in recent years, all of which are discussed in detail at appropriate points later in this book. The table places these innovations in context with key technological developments and important contemporary economic/political events. Scholars studying the process of financial innovation believe it is no coincidence that a wave of innovation has occurred in the past two decades. Financial economist and Nobel Laureate Merton Miller argues that before the mid- to late 1960s, the country was preoccupied with more pressing concerns: global warfare and economic depression threatened the nation's survival and naturally dominated the thoughts of managers and regulators alike. But as the nation recovered from these traumas, regulatory taxes imposed during an earlier era began to seem more important. The new period of relative prosperity and security coincided with the rise to prominence of tools that are now standard in the financial markets—video screens, calculators, and computers. Thus, the antithesis is driven by economic and technological changes as well as by the attitudes of regulators and the regulated.

TECHNOLOGICAL INNOVATIONS AND THE ANTITHESIS BEFORE 1980. Computer technology has affected many aspects of business systems and personal habits. During the 1970s, the ability to analyze large quantities of information quickly and efficiently and to transmit it rapidly raised the expectations of customers

---

[4] Summary discussions of the economic costs of avoidance behavior are available in "The Depository Institutions . . . Act" 1980; and Gilbert 1986.

[5] The role of technology in the regulatory dialectic was initially identified by Kane; more elaborate discussion has appeared in subsequent studies. See Broaddus 1985; Van Horne 1985; and Finnerty 1988.

TABLE 2.2	**Timing and Context of Selected Financial Innovations**

Regulatory avoidance is often manifest in financial innovations devised by the regulated. In turn, financial innovations are encouraged by technological and economic change, as seen from the increase in the number of financial innovations in the past 20 years.

Decade	Financial Innovation	Technological Innovation	Economic/Political Environment
1920s			Stock market crash
1930s			Bank holiday
			Great Depression
			World War II begins

Major Laws and Policies Forming the Thesis of the Dialectic Are Instituted.

Decade	Financial Innovation	Technological Innovation	Economic/Political Environment
1940s			World War II ends
			Interest rates controlled by Federal Reserve System
1950s		Television	Federal Reserve System/Treasury "Accord": Controls lifted
			Cold War
			Korean War
1960s	Eurodollar deposits	Mainframe computer	Vietnam War escalates
	Bank credit cards		
	Federal funds market		
	Negotiable CDs		
1970s	Financial futures	Hand-held financial calculator	Gold standard abandoned: Exchange rates float
	Automated teller machines		Vietnam War ends
	Money market mutual funds		Oil embargo
	Adjustable rate mortgages		Double-digit inflation
	Negotiable order of withdrawal (NOW) accounts		Change in Federal Reserve System's open-market policies
	Discount brokerage accounts		
	Options		
	Junk bonds		
1980s	Interest rate swaps	Microcomputer	Double-digit inflation ends
	Zero-coupon bonds	Fax machine	Stock market crash
	24-hour securities trading		Collapse of commercial real estate market
	"Program" trading		
	Universal/variable life insurance		
	Off–balance sheet guarantees		
	Securitization		
1990s	Global futures trading		Corporate "downsizing"
			Low interest rates
			Free-trade agreements proposed

at financial institutions. Demand grew rapidly for customer services such as cash management and electronic banking.

Not all financial institutions were able to respond to these demands quickly. Depository institutions, in particular, were slowed by legal limitations. For example, the installation of electronic banking equipment at grocery stores and shopping centers was initially challenged on grounds that such facilities were the equivalent of branch banks. In states with limited-branching laws, electronic banking was delayed. Similarly, Reg Q interfered with introduction of cash management services by depository institutions, while securities firms were free to pioneer the development of these programs.

ECONOMIC CHANGE AND THE ANTITHESIS BEFORE 1980. Economic change also contributed to changing customer demands. During the late 1970s and early 1980s, high inflation and record-setting interest rates stimulated demand by businesses and individuals for investments offering protection against increased risk. Even financially unsophisticated customers resisted deposit accounts paying below-market interest rates. Savers were willing to forgo the safety of insured deposits in search of higher and more flexible returns.

As with technological innovations, some financial institutions faced more severe restrictions than others in their efforts to respond to investors' desires for savings alternatives. Strategies available to depository institutions were especially limited. Depositors whose savings were too small to invest directly in higher-return but low-risk securities, such as Treasury bills, could not be served by depositories. In contrast, money market mutual funds could offer liquid accounts with flexible rates of return. Critics of existing regulations argued that it was unfair to impose below-market interest rate ceilings on deposit accounts heavily used by small savers. These developments were part of the antithesis leading to regulatory adjustments in 1978 and thereafter.

THE SYNTHESIS: REGULATORY ADJUSTMENTS

Regulation of financial institutions is dynamic. Forces for change arise in part from the objectives of managers and owners of regulated institutions, but change is also market-driven. After a period of delay and analysis, regulations are adjusted. As long as any regulatory restrictions remain—and it is certain that they will—the dialectic continues. Synthesis in the regulatory dialectic is only a temporary equilibrium, because legal revisions immediately provoke new avoidance behavior. One cycle's synthesis is the next cycle's thesis.

Since 1978, regulatory changes have been introduced rapidly. Between 1978 and 1980, the actions of depository regulators were tentative, consisting of incremental changes in deposit regulations. By the end of 1982, however, Congress had lightened or eliminated many of the restrictions mentioned earlier. Those changes, in turn, affect the competitive position of other financial institutions, as depositories expand product lines and market areas. Five laws culminating this period of regulatory synthesis are the **DIDMCA,** the **Garn-St Germain Depository Institutions Act of 1982 (G-St G),** the **Competitive Equality Banking Act of 1987 (CEBA),** the **Financial Institutions Reform, Recovery, and Enforcement Act of 1989 (FIRREA),** and the **Federal Deposit Insurance Corporation Improvement Act of 1991 (FDICIA).** They and remaining regulations from a prior era are now the new thesis.

Before these laws can be appreciated, however, it is necessary to review the regulatory structure under which financial institutions have traditionally operated. The following discussion provides an overview of decision areas addressed by financial institution regulators. More detailed treatment of specific regulations is reserved for subsequent chapters.

DEPOSITORY INSTITUTIONS

Regulations for depository institutions affect almost every aspect of operations. The complexity of the regulatory process extends beyond the quantity of regulations. Not only are the rules numerous, so are the regulators.

WHO ARE THE REGULATORS?

The federal regulatory structure is so complex that one institution may be answerable to four or five different agencies.

COMMERCIAL BANKING. Banks may obtain an operating charter at the federal or state level. Those in the first group are **national banks,** and those in the latter are **state banks.** Many regulations for national banks are made and enforced by the **Comptroller of the Currency.**

The Comptroller was created in the **National Currency Act of 1863,** and additional powers were given to the office in the **National Banking Act of 1864.** Together, these laws established standards a bank had to meet before receiving a national charter. They also promoted the development of a uniform currency by authorizing national bank notes that could be issued only by banks with federal charters. Although public confidence in the notes encouraged many state-chartered banks to switch to federal charters, other state banks remained viable by popularizing demand deposit accounts and encouraging customers to accept checks as an alternative to currency for the payment of bills. The current **dual banking system,** in which both states and the federal government issue bank charters, is traced to this period.

The **Federal Reserve System (the Fed)** supervises federally chartered institutions, which must be members of the Fed, and state-chartered banks choosing Fed membership voluntarily. The Fed was created by the **Federal Reserve Act of 1913** to ensure the existence of both a flexible payments system and a lender of last resort for troubled banks. The Fed's role in setting monetary policy and providing leadership in the international financial markets is so important that it is the subject of the next chapter.

State-chartered banks also must comply with the regulations of banking authorities in the state. All banks are eligible to purchase deposit insurance from the **Bank Insurance Fund (BIF)** of the **Federal Deposit Insurance Corporation (FDIC);** the FDIC was created in the Glass-Steagall Act. Fed member banks must be insured by the FDIC. If a bank purchases insurance, it must comply with rules set by the FDIC.

Because the three major federal banking regulators—the Comptroller, the Fed, and the FDIC—arose at different times to serve different purposes, they are independent of one another. They are not always legally required to coordinate their actions, and conflicts and even competition exist among them, adding an additional dimension to the regulatory dialectic.

THRIFTS. Like commercial banks, thrifts may have either state or federal charters. FIRREA mandated a major restructuring of the federal regulatory and insurance functions for the thrift industry, the most notable of which was the abolition of the **Federal Home Loan Bank Board (FHLBB)** and the **Federal Savings and Loan Insurance Corporation (FSLIC).** These agencies, created in the **Federal Home Loan Bank Act of 1932** and the **National Housing Act of 1934,** had composed the federal chartering, regulatory, and insurance authority for thrifts for more than 50 years.

FIRREA created an even more complex supervisory structure. The regulatory authority for federally chartered thrifts now rests with the **Office of Thrift Supervision (OTS),** which was established within the Treasury Department but operates independently of the Secretary of the Treasury. Federal deposit insurance for thrifts is now provided by a newly created **Savings Association Insurance Fund (SAIF),** a subsidiary of the FDIC. The Federal Reserve Board continues to set reserve requirements on deposits held by thrift institutions.

CREDIT UNIONS. Credit Unions (CUs) also operate under a dual chartering system. The major federal credit union regulator is the **National Credit Union Administration (NCUA).** CUs may purchase deposit insurance from the **National Credit Union Share Insurance Fund (NCUSIF),** established in the 1970 Amendments to the National Credit Union Act, or from individual state funds. Reserve requirements on deposits are enforced by the Federal Reserve Board.

WHAT IS REGULATED?

Table 2.3 on pages 30–32 provides a summary, prepared by the Federal Reserve Bank of New York, of regulated management areas and the agencies responsible for monitoring institutions' behavior in each area. That compilation provides convincing evidence of the extent of the restrictions and the complexity of the structure. For example, 12 categories of control are identified, ranging from initial entry into an industry (chartering and licensing) to customer relationships (consumer protection).[6]

Table 2.3 identifies the agencies with which a single institution interacts. Consider, for example, a state-chartered S&L, row F(ii) in the table. Five state or federal authorities either set the rules for its operations, enforce the rules, or do both. For instance, a state savings institution gets its charter from a state agency, but its ability to branch or acquire other institutions is under the control of both state authorities and the OTS. Its regional Federal Home Loan (FHL) Bank serves as a source of liquidity and provides funds for housing finance under terms established by FIRREA. Both the state and the OTS may conduct periodic examinations of the institution's financial condition and operations. The Federal Reserve Board determines the S&L's reserve requirements on deposits, and these deposits may be insured by the FDIC (through its SAIF division) or by a nonfederal insurance fund. If insured by SAIF, the thrift is subject to additional regulations the FDIC may choose to impose at any time to preserve the insurance fund's financial health.

---

[6]Discussion of the details of these regulations is reserved for the chapters devoted to the specific management areas. For example, regulations governing expansion are covered in Chapter 4, reserve requirements in Chapter 13, and deposit restrictions in Chapter 16.

TABLE 2.3   **Depository Institutions and Their Regulators**

The regulatory structure for depository institutions is based on a dual banking system, in which both states and the federal government can issue charters. A single institution may be supervised by state and by several federal regulators, depending on the activities in which it is engaged.

| | Chartering and Licensing | Branching | |
		Intrastate	Interstate
A. National Banks	Comptroller	Comptroller	(2)
B. State Member Banks	State authority	Federal Reserve and state authority	(2)
C. Insured State Nonmember Banks	State authority	FDIC and state authority	(3)
D. Noninsured State Banks	State authority	State authority	(3)
E. Savings Banks			
(i) Federal Mutual	OTS	OTS	OTS
(ii) State Mutual	State authority	FDIC and state authority	FDIC and state authority
F. Savings and Loan Associations			
(i) Federal	OTS	OTS	OTS
(ii) State	State authority	OTS and state authority	OTS and state authority
G. Credit Unions			
(i) Federal	NCUAB	(1)	(1)
(ii) State	State authority	State authority	State authority

EXAMINATION PROCESS. The previous example highlights the fact that a major function of depository institution regulators is examining the financial condition and operations of the firms they supervise. At the federal level, the **Federal Financial Institutions Examination Council (FFIEC)** coordinates procedures for assuring compliance with a variety of regulations. The FFIEC consists of representatives from the Board of Governors of the Fed, the FDIC, the OTS, the NCUA, and the Comptroller of the Currency. It controls requirements for financial reports and disclosures that institutions must make to regulators, negotiates sharing of information between state and federal agencies, and even provides training programs for examiners of the member agencies.

Examinations performed by the regulators consist of on-site visits by agency personnel, who conduct audits of policies and procedures used to grant loans, purchase and sell securities, process deposits, manage cash, and keep financial records. Typically, from one to four examiners remain at an institution for a month or more. The frequency of examinations varies with the existing condition of a depository. For example, a small institution with unchanged ownership and a clean bill of health in its most recent examination may be visited every 18 months. Supervisors must examine other institutions, either larger or with specified deficiencies, at least once a year. Since 1993, regulators have used a set of so-called **tripwires** to identify unsafe or unsound banking practices. These tripwires establish minimum standards for virtually every area under management's influence or control.

Four federal regulators—the Fed, the FDIC, the Comptroller of the Currency, and the NCUA—use a uniform rating system known by the acronym **CAMEL.** This system uses 1 to 5 (best to worst) assessments of the institution's capital, assets, management, earnings, and liquidity. The OTS has a separate,

TABLE 2.3 *CONTINUED*

Mergers, Acquisitions, and
Consolidations

Intrastate	Interstate	Reserve Requirements	Access to the Discount Window	Deposit Insurance
A. Federal Reserve and Comptroller (4)	(5)	Federal Reserve	Federal Reserve	FDIC (BIF)
B. Federal Reserve and state authority (4)	(5)	Federal Reserve	Federal Reserve	FDIC (BIF)
C. FDIC and state authority (4)	(5)	Federal Reserve	Federal Reserve	FDIC (BIF)
D. State authority (4)	State authority	Federal Reserve	Federal Reserve	None or state insurance fund
E. (i) OTS and FDIC (4)	(5)	Federal Reserve	Federal Reserve	FDIC (SAIF)
(ii) FDIC and state authority (4)	(5)	Federal Reserve	Federal Reserve	FDIC (BIF) or state insurance fund
F. (i) OTS and FDIC (4)	(5)	Federal Reserve	Federal Home Loan Bank and Federal Reserve	FDIC (SAIF)
(ii) OTS, FDIC, and state authority (4)	(5)	Federal Reserve	Federal Home Loan Bank and Federal Reserve	FDIC (SAIF) or state insurance fund
G. (i) NCUA Board	(5)	Federal Reserve	Central Liquidity Facility and Federal Reserve	NCUSIF
(ii) NCUA Board and state authority (4)	(5)	Federal Reserve	Central Liquidity Facility and Federal Reserve	NCUSIF or state insurance fund

very similar system known as **MACRO.** The composite ratings are one basis for determining how often examiners arrive and even whether regulators can restrict institutions from activities available to safer depositories. Other examiners, such as state regulators, may operate on different schedules.

DOES THIS STRUCTURE MAKE SENSE?

Few disagree that the activities of regulatory agencies are duplicative. In 1974, Arthur Burns, then Chairman of the Board of Governors of the Federal Reserve, called the bank regulatory system "a jurisdictional tangle that boggles the mind."[7] Beginning with the Hoover Commission in 1949, considerable resources have been devoted to analyzing the system and

recommending reforms. A recent effort was the Task Group on Deregulation of Financial Services, headed by then Vice-President George Bush (and more commonly known as the Bush Task Group), which made its recommendations to Congress in 1984.

Some studies have advocated consolidating supervisory power in a single agency, whereas others have warned against giving any single organization too much power. The Bush Task Group did not recommend complete consolidation but instead suggested reorganizing agencies along functional lines, giving one agency the authority over federal deposit insurance, another over examination and supervision, and so forth. As with earlier reports, however, Congress delayed action on the proposals. Interestingly, major opponents of reorganization included some regulated institutions, which enjoyed the protection of existing agencies, as Kane's dialectic predicts.[8]

---

[7] See Johnson 1984.

[8] For more information, see Johnson 1984 and Gilbert 1984.

TABLE 2.3 *CONTINUED*

	Supervision and Examination	Prudential Limits, Safety, and Soundness	Consumer Protection	
			Rulemaking	Enforcement
A. National Banks	Comptroller	Comptroller	Federal Reserve	Comptroller
B. State Member Banks	Federal Reserve and state authority	Federal Reserve and state authority	Federal Reserve and state authority	Federal Reserve and state authority
C. Insured State Non-member Banks	FDIC and state authority	FDIC and state authority	Federal Reserve and state authority	FDIC and state authority
D. Noninsured State Banks	State authority	State authority	Federal Reserve and state authority	State authority and Federal Trade Commission
E. Savings Banks				
(i) Federal Mutual	OTS and FDIC	OTS and FDIC	Federal Reserve and OTS	OTS
(ii) State Mutual	FDIC and state authority	FDIC and state authority	Federal Reserve, OTS, and state authority	FDIC, state authority, or OTS
F. Savings and Loan Associations				
(i) Federal	OTS and FDIC	OTS and FDIC	Federal Reserve and OTS	OTS
(ii) State	OTS, FDIC, and state authority (6)	FDIC or state authority	Federal Reserve, OTS, and state authority	OTS, FDIC, or state authority
G. Credit Unions				
(i) Federal	NCUA Board	NCUA Board	Federal Reserve and state authority	NCUA Board
(ii) State	State authority	State authority	Federal Reserve and state authority	State authority

(1) Federal CUs are not required to receive approval from the NCUA Board before opening a branch.
(2) Although the McFadden Act prevents interstate branching by national banks and state member banks, banks can provide certain services on an interstate basis.
(3) The McFadden Act's interstate branching restrictions are generally not applicable to noninsured state banks and insured state nonmember banks.
(4) Regulators' involvement varies, depending on characteristics of merged or acquired firms.
(5) The McFadden Act prevents interstate branching by national banks and state member banks. The G-St G provided the initial statutory framework for interstate and interindustry acquisitions or mergers of failing federally insured depository institutions. FIRREA permitted the FDIC and the Fed to approve interstate, interindustry mergers and acquisitions of both failing and healthy depositories.
(6) Federally insured state S&Ls are supervised and examined by the OTS and the FDIC, nonfederally insured state S&Ls by the OTS and state authority.

Source: Adapted from Federal Reserve Bank of New York, *Depository Institutions and Their Regulators,* 1988; updated by authors.

Although Congress failed to act on restructuring soon after the Bush Task Group report, developments in the national and international financial markets continued to make regulatory reform a priority among many regulators, managers, and academics for the remainder of the 1980s and into the 1990s. The most recent proposal, issued in 1993 by the National Commission on Financial Institution Reform, Recovery, and Enforcement, went so far as to recommend that

thrift institutions (and their regulators) be eliminated altogether, that the Comptroller of the Currency be abolished, and that eligibility for deposit insurance be limited to so-called **monetary service companies.** These special-purpose firms would be affiliates of commercial banks but would be permitted to invest customers' deposits only in low-risk, short-term assets, such as Treasury bills and federal agency securities. Under this proposal, other financial institutions could accept uninsured deposits, make risky investments with those funds, and enjoy relatively less regulation. As this proposal suggests, the focus of most reports has shifted from eliminating regulatory duplication as an end in itself toward making depositories (and especially commercial banks) more competitive with less-regulated foreign banks and domestically chartered securities and insurance firms and, at the same time, maintaining the safety and soundness of the banking system.[9]

However, Congress's attention has often been diverted from long-run change in the regulatory structure to recurring financial crises. As explained in more detail later in the chapter, FIRREA followed one of the suggestions of the Bush Task Group by consolidating the administration of the deposit insurance agencies under the FDIC. Nonetheless, FIRREA was widely perceived as merely a stopgap approach to regulatory reform; indeed, it created more new regulatory agencies than it eliminated. When Congress returned its attention to the banking industry in FDICIA, lobbyists for different special interest groups, including the insurance and securities industries, successfully blocked once again any sweeping changes in bank powers and regulatory structure. These issues are discussed in greater detail at several points later in the book.

FINANCE COMPANIES

In contrast to depositories, the sources and uses of funds of finance companies are not heavily regulated at the federal level. These institutions raise funds in the debt markets rather than from deposits and do not have to meet federal reserve requirements or other asset restrictions. Some experts believe that finance companies' recent ability to compete with greater success against commercial banks is the result of technological and financial innovations that have aided them in raising funds efficiently.[10]

LICENSING RESTRICTIONS

Finance companies must seek permission from state authorities to open new offices. They enjoy more freedom than banks or thrifts to expand across state lines, however, because there is no federal restriction on interstate operations. In most states, a request to open a new office is evaluated by the **"convenience and advantage" rule,** which holds that expansion should occur only if the community will benefit. As a result, limitations on competition within individual states or communities may exist.[11]

CONSUMER PROTECTION LEGISLATION

Finance companies face other regulations as well. An extensive body of consumer protection legislation has accumulated since 1968 and affects the managerial decisions of finance companies and other consumer lenders. In the finance company industry, the responsibility for monitoring compliance with consumer protection laws such as the **Consumer Credit Protection (Truth-in-Lending) Act of 1968** and **Equal Credit Opportunity Act of 1974** lies with the Federal Trade Commission.

Federal regulations have focused on equality in the availability of credit and on the completeness, accuracy, and uniformity of information disclosed to potential borrowers. At the state level, regulations concentrate on the rate of interest charged. In recent years, attention has focused on state **usury ceilings,** which are legal limitations on lending rates. When market interest rates rise significantly above the usury ceilings, as they did in the early 1980s, severe problems for lenders are created, and the amount of available credit is restricted.

Again, in the spirit of Kane's regulatory dialectic, state regulations were modified in the 1980s, necessitated by market conditions or by regulatory actions at the federal level. For example, in 1980, federal law removed usury ceilings from residential mortgage loans unless states overrode the action by 1983; most states did not. Many states increased or removed usury

---

[9] For details on these and other recent proposals, see "Regulators, Congress Are Cited by Panel for Thrift Debacle," *The Wall Street Journal,* July 28, 1993, C20; Robert Litan, "Deposit Insurance, Gas on S&L Fire," *The Wall Street Journal,* July 29, 1993, A14; Robyn Meredith, "U.S. Panel: Scrap S&Ls, Cut Insurance," *American Banker,* July 28, 1993, 1, 18; Sellon 1988; Gilbert 1988; and Greenspan 1988.

[10] See Gorton and Pennacchi 1992.

---

[11] Although the absence of a federal chartering agency removes one layer of regulation, it also means that if a firm is denied a charter at the state level, no recourse is available. The resulting competitive effect of this and other state restrictions is explored more fully in Selden 1981.

ceilings on personal loans after market interest rates rose to historic highs in 1980 and 1981.

INSURANCE COMPANIES

Life insurers and property/liability insurers have a regulatory system that falls somewhere in between those of depository institutions and finance companies. The **McCarran-Ferguson Act of 1945** gave the federal government the right to regulate insurance companies.[12] Congress agreed, however, that the right to impose federal regulations would not be exercised until 1948 and would not be exercised at all if states adequately established and enforced standards for the industry. Thus, the legal basis for federal regulation of insurers exists, but for all practical purposes insurers operate at the direction of state agencies. Commissioners of insurance in each state wield considerable power individually and exert influence collectively through the **National Association of Insurance Commissioners (NAIC),** an organization with no legal power but with substantial political clout.

Recent increases in the cost of property/liability insurance have renewed calls for federal regulation of that industry or, at a minimum, for tighter regulation at the state level. The McCarran-Ferguson Act recognized that insurers often pool data on the frequency and causes of their customers' accidents, natural disasters, fires, and so forth to establish statistical data bases that can be used to assist in pricing insurance policies. Yet federal antitrust laws prohibit data sharing by competitors in most industries on the grounds that it can lead to collusion and price fixing. Thus, McCarran-Ferguson specifically exempts insurers from federal antitrust laws unless firms can be shown to be engaged in "boycott, coercion, or intimidation" as a result of data sharing.

State regulators are supposed to ensure that these prohibited activities do not occur, but in the late 1980s,

some critics charged that oversight of the insurance industry was too lax. By November 1988, charges of unfair pricing in the property/liability segment of the industry were widespread in some states, including California, where voters decided the cost of automobile insurance was too high and passed **Proposition 103.** This referendum mandated a substantial reduction in the price of some insurance policies issued in that state.

The success of Proposition 103 encouraged other consumer advocates to challenge the antitrust provisions of McCarran-Ferguson and to advocate the law's repeal, substituting instead direct federal regulation of the industry. Responding to criticisms of laxity and inadequate expertise among state regulators and hoping to avert federal regulation of the industry, the NAIC developed an accrediting system for state insurance regulators. The system did not, however, quiet Congressional critics of the industry. These developments are discussed in greater detail in Chapter 24.

LICENSING AND SOLVENCY REQUIREMENTS

Regulatory structure aside, a number of similarities exist in the scope and focus of regulations with which insurers and depository institutions must comply. For example, strict standards designed to protect the solvency of insurers are applied in granting company licenses. After entry is granted, annual financial statements are closely scrutinized, and insurers are subject to frequent examinations. Finally, analogous to deposit insurance agencies, insolvency guarantee funds are established in all states to protect policyholders should an insurer go bankrupt.

RATE REGULATION

A considerable amount of time is devoted to rate regulation. Generally, regulators agree that rates charged by insurers, when combined with income from investments, must be sufficient to cover the potential liabilities of the firm. At the same time, rates must not be excessive or discriminate unfairly. Although insurers must differentiate between high-risk and low-risk customers and charge accordingly, regulations attempt to prevent rate discrimination not justified by differing levels of risk. The approach that state legislators and commissioners of insurance take

---

[12] Before 1945, the insurance regulatory structure was based on the ruling of the Supreme Court in *Paul v. Virginia,* 75 U.S. 168, 8 Wall 168, 19 L Ed 357 (1869), that insurance was not interstate commerce and was therefore not subject to federal regulation. Thus, no federal regulatory structure existed when the McCarran-Ferguson Act was passed. More details on the McCarran-Ferguson Act can be found in "Open Season on an Old Law," *Journal of American Insurance* 63 (First Quarter 1987): 8–12.

toward achieving ideal rates differs from state to state and varies according to the category of insurer.

Generally, the policy premiums life insurers may charge are not directly controlled, but standards designed to guarantee sufficient reserves to cover future claims are imposed in most states. Thus, the regulations establish a floor for policy rates, because insurers must set rates high enough to generate the required reserves. For property/liability insurers, state regulations on policy rates are more extensive. Most states require property/liability insurers to obtain the approval of regulators before increasing policy rates.[13]

PRODUCT REGULATION

Just as depository institutions have operated under asset and deposit restrictions for many years, insurers must comply with limitations on the types of policies they can offer. In many states, insurers must seek the approval of the insurance commissioner before they can sell new products. The close scrutiny is intended to protect customers against unfair policy provisions and to protect the insurance firm from commitments that may undermine its financial stability.

ASSET STRUCTURE

Insurers' investments are also regulated. State insurance codes specify permissible categories and quality grades of assets. Many states restrict the percentage of firms' total assets that may be invested in specific types of securities, such as common stock. Despite these restrictions, however, the spotlight focused on the industry in the early 1990s, when several large insurers with extensive junk bond and commercial real estate holdings failed, leaving policyholders stranded. These events strengthened Congressional interest in federal regulation of insurers.

PENSION FUNDS

Pension funds operate under contractual savings agreements that obligate them to pay retirement benefits to workers. The pension plans of private corpora-

tions are subject to the **Employee Retirement Income Security Act,** passed by Congress in 1974 and more commonly known as **ERISA.**

INVESTMENT MANAGEMENT

ERISA covers almost all areas of pension fund management. Two provisions set standards for **vested benefits** to plan participants and for funding a plan so that assets are equal to accrued liabilities. Vested benefits are those to which employees are entitled even if they leave the firm before retirement. ERISA requires early vesting of benefits and ensures that most employees are 100 percent vested after 15 years of service.

ERISA also sets standards for employer contributions in relation to the fund's investment income and benefit liabilities. Generally, ERISA attempts to ensure that employers work toward making pension assets equal to the fund's obligations. Pension fund managers have **fiduciary responsibility** for investment of assets, and they are required to act solely in the interests of the fund's beneficiaries.

PENSION INSURANCE

Another ERISA provision, also designed to protect the financial interests of fund members, established an insurance fund to guarantee that benefits are paid to eligible members even if a pension plan defaults on its obligations. This federal insurance agency is called the **Pension Benefit Guaranty Corporation (PBGC)** and is funded by assessments on an employer according to the number of employees covered and the riskiness of the fund's assets. To ensure the continuing financial stability of pension funds, the law imposes requirements for extensive and frequent reporting and disclosure. As explained in Chapter 25, federal pension insurance has been plagued by many of the same difficulties as federal deposit insurance, evoking considerable concern among regulators and retirees whose future income may be in jeopardy.

INVESTMENT COMPANIES

Investment companies act as portfolio managers for those to whom they sell ownership shares. Because investment company shares are sold publicly and

---

[13] For an exhaustive review of the effect of rate regulation on property/liability firms, see Harrington 1984.

because many of their assets are publicly traded, investment companies must comply with federal securities laws. The obligations of fund managers to shareholders are also defined by federal and state laws.

FEDERAL SECURITIES LAWS

The issuance of ownership shares by investment companies and the frequency and accuracy of their financial reports are monitored by the **Securities and Exchange Commission (SEC),** under the authority of the Securities Act of 1933 and the Securities Exchange Act of 1934. Many provisions affecting investment companies also apply to other firms that issue securities for sale to the public. Some provisions address investment companies specifically, however, to ensure regular and truthful disclosures to existing and potential shareholders.

The Securities Act of 1933 focused on new issues, requiring firms to provide full and accurate information about their financial positions and about new securities offered. The Securities Exchange Act of 1934 established the SEC as the chief regulator of the securities markets and requires regular disclosure of financial information by firms with publicly traded securities.

Securities laws are rooted in the belief that access to information is the best guarantor of the public interest. Depository institution legislation, in contrast, has produced elaborate regulatory systems for gathering information, much of which is unavailable to the public. The securities and investment company industries operate with a strong system of self-regulation through trade organizations, whereas depository trade organizations are more like political action groups, seeking to preserve existing laws or to promote new legislation.

REGULATIONS ON SOURCES AND USES OF FUNDS

The Investment Company Act of 1940 and subsequent amendments, and the **Investment Advisers Act** of the same year, are the foundation for specific regulations governing investment companies. These laws identify responsibilities of investment advisers and fund managers. For example, the use of financial leverage is limited. Also, mutual fund managers must obtain shareholder approval of a change in investment objectives, so shareholders are guaranteed at least some degree of control over the risk exposure and return potential of the funds.

The Investment Company Act also imposed diversification requirements to protect shareholders against the risk of total loss. Investment companies may invest no more than 5 percent of their assets in any one firm and may hold no more than 10 percent of the outstanding voting shares of a company. These restrictions apply to 75 percent of an investment company's portfolio; the remaining 25 percent is exempted to encourage investment in smaller businesses.

Another influence on managers is the exemption of investment company income from federal taxes if at least 90 percent of net capital gain income and 97 percent of dividend and interest income are distributed to shareholders. Taxes are paid only by individual shareholders, and no taxes are assessed on the fund, an approach to taxation known as the **conduit theory.** Finally, the federal regulatory and tax codes are supplemented by state codes placing additional responsibilities on fund managers.

In contrast to savings at depository institutions, pension funds, or insurance firms, funds entrusted to investment companies have no guarantee of recovery in case of fund failure. The goal of regulation is to ensure availability of truthful information. If investors make a bad choice of investment companies, however, no federal or state insurance will mitigate the loss.

SECURITIES FIRMS

Like investment companies, securities firms are subject to SEC scrutiny under the Securities Exchange Act and its amendments. The act established maximum levels of indebtedness for securities dealers and gave the Fed the authority to set **margin requirements** governing loans by securities firms to customers for the purchase of securities. In addition, securities firms are prohibited from using inside information about firms to profit at the expense of the public. Firms selling investment advice to clients are subject to the Investment Advisers Act of 1940, which seeks to prevent fraudulent practices. The scope of a firm's operations determines additional constraints to which it is subject. For example, members of the New York Stock Exchange must conform to the self-regulating rules of the exchange. The **National Association of Securities Dealers (NASD)** is a self-regulating body for all brokers and dealers interacting with the public.

The industry operates under Congressional objectives for a national securities market articulated in the **Securities Acts Amendments of 1975.** This legislation directed the SEC to promote a fully competitive trading system under which investors nationwide have equal and instantaneous access to information. Historic practices concentrating trades in a few locations, such as New York City, would be eliminated. Although progress has been made toward this goal, it has yet to be fully achieved.

Before 1970, the daily volume of transactions processed by securities firms was relatively small, and all facets of each transaction were handled manually, including the physical transfer of securities between buyer and seller. As in other financial industries, however, fading memories of the Great Depression gave rise to increased investment activity. In 1968 and 1969, several securities firms failed under the burden, and customers' securities were discovered missing. To promote public confidence in the industry, Congress passed the **Securities Investor Protection Act** in 1970, mandating the creation of the **Securities Investor Protection Corporation (SIPC).** The SIPC is an industry-funded organization providing reimbursement to customers of securities firms if their securities or cash are missing when an affiliated firm fails. Although initiated by Congress, the SIPC's promises to investors are not guaranteed by the federal government, and it has no legal regulatory powers. Instead, it is a visible symbol of the industry's obligation to self-regulation.

Whether securities firms will continue to enjoy the relative freedom that many depository institutions seek is an important question. The last half of the 1980s found the industry's integrity battered. Between 1985 and 1991, several major scandals, led by disclosures discrediting junk bond king Michael Milken, rocked the industry as a result of **insider trading**—transactions in which corporate managers, directors, or their securities advisors illegally profit from private information affecting the value of a firm's securities. Some observers blamed self-interested computerized trading by securities firms for the stock market crash of October 1987. In 1991, Salomon Brothers, a major securities firm, admitted to manipulating the Treasury securities market for its own benefit.

Incidents such as these evoked cries for greater government regulation. Congress responded to some of the criticisms with the passage of the **Insider Trading and Securities Fraud Enforcement Act of 1988,** more commonly known as the **Insider Trading Act.** The legislation established deterrents to insider trading by setting stronger penalties for violators and requiring firms to develop formal policies to prevent abuses. The act also increased federal agencies' ability to enforce regulations. The Salomon Brothers' scandal resulted in rule changes in the Treasury securities market.

Despite the recognized need for closer scrutiny of securities activities, global market forces have increased competition from foreign firms and caused many experts to warn against shackling the industry with additional, costly regulatory taxes. Furthermore, as discussed earlier, technological change cannot be regulated away, and attempts to prevent securities firms from using today's computerized trading strategies are likely to lead only to different, unregulated strategies tomorrow.

ORIGINS OF FINANCIAL INNOVATION AND REGULATORY REFORM IN THE 1980s

The discussion of the regulatory dialectic introduced forces producing regulatory reform including financial market changes and regulatory avoidance behavior. No example of the confluence of these forces and the regulatory response is clearer than events leading to two of the most important pieces of financial legislation of the 1980s, DIDMCA and Garn-St Germain.

By 1980, the need for reforms was widely recognized. As noted, several government commissions had studied the problems of financial institutions and recommended revisions in the regulatory structure. Congress, however, failed to respond with substantive changes. As problems motivating the formation of those study groups reappeared in the late 1970s, federal legislators again turned their attention to the possibility of regulatory reform.[14] These problems

---

[14] More details on the problems that precipitated formation of these commissions, as well as a discussion of their recommendations, are available in several sources, including West 1982; "The Depository Institutions . . . Act" 1980; and Shull 1981.

stimulated antithetical forces that culminated in major regulatory revisions.

ECONOMIC CONDITIONS

As 1980 approached, inflation and interest rates were reaching historically high levels. Uncertainty about future interest rates was great, arising from expected inflation and fears that changes in the Fed's approach to monetary policy would increase rate volatility.

When unusual uncertainty about future economic conditions exists, financial market participants respond by demanding investments that reduce their risk exposure. A rigid regulatory structure prevents financial institutions from responding to customer demands rapidly and, in some cases, prevents any response at all. Regulatory restrictions may also prevent managers of financial institutions from making investment decisions necessary to protect the stability and level of the institution's income.

INTEREST RATE CEILINGS

As mentioned earlier, by the late 1970s, Reg Q ceilings were lower than market interest rates. As a result, depositors withdrew funds to invest in instruments with the potential to earn a higher rate of return. When funds are removed from financial institutions in favor of direct investments, the phenomenon is known as **disintermediation.**

Large commercial banks had developed regulation-avoidance strategies to prevent large depositors from disintermediating. Small savers, however, had few alternatives except to try other financial institutions such as mutual funds, on which returns were tied to market conditions. In other words, depositories were also subject to **cross-intermediation,** or the transfer of funds from one financial intermediary to another. In the 1970s, many investment companies had introduced money market mutual funds (MMMFs), whose assets were invested in short-term securities. MMMFs offered liquidity through checkwriting privileges and a relatively low level of risk, because fund portfolios included a large proportion of U.S. government securities. More important, their rate of return was not controlled by Reg Q.

INITIAL REGULATORY RESPONSE TO BINDING CEILINGS. Beginning in 1978, regulators made several "patchwork" attempts to revise regulations that had contributed to disintermediation and cross-intermediation. New types of deposit accounts (discussed in more detail in Chapter 16) were permitted, each designed to allow small savers to earn market rates of interest or to earn a modest return on checking account balances.

Although the new accounts were popular, they could not stem the tide of disintermediation as interest rates soared to unprecedented levels in late 1979. Furthermore, the right of federal regulators to introduce deposit innovations without explicit Congressional action was challenged, and eventually a Court of Appeals ruling established a January 1, 1980, deadline for eliminating the innovations unless Congress acted. Although final action was not forthcoming by that date, Congress extended the life of the new deposits temporarily, to expire March 31, 1980.[15]

DECLINING FED MEMBERSHIP

Additional acts of regulatory avoidance in the late 1970s added to the need for reform legislation by 1980. Before then, only commercial banks that were members of the Fed were required to keep nonearning reserves at regional Federal Reserve Banks. Reserve deposits are intended to provide an institution with sufficient liquid funds to meet customers' deposit withdrawals and to assist the Fed in controlling lending. Nonmember banks, thrifts, and CUs were not subject to the same kinds of reserve requirements. As interest rates rose, the opportunity cost of nonearning reserves was more and more burdensome for member banks.

To the dismay of Fed officials, an increasingly large number of banks resigned Fed membership, and most new banks chose to obtain state charters to avoid the Fed's reserve requirements. The Fed argued that as the proportion of deposits held by member banks declined, the effectiveness of reserve requirements as a tool of monetary policy declined. Fed officials pressured Congress to introduce a more equitable system.

---

[15] For more details on these events, see Kent W. Colton, "Financial Reform: A Review of the Past and Prospects for the Future," invited research working paper, #37, Federal Home Loan Bank Board, September 1980.

DECLINING PROFITABILITY

Some financial institutions needed more flexibility to protect against interest rate risk, just as individual and corporate investors did. Once again, however, regulations prevented them from adjusting asset portfolios quickly in response to market conditions. For example, profits in the thrift industry suffered because institutions were, to comply with regulations, heavily invested in long-term, fixed-rate mortgages. As thrifts incurred higher interest expenses on new deposit accounts, they needed to increase returns on assets. They had little ability to diversify, however, especially in comparison with commercial banks, and their profits declined at an alarming rate.[16]

Insurers also had problems. Consumers no longer demanded traditional life insurance products. Property/liability insurers suffered because inflation increased their claims expenses more rapidly than they could increase income. These pressures, too, called for regulatory changes.

TECHNOLOGICAL INNOVATION

The influence of technology was also great. Computers made it possible to analyze large quantities of data efficiently and revolutionized the availability of information. **Electronic funds transfers,** or movement of funds by electronic impulse rather than by paper check or other traditional methods, were increasing. As a result, financial institutions could offer more services and respond more rapidly to market conditions than ever before, and their demands for the power to diversify services became increasingly forceful.

In the face of technology, regulations began to seem antiquated. As information systems enabled some participants in the financial markets, such as securities firms, to respond almost instantaneously to changes in interest rates or other market conditions, restrictive regulations on others, such as depositories, appeared anticompetitive. Said Henry Wallich, member of the Board of Governors of the Federal Reserve, "Deregulation has been driven . . . by technological innovation. Anticompetitive practices have had to be abandoned, on pain of being circumvented; bureau-

cratic resistance had to yield to the pressures of the market."[17]

COMPETITIVE INEQUITIES: THE CALL FOR A "LEVEL PLAYING FIELD"

Depository institutions saw their competitors grow in number. Investment companies, insurance companies, securities firms, and even diversified firms such as Sears, Roebuck introduced financial products that encroached on territory previously controlled by depositories. The latter grew more vocal in their demands for regulatory reform, arguing that they labored under restrictions not faced by competitors. For example, while Merrill Lynch and Sears were free to offer services nationwide, many depositories could not even open a branch in the next county, let alone another state. Even though competitors could offer a wide variety of financial products, services offered by a depository were limited. Protestors called for a **"level playing field"** a set of rules allowing them to compete on an equal footing.

CHANGING VIEWS ON REGULATION: DOES IT REALLY PROMOTE SAFETY?

A final catalyst for change was more subtle. As memories of the financial crisis of the 1930s faded, some researchers believe that regulators may have modified their views on the rationale for regulation.[18] For example, recognition grew that interest rate ceilings had a destabilizing effect on the economy, provoking reevaluation of regulations intended to prevent competition among depositories. Furthermore, it was apparent that forcing specialization on institutions such as S&Ls did not ensure their stability or solvency. The deterioration of the financial position of the thrift industry was one more incentive to examine the philosophy that had traditionally guided regulators. It was no longer clear that regulations promoted institutional safety; the possibility arose that regulations might actually make institutions riskier.

---

[16] A good summary of the plight of the thrift institutions before DIDMCA is available in Brock 1980 and White 1991.

[17] Henry C. Wallich, "A Broad View of Deregulation," unpublished remarks at the Conference on Pacific Basin Financial Reform, Federal Reserve Bank of San Francisco, San Francisco, California, December 1984, 3.

[18] References to the changing regulatory philosophy are found in Cargill and Garcia 1985 and West 1982.

DIDMCA

These factors led Congress to enact the landmark Depository Institutions Deregulation and Monetary Control Act on March 31, 1980, the day depositories' authority to offer new deposit accounts was to expire. The act was considered the most significant financial legislation since the Federal Reserve Act of 1913 and the many acts of the 1930s.

DIDMCA had two major components evident in its name: 1) deregulation of depository institutions; and 2) improved monetary control. The deregulation provisions allowed more competition among depositories while improving financial services for small savers. The monetary control provisions improved the effectiveness of the Fed's responses to changing economic conditions and equalized the monetary policy burden among depositories.

DEPOSITORY INSTITUTIONS DEREGULATION

The deregulation part of the act did not actually deregulate depository institutions. Many experts refer to it as "*re*-regulation." Nevertheless, DIDMCA introduced important changes in sources and uses of funds for depository institutions.

The ramifications of DIDMCA are broad and are examined in detail in subsequent chapters. The following paragraphs highlight only a few of the consequences, and Table 2.4 summarizes the act. The word "Title" in the table is a legal term indicating a major section of a law.

ELIMINATION OF DEPOSIT INTEREST RATE CEILINGS. Title II of DIDMCA provided for the phase-out of interest rate ceilings on deposits over a 6-year period ending March 31, 1986. The intent was to provide an orderly transition to market interest rates on deposits. Legislators' introductory remarks to Title II reveal the belief that the ceilings discouraged savings, created inequities for small savers, and had not achieved desired economic goals.[19]

NEW SOURCES OF FUNDS. Title III authorized all banks and thrifts to offer interest-bearing **transactions accounts,** or accounts on which an unlimited number of checks can be written, to individuals and nonprofit organizations. In banks and thrifts, they are called **negotiable orders of withdrawal (NOWs),** and in CUs, **share drafts.** Interest-bearing checking had been prohibited nationwide since Glass-Steagall in 1933. In a provision with wide-ranging effects unforeseen at the time, Title III also increased federal deposit insurance coverage from $40,000 to $100,000 per account holder per institution. In the years since DIDMCA, many observers have concluded that raising the limit was one of the most serious legislative errors of all time.

NEW USES OF FUNDS. Many blamed the precarious financial position of the thrift industry on its inability to diversify asset portfolios. To provide relief, Congress allowed savings institutions to invest in a wider variety of nonmortgage instruments, such as consumer loans, commercial paper, investment company shares, and education loans. The intent of Congress was to allow thrifts to achieve a better balance between asset and liability maturities. The importance of maturity matching for institution management is discussed at many points later in this book.

To further strengthen their competitive position, the law allowed savings institutions to offer credit card and trust services. Savings banks were permitted to make commercial loans and, for the first time, to accept **demand deposits,** or noninterest-bearing checking accounts, in conjunction with corporate loan relationships. Although these provisions allowed thrifts to diversify to an unprecedented degree, their uses of funds remained more restricted than funds sources. Congress also preempted state usury ceilings on certain categories of loans so that thrifts and CUs could charge rates that were more closely aligned with their costs of funds.

MONETARY CONTROL

The first title of DIDMCA addressed monetary policy. The intent was to strengthen the Fed's monetary policy responses, the mechanics of which are discussed in the next chapter.

UNIVERSAL RESERVE REQUIREMENTS. To arrest the decline in Fed membership, Congress extended reserve requirements to all depositories offering trans-

[19] See "The Depository Institutions . . . Act" 1980.

TABLE 2.4	Provisions of the Depository Institutions Deregulation and Monetary Control Act of 1980

DIDMCA brought about the most sweeping changes in financial regulation since the 1930s. Its main effects were to deregulate deposit accounts, to extend the same reserve requirements to all depositories, to broaden the asset choices of thrifts, and to increase deposit insurance coverage.

Title I: Monetary Control Act of 1980
Phased in reserve requirements on transactions accounts at all depository institutions; authorized the Fed to impose supplemental interest-bearing reserve requirements if necessary; extended discount window borrowing privileges and other Fed services to any depository institution issuing transactions accounts or nonpersonal time deposits; mandated the development of a fee structure for Fed services

Title II: Depository Institutions Deregulation Act of 1980
Provided for the orderly phase-out and ultimate elimination of interest rate ceilings on deposit accounts

Title III: Consumer Checking Account Equity Act of 1980
Authorized interest-bearing transactions accounts at all depositories; increased federal deposit insurance coverage from $40,000 to $100,000

Title IV: Expanded Powers for Thrifts
Allowed federally chartered S&Ls to invest in consumer and other loans, commercial paper, corporate bonds, and mutual funds; authorized federal thrifts to issue credit cards; increased powers for savings banks, including demand deposit accounts to commercial loan customers

Title V: Preemption of State Interest Rate Ceilings
Eliminated state usury ceilings on residential mortgage loans; tied ceiling rates on business and agricultural loans of $25,000 or more to the Fed discount rate; gave states until April 1, 1983, to reinstate usury ceilings on these loan categories; overrode state laws imposing ceilings on deposit interest rates

Title VI: Truth-in-Lending Simplification
Revised the Truth-in-Lending Act to make it easier for creditors to comply with disclosure requirements; gave consumers additional rights in case of false disclosure

Title VII: Amendments to the National Banking Laws
Miscellaneous provisions on national banks and bank holding companies

Title VIII: Financial Regulation Simplification Act of 1980
Required regulators to limit regulations to those "for which a need has been established" and to minimize compliance costs

Title IX: Foreign Control of U.S. Financial Institutions
Imposed a moratorium until July 1, 1980, on foreign takeover of U.S. financial institutions

actions accounts. To improve the Fed's ability to monitor the economy, Congress authorized the Board to require regular reports on assets and liabilities.[20] The incentive for banks to resign from the Fed disappeared because electing nonmembership no longer offered an escape from the burden of reserve requirements.

Some relief was available to member banks, however, because the act reduced the required percentage of deposits to be kept on reserve. Recognizing the reserve management problems depositories would face, Congress set a phase-in period for the new regulations. The reserves continue to be noninterest-bearing.[21] Details on implementation of Title I are presented in Chapter 13.

[20] In practice, severe problems arose in trying to monitor the assets and liabilities of almost 40,000 depository institutions. After those data collection and analysis problems were recognized, the first $2 million in transactions deposits were exempted from required reserves. In effect, that ruling entirely exempted a large number of smaller depositories, especially CUs, and was made permanent by Congress in the Garn-St Germain Act. The amount of reservable liabilities subject to the 0 percent requirement is adjusted annually using a formula stipulated by Congress.

[21] Normally, marginal reserve requirements range from 3 percent to a maximum of 10 percent. A provision allows the Fed to impose a supplemental requirement of up to 4 percent under specified conditions, but the Fed is required to pay interest on those supplemental reserves.

UNIVERSAL ACCESS TO FEDERAL RESERVE SERVICES. Whereas holding nonearning reserves had been a major cost of Fed membership, the ability to borrow from the Fed (to use the **discount window**) and to obtain free services such as check-clearing and securities safekeeping were offsetting benefits. Once reserve requirements were extended to all institutions, Congress directed the Fed to make services available to all depositories and to charge for services that had previously been free. All depository institutions were granted the right to use the discount window or to purchase Fed check-clearing or other services.[22] The same fee structure applies to both members and nonmembers.

AFTER DIDMCA: CONTINUING NEED FOR REFORM

The monumental changes introduced by DIDMCA produced no overnight miracles. The act included phase-in periods for several provisions, and changes in the asset structure of thrifts could not be accomplished quickly. In the context of the regulatory dialectic, DIDMCA did not produce a synthesis. Additional pressures for change began even before final passage of DIDMCA and continued to gain momentum afterward.[23]

CRISIS IN THE THRIFT INDUSTRY: ROUND ONE

Despite DIDMCA, thrifts' profitability continued to decline at an alarming rate. In 1981, the FHLBB authorized thrifts to offer adjustable-rate mortgages, hoping the industry would be able to earn interest revenues above interest expenses. But market interest rates, especially on short-term deposits, remained high well into 1982, and the cost of funds to many S&Ls

remained above the rate of return on assets. Operating losses mounted, and massive failures were predicted.[24]

The prospects of a high failure rate alarmed regulators, because both they and Congress doubted whether the resources of the FSLIC were sufficient to protect insured depositors. The status of the industry reached crisis proportions, causing Congress to move more rapidly than usual toward new legislation.

CONTINUING GROWTH OF MONEY MARKET FUNDS

Despite plans to phase out Reg Q interest ceilings, the migration of funds from depository institutions to MMMFs continued. Depositories still could not compete with the high rates, convenience, and liquidity offered by MMMFs. Leaders in the bank and thrift industries continued to call for freedom to develop deposit accounts that would effectively counteract the outflow of funds.

PRESSURE FOR GEOGRAPHICAL EXPANSION

DIDMCA did not address the limits on geographical expansion by banks and thrifts. But depositories' call for a level playing field included the desire to broaden geographical markets, especially as nondepository competitors moved into areas previously served primarily by depositories.

At the same time, regulators found that geographical constraints limited their ability to deal with troubled institutions. The FSLIC had begun relying more heavily on forced mergers for failing thrifts. Instead of closing a failing thrift, the FSLIC found a stronger institution with which to merge it, thereby avoiding immediate payments to insured depositors. The FSLIC had difficulty finding merger partners located near several large institutions, raising the possibility of a need for interstate mergers. The prospect of high failure rates put regulators and the industry on the same side of the geographic expansion question. In this case, it was clear that regulation had a destabilizing effect.

---

[22] In FDICIA, discount window privileges were extended to securities firms. In practice, the Fed has been reluctant to loan to any institutions but member commercial banks, and it encourages others to borrow from their primary regulators. More details are provided in Chapter 13.

[23] A discussion of the period between DIDMCA and the passage of Garn–St Germain is provided in Chapter 5 of Cargill and Garcia 1985. The material in this section draws on their analysis.

[24] The extent of the financial crisis in the S&L industry was documented in Carron 1982. Carron's predictions of high failure rates in the industry were widely quoted.

TABLE 2.5	**Provisions of the Garn-St Germain Depository Institutions Act of 1982**

Passage of G-St G was hastened by an earnings crisis in the thrift industry. The law provided for interstate acquisitions and other measures to aid regulators of failing institutions. It further deregulated thrifts' asset portfolios and expanded the types of accounts depositories could offer.

Title I: The Deposit Insurance Flexibility Act
  Gave the FDIC, FSLIC, and NCUSIF expanded options to handle failing institutions; established a priority system for emergency acquisition of insolvent depositories, permitting interstate, interindustry acquisitions as a last resort

Title II: The Net Worth Certificate Act
  Permitted the FSLIC and FDIC to issue net worth certificates to provide capital assistance to qualifying S&Ls and savings banks

Title III: The Thrift Institution Restructuring Act
  Gave federal thrifts broader investment powers, including commercial loans up to 10 percent of total assets by 1984; increased the permissible percentage of consumer loans from 20 percent to 30 percent of total assets; authorized the creation of an account directly competitive with MMMFs (later named the MMDA) for all depositories; overrode state laws preventing the enforcement of due-on-sale clauses in mortgages; permitted S&Ls to offer demand deposits to commercial loan customers; increased chartering flexibility for thrifts

Title IV: Provisions Relating to National and Member Banks
  Increased the amount that could be loaned to a single borrower; exempted small institutions from reserve requirements

Title V: Credit Union Amendments
  Streamlined the regulatory process for federal CUs; expanded CUs' real estate lending powers; increased their authority to invest in government securities

Title VI: Amendment to the Bank Holding Company Act
  Prohibited BHCs from selling or underwriting insurance

Title VII: Miscellaneous
  Authorized the issuance of NOW accounts and share drafts to state and local governments

Title VIII: The Alternative Mortgage Transaction Act of 1982
  Permitted state-chartered institutions to offer the same types of adjustable-rate mortgages authorized for federally chartered institutions, unless overridden by new state laws within 3 years

THE GARN-ST GERMAIN DEPOSITORY INSTITUTIONS ACT OF 1982

The Garn-St Germain Act became law in October 1982. In a summary of the legislation, the research staff of the Federal Reserve Bank of Chicago called G-St G "primarily a rescue operation of the S&Ls and mutual savings banks."[25] At the same time, however, it continued the deregulation of depositories and offered new alternatives for small savers. A summary is given in Table 2.5, and highlights are discussed in the following paragraphs.

[25] Several summaries of the act's provisions are available. See Federal Reserve Bank of New York, *Capsule,* Special Issue, No. 27, January 1983; Garcia 1983; and Cargill and Garcia 1985.

SOURCES OF FUNDS

G-St G allowed banks and thrifts to offer a deposit account specifically designed to compete with MMMFs. The **money market deposit account (MMDA)** had an interest rate similar to the yield on money market funds, with the advantage of FDIC, FSLIC, or NCUSIF insurance. Other provisions made NOW accounts available to a wider clientele, although not to businesses, and allowed S&Ls to offer demand deposits to corporate borrowers.

ADDITIONAL POWERS FOR BANKS AND THRIFTS

Some provisions were designed to strengthen thrift institutions. Federally chartered S&Ls were permitted to make commercial loans and to invest a larger proportion of assets in consumer loans than was allowed by DIDMCA. Thrifts were also allowed to invest in securities that were issued by state and local governments.

Garn-St Germain also gave thrifts flexibility in changing their charter and ownership form. They were permitted to convert from state to federal charter, or vice versa; to switch between S&L and savings bank charters; and to switch forms of ownership. Thrifts were also given relief from remaining limitations on adjustable-rate mortgages and were permitted to enforce due-on-sale provisions in mortgage loan contracts.[26]

EMERGENCY POWERS FOR REGULATORS

The FDIC and the FSLIC were given broad powers to assist troubled banks and thrifts. The assistance could be loans to or deposits in financially troubled institutions or the assumption or purchase of some of their assets and liabilities.

NET WORTH CERTIFICATES. The insurers were also temporarily authorized to issue a new form of support known as a **net worth certificate.** Although essentially a bookkeeping transaction, net worth certificates were intended to prevent an institution's insolvency and outright failure. The accounting rules devised by regulators in conjunction with net worth certificates conflicted with generally accepted accounting principles prescribed by the Financial Accounting Standards Board and gave rise to major controversies that plagued the financial system into the 1990s. Details are provided in Chapter 17.

ARRANGING EMERGENCY ACQUISITIONS. The FDIC, FSLIC, and federal CU regulators were authorized to arrange interstate and interindustry mergers if suitable partners could not be found within the state

and/or industry.[27] Regulators were first required to attempt to merge firms in the same industry in the same state. If a suitable partner could not be found, an out-of-state institution could be sought. If intraindustry efforts failed, regulators were to seek an acquiring firm within the same state, with an interstate, interindustry merger as the last resort. These emergency powers could be applied in the case of failing thrift institutions of any size, but only in the case of faltering commercial or savings banks with assets of more than $500 million.

1982 TO 1987: THE DIALECTIC CONTINUES

As was true of DIDMCA, Garn-St Germain left important questions either partially or completely unanswered, and there was little doubt that the cat-and-mouse game would continue. Many points of controversy between institutions and regulators and among institutions continued to percolate; major ones are summarized in this section.

REMOVAL OF GEOGRAPHIC RESTRICTIONS

Although Garn-St Germain gave the federal stamp of approval to interstate expansion in emergencies, no power was given to *healthy* institutions to broaden markets. In the years immediately after Garn-St Germain, however, state governments acted where Congress did not. In some states, legislators invited out-of-state banks to enter their borders. Other states approved reciprocal laws, allowing out-of-state banks to enter if the opportunity was reciprocated in their home states. In some areas, such as New England, the Southeast, and the Midwest, groups of states formed **regional compacts,** or reciprocal agreements among participating states.

The desire to compete in interstate markets was a strong incentive to avoid regulations. A favorite

[26] A due-on-sale clause requires the borrower to repay the mortgage loan in its entirety if the home is sold before the loan has been completely repaid. Without the clause, the new owner may be able to assume the remaining balance of the mortgage loan, without renegotiating the interest rate. S&Ls argued their need to enforce due-on-sale clauses, enabling them to get older loans made at low interest rates off the books.

[27] Actually, more than one emergency takeover had been arranged and approved before G-St G was passed. The first was an interstate acquisition of S&Ls in California, New York, and Florida. The most controversial decision, however, was to allow an interindustry acquisition in which Citicorp acquired Fidelity Federal Savings and Loan (California) in mid-1982.

strategy by depositories and nondepositories alike in the mid-1980s, discussed in more detail in Chapter 4, was to open **limited-service banks,** also known as **nonbank banks.** These firms looked and acted like banks but were sufficiently different to circumvent the regulatory and legal definitions of a bank. Although the Fed opposed nonbank banks, the courts upheld their existence. Other federal regulators took a more positive view toward nonbank banks than did the Fed, and institutions themselves were divided on the issue.

DIVERSIFICATION BY DEPOSITORY INSTITUTIONS

Commercial banks also were dissatisfied with their limited ability to compete in diversified product markets. In particular, G-S prohibitions against involvement by national banks in the securities markets were the target of bankers' ire in the light of inroads made by securities firms into banking territory. Depositories were also eager to enter the insurance business, from which they had been, for the most part, historically restricted.

At the state level, again, deregulation moved more quickly. By 1987, several states allowed state-chartered banks to sell or even to underwrite insurance. Some states allowed banks to own insurance companies, and many state-chartered banks, thrifts, and CUs engaged in brokerage activities. National banks entered the securities business through the acquisition of discount brokers in the early 1980s, followed by the Fed's authorization in 1986 of full-service brokerage for institutional customers. In the summer of 1987, the Fed permitted bank holding companies to underwrite selected debt securities under limited conditions. Nevertheless, underwriting corporate bonds and stock and offering full-service brokerage for consumers continued to elude most banks. Ironically, as depositories gained new markets in the securities industry to escape one set of regulations, the SEC attempted to expand its authority over depositories.

CRISIS IN THE THRIFT INDUSTRY: ROUND TWO

While many commercial banks concentrated their energies on lowering barriers to geographic and product expansion and rivals in the insurance and securities industry focused on keeping banks at bay, thrift institutions and their regulators were increasingly preoccupied with the second industry earnings crisis of the decade. Although the industry's sharp profitability decline before G-St G had systemic causes largely beyond the control of individual managers, the new wave of thrift insolvencies had more ominous origins. As noted in Chapter 1, some states, particularly Texas and California, had moved to allow state-chartered S&Ls to diversify their assets well beyond the guidelines established for federally chartered institutions in G-St G. Some thrift managers made bad—even fraudulent—investment decisions that drove their institutions into insolvency, straining the FSLIC's resources, already drained as a result of the crisis of the early 1980s, beyond their limits. Although about 85 percent of the institutions in the industry remained solvent—at least according to regulators' accounting rules—the magnitude of losses in the remaining 15 percent was overwhelming.

By the end of 1986, the FSLIC itself was declared insolvent by the General Accounting Office. Losses mounted daily, but the deposit insurer was unable to close troubled institutions because it either lacked the funds to pay off depositors or was unable to arrange a merger under G-St G guidelines. The Reagan administration proposed a recapitalization plan for the agency that fell far short of the insurer's real needs, but Congressional inaction on even this modest plan was the order of the day. Several prominent Congressmen had close ties with thrifts in Texas and California, blocking actions that would have allowed the FSLIC to recover fast enough to attack the real roots of the problem. To some, the situation evoked images of the Emperor Nero fiddling while Rome burned.[28]

BANK FAILURES ALSO CHALLENGE REGULATORS

Although national attention was focused primarily on the thrift crisis, the banking industry was not immune to problems. In particular, the agricultural

---

[28] Typical discussions of the situation include Martin Mayer, "S&Ls Seduce Congress—It's a Scandal," *The Wall Street Journal,* June 30, 1987, 26; John E. Yang, "Congress's Plan to Aid S&L Insurance Fund Could Aggravate Ills," *The Wall Street Journal,* July 22, 1987, 1, 15; and White 1991.

banking sector suffered severe strains in the mid-1980s; many institutions failed, and others reported record loan losses. At the same time, losses on loans to developing nations staggered some of the nation's largest banks. Most serious were the effects of economic problems in Texas, which led to the failure or near-failure of almost all the largest banks in that state, including First Republic and M Corp.

THE COMPETITIVE EQUALITY BANKING ACT OF 1987

Finally, as a result of mounting public concern about the safety of deposits, Congress passed the Competitive Equality Banking Act in August 1987. The law's provisions are summarized in Table 2.6.[29] Ironically, most experts believe it promoted anything but competition and equality.

Title I of CEBA was Congress's answer to institutions' attempts to expand geographically by forming special nonbank entities not subject to existing regulations. Although it closed the loophole in the previous legal definition of "bank" and thus prevented the formation of additional, less-regulated nonbank banks, Title I protected nonbank banks in existence before March 1987. Thus, many observers believe the law perpetuated competitive *in*equality. Similarly, Title II merely prolonged indecision on new powers for banks until at least March 1988, rather than attempting to provide a long-term resolution to the controversy. Together, these two provisions virtually guaranteed that the antithesis of the dialectic would continue after CEBA.

Title III of CEBA addressed the thrift crisis. Through special financing arrangements, it authorized the injection of nearly $11 billion of new funds into the FSLIC. Unfortunately, however, by the time CEBA was passed, most experts estimated the cost of resolving the industry's problems and restoring the FSLIC to health at between $50 billion and $100 billion. Again, it was clear that the instability in the financial system would continue virtually unabated despite CEBA's passage.

Titles IV and V merely reinforced that view. Together, they mandated continued "go slow" approaches by the regulators in their attempts to close insolvent institutions in economically troubled areas. One of the nation's most troubled areas at that time was Texas, where the thrift crisis was concentrated. Observers attributed the troubles of some Texas thrifts at least partially to mismanagement rather than solely to local economic difficulties. Yet Title IV gave many of these institutions further breathing room; its inclusion in the bill was at the insistence of then-Speaker of the House Jim Wright, who hailed from Texas.

Title VII attempted to provide some relief to agricultural banks, under the assumption that the farming economy would soon stabilize. The rest of CEBA consisted primarily of a variety of rather specific consumer-oriented provisions addressed in appropriate sections later in the book. Title IX, however, is noteworthy. Congress chose to reaffirm that the "full faith and credit" of the U.S. Treasury stood behind insured deposits. The thrift crisis had reached such alarming proportions that virtually the entire industry was experiencing sharp deposit withdrawals, threatening even healthy thrifts. Congress hoped that a renewed guarantee of deposit insurance would stem the flow.

BEYOND CEBA

In the fall of 1987, the nation's attention was temporarily diverted to the October 19 stock market crash, when the value of major stock indexes fell more than 20 percent in 1 day. All eyes turned toward the securities industry, and, for a brief time at least, depository institutions seemed pleased to point out that most had virtually no involvement in the stock market. Several commissions studied potential reform of the securities markets, continuing their work into 1988.

To no one's surprise, the March 1, 1988, moratorium on additional banking powers imposed in Title II of CEBA expired without more legislation. The stock market began to rebound slowly toward its precrash level. Shortly, in an effort to assist domestic institutions in their escalating competition with foreign banks, the Fed began to approve further securities activities for banks. By 1989, these powers included even the underwriting of small amounts of corporate bonds, an activity prohibited since 1933. The Fed promulgated strict rules on so-called **firewalls** between commercial banks and their securities units, designed to prevent potential difficulties in securities

---

[29] Details on CEBA are found in Smith and Dietz 1988; and U.S. League of Savings Institutions, *Special Management Bulletin,* S-261, October 16, 1987.

TABLE 2.6	Provisions of the Competitive Equality Banking Act of 1987

CEBA was but a short-run answer to several issues facing the financial system. It authorized additional funds to assist the FSLIC with the continuing thrift crisis, but the problem was much larger than the law recognized. CEBA also prohibited the spread of nonbank banks and temporarily postponed action on further expansion of banking powers.

Title I: Financial Institutions Competitive Equality Act
Expanded the definition of "bank" to include any institution insured by the FDIC (did not apply to 168 nonbank banks in existence on March 5, 1987); permitted nonbank banks to acquire failing savings institutions; clarified regulations applying to thrift holding companies

Title II: Moratorium on Certain Nonbanking Activities
Prohibited federal bank regulators from approving new securities, real estate, or insurance activities until March 1, 1988, beginning retroactively on March 5, 1987; brought state-chartered banks that were not members of the Fed under G-S with regard to affiliation with securities firms; limited the securities activities of thrifts until March 1, 1988, unless those activities were in place before March 5, 1987

Title III: FSLIC Recapitalization Act
Authorized the FHL Bank System to borrow up to $10.825 billion, collateralized by zero-coupon Treasury securities, to assist the FSLIC; permitted assessment of FSLIC institutions to service the authorized debt; phased out the special assessment of FSLIC-insured institutions in effect since 1985; specified circumstances under which "exit fees" could be charged to institutions departing the FSLIC; established an FSLIC oversight committee

Title IV: Thrift Industry Recovery Act
Required regulators to forbear in closing troubled savings institutions during the period in which FSLIC recapitalization occurred, provided an institution's problem could be attributed to economic conditions; required uniform, generally accepted accounting standards for commercial banks and savings institutions by 1993

Title V: Financial Institutions Emergency Acquisitions Act
Extended the net worth certificate program for 5 years; made G-St G emergency acquisition powers permanent; equalized emergency acquisition rules for commercial banks and savings institutions

Title VI: Expedited Funds Availability Act
By September 1, 1990, required depositories to make funds from local deposits available to customers within 1 business day

Title VII: Credit Union Amendments
Provided the NCUA with additional powers to regulate CUs more closely

Title VIII: Loan Loss Amortization
Instituted special provisions for banks in agricultural areas, permitting them to write off selected loan losses over an extended period

Title IX: Full Faith and Credit of Federally Insured Depository Institutions
Reaffirmed the Congress's intent to provide federal insurance for all qualifying depositors up to the legal limit

Title X: Government Checks
Required depository institutions to cash government checks for customers

Title XI: Interest to Certain Depositors
Ordered the FDIC to pay a specific rate of interest to depositors of a New York bank it had previously closed

Title XII: Miscellaneous Provisions
Mandated a study of junk bonds; required lenders to designate and disclose a cap on adjustable rate loans

operations from posing risk to the deposit insurance funds. The rules included prohibitions on sharing of facilities, staff, or marketing.[30] Alan Greenspan, Chairman of the Federal Reserve Board, asked Congress to repeal remaining G-S provisions, including those against the underwriting of corporate stock by commercial banks and against the provision of banking services by securities firms. President Bush indicated his support for similar actions, as did the Chairman of the SEC, provided that the agency was

[30] Paul Duke, Jr., "Fed Moves to Allow Banks to Underwrite Corporate Debt; Equity Powers Withheld," *The Wall Street Journal*, January 19, 1989.

given jurisdiction over the securities activities of banks.

In the absence of federal legislation, regulators in several states also moved to give resident banks additional securities, insurance, and even real estate investment powers. An FDIC study in late 1988 found, in fact, that 22 states permitted real estate development by banks, five allowed insurance underwriting, and eight sanctioned securities underwriting. Supporters of greater powers for banks used findings such as these to stress the benefits of the dual banking system.[31]

CRISIS IN THE THRIFT INDUSTRY, ROUND THREE: DOWN FOR THE COUNT?

As foreseen, the thrift crisis continued unabated after CEBA; in fact, the problems escalated. The FHLBB launched a massive new program to find buyers for troubled thrifts, requiring that the acquirers inject cash into institutions in exchange for long-term government assistance and substantial tax breaks. But nothing seemed to stem the wave of red ink. Lobbyists for the thrift industry continued to oppose solutions that would result in closing large numbers of institutions. By December 1988, the situation at the FSLIC was so desperate that the FHLBB was accused of virtually giving away thrifts to wealthy investors who stood to make millions on the deals.[32]

In February 1989, President Bush announced a plan to rescue the FSLIC and to eliminate loopholes in depository institution regulation that had permitted the abuses in the thrift industry to occur. He immediately directed the FDIC, which had substantially more resources than the FSLIC (although clearly not enough to solve the problem), to close or to merge as many insolvent thrifts as possible. Other parts of the plan,

requiring Congressional action, were delayed for several months. Meanwhile, thrift industry losses mounted at a rate exceeding $10 million per day. By the summer of 1989, the FDIC had taken over more than 200 thrifts. The cost of resolving the crisis was pegged as high as $285 billion, almost triple the highest estimate at the time of CEBA 2 years earlier and almost 30 times the amount Congress had authorized to help the FSLIC in Title I of that law.[33]

FIRREA

On August 9, 1989, after considerable bickering among Bush administration officials, the Senate, and the House of Representatives, President Bush signed FIRREA, saying, "Plenty of work lies ahead. Thank you all very much, and now I'm proud to sign this monster." Bush was actually referring to the physical size of the act, which encompassed more than 1,000 pages and was stacked a foot high in front of him.[34] Ironically, "monster" is an appropriate descriptor for many of FIRREA's provisions, which horrified most financial experts.

Table 2.7 summarizes FIRREA. Congress's intent clearly was to punish the thrift industry and the FHLBB for the insolvency of the FSLIC. At the same time, legislators chose to ignore their own role in ducking the crisis throughout the mid-1980s and failed to address what many view as the root cause of depository institutions' difficulties: a generous deposit-insurance system which was not tied to the riskiness of insured institutions. Instead of recognizing the potential risk-reduction benefits of a diversified asset portfolio, well established in finance theory, legislators turned back the "regulatory clock" to a time preceding DIDMCA.[35]

Title I summarizes the purposes the act was intended to accomplish. Title II is one of the most important provisions. It established the authority of the

[31] Robert E. Taylor, "Fed Moves to Require Bank Units to Seek Its Approval for Any Outside Businesses," *The Wall Street Journal,* November 22, 1988, A6.

[32] Details on the condition of the industry and its causes are found in Brumbaugh 1988; Kane 1989b; Dotsey and Kuprianov 1990; White 1991; and in three articles by David B. Hilder: "Insolvent S&Ls Stay Open, Losing Billions, Despite Disposal Plan," *The Wall Street Journal,* November 16, 1987, 1, 17; "Thrift-Industry Crisis May Force an Overhaul of Deposit Insurance," *The Wall Street Journal,* July 29, 1988, 1, 6; and "Are Big S&L Rescues Giveaways to Buyers? Questions Are Growing," *The Wall Street Journal,* December 30, 1988. Also informative is Jill Abramson, "S&L Mess Isn't All Bad, at Least for Lawyers Who Were Regulators," *The Wall Street Journal,* January 31, 1989, A1, A16.

[33] Paulette Thomas, "GAO Puts Cost of S&L Rescue at $285 Billion," *The Wall Street Journal,* May 22, 1989, A5.

[34] Terry Atlas, "S&L Bailout Bureaucracy Off and Running," *Chicago Tribune,* August 10, 1989, Sec. 3, 1, 2.

[35] For more details on FIRREA, see "Conference Report on H.R. 1278, Financial Institutions Reform, Recovery, and Enforcement Act, 1989," *Congressional Record—House of Representatives,* August 4, 1989; Brewer 1989; Bush and Marshall 1989; and Neuberger 1989.

TABLE 2.7	**Provisions of the Financial Institutions Reform, Recovery, and Enforcement Act of 1989**

FIRREA was passed in response to the financial crisis of the FSLIC. The law abolished existing federal thrift regulators, created a new supervisory structure, and transferred thrift deposit insurance to the FDIC. The law was viewed as being punitive toward the thrift industry and shortsighted in its failure to address more fundamental questions.

Title I: Purposes
Summarized Congressional intentions to strengthen the thrift industry through improved supervision and stricter regulatory standards, to place the FDIC on sound financial footing, and to promote a safe and stable system of affordable housing finance

Title II: Federal Deposit Insurance Corporation
Designated the FDIC (with its BIF and SAIF divisions) as the sole federal deposit insurer for banks and thrifts; restricted thrifts' junk bond and real estate investments; gave FDIC increased authority over state-chartered thrifts

Title III: Savings Associations
Created the OTS under the Department of the Treasury as the new principal thrift regulator; required thrift institutions to adhere to capital standards "no less stringent" than those of national banks; increased enforcement powers of FDIC and OTS over insolvent or *potentially* insolvent institutions; mandated uniform accounting rules for banks and thrifts; increased percentage of mortgage assets thrifts must hold to avoid stricter regulations

Title IV: Transfer of Functions, Personnel, and Property
Abolished FSLIC and FHLBB and transferred their regulatory functions to other agencies

Title V: Financing for Thrift Resolution
Created the Resolution Trust Corporation, the Resolution Funding Corporation, and the Oversight Board to dispose of insolvent thrifts

Title VI: Thrift Acquisition Enhancement Provisions
Permitted BHCs to acquire healthy thrifts

Title VII: Federal Home Loan Bank System Reforms
Created the Federal Housing Finance Board to oversee the 12 district FHL Banks; required the FHL Banks to promote "affordable housing" and community investment programs; removed all thrift supervisory authority from the FHL Banks

Title VIII: Bank Conservation Act Amendments
Clarified procedures related to bank conservatorships

Title IX: Regulatory Enforcement Authority
Stiffened penalties for depository institution managers and directors who commit fraudulent acts

Title X: Studies of Federal Deposit Insurance, Banking Services, and the Safety and Soundness of Government-Sponsored Enterprises
Mandated studies on federal deposit insurance, cost and availability of retail banking services, and capital adequacy of government-sponsored organizations

Title XI: Real Estate Appraisal Reform Amendments
Required regulators to develop and enforce minimum standards for property appraisal

Title XII: Miscellaneous Provisions
Addressed community reinvestment, CUs, consumer protection, and other matters

Title XIII: Participation by State Housing Finance Authorities and Nonprofit Entities
Permitted state agencies to buy mortgage-related assets from the Resolution Trust Corporation or FDIC

Title XIV: Tax Provisions
Lowered tax benefits to acquirers of failed or failing thrifts

FDIC over all federally insured thrifts. Although not actually merging the finances of the FSLIC and the FDIC (separate accounting is maintained by BIF and SAIF), the law consolidated the administration of federal deposit insurance and greatly increased the supervisory and enforcement powers of the FDIC.

Another section of Title II eliminated the ability of federally insured thrifts (whether federally or state chartered) to invest in junk bonds and reduced the permissible amount of commercial real estate mortgages. Unless they pass stringent tests imposed by the FDIC, state-chartered institutions are prohibited from engaging in activities barred to federally chartered thrifts. These provisions were attempts to gain better supervisory control over the riskiness of thrift assets, but many observers have noted that they also were an assault by Congress on the principle of a dual banking system.

Unhappy with the three-member FHLBB's oversight of the industry in the 1980s, Congress, in Title III, created a new thrift regulatory agency, the Office of Thrift Supervision (OTS), consisting of only one director. Political pressure exerted by Senator Jake Garn (co-author of the 1982 act) succeeded, and M. Danny Wall, the existing Chairman of the FHLBB, was named as head of the OTS. Within 6 months of the passage of FIRREA, however, Wall resigned under heavy Congressional criticism.

Another part of Title III, which increased federally insured thrifts' capital requirements by ruling that they could be "no less stringent" than those for national banks, was initially greeted more positively by observers of the thrift crisis than perhaps any provision of FIRREA. Title III also strengthened regulators' abilities to halt risky practices in thrift institutions *before* their capital is totally depleted. It became quickly apparent, however, that the phrase "no less stringent" could not be clearly interpreted, given the web of bank capital regulations in effect in 1989, as well as changes scheduled for the banking industry by 1992. Many months passed before regulators decided how to implement the new thrift capital standards. Title III also changed the so-called **qualified thrift lender (QTL)** test, used to determine whether a depository institution enjoys regulatory and tax advantages given to thrifts but not to banks. The revised QTL required thrifts to hold at least 70 percent of their portfolio assets in mortgage-related investments, reducing their abilities to diversify holdings. Amendments to FIRREA in 1991 lowered the required percentage to 65.

Title IV was a technical provision, formally abolishing the old regulatory structure and transferring its functions to the newly created structure. Title V outlined a controversial and incredibly complex plan for salvaging or liquidating the nearly 250 insolvent institutions the FDIC had acquired since early 1989, plus any subsequent insolvencies. To avoid increasing the federal deficit, Title V established an "off budget" agency **(Resolution Funding Corporation,** or **REFCORP)** to sell bonds to raise cash to meet obligations previously incurred by the FSLIC. Cash raised by REFCORP was to be transferred to the **Resolution Trust Corporation (RTC),** which was to manage the disposition of insolvencies. Repayment of REFCORP's debt is to be through a combination of Treasury borrowing (thus, taxpayer financing) and contributions from healthy members of the thrift industry. Complicating the regulatory scene was the Oversight Board, a committee consisting largely of Cabinet members and regulators, which formulates the overall strategy of the RTC and REFCORP. The FDIC was made the "exclusive manager" of the RTC's day-to-day operations, and the FDIC's Chairman was also given the title of Chairman of the RTC. (In 1991, Congress reduced somewhat the power of the FDIC Chairman when it authorized a separate Chief Executive Officer for the RTC, changed the name of the board to the Thrift Depositor Protection Oversight Board, and expanded its size to seven members.) At the time FIRREA was passed, lawmakers acknowledged that the disposition cost was sure to be about $160 billion; independent estimates were much higher. Also, many observers doubted that the solvent portion of the industry could shoulder the financial burden of its failed counterparts, suggesting that the law might actually produce more failures than would have occurred without its passage.

Commercial banks reacted positively to Title VI of FIRREA, which permitted them to acquire healthy thrifts across state lines. In another assault on duality, the Fed quickly indicated that, pursuant to FIRREA, it would entertain applications for interindustry, interstate mergers even if state laws did not provide for such combinations. Title VI thus permitted banks to enter states from which they had previously been barred by acquiring healthy thrifts, then converting an acquired institution's charter to a bank charter.

The last major provision of FIRREA, Title VII, substantially altered the role of the FHL Banks. Despite the abolition of the FHLBB, the 12 district banks remain to provide emergency loans to thrifts in their regions and to develop and administer programs for "affordable housing" and "community-oriented lending." Through these programs, the FHL Banks are to provide loans to thrifts, which in turn are to make the funds available to low- and moderate-income families to purchase homes. Yet another bureaucracy, in the form of the **Federal Housing Finance Board (FHFB),** oversees the 12 FHL Banks. The remainder of FIRREA consists of relatively minor technical provisions, identified briefly in Table 2.7.

Figure 2.1 outlines the new regulatory structure which was created by FIRREA. The simplified structure drawn in Panel A reveals that the banking industry was affected only minimally through the creation of BIF as a division of the FDIC. Panel B of Figure 2.1 reproduces the full heights that the complexity of thrift regulation reached under FIRREA. On studying this chart, the editors of *The Wall Street Journal* commented: "We doubt that we can add much to what any rational person would think of the . . . flowchart."[36] The major impact on the regulation of savings institutions is evident, however. The new OTS agency has extensive authority, and the FHL Bank system is now subordinate to the OTS with a substantially reduced sphere of influence. Deposit insurance for savings institutions is now provided by SAIF. The FHLBB and the FSLIC no longer exist.

Recall that President Bush noted, on signing FIRREA, that "plenty of work lies ahead." His comment can safely be characterized as an understatement. Even before the law was signed, little doubt existed that additional major legislation aimed at financial institutions would be necessary, because of both the solutions Congress proposed and the problems it failed to address in FIRREA. As early as January 1990, the *American Banker,* the major daily publication for the banking industry, featured the page-one headline "2d Thrift Bill Takes Shape, But Congress Is Reluctant." By April 1990, the General Accounting Office stated that the cost of the bailout would be at least $325 billion and could possibly exceed an incredible *$500 billion.* There was also mounting concern about the effects of FIRREA on the future profitability of healthy thrifts.[37]

Also overhanging the financial system were questions of commercial bank powers, international competition, and reform of the regulatory structure. FIRREA reversed some previous elements of deregulation, imposed even greater overlap in regulatory authority, and ignored important existing sources of institutions' antithetical behavior. In terms of the dialectic, it was perhaps as far from synthesis as any law could have been.

DEJÀ VU ALL OVER AGAIN

Because FIRREA failed to address comprehensively the systemic flaws in federal deposit insurance, few experts were surprised that the newly restructured FDIC almost immediately encountered problems ominously reminiscent of the FSLIC's several years earlier. A recession beginning in the summer of 1990 accelerated banks' losses from already shaky commercial real estate loans. Drowning in a sea of bad loans, some institutions tightened credit standards, resulting in widely publicized fears of a "credit crunch" under which even creditworthy borrowers might be turned away. Although many experts were skeptical that a crunch really existed, plummeting consumer confidence dried up "good" loan demand in virtually every region.

In this uncertain environment, nearly 300 commercial banks failed in 1990 and 1991, and the cost of handling the failures eroded BIF's available funds from $15 billion to almost nothing. With a host of new bank closures predicted through 1993, forecasters estimated that BIF would soon be insolvent unless new sources of cash emerged. At first, FDIC officials announced they would use their authority under FIRREA to raise insurance premiums high enough to cover anticipated needs, but experts quickly noted that such a drastic increase might be enough to drive marginal institutions into failure, defeating regulators' purpose. The Bush administration briefly toyed with selling stock in the FDIC to insured banks (and requiring banks to buy it!), but that idea fared no better, nor did a plan for a huge one-time special assessment of insured banks. Between January and May 1991, 31 bank reform bills were introduced in the U.S. Senate alone. Most addressed the deposit insurance system but also proposed additional ways of shoring up the weak banking industry, either by expanding bank powers to generate new sources of income or by loosening G-S

[36] "Uncle Sam's House Sale," *The Wall Street Journal,* February 23, 1990, A10.

[37] Robert M. Garsson, "2d Thrift Bill Takes Shape, But Congress Is Reluctant," *American Banker,* January 22, 1990, 1, 17; Garsson, "Bailout to Cost $325 Billion, GAO Reports," *American Banker,* April 9, 1990, 2.

FIGURE 2.1   **Bank and Thrift Regulatory Structure**

FIRREA resulted in major changes to the thrift regulatory structure as shown in Panel A. The OTS was created to regulate savings institutions, and deposit insurance was transferred to the SAIF of the FDIC. The FHLBB and FSLIC were abolished. Panel B identifies the true complexity of the functional relationships.

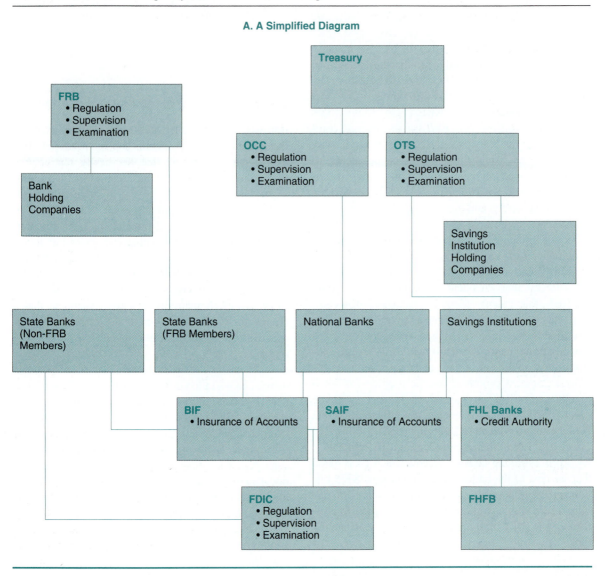

A. A Simplified Diagram

restrictions on who could and could not invest in banks.[38]

Meanwhile, the RTC, to no one's surprise, found by the fall of 1990 that the funding initially provided in FIRREA was far less than required to dispose of the

---

[38] Garcia 1991; Dean Foust, "How Deep Is the Hole?" *Business Week,* December 9, 1991, 30–32; Kenneth H. Bacon, "Administration Weighs Plan on FDIC Stock," *The Wall Street Journal,* November 28, 1990, A3; Fred R. Bleakley, "FDIC May Assess One-Time Premium if the Pace of Bank Failures Increases," *The Wall Street Journal,* November 5, 1990, A2.

FIGURE 2.1 *CONTINUED*

B. The S&L Maze

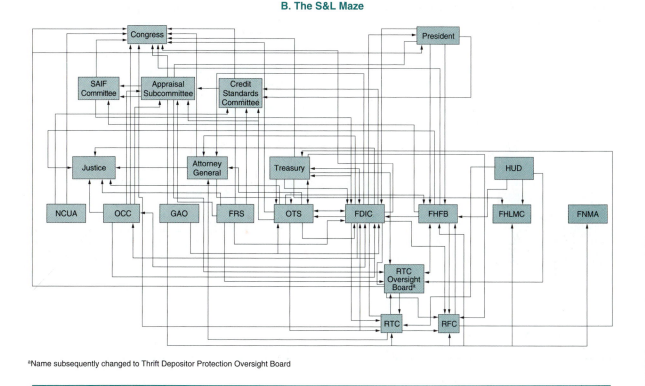

[a]Name subsequently changed to Thrift Depositor Protection Oversight Board

Source: Adapted by the authors from Ernst and Young, *Current Issues in the Financial Services Industry,* October 1989, p. 24; "The S&L Maze," *The Wall Street Journal,* February 23, 1990, A10.

assets of the many failed and failing S&Ls for which it was responsible, and its officials sought additional borrowing authority. Public outrage at the bailout continued to run high, and considerable partisan bickering between a Republican administration and a Democratic Congress, both seeking to avoid blame, delayed action for many months. But by the fall of 1991, it was clear that additional funding for the RTC was required if efforts to "clean up" the thrift industry were to continue.

FDICIA

The funding crises at BIF and the RTC served as catalysts for the next step in the regulatory dialectic, signed by President Bush on December 19, 1991. To assure

assistance to the FDIC before it formally was declared insolvent, both legislators and administration officials were forced to abandon efforts to address the more controversial issues of expanding bank powers and streamlining the regulatory structure. FIRREA had clearly shown Congress's ire at thrift regulators and especially at thrift managers. Although providing borrowing authority for the FDIC, in FDICIA Congress revealed its extreme displeasure with bank regulators by imposing unprecedented measures to restrict their judgment in evaluating institutions' safety and soundness. Although some experts, such as Professor Kane (who had long charged regulators with **"regulatory malpractice"**) welcomed many of FDICIA's provisions, others believed it went too far in prescribing actions regulators must take. Several of the rules it mandated, described only briefly in the following

TABLE 2.8 **Provisions of the Federal Deposit Insurance Corporation Improvement Act of 1991**

FDICIA was passed amidst growing concern about the financial condition of the FDIC and the problems left unattended in FIRREA. The new law imposed risk-adjusted deposit insurance premiums and detailed rules of conduct on both regulators and depositories to prevent reoccurrence of the crises of the 1980s.

Title I: Safety and Soundness
Increased the borrowing authority of the FDIC; established minimum level for the FDIC's reserves; mandated specific examination schedules for depositories and created "tripwire" system for detecting problem institutions; strengthened financial reporting rules for insured firms, including use of generally accepted accounting principles, market valuation of assets and liabilities, and complete analysis of contingent obligations; required regulators to take prompt corrective action against unsound firms; insisted that regulators resolve institution failures in the least costly manner

Title II: Regulatory Improvement [Foreign Banks and Consumer Protection]
Strengthened Fed's authority over expansion or termination of foreign banking operations in the United States; required foreign banks accepting small deposits in the United States to obtain federal deposit insurance; reduced deposit insurance premiums to institutions offering low-cost checking accounts to consumers; encouraged institutions' involvement in "distressed" communities; imposed uniform disclosure of deposit account rates and fee schedules

Title III: Regulatory Improvement [Deposit Insurance]
Limited institutions' ability to take excessive risks in attracting new deposits; mandated risk-based federal deposit insurance premiums, effective no later than January 1, 1994; unless federal regulators approve, restricted the activities of state-chartered banks to those permitted to federally chartered banks; required periodic review of regulators' minimum capital standards

Title IV: Miscellaneous Provisions
Different technical policies relating to interbank funds transfers, rights to financial privacy, the QTL test for thrifts, discount window borrowing, and real estate appraisal

Title V: Depository Institution Conversions
Changed rules under which merged institutions obtain federal deposit insurance

paragraphs and in Table 2.8, were laid out in truly microscopic detail in the text of the law. This approach contrasted with much previous financial legislation in which Congress left the determination of most policy details to regulatory agencies.[39]

In lengthy and comprehensive Title I, Congress gave the FDIC the authority to borrow up to $30 billion from the U.S. Treasury to be repaid over the 15

years after the passage of the bill. The agency was also permitted to borrow additional funds from the **Federal Financing Bank,** an established source of working capital for federal agencies, according to a formula based on the FDIC's assets. BIF may charge whatever premiums or assessments are necessary to repay its loans. Furthermore, Congress mandated that the agency's reserves must be rebuilt over the next 15 years to a level equal to 1.25 percent of insured deposits.

FDICIA established a universal examination schedule for depositories of either every 12 or every 18 months, depending on the size and condition of an institution. The tripwire system that examiners must use to determine their ratings of particular management areas also originated in FDICIA. (These provisions were discussed earlier in the chapter in the section on examinations.) Except for the very smallest, all insured institutions must have annual independent audits, the results of which must be made available to the public. Depositories must also use generally accepted accounting principles unless regulators specify even

[39] Details of FDICIA are contained in 102nd Congress, PL 102-242, "Federal Deposit Insurance Corporation Improvement Act of 1991," December 19, 1991. Further discussion can be found in "Summary of Federal Legislation," *Banking Legislation and Policy* (Federal Reserve Bank of Philadelphia), 10 (October–December 1991), 1–4; Muckenfuss et al. 1992; Kenneth H. Bacon, "The New Banking Law Toughens Regulation, Some Say Too Much," *The Wall Street Journal,* November 29, 1991; Alan Greenspan, "Putting FDICIA in Perspective," remarks at the 1992 Conference on Bank Structure and Competition, Federal Reserve Bank of Chicago, May 7, 1992. Updated information on regulatory revisions and the implementation of FDICIA provisions may be found in "Recent Developments Affecting Financial Institutions," a regular feature of the *FDIC Banking Review.*

more conservative reporting methods. The intent of this provision was to eliminate potentially deceptive practices, such as the net worth certificates permitted in the Garn-St Germain Act. Congress also required regulators to develop new accounting standards in several controversial areas, including disclosure of the market value of assets and liabilities and full reporting of obligations that have traditionally not appeared on a firm's balance sheet. These requirements are discussed in greater detail at several points later in the book. Many analysts believe the considerable attention FDICIA paid to accounting practices came at the urging of officials in the General Accounting Office, frequent critics of regulators in the 1980s.

In a provision some observers, including Federal Reserve Chairman Alan Greenspan, called "micromanagement" by Congress, FDICIA required regulators to classify institutions according to a combination of their CAMEL or MACRO ratings and their capital-to-assets ratios. Any depository that does not meet minimum capital requirements must provide regulators with a plan to bring net worth up to standards, and regulators must impose a variety of operating restrictions on such institutions. Regulators also must take drastic immediate action against depositories with very low capital ratios or low CAMEL or MACRO ratings, including limiting the ability of these institutions to borrow from the Fed to stay afloat. These provisions are described in more detail in Chapter 17. This group of **prompt corrective action (PCA)** provisions, which stripped regulators of much of the customary discretion they used in handling troubled financial institutions, were widely perceived as punishment for excessive and costly forbearance by regulators throughout the 1980s. It is interesting to note that many of the forbearance procedures had been mandated by Congress itself in G-St G and CEBA.

Title I also required regulators to choose the least costly method for resolving depository institution failures. They may not, however, keep insolvent institutions artificially alive to reduce FDIC costs in the short run. As of 1995, regulators may no longer protect uninsured deposits to avoid the failure of large institutions, bringing to an end the controversial 1980s policy that held that some institutions are **"too big to fail."** Still, at the urging of regulators, Congress permitted exceptions to the new rule if regulators and the President agree that uninsured depositors must be protected

in a given situation to prevent the failure of other institutions (the **"systemic risk" exception**).

Unlike FIRREA, which focused solely on domestically chartered institutions, Title II of FDICIA addressed supervision of foreign banks operating in the United States. The Fed was given increased powers to approve or deny their entrance and expansion and was also given greater authority to terminate their operations. According to FDICIA, foreign banks that are not subject to comprehensive examination and supervision by home country regulators may not operate in the United States. Although existing foreign banks were exempted, Congress required new foreign banks that accept deposits of $100,000 or less to obtain federal deposit insurance. These provisions were reactions to the 1991 **Bank of Credit and Commerce International (BCCI)** scandal in which thousands of small depositors worldwide lost nearly $20 billion as a result of egregious fraud and mismanagement. (Because BCCI offices in the United States did not accept deposits, U.S. depositors were spared losses in the crisis.)[40]

Although most of FDICIA was intended to tighten supervision of institutions to prevent future collapses of the deposit insurance system, a few provisions in Title II were directed at consumer protection. Noteworthy is the **truth-in-savings** provision. Just as all institutions must inform borrowers of their credit costs on a comparable basis to facilitate "shopping" for credit, they must now provide uniform comparative information on deposit rates for savers. The law provided special benefits to institutions that offer inexpensive deposit accounts for low-income customers and encouraged lending to households and businesses in communities that are experiencing economic distress.

Title III contained additional specific directives to reduce risk to the deposit insurance system. Insured institutions were prohibited from paying excessive interest rates or engaging in risky and aggressive programs to attract new deposits, practices many believe contributed to the thrift debacle. In a major departure

---

[40] The worldwide regulatory nightmares created by the BCCI scandal are discussed in David Lascelles et al., *Behind Closed Doors,* London: The Financial Times, 1991; and Statements to Congress by J. Virgil Mattingly, Jr., William Taylor, and E. Gerald Corrigan, *Federal Reserve Bulletin* 78 (November 1991): 902–920.

from historical practice, Congress required regulators to develop a system of risk-based deposit insurance, not merely to study the issue once again. The new system, effective January 1, 1994, is discussed fully in Chapter 16.

Erosion of the dual banking principle, clearly a part of FIRREA, continued in FDICIA, as Congress decided that state-chartered commercial banks may not engage in any activities prohibited to national banks without specific FDIC approval. In response to pressure on Congress from the insurance industry, especially noteworthy was the Title III provision rolling back, with selected exceptions, banks' hard-won permission to underwrite insurance in several states.

As is usual in such legislation, Title IV of FDICIA contained a number of technical provisions addressing smaller, more specialized problems. Of interest to thrift managers was one addressing the QTL test. Recall that FIRREA required thrifts to hold a larger proportion of mortgage-related assets than both DIDMCA and G-St G had permitted. FDICIA reduced the proportion somewhat (from 70 to 65 percent) but did not return it to pre-1989 levels. However, the new law made it easier for thrifts to meet the QTL test by broadening the definition of mortgage-related investments. The percentage of total assets thrifts may devote to consumer loans was increased to 35 percent. Title IV also permitted the Fed to provide discount window loans to nonbanking firms, including securities firms. Ordinarily, however, nonbank borrowers should have exhausted all other sources of funds before coming to the Fed.

The fifth and last title of FDICIA ended the string of legislation begun in G-St G by removing restrictions on bank and thrift mergers that remained after FIRREA. Now any bank or thrift may acquire or be acquired by any other bank or thrift, regardless of charter type or financial condition, provided the merger or acquisition complies with other merger laws and regulations.

RTC REFINANCING, RESTRUCTURING, AND IMPROVEMENT

In a companion piece of minor legislation passed almost simultaneously to FDICIA, Congress both ap-

propriated $25 billion in additional funds for the RTC (an amount that later proved to be insufficient) and increased the agency's borrowing authority. As noted earlier, the structures of the OTS and the RTC, originally established in FIRREA, were changed slightly.

THE IMPOSSIBLE DREAM: A LAW IN PURSUIT OF THE LAST LOOPHOLE

Readers may recall the opening quotation to this chapter, in which a prominent banker suggested that financial regulation in the United States was moving in the heavy-handed direction followed for many years in the former Soviet Union. These remarks were, in fact, that banker's response to the detailed scrutiny of institutions and regulators Congress imposed in FDICIA. Many of the law's most sweeping provisions were not effective until months or even years after FDICIA was passed, so it is too soon to know whether Congress's aim to close virtually all remaining loopholes in the deposit insurance system has succeeded. By the beginning of 1993, however, writers for the *American Banker* had already dubbed FDICIA the "red tape act." They noted that bankers had changed their legislative priorities from securing new powers to rolling back the regulatory taxes FDICIA imposed. Students of the regulatory dialectic understand that, no matter how many existing doors may be closed by one law, financial and technological innovations are busy opening others.

CONTINUING REGULATORY CONCERNS

No matter how much legislation had been passed since 1980, the pressure for additional changes will remain. While regulated institutions push for freedom to compete, regulators and lawmakers are still concerned about safety and soundness and about overlapping regulatory authority.

As both FIRREA and FDICIA underscore, the gradual removal of some restrictions for depository and other financial institutions does not imply that government officials believe in complete deregulation. Instead, efforts are directed toward increasing the effectiveness and fairness of regulation. Regulators are also sometimes mindful of the possibility that regulations may actually increase rather than decrease risk.

MEASURING RISK

Risk-based deposit insurance and risk-based capital requirements, both products of recent legislation, mean that regulators must be able to reduce a complex set of financial characteristics to a small number of categories into which institutions can be slotted. Sharp disagreements continue between regulators and industry personnel and among regulators themselves on the most appropriate techniques for quantifying risk. These debates will undoubtedly flourish in the 1990s.

SECURITIZATION. Many intermediaries have turned from a buy-and-hold management strategy, in which they collect funds from customers, then invest them in financial assets held until maturity. Instead, institutions seek flexibility to sell financial assets to other investors should operating needs or economic conditions dictate a change in strategy. Although some financial assets, such as stocks, bonds, and mortgages, have well-developed resale markets, others, such as consumer and commercial loans, have not until very recently. **Securitization** is the name given to attempts by financial institutions to create new securities suitable for resale out of assets that would otherwise be held to maturity. As these markets emerge, institutions are exposed to new kinds of risks. Securitization is explored in Chapter 19.

IMPACT OF TECHNOLOGY. The risks to which institutions are exposed change as technology changes. Traditional examinations of the safety and soundness of financial institutions focus on balance sheets and income statements, as well as on subjective assessments of the quality of management. Technology enables institutions to enter and leave financial markets virtually instantaneously, assuming risks on a given day that may never appear on a balance sheet or arise in an examiner's conversation with a manager. The pace and sophistication of technological change now challenge managers' and regulators' abilities to understand, much less to control, the level of risk to which institutions are exposed. Some experts believe that measuring and controlling the risks posed by technology are the most difficult problems facing regulators of financial institutions today.[41]

CONTINGENT LIABILITIES. Besides instantaneous risks posed by technology, institutions are exposed to ongoing risks not reported in accounting records. For example, some institutions offer as regular services advance commitments to lend or to pay the debts of customers who go into default. These **contingent liabilities,** sometimes called **off–balance sheet items** because they have not traditionally appeared in financial statements, may or may not require cash outflows from the institution. Under pre-FDICIA accounting rules, these items were not reported as obligations on the balance sheet. Because some institutions have billions of dollars of contingent liabilities, they were of growing concern to regulators. A first step was taken in the late 1980s with the **Basle Accord,** which explicitly considers off–balance sheet items in the determination of required capital. The Basle Accord was a major effort by regulators from 12 Western nations to coordinate their policies. The agreement established capital requirements based on the risk of individual institutions and is discussed in detail later in this book. FDICIA went further by requiring regulators and accountants to develop specific methods for reporting contingent liabilities. The law stopped short, however, of setting limits on their use. Other complexities remain to be addressed, as discussed in Chapters 17 and 22.

GLOBALIZATION OF FINANCIAL MARKETS

At several points earlier in the chapter, increasing international competition among financial institutions has been stressed. U.S. institutions now operate around the world, just as do foreign firms. Managers must understand exchange rate fluctuations, interest rate differentials among countries, international supervisory agencies, and the varying cultural attitudes toward banking and financial management that they may encounter in the course of routine business. These and

[41] For more discussion of these points, see Goodman 1986 and Corrigan 1986.

other facets of the global financial markets are discussed throughout the text. Regulators, too, must consider the effect of new policies abroad as well as at home. The importance of international policy coordination is so great, in fact, that it is addressed in more detail in the next chapter.

RENEWED EMPHASIS ON BUSINESS ETHICS

The public did not ignore headlines of scandal and greed in financial institutions during the late 1980s. Even the seemingly invincible—Michael Milken, until 1988 a kingpin at Drexel Burnham Lambert (a prominent securities firm), and Jim Wright, Speaker of the House of Representatives until the summer of 1989—were brought down by charges of unethical financial dealings, and scores of lesser-known thrift, insurance, and securities industry personnel were accused of fraud. In 1992, former Secretary of Defense Clark Clifford was indicted in connection with the BCCI scandal. These examples by no means exhaust the list of managers, regulators, and politicians whose behavior has been called into question since 1985. There is little doubt that new standards of conduct and integrity will be expected of future managers, and policies and procedures of institutions and regulators will, in turn, be affected.

CHANGES IN THE REGULATORY STRUCTURE

Events of recent years suggest that reform of the regulatory system itself cannot be ignored. The most obvious indicator is the risk posed to the current structure by perpetuating the weaknesses of the deposit insurance system, despite considerable attention from Congress since 1987. Events have also led to calls for regulatory reform in the insurance, pension fund, and securities industries. The globalization of financial markets, technological developments, and renewed emphasis on ethical behavior affect not only the substance of regulations but also how and by whom they are administered.

As suggested in earlier sections, another factor driving the need for regulatory reform is the substantial economic burden of maintaining the current complex, duplicative supervisory structure. For example, a

1992 study by the Federal Financial Institutions Examination Council estimated the cost to the banking and thrift industries of complying with pre-FDICIA regulation averaged between $7.5 billion and $17 billion per year. Because FDICIA increased regulatory taxes as much as any financial legislation in recent years, this cost can only accelerate as all its provisions take effect. Whether institutions' resources are best put to such uses, or whether opportunities for more productive resource allocation can and should be provided, are questions Congress must consider in this decade.[42]

Finally, an important issue facing regulators and managers is whether some institutions in the increasingly global and deregulated environment perform a unique economic role that no other institution can play: The question "Are banks special?" is often posed. If the consensus answer is yes, a structure that treats banks differently from other institutions will continue. If the answer is no, a more integrated regulatory structure is likely.

Thus, the stage is set for another chapter of the regulatory dialectic, as old rules meet new forms of regulatory avoidance, financial and technological innovations, and economic change. In turn, a new antithesis will arise, and a new synthesis will follow as financial institutions move into the twenty-first century.

SUMMARY

Financial institutions have historically been tightly regulated, although specific rules evolve as part of the regulatory dialectic. According to this concept, regulators articulate a set of regulations and the rationale (thesis); regulated firms respond by attempting to avoid regulations (antithesis); and a new set of regulations emerges (synthesis) as a result of these actions. In the course of the dialectic, financial innovation and technical and economic change exert strong influences on the outcome. The dialectic has been especially evident in recent years.

Depository institutions have received the most attention from regulators. Over the years, a dual regu-

---

[42] Kenneth H. Bacon, "Rules Cost Banks, Thrifts $7.5 to $17 Billion Annually, Panel Says," *The Wall Street Journal,* December 16, 1992, A2.

latory structure at the state and federal levels has emerged. Although repeated concern has been expressed about overlapping authority, Congress has not yet enacted any proposals to simplify the bureaucracy. Nondepository institutions are also regulated, but to a lesser extent. Most regulations governing finance companies are established at the state level and are less complex than those for depositories. Insurance companies are also governed by state regulators, and the scope of regulation is substantial. Pension funds, investment companies, and securities firms are regulated by major federal statutes and by states.

The two most important regulatory reforms in the early 1980s were DIDMCA and G-St G. These laws removed some restrictions on depositories' asset choices and on their sources of funds and increased similarity in the regulation of banks, thrifts, and credit unions. Regulators were also given more flexibility to handle failing institutions.

Almost immediately, however, forces for additional change were at work, spurred by the crisis in the thrift industry. In 1987, CEBA was passed, but it proved to be "too little, too late" to rescue the ailing FSLIC and served only to postpone more drastic action until 1989. FIRREA, passed in 1989, was a punitive law that did little to solve the systemic problems of deposit insurance and failed to address the question of appropriate bank powers. In 1991, FDICIA attempted to reform the deposit insurance system, reign in risk-taking behavior of depository institution managers, and require regulators to be more aggressive in enforcing restrictions. Congress, however, once against avoided important decisions on bank powers and regulatory restructuring. Current issues include continued diversification of depository institutions' operations; better ways of measuring and controlling the risks taken by financial institutions, including the impact of securitization and contingent liabilities; reform of the regulatory structure; the regulation of institutions with international operations; and the renewed emphasis on ethical behavior. Only one thing is certain: Change is inevitable.

QUESTIONS

1. Explain in your own words the meaning of the "regulatory dialectic." Describe the three stages of the dialectic, and provide a historical example of each. Using current publications, identify a recent regulatory decision and explain the reaction of financial institutions to it.

2. Explain regulatory avoidance. In your opinion, what is currently the most restrictive regulation placed on commercial banks? Find a recent example of the reaction of a member of the banking industry to this restriction.

3. How is the process of financial innovation linked to regulation and the regulatory dialectic? Give an example of a recent financial innovation, and explain whether the incentive for its development is traced to regulatory avoidance, new technology, economic conditions, or other causes.

4. From Table 2.2, choose a recent financial innovation. How are developments in the economic/political environment related to the innovation? In general, how would you characterize economic and technological conditions that are conducive to financial innovation?

5. Based on emerging technology, economic conditions, and forecasts for the rest of the 1990s, do you predict numerous or few financial innovations in this decade? Explain.

6. Do you agree with Professor Kane's opinion that the goals and objectives of legislators and financial institution regulators changed in the 1960s and 1970s from safety and soundness to limiting competition? Why or why not? How would you characterize the intent of legislators and regulators as demonstrated in FIRREA and FDICIA?

7. During the 1980s, significant progress was made toward easing the regulatory burden of financial institutions. Discuss the rationale for revising regulations, many of which had their origin in the post-depression years.

8. A noted columnist in *The Wall Street Journal* recently wrote, "Banks . . . like to shop around for the best regulation." Discuss the regulatory structure for commercial banks and thrifts in this context. What purpose does each regulator serve? In your opinion, does there appear to be unnecessary duplication or overlap? Why or why not?

9. What explanations can you offer for the long-standing tradition of concentrating insurance regulation at the state rather than at the federal level? Do you believe other industries, such as banks, pension funds, or investment companies, could be effectively regulated only by the states?

10. Explain the impact of the McCarran-Ferguson Act on insurance pricing and the application of antitrust legislation to insurers. How did California's Proposition 103 present a challenge to the spirit of the McCarran-Ferguson law?

11. Briefly discuss the safeguards for employees included in the Employee Retirement Income Security Act (ERISA). What is the role of the Pension Benefit Guaranty Corporation (PBGC)?

12. Provide several examples of the types of regulations imposed on investment companies to control the risk exposure of shareholders.

13. In the 1970s and 1980s, Congress created regulatory safeguards to supplement the self-regulation already existing in the securities industry. What motivated these laws, and how did they restrict the activities of securities firms? What is insider trading, and what was its importance in the 1980s?

14. In the late 1980s and early 1990s, two prominent securities firms—Drexel Burnham Lambert and Salomon Brothers—were involved in financial scandals. Find a newspaper or journal article analyzing one of these incidents. Do you anticipate a need for further legislation affecting the securities industry? Why?

15. Give an example of a regulatory restriction that hindered depository institutions' responses to changes in economic or technological developments in the 1980s.

16. Explain how DIDMCA and Garn-St Germain changed asset and deposit management in depository institutions.

17. Explain the events and conditions that led to the creation of Garn-St Germain and CEBA. How did the deterioration in the financial condition of the thrift industry and the FSLIC serve as an incentive for rapid Congressional action?

18. Both Garn-St Germain and CEBA included provisions responding to the financial difficulties in the bank and thrift industries. Briefly summarize the powers given to regulators to assist troubled institutions. In retrospect, were these provisions appropriate courses of action? Why or why not?

19. Many observers viewed the CEBA provisions on nonbank banks and nonbanking activities of commercial banks as a reversal of the trend toward deregulation. Briefly explain these points of the legislation. Do you believe they conflicted with the direction set in DIDMCA and Garn-St Germain? Why or why not? How may they have contributed to the regulatory dialectic?

20. Explain the regulatory structure created in FIRREA to replace the supervisory and insurance functions of the FHLBB and FSLIC. What are the advantages and disadvantages of this new structure?

21. What is the QTL test as revised by FIRREA (and again by FDICIA)? How does this requirement affect a thrift's ability to diversify its portfolio? What are the potential consequences on an institution's riskiness?

22. Some observers believe that FIRREA may have created more problems than it resolved. Choose an area of depository institution regulation that you believe has been negatively affected by FIRREA, and explain why. In your opinion, what was FIRREA's wisest provision? Why?

23. What developments, beginning almost immediately after FIRREA, prompted the passage of FDICIA? Do you believe FDICIA responded adequately? Why or why not?

24. What are CAMEL and MACRO ratings? How are they used in evaluating depository institutions? Explain how FDICIA's tripwires strengthen the examiners' hands.

25. Regulations are the rules under which financial institutions may operate, while supervision determines enforcement of those rules. Do you attribute the deposit insurance crisis primarily to shortcomings in regulations or supervision? Explain.

26. Explain FDICIA's Prompt Corrective Action (PCA) provision. Why did Congress consider such a measure to be necessary?

27. Do you believe different policies should be applied to large versus small institutions that are failing? Why?

28. Some provisions in FDICIA were intended to solve permanently the financial problems of the deposit insurance system. What measures did Congress enact for this purpose?

29. Choose two of the areas of continuing regulatory concern discussed in the last part of the chapter. Which one of these issues do you think will precipitate the next major congressional action? Using current publications, find a reference to or discussion of these issues by a legislator, regulator, or practitioner.

30. Define the following terms:
   - dual banking system
   - regulatory avoidance
   - usury ceilings
   - vested benefits
   - conduit theory of taxation
   - disintermediation
   - cross-intermediation
   - electronic funds transfers
   - "level playing field"
   - securitization
   - firewalls
   - Federal Financial Institutions Examination Council (FFIEC)
   - regulatory taxes
   - Basle Accord
   - tripwires
   - contingent liabilities

SELECTED REFERENCES

Brewer, Elijah, III. "Full-Blown Crisis, Half-Measure Cure," *Economic Perspectives* (Federal Reserve Bank of Chicago) 13 (November/December 1989): 2–17.

Broaddus, Alfred. "Financial Innovation in the United States—Background, Current Status and Prospects." *Economic Review* (Federal Reserve Bank of Richmond) 71 (January/February 1985): 2–22.

Brock, Bronwyn, "Regulatory Changes Bring New Challenges to S&Ls, Other Depository Institutions." *Voice* (Federal Reserve Bank of Dallas) (September 1980): 5–9.

Brumbaugh, R. Dan, Jr. *Thrifts Under Siege.* Cambridge, MA: Ballinger Publishing Company, 1988.

Bush, Vanessa, and Katherine Marshall. "The Law: The Business Reviews a New Script." *Savings Institutions* 110 (October 1989): 30–35.

Cargill, Thomas F., and Gillian Garcia. *Financial Reform in the 1980s.* Stanford, CA: Hoover Institution Press, 1985.

Carron, Andrew S. *The Plight of the Thrift Institutions.* Washington, DC: The Brookings Institution, 1982.

"Conference Report on H.R. 1278, Financial Institutions Reform, Recovery, and Enforcement Act, 1989." *Congressional Record—House of Representatives,* August 4, 1989.

Corrigan, E. Gerald. "Bank Supervision in a Changing Financial Environment." *Quarterly Review* (Federal Reserve Bank of New York) 10 (Winter 1985–1986): 1–5.

"The Depository Institutions Deregulation and Monetary Control Act of 1980." *Economic Perspectives* (Federal Reserve Bank of Chicago) 4 (September/October 1980): 3–23.

Dotsey, Michael, and Anatoli Kuprianov. "Reforming Deposit Insurance: Lessons from the Savings and Loan Crisis." *Economic Review* (Federal Reserve Bank of Richmond) 76 (March/April 1990): 3–28.

Finnerty, John D. "Financial Engineering in Corporate Finance: An Overview." *Financial Management* 17 (Winter 1988), 14–33.

Flood, Mark D. "Two Faces of Financial Innovations." *Review* (Federal Reserve Bank of St. Louis) 74 (September/October 1992): 3–17.

Garcia, Gillian. "The Condition of the Bank Insurance Fund: A View from Washington." In *Proceedings from a Conference on Bank Structure and Competition.* Chicago: Federal Reserve Bank of Chicago, 1991: 50–69.

Garcia, Gillian, et al. "The Garn-St Germain Depository Institutions Act of 1982," *Economic Perspectives* (Federal Reserve Bank of Chicago) 7 (March–April 1983): 2–31.

Germany, J. David, and John E. Morton, "Financial Innovation and Deregulation in Foreign Industrial Countries." *Federal Reserve Bulletin* 71 (October 1985): 743–753.

Gilbert, Gary G. "An Analysis of the Bush Task Group Recommendations for Regulatory Reform." *Issues in Bank Regulation* 7 (Spring 1984): 11–16.

Gilbert, R. Alton. "Requiem for Regulation Q: What It Did and Why It Passed Away." *Review* (Federal Reserve Bank of St. Louis) 68 (February 1986): 22–37.

———. "A Comparison of Proposals to Restructure the Financial System." *Review* (Federal Reserve Bank of St. Louis) 70 (July/August 1988): 58–73.

Goodman, Laurie S. "The Interface between Technology and Regulation in Banking." In *Technology and the Regulation of Financial Markets,* edited by Anthony Saunders and Lawrence J. White, 181–186. Lexington, MA: DC Heath and Co., 1986.

Gorton, Gary, and George Pennacchi. "Nonbanks and the Future of Banking." *Proceedings of a Conference on Bank Structure and Competition.* Chicago: Federal Reserve Bank of Chicago, 1992.

Greenspan, Alan. "An Overview of Financial Restructuring." *The Financial Services Industry in the Year 2000.* Chicago: Federal Reserve Bank of Chicago, 1988: 3–9.

Harrington, Scott. "The Impact of Rate Regulation on Prices and Underwriting Results in the Property-Liability Insurance Industry: A Survey." *Journal of Risk and Insurance* 51 (December 1984): 577–623.

Johnson, Verle B. "Reorganization?" *Weekly Letter* (Federal Reserve Bank of San Francisco), March 2, 1984.

Kane, Edward J. "Good Intentions and Unintended Evil: The Case Against Selective Credit Allocation." *Journal of Money, Credit, and Banking* 9 (February 1977): 55–69.

———. "Accelerating Inflation, Technological Innovation, and the Decreasing Effectiveness of Banking Regulation." *Journal of Finance* 36 (May 1981): 355–367.

———. "Technology and the Regulation of Financial Markets." In *Technology and the Regulation of Financial Markets,* edited by Anthony Saunders and Lawrence J. White, 187–193. Lexington, MA: DC Heath and Co., 1986.

———. "Changing Incentives Facing Financial-Services Regulators." *Journal of Financial Services Research* 2 (1989a): 265–274.

———. *The S&L Insurance Mess: How Did It Happen?* Washington, DC: The Urban Institute Press, 1989b.

Kelley, Michael C., and Frederick T. Furlong. "Bank Regulation and the Public Interest." *Economic Review* (Federal Reserve Bank of San Francisco) (Spring 1986): 55–71.

Kopcke, Richard W., and Richard E. Randall, Ed. *The Financial Condition and Regulation of Insurance Companies.* Boston: Federal Reserve Bank of Boston, 1991.

Lash, Nicholas. *Banking Laws and Regulations.* Englewood Cliffs, NJ: Prentice-Hall, 1987.

Martin, Preston, and Bryon Higgins. "The World Financial Scene: Balancing Risks and Rewards." *Economic Review* (Federal Reserve Bank of Kansas City) 71 (June 1986): 3–9.

Miller, Merton H. "Financial Innovation: The Last Twenty Years and the Next." *Journal of Financial and Quantitative Analysis* 21 (December 1986): 459–471.

Muckenfuss, Cantwell F., III, Robert C. Eager, and Clark H. Nielsen. "The Federal Deposit Insurance Corporation Improvement Act of 1991." *Bank Management* (January 1992), 37–44.

Myers, Forest, and Catharine Lemieux. "Three Decades of Banking." *Annual Banking Studies* (Federal Reserve Bank of Kansas City) (1991): 1–27.

Neuberger, Jonathon. "FIRREA and Deposit Insurance Reform," *Weekly Letter* (Federal Reserve Bank of San Francisco), December 1, 1989.

Rhoades, Stephen A., and Donald T. Savage. "Controlling Nationwide Concentration under Interstate Banking." *Issues in Bank Regulation* 9 (Autumn 1985): 34–40.

Selden, Richard T. "Consumer-Oriented Intermediaries." In *Financial Institutions and Markets,* 2d ed., edited by Murray E. Polakoff and Thomas A. Durkin, 207–212. Boston: Houghton Mifflin, 1981.

Sellon, Gordon H., Jr. "Restructuring the Financial System: Summary of the Bank's 1987 Symposium." *Economic Review* (Federal Reserve Bank of Kansas City) 73 (January 1988): 17–28.

Shull, Bernard. "Economic Efficiency, Public Regulation, and Financial Reform: Depository Institutions." In *Financial Institutions and Markets,* 2d ed., edited by Murray E. Polakoff and Thomas A. Durkin, 671–702. Boston: Houghton Mifflin, 1981.

Silber, William. "The Process of Financial Innovation." *American Economic Review* 73 (May 1983): 89–95.

Smith, Brian W., and Phyllis P. Dietz, "The Competitive Equality Banking Act: What's in a Name." *The Bankers Magazine* 171 (January–February 1988): 18–23.

Spong, Kenneth. *Banking Regulation: Its Purposes, Implementation, and Effects.* 3d ed. Kansas City: Federal Reserve Bank of Kansas City, 1990.

Van Horne, James C. "Of Financial Innovations and Excesses." *Journal of Finance* 40 (July 1985): 621–631.

West, Robert Craig. "The Depository Institutions Deregulation Act of 1980: A Historical Perspective." *Economic Review* (Federal Reserve Bank of Kansas City) 67 (February 1982): 3–13.

White, Lawrence J. *The S&L Debacle.* New York: Oxford University Press, 1991.

*For years, the secrecy surrounding the [Federal Reserve's] meetings
has only served to give rise to a rumor-and-leak industry
that benefits certain market players over others.*
Congressman Henry Gonzales (1992)

CHAPTER

3

THE FEDERAL
RESERVE
SYSTEM AND
INTERNATIONAL
POLICY
COORDINATION

In early 1989, members of the United Auto Workers received a
pamphlet distributed by the union to express its dismay with the Federal
Reserve System (Fed). The Fed had recently announced a campaign to
fight potential inflation by increasing interest rates. A cartoon showed a
wealthy capitalist poring over the financial pages. "The money market
is up! Again!" said he to his expensively dressed wife. "Now we can
afford that Mercedes! Thanks a *million,* Alan Greenspan!"

It is unlikely that the Chairman of the Board of Governors of the
Fed, to whom the cartoon referred, was amused. But it and similar barbs
may eventually get his attention. In 1992, for example, Fed officials
briefly considered the possibility that their most closely scrutinized gath-
erings could be videotaped and made available to the public. The Fed's
critics quickly endorsed the idea, saying it was a step in the right direction. But Fed officials later decided that such a plan would constrain the
"free flow" of ideas and determined to maintain their policy of releas-
ing only summaries of their meetings. As the quote from Representative
Gonzales suggests, Fed officials routinely are the targets of public criticism for allegedly favoring one segment of society or one political interest group over another. Professional "Fed watchers" attempt to divine
the future direction of interest rates—and thus the best management
strategies for institutions to follow—from even the seemingly most
inconsequential remarks by the Chairman. Why does such an august
institution have such a controversial yet influential role? The purpose of
this chapter is to answer that question by exploring the Fed beyond the
supervisory and regulatory functions discussed in Chapter 2. In particular, the focus is on the Fed's role as a lender of last resort, guardian of
the nation's payments system, architect of monetary policy, and a major
participant in the international regulatory scene. Amidst the rapid technological and economic changes in the last decade, the Fed's place in
the financial environment has become even more important, and it will
undoubtedly increase as globalization of financial markets progresses.[1]

---

[1] Alan Murray and Tom Herman, "Why the Fed's Efforts to Forestall Inflation Have Thus Far
Failed," *The Wall Street Journal,* March 29, 1989, A1, A8; and Claudia Cummins, "House
Panel Scrutinizing Minutes of Fed's District Bank Meetings," *American Banker,* November 3,
1992, 2; Bart Fraust, "Fed's Secrecy Comes Under More Scrutiny," *American Banker,* July
26, 1993, 1, 16.

WHY THE FED?

Although the nation is well into its third century, the Fed only recently celebrated its seventy-fifth anniversary, having been created in a law signed by President Woodrow Wilson on December 23, 1913. Thus, for most of its history, this country operated without such an organization.[2] Yet few managers envision a future without the Fed. Clearly, then, inadequacies existed in the financial system before 1913 that the Fed has addressed successfully, even if not to everyone's complete satisfaction.

A BRIEF HISTORY OF PRE-FED DAYS

Historians identify the most important recurring and interrelated financial problems plaguing the nation before the Fed as 1) an unsatisfactory currency, 2) a deficient payments system for transferring funds from one party to another, and 3) periodic panics that led to the failure of large numbers of banks.[3] Resolving each of these problems was an important objective to the framers of the Federal Reserve Act.

THE MONEY SUPPLY PROBLEM. As noted in the previous chapter, the National Currency Act of 1863 and the National Banking Act of 1864 attempted to solve problems created by lack of a uniform currency by authorizing the formation of federally chartered banks that could issue national bank notes. To promote the public's confidence in accepting them as legal tender for transactions, national bank notes had to be collateralized by U.S. government securities. In the decades to follow, the U.S. Treasury also issued a fixed quantity of paper money, backed by gold and silver.

Although this system clearly improved confidence in paper money, promoted growth in the number and size of financial transactions, and encouraged interstate commerce, problems remained. The number of Treasury notes outstanding was tied directly to gold and silver reserves, and the number of national bank notes was tied to the volume of Treasury securities outstanding. Thus, such a currency was *inelastic;* the volume available was incapable of changing spontaneously as the economy changed.

THE PAYMENTS PROBLEM. Additional pre-Fed difficulties related to a lack of confidence in the nation's payments system. Not only do people require assurances that money used to conduct transactions has value, they also must know that they can rely on financial institutions to transfer funds from one party to another efficiently, honestly, and reasonably quickly. Without a strong authority to enforce minimum levels, some banks did not keep enough reserves to cover customers' withdrawals, and others failed to provide for effective, fairly priced methods of clearing checks.

THE "PANIC" PROBLEM. Economic cycles, coupled with unsettling questions about the value of currency, whether there was enough of it, and whether funds transfers would be carried out as promised, led to periodic financial panics. At these times, banks failed when they were unable to meet withdrawals on demand. The failure of some banks created a drain on others, causing them to fail as well.

The Bank of England successfully served its homeland as a **lender of last resort**—a central bank that could and would supply liquidity to other banks in emergencies. Because of Americans' distrust of centralized authority and their reluctance to emulate Great Britain, however, no such institution existed in the United States. Thus, the banking system went through periods of severe contraction. A particularly drastic panic in 1907 caused political leaders to conclude that opposition to a central bank was no longer in the nation's best interests. It took 6 years more, however, to devise the political solutions necessary to create the Federal Reserve System.

ORGANIZATION OF THE FEDERAL RESERVE SYSTEM

The law authorizing the Fed was an artful compromise between advocates of a strong central bank with sweeping authority to supervise the money sup-

---

[2]Forerunners of the Fed included the First and Second National Banks of the United States; the charter for the latter expired in 1836. Although intended to have functions similar to the Bank of England, which many credited with promoting financial stability in Great Britain, these two institutions were widely distrusted by many Americans who feared concentration of financial power in a central bank.

[3]This discussion draws on the views of James Parthemos as expressed in "The Origins of the Fed" 1988; "The Federal Reserve Act of 1913" 1988; Spong 1990; and Kindleberger 1989. (References are listed in full at the end of this chapter.)

ply and the payments system and those who feared that such a bank would support large institutions located in urban areas and ignore the needs of small, rural ones. The cornerstone of this compromise was the creation of not one but 12 Federal Reserve Banks and more than 20 additional branches, located throughout the nation as indicated in Figure 3.1. Funds to begin district banks' operations were contributed by private-sector banks choosing to become members of the Fed. All national banks were required to be members, but membership was available to state-chartered institutions on a voluntary basis. A seven-member Board of Governors, located in Washington, D.C., was charged with coordinating the activities of the district banks. The geographic origin of persons appointed to the Board was, and still is, required to be diverse.

In the early days, the regional banks had considerably more authority than they have today. They could set the rate at which they would lend to banks in their districts (the **discount rate**) without consultation with the Board; now, Board approval is required. The district banks were also originally envisioned to be the primary loci for influencing the nation's money supply.

Events subsequently proved this approach to be unworkable, and today monetary policy is centralized in a single committee dominated by the seven Board members. As a result, the district banks and their branches play a less important policy role than originally envisioned (although they are active in assisting with funds transfers), and the Fed has gradually moved away from the original intent that it be the world's only *de*centralized central bank.

THE FED AS A FINANCIAL INSTITUTION

The Fed is a critical policy-making entity and a regulator of others, but it is also a financial institution: Its assets are primarily financial assets on which it earns interest revenues. An examination of a recent consolidated balance sheet from the Fed, shown in Table 3.1, is a useful way to understand the Fed's primary functions today and their relative importance to financial institutions management.

TABLE 3.1	Balance Sheet of the Federal Reserve System, Year-end 1991

The Fed's balance sheet reflects its important responsibilities. Particularly notable are its securities portfolio, the vehicle through which it conducts open market operations; Federal Reserve notes, which serve as the nation's currency; and deposits of depository institutions, which are the reserves of the nation's banking system.

		Dollars in Billions	% of Total
Assets			
Gold certificates and coin		$ 21.605	6.12
Loans to depository institutions	$ 0.218		
Federal agency securities	6.598		
Treasury securities	281.831		
Total loans and securities		288.647	81.75
Items in process of collection		8.285	2.35
Other assets		34.524	9.78
Total assets		$353.061	100.00
Liabilities and Net Worth			
Federal reserve notes		$287.906	81.55
Deposits of depository institutions	29.413		
Other deposits	20.371		
Total deposits		49.784	14.10
Other liabilities		10.068	2.85
Capital		5.303	1.50
Total liabilities and capital		$353.061	100.00

Source: Prepared by the authors with data from the Board of Governors of the Federal Reserve System, *78th Annual Report* (Washington, DC: Board of Governors of the Federal Reserve System, 1991), 244–245.

FIGURE 3.1 Federal Reserve Banks and Branches

The dispersion of district banks and branches around the country reflects a political compromise by the framers of the Fed, who recognized the need for a central banking system but feared concentration of financial power. The numbers and corresponding letters assigned to a district appear on Federal Reserve notes issued in that district.

ASSETS OF THE FEDERAL RESERVE SYSTEM

Clearly the largest asset of the Fed is its holdings in U.S. Treasury and federal agency securities. Almost as an afterthought, the Federal Reserve Act gave the Fed the power to own and trade these assets. The inclusion of that power is fortuitous indeed, because the trading of government securities—called **open market operations**—is the single most important tool in the Fed's conduct of monetary policy. It is discussed in more detail in subsequent sections.

Other asset accounts are much less significant on the balance sheet but arise nonetheless as the Fed carries out important responsibilities. For example, the Fed occasionally buys and sells gold, often to assist the Treasury in international transactions. The Federal Reserve Banks do not physically store precious metals, so the "gold certificates and coin" account represents the Fed's claim on bullion stored in federal depositories, such as that at the U.S. Army installation at Fort Knox, Kentucky. The "loans to depository institutions" account symbolizes another major Fed activity—its role as lender of last resort. This role is discussed in more detail later.

As noted, the Fed is also responsible for promoting an effective and efficient payments system. The "items in the process of collection" account is the dollar amount of uncleared checks in process at the time this balance sheet was prepared. Although the volume on any one day is relatively small, as shown in Table 3.1, the volume of funds transfers passing through the Federal Reserve Banks annually is staggering—running well into the trillions of dollars. The Fed's role in the payments system is discussed in more detail later in this chapter and in the material on electronic funds transfers in Chapter 20. The "other assets" account primarily represents physical facilities.

LIABILITIES AND CAPITAL OF THE FEDERAL RESERVE SYSTEM

The largest liabilities of the Fed by far are Federal Reserve notes in circulation––the paper money Americans use for millions of transactions daily. The 1913 Act called for replacing national bank notes with Federal Reserve notes. Originally, the Fed's notes had to be backed partially by gold and partially by other assets (not including government securities), so there were still limitations to the total volume of currency

that could be issued. Gradually, the asset categories that could be used as backing for Federal Reserve notes were broadened. Today, the Fed recognizes many forms of money besides currency and is not bound by a particular formula in determining the amount of its notes outstanding as a proportion of total media of exchange. Issued by each district bank (Figure 3.1 shows the letter of the alphabet that appears on currency issued in a district), worn notes must be retired from circulation frequently, and currency production costs are among the largest expenses of the Fed.

The account "deposits of depository institutions" reflects two of the Fed's main functions—that of regulator and that of architect of monetary policy. As mentioned in the previous chapter, the Depository Institutions Deregulation and Monetary Control Act of 1980 (DIDMCA) authorized the Fed to establish universal reserve requirements for all depositories. These reserves—the deposits of depository institutions shown on the Fed's balance sheet—serve both as assurance that individual institutions are liquid enough to meet normal operational needs and also as targets for the Fed's monetary policy activities. Reserves are discussed in more detail later in this chapter and in Chapter 13 on liquidity management in depositories.

"Other liabilities" comprise a collection of relatively small obligations of the Fed, including accounts payable that arise in the normal course of business. The "capital" account represents the contributions of member institutions, on which they earn a flat 6 percent dividend, plus a relatively small accumulated surplus. As a financial institution, the Fed has been quite "profitable" in recent years. In 1991 for example, it earned a net income of $21.124 billion. After paying a 6 percent dividend to member banks and retaining a small sum, the Fed turned over $20.778 billion to the Treasury. It considered this payment to the Treasury a form of interest on its outstanding Federal Reserve notes.[4]

THE FED AS GUARDIAN OF THE PAYMENTS SYSTEM

Even in the 1990s, methods of funds transfers used for centuries persist; most Americans use both currency and checks to execute transactions daily. They never

---

[4] See Board of Governors 1991, 256–261.

wonder whether a dollar bill received in Denver will be the equivalent of 100 cents in Boston the next day, nor do they worry about whether a check to the utility company written on a local bank account will be accepted by the utility's bank at face value (assuming there are enough funds in the account to honor the check). It was not always so, and the Fed has been instrumental in eliminating skepticism, and even panic, about whether the payments system will function predictably.

The Federal Reserve Act charged the Fed with improving the check-clearing process, especially between distant points. As a first step, member banks were required to clear checks drawn on other banks at face value, a practice by no means universal before 1913. Among other major improvements was the development in 1918 of **Fedwire,** whereby member banks could transfer funds to and from one another by telegraph, free of charge. Today, many types of electronic funds transfers occur, and the Fed led the way in their development, although checks and wire transfers (no longer free) are still common. In 1991, for example, the Fed cleared almost 19 billion paper checks, handled more than 66 million wire transfers, and processed more than 1 billion commercial transfers electronically. Privately owned and operated funds transfer systems also exist, providing interesting (and not altogether friendly) competition among regulators and the regulated. Acknowledging allegations from banks that it was an unfair competitor, the Fed announced in 1990 that it would begin to reduce—but certainly not eliminate—its involvement in funds transfers and to allow the private sector to earn more of the rewards (but bear more risk). More details are provided in Chapter 20.[5]

DAYLIGHT OVERDRAFTS

Currently, **daylight overdrafts** reflect a banking practice that some experts believe poses a growing risk to the payments system. Daylight overdrafts arise when depository institutions overdraw their reserve deposit accounts at the Fed while making transfers through Fedwire during the course of a business day. Although the Fed has yet to lose money as a result, the

volume of overdrafts is so large (averaging $112 billion daily in 1987) that the Fed now requires institutions to have internal policy limits on the amount of overdrafts incurred in any one day. Since 1991, it has required collateral for certain types of overdrafts. The Fed limits the dollar volume of overdrafts it will process for institutions, especially those under financial stress. In April 1994, the Fed will begin charging institutions when daylight overdrafts occur in their reserve and clearing accounts.[6]

Privately owned payments systems, such as Clearing House Interbank Payments System (**CHIPS**) in New York City, are also exposed to losses from members' daylight overdrafts. CHIPS members include about 130 important domestic and foreign banks, which routinely exchange large volumes of funds and securities among themselves. Although the Fed would absorb a loss should an overdrawn bank fail while using its systems, CHIPS members would have to bear the losses themselves in case of the failure of an overdrawn CHIPS user. Cognizant of this risk, the Fed requires that institutions include both CHIPS and Fedwire transactions in establishing their policy limits on daylight overdrafts.

THE FED AS LENDER OF LAST RESORT

The Fed's first test as a lender of last resort did not come for more than 15 years, when the 1929 stock market crash and the Great Depression that followed resulted in a series of bank failures. Many borrowers defaulted on bank loans, and depositors responded to the economic uncertainty by attempting to withdraw their bank deposits in cash. To obtain cash to meet depositors' demands, banks were forced to dump large quantities of their government securities holdings into the financial markets at "fire sale" prices, further weakening their financial positions. Intended as a recourse for member banks needing cash, the Fed was slow to react to the crisis. Economic historians, although not in complete agreement, attribute the Fed's disappointing performance to inadequate tools, to a

[5] See Board of Governors 1991, 227–229; Jeanne Iida, "Fed Planning to Privatize Funds-Transfer Operations," *American Banker,* May 3, 1990, 1, 3.

[6] For further discussion of payments system risks, see Gilbert 1989; Belton et al. 1987; Summers 1991; Juncker and Summers 1991; Baer and Evanoff 1990; and *Fed Wire* (Federal Reserve Bank of Chicago) (February 1993).

lack of understanding of the economic system's needs, or to both.[7] By 1933, nearly 9,000 banks had failed, almost half those in existence in 1929.

As noted in Chapter 2, much Depression-era legislation is now viewed by experts as outmoded and even based on erroneous interpretations of the events of the time. At least one legislative response to the Depression, however, established procedures that remain the foundation of some of the Fed's current activities. The Banking Act of 1935 made permanent several changes in Fed procedures that had been introduced as temporary measures in 1932 and 1933. Notably, the Fed was allowed more latitude in deciding what collateral to accept from banks wishing to borrow at the so-called discount window. (Discount windows are not physical locations but merely procedures through which financial institutions can borrow through the Fed.) The policies governing the Fed's discount window lending are stipulated in Regulation A, which is explained in more detail in Chapter 13.

The Fed's actions in more recent financial market crises have been almost universally praised. For example, in the aftermath of the stock market crash of 1987, the Fed received high marks for its responsiveness. By standing ready to buy unlimited quantities of government securities from banks that needed cash, and by clearly and frequently communicating its intention to do so, the Fed maintained liquidity in the financial system, and not one bank failure was attributed to the crash. Subsequent analysis has led experts to conclude that the Fed balanced successfully its monetary policy objectives with its actions as lender of last resort.[8]

WHOM SHOULD A LENDER OF LAST RESORT PROTECT?

Today, the proper role of a lender of last resort is receiving renewed attention, primarily because of the thrift crisis and the failure of several large banks in the 1980s. Classical lender-of-last resort theory holds that the objective of such institutions should be 1) to protect the *aggregate* money supply, not the safety of individual institutions; 2) to lend only to well-managed institutions with temporary cash needs; 3) to allow poorly managed institutions to fail; 4) to require good collateral for all loans; and 5) to announce those conditions well in advance of a crisis so that market participants know what to expect.[9] The Fed departed from these principles in 1974 in the case of Franklin National Bank, a large New York institution whose impending failure the Fed attempted to "manage" to avoid hurting other large banks. This limited action had a happy ending, in that the collapse of other large banks was averted, and Franklin National was merged with a large European bank shortly thereafter. The Fed sustained no losses. Similar lending by the Fed helped to avert a banking crisis in the collapse of Continental Illinois National Bank 10 years later.

Observers have noted, however, that by keeping hundreds of failing thrift institutions afloat since the early 1980s, regulators, including the Fed, have departed from these principles even more drastically. Concern escalated in April 1989, when the Fed lent $70 million to a bankrupt but still operating thrift institution that had *no* collateral because its parent company had previously transferred all its good assets to other subsidiaries before declaring bankruptcy. Thus, there were no apparent prospects for repayment but, instead, only continuing withdrawals by the thrift's customers as their confidence deteriorated. During the same period, the Fed agreed to make similar loans to at least eight other thrifts. Most experts view discount window lending under these conditions as unwise and certainly not in keeping with the intent of lender-of-last-resort legislation. In the Federal Deposit Insurance Corporation Improvement Act (FDICIA), Congress attempted to curtail such practices by prohibiting the Fed from extending discount window loans to institutions in poor financial condition with no prospects of recovery.[10]

---

[7] See, for example, Friedman and Schwartz 1963; Todd 1988; Wheelock 1989; and Bordo 1990.

[8] See Robinson 1992; and Alan Murray, "Fed's New Chairman Wins a Lot of Praise on Handling the Crash," *The Wall Street Journal,* November 25, 1987, 1, 7. The Fed was also praised for its handling of a crisis in the commercial paper market in 1970. For an account of its actions, see Evelyn Hurley, "The Commercial Paper Market," *Federal Reserve Bulletin* 63 (June 1977): 525–536.

---

[9] A history of lender-of-last-resort theory is found in Humphrey March/April 1989.

[10] Paulette Thomas, "Fed, Fulfilling Pledge, Advances Funds to Lincoln S&L as Lender of Last Resort," *The Wall Street Journal,* April 25, 1989, A2; Smith and Wall 1992; and Schwartz 1992.

THE FED AS ARCHITECT OF MONETARY POLICY

Perhaps the single most important responsibility of the Fed, and the one for which it most often receives criticisms such as those cited at the beginning of the chapter, is the conduct of monetary policy. **Monetary policy** encompasses the Fed's attempts to influence both the money supply and the level of interest rates. This section identifies the goals of monetary policy, the primary methods by which the Fed attempts to achieve those goals, and the main effects of monetary policy on financial institutions management.

GOALS OF MONETARY POLICY

Controlling the money supply is not an end in itself. Instead, most economists believe that there is a relationship between money and other important economic variables such as interest rates (and their effect on the supply and demand for credit), inflation, employment, national income, and currency exchange rates. Thus, the ultimate goal of monetary policy is to promote a healthy economy as evidenced by low inflation, a satisfactory rate of growth in output, full employment, and an acceptable balance of trade between the United States and other countries. The importance of particular goals may change, as when Congress placed special emphasis on jobs in the Full Employment and Balanced Growth Act of 1978, which requires the Fed to report to Congress semiannually on the impact of its policies on the unemployment rate and other economic measures. Also the goals of monetary policy sometimes conflict; for example, a booming economy with a low jobless rate may lead to inflation and high interest rates. Nonetheless, the goals listed earlier are generally accepted.

FIRST THINGS FIRST: WHAT IS MONEY?

Successful monetary policy cannot be conducted unless the Fed can define and measure money. Economists agree that "money" as an abstract concept is something accepted as a medium of exchange that holds its value. In a modern financial system, this definition can apply to a wide variety of financial instruments. For example, currency, checking accounts, money market accounts, and even savings accounts in certain situations can all be used to make transactions. Recognizing this, the Fed has several categories of money (called the **monetary aggregates**) that can be used as the targets of its monetary policy operations. Recent definitions of main categories are summarized in Table 3.2. The most fundamental type of money is the **monetary base,** consisting of currency and reserves of depository institutions held within the Fed. Closely related is the narrowest monetary aggregate, M1, which adds checking accounts to the monetary base. M2 adds other interest-bearing accounts that are relatively liquid, and M3 and L are yet broader measures.[11] Each of the components of the monetary aggregates is defined in more detail in later chapters.

Economists also attempt to measure **money multipliers,** or relationships between the monetary base and the monetary aggregates, determined by the complex interaction of reserve requirements and public and institutional preferences for holding money. Recent research indicates, for example, that the multiplier between the monetary base and M2 during the period 1980–1988 ranged between 10 and 12; that is, for every $1 change in the monetary base, a $10 to $12 change in M2 would have been expected.[12] Unfortunately for the smooth conduct of monetary policy, money multipliers change as a result of economic changes and financial and technical innovation, adding more uncertainty to the policy-making process.

Deciding which of the "moneys" to target to achieve ultimate monetary policy goals is not easy. A desirable target should be clearly related to important economic variables *and* should be within the Fed's ability to influence directly without undesirable economic side effects. Economists debate the question vigorously, without consensus. For example, many experts believe that M2 currently has the most stable relationship with ultimate policy variables, although that relationship is far from certain.[13] However, the monetary base is the most easily controlled measure of

---

[11] Definitions of money have received intense scrutiny in recent years. See, for example, Walter 1989; Osborne 1985; and Wenninger and Partlan 1992.

[12] See Cox and Rosenblum 1989. Derivation and complete analysis of money multipliers are not within the scope of this text. A representative discussion is found in Frederic S. Mishkin, *The Economics of Money, Banking, and Financial Markets.* (Glenview, IL: Scott, Foresman, 1989).

[13] Recently, for example, **P-star (P*),** a predictor of the relationship between the current level of M2 and future inflation, has become a widely watched indicator of the success of monetary policy in controlling inflation. For more details, see Humphrey July/August 1989 and Carlson 1989.

TABLE 3.2   Components of the Monetary Base and Monetary Aggregates

In today's sophisticated financial markets, many things qualify as money because they have lasting value and can be used to make transactions. The narrowest definition is the monetary base, but several broader monetary aggregates also exist. Deciding which definition is best for monetary policy purposes is difficult.

Monetary Base
   Currency in circulation (Federal Reserve notes, coins, U.S. Treasury certificates)
   Reserve deposits of financial institutions

Aggregate Measures of the Money Supply
   M-1
      Cash held by the public
      Travelers checks of nonbank issuers
      Demand deposits at commercial banks
      Negotiable Order of Withdrawal (NOW) and Super NOW accounts
      Automatic transfer service accounts
      Credit Union share draft accounts
      Demand deposits at thrift institutions
   M-2
      M-1 plus
         Overnight repurchase agreements
         Overnight Eurodollars
         Money market deposit accounts (MMDAs)
         Most money market fund balances
         Savings and small time deposits at depository institutions
   M-3
      M-2 plus
         Large time deposits at depository institutions
         Longer-term repurchase agreements and Eurodollars
   L
      M-3 plus
         Liquid assets held by U.S. residents (such as Treasury bills, bankers' acceptances, commercial paper, U.S. savings bonds)

Source: Federal Reserve Bulletin 79 (July 1993), A4.

money, and changes in the monetary base should, through the multiplier effect, result in changes in M2. Some argue, however, that manipulation of the monetary base could have undesirable effects on interest rates. Deregulation, increasing globalization, and shocks to the economic system—such as the stock market crash of 1987 and the 1989 crisis in the thrift industry—further confuse the relationship between measures of money and monetary policy goals, ensuring continuation of the debate over appropriate targets.

MONEY OR INTEREST RATES?

Another important issue complicates the monetary policy landscape. Some economists argue that the best way to achieve ultimate economic goals is not for the Fed to focus directly on money, however defined, but rather to establish *interest rate* targets and to manage the monetary aggregates to achieve these rate targets. According to this belief, if interest rates are at desirable levels, one can conclude that acceptable levels of economic growth, inflation, employment, and trade will follow. In this view, the level of any particular monetary aggregate is important only insofar as it increases or decreases interest rates beyond target levels.[14]

In recent years, the Fed itself has seemed to vacillate over whether monetary aggregates or interest rates were its true policy targets. Although public statements by Fed officials consistently have stressed monetary aggregates, "Fed watchers" universally believe that during the 1970s, monetary policy was really directed at maintaining interest rate levels by control of the **federal funds rate,** the interest rate that depository institutions charge on the excess reserves they lend to one another. In October 1979, however, with inflation rising precipitously, the Fed took an abrupt turn toward focusing on monetary aggregates regardless of the effect on interest rates. But recent statements by Fed Chairman Greenspan suggest that interest rates are once again the primary monetary policy target.

The perception that the Fed cannot decide what targets are best arises from the fact that the Fed is buffeted by political as well as economic pressures in setting monetary policy. For example, many politicians, including presidents, focus on interest rates because they are highly visible symbols of the economy's performance. Thus, a monetary policy that targets monetary aggregates exclusively is unlikely to be popular with prominent politicians if it leads, for example, to high mortgage rates. Similarly, inflation is not politically popular, so a policy that targets interest rates but leads to inflationary monetary growth will also not win friends. Although the Fed is nominally independent of politics, the members of the Board are appointed by the President, and the Chairman must report regularly

---

[14] These arguments are summarized in Motley and Runyon 1981; Bohne 1987; and Roberds 1992.

to Congress. Thus, many expert Fed watchers believe that the political climate influences monetary policy as much as does economic theory. Further complicating monetary policy is the Fed's regulatory role. Some observers believe the Fed may delay or forgo certain monetary policy actions if these actions would adversely affect institutions it regulates.[15]

TOOLS OF MONETARY POLICY

Regardless of the economic and political difficulties, decisions about monetary policy must be, and are, made; then policy directives must be put in motion. The current structure through which monetary policy is implemented has its roots in post-Depression legislation. The Banking Act of 1935 made permanent the **Federal Open Market Committee (FOMC),** although similar groups had existed since the early 1920s. The FOMC is the body through which all important policy decisions are made. It consists of the seven members of the Board of Governors and of the presidents of five district Federal Reserve Banks.[16] Besides deciding the appropriate targets of monetary policy activities, the FOMC has, since the 1970s, identified specific quantitative objectives, such as the rate of growth in the monetary aggregates. Finally, it considers how one of the major policy tools—buying and selling of government securities in the financial markets (open market operations)—should be conducted.

In addition to open market operations, the Fed has two other means by which to pursue its desired monetary policy targets: changing reserve requirements for depository institutions and changing the discount rate. Although some disagree, most experts believe that these tools are relatively insignificant in monetary policy (even though they are important for other reasons).[17] Increasing or decreasing the amount

of required reserves would have an instantaneous effect on the money supply, but the resulting expansion or contraction could be quite drastic. Thus, changes in reserve requirements are seldom used to change the money supply. A recent exception was the Fed's 1992 decision to lower, from 12 to 10 percent, the maximum proportion of selected deposits institutions must hold as reserves at the Fed. The Fed could also attempt to increase (or decrease) the level of reserves available to the banking system by lowering (or raising) the discount rate to influence the level of borrowing by depository institutions, an approach it followed many times during the recession of the early 1990s. Yet the Fed cannot force institutions to borrow, nor, as lender of last resort, can it easily refuse qualifying loan applications even if they conflict with monetary policy objectives. Thus, the subsequent discussion focuses exclusively on open market operations.

HOW OPEN MARKET OPERATIONS INFLUENCE THE MONEY SUPPLY AND INTEREST RATES. The effect of open market operations was discovered accidentally in the early days of the Fed, as individual district banks purchased and sold government securities to increase their income. The impact of these activities on the monetary base was immediate. When district banks accepted payment for the securities they sold, reserve accounts of purchasers were debited, decreasing total reserves in the banking system; when the Fed purchased securities, reserves were injected into the system. A simplified example of the effect of transactions such as these is illustrated in Figure 3.2. When the Fed sells securities to a commercial bank, as shown in Panel A of Figure 3.2, the bank's reserves—and thus the monetary base and monetary aggregates—decrease. The decline in the money supply causes an increase in interest rates. When the Fed purchases securities in open market operations (Panel B), the opposite occurs: bank reserves and the money supply grow, while interest rates decline.

It soon was apparent that sales and purchases of government securities by Federal Reserve Banks should be managed to avoid unplanned contractions or expansions of the monetary base and, thus, of other monetary aggregates. Eventually, the authority to manage open market purchases and sales was vested in the FOMC, which implements the entire System's plans through a trading desk at the Federal Reserve Bank of

---

[15] See Cargill 1989 and Kane 1982.

[16] The early history of open market operations is described in Sproul 1989. Other accounts of monetary policy before the 1970s can be found in Wallich 1979; and Crabbe 1989. In recent years, the district presidents have become more outspoken and influential. See Alan Murray, "Fed Banks' Presidents Hold Private Positions But Major Public Role," *The Wall Street Journal,* August 1, 1991, A1, A7.

[17] For a defense of reserve requirements and the discount rate as effective tools of monetary policy, see Meulendyke 1992; Weiner 1992; and Sellon 1984.

FIGURE 3.2   Effects of Open Market Operations on Bank Reserves

A sale of securities by the Fed decreases the level of reserves and thus the monetary base. A purchase of securities by the Fed has the opposite effect.

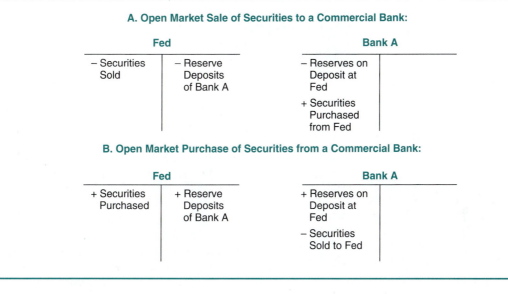

A. Open Market Sale of Securities to a Commercial Bank:

Fed		Bank A	
– Securities Sold	– Reserve Deposits of Bank A	– Reserves on Deposit at Fed	
		+ Securities Purchased from Fed	

B. Open Market Purchase of Securities from a Commercial Bank:

Fed		Bank A	
+ Securities Purchased	+ Reserve Deposits of Bank A	+ Reserves on Deposit at Fed	
		– Securities Sold to Fed	

New York. In between FOMC meetings, members of the Board staff and at least one member of the FOMC talk with the trading desk daily.[18]

The FOMC meets several times a year to review progress toward annual targets and to provide short-run direction to the trading desk. To avoid undue interference from politicians and overreaction from the financial markets, the FOMC doesn't release minutes of its meetings until some time later. This delay does not stop Fed watchers from speculating about changes in monetary policy and from attempting to divine the "true" motivations for the current activities of the New York trading desk.

MONETARY POLICY: A SUMMARY

Theorized relationships among monetary policy goals, targets, and tools are summarized in Figure 3.3, which was designed by economists at the Federal Reserve Bank of Dallas. The three policy tools are shown at left. Actions resulting from the tools are directed at

some type of target, and the figure illustrates that either the monetary base or a broader monetary aggregate could be chosen. This particular graphic is drawn under the assumption that monetary policy will be focused on a measure of money. As noted previously, an interest rate target may be, and sometimes is, substituted for a monetary target if the Fed believes that it is appropriate for the current environment. Finally, the supply of money resulting from these activities interacts with the demand for money, and, ideally, ultimate policy goals are achieved. Unfortunately, the path is straight in theory but winding in practice, and along the way, the Fed sometimes catches financial institutions managers by surprise. This point is illustrated in the next section.

MONETARY POLICY AND ASSET/LIABILITY MANAGEMENT

A good way to understand how monetary policy affects financial institutions is to recall that asset/liability management involves managing the spread (the difference between interest earned on assets and the interest

---

[18] Detailed discussions of the translation of policy targets into open market actions are found in Meek 1982; Gilbert 1985; Meulendyke 1988; and Garfinkel 1989.

FIGURE 3.3   **Relationships among Monetary Policy Goals, Tools, and Targets**

The path between the tools of monetary policy (directed at either intermediate monetary targets or interest rates) and ultimate policy goals seems direct in theory but is difficult to find in practice.

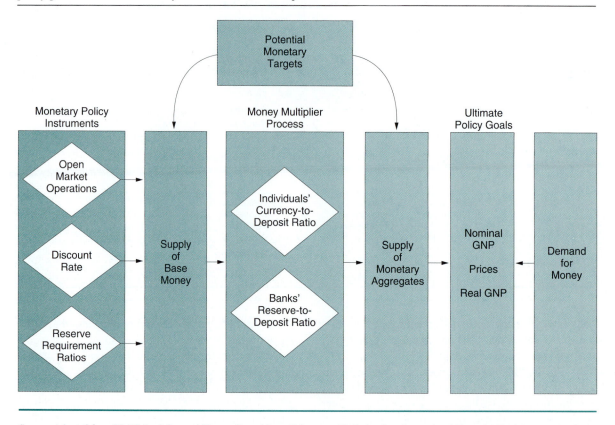

Source: Adapted from W. Michael Cox and Harvey Rosenblum, "Money and Inflation in a Deregulated Financial Environment: An Overview," *Economic Review* (Federal Reserve Bank of Dallas) (May 1989), 2.

---

cost of liabilities) as well as the associated risk (variability) in the spread. Thus, anything that affects the level and variability of interest rates has a direct effect on management.

Figure 3.4 diagrams the way in which a commercial bank's (or any large institution's) asset/liability policies might be influenced by monetary policy decisions. Specific lending, investment, and liability management policies are established only after a review of the institution's existing and projected financial position (by means of the balance sheet) and a forecast of interest rates (which is predicated on a forecast of monetary policy decisions). Unexpected changes in monetary policy, or a monetary policy that

produces unexpected changes in interest rates, can be hazardous to a financial institution's health.

THE CLASSIC EXAMPLE: OCTOBER 1979

Few situations provide a more vivid example of the effect of differences in monetary policy on financial institutions than the Fed's change, in October 1979, from a policy that concentrated primarily on interest rates to one that attempted to control inflation, regardless of the effect on interest rates. Under the policy in effect before October, the Fed specified a relatively narrow range for the federal funds rate, then

FIGURE 3.4	**Effects of Monetary Policy on Asset/Liability Management**

Monetary policy affects asset/liability management through the interest rate forecasts that managers use to plan loan, investment, and liability management activities.

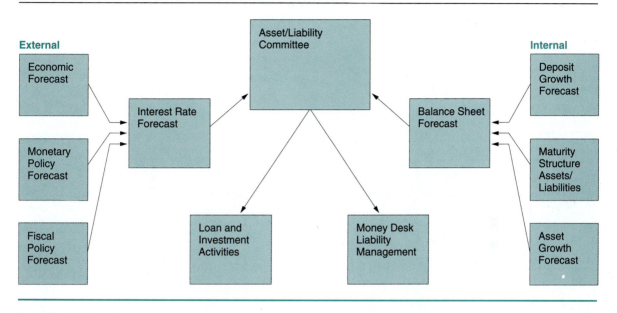

Source: Paul Meek, *U.S. Monetary Policy and Financial Markets* (New York: Federal Reserve Bank of New York, 1982), 42.

directed the trading desk to buy and sell securities in the financial markets to keep the rate within the target range. In September 1979, for example, the target range for the federal funds rate was 11¼ to 11¾ percent.[19] Interest rate volatility was relatively low, and the level of rates, although climbing at the time of the change, was soon to seem relatively modest.

By October, the FOMC concluded that monetary growth under the existing policy was too rapid, resulting in unacceptable levels of inflation. The trading desk was instructed to focus on targets for the monetary aggregates, letting the federal funds rate move more freely. Although targets for the funds rate continued to be set, they were much wider than under the previous policy. For example, by December 1980, the FOMC's federal funds rate target range was between 15 and 20 percent.

Figure 3.5 traces the trend in selected short-term

interest rates before and after October 1979. Many financial institution managers found both the level and volatility of rates after the monetary policy change to be astonishing. Eventually, banks' best customers were offered loans at an interest rate of 21½ percent, and mortgage rates also reached historical highs. Business activity virtually ground to a halt, resulting in an economic recession. But inflation was licked, and the Fed's Chairman, Paul Volcker, was unapologetic.

The 1979 change sparked an unprecedented wave of attention to interest rate risk management tools—attention that persists today and is the basis for much of the rest of this book. Managers' continuing concern with risk management is well advised: recent research shows that potential risk-reduction benefits available to depositories (and especially to thrifts) after the passage of DIDMCA in 1980 were more than offset by the increase in interest rate volatility from the Fed's 1979 monetary policy change.[20] The policy

---

[19] FOMC targets are reported in minutes of committee meetings and appear in the press and several Fed publications.

[20] See Aharony, Saunders, and Swary 1988.

FIGURE 3.5   **Short-Term Interest Rates before and after a Change in Monetary Policy**

Before October 1979, the Fed's monetary policy targeted interest rates, but for several years afterward, monetary policy focused on the monetary aggregates, allowing interest rates to move more freely. The level and volatility of interest rates changed dramatically, greatly increasing managers' concern for interest rate risk management.

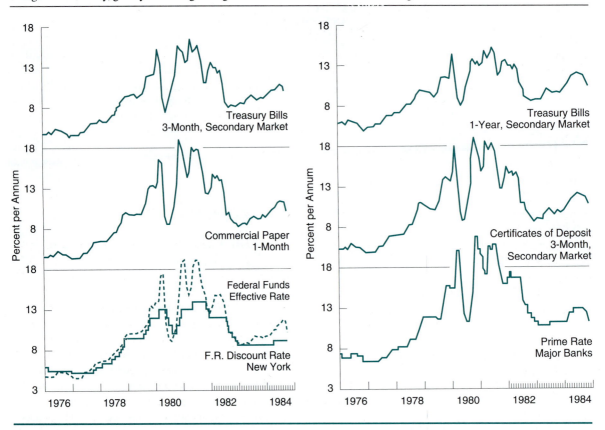

Source: Board of Governors of the Federal Reserve System, *Federal Reserve Chart Book,* November 1984, 72.

change also sparked an unprecedented wave of "Fed-bashing" that persisted for several years. One cartoon, widely circulated in late 1981, showed the Federal Reserve Board in medical attire, operating on a patient (the U.S. economy) and using high interest rates as the surgical tool. The caption read, "Congratulations, Doctor! It was a good operation on inflation . . . too bad the patient died."

Fortunately, reports of the patient's death were premature, and by 1982, Fed watchers had noted that the FOMC's target ranges for the federal funds rate were again narrower. For example, in December 1988, the FOMC's announced range was between 7 percent and 11 percent, but actual variations in the rate were much smaller. Financial institutions managers have learned, however, that they can never again afford to take monetary policy effects lightly.

THE FED AND INTERNATIONAL POLICY COORDINATION

The Fed is not a domestic institution only; it affects, and is affected by, the larger world. This international dimension further complicates the Fed's attempts to conduct monetary policy and to regulate financial institutions operating in the United States.

THE GOLD STANDARD

International responsibilities are not new for the Fed. From its inception, it was charged with managing the United States's adherence to the **gold standard.** For decades before the formation of the Fed, the United States and several other countries had agreed to honor gold as the definitive standard of value and to maintain a fixed exchange rate between their currencies based on gold. After 1913, when the Fed's monetary policy responsibilities were mandated, it was required to tie the expansion of the monetary base in the United States to the nation's supply of gold. As the world's supply of gold changed and as this country's share of that supply fluctuated, the U.S. money supply would then also change, whether or not other domestic economic conditions warranted it. Some economic historians, in fact, attribute the Fed's failure to provide sufficient reserves to illiquid U.S. banks between 1929 and 1933 to its overriding loyalty to the gold standard.

Events of the Great Depression made it clear that the gold standard was no longer workable, although fixed exchange rates between dollars and other currencies, based in part on gold reserves, existed from 1945 to 1971. In 1971, President Richard M. Nixon set in motion the transition to a "floating" system of exchange rates unrelated to gold in any way.[21] That does not mean, however, that the Fed's international responsibilities in the exchange markets have ended. More and more, in fact, the Fed is required to coordinate its policies with those of central banks around the world.[22]

INTERNATIONAL COORDINATION AND MONETARY POLICY

Any discussion of monetary policy leads inevitably to a discussion of the Fed in the international financial markets. Recall that one of the goals of monetary policy is to promote a satisfactory trade balance between the United States and other nations, meaning that the Fed must be concerned about rates of exchange between U.S. dollars and the currencies of other countries. How does monetary policy affect exchange rates?

A full discussion of exchange rate determination is deferred until Chapter 6, but basic principles are useful at this point. Under a floating exchange rate system, familiar supply-demand relationships apply in the currency markets. Increased demand for U.S. dollars (which occurs if U.S. interest rates are high compared with those in other countries) pushes up the value of the dollar as investors seek to take advantage of high returns on dollar-denominated financial assets. When the value of the dollar rises, goods that U.S. firms hope to export become more expensive for purchasers in Japan, Germany, or other countries. Thus, U.S exports may drop, causing the trade balance between the United States and other nations to become unfavorable. If, for different reasons—say, because of concern about inflation at home—the Fed takes monetary policy actions that cause interest rates to increase even more, the imbalance in trade may worsen.

G-5 AND G-7 AGREEMENTS. Conflicts between these two *domestic* goals—keeping inflation down and promoting a favorable export climate—are not the only ones the Fed faces as it takes monetary policy actions. In 1985, the United States and four other nations—called the Group of Five (G-5)—agreed to coordinate efforts to keep the U.S. dollar within a specified trading range relative to the currencies of other countries; in 1987, the Group of Five was expanded to the **Group of Seven (G-7).**[23] The actual range, which is considered "top secret" by the G-7 group, is one they believe is in the best interests of the nations collectively. It is thought by experts to be a very flexible target rather than a narrow one.

To carry out the agreement, central banks in the G-7 nations buy or sell dollars in the exchange markets whenever the dollar's value threatens to break through the range. When open market purchases and sales of dollars fail to reverse what the group considers an undesirable trend, the non-U.S. G-7 central banks sometimes attempt to increase or decrease interest rates in their own countries to counteract differentials between U.S. and non-U.S. interest rates. If the Fed decides to change its monetary policy approach for reasons unrelated to the G-7 agreement, that change can conflict with actions the other central banks are simultaneously

---

[21] See Crabbe 1989; for more information on exchange rates from World War II to the 1970s, see Hayes 1989.

[22] Kasman 1992 finds similarities in monetary policy procedures of central banks in 6 countries. Stevens 1992 compares rules and regulations in 4 countries.

[23] The G-7 nations are the United States, Canada, France, Great Britain, Italy, Japan, and Germany. Canada and Italy were not included in the Group of Five.

taking, thus frustrating policy coordination. Fed watchers continually monitor the Fed to determine whether, in a conflict, it places domestic or international objectives ahead. Although it is too early in the process of international policy coordination to draw firm conclusions, many observers believe the Fed has favored domestic policy needs thus far. The same seems to be true of central bankers in the other G-7 nations.[24]

INTERNATIONAL COORDINATION OF FINANCIAL INSTITUTIONS REGULATION

Not only does the intertwining of domestic monetary policy with the foreign exchange markets require the Fed to devote more attention to international issues, but technological and financial innovations spurring regulatory revisions in the United States have implications for international regulatory reform as well.

GLOBALIZATION IS INCREASING. As Fed Chairman Alan Greenspan noted, in recent years technology has permitted many products to be downsized, greatly reducing the cost of shipping between countries. Increased international trade means increased demands on institutions to facilitate financing. Recent advances in technology also permit the rapid transmission of financial information, bringing the financial markets of many countries closer together. The world's financial markets are becoming increasingly integrated; integration means closer communication and greater competition among financial institutions worldwide.[25]

When financial institutions interact internationally, the pressure for domestic regulatory adjustments

increases. If regulators establish restrictive rules in the United States, the regulatory dialectic suggests an immediate incentive for markets to move to countries with more accommodating rules. A chain of responses by regulators is then initiated. One possible result is a reciprocal agreement giving foreign banks in the United States powers that U.S. banks are seeking abroad. Then, to avoid the perception that foreign banks in the United States have special privileges prohibited to domestic banks, rules for the latter may be changed. Similarly, U.S. markets cannot flourish if some domestic institutions, such as securities firms, are permitted to engage in international transactions that give them advantages over their domestically chartered competitors, such as commercial banks; thus, rules governing domestic institutions' relationships with one another may also change. In recent years, the proper regulatory response to international events has been debated extensively.

REGULATORY RESPONSES TO GLOBALIZATION. As early as 1919, the **Edge Act** recognized the need for competitive equality among domestic and foreign banks by permitting banks to establish operations outside their home territories to conduct international banking. At that time, branching by out-of-state commercial banks was restricted in most states, so the Edge Act was an early loosening of regulations in the face of competitive pressures. Edge Corporations also have been permitted to invest in a greater variety of assets than banks conducting business solely within the United States; they are, however, subject to some domestic banking regulations, such as reserve and minimum capital requirements. In 1991 the Fed amended its rules to permit Edge Corporations to provide domestic banking services to foreign persons and governments.

Other steps toward uniform banking regulations in the United States were taken in the **International Banking Act of 1978,** under which foreign banks operating in the United States were required to purchase deposit insurance and to choose a home state and operate under its branching laws. Because most states continued to prohibit interstate branching at that time, Congress's intent was not to loosen restrictions on domestic banks but to tighten them on foreign banks. One main exception to that intent subsequently returned to haunt the Congress a decade later: The Inter-

---

[24] See, for example, Alan Murray and Walter S. Mossberg, "Raising Discount Rate, Fed Puts Inflation War Ahead of Dollar Policy," *The Wall Street Journal,* August 10, 1988, 1, 8; Alan Murray and Michael R. Sesit, "As Dollar Marches On, Central Banks Prepare Big New Intervention," *The Wall Street Journal,* May 19, 1989, A1–A2; David Wessel and Terence Roth, "As Central Banks Go Their Own Ways, Global Tensions Rise," *The Wall Street Journal,* August 3, 1992, A1, A9; Clay Chandler, "Japan's Central Banker Begins to Win Praise for Saving Its 'Soul,' " *The Wall Street Journal,* June 15, 1993, A1, A5; and Michael Sesit, Glenn Whitney, and Terence Roth, "German Stance on Rates Sends ERM to Brink," *The Wall Street Journal,* July 30, 1993, C1, C13.

[25] See Espinosa and Yip 1993; Pavel and McElravey 1990; "A Survey of World Banking," *The Economist,* May 2, 1992; Spong 1990; Abken 1991; and Corrigan 1992.

national Banking Act exempted 15 large foreign banks from Glass-Steagall prohibitions against the underwriting of corporate debt and equities by commercial banks. Thus, by the late 1980s, both domestic commercial banks and securities firms were losing business to the 15 foreign banks that could provide both types of financial services.[26]

The restrictions imposed on foreign banks were not popular in those banks' countries of origin, so in response to criticisms of the International Banking Act, the Fed in 1981 authorized domestic and foreign banks to establish **international banking facilities (IBFs).** These are entities formed to conduct business solely with international customers. Unlike Edge Corporations, IBFs are not subject to reserve requirements, nor are the deposits taken eligible for deposit insurance. The Fed made IBFs relatively inexpensive to establish. They need not be separate physical facilities but, rather, just separate bookkeeping entities. IBFs have proved to be popular.[27]

In the wake of the scandal over the Bank of Credit and Commerce International (BCCI), Congress included in FDICIA the **Foreign Bank Supervision Enhancement Act (FBSEA),** directing the Fed to impose more stringent regulations on foreign banks operating in the United States. FBSEA requires Fed approval of the establishment of all new branches or agencies of foreign banks. The Fed must also determine whether foreign banks can enter the United States by evaluating the home country supervisor's procedures for monitoring and controlling the institution's *worldwide* operations, including relationships between banks and nonbank affiliates. (The term used for this worldwide scrutiny is **comprehensive consolidated supervision.**) The extent to which the home country supervisor enforces safety and soundness regulations on all the bank's activities is also important.

A further restriction imposed by the Act mandates that all banks accepting domestic retail deposits under $100,000 purchase deposit insurance. Finally, the Fed requires from foreign institutions details on secrecy laws in their home countries that might prohibit them from providing the Fed with complete financial information. If Fed officials believe that foreign laws interfere substantially with adequate disclosure in the United States, they may deny entry to a foreign institution. Effects of FBSEA were soon apparent; between its passage in late 1991 and April 1993, the Fed approved only three applications from foreign banks to open U.S. offices.[28]

CONTINUING PRESSURE FOR POLICY COORDINATION IN THE 1990S. These laws and regulations, although intended to equalize treatment of commercial banks in the United States, do not consider the impact of other countries' laws and regulations on U.S. institutions. Pressure is increasing for uniformity of treatment, regardless of country. Regulators in several other nations with which U.S. institutions are linked through global markets have been less restrictive than U.S. regulators for several years. Most impose fewer balance sheet constraints on commercial banks and had acted to deregulate deposit interest rates long before the 1986 demise of Regulation Q (Reg Q) mandated by DIDMCA.[29]

Table 3.3 summarizes major regulatory differences that existed between the United States and other Group of Ten (G-10) nations in the early 1990s.[30] Those countries identified as having "universal" regulatory systems permit banks to provide virtually all types of financial services or products, including securities and insurance. Those with "blended" systems permit some diversification by banks but maintain a degree of separation (that is, require firewalls of varying thickness) between traditional commercial banking activities and other operations. Recall from Chapter 2 that firewalls are regulatory limitations on the extent to which banking and nonbanking activities can be conducted within the same organization. Their purpose is to keep financial crises arising in the conduct of nonbanking activities from spreading to banking and thus imposing costs on the deposit insurance system. Note that the United States is more restrictive

---

[26] Deirdre Fanning, "Set Us Free," *Forbes,* February 23, 1987, 94–96.

[27] See White 1982; Chrystal 1984; Houpt 1988; and Board of Governors 1991, 211.

[28] See Misback 1993 and James R. Kraus, "Foreign Banks Face Hurdles," *American Banker,* April 19, 1993, 2A.

[29] See Germany and Morton 1985; Sellon 1988; Cumming and Sweet 1987–88; and Frankel and Morgan 1992.

[30] Readers may be surprised to learn that there are 11 countries and one territory in the Group of 10: the G-7 nations, plus Belgium, the Netherlands, Sweden, Switzerland, and the Grand Duchy of Luxembourg.

TABLE 3.3	Comparison of Bank Regulations in the G-10 Countries

Although few G-10 nations give securities firms access to discount window and payments system privileges, U.S. regulators make it more difficult for commercial banks to engage in securities activities than do regulators in other nations. U.S. institutions are subject to regulation by a variety of agencies, whereas other countries limit the number of banking and securities regulators to one or two.

Country	Form of Bank/Securities Integration			Number of Banking and Securities Regulators	Access to Central Bank Lending		Access to Central Bank Payments System	
	Within Bank	Thin Fire-walls	Thick Fire-walls		Depositories	Depositories and Securities Firms	Depositories	Depositories and Securities Firms
Universal System								
France	x			One	x		x	
Germany	x			One	x		x	
Italy	x			One	x		x	
The Netherlands	x			One	x		x	
Switzerland	x			One	x		x	
Blended System								
Belgium		x		One	x		x	
Canada		x		Two		x	x	
Japan		x[a]		Two		x		x
Sweden		x		One	x		x	
United Kingdom		x		Two	x		x	
United States			x	Multiple		x	x	

[a] Banks permitted to invest in, and bank subsidiaries permitted to underwrite, equity securities; equity brokerage prohibited to banks and bank subsidiaries.
Sources: Adapted from Cumming and Sweet 1987–88; Robert H. Dugger et al., "EC 1992: The Financial Competitiveness Implications," paper presented at the 26th Annual Conference on Bank Structure and Competition, Chicago, Illinois, May 1990; and Frankel and Morgan 1992.

than most other G-10 nations and requires institutions to report to more regulators. Only Japan allows securities firms both discount window and payments system privileges; however, like the U.S., Japan is considered to be more adamant than other G-10 nations about separating banking and the securities business. Although financial regulations in Japan have liberalized in the 1990s, they are still less progressive than in other developed economies.

Financial crises among so-called **less developed countries (LDCs)**—such as many in Latin and Central America, Africa, and parts of Asia—have added to the pressure for international policy coordination. Many large financial institutions in the United States, Europe, and Japan lent billions to LDCs during the 1980s, loans that began to look very risky as domestic financial conditions in many LDCs deteriorated. Government officials in the G-7 nations recognized the need to work together to avert the collapse of

major banks as a result of defaults by LDCs and simultaneously to buy time for the LDCs' governments to emerge from their financial crises with stronger economies.

THE EUROPEAN COMMUNITY. Perhaps the strongest impetus that U.S. regulators have been given to participate in international policy coordination was the decision by the 12 members of the **European Community (EC)** to remove all internal barriers among themselves to trade, travel, and employment after December 31, 1992.

In the Second Banking Directive of 1989, uniform regulations for financial institutions were outlined. The EC agreed on permissible banking powers, including securities but not insurance activities, and established the principle that an institution, once it is authorized by its home country to operate as a bank, may operate as a bank anywhere in the EC without formal approval from the host government. The rules also include **national treatment,** a policy under which a financial institution from a non-EC country will be granted full competitive powers within the EC as long as EC banks are allowed to operate in the other country on an equal footing with that nation's domestic institutions. Thus, regulations in all countries need not be identical; as long as EC banks are not at a competitive disadvantage when operating in other countries, non-EC banks will not be at a disadvantage in European markets. Finally, a pan-European central bank (initially nicknamed the **Eurofed**), with authority over the central banks of EC nations, was proposed in 1990. As the early name suggests, EC officials carefully studied the U.S. Fed when developing the proposal for the **European Central Bank.**

Perhaps the most dramatic financial development accompanying Europe 1992 was the decision by EC nations to consider abandoning separate currencies and forming a **European Monetary Union (EMU)** with a common currency, the **European Currency Unit (ECU).** This agreement, known as the **Maastricht Accord** (for the city in the Netherlands in which it was signed), originally called for the ECU to be operational as early as 1996 and no later than 1999. Monetary policy governing the ECU would be the responsibility of the European Central Bank. Each country would also create an independent central bank, governors of which would participate in ECB decision making. This system would be analogous to District Bank/Board of Governors relationships within the Fed. At some point, the rate at which each unit of existing European currency (for example, the British pound, the French franc, and the German Deutschmark) would be exchanged into ECUs would be determined. This process could no doubt be facilitated by the presence, since 1986, of an ECU-denominated bond market within the EC.[31] The ambitious 1996 target date is unlikely to be achieved because most EC nations have had to emphasize domestic economic concerns more than international policy coordination. In some EC countries, voters have shown initial resistance to eliminating individual currencies. Nevertheless, the pros-

pect of the economic unification of Europe will continue to reinforce to U.S. financial institutions the probability of increased international competition.

For example, European financial institutions, spurred by the 1992 agreement, moved quickly to restructure. By the end of 1988, nearly 400 banks and other financial firms in Europe had merged to position themselves for expansion, and the merger wave continued well into the 1990s. New products were devised, and joint marketing of existing product lines became popular. Some experts estimate that the cost of financial services for Europeans may decline by as much as 10 percent due to increased competition.[32]

Fed officials, greatly concerned about the viability of U.S. institutions in foreign markets, began in 1987 to encourage international regulatory cooperation. Although supportive of the removal of Glass-Steagall prohibitions against the mixing of commercial and investment banking, the Fed seeks to limit the risks to the deposit insurance system from exposure to potential losses if depositories are permitted to engage in securities activities. Accordingly, as noted in Chapter 2, the Fed was influential in passage of the Basle Agreement in 1987, under which commercial banks' minimum capital requirements are uniform in the G-10 nations.

Other differences may be more difficult to reconcile. For example, most countries do not offer governmentally provided deposit insurance. Although (as discussed in detail in Chapter 16) some economists believe it is not really needed, most observers agree that elimination of the U.S. system of deposit insurance is unlikely. Still other experts warn of the danger of relying on international policy coordination and regulation as a substitute for market-determined solutions to economic problems. Thus, the Fed's challenge is to promote competitive equality with other countries while maintaining free markets and preserving the unique features of the U.S. system. Regulation and economic policy in the international arena are certain to play a major role in the regulatory dialectic of the future.

---

[31] Carl W. Walsh, "EMU and the ECB," *Weekly Letter* (Federal Reserve Bank of San Francisco), June 5, 1992; Chriszt 1991; and Carré and Johnson 1991.

[32] For more information on the EC 1992 agreement, see "A Survey of World Banking"; Boucher 1991; Feldberg 1990; Weatherstone 1989; Wormuth 1989; Bennett and Hakkio 1989; Adamantopoulous 1989; and Key 1989.

SUMMARY

Although there are many financial institution regulators, the Fed's influence is the most pervasive. As the central bank of the United States, the Fed is charged with issuing currency, maintaining a well-functioning payments system, serving as a lender of last resort to institutions with liquidity problems, and developing and executing monetary policy that promotes the nation's economic well-being. The Fed must also coordinate its regulatory and monetary activities with central banks around the world. As might be expected, given the degree of evolution and globalization in financial markets, each of these tasks has become increasingly complex in recent years.

In administering the payments system, the Fed finds that more and more funds are transferred by electronic means, and the daylight overdrafts of large banks pose new risks. Increasing numbers of depositories have called on the Fed's discount window, raising questions about its proper role as a lender of last resort. Yet monetary policy poses perhaps the stiffest challenges for the Fed. Major players in monetary policy decisions are members of the FOMC who periodically determine how the Fed's purchases and sales of government securities will be conducted. Unfortunately for the FOMC, it is more difficult than ever to define "money," and the relationships between different measures of money and desirable economic outcomes are tenuous. Whether the money supply ought to be targeted directly or whether interest rates are the appropriate targets are questions that the Fed and its critics debate. Through their effects on interest rates, monetary policy decisions have a substantial impact on financial institutions' asset/liability management decisions.

An issue of growing importance is the Fed's need to coordinate monetary policy and regulatory initiatives with central banks in other countries. Recent currency exchange agreements between the United States and other G-7 nations affect the value of the U.S. dollar and the way in which monetary policy is conducted and interpreted. The degree to which U.S. regulations are more or less restrictive than those abroad determines the degree to which U.S. institutions and markets can compete. Although central banks have made strides toward greater policy coordination since the late 1980s, the U.S. financial system continues to be less integrated than those of other major powers. This fact is sure to influence the Fed's behavior, and thus the management of financial institutions, during the 1990s and beyond.

QUESTIONS

1. The Federal Reserve System was created by Congress in 1913 to solve several persistent economic problems, two of which were inadequate control over the money supply and uncertainties in the payments system. Explain briefly the nature of these problems, and describe how the powers of the Fed were designed to solve them.

2. The Fed is sometimes called a decentralized central bank. Explain the structure of the Fed in this context. What political and economic forces provided the motivation for this structure? Has the balance of power shifted toward or away from the Board of Governors since the system was created? Explain.

3. What is a Federal Reserve note? Do you have any? To what extent is the quantity of Federal Reserve notes issued tied to the amount of gold or other assets held by the Fed? Does the current system reflect an elastic or an inelastic currency? Why?

4. Suppose you were hired by the Fed as a consultant to evaluate the safety and stability of the payments system. How would you describe the characteristics of an ideal system? What are daylight overdrafts, and what risks to the payments system do they present? What incentives and disincentives motivate institutions to use daylight overdrafts?

5. An important activity of the Federal Reserve is serving as the lender of last resort. What is the meaning of this term, and how does this Fed power contribute to the stability of the banking system? Ideally, under what circumstances should the Fed lend money to an institution experiencing liquidity difficulties? In your opinion, was the Fed's support of problem thrifts in the late 1980s consistent with the theoretical objectives of a lender of last resort? Why or why not?

6. One of the Fed's important functions is to implement monetary policy. What are the long-term objectives of monetary policy? Is the Fed always free to set its own targets for the level of economic activity and growth? Provide an example to support your answer.

7. The discount window and the discount rate are important in the implementation of monetary policy and in the Fed's role as lender of last resort. Explain how the discount window functions. How may management of the discount rate create conflicts between monetary policy goals and obligations as lender of last resort?

8. Should the Fed be required to publish verbatim transcripts of its deliberations on open market operations? If so, what are the benefits? If not, what are the potential dangers of such public disclosure?

9. Economists have never agreed on a single definition of money. Develop your own general definition of money and its purpose. What monetary aggregate best matches your definition? Is the monetary base a better match for your definition? Why or why not?

10. Suppose that it is your job to develop a procedure for controlling the money supply. Your salary and benefits depend on your success in keeping money within a target range. Would you prefer to use as your definition the monetary base or M2? Why? Now suppose instead that your future depends on your success in controlling inflation and the rate of growth in GNP. Under these circumstances, which definition of money would you choose to watch most closely, and why?

11. The FOMC has just voted unanimously to sell $100 million in government securities to dealers, who in turn will sell them to First National Bank. Explain how this transaction will affect 1) the total assets of First National Bank, 2) the assets and liabilities of the Fed, and 3) the monetary base. What is the role of money multipliers in determining the potential effect on M2?

12. In addition to open market operations, the Fed has two other monetary policy tools. Describe these two tools, and explain why some experts view them as less effective than the work of the FOMC. How does the Fed's obligation to protect the safety and soundness of the financial system complicate the use of these second and third monetary policy tools?

13. In October 1979, the Fed made an important change in monetary policy procedures by switching its focus from the money supply to interest rates as the principal policy target. Explain the subsequent effects on interest rates and the rate of inflation. What has been the lasting effect on financial management techniques in financial institutions? Why?

14. Survey current periodicals and newspapers for a recent report on the Fed's monetary policy decisions. What is the author's evaluation of the effectiveness of recent Fed decisions? What policy tools are mentioned? In the author's opinion, what intermediate target (i.e., money supply or interest rates) is the Fed currently using to guide policy decisions?

15. For several decades prior to 1971, the rate of exchange between the currencies of many countries was related to the value of gold. Is the floating system introduced in 1971 related in any way to gold? If not, what factors influence currency exchange rates? How do the activities of the G-7 countries reduce variability in exchange rates?

16. Explain the term "globalization." Describe at least two recent developments contributing to globalization. Provide an example of the way globalization has increased the need for international coordination of the regulations under which financial institutions operate.

17. The Edge Act and later legislation included provisions that contributed to a balance of power between domestic and international institutions. Compare and contrast Edge Corporations and International Banking Facilities, and explain how they promote international banking activities.

18. What was the reaction of international banks operating in the United States to the restrictive provisions imposed on them by the International Banking Act of 1978? Evaluate these developments in the context of the regulatory dialectic. What was the response of the Fed?

19. Since December 31, 1992, the European Community has made progress toward creating a single market. Explain the expected impact of this economic agreement on the market for financial services in Europe. Why might a single European market place pressure on regulators in the United States to modify long-standing laws and policies?

20. Explain how a more integrated European economic environment may hasten the demise of Glass-Steagall.

21. Do you believe it is appropriate for U.S. regulators to change policies to conform with international standards? What are the benefits to U.S. financial institutions and the U.S. financial system from such policy coordination? Can you think of any circumstances under which major changes in the regulation of capital, deposit insurance, or the scope of banking activities, for example, might pose new risks for the U.S. economy? If so, how can regulators respond to those risks in light of the increasing pressure from globalization?

22. Using your library resources, find a recent article reporting on the status of the unified European Community or the European Monetary Union. In the author's opinion, how close has the European Community really come to removing all economic barriers between the member countries? What difficulties have impeded realization of that ultimate goal? What are the implications for U.S. financial institutions seeking global markets?

23. FDICIA strengthened the Fed's control of foreign banks. Explain the regulatory changes brought about because of that law.

SELECTED REFERENCES

Abken, Peter A. "Globalization of Stock, Futures, and Options Markets." *Economic Review* (Federal Reserve Bank of Atlanta) 76 (July/August 1991): 1–22.

Adamantopoulous, Constantinos G. "A Single Market for Financial Services in 1992." *Journal of Business and Society* 2 (Spring 1989): 49–59.

Aharony, Joseph, Anthony Saunders, and Itzhak Swary. "The Effects of DIDMCA on Bank Stockholders' Returns and Risk." *Journal of Banking and Finance* 12 (September 1988): 317–331.

Baer, Herb L., and Douglas D. Evanoff. "Payments System Risk in Financial Markets that Never Sleep." *Economic Perspectives* (Federal Reserve Bank of Chicago) 14 (November/December 1990): 2–15.

Belton, Terrence M., et al. "Daylight Overdrafts and Payments System Risk." *Federal Reserve Bulletin* 73 (November 1987): 839–852.

Bennett, Thomas, and Craig S. Hakkio. "Europe 1992: Implications for U.S. Firms." *Economic Review* (Federal Reserve Bank of Kansas City) 74 (April 1989): 3–17.

Board of Governors of the Federal Reserve System. *78th Annual Report.* Washington, DC: Board of Governors of the Federal Reserve System, 1991.

Bohne, Edward G. "Is There Consistency in Monetary Policy?" *Business Review* (Federal Reserve Bank of Philadelphia) (July/August 1987): 3–8.

Bordo, Michael D. "The Lender of Last Resort: Alternative Views and Historical Experience." *Economic Review* (Federal Reserve Bank of Richmond) 76 (January/February 1990): 18–29.

Boucher, Janice L. "Europe 1992: A Closer Look." *Economic Review* (Federal Reserve Bank of Atlanta) 76 (July/August 1991): 23–38.

Cargill, Thomas. *Central Bank Independence and Regulatory Responsibilities: The Bank of Japan and the Federal Reserve.* New York: Salomon Brothers Center for the Study of Financial Institutions, 1989.

Carlson, John B. "The Indicator P-Star: Just What Does It Indicate?" *Economic Commentary* (Federal Reserve Bank of Cleveland), September 15, 1989.

Carré, Hervé, and Karen Johnson. "Progress Toward a European Monetary Union." *Federal Reserve Bulletin* 77 (October 1991): 769–783.

Chriszt, Michael J. "European Monetary Union: How Close Is It?" *Economic Review* (Federal Reserve Bank of Atlanta) 76 (September/October 1991): 21–27.

Chrystal, K. Alec. "International Banking Facilities." *Review* (Federal Reserve Bank of St. Louis) 66 (April 1984): 5–11.

Corrigan, E. Gerald. "Challenges Facing the International Community of Bank Supervisors." *Quarterly Review* (Federal Reserve Bank of New York) 17 (Autumn 1992): 1–9.

Cox, W. Michael, and Harvey Rosenblum. "Money and Inflation in a Deregulated Financial Environment: An Overview." *Economic Review* (Federal Reserve Bank of Dallas) (May 1989): 1–19.

Crabbe, Leland. "The International Gold Standard and U.S. Monetary Policy from World War I to the New Deal." *Federal Reserve Bulletin* 75 (June 1989): 423–440.

Cumming, Christine M., and Lawrence M. Sweet. "Financial Structure of the G-10 Countries: How Does the United States Compare?" *Quarterly Review* (Federal Reserve Bank of New York) 12 (Winter 1987–88): 14–25.

Espinosa, Marco and Chong K. Yip. "International Policy Coordination: Can We Have Our Cake and Eat It Too?" *Economic Review* (Federal Reserve Bank of Atlanta) 78 (May/June 1993): 1–12.

Feldberg, Chester B. "Competitive Equality and Supervisory Convenience." *Economic Perspectives* (Federal Reserve Bank of Chicago) 14 (May/June 1990): 30–32.

Frankel, Allen B., and Paul B. Morgan. "Deregulation and Competition in Japanese Banking." *Federal Reserve Bulletin* 78 (August 1992): 579–593.

Friedman, Milton, and Anna J. Schwartz. *A Monetary History of the United States, 1867–1960.* Princeton, NJ: Princeton University Press, 1963.

Garfinkel, Michelle R. "The FOMC in 1988: Uncertainty's Effects on Monetary Policy." *Review* (Federal Reserve Bank of St. Louis) 71 (March/April 1989): 16–33.

Germany, J. David, and John E. Morton. "Financial Innovation and Deregulation in Foreign Industrial Countries." *Federal Reserve Bulletin* 71 (October 1985): 743–753.

Gilbert, R. Alton. "Operating Procedures for Conducting Monetary Policy." *Review* (Federal Reserve Bank of St. Louis) 67 (February 1985): 13–21.

————. "Payments System Risk: What Is It and What Will Happen if We Try to Reduce It?" *Review* (Federal Reserve Bank of St. Louis) 71 (January/February 1989): 3–17.

Hayes, Alfred E. "The International Monetary System—Retrospect and Prospect." *Quarterly Review* (Federal Reserve Bank of New York), special 75th anniversary issue (1989): 29–34.

Houpt, James V. "International Trends for U.S. Banks and Banking Markets." *Federal Reserve Bulletin* 74 (May 1988): 289–290.

Humphrey, Thomas M. "Lender of Last Resort: The Concept in History." *Economic Review* (Federal Reserve Bank of Richmond) 75 (March/April 1989): 8–16.

_____. "Precursors of the P-Star Model." *Economic Review* (Federal Reserve Bank of Richmond) 75 (July/August 1989): 3–9.

Juncker, George R., and Bruce J. Summers. "A Primer on the Settlement of Payments in the United States." *Federal Reserve Bulletin* 77 (November 1991): 847–858.

Kane, Edward J. "Selecting Monetary Targets in a Changing Financial Environment." In *Monetary Policy Issues in the 1980s,* 181–206. Kansas City: Federal Reserve Bank of Kansas City, 1982.

Kapstein, Ethan B. *Surpervising International Banks: Origins and Implications of the Basle Accord.* Princeton University; Essays in International Finance, Number 185, December 1991.

Kasman, Bruce. "A Comparison of Monetary Policy Operating Procedures in Six Industrial Countries." *Quarterly Review* (Federal Reserve Bank of New York) 17 (Summer 1992): 5–24.

Key, Sidney J. "Mutual Recognition: Integration of the Financial Sector in the European Community." *Federal Reserve Bulletin* 75 (September 1989): 591–609.

Kindleberger, Charles P. *Manias, Panics, and Crashes: A History of Financial Crises.* Rev. ed. Basic Books, 1989.

Meek, Paul. *U.S. Monetary Policy and Financial Markets.* New York: Federal Reserve Bank of New York, 1982.

Meulendyke, Ann-Marie. "A Review of Federal Reserve Policy Targets and Operating Guides in Recent Decades." *Quarterly Review* (Federal Reserve Bank of New York) 13 (Autumn 1988): 6–17.

_____. "Reserve Requirements and the Discount Window in Recent Decades." *Quarterly Review* (Federal Reserve Bank of New York) 17 (Autumn 1992): 25–43.

Misback, Ann E. "The Foreign Bank Supervision Enhancement Act of 1991." *Federal Reserve Bulletin* 79 (January 1993): 1–10.

Motley, Brian, and Herbert Runyon. "Interest Rates and the Fed." *Weekly Letter* (Federal Reserve Bank of San Francisco), February 20, 1981.

Osborne, Dale K. "What Is Money Today?" *Economic Review* (Federal Reserve Bank of Dallas) (January 1985): 1–15.

Parthemos, James. "The Origins of the Fed." *Cross Sections* (Federal Reserve Bank of Richmond) 5 (Fall 1988): 9–11.

_____. "The Federal Reserve Act of 1913 in the Stream of U.S. Monetary History." *Economic Review* (Federal Reserve Bank of Richmond) 74 (July/August 1988): 19–28.

Pavel, Christine, and John N. McElravey. "Globalization in the Financial Services Industry." *Economic Perspectives* (Federal Reserve Bank of Chicago) 14 (May/June 1990): 3–18.

Roberds, William. "What Hath the Fed Wrought? Interest Rate Smoothing in Theory and Practice." *Economic Review* (Federal Reserve Bank of Atlanta) 77 (January/February 1992): 12–24.

Robinson, Kenneth J. "Banking Difficulties and Discount Window Operations: Is Monetary Policy Affected?" *Financial Industry Studies* (Federal Reserve Bank of Dallas) (August 1992): 15–23.

Schwartz, Anna J. "The Misuse of the Fed's Discount Window." *Review* (Federal Reserve Bank of St. Louis) 74 (September/October 1992): 58–69.

Sellon, Gordon H., Jr. "The Instruments of Monetary Policy." *Economic Review* (Federal Reserve Bank of Kansas City) (May 1984): 3–20.

_____. "Restructuring the Financial System: Summary of the Bank's 1987 Symposium." *Economic Review* (Federal Reserve Bank of Kansas City) 73 (January 1988): 17–28.

Smith, Stephen D., and Larry D. Wall. "Financial Panics, Bank Failures, and the Role of Regulatory Policy." *Economic Review* (Federal Reserve Bank of Atlanta) 77 (January/February 1992): 1–11.

Spong, Kenneth. *Banking Regulation: Its Purposes, Implementation, and Effects.* 3d ed. Kansas City: Federal Reserve Bank of Kansas City, 1990.

Sproul, Allan. "Reflections on a Central Banker." *Quarterly Review* (Federal Reserve Bank of New York), special 75th anniversary issue (1989): 21–28.

Stevens, E. J. "Comparing Central Banks' Rulebooks." *Economic Review* (Federal Reserve Bank of Cleveland) 28 (1992 Quarter 3): 2–15.

Summers, Bruce J. "Clearing and Payments Systems: The Role of the Central Bank." *Federal Reserve Bulletin* 77 (February 1991): 81–91.

Todd, Walker F. "Lessons of the Past and Prospects for the Future in Lender of Last Resort Theory." In *Proceedings of a Conference on Bank Structure and Competition,* 533–560. Chicago: Federal Reserve Bank of Chicago, 1988.

Wallich, Henry C. "The Role of Operating Guides in U.S. Monetary Policy." *Federal Reserve Bulletin* 65 (September 1979): 679–691.

Walter, John R. "Monetary Aggregates: A User's Guide." *Economic Review* (Federal Reserve Bank of Richmond) 75 (January/February 1989): 20–28.

Weatherstone, Dennis. "A U.S. Perspective on Europe 1992." In *New York's Financial Markets: The Challenges of Globalization,* edited by Thierry Noyelle, 115–118. Boulder, CO: Westview Press, 1989.

Weiner, Stuart E. "The Changing Role of Reserve Requirements in Monetary Policy." *Economic Review* (Federal Reserve Bank of Kansas City) 77 (Fourth Quarter 1992): 45–63.

Wenninger, John, and John Partlan. "Small Time Deposits and the Recent Weakness in M2." *Quarterly Review* (Federal Reserve Bank of New York) 17 (Spring 1992): 21–35.

Wheelock, David C. "The Fed's Failure to Act as Lender of Last Resort during the Great Depression, 1929–1933." In *Proceedings of a Conference on Bank Structure and Competition,* 154–176. Chicago: Federal Reserve Bank of Chicago, 1989.

White, Betsy Buttrill. "Foreign Banking in the United States: A Regulatory and Supervisory Perspective." *Quarterly Review* (Federal Reserve Bank of New York) 7 (Summer 1982): 48–58.

Wormuth, Diana. "Europe Gets Ready for a New Era." *Best's Review* (Property/Casualty Edition) 90 (November 1989): 22–28.

I believe we are going to see national banking in the United States by the end of the decade, probably within the next five years. I want to be able to take advantage of what is coming.

Richard Rosenberg
CEO, Bank America (1991)

———

In Denver, Colorado, dentist Ronald Yaros has personal experience with the effects of interstate expansion in the banking industry. Dr. Yaros had banked with United Banks of Colorado for more than a decade, but in 1991, Norwest Corporation, headquartered in Minnesota, acquired United Banks. In the first year after the acquisition, Dr. Yaros had three different loan officers; when the loan on his vacation home matured, he was informed that Norwest did not serve that part of the state, and he was forced to seek another lender. Next, his line of credit was cut. Finally, believing that the loan officers serving his account had little understanding of either his financial position or his financial needs, Dr. Yaros transferred his business to a small, locally owned community bank and has been much happier.[1]

The rapid growth in interstate acquisitions by bank holding companies all across the nation has generated extensive debate about the potential effects on customers and the banking industry. Some fear that the experiences of Dr. Yaros will become quite common and that local community needs, small businesses, and individuals will not be well served. Others argue that the acquiring banks will continue to provide as good or better service. An equally important question is the effects on the financial health of the banking industry. Interstate expansion continues the trend toward concentrating assets in the control of fewer institutions. Will this strengthen the industry or weaken it as smaller, independently owned banks disappear? Although the answers to these questions have not emerged, little doubt remains about the importance of geographical expansion and other structural issues. A major reason financial institutions differ from nonfinancial firms is that most of their assets are financial claims against others. But many financial institutions are also different because of the ways they raise funds, because of who benefits from the profits, because of where they can locate, and because of whom they can serve. These factors have led to differences in organizational structure explored in some detail in this chapter.

———

[1] Steven Lipin and Marj Charlier, "As National Banking Nears, Mergers Sweep Across State Borders," *The Wall Street Journal,* June 22, 1992, A1, A4.

EQUITY VERSUS NET WORTH

Almost all nonfinancial businesses are organized with an equity investment by one or several persons. Webster's *Ninth New Collegiate Dictionary* defines *equity* as "a risk interest or ownership right in a property." Individuals with equity in a business may be sole owners, as in a proprietorship, with full personal liability for any debt obligations of the business; may share ownership and legal liability with others, as in a partnership; or may have an ownership interest but no personal responsibility for the firm's debt obligations, as in a corporation.

EQUITY IS OWNERSHIP

The "ownership right" part of Webster's definition means that those with equity in a business are entitled to all **residuals,** or profits remaining after the debt of the organization is serviced. Residual profits may be paid to owners in the form of cash dividends or retained in the business to support future operations; in either case, under current tax laws, they are subject to corporate and personal income taxes. Even if earnings are retained, each owner holds claim to a proportionate amount and may realize cash if shares are sold to new owners.

The "risk interest" part of Webster's definition of equity means that residuals may not exist, as the owners of Braniff Airlines found when the firm went bankrupt in 1982, 1989, and again in 1992. However, residuals may be larger than ever imagined, as long-term owners of Wal-Mart have learned. Because such potential variability is risk, holders of equity are subject to considerable risk. Yet their willingness to invest makes the very existence of a business possible. Not surprisingly, then, much of finance theory has been devoted to understanding and improving the risk/expected return relationship for equity holders of nonfinancial firms.

BUT NOT ALL OWNERSHIP IS EQUITY

Financial institutions as a group are unusual because not all of them are organized with equity ownership interests. As noted in Chapter 1, some are mutually organized, including most savings and loan associations (S&Ls), savings banks, and insurance companies. Thrift depositors or insurance policyholders are the "owners" of the business. Their initial deposits or policy premium payments provide the funds from which the institution begins operations. Profits earned from investment of these funds are then returned to customers of the organization in the form of interest on deposits or refunds on past premiums paid. Unlike shareholder-owned businesses, in which an owner may sell shares to realize capital gains, profits not distributed to owner-members of a mutual organization are available for use only by the institution itself. Profits retained are subject to corporate taxes in the year earned, but profits paid to members are taxable at the personal level.

NOT-FOR-PROFIT ORGANIZATIONS

Still other financial institutions, such as credit unions (CUs), are organized on a **not-for-profit** basis. Not-for-profit organizations provide goods or services at below-market or no cost to specific groups of beneficiaries. The organization either distributes income earned in excess of expenses to the beneficiary group in the form of increased services and/or refunds for previous payments or else retains the income to provide a cushion against potential losses. There are no residual claimants. Because not-for-profit organizations are presumed to be charitable, they do not pay taxes, even if they retain excess income.[2]

CONCEPT AND MEASUREMENT OF NET WORTH

Although financial institutions may differ because of the presence or absence of equity ownership interests, all have one thing in common: Each institution must focus attention on its **net worth (NW),** or the difference between the market value of its assets and the market value of its liabilities. Net worth is the cushion between bankruptcy and continued existence.

---

[2] Federal CUs are not the only financial institutions with earnings untaxed at the institutional level. The earnings of investment companies and pension funds are treated similarly. Because investment companies and pension funds lack the charitable objectives of CUs, however, they are not considered not-for-profit institutions, even though they receive similar tax treatment.

It is defined as the amount by which total asset (TA) value can decline before it will be exceeded by the total value of liabilities:

$$NW = TA - TL$$

Net Worth = Value of Assets − Value of Liabilities

This definition simply restates the basic balance sheet identity for an organization:

$$TA = TL + NW$$

Value of Assets = Value of Liabilities + Net Worth

In institutions with equity owners, managerial attention to net worth is equivalent to preserving owners' interests. In mutual and not-for-profit institutions, attention to net worth, although not directly for the benefit of a specific residual group, is necessary to ensure that the members and beneficiary groups of the institution can continue to be served. Consequently, asset/liability management techniques are designed to assist managers in achieving the institution's net worth objectives, regardless of its specific organizational form.

ROLE OF NET WORTH IN ASSET/LIABILITY MANAGEMENT

Specific net worth objectives guiding asset/liability management decisions usually include both a target rate of return and a desired ratio of net worth to total assets. The target rate of return is expressed as the return on net worth (RONW), or the ratio of expected net income (NI) to net worth:

$$RONW = \frac{Net\ Income}{Net\ Worth} \qquad \frac{NI}{NW}$$

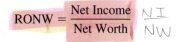

In stockholder-owned institutions, net worth is synonymous with common equity, and return on net worth is usually called return on equity (ROE).[3]

The target ratio of net worth to total assets may be expressed directly as that ratio or as its reciprocal, called the **net worth multiplier:**

leverage

$$Net\ Worth\ Multiplier = \frac{Total\ Assets}{Net\ Worth} \qquad \frac{TA}{NW}$$

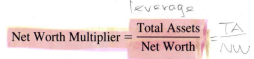

These and other important financial statement relationships are illustrated in Figure 4.1. Ideally, according to its definition, net worth should be calculated as the amount by which *asset market* values exceed *liability market* values. In practice, because market values for some assets and liabilities may be unavailable, book values are often used.

The relationships illustrated in Figure 4.1 can be used to demonstrate how RONW targets affect the target net interest margin (NIM) and thus affect asset/liability management strategies. First, note that NI can be defined mathematically as:

$$NI = [(IR - IE) - NIE] \times (1 - t) \qquad [4.1]$$

Net noninterest expense (NIE) is the difference between noninterest income and noninterest expense.

It follows that the spread (IR − IE) is

$$(IR - IE) = [NI \times 1/(1 - t)] + NIE \qquad [4.1A]$$

Dividing both sides of Equation 4.1A by total assets, one can see that the NIM is also directly related to return on assets (ROA):

$$NIM = \frac{(IR - IE)}{TA} = \left[\frac{NI}{TA} \times \frac{1}{(1-t)} \right] + \frac{NIE}{TA} \qquad [4.2]$$

Figure 4.1 also illustrates that RONW = ROA × the net worth multiplier (TA/NW). Thus, rearranging that relationship,

$$ROA = (RONW) \times \left(\frac{1}{NWM}\right) \qquad [4.3]$$

$$\frac{NI}{TA} = \left[\frac{NI}{NW} \times \frac{NW}{TA} \right]$$

FIGURE 4.1   Financial Statement Relationships

One of an institution's important financial management objectives is to plan for an adequate return on net worth (RONW). Ultimately, RONW is a result of decisions about assets, liabilities, revenues, and expenses. If the net interest margin is not sufficient, RONW objectives will not be met.

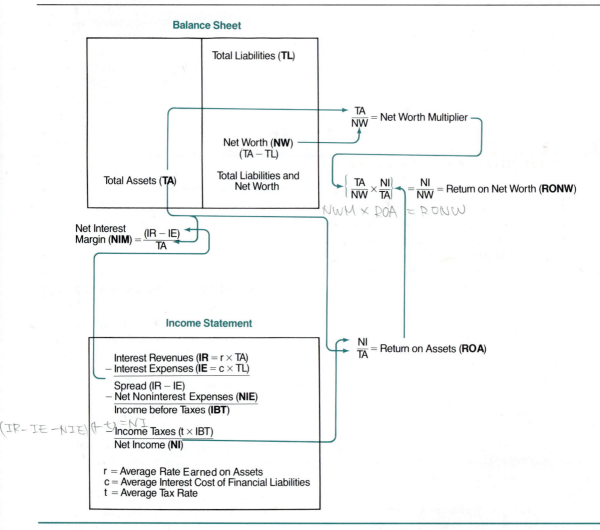

Balance Sheet

Total Liabilities (**TL**)

$\dfrac{TA}{NW}$ = Net Worth Multiplier

Net Worth (**NW**)
(TA − TL)

Total Assets (**TA**)

Total Liabilities and Net Worth

$\left\{ \dfrac{TA}{NW} \times \dfrac{NI}{TA} \right\} = \dfrac{NI}{NW}$ = Return on Net Worth (**RONW**)

NWM × ROA = RONW

Net Interest Margin (**NIM**) $= \dfrac{(IR - IE)}{TA}$

Income Statement

$\dfrac{NI}{TA}$ = Return on Assets (**ROA**)

Interest Revenues (**IR** = r × TA)
− Interest Expenses (**IE** = c × TL)
_____
Spread (IR − IE)
− Net Noninterest Expenses (**NIE**)
_____
Income before Taxes (**IBT**)
− Income Taxes (t × IBT)
_____
Net Income (**NI**)

$(IR - IE - NIE)(1-t) = NI$

r = Average Rate Earned on Assets
c = Average Interest Cost of Financial Liabilities
t = Average Tax Rate

[a] As noted in Chapter 1, some sources prefer to use earning assets rather than total assets as the denominator in the NIM equation. This book, however, uses total assets throughout.

Substituting Equation 4.3 into Equation 4.2 shows that

$$\left[RONW \times \left(\frac{1}{NWM}\right) \times \frac{1}{(1-t)} \right]$$

$$NIM = \left[\frac{NI}{NW} \times \frac{NW}{TA} \times \frac{1}{(1-t)} \right] + \frac{NIE}{TA} \qquad [4.4]$$

Equation 4.4 demonstrates that the target NIM is a function of the target RONW (NI/NW) and the ratio of

net worth to assets (NW/TA), which is the reciprocal of the net worth multiplier. Not surprisingly, the equation also shows that the target NIM must be high enough to cover taxes and net noninterest expenses.

Once management has established net worth targets, a target for the NIM is also implied, given values for existing assets, liabilities, and net worth. For example, if the target RONW is 18 percent; if the desired ratio of net worth to total assets is 8 percent (implying a net worth multiplier of 12.5); if the ratio of net non-interest expense to assets is 1 percent; and if the tax rate is 34 percent, then the minimum NIM necessary to achieve those targets is 3.2 percent:

$$\text{Target NIM} = 0.18 \times 0.08 \times [1/(1 - 0.34)]$$
$$+ 0.01 = 0.032 = 3.2\%$$

Daily decisions concerning asset and liability management must be made with this target in mind if RONW goals are to be achieved.

(citicorp)

BANK HOLDING COMPANIES

Although the basic forms of financial institutions are stock, mutual, and not-for-profit, additional organizational arrangements arise from the basic structures. Each form and its variations have implications for financial management. In particular, the form can affect an institution's growth potential, its ability to raise capital, its opportunities to diversify operations, and its taxation.

Many financial institutions are shareholder-owned, including all commercial banks, all finance companies, many securities firms, some S&Ls and savings banks, and some insurance companies. The primary disadvantage of the corporate form of ownership is double taxation of earnings, once at the corporate level and then again when paid as dividends to owners. The primary advantage is the ability to raise funds more easily than in other organizational forms through the sale of new shares or through access to the commercial paper and bond markets.

Shareholder-owned institutions are also able to take advantage of another organizational arrangement called the **holding company.** Holding companies are businesses formed to acquire the stock of other companies to control their operations. Because commercial bank holding companies (BHCs) are subject to special regulatory treatment, they are discussed in more detail than holding companies formed by other financial institutions.

GROWTH OF BHCS

In the past several decades, commercial banks have increasingly turned to the BHC form of organization, in which controlling interest in the stock of one or several banks—called **subsidiaries**—is owned by a holding company. The stock of the BHC is owned by shareholders. BHCs are also permitted to own non-bank subsidiaries, provided that they obtain regulatory approval.

In the 1980s, the trend toward formation of holding companies accelerated, encompassing small and large banks alike; regulators approved as many as 400 new BHC applications in some years. Between the late 1970s and the early 1990s, the number of BHCs grew at a rate of almost 9 percent annually, reaching a total of nearly 6,500 at the end of 1991. These BHCs controlled more than 93 percent of the assets in insured commercial banks operating in the United States.[4]

REGULATION OF BHCS

Under current law, "controlling interest" in a bank is presumed to exist if a holding company owns 25 percent or more of the bank's voting stock. Controlling interest is presumed not to exist if less than 5 percent of the voting stock is owned. Ownership proportions of at least 5 percent but less than 25 percent are evaluated on a case-by-case basis by officials of the Federal Reserve System (Fed). If more than 85 percent of the stock of a subsidiary is owned by a holding company, dividends paid by the subsidiary to the holding company are not subject to federal taxation when earned by the subsidiary. For this reason, most subsidiaries are fully owned by BHCs.

All BHC activities are regulated by the Fed, regardless of whether the banks owned by the holding company are member banks. The Bank Holding Company Act of 1956 and its 1970 Amendments are the primary sources of existing BHC regulations. Together, they authorize the Federal Reserve Board to approve all applications for formation of BHCs and for acquisition of bank and nonbank subsidiaries. These laws also control the geographic expansion of BHCs.

The 1970 Amendments defined a "bank" for the purposes of BHC regulation as an institution that accepted demand deposits *and* made commercial loans. The Garn-St Germain Act (G-St G) amended the definition by stating that institutions insured by the

---

[4] See Board of Governors 1991, 208, 217. (References are listed in full at the end of this chapter.)

Federal Savings and Loan Insurance Corporation (FSLIC) or chartered by the Federal Home Loan Bank Board (FHLBB) were not banks, regardless of their activities. The Competitive Equality Banking Act (CEBA) of 1987 redefined "bank." CEBA stated that a bank is any institution whose deposits are insured by the Federal Deposit Insurance Corporation (FDIC). Since the Financial Institutions Reform, Recovery, and Enforcement Act (FIRREA), this definition has been applied to institutions insured by the Bank Insurance Fund (BIF). Although there are other definitions of *bank* in law, these meanings have been an important focus of the continuing dialectic between BHCs and their regulators, as explained later in the chapter.[5]

BHC regulations are a separate part of the regulatory structure of banking, imposed in addition to other bank regulations. Despite this additional layer of supervision, the primary motivation for the trend toward BHCs is an attempt by banks to avoid other federal and state regulations that have historically prevented them from raising capital, diversifying their product offerings, or expanding geographically.

RAISING CAPITAL

As noted in Chapter 2 and discussed in more detail in Chapter 17, regulators establish minimum capital standards for commercial banks, requiring that net worth be a specified minimum proportion of total assets. These standards affect the possible rate of expansion by individual banks, because for every dollar by which assets and deposits increase, net worth must also increase. For example, if a bank's equity capital must equal at least 8 percent of total assets, 8 cents of every dollar increase in assets must be financed by retaining earnings or by selling new stock, even though management might prefer to finance expansion solely by increasing deposits. Although BHCs are also subject to minimum capital standards, equity capital from nonbank affiliates of the BHC is currently included in the calculation of overall BHC capital. Therefore, affiliation with a BHC whose nonbank subsidiaries have

[5] For a review of the legal history of the word *bank* from the BHC Act of 1956 through the Garn-St Germain Act, see DiClemente 1983. The CEBA definition is discussed in Smith and Dietz 1988.

FIGURE 4.2 **Downstreaming: BHC Leverage as a Source of Bank Equity Capital**

The holding company structure allows a parent organization to borrow money, then to downstream that borrowed money as new equity in a subsidiary bank.

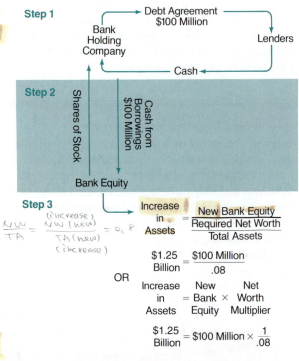

$$\frac{NW}{TA} = \frac{NW\ (new)\ (increase)}{TA\ (new)\ (increase)} = 0.8$$

$$\frac{\text{Increase in Assets}}{} = \frac{\text{New Bank Equity}}{\frac{\text{Required Net Worth}}{\text{Total Assets}}}$$

$$\frac{\$1.25}{\text{Billion}} = \frac{\$100\ \text{Million}}{.08}$$

OR

$$\text{Increase in Assets} = \text{New Bank Equity} \times \text{Net Worth Multiplier}$$

$$\frac{\$1.25}{\text{Billion}} = \$100\ \text{Million} \times \frac{1}{.08}$$

---

relatively high capital ratios can assist a bank in expansion without jeopardizing its position with regulators.

The potential assistance provided by holding company affiliation is illustrated in Figure 4.2. If a commercial bank is owned by a holding company, the BHC may borrow money under its own name, then invest the borrowed funds as equity capital in the bank, a practice known as **downstreaming**. As long as the BHC maintains its own required capital ratio, funds borrowed by the holding company may be used to meet the bank's capital needs in an expansion. In Step 1 of the figure, a BHC borrows an additional $100 million. In Step 2, the BHC downstreams those funds as equity capital to a subsidiary bank with an 8 percent required ratio of net worth to total assets. Finally, in

100 million (= 0.1 billion)

the third step, the bank uses the funds, as well as $1.15 billion additional deposits, to finance a 1.25 billion ($100 million divided by 0.08) increase in assets while still meeting regulatory capital standards.

This so-called **double leverage** substantially reduces the amount of equity capital required for the holding company to control a large dollar volume of bank assets. Also, the level and riskiness of expected RONW are greatly affected by the extent to which financial institutions are leveraged. A numerical illustration of the magnifying impact of leverage on RONW is provided in the appendix to this chapter.

PRODUCT DIVERSIFICATION

Chapter 2 explains that banks' product offerings historically have been limited by regulation. The Glass-Steagall Act (G-S), for example, prohibited Fed member banks *and* their affiliates, such as subsidiaries of the same holding company, from underwriting securities. Although the G-S restrictions have been loosened in recent years, they remain in effect against some underwriting activities.

Except for securities underwriting, however, federal legislation on whether banks should be permitted to engage in other activities besides accepting deposits and making loans has been less specific. The National Currency Act of 1863 stated that banks were allowed "all such incidental powers . . . necessary to carry on the business of banking."[6] This language is broad enough to have allowed widely varying interpretations by regulators over the years. Consequently, activities as diverse as leasing operations and the offering of travel services have been authorized as permissible "incidental powers." Still, when national banks actually engage in these incidental powers, they compete directly with other businesses, a more vulnerable position for banks than some managers and owners (and, especially, than some regulators) may wish.

A holding company gives banking organizations a way to engage in nonbanking activities without directly involving the bank subsidiary and, presumably, without exposing the deposit insurance funds to additional risk. For example, by operating a nonbank subsidiary in the leasing or brokerage business, the BHC gives its shareholders the benefit of the income generated by the nonbank subsidiary and also subjects them to the riskiness of that income stream. Depositors in banking subsidiaries, however, are not directly exposed to risks associated with nonbank subsidiaries. At the extreme, the failure of a nonbank subsidiary could theoretically have no effect on bank subsidiaries of the same BHC. The idea that bank and nonbank subsidiaries from the same BHC can be operated without affecting one another is called **corporate separateness.** Evidence on whether corporate separateness exists in practice is addressed later in the chapter.

Under Federal Reserve Board **Regulation Y (Reg Y),** the Board may allow BHCs to form or acquire nonbank subsidiaries *if* these nonbank subsidiaries are "so closely related to banking or managing or controlling banks as to be a proper incident thereto."[7] The words *closely related* and *proper incident thereto* are subject to the same latitude in interpretation as the words *incidental powers.* Thus, the list of permissible activities has grown as different interpretations have been made.

Table 4.1 reports nonbank activities that had been permitted and denied to BHCs as of the early 1990s. The left section includes activities that have been specifically approved under Reg Y. BHCs desiring to offer these services may do so upon approval by a regional Federal Reserve Bank. The middle section includes activities permitted by special order of the Board of Governors but not officially authorized by Reg Y. BHCs must apply directly to the Board for approval of these activities. The right section includes activities the Board has denied to BHCs. (Some of them have been approved by the Comptroller of the Currency for national banks themselves but not by the Fed for BHCs.) For example, BHCs attempting to establish direct life or property/liability underwriting subsidiaries have been unsuccessful, consistent with the general prohibition of banks and BHCs from underwriting "risky" ventures. In contrast, offering insurance in connection with lending activities ("credit life") was permitted, as were selected securities underwriting activities.

---

[6] See Shull 1981.

---

[7] This phrase is from Section 4(c)8 of the 1970 BHC Amendments. Since that time, nonbank activities permitted to BHCs are often referred to as "4(c)8 activities."

TABLE 4.1	**Permissible Nonbank Activities for Bank Holding Companies**

The nonbank activities of BHCs are controlled by the Fed. Although the list of permissible activities has lengthened in recent years, many activities—especially those related to securities and insurance underwriting—remain prohibited to commercial banking organizations.

Activites Permitted by Regulation

1. Making, acquiring, or servicing loans such as would be made by the following companies:
   - consumer finance
   - credit card
   - mortgage
   - commercial finance
   - factoring
2. Operating an industrial or Morris Plan bank or other industrial loan company
3. Performing trust company or fiduciary activities
4. Investment or financial advising
5. Full payout leasing of personal or real property
6. Investments in community welfare projects
7. Data processing services
8. Acting as insurance agent or broker primarily in connection with credit extensions
9. Underwriting credit life, accident, and health insurance
10. Courier services
11. Management consulting to depository institutions
12. Issuance and sale at retail of money orders with a face value of not more than $1,000, U.S. savings bonds, and travelers checks
13. Real estate and personal property appraisal
14. Arranging commercial real estate equity financing
15. Full-service securities brokerage
16. Underwriting and dealing in U.S. government obligations and money market instruments
17. Foreign exchange advisory and transactional services
18. Futures commission merchant
19. Investment advice on financial futures and options on futures
20. Consumer financial counseling
21. Tax planning and preparation
22. Check-guaranty services
23. Operating a collection agency
24. Operating a credit bureau

Activities Permitted by Order

1. Operating a "pool reserve plan" for loss reserves of banks for loans to small businesses
2. Operating an S&L type business in Rhode Island
3. Operating certain state stock savings banks
4. Buying and selling gold and silver bullion and silver coin for the account of customers
5. Operating an Article XII New York Investment Company
6. Performing commercial banking functions at off-shore locations
7. Offering negotiable order of withdrawal (NOW) accounts

8. Operating an S&L whose activities are limited to those approved for banks
9. Issuance and sale of variably denominated payment instruments (maximum face value of $10,000)
10. Operating a chartered bank that does not both take demand deposits and make commercial loans
11. Providing financial feasibility studies for specific projects of private corporations; valuations of companies and large blocks of stock for a variety of purposes; expert witness testimony on behalf of utility companies in rate cases
12. Providing advice regarding loan syndications, advice in connection with merger, acquisition/divestiture, and financing transactions for nonaffiliated financial and nonfinancial institutions; valuations for nonaffiliated financial and nonfinancial institutions; fairness opinions in connection with merger, acquisition, and similar transactions for nonaffiliated financial and nonfinancial institutions
13. Executing and clearing futures contracts on stock indexes and options on such futures contracts
14. Advisory services with respect to futures contracts on stock indexes and options on futures contracts
15. Credit card authorization services and lost or stolen credit card reporting services
16. Acting as a broker's broker of municipal securities
17. Employee benefits consultant
18. Student loan servicing activities
19. Offering the combination of securities brokerage services and related investment advice to institutional customers
20. Printing and selling checks
21. Cash management services
22. Acting as agent and adviser to issuers of commercial paper in connection with the placement of such paper with institutional purchasers
23. Underwriting and dealing in, to a limited extent, municipal bonds, mortgage-related securities, consumer-receivable related securities, and commercial paper
24. Provision of financial office services
25. Operating a proprietary system for trading put and call options on U.S. Treasury securities
26. Retention of a thrift after the thrift's parent is acquired by a new BHC
27. Acquisition of a healthy savings bank that qualifies as a commercial bank on the basis of its commercial loans and demand deposits
28. Permitting a nonprofit tax-exempt college to become a BHC and engage in college activities, including fund raising incidental to educational activities, but requiring the college to divest real estate received as gifts

TABLE 4.1 *CONTINUED*

29. Consulting and management services to insolvent thrifts
30. Corporate bond trading

Activities Prohibited

1. Insurance premium funding
2. Underwriting life insurance that is not related to credit extension
3. Real estate brokerage
4. Land investment or real estate development
5. Real estate syndication
6. Management consulting to nondepository firms
7. Property management services
8. Operating a travel agency
9. Contract data entry services
10. Underwriting property/liability insurance

11. Dealing in platinum and palladium
12. Engaging in pit arbitrage
13. Public credit ratings on bonds, preferred stock, and commercial paper
14. Acting as a specialist in French franc options on the Philadelphia Stock Exchange
15. Selling title insurance
16. Sale of certain thrift notes
17. Oil and gas activities
18. Timber brokerage activities
19. Sale of level-term credit life insurance
20. Acceptance of deposit accounts linked to credit card accounts
21. Selling auto club memberships

Source: Adapted from King, Tschinkel, and Whitehead 1989, 48–50; *Federal Reserve Bulletin,* various issues.

INTERSTATE EXPANSION

Between 1864 and 1927, national banks were prohibited from branching at all. Since 1927 and the passage of the McFadden-Pepper Act, individual banks have been subject to geographic expansion laws passed by the states in which their main office is located, regardless of the type of charter the bank holds. Specifically, this has meant that individual banks could not open branch offices within a state unless permitted by state law. Furthermore, individual banks cannot open offices outside their home states unless permitted by the laws of the other states. Although almost all states now allow entry by nonresident banks, one still prohibits the establishment of banking offices by banks domiciled in another state.

Some state laws permitting entry by out-of-state banks do so only on a limited basis by agreement with specific, usually neighboring, states. These compacts are anchored on the concept of reciprocity within limited geographic areas. Their major intent has been to promote the growth and development of banks within a region while excluding the entry of large banks from other states. Although banks in states excluded from regional compacts fought to have them declared illegal, the Supreme Court upheld the constitutionality of regional banking in 1985.[8] Figure 4.3 identifies states with either regional or nationwide banking as of 1993.

Besides being affected by state laws, BHCs are also subject to geographic restrictions in the BHC Act and its Amendments. Although they may not have banking subsidiaries in states that do not specifically permit entry by out-of-state BHCs, BHC legislation defined *bank* very narrowly until recently. Organizations either accepting demand deposits or making commercial loans, but not both, were not subject to BHC restrictions. It is not surprising, therefore, that thousands of out-of-state nonbank BHC subsidiaries were established by BHCs headquartered in other states.

Besides establishing nonbank subsidiaries according to Reg Y, BHCs used other legal means to do so. When the BHC Act of 1956 was passed, BHCs with existing out-of-state subsidiaries were permitted to retain them under a grandfather clause. Also, BHCs are permitted to have **loan production offices (LPOs)** out of state. Negotiations for commercial loans occur through LPOs, but no funds are dispensed. Finally, as noted in Chapter 3, BHCs may maintain banking offices out of state to pursue international business; these offices are called Edge Corporations.

Efforts by institutions to expand the geographic scope of their banking activities in the 1980s provide a particularly vivid example of the regulatory dialectic

---

[8] See Clair and Tucker 1989; Whitehead 1985; Richard 1985; "Supreme Court Ruling Supports Regional Banks," *The Wall Street Journal,* June 11, 1985, 3, 14; G. David Wallace, "Nationwide Banking: A Welcome Mat—Not a Slammed Door," *Business Week,* June 24, 1985, 90–91; Baer and Gregorash 1986.

FIGURE 4.3   **Interstate Banking Laws as of mid 1993**

Most states now permit entry by out-of-state banks nationwide, although some require reciprocal agreements. Others permit entry by nonresident banks from selected states only. Only one state (Hawaii) prohibits interstate banking.

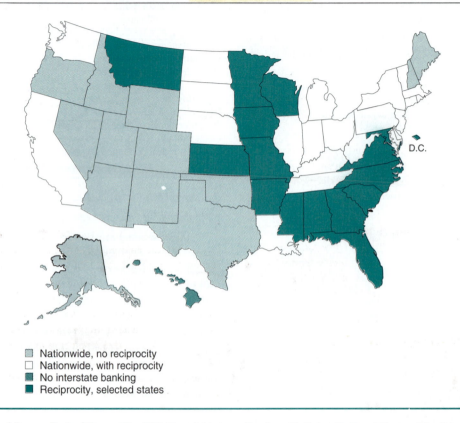

- Nationwide, no reciprocity
- Nationwide, with reciprocity
- No interstate banking
- Reciprocity, selected states

Source: Federal Reserve Bank of Kansas City, *1992 Financial Industry Trends,* p. 31; Robert B. Cox, "Montana May Join 48 Others With Interstate Banking Laws," *American Banker,* April 14, 1993, 12.

---

in action. By 1984, the attention of regulators, bankers, and economists alike was focused on nonbank, or limited-service, banks. Although organizations that accepted deposits or made commercial loans (but not both) were formed as early as 1933, attention to this type of financial institution was heightened in the 1980s.[9] In 1980, the Comptroller of the Currency permitted Gulf and Western Industries to purchase Fidelity National Bank of Concord, California, after selling the bank's commercial loans. Several similar acquisitions were approved, but the 1983 request by Dimen-

sion Financial Corporation to charter 31 *new* nonbank banks drew nationwide attention to the phenomenon. The Fed declined to approve these requests, and Dimension sued.[10]

In January 1986, the Supreme Court ruled that the Fed had exceeded its authority by attempting to halt the expansion of nonbank banks. Although the court stated there is "much to be said" for the regulation of financial institutions, including those that are the "functional equivalent" of banks, it stated that the power to do so belonged to Congress alone. The Fed

---

[9] See Jacobe 1985.

[10] See Moulton 1985.

subsequently recommended to Congress that an unambiguous definition of *bank* be developed, such as "any institution insured by the FDIC," so that institutions conducting similar activities would be subject to the same regulations.

Congress finally agreed, and in CEBA, it defined a bank as the Fed suggested. This definition halted the formation of new nonbank banks as a way to circumvent interstate branching restrictions. Still, more than 150 of them chartered before CEBA were grandfathered, remaining as reminders of the regulatory dialectic. And only 2 years after CEBA, Congress opened a new route for interstate expansion in FIRREA when it decreed that BHCs could acquire healthy out-of-state thrift institutions virtually without restriction.

Lately, the controversy over nonbank banks has heated up again. Although CEBA and FIRREA may seem to have eliminated this route for escaping federal banking laws, previously-existing (now CEBA-grandfathered) nonbank banks have proved to be bigger obstacles to regulatory control than once anticipated. In the early 1990s, several large industrial and nonbank corporations (such as Sears Roebuck, Merrill Lynch, AT&T, and General Motors) began purchasing so-called **industrial loan companies** in Utah. Following the 1987 failure of their private deposit insurance system, these state-chartered entities (which can no longer be newly chartered under Utah law) became eligible to apply for federal deposit insurance. Still, because they are technically not banks or thrifts, they are not subject to G-S restrictions barring their acquisition by industrial or nonbanking firms. And since no laws prevent Sears or AT&T, for example, from branching anywhere they wish, several of the acquiring firms have quickly made plans to have their new Utah-based industrial loan affiliates operate nationwide. BHCs, clearly barred by G-S and CEBA from acquiring these firms, immediately cried "Foul!" and claimed they were facing unfair competition from nonfinancial firms. Observers noted with approval that the FDIC has thus far used the tougher supervisory authority it gained in FDICIA to move swiftly and aggressively to control industrial loan companies' growth rates and product offerings. But corporate acquirers have made it clear that they believe the FDIC is overstepping its authority and have expressed intentions to make the FDIC "back off." The dialectic continues.[11]

IMPLICATIONS OF INTERSTATE EXPANSION FOR BANKING STRUCTURE AND PERFORMANCE

Although interstate banking is a relatively new phenomenon, observers have noted some of its potentially important implications for the industry's future structure and performance.

SUPERREGIONALS. The formation of regional compacts in the mid-1980s gave rise to a new group of BHCs dubbed the **superregionals,** several of which had grown to be among the largest BHCs in the nation by 1990. These BHCs—such as NationsBank, with home offices in Charlotte, North Carolina; Banc One, headquartered in Columbus, Ohio; and Fleet Financial Group, based in Providence, Rhode Island—expanded rapidly under the protection of regional bans that kept out giant BHCs located in New York and California. By the time many of the regional agreements gave way to full interstate banking, the superregionals were major players on the national banking scene. Their strength consists primarily of loans to small and medium-sized corporations and to consumers, two of the important banking markets of the future. Unlike the biggest BHCs, the superregionals are not heavily burdened with loans to developing countries, which, as discussed in Chapter 14, have proved to be exceptionally risky in recent years.[12]

BHC PROFITABILITY. Managers and shareholders are also keenly interested in whether interstate banking will be the key to higher returns on net worth. It is too early to tell for sure about the new wave of interstate

[11] Tim Carrington, "Freeze on New Consumer Banks Renewed, but Comptroller Prods Congress to Act," *The Wall Street Journal,* May 10, 1984; Monica Langley, "Rival Bank Regulators Agree Only to Disagree on Most Major Issues," *The Wall Street Journal,* January 23, 1985; Stephen Wermiel and Monica Langley, "Top Court Clears Limited-Service Banks and Deals Major Blow to Power of Fed," *The Wall Street Journal,* January 23, 1986, 4; Peter Pae, "Corporate Giants Buy Tiny Thrifts in Utah in Bid to Start Banks," *The Wall Street Journal,* November 17, 1992, A1, A4.

[12] See Steven Lipin and Marj Charlier, "As National Banking Nears, Mergers Sweep Across State Borders," *The Wall Street Journal,* June 22, 1992, A1, A4; Robert Guenther, "Some Regional Banks Grow Rapidly, Reach Major League Status," *The Wall Street Journal,* October 1, 1987, 1, 18; and Andrews and Milligan 1985. Rose 1989 provides a comprehensive review of relevant issues.

expansion, but recent research provides interesting findings related to the question. As noted earlier, the BHC Act of 1956 "grandfathered" interstate banking operations in existence before the law was passed, although it barred the spread of BHCs interstate after that time. In a study using data from 1960 through 1983, researchers compared the profitability and market share of grandfathered interstate BHCs to BHCs not permitted to expand interstate. They found no evidence that the grandfathered BHCs had a competitive advantage over banks in single-state markets; neither did the interstate banks do worse than their in-state competitors. Other research indicates that small banks may, in fact, face greater competition when larger out-of-state banks enter their markets. The effects differ, however, depending on the competitive environment existing before the onset of interstate banking. Still, some observers have expressed concern that interstate banking will allow large multistate BHCs to dominate smaller banks. But other studies argue that preventing interstate banking disadvantages consumers and contributes to regional economic declines because it keeps banks from diversifying to offset local economic conditions that can lead to bank failures. Research on the topic will no doubt continue.[13]

MORE ON CORPORATE SEPARATENESS: FACT OR FICTION?

As noted earlier, the doctrine of corporate separateness holds that, because the legal organization of BHCs makes their subsidiaries separate corporate entities, the financial problems of one should theoretically have no effect on others. Whether corporate separateness is synonymous with economic and financial separateness, however, is debatable. Connections between holding company affiliates may be subtle and even undetectable by outsiders. Suppose, for example, that BHC management diverts resources that could just as easily be used in a bank subsidiary to a troubled holding company affiliate; that an affiliate provides services to a bank at a higher price than would be charged in the open market; or that public confidence

in a bank is eroded by the failure of an affiliated bank or nonbank. Even though Federal Reserve Board regulations limit the activities of BHC subsidiaries and regulate transactions between affiliates of the same BHC, some observers argue that these regulations cannot address the potential problem of a bank run caused by the failure of an affiliated subsidiary. In addition, under the current rules, few believe that the Fed or other regulators would fail to assist a bank that was weakened because of problems elsewhere in the holding company. Experts also note that for the purpose of credit ratings, holding companies tend to be viewed as one entity; that is, the parent holding company's financial condition is considered when providing a credit rating for a subsidiary's debt, even if the two firms are legally separate companies.[14]

Empirical evidence seems to support these arguments.[15] For example, a recent survey of **multibank holding companies (MBHCs)**—BHCs with more than one bank subsidiary—indicated that the budgeting, capital management, and portfolio management policies of their bank subsidiaries were highly centralized and that the degree of centralization has increased over time. Centralized management of nonbank subsidiaries has been documented, as well as the tendency of BHC management to rely on the resources of the entire organization to prevent the failure of an individual subsidiary. Some studies show that affiliation with BHCs seems to result in shifts among subsidiary banks to relatively riskier loans, lower levels of liquidity, and lower capital ratios. Although not directly examining corporate separateness, a recent study at the Fed found that nonbank affiliates of BHCs were more profitable but had riskier assets than bank subsidiaries of the same holding company. The authors also found that the probability of insolvency was greater in nonbank subsidiaries and noted it was likely that the parent company would provide capital assistance to a subsidiary in financial difficulty.

Despite this evidence, there is, by no means, agreement that BHCs should be prohibited from own-

---

[13] See Goldberg and Hanweck 1988; Laderman and Pozdena 1991; Gunther 1992; and Calem 1993.

[14] See Wall 1984.

[15] The evidence includes Liang and Savage 1990; Pozdena 1988; Whalen 1981–1982; Eisenbeis 1983; Chase and Mingo 1975; Cornyn and Talley 1983; and Frieder and Apilado 1982.

Affiliation more risk more profit

Subsidiary less risk less

ing nonbank subsidiaries. Some analysts argue that because financial market participants view BHCs as single entities, BHC affiliation may decrease the soundness of banks to the extent that affiliated subsidiaries engage in risky activities.[16] Yet others believe that the benefits of BHC affiliation, particularly the potential for reducing risk through geographic diversification, may outweigh the potential risk increases, at least from a shareholder's perspective.[17]

Still others note that, regardless of riskiness, BHCs should not be prohibited from owning nonbanking subsidiaries, because that action would simply make them unable to compete with other firms, especially foreign banks. Instead, regulators should direct efforts toward requiring thicker "firewalls" between bank and nonbank subsidiaries to make sure that the principles of corporate *and* economic separateness hold. Banking activities would then be narrowly limited and strictly supervised by regulators, and BHCs would be required to offer all nonbanking services through subsidiaries in no way protected by deposit insurance. With better firewalls, according to this view, BHCs whose managers and owners decide to pursue expansion into nonbanking products and services, such as securities and insurance, would then bear the risks—and reap the potential rewards—of those services themselves. Even supporters of this argument acknowledge the tension between the existence of firewalls and the potential for institutions to reap the promised benefits of expanded powers. The thicker the firewalls, the greater the protection for the deposit insurance system, but also the more difficult for BHCs to obtain the full benefits of diversification.

As an added complication, the Fed has followed a policy in its regulation of BHCs that runs counter to corporate separateness. This policy is known as the **source of strength doctrine** and requires the holding company to be a source of financial and managerial support to its subsidiary bank(s). Rather than promoting separation by firewalls, the source of strength policy implies a close relationship between the parent and

the subsidiary. Congress took a similar approach in FDICIA when it required holding companies to guarantee plans to restore capital in undercapitalized subsidiary banks. Thus, the optimal relationship between holding companies and subsidiary banks continues to be debated energetically.[18]

The one thing on which experts do agree is that more research is needed into the relationships among BHC affiliation, nonbank activities, and the riskiness of banking organizations. Because the size of banking organizations increases with holding company affiliation and because the failure of large banks is a greater shock to the financial system than the failure of smaller banks, the issue will remain critical as deregulation of the financial system proceeds.

HOLDING COMPANIES: NONBANK FINANCIAL INSTITUTIONS

Many shareholder-owned nonbank financial institutions—such as stockholder-owned savings and loans, finance companies, and insurance companies—are affiliated with holding companies. For many of these institutions, laws governing nonbank holding companies are considerably less restrictive than those governing BHCs. For example, there are no federal requirements that subsidiaries of insurance holding companies must engage in activities "closely related" to the insurance business. As a consequence, stockholder-owned insurers are partially or fully owned by firms in industries such as retailing; Sears, Roebuck and Company's Allstate Insurance subsidiary is a good example. Many finance companies, too, are part of holding company organizations diversified well beyond financial services.

FIRREA placed new restrictions on thrift holding companies. They must now notify the Office of Thrift Supervision (OTS) and the FDIC of intended acquisitions or planned new activities in current subsidiaries; if regulators conclude that new activities or acquisitions could endanger the institution's stability

---

[16] See Cornyn and Talley 1983, 36–37. For an exhaustive review of this point, see Cornyn, Hanweck, Rhoades, and Rose 1986.

[17] See Benston 1991; Brewer 1988; Eisenbeis, Harris, and Lakonishok 1984; and Wall November 1986.

[18] See Mester 1992 for a comprehensive review of these arguments. Further discussion is found in Gilbert 1991; Keeton 1990; Greenspan 1990; Keeley and Bennett 1989; Gilbert 1988; Corrigan 1987; and Keehn 1989.

or the safety of the deposit insurance system, permission can be denied. Furthermore, thrift holding companies whose portfolios fail to meet FIRREA's "qualified thrift lender (QTL)" test can subsequently be brought under more stringent BHC regulations.

GEOGRAPHIC EXPANSION WITHOUT HOLDING COMPANIES

Although stockholder-owned financial institutions, especially banks, have found the holding company form of organization increasingly attractive in recent years, alternative methods of geographic expansion exist. These methods are used in addition to, or in place of, holding company formation, depending on state law and on the objectives of the parent organization.

INTRASTATE BRANCHING

Not long ago, a central issue in the regulatory dialectic was whether commercial banks should be allowed to open more than one branch office within their home states. As recently as 1974, only 19 states permitted statewide branching by resident banks. A classic article analyzing the pros and cons of intrastate branching called it the "perennial issue," referring to the fact that for more than a century the debate had raged continuously among small banks, large banks, and regulators.[19] Most small, rural institutions were opposed to branch banking, arguing that they would be unfairly disadvantaged if "big city" banks were allowed to operate anywhere they wanted. Supporters of branch banking argued that it was safer, noting that most bank failures during the Great Depression were in states that prohibited branch banking (so-called **unit banking states**).

Gradually, supporters of branch banking prevailed, and by 1993, statewide branching by commercial banks was permitted in 44 states; branching within a limited area was permitted in the other six.[20] Many legislatures heeded complaints by bankers about unfair competition from rival institutions without intrastate branching restrictions; many also believed large banks' arguments that, under branch banking, funds could move more efficiently to areas of greatest need. Legislators in some states also saw liberalization of branching laws as a way of preventing failures; by permitting branch banking, weaker unit banks could become branches of stronger firms instead.

Although these data might seem to imply that branching is now a completely irrelevant issue for financial institutions' managers, that is not the case. In states that prohibit formation of multibank holding companies (MBHCs), branch banking may be the only way to operate in a desired geographic market. Even if MBHCs are permitted, branching may be a less costly way to expand in-state. Finally, branching raises questions of **economies of scale** in financial institutions— that is, questions about whether increasing an institution's size will lower the cost of its products and services and whether there is, in fact, an optimal size for financial firms. Because economies-of-scale questions arise not only in connection with branching but also in relation to other forms of expansion by institutions, they are discussed in a separate section later in the chapter.

CHAIN BANKING

As noted, not all states allow MBHCs, thereby preventing the operation of several banks under one umbrella organization. This prohibition has not, however, prevented other ways of affiliating several banks or one-bank holding companies. One of the most common arrangements is **chain banking.** Chain banking occurs when one investor owns 5 percent of the voting stock in one or more individual banks *and* holds a managerial post in each bank, or when an individual or group owns at least 10 percent of the voting shares of two or more banks. In a few instances, chain-banking organizations have been formed by individuals with common ownership shares in two or more one-bank holding companies.

Because of the more informal structure of chain banking, the independent identity of each bank is maintained to a greater degree than in an MBHC, yet a single investor or group is able to control a substantial amount of banking assets. Furthermore, chain-banking organizations not involving holding companies are not subject to BHC geographic restrictions, so chains can cross state lines, regardless of state laws on

---

[19] See Mote 1974. Mote's article contains an interesting and comprehensive history of theory and evidence on the subject.

[20] The effects of liberalized branching laws on statewide and local banking markets are discussed in Amel and Jacowski 1989.

interstate banking. Also, reporting requirements are not stringent, so less is known about the performance of chain banks than about BHCs.[21]

FRANCHISING

Another alternative to a holding company is the franchise, under which an independent financial institution leases the right to use the name and marketing programs of a larger umbrella organization. The first application of franchising to financial institutions is attributed to First Interstate Bancorp, one of the interstate banking organizations grandfathered under BHC legislation. In 1982, First Interstate began leasing the use of its name and promotional strategies to independent banks around the nation. A franchising institution must change its name to First Interstate Bank of [its town] but does not become a member of the holding company. The objective of franchisees is to obtain the benefits of association with a large banking organization, such as a wide range of marketing and other managerial talents, while still retaining operational independence.[22]

Thrift institutions also participate in franchising. The leader in the thrift franchise movement was First Nationwide Network, which leased the right to the phrase "a member of the First Nationwide Network" and made available a host of management support systems. In 1990, the name was changed to U.S. Banking Alliance, and network membership opportunities were extended to community banks. As with the First Interstate franchise, U.S. Banking Alliance appeals to smaller institutions hoping to compete successfully as independent firms.

MUTUALLY OWNED INSTITUTIONS

Unlike stockholder institutions, mutually organized firms, such as thrifts and insurers, are "owned" by their customers. Depositors, policyholders, or borrowers become owners when they initiate a business relationship with the institution.

DISTRIBUTION OF MUTUAL INSTITUTIONS

Table 4.2 provides information on the number of shareholder-owned versus mutually owned thrifts and life insurance companies. For reasons explored later, the number of stock companies has been increasing in recent years. Nonetheless, most S&Ls, savings banks, and property/liability insurers (for which data are not shown in the table), are mutually owned. Most life insurers are organized as stockholder-owned corporations, although the largest firms in the industry are mutually organized. The opposite is true for S&Ls; most are mutuals but the largest are shareholder-owned.

ORIGIN AND CHARACTERISTICS OF MUTUAL OWNERSHIP

The primary rationale for the mutual form of organization is that it presumably ensures that an institution will operate for the benefit of its customers, who have supplied the majority of funds and depend on it for service and security. In the United States, this

TABLE 4.2	Ownership Form in the Thrift and Life Insurance Industries

Most firms in the thrift industry are mutually owned, although many large firms are stockholder-owned. Mutual ownership has limited the industry's ability to raise additional external capital. The opposite prevails in the life insurance industry, where the largest firms are mutually owned.

	Federally Insured Savings Institutions[a]	
	Number	**Percent**
Mutual	1,588	58.0
Stock	1,162	42.0
Total	2,750	100.0
	Life Insurance Companies[b]	
	Number	**Percent**
Mutual	117	5.6
Stock	2,078	94.4
Total	2,195	100.0

[a] March 31, 1991 data. Does not include 204 thrifts consigned to the RTC.
[b] 1990 data.
Sources: National Council of Savings Institutions, *Economic Insight,* August 1991; American Council of Life Insurance, *1991 Life Insurance Fact Book.*

---

[21] For more information on chain banks, see Federal Reserve Bank of Kansas City 1983, 9–11; and Cyrnak 1986.

[22] See Eickhoff 1985 and Carner 1986–1987.

rationale dates to the early 1800s, when consumer-oriented financial institutions appeared for the first time. Instead of focusing exclusively on profits, managers of mutual institutions supposedly make decisions that meet their customers' needs better.[23]

OWNERS' RIGHTS. Ownership rights in a mutual organization are considerably different from those in a stockholder-owned firm. In both instances, the owners have a right to elect a board of directors to monitor management's performance. But potential control over management is stronger in a stockholder-owned firm. First, because ownership rights in a mutual institution cannot be sold to another party (in legal language, they are nonnegotiable), there is little chance that anyone can obtain enough influence to control the outcome of elections. Furthermore, in some thrift institutions, owners are asked to sign away their rights to vote at the time they open an account or take out a loan, in effect giving managers a permanent proxy. Some observers of thrifts have stated, in fact, that a mutual organization often results in a "self-perpetuating" board. Further, although owners of a mutually organized company theoretically have a pro rata claim on the institution's retained earnings, they have no way to exercise that claim. Because there are no negotiable ownership shares, no capital gains can be earned. An owner who cancels a policy or closes a deposit account also cancels the right to this pro rata share. Finally, mutually owned institutions are not legally required to disclose as much detail about their financial condition as are stockholder-owned firms. Thus, depositors or policyholders may lack access to information about the safety and soundness of their institutions.

PERFORMANCE OF MUTUAL FIRMS. As a result of these differences, some argue that managers have more latitude in mutual organizations than in stockholder-held firms. Whether or not this latitude is good depends on its effect on institutional performance relative to the performance of similar stockholder-owned institutions. Much of the research evidence on this point has been accumulated for S&Ls. Some scholars

have hypothesized that stock associations should be more cost-efficient and more profitable, because of managers' fear of removal by shareholders if costs are excessive and profits inferior. Agency theory, discussed in Chapter 1, suggests that mutually owned associations, in which owners' monitoring costs are likely to be higher, may permit managers to exercise their own preferences to a greater degree than in stockholder-owned institutions. Furthermore, because of the possibility of managerial benefits from stock options in stockholder-owned associations, those managers should be more aggressive and willing to take more risks than managers of mutually owned firms. Finally, because mutual associations have only one source of net worth—earnings retained from profitable operations—stock associations have been hypothesized to be better capitalized than mutuals. Yet, other researchers, while acknowledging that mutuals' managers may have greater latitude, have hypothesized that they may also have considerable incentive to be efficient: If their institutions fail, they will be out of their jobs.

Tests of these hypotheses have yielded mixed results. Generally, researchers have concluded that stock associations are riskier and more aggressive because they grow at faster rates, but they are not necessarily more efficient or more profitable than their mutual counterparts.[24]

In the 1980s, when the thrift industry as a whole was unprofitable, events demonstrated that one key difference between mutuals and stocks—their ability to raise capital—is important. When profits are negative and retained earnings are reduced, mutual associations have no way to replenish lost net worth. If losses persist, mutual thrift institutions may be forced into a position of negative net worth, eventually leading to failure. Similar profitability difficulties, as well as tax considerations, have troubled mutually owned insurance companies. More and more, the thrift and insurance industries have turned to **conversion,** a procedure through which an institution's organizational structure changes from mutual to stock.

---

[23] See Blyn 1981, 40–41; and Smith and Stutzer 1990.

[24] Discussions of mutual versus stock S&L performance can be found in Simpson and Kohers 1979; Woerheide 1984, 29–31; "Well-Run Mutuals Deserve the Needed Latitude to Succeed," *Savings Institutions* 112 (May 1991): 14–15; Akella and Greenbaum 1988; Fields 1988; Mester 1993; Cebenoyan et al 1993.

CONVERSION: THE THRIFTS

In the 1980s more than 500 thrifts converted from the mutual to the stock form of ownership, a rapid rate compared with the past. Many observers expect the pace to continue as thrifts struggle to meet the more stringent capital requirements imposed by FIRREA and FDICIA.[25] Requirements for conversion are strictly defined by the OTS and are intended to promote conversions while limiting the possibility that only a few individuals can benefit at the expense of others.[26] The process involves the preparation of a conversion plan by management with the approval of directors, regulators, and most owner-depositors. Stock sold in a conversion is first offered to eligible depositors, none of whom may purchase more than 5 percent of the new stock. Depositors not interested in the stock may not sell their rights to those who are.

Few studies have evaluated the results of recent thrift conversions. However, an analysis of converted thrifts in New England concluded that they were less profitable than their mutual counterparts. Unfortunately, their managers invested heavily in commercial real estate shortly before that market collapsed. The author noted that all thrifts in the region had similar opportunities, but managers eager to take more risk chose to convert. Thus, conversion allows some institutions greater access to capital but does not ensure that managers will make good investment decisions. Another recent study found that the proportion of stock owned by managers of a converted institution greatly influences whether they engage in expense-preference behavior. The more stock managers acquire, the more likely they are to favor on-the-job perquisites for themselves, and, thus, the more similar is their behavior to that of managers in mutual thrifts. When managers of converted thrifts own relatively little stock, nonmanager-owners can exert greater control on the institution's expenses.[27]

CONVERSION: THE INSURERS

The insurance industry, too, has faced profitability problems recently because changing consumer preferences, increasing litigation of claims, inflation, and changing interest rates have required large cash outflows. Like their thrift counterparts, mutual insurers have faced pressures from reduced net worth caused by low or negative earnings. Consequently, they, too, have considered conversion as a survival strategy. Several property/liability insurers have converted since 1984, and in 1984, the first application in 80 years for conversion of a mutual life insurer was filed by Union Mutual Life with the Maine insurance commission. Especially noteworthy was the 1992 conversion by Equitable Life Assurance Society, the fourth largest firm in the industry.[28]

Motivation for conversion was fueled by the Tax Reform Act of 1984, which lowered the amount of tax-deductible "dividends" that can be paid to policyholder-owners of mutual insurers. Because the tax deductibility of these dividends was a major reason for the popularity of the mutual form of organization, its attractiveness was thought to have been considerably reduced. The first few years under the 1984 law, however, were not as burdensome for mutuals as predicted.[29]

Because the regulation of insurers rests largely at the state, rather than federal, level, there is no uniform procedure for conversion analogous to the policies governing thrifts. Observers of recent conversions suggest that managers and some policyholders may

---

[25] From 1945 to 1955, when there were few restrictions on conversion, only 30 thrifts converted. From 1955 to 1974, conversions were prohibited altogether. Even though restrictions were removed after 1974, few conversions occurred until the financial crisis in the industry beginning in 1980. See Dunham 1985 and Simons 1992.

[26] FHLBB, "Conversions from Mutual to Stock Form and Acquisitions of Control of Insured Institutions," 12 CFR Parts 543, 546, 552, 562, 563, 563b, and 574, October 17, 1986; and U.S. League of Savings Institutions, "Conversions from Mutual to Stock Form and Acquisitions of Control of Insured Institutions," *Special Management Bulletin,* August 28, 1987.

[27] See Simons 1992.

[28] Dan Baum, "Union Mutual's Plan to Be Stock Owned Leads to Suits Against Some Agents and a Proxy Fight," *The Wall Street Journal,* February 26, 1985; Laura Meadows, "Minuet in Maine," *Forbes,* November 18, 1985, 208; Susan Pullian, "Equitable Life to Convert to Stock-Owned Company," *The Wall Street Journal,* December 12, 1990, A3; and Greg Steinmetz, "Equitable Sets Offering Price Below Target," *The Wall Street Journal,* July 15, 1992, A4.

[29] Murray 1985; and Jeffrey H. Birnbaum, "Tax Battle between Stocks and Mutual Insurers, a Dispute Nearly 80 Years Old, Is Set to Resume," *The Wall Street Journal,* April 25, 1989, A30.

gain more from conversion than others and that state officials should, therefore, closely scrutinize conversion plans. Other research indicates that life insurance conversions are more likely to be motivated by a need to improve economic efficiency rather than by one group's desire to increase its wealth at the expense of others. Equitable's decision to convert was clearly spurred by net worth constraints, and some experts have predicted that the number of insurers will decline (or even disappear altogether) as a result of the heightened need for capital in a more competitive environment. Observers have also noted that international insurance firms—particularly those in the European Community—are increasingly interested in the U.S. markets, as evidenced by Group AXA's investment in Equitable. Such international firms could create a strong market for the shares of converted mutuals. If these trends continue, the insurance industry is in for major structural change.[30]

HOLDING COMPANIES FOR MUTUAL THRIFTS

CEBA ushered in a new organizational form for mutually owned thrift institutions. Previously unable to form holding companies, they may now do so. The unusual procedure involves a mutual thrift's first transferring assets, insured liabilities, and capital to a newly formed stockholder-owned savings bank subsidiary. Common stock in the new subsidiary bank can be sold to the public to raise additional capital. The mutual institution (now the parent holding company with the same management and board as before) can retain operating control over the new bank by simply continuing to hold at least 51 percent of the shares. The parent company can also invest in other stockholder-owned thrifts.

It is too early to tell whether this experiment will attract more capital to mutual firms, although that was clearly Congress's intent in passing the original enabling legislation and in strengthening it in FIRREA. The first successful market test of the provision was conducted by Peoples Bank in Bridgeport, Connecticut, which formed a mutual holding company in 1989;

the institution attracted $55 million in new equity capital. Recently, observers have noted that the mutual holding company provides a way to retain the mutual form of organization while giving stock-option incentives to management. If so, mutual holding companies may help to reduce agency costs.[31]

SERVICE CORPORATIONS: THE HOLDING COMPANY ALTERNATIVE

Alternative structures besides holding companies permit thrift mutuals (and stock institutions, too, if they so desire) to diversify outside their traditional functions of accepting deposits and making mortgage loans.

Since the 1950s, S&Ls with federal charters have been permitted to form **service corporations (SCs)** to conduct diversified lines of business. An SC is formed when one or more associations purchase the stock of a new organization. The associations, as residual owners of the SC, are entitled to all profits from its operations. The amount invested in SCs is limited to 3 percent of a thrift's total assets. Although laws vary from state to state, similar arrangements exist for mutual insurance companies to form subsidiaries by using some of their assets to purchase stock in affiliated stockholder-owned organizations.

Typically, investment in SCs has been less than 2 percent of the S&L industry's assets. SC activities include real estate development and property management, insurance agency and brokerage services, appraisal services, data processing services, and consumer lending. Little long-term evidence is available on the effect of SCs on institutional profitability.[32]

---

[30]Heimann 1984; McNamara and Rhee 1992; "AXA Feels Equitable," *The Economist,* May 30, 1992, 78–79; and Russ Banham, "Tough Times, Tough Choices," *Insurance Review,* September 1992, 24–27.

[31]U.S. League of Savings Institutions, "The Competitive Equality Banking Act of 1987," *Special Management Bulletin,* October 16, 1987; Resa W. King, "The Shape of Thrifts to Come?" *Business Week,* September 18, 1989, 102; "Mutual Holding Companies May Be a Growing Trend," *Savings Institutions* 110 (December 1989): 6–7; Tom Parliment, "To Raise Capital, Consider A Mutual Holding Company," *Savings Institutions* 112 (May 1991): 52–53; and Phillip Britt, "Mutual Holding Companies Unlock Needed Capital," *Savings Institutions* 113 (January 1992): 9; and Brian Nixon, "Going Full Stock or Mutual Stock," *Savings and Community Banker* 2 (February 1993): 22–26.

[32]Pat Allen, "Service Corporations Fight for Earnings," *Savings Institutions* 108 (May 1987): 42–49; "Service Corporations Are Ideal Diversification Tool," *Savings Institutions* 104 (October 1983): 52–55; and Harold B. Olin, "Service Corporations Help the Business Diversify," *Savings Institutions* 105 (April 1984): 120–127.

NOT-FOR-PROFIT INSTITUTIONS

The third main organizational structure in financial institutions is the not-for-profit form. Credit Unions (CUs) are currently the only major financial group with this structure. CUs are similar to mutually owned institutions with two major exceptions: Membership in CUs is restricted by law to those with a common bond, and profits retained by federal CUs to increase the net worth of the organization are not taxable.

The **common bond** requirement for membership in a CU—usually a tie formed as a result of occupational, religious, or social affiliations—is related to the cooperative motivation that theoretically underlies the formation of mutual financial institutions. Because federal CUs are exempt from taxation based on the purported strength of this cooperation, the common bond requirement is intended to ensure that the spirit of colleague helping colleague is a reality. In practice, the interpretation of the phrase *common bond* has been expanded over the years, and it is now quite liberal.

CU members are "owners" of the organization. In fact, their savings are called "shares," although these shares are more like deposits than stock because they are eligible for federal deposit insurance. As in mutuals, members cannot sell shares to profit from capital gains. Also like mutuals, CUs must maintain sufficient net worth (called "reserves") from earnings retention to withstand a potential decline in asset values; they have no other source of equity-like capital. Nevertheless, their tax exemption may enable federal CUs to charge lower loan rates, yet achieve the same additions to net worth as a comparably sized S&L or savings bank.

SERVICE ORGANIZATIONS

Federal CUs can form **credit union service organizations (CUSOs)** on a for-profit basis. As with thrift service corporations, investment in CUSOs is limited, although the restriction is expressed as a percentage of a CU's net worth, not of its assets. CUSOs enable CUs to earn income from sources that would be prohibited without the CUSO, such as insurance, brokerage, and financial planning services. The small size of most CUs has prevented them from using CUSOs up to this point, although managers in larger CUs

found them to be an attractive diversification vehicle in the 1980s.[33]

ECONOMIES OF SCALE AND SCOPE

As noted earlier, managers must be able to evaluate alternative organizational structures not only because of their relative regulatory advantages and disadvantages but also because answers to questions about firm structure (and its close relative, firm size) may affect financial performance. Are banks that can grow by branching more or less efficient than small unit banks? Are MBHCs with both bank and nonbank subsidiaries more or less efficient than banks and nonbanks operating separately? Is a thrift with $15 billion in assets able to provide loans at lower cost than a thrift with only $500 million in assets? These and similar questions are asked in an extensive body of research on financial institutions—studies of economies of scale and scope.

ECONOMIES OF SCALE AND SCOPE ILLUSTRATED

Economies of scale occur when the average cost of producing a product or service declines as the amount produced increases. Economies of scope occur when the cost of producing two or more products jointly is less than the cost of producing an equivalent quantity of each product separately. Economies of scale and scope are by no means mutually exclusive, and Table 4.3 provides a numerical illustration of each.

Suppose that Bank A decides to make only commercial loans. It purchases a computer and hires two loan officers, thus incurring fixed costs. Bank A will also have variable costs, such as interest paid on funds with which to make loans; these costs will increase as the size of the loan portfolio increases. Bank A may be able to make 400 commercial loans at a lower average cost than if it made only 100 loans, because the computer's cost and the loan officers' salaries would be spread over a greater number of loans. If Bank B across the street made only consumer loans, it might

---

[33] "CUSOs Open New Service Areas," *Credit Union Magazine* 50 (November 1984): 8–14; and "Leagues and Regulators Take a Hard Look," *Credit Union Magazine* 50 (December 1984): 42–45.

TABLE 4.3   Economies of Scale and Scope

Both banks A and B are subject to economies of scale, because at certain levels of lending, the average cost per loan declines. Bank B is subject to diseconomies of scale as well; if it makes more than 200 loans, the average loan cost rises. At certain levels of output, economies of scope are also present. It costs less to make both commercial and consumer loans than to make an equivalent amount of each type separately.

A. Bank A (Commercial Loans Only)			B. Bank B (Consumer Loans Only)		
No. of Loans	Total Cost	Average Cost	No. of Loans	Total Cost	Average Cost
0	$ 12,000		0	$ 12,000	
100	60,000	$600	100	52,000	$520
200	100,000	500	200	100,000	500
300	132,000	440	300	156,000	520
400	156,000	390	400	220,000	550
Economies of scale at all levels			Economies of scale at some, but not all, levels		

C. Both Commercial and Consumer Loans

No. of Loans (Commercial)	No. of Loans (Consumer)	Total Cost if Made Jointly	Total Cost if Made Separately
100	100	$102,000	$112,000
	200	152,000	160,000
	300	210,000	216,000
	400	276,000	280,000
200	100	144,000	152,000
	200	196,000	200,000
	300	256,000	256,000
	400	324,000	320,000
300	100	178,000	184,000
	200	232,000	232,000
	300	294,000	288,000
	400	364,000	352,000
400	100	204,000	208,000
	200	260,000	256,000
	300	324,000	312,000
	400	396,000	376,000
Economies of scope for some combinations of commercial and consumer lending but not for all			

Source: Adapted from Mester 1987, 20–21.

also find, for the same reasons, that the average cost of 200 loans would be lower than the average cost of only 100. In each case, economies of scale would exist, as illustrated at the top of Table 4.3. It is important to recognize, however, that economies of scale might exist only for selected ranges of loan volume. For example, even if the average cost of making 200 consumer loans were lower than the average cost of 100, the average cost of 300 loans might not be lower still. Perhaps a new computer or another loan officer would be needed, increasing the average cost per loan; there could then be *dis*economies of scale, as is shown in the table when Bank B makes more than 200 consumer loans.

Suppose further that if either bank makes both commercial and consumer loans, the *total* cost is lower than if each institution continues to make only one type of loan. If the same computer and loan officers could be used for both operations, economies of scope could exist, and a diversified bank would be more efficient than a single-product institution. This situation is illustrated at the bottom of Table 4.3. Again, economies of scope might not exist for all levels of lending. In the example, it would cost more for a diversified bank to make 400 commercial and 400 consumer loans ($396,000) than it would for two single-product banks to make 400 specialized loans each ($156,000 + $220,000 = $376,000). But the table also shows that some lending combinations are less costly if produced jointly; for example, it would cost less for one bank to make 200 commercial *and* 200 consumer loans ($196,000) than it would for each bank to make 200 of only one type ($100,000 + $100,000 = $200,000).

ECONOMIES OF SCALE AND SCOPE IN THE "REAL WORLD"

For decades, researchers have attempted to determine whether economies of scale and scope exist for depositories. Although controversy remains about the proper way to measure the output of depositories (for example, are deposits inputs or outputs of a bank?), consensus is forming around a few conclusions. The findings provide guidance not only for managers concerned with the advisability of changing firm size, structure, or both but also for regulators attempting to tackle many of the thorny issues discussed in this and other chapters.[34]

BIGGER IS SOMETIMES—BUT NOT ALWAYS— BETTER. Some researchers believe that economies of scale exist for very large institutions—even those with assets of several billion dollars. But many studies indicate that economies may exist only for firms with less than $100 million in deposits; above that threshold, scale economies are no longer significant. This finding suggests that if managers generally seek to use resources efficiently and if the marketplace rewards firms that do, the financial system is unlikely to be dominated by a few large institutions. All studies indicate that regulations that serve to keep institutions relatively small, such as limitations on branching, are ill-advised, because they may prevent customers from enjoying the scale economies that do exist.

WHAT ABOUT DIVERSIFICATION? It is more difficult to generalize about economies of scope. Even though this line of research is newer than the literature on economies of scale, most studies were conducted before significant product deregulation for depositories.

Thus, research is needed that examines possible complimentarities between banking and nonbanking services, not just between different combinations of banking products.

Existing studies suggest that economies of scope may exist for some combinations of banking products but not for others. The lack of agreement implies that although one cannot state with certainty that diversified firms are good, neither are they likely to be dangerous to the financial system. The research also suggests that because economies of scope have not been found on a wide scale, financial firms that choose to specialize in a limited range of products or services may not be at a disadvantage when competing with more diversified counterparts. Given existing pressures for continued product deregulation in the banking, insurance, and securities industries, many experts consider economies of scope to be among the most researchable issues in financial institutions management in the next decade.[35]

COMPARATIVE TAXATION OF FINANCIAL INSTITUTIONS

Taxation of financial institutions is based largely on institutional structure. Because it is impossible to summarize all state tax laws, this section is confined to differences in federal taxation among institutions. Like all entities subject to taxation, financial institutions are concerned with three types of tax provisions: tax rates, or the percentage of taxable income paid in taxes; tax deductions, or expenses that may be deducted from income before taxable income is calculated; and tax credits, or direct deductions from taxes owed. Differences in any of these areas can cause the taxation of institutions to differ substantially. As with other issues, the financial community disagrees on which institutions benefit most from the tax system.

The federal tax system has undergone several major changes since the mid-1970s, with revisions in 1976, 1978, 1981, 1982, 1984, 1986, and 1993. Until 1986, the thrust of these changes was to lower the proportion of total federal revenues generated by corporations as compared with individuals. In the Tax

---

[34]Excellent summaries of this literature and of the methodological questions facing researchers are found in Berger, Hunter, and Timme 1993; Berger and Humphrey 1992; Clark 1988; Mester 1987; Benston, Hanweck, and Humphrey 1982; Evanoff and Israelevich 1991; and Humphrey 1990.

[35]See Mester 1990.

Reform Act of 1986, that trend was reversed with the elimination of several provisions beneficial to business in general and to specific financial institutions. Because tax rates were lowered in 1986, however, institutions without special privileges reducing taxable income were not necessarily harmed by the legislation. Although corporate tax rates were raised slightly in 1993, it is too early to assess the effect of this increase on financial institutions.

Clearly, taxation requires continuing attention, and managers must always consult the most recent information before making a financial decision involving taxes. Furthermore, federal taxation is so complex that volumes are required to explain the subject fully. Nonetheless, brief summaries of existing regulations are useful for illustrating the tax environment in which institutions operate.

TAXATION OF DEPOSITORIES

Although the three types of depositories have many similarities, they are subject to strikingly different tax treatments.

THRIFTS. For many years most thrifts were not only permitted to deduct ongoing interest and operating expenses from taxable income, but they were also permitted to transfer nontaxable yearly additions to their bad-debt reserves. Thrifts paid a very small proportion of income in taxes, especially compared with commercial banks, which were not permitted such a generous bad-debt deduction.

Under prodding from the commercial banking industry, thrifts' bad-debt deductions were limited, most recently in 1986, resulting in an upward drift in the percentage of taxes they have paid. Additional changes in tax laws in 1969 tied thrifts' bad-debt deductions to the percentage of assets in housing-related investments (the QTL test). The required percentage of housing-related investments has changed several times in the past decade; most recently, FDICIA set it at 65 percent. This tie-in between thrift investments and tax provisions reduces the diversification potential of thrifts wishing to take advantage of available tax deductions. In recent years, when many thrifts have experienced losses, the industry as a whole has paid few taxes. Exemption from taxes for that reason is not good news.

COMMERCIAL BANKS. The taxation of commercial banks does not differ materially from that of nonfinancial corporations, but banks' ability to use tax shelters for many years resulted in a relatively low proportion of income actually paid in taxes. In fact, the tax burden of commercial banks steadily declined for several decades before 1986, because they invested relatively heavily in securities on which income is tax-exempt. Although tax-exempt securities have lower pretax returns, the tax savings can easily make up the difference for many institutions. Thrifts' inability to shift asset structures away from housing-related assets has prevented them from taking full advantage of tax-exempt securities.

In 1986, commercial banks were among the industries targeted for tax increases, as Congress phased out relatively generous bad-debt deductions for large banks and eliminated other deductions that encouraged banks' investments in municipal bonds. In general, income from municipal bonds remained tax-exempt to investors, including banks. However, all businesses became subject to a strictly enforced minimum tax, and banks with exceptionally large amounts of tax-exempt income can now be required to pay taxes on some of it. Finally, tax deductions for taxes paid on income earned in foreign countries were curtailed by the 1986 legislation, increasing the taxes of banks with international operations.

Although bankers complained about Congress's apparent intention to target the banking industry for higher taxes, the experience of the first several years under the 1986 tax law suggests that banks adjusted well to the lost benefits. Tax-exempt securities have declined as a proportion of banks' total securities holdings (by 17 percent in the first year alone), but the benefits of lower overall tax rates appear to have offset the decline in tax-exempt income.[36] Most experts believe that banks will continue to adapt portfolios to new tax laws as the need arises.

CREDIT UNIONS. During the first 3 years of their existence, federal CUs paid state taxes, but technical differences between CU shares and deposits meant that their tax burden was quite high in some states. In 1937, Congress decided that the cooperative movement was

---

[36] See Neuberger 1988.

best served by exempting federal CUs from taxation. This tax exemption has been under renewed scrutiny in recent years but survived tax reforms in 1986 and 1993. Opponents argue that the increasingly loose common bond requirements on CU membership are eroding the principal reason for their not-for-profit status, and that exemption from taxes represents a subsidy of CUs by taxpayers.[37]

TAXATION OF INSURANCE COMPANIES

Tax provisions applying to insurers differ from those applying to depositories. Also, different types of insurers face different tax laws.

LIFE INSURERS. The income of an insurance company comes from two sources: sale of policies, and income from investments made by the insurer when cash inflows from sales exceed cash needed to pay claims. State regulations require insurers to estimate the rate of return they expect on their investments and to use the estimate to set policy fees, or **premiums,** under the theory that premiums charged policyholders can be lower if investment income is higher. However, conservative rules in most states allow insurers to estimate their investment income at a much lower level than has actually been earned in recent years. Consequently, a major issue in insurance company regulation is how investment income should be estimated and taxed.

The taxation of life insurers has undergone major changes since 1984.[38] Before that time, taxes were based on a 1959 law that taxed investment income actually earned *in excess* of estimated investment income. For many years, life insurer taxes were low relative to those of other financial institutions, because investment income seldom exceeded estimated income by a large amount. As market interest rates rose, creating large discrepancies between estimates of investment income and actual earnings, life insurers paid higher and higher taxes.

By 1984, Congress decided that the 1959 law was obsolete. Therefore, a provision taxing life insurers on net income from investments was passed in the Tax Reform Act of 1984. (Net investment income is income after the deduction of portfolio management expenses.) Although the law improved the position of life insurers as compared with many other financial institutions, it also created some inequities between mutual and stock insurers.

To understand the source of this inequity, it is necessary to know that insurers sometimes refund a portion of premiums paid by policyholders. These premium rebates are paid in years in which investment income is especially good. Stockholder-owned life insurers may consider premium rebates as tax-deductible expenses. Because the policyholders of mutuals are owners, however, the new law does not permit mutuals to deduct all premium rebates. Permissible deductions are governed by a complex formula based on the proportion of industry assets held by mutual firms. As a result of the 1984 law, industry observers estimated that total taxes paid by the industry would increase, because most of the industry's assets are held by a few large mutuals. In 1986, however, the lowering of tax rates offset the loss of deductions in the 1984 law. In fact, the combined effects of the 1984 and 1986 laws have thus far not been particularly negative for life insurers, and mutual firms—the largest in the industry—have not borne nearly as high a tax burden as Congress expected when it revised the law.

PROPERTY/LIABILITY INSURERS. With the exception of very small firms, property/liability insurers have enjoyed few of the tax benefits of their life counterparts, facing instead the same tax structure faced by nonfinancial corporations. Like life insurers, their income arises from premiums and from investments. Without the favorable tax treatment historically given to life insurers, property/liability insurers chose to invest heavily in securities providing tax-exempt income. Recently, however, rapidly accelerating policy claims have produced large losses in some years, making investment income even more important for overall company profitability. As discussed in Chapter 24, the decline in earnings has decreased the attractiveness of tax-exempt securities. Consequently, the tax treatment of the industry has always had a strong impact on its asset/liability management strategies.

---

[37] See Moody and Fite 1971, Chapter 10; Pearce 1984, 18; and Phil Gasteyer, "New Challenges Threaten Credit Union Advantages," *Savings Institutions* 112 (November 1991): 17.

[38] This section draws on parts of Kopcke 1985; and Birnbaum, "Tax Battle between Stock and Mutual Insurers."

Tax reform in 1986 was generally interpreted as unfavorable for property/liability insurers because they lost the ability to defer some tax payments by using special accounting methods. Also, property/liability firms, like commercial banks, are now subject to the minimum tax provision.

TAXATION OF OTHER FINANCIAL INSTITUTIONS

Federal taxation of other financial institutions also substantially affects their management strategies. Most finance companies and securities firms are taxed identically to nonfinancial firms, so the lowering of tax rates in 1986 benefited them, although finance companies lost some of their favorable bad-debt deductions. In contrast, the income of pension funds is not taxed until paid to employees on resignation or retirement. At that time, the employee's personal tax rate is the relevant rate. Although pension funds are not classified as not-for-profit organizations, because their beneficiaries have enforceable claims on the fund's assets, their freedom from taxes makes tax-exempt securities unattractive. Other tax-related issues have little relevance for pension funds.

Mutual funds and other investment companies also enjoy favorable tax treatment at the fund level, thanks to Subchapter M of the Internal Revenue Code. Shareholders pay personal taxes on income from their shares, provided that the funds pass along at least 97 percent of ordinary income and 90 percent of net capital gain income to investors. The investment company itself pays no taxes, based on the conduit theory introduced in Chapter 2. Although other laws and regulations limit the flexibility with which mutual fund assets can be managed, taxation is not the source of major restrictions.

SUMMARY

This chapter has explored key structural issues for financial institutions, such as the way they raise funds, the beneficiaries of their profits, and their taxation.

Many institutions are mutually organized, including most thrifts and many insurance companies. As a result, customers are the "owners" of the business. CUs are unusual because they are organized on a not-for-profit basis and exist to provide goods or services at below-market cost to members with a common bond.

The holding company form of ownership is important for financial institutions, particularly commercial banks. BHCs have become increasingly popular because they provide access to capital, potential for diversification and geographic expansion, and the benefits of financial leverage. These benefits are monitored by the Federal Reserve Board. In the 1980s, BHCs gained new powers to expand interstate operations, resulting in the emergence of superregionals.

The effect of BHCs on the safety and soundness of institutions, however, remains controversial. Regulators persist in requiring firewalls between bank and nonbank subsidiaries. The potential for economies of scale and scope in MBHCs also continues to be a topic of great concern.

Banks also expand geographically through branches, although some unit banking states still exist. Chain banking, franchising, and service corporations are also growing in popularity, but because they provide more limited benefits than BHCs, they are not as closely regulated.

It is generally agreed that managers of mutual firms have more latitude than those of stockholder-owned firms, but profitability difficulties have troubled many mutually owned firms. Increasingly, mutuals are considering conversion, a procedure by which the ownership of an institution is transferred from customers to shareholders.

Finally, financial institutions are subject to special federal tax provisions that affect asset/liability management. Some institutions pay taxes at a relatively low rate, whereas others enjoy few tax privileges.

APPENDIX

4A

EFFECT OF LEVERAGE ON RETURN ON NET WORTH

Financing with borrowed funds instead of equity affects the level and variability of returns to shareholders. Because financial institutions rely heavily on liabilities, the effect of leverage is important.

Suppose that a bank has assets of $10 million, with equity of $1 million. The ratio of net worth to total assets is 10 percent, so the net worth multiplier is 10. Net noninterest expenses are $100,000, and the bank's marginal tax rate is 34 percent.[1] Return on net worth (RONW) can be estimated under several earnings levels:

Interest Revenues (IR)	$880,000	$1,000,000	$1,100,000
Interest Expense (IE):			
8% × Total Liabilities (TL)	720,000	720,000	720,000
Net Noninterest Expenses (NIE)	100,000	100,000	100,000
Income before Taxes	$ 60,000	$ 180,000	$ 280,000
Taxes (34%)	20,400	61,200	95,200
Net Income (NI)	$ 39,600	$ 118,800	$ 184,800
IR/Total Assets (TA)	8.8%	10.0%	11.0%
RONW (Net Income/ Net Worth)	4.0%	11.9%	18.5%

If another bank has assets of $10 million with equity of $750,000, its ratio of net worth to total assets is 7.5 percent. Under the same levels of IR and at the same cost of borrowed funds, the following is calculated:

Interest Revenues (IR)	$880,000	$1,000,000	$1,100,000
Interest Expense (IE):			
8% × Total Liabilities (TL)	740,000	740,000	740,000
Net Noninterest Expenses (NIE)	100,000	100,000	100,000
Income before Taxes	$ 40,000	$ 160,000	$ 260,000
Taxes (34%)	13,600	54,400	88,400
Net Income (NI)	$ 26,400	$ 105,600	$ 171,600
IR/Total Assets (TA)	8.8%	10.0%	11.0%
RONW (Net Income/ Net Worth)	3.5%	14.1%	22.9%

For a $10 million bank with equity of $500,000 (a ratio of net worth to total assets of 5 percent), the figures below are found.

The data below reveal that the lower the ratio of net worth to total assets (that is, the more the bank is leveraged), the greater the variation in RONW as interest revenues vary. If interest revenues vary between $880,000 and $1,100,000, the bank with Net Worth/Total Assets equal to 10 percent can expect RONW to vary between 4 and 18.5 percent; the bank with NW/TA equal to 5 percent can expect RONW to range from less than 3 to more than 31 percent. A graph makes comparison clearer. In Figure 4A.1 the relationship between IR/Total Assets and RONW is represented by a different line for each bank.

Interest Revenues (IR)	$880,000	$1,000,000	$1,100,000
Interest Expense (IE):			
8% × Total Liabilities (TL)	760,000	760,000	760,000
Net Noninterest Expenses (NIE)	100,000	100,000	100,000
Income before Taxes	$ 20,000	$ 140,000	$ 240,000
Taxes (34%)	6,800	47,600	81,600
Net Income (NI)	$ 13,400	$ 92,400	$ 158,400
IR/Total Assets (TA)	8.8%	10.0%	11.0%
RONW (Net Income/ Net Worth)	2.7%	18.5%	31.7%

Because of the potential benefits to shareholders when earnings are strong, managers of financial institutions often choose to use leverage to its maximum possible level. Accompanying the higher expected rates of return, however, is greater risk. If earnings prospects are poor, shareholders in more highly leveraged institutions are worse off than they would be in

---

[1] As this edition was going to press, Congress increased the highest corporate tax rate from 34 to 35 percent. This example reflects tax rates before 1993.

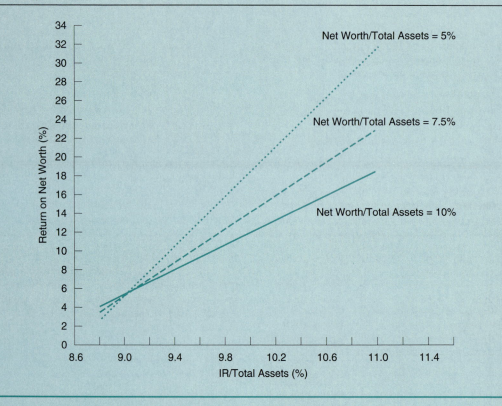

FIGURE 4A.1 Leverage and RONW

The bank with the most leverage (and the least net worth) will have the highest RONW if earnings are high but the lowest RONW if earnings are low.

more conservatively managed firms. No matter what the level of earnings, interest expense must be paid, and noninterest expenses will also be incurred. If asset returns are insufficient to pay interest, shareholders not only have no residual profits, but their retained earnings also would be reduced by the amount of the loss.

QUESTIONS

1. Compare and contrast, for mutual and stock organizations: a) the rights and the risk exposure of owners; and b) the distribution of residual profits.

2. What is the net worth multiplier? Explain the change in the relationship between the return on assets (ROA) and the return on net worth (RONW) as the net worth multiplier gets larger.

3. Explain how the target net interest margin (NIM) can be determined once an institution's managers have set a desired goal for RONW.

4. What are loan production offices? Edge Corporations? Why have they been important competitive tools for growth-oriented banks?

5. What is a bank holding company? What is the nature of the relationship between a holding company and its subsidiaries? Explain the potential benefits available to banks through the holding company form of ownership.

6. Part of the antithesis in the regulatory dialectic has been the efforts of some BHCs to expand their scope of activities into areas previously denied to banking, such as securities underwriting. Briefly summarize arguments opposing bank entry into such activities. What is meant by corporate separateness? By the source of strength doctrine? Which of these doctrines do you believe should govern the relationship between the BHC subsidiaries? Explain.

7. What are nonbank banks and why were they formed? How were they affected by CEBA? What are industrial loan companies? In your opinion, do they upset the competitive balance in the banking industry? Explain.

8. In some states, multibank holding companies are prohibited. For banks in those states, what arrangements allow the operation of several banks under one organization? Compare these structures to that of a holding company.

9. Compare the benefits and disadvantages of bank expansion through holding company acquisition to expansion through a branching network. What economic principles finally eliminated the unit banking concept?

10. What laws on bank branching and expansion of bank holding companies exist in your state? Have these laws changed in recent years, or are additional changes anticipated in the future? If so, why?

11. Distinguish between economies of scale and economies of scope. Explain how both types of cost benefits could arise in holding companies. Have these benefits been confirmed through empirical research? Under what circumstances might diseconomies of scale be realized?

12. What is meant by conversion? Why have some firms considered conversion, and what potential controversies arise in the process? Find an article on a thrift or insurer that has converted recently. What advantages and disadvantages of conversion are evident in the article?

13. Briefly summarize research on the results of thrift and life insurer conversions. Would you favor more conversions in the future? Why or why not?

14. What are mutual holding companies?

15. Compare a service corporation to a nonbank subsidiary of a bank holding company. Explain which organizational form you believe to be more beneficial to an institution.

16. How does the organizational form of credit unions affect the ownership, management, and taxation of the institution? Do you support continuation of the tax-exempt status of federal credit unions, which has been criticized recently? Explain.

17. Compare the taxation of life insurers with that of property/liability insurers.

18. What similarities can you identify in the tax provisions applied to investment companies and pension funds? How do these tax policies affect their financial management strategies?

PROBLEMS

1. The board of directors of First Federal Savings has approved target rates of return for shareholders:

Target return on net worth	16%
Target net worth multiplier	12
Tax rate (t)	35%
Total assets	$850,000,000
Interest expense	$80,000,000
Net noninterest expense	$11,500,000

a. What should be the target net interest margin for the planning period?
b. What before-tax interest revenues must be earned to allow First Federal to meet its financial goals?
c. Suppose interest revenues fall 10 percent below the target figure calculated in Part b. What return on net worth will the thrift actually earn?

2. An assignment for management trainees at Bank U.S. is to estimate the return to shareholders under the following conditions:

Net interest margin	4.2%
Net worth multiplier	11
Tax rate (t)	35%
Net noninterest expense	$40,000,000
Total assets	$1,750,000,000

    a.   What will be the bank's return on net worth?

    b.   If the bank's board of directors decides to increase the net worth multiplier to 12, what will be the expected return on net worth?

3. Heartland Savings is preparing a financial plan based on the following data:

Target RONW	15%
Tax rate (t)	35%
Total assets	$700,000,000
Total liabilities	$640,000,000

    a.   What is the current net worth multiplier?

    b.   If the current net worth multiplier is optimal, what before-tax income must the thrift earn to meet its target return on net worth?

    c.   What is the thrift's target net interest margin, assuming that net noninterest expense is 1.1 percent of total assets?

4. A BHC subsidiary has ambitious growth targets. The bank currently has a minimum capital requirement of 8.0 percent and wants to expand total assets by $300 million.

    a.   If the bank takes advantage of double leverage, how much must the BHC borrow and downstream to the bank to provide capital support for the expansion plan?

    b.   Suppose a change in the bank's asset portfolio causes regulators to lower the allowed net worth multiplier to 11. By how much will the bank be able to expand total assets if the BHC borrows $95 million and invests the proceeds in new bank equity?

5. The board of directors of a rapidly expanding regional bank has requested a presentation on the relationship between financial leverage and return on net worth. The bank has assets of $2 billion and a net worth multiplier of 10. Net income in the coming year is expected to be between 1.2 percent and 2.0 percent of total assets.

    a.   At the bank's current capital level, what is the expected range for RONW?

    b.   The new chief financial officer (CFO) hopes to persuade the directors to operate aggressively and to increase the net worth multiplier to 12. If they do, interest expense will rise because of the higher level of borrowed funds. The estimated range of NI/TA changes to a low of 0.5 percent and a high of 1.9 percent. What will be the resulting range for RONW?

    c.   Based on these estimates, what recommendation should the directors follow?

6. A small regional bank has total assets of $500 million and a ratio of net worth to total assets of 10 percent. A competitor of equal size has 8 percent net worth. Both managers are estimating returns, and both forecast interest revenues ranging from 7 percent to 13 percent of total assets. Interest costs for both firms are expected to average 9 percent of total liabilities. For illustrative purposes, ignore tax effects.

    a.   Calculate the potential range of net income and RONW for each bank. (**Hint:** Use the "What if" feature of your spreadsheet program.)

    b.   Graph the relationship between IR/TA and RONW for each bank.

    c.   Which shareholders will be better off in an economic downturn? Which owners will benefit under a strong economy?

    d.   If you placed a high probability on earning interest revenues of 10 percent of total assets, which capitalization plan would shareholders prefer?

7. Fourth/Third National Bank reports the following functional cost data for its Commercial & Industrial (C&I) and commercial real estate loan portfolios:

Number of Loans	**Total Cost**
C&I Loans:	
50	$ 75,000
150	200,000
300	350,000
500	500,000

Number of Loans	Total Cost
Commercial Real Estate Loans:	
50	$ 90,000
150	240,000
300	515,000
500	900,000

Combined Costs:

Number of C&I Loans	Number of Commercial Real Estate Loans	Total Cost
50	50	$150,000
	150	325,000
150	50	$280,000
	150	435,000

a. Does the bank realize economies of scale at higher volumes of C & I loans? Of commercial real estate loans? Explain.

b. Does the bank benefit from economies of scope by having both types of loans in its portfolio? Why or why not?

SELECTED REFERENCES

Akella, Srinivas R., and Stuart I. Greenbaum. "Savings and Loan Ownership Structure and Expense-Preference." *Journal of Banking and Finance* 12 (September 1988): 419–437.

Amel, Dean F., and Michael J. Jacowski. "Trends in Banking Structure since the Mid-1970s." *Federal Reserve Bulletin* 75 (March 1989): 120–133.

Andrews, Suzanna, and John W. Milligan. "Here Come the Super-Regionals." *Institutional Investor* 19 (December 1985): 74–82.

Baer, Herbert, and Sue F. Gregorash. *Toward Nationwide Banking: A Guide to the Issues.* Chicago: Federal Reserve Bank of Chicago, 1986.

Benston, George J. "Analyzing the Case Against Commercial Firms Owning Banks." *Banking Policy Report,* August 5, 1991: 4.

Benston, George J., Gerald A. Hanweck, and David B. Humphrey. "Scale Economies in Banking: A Restructuring and Reassessment." *Journal of Money, Credit, and Banking* 14 (November 1982): 435–456.

Berger, Allen N., and David B. Humphrey. "Competition, Efficiency, and the Future of the Banking Industry." *Proceedings of the Conference on Bank Structure and Competition.* Chicago: Federal Reserve Bank of Chicago, 1992.

Berger, Allen N., William C. Hunter, and Stephen G. Timme. "The Efficiency of Financial Institutions: A Review and Preview of Research Past, Present, and Future." *Journal of Banking and Finance* 17 (forthcoming 1993).

Blyn, Martin R. "The Evolution of the U.S. Money and Capital Markets and Financial Intermediaries." In *Financial Institutions and Markets,* 2d ed., edited by Murray E. Polakoff and Thomas A. Durkin, 31–45. Boston: Houghton Mifflin, 1981.

Board of Governors of the Federal Reserve System. *Annual Report, 1991.* (Washington, DC: Board of Governors of the Federal Reserve System, 1991).

Boyd, John H., and Stanley L. Graham. "Risk, Regulation, and Bank Holding Company Expansion into Nonbanking." *Quarterly Review* (Federal Reserve Bank of Minneapolis) 10 (Spring 1986): 2–17.

Brewer, Elijah, III. "A Note on the Relationship between Bank Holding Company Risk and Nonbank Activity." Staff memorandum 88-5. Federal Reserve Bank of Chicago, 1988.

Brown, Donald M. "Bank Holding Company Performance Studies and the Public Interest: Normative Uses for Positive Analysis?" *Review* (Federal Reserve Bank of St. Louis) 65 (March 1983): 26–34.

Calem, Paul S. "The Proconsumer Argument for Interstate Branching." *Business Review* (Federal Reserve Bank of Philadelphia)(May/June 1993): 15–29.

Carner, William J. "An Analysis of Franchising in Retail

Banking." *Journal of Retail Banking* 8 (Winter 1986–1987): 57–66.

Carter, Richard B., and Roger D. Stover. "The Effects of Mutual to Stock Conversions of Thrift Institutions on Managerial Behavior." *Journal of Financial Services Research* 4 (1990): 127–144.

Cebenoyan, A. Sinan, Elizabeth A. Cooperman, Charles A. Register, and Sylvia C. Hudgins. "The Relative Efficiency of Stock vs. Mutual S&Ls: A Stochastic Cost Frontier Approach." *Journal of Financial Services Research* 7 (forthcoming 1993).

Chase, Samuel B., Jr., and John J. Mingo. "The Regulation of Bank Holding Companies." *Journal of Finance* 30 (May 1975): 281–292.

Clair, Robert T., and Paula K. Tucker. "Interstate Banking and the Federal Reserve: A Historical Perspective." *Economic Review* (Federal Reserve Bank of Dallas) (November 1989): 1–20.

Clark, Jeffrey A. "Economies of Scale and Scope at Depository Financial Institutions: A Review of the Literature." *Economic Review* (Federal Reserve Bank of Kansas City) 73 (September/October 1988): 16–33.

Cornyn, Anthony G., and Samuel H. Talley. "Activity Deregulation and Bank Soundness." *Proceedings of a Conference on Bank Structure and Competition.* Chicago: Federal Reserve Bank of Chicago, 1983: 28–31.

Cornyn, Anthony, Gerald Hanweck, Stephen Rhoades, and John Rose. "An Analysis of the Concept of Corporate Separateness in BHC Regulation from an Economic Perspective." *Proceedings of a Conference on Bank Structure and Competition.* Chicago: Federal Reserve Bank of Chicago, 1986: 174–212.

Corrigan, E. Gerald. "A Framework for Reform of the Financial System." *Quarterly Review* (Federal Reserve Bank of New York) 12 (Summer 1987): 1–8.

Cyrnak, Anthony W. "Chain Banks and Competition: The Effectiveness of Federal Reserve Policy since 1977." *Economic Review* (Federal Reserve Bank of San Francisco) (Spring 1986): 5–15.

DiClemente, John J. "What Is a Bank?" *Economic Perspectives* (Federal Reserve Bank of Chicago) 7 (January/February 1983): 20–31.

Dunham, Constance. "Mutual-to-Stock Conversion by Thrifts: Implications for Soundness." *New England Economic Review* (Federal Reserve Bank of Boston) (January/February 1985): 31–45.

Eickhoff, Gerald. "Going Interstate by Franchises or Networks." *Economic Review* (Federal Reserve Bank of Atlanta) 70 (January 1985): 32–35.

Eisenbeis, Robert. "How Should Bank Holding Companies Be Regulated?" *Economic Review* (Federal Reserve Bank of Atlanta) 68 (January 1983): 43–47.

Eisenbeis, Robert A., Robert S. Harris, and Josef Lakonishok. "Benefits of Bank Diversification: The Evidence from Shareholder Returns." *Journal of Finance* 39 (July 1984): 881–892.

Evanoff, Douglas D., and Philip R. Israelevich. "Productive Efficiency in Banking." *Economic Perspectives* (Federal Reserve Bank of Chicago) 15 (July/August 1991): 11–32.

Federal Reserve Bank of Kansas City. "Report on Chain Banking Organizations in Kansas, Nebraska, and Oklahoma." *Banking Studies* 1 (1983).

Fields, Joseph A. "Expense Preference Behavior in Mutual Life Insurers." *Journal of Financial Services Research* 1 (January 1988): 113–129.

Frieder, Larry A., and Vincent P. Apilado. "Bank Holding Company Research: Classification, Synthesis, and New Directions." *Journal of Bank Research* 13 (Summer 1982): 80–95.

Gilbert, R. Alton. "A Comparison of Proposals to Restructure the U.S. Financial System." *Review* (Federal Reserve Bank of St. Louis) 70 (July/August 1988): 58–73.

————. "Do Bank Holding Companies Act as 'Sources of Strength' for Their Bank Subsidiaries?" *Review* (Federal Reserve Bank of St. Louis) 73 (January/February 1991): 3–18.

Goldberg, Lawrence J., and Gerald A. Hanweck. "What We Can Expect from Interstate Banking." *Journal of Banking and Finance* 12 (March 1988): 51–67.

Greenspan, Alan. "Subsidies and Powers in Commercial Banking." *Proceedings of the Conference on Bank Structure and Competition.* Chicago: Federal Reserve Bank of Chicago, 1990: 1–8.

Gunther, Jeffrey W. "The Movement Toward Nationwide Banking." *Financial Industry Studies* (Federal Reserve Bank of Dallas) (December 1992): 1–9.

Heimann, John. "Market-Driven Deregulation of Financial Services." *Economic Review* (Federal Reserve Bank of Atlanta) 69 (December 1984): 36–41.

Humphrey, David B. "Why Do Estimates of Bank Scale

Economies Differ?" *Economic Review* (Federal Reserve Bank of Richmond) 76 (September/October 1990): 38–50.

Hunter, William C., and Stephen G. Timme. "Does Multiproduct Production in Large Banks Reduce Costs?" *Economic Review* (Federal Reserve Bank of Atlanta) 74 (May/June 1989): 2–9.

Jacobe, Dennis. "Nonbank Banks: A Prescription for Disaster." *Savings Institutions* 106 (March 1985): 70–76.

Karna, Adi S., and Duane B. Graddy. "Bank Holding Company Leverage and the Return on Stockholders' Equity." *Journal of Bank Research* 13 (Spring 1982): 42–48.

Keehn, Silas. *Banking on the Balance: Powers and the Safety Net.* Chicago: Federal Reserve Bank of Chicago, 1989.

Keeley, Michael C., and Barbara A. Bennett. "Corporate Separateness." *Weekly Letter* (Federal Reserve Bank of San Francisco), June 3, 1989.

Keeton, William R. "Bank Holding Companies, Cross-Bank Guarantees, and Source of Strength." *Economic Review* (Federal Reserve Bank of Kansas City) (May/June 1990): 54–67.

King, B. Frank, Sheila L. Tschinkel, and David D. Whitehead. "Interstate Banking Developments in the 1980s." *Economic Review* (Federal Reserve Bank of Atlanta) 74 (May/June 1989): 35–38.

Kopcke, Richard W. "The Federal Income Taxation of Life Insurance Companies." *New England Economic Review* (Federal Reserve Bank of Boston) (March/April 1985): 5–19.

Laderman, Elizabeth S., and Randall J. Pozdena. "Interstate Banking and Competition: Evidence from the Behavior of Stock Returns." *Economic Review* (Federal Reserve Bank of San Francisco) (Spring 1991): 32–47.

Liang, J. Nellie, and Donald T. Savage. "The Nonbank Activities of Bank Holding Companies." *Federal Reserve Bulletin* 76 (May 1990): 280–292.

Masulis, Ronald W. "Changes in Ownership Structure: Conversions of Mutual Savings and Loans to Stock Charter." *Journal of Financial Economics* 18 (March 1987): 29–59.

McNamara, Michael J., and S. Ghon Rhee. "Ownership Structure and Performance: The Demutualization of Life Insurers." *Journal of Risk and Insurance* 59 (June 1992): 221–238.

Mengle, David L. "The Case for Interstate Branch Banking." *Economic Review* (Federal Reserve Bank of Richmond) 76 (November/December 1990): 3–17.

Mester, Loretta J. "Efficient Production of Financial Services: Scale and Scope Economies." *Business Review* (Federal Reserve Bank of Philadelphia) (January/February 1987): 15–25.

———. "The Costs of Traditional and Nontraditional Banking." *Proceedings of the Conference on Bank Structure and Competition.* Chicago: Federal Reserve Bank of Chicago, 1990: 170–174.

———. "Banking and Commerce: A Dangerous Liaison?" *Business Review* (Federal Reserve Bank of Philadelphia) (May/June 1992): 17–29.

———. "Efficiency in the Savings and Loan Industry." *Journal of Banking and Finance* 17 (April 1993).

Moody, J. Carroll, and Gilbert C. Fite. *The Credit Union Movement.* Lincoln: University of Nebraska Press, 1971.

Mote, Larry R. "The Perennial Issue: Branch Banking." *Business Conditions* (Federal Reserve Bank of Chicago) (February 1974): 3–23.

Moulton, Janice M. "Nonbank Banks: Catalyst for Interstate Banking." *Business Review* (Federal Reserve Bank of Philadelphia) (November/December 1985): 3–18.

Murray, Gregory E. "Demutualization of Insurance Companies—Advantages and Disadvantages." *Journal of the American Society of Chartered Life Underwriters* 39 (January 1985): 52–54.

Neuberger, Jonathan A. "Tax Reform and Bank Behavior." *Weekly Letter* (Federal Reserve Bank of San Francisco), December 16, 1988.

Neubig, Thomas S. "The Taxation of Financial Institutions after Deregulation." *National Tax Journal* 37 (September 1984): 351–359.

Ornstein, Franklin. *Savings Banking: An Industry in Change.* Reston, VA: Reston Publishing Co., 1985.

Pearce, Douglas K. "Recent Developments in the Credit Union Industry." *Economic Review* (Federal Reserve Bank of Kansas City) 69 (June 1984): 3–19.

Pozdena, Randall Johnston. "Banks Affiliated with Bank Holding Companies: A New Look at Their Performance." *Economic Review* (Federal Reserve Bank of San Francisco) (Fall 1988): 29–40.

Richard, Robert A. "States' Interstate Banking Initiatives."

Economic Review (Federal Reserve Bank of Atlanta) 70 (March 1985): 20–22.

Rose, Peter S. *The Interstate Banking Revolution.* New York: Quorum Books, 1989.

Savage, Donald T. "Interstate Banking Developments." *Federal Reserve Bulletin* 73 (February 1987): 79–92.

Shull, Bernard. "Economic Efficiency, Public Regulation, and Financial Reform: Depository Institutions." In *Financial Institutions and Markets,* 2d ed., edited by Murray E. Polakoff and Thomas A. Durkin, 671–702. Boston: Houghton Mifflin, 1981.

Simons, Katerina. "Mutual-to-Stock Conversions by New England Savings Banks: Where Has All the Money Gone?" *New England Economic Review* (Federal Reserve Bank of Boston) (March/April 1992): 45–53.

Simpson, Gary W., and Theodor Kohers. "The Effects of Organizational Form on Performance in the Savings and Loan Industry." *Financial Review* 14 (Fall 1979): 1–14.

Smith, Brian, and Phyllis P. Dietz. "The Competitive Equality Banking Act: What's in a Name?" *The Bankers Magazine* 171 (January–February 1988): 18–23.

Smith, Bruce D., and Michael J. Stutzer. "Adverse Selection, Aggregate Uncertainty, and the Role for Mutual Insurance Contracts." *Journal of Business* 63 (1990): 493–510.

Wall, Larry D. "Insulating Banks from Non-Bank Affiliates." *Economic Review* (Federal Reserve Bank of Atlanta) 69 (September 1984): 18–27.

———. "Nonbank Activities and Risk." *Economic Review* (Federal Reserve Bank of Atlanta) 71 (October 1986): 19–34.

———. "Risk and BHC Nonbank Activities." *Economic Review* (Federal Reserve Bank of Atlanta) 71 (November 1986): 10–15.

Whalen, Gary. "Operational Policies of Multibank Holding Companies." *Economic Review* (Federal Reserve Bank of Cleveland) (Winter 1981–1982): 20–31.

Whitehead, David D. "Interstate Banking: Probability or Reality?" *Economic Review* (Federal Reserve Bank of Atlanta) 70 (March 1985): 6–19.

Woerheide, Walter J. *The Savings and Loan Industry.* Westport, CT: Quorum Books, 1984.

*There are as many different ways to calculate interest
as there are to skin a cat.*
Robert K. Heady
Publisher, *Bank Rate Monitor* (1989)

———————————

The U.S. government is the largest and most frequent borrower in the entire world. Despite fast-paced innovations in most financial markets, the systems used by the Treasury to issue its debt securities have changed very little in recent decades. In the aftermath of the 1991 Salomon Brothers illegal trading scandal, the Treasury markets have been subjected to intensive scrutiny, and some fascinating information has been revealed, including the influence of Wall Street professionals on the borrowing decisions of the Treasury.

For example, the Treasury Department regularly looks to its advisors on Wall Street to fill important jobs as they become vacant. Also, a little-known group called the Treasury Borrowing Advisory Committee, composed of Wall Street bond and money market dealers, exerts a great deal of influence on the quantity and maturity of government securities issued. This group travels to Washington four times a year and, until 1992, enjoyed a preliminary view of the government's quarterly borrowing needs.

A closer look at the rituals of this advisory committee sheds some light on the Treasury market's resistance to change. Every briefing of the committee by the Treasury is followed by a meeting with the full membership of the Board of Governors of the Federal Reserve System (Fed). The committee members recess for lunch at a famous Washington hotel and then reconvene to prepare their recommendations to the Treasury. After this busy day, they enjoy a dinner at the same hotel. Every detail of this schedule has become a structured routine; the hotel never changes, and even the menu for the advisory committee's meals is always the same: salmon for lunch and lamb chops for dinner.[1] Many observers believe the Treasury's management of the federal debt has been similarly resistant to innovation.

Of course, Treasury securities are but one of many investments that individuals and financial institutions must compare. Across the wide spectrum of primary and secondary securities are many different conventions for calculating and quoting expected rates of return. Although,

———————————

[1] David Wessel, "The Bond Club: Treasury and the Fed Have Long Caved in to 'Primary Dealers,'" *The Wall Street Journal,* September 25, 1991, A1, A6.

as the previous chapters emphasize, regulation and legislation are important environmental influences on asset/liability management, they are by no means the only ones. Institutional managers must also be familiar with the markets for financial assets and liabilities. In particular, because asset/liability management involves close attention to the net interest margin, managers must understand methods for calculating asset yields and liability costs accurately.

A discussion of financial instruments can be divided conceptually in many ways—according to their size or their cash flow characteristics, for example. By convention, however, financial instruments are most often categorized by original maturity. Securities with original maturities of one year or less are **money market,** or short-term, investments; those with original maturities in excess of one year are **capital market,** or long-term, securities. This chapter follows the tradition of emphasizing time. Because time is an important dimension, calculation of market yields requires an understanding of the time value of money. Students wishing to review the mathematics should read the appendix to this chapter before proceeding.

Although many more financial instruments exist, the main ones with which institutions are involved, and significant issues relating to their yields, are explained here.[2] More specialized instruments important to particular institutions are introduced later in the text.

---

[2] The definition of financial institutions in Chapter 1 stressed their activities on both the asset and liability sides of the balance sheet. They are thus concerned with both the *returns* (called *yields,* by convention) on institutional assets and the *costs* of institutional liabilities. For brevity, the term *yield* is used throughout this discussion. Also, all calculations ignore transaction costs and taxes, unless specifically noted in the text.

ISSUES AFFECTING THE CALCULATION OF MONEY MARKET YIELDS

As noted, financial markets are traditionally divided into those for securities with maturities of one year or less (money markets) and those for securities with longer maturities (capital markets). Separating the markets into categories based on original maturity might seem to reduce the necessary yield calculations to only two—one for short-term and one for long-term securities. Unfortunately, this is not the case, although many of the required formulas generalize to more than one instrument. Issues affecting calculation of money market yields are considered in this section.

DIFFERENT ORIGINAL MATURITIES

Even within 1 year, financial instruments have many possible original maturities. Treasury bills (T-bills) may be issued for 91 or 182 days, or a bank may issue a short-term deposit to a corporation for a "customized" original maturity exactly equal to the length of time the business expects to have extra cash.

DIFFERENT HOLDING PERIODS

Holders of short-term securities may sell them before the original maturity date. For example, the original investor in a 91-day T-bill may hold it for only 23 days, selling it to a purchaser who anticipates its maturity in 68 days. The same bill provides a yield to both investors, but each yield is based on a different maturity.

DIFFERENT MARKET TRADITIONS

Even in the electronic age, traditional methods persist for calculating money market yields, dating to periods in which hand-held calculators and computers were unavailable. Some yield quotations for T-bills, for example, are based on a 360-day year, and investors must recognize this before using such a yield in making financial decisions.

DIFFERENT CASH FLOW CHARACTERISTICS

Finally, short-term financial instruments may have different cash flow characteristics, even when they have the same initial maturities or holding periods. For example, a 6-month loan by a finance company to a customer is an **interest-bearing security,** but commercial paper owned by the same company is a **discount security.** In lending to a customer, the finance company advances cash and expects to receive monthly cash interest payments *and* the principal amount at maturity. When purchasing commercial paper, the finance company advances cash to the business issuing the paper and expects to receive a single cash payment of a higher amount at maturity. Differences in the timing of cash benefits affect the finance company's yields.

CALCULATING ANNUAL YIELDS

Yield comparisons considering these factors are facilitated by converting rates of return on instruments with different maturities, holding periods, and cash flows to **effective annual yields.** The effective annual yield (y^*) on an investment is the compound rate of return an investor would earn, given the asset's cash flow characteristics, if the investor held it for exactly 365 days (366 days in leap years).

It is useful to separate calculations of effective annual yields on short-term securities into two categories: 1) yields for discount securities, defined as those requiring a single cash outflow from the investor, followed by a single cash inflow at a later date; and 2) yields for short-term securities with more than one cash inflow to the investor during the time the security is held.

ANNUAL YIELD WITH NO COMPOUNDING

The equation for y, the annual yield on a discount instrument *without* considering compound interest, is

[5.1]

$$y = \frac{\text{Par (or } P_1) - P_0}{P_0} \times \frac{365}{n}$$

where

P_0 = amount initially invested;

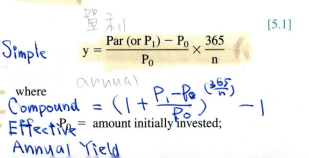

Par (or P_1) = par value at maturity (Par) or price received if sold before maturity (P_1);

   n = number of days until maturity or until sold.

The equation states that the annual yield on an investment is equal to the dollars earned over the period during which the investment is held ($P_1 - P_0$), expressed as a percentage of the dollars invested (P_0), multiplied by the number of times during the year that the amount could potentially be earned. Another way to think about this annual yield is as the periodic rate of return earned times the number of periods in a year.

EFFECTIVE ANNUAL YIELD

Considering the additional possibility of earning interest on one period's returns during the following periods—that is, considering the possibility of compounding over a full year—the effective annual yield on a discount instrument is

[5.2]

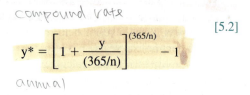

compound rate

$$y^* = \left[1 + \frac{y}{(365/n)} \right]^{(365/n)} - 1$$

annual

Equation 5.2 is a variation of the basic intrayear compounding formula from Appendix 5A—Equation 5A.2—with the number of compounding periods per year (m) expressed as 365/n.

DISCOUNT SECURITIES AND THEIR YIELDS

Many types of short-term discount securities exist. The most important for financial institutions are T-bills, commercial paper, repurchase agreements (repos), bankers' acceptances, and some short-term commercial loans. A brief description of these securities and appropriate yield calculations are given in this section. Financial institutions participate in both **primary markets,** the markets for original issuance, and **secondary markets,** the markets for resale of these instruments.

TREASURY BILLS

T-bills are short-term debt obligations of the U.S. government.

CHARACTERISTICS OF T-BILLS AND THEIR MARKETS. T-bills are usually issued with one of three original maturities—91 days (13 weeks), 182 days (26 weeks), or 364 days (52 weeks). Bills with irregular maturities, called **cash management bills,** are sometimes issued in minimum denominations of $1 million to raise cash in anticipation of future tax receipts.

T-bills are sold in minimum denominations of $10,000 to high bidders in weekly auctions conducted by the Federal Reserve Bank of New York. These auctions are the primary market for T-bills. Bids are expressed as a percentage of the bills' par value. For example, a discount bid of 95.556 on 26-week bills indicates the bidder's willingness to pay that percentage of par. Because bills are sold on a discount basis, purchasers' yields are based on the difference between what they pay for the bills (P_0) and the face value (Par) and on the length of time the bills are held (n). Yield calculations vary somewhat, depending on whether n exceeds 182 days, but most bills are issued with 182-day or shorter maturities. Therefore, all calculations that follow pertain to bills with shorter maturities.[3]

---

[3] As of spring 1992, for example, the total volume of 91- and 182-day bills outstanding was about $420 billion, compared with about $164 billion outstanding in 52-week bills. These statistics are reported periodically in the *Treasury Bulletin* under "Public Debt Operations."

The formula for the yield on a discount security with a maturity exceeding 182 days is

[5.1a]

$$y = \frac{\sqrt{b^2 - 4ac} - b}{2a}$$

$$a = [n/(2 \times 365)] - 0.25$$

$$b = n/365$$

$$c = \frac{P_0 - Par}{P_0}$$

For a derivation of this formula, see either Stigum, 1981, 34–35, or Trainer, 1982, 16–18, 32–33. (References are listed in full at the end of this chapter.)

The equation takes into account the fact that the proceeds from "long" discount bills are not available for reinvestment at the end of 6 months so they are not directly equivalent to long-term securities paying interest semiannually. Because the yield in Equation 5.1 compares discount securities with interest-bearing securities that pay interest on an intrayear basis, it is not appropriate for "long" discount securities.

Figure 5.1 illustrates the main ownership categories of T-bills and other Treasury securities since 1960. The growth in total federal debt since the mid-1970s is apparent, as is the role of financial institutions in these markets. Although "private domestic nonfinancial" owners (a category including individual investors) hold a great deal of federal debt, commercial banks and "private nonbank financial" owners (all other financial institutions) hold more. In particular, the role of nonbank financial institutions has increased dramatically since 1980.

Markets for Treasury securities are facilitated by the activities of about 40 large securities dealers who stand ready to purchase Treasury securities at every auction and who often act as buyers and sellers in the secondary market.[4] These dealers are the institutions with whom the Fed frequently trades in carrying out open market operations. In 1985, the New York Fed established voluntary financial guidelines for primary dealers, but many small secondary market dealers remained untouched by even voluntary standards for financial soundness. In 1986, as monthly trading volume in the secondary market for Treasury securities approached $2 trillion, Congress enacted the first comprehensive regulation of the Treasury securities markets, including the activities and financial condition of primary and secondary market dealers. Under the **Government Securities Act of 1986,** the Fed retained its authority over primary dealers. The U.S. Treasury was authorized to set financial standards for secondary market dealers; these standards are enforced by either the Federal Deposit Insurance Corporation (FDIC), the Comptroller of the Currency, the Fed, the Office of Thrift Supervision (OTS), or the Securities and Exchange Commission (SEC), depending on the organizational structure of the dealer.[5]

The Government Securities Act of 1986 did not silence critics of the dealer system. In recent years, because federal budget deficits have increased the Treasury's borrowings considerably, the privileges accompanying the prestigious role of primary dealer have been attacked by those inside and outside government. In particular, attention has been focused on the fact that information on the prices at which primary dealers trade Treasury securities with one another—even in the secondary market—is generally unavailable to other investors. Because primary dealers are involved in about 75 percent of the *$100 billion* daily trading volume, the price information they withhold is not insignificant to investors in the remaining 25 percent of the market. Both the General Accounting Office (GAO) and the Justice Department have investigated whether the dealers' greater access to information gives them a competitive advantage over other traders. The GAO's initial approach was to ask primary dealers to change their practices voluntarily, but by the late 1980s, they had shown little inclination to do so.

A series of incidents in 1991 involving illegal bidding at several Treasury note auctions by securities giant Salomon Brothers brought the privileges of primary dealership to worldwide attention. Treasury auction rules are intended to prevent a single bidder from receiving more than 35 percent of any issue. At one May 1991 auction, Salomon, in an effort to corner the market, submitted false bids in its customers' names and won more than 90 percent of a 2-year Treasury note issue. Because Salomon virtually controlled the supply of that issue, the firm profited handsomely when it faced virtually no price competition from other dealers as it sold the cornered securities in the secondary market.

Disclosure of Salomon's unethical bidding launched investigations into auction procedures. Analysts' reports suggested that not only did Salomon submit false bids on several occasions but that primary dealers in general had opportunities—and considerable incentives—to collude with one another before submitting bids at Treasury auctions. Although many observers initially predicted the demise of the primary dealer system and others called for stringent government regulation of auctions, actual changes were rather modest. Despite Salomon's embarrassing revelations (for which it was fined $290 million but not removed from the roll of primary dealers), regulators concluded that "the government securities market is too important a national resource and works too well

---

[4]For many years, 36 firms were designated Treasury securities dealers. In 1986, the Fed stunned many observers when it announced the addition of several large Japanese securities firms to the ranks of primary Treasury securities dealers. There were more than a dozen foreign firms by 1989, including six from Japan.

[5]Before Congress acted, many people were unhappy about the lack of regulation. See Balazsy 1986, Syron and Tschinkel 1985, Tschinkel 1985, and Rosengren 1986. The Treasury's regulations are outlined in Federal Home Loan Bank System, *Thrift Bulletin* TB 27, May 24, 1989.

FIGURE 5.1   ## Ownership of U.S. Securities

The growth in the volume of Treasury securities outstanding has been extremely rapid since the mid-1970s. During this period, nonbank financial institutions, especially securities brokers and dealers, have become major participants in the market.

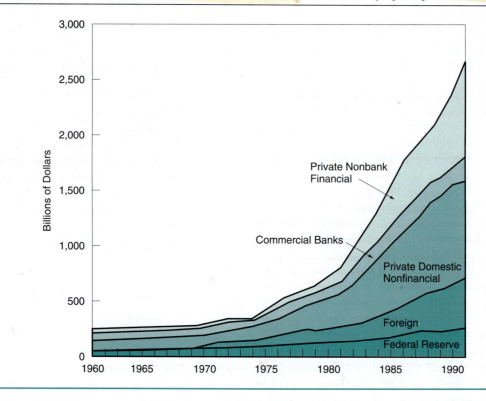

Source: Board of Governors of the Federal Reserve System, *Flow of Funds*, Q1, 1992, June 11, 1992.

---

to be put at risk by regulatory change for the sake of change."[6]

As with much securities regulation in the United States, regulators concluded that the best guarantor of a fair market is more competition. Therefore, the Fed now permits a wider range of investors to place bids at Treasury auctions, increasing the competition faced by primary dealers. The Fed also allows more small firms to act as secondary Treasury dealers. It has accelerated automation of Treasury auctions so that bidders now submit bids electronically. Thus, securities prices are available much more quickly than under the antiquated handwritten bid system used before 1993.

The quotation is from David W. Mullins, Jr., Vice Chairman of the Board of Governors of the Federal Reserve System, in testimony before Congress on February 3, 1992. Discussion of alternative auction techniques is included in E. J. Stevens, "Auctioning Treasury Securities," *Economic Commentary* (Federal Reserve Bank of Cleveland), June 15, 1992; Reinhart 1992; Chari and Weber 1992; Kevin G. Salwen and John Connor, "Treasury to Try 'Dutch' System at Its Auctions," *The Wall Street Journal,* September 4, 1992, C1, C17; Thomas T. Vogel, Jr., "Dutch Auctions Appear to be Mixed Blessing for U.S.," *The Wall Street Journal,* January 4, 1993, C1, C17.

---

[6] Accounts of the Salomon incidents are numerous, including Michael Siconolfi et al., "Salomon's Admission of T-Note Infraction Gives Market a Jolt," *The Wall Street Journal,* August 12, 1991; "Hidden Bonds: Collusion and Price Fixing in Market for Treasury Securities Have Been Rife for Years," *The Wall Street Journal,* August 19, 1991; and E. Gerald Corrigan, "Statement to Congress, September 4, 1991," *Federal Reserve Bulletin* 78 (November 1991): 887–902.

Finally, in an important experiment begun in 1992, the Fed instituted a **single-price,** or **Dutch, auction system** for selected 2-year and 5-year Treasury notes. In a traditional Treasury auction, securities are allocated to the highest bidders, in descending order of the prices they bid, until all securities to be issued are awarded. Thus, winning bidders for the same security pay different amounts, and the highest bidder knows that he or she is paying more than competing investors, a phenomenon known as the **winner's curse.** In a Dutch auction, however, all winning bidders pay the same price. Many experts believe that the traditional bidding system encourages primary dealers, who must bid at every auction, to collude in their efforts to minimize the winner's curse. The traditional system may also encourage cornering: Winning bidders may attempt to compensate for the winner's curse by earning excess profits as they resell securities they have won at the auction. Although this limited experiment was still in progress as this chapter was completed, initial reports were favorable. Some experts predict that the Dutch auction approach will be extended to most primary Treasury markets by the latter half of the decade.

INFORMATION FROM A TRADITIONAL TREASURY BILL AUCTION.

Figure 5.2 contains information on a typical group of new T-bill issues in 1992. The information is published on Tuesdays following regularly scheduled Monday auctions. These data are for bills auctioned on August 31, 1992. In this auction, as usual, many more bids were submitted than could be accepted, based on the volume of bills the Treasury had decided to sell.

Noncompetitive bids are applications to regional Federal Reserve Banks to purchase less than $1 million face value of bills, usually from individual investors and small institutions. Noncompetitive bidders are assured of receiving bills, but the price they pay is determined by the average competitive bid that is ultimately accepted. Winning competitive bidders are those willing to pay the highest percentage of par value. Thus, noncompetitive bidders know their bids will be accepted but are unsure of the price, whereas competitive bidders know the price they will pay if they win but have no guarantee of delivery.

Published information on T-bill auctions includes the average, high, and low prices paid for bills; the "rate." more formally called the **bank discount**

FIGURE 5.2   Results of a Typical Treasury Bill Auction in 1992

Results of weekly T-bill auctions are reported in major newspapers. Data include the volume sold, the average price, and the discount and coupon equivalent yields to purchasers. For comparative purposes, financial institutions must understand how to convert these yields into effective annual yields.

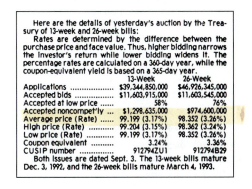

Here are the details of yesterday's auction by the Treasury of 13-week and 26-week bills:
Rates are determined by the difference between the purchase price and face value. Thus, higher bidding narrows the investor's return while lower bidding widens it. The percentage rates are calculated on a 360-day year, while the coupon-equivalent yield is based on a 365-day year.

	13-Week	26-Week
Applications	$39,344,850,000	$46,926,345,000
Accepted bids	$11,603,915,000	$11,603,545,000
Accepted at low price	58%	76%
Accepted noncompet'ly	$1,298,635,000	$974,600,000
Average price (Rate)	99.199 (3.17%)	98.352 (3.26%)
High price (Rate)	99.204 (3.15%)	98.362 (3.24%)
Low price (Rate)	99.199 (3.17%)	98.352 (3.26%)
Coupon equivalent	3.24%	3.36%
CUSIP number	912794ZU1	912794B29

Both issues are dated Sept. 3. The 13-week bills mature Dec. 3, 1992, and the 26-week bills mature March 4, 1993.

Source: The Wall Street Journal, September 1, 1992, C17.

rate; and the **coupon-equivalent** or **bond-equivalent yield;** these terms are defined later. CUSIP is an acronym for the Committee on Uniform Securities Identification Procedures; Treasury securities and many other securities have an identifying CUSIP number assigned by Standard and Poors (S&P), a securities rating company.

EFFECTIVE ANNUAL YIELD ON T-BILLS. Suppose a small commercial bank paid the average price of 99.199 percent for a $10,000, 91-day bill. The annual yield expected if the bill is held to maturity is found from Equation 5.1:

$$y = \frac{\$10,000 - \$9,919.90}{9,919.90} \times \frac{365}{91} = 3.24\%$$

The same answer results from using percentages of par value instead of dollar values for P_0 and Par:

$$y = \frac{100 - 99.199}{99.199} \times \frac{365}{91} = 3.24\%$$

The annual yield calculated either way is reported in Figure 5.2 as the coupon-equivalent, or bond-equivalent, yield. It is the annualized rate of return to the bank, *without* considering the possibility of earning interest on reinvested profits (Par − P_0) at the end of 91 days. By definition, there is always an inverse relationship between T-bill prices and their yields, made clear in Equation 5.1.

If compounding is considered, the effective annual yield on the bill can be calculated from Equation 5.2:

$$y^* = \left[1 + \frac{0.0324}{(365/91)}\right]^{(365/91)} - 1$$

$$= 0.0328 = 3.28\%$$

If the bill is not held to maturity but instead is sold after 7 weeks (49 days) at a price of 99.250 percent, the bond-equivalent and effective annual yields earned by the bank are:

$$y = \frac{99.250 - 99.199}{99.199} \times \frac{365}{49} = 3.83\%$$

$$y^* = \left[1 + \frac{0.0383}{(365/49)}\right]^{(365/49)} - 1$$

$$= 0.0389 = 3.89\%$$

When the effective annual yield is calculated using an initial purchase price P_0 and a known sales price P_1, the result is the annualized **holding-period yield.**

It is important to remember that whenever an institution uses information available at the time of an investment to compute an effective annual yield, the results of Equations 5.1 and 5.2 are *expected* (or *ex ante*) annual rates of return. Unless reinvestment rates at the time of a bill's maturity or sale are exactly the same as they were at the time of the original purchase, the expected annual yield will vary from the actual (or *ex post*) yield over a 365-day period. Even annualized holding-period yields, based on actual purchase and sales prices, are not guaranteed over a 365-day period. The example was based on an initial holding period of 49 days, and market conditions for the rest of the year may differ from those that prevailed during the holding period. Nonetheless, because all investment decisions are made *ex ante,* it is useful to have methods for com-

paring expected yields on different alternatives before deciding to commit cash.

BANK DISCOUNT YIELD. It is also important to distinguish the effective annual yield from another yield always computed on T-bills. Money market participants are familiar with bank discount yields—the "rates" given in Figure 5.2. This traditional method for quoting bill yields dates to 1929 when T-bills were first sold. At that time, traders found it easier to make computations considering a year as 360 days. The formula for calculating the bank discount yield (d) on T-bills is

[5.3]

$$d = \frac{\text{Par} - P_0}{\text{Par}} \times \frac{360}{n}$$

The bank discount yield on a 91-day bill bought at the average price of 99.199 on August 31, 1992, and held to maturity is:

$$d = \frac{100 - 99.199}{100} \times \frac{360}{91} = 3.17\%$$

There are two main differences between Equations 5.1 and 5.2 and Equation 5.3; one is the 365- versus 360-day year. Also, the bank discount method assumes that the investor's return is calculated as a percentage of the par value, whereas Equations 5.1 and 5.2 assume that the investor's yield is calculated based on the amount invested. The traditional bank discount is thus theoretically incorrect and underestimates the expected rate of return on T-bills, given market conditions at the time of a purchase.

Nonetheless, the bank discount method of quoting bill yields persists in the money markets. For this reason, it is useful to be able to convert a bank discount quotation directly into the corresponding bond-equivalent yield. A formula for making this conversion is[7]

[5.4]

$$y = \frac{365d}{360 - dn}$$

Applying Equation 5.4 to the discount yield of 3.17 percent results in the bond equivalent yield found earlier for a bill selling at 99.199 percent of par:

$$y = \frac{365\,(0.0317)}{360 - (0.0317 \times 91)}$$

$$= 0.0324 = 3.24\%$$

This yield can then be converted to the effective annual yield using Equation 5.2.

USING THE DISCOUNT YIELD TO DETERMINE A T-BILL PRICE. Another reason to understand how the conventional bank discount yield is calculated is that it enables investors to determine the secondary market price for T-bills should they wish to sell or buy bills after their original issue. Figure 5.3 shows data on T-bill yields in the secondary market on August 31, 1992.

Besides the maturity date of the bills, the prices at which dealers were willing to buy (the **bid price**) and sell them (the **asked price**) are given on a bank discount basis. Asked yields are lower than bid yields. Because there is an inverse relationship between bill prices and yields, dealers were selling bills at higher prices (lower yields to buyers) than the prices at which they were willing to buy them. The spread between dealers' bid and asked prices is their anticipated profit.

Suppose that on August 31, a savings and loan association (S&L) wished to purchase a T-bill maturing on October 1 ($n = 31$ days). If dealers quote buyers

---

[7]If D equals the dollar discount from par, then $D = Par - P_0$, and $P_0 = Par - D$. Substituting for P_0 in the formula for the bond equivalent yield (Equation 5.1),

[5.1b]

$$y = \frac{Par - (Par - D)}{Par - D} \times \frac{365}{n}$$

$$y = \frac{D}{Par - D} \times \frac{365}{n}$$

Equation 5.3 can also be solved for D:

$$d = \frac{D}{Par} \times \frac{360}{n}, \text{ so } D = d \times Par \times \frac{n}{360}$$

Substituting for D in equation 5.1b,

$$y = \frac{d \times Par \times (n/360)}{Par - [d \times Par \times (n/360)]} \times \frac{365}{n}$$

This expression can then be reduced to Equation 5.4.

FIGURE 5.3   **Treasury Bills: Secondary Market Information**

Secondary market yields on T-bills maturing at various dates are published daily. The bid price is the price at which investors can sell to dealers, whereas the asked price is the price investors must pay dealers. The "yield" quoted is the bond equivalent yield, based on the asked price.

Maturity	Days to Mat.	Bid	Asked	Chg.	Ask Yld.
Sep 03 '92	1	3.22	3.12	+0.12	3.16
Sep 10 '92	8	3.11	3.01	+0.02	3.05
Sep 17 '92	15	3.10	3.00	+0.02	3.05
Sep 24 '92	22	3.07	2.97	+0.02	3.02
Oct 01 '92	29	3.00	2.96	-0.02	3.01
Oct 08 '92	36	3.09	3.05	-0.01	3.10
Oct 15 '92	43	3.11	3.07	....	3.12
Oct 22 '92	50	3.12	3.08	+0.01	3.14
Oct 29 '92	57	3.11	3.07	....	3.13
Nov 05 '92	64	3.13	3.11	....	3.17
Nov 12 '92	71	3.14	3.12	-0.01	3.18
Nov 19 '92	78	3.15	3.13	....	3.20
Nov 27 '92	86	3.16	3.14	....	3.21
Dec 03 '92	92	3.16	3.14	....	3.21
Dec 10 '92	99	3.16	3.14	-0.01	3.21
Dec 17 '92	106	3.16	3.14	-0.01	3.22
Dec 24 '92	113	3.17	3.15	-0.01	3.23
Dec 31 '92	120	3.15	3.13	....	3.21
Jan 07 '93	127	3.17	3.15	....	3.23
Jan 14 '93	134	3.20	3.18	+0.01	3.27
Jan 21 '93	141	3.20	3.18	....	3.26
Jan 28 '93	148	3.21	3.19	-0.01	3.28
Feb 04 '93	155	3.23	3.21	+0.01	3.30
Feb 11 '93	162	3.23	3.21	....	3.31
Feb 18 '93	169	3.24	3.22	+0.01	3.31
Feb 25 '93	176	3.24	3.22	....	3.32
Mar 11 '93	190	3.24	3.22	....	3.32
Apr 08 '93	218	3.25	3.23	....	3.33
May 06 '93	246	3.26	3.24	....	3.34
Jun 03 '93	274	3.27	3.25	....	3.34
Jul 01 '93	302	3.30	3.28	+0.01	3.40
Jul 29 '93	330	3.32	3.30	....	3.42
Aug 26 '93	358	3.33	3.31	....	3.44

Source: The Wall Street Journal, September 1, 1992, C16.

a discount yield of 2.96 percent, what must the S&L pay? The price is determined by solving Equation 5.3 for P_0:

[5.5]

$$P_0 = Par \times \left[1 - \frac{dn}{360} \right]$$

$$= 100 \times \left[1 - \frac{0.0296\,(31)}{360} \right]$$

$$= 99.745\% \text{ of par}$$

Using Equation 5.1, the bond-equivalent yield to the S&L is

$$y = \frac{100 - 99.745}{99.745} \times \frac{365}{31} = 3.01\%$$

This is, in fact, the "yield" on this bill shown in Figure 5.3. Thus, the yields quoted in the secondary market for T-bills are coupon or bond equivalents based on the asked price.

The same equations are used to determine the current market price of commercial paper, bankers' acceptances, and other securities on which primary and secondary market yields are customarily quoted on a bank discount basis.

REPURCHASE/REVERSE REPURCHASE AGREEMENTS

Repurchase agreements (repos) and **reverse repos** are money market transactions in which securities (usually Treasury securities) are sold by one party to another, with the agreement that the seller will repurchase the securities at a specified price on a specified date.

CHARACTERISTICS OF REPOS AND THEIR MARKETS. Whether the transaction is considered a repo or a reverse repo depends, by convention, on whether an institution is the seller or the buyer in the transaction. Unfortunately, even among financial institutions, the terminology is confusing, with the "repo" designation given to the seller's side in some industries and the buyer's side in others. Managers must be alert to the contexts in which the labels *repo* and *reverse repo* are used. Figure 5.4 illustrates the mechanics of several hypothetical repo/reverse repo agreements.

In Transaction 1, a large securities dealer sells Treasury securities to a commercial bank, with the agreement that the dealer will buy them back in 30 days. The dealer considers the transaction a repo; the bank considers it a reverse repo. From the bank's point of view, it is, in effect, lending the dealer money for 30 days with the securities pledged as collateral. Transaction 3 is similar, except the counterparty to the

---

FIGURE 5.4   **Repurchase and Reverse Repurchase Agreements**

Repurchase agreements are short-term loans collateralized by government securities. A borrower temporarily sells securities to a lender, with an agreement to buy them back on a given date. Although custom varies, this figure uses *repo* to refer to the seller's (borrower's) side of the transaction and *reverse repo* to refer to the investor's (lender's) side of the transaction.

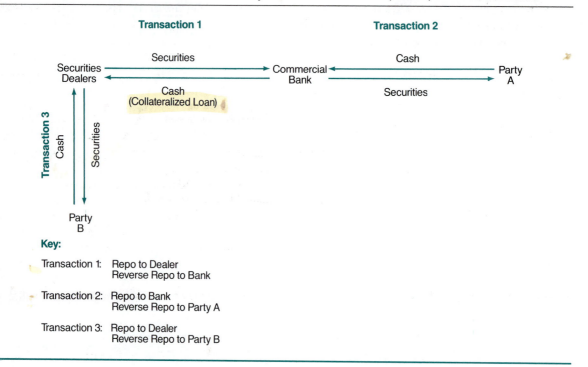

Key:

Transaction 1:   Repo to Dealer
                 Reverse Repo to Bank

Transaction 2:   Repo to Bank
                 Reverse Repo to Party A

Transaction 3:   Repo to Dealer
                 Reverse Repo to Party B

dealer is another institution or individual. Transaction 2 illustrates an agreement in which the bank promises to repurchase securities from one of its own customers; the bank views this transaction as a repo, the customer as a reverse repo.

Repurchase agreements are commonly used by large government securities dealers to finance their inventories, and the daily volume of repurchase agreements sometimes reaches $1 trillion. Many transactions have maturities as short as 1 day. Therefore, financial institutions have ample opportunities to earn profits on temporarily idle cash by taking the other side of these transactions—that is, by advancing funds through reverse repos.

Repos are also used by the Fed as part of open market operations to decrease temporarily the amount of reserves available in the banking system. The Fed does this by selling Treasury securities to banks with agreements to repurchase them later. Conversely, the Fed can increase bank reserves temporarily if it buys Treasury securities from banks under agreement that the banks will later repurchase them. Such transactions take place in a large and well-developed market and are substitutes for direct purchases and sales of Treasury securities.

The repo/reverse repo market is not without its risks. In the mid-1980s, crises in several depository institutions were precipitated by the collapse of government securities dealers with whom the depositories had large reverse repos. Although the recent regulation of Treasury securities dealers is intended to prevent such incidents in the future, there is no guarantee that a seller will fulfill its obligations to repurchase. Also, no secondary market exists for reverse repos. Before an institution makes repos and reverse repos major features of its asset/liability management strategies, both the risk and return dimensions of the agreements must be fully appreciated. More information on the use of repos/reverse repos is given in Chapters 13 and 16.[8]

EFFECTIVE ANNUAL YIELD ON REPOS/REVERSE REPOS. In Figure 5.4 (Transaction 1), the bank's expected dollar return on its reverse repo is the difference between the amount initially advanced to the dealer

and the price at which the dealer will repurchase the securities in 30 days. That dollar return can be converted into both an annual yield and an effective annual yield using Equations 5.1 and 5.2.

By convention, yields available on reverse repos are quoted on a bank discount basis. For example, suppose the discount yield on overnight reverse repos is quoted as 9.85 percent. The effective annual yield (y^*) to an institution engaging in repeated similar transactions is 10.50 percent, found first by converting the bank discount yield to an annual yield (y) using Equation 5.4, then using Equation 5.2. On an overnight repo, $n = 1$.

$$y = \frac{365(0.0985)}{360-(0.0985 \cdot 1)} = 0.0998954$$

$$y^* = \left(1 + \frac{0.099854}{(365/1)}\right)^{\left(\frac{365}{1}\right)} - 1 = 10.50\%$$

COMMERCIAL PAPER

Another short-term investment of interest to many financial institutions is **commercial paper.** For many years, commercial paper could be defined quite clearly as short-term, unsecured borrowing by major U.S. corporations. Unfortunately, such a straightforward definition no longer holds. Traditional, blue-chip firms continue to dominate, but several smaller, lesser-known companies have issued commercial paper since the late 1980s, including some backed by collateral. And as with most financial markets, much of the commercial paper action is now international; the Euro-commercial paper market, centered in London, is booming. Thus, commercial paper is perhaps now best defined simply as corporations' short-term borrowings in the open market. Note that the "short-term" part of the definition has not changed. Commercial paper has a maturity of less than 9 months, because issues of longer maturity sold in the United States must be registered with the SEC, increasing the borrower's cost and the time required to raise funds.[9]

Commercial banks, S&Ls, insurance companies, mutual funds, and other large financial institutions are main purchasers of commercial paper. The paper is almost always bought on a discount basis and redeemed at par on maturity. Minimum denominations are usually higher than for T-bills, ranging from $25,000 upward, depending on whether the purchase is made through a dealer or directly from the borrowing firm.

---

[8] A summary of the problems in the repo market in the mid-1980s can be found in Stevens 1987.

[9] For more information about recent changes in the commercial paper market, see Stigum 1990; Segall 1987; McCauley and Hargraves 1987; Post 1992.

Like other money market securities, commercial paper provides investors with short-term opportunities to invest cash. The secondary market for commercial paper is somewhat limited, however, compared with the secondary markets for T-bills. Therefore, most commercial paper is held to maturity. Occasionally, the borrower is willing to repurchase its paper before maturity (that is, to repay the loan early). Securities dealers are increasingly willing to purchase paper from initial investors. These activities maintain liquidity in the commercial paper market, ensuring that it continues. Also, the growth of money market mutual funds (MMMFs) has enlarged the market. In 1991, for example, MMMFs held almost $188 billion in commercial paper, more than 40 percent of the funds' total assets.[10]

Figure 5.5 reproduces information on the money markets from the financial pages of September 1, 1992. Besides summarizing the average bank discount yields on the Treasury auction of the day before, previously shown in Figure 5.1, market information is given for other important short-term instruments, including commercial paper. Two quotes are given for commercial paper, one for paper sold directly by an issuer to investors and one for paper sold through dealers.

Suppose a large life insurance firm anticipates idle cash for the next 90 days and approaches a dealer to purchase commercial paper. The dealer quote is shown as 3.40 percent on a bank discount basis. What price must the insurer pay, and what is the effective annual yield? Solving for the price using Equation 5.5, the insurance firm must pay 99.15 percent of par, for an effective annual yield (y^*) of 3.53 percent, calculated using Equations 5.1 and 5.2.

$$y = 100\left[1 - \frac{(0.034)(90)}{360}\right] = 99.15\%$$

$$y = \frac{100 - 99.15}{99.15} \times \frac{365}{90} = 3.4796\%$$

$$y^* = \left[1 + \frac{(0.034768)(90)}{365}\right] = $$

$$= 3.52\%$$

BANKERS' ACCEPTANCES

Other short-term securities of global importance are **bankers' acceptances.** They are short-term credit agreements, often called **time drafts,** through which international trade is financed. Because sellers often

FIGURE 5.5 Money Market Yield Quotations

Current rates on a variety of money market instruments are published daily in major newspapers. Most rates are quoted on a bank discount basis, so investors must understand how to convert those rates to effective annual yields.

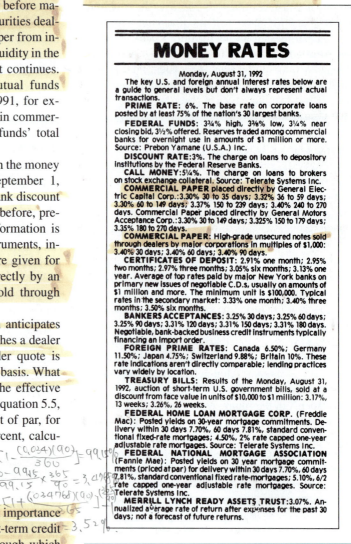

MONEY RATES

Monday, August 31, 1992

The key U.S. and foreign annual interest rates below are a guide to general levels but don't always represent actual transactions.

PRIME RATE: 6%. The base rate on corporate loans posted by at least 75% of the nation's 30 largest banks.

FEDERAL FUNDS: 3¾% high, 3⅜% low, 3¼% near closing bid, 3½% offered. Reserves traded among commercial banks for overnight use in amounts of $1 million or more. Source: Prebon Yamane (U.S.A.) Inc.

DISCOUNT RATE: 3%. The charge on loans to depository institutions by the Federal Reserve Banks.

CALL MONEY: 5¼%. The charge on loans to brokers on stock exchange collateral. Source: Telerate Systems Inc.

COMMERCIAL PAPER placed directly by General Electric Capital Corp.: 3.30% 30 to 35 days; 3.32% 36 to 59 days; 3.30% 60 to 149 days; 3.37% 150 to 239 days; 3.40% 240 to 270 days. Commercial Paper placed directly by General Motors Acceptance Corp.: 3.30% 30 to 149 days; 3.325% 150 to 179 days; 3.35% 180 to 270 days.

COMMERCIAL PAPER: High-grade unsecured notes sold through dealers by major corporations in multiples of $1,000: 3.40% 30 days; 3.40% 60 days; 3.40% 90 days.

CERTIFICATES OF DEPOSIT: 2.91% one month; 2.95% two months; 2.97% three months; 3.05% six months; 3.13% one year. Average of top rates paid by major New York banks on primary new issues of negotiable C.D.s, usually on amounts of $1 million and more. The minimum unit is $100,000. Typical rates in the secondary market: 3.33% one month; 3.40% three months; 3.50% six months.

BANKERS ACCEPTANCES: 3.25% 30 days; 3.25% 60 days; 3.25% 90 days; 3.31% 120 days; 3.31% 150 days; 3.31% 180 days. Negotiable, bank-backed business credit instruments typically financing an import order.

FOREIGN PRIME RATES: Canada 6.50%; Germany 11.50%; Japan 4.75%; Switzerland 9.88%; Britain 10%. These rate indications aren't directly comparable; lending practices vary widely by location.

TREASURY BILLS: Results of the Monday, August 31, 1992, auction of short-term U.S. government bills, sold at a discount from face value in units of $10,000 to $1 million: 3.17%, 13 weeks; 3.26%, 26 weeks.

FEDERAL HOME LOAN MORTGAGE CORP. (Freddie Mac): Posted yields on 30-year mortgage commitments. Delivery within 30 days 7.70%, 60 days 7.81%, standard conventional fixed-rate mortgages; 4.50%, 2% rate capped one-year adjustable rate mortgages. Source: Telerate Systems Inc.

FEDERAL NATIONAL MORTGAGE ASSOCIATION (Fannie Mae): Posted yields on 30 year mortgage commitments (priced at par) for delivery within 30 days 7.70%, 60 days 7.81%, standard conventional fixed-rate mortgages; 5.10%, 6/2 rate capped one-year adjustable rate mortgages. Source: Telerate Systems Inc.

MERRILL LYNCH READY ASSETS TRUST: 3.07%. Annualized average rate of return after expenses for the past 30 days; not a forecast of future returns.

Source: The Wall Street Journal, September 1, 1992, C17.

---

[10]Investment Company Institute, *1992 Mutual Fund Fact Book,* 114. Several commercial paper defaults in the late 1980s prompted the SEC to restrict the amount of so-called "second tier" (low rated) commercial paper an MMMF can hold. Before 1991, no such limitations existed.

have difficulty assessing the creditworthiness of overseas customers, they may be more comfortable if the buyer's bank agrees to guarantee payment for goods ordered.

CREATION OF A BANKERS' ACCEPTANCE. The complicated steps leading to the creation of a bankers' acceptance are illustrated in Figure 5.6.[11] Suppose an importer orders goods and simultaneously applies to his or her bank, Chase Manhattan, for financing (Steps 1–2). Typically, the financing request is for a letter of credit (L/C in the figure), certifying that the bank will stand behind the importer. If the financing request is approved, Chase notifies the exporter's bank that payment will be forthcoming (Steps 3–4). On guarantee of payment, the exporter sends the goods and forwards shipping documents and a draft (authorization for payment) with a specific payment date (hence the origin of the phrase "time draft") to his or her own bank. That bank, in turn, passes the draft and shipping information to Chase (Steps 5–7).

On receipt of the papers, Chase will stamp the draft "Accepted" (Step 8). At this point, the draft becomes a bankers' acceptance (B/A in the figure); Chase has accepted unconditional responsibility for payment on the due date to whoever holds the acceptance at that time. Of course, Chase plans to collect from the importer. If Chase sends funds to the exporter's bank on receipt of the draft, it will discount the draft, paying less than the face amount (also Step 8) in exchange for providing funds before the goods are received. The money may or may not be immediately sent to the exporter by the exporter's bank (Step 9). At this point, the acceptance remains in Chase's hands.

BANKERS' ACCEPTANCES AS MONEY MARKET INSTRUMENTS. If Chase has already advanced funds and wants to recover them before the importer pays, it may sell the acceptance to money market investors (Steps 11–12). At this point, the purchaser of an acceptance has the promise of two parties, the importer and Chase, that the acceptance will be paid at maturity. For this reason, the acceptance is sometimes called **two-name paper.**

Acceptances are sold to money market investors at a discount from the face amount. As with other discounted securities, the purchaser of the acceptance expects to receive the face amount at maturity. On sale of the acceptance, Chase is no longer financing the importer's transaction; the money market investor is. When the acceptance matures, the importer pays Chase for the goods, and the funds are paid to the acceptance holder (Steps 13–15). Thus, bankers' acceptances serve not only as short-term assets to money market investors but also as short-term sources of funds to large banks that finance international transactions.

Because of the relative security of two-name paper, bankers' acceptances gained popularity in the 1970s and early 1980s. In fact, the dollar volume of acceptances traded grew more than 1,000 percent between 1972 and 1982. The market peaked in 1984, however, and by 1991, because importers had turned to other sources of financing and because banks had become more reluctant to accept the liability accompanying bankers' acceptances, volume outstanding had fallen well below its 1982 level.[12]

EFFECTIVE ANNUAL YIELD ON BANKERS' ACCEPTANCES. If the manager of a large MMMF wished to purchase 60-day bankers' acceptances as part of the fund's portfolio, Figure 5.5 indicates that on August 31, 1992, a dealer would have quoted a yield of 3.25 percent. Knowing that the quotation is on a bank discount basis, the fund manager could have used Equations 5.5, 5.1, and 5.2 to determine the price of the acceptances and the effective annual yield expected on the transaction. The resulting price is 99.458 percent, with an effective annual yield (y^*) of 3.37 percent.

COMMERCIAL LOANS WITH DISCOUNTED INTEREST

Another short-term use of funds for some financial institutions is commercial lending, and some commercial loan yields are analogous to yields on discounted money market instruments. If lenders require interest on a loan to be paid in advance instead of at maturity, the arrangement is called a **discounted loan.** For example, suppose a small bank agrees to loan a

---

[11] Figure 5.6 assumes that the importer and the importer's bank are in the United States, so the U.S. bank is the "accepting" bank. Bankers' acceptances are also used when U.S. firms are exporters. Even in these cases, however, U.S. banks are most often the accepting banks, although the process by which the acceptance is created differs somewhat. See Hervey 1983.

[12] See Jensen and Parkinson 1986; Board of Governors of the Federal Reserve System, *Flow of Funds,* Q1, 1992, June 11, 1992; LaRoche 1993; and Stigum 1990.

| FIGURE 5.6 | Example of Bankers' Acceptance Financing of U.S. Imports: A Bankers' Acceptance Is Created, Discounted, Sold, and Paid at Maturity |

Mechanically speaking, bankers' acceptances are among the most complex money market instruments. In this example, a banker's acceptance is created as a result of a purchase of imported goods by a U.S. firm. The purchaser's bank, assumed to be Chase Manhattan, initially extends credit to pay for the goods. Chase, in turn, borrows the funds from a money market investor by issuing a bankers' acceptance. When the acceptance matures, Chase repays the investor, using funds repaid to it by the importer.

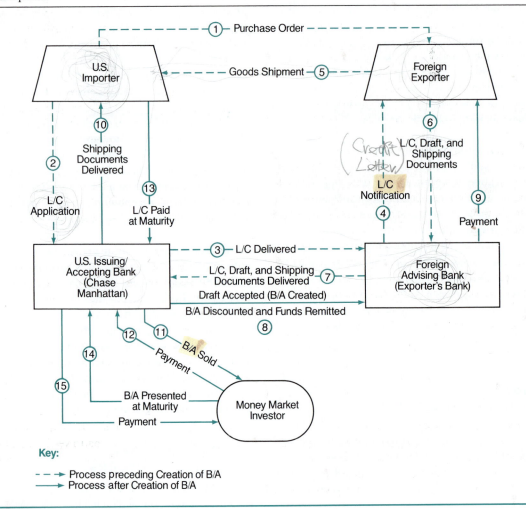

Key:

- - - ► Process preceding Creation of B/A
———► Process after Creation of B/A

Source: Adapted by the authors from Eric Hill, "Bankers' Acceptances," in *Instruments of the Money Market* (Richmond, Va.: Federal Reserve Bank of Richmond, 1986), 127.

local business $15,000 for 180 days at an annual rate of 12 percent; interest is to be paid in advance. What is the effective annual yield to the bank on this transaction?

The interest owed by the borrower is 180/365 of the annual interest, or $(180/365) \times 12\% \times \$15,000 =$ $888.[13] The bank is really advancing only $15,000 −

---

[13] Some banks calculate interest charges on the basis of a 360-day year, then multiply by 365/360. Using this method in this example, the interest charges would be: $(180/360) \times 12\% \times \$15,000 = \$900 \times 365/360 = \$912.50$. Calculating interest charges in this way increases the effective annual yield (and the borrower's cost).

$888 = $14,112 to the firm, expecting repayment of the full $15,000 in 180 days. Using Equation 5.1, the annual yield (y) is

$$y = \frac{\overset{Par}{\$15,000} - \overset{Po}{\$14,112}}{\underset{Po}{\$14,112}} \times \frac{365}{180} = 12.76\%$$

The effective annual yield (y^*) on loans of this type would be 13.17 percent, found by using Equation 5.2.

$$13.17\% = \left[1 + \frac{(12.76\%)(180)}{365}\right]^{\left(\frac{365}{180}\right)} - 1$$

SHORT-TERM INTEREST-BEARING SECURITIES

Although many short-term instruments are discounted, several are interest-bearing. Among the most important are negotiable certificates of deposit (CDs) and Eurodollar CDs. Interest-bearing securities provide returns to investors in two ways: repayment of face value and interest earned on the face value. When interest and face value are paid simultaneously, the effective annual yield on an interest-bearing security is calculated in the same way as the effective annual yield on a discount security, because the face value and interest are, in effect, a single payment. The effective annual yield on several instruments of this type is considered in the following discussion.

NEGOTIABLE CERTIFICATES OF DEPOSIT

As Chapter 2 explains, while Regulation Q (Reg Q) was in effect, it was often difficult for banks to retain large depositors. In times of relatively high interest rates, corporate depositors could earn more and obtain greater liquidity by investing directly in T-bills. In 1961, long before the Depository Institutions Deregulation and Monetary Control Act (DIDMCA) removed Reg Q ceilings, large banks, led by First National City Bank of New York (now Citibank), created a new deposit designed to please the corporate customer. Called **negotiable CDs,** they had large face values (a legal minimum of $100,000 but in practice usually more than $1 million). They could be sold in a secondary market in case the original depositor needed cash before maturity and had higher ceil-

ings than many traditional deposits. In 1973, Reg Q ceilings were removed altogether from negotiable CDs, making them even more attractive to corporate customers.

Almost without exception, negotiable CDs have original maturities of less than 1 year and have a **coupon** or **stated rate,** which is the annual interest expressed as a percentage of par value. Interest calculations assume a 360-day year. By convention, interest and principal are both paid at maturity. Although market rates are now available on all types of deposits, negotiable CDs are still popular with some large investors because of the secondary market. The market has shrunk dramatically in recent years, however, as troubles in the banking industry caused investors to turn to less risky short-term instruments.

INNOVATIONS IN THE CD MARKET. Recent innovations in the negotiable CD market include variable-rate CDs, on which the maturity is fixed but the interest rate varies every 30 days. Also, Eurodollar CDs—which are dollar-denominated negotiable CDs issued primarily by London-based branches of American, Japanese, British, or other foreign banks—have gained popularity.[14] The major purchasers of these CDs are large businesses or large financial institutions seeking temporary returns on idle cash.

The secondary market for Eurodollar CDs is smaller than the secondary market for negotiable CDs issued in the United States; both markets, however, have declined substantially since the late 1980s. Because the first $100,000 of each domestic negotiable CD is eligible for federal deposit insurance, yields are usually higher on Eurodollar CDs than on domestic CDs, although the spread has narrowed in recent years as domestic CDs have been viewed as increasingly risky.

EFFECTIVE ANNUAL YIELD ON NEGOTIABLE CDS. Figure 5.5 indicates typical negotiable CD coupon rates prevailing in August 1992. If an investor had purchased a 180-day negotiable CD with a face value of $1 million and a coupon rate of 3.50 percent, what was

---

[14] Eurodollar CDs are different from Eurodollar *time* deposits, which are deposits for which there is no secondary market. The latter are discussed in Chapter 16. For an extensive discussion of recent developments in the CD market, see Stigum 1990.

the effective annual yield? Because negotiable CDs are interest-bearing but have the cash flow characteristics of discount securities, Equations 5.1 and 5.2 can be used to determine y^*. The trick is to remember that interest on negotiable CDs is paid on the basis of a 360-day year, so in 180 days, an investor will earn interest of $(3.50\%/360) \times 180 \text{ days} = 1.75\%$ (*not* $3.50\%/365 \times 180$ days). P_1 is

$$P_1 = \$1,000,000 + \$1,000,000 (0.0175)$$
$$= \$1,017,500$$

There are still 365/180, or 2.0278 possible 180-day periods in a 365-day year; therefore the annual yield (y) expected on the CD is 3.61 percent, and the effective annual yield (y^*) is 3.64 percent. Conventions followed for quoting interest and calculating yields in the Eurodollar CD market are identical to those in the domestic market.

FEDERAL FUNDS

If depository institutions have cash reserves in excess of those required by the Fed, one possible outlet is to lend them to other institutions needing funds to meet their own reserve requirements. First defined in Chapter 3, excess reserves lent by one institution to another are **federal funds (fed funds);** they are the assets of the lending institution and liabilities of the borrowing firm. Typically, fed funds transactions are very short-term; in fact, many are overnight, similar to repo/reverse repo agreements.

Fed funds are borrowed either through direct negotiation with the lending institution or through New York brokers. The lending institution instructs the Fed or its own bank to transfer the agreed-on balances to the borrower. Because most fed funds transactions are overnight, the transaction is reversed the next day, including 1 day's interest.

EFFECTIVE ANNUAL YIELD ON FED FUNDS. The fed funds rate, like a negotiable CD rate, is quoted on the basis of a 360-day year, and interest is added to the principal to determine the total required repayment. For example, suppose an S&L agreed to sell a large commercial bank $100 million of fed funds overnight

at a quoted rate of 3.625 percent. The amount the borrower must repay the seller on the following day is

$$P_1 = P_0 + (i \times P_0 \times n/360)$$
$$P_1 = \$100,000,000$$
$$\quad + (0.03625 \times \$100,000,000 \times 1/360)$$
$$= \$100,010,069$$

The effective annual yield (y^*) is then found from Equations 5.1 and 5.2. The annual yield is 3.64 percent; the effective annual yield is 3.74 percent.

SHORT-TERM INTEREST-BEARING LOANS

Many financial institutions make short-term loans to individuals or businesses requiring periodic payment of interest, with repayment of principal on maturity. One example is a 12-month, $10,000 loan by a life insurance company to a policyholder, requiring quarterly interest payments at a 12 percent stated rate. It is easier to compare the yield on loans of this type with those on other financial assets if the effective annual yield is calculated. In doing so, the intrayear compounding equation developed in Appendix 5A is useful.

In this example, the annual interest rate of 12 percent translates into a quarterly rate of 3 percent; because there are four quarters per year, the effective annual yield is

$$y^* = \left(1 + \frac{i}{m}\right)^m - 1 \qquad [5.6]$$

where i = stated annual interest rate and
m = number of periods interest is
earned during a year.

$$y^* = \left(1 + \frac{0.12}{4}\right)^4 - 1 = 0.1255 = 12.55\%$$

Equation 5.6 is conceptually identical to Equation 5.2; differences arise only because of the terminology applied to interest-bearing versus discount securities. Thus, no matter what the investment, a financial institution manager can calculate yields that make it easy to compare a range of alternatives. Commonly quoted figures such as bank discount rates or nominal rates do not allow accurate comparisons.

CAPITAL MARKET INSTRUMENTS AND YIELDS: DEBT SECURITIES

Most financial institutions also make long-term investments. By definition, long-term assets are those with original maturities exceeding 1 year, a definition obviously encompassing many possible time horizons. Thus, there is a need for some standard period over which to calculate effective yields. Although any time period could be chosen, 1 year is commonly used.

Cash returns from long-term securities come in a variety of forms: as a single payment several years after the initial investment, as a series of equal periodic payments, or as a series of unequal cash payments. This variety again causes a need for some standardization of yield calculations. Fortunately, however, there is one approach that can be used to calculate y^* on a long-term investment of any maturity and with any cash flow characteristics. Assuming annual cash inflows, the effective annual yield on a long-term investment can be found by solving Equation 5.7 for y^*. Modifications are necessary when compounding occurs more than once a year; these are presented later.

[5.7]

$$(NPV) \quad P_0 = \sum_{t=1}^{N} \frac{C_t}{(1 + y^*)^t}$$

where P_0 = investor's cash outflow (analogous to purchase price of a discount security);
C = periodic cash inflows (interest and/or principal);
t = sub- or superscript denoting an individual time period;
N = number of periods until maturity (or until sold).

The effective annual yield to the lender calculated from Equation 5.7 is the **internal rate of return** on the investment. It is the annualized interest rate that

equates the present value of the cash outflow required to the present value of the cash inflows expected.

Unless there is a single cash inflow or unless the cash inflows are equal or perpetual, the determination of y^* is a trial-and-error iterative process. The analyst uses successively smaller changes in y^* until a rate is found at which the present value of the cash inflows equals the cash outflow required. (See Appendix 5A for examples.) Although formerly a tedious endeavor, the availability of financial analyst calculators and microcomputers makes determining y^* almost instantaneous. Examples of investments for which Equation 5.7 is appropriate are coupon bonds, zero-coupon bonds, mortgages, and long-term loans with add-on interest charges.

COUPON BONDS

Coupon bonds are long-term debt instruments. They are issued by the Treasury (called **T-notes** with initial maturities of 10 years or less and **T-bonds** with longer maturities); by agencies such as the Federal Home Loan Banks, not directly funded by the Treasury but authorized to sell bonds to carry out their responsibilities; by foreign governments; by states, municipalities, and counties; and by domestic and international firms of all types.

CHARACTERISTICS OF BONDS AND THEIR MARKETS. An investor in coupon bonds pays an initial price in exchange for periodic interest payments and repayment of the par value at maturity. Most bonds have a coupon rate that does not vary, no matter how long the time to maturity. The original maturity of bonds varies greatly, depending on the prevailing level of interest rates when a bond is issued.

Bonds may be purchased when originally issued or at a later date in the secondary markets. The secondary market for U.S. Treasury notes and bonds is quite large; secondary markets for other types of bonds are smaller. As a result of the larger secondary market and the guarantee against default provided by the taxing power of Congress and the money-creation power of the Fed, T-notes and T-bonds provide lower effective yields than their non-Treasury counterparts.

Many special features are associated with bond issues, each designed to appeal to different types of investors. For example, interest on **municipal bonds**—bonds of states, municipalities, counties, port authorities, and other nonfederal governmental entities—is not taxed at the federal level, making them attractive to investors in higher tax brackets and providing local governments with relatively low-cost funds. Still other bonds have variable coupon rates that adjust with changes in market conditions; these appeal to investors who anticipate increases in interest rates. Some corporate bonds are convertible to the common stock of the issuing corporation and are designed to appeal to investors who may wish to share in the growth prospects of the company.

Eurobonds. In recent years, the **Eurobond market** has gained prominence. Although Eurobonds were originally defined as dollar-denominated bonds issued outside the United States, globalization has made that definition inadequate. Today, Eurobonds are more accurately defined as bonds issued outside the issuer's home country to investors who are not citizens of the home country. The number of bonds issued by U.S. firms—Eurodollar bonds—declined in the 1980s, but market growth occurred from issuance by non-U.S. firms, and the volume outstanding was estimated at $750 billion in mid-1988. Financial innovations have made the Eurobond market so attractive that by 1993 U.S. and non-U.S. firms together were issuing these bonds at a volume in excess of $400 billion per year.

These instruments have several advantages to borrowers, not the least of which is absence of regulation either by the home country *or* by the countries in which they are sold. As a result, Eurobonds can be issued quickly if the need arises. Investors, too, find Eurobonds attractive; for example, non-U.S. investors are exempt from federal tax on their Eurobond holdings (although they might be subject to taxation in their own countries). The tax-exempt feature also means that borrowers are often able to pay lower interest rates than if bonds were issued in the home country. Additional differences between Eurobonds and many bonds issued in the United States include the frequency of interest payments (annually for Eurobonds versus semiannually for domestic bonds) and the fact that Eurobonds are almost entirely directly placed rather than sold through public auction.

Of course, no financial instrument is perfect. Ironically, the main problem Eurobond investors face is the absence of regulation. Should a Eurobond issuer default, it could be difficult to settle legal claims, because it is not altogether clear what country would have jurisdiction. To compensate for this risk, investors demand a high degree of creditworthiness from Eurobond issuers. Thus, the market is dominated by blue-chip firms. Some research also indicates that despite the lack of regulation, total issuance costs can be comparatively high because issue arrangements must be made outside the home country. Nonetheless, experts predict that Eurobonds will continue to be an important global market.

Other recent developments in the international bond markets include the appearance of **global bonds** and **ECU bonds.** Global bonds are issued simultaneously in several countries at once and are denominated in a single currency, usually the U.S. dollar. They are attractive to issuers because the large number of investors involved allows negotiation of lower interest rates. ECU bonds, first created in the early 1980s, are denominated in European currency units. The market grew rapidly through 1991, but its future is expected to be closely tied to the success of the Maastricht Treaty.[15]

Effective Annual Bond Yield Illustrated: Municipal Bonds. Calculating the effective annual yield on a coupon bond is a straightforward application of Equation 5.7. It is illustrated here for a bond listed in Figure 5.7, which provides data on prices of selected tax-exempt bond issues as of August 31, 1992. Most of these issues are **revenue bonds;** they will be repaid out of proceeds from the specific revenue-generating projects that they were sold to finance, such as toll roads. A few of those listed are **general obligation bonds (GOs),** to be repaid from the general funds of the issuing entity. Both revenue bonds and GOs are members of the municipal bond family.

The municipal bond market has been among the most adversely affected by recent legal and regulatory

[15] For more on the global bond markets, see Kidwell, Marr, and Thompson 1985; Plaut 1988; Thomas T. Vogel, Jr., "Matsushita Electric's Planned $1 Billion Issue May Open Up Access to Issuance of Global Bonds," *The Wall Street Journal,* June 8, 1992, C1, C17; "The Resurrection of ECU Bonds," *The Economist,* April 24, 1993, 81; Constance Mitchell, "'Funnies' Spark Light-Hearted Revival In Once-Sedate Market for Eurobonds," *The Wall Street Journal,* March 24, 1993, C1, C25.

| **FIGURE 5.7** | **Secondary Market Information on Tax-Exempt Bonds** |

Daily price and yield information for actively traded tax-exempt securities is available in the financial pages. Data include coupon rates and maturity dates as well. The yield is the yield to maturity based on the bid price.

TAX-EXEMPT BONDS

Representative prices for several active tax-exempt revenue and refunding bonds, based on institutional trades. Changes rounded to the nearest one-eighth. Yield is to maturity. n-New. Source: The Bond Buyer.

ISSUE	COUPON	MAT	PRICE	CHG	BID YLD	ISSUE	COUPON	MAT	PRICE	CHG	BID YLD
Bass Brook Minn	6.000	07-01-22	95⅞	− ⅛	6.30	NYC Muni Wtr Fin Auth	6.000	06-15-17	94	...	6.49
Calif Dept of Wtr Res	6.125	12-01-13	98½	+ ⅛	6.25	NYS Med Care Fin Agcy	6.200	08-15-22	98⅛	...	6.34
Charlotte Hosp Auth NC	6.250	01-01-20	98⅜	...	6.36	NYS Pwr Auth	6.250	01-01-23	99½	...	6.29
Chgo GO Ser 92 Proj A	5.875	01-01-22	93⅜	+ ⅛	6.37	Okla Tpke Auth					
Chgo III Arpt Ser 92A	6.000	01-01-18	93⅜	+ ⅛	6.51	Ser92C&E	6.250	01-01-22	99¾	...	6.27
Farmngtn NM Util Sys	5.750	05-15-13	93½	+ ⅛	6.31	Osceola Co Fla Transp	6.100	04-01-17	97⅜	+ ¼	6.29
Fla Mun Pwr Agcy	5.500	10-01-12	91¼	+ ¼	6.27	P R Hwy & Transp Auth	6.500	07-01-22	100⅛	+ ⅛	6.49
Fla Mun Pwr Agcy	5.700	10-01-16	92⅞	+ ⅜	6.27	P R Hwy & Transp Auth	6.625	07-01-18	101⅛	...	6.54
Fla St Bd of Ed	6.000	06-01-22	96⅛	+ ⅛	6.28	P.R. G.O. Pub Imprvmt	6.800	07-01-21	103⅛	...	6.56
Intermtn Pwr Agcy Utah	6.000	07-01-12	96½	+ ⅜	6.35	P.R. Pub Bldg Auth	6.875	07-01-21	103⅜	+ ⅛	6.62
Jacksonville Elec Fla	5.750	10-01-12	93¾	+ ⅛	6.30	PR Pub Imprvmt 1993	6.000	07-01-22	94⅜	...	6.42
Kans Dept Trans Ser92	6.500	03-01-12	101⅞	+ ⅛	6.33	S.C. Pub Serv Rev	6.625	07-01-31	100⅞	...	6.56
LA Dept Wtr & Pwr	6.000	08-15-32	95⅛	+ ⅛	6.33	Salt Lake City Utah 92	6.250	02-15-23	97⅞	+ ⅛	6.41
Metro Seattle Swr	6.200	01-01-32	96½	+ ⅛	6.45	Salt River Agri Imprvmt	6.000	01-01-13	96½	+ ¼	6.31
N.J. Turnpike Au Ser 91	6.200	01-01-18	98½	+ ⅛	6.32	San Antonio Texas	5.750	08-01-13	93½	+ ⅛	6.30
NJ Hwy Auth Ser 9	6.000	01-01-16	96⅞	+ ¼	6.26	SCAPPA Sub Ref Rev	6.125	07-01-18	97½	...	6.32
NJ Hwy Auth Ser 9	6.250	01-01-14	99⅜	+ ¼	6.31	Sikeston Mo Elec Sys	6.250	06-01-22	99⅛	+ ¼	6.32
NY Tnsp Auth commuter	6.125	07-01-12	98¾	...	6.23	TBTA Ser 92	6.000	01-01-15	97¼	+ ⅛	6.22
NY Trnsp Auth com-						Univ of Pittsburgh	6.125	06-01-21	97⅜	...	6.32
muter	6.250	07-01-17	99½	...	6.29	Va Pub Bldg Auth	5.750	08-01-12	93¾	+ ⅛	6.30
NYC Muni Wtr Fin Auth	5.750	06-15-18	93½	...	6.26	Washn Hlth Care Fac	5.750	08-15-22	91⅜	+ ¼	6.40

Source: The Wall Street Journal, September 1, 1992, C11.

changes. As noted in Chapter 4, the Tax Reform Act of 1986 reduced the attractiveness of municipal bonds to commercial banks. The same law also greatly restricted the purposes for which municipal securities, which have historically been low-cost sources of financing for state and local governments, can be issued. Furthermore, in 1988, the Supreme Court struck down South Carolina's challenge to Congress's right to regulate municipals, paving the way for what many experts predicted would be elimination of the tax-exemption to reduce the federal budget deficit. By 1993, however, Congress had taken no action to change the taxation of municipals, despite continuing criticism of the policy and the loss of much-needed federal tax revenues. Demand for municipals remained strong among high-income investors, and municipal bond mutual funds enjoyed substantial growth in the early 1990s.[16]

Suppose that a property/liability insurer purchased a City of Chicago GO bond and planned to hold

[16]Recent analyses of the municipal bond market include Howard Gleckman and David Zigas, "It's Open Season on Tax-Exempt Bonds," *Business Week,* May 2, 1988, 38–40; Fortune 1991; and Fortune 1992.

it until maturity. Figure 5.7 indicates that, to the nearest whole year, the bond had 30 years to maturity at that time (a maturity date of 01-01-22, or January 1, 2022) and paid an annual coupon rate of 5.875 percent of par. The price was 93⅜, or 93.375 percent of par. Assuming a typical par value of $1,000 and annual interest payments, the effective annual yield to the insurance company is found by solving Equation 5.7 for y^*. Because the annual coupon payments are an annuity of $58.75 per year, the right-hand side of Equation 5.7 can be expanded to incorporate the computational efficiency of the present value of an annuity formula (Equation 5A.7 in the appendix to this chapter):

$$\$933.75 = \$58.75 \left[\frac{1 - \frac{1}{(1 + y^*)^{30}}}{y^*} \right] + \frac{\$1,000}{(1 + y^*)^{30}}$$

Through a trial-and-error process or with a calculator or microcomputer, the following solution results:

$$y^* = 0.0638 = 6.38\%$$

Except for rounding, this is the same as the yield shown in Figure 5.7.

ADJUSTING FOR TAX EFFECTS

In the case of tax-exempt bonds, an adjustment must be made to make their effective yields (y^*_{TE}) comparable to the effective annual yield on taxable investments. Because no federal tax will be paid on the cash inflows, their effective yield must be put on a **tax-equivalent basis.** Assuming the insurer is in the 35 percent marginal tax bracket (tr), the tax-equivalent effective annual yield on tax-free securities is

[5.8]

$$y^*_{TE} = \frac{y^*}{(1 - tr)}$$

$$y^*_{TE} = \frac{0.0638}{(1 - 0.35)} = 0.0982 = 9.82\%$$

Earning an effective yield of 6.38 percent on a tax-exempt security is equivalent to earning 9.82 percent on a taxable security and paying tax at 35 percent. All things equal, the higher the investor's tax bracket, the higher the tax-equivalent yield of a given tax-exempt security.

HOLDING-PERIOD YIELD ON A COUPON BOND. As with short-term securities, the effective annual yield (often called the **yield to maturity (YTM)** on a bond) is only an expected yield. The actual yield on a long-term investment depends on many factors unknown at the time the investment is made, such as whether expected cash flows are actually paid or whether the investor holds the investment to maturity. If the insurer sells the Chicago bond before maturity, perhaps in 1998, the actual annualized holding-period yield earned during the 5 years can be calculated. Assuming a sales price of $950, Equation 5.7 can be used to determine the insurer's holding-period yield by substituting the selling price for C_N. An annualized holding-period yield of 6.18 percent results. Again, this can be converted to its tax-equivalent basis using Equation 5.8; y^*_{TE} under these assumptions is 9.51 percent.

EFFECT OF INTRAYEAR INTEREST PAYMENTS. Usually, the total annual interest required on bonds is paid in two equal semiannual payments, and the effective annual yield to the lender is increased because some of the cash flows are received sooner than if interest were paid annually. Under these circumstances, Equation 5.7 is first used to calculate a *periodic* yield (y_P). That periodic (semiannual in this case) rate is then converted into an effective annual rate using Equation 5.6, the intrayear compounding equation.

If the 30 year, 5.875 percent Chicago bonds paid interest semiannually, the purchaser would receive 60 (N) interest payments of $29.38 each, plus the principal repayment at the end of 60 6-month periods.

$$\$933.75 = \$29.38 \left[\frac{1 - \dfrac{1}{(1 + y_P)^{60}}}{y_P} \right] + \frac{\$1,000}{(1 + y_P)^{60}}$$

By trial-and-error solution, $y_P = 0.0319 = 3.19\%$, and $y^* = (1 + 0.0319)^2 - 1 = 0.0647$, or 6.47%.

Again, the effective yield calculations are conceptually similar, regardless of the financial instrument involved. Although notation may vary to account for the differing cash flow patterns found with money and capital market investments, in all cases the effective annual yield is found by identifying a periodic rate of return and compounding it over the number of such periods in a year.

ZERO-COUPON BONDS

Zero-coupon bonds are long-term debt instruments promising a single higher cash inflow at maturity in exchange for the initial purchase price. No periodic interest payments must be made by the borrower; hence the name *zero-coupon.* They are the long-term analogs of short-term discount securities. In the 1980s, zero-coupon bonds gained popularity with borrowers anxious to avoid the periodic cash payments required to service coupon bonds. From the lender's point of view, even though no interest payments are actually received, taxes must be paid as if cash returns were earned each year. "Zeros" are thus most popular with tax-exempt investors, such as pension funds or investment companies.

FIGURE 5.8 **New York Exchange Bond Quotations**

Price information for bonds traded on the New York Exchange is reported daily, including the number of bonds traded (notice how few) and the closing price. The yield quoted is not the yield to maturity (the effective annual yield) but rather the current yield—the coupon rate divided by the current price as a percentage of par. In the case of zero-coupon bonds, the yield column is blank.

NEW YORK EXCHANGE BONDS

Quotations as of 4 p.m. Eastern Time
Monday, August 31, 1992

BONDS	CUR YLD	VOL	CLOSE	NET CHG	BONDS	CUR YLD	VOL	CLOSE	NET CHG
CmwE 8s03	7.9	50	101¾	+ ¼	MarO 9½94	9.0	142	105⅝	...
CmwE 8¾05	8.4	10	104	+ ⅝	MarO 9¾99	9.0	23	108½	+ ⅝
CmwE 9⅜04	9.1	20	103⅛	− ⅜	Marriott zr06	...	21	33	− ¼
CmwE 8⅛07J	8.0	50	101½	+ ¾	Masco 5¼12	cv	30	87	+ ¾
CmwE 8¼07	8.1	12	101¾	− ⅛	v|McCro 7½s94f	...	4	15⅞	+ ¼
CmwE 9⅛08	8.8	25	104	− ⅝	v|McCro 7⅝s97f	...	50	17	+ 1
ConrPer 6¾01	cv	25	93	+ ½	v|McCro 7¾95f	...	10	16	− ⅜
Consec 12¾97	11.9	20	106⅞	...	McDnl 8⅞19	8.4	10	105⅛	+ ⅛
ConEd 7.9s01	7.7	15	102⅛	...	McDnlDg 7⅞97	8.0	14	99	+ ⅛
ConEd 7.9s02	7.7	3	102⅛	− ¼	McDnlDg 8¼93	8.2	8	$100\tfrac{17}{32}$	− $1\tfrac{15}{32}$
ConEd 7¾03	7.6	12	101⅝	...	McDnlDg 8⅝97	8.5	22	101¾	+ ¾
CnNG 7¾96	7.7	50	100¾	− 1¼	McDnlDg 9s93	8.9	20	$100\tfrac{29}{32}$	+ $\tfrac{13}{32}$
ConNG 7¼15	cv	10	108½	− ¼	Mead 6¾12	cv	119	98½	...
CnPw 6⅞98	6.9	4	99½	+ 1	MesaCap na96	...	25	88½	+ ½
CnPw 7⅝99	7.6	32	100⅞	+ ⅝	MesaCap 13½99	14.4	35	94	...
CnPw 7½02J	7.6	35	98¾	+ ⅛	MichB 7s12	7.2	4	97⅜	+ ⅛
CnPw 9s06	8.7	15	102⅞	...	MidlBk 11.35s93	11.2	51	101½	− ½
CnPw 8⅞07	8.6	19	102⅞	− ⅜	MKT 5½33f	...	16	51	+ 1½
CnPw 8⅝07	8.3	10	103⅞	+ ⅜	MKT 5½33fr	...	10	50	...
vjCtlInf 9s06f	cv	64	7⅞	− ⅝	MPac 4¾30f	...	38	58¼	+ 1½
CoopCo 10⅝05	cv	35	84¾	− ¼	MPac 5s45f	...	20	61	+ ½
CrayRs 6⅛11	cv	110	77	+ ⅝	Mobil 8⅝94	8.1	65	107	− ⅛
CumE 8⅞95	8.9	25	99⅝	− 1⅝	MobO 7⅜01	7.3	4	101⅛	+ ⅝
CumE zr05	...	30	37	...	Monog 11s04	11.7	1	94	− ⅞
Dana dc5⅞06	cv	50	85	+ 1	Mons 9⅛00	8.9	6	102½	...
DatGen 8⅜02	9.7	37	86½	+ 1	Moran 8¾08f	cv	10	71	...
DataGn 01	cv	15	84	...	MorKnd zrcld	...	1	40½	− ⅛
Datpnt 8⅞06	cv	5	63⅛	− ⅜	Motrla zr09	...	6	41	+ ½
DeereCa 9.35s03	9.2	5	101½	+ 1	MtSTI 7⅜11	7.6	15	97¼	− 1
DetEd 6s96	6.0	15	99¼	+ ¼	MtSTI 8s17	8.0	178	100	...
DetEd 6.4s98	6.5	29	98½	+ ⅛	MtSTI 8⅝18	8.3	10	104⅜	+ ⅜
DetEd 8⅛01	8.0	14	101	− 2	NCNB 11⅛cld	...	20	$100\tfrac{1}{16}$	...
DetEd 7½03	7.5	1	100	− 1	NJBTl 7¼11	7.4	63	97¾	...
Disney zr05	...	121	46⅞	− ⅛	NJBTl 7¾13	7.7	16	101¼	+ 1¾
DmBk 7¾96	7.7	10	100¼	+ ½	NJBTl 8¼16	8.0	10	103⅝	+ ⅝
Dow 6.70s98	6.7	52	100	− ⅛	NConv 9s08f	cv	23	45	...
duPnt 8.45s04	8.2	15	103¼	− ⅛	NtEdu 6½11	cv	36	70	...
duPnt 8½06	8.2	1	103½	− ⅜	NavFin 7⅝93	7.9	142	96¼	+ ¼

Source: The Wall Street Journal, September 1, 1992, C15.

Applying Equation 5.7 to zero-coupon bonds is straightforward algebra. There is but a single cash inflow, the present value of which must be equated to the investor's cash outflow.[17] Based on data from Figure 5.8, the zero-coupon bonds of Marriott Corporation maturing in 2006 were selling for 33 (33 percent of par) at the close of trading on August 31, 1992. If the bonds have a par value of $1,000, the effective annual yield is found by direct solution of Equation 5.7 for y^*:

$$\$330.00 = \frac{\$1{,}000}{(1 + y_P)^{28}}$$

$$(1 + y_P)^{28} = (\$1{,}000/\$330.00) = 3.0303$$

$$y_P = \sqrt[28]{3.0303} - 1$$

$$y_P = .0404 = 4.04\%$$

$$y^* = (1 + .0404)^2 - 1 = .0824 = 8.24\%$$

[17] Even though the bond has no periodic cash flows, the YTM is calculated assuming semiannual periods, just as is done with a coupon bond.

MORTGAGES

Mortgages are debt instruments collateralized by real property. The property is classified as residential if it is a one- to four-family dwelling, or commercial if it is for business use or its residential capacity exceeds four families. The residential mortgage debt of individual homeowners is one of the largest single categories of private debt in the United States. Major institutional lenders in the residential mortgage market are discussed at several points later in the text.

Few financial markets have undergone such dramatic changes as have the primary mortgage markets since 1980. In general, mortgages have fixed or variable interest rates and usually carry maturities of 15 years or more.[18] Although recently many lenders have desired variable rates or shorter maturities on new mortgages, most existing mortgages have fixed rates. The typical fixed-rate mortgage requires the borrower to make equal monthly payments, including interest owed for the month plus repayment on the principal balance. Repayment schedules (called **amortization schedules**) are prepared so that both parties know the exact principal balance outstanding at any time.

Table 5.1 presents parts of the amortization schedule for a 20-year fixed-rate $100,000 mortgage with an annual interest rate of 14.5 percent, or $14.5/12 = 1.2083$ percent per month. If a borrower makes each monthly payment for the entire life of the mortgage, the present value of the payments, discounted at the monthly interest rate, will equal the original principal amount of the mortgage. As shown in Appendix 5A, these monthly mortgage payments are determined by solving the present value of an annuity equation (Equation 5A.7) for the required annuity amount.

EFFECTIVE ANNUAL YIELD ON MORTGAGES. An issue of special interest is the widespread practice in the residential mortgage market of charging borrowers **mortgage points.** Each mortgage point is 1/100 of the principal balance of the loan; points must be paid in cash to the lender at the time mortgage contracts are signed. Because they reduce the net amount the lender

advances to the borrower, they increase borrowers' costs and lenders' yields.

If an S&L charges 2½ points on the $100,000 20-year mortgage with a 14.5 percent fixed interest rate, the lender actually advances a net loan of $100,000 - (0.025 \times \$100,000) = \$97,500$, even though the borrower must repay the full $100,000. As shown in Table 5.1, monthly payments on this mortgage are $1,280. The monthly yield (y_P) is found from Equation 5.7, and Equation 5.6 is used to convert this monthly yield into an effective annual yield of 16.08 percent:

$$\$97,500 = \sum_{t=1}^{240} \frac{\$1,280}{(1 + y_P)^t}$$

$$= \$1,280 \left[\frac{1 - \dfrac{1}{(1 + y_P)^{240}}}{y_P} \right]$$

$$y_P = 0.0125 = 1.25\%$$

$$y^* = (1 + 0.0125)^{12} - 1 = 16.08\%$$

EFFECT OF PREPAYMENTS ON YIELDS. Because most mortgages are prepaid by borrowers, institutional managers with large mortgage portfolios should estimate the effective annual yield assuming payment before maturity. Suppose the $100,000 mortgage in Table 5.1 is expected to be prepaid in 5 years when the borrower sells the house on which the mortgage is held. The amortization schedule indicates that after 60 monthly payments have been made, the principal balance is just over $93,738. Thus, the lender's anticipated cash flow when prepayment is expected consists of a monthly annuity with a lump-sum prepayment at the end.

As shown on the following page, the effective yield is higher than if the mortgage were not prepaid, because the lender receives the return of the principal balance sooner. Still, lenders do not always welcome prepayments, because they must then incur the costs of finding alternate uses for the funds. Also, many borrowers prepay mortgages in periods when interest rates have fallen, because they can refinance their homes at lower mortgage rates. Lenders, after receiving repayment of funds earlier than expected, find they must reinvest them in loans carrying lower annual yields. Using Equations 5.7 and 5.6, the yield on the prepaid loan is

---

[18] Discussion of the many new mortgage instruments available is in Chapter 15. Further, the secondary market for mortgages is one of the fastest growing and most complex of all the financial markets. These markets, the mortgage-backed securities developed by market participants, and the use of secondary mortgage markets as an asset/liability management tool are discussed in Chapter 19.

TABLE 5.1   **Mortgage Amortization Schedule**

A loan's amortization schedule identifies how each payment is allocated between principal and interest and shows the remaining principal balance. In this example, as in the case of most mortgages, interest is paid only on the unpaid balance at the beginning of the month. Thus, as more payments are made, monthly interest charges decline.

Monthly Payments: $1,280 (1)		Initial Balance: $100,000 (2)	Initial Maturity: 20 years (3)	Points: 2½ (4)	Interest Rate: 14.5% (5)
Month	Payment	Beginning Balance	Interest $(0.145/12) \times (2)$	Principal Paid (1)—(3)	End-of-Month Balance (2)—(4)
1	$1,280	$100,000.00	$1,208.33	$ 71.66	$99,928.34
2	1,280	99,928.34	1,207.47	72.53	99,855.81
3	1,280	99,855.81	1,206.59	73.41	99,782.40
4	1,280	99,782.40	1,205.70	74.29	99.708.10
5	1,280	99,708.10	1,204.81	75.19	99,632.91
6	1,280	99,632.91	1,203.90	76.10	99,556.81
7	1,280	99,556.81	1,202.98	77.02	99,479.79
8	1,280	99,479.79	1,202.05	77.95	99,401.84
9	1,280	99,401.84	1,201.11	78.89	99,322.95
10	1,280	99,322.95	1,200.15	79.85	99,243.11
50	1,280	95,247.33	1,150.91	129.09	95,118.24
51	1,280	95,118.24	1,149.35	130.65	94,987.59
52	1,280	94,987.59	1,147.77	132.23	94,855.36
53	1,280	94,855.36	1,146.17	133.83	94,721.53
54	1,280	94,721.53	1,144.55	135.45	94,586.08
55	1,280	94,586.08	1,142.92	137.08	94,449.00
56	1,280	94,449.00	1,141.26	138.74	94,310.26
57	1,280	94,310.26	1,139.58	140.42	94,169.84
58	1,280	94,169.84	1,137.89	142.11	94,027.73
59	1,280	94,027.73	1,136.17	143.83	93,883.90
60	1,280	93,883.90	1,134.43	145.57	93,738.33
230	1,280	13,110.45	158.42	1,121.58	11,988.87
231	1,280	11,988.87	144.87	1,135.13	10,853.73
232	1,280	10,853.73	131.15	1,148.85	9,704.89
233	1,280	9,704.89	117.27	1,162.73	8,542.16
234	1,280	8,542.16	103.22	1,176.78	7,365.38
235	1,280	7,365.38	89.00	1,191.00	6,174.38
236	1,280	6,174.38	74.61	1,205.39	4,968.98
237	1,280	4,968.98	60.04	1,219.96	3,749.03
238	1,280	3,749.03	45.30	1,234.70	2,514.33
239	1,280	2,514.33	30.38	1,249.62	1,264.72
240	1,280	1,264.72	15.28	1,264.72	0.00

$$\$97,500 = \$1,280 \left[\frac{1 - \dfrac{1}{(1 + y_P)^{60}}}{y_P} \right]$$

$$+ \frac{\$93,738}{(1 + y_P)^{60}}$$

$$y_P = 0.0127 = 1.27\%$$

$$y^* = (1 + 0.0127)^{12} - 1 = 16.35\%$$

ADD-ON LOANS

   Some long-term loans are made with **add-on interest.** Automobile and other consumer loans by finance companies, commercial banks, credit unions (CUs), and S&Ls are frequently made on this basis. Add-on interest means that the total interest owed on the loan, based on the annual stated interest rate, is added to the initial principal balance *before* determining periodic payments. If, for example, an individual borrows $8,000 to purchase a car, must make monthly payments for 36 months, and is quoted a 10 percent add-on rate by a finance company, the 10 percent stated annual interest will be added to the $8,000 principal before monthly payments are calculated. In this example, $2,400 will be added on (10% × $8,000 × 3 years), for a total initial balance of $10,400. Periodic payments are then calculated by dividing the $10,400 by the number of payments to be made, resulting in cash payments of $10,400/36 = $288.89 per month. In effect, the lender is advancing $8,000 cash at the time the loan is made in exchange for 36 annuity payments of $288.89.

The effective annual yield on this loan is calculated by using Equations 5.7 and 5.6. The monthly yield (y_P) is 1.49 percent, and y^* is 19.42 percent. Unlike a mortgage, an add-on loan requires the borrower to pay interest on more than just the remaining unpaid balance of the original loan. During the first year, the borrower will pay the lender 12 × $288.89 = $3,466.68 in total payments—almost half the original amount borrowed. Even after interest owed during the first year is deducted, the borrower retains use of much less than the $8,000 originally borrowed. Yet, the interest owed in both the second and third years is 10 percent of $8,000. Because interest is paid on the full principal balance after much of it has been repaid, add-on loans produce some of the biggest differences between stated and effective rates among financial assets. Federal consumer-protection laws require lenders to inform borrowers of the effect of add-on interest.[19]

CAPITAL MARKET INSTRUMENTS AND YIELDS: EQUITY SECURITIES

Although the classification of securities into money or capital market categories is based on original maturity, two securities—preferred and common stock—have no maturity date and therefore defy a strict application of this definition.[20] Both securities signify that the holder is not entitled to legal repayment of principal but has a residual claim on the issuing firm. They are long-term claims on the firm's assets and income and are traded in capital markets.

PREFERRED STOCK

Preferred stockholders pay an initial price for the security in exchange for expected cash dividends and/or the possibility of selling the stock at a higher price in the future. Dividends to preferred stockholders are almost always specified by the issuing firm as a dollar amount per year or as a stated percentage of the par value of the stock. The par value of preferred, however, is not an amount preferred stockholders expect to receive at a specified date, although it is the maximum per share a preferred stockholder can expect to receive if a company is liquidated. Preferred dividends are not legal obligations of the issuing firm, but they must be paid before any dividends are paid to common shareholders. Thus, unlike missing bond interest payments, failing to pay preferred dividends in a given year cannot usually force a firm into bankruptcy. Preferred stock is attractive to corporate investors, because under current tax laws, 70 percent of the dividends on the preferred stock of another company are tax-exempt. As yields in the debt markets fell precipitously in the early 1990s, investors' willingness to purchase preferred stock rose substantially, and a record volume of preferred shares was issued in 1991.

EFFECTIVE ANNUAL YIELD ON PREFERRED STOCK. Because most preferred dividends are fixed indefinitely, expected cash returns on preferred stock are perpetual annuities. Therefore, the expected annual yield on preferred stock is easily estimated from Equation 5.9, a restatement of Equation 5A.10 in the appendix to this chapter.

[5.9]

$$y^* = \frac{C_1}{P_0}$$

---

[19] Federal truth-in-lending legislation does not require the effect of compounding to be reported. To meet disclosure requirements, the monthly rate of 1.49 percent in the example would be converted to an annual rate (y) of 1.49 × 12 = 17.88%. The lender's effective yield (y^*) is higher, as previously shown.

[20] Occasionally preferred stock is issued with stated maturity dates—usually by financial institutions—and called "limited life" preferred. These securities are classified as liabilities of the issuer, not as equity instruments.

According to Figure 5.9, on August 31, 1992, the preferred stock of Texas Instruments closed at 33⅝. Unlike bond quotes, prices on preferred and common stock are quoted as dollar figures, so the price is $33.63. The annual dividend was $2.26. Therefore, the expected annual yield to a purchaser who bought the stock at $33.63 and held it indefinitely would be

$$y^* = \frac{\$2.26}{\$33.63} = 6.72\%$$

COMMON STOCK

Common stock entitles the holder to profits after employees, creditors, and preferred stockholders have been paid. In case of liquidation, all proceeds from the sale of assets go to common shareholders after the same prior claimants have been satisfied.

Returns to common shareholders are earned from cash dividends and proceeds from the resale of the stock. Like preferred stock dividends, common stock dividends are not legal requirements of issuing firms. Unlike preferred stockholders, however, common shareholders have the potential for substantial dividend increases if the issuing firm's earnings prospects are favorable. Expectations of increased earnings also increase the market value of the firm's stock, enabling common shareholders to profit from the sale of their shares at an appreciated price in the future. A firm's prospects may decline, but most investors purchase common stock in anticipation of a positive rate of return.

Few topics in finance have received more attention in the past 20 years than the estimation of expected rates of return on common stock. In the absence of universal agreement on the best approach for making such estimates, several widely accepted approaches are advocated in the academic literature and used in practice. Two important ones are examined in the following paragraphs.

EFFECTIVE ANNUAL YIELD ON COMMON STOCK: CONSTANT GROWTH MODEL. In theory, the effective annual yield on common stock is estimated in the same way as the return on other types of investments; it is the discount rate that equates the present value of the expected cash benefits to the purchase price. A major complication, however, is that future cash flows are

FIGURE 5.9 **New York Stock Exchange Quotations**

Daily New York Stock Exchange listings include information on price performance over the past year, as well as high, low, and closing prices for the previous day. Also provided are the number of securities traded (note how much larger than for bonds), the most recent annualized dividend, the dividend yield (dividend/closing price), and the ratio of closing price to most recent annualized earnings.

NEW YORK STOCK EXCHANGE COMPOSITE TRANSACTIONS

52 Weeks Hi	52 Weeks Lo	Stock	Sym	Div	Yld %	PE	Vol 100s	Hi	Lo	Close	Net Chg
6	3	Terraind	TRA	...	12	188	5	4⅞	5	+ ⅛	
20⅜	10	Teradyne	TER	...	16	369	12¾	12⅝	12⅝	...	
7¼	4	Tesoro	TSO	...	...	94	4⅛	4	4	...	
14⅛	10	Tesoro pf		...	...	8	11⅛	11⅛	11¼	...	
66⅞	55½	Texaco	TX	3.20	4.9	18	5606	65⅞	65½	65¾	+ ⅜
54½	51⅞	Texaco pfC		3.78e	7.1	...	19	53⅛	52½	53⅛	+ ½
25¼	18	Texind	TXI	.20	1.0109	18	20⅝	20½	20⅝	+ ⅛
42⅜	26	Texinstr	TXN	.72	1.9	...	2193	38⅞	38⅛	38⅝	– ¼
36¾	27½	Texinstr pf		2.26	6.7	...	136	33⅞	33½	33⅝	– ¼
23¼	17	TexPacTr	TPL	.40	2.2	34	7	17⅞	17⅝	17⅞	+ ¼
43¾	37	TexUtil	TXU	3.04	7.1	...	6094	43¼	42⅜	43	– ¼
9¼	3⅞	Texfiind	TXF		...	9	162	8½	7¾	8⅛	...
10¾	9¼	Texfiind pf		1.00	9.8	...	6	10⅜	10¼	10¼	– ⅜
40¼	32⅞	Textron	TXT	1.12	3.1	10	619	37	36½	36½	– ⅝
9⅜	7½	ThaiCapFd	TC	.25e	3.0	...	142	8⅜	8¼	8⅜	+ ⅛
18½	13¾	ThaiFd	TTF	.68e	4.5	...	53	15⅛	15	15	– ¼
47½	37½	ThermoElec	TMO	...	19	404	39⅜	39	39⅜	+ ½	
21¼	13¾	Thiokol	TKC	.40	2.5	5	47	16⅛	16	16½	...
65⅜	50⅜	ThomBetts	TNB	2.24	3.5	22	312	64¾	63¾	64¾	+ ⅛
x 14⅛	9	Thomind	TII	.40	4.3	26	x43	9¾	9¼	9¼	– ⅜
19½	11½	ThomsAdv	TAG	1.90e	12.0	8	38	16¼	15¾	15⅞	– ⅜
s 19½	7	ThorInd	THO	.12	1.0	13	203	12½	12¼	12¼	– ¼
▲ 18¼	9⅞	Tidewtr	TDW	.08e	.4	46	3935	18⅝	18	18½	+ ½
52⅞	23¼	Tiffany	TIF	.28	1.1	15	1000	26½	26¼	26⅛	– ⅜
17⅜	7⅞	Timberlnd	TBL	...	17	48	15	14¾	14⅞	– ⅛	
116¾	77¾	TimeWarner	TWX	1.00	1.0	...	1006	104½	103⅜	103½	– ¼
29½	19¾	TimeWarner wi		...	...	32	26¾	26	26½	– ⅛	
52¼	41¾	TimeWarner pfC		4.38	8.5	...	342	51⅞	51½	51¾	– ⅛
55	41	TimeWarner pfD		5.50t	10.0	...	138	55	54¾	54¾	...
38⅜	25½	TimesMir	TMC	1.08	3.2	24	980	33½	32⅞	33⅜	+ ⅜

Source: The Wall Street Journal, September 1, 1992, C5.

more difficult to estimate for stock than for other financial assets. A way of simplifying estimation is to assume that cash benefits will grow at a constant rate, then to estimate a price at which the stock can be sold at the end of the planned holding period.

As shown in Figure 5.9, the common stock of Texas Instruments closed at 38⅝ on August 31, 1992.

Suppose that the manager of a pension fund planned to purchase the stock at this price and anticipated that cash dividends would grow at an annual rate of 9 percent over their most recent level of $0.72 per share.[21] After 5 years, the manager plans to sell the stock and estimates that the selling price will be $48. Equation 5.7 is used to estimate the effective annual yield, based on these cash flow estimates:

$C_1 = \$0.72\,(1.09)\quad = \$0.78$

$C_2 = \$0.72\,(1.09)^2 = \$0.86$

$C_3 = \$0.72\,(1.09)^3 = \$0.93$

$C_4 = \$0.72\,(1.09)^4 = \$1.02$

$C_5 = \$0.72\,(1.09)^5 = \$1.11$, plus the anticipated $48 sales price = $49.11

$$\$38.63 = \sum_{t=1}^{5} \frac{C_t}{(1 + y^*)^t}$$

$$y^* = 0.0665 = 6.65\%$$

If, instead, the pension fund manager planned to hold Texas Instruments shares indefinitely, the cash dividends would be a perpetually growing annuity. The effective annual yield with an indefinite holding period can be found from Equation 5A.11 in the appendix. For the Texas Instruments stock purchased at $38.63, y^* is

$$y^* = \frac{\$0.72\,(1.09)}{\$38.63} + 0.09$$

$$= 0.1103 = 11.03\%$$

EFFECTIVE ANNUAL YIELD: CAPITAL ASSET PRICING MODEL. Many analysts believe that there is a better approach to estimating the expected return on common stock, particularly for investors holding large, widely diversified portfolios. This approach focuses on a firm's sensitivity to systemwide economic factors that could alter its earnings prospects, such as changes in monetary policy, fiscal policy, or the overall rate of economic growth. A measure of this sensitivity is the stock's **beta coefficient (β).** The beta for stock j is defined in statistical terms as the covariance (cov) of its

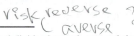

expected return (r_j) with the expected return on the **market portfolio (r_m),** divided by the variance of returns on the market portfolio (σ_m^2). The market portfolio is a large, diversified portfolio.

[5.10]

$$\beta_j = \frac{\text{cov}\,(r_j,\, r_m)}{\sigma_m^2}$$

Beta coefficients are estimated in several ways; the most common is regression analysis. Figure 5.10 illustrates a regression line between monthly returns (dividends plus price appreciation or depreciation) on the common stock of IBM and monthly returns on the S&P 500 from January 1983 through December 1987. The slope of the line (0.704) is an estimate of the stock's beta. This estimate of beta can then be adjusted for any anticipated changes.[22] The more sensitive a stock's expected returns to general market conditions, the higher the stock's beta. A beta close to 1 indicates average sensitivity. A beta of 0.704 indicates less-than-average sensitivity to market factors.

According to the **capital asset pricing model (CAPM),** expected returns on common stocks are linearly related to their betas, as expressed in Equation 5.11:

[5.11]

$$r_j = r_f + (r_m - r_f)\,\beta_j$$

Theoretically, r_f is the expected return on an investment without risk—that is, without potential variation in expected cash inflows. The expression

---

[21] This historical dividend growth rate and the beta coefficient for Texas Instruments are from the July 31, 1992, report on the firm in *Value Line Investment Survey.*

[22] Besides adjusting for changes in the relationship as a result of factors specific to a firm (such as a merger or divestiture), one must adjust for the tendency of betas in general to change over time. For further discussion, see Blume 1975.

Betas are also sensitive to the time period over which they are measured. For example, the 60-month period illustrated in Figure 5.10 includes October 1987 when the return on the S&P 500 Index was *negative* 27.5 percent but the return on IBM stock was "only" negative 18.7 percent (note the data point at the lower left of Figure 5.10). The fact that IBM's stock fell less dramatically than the market as a whole and the fact that monthly returns for October 1987 are so atypical (they are "outliers" in statistical terms) greatly influence estimates of IBM's beta during this period. For most of the late 1980s and early 1990s, for example, IBM's beta coefficient, estimated through simple regression, was about 0.9. Professional analysts use sophisticated adjustments to "raw" betas such as that shown in Figure 5.10 to avoid drawing unwarranted conclusions about a stock's sensitivity compared with that of the market.

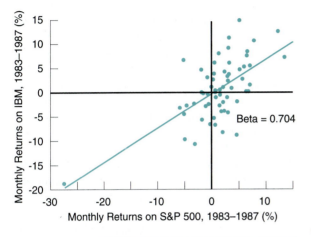

FIGURE 5.10   Using Regression to Estimate Beta

An investment's beta coefficient, a measure of its sensitivity to systemwide economic factors, is estimated by regressing periodic returns on the investment against returns on a portfolio mirroring the market as a whole over the same period. The slope of the regression line—an estimate of how the investment's returns change as the market changes—is the investment's beta.

$(r_m - r_f)$ in CAPM is the expected **market risk premium.** CAPM holds that the expected return on an investment is directly and solely proportional to its sensitivity to systematic changes in the financial markets, as measured by the beta coefficient.[23]

No investment's returns are so predictable that they are literally free of any potential variation, but most managers assume that short-term Treasury securities are essentially risk-free. Returning to the Texas Instruments example, a user of CAPM would estimate the expected return on Texas Instruments common

stock based on the stock's beta, the risk-free rate, and the market risk premium. Figure 5.3 indicates that as of August 31, 1992, the bond-equivalent yield on a T-bill maturing in 10 days (September 10, 1992) was 3.05 percent, for an effective annual yield, using Equation 5.2, of 3.09 percent.[24] An estimate of the expected market risk premium $(r_m - r_f)$, based on 67 years of data from the financial markets, is 8.6 percent.[25] *Value Line Investment Survey* reported in July 1992 that the beta of Texas Instruments stock was 1.55—that is, that the stock was expected to show above-average sensitivity to general market movements. Using Equation 5.11, a CAPM estimate of the expected 1-year rate of return on Texas Instruments stock, as of July 1992, is

$$r_{TI} = 3.09\% + (8.60\%)\,1.55 = 16.42\%$$

CAPM provides an alternative way to estimate the expected annual return on common stock for managers of widely diversified portfolios. Under those conditions, it can be argued that estimating individual cash flows for each stock is tedious, time-consuming, and not worth the effort required. The degree to which CAPM is an adequate replacement for individual security analysis is debatable, for not all experts agree that the sensitivity of a stock to common market factors is the only important determinant of its expected return. Nonetheless, CAPM remains a widely used alternative to other models.

WHAT DETERMINES YIELDS?

The discussion has focused thus far on the mechanics of calculating yields, stressing the importance of comparing returns on an equivalent basis. Clearly, effective annual yields depend on the size of the cash outflows required and the size and timing of the cash inflows expected. If either the cash outflow required (the price) or the benefits to be received change, an effective yield

---

[23] Initial development of CAPM is attributed to Jack Treynor in an unpublished paper; Sharpe 1964; and Lintner 1965.

Since then, the theory has been subjected to voluminous empirical examination, refinement, and criticism. Thorough explication of these efforts is beyond the intent of this book. Empirical tests of CAPM are typified by Fama and McBeth 1973. A comprehensive look at practical applications of the model can be found in Harrington 1983, while criticisms of and alternatives to the model are found in Ross 1976 and Roll 1977. A summary of criticisms written for practitioners is Wallace 1980. Most recently, Fama and French (1992) seriously questioned CAPM's hypothesized relationship between beta and returns; no alternative theory was proposed, however.

---

[24] *Value Line* estimates stock betas by regressing weekly returns on a stock against weekly returns on a market portfolio. Carleton argued that the annualized risk-free return used in CAPM should be based on the data interval that generated the beta. This suggests that if *Value Line* betas are used, the return on a 1-week Treasury security should be used to estimate the annualized risk-free rate. For this example, a 10-day maturity was used in the absence of a 7-day bill. See Carleton 1978.

[25] See Ibbotson Associates 1993, 128.

changes. But what is the underlying factor that determines the price, given the cash flows the investor expects to receive? All else being equal, it is the investment's risk.

SOURCES OF RISK

What are some sources of potential variability? The main ones are the possibility of default, illiquidity, changes in interest rates, and market factors.

DEFAULT. One possibility is that a borrower will **default** on a financial obligation by failing to pay interest, principal, or both. Some financial instruments are considered to be virtually free of the risk of default, although others, such as unsecured personal loans, are subject to considerable default risk. Because Treasury securities are backed by the taxing and money-creation power of the federal government, they are free of default risk, and it is in this sense that they are considered risk-free investments.

ILLIQUIDITY. The existence of secondary markets for investments and the size of those markets also affect an investor's assessment of risk. An investor wishing to sell a financial asset quickly obviously needs a market in which to sell it. The larger the market, the greater the seller's opportunity to obtain cash easily without substantial loss of value—that is, the greater the **liquidity.**

CHANGES IN INTEREST RATES. Another source of potential variability is changes in market interest rates. If interest rates change, the reinvestment rate for cash received from an investment will change. Also, as explained in Chapter 8, the price at which an investment can be sold in the future is affected by changes in market rates. The **interest rate risk** faced by an investor depends on many features of a security, including the stated interest rate and the term to maturity.

MARKET FACTORS. A final risk is the sensitivity of an asset's returns to factors affecting the entire financial system. This risk, emphasized in CAPM, is **systematic** or **market risk.** Sources are political, legal, fiscal, and national and international economic conditions.

EFFECT OF RISK ON YIELDS

In general, investors, including financial institutions, are **risk averse.** Risk aversion means that investors will pay less for the opportunity of receiving cash flows with high potential variability than for cash flows of the same expected size but lower risk. Given two investments with equal expected cash inflows, if investors pay less for the opportunity to receive the riskier flows, the expected yield on the riskier investment is higher.

For example, Figure 5.8 presents details on zero-coupon bonds, maturing in 2005, issued by Cummins Engine and Disney. On August 31, 1992, the Cummins Engine bonds closed at 37 and the Disney bonds closed at 46⅞. Assuming a $1,000 par value for each bond, an investor would have paid $370 for the Cummins bond but $468.75 for the Disney bond; yet both had the same maturity date and the same expected cash inflow. The effective annual yields on the two investments, using Equation 5.7 and the procedure illustrated for zero-coupon bonds, are 6.00 percent for the Disney bond and 7.95 percent for the Cummins Engine bond.

Although the effective annual yield on the Cummins bond was higher than the effective annual yield on the Disney bond, investors did not consider the Cummins bond "better." In fact, they were willing to pay *less* for it than for a virtually identical bond from Disney. Because these effective yields are *expected* yields only, the lower price for the Cummins bond reflects the financial market's assessment that it was riskier than the Disney bond. Because the only cash flow expected from either bond is the par value in 2005, the lower price for the Cummins bond was due to greater probability of default on that bond or to lower marketability. Risk-averse participants in the bond markets enforced their belief that the Cummins bond was riskier by paying a lower price, increasing its expected annual yield.

Risk aversion does not mean that investors are unwilling to accept investments with potentially variable returns; it simply means they will pay less for them than for comparable ones with less potential variation. The principle of expecting a higher rate of return (paying a lower price) based on the riskiness of an investment is the **risk/expected return trade-off.**

Throughout the text, the concept of risk as variability, its sources, its measurement, and its management are illustrated as asset/liability management is explored. It is important to remember that although the mechanics of yield calculations are necessary tools for the financial manager, risk assessment is equally important.

SUMMARY

Financial instruments can be categorized by their initial maturity. Securities with an initial maturity of 1 year or less are money market instruments, and those with longer initial maturities are capital market securities.

Care must be taken in calculating yields on money market securities, because many are traded on a discount basis, and market conventions differ. All quoted yields must be converted to effective annual yields. The equations in this chapter demonstrate similarities in yield calculations for several short-term securities, including T-bills, repurchase agreements, reverse repos, commercial paper, bankers' acceptances, negotiable CDs, fed funds, and discounted loans.

To analyze investments with more than 1 year to maturity, cash flows must be estimated and the internal rate of return determined. The effective yield on coupon bonds, zero-coupon bonds, mortgage loans, and add-on consumer loans is calculated similarly. A tax adjustment may be necessary because of the special characteristics of some long-term instruments, such as municipal bonds. Caution must also be taken to recognize features of mortgage and add-on loans that make effective yields higher than stated rates.

The final category of instruments is equity securities. Preferred stock returns are estimated as perpetual annuities. Returns on common stock investments are more difficult to estimate. Two ways of estimating expected yields on common stock are the constant dividend growth model and the Capital Asset Pricing Model.

Equally important are factors affecting the level of risk, or potential variability, in returns. Sources of variability include the possibility of default, illiquidity, and exposure to interest rate and systematic (or market) risk. Investors, who are generally risk averse, will pay less for and require higher returns on more risky investments, a relationship known as the risk/expected return trade-off.

QUESTIONS

1. How do money market securities and capital market securities differ?

2. Your father's company is considering several investment alternatives: a $25,000, 13-week T-bill; $100,000, 90-day commercial paper; a $30,000, 60-day bankers' acceptance; and a $75,000, 180-day discounted commercial bank loan. Without doing any calculations, explain the steps you would follow to choose the investment with the highest rate of return.

3. Distinguish between discount securities and interest-bearing securities, and explain the differences in estimating rates of return on the two types of instruments.

4. What is the difference between an annualized holding-period yield and an *ex ante* yield?

5. Find a report of the most recent Treasury bill auction. What was the average yield on a discount basis? The average coupon-equivalent yield? Explain the difference in the two yield quotations. Which yield is a better *ex ante* estimate of return? Why?

6. How did the Salomon Brothers' illegal activity in the Treasury market in 1991 affect the competitive balance in the Treasury securities markets? What steps have been taken to prevent future price manipulations?

7. Explain the difference between traditional Treasury auctions and the single-price or Dutch-auction experiment begun in 1992. What are the potential benefits of the new system? Find a recent evaluation of the effectiveness of the Dutch-auction system.

8. What is a repurchase agreement (repo)? Compare and contrast repos and reverse repos.

9. If an investor holding commercial paper needs to sell it before its maturity date, what options are available? How has the commercial paper market changed in recent years?

10. What are bankers' acceptances? At what point does a bankers' acceptance become a money market instrument? Compare the riskiness of bankers' acceptances to that of other money market securities.

11. Explain the origin of negotiable certificates of deposit. Why has their popularity declined recently?

12. What is a Eurobond? Why are they increasingly popular? How do they compare to global and ECU bonds?

13. By reviewing recent periodicals, assess the current status of the municipal bond market. Has Congress or any court decision changed the taxation of municipal securities or altered the discretion of municipalities to issue them?

14. Compare and contrast the characteristics of coupon bonds and zero-coupon bonds, and explain how these differences affect yield calculations.

15. What are points on a mortgage loan? How do they affect borrower costs?

16. If you are offered an add-on loan, would you pay more or less interest than on a loan with the same stated rate but amortized like a mortgage loan? Explain.

17. Investment advisors for the Twenty-First Century Growth Fund are considering purchasing shares of Ameritech Co. If the constant growth model is used to estimate the stock's yield, what assumptions are made about future cash flows? For what types of firms might these assumptions be reasonable? In what situations would you discourage use of the constant growth model?

18. Suppose Twenty-First Century Growth uses CAPM to estimate the yield on Ameritech. What is the interpretation of the beta coefficient? What are its limitations?

19. Evaluate the relative benefits and disadvantages of the constant growth model and the CAPM.

20. The riskiness of an investment affects investors' required yield and the purchase price. Explain the sources of potential variability affecting required rates of return. All else equal, as riskiness increases, in what direction do prices change? Required yields? Why?

PROBLEMS

1. Use the Treasury bill auction data given in Figure 5.2 to identify the following:
   a. The total dollar amount of 13-week Treasury bills sold at the auction;
   b. The total dollar amount of 13-week T-bills sold at the low price;
   c. The price noncompetitive bidders paid per $10,000, 26-week T-bill;
   d. The bond-equivalent yield on 13-week T-bills.

2. State College's Credit Union bid noncompetitively for a $10,000, 91-day T-bill. The high price at the auction was 98.932, the low price was 98.545, and the average price was 98.625.
   a. Calculate the bond-equivalent yield and the effective annual yield that the credit union will earn if the bill is held to maturity.
   b. What holding-period yield will the credit union earn if the bill is sold after five weeks at a price of 99.125?

3. A 13-week T-bill yields a bank discount rate of 7.85 percent. What price must a commercial bank pay to purchase this T-bill from a dealer? What is the bond-equivalent yield on the bill? What is the effective annual yield?

4. What is the effective annual yield on a 52-week Treasury bill selling at 93.275? The bank discount yield?

5. Using newspaper advertisements or other sources, gather information about rates currently being paid by local financial institutions on various certificates of deposit. Based on the frequency of compounding, convert the stated rates to effective annual yields.

6. On August 31, 1992, a small thrift purchased a Treasury bill maturing on November 12, 1992. Using Figure 5.3, calculate the effective annual yield that the thrift earned by holding the bill to maturity.

7. The discount yield on a 10-day, $100,000 reverse repurchase agreement is quoted in the market as 5.95 percent. Use Equation 5.4 to calculate the expected annual yield to an institution that engages in this transaction. Calculate the purchase price using Equation 5.5, and then verify your first answer using Equation 5.1. What is the effective annual yield to the institution?

8. Snow City Bank offered Carla Houx a $20,000 discounted loan to expand her restaurant's seating capacity. The loan has a 1-year maturity with a stated annual rate of 8.9 percent. What is the effective annual yield to the bank?

9. The comptroller of Software Sophisticates Company plans to invest $4 million in a negotiable certificate of deposit for 180 days. Gotham National Bank offers a rate of 6.20 percent. What is the effective annual yield on the CD?

10. The Midwest Construction Credit Union offers short-term vacation loans to its members at an annual rate of 8.55 percent. Equal monthly payments of interest and principal are required. If you take out a 6-month, $6,000 loan, what will your monthly payments be?

11. Find the results of the most recent Treasury auction in *The Wall Street Journal* or other newspaper; find the most recent "Money Rates" column as well. Using that information, calculate the effective annual yields on 91-day T-bills, 3-month CDs, 90-day commercial paper, and 90-day bankers' acceptances. What factors explain the yield differences you find?

12. Financial Security Corporation purchased a general obligation bond issued by the State of Arkansas at 97 percent of par. The $1,000 par bond carries a coupon rate of 6.85 percent and matures in 15 years. Interest is paid semiannually. The marginal tax rate for Financial Security is 35 percent. Calculate the tax-equivalent yield to maturity for the bond. If Financial Security sells the bond for $881.64 at the end of 5 years, what is the tax-equivalent, holding-period yield?

13. A local bank offers a 1-year CD at a stated interest rate of 9.5 percent. A federal savings bank and your credit union offer identical 1-year rates. However, the bank compounds interest semiannually, the savings bank quarterly, and the credit union daily. Calculate the effective annual yield available from each institution.

14. On January 1, 1995, Beta Corporation's zero-coupon bonds, which mature on December 31, 2012, are selling for $34\frac{3}{8}$. What is the effective annual yield to an investor who buys the bond on that date and holds the bond until maturity?

15. Home State offers certificates of deposit for an initial investment of $425. The $1,000 CDs mature in 12 years. What is their effective annual yield?

16. Federal Savings and Loan Association offers you a $150,000, 30-year mortgage with a 9.7 percent fixed interest rate. The S&L charges $3\frac{1}{2}$ points on the loan. If you accept this loan, what will your monthly loan payments be? Prepare an amortization schedule for the first 5 years. What is your principal balance after 60 payments?

17. The Cagles just signed the papers for a $16,000 car loan. They will make 60 equal monthly payments at a 10.2 percent add-on rate. What will their monthly payments be? What effective annual yield will the bank earn on this loan?

18. Sherman Mortgage Company analysts are evaluating a secondary mortgage market investment. The mortgage has a 25-year term to maturity, carries a 10 percent interest rate on the $100,000 principal, and is expected to be prepaid in 12 years. (In other words, the investment is realistically expected to have a 12-year life, with a substantial cash inflow at that time.) The monthly payment on the mortgage is $908.70.
   a.   If the mortgage is prepaid at the end of 12 years, what cash inflow will Sherman receive?
   b.   If the company currently requires 10.25 percent on this investment, what is the maximum amount that should be paid for the mortgage? (Hint: Consider the present value of future cash flows.)

19. Hatton Investment Company analysts advise the purchase of a 5-year annuity. The initial investment is $8,000; the annuity will provide cash flows of $950 semiannually. The first payment will be received 6 months after the initial investment. What annual rate of return would you earn if you followed the analysts' advice?

20. The Lowry Corporation's Series A preferred stock is trading at $67. The stock carries an 8 percent dividend on a par value of $100. What is the effective annual yield on the stock?

21. The manager of a major pension fund might invest in the common stock of American Laser Disk, Inc. The stock's current market price is $31.75. The annual dividend on the stock 9 years ago was $0.25, and it has grown at a constant rate to the present dividend of $1.00. This growth rate is expected to continue. If the pension fund manager has no future plans for selling the stock once it is purchased, what is the effective annual yield on a share of American Laser Disk's common stock? (Hint: Use Equation 5A.1 to find the growth rate.)

22. A large life insurance company is planning to invest in Classic Car Corporation's common stock, which is currently trading at $33 per share. Common stock dividends 5 years ago were $1.20 per share; last year, the corporation paid an annual dividend of $2.35.
   a.   After 7 years, the insurance company expects to sell the stock at an estimated price of $44. What is the effective annual yield on this investment?
   b.   What is the estimated annual yield if the company owns the stock for an indefinite period of time?
   c.   What is the effective annual yield if the stock is sold for $28 in 7 years?

23. The manager of a major pension fund purchased a $1,000 par corporate bond at 98.25 percent of par. The bond carries a coupon rate of 10.50 percent and matures in 20 years. Interest is paid semiannually.

    a.   Calculate the yield to maturity for the bond.

    b.   If the pension fund manager sells the bond at the end of 7 years for $940, what is the holding-period yield on the investment?

24. The Omega Savings and Loan is currently offering 25-year fixed-rate mortgages at 11.5 percent.

    a.   If you borrow $225,000 to purchase the home of your dreams, the S&L will charge you 2½ points on the loan. Calculate the monthly payment required to amortize the loan and the amortization schedule for the first 3 years.

    b.   Suppose that the institution will charge only 2 points if the interest rate increases to 13.75 percent. What is the effective annual yield and the new 3-year amortization schedule?

    c.   If the stated interest rate is only 12.25 percent, how many points would Omega have to charge to earn the same effective yield as on the 13.75 percent mortgage? Would it be reasonable for the lender to charge this many points to compensate for the lower interest rate? (Hint: Find the monthly payments at the 12.25 percent rate, then work from there.)

25. Elixir Corporation's beta is 1.3, the expected return on the market is 13 percent, and the risk-free rate is 7.5 percent.

    a.   What is the expected return on Elixir's common stock?

    b.   Suppose that an analyst estimates Elixir's expected return at 12 percent. If the analyst is using the previous r_m and r_f estimates, what is the analyst's estimate of the firm's beta?

26. Find the most recent estimate of Texas Instruments Corporation's beta coefficient from *Value Line* or another investment publication. Using current information on Treasury security rates and an estimate of the market risk premium, calculate the expected annual return on Texas Instruments' stock using the Capital Asset Pricing Model. Do the same for the stock of Wal-Mart. What factors account for the difference in expected returns for the two firms?

SELECTED REFERENCES

Balazsy, James J. "The Government Securities Market and Proposed Regulation," *Economic Commentary* (Federal Reserve Bank of Cleveland), April 1, 1986.

Blume, Marshall. "Betas and Their Regression Tendencies." *Journal of Finance* 30 (June 1975): 785–796.

Carleton, Willard T. "A Highly Personal Comment on the Use of the CAPM in Public Utility Rate Cases." *Financial Management* 7 (Autumn 1978): 57–59.

Chari, V. V., and Robert J. Weber, "How the Treasury Should Auction Its Debt." *Quarterly Review* (Federal Reserve Bank of Minneapolis) 16 (Fall 1992): 3–12.

Cook, Timothy Q., and Timothy D. Rowe, eds. *Instruments of the Money Market*. 6th ed. Richmond, VA: Federal Reserve Bank of Richmond, 1986.

Fama, Eugene F., and Kenneth R. French. "The Cross-Section of Expected Stock Returns." *The Journal of Finance* 47 (June 1992): 427–465.

Fama, Eugene F., and James D. McBeth. "Risk, Return, and Equilibrium: Empirical Tests." *Journal of Political Economy* 81 (May 1973): 607–636.

Fortune, Peter. "The Municipal Bond Market, Part I: Politics, Taxes, and Yields." *New England Economic Review* (Federal Reserve Bank of Boston) (September/October 1991): 13–36.

———. "The Municipal Bond Market, Part II: Problems and Policies." *New England Economic Review* (Federal Reserve Bank of Boston) (May/June 1992): 45–64.

Harrington, Diana R. *Modern Portfolio Theory and the Capital Asset Pricing Model: A User's Guide.* Englewood Cliffs, NJ: Prentice-Hall, 1983.

Hervey, Jack L. "Bankers' Acceptances Revisited." *Economic Perspectives* (Federal Reserve Bank of Chicago) 7 (May/June 1983): 21–31.

Ibbotson Associates. *Stocks, Bonds, Bills, and Inflation: 1993 Yearbook.* Chicago: Ibbotson Associates, 1993.

Jensen, Frederick H., and Patrick M. Parkinson. "Recent Developments in the Bankers' Acceptance Market." *Federal Reserve Bulletin* 72 (January 1986): 1–12.

Kidwell, David S., M. Wayne Marr, and G. Rodney Thompson. "Eurodollar Bonds: Alternative Financing for U.S. Companies." *Financial Management* 14 (Winter 1985): 18–27.

LaRoche, Robert K. "Bankers Acceptances." *Economic Quarterly* (Federal Reserve Bank of Richmond) 79 (Winter 1993): 75–85.

Lintner, John. "The Valuation of Risk Assets and the Selection of Risky Investments in Stock Portfolios and Capital Budgets." *Review of Economics and Statistics* 47 (February 1965): 13–37.

McCauley, Robert N., and Lauren A. Hargraves. "Eurocommercial Paper and U.S. Commercial Paper: Converging Money Markets?" *Quarterly Review* (Federal Reserve Bank of New York) 12 (Autumn 1987): 24–35.

Plaut, Steven. "The Eurobond Market—Its Use and Misuse." *Weekly Letter* (Federal Reserve Bank of San Francisco), June 10, 1988.

Post, Mitchell A. "The Evolution of the U.S. Commercial Paper Market Since 1980." *Federal Reserve Bulletin* 78 (December 1992): 879–891.

Reinhart, Vincent. "An Analysis of Potential Treasury Auction Techniques." *Federal Reserve Bulletin* 78 (June 1992): 403–413.

Roll, Richard. "A Critique of the Asset Pricing Theory's Empirical Tests, Part I: On Past and Potential Testability of the Theory." *Journal of Financial Economics* 4 (March 1977): 129–176,

Rosengren, Eric S. "Is There a Need for Regulation in the Government Securities Market?" *New England Economic Review* (Federal Reserve Bank of Boston) (September/October 1986): 29–40.

Ross, Stephen. "The Arbitrage Theory of Capital Asset Pricing." *Journal of Economic Theory* 13 (December 1976): 341–360.

Segall, Patricia. "Commercial Paper: New Tunes on an Old Instrument." *Journal of Commercial Bank Lending* 69 (April 1987): 16–23.

Sharpe, William F. "Capital Asset Prices: A Theory of Market Equilibrium Under Conditions of Uncertainty." *Journal of Finance* 19 (September 1964): 425–442.

Stevens, E. J. "Seeking Safety." *Economic Commentary* (Federal Reserve Bank of Cleveland), April 15, 1987.

Stigum, Marcia. *Money Market Calculations: Yields, Breakevens, and Arbitrage.* Homewood, IL: Dow Jones-Irwin, 1981.

———. *The Money Market.* Homewood, IL: Dow Jones-Irwin, 1990.

Syron, Richard, and Sheila L. Tschinkel. "The Government Securities Market: Playing Field for Repos." *Economic Review* (Federal Reserve Bank of Atlanta) 70 (September 1985): 10–19.

Trainer, Richard D. C. *The Arithmetic of Interest Rates.* New York: Federal Reserve Bank of New York, 1982.

Tschinkel, Sheila L. "Overview." *Economic Review* (Federal Reserve Bank of Atlanta) 70 (September 1985): 5–9.

Wallace, Anise. "Is Beta Dead?" *Institutional Investor* 14 (July 1980): 22–30.

APPENDIX 5A
THE MATHEMATICS OF COMPOUND AND PRESENT VALUE

The mathematics of compound and present value underlying effective annual yields are formal expressions of the intuitive notion that if cash is invested today and not used for consumption purposes, it should accumulate to a higher sum over time. Otherwise, postponing consumption would not be worth it, and no one would invest. The accumulation occurs through periodic interest paid on the initial investment.

COMPOUND (FUTURE) VALUE

If an initial amount is invested for several periods and if subsequent interest is earned on past interest as well as on the initial amount, **compound interest,** or interest on interest, is involved. The longer the investment horizon and the higher the rate of interest each period, the higher the accumulated sum. A less intuitive but conceptually identical expression of this idea is as follows: Given an expected rate of interest, the present value of a future cash flow is lower than the future cash flow. An even more formal mathematical expression of the same idea is the basic compound interest equation:

$$C_N = C_0 (1 + k)^N \qquad [5A.1]$$

where C_0 = initial sum invested;
C_N = future sum accumulated;
k = annual rate of interest;
N = number of years during which cash is invested.

Equation 5A.1 permits an investor to calculate the future cash benefit expected from an initial investment, given any levels of k and N. For selected levels of these two variables, tables containing values of $(1 + k)^N$ and several other time-value-of-money formulas are provided at the end of the book. Equation 5A.1 assumes that interest earned during a year is paid at the end of each year. For investments in which part of the annual interest is earned before the end of each year—for example, semiannually or quarterly—the basic compound interest equation is modified to include **intrayear compounding:**

$$C_N = C_0 (1 + k/m)^{Nm} \qquad [5A.2]$$

where m = number of compounding periods per year.

Effective annual yields in Chapter 5 consider intrayear compounding.

PRESENT VALUE

Often a different sort of problem occurs: An investor has the opportunity to receive future cash benefits whose size and timing can be estimated and must decide how much to pay for the opportunity. Here, present value is important. The present value of a future sum is the amount that must be invested initially, given an expected interest rate, to accumulate to the future sum. The expression for the present value of a future sum is the algebraic equivalent of Equation 5A.1. The higher the expected interest rate and the further in the future the cash benefit is expected, the lower its present value.

$$C_0 = \frac{C_N}{(1 + k)^N} \qquad [5A.3]$$

If total annual interest will be divided into m payments during the year, the present value of a future cash flow is

$$C_0 = \frac{C_{Nm}}{(1 + k/m)^{Nm}} \qquad [5A.4]$$

PRESENT VALUES CAN BE ADDED

Present values are additive; that is, if several future cash flows are expected, their total present value is the sum of the present values of the individual future sums:

$$C_0 = \frac{C_1}{(1 + k)^1} + \frac{C_2}{(1 + k)^2} + \cdots + \frac{C_N}{(1 + k)^N}$$

which is simplified to

$$C_0 = \sum_{t = 1}^{N} \frac{C_t}{(1 + k)^t} \qquad [5A.5]$$

where

t = sub- or superscript denoting the specific period at the end of which a sum is expected.

For intrayear compounding, Equation 5A.5 is modified:

$$C_0 = \sum_{t = 1}^{Nm} \frac{C_t}{(1 + k/m)^t} \qquad [5A.6]$$

STREAMLINING THE CALCULATIONS: IDENTIFYING SPECIAL CASH FLOW PATTERNS

Equations 5A.5 or 5A.6 permit one to calculate the present value of a series of future benefits no matter how many individual sums are involved, no matter what their size, and no matter when they are expected.

Many investment opportunities, however, return benefits in distinct patterns. Recognizing those patterns simplifies the calculation of present value.[1]

THE ANNUITY

Among the most common special cash flow patterns is the **annuity,** a series of equal future cash flows occurring at the end of each of a finite number of periods. When an investment offers cash benefits in annuity form, its present value is

[5A.7]

$$C_0 = C_1 \left[\frac{1 - (1 + k)^{-N}}{k} \right]$$

$$= C_1 \left[\frac{1 - \dfrac{1}{(1 + k)^N}}{k} \right]$$

PERPETUAL ANNUITIES

If the equal cash inflows are expected to occur indefinitely, the cash flow stream is a **perpetual annuity,** or **perpetuity.** For a perpetuity, N approaches infinity, and $[1/(1 + k^N]$ approaches 0. Thus, the present value of a perpetuity is equal to

[5A.8]

$$C_0 = \frac{C_1}{k}$$

If the cash flows are not equal but occur at equal time intervals and are expected to *grow* at a constant rate (g) indefinitely, the cash flow stream is a **growing perpetuity.** The present value of a growing perpetuity is

[5A.9]

$$C_0 = \frac{C_1}{k - g}$$

---

[1] The derivations of formulas in this appendix are presented in many sources. Interested readers may examine a source such as Eugene F. Brigham and Louis C. Gapenski, *Intermediate Financial Management,* 4th ed. (Chicago: Dryden Press, 1993), Chapter 3 and Appendix A.

FINDING AN UNKNOWN INTEREST RATE

The problems considered so far assume that someone already knows the relevant interest rate and seeks a future or present value. Many investors, however, ask a different kind of question. They know the initial cash investment required and the benefits expected but do not know the annual interest rate implied by the cash flows. The problem is to estimate an expected annual rate of return. Fortunately, previous formulas can be used; the proper equation must be solved for k.

DIRECT SOLUTION FOR k

For an investment with a single cash outflow and a single cash benefit at the end of N periods, the implicit annual rate of return is found by solving Equation 5A.3 for k:

$$C_0 = \frac{C_N}{(1 + k)^N}$$

$$(1 + k)^N = C_N/C_0$$

$$k = \sqrt[N]{C_N/C_0} - 1$$

For example, suppose that by investing $675 today, an investor expects to receive $1,000 at the end of 5 years. The expected annual rate of return is

$$(1 + k)^5 = C_5/C_0$$

$$(1 + k)^5 = \$1,000/\$675 = 1.48148$$

$$k = \sqrt[5]{1.48148} - 1$$

$$= 0.08178$$

$$= 8.178\%$$

Investments with perpetual cash benefit streams also lend themselves to a direct solution for k, using either Equations 5A.8 or 5A.9. The implied annual interest rate on an investment in a perpetuity is

[5A.10]

$$k = \frac{C_1}{C_0}$$

For a growing perpetuity, the implicit interest rate is

$$k = \frac{C_1}{C_0} + g \qquad [5A.11]$$

TRIAL-AND-ERROR SOLUTION FOR *k*

Unfortunately, if neither a single cash inflow nor a perpetual series of benefits is involved, finding the implied rate of return is a trial-and-error process. The analyst must try different values for *k* in Equations 5A.5, 5A.6, or 5A.7, depending on whether an annuity and/or intrayear interest payments are expected. The goal is to find an interest rate that equates the present value of the cash benefits to the cash outflow required.

To exemplify the trial-and-error process, suppose that an investment of $500 today is expected to produce benefits of $200 per year at the end of each of 4 years:

$$C_0 = C_1 \left[\frac{1 - \frac{1}{(1+k)^N}}{k} \right]$$

$$\$500 = \$200 \left[\frac{1 - \frac{1}{(1+k)^4}}{k} \right]$$

Trying 20 percent (0.20) in Equation 5A.7 produces an inequality; the present value of the four $200 payments is $517.75. Because their present value is too high at a discount rate of 20 percent, a higher value for *k* should be tried; the mathematics of present value make it clear that a present value will be lower at a higher discount rate. At 21 percent, the present value of the four $200 payments is $508.09, still too high; and at 22 percent, it is $498.73. Thus, a precise value for *k* is between 21 percent and 22 percent. Further refinement results in a *k* of 21.86 percent.

CALCULATOR SOLUTIONS FOR *k*

Fortunately, financial analyst calculators and microcomputers provide virtually instantaneous solutions to rate-of-return problems. The illustrations that follow are based on the Sharp Business/Financial Calculator. Similar procedures are used for calculators manufactured by other firms.

To find the implied rate of return on a $200, 4-year annuity requiring an initial $500 investment, the following steps can be taken:

1. Press the 2ndF and Mode keys until FIN appears in the display.

2. Enter 500, then press the +/− and PV keys. (Entering the initial investment, or present value, as a negative number is a requirement on the Sharp but not on all calculators.)

3. Enter 4 and press the *n* key, then enter $200 and press the PMT key.

4. Press the COMP and *i* keys. After about 2 seconds, the number 21.86227 will appear in the display, indicating an annual rate of return over the 4-year period of slightly over 21.86 percent. Although the mathematics of compound and present value require that interest rates be expressed as decimals, financial calculators usually work with interest rates in nondecimal form to facilitate entry or interpretation by the user.

A similar procedure is used to find the implied rate of return if the investment problem involves a single cash outflow followed by only a single cash inflow at a later time. A direct algebraic solution to such a problem was illustrated on page 153 using Equation 5A.3. The same problem on a Sharp calculator could be solved as follows:

1. Enter 675, then press the +/− and PV keys.

2. Enter 5 and press the *n* key, then enter $1,000 and press the FV key. If you have just completed an annuity problem, enter 0 and press PMT to clear the payment register.

3. Press the COMP and *i* keys. Shortly, the number 8.178074 will appear in the display.

It is not difficult to understand why financial calculators and computers are considered essential tools for financial analysts and managers everywhere. These tools are not substitutes for understanding the mathematical and financial concepts addressed in Chapter 5, but they provide assistance in applying those concepts easily, quickly, and productively.

PART TWO

INTEREST RATE THEORIES AND INTEREST RATE RISK

- INTEREST RATES, EXCHANGE RATES, AND INFLATION: THEORIES AND FORECASTING

- THE TERM STRUCTURE OF INTEREST RATES

- INTEREST RATE RISK

- INTEREST RATE RISK MANAGEMENT: DURATION

- INTEREST RATE RISK MANAGEMENT: INTEREST RATE AND FOREIGN CURRENCY FUTURES

- INTEREST RATE RISK MANAGEMENT: INDEX FUTURES AND OPTIONS

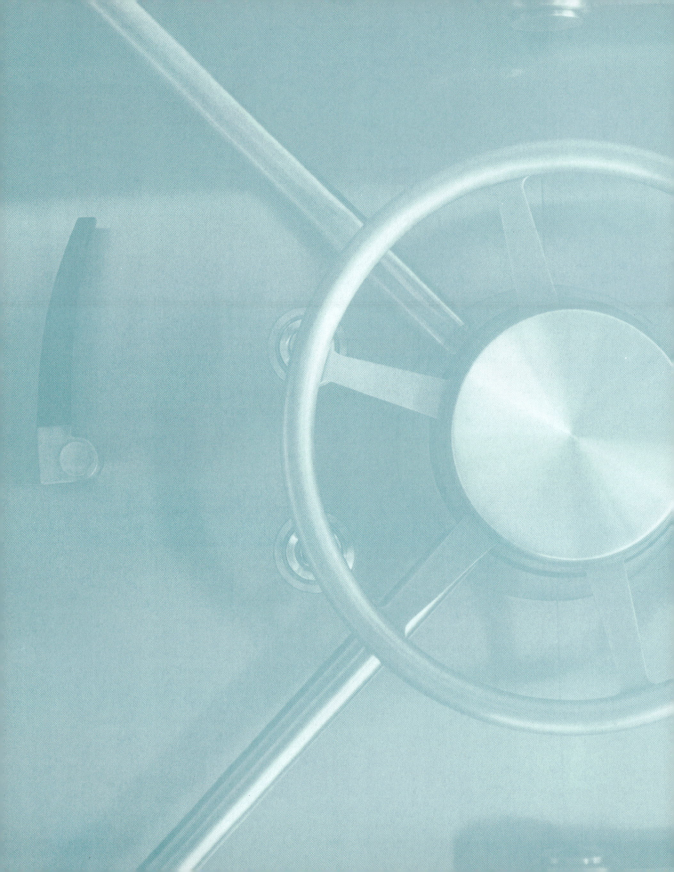

The lesson is, if you believe economists can predict the future, then you also believe in the Tooth Fairy and Santa Claus.

Amitai Etzioni
Professor, George Washington University (1989)

Forecasting interest rates and other economic measures has long been regarded as an inexact science. In mid-1992, *The Economist* introduced an analysis of the performance of economic forecasters in the early 1990s with a favorite joke. The story goes that Albert Einstein, while waiting to enter the gates of heaven, begins a conversation with three others waiting with him. He asks their IQs. The first answers 190, to which Einstein responds with enthusiasm about wanting to discuss his theory of relativity. The second answers 150, and Einstein suggests they will be able to talk about the prospects for world peace. The third mumbles 50; after a pause, Einstein asks, "So what's your forecast for economic growth for next year?"[1]

Interestingly, the analysis that followed this unflattering view of economic forecasters was not particularly negative. In fact, it noted that despite the complexities introduced by financial deregulation, technology, and globalization, the accuracy of economic forecasts did not decline substantially in the late 1980s and early 1990s from levels in earlier decades. The discussion concluded with the recognition that economic forecasting will never achieve 100 percent accuracy, and that attempting to predict the future of the economy and interest rates will continue to be a challenge.

Preceding chapters have introduced unique characteristics of financial institutions, including the predominance of financial assets and liabilities and the resulting emphasis on the net interest margin (NIM). Thus, the interest rate environment is one of the most important influences on asset/liability decisions and institutional performance. Key determinants of success are managers' abilities to understand movements in interest rates and inflation and to interpret forecasts. And, although all financial institution managers must respond to interest rate changes, growing globalization of financial markets creates additional requirements for some; they must make asset/liability decisions in reaction to changes in the value of the dollar compared with other currencies. Fortunately, managers have access to a growing array of risk management tools; but they must first understand the theories underlying interest rate and exchange rate movements.

CHAPTER

6

INTEREST RATES, EXCHANGE RATES, AND INFLATION: THEORIES AND FORECASTING

---

[1] "The Future Is Not What It Used To Be," *The Economist,* June 13, 1992, 75.

WHY THEORIES ARE IMPORTANT TO MANAGERS

Managers are rarely theoreticians; instead, they spend their time analyzing and making decisions critical to the future of their institutions. These decisions rely on often conflicting opinions about the direction of the economy and interest rates, nationally and internationally. To make better decisions, managers must be able to evaluate available data and forecasts. Those evaluations, in turn, require knowledge of the principles on which forecasts are based.

For example, the manager of the investment portfolio of a life insurance company can invest in variable-coupon bonds, zero-coupon bonds, or traditional fixed-rate instruments, among many other choices. The manager's expectations about interest rate movements will certainly influence the decision. In a period of declining rates, a variable-coupon instrument will be unattractive, but a zero-coupon bond will lock in a higher rate if intermediate cash flows are not important. A bond denominated in British pounds will be undesirable if the value of the pound is expected to fall. Similarly, raising funds also must be guided by forecasts.

Often economists are unable to agree about the future direction of economic variables, and managers must exercise judgment in evaluating available forecasts. This chapter and the next examine the economic, political, and behavioral factors that influence interest rates and exchange rates. These theories provide the foundation on which economic forecasters base their expectations about interest and exchange rate changes, which also affect managerial evaluation and decision making.

A HISTORICAL LOOK AT INTEREST RATES

Although interest rates are always changing, they have been particularly volatile over the past 15 years, reaching historically high levels in 1980 and 1981. Ten years later, short-term Treasury securities were at their lowest yields since the early 1960s, and interest rates on some savings accounts at banks and thrifts hovered at Great Depression levels. Figure 6.1A traces yields on long-term bonds in several different default risk classes over the period 1925–1989. Although an up-

ward trend began in the late 1960s, rates rose rapidly in late 1979 and peaked about 2 years later, fueled by expectations of high inflation and government deficits. As discussed in Chapter 3, the Federal Reserve System's (Fed's) famous October 1979 change away from targeting interest rates as a part of monetary policy also led to greater rate volatility during the early 1980s. Even though yields declined in 1982, as inflation subsided, the volatility continued through the end of the decade. Figure 6.1B illustrates the course of rates in several long-term financial markets from 1990 to mid-1992. The downward trend depicted at the end of Figure 6.1A continued, although the path was clearly not smooth and predictable from month to month. Short-term rates, not shown in either Figure 6.1A or B, plunged even more dramatically in the early 1990s. Financial institutions find this environment a continuing challenge to their managers' skills.[2]

Some institutions have maintained good performance records, but many firms have faltered or failed. For example, at the end of 1987, First Bank System, Inc., at that time the nation's sixteenth largest bank holding company (BHC), announced a loss on its investment portfolio of more than $700 million. The reason? According to *The Wall Street Journal,* management's mistake was "betting heavily the wrong way on interest rates." Fortunately, the outlook is almost always brighter for institutions that successfully navigate choppy interest rate waters. In 1992, for example, Boatmen's Bankshares Inc. of St. Louis enjoyed hefty profits because, according to Chairman Andrew Craig, "We structured the balance sheet in anticipation of a downturn in rates."[3]

THE GENERAL LEVEL OF INTEREST RATES

Theories of interest rate determination follow several conventions. First, models usually focus on determination of the *equilibrium* level of interest. Equilibrium

---

[2] See Becketti and Sellon 1990 and Fortune 1989. (References are listed in full at the end of this chapter.)

[3] Jeff Bailey, "First Bank System Says Bond Portfolio Fell $700 Million as Interest Rates Rose," *The Wall Street Journal,* October 14, 1987, 17; Fred R. Bleakley, "Banks, Thrifts Scored as Interest Rates Fell, But Difficulties Loom," *The Wall Street Journal,* February 2, 1992, A1, A6.

FIGURE 6.1 **Long-Term Bond Yields (Periodic Averages)**

Over time, interest rates are variable. Although there are many different financial markets, interest rates in all markets tend to move in the same general direction at the same time.

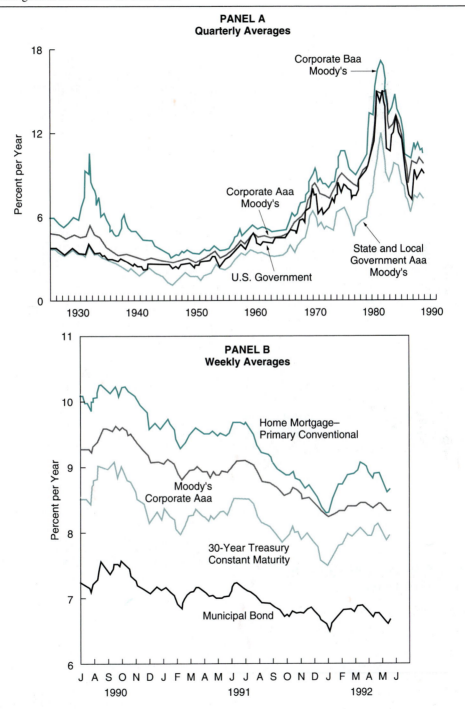

Source: Board of Governors of the Federal Reserve System, *1989 Historical Chart Book,* 97; Federal Reserve Bank of Cleveland, *Economic Trends.*

is a state of rest or the absence of forces for change. Actually, the financial markets are seldom, if ever, in equilibrium but are in the process of approaching equilibrium as they respond to the numerous factors that cause an imbalance between supply and demand.

Second, economic models rely on several assumptions required to simplify the real world. The objective is to develop a useful explanation without omitting factors crucial to achieving the purpose of the model.

Finally, theories explaining the general level of interest rates do just that: They focus on *the* rate of interest. Obviously, there are many interest rates, as Figure 6.1 illustrates, and many other interest rates are not shown there. Chapter 5 points out that differences in yields reflect term to maturity, default risk, taxability, and other characteristics of the underlying security. Still, compared over time, yields on securities tend to move in the same general direction. Although the correlation is not perfect, it is strong enough that economists are justified in focusing on *one* interest rate to build a model that explains movements in *all* rates.

LOANABLE FUNDS THEORY

Several compatible theories attempt to explain interest rate movements, although they are not equally useful for forecasting changes in rates. The **loanable funds theory** focuses on the amount of funds available for investment (the supply of loanable funds) and the amount of funds that borrowers want (the demand for loanable funds). It is particularly adaptable for use in forecasting and, therefore, is the one on which the discussion concentrates.

THE SUPPLY OF LOANABLE FUNDS

The loanable funds theory categorizes borrowers and lenders into four distinct types: households or consumers, businesses, governments, and the foreign sector. Governments supply almost no loanable funds, but it is important to understand the forces affecting the savings decisions of individuals, businesses, and foreign investors.

THE EXPECTED RATE OF RETURN AND THE DECISION TO SAVE. Economic units always have several choices for disposition of funds. They can *spend* money on consumable goods; they can *save* money by investing in financial assets; or they can choose to hold, or *hoard,* money. The motivation for consumption is self-evident. But once the amount of consumption has been determined, there is still a choice between investing and holding money.

A key motivation for saving is the expected rate of return. Because investors have a **time preference for consumption,** they will reduce current consumption to save money only if they receive some reward for doing so. That reward is the expected rate of interest, which must always be positive to induce substantial postponement of consumption. Economists have also identified several other motivations for savings, discussed shortly, which suggest that some funds will be saved even if the expected rate of interest is zero.

Holding or hoarding cash requires postponement of consumption but, unlike saving, does not provide a positive rate of return. So why does anyone hold cash balances? Three motivations have been identified: the **transactions demand,** the **precautionary demand,** and the **speculative demand.**[4] Because individuals and businesses cannot always assume that the timing of cash inflows and cash expenditures will coincide, they usually need to maintain ready access to cash to handle transactions. Also, some cash will be held as a precaution against unforeseen contingencies. Neither of these motivations is tied to the expected rate of interest.

The third demand for money—the speculative motivation—*is* sensitive to expected interest rates and is therefore especially important in understanding the supply of loanable funds. In the face of high expected rates on financial assets, funds suppliers will reduce cash balances as they invest; with low expected rates of return, they will hold cash in anticipation of better opportunities later. Thus, the expected rate of return is

---

[4]These motivations for holding cash were introduced by the renowned economist John Maynard Keynes in *The General Theory of Employment, Interest, and Money* (1936). Actually, Keynes used them in the liquidity preference theory, an explanation of interest rates that is separate but compatible with the loanable funds theory. The liquidity preference theory focuses on the supply and demand for money, whereas the loanable funds theory focuses on the supply and demand for credit. Once consumption is determined, a household's decisions to hold cash (demand money) or to lend (supply credit) are not independent of one another; deciding to do more of one means deciding to do less of the other. Thus, it is easy to see how theories on the determination of interest rates can be approached by looking at either money or loanable funds.

important in the decision to reduce speculative cash balances, increasing the supply of loanable funds.

OTHER FACTORS INFLUENCING HOUSEHOLDS. These relationships lead to a better but still incomplete understanding of the amount of funds available for borrowing. Factors other than interest rates affect the savings decision. For example, most people voluntarily save for future needs, either because they recognize that illness or other emergencies could jeopardize their financial position or because they will need funds to support themselves after retirement. Other people may be involved in involuntary savings programs, such as social security or required retirement programs for state and federal employees.

The income of a household is also significant. Low-income families often spend all available funds on the basic necessities of life, leaving nothing for alternative uses. At the opposite end of the spectrum, high-income families may be unable to consume all available funds even if they want to, so they must invest regardless of the expected interest rate.

OTHER FACTORS INFLUENCING BUSINESSES. Although businesses are usually demanders, they also supply some loanable funds. The primary sources of these funds are the depreciation tax shield and retained earnings from profitable past operations. Expected interest rates may have some bearing on the decisions of businesses to save by investing in financial assets, but other important factors are potential real asset investments, the nature of the business enterprise, and the philosophy of the firm's managers and owners.

THE MONEY SUPPLY. The supply of loanable funds is affected by changes in the total money supply (ΔM), which is influenced by Fed policy. An increase in the money supply makes more funds available for saving after consumption is satisfied.

THE FOREIGN SECTOR. Funds available domestically are also influenced by the behavior of foreign investors. The key factor influencing funds provided by the foreign sector is not simply the expected rate of interest in the United States, but the difference between that rate and the expected rate available in other countries. This relationship is explained in more detail later.

THE SUPPLY OF LOANABLE FUNDS ILLUSTRATED. The combined impact of these influences on the supply

of loanable funds is shown in Figure 6.2. The supply curve (S_{LF}) is positively related to the expected rate of interest; that is, the quantity supplied is larger as the interest rate increases, but only moderately so. Even at a zero rate of interest, the supply of loanable funds exceeds zero because of nonrate factors influencing the savings decision.

The household sector is the only *net* supplier of loanable funds; that is, in a given period, households save more than they demand in the credit markets. For that reason, the borrowings of the household sector are usually netted against savings, and the S_{LF} curve is net of loanable funds demanded by households. Using this approach, households' savings equals income minus consumption minus household borrowing.

THE DEMAND FOR LOANABLE FUNDS

The forces determining the demand for loanable funds—the total funds that households, businesses, government units, and the foreign sector want to borrow—is tied much more closely to expected interest rates than is the supply.

THE EFFECT OF EXPECTED INTEREST RATES ON BORROWING. Most business borrowing is sensitive to expected interest rates. The funds raised by nonfinancial firms will depend on their optimal budgets for investment in real assets. An optimal capital budget reflects a firm's investment opportunities. It occurs at the point where the marginal returns from investing in real assets are equal to the marginal costs of raising the funds, and the net present value of incremental investments is zero. At lower rates of interest, the capital budget will be larger, because a lower discount rate will be used for calculating net present value.[5] The investment opportunity schedule and the resulting

---

[5] The net present value (NPV) of a capital investment is defined as the discounted sum of future, after-tax cash flows minus the present value of the initial cash outlay:

$$NPV = \sum_{t=1}^{N} \frac{C_t}{(1+i)^t} - C_0$$

As i, the required rate of return, gets smaller, the NPV of a given project gets larger. Thus, at lower discount rates, more projects may be acceptable under this decision criterion. See the appendix to Chapter 5 for a more detailed discussion of discounted cash flows and Chapter 20 for more information on NPV.

FIGURE 6.2   **Supply of Loanable Funds**

The willingness of households, businesses, governments, and the foreign sector to supply loanable funds increases as the expected interest rate increases.

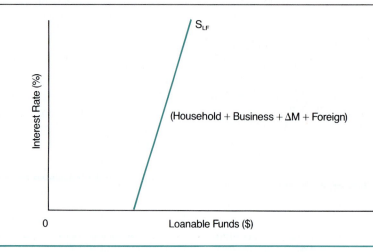

demand for loanable funds (D_{LF}) are inversely related to expected interest rates.

NONINTEREST FACTORS. As with the supply of loanable funds, noninterest factors motivate the demand for borrowing. For example, government units at the local, state, and federal levels often must borrow regardless of interest rates. Governments borrow whenever they face budget deficits or when they need to finance major construction of roads or government buildings.[6] In fact, government demand for credit is relatively inelastic with respect to interest rates.

DEMAND BY THE FOREIGN SECTOR. Foreign borrowers also seek funds in the domestic credit markets. Foreign business borrowers are motivated by the same factors affecting domestic firms, but differences between interest rates in the United States and those abroad will determine where borrowing actually occurs. Foreign governments also borrow in U.S. mar-

kets for the same reasons that U.S. governmental units borrow. Recently, in fact, the domestic demand for loanable funds by foreign governments has been substantial.[7]

THE DEMAND FOR LOANABLE FUNDS ILLUSTRATED. The demand schedule (D_{LF}) for loanable funds in Figure 6.3 is for total business, government, and foreign borrowing. As noted earlier, households do borrow, but their demand is usually netted against the funds they supply and is not included in the aggregate demand for loanable funds.

THE RATE OF INTEREST

The loanable funds theory follows classical supply/demand analysis and explains the equilibrium rate of interest as the point of intersection of the supply and demand schedules. In Figure 6.4, the $i*$ and $Q*$ represent the equilibrium rate of interest and the equilibrium quantity of loanable funds. Many analysts use the loanable funds framework to explain and anticipate the movement of interest rates.

---

[6] Many experts argue that the relationship between borrowing and interest rates is not the same for state and local governments as it is for the federal government, under the assumption that the former are more flexible in spending decisions and may postpone some projects to be financed by borrowing if interest rates are high. In addition, some state or municipal statutes actually prohibit government units from borrowing if expected interest rates exceed a certain critical level. For further discussion, see Polakoff 1981, 494.

[7] In recent years, the foreign sector as a whole has been a net supplier of funds to the U.S. credit market. In the past, however, it was a net borrower. See Board of Governors of the Federal Reserve System, *Flow of Funds Accounts,* Financial Assets and Liabilities, First Quarter 1992.

FIGURE 6.3   **Demand for Loanable Funds**

The willingness of businesses, governments, and the foreign sector to borrow funds decreases as the expected interest rate increases.

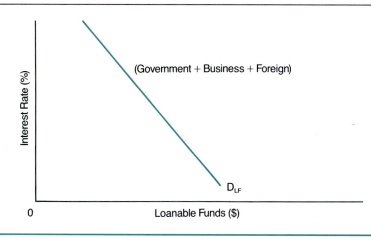

FIGURE 6.4   **Equilibrium Rate of Interest**

The equilibrium level of interest rates is the rate at which the quantity of loanable funds demanded equals the quantity of loanable funds supplied.

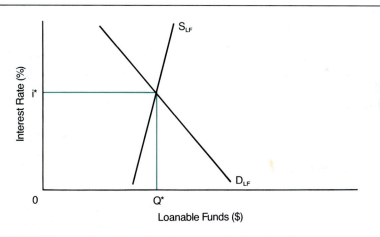

LOANABLE FUNDS THEORY AND INTEREST RATE FORECASTING

Because the loanable funds theory explains the rate of interest as the point of intersection between supply and demand curves, political, economic, or behavioral fac-

tors shifting either curve are expected to result in a change in interest rates.

CHANGES IN SUPPLY OR DEMAND

What forces could shift the supply or the demand curve? Government fiscal policy is one important force. The size of the federal budget deficit affects the demand for loanable funds. The more federal expenditures exceed federal revenues, the more frequently the government must enter the credit markets. Unless the change in government borrowing is offset by an equal and opposite change in demand for loanable funds by other sectors, the demand curve must shift, and the rate of interest will be higher. Furthermore, the supply curve may also be affected, as anticipated increases in government borrowing cause funds suppliers to increase their speculative balances in anticipation of higher interest rates.

Another fiscal policy, taxation, also has the potential for shifting the supply or demand curves. For example, an increase in corporate taxes reduces after-tax profits and thereby reduces the incentive for additional business spending. Smaller capital budgets lower the demand for borrowed funds.

Monetary policy, through its effect on the money supply, also affects interest rates. For example, an increase in the money supply relative to money demand leads to higher levels of savings, shifting the supply curve to the right. This subsequently leads to a lower interest rate, at least in the short run.[8] Research suggests another monetary policy effect: Volatility in money growth may lead to higher interest rates because it precipitates a reduction in the supply of loanable funds. High variability in monetary growth increases investors' uncertainty about future rates of return on financial assets. In response to that uncertainty, the suppliers of loanable funds will choose to hold more money, and the supply curve will shift to the left. Borrowers may also respond by reducing their demand for funds as they grow more uncertain about their borrowing costs.[9]

A shift in the demand curve could also result from a change in the state of the economy. As the economy moves into a recession, customer demand drops off, inventory surpluses accumulate, and expansion plans are postponed. Capital expenditures and the need for funds to support them decline.

FORECAST OF FUTURE INTEREST RATES ILLUSTRATED

Suppose a recession is anticipated. The forecaster expects the quantity of funds required by the business community to decline in anticipation of reduced consumer demand. At the same time, estimates of lower federal tax revenues, as unemployment rises, lead to a forecast of larger deficits. The government sector, therefore, will demand more loanable funds.

In practice, an interest rate forecast requires detailed identification of all potential changes and their magnitude. As shown in Figure 6.5, if the increase in governments' demand for funds (ΔD_G) is greater than the decrease in demand by the business sector (ΔD_B), then net demand will increase, the demand curve will shift to the right, and the new equilibrium interest rate (i') will be higher. If the decrease in business demand is greater than the increase in government demand ($\Delta D_B > \Delta D_G$), aggregate demand for loanable funds will decline, the demand curve will shift to the left, and the forecast will be for a new lower equilibrium rate of interest. The supply curve also may shift as a result of changing conditions. This, too, would affect anticipated movements in interest rates.

INFLATION AND THE LEVEL OF INTEREST RATES

The rate of inflation was of particular concern in the 1980s because of the volatility in and high levels of several different measures of price changes. By the early 1990s, a decline in annual inflation rates had some economists studying and writing about **disinflation,** or a reduction in the inflation rate to zero.[10] Because anticipated changes in the purchasing power of the dollar affect investors' yields, price-level changes have a role in theories of the general level of interest rates.

To illustrate, suppose a student's parents are saving for a graduation gift to be presented in 1 year. They

---

[8]This effect is somewhat controversial; some analysts argue that growth in the money supply will lead to higher inflation so that the long-term effect on interest rates is uncertain. The effects of inflation are examined in subsequent sections.

[9]Mascaro and Meltzer 1983.

[10]Croushore (1992) reviews the arguments for and against the Fed's trying to reduce inflation to 0 percent and provides a comprehensive bibliography. See also Lawrence B. Lindsey, "The Case for Disinflation," *Economic Commentary* (Federal Reserve Bank of Cleveland), March 15, 1992.

FIGURE 6.5   **Shifts in the Demand Curve and Changes in the Equilibrium Rate of Interest**

If the demand for loanable funds increases, the equilibrium level of interest rates will increase. If the demand for loanable funds decreases, the equilibrium level of interest rates will fall.

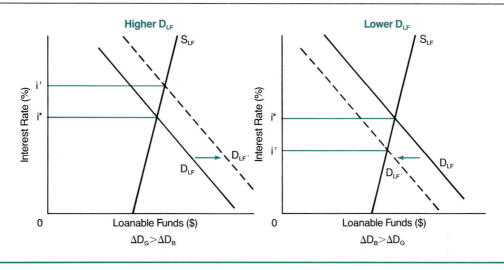

are considering a 1-year, $2,500 bank certificate of deposit in a federally insured institution, expected to yield 9 percent. The expected yield at the time of investment is the **nominal return.** If there is no inflation during the coming year, the *ex post* **real return** will also be 9 percent. But if the price level increases during the year, the *ex ante* yield of 9 percent will not be the *ex post* real return. Even if the depository institution pays the promised yield of 9 percent, the real rate of return will be lower because the purchasing power of the dollar has declined. The $2,500 principal repayment will not purchase the same quantity of goods as it would have a year earlier, and the $225 in interest received will not be enough to make up the difference while still providing an annual return of 9 percent.

INFLATION AND FINANCIAL INNOVATION

If inflation were uncommon, participants in the financial markets would pay relatively little attention to it in forecasting future events. Charts of historic movements in the Consumer Price Index (CPI) and the Producer Price Index (PPI) in Figure 6.6 demonstrate, however, that neither borrowers nor lenders can afford to ignore price levels and their potential impact on returns and costs.[11] Many observers have noted, in fact, that the demand for new financial products in recent years can be attributed at least partially to expectations of inflation. Examples are adjustable-rate bonds and mortgages, zero-coupon bonds, deposit accounts that pay variable rates of interest, universal life insurance policies, interest rate swaps, and inflation futures contracts. An entirely new type of financial institution, the money market mutual fund (MMMF), was created to allow investors to obtain yields that vary with daily changes in market conditions. Major deregulation of the financial system, through the Depository Institutions Deregulation and Monetary Control Act (DIDMCA), the Garn-St Germain Act, and changes in state laws, have permitted institutions to meet this inflation-driven demand.

---

[11] There is no general agreement on how to measure inflation. The most widely used measures are the CPI, the PPI, and the implicit Gross National Product (GNP) Price Deflator. The first two track changes in the price level of "market baskets" of goods; the third attempts to reflect price changes in all components of the GNP. A good discussion of the PPI and the GNP Price Deflator is in Wallace and Cullison 1979. For a description of the current components of the CPI, which has been undergoing revisions since 1981, see the monthly issues of "The CPI Detailed Report," U.S. Department of Labor, Bureau of Labor Statistics.

FIGURE 6.6 **Comprehensive Price Measures: CPI and PPI**

Inflation rates change over time. There are also many different ways of measuring inflation, such as the CPI, which focuses on the prices of goods most important to households, and the PPI, which tracks prices of goods especially important to businesses.

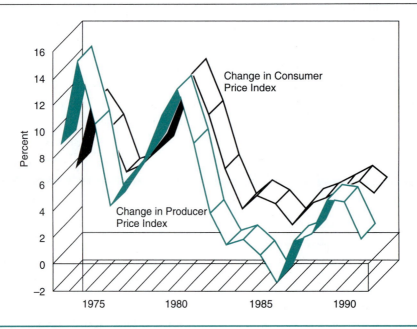

Source: Federal Reserve Bank of St. Louis, *Annual U.S. Economic Data.*

MORE ABOUT REAL AND NOMINAL RATES

It seems reasonable to assume that if inflation is anticipated during the coming year, lenders will build in some protection against the decline in purchasing power of their dollars by increasing their required *ex ante* rate of return. The size of the premium for expected inflation and the way that it is determined have been the subjects of much theoretical and empirical investigation. Before examining those efforts, however, the meaning of the terms *real* and *nominal* must be further clarified. The real rate of interest is the rate of exchange between present and future *goods*, whereas the rate of exchange between present and future *dollars* is the nominal rate of interest. In the absence of inflation, real and nominal rates are equal.[12]

For example, suppose the real rate of interest is 12 percent. The price of a music video is $10 and is not expected to change for at least 1 year. An owner of 100 tapes is considering including them in a transaction. She could sell them today for $1,000 and invest the money at 12 percent, accumulating $1,120 by the end of the year. However, she could lend the 100 tapes to someone today, on the condition that she will be repaid with 112 tapes at the end of the year. The yield on the exchange of both dollars and goods would be 12 percent; in other words, the nominal and the real rates of interest would be equal. The owner of the tapes will be equally well off in 1 year, regardless of which arrangement she makes:

$$\frac{\$1,120 - \$1,000}{\$1,000} = \text{12\% on exchange of dollars for dollars}$$

$$\frac{112 \text{ tapes} - 100 \text{ tapes}}{100 \text{ tapes}} = \text{12\% on exchange of goods for goods}$$

[12] This discussion draws on the work of Santoni and Stone March 1981.

The purchasing power of the two transactions is the same, because the dollar-for-dollar exchange permits the lender to purchase $1,120/$10 = 112 videotapes in 1 year, the same number that she would have if she simply exchanged tapes directly.

But suppose the price of videotapes is expected to rise by 2 percent during the year, to $10.20. If this price change is accurately foreseen before any exchanges occur, a 12 percent nominal interest rate will no longer be adequate to protect lenders' purchasing power. The exchange of dollars would still result in $1,120 at the end of the year, but that amount would no longer be equivalent to 112 videotapes, since the price of 112 tapes would be 112 × ($10 × 1.02) = $1,142 by the end of 1 year.

Compared with a 12 percent return on the exchange of goods, the return on the exchange of dollars would be lower. The 112 tapes received in a tape-for-tape exchange exceed the 110 tapes ($1,120/$10.20) that could be purchased in 1 year if dollars were exchanged for dollars at a 12 percent nominal rate. In fact, to equate the return on the two media of exchange, the nominal rate must be slightly more than 14 percent:

$$\frac{\$1,142 - \$1,000}{\$1,000} = \text{14.2\% nominal rate required to purchase 112 tapes in 1 year}$$

The nominal rate of interest must be equal to the real rate *plus* a premium for expected inflation if the lender is to be equally well off regardless of which transaction she chooses. Furthermore, if the 2 percent price change is not anticipated and the nominal rate is not adjusted, the realized *ex post* return on a dollar-for-dollar exchange will be less than 12 percent. Because the $1,120 received at the end of the year will now purchase only 110 videotapes, the *ex post* return, adjusting for the loss of purchasing power, is 10 percent:

$$\frac{110 - 100}{100} = 10\%$$

THE FISHER EFFECT

Although the basic principles of this real/nominal effect were first suggested in the eighteenth century, a twentieth-century economist, Irving Fisher, is

widely credited with laying the foundation for the study of the relationship between interest rates and expected inflation.[13] That relationship, now frequently called the **Fisher effect,** is summarized as follows: The nominal rate of interest reflects the real rate of interest and a premium based on the *expected* rate of inflation.[14] Stated as an equation,

$$1 + i_N = (1 + i_R)[1 + E(P)] \qquad [6.1]$$
$$1 + i_N = 1 + i_R + E(P) + i_R E(P)$$
$$i_N = i_R + E(P) + i_R E(P)$$

where i_N = nominal rate;
i_R = real rate;
$E(P)$ = *expected* rate of inflation.

When the Fisher theory is applied to the problem of deciding on a nominal rate for the videotape transaction under the expectation of 2 percent inflation, the result, using Equation 6.1, is 14.2 percent, the same rate determined earlier:

$$1 + i_N = (1 + 0.12)(1 + 0.02)$$
$$i_N = 1.142 - 1 = 14.2\%$$

Often, analysts follow the convention of eliminating the cross-product term, $i_R \times E(P)$, and the nominal rate is simply expressed as the sum of the real rate and the expected rate of inflation:

$$i_N = i_R + E(P) \qquad [6.2]$$
$$= 0.12 + 0.02 = 14\%$$

---

[13] For a discussion of the development of the theory of real and nominal rates, including Fisher's forerunners and his own contributions, see Humphrey 1983.

[14] Economists have studied several relationships between yields and price levels. Fisher was interested in the relationship between security yields and *changes* in the price level. Another researcher, A. H. Gibson, studied the relationship between the actual level of prices and yields, noting that when prices are relatively high, so are interest rates, and when prices are low, yields also tend to be low. No conclusion has been reached about whether the Gibson relation is consistent with or in conflict with the Fisher effect. See Gibson 1923; Shiller and Siegel 1977; and John H. Wood and Norma L. Wood, *Financial Markets* (San Diego, CA: Harcourt Brace Jovanovich, 1985): 579–586.

FIGURE 6.7   **Inflation and the Equilibrium Rate of Interest**

According to the Fisher theory of interest rates and inflation, if inflation is anticipated, the nominal equilibrium level of interest rates (i_N) will equal the real rate (i_R) plus a premium equal to the expected rate of inflation $[E(P)]$.

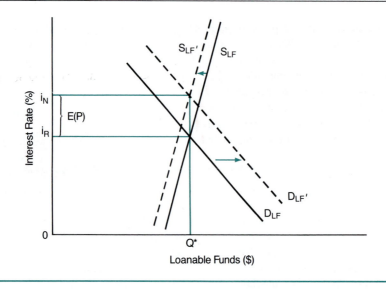

The convention is justified by the argument that the cross-product term, especially for low values of i_R and $E(P)$, is so small that it does not make a material difference in the rate estimate. When the cross-product term is ignored, there is a one-to-one relationship between expected inflation and the amount by which the nominal rate exceeds the real rate.

EXPECTED INFLATION AND THE LOANABLE FUNDS THEORY

Changes in nominal interest rates can be examined in the context of the loanable funds theory. An anticipated increase in price levels means that savers (the suppliers of loanable funds) will require a higher nominal rate of return $[i_R + E(P)]$ at every quantity of loanable funds supplied. This change means that the original curve S_{LF} must shift to the left, to $S_{LF'}$. At the same time, however, borrowers (the demanders of loanable funds) will be willing to pay the higher nominal rate, realizing that they will be repaying their loans in "cheaper dollars," so the demand curve D_{LF} will shift to $D_{LF'}$.

The result is a new point of intersection at a higher nominal rate of interest. The increase in nominal interest rates, or the inflationary premium, is equal to the expected rate of inflation, as shown in Figure 6.7. A key point is that the *real* rate of interest remains unchanged. The Fisher theory implicitly assumes that even in the face of inflationary expectations, the real rate, or the rate at which goods can be exchanged for goods, is unaffected.

EVALUATION OF THE FISHER THEORY

Fisher's theory is intuitively appealing and widely cited. During the 1980s, as inflation approached a modern peak of 13.6 percent in 1980 and Treasury bill (T-bill) yields were on their way to levels as high as 15.51 percent in the summer of 1981, the link between the two was emphasized even more than usual. Without actual reference to the Fisher theory, Fed officials publicly blamed high interest rates on inflation. Then-

Chairman Paul Volcker stated, "When the money supply is brought clearly under control and expectations of inflation dissipate, interest rates will tend to decline." His predecessor, G. William Miller, made a similar reference, stating, ". . . the recent and expected inflation also has been an extremely important factor underlying the increase in interest rates. . . ."[15] More recently, the Bush administration's chief economist, Michael Boskin, also acknowledged the linkage by stating, "The best step we can take to reduce pressure on inflation and interest rates is to negotiate a credible deficit-reduction package promptly."[16] (This statement is also an implicit acceptance of the loanable funds theory.)

HISTORICAL RELATIONSHIPS

Empirical research on past interest rate movements and the rate of inflation has also been used to support the Fisher theory. Tracking historical changes in a rate-of-inflation measure such as the CPI against an interest rate measure almost always results in a positive correlation. For example, during the period 1966–1979, the correlation coefficient between the prime rate and the GNP Price Deflator was .70; when the commercial paper rate was used as the measure of interest rates, the correlation was .81.[17] A graphical comparison of these data over time, provided in Figure 6.8, emphasizes those findings. Although the relationship has been stronger in some periods than others, it encourages belief in the Fisher effect.

Findings such as these are interesting, but they do not prove the Fisher theory. First, observed correlation does not guarantee causality. Some unknown factor or factors could be affecting both interest rates and inflation in a similar fashion so that they appear to be related to one another but are actually both related to other things. In addition, these findings focus on historical inflation rates, whereas the Fisher effect addresses expected inflation rates.

---

[15] See Cox 1980.

[16] David Wessel and Tom Herman, "Interest Rates Head Up Across the Board, but Brady Discounts New Inflation Fears," *The Wall Street Journal,* February 24, 1989, A2.

[17] See Cox 1980, 22.

MEASUREMENT PROBLEMS

Efforts to validate the hypothesized relationship are confounded by several obstacles. The first is the accurate measurement of variables in the Fisher equation. Neither the real rate of interest nor the expected rate of inflation is empirically observable; both must be estimated in some manner, because one can observe only the nominal rate of interest at any time. (Despite measurement difficulties, researchers and expert observers generally assume it to be in the range of 2–4 percent.)

Proxy measurements for expected inflation have often been based on historical values. Fisher himself was the first in a long line of investigators. One of his conclusions was that investors' expectations of inflation are often inaccurate. Using historical data, Fisher calculated *ex post* real rates of return by subtracting *ex post* inflation rates from nominal rates:

$$I_R = i_N - P \qquad [6.3]$$

where I_R = ex post real rate;
P = ex post rate of inflation.

Fisher found that *ex post* real rates were not stable. Because he believed that *ex ante* real rates were constant, he interpreted fluctuations in *ex post* real rates to mean that the markets' inflationary expectations were consistently incorrect. In later tests, he concluded that inflation premiums imposed by the markets were strongly influenced by past rates of inflation and that past price changes were inadequate estimates of future inflation.[18]

Recent *ex post* analyses confirm that if the Fisher theory is true, inaccurate inflationary expectations persist. For example, Figure 6.9 shows that during the period 1960–1986, the *ex post* real rate on 3-month T-bills was sometimes negative. This means that nominal rates were less than actual rates of inflation in some years.

Based on Fisher's early conclusions, researchers have focused on better ways of estimating the *ex ante*

---

[18] A review of Fisher's initial empirical research is provided in Humphrey 1983.

FIGURE 6.8	**Inflation and Interest Rates: Historical Relationships**

Interest rates in both short- and long-term financial markets have been strongly correlated with actual inflation rates.

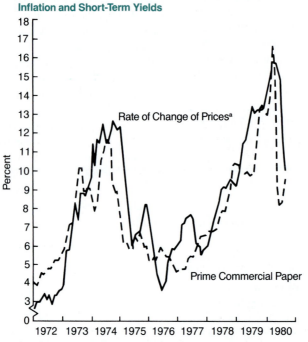

Inflation and Short-Term Yields

Rate of Change of Prices[a]

Prime Commercial Paper

[a]Compounded annual rates of change in the consumer price index over the previous six months.

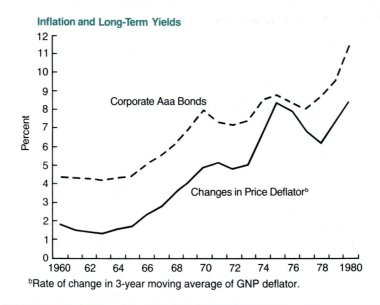

Inflation and Long-Term Yields

Corporate Aaa Bonds

Changes in Price Deflator[b]

[b]Rate of change in 3-year moving average of GNP deflator.

Source: Norman N. Bowsher, "Rise and Fall of Interest Rates," *Review* (Federal Reserve Bank of St. Louis) 62 (August/September 1980): 18–19.

FIGURE 6.9   *Ex Post* **Nominal and Real Interest Rates on 3-Month T-Bills: 1960–1986**

If the actual *(ex post)* rate of inflation during a period exceeds the premium for expected *(ex ante)* inflation incorporated in nominal interest rates, the *ex post* real rate will be negative.

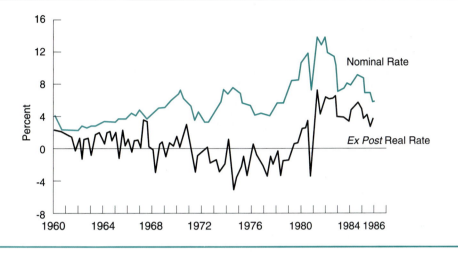

Source: Adapted from Carl E. Walsh, "Three Questions Concerning Nominal and Real Interest Rates," *Economic Review* (Federal Reserve Bank of San Francisco) (Fall 1987): 7.

real rate and inflationary expectations. Estimates of real rates have included yields on T-bills, high-grade corporate bonds, and equity securities. Actual figures or lagged averages of one of several inflation measures, such as the CPI or the GNP Price Deflator, have been used to estimate the inflationary premium. An alternative measure of inflationary expectations is a compilation of experts' forecasts of inflation, sometimes published in major newspapers. Not surprisingly, there is no uniform agreement on measurement or methodology, and the research findings are contradictory.[19]

STABILITY OF THE REAL RATE

Another concern about the Fisher theory is its assumption that the real rate itself is unaffected by the expected rate of inflation and therefore remains stable. Research attention has focused increasingly on that as-

sumption. Some economists argue that inflationary expectations affect not only the nominal rate but also the real rate. They suggest that an increase in inflationary expectations will cause people to change their asset holdings, reducing the amount of cash held in the short run because of an expected decline in its purchasing power and increasing the amount of interest-bearing assets. This adjustment will cause the supply curve to shift to the *right* (to $S_{LF'}$), indicating that more funds are available. The result, shown in Figure 6.10, is that the real rate of interest falls from i_R to i_R'. This theory contrasts with the traditional result shown in Figure 6.7, where the supply of loanable funds was presumed to be reduced when inflation is expected.[20]

According to this theory, if Equation 6.1 or 6.2 is used to estimate the new nominal rate, expected inflation would be added to this lower real rate, not to the original one. The nominal rate of interest thus changes less than the rate of expected inflation,

---

[19] Examples of attempts to measure inflationary expectations and/or the real rate can be found in Fama 1975, Carlson 1977, Mullineaux and Protopapadakis 1984, and Leonard and Solt 1986.

[20] Mundell 1963 and Tobin 1965. Recent empirical work also casts doubt on the stability of the real rate. See Rose 1988.

FIGURE 6.10   **Inflationary Expectations and the Real Rate of Interest**

Challengers of the Fisher theory argue that real rates are also affected by expected inflation. Thus, the supply of loanable funds may increase if inflation is anticipated, resulting in a decrease in the real rate.

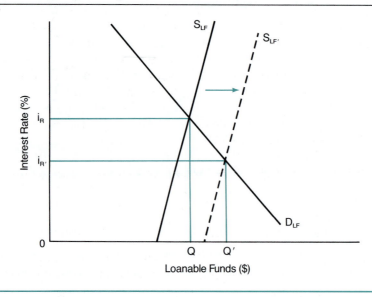

because the inflationary premium is partially offset by a lower real rate of interest.

THE TAX EFFECT

Another complicating factor is income taxes, which are levied on nominal rather than real returns. Several researchers argue that changes in inflationary expectations cause investors to act to protect *after-tax* real returns.[21] For example, suppose that the before-tax *ex ante* real rate is 4 percent. For an investor in the 28 percent marginal tax bracket, an after-tax real rate of $4\% \times (1 - 0.28) = 2.88\%$ would be expected in the absence of inflation.

Now suppose that inflation is expected to be 4 percent. The Fisher theory would project nominal rates

at 8 percent. If nominal yields rise only to that level, however, the expected real after-tax return would fall to $[8\% \times (1 - 0.28)] - 4\% = 1.76\%$. Anticipation of this tax effect exerts a new upward pressure on the nominal rate, suggesting that the change in nominal yields will actually be greater than that predicted by Fisher. To protect after-tax real returns to an investor with a 28 percent tax rate (t), the nominal yield must increase by $[E(P)]/(1 - t)$:

$$i_N = i_R + [E(P)/(1 - t)] \tag{6.4}$$

$$i_N = 4\% + [4\%/(1 - 0.28)] = 9.56\%$$

At this nominal rate, the after-tax real return would be $[9.56\% \times (1 - 0.28)] - 4\% = 2.88\%$, as the investor expected in the absence of inflation.

In recent years, some portions of the personal tax code have been rewritten to lessen the effect of inflation. The inflation adjustments, however, are based on *ex post* rather than *ex ante* inflation rates. Thus, the

[21] Key proponents of the tax effect are Darby 1975 and Feldstein 1976.
     A discussion of the potential impact of changing inflationary expectations on the real rate and the subsequent tax effects is provided in Holland 1984.

problem of protecting *ex ante* after-tax yields remains.[22]

THE DEBATE CONTINUES

Several researchers have supported the one-for-one relationship and the stable real rate of interest of the Fisher hypothesis. In contrast, other studies have concluded that inflationary expectations have a weaker impact; estimates of the effect of a 1 percent change in inflationary expectations on the nominal rate range from 0.65 to 0.9 percent. Finally, the effect of taxes suggests that inflation has more than a one-for-one impact on nominal rates. Thus, many questions remain about how to measure the effect of expected inflation. Experts agree, however, that inflationary expectations play such a large role in the financial markets and in the management of financial institutions that economists will (and should) continue work toward resolving these measurement problems.[23]

One economist has provided an interesting graphical description of the problem. In a world of perfect foresight where people are "omniscient agents" and the real rate of interest is stable, the nominal rate would exactly and immediately respond at t_1 and t_2 to changes in inflation, adjustments represented by the solid lines in Figure 6.11. But with ordinary mortals, the adjustment is less exact and slower, as represented by the dotted lines. So nominal rates established by ordinary mortals will differ from those that would be established in markets full of omniscient agents. And although gods would earn a constant real rate, the real rate that mortals earn would not be constant.

---

[22] Equation 6.4 is based on the version of the Fisher effect specified in Equation 6.2, so it does not consider the cross-product term. If the cross-product term were included, the nominal rate necessary to produce a desired real after-tax rate would be

[6.4a]

$$i_N = i_R + \frac{E(P) + i_R\, E(P)}{(1 - t)}$$

In this example, the nominal rate necessary to produce the expected 2.88 percent after-tax real rate, using Equation 6.4a, would be 9.78 percent. For more discussion, see Gordon J. Alexander and William Sharpe, *Fundamentals of Investments,* (Englewood Cliffs, NJ: Prentice-Hall, 1989), 102; and Peek 1988.

[23] For further details, see Fama 1975 and Santoni and Stone November 1981. Contrasting views are found in Yohe and Karnosky 1969 and Friedman 1980. Reviews of several studies are found in Taylor 1982, Wood 1981, and Van Horne 1984.

ACCURACY OF INTEREST RATE FORECASTING

As the opening paragraphs to this chapter suggest, the life of a forecaster of interest rates and inflation is difficult. Many variables must be considered before rates are predicted, and each variable is a possible source of error. Another problem is that forecasters cannot stop with a prediction of *the* rate of interest but are expected to estimate several different rates. At commercial banks, movements in T-bill and negotiable certificate of deposit (CD) rates are of great concern. At a savings institution, trends in mortgage rates are just as crucial. Managers of insurance companies are interested in long-term bond yields, as are mutual fund and pension fund managers. Finance company managers focus on interest rates on consumer credit and commercial paper.

PROFESSIONAL FORECASTS BASED ON THE LOANABLE FUNDS THEORY

The loanable funds framework is widely used by professional forecasters. They project changes in interest rates based on an analysis of credit demand by sector and by type of security offered as well as on the amount of loanable funds supplied and the types of securities investors will prefer. Resulting forecasts are crucial to managers who must choose what securities to issue or to purchase from among a variety with fixed and variable rates and different maturities.

Salomon Brothers' annual *Prospects for the Credit Markets* is perhaps the most widely quoted example of this approach to rate forecasting, but the American Council of Life Insurance, Morgan Guaranty Trust Company, Prudential Insurance Company, and others also make their forecasts available to financial intermediaries. Other analysts supply forecasts only on a proprietary basis. Large financial institutions often have staff economists who develop forecasts for managers. Managers of smaller firms gather information from many professional forecasters to assist in formulating asset/liability strategies appropriate for the interest rate environment.

A SIMPLE FORECASTING MODEL ILLUSTRATED

Most forecasting models used by economists are extremely complex and cannot be shown effectively in

---

FIGURE 6.11   **Responses of Market Participants to Changes in Expected Inflation**

Because financial market participants are mortal and lack perfect foresight, the nominal rates that mortals earn do not perfectly protect them against inflation. Thus, the real rates they earn are not constant.

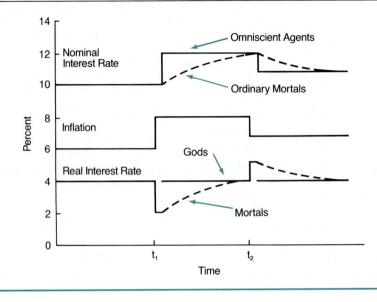

Source: John H. Wood, "Interest Rates and Inflation: An Old and Unexplained Relationship," *Economic Review* (Federal Reserve Bank of Dallas) (January 1983): 21.

a text of this scope. For example, in estimating changes in the supply and demand for credit—which, in turn, are used for estimating changes in interest rates—forecasters must collect data on a wide variety of economic variables that might affect the spending, borrowing, and saving behavior of households, businesses, governments, and the foreign sector. When a forecasting model is initially developed, historical data are examined to determine underlying structural relationships among variables. Sophisticated quantitative techniques, especially regression analysis and its variants, are used for this purpose. Recently, vector autoregressive (VAR) models, which attempt to forecast an economic variable on the basis of its own past behavior without considering other variables, have also become popular. Regardless of a forecaster's preferred methodology, statistically significant historical information, if any, is then used as the basis for forecasting future changes in interest rates.[24]

A study by two economists at the Federal Reserve Bank of St. Louis is a greatly simplified example of forecasting with multivariate regression analysis.[25] They were interested in determining whether *unexpected* announcements by federal officials of changes in key economic variables could be used as the basis of forecasting yields on 3-month and 30-year Treasury securities. Using data from 1980 through 1987, they developed the following model:

$$\Delta i_t = \alpha + \beta_1 \Delta MS_t + \beta_2 \Delta CPI_t + \beta_3 \Delta PPI_t + \beta_4 \Delta U_t + \beta_5 \Delta IP_t + \beta_6 \Delta TB_t + \epsilon$$

where Δi = observed change in interest rates;

ΔMS = unexpected change in M_1, a money supply measure;

ΔCPI = unexpected change in the CPI;

ΔPPI = unexpected change in the PPI;

---

[24] VAR models are discussed and illustrated in Eugeni, Evans, and Strongin 1992; and in "The Future Is Not What It Used To Be," *The Economist,* June 13, 1992, 75.

[25] Dwyer and Hafer 1989.

ΔU = unexpected change in the unemployment rate;

ΔIP = unexpected change in industrial production;

ΔTB = unexpected change in the trade balance;

α = intercept term;

ϵ = random error term;

and t = subscript denoting a time period.

This model attempts to explain interest rate changes using measures of the money supply (MS), inflation (CPI and PPI), the level of business activity (U and IP), and activity involving the foreign sector (TB)—all important components of the theoretical interest rate models discussed earlier in the chapter.

DATA COLLECTION AND ANALYSIS. Initially, the two economists collected data to measure each of the variables, itself a very complex process. For example, to determine the *unexpected* change in M_1 included in the government's announcement of the level of M_1 in period t, they first had to collect data on *expected* changes. They used surveys of the expectations of a group of securities dealers and other market professionals; they then calculated the differences between respondents' expectations and the actual value for M_1 to determine unexpected changes during a period. A similar process was used for each variable.

After data collection, the study used regression analysis to determine if any or all explanatory variables were significantly related to changes in interest rates on Treasury securities. The authors concluded that, disappointingly, there was little consistent relation among the variables during the period 1980–1987, although some variables were significantly related to interest rate changes in individual years. Thus, they did not recommend that market participants forecast future interest rates solely by examining the data included in their model. Nonetheless, their approach is typical of that used by many interest rate forecasters.

WHY IS FORECASTING SO DIFFICULT?

The underlying problem with forecasting is that no matter how well someone understands the factors that cause interest rates to move, such as supply, demand, and expected inflation, predicting just when and in what magnitude those factors will change is virtually impossible. As a result, as noted in the opening paragraphs of this chapter, forecasts are often less than accurate.[26] For several years, *Institutional Investor (II)* evaluated the forecasts of 50 well-known economists. After calculating the difference between the economists' predictions of different rates for a future date and actual rates as of that date, the publication ranked the economists in order of accuracy. Recent results provide excellent examples of the difficulties inherent in the profession. The forecaster who ranked first on forecasts of four key rates in 1988 was the same individual who ranked *forty-seventh* on those rate predictions in 1989! *The Wall Street Journal,* which also publishes semiannual polls of economists' forecasts, reported in 1993 that the economist who ranked first for accuracy in 1991 was "dead last" the next year.[27]

It is not uncommon to see economists' seemingly inaccurate forecasting records addressed in the popular press. For example, in late 1988, a writer for *Forbes* magazine titled an article on the subject "Them That Can, Do; Them That Can't, Forecast" (a variation on an old saying about college professors). However, it is interesting to contemplate other reasons, besides economists' alleged incompetence, that could lead to differences between published forecasts and subsequent reality. If someone is an exceptionally accurate forecaster in a competitive economy, why *should* he or she share secrets to forecasting success? The **efficient markets hypothesis,** a cornerstone of finance theory, holds that financial markets reflect all publicly available information immediately after it becomes known. In reasonably efficient markets, only those participants with private sources of information or with superior information-processing models unknown to other participants are in a position to earn

---

[26] The perils of economic forecasting are discussed in more detail in Van Dyke 1986 and Taylor 1992. A recent study at the Federal Reserve Bank of Cleveland showed that households' forecasts of inflation are more accurate than forecasts of professional economists. See Bryan and Gavin 1986. Some argue, however, that economists are improving through the use of techniques such as VAR. See "The Future Is Not What It Used to Be."

[27] Urang 1988 and 1989; Tom Herman, "How to Profit From Economists' Forecasts," *The Wall Street Journal,* January 22, 1993, C1, C6.

potentially superior profits. Thus, if an economist is an exceptionally successful forecaster, it is not in his or her best interests to reveal that fact to others. It could be that the most successful forecasters keep the lowest public profile.[28]

The difficulties that managers face in obtaining accurate forecasts explain why even sophisticated forecasts must be accompanied by a variety of strategies for managing interest rate risk. Whether a financial institution generates its own forecasts or uses the opinions of other experts, the predictions are often wrong. This element of uncertainty presents managers with several dilemmas. First, they must decide whether to commit the entire institutional strategy to one interest rate scenario or whether to adapt asset and liability accounts on an individual basis. For example, in response to a forecast of rising rates, should a savings and loan association (S&L) make variable-rate loans; offer long-term, fixed-rate deposits; and shorten the maturity of its securities portfolio—all at the same time? Or should the new policies affect only a certain proportion of the loan portfolio? These choices, in turn, suggest a second key decision—the extent to which asset/liability policies will involve hedging, or protective strategies to reduce the effect of inaccurate forecasts. This alternative for managing interest rate risk is explored in detail in chapters to follow.

CURRENCY EXCHANGE RATES

Financial institutions active in international markets face **exchange rate risk,** or variability in NIM caused by fluctuations in currency exchange rates. Exchange rate risk increased significantly in 1971 when, as explained in Chapter 3, the United States officially abandoned the gold standard and allowed its currency exchange rate to float. Although many other currencies had been pegged to the value of the U.S. dollar, since 1973 most have been allowed to float. As a result, institutions that have foreign branches, issue bankers' acceptances, purchase foreign securities, accept deposits in foreign currencies, or provide loans in the international markets are exposed to exchange rate risk.

Figure 6.12 tracks exchange rates for two foreign currencies against the U.S. dollar between 1990 and 1992. The fluctuations, which are typical of any period, illustrate the uncertainty faced in international finance. For example, during this relatively short period, the graph shows that a U.S. dollar could have been exchanged for more than 155 Japanese yen at one time, only to be worth as little as 123 yen less than 2 years later. The rates plotted are **spot rates**—that is, rates for immediate exchanges between currencies. In the foreign exchange markets, spot rates are distinguished from **forward rates**—rates agreed on today for currency exchanges occurring at a future date. Differences between forward and spot rates are illustrated later.[29]

EXCHANGE RATE RISK

Whenever a financial institution negotiates an international transaction involving a transfer of funds at a later date, so that the rate at which foreign currencies and U.S. dollars will be exchanged is unknown when the transaction is negotiated, exchange rate risk is present. For example, suppose that a U.S. bank agreed in August 1992 to finance a U.S. importer of Swiss chocolates. The cost of the imported chocolates, in Swiss francs (SF), was 25 million; the bank did not actually have to provide the funds until September 14, 1992. As shown in Figure 6.13 (page 178) under the column labeled "U.S. $ equiv.," the spot exchange rate prevailing on Thursday, August 13, 1992, was

$$\$/SF = 0.7645$$

In other words, one Swiss franc would buy 0.7645 U.S. dollars—the **direct rate,** or dollars per unit of foreign currency. Under the column headed "Currency per U.S. $," the spot rate is quoted as an **indirect rate,** or units of foreign currency per dollar:

$$SF/\$ = 1.3080$$

Thus, one U.S. dollar would buy 1.3080 Swiss francs. Direct and indirect rates are reciprocals.

---

[28]Ronald Bailey, "Them That Can, Do; Them That Can't, Forecast," *Forbes,* December 26, 1988, 94–100; and Belongia 1987.

[29]Details on the microstructure of foreign exchange markets and illustrative transactions (using the colorful vocabulary of the markets) are found in Flood 1991.

FIGURE 6.12   ### Spot Exchange Rates, 1990–1992

Exchange rates among currencies fluctuate, sometimes considerably. In recent years, the value of the U.S. dollar has changed frequently in relation to other major currencies.

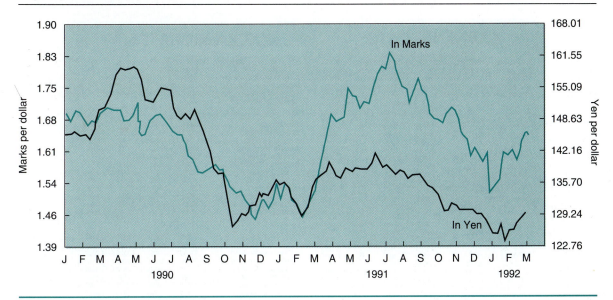

Source: Federal Reserve Bank of Cleveland, *Economic Trends.*

If the funds transfer had occurred in August 1992, the bank would have lent

$$SF25,000,000/1.3080 = \$19,113,150$$

The bank faced uncertainty because the SF25,000,000 was not to be paid until a month later, and the actual dollar commitment could be more or less than $19,113,150. In fact, Figure 6.13 shows that on Monday, September 14, 1992, the direct spot rate was 0.7596 and the indirect spot rate was 1.3165. The value of the dollar had risen, and SF25,000,000 cost only $18,989,746. In this example, the bank benefited from an increase in the value of the dollar relative to the Swiss franc, but it could just as easily have seen a depreciation in the value of the dollar. In fact, Figure 6.13 shows that, had the SF25,000,000 been due only 1 trading day earlier, on Friday, September 11, the bank would have owed SF25,000,000/1.2850 = $19,455,253—*more* than at the time of the original transaction. The considerable increase in the value of the dollar in a single day resulted from a discount rate

reduction by the German central bank early on September 14. As explained in a later section, changes in relative interest rates among major economies often lead to changes in the relative values of their currencies on the worldwide market. In this instance, the U.S. dollar increased in value as German interest rates fell. Because they can rarely forecast with precision the actions of regulators or other market participants over whom they have no control, financial institutions managers face exchange rate variability, such as that illustrated here, whenever they engage in international commerce.[30]

THE FORWARD CURRENCY MARKET

A discussion of exchange rate risk would be incomplete without mention of a mechanism heavily

---

[30] The colorful activities of currency traders in several large U.S. commercial banks are profiled in Randall Smith, "How Currency Traders Play for High Stakes against Central Banks," *The Wall Street Journal,* September 18, 1992, A1, A5.

FIGURE 6.13   Foreign Exchange Rates

Spot and forward exchange rates between the U.S. dollar and other currencies are reported daily in the financial pages. Both direct (U.S. $ equiv.) and indirect (currency per U.S. $) rates are listed.

EXCHANGE RATES

Thursday, August 13, 1992
The New York foreign exchange selling rates below apply to trading among banks in amounts of $1 million and more, as quoted at 3 p.m. Eastern time by Bankers Trust Co., Telerate and other sources. Retail transactions provide fewer units of foreign currency per dollar.

Country	U.S. $ equiv. Thurs.	U.S. $ equiv. Wed.	Currency per U.S. $ Thurs.	Currency per U.S. $ Wed.
Argentina (Peso)	1.01	1.01	.99	.99
Australia (Dollar)	.7180	.7170	1.3928	1.3947
Austria (Schilling)	.09712	.09709	10.30	10.30
Bahrain (Dinar)	2.6522	2.6522	.3771	.3771
Belgium (Franc)	.03341	.03317	29.93	30.15
Brazil (Cruzeiro)	.00023	.00023	4397.00	4356.00
Britain (Pound)	1.9345	1.9300	.5169	.5181
30-Day Forward	1.9238	1.9192	.5198	.5211
90-Day Forward	1.9019	1.8970	.5258	.5271
180-Day Forward	1.8705	1.8657	.5346	.5360
Canada (Dollar)	.8375	.8388	1.1940	1.1922
France (Franc)	.20212	.20161	4.9475	4.9600
30-Day Forward	.20094	.20045	4.9767	4.9887
90-Day Forward	.19859	.19806	5.0355	5.0490
180-Day Forward	.19524	.19478	5.1220	5.1340
Germany (Mark)	.6873	.6832	1.4550	1.4637
30-Day Forward	.6835	.6794	1.4630	1.4719
90-Day Forward	.6763	.6722	1.4787	1.4877
180-Day Forward	.6659	.6619	1.5017	1.5107
Greece (Drachma)	.005556	.005540	180.00	180.50
Hong Kong (Dollar)	.12931	.12953	7.7335	7.7200
South Korea (Won)	.0012703	.0012703	787.20	787.20
Spain (Peseta)	.010715	.010685	93.32	93.59
Sweden (Krona)	.1881	.1881	5.3175	5.3175
Switzerland (Franc)	.7645	.7567	1.3080	1.3215
30-Day Forward	.7613	.7536	1.3135	1.3270
90-Day Forward	.7547	.7470	1.3250	1.3386
180-Day Forward	.7454	.7381	1.3415	1.3548
Taiwan (Dollar)	.040193	.040209	24.88	24.87
Thailand (Baht)	.03951	.03951	25.31	25.31
Turkey (Lira)	.0001438	.0001439	6952.00	6951.00
United Arab (Dirham)	.2723	.2723	3.6725	3.6725
Uruguay (New Peso)				
Financial	.000315	.000315	3175.01	3175.01
Venezuela (Bolivar)				
Floating rate	.01508	.01507	66.32	66.34
SDR	1.44862	1.44633	.69031	.69141
ECU	1.39750	1.39120	....	....

Special Drawing Rights (SDR) are based on exchange rates for the U.S., German, British, French and Japanese currencies. Source: International Monetary Fund.
European Currency Unit (ECU) is based on a basket of community currencies.

EXCHANGE RATES

Monday, September 14, 1992
The New York foreign exchange selling rates below apply to trading among banks in amounts of $1 million and more, as quoted at 3 p.m. Eastern time by Bankers Trust Co., Telerate and other sources. Retail transactions provide fewer units of foreign currency per dollar.

Country	U.S. $ equiv. Mon.	U.S. $ equiv. Fri.	Currency per U.S. $ Mon.	Currency per U.S. $ Fri.
Argentina (Peso)	1.01	1.01	.99	.99
Australia (Dollar)	.7337	.7263	1.3630	1.3768
Austria (Schilling)	.09558	.09823	10.46	10.18
Bahrain (Dinar)	2.6522	2.6522	.3771	.3771
Belgium (Franc)	.03265	.03351	30.63	29.84
Brazil (Cruzeiro)	.00018	.00019	5411.00	5354.00
Britain (Pound)	1.8900	1.9250	.5291	.5195
30-Day Forward	1.8790	1.9136	.5322	.5226
90-Day Forward	1.8574	1.8900	.5384	.5291
180-Day Forward	1.8263	1.8557	.5476	.5389
Canada (Dollar)	.8241	.8224	1.2135	1.2160
France (Franc)	.19845	.20331	5.0390	4.9185
30-Day Forward	.19732	.19181	5.0680	5.2135
90-Day Forward	.19505	.19963	5.1270	5.0092
180-Day Forward	.19196	.19617	5.2095	5.0975
Germany (Mark)	.6725	.6916	1.4870	1.4460
30-Day Forward	.6689	.6877	1.4949	1.4541
90-Day Forward	.6622	.6803	1.5101	1.4699
180-Day Forward	.6530	.6700	1.5315	1.4926
Greece (Drachma)	.005397	.005556	185.30	180.00
Hong Kong (Dollar)	.12932	.12937	7.7330	7.7300
South Korea (Won)	.0012723	.0012749	785.95	784.40
Spain (Peseta)	.010386	.010639	96.28	93.99
Sweden (Krona)	.1837	.1891	5.4435	5.2895
Switzerland (Franc)	.7596	.7782	1.3165	1.2850
30-Day Forward	.7568	.7753	1.3213	1.2898
90-Day Forward	.7519	.7696	1.3300	1.2994
180-Day Forward	.7447	.7614	1.3428	1.3133
Taiwan (Dollar)	.039984	.040096	25.01	24.94
Thailand (Baht)	.03959	.03981	25.26	25.12
Turkey (Lira)	.0001366	.0001414	7319.00	7070.00
United Arab (Dirham)	.2723	.2723	3.6725	3.6725
Uruguay (New Peso)				
Financial	.000307	.000306	3254.00	3265.01
Venezuela (Bolivar)				
Floating rate	.01476	.01477	67.75	67.72
SDR	1.44847	1.46759	.69038	.68139
ECU	1.35710	1.39800	....	....

Special Drawing Rights (SDR) are based on exchange rates for the U.S., German, British, French and Japanese currencies. Source: International Monetary Fund.
European Currency Unit (ECU) is based on a basket of community currencies.

Source: The Wall Street Journal, August 14, 1992, C13; September 15, 1992, C15.

used by investors, nonfinancial firms, and financial institutions to reduce the uncertainty about exchange rates during a planning period—the **forward currency market.** A forward exchange is an agreement between two parties to exchange a specified amount of one currency for another, at a specified future date, at a specified rate of exchange. The forward rate that is agreed on may differ from the spot rate at the time of negotiation and also from the spot rate at the time the exchange actually occurs.

Forward rates are quoted daily along with spot rates; for many currencies, rates for 30-, 90-, and 180-day forward exchanges are reported. In Figure 6.13, all three forward rates are quoted for the Swiss franc. As of August 13, 1992, the direct forward rates were less than the spot rate. If the U.S. bank, in its agreement to finance the Swiss chocolate importer, had wanted to lock in a rate in the forward market, it could have negotiated an agreement at the 30-day forward rate. Reported in the row below the spot rate, the 30-day direct and indirect forward rates prevailing on August 13 were

$$\$/SF = 0.7613$$
$$SF/\$ = 1.3135$$

In other words, in August the bank could have guaranteed that in September, the SF25,000,000 it had to provide to the importer would represent an investment, in dollars, in the amount of

$$SF25,000,000/1.3135 = \$19,033,118$$

The forward rate was favorable compared with August's spot rate, and it was a figure on which the bank could base its plans. The uncertainty about the dollar commitment in August would have been eliminated. As can be seen from the rates reported in Figure 6.13, however, a forward transaction would have locked the bank into an exchange rate less desirable than the spot rate that actually prevailed on September 14, 1992. Still, the potential for a favorable movement in rates could have been traded for certain knowledge of the rate of exchange.

On average, forward rates are reasonably good indicators of future spot rates, so in this instance managers might have predicted that spot rates in September would be less than those in August. But averages, by definition, are based on the results of many transactions occurring above and below the mean. In this case, in fact, spot rates in September were actually less than the 30-day forward rate predicted. As these examples suggest, to determine whether spot or forward exchange transactions are appropriate, managers must understand the reasons behind exchange rate fluctuations.

THEORIES OF EXCHANGE RATE DETERMINATION

Exchange rate variability has been the focus of much academic research. Some theories focus on supply/demand relationships for goods and services; oth-

ers focus more specifically on comparative inflation rates or interest rates among nations.

SUPPLY AND DEMAND FOR GOODS AND SERVICES. A fundamental factor influencing exchange rates is the demand for goods and services produced in one country relative to the demand for goods and services produced in another. Imbalances may lead to trade or balance-of-payments deficits that eventually affect currency exchange rates. Suppose, for example, that the demand for California wine in France is greater than the demand for French wine in the United States. The demand for U.S. dollars with which to buy California wine will exceed Americans' demand for French francs to buy French wine. An excess supply of French francs will develop in the currency markets, and the value of the franc will fall. The reverse would apply if Americans demanded relatively more French wine; the value of the dollar would fall compared with the franc. In summary, an increase in the demand for a country's goods and services should lead to an increase in the value of its currency, and a decrease in demand for its goods and services should lead to currency depreciation.

Under a managed floating exchange rate system, such as that described in Chapter 3, trade imbalances leading to exchange rate fluctuations are somewhat self-correcting. If the value of the French franc falls because the French are exchanging their money to buy California wine, California wine will begin to seem more expensive. Even if the dollar price of California wine does not change, subsequent wine purchases by the French will cost more because more francs will be required to purchase the same amount of dollars. Eventually, the demand for California wine may diminish among the French and they will begin to purchase more French wine. As fewer francs are changed into dollars, the supply of francs in the currency markets will fall, and the value of francs will rise relative to the dollar.

RELATIVE INFLATION RATES. The previous illustration assumed no change in the dollar prices of California wines, but changes in the prices of goods *do* occur. The **purchasing power parity theorem** ties exchange rates to differential inflation rates across countries. The theorem states that relatively high inflation in one country will be accompanied by a *depreciation* of its currency relative to currencies in countries with lower inflation rates. In other words, there is an inverse relationship between differences in inflation rates and changes in currency values.

Suppose that a drought in the United States greatly reduces harvests on most agricultural products, including chardonnay grapes, which are used to produce some of California's finest white wines. Even with no increase in demand, the price of California wine will increase, along with the price of most goods dependent on agriculture. More francs must be exchanged to import California wines and other U.S. products, not because the exchange rate has changed, but because U.S. prices have increased. If French goods of comparable quality are less expensive because they escape the drought, French *and* U.S. citizens will increase their demand for French products. As more dollars are exchanged for francs, and fewer francs are exchanged for dollars, the value of the dollar will fall. The purchasing power parity theorem holds that the value of the dollar will decline because inflation in the United States exceeds that in France.

RELATIVE INTEREST RATES. Yet another theory suggests that exchange rates are closely tied to interest rates. The previous theories have focused on consumption goods and services, but currencies also travel among countries as a result of the purchase and sale of financial assets. The **interest rate parity theorem** asserts that interest rates and exchange rates are interdependent: If interest rates in one country differ from those in another, supply and demand for the currencies of the two countries can be affected. According to this theory, when interest rates in the United States are high relative to those in other countries, foreign investors will demand U.S. dollars so that they can take advantage of more desirable rates of return. Exchange rates will then adjust to reflect the interest rate differentials; in this example, the value of the dollar will increase as demand exceeds supply.

The increase in the value of the dollar shown in Figure 6.13 between September 11 and September 14, 1992, is a concrete example of the workings of interest rate parity. As the top panel of Figure 6.14 shows, for many months before September 1992, the German discount rate had been rising as Japanese and U.S. central bank rates were falling. Market rates in the three countries followed the lead of central bank rates, as the bottom panel of Figure 6.14 depicts. Thus, investors all over the world were changing U.S. dollars into Deutschmarks to take advantage of high yields on German securities. Central banks in other European countries had kept their interest rates high, too, to maintain their currencies' values relative to the Deutschmark. But many of these countries were mired in recessions, so the higher rates were hurting them domestically even as they helped in the foreign exchange markets. Finally, under pressure from its G-7 partners, the German central bank cut its discount rate by ¼ percent. (The change is not shown in the figure.) Because the spread between U.S. and German rates narrowed, the immediate reaction in world markets was to increase the value of the U.S. dollar. Although the longer-run effects of the German bank's action are more complex and beyond the intent of this chapter, the importance of relative interest rates to exchange rate determination is clear.

A COMPLEX PUZZLE. It is obvious that integrating these three explanations of changes in currency exchange rates requires some thought. Thus far, one can conclude that greater demand for a nation's goods and services leads to appreciation in the value of its currency, assuming no change in the price level. But this limited scenario is insufficient when inflation or deflation occurs. The purchasing power parity theorem says that higher inflation in one country will lead to a *depreciation* of its currency, and the interest rate parity theorem states that higher interest rates in a country will lead to *appreciation* of its currency. Yet the Fisher effect says that inflation rates and interest rates are directly related!

What may seem confusing can actually be resolved by recalling the Fisher theory's distinction between nominal and real rates of interest. Suppose that nominal rates in the United States increase as a result of expected inflation. Although the interest rate parity theorem would seem to predict that the U.S. dollar would appreciate as a result of higher interest rates, the purchasing power parity theorem helps managers recognize that increases in interest rates caused by inflation will ultimately result in depreciation, not appreciation, of the U.S. dollar. However, relatively high U.S. nominal rates resulting from an increase in the real rate—signifying greater potential return on investment in goods and services—should strengthen the

FIGURE 6.14	**Relative Interest Rates in Germany, Japan, and the United States**

During the early 1990s, the German central bank raised its discount rate as central banks in the United States and Japan lowered theirs. Market interest rates in the three countries followed the lead of central bank rates. These differences in interest rates affected currency exchange rates.

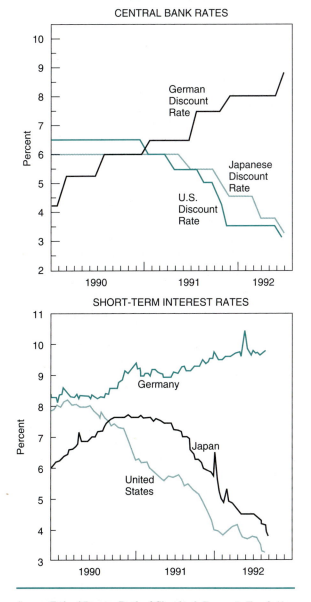

Source: Federal Reserve Bank of Cleveland, *Economic Trends* (August 1992): 18.

value of the dollar, as investment in U.S. assets is seen as being more desirable.[31]

THE ROLE OF EXPECTATIONS. Finance experts recognize that no forecasts are complete without a role for expectations. Some of the ideas discussed previously focus on market participants' reactions to what *is,* but both consumers and investors also react to what they believe *will be.* Indeed, the existence of the forward market is a testimony to the influence of expectations in foreign currency exchanges. The role of expectations is so important in interest rate (and thus exchange rate) forecasting, in fact, that it is explored in greater detail in the next chapter.

SUMMARY

Because the net interest margin is the key variable in asset/liability management, understanding the behavior of interest rates is important. In increasingly global markets, the NIM is also affected by the value of one currency relative to others. This chapter discussed the general level of interest rates and currency exchange rates.

Because all interest rates tend to move in the same direction, a forecast for the general level of interest rates is a starting point for estimating future rates on specific assets and liabilities. The most widely used explanation for movements in the general level is the loanable funds theory, based on the motivations for saving and borrowing. Although other factors also affect the decision, the dollar amount individuals are willing to save is positively related to interest rates, and the demand for borrowing is inversely related to interest rates. The equilibrium general level of interest rates is determined by the intersection of the supply and demand curves for loanable funds.

Economists have also hypothesized that expected inflation influences the general level of interest rates. In fact, the Fisher effect suggests that nominal market rates of interest reflect a real rate of interest plus a premium equal to the expected rate of inflation.

---

[31] Further discussion of the parity theorems is found in Kubarych 1983, Shapiro 1983, and Giddy and Dufey 1975. Reconciling the theories is considered in Reuven Glick, "Global Interest Rate Linkages," *Weekly Letter,* Federal Reserve Bank of San Francisco, May 25, 1990; and Strongin 1990.

Although this theory is difficult to validate empirically, most researchers agree that inflationary expectations affect the general level of rates.

Because they attempt to predict an unknown future, interest rate forecasts, no matter how carefully made, are subject to error. So, besides theories, financial institution managers must be aware of techniques to minimize the impact of forecasting errors on the institution's performance.

Exchange rate risk, or variability in the rate at which one currency can be converted to another, is significant for all institutions participating in international markets, particularly for those that negotiate transactions today for execution at a later date. Such transactions may occur either at subsequent spot rates or at forward rates determined today. Several theories have been advanced to explain exchange rate variability. In general, the value of a nation's currency should increase if demand increases for its goods and services or if interest rates are relatively high compared with those in other countries. The value of a country's currency should decrease, however, if its rate of inflation is relatively high. Both interest rates and exchange rates are influenced not only by contemporary developments but also by market participants' expectations of the future.

QUESTIONS

1. Describe the direction and volatility of interest rate movements during the last two years. Discuss the expected effects of this interest rate environment on financial institution management.

2. What choices are available to institutions (or others) for the use of funds? Why would anyone hold cash balances? Do interest rates affect these motives? If so, how?

3. What economic sector is a net supplier of loanable funds? How are savings decisions of this sector affected by noninterest factors?

4. A 1989 survey of consumer savings patterns in the United States revealed that Americans saved only 4.2 percent of disposable income in 1988, compared to 7.5 percent in 1981 and 9.4 percent in 1973. Based on your knowledge of the loanable funds theory, explain the potential impact of this trend on U.S. interest rates (assuming no increase in loanable funds from international investors). Find a recent article on Americans' propensity to save. Has the rate of savings increased or decreased since the late 1980s?

5. Explain why the federal government's demand for loanable funds is relatively inelastic with respect to interest rates.

6. How is the business sector's demand for loanable funds related to interest rates? Why? If corporate taxes are lowered, how would the demand curve for loanable funds be affected?

7. Find a recent forecast of interest rates. On what factors or theories were the forecasts based?

8. Distinguish between the nominal rate and the real rate of interest. How does inflation affect the real, *ex post* rate of return to investors?

9. Could the *ex ante* real rate of return to an investor be negative? Could the *ex post* real rate be negative? Explain.

10. Explain Fisher's theory of the relationship between the nominal rate of interest and expected inflation. Explain whether you agree with the following statement: A 0.9 correlation between *ex post* T-bill rates and *ex post* inflation proves that the Fisher theory is true.

11. Explain why Fisher's belief that the *ex ante* real rate of interest is constant has become controversial.

12. Assume that investors adjust required nominal rates based on expected inflation as Fisher hypothesized. Does this adjustment assure an investor that the after-tax real return will be protected from inflation? Why or why not?

13. Using the CPI as the measure of inflation, calculate the *ex post* real rate of return on 3-month T-bills over a recent period. Using a current forecast of inflation, determine the current *ex ante* real rate on 3-month T-bills.

14. A Kansas savings institution introduced a CD in 1988 that paid a fixed rate of 3 percent plus adjustments based on changes in the Consumer Price Index. If you accepted Fisher's hypothesis and also believed that past inflation is an accurate predictor of future inflation, would you have any preference for this CD? Why or why not?

15. Interest rate forecasters are often criticized for their somewhat less-than-accurate predictions. Explain some of the difficulties economists face in developing forecasts. How might you use the efficient markets hypothesis to explain a forecaster's performance?

16. What is the difference between spot and forward rates in the foreign currency markets? How does a forward exchange agreement assist market participants in reducing their exchange rate risk exposure?

17. How do changes in the supply of and demand for goods and services affect exchange rates between the currencies of two countries?

18. Under the purchasing power parity theorem, explain how and why a decline in the rate of inflation in the United States affects the value of the dollar in relation to the currencies of countries with higher rates of inflation.

19. Under the interest rate parity theorem, how is the value of a currency affected when the nation's interest rates are relatively higher than those of other countries? Does this relationship hold for real rates, nominal rates, or both? Why?

PROBLEMS

1. Graph the supply and demand curves for loanable funds. What is meant by the equilibrium rate of interest?

2. Using the graph from Problem 1, show the effect on the equilibrium rate of interest if government borrowing increases while the demand for loanable funds from other sectors remains constant.

3. If the demand for loanable funds by the business sector decreases because of a recession, and the demand for loanable funds by the government increases but by a smaller amount, how will the equilibrium interest rate be affected? Sketch the change on the same graph used in Problems 1 and 2.

4. Within the framework of the loanable funds theory, illustrate how inflation affects the equilibrium rate of interest.

5. Your mother received an inheritance from the estate of a great aunt consisting of 11 small diamonds valued at $800 each. She has considered selling the diamonds and investing the $8,800 in a bank CD for 1 year.
   a. A dealer in precious stones has offered to take your mother's diamonds now and give her back 12 diamonds at the end of 1 year. If you assume stable market values, what CD rate would be required to make her indifferent between the two alternatives?
   b. Suppose your mother expected the value of the diamonds to be $825 at the end of the year. What change in the CD rate should occur, given inflationary expectations?

6. Using the original statement of the Fisher equation (Equation 6.1), calculate the nominal yield required by investors when the real rate of interest is 4 percent and the expected inflation rate is 5 percent. What will be the after-tax real rate of return to an investor in the 28 percent tax bracket who invests at this nominal rate?

7. Your favorite uncle has asked you for assistance. He requires a real return before taxes of 4.5 percent; based on prevailing inflationary expectations, he is offered a nominal annual rate of 10 percent. At the end of the year, however, he calculates his after-tax real rate of return, using a 28 percent tax rate, to be only 2.5 percent.
   a. If your uncle expected to earn a real after-tax rate of return of 4.5 (1 − 0.28) = 2.79 percent, what rate of inflation was he expecting? (Ignore the cross product in the Fisher equation.)
   b. Considering the fact that his actual after-tax real rate of return was 2.5 percent, what was the *ex post* rate of inflation?

8. Several years ago, a Texas bank offered a 30-year CD with an annual return indexed to inflation. The rate offered was the annual percentage increase in the CPI plus 4 percent. Suppose that you are in the 28 percent marginal tax bracket and require a 5 percent real return after taxes. Suppose also that the annual inflation rate last year was 3 percent, so this year's annual rate on the CD investment is set at 7 percent.
   a. Show the after-tax real return you would earn, assuming that the inflation rate stays at 3 percent.
   b. What *ex ante* nominal rate should you require to keep your after-tax real yield at 5 percent?

9. Refer to the exchange rates on August 13, 1992, shown in Figure 6.13.
   a. Suppose your firm needed to pay a French exporter for goods received. The bill is 750,000 French francs. What was the cost in dollars on August 13?
   b. If, on the same day, a Japanese corporation needed to pay your firm $3.5 million, what was the cost in yen?

10. A midwestern auto dealer must convert $2 million into yen to buy Japanese cars priced at 220 million yen.
   a. What is the direct rate of exchange between dollars and yen?
   b. What is the indirect exchange rate?

11. Suppose that the importer in Problem 10 had earlier locked in a forward exchange agreement at a direct rate of 0.0094. Under that agreement, how many U.S. dollars must be converted to cover the cost of the imported automobiles?

SELECTED REFERENCES

Barth, James R., and Michael D. Bradley. "On Interest Rates, Inflationary Expectations and Tax Rates." *Journal of Banking and Finance* 12 (June 1988): 215–220.

Becketti, Sean, and Gordon H. Sellon, Jr. "Has Financial Market Volatility Increased?" In *Financial Market Volatility and the Economy,* 3–16, Research Division, Federal Reserve Bank of Kansas City, 1990.

Belongia, Michael T. "Predicting Interest Rates: A Comparison of Professional and Market-Based Forecasts." *Review* (Federal Reserve Bank of St. Louis) 69 (March 1987): 9–15.

Bryan, Michael F., and William T. Gavin. "Comparing Inflation Expectations of Households and Economists: Is a Little Knowledge a Dangerous Thing?" *Economic Review* (Federal Reserve Bank of Cleveland) (Quarter 3 1986): 14–19.

Carlson, John A. "Short-Term Interest Rates as Predictors of Inflation: Comment." *American Economic Review* 67 (June 1977): 469–475.

Clarida, Richard D., and Benjamin M. Friedman. "The Behavior of U.S. Short-Term Interest Rates since October 1979." *Journal of Finance* 39 (July 1984): 671–682.

Cox, William N., III. "Interest Rates and Inflation: What Drives What?" *Economic Review* (Federal Reserve Bank of Atlanta) 65 (May/June 1980): 20–23.

Croushore, Dean. "What Are the Costs of Disinflation?" *Business Review* (Federal Reserve Bank of Philadelphia) (May/June 1992): 3–16.

Darby, Michael R. "The Financial and Tax Effects of Monetary Policy on Interest Rates." *Economic Inquiry* 12 (June 1975): 266–276.

Dwyer, Gerald P., Jr., and R. W. Hafer. "Interest Rates and Economic Announcements." *Review* (Federal Reserve Bank of St. Louis) 71 (March/April 1989): 34–46.

Eugeni, Francesca, Charles Evans, and Steven Strongin. "Making Sense of Economic Indicators: A Consumer's Guide to Indicators of Real Economic Activity." *Economic Perspectives* (Federal Reserve Bank of Chicago) 16 (September/October 1992): 2–32.

Fama, Eugene A. "Short-Term Interest Rates as Predictors of Inflation." *American Economic Review* 65 (June 1975): 269–282.

Feldstein, Martin, "Inflation, Income Taxes and the Rate of Interest: A Theoretical Analysis." *American Economic Review* 66 (December 1976): 809–820.

Fisher, Irving. *The Theory of Interest.* New York: Macmillan, 1930.

Flood, Mark D. "Microstructure Theory and the Foreign Exchange Market." *Review* (Federal Reserve Bank of St. Louis) 73 (November/December 1991): 52–70.

Fortune, Peter. "An Assessment of Financial Market Volatility: Bills, Bonds, and Stocks." *New England Economic Review* (Federal Reserve Bank of Boston) (November/December 1989): 13–28.

Friedman, Benjamin. "Price Inflation, Portfolio Choice and Nominal Interest Rates." *American Economic Review* 70 (March 1980): 32–48.

Gibson, A. H. "The Future Course of High Class Investment Values." *Bankers Magazine* (London) 115 (January 1923): 15–34.

Giddy, Ian H., and Gunter Dufey. "The Random Behavior of Flexible Exchange Rates." *Journal of International Business Studies* 6 (Spring 1975): 1–32.

Hakkio, Craig S. "Interest Rates and Exchange Rates—What Is the Relationship?" *Economic Review* (Federal Reserve Bank of Kansas City) 71 (November 1986): 33–43.

Holland, A. Steven. "Real Interest Rates: What Accounts for Their Recent Rise?" *Review* (Federal Reserve Bank of St. Louis) 66 (December 1984): 18–29.

Humphrey, Thomas M. "The Early History of the Real/Nominal Interest Rate Relationship." *Economic Review* (Federal Reserve Bank of Richmond) 69 (May/June 1983): 2–10.

Keane, Michael P., and David E. Runkle. "Are Economic Forecasts Rational?" *Quarterly Review* (Federal Reserve Bank of Minneapolis) 13 (Spring 1989): 26–33.

Keynes, John Maynard. *The General Theory of Employment, Interest, and Money.* New York: Harcourt, Brace, and World, 1936.

Kubarych, Roger M. *Foreign Exchange Markets in the United States,* 2d ed. New York: Federal Reserve Bank of New York, 1983.

Leonard, David C., and Michael E. Solt. "Recent Evidence on the Accuracy and Rationality of Popular Inflation Forecasts." *Journal of Financial Research* 9 (Winter 1986): 281–290.

Mascaro, Angelo, and Allen H. Meltzer. "Long- and Short-Term Interest Rates in a Risky World." *Journal of Monetary Economics* 12 (November 1983): 485–518.

McNees, Stephen K. "Consensus Forecasts: Tyranny of the Majority?" *New England Economic Review* (Federal Reserve Bank of Boston) (November/December 1987): 15–21.

Mullineaux, Donald J., and Aris Protopapadakis. "Revealing Real Interest Rates: Let the Market Do It." *Business Review* (Federal Reserve Bank of Philadelphia) (March/April 1984): 3–8.

Mundell, Robert. "Inflation and Real Interest." *Journal of Political Economy* 71 (June 1963): 280–283.

Peek, Joe. "Inflation and the Excess Taxation of Personal Interest Income." *New England Economic Review* (Federal Reserve Bank of Boston) (March/April 1988): 46–52.

Polakoff, Murray E. "Loanable Funds Theory and Interest Rate Determination." In *Financial Institutions and Markets.* 2d ed., edited by Murray E. Polakoff and Thomas A. Durkin, 483–510. Boston: Houghton Mifflin, 1981.

Rose, Andrew K. "Is the Real Rate Stable?" *Journal of Finance* 43 (December 1988): 1095–1112.

Rosenblum, Harvey, and Steven Strongin. "Interest Rate Volatility in Historical Perspective." *Economic Perspectives* (Federal Reserve Bank of Chicago) 7 (January/February 1983): 10–19.

Santoni, G. J., and Courtenay C. Stone. "Navigating Through the Interest Rate Morass: Some Basic Principles." *Economic Review* (Federal Reserve Bank of St. Louis) 63 (March 1981): 11–18.

Santoni, G. J., and Courtenay Stone. "What Really Happened to Interest Rates?" *Economic Review* (Federal Reserve Bank of St. Louis) 63 (November 1981): 3–14.

Shapiro, Alan C. "What Does Purchasing Power Parity Mean?" *Journal of International Money and Finance* (December 1983): 295–318.

Shiller, Robert J., and Jeremy J. Siegel. "The Gibson Paradox and Historical Movements in Real Interest Rates." *Journal of Political Economy* 85 (October 1977): 891–907.

Strongin, Steven. "International Credit Market Connections." *Economic Perspectives* 14 (July/August 1990): 2–10.

Taylor, Herbert. "Interest Rates: How Much Does Expected Inflation Matter?" *Business Review* (Federal Reserve Bank of Philadelphia) (July/August 1982): 3–12.

————. "The Livingston Surveys: A History of Hopes and Fears." *Business Review* (Federal Reserve Bank of Philadelphia) (January/February 1992): 15–27.

Tobin, James. "Money and Economic Growth." *Econometrica* 33 (October 1965): 671–684.

Urang, Sally. "The Economists' Scoreboard." *Institutional Investor* 22 (March 1988): 251–256, and 23 (March 1989): 211–216.

Van Dyke, Daniel T. "Why Economists Make Mistakes." *Bankers Magazine* 169 (May/June 1986): 69–75.

Van Horne, James C. *Financial Market Rates and Flows,* 2d ed. Englewood Cliffs, NJ: Prentice-Hall, 1984.

Wallace, William H., and William E. Cullison. *Measuring Price Changes,* 4th ed. Richmond, VA: Federal Reserve Bank, 1979.

Wood, John H. "Interest Rates and Inflation." *Economic Perspectives* (Federal Reserve Bank of Chicago) 5 (May/June 1981): 3–12.

Yohe, William P., and Denis Karnosky. "Interest Rates and Price Level Changes, 1952–1969." *Review* (Federal Reserve Bank of St. Louis) 51 (December 1969): 18–39.

If I had to pick one indicator, it would be the yield curve.
It hasn't missed in a century. Every time the yield curve is inverted,
a contraction has followed on average a year later.
Raymond Dalio
Bridgewater Group (1989)

An investor with idle funds in mid-1989 would have faced nothing but frustration in soliciting professional advice about how long to invest those funds. Consider the recommendations given *simultaneously* to a reporter for *The Wall Street Journal:* "Shorter is better right now," said Michael D. Hirsch, chief investment officer of Republic Bank of New York. "People should be lengthening their maturities now," advised James Riepe, director of investment services at T. Rowe Price, a large mutual fund group. "Intermediate-term bonds offer the possibility of price appreciation and good rates," opined William E. Donoghue, chairman of Donoghue Organization, an investment research group. The reason behind the confusion? The yield curve, often used as an indicator of the course of future interest rates, was "flat"—that is, expected rates of return were almost equal regardless of how long one invested one's money.[1] This situation made economic forecasting even more difficult than usual.

The previous chapter points to the importance of understanding how both the supply and demand for credit and inflationary expectations affect the general level of interest rates. The preceding paragraph, as well as the opening quotation, point to another important influence on institutional performance—the **term structure of interest rates,** often called the **yield curve.** All else equal, the term structure of interest rates is the relationship, at a specific time, between yields on securities and their maturities. For example, yields on 182-day Treasury bills (T-bills) almost always differ from those on 25-year Treasury bonds (T-bonds).

Just as there are theories explaining how the general level of interest rates is determined, there are also theories explaining the term structure. Because financial institutions simultaneously participate in the markets for securities of many different maturities, theories of the term structure can assist managers in making decisions that commonly confront them. Some of these decisions are illustrated later in the chapter.

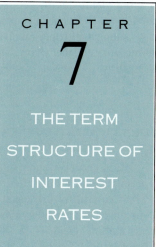

CHAPTER

7

THE TERM
STRUCTURE OF
INTEREST
RATES

---

[1] Georgette Jasen, "High-Yield Hunters Now Face a Decision," *The Wall Street Journal,* May 3, 1989, C1.

THE TERM STRUCTURE DEFINED: A CLOSER LOOK

As noted, the term structure of interest rates is the relationship between security yields and maturities, *all else equal.* "All else equal" is an important qualifying phrase. To isolate the impact of maturity on yield, one must remove potential effects of other factors. Comparing a bank's existing yields on a 6-month T-bill and a 20-year loan to a developing nation would say little about the effect of maturity on yields but a great deal about default risk. It would also be wrong to compare a T-bill yield with the tax-exempt yield on bonds of the City of Dallas or to compare General Motors' 90-day commercial paper rate with the yield on its preferred stock and then draw conclusions about the effect of maturity on expected return.

IDENTIFYING THE EXISTING TERM STRUCTURE

It is generally agreed that comparing yields on Treasury securities of different maturities is the best way to control for extraneous factors. Existing term structures are obtained by observing spot rates—current market yields—on T-bills, Treasury notes (T-notes), and T-bonds. A daily listing of yields and maturities is found in the "Treasury Issues" column of major newspapers; an example is shown in Figure 7.1. The few Treasury issues that are callable or have special estate tax features, called flower bonds, must be eliminated. The $3\frac{1}{2}$ percent bond maturing in 1998, yielding 3.60 percent and highlighted in the figure, is one such example. Standardized calculations must be used so that bank discount yields are not erroneously compared with bond-equivalent yields.[2]

A HISTORICAL LOOK AT TERM STRUCTURES

Just as the general level of interest rates differs over time, so does the term structure. In March 1989, for example, yields on short-term Treasury securities exceeded those on long-term Treasuries. A plot of this relationship is shown in Figure 7.2. A yield curve with this shape is often described as **downward-sloping** or **inverted.** In contrast, Figure 7.3 shows an upward-sloping relationship in March 1992. Figure 7.4 shows an almost constant relationship between yields and maturities in December 1988.

Figure 7.5 on page 193 gives a long-term view of short- and long-term rates, showing yields on T-bills and T-bonds over a period of approximately 20 years. During this period, no single relationship between short- and long-term rates prevailed although short-term rates exceeded long-term rates most of the time. In fact, the prevalence of upward-sloping yield curves during much of the early twentieth century led to their being dubbed **"normal" yield curves,** which is why downward-sloping curves have been called "inverted."[3]

A financial institution manager aware of these facts can be certain of one thing: Because both short- and long-term financial markets are part of the environment, one must understand reasons for yield differences based on maturity and learn to anticipate changes in current relationships.

THE TERM STRUCTURE AND THE GENERAL LEVEL OF INTEREST RATES

Another feature of Figure 7.5 is important because it suggests a historical relationship between the general level of economic activity and the shape of the yield curve. The dates labeled on the graph denote months when there were peaks in the business cycle.[4] At these times, such as the early 1970s, a downward-

---

[2]For a theoretically correct determination of the "true" term structure, the securities used should all be pure discount, zero-coupon bonds of varying maturities. The growing market for stripped Treasury securities, discussed in Chapter 9, may eventually introduce new practices, but currently coupon-bearing as well as discount security yields are used to estimate existing term structures, especially when the analyst is fitting a curve visually. Also, bonds with different coupon rates are usually used to construct a yield curve, causing some distortion. The relationship between coupon rate, maturity, and yield to maturity is discussed in Chapters 8 and 9.

[3]Inverted yield curves appeared more frequently in the 1970s and early 1980s than in previous periods, although they are not evident in Figure 7.5, which shows only annual averages.

[4]Peaks shown are as delineated by the National Bureau of Economic Research, U.S. Department of Commerce, *Business Conditions Digest.*

FIGURE 7.1 **Treasury Bonds, Notes, and Bills**

Yields of Treasury securities of varying maturities are found in the daily financial pages. These data are the basis for estimating the current shape of the yield curve.

TREASURY BONDS, NOTES & BILLS

Thursday, September 17, 1992

Representative Over-the-Counter quotations based on transactions of $1 million or more.

Treasury bond, note and bill quotes are as of mid-afternoon. Colons in bid-and-asked quotes represent 32nds; 101:01 means 101 1/32. Net changes in 32nds. n-Treasury note. Treasury bill quotes in hundredths, quoted on terms of a rate of discount. Days to maturity calculated from settlement date. All yields are to maturity and based on the asked quote. Latest 13-week and 26-week bills are boldfaced. For bonds callable prior to maturity, yields are computed to the earliest call date for issues quoted above par and to the maturity date for issues below par. *-When issued.

Source: Federal Reserve Bank of New York.

U.S. Treasury strips as of 3 p.m. Eastern time, also based on transactions of $1 million or more. Colons in bid-and-asked quotes represent 32nds; 101:01 means 101 1/32. Net changes in 32nds. Yields calculated on the asked quotation. ci-stripped coupon interest. bp-Treasury bond, stripped principal. np-Treasury note, stripped principal. For bonds callable prior to maturity, yields are computed to the earliest call date for issues quoted above par and to the maturity date for issues below par.

Source: Bear, Stearns & Co. via Street Software Technology Inc.

GOVT. BONDS & NOTES

Rate	Maturity Mo/Yr	Bid	Asked	Chg.	Ask Yld.
8 1/8	Sep 92n	100:05	100:07	....	0.00
8 3/4	Sep 92n	100:06	100:08	....	0.00
9 3/4	Oct 92n	100:16	100:18	....	1.12
7 3/4	Oct 92n	100:17	100:19	....	2.21
7 3/4	Nov 92n	100:23	100:25	....	2.44
8 3/8	Nov 92n	100:26	100:28	− 1	2.43
10 1/2	Nov 92n	101:05	101:07	− 1	2.24
7 3/8	Nov 92n	100:27	100:29	....	2.56
7 1/4	Dec 92n	101:06	101:08	....	2.62
9 1/8	Dec 92n	101:23	101:25	....	2.54
8 3/4	Jan 93n	101:26	101:28	....	2.71
7	Jan 93n	101:14	101:16	+ 1	2.75
4	Feb 88-93	99:26	100:10	+10	3.19
6 3/4	Feb 93	101:17	101:21	....	2.54
7 7/8	Feb 93	101:31	102:03	+ 1	2.56
8 1/4	Feb 93n	102:02	102:04	− 1	2.85
8 3/8	Feb 93n	102:04	102:06	....	2.81
10 7/8	Feb 93n	103:04	103:06	− 1	2.78
6 3/4	Feb 93n	101:21	101:23	....	2.80
7 1/8	Mar 93n	102:04	102:06	....	2.89
9 5/8	Mar 93n	103:15	103:17	....	2.80
7 3/8	Apr 93n	102:14	102:16	....	2.89
7	Apr 93n	102:12	102:14	+ 1	2.93
7 5/8	May 93n	102:29	102:31	....	2.98
8 5/8	May 93n	103:18	103:20	....	2.96
10 1/8	May 93n	104:17	104:19	....	2.94
6 3/4	May 93n	102:16	102:18	....	2.98
7	Jun 93n	102:31	103:01	....	3.02
8 1/8	Jun 93n	103:27	103:29	....	2.99
7 1/4	Jul 93n	103:09	103:11	....	3.07
6 7/8	Jul 93n	103:04	103:06	....	3.09
8	Aug 93n	104:08	104:10	+ 1	3.10
8 5/8	Aug 93	104:27	104:29	+ 1	3.06
8 3/4	Aug 93n	104:29	104:31	....	3.11
11 7/8	Aug 93n	107:23	107:25	....	3.05
6 3/8	Aug 93n	102:30	103:00	....	3.12
6 1/8	Sep 93n	102:29	102:31	....	3.16
8 1/4	Sep 93n	105:02	105:04	....	3.13
7 1/8	Oct 93n	104:02	104:04	....	3.16
6	Oct 93n	102:29	102:31	....	3.25
7 3/4	Nov 93n	104:31	105:01	....	3.26
8 5/8	Nov 93	105:31	106:01	....	3.24
9	Nov 93n	106:12	106:14	....	3.25
11 3/4	Nov 93n	109:15	109:17	− 1	3.24
5 1/2	Nov 93n	102:16	102:18	....	3.29
5	Dec 93n	102:01	102:03	+ 1	3.31
7 5/8	Dec 93n	105:09	105:11	....	3.31
7	Jan 94n	104:18	104:20	....	3.38
4 7/8	Jan 94n	101:28	101:30	....	3.40
6 7/8	Feb 94n	104:19	104:21	....	3.44
8 7/8	Feb 94n	107:11	107:13	....	3.41
9	Feb 94	107:17	107:21	....	3.36
5 3/8	Feb 94n	102:20	102:22	....	3.45
5 3/4	Mar 94n	103:08	103:10	....	3.50
8 1/2	Mar 94n	107:10	107:12	....	3.49
7	Apr 94n	105:05	105:07	....	3.54
5 3/8	Apr 94n	102:22	102:24	....	3.60
4 1/8	May 89-94	100:08	100:24	− 2	2.95
7	May 94n	105:09	105:11	+ 2	3.63
9 1/2	May 94n	109:09	109:11	+ 2	3.62
13 1/8	May 94n	115:06	115:08	− 1	3.53
5 1/8	May 94n	102:12	102:14	+ 1	3.63
5	Jun 94n	102:06	102:08	+ 1	3.68
8 1/2	Jun 94n	108:06	108:08	....	3.66
8	Jul 94n	107:14	107:16	+ 1	3.69
4 1/4	Jul 94n	100:27	100:29	+ 1	3.74
6 7/8	Aug 94n	105:19	105:21	....	3.76
8 5/8	Aug 94n	108:25	108:27	....	3.76
8 3/4	Aug 94	109:01	109:05	+ 1	3.71
12 5/8	Aug 94n	116:06	116:08	....	3.69
4 1/4	Aug 94n	100:25	100:27	+ 1	3.80
8 1/2	Sep 94n	109:01	109:03	+ 1	3.79
9 1/2	Oct 94n	111:00	111:02	....	3.88
6	Nov 94n	104:06	104:08	+ 2	3.92
8 1/4	Nov 94n	108:24	108:26	....	3.94
10 1/8	Nov 94	112:19	112:21	+ 1	3.93
11 5/8	Nov 94n	115:21	115:23	....	3.93
7 5/8	Dec 94n	107:28	107:30	+ 1	3.94
8 5/8	Jan 95n	110:01	110:03	+ 2	4.02
3	Feb 95	99:18	100:18	+21	2.76
5 1/2	Feb 95n	103:04	103:06	+ 2	4.09
7 3/4	Feb 95n	108:07	108:09	+ 1	4.09
10 1/2	Feb 95	114:15	114:17	+ 1	4.08
11 1/4	Feb 95n	116:05	116:07	+ 1	4.09
8 3/8	Apr 95n	110:02	110:04	+ 2	4.17
5 7/8	May 95n	104:02	104:04	+ 1	4.21
8 1/2	May 95n	110:19	110:21	+ 3	4.21
10 3/8	May 95	115:07	115:09	+ 2	4.22
11 1/4	May 95n	117:11	117:13	+ 1	4.24
12 5/8	May 95	121:00	121:04	+ 1	4.13
8 7/8	Jul 95n	111:30	112:00	+ 2	4.31
4 5/8	Aug 95n	100:24	100:26	+ 2	4.32
8 1/2	Aug 95n	111:04	111:06	+ 3	4.35
10 1/2	Aug 95n	116:16	116:18	+ 2	4.36
8 5/8	Oct 95n	111:25	111:27	+ 2	4.45
8 1/2	Nov 95n	111:19	111:21	+ 3	4.49
9 1/2	Nov 95n	114:17	114:19	+ 2	4.48
11 1/2	Nov 95	120:10	120:14	+ 2	4.47
9 1/4	Jan 96n	114:00	114:02	+ 3	4.63
7 1/2	Jan 96n	108:26	108:28	+ 3	4.62
7 7/8	Feb 96n	109:29	109:31	+ 2	4.67
8 7/8	Feb 96n	113:01	113:03	+ 2	4.67
7 1/2	Feb 96n	108:25	108:27	+ 2	4.69
7 3/4	Mar 96n	109:19	109:21	− 1	4.74
9 3/8	Apr 96n	114:28	114:30	+ 1	4.77
7 5/8	Apr 96n	109:08	109:10	+ 1	4.79
7 3/8	May 96n	108:14	108:16	+ 1	4.81
7 5/8	May 96n	109:09	109:11	+ 1	4.83
7 7/8	Jun 96n	110:07	110:09	+ 1	4.86
7 7/8	Jul 96n	110:05	110:07	....	4.91
7 7/8	Jul 96n	110:05	110:07	+ 1	4.94
7 1/4	Aug 96n	108:02	108:04	+ 1	4.96
7	Sep 96n	107:05	107:07	....	5.00
8	Oct 96n	110:23	110:25	....	5.03
6 7/8	Oct 96n	106:22	106:24	+ 1	5.04
7 1/4	Nov 96n	107:31	108:01	....	5.08
6 1/2	Nov 96n	105:07	105:09	....	5.09
6 1/8	Dec 96n	103:27	103:29	+ 2	5.10
8	Jan 97n	110:27	110:29	+ 1	5.15
6 1/4	Jan 97n	104:02	104:04	+ 1	5.18
6 3/4	Feb 97n	105:29	105:31	+ 1	5.23
6 7/8	Mar 97n	106:10	106:12	+ 1	5.27
8 1/2	Apr 97n	112:23	112:25	....	5.31
6 7/8	Apr 97n	106:09	106:11	....	5.31
8 1/2	May 97n	112:30	113:00	− 1	5.31
6 3/4	May 97n	105:25	105:27	+ 2	5.33
6 3/8	Jun 97n	104:08	104:10	+ 1	5.34
8 1/2	Jul 97n	113:02	113:04	....	5.37
5 1/2	Jul 97n	100:19	100:21	+ 2	5.34
8 5/8	Aug 97n	113:23	113:25	+ 1	5.39
5 5/8	Aug 97n	101:01	101:03	− 1	5.37
8 3/4	Oct 97n	114:12	114:14	....	5.45
8 7/8	Nov 97n	115:01	115:03	....	5.47
7 7/8	Jan 98n	110:18	110:20	− 1	5.54
8 1/8	Feb 98n	111:25	111:27	− 1	5.56
7 7/8	Apr 98n	110:21	110:23	....	5.61
7	May 93-98	102:18	102:26	....	2.61
9	May 98n	116:01	116:03	....	5.63
8 1/4	Jul 98n	112:12	112:14	− 1	5.71
9 1/4	Aug 98n	117:13	117:15	− 1	5.72
7 1/8	Oct 98n	106:26	106:28	− 2	5.77
3 1/2	Nov 98	98:14	99:14	+ 6	3.60
8 7/8	Nov 98n	115:22	115:24	....	5.79
6 3/8	Jan 99n	102:23	102:25	+ 1	5.84
8 7/8	Feb 99n	115:23	115:25	....	5.88
7	Apr 99n	105:28	105:30	− 2	5.90
8 1/2	May 94-99	107:06	107:14	− 5	3.81
9 1/8	May 99n	117:08	117:10	....	5.94
6 3/8	Jul 99n	102:17	102:19	− 1	5.91
8	Aug 99n	111:05	111:07	− 2	5.99
7 7/8	Nov 99n	110:14	110:16	− 2	6.04
7 7/8	Feb 95-00	107:17	107:21	....	4.48
8 1/2	Feb 00n	114:00	114:02	− 1	6.11
8 7/8	May 00n	116:08	116:10	+ 1	6.17
8 3/8	Aug 95-00	109:26	109:30	....	4.67
8 3/4	Aug 00n	115:15	115:17	− 1	6.23
8 1/2	Nov 00n	114:00	114:02	+ 3	6.27
7 3/4	Feb 01n	109:03	109:05	+ 2	6.33
11 3/4	Feb 01	135:03	135:07	+ 1	6.29
8	May 01n	110:21	110:23	+ 2	6.37
13 1/8	May 01	144:30	145:02	+ 2	6.29
7 7/8	Aug 01n	109:24	109:26	+ 2	6.41
8	Aug 96-01	108:21	108:25	+ 3	5.47
13 3/8	Aug 01	147:14	147:18	+ 2	6.31
7 1/2	Nov 01n	107:04	107:06	+ 2	6.45
15 3/4	Nov 01	164:15	164:19	+ 3	6.34
14 1/4	Feb 02	154:31	155:03	+ 1	6.37
7 1/2	May 02n	107:10	107:12	+ 2	6.46
6 3/8	Aug 02n	99:27	99:29	+ 2	6.39
11 5/8	Nov 02	137:25	137:29	+ 2	6.47
10 3/4	Feb 03	131:10	131:14	+ 2	6.54
10 3/4	May 03	131:20	131:24	+ 1	6.56
11 1/8	Aug 03	134:29	135:01	+ 4	6.57
11 7/8	Nov 03	141:01	141:05	+ 2	6.60
12 3/8	May 04	145:27	145:31	+ 3	6.65
13 3/4	Aug 04	157:14	157:18	+ 1	6.67
11 5/8	Nov 04	139:31	140:03	+ 3	6.74
8 1/4	May 00-05	110:22	110:26	....	6.44
12	May 05	143:27	143:31	+ 2	6.77
10 3/4	Aug 05	133:14	133:18	+ 3	6.80
9 3/8	Feb 06	122:11	122:15	+ 3	6.79
7 5/8	Feb 02-07	106:16	106:20	− 1	6.67
7 7/8	Nov 02-07	108:10	108:14	+ 7	6.72
8 3/8	Aug 03-08	111:31	112:03	+ 3	6.79
8 3/4	Nov 03-08	114:25	114:29	....	6.82
9 1/8	May 04-09	117:20	117:24	− 5	6.88
10 3/8	Nov 04-09	128:09	128:13	....	6.89
11 3/4	Feb 05-10	139:29	140:01	+ 2	6.90
10	May 05-10	125:24	125:28	+ 4	6.90
12 3/4	Nov 05-10	149:27	149:31	+ 1	6.91
13 7/8	May 06-11	160:21	160:25	+ 3	6.92
14	Nov 06-11	163:02	163:06	+ 3	6.92
10 3/8	Nov 07-12	130:18	130:22	+ 2	7.05
12	Aug 08-13	146:14	146:18	+ 2	7.08
13 1/4	May 09-14	159:15	159:19	+ 3	7.09
12 1/2	Aug 09-14	152:13	152:17	+ 3	7.11
11 3/4	Nov 09-14	145:07	145:11	+ 5	7.13
11 1/4	Feb 15	143:01	143:03	+ 1	7.31
10 5/8	Aug 15	136:05	136:07	− 1	7.34
9 7/8	Nov 15	127:29	127:31	+ 3	7.34
9 1/4	Feb 16	120:28	120:30	+ 2	7.36
7 1/4	May 16	98:16	98:18	+ 3	7.38
7 1/2	Nov 16	101:06	101:08	+ 2	7.39
8 3/4	May 17	115:13	115:15	+ 2	7.38
8 7/8	Aug 17	116:28	116:30	+ 2	7.38
9 1/8	May 18	119:28	119:30	+ 2	7.38
9	Nov 18	118:16	118:18	+ 3	7.39
8 7/8	Feb 19	117:02	117:04	+ 3	7.39
8 1/8	Aug 19	108:12	108:14	+ 4	7.40
8 1/2	Feb 20	112:25	112:27	+ 3	7.40
8 3/4	May 20	115:25	115:27	+ 2	7.40
8 3/4	Aug 20	115:26	115:28	+ 4	7.40
7 7/8	Feb 21	105:18	105:20	+ 2	7.40
8 1/8	May 21	108:18	108:20	+ 2	7.40
8 1/8	Aug 21	108:18	108:20	+ 3	7.40
8	Nov 21	107:07	107:09	+ 2	7.39
7 1/4	Aug 22	98:30	99:00	+ 3	7.33

TREASURY BILLS

Maturity	Days to Mat.	Bid	Asked	Chg.	Ask Yld.
Sep 24 '92	3	2.65	2.55	+0.03	2.59
Oct 01 '92	10	2.59	2.49	....	2.53
Oct 08 '92	17	2.73	2.63	+0.03	2.67
Oct 15 '92	24	2.73	2.63	+0.04	2.67
Oct 22 '92	31	2.81	2.77	+0.01	2.82
Oct 29 '92	38	2.79	2.75	+0.01	2.80
Nov 05 '92	45	2.82	2.78	+0.01	2.83
Nov 12 '92	52	2.82	2.78	−0.01	2.83
Nov 19 '92	59	2.84	2.82	−0.01	2.88
Nov 27 '92	67	2.85	2.83	....	2.88
Dec 03 '92	73	2.88	2.86	−0.01	2.92
Dec 10 '92	80	2.88	2.86	−0.01	2.92
Dec 17 '92	**87**	**2.88**	**2.86**	**−0.02**	**2.93**
Dec 24 '92	94	2.88	2.86	−0.01	2.92
Dec 31 '92	101	2.84	2.82	−0.02	2.88
Jan 07 '93	108	2.88	2.86	−0.02	2.92
Jan 14 '93	115	2.89	2.87	−0.03	2.94
Jan 21 '93	122	2.91	2.89	....	2.96
Jan 28 '93	129	2.91	2.89	−0.01	2.96
Feb 04 '93	136	2.92	2.90	....	2.97
Feb 11 '93	143	2.92	2.90	−0.01	2.98
Feb 18 '93	150	2.93	2.91	....	2.99
Feb 25 '93	157	2.93	2.91	....	2.99
Mar 04 '93	164	2.93	2.91	....	2.99
Mar 11 '93	171	2.91	2.89	−0.01	2.97
Mar 18 '93	**178**	**2.92**	**2.90**	**−0.01**	**2.98**
Apr 08 '93	199	2.93	2.91	....	2.99
May 06 '93	227	2.95	2.93	−0.01	3.02
Jun 03 '93	255	2.95	2.93	−0.01	3.02
Jul 01 '93	283	3.00	2.98	+0.01	3.08
Jul 29 '93	311	3.02	3.00	....	3.10
Aug 26 '93	339	3.03	3.01	....	3.12

Source: The Wall Street Journal, September 18, 1992, C14.

FIGURE 7.2 | **Yields of Treasury Securities, March 31, 1989**

The yield curve in March 1989 was downward-sloping, or inverted: Short-term rates were higher than long-term rates.

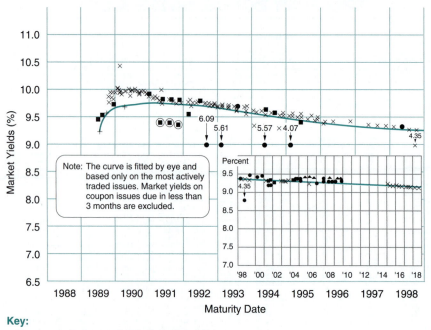

Note: The curve is fitted by eye and based only on the most actively traded issues. Market yields on coupon issues due in less than 3 months are excluded.

Key:
× Fixed maturity coupon issues less than 12%.
■ Fixed maturity coupon issues of 12% or more.
● Callable coupon issues less than 12%.
▲ Callable coupon issues of 12% or more.
  Note: Callable issues are plotted to the earliest call date when prices are above par and to maturity when prices are at par or below.
+ Bills. Coupon equivalent yield of the latest 13-week, 26-week, 52-week bills.

Source: Treasury Bulletin, June 1989, 55.

sloping yield curve has been common. During periods of sluggish economic performance, such as the mid-1970s, the yield curve is usually upward-sloping. This pattern was repeated when an inverted curve before July 1981 was followed by a "normal" one as the 1981–1982 recession took hold.[5]

The next downward-sloping curve appeared for a brief period in 1989 (recall Figure 7.2), although it is not seen in the annual averages plotted in Figure 7.5. At the time, some economists suggested that an inverted term structure might no longer signal a recession. Previously, recessions were the only times that market participants seemed to expect interest rates to decline. But surveys of financial institution managers in the late 1980s revealed expectations of a prolonged decline in the rate of inflation, particularly relative to inflation in the early part of the decade. Some experts suggested that the downward-sloping curve meant only that a smaller inflationary premium would be built into future short-term rates, not that a recession

---

[5] From the beginning of World War II until 1951, Federal Reserve policies actually kept the term structure independent of the level of economic activity. Controls were lifted by President Harry Truman making rates free to move according to the supply of and demand for funds. For more discussion of this policy and the accord that brought it to an end, see Wallich and Keir 1979. (References are listed in full at the end of this chapter.)

FIGURE 7.3 Yields of Treasury Securities, March 31, 1992

The yield curve in early 1992 was upward-sloping, or normal: Short-term rates were lower than long-term rates.

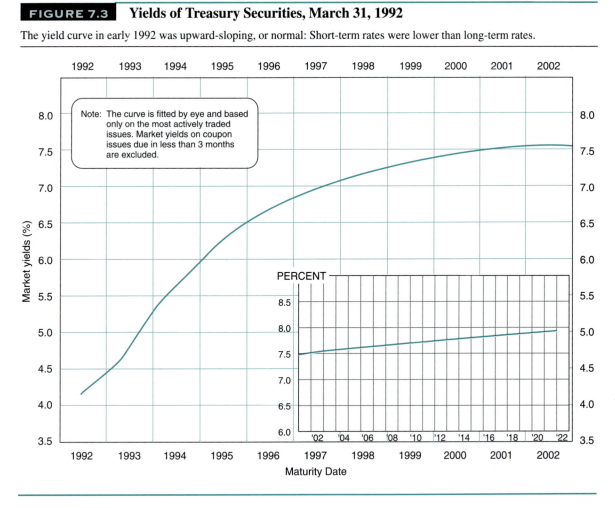

Source: Treasury Bulletin, June 1992, 78.

was at hand.[6] This alternate interpretation of the inverted yield curve proved, of course, to be incorrect. The U.S. economy fell into a prolonged recession in the early 1990s, confirming once again the difficulties encountered by economic forecasters.

A different perspective on historical term structures is shown in Figure 7.6. When the general level of rates has been relatively high, term structures have tended to slope downward, and they have sloped upward when the general level has been relatively low.

From 1900 to 1929, as the general level of rates drifted upward, yield curves gradually changed shape from flat to inverted. From 1930 to 1981, as rates gradually moved higher, yield curves also shifted from upward-sloping to downward-sloping. Scholars have inferred from curves such as those illustrated in Figure 7.6B that the financial markets may periodically revise their opinions of what represents a high general level. Before the 1930s, for example, a 7 percent short-term rate may have been considered high, although by the 1970s, such a rate was considered relatively low. In this context, the 1982 normal curve was an aberration from recent history. As Figures 7.2, 7.3, and 7.4

[6] See Furlong 1989 and Stevens 1989.

FIGURE 7.4   **Yields of Treasury Securities, December 31, 1988**

The yield curve in late 1988 was almost flat: Short-term and long-term rates were approximately equal.

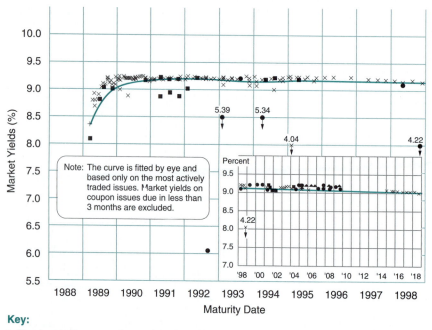

Key:

× Fixed maturity coupon issues less than 12%.
■ Fixed maturity coupon issues of 12% or more.
● Callable coupon issues less than 12%.
▲ Callable coupon issues of 12% or more.
  Note: Callable issues are plotted to the earliest call date when prices are above par
  and to maturity when prices are at par or below.
+ Bills. Coupon equivalent yield of the latest 13-week, 26-week, 52-week bills.

Source: Treasury Bulletin, March 1989, 59.

indicate, during the late 1980s and early 1990s the general level of interest rates fell and yield curve levels appeared similar to those from the 1960s and 1970s.

One important difference observed in the early 1990s, however, was the extremely steep slope of the yield curve. As shown in Figure 7.7, although short-term interest rate levels were similar to those prevailing in the 1960s, the relative differential between short-term and long-term rates was most unusual. By August 1992, when the yield on 3-month T-bills was just above 3 percent, the yield on 30-year T-bonds was more than twice that, at 7.3 percent. Experts attributed this differential to investor uncertainties about long-

term economic conditions, including the outlook for inflation and stability in the world currency markets.[7]

UNBIASED (PURE) EXPECTATIONS THEORY

Historical patterns and the reasons for their existence provide clues about when to expect shifts in the term structure, but they are no substitute for a theoretical

[7] For more discussion, see Wood 1983; Blalock 1993; and Cogley 1993.

| FIGURE 7.5 | **Long- and Short-Term Interest Rates** |

Short-term rates have been lower than long-term rates most of the time in this century. Periods when short-term rates were higher have often coincided with peaks in the business cycle, leading to subsequent recessions.

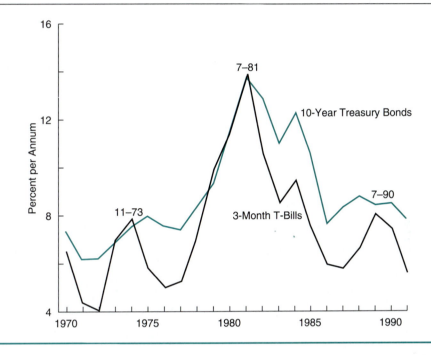

Source: Board of Governors of the Federal Reserve System, *Federal Reserve Bulletin,* various issues.

understanding of the yield curve. Understanding how the term structure is determined is complicated by economists' lack of agreement on any single explanation. The existence of several theories should not be discouraging, however, because each provides insights the others lack. The body of knowledge is valuable for managers who make decisions involving assets and liabilities of different maturities.

Perhaps the most influential of the term structure theories is the **unbiased (pure) expectations theory,** which holds that observable long-term yields are the average of expected, but directly unobservable, short-term yields.[8] For example, this theory argues that the

spot rate on 20-year T-bonds is the average of expected annual yields on short-term Treasury securities over the next 20 years. Theoretically, there is no best definition of "short-term" or "long-term." For simplicity, most of the following examples define short-term as 1 year; however, the pure expectations theory also holds that the observed yield on 1-year securities is the average of expected rates on shorter-maturity securities during the year. *Short-* and *long-term* can therefore be defined as the decision maker desires.

ASSUMPTIONS OF THE PURE EXPECTATIONS THEORY

The pure expectations theory rests on important assumptions about investors (lenders or demanders of securities) and markets:

1. All else equal, investors are indifferent between owning a single long-term security or a series of

---

[8] Irving Fisher, discussed in the previous chapter in connection with inflation and the general level of rates, is often credited with the first statement of the pure expectations hypothesis in 1896. The theory was not fully developed until several decades later, however, when both J. R. Hicks (1946) and Frederick Lutz (1940) pursued it. More recent discussions are found in Malkiel 1966 and Meiselman 1962.

FIGURE 7.6   **Yield Curves for High-Grade Corporate Bonds, 1900–1929 and 1930–1982**

When the general level of interest rates is relatively high, yield curves are usually downward-sloping. When the general level is relatively low, the yield curve often slopes upward.

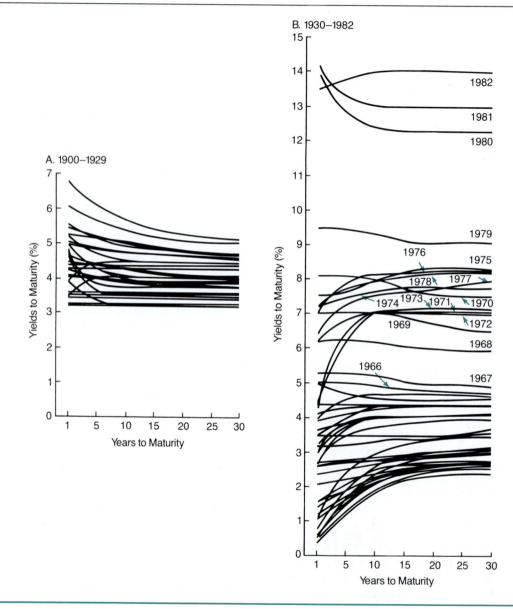

Source: John Wood, "Do Yield Curves Normally Slope Up? The Term Structure of Interest Rates, 1862–1982," *Economic Perspectives* (Federal Reserve Bank of Chicago) 7 (July/August 1983): 18.

FIGURE 7.7   **Yields of Treasury Securities, 1991 and 1992**

The term structure of interest rates exhibited a very steep slope in 1991 and 1992, presenting a strong contrast to earlier periods when the differential between short-term and long-term rates was much smaller.

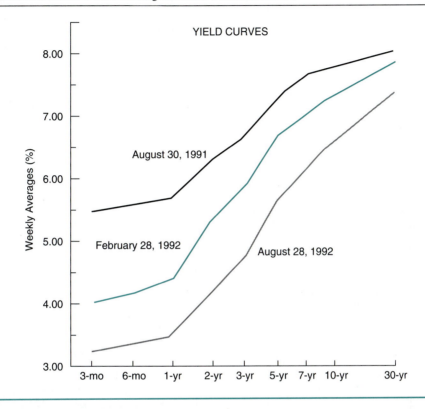

Source: Economic Trends (Federal Reserve Bank of Cleveland) (September 1992): 5.

short-term securities over the same time period. In other words, maturity alone does not affect investors' choice of investments.

2. All investors hold common expectations about the course of short-term rates.

3. On average, investors are able to predict rates accurately. Their expectations about future rates are unbiased in the *statistical* sense—they are neither consistently low nor consistently high.

4. There are no taxes, information costs, or transaction costs in the financial markets. Investors are free to exchange securities of varying maturities quickly and without penalty.

The main implication of the pure expectations theory follows directly from these assumptions. *For a*

given holding period, the average expected annual yields on all combinations of maturities will be equal.[9] For example, the theory holds that the average annual yield on a series of 1-year investments over a specific 5-year period will be the same as the average annual yield on a single 3-year investment followed by two 1-year investments *and* the same as the average annual yield on a single 5-year security. Because investors are assumed to be indifferent about the maturity of their holdings and because they have common and accurate predictions about future rates, they will demand

---

[9]Recently, some scholars have argued that this implication holds strictly only for a specific holding period of instantaneous duration and that it is incompatible with other versions of the expectations hypothesis, such as the statement that long-term spot rates are the average of expected short-term rates. See Cox, Ingersoll, and Ross 1981.

securities at prices that equalize average annual yields over the period. Investors simply have no incentive to prefer one combination of maturities over another. Annual yields currently available on long-term securities will be the average of expected annual yields on shorter-term instruments.

MATHEMATICS OF THE PURE EXPECTATIONS THEORY

Mathematically, the theory is expressed by the following formula:

$$1 + {}_1\bar{i}_n = \sqrt[n]{\prod_{t=1}^{n} (1 + {}_t\tilde{i}_1)} \qquad [7.1]$$

$$= \sqrt[n]{(1 + {}_1\tilde{i}_1)(1 + {}_2\tilde{i}_1) \cdots (1 + {}_n\tilde{i}_1)}$$

The "average" of rates referred to earlier is not the simple arithmetic average; the symbol $\prod$ directs the user to multiply, not add, a series of expressions from $t = 1$ to $t = n$. The left subscript in each term identifies the beginning of a particular time period. The right subscript in each term indicates the maturity to which a particular yield applies. Thus, for example, the term $(1 + {}_2\tilde{i}_1)$ refers to 1 plus the 1-year (right subscript) yield as of the beginning of period 2 (left subscript). Equation 7.1 states that the *observed* yield in period 1 $({}_1\bar{i}_n)$ on an n-period security is the **geometric average** of a series of one-period *expected* yields $({}_t\tilde{i}_1)$ from period 1 to period n. The geometric average is calculated by taking the n-th root of the *product* of (1 + expected one-period yields) and subtracting 1 from the root. This calculation assumes reinvestment, at rate ${}_t\tilde{i}_1$, of all proceeds throughout the holding period. In practice, the one-period yield currently observed in the securities market is used as the one-period expected yield at $t = 1$; that is, ${}_1\tilde{i}_1 = {}_1\bar{i}_1$.[10]

Table 7.1 contains investors' expectations for 1-year yields during the period January 1994 to January 1998. The first three columns are used in the following

examples. The fourth column of liquidity premiums is used later.

According to the unbiased expectations theory and from these expectations alone, Equation 7.1 gives the following yield to maturity on a 4-year Treasury security bought in January 1994 (the beginning of period 1) and maturing in January 1998:

$$1 + {}_1\bar{i}_n = \sqrt[n]{\prod_{t=1}^{n} (1 + {}_t\tilde{i}_1)}$$

$$1 + {}_1\bar{i}_4 = \sqrt[4]{\prod_{t=1}^{4} (1 + {}_t\tilde{i}_1)}$$

$$1 + {}_1\bar{i}_4 = \sqrt[4]{(1.0850)(1.0950)(1.1100)(1.1175)}$$

$${}_1\bar{i}_4 = 1.10180 - 1 = 0.10180 = 10.180\%$$

Given the same set of expectations and again using Equation 7.1, it is possible to calculate spot yields on securities with 2- and 3-year maturities as of January 1994:

$$1 + {}_1\bar{i}_2 = \sqrt{(1.0850)(1.0950)}$$

$${}_1\bar{i}_2 = 1.08999 - 1 = 0.08999 = 8.999\%$$

$$1 + {}_1\bar{i}_3 = \sqrt[3]{(1.0850)(1.0950)(1.1100)}$$

$${}_1\bar{i}_3 = 1.09662 - 1 = 0.09662 = 9.662\%$$

The unbiased expectations theory implies that investors' expectations of rising short-term yields will result in an upward-sloping yield curve for Treasury securities as of January 1994, as shown in Figure 7.8.

If the pure expectations theory is correct, the average annual yield an investor could obtain over the period 1994–1998 is the same, regardless of the investment strategy chosen. If the investor decides to buy four 1-year securities, the average annual yield over the holding period (i_H) will be 10.180 percent. If, instead, the investments are a 2-year security in January 1994 (annual yield of 8.999 percent) and two successive 1-year T-bills in 1996 and 1997 (expected yields of 11.000 percent and 11.750 percent, respectively), the average annual yield for this strategy is

$$1 + i_H = \sqrt[4]{(1.08999)(1.08999)(1.11000)(1.11750)}$$

$$i_H = 1.10180 - 1 = 10.180\%$$

Or, if an investor buys a 3-year T-note in 1994 (annual

---

[10] The notation for pure expectations mathematics is invariably confusing. Present and compound value calculations usually emphasize end-of-period cash flows, so $t = 1$ usually means the end of period 1 and $t = n$ means the end of period n. That usage prevails in most chapters in this book. The pure expectations theory focuses on beginning-of-period expectations, however, so $t = 1$ means the beginning of period 1 (or the end of period 0), and the notation $t = n$ means the beginning of period n.

TABLE 7.1	**Observed and Expected 1-Year Yields and Premiums as of January 1994**

These hypothetical data on observed and expected 1-year rates and liquidity premiums can be used to estimate the shape of a yield curve.

Bill Purchased	Bill Matures	Observed or Expected Annual Yield (%)	Liquidity Premium (%)
January 1994	January 1995	8.50% observed ($_1\bar{i}_1$)	0.00% (on 1-year security)
January 1995	January 1996	9.50% expected ($_2\bar{i}_1$)	0.35% (on 2-year security)
January 1996	January 1997	11.00% expected ($_3\bar{i}_1$)	0.45% (on 3-year security)
January 1997	January 1998	11.75% expected ($_4\bar{i}_1$)	0.50% (on 4-year security)

$$1 +_1\bar{i}_3 = \sqrt{(1.085)(1.095)(1.11)} = 1.09662$$

yield of 9.662 percent), followed by a 1-year bill in 1997 (11.750 percent expected yield), the average annual yield for the holding period is

$$1 + i_H = \sqrt[4]{(1.09662)(1.09662)(1.09662)(1.11750)}$$

$$i_H = 1.10180 - 1 = 10.180\%$$

Under the assumptions of investor indifference to maturity and unbiased expectations of future short-term rates, any combination of maturities over the period will result in an average annual yield of 10.180 percent. This will be true as long as all proceeds are reinvested and expectations of future rates remain constant during the period. In other words, the 10.180 percent average 4-year yield would be expected as long as investors do not revise their 1-year predictions for 1996, for example, at some point after 1994.

MODIFICATIONS OF THE UNBIASED EXPECTATIONS THEORY

The unbiased expectations theory succinctly explains the shape of any term structure: Lenders' expectations

FIGURE 7.8	**Hypothetical Observed Yield Curve, January 1994**

Because long-term yields are the average of expected short-term yields, if short-term rates are expected to increase, the pure expectations theory holds that the term structure will be upward-sloping.

$$1 +_1\bar{i}_2 = \sqrt{(1.085)(1.095)}$$
$$_1\bar{i}_2 = 8.999\%$$

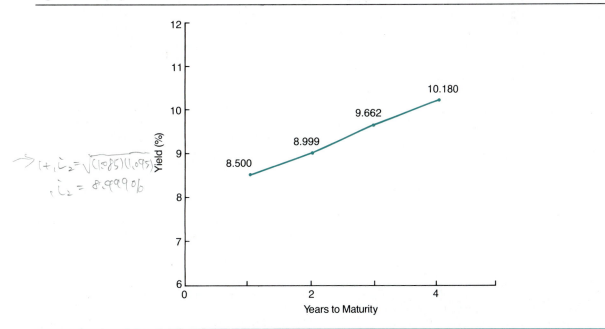

of rising short-term rates produce an observable upward-sloping yield curve; expectations of falling short-term rates produce a downward-sloping term structure; and expectations of unchanging rates produce a flat yield curve. Changes in the shape of the curve over time, such as those implied by Figures 7.5, 7.6, and 7.7, can be easily explained by changes in expectations. Also, the theory appeals to researchers because its mathematical form provides testable hypotheses as well as the opportunity to develop models for predicting interest rates.

CRITICISMS OF THE UNBIASED EXPECTATIONS THEORY

The theory is not without its critics, however, who focus on its restrictive assumptions as serious shortcomings. In particular, investors' assumed indifference between short- and long-term securities ignores the fact that a long-term investment may be riskier than a series of short-term investments. Risk, brought about by the passage of time alone, is rarely a matter of indifference. Even for two securities of the same issuer with equal initial default risk, the probability of default may increase on the long-term security over time. Furthermore, investors are never certain that personal circumstances will allow them to follow initial investment strategies throughout the holding period. If emergencies arise, they may have to sell long-term securities at a loss when forced to abandon their initial plans.[11]

A second assumption that troubles critics is that, according to the theory, issuers of securities have no influence on the term structure. This appears to contradict the negotiation process that actually occurs between borrowers and lenders in many financial markets. It is important to remember that no theory should be judged on the realism of its assumptions. The test of a theory is how well it explains "real world" relationships, and the theory enjoys some qualified empirical support. However, these criticisms have led to some theoretical modifications.

THE LIQUIDITY PREMIUM HYPOTHESIS

The belief that most investors find long-term securities to be riskier than short-term securities has led to the **liquidity premium hypothesis.** According to this theory, today's long-term rates reflect the geometric average of intervening expected short-term rates *plus* a premium that investors demand for holding long-term securities instead of a series of short-term, less risky investments. The hypothesized effect of these liquidity premiums—also called **term premiums**—on the term structure can be illustrated by considering the fourth column of Table 7.1.[12]

Using the unbiased expectations theory, spot rates of 8.99 percent, 9.66 percent, and 10.18 percent were calculated earlier for 2-, 3-, and 4-year maturities. According to the liquidity premium hypothesis, the following yields would be observed instead, using Equation 7.1 with the premium added:

$$1 + {}_1\bar{I}_2 = \sqrt{(1.0850)(1.0950 + 0.0035)}$$
$${}_1\bar{I}_2 = 1.0917 - 1 = 0.0917 = 9.17\%$$

$$1 + {}_1\bar{I}_3 = \sqrt[3]{\begin{array}{c}(1.0850) \times (1.0950 + 0.0035) \\ \times (1.1100 + 0.0045)\end{array}}$$
$${}_1\bar{I}_3 = 1.0993 - 1 = 0.0993 = 9.93\%$$

$$1 + {}_1\bar{I}_4 = \sqrt[4]{\begin{array}{c}(1.0850) \times (1.0950 + 0.0035) \\ \times (1.1100 + 0.0045) \times (1.1175 \\ + 0.0050)\end{array}}$$
$${}_1\bar{I}_4 = 1.1050 - 1 = 0.1050 = 10.50\%$$

Because investors are no longer indifferent among maturities, the same expectations are supplemented by a premium for holding long-term securities. As shown in Figure 7.9, this term structure has a steeper slope than the term structure illustrated in Figure 7.8, which

---

[11] For an investor who holds the investment throughout the planned holding period, another element of risk must be considered—the potential for *unexpected* changes in short-term yields. If such changes occur, the investor faces uncertainty from periodic reinvestment rates. This source of risk is discussed in more detail in Chapter 8.

[12] Presentations of the liquidity premium hypothesis can be found in Hicks 1946; and Kessel 1965.

Although it is easy to incorporate given liquidity premiums into the basic pure expectations equation, it is more difficult to specify the structure of liquidity premiums themselves. Scholars disagree about how to model them, but for illustrative purposes, liquidity premiums in these examples are considered to increase with time. A brief review of alternative specifications is provided later in the chapter.

FIGURE 7.9   **Hypothetical Yield Curve with Liquidity Premiums**

If short-term rates are expected to increase and if investors demand a premium for holding long-term securities, long-term yields will be higher than if expectations alone are considered.

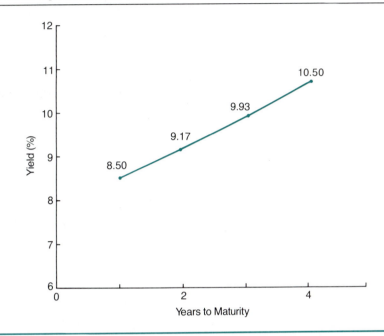

was based on the same expectations but assumed no liquidity premiums.

A general restatement of the term structure including liquidity premiums is seen in Equation 7.2:

$$(1 + {}_1\bar{\imath}_n) = \sqrt[n]{\prod_{t=1}^{n} (1 + {}_t\bar{\imath}_1 + L_t)} \qquad [7.2]$$

where

L_t = liquidity premium for holding a t-period security instead of a 1-year security. By definition, $L_1 = 0$.

The liquidity premium hypothesis does not rule out the possibility of downward-sloping yield curves, although some economists believe that it explains why they are less common. If investors expect future short-term rates to fall sharply, the pure expectations theory holds that a steeply downward-sloping curve should be observed in the spot markets. If investors also demand a premium for investing long-term, the observed yield curve might still be inverted, but it would be more gently sloped than if determined by expectations alone, as shown in Figure 7.10.

It is even possible, according to the liquidity premium hypothesis, that a yield curve reflecting expectations of falling rates could appear to be upward-sloping if investors demanded a relatively high premium on long-term issues. Such a situation is illustrated in Figure 7.11.

INCORPORATING THE ROLE OF LENDERS

Other theories of the term structure are distinguished from the pure expectations approach because they include a role for lenders in the determination of spot rates, and they discard the assumption of indifference between maturities.

THE MODIFIED EXPECTATIONS THEORY. One theory is sometimes called the **modified expectations theory**

FIGURE 7.10   Pure Expectations and Liquidity Premiums

If short-term rates are expected to decrease sharply and if investors also demand a premium for holding long-term securities, the slope of the yield curve will be less steep than if expectations alone are considered.

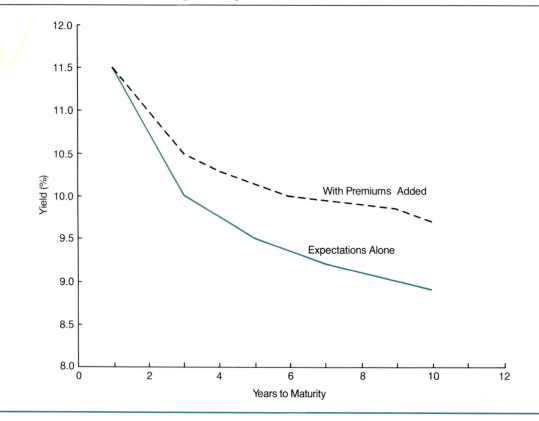

to reflect support for the idea that expectations of future rates do, in fact, determine today's yields.[13] As this argument goes, if interest rates are expected to rise in the future, lenders may wish to lend short-term to avoid locking in today's lower spot rates. Such a long-term commitment would not only prevent reinvestment of principal at the expected higher rates, but it also would subject lenders to capital losses should they sell their investments before maturity. However, borrowers will wish to borrow long-term to avoid expected higher interest costs.

According to the theory, the common expectations of borrowers and lenders and their conflicting maturity preferences put pressure on long-term rates,

producing an upward-sloping curve. Conversely, when all parties expect interest rates to fall, lenders wish to lend long, but borrowers prefer to roll over a series of short-term loans at progressively lower expected rates. This places upward pressure on short-term rates, resulting in an inverted term structure. Thus, the conclusions of the modified expectations theory are the same as those for the unbiased expectations theory: Expectations of rising rates produce an upward-sloping curve, while expectations of falling rates produce a downward-sloping relationship. The main difference between the theories is the motivations determining spot rates.

THE SEGMENTED MARKETS THEORY. Relying heavily on the existence of market imperfections, the **segmented markets theory** argues that there really is

---

[13] Smith 1960. The modified expectations theory produces the same mathematical model as the pure expectations theory (Equation 7.1).

| FIGURE 7.11 | **Transformation of an Inverted Curve** |

If short-term rates are expected to decrease slightly and if investors also demand a premium for holding long-term securities, the yield curve could be slightly upward-sloping.

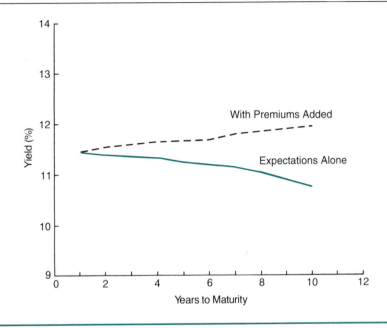

no term structure. The segmentation theory has gained especially strong support among market participants.[14] It suggests that different spot rates on long- and short-term securities are explained not by any common set of market expectations, nor by a liquidity premium to induce lenders to switch from short- to long-term securities, but rather by separate supply/demand interactions in the financial markets. According to this theory, short-term yields result from interactions of individuals and institutions in the short-term market segment; the same is true of yields on long-term securities. Because laws, regulations, or institutional objectives prevent many market participants from borrowing or lending in every segment, some maturities are of little concern.

One justification for the segmented markets theory is that it reflects the preference of financial institutions to match the maturities of their assets and liabilities. Commercial banks, for example, have traditionally concentrated on lending in the short-term markets while obtaining funds from depositors in that same segment of the market. Similar segmented supply/demand factors may affect long-term rates. Life insurance firms expect long-term payment inflows from customers and invest those funds heavily in instruments with long maturities.

According to the segmented markets theory, what might seem to be a downward-sloping yield curve is really many distinct—and theoretically unrelated—market interactions, as shown in Figure 7.12. Notice the similarities between this hypothetical curve and the actual term structure of interest rates shown in Figure 7.13. For example, proponents of the market segmentation theory believe that the yield curve on December 31, 1969, clearly reveals distinct financial market segments. This theory has implications for interest rate forecasting that are quite distinct from those of the expectations hypothesis. It returns forecasting solely to supply/demand in market segments and relies on forecasting methods similar to those discussed in Chapter 6.

[14] See Culbertson 1957.

FIGURE 7.12   **Yields in Segmented Markets**

The segmented markets theory holds that the term structure is not continuous. Instead, supply and demand in separate financial markets determine the yields in those markets.

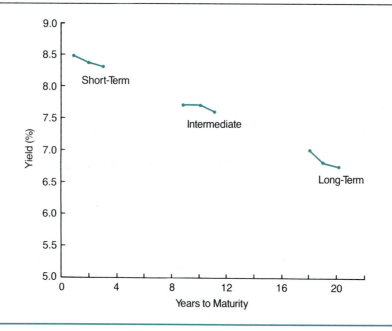

THE PREFERRED HABITAT THEORY. Closely related to the segmented markets theory is the **preferred habitat theory,** which assumes that although investors may strongly prefer particular segments of the market, they are not necessarily locked in to those segments. These strong preferences for certain maturities arise not from legal or regulatory reasons but, rather, from *consumption* preferences.[15] In other words, investors' time preferences for spending versus saving influence their choice among securities. They will lend in markets other than their preferred one, but only if a premium exists to induce them to switch. This argument differs from the liquidity premium theory in that it does not assume that all lenders prefer short-term securities to long-term ones. There may well be lenders who prefer to lend long but who can be induced to lend short for a yield premium, or vice versa.

---

[15] See Modigliani and Sutch 1966. Cox, Ingersoll, and Ross (1981) argued instead that risk aversion, not time-related consumption preferences, will create preferred habitats. In particular, they interpreted a habitat "as a stronger or weaker tendency to hedge against changes in the interest rate" (p. 786).

Although the preferred habitat theory recognizes that some lenders may not be persuaded to depart from their preferred habitats at any price, it holds that the markets are only partially segmented because many participants *are* willing to switch maturities if properly rewarded. Short- and long-term yield differentials are only partially explained by the expectations hypothesis; supply/demand imbalances in various markets may result in positive or negative premiums added to the pure expectations rate to induce shifts from one segment to another. Thus, the preferred habitat theory differs from the segmented markets theory in the following ways:

1. It relies less on the maturity preferences of the suppliers of securities in the determination of spot rates.
2. It acknowledges that many investors consider developments across the spectrum of maturities before making their decisions.

EMERGING THEORIES OF THE TERM STRUCTURE. Since the mid-1980s, several new formulations of the term structure have emerged. While still in their for-

| FIGURE 7.13 | **Yields of Treasury Securities, December 31, 1969** |

The shape of the yield curve in December 1969 has been used by some as support for the segmented markets theory; yields seemed to cluster rather than being continuously distributed across the spectrum of maturities.

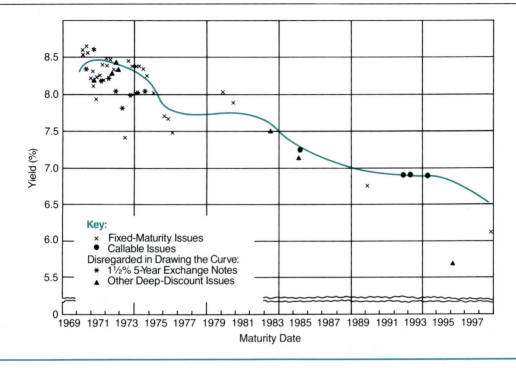

Source: Treasury Bulletin, January 1970, 83.

mative stages and yielding conflicting results in empirical tests, these models are gaining support in some circles at the expense of the expectations theory and its modifications.[16] They have by no means supplanted the more traditional theories, however.

Best known of the new models is the work of Cox, Ingersoll, and Ross. Their model bears some similarity to the expectations theory in that it, too, recognizes the influence of interest rate expectations. The newer approach, however, focuses on the factors determining those expectations, such as inflation, uncertainty, and productivity.

Researchers continue to explore adjustments, applications of, and empirical verification of the new

models, although their complexity has made empirical testing difficult. Experts agree that investigation of these term structure theories will continue to be a fertile area of research.

EMPIRICAL TESTS OF THE TERM STRUCTURE THEORIES

A full review of empirical tests of term structure theories would fill a book, because research interest in the subject spans almost a century. Nonetheless, no single theory has prevailed.

A FAMILIAR RESEARCH PROBLEM: MEASURING EXPECTATIONS

As the oldest of the theories, the pure expectations model has received the greatest attention. Particularly troublesome, however, is a problem also faced

---

[16] See Cox, Ingersoll, and Ross 1981; Cox, Ingersoll, and Ross 1985; and Ho and Lee 1986. Abken 1990 offers a comprehensive summary and evaluation of the newer models and results of empirical tests.

in tests of the Fisher effect—measuring market expectations to be compared with subsequent actual rates. Researchers have used several alternatives. Some have used *ex post* rates as a proxy for expected rates. The conclusions are similar to those drawn by students of the Fisher theory: Even though, after the fact, expectations are not always correct, they still influence observed term structures.[17]

For example, some researchers have developed an "error learning" model, which argues that investors continually revise their expectations in response to earlier errors. This model implies that past and present experiences affect investors' response to new information. Other researchers have argued that investors' expectations are "regressive"—that is, when the general level of rates is high, people expect them to fall, and when the general level is low, they expect rates to increase.

Quite a different approach uses interest rate forecasts of professional investors and analysts as proxies for interest rate expectations. Some researchers have also recognized that the financial futures markets may provide a good method for estimating interest rate expectations and have turned to those markets for continuation of empirical tests. Others have investigated the influence of monetary policy on expectations and the slope of the yield curve.[18] Regardless of the chosen measurement, many studies of the U.S. Treasury securities market have concluded that expectations play a major role in determining the term structure.[19]

Research on the expectations theory increasingly reflects globalization of financial markets. Scholars have noted that investors' expectations may be directed not only toward rates in their home country but also toward rates in other financial markets in which they customarily interact. Thus, some recent studies

have tested the expectations theory on contemporaneous data from several countries. Although the evidence by no means supports a definite conclusion that long-term rates in one country reflect expectations of short-term rates in other countries, this avenue of term structure research will undoubtedly be continued in the next decade.[20]

EVIDENCE ON LIQUIDITY PREMIUMS

Many researchers have concluded that investors also demand liquidity premiums, although they do not agree on the nature of these premiums. The disagreement centers on whether the premium demanded by investors is affected by the general level of interest rates (that is, whether the premium increases or decreases when rates are considered to be relatively high or low) and whether it is stable or rises monotonically with maturity. There is considerable evidence that the liquidity premium *does* vary with the general level of interest rates, but there is no agreement on whether the relationship is positive or negative.[21] In other words, some research indicates that when rates are higher than normal, the liquidity premium required by investors is smaller than usual, whereas other results suggest that it is larger.

The debate over the nature of the liquidity premium has implications for tests of the expectations hypothesis and for its usefulness as a forecasting model. Because it is difficult to determine the size and pattern of liquidity premiums, it is difficult to isolate an expected "pure" interest rate from a premium attached to it. Some research has suggested that liquidity premiums range from 0.54 to 1.56 percent, but other studies have concluded that premiums are less than 0.50 percent, even for long maturities. Some researchers have even concluded that liquidity premiums decrease, rather than increase, with maturity.[22]

---

[17] Examples of these studies include Van Horne 1965; Kessel 1965; Meiselman 1962; Wood 1983; Walz and Spencer 1989; Froot 1989; and Dua 1991.

[18] See Kane and Malkiel 1967; Friedman 1979; Hafer and Hein 1989; and Cook and Hahn 1990.

[19] There are serious critics. For example, one study concludes that the use of the simple expectations theory "to forecast the direction of future changes in the interest rate seems worthless." See Schiller, Campbell, and Schoenholtz 1983. Belongia and Koedik (1988) also fail to find support for the expectations hypothesis.

---

[20] See Belongia and Koedik 1988; and Kool and Tatom 1988.

[21] See Nelson 1972; Van Horne 1965; Friedman 1979; and Dua 1991.

[22] For further information on empirical research addressing the liquidity premium hypothesis, see McCulloch 1975; Lee, Maness, and Tuttle 1980; Roll 1970; and Throop 1981.

RESEARCH ON SEGMENTED MARKETS AND PREFERRED HABITATS

Research on the segmented markets and preferred habitat theories is extremely contradictory. Some researchers have reported findings of discontinuities in the yield curve, supporting the market segmentation theory; some have concluded that preferred habitats exist.[23] In contrast, other studies, including those supporting the expectations and liquidity premium theories, argue that the financial markets function more efficiently than the segmented markets theory or preferred habitat theory recognizes. In other words, investors are more willing to move funds back and forth between maturities to maximize returns than either of these theories implies.

APPLICATION OF TERM STRUCTURE THEORIES TO FINANCIAL INSTITUTIONS MANAGEMENT

Most managers do not personally intend to resolve these theoretical and empirical debates, but they are interested in using the fruits of research to make better decisions. Fortunately, although no one has written the definitive word on yield curves, ample insights are available from existing theory to assist a knowledgeable manager. Some of the most important problems for which term structure theories are useful are illustrated in the following discussion.

It is important to appreciate the perspective from which managers view the term structure. Instead of confronting the raw material of yield curves—investors' expectations, liquidity premiums, supply/demand relationships in the financial markets—managers observe the finished products, such as the actual term structures depicted in Figures 7.2 through 7.4. Term structure theories attempt to explain how observed term structures came about. The information a manager obtains by applying theory to an existing yield

curve can assist in making decisions, such as forecasting interest rates, setting a mortgage loan rate, or trading securities for the institution's portfolio.

INTEREST RATE FORECASTING

Of particular importance to interest rate forecasting is the pure expectations theory. The mathematical expression of the pure expectations theory itself provides a forecasting model. To illustrate, suppose that in June 1994, the spot Treasury yields shown in Table 7.2 for a 5-year maturity horizon are observed.

FORWARD RATES. According to the pure expectations theory, the 2-year spot rate (that is, the existing yield on a security maturing in June 1996) is the geometric average of the expected yield on a 1-year Treasury security (a rate that *can* be directly observed from the existing yield curve) and the expected annual yield on 1-year securities as of June 1995 (a rate not directly observable). That relationship was modeled mathematically in Equation 7.1.

Using data from Table 7.2,

$$1 + {}_1\tilde{i}_2 = \sqrt{(1 + {}_1\tilde{i}_1)(1 + {}_2\tilde{i}_1)}$$
$$1 + 0.1185 = \sqrt{(1.1250)(1 + {}_2\tilde{i}_1)}$$

where ${}_2\tilde{i}_1$ = unobservable expected 1-year rate at the beginning of period 2.

If the pure expectations theory is correct, one can infer the expected 1-year rate at the beginning of period 2 by solving Equation 7.1 for ${}_2\tilde{i}_1$.

---

[23] See Modigliani and Sutch 1966. Also see Dobson, Sutch, and Vanderford 1976; Echols and Elliott 1976; Roley 1981; and Heuson 1988.

TABLE 7.2	Hypothetical Spot Rates on Treasury Securities as of June 1994

These hypothetical data on observed yields can be used to infer 1-year forward rates.

Maturity Date	Spot Yield (%)	Notation
June 1995	12.50%	${}_1\tilde{i}_1$
June 1996	11.85%	${}_1\tilde{i}_2$
June 1997	11.00%	${}_1\tilde{i}_3$
June 1998	10.90%	${}_1\tilde{i}_4$
June 1999	10.50%	${}_1\tilde{i}_5$

[7.3]
$$(1 + {}_1\bar{\imath}_2)^2 = (1 + {}_1\bar{\imath}_1)(1 + {}_2\bar{\imath}_1)$$

$$1 + {}_2\bar{\imath}_1 = (1 + {}_1\bar{\imath}_2)^2/(1 + {}_1\bar{\imath}_1)$$

$$1 + {}_2\bar{\imath}_1 = (1.1185)^2/1.1250 \qquad \text{foward rate}$$

$$1 + {}_2\bar{\imath}_1 = 1.1120 - 1 = 0.1120 = 11.20\%$$

An implied expected rate calculated from an existing yield curve is a **forward rate.** The 1-year forward rate at the beginning of period 2 is 11.20 percent. This rate is expected to prevail on investments made in June 1995 and maturing in June 1996. It is lower than the 1-year T-bill yield in 1994, because the spot yields in Table 7.2 suggest market expectations for falling rates. If an institution's managers use the pure expectations theory, this forward rate can serve as a specific forecast for short-term T-bill rates for June of 1995.

The general formula for a 1-year forward rate as of the beginning of period t is

[7.4]
$$1 + {}_t\tilde{\imath}_1 = (1 + {}_1\bar{\imath}_t)^t/(1 + {}_1\bar{\imath}_{t-1})^{t-1}$$

Equation 7.4 allows calculation of the 1-year forward rate as of the beginning of any future period (t). It is more useful than Equation 7.3, which solves only for the 1-year forward rate as of the beginning of period 2.

INCORPORATING LIQUIDITY PREMIUMS. Many managers may not accept the unbiased expectations theory as the only explanation for the term structure. Fortunately, it is possible to incorporate liquidity premiums into a forecasting model. If liquidity premiums exist, spot rates for 2-, 3-, 4-, and 5-year securities in Table 7.2 are affected not only by expectations but also by premiums on long-term investments.

For example, suppose a manager believes that investors expect a premium of 0.5 percent for holding a 2-year security in 1994. That belief can be incorporated into a forecast of future short-term rates by solving Equation 7.2 for the forward rate as of the beginning of period 2:

[7.5]
$$1 + {}_1\bar{\imath}_2 = \sqrt{(1 + {}_1\bar{\imath}_1)(1 + {}_2\bar{\imath}_1 + L_2)}$$

$$1 + {}_2\bar{\imath}_1 = [(1 + {}_1\bar{\imath}_2)^2/(1 + {}_1\bar{\imath}_1)] - L_2$$

Under the assumption of liquidity premiums, the estimate for the forward rate in June 1995 becomes

$$(1.1185)^2 = (1.1250)(1 + {}_2\bar{\imath}_1 + 0.005)$$

$$1 + {}_2\bar{\imath}_1 + 0.005 = (1.1185)^2/(1.1250)$$

$$1 + {}_2\bar{\imath}_1 + 0.005 = 1.1120$$

$$1 + {}_2\bar{\imath}_1 = 1.1120 - 0.005 = 1.1070$$

$${}_2\bar{\imath}_1 = 0.1070 = 10.70\%$$

This 1-year rate expected to prevail in 1995 is lower than the forward rate of 11.20 percent calculated earlier with only the pure expectations theory as a basis for forecasting. The difference is the assumed liquidity premium required for 2-year loans. If liquidity premiums exist, their effect on actual long-term rates will cause the results of Equations 7.3 or 7.4 to be biased upward. Equation 7.5 adjusts for that bias.

Using the pure expectations theory with liquidity premiums, the general equation for calculating the 1-year forward rate in period t is

[7.6]
$$1 + {}_t\tilde{\imath}_1 = [(1 + {}_1\bar{\imath}_t)^t/(1 + {}_1\bar{\imath}_{t-1})^{t-1}] - L_t$$

Equation 7.6 allows estimation of the forward rate as of the beginning of any future period, adjusted for a liquidity premium. In contrast, Equation 7.5 applies only to the forward rate as of the beginning of period 2.

SETTING INSTITUTIONAL INTEREST RATES

A financial institution manager frequently faces simultaneous decisions about short- and long-term interest rates. For example, if short-term deposits such as 1-year certificates of deposit (CDs) are to be used to finance long-term assets such as mortgages, care must be taken to establish both rates so that the cost of financing does not exceed the yield on the mortgages. Using the pure expectations theory, a manager who observes an upward-sloping Treasury security term structure can infer that most investors expect increasing short-term rates over the next several periods. The cost of 1-year CDs is therefore likely to increase during the period when mortgage loans made today have a constant yield.

According to the liquidity premium theory, existing Treasury rates may also include liquidity premiums, and the manager may also believe that a premium for default risk should be required for holding mortgages instead of Treasury securities. Furthermore, the segmented markets and preferred habitat theories suggest that competitive pressures from other depository institutions should be considered in setting both rates. For example, if there is strong competition for 1-year CDs, a savings and loan association (S&L) may be forced to pay an even higher yield than the expectations hypothesis would suggest.

ESTIMATING THE COST OF DEPOSITS. Sample calculations and estimations involved in this decision are provided in Table 7.3. For simplicity, it is assumed that mortgages made today will mature in 5 years. Since the source of funds is 1-year CDs, the manager would

begin by calculating a series of 1-year forward rates implied in the existing yield curve, using Equation 7.4. Using Equation 7.6, liquidity premiums embedded in the current term structure would be removed to avoid overestimating expected 1-year CD rates in future periods. Because the institution plans to issue 1-year CDs each year, it would not have to offer liquidity premiums to its depositors.

The resulting series of forward rates (given in Column 5) is used to set initial and anticipated 1-year CD rates. Specifically, the initial CD rate is based on the first rate in this series (8 percent), with subsequent forward rates serving as the basis for estimating the future annual interest cost of the deposits. After obtaining these costs, the manager would increase them as needed to account for the administrative costs of servicing deposits (Column 6). In addition, adjustments might be made to account for premiums necessary to

---

TABLE 7.3   Using Term Structure Theories to Set Institutional Interest Rates

These hypothetical data on observed yields, liquidity premiums, administrative costs, risk premiums, and profit markups can be used to estimate the appropriate rate to charge on a mortgage loan.

(1) Maturity (Years)	(2) Observed Yield on Treasury Securities	(3) Unadjusted 1-Year Forward Rate (from Equation 7.4)	(4) Estimated Liquidity Premium	(5) Estimated 1-Year Rate with Liquidity Premium Removed (Column 3 – Column 4)
1	0.0800	0.0800	0.0000	0.0800
2	0.0825	0.0850	0.0050	0.0800
3	0.0950	0.1204	0.0100	0.1104
4	0.1025	0.1253	0.0250	0.1003
5	0.1100	0.1405	0.0350	0.1055

(6) Annual CD Cost (Column 5 + Administrative Markup of 0.25% per Year)	(7) Estimated Premium Required to Hold Mortgages	(8) Estimated Annual Required Return (Column 6 + Column 7 + Profit Markup of 0.75% per Year)
0.0825	0.0100	0.1000
0.0825	0.0250	0.1150
0.1129	0.0300	0.1504
0.1028	0.0400	0.1503
0.1080	0.0450	0.1605

(9)
Estimation of Required Annual Yield on Mortgages
(Using Equation 7.1 on Data from Column 8)

$$i_m = \sqrt[5]{(1.1000)(1.1150)(1.1504)(1.1503)(1.1605)} - 1$$

$$i_m = 0.1350 = 13.50\%$$

meet competitors' offerings. Column 6 contains estimated total interest plus noninterest costs of issuing 1-year CDs each year for 5 years.

SETTING THE MORTGAGE RATE. The manager would then set the 5-year mortgage rate by estimating the risk premium necessary to compensate the institution for holding mortgages (Column 7). Finally, a desired profit markup of 0.75 percent per year is added to allow for a return to owners in a stockholder-owned firm or to provide for additions to net worth in a mutual institution. The resulting figures in Column 8 are the estimated annual returns required to cover all costs, including the cost of funds, noninterest costs, and a target rate of profit. Finally, the geometric average of the five rates is calculated, using Equation 7.1. This rate, 13.50 percent in Table 7.3, is the appropriate annual interest rate to charge on a mortgage made at the beginning of the 5-year period. If the institution earns 13.50 percent annually for 5 years and if actual costs equal estimates, the desired profit markup over the life of the mortgage will be earned. Of course, an institution's ability to charge this rate is constrained by competition, but competing institutions would also be aware of the need to recover long-term costs.

It is important to remember that even such careful forecasting and rate setting include a great deal of uncertainty. As the review of empirical research suggested, expectations embedded in the term structure are not always fulfilled, and additional sources of error are introduced in the estimation of the liquidity premium. Such errors can be costly, because once the long-term mortgage rate has been established, it may not be subject to renegotiation, and profits will disappear if interest rates move to such a high level that costs cannot be recovered. Many thrift institutions, in particular, learned this lesson the hard way in the early 1980s. Institutions must also maintain sufficient flexibility to respond when forecasts prove to be incorrect. Increasingly sophisticated techniques for managing interest rate risk are discussed in chapters that follow.

MANAGING THE SECURITIES PORTFOLIO

Term structure theories are also useful in managing the institution's securities portfolio. A common trading strategy is searching for undervalued or over-

valued securities. This strategy assumes that, although the pure expectations theory applies in general and investors price securities to make the expected annual yield the same regardless of the maturities selected over a holding period, the markets are sometimes in temporary disequilibrium. According to this line of thinking, if a security's yield exceeds those on securities of equal maturity and risk, the security is underpriced. If the institution does not own the security, it can purchase it immediately. When the market returns to equilibrium, the price of the security should rise, lowering its yield to the appropriate level. The institution can expect to profit from the capital gain.

Conversely, if a security's yield is less than those on securities of comparable maturity, the security is overpriced and should be sold. The pure expectations theory suggests that its price will fall as the market returns its yield to the level proper for its maturity. Analysts sometimes attempt to identify under- or overvalued securities in the Treasury market, for example, by studying yield curves such as the one in Figure 7.2. The issues circled left of the center of the graph have lower yields than securities of similar maturity (approximately 2 years). A manager who believed that the market was in temporary disequilibrium would sell the issues before the anticipated drop in price increased their yields.

Such a strategy would reflect not only a belief that the pure expectations theory correctly describes interest rate movements in the long run but also a recognition of the role of **arbitrage** in the financial markets. Arbitrage is trading to profit from temporary price discrepancies in otherwise identical assets. As noted, the pure expectations theory assumes that investors are indifferent among equally risky securities of varying maturities. If the theory is correct, investors holding the relatively lower-yielding 2-year securities circled in Figure 7.2 would possess arbitrage opportunities. They could attempt to improve returns by selling the circled securities and either purchasing higher-yielding 2-year securities *or* purchasing a series of shorter-term securities over a 2-year period. These arbitrage selling and buying activities would, in turn, cause the price of the circled securities to decline and the prices of purchased securities to rise. Because of the inverse relationship between prices and yields, the expected return to subsequent owners of the circled securities would rise. Ultimately, then, the actions of arbitrage traders should cause the yields on securities of similar maturity to converge.[24] The relationship between prices and yields is explored further in the next chapter.

SUMMARY

The term structure of interest rates is the relationship at a specific time between the yields and maturities of securities of comparable default risk. Historically, this relationship has varied. The variation is related both to the general level of interest rates and to the pace of economic activity.

Economists have developed several theories to explain term structures. Researchers agree that the financial markets' expectations of future short-term rates play a large role in determining existing yields on long-term securities. Other factors, such as possible investors' preferences for liquidity, their policies and attitudes, or regulation in the financial markets, appear to have less influence on the term structure.

Knowledge of term structure relationships is useful in asset/liability management. Understanding the role of expectations allows managers to develop interest rate forecasts to use in institutional planning and in trading strategies for the securities portfolio. Also, knowledge of expectations, liquidity preferences, and supply/demand interactions can help managers establish the prices of financial products such as deposits and loans.

QUESTIONS

1. Explain the term structure of interest rates and the relationships measured. Why must all securities plotted on a given term structure have equal default risk?

2. Historically, what has been the relationship between the slope of the yield curve and the level of economic activity?

---

[24] This discussion refers to arbitrage in general and not to a specific trading strategy used by some securities firms called "yield-curve arbitrage." The latter phrase refers to simultaneous trading in short-term interest rate futures and long-term bonds to profit from the fact that short-term interest rates (thus, the "short" end of the yield curve) fluctuate more than long-term rates. For more information, see Craig Torres, " 'Yield-Curve Arbitrage' Rewards the Skillful," *The Wall Street Journal,* July 27, 1989, C1, C10.

Between the slope of the yield curve and the general level of interest rates?

3. In a recent issue of *The Wall Street Journal* or other major newspaper, find yield quotations for U.S. Treasury securities. Using data for T-bills, bonds, and notes, sketch the prevailing term structure.

4. According to the pure expectations theory, what determines the slope of the term structure of interest rates? On what important assumptions is this theory based? Using this theory, what expectations about future interest rates are reflected in the term structure you plotted for Question 3?

5. An investor who accepts the pure expectations theory and its underlying assumptions has been offered two 6-year investment plans. One plan is a series of three 2-year instruments, whereas the other plan is a series of six 1-year T-bill purchases. Ignoring any fees and assuming no liquidity premiums, which alternative would be preferable? Why?

6. Explain how the liquidity premium hypothesis differs from the pure expectations theory. Which of the pure expectations assumptions is rejected under the liquidity premium hypothesis?

7. Assume that the yield curve you plotted in Question 3 includes liquidity premiums that gradually increase as maturity increases. Sketch an estimate of the prevailing pure expectations term structure.

8. According to the modified expectations theory, what role do borrowers play in determining the relationship between short-term and long-term interest rates?

9. What market imperfections are recognized in the segmented markets hypothesis? What are its assumptions about the maturity preferences of borrowers and lenders?

10. How does the preferred habitat theory characterize the maturity preferences of borrowers and lenders? Under what conditions will investors switch from one maturity to another? Does the preferred habitat theory support the concept of a continuous yield curve? Why or why not?

11. Which theory of the term structure do you find most plausible? Which is the least plausible? By integrating ideas from all term structure theories, state briefly how you believe the term structure is determined.

12. Briefly summarize the difficulties in measuring interest rate expectations and liquidity premiums for tests of the pure expectations theory.

13. Explain how estimates of forward rates may be used by financial institution managers as they set long-term loan and deposit rates.

PROBLEMS

1. Your financial planning consultant has adopted the followed expectations for short-term interest rates:

1-year rate prevailing January 1995: 6.7%
1-year rate prevailing January 1996: 7.8%

Based on these expectations and assuming no liquidity premiums, what rate does your consultant expect you to earn on a 2-year security purchased in January 1995?

2. Your mother, who watches her investments closely, has sent a newsletter reporting yields currently available on various Treasury securities. As of January 1, 1994, a T-bond with exactly 3 years to maturity carries a yield of 7.65 percent, while a 4-year bond (maturing January 1, 1998) offers a yield of 7.30 percent. Assuming no liquidity premiums, what is the 1-year forward rate expected to prevail as of January 1, 1997 (the beginning of Year 4)?

3. If you estimate that a liquidity premium of 0.0025 (0.25 percent) on a 4-year investment is included in the yields quoted in Problem 2, what is your revised estimate of the 1-year forward rate expected to prevail at the beginning of Year 4?

4.

Treasury Bill Purchased	Treasury Bill Matures	Expected Annual Rate %
January 1995	January 1996	9.35% (observed)
January 1996	January 1997	8.95
January 1997	January 1998	8.15
January 1998	January 1999	7.50

a. Using the preceding information and the pure expectations hypothesis, calculate the yield to maturity as of January 1995 for each of the following:
  1) a 2-year security
  2) a 3-year security
  3) a 4-year security
b. Using your calculations in Part a, sketch the term structure of interest rates prevailing in January 1995.
c. Calculate the expected average annual yield for each of the following investment strategies:
  1) investment in a 2-year security followed by investment in a 2-year security
  2) investment in a series of four 1-year T-bills
d. Explain how your answers to Part c support the pure expectations theory.

5.

Treasury Bill Purchased	Treasury Bill Matures	Expected Annual Rate %	Liquidity Premium as of June 1996 %
June 1996	June 1997	4.25% (observed)	0.00%
June 1997	June 1998	5.95	0.15 (on 2-year security)
June 1998	June 1999	6.75	0.25 (on 3-year security)
June 1999	June 2000	7.95	0.30 (on 4-year security)

a. Based on the preceding information and using the pure expectations and liquidity premium hypotheses, calculate the yield to maturity as of June 1996 for each of the following:
  1) a 2-year Treasury security
  2) a 3-year security
  3) a 4-year security
b. Using your calculations in Part a, sketch the observed term structure of interest rates as of June 1996.

c. Calculate the expected annual yield for each of the following investment strategies:
   1) investment in a 4-year Treasury security
   2) purchase of a 1-year T-bill followed by investment in a 3-year Treasury security
   3) investment in a series of four 1-year T-bills

6.

Treasury Bill Purchased	Treasury Bill Matures	Expected Annual Rate %
June 1994	June 1995	6.75% (observed)
June 1995	June 1996	7.30
June 1996	June 1997	8.05
June 1997	June 1998	8.95

a. Calculate the expected average annual yield for each of the following investment strategies:
   1) investment in a series of three 1-year securities, with the investments made in June of each year from 1994 through 1996 (beginning of the month)
   2) investment in a 2-year security in June 1994 followed by investment in a 1-year T-bill in June 1996
b. Calculate the expected average annual yield for each of the following investment strategies:
   1) investment in a 1-year security in June 1994 followed by investment in a 3-year security in June 1995
   2) investment in a series of four 1-year T-bills, with the investments made in June of each year from 1994 through 1997
c. Recalculate your answers for Parts a and b under the liquidity premium hypothesis, given the following liquidity premiums as of June 1994:

Maturity of Security	Liquidity Premium
1 Year	0.00%
2 Years	0.12
3 Years	0.18
4 Years	0.22

7. Assume it is now May 1995 and that the following yields prevail:

Treasury Security Maturity Date	Spot Yield as of May 1995 %
May 1996	11.05%
May 1997	10.50
May 1998	10.05
May 1999	9.45
May 2000	8.95

a. Calculate the 1-year forward rate as of May 1998 (the beginning of Period 4).
b. Calculate the 1-year forward rate as of May 1997 (the beginning of Period 3).

8. For these problems, use the information on maturity dates and spot yields from Problem 7 and the liquidity premiums in the following table:
a. Calculate the 1-year forward rate with liquidity premium removed as of May 1998 (the beginning of Period 4).
b. Calculate the 1-year forward rate with liquidity premium removed as of May 1999 (the beginning of Period 5).

Maturity of Security	Liquidity Premium as of May 1995 %
1 Year	0.00%
2	0.15
3	0.21
4	0.26
5	0.29

9. The president of a community bank in the Southwest is in the process of setting rates on 1-year certificates of deposit and on 4-year, fixed-rate automobile loans, in which newly-acquired funds will be invested. The yield curve is presently upward sloping, suggesting that these fixed-rate loans should be priced carefully. Based on the following information and the pure expectations hypothesis, what rate should the bank charge on a 4-year loan? (Hint: Calculate the expected rates for future 1-year CDs first.) Assume liquidity premiums equal 0.

Treasury Securities:

Maturity	Observed Annual Yield %
1 Year	4.50
2	5.25
3	5.75
4	6.50

Administrative Markup:

$1\frac{1}{2}$% per year

Risk Premiums Required for Holding Auto Loans:

Year 1	2.0%
Year 2	2.5
Year 3	3.0
Year 4	3.5

10. A commercial bank is evaluating its charges on 5-year balloon mortgages. The mortgage rate is fixed for 5 years, but the bank acquires funds primarily by issuing 1-year CDs. Using the following information, estimate rates for future CDs and the appropriate 5-year mortgage rate.

Treasury Securities:

Maturity	Observed Yield
1 Year	9.00%
2 Years	9.75
3 Years	10.15
4 Years	10.95
5 Years	11.40

Administrative Cost Percentage (Markup) on CDs:

1% per year

Estimated Risk Premiums Required for Holding Mortgages:

Year 1	1.0%
Year 2	1.8
Year 3	2.5
Year 4	3.2
Year 5	3.8

In addition to this information, bank management estimates that the following liquidity premiums are included in observed long-term yields:

Maturity	Premium
1 Year	0.00%
2	0.10
3	0.16
4	0.21
5	0.25

SELECTED REFERENCES

Abken, Peter. "Innovations in Modeling the Term Structure of Interest Rates." *Economic Review* (Federal Reserve Bank of Atlanta) 65 (July/August 1990): 2–27.

Belongia, Michael T., and Kees G. Koedik. "Testing the Expectations Model of the Term Structure: Some Conjectures on the Effects of Institutional Changes." *Review* (Federal Reserve Bank of St. Louis) 70 (September/October 1988): 37–45.

Blalock, Joseph. "Whither the Yield Curve?" *Savings and Community Banker* 2 (April 1993): 36–38.

Cogley, Timothy. "Interpreting the Term Structure of Interest Rates." *Weekly Letter* (Federal Reserve Bank of San Francisco) (April 16, 1993).

Cook, Timothy, and Thomas Hahn. "Interest Rate Expectations and the Slope of the Money Market Yield Curve." *Economic Review* (Federal Reserve Bank of Richmond) 76 (September/October 1990): 3–26.

Cox, John C., Jonathan E. Ingersoll, Jr., and Stephen A. Ross. "A Re-Examination of Traditional Hypotheses about the Term Structure of Interest Rates." *Journal of Finance* 36 (September 1981): 769–799.

——— "A Theory of the Term Structure of Interest Rates." *Econometrica* 53 (March 1985): 385–408.

Culbertson, John M. "The Term Structure of Interest Rates." *Quarterly Journal of Economics* 71 (November 1957): 485–517.

Dobson, Steven W., Richard C. Sutch, and David E. Vanderford. "An Evaluation of Alternative Empirical Models of the Term Structure of Interest Rates." *Journal of Finance* 31 (September 1976): 1035–1065.

Dua, Pami. "Survey Evidence on the Term Structure of Interest Rates." *Journal of Economics and Business* 43 (1991): 133–142.

Echols, Michael E., and J. Walter Elliott. "Rational Expectations in a Disequilibrium Model of the Term Structure." *American Economic Review* 66 (March 1976): 28–44.

Friedman, Benjamin M. "Interest Rate Expectations versus Forward Rates: Evidence from an Expectations Survey." *Journal of Finance* 34 (September 1979): 965–973.

Froot, Kenneth A. "New Hope for the Expectations Hypothesis of the Term Structure of Interest Rates." *Journal of Finance* 44 (June 1989): 283–305.

Furlong, Frederick T. "The Yield Curve and Recessions." *Weekly Letter* (Federal Reserve Bank of San Francisco), March 10, 1989.

Hafer, R. W., and Scott E. Hein. "Comparing Futures and Survey Forecasts of Near-Term Treasury Bill Rates." *Review* (Federal Reserve Bank of St. Louis) 71 (May/June 1989): 33–42.

Heuson, Andrea J. "The Term Premia Relationship Implicit in the Term Structure of Treasury Bills." *Journal of Financial Research* 11 (Spring 1988): 13–20.

Hicks, J. R. *Value and Capital.* London: Oxford University Press, 1946.

Ho, Thomas, and Sang-Bin Lee. "Term Structure Movements and Pricing Interest Rate Contingent Claims." *Journal of Finance* 41 (December 1986): 1011–1029.

Kane, Edward J., and Burton G. Malkiel. "The Term Structure of Interest Rates: An Analysis of a Survey of Interest Rate Expectations." *Review of Economics and Statistics* 49 (August 1967): 343–355.

Kessel, Reuben A. *The Cyclical Behavior of the Term Structure.* New York: National Bureau of Economic Research, 1965.

Kool, Clemens J. M., and John A. Tatom. "International Linkages in the Term Structure of Interest Rates." *Review* (Federal Reserve Bank of St. Louis) 70 (July/August 1988): 30–42.

Lee, Wayne, Terry S. Maness, and Donald Tuttle. "Non-Speculative Behavior and the Term Structure." *Journal of Financial and Quantitative Analysis* 15 (March 1980): 53–83.

Lutz, Frederick. "The Structure of Interest Rates." *Quarterly Journal of Economics* 30 (November 1940): 36–63.

Malkiel, Burton. *The Term Structure of Interest Rates: Theory, Empirical Evidence, and Applications.* Princeton, NJ: Princeton University Press, 1966.

McCulloch, Huston J. "An Estimation of the Liquidity Premium Hypothesis." *Journal of Political Economy* 83 (January/February 1975): 95–119.

Meiselman, David. *The Term Structure of Interest Rates.* Englewood Cliffs, NJ: Prentice-Hall, 1962.

Modigliani, Franco, and Richard Sutch. "Innovation in Interest Rate Policy." *American Economic Review* 66 (May 1966): 178–197.

Nelson, Charles R. *The Term Structure of Interest Rates.* New York: Basic Books, 1972.

Roley, V. Vance. "The Determinants of the Treasury Yield Curve." *Journal of Finance* 36 (December 1981): 1103–1126.

Roll, Richard. *The Behavior of Interest Rates.* New York: Basic Books, 1970.

Schiller, Robert J., John Y. Campbell, and Kermit L. Schoenholtz. "Forward Rates and Future Policy: Interpreting the Term Structure of Interest Rates." In *Brookings Papers on Economic Activity, I: 1982* (Washington, DC: Brookings Institution, 1983): 173–223.

Smith, Warren L. *Debt Management in the United States.* Study Paper 19, Joint Economic Committee of the 86th Congress, January 1960.

Stevens, E. J. "Is There a Message in the Yield Curve?" *Economic Commentary* (Federal Reserve Bank of Cleveland), March 15, 1989.

Throop, Adrian. "Interest Rate Forecasts and Market Efficiency." *Economic Review* (Federal Reserve Bank of San Francisco) (Spring 1981): 29–43.

Van Horne, James. "Interest Rate Risk and the Term Structure of Interest Rates." *Journal of Political Economy* 73 (August 1965): 344–351.

Wallich, Henry C., and Peter M. Keir. "The Role of Operating Guides in U.S. Monetary Policy: A Historical Review." *Federal Reserve Bulletin* 65 (September 1979): 679–691.

Walz, Daniel T., and Roger W. Spencer. "The Informational Content of Forward Rates: Further Evidence." *Journal of Financial Research* 12 (Spring 1989): 69–81.

Wood, John H. "Do Yield Curves Normally Slope Up? The Term Structure of Interest Rates, 1862–1982." *Economic Perspectives* (Federal Reserve Bank of Chicago) 7 (July/August 1983): 17–23.

How much risk to take on interest rates is one of the biggest decisions a bank makes.
Steven Elliott
Chief Financial Officer, Mellon Bank (1992)

As the preceding quotation from an officer of one of the nation's largest banks suggests, some of the most important decisions managers of financial institutions make are based on factors well beyond their control, such as the direction of market interest rates. Many managers faced a critical dilemma in the early 1990s as market rates fell to levels not seen in three decades or more, while at the same time the upward-sloping term structure was much steeper than usual—that is, the spread between what could be earned on long- versus short-term assets was relatively large. Decision-makers at Collective Savings Bank in Egg Harbor, New Jersey, decided to structure the institution's assets on the assumption that the rate decline was temporary: they chose a preponderance of short-term investments so as not to be "locked in" if rates rose suddenly. But managers of other depositories, such as Boatmen's Bancshares in St. Louis, took an entirely opposite tack and lengthened asset maturities to take advantage of the high spread between long- and short-term rates. Considering how many of each bank's asset returns and liability costs were affected by these decisions about an unknowable future, the risks of betting wrong were enormous for both groups of managers.[1]

CHAPTER

8

INTEREST RATE

RISK

---

[1] Fred R. Bleakley, "Bank, Thrifts Scored as Interest Rates Fell, But Difficulties Loom," *The Wall Street Journal,* February 12, 1992, A1, A6.

INTEREST RATE RISK DEFINED

Risk is a fact of life. Previous chapters have defined risk as potential variation in the returns from an investment and have briefly identified its sources in the financial markets. This chapter explains and illustrates one of the most significant risks faced by financial institutions today: potential variation in returns caused by unexpected changes in interest rates, or **interest rate risk.**

Note the use of the word *unexpected.* As indicated in the last two chapters, investors can—and, according to empirical tests, do—incorporate *expected* changes in interest rates into their investment decisions. The risk they face, then, arises not from changes they *correctly* anticipate at the time investment decisions are made but from changes they do not anticipate. Because even the most astute forecasters err, no investors are protected against potential variation in returns, even if forecasting is a part of their decision making.

THE PRICE/YIELD CONNECTION

Although unexpected changes in interest rates affect virtually all financial instruments, they do not affect them equally. Differences in interest rate risk occur because of the type of instrument, the maturity, the size and timing of cash inflows, and the planned holding period relative to the asset's maturity. To understand interest rate risk, however, it is first necessary to understand fundamental principles of financial asset prices.

INDIVIDUAL INVESTORS CANNOT CHANGE PRICES

Chapter 5 noted that most financial markets are characterized by many participants and much publicly available information. Generally, an individual investor, as only one of many buyers and sellers, is unable to influence the price of a financial asset. A manager considering the purchase of a Treasury bill (T-bill) knows that an institution must pay the going market price; it is futile to expect a lower price than other market participants are willing to pay at the time. Conversely, the manager need not fear paying more than other buyers of the same T-bill at the same time.

SUPPLY/DEMAND IS IMPORTANT

It is also clear, from casual observation of the financial pages of any newspaper, that market prices of financial assets change frequently. Thus, knowing the price of a T-bill one day does not mean that one will know it the next day or even later in the same day. A successful manager must understand factors associated with price changes.

Basic microeconomic theory establishes the influence of supply and demand in setting nonfinancial market prices. Financial assets, too, are affected by these forces. Actually, two supply/demand relationships are at work. One is the supply of and demand for a particular financial asset. Generally, the larger the quantity of a financial asset relative to similar assets, the lower its price. Thus, a corporation's sale of new stock often results in a decline in price as supply increases.

But a broader supply/demand relationship is also important, as seen in Chapter 6. For example, an increase in the total supply of loanable funds, with no increase in the demand for borrowing, will result in higher financial asset prices in general as more lenders bid for the right to hold the existing stock of financial assets instead of cash. Because new financial assets are always being created and existing ones eliminated as borrowers repay previous liabilities, prices often change as a result of changes in overall supply and demand.

RISK IS IMPORTANT, TOO

Yet prices are determined by more than total supply and demand. As noted in Chapter 5, all else equal, the price of a riskier asset will be lower than that of a less risky one because most financial market participants are risk-averse. Risk aversion causes investors to demand higher expected rates of return from riskier investments.

PUTTING THEM TOGETHER

The effects of these influences on security prices are incorporated in a mathematical relationship explained in Chapter 5 as the general equation for the effective annual yield on a financial asset:

$$P_0 = \sum_{t=1}^{N} \frac{C_t}{(1 + y^*)^t}$$

Although this equation was used as an *implicit* formula for the effective yield, it is also an *explicit* expression for the price of a financial asset. Specifically, it states that the price of an asset is equal to the present value of its future cash benefits, discounted at y^*, the rate of return that the financial markets require for the riskiness of the asset. This expression reveals the relationship between price and yield.

PRICES AND YIELDS CHANGE SIMULTANEOUSLY. It is evident that, all else equal, price changes must be accompanied by yield changes, and vice versa. However, one does not cause the other; they change simultaneously, both resulting from changes in underlying economic conditions. For example, suppose the supply of securities declines. If there is no shift in the demand curve for securities, the price of financial assets will rise. This situation is illustrated in Figure 8.1A. A purchaser of financial assets at the new higher price expects a lower annual yield than before the price increase.

The supply of securities is also the demand for loanable funds, just as demand for securities reflects the willingness to supply loanable funds. A decrease in the supply of securities corresponds to a decrease in the demand for loanable funds. Should this occur, as shown in Figure 8.1B, the market yield will decline. Thus, both the prices of financial assets and their expected yields change simultaneously but in opposite directions. The price/yield relationship before and after a change in the demand for securities (or the supply of loanable funds) is illustrated in Figure 8.1C and D.

INCLUDING RISK IN THE RELATIONSHIP. Suppose that increasing tension between the United States and Cuba makes investors more risk-averse. If they expect the tension to lead to greater economic uncertainty, the slope of the risk/expected return relationship will

change, and the investors will expect greater rewards for bearing risk at all levels, as illustrated in Figure 8.2. If investors previously expected an effective annual yield of y_1^* on an investment with a perceived level of risk designated by point A, but an increase in risk aversion increases the yield to y_2^*, the price of securities with that degree of risk will fall. Supply/demand relationships and risk aversion can change at the same time. If so, prices and yields will still change simultaneously in opposite directions.

THE PRICE/YIELD RELATIONSHIP ILLUSTRATED

Figure 8.3 presents information about several bonds traded on Wednesday, April 8, and Thursday, April 9, 1992. The figure focuses on bonds issued by RJR Nabisco (RJR Nb), famous as a result of one of the largest and most controversial leveraged buyouts of the late 1980s. RJR Nabisco bonds traded on those dates had coupon rates that varied from 0 (zr) percent to $17\frac{3}{8}$ percent, and their maturity dates ranged from 1998 to 2009; in other words, the size and timing of their promised cash flows varied. Some of the coupon rates were quite high, because investors believed the firm's considerable debt made it riskier than less leveraged firms. Still, although all RJR Nabisco bonds were roughly equal in default risk, they sold at different prices and yields on Wednesday, April 8.

Focusing on two specific issues, the $13\frac{1}{8}$ of 01 and the $13\frac{1}{2}$ of 01, and assuming a par value of $1,000, annual interest payments, and exactly 9 years to maturity, it is possible to calculate their yields to maturity as of April 8[2]:

$$\$1,017.50 = \sum_{t=1}^{9} \frac{\$131.25}{(1 + y^*)^t} + \frac{\$1,000.00}{(1 + y^*)^9}$$

$$y^* = 12.79\%$$

$$\$1,170.00 = \sum_{t=1}^{9} \frac{\$135.00}{(1 + y^*)^t} + \frac{\$1,000.00}{(1 + y^*)^9}$$

$$y^* = 10.49\%$$

---

[2] Specific maturity and interest payment dates for most publicly traded bonds are available in publications such as *Moody's Bond Record*.

FIGURE 8.1   **Relationship between Security Prices and Market Prices**

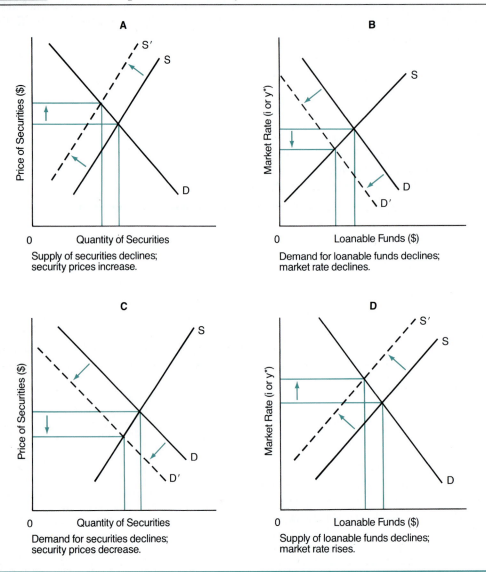

A

Supply of securities declines;
security prices increase.

B

Demand for loanable funds declines;
market rate declines.

C

Demand for securities declines;
security prices decrease.

D

Supply of loanable funds declines;
market rate rises.

On Thursday, April 9, the Federal Reserve Board announced it was decreasing the discount rate from 4 percent to 3.75 percent. Economic growth had been sluggish for many months, and Federal Reserve System (Fed) watchers interpreted the move as an effort to encourage consumers and businesses to borrow. Although the discount rate is an administered, and not a market, rate, the Fed's message was that it was de-

creasing the price of loanable funds for financial institutions eligible to use the discount window, spurring them to cut their own lending rates. On the next business day, a headline in *The Wall Street Journal* read: "Federal Reserve Pushes Down Interest Rates." (Financial institutions do not always take hints from the Fed. In this instance, most banks did not cut their lending rates, believing they were already low enough that

FIGURE 8.2   **Effect of a Change in Market Yields Caused by a Change in Risk Aversion**

When political or economic factors cause investors to become more risk-averse, the slope of the risk/expected return relationship shifts upward, and investors expect a higher rate of return for each level of risk assumed.

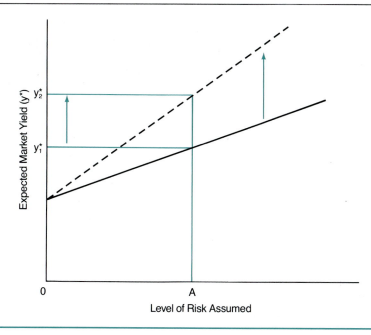

anyone wanting to borrow could do so. But some banks used the Fed's rate cut as an opportunity to decrease the rates they paid savers on their certificates of deposits!)[3]

What reaction would be predicted in the market for RJR Nabisco bonds? With falling interest rates, investors would expect the prices of bonds to rise. Because neither the maturity dates nor the cash inflows from the two RJR Nabisco bonds would change with the Fed's announcement, the prices of these bonds would be expected to increase to bring their yields into line with new market conditions.[4] In fact, these movements did occur, as illustrated by trading data on Thursday, April 9:

$$101\tfrac{7}{8} = 101.875, \quad 13\tfrac{1}{8}01 = 13.125$$

$$\$1{,}018.75 = \sum_{t=1}^{9} \frac{\$131.25}{(1 + y^*)^t} + \frac{\$1{,}000.00}{(1 + y^*)^9}$$

$$y^* = 12.76\%$$

$$117\tfrac{3}{8} = 117.3759, \quad 1350 1 = 13.5$$

$$\$1{,}173.75 = \sum_{t=1}^{9} \frac{\$135.00}{(1 + y^*)^t} + \frac{\$1{,}000.00}{(1 + y^*)^9}$$

$$y^* = 10.43\%$$

---

[3] David Wessel, "Federal Reserve Pushes Down Interest Rates," *The Wall Street Journal,* April 10, 1992, A2, A18. Because the discount rate is an administered rate, the relationship between market-determined rates and the discount rate is not uniform. In this instance, some market decreases (such as CDs) and the discount rate decrease coincided, although at other times, the Fed has, to meet monetary policy objectives, changed the discount rate in an opposite direction from recent market rate changes. See John H. Wood and Norma L. Wood, *Financial Markets.* (San Diego: Harcourt Brace Jovanovich, 1985), 235–240.

---

[4] As mentioned in Chapter 5, variable-rate bonds have coupons that change over the time to maturity, usually in conjunction with the movement of a specified interest rate index. It is possible, therefore, that the expected cash benefits from some bonds could change with a change in market yields. Variable-rate bonds are the exception, however, rather than the rule. The impact of variable-rate financial assets and liabilities is explored in later chapters.

FIGURE 8.3 **RJR Nabisco Bond Prices: April 8 and April 9, 1992**

Bond values reacted to the Federal Reserve Board's April 9 announcement of a decrease in the discount rate. Between April 8 and April 9, 1992, the market values of most bonds rose as market interest rates fell.

NEW YORK EXCHANGE BONDS

Wednesday, April 8, 1992

CORPORATION BONDS
Volume, $44,870,000

Bonds	Cur Yld	Vol	Close	Net Chg
AForP 5s30	9.0	22	55⅝	+ ¾
AMR 9s16	8.8	5	101⅞	+ 1
Advst 9s08	cv	29	88¾	− 1¼
AetnLf 8⅛07	8.3	10	98⅛	...
AlaP 9s2000	8.7	10	103	...
AlaP 7¾s02	7.9	19	97⅞	+ ⅛
AlaP 8⅞s03	8.7	5	102	...
AlaP 8¼s03	8.1	1	102⅜	+ 2
AlaP 9¾s04	9.3	30	105	+ ½
AlaP 8¾07	8.6	40	101¾	...
AlskAr 6⅞14	cv	46	79½	+ ½
AlskAr zr06	...	37	32¾	− ½
AlldC zr98	...	33	59⅞	+ ¼
AlldC zr92	...	11	97 17/32	...
AlldC zr96	...	43	76¼	− ½
AlldC zr2000	...	35	50¾	+ ¼
AlldC zr99	...	10	55⅛	+ 1⅛
AlldC zr09	...	70	22⅛	− ⅜
Allwst 7¼14	cv	28	86	− 1
ACyan 7⅜01	7.5	11	98	− 1
AmStor 01	cv	113	98¼	− ½
ATT 5⅝95	5.7	5	98¼	+ ⅜
ATT 5½97	5.9	11	94	+ ¼
ATT 6s00	6.7	55	89¾	− ½
ATT 5⅛01	6.2	4	82½	...
ATT 7s01	7.4	814	94⅞	− ⅛
ATT 7⅛03	7.5	101	94¾	...
ATT 8⅝26	8.6	941	99⅞	− ½
ATT 8⅝31	8.6	240	100½	...
ATT 7⅛02	7.4	115	96	− ⅜
ATT 8⅛22	8.4	504	96⅞	− ¼
v|Ames 10s95f	...	10	17¼	...
v|Ames 7½14f	cv	30	3⅜	− ⅝
Amoco 8⅝16	8.3	25	103⅜	+ ⅜
AmocoCda 7⅜13	7.1	17	104	− 1
Andarko 6¼14	6.6	78	94	− ⅞
Anhr 8s96	7.8	7	102¼	...
Anhr 8⅝16	8.6	33	100¼	− 1¼
Apache 7½00	cv	104	104	...
Arml 13½94	12.8	12	105⅝	+ ⅝
AshO 8.8s00	8.7	2	100¾	− ⅛
AshO 8.2s02	8.2	32	100¼	+ ¼
AshO 11.1s04	10.5	2	105⅝	+ ⅛
AshO 6¾14	cv	71	88½	...
PhilEl 6½93	6.5	23	100¼	+ 1/16
PhilEl 6⅛97	6.5	15	94	− ½
PhilEl 9s95	8.8	30	101¾	+ ⅝
PhilEl 7½98	7.6	21	98¾	+ ¼
PhilEl 11s00	10.6	12	103¾	− ¼
PhilEl 8⅝07	8.5	25	101¾	...
PhilEl 11s11	10.2	5	107½	− ¼
PhilP 8⅞00	8.8	23	100⅜	...
PhilP 12¼12	11.2	26	109	+ ⅞
PiedNG 8⅝97	8.5	3	101	+ 2¾
Pier1 6⅞02	cv	23	100¼	− ½
Pittstn 9.2s04	cv	10	100¼	...
PogoP 8s05	cv	40	78	...
PopeTl 6s12	cv	31	87	...
PotEl 8⅜09	8.3	10	101⅜	+ 1⅛
PotEl 8¾16	8.6	15	102¼	...
v|PrmM 6⅝11f	cv	70	17½	− 1½
v|PrmM 7s13f	cv	23	19	+ ⅜
ProcG 8¼05	8.2	3	101⅛	− ¾
PSInd 7⅝01	7.8	5	97¼	− ¾
PSInd 8s04	8.2	1	97⅛	− 1⅞
PSEG 8¾16	8.6	10	101⅜	− ⅝
PSEG 8¾94	8.6	10	101¼	...
PSEG 9¾20	9.0	1	108⅞	+ 2¼
QuaStC 9s95	8.9	65	101¼	...
RJR Nb 17⅜09	9.7	10	179	...
RJR Nb 13⅛01	12.9	586	101¾	...
RJR Nb na15s01	...	140	126⅛	...
RJR Nb 13½01	11.5	351	117	− ¼
RJR Nb zr01	...	2686	92	...
RJRNC 10½98	9.5	55	110⅜	− ⅜
RJR Nb 8.3s99	8.3	230	100¼	− ⅛
RJR Nb 8¾04	8.8	404	99⅝	...
RalsP 9½16	9.1	5	104	...
RalsP 9⅝16	9.1	5	103	+ ½
RapA72 7s94f	...	6	⅞	− ⅛
v|RapA69 7s94f	...	14	¾	+ ⅛
v|RapA 10¾03f	...	9	1	...
RelFncl 11⅜08	12.1	67	94	+ ¼
RelGp 9⅞98	10.8	5	91¾	+ ¾
RelGp 14s96	13.6	76	102⅞	− 1⅛
RelGp 11s96	12.2	298	90	− ½
v|RepStl 8.9s95f	...	10	15	...

NEW YORK EXCHANGE BONDS

Thursday, April 9, 1992

CORPORATION BONDS
Volume, $55,190,000

Bonds	Cur Yld	Vol	Close	Net Chg
AExC 11¾12	10.9	3	107¾	− 1½
AMR 9s16	9.0	367	100	− 1⅞
Adien 15s99	20.5	3	73	− 1¾
Advst 9s08	cv	3	90	+ 1¼
AetnLf 8⅛07	8.2	5	98¾	+ ⅝
AlaBn 4.85s99t	4.9	10	98⅞	+ ⅛
AlaP 9s2000	8.7	15	103	...
AlaP 8½s01	8.3	20	102	+ ½
AlaP 7¾s02	7.9	5	98	+ ⅛
AlaP 8¼s03	8.0	125	102¾	+ ⅜
AlaP 9¾s04	9.3	35	104½	− ½
AlaP 8¾07	8.6	5	101⅝	− ⅛
AlskAr 6⅞14	cv	52	81	+ 1½
AlskAr zr06	...	210	32¾	...
AlldC zr92	...	99	97 17/32	...
AlldC zr96	...	35	76¾	+ ½
AlldC zr2000	...	92	50⅝	− ⅛
AlldC zr97	...	5	67	+ 1⅛
AlldC zr03	...	5	38¼	− ¼
AlldC zr05	...	10	31	− 1
AlgLud 02	cv	20	100½	− 1½
Allwst 7¼14	cv	41	85	− 1
AAir-dc6¼96	6.7	8	93½	− 1½
AmStor 01	cv	66	98	− ¼
ATT 5⅝95	5.7	140	98¼	...
ATT 5½97	5.9	60	93⅞	− ⅛
ATT 6s00	6.7	4	89⅞	+ ⅛
ATT 5⅛01	6.2	11	82¾	+ ¼
ATT 7s01	7.4	1015	95⅛	+ ¼
ATT 7⅛03	7.5	655	94⅞	+ ⅛
ATT 8⅝26	8.6	2366	100½	+ ⅝
ATT 8⅝31	8.6	70	100¼	− ¼
ATT 7⅛02	7.4	95	96⅜	+ ⅜
ATT 8⅛22	8.4	1049	97¼	+ ⅜
v|Ames 7½14f	cv	25	3½	+ ⅛
Amoco 6s98	6.4	5	94⅛	− ⅝
Amoco 8⅜05	8.3	5	100½	− ¾
Amoco 7⅞07	7.8	1	100½	+ ¼
PhilEl 6½93	6.5	20	100¼	...
PhilEl 9s95	8.8	20	102	+ ¼
PhilEl 8¼96	8.2	15	100½	− 1
PhilEl 8½04	8.3	9	102	+ 1½
PhilEl 9⅛08	8.9	10	103	− ¼
PhilEl 10¼16	9.5	8	108⅛	...
PhilP 8⅞00	8.8	10	100⅜	...
PhilP 11¼13	10.5	3	107½	− ½
Pier1 6⅞02	cv	40	99	− 1¼
PopeTl 6s12	cv	1	87	...
PotEl 7¾s07	7.8	10	99¼	+ ¾
PotEl 8⅜09	8.2	10	102⅛	+ ¾
PotEl 8¾16	8.6	10	102	− ¼
PotEl 7s18	cv	10	97½	− ½
v|PrmM 7s13f	cv	10	18	− 1
ProcG 8¼05	8.2	50	101⅛	...
PSInd 7⅝01	7.9	20	97⅛	− ⅛
PSInd 7s02	7.6	50	92½	...
PSEG 7½96	7.4	18	100¾	+ ⅛
PSEG 8¾16	8.6	16	101⅝	...
PSEG 8¾94	8.6	10	101¼	...
RJR 7⅜01	8.0	18	92⅛	− ½
RJR Nb 17⅜09	9.7	69	179	...
RJR Nb 13⅛01	12.9	72	101⅞	+ ⅛
RJR Nb na15s01	...	1787	126½	+ ⅜
RJR Nb 13½01	11.5	50	117⅜	+ ⅜
RJR Nb zr01	...	5451	91⅞	− ⅛
RJRNC 10½98	9.5	193	110¾	+ ⅜
RJR Nb 8.3s99	8.2	180	100¾	+ ½
RJR Nb 8¾04	8.8	305	99⅞	+ ¼
RalsP 9s96	8.6	5	105¼	− ½
RalsP 9⅝16	9.1	5	103	...
RapA72 7s94f	...	3	⅞	...
v|RapA69 7s94f	...	10	¾	...
v|RapA 10¾03f	...	81	1⅛	+ ⅛
RelGp 9⅞98	10.8	5	91¾	...
RelGp 14s96	13.7	10	102	− ⅞

Source: The Wall Street Journal, April 9, 1992, C16; April 10, 1992, C18.

Because both bonds matured in 9 years, term structure effects did not account for their yield differences. Nor did the prices of the two bonds change by the same dollar amount or by the same percentage of the April 8 price. The price of the 13⅛ bond rose by $1.25, or 0.123 percent, whereas the price of the 13½ bond rose by $3.75, or 0.321 percent.

The reason for these differences is related to the bonds' differing coupon rates and initial yields compared with new market rates and is explored later. For now, the important point is that Figure 8.3 shows that the upward bond price movements held for almost all RJR Nabisco bonds traded both on April 8, before the rate cut, and on April 9, after the rate decrease. (The zero-coupon bond with "−" in the price change column either was not traded after the discount rate change or may have been affected by unique supply/demand factors. The trading volume for that bond was, in fact, quite high on April 9.) This is a direct example of one of the most important economic principles in the financial markets: *When market yields fall unexpectedly, the prices of existing financial assets rise; when market yields rise unexpectedly, the prices of existing financial assets fall.*

The inverse relationship between prices and yields holds for all types of financial assets, although it is particularly important for assets with fixed future cash benefits, such as discount securities, coupon bonds, or annuities. Because both asset yields and liability costs are affected by this principle, managers cannot manage the net interest margin (NIM) well without understanding it. The remainder of this chapter and the next explore the implications of the price/yield relationship for specific types of securities with different cash flow characteristics and different maturities.

THE TWO SIDES OF INTEREST RATE RISK

Another question arises from the events surrounding the change in the Fed's discount rate: To what extent did the effects of the cut represent interest rate risk to the holders of the RJR Nabisco bonds? The answer depends on the bondholder's investment planning horizon.

EFFECT ON AN INVESTOR PLANNING TO HOLD TO MATURITY

For an owner on April 8 planning to hold RJR Nabisco bonds until maturity, the price change *per se* would have no effect, because $1,000 would be expected at maturity both before and after the discount rate cut. For such an investor, a significant influence on investment returns is the rate at which periodic cash flows received *before* maturity can be reinvested. Because market conditions changed with the discount rate increase, the rate at which periodic interest payments could be reinvested would have changed on April 9. To the extent that the change was unexpected, a bondholder was exposed to interest rate risk. Assuming no additional market changes until the bond's maturity (a bold assumption), an investor's *realized* annual rate of return would not be the same as the *expected y** as of April 8; it would be lower.

Table 8.1 presents the details of this situation. The April 8 price of the 13⅛ bond was $1,017.50, and the expected annual yield was 12.79 percent. Assuming no change in market yields until maturity, a bondholder could have expected to reinvest intermediate coupon payments at a yield of 12.79 percent. Under that assumption, the bondholder could calculate the value of each cash inflow plus earnings from reinvestment until 2001. For example, using Equation 5A.1, the basic compound interest equation, the 1993 interest payment of $131.25, reinvested at an annual rate of 12.79 percent for the 8 remaining years of the bond's life, would grow to $343.69 by 2001:

compound rate
$$\$131.25 \times 1.1279^8 = \$343.69$$

The total value of all reinvested cash flows plus the cash flows expected in 2001—that year's interest payment and the par value to be repaid in that year—would have been $3,005.07. As shown at the bottom of Table 8.1, the realized rate of return would have been 12.79 percent: The original $1,017.50 investment in April 1992 would have had a value of $3,005.07 by 2001, a compound annual rate of return of 12.79 percent.

After the decrease in the discount rate, the expected reinvestment rate fell to 12.76 percent, the bond's new yield to maturity. If all intermediate cash

TABLE 8.1   Effect of a Change in the Reinvestment Rate on Realized Yields

For investors planning to hold bonds until maturity, changes in market interest rates affect the rate at which cash flows from bonds can be reinvested. When market yields fell in April 1992, the potential realized yield also fell, reflecting a lower reinvestment rate.

Year Cash Received or (Invested)	Years to 2001	Cash Flow	Value of Cash Flow in 2001 if Reinvested at 12.79% (Original y*)	Value of Cash Flow in 2001 if Reinvested at 12.76% (New y*)
1992	9	($1,017.50)	—	—
1993	8	131.25	$ 343.69	$ 343.11
1994	7	131.25	304.72	304.27
1995	6	131.25	270.18	269.83
1996	5	131.25	239.55	239.29
1997	4	131.25	212.39	212.21
1998	3	131.25	188.31	188.19
1999	2	131.25	166.96	166.89
2000	1	131.25	148.03	148.00
2001	0	1,131.25	1,131.25	1,131.25

Total Value of Cash Flows in 2001[a]: $3,005.07

Total Value of Cash Flows in 2001: $3,003.04

Realized Annual Yield over 9 Years:
$$\sqrt[9]{\$3,005.07/\$1,017.50} - 1 = 12.79\%$$

Realized Annual Yield over 9 Years:
$$\sqrt[9]{\$3,003.04/\$1,017.50} - 1 = 12.78\%$$

[a]Column does not sum to total because of rounding.

flows were reinvested at that rate, total accumulated value would be $3,003.04 as of 2001. The realized compound annual yield on the $1,017.50 investment would be 12.78 percent, lower than the expected annual yield before market conditions changed. Although the difference may seem small when only one bond is involved, $1/100$ of a percent makes a big difference to investors holding millions, or even billions, of dollars of assets.

REINVESTMENT RISK AND FINANCIAL INSTITU- TIONS. Financial institutions have so many interest-bearing assets and liabilities that the effect of changing reinvestment rates is very important to them. Changing reinvestment rates for investors mean changing costs for financial institutions. If market yields fall unexpectedly, the interest costs of a financial institution will fall if it has incurred variable rate liabilities. If market rates rise unexpectedly, the reverse is true. Either way, the net interest margin is subject to unexpected variation.

EFFECT ON AN INVESTOR PLANNING TO SELL BEFORE MATURITY

What about an owner who planned all along to sell the 13⅛ RJR Nabisco bond at the opening of trading on April 10, expecting market conditions to remain unchanged? The price change *would* cause the realized return to differ from the original y*, because the sales price would be $1.25 higher than anticipated. However, the investors' expected return would *not* have been affected by the change in the rate at which the bond's interest payments could be reinvested after the discount rate decrease, because the holder never planned to receive those payments in the first place.

REINVESTMENT RISK VERSUS PRICE RISK

Thus, interest rate risk has two facets: potential variation from unexpected changes in the rate at which intermediate cash flows can be reinvested—**reinvestment risk**—and potential variation from unexpected changes in market prices of financial assets—**market value** or **price risk.** For a given change in market conditions, the two types of interest rate risk have opposite effects. A decline in market rates lowers reinvestment rates but increases prices; an increase in market rates improves reinvestment rates but decreases prices. It is not surprising, then, that interest rate risk is so hard to manage successfully.

EFFECT OF INTEREST RATE CHANGES ON DEBT SECURITIES

Financial institution balance sheets have become more similar in recent years, but different types of institutions still focus on different instruments. Even though the general price/yield relationship is illustrated in graphs such as Figure 8.1, the impact of unexpected changes in interest rates varies from instrument to instrument.

BOND THEOREMS

In 1962, as part of an article on the term structure of interest rates, Burton Malkiel proposed and proved mathematically a series of theorems on the relationship between the yields and prices of fixed-income securities. These theorems have become known simply as "the bond theorems."[5] Using calculus, Malkiel differentiated a bond price equation, similar to Equation 5.7, with respect to yield and maturity and drew the following conclusions:

THEOREM I. *Bond prices move inversely to bond yields.* The implications of Theorem I were explained earlier in this chapter.

THEOREM II. *Holding the coupon rate constant, for a given change in market yields, percentage changes in bond prices are greater the longer the term to maturity.*[6] To illustrate, consider two $1,000 bonds with 12 percent coupon rates, one with 15 years to maturity and one with 5 years to maturity. If the expected yield for bonds in this risk class is 12 percent and the term structure is flat, both will sell at par because the present value of the future cash flows, discounted at 12 percent, is $1,000. If market yields rise to 14 percent, the resulting bond prices will be:

$$\$931 = \sum_{t=1}^{5} \frac{\$120}{(1.14)^t} + \frac{\$1,000}{(1.14)^5}$$

$$\$877 = \sum_{t=1}^{15} \frac{\$120}{(1.14)^t} + \frac{\$1,000}{(1.14)^{15}}$$

The price of the 5-year bond will fall to $931, whereas the 15-year bond will sell for only $877. The percentage change in the price of the 5-year bond is 6.9 percent; for the 15-year bond, the price decline is 12.3 percent. If market yields fall to 11 percent, the price of the 5-year bond will rise to $1,037, a 3.7 percent increase. The 15-year bond price will increase to $1,072, a change of 7.2 percent. In both instances, the price of the 15-year bond changes by a larger percentage than the price of the 5-year bond, as stated formally in Theorem II. For any given change in market yields away from 12 percent, this is true.

An interesting historical look at the implications of Theorem II is provided in Figure 8.4, which shows yearly rates of return—interest income plus price changes as a percentage of value at the beginning of the year—for portfolios of long-term government bonds and T-bills.[7] Beginning at the left side, each bar represents a realized 1-year rate over the period 1926–1992. The series of annual returns is more variable for the long-term government bond portfolio than for

---

[5] Differences between the two main types of debt securities—discount and coupon-bearing—are examined in Chapter 5. They also have an important similarity in that the purchaser who holds them to maturity knows in advance the dollar amounts of the expected cash benefits from both types of instruments. Therefore, in this section they are discussed together under the generic term *bonds*. The bond theorems are discussed and proved on pp. 201–206 of Malkiel 1962. (References are listed in full at the end of this chapter.)

[6] Theorem II is true for bonds selling at or above par at the time of a change in market yields, but not for all discount bonds. Malkiel observed this but did not examine why it was so, as other authors have done subsequently. Chapter 9 develops a more general relationship between the prices and yields of bonds selling at all levels—below, at, and above par.

[7] These series are two of several historical portfolio returns presented in Ibbotson Associates 1993.

FIGURE 8.4   **Year-by-Year Returns on Treasury Bonds and Bills, 1926–1992**

When 1-year returns on short-term T-bills and long-term T-bonds are compared over a historical period, the greater risk, or variability, in returns on the longer-term securities is evident.

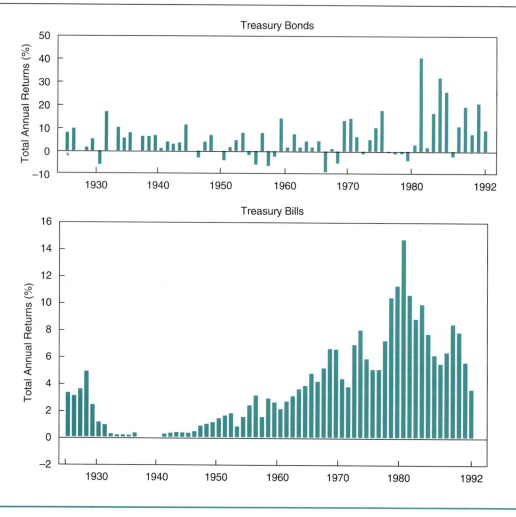

Source: Ibbotson Associates, *Stocks, Bonds, Bills and Inflation: 1993 Yearbook.* (Chicago: Ibbotson Associates, 1993), 49, 57.

T-bills. The figure demonstrates Theorem II's statement that, holding default risk constant, long-term bonds are more subject to market value risk than short-term securities.

THEOREM III. *The percentage price changes described in Theorem II increase at a decreasing rate as N increases.* In other words, the longer the time to maturity, the less the *difference* in percentage price changes. For example, when yields change, the prices

of 15-year bonds change by a greater percentage than the prices of 10-year bonds, but the *difference* is less than the *difference* between the price changes of a 5-year bond and a 10-year bond.

Figure 8.5 plots the prices of 5-, 10-, and 15-year, 12 percent coupon bonds at market yields ranging from 1 percent to 24 percent. Because the slopes of the lines are the *rates* (percentages) at which prices change as yields change, lines with similar slopes depict bonds with similar percentage price

FIGURE 8.5   Bond Theorems III and IV: As *N* and *y** Increase, Percentage Price Changes Decrease

Although the values of bonds with longer maturities are more adversely affected by changes in market yields, the percentage price changes occur at a decreasing rate at higher market yields and for bonds with longer terms to maturity.

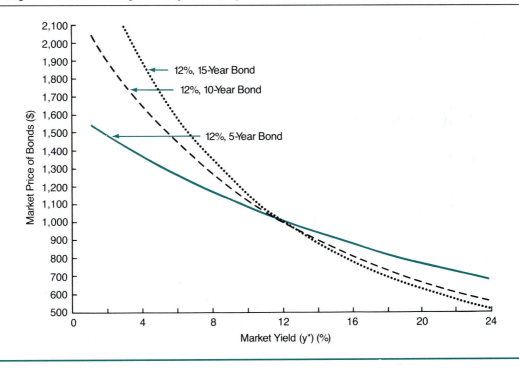

changes as yields change. The slopes of the lines for price changes of 10- and 15-year bonds are more similar than the slopes of the 5- and 10-year lines. The 15-year line is the steepest of all, as Theorem II suggests, and the 5-year line is the flattest.

Higher coupon, lower risk, sooner return

THEOREM IV. *Holding* N *constant and starting from the same market yield, equal yield changes up or down* do not *result in equal percentage price changes. A decrease in yield increases prices more than an equal increase in yield decreases prices. In more formal terms, price changes are asymmetric with respect to changes in yield.* For example, consider the effect of equal increases and decreases in market yields on the price of a 12 percent coupon, 8-year bond. If market yields start at 12 percent and increase to 14 percent, the price of the bond will fall from $1,000 to $907, a decrease of 9.3 percent. If market yields instead fall to 10 per-

cent, the bond's price will increase to $1,107, a percentage increase of 10.7 percent.

Figure 8.5 shows this asymmetric relationship for each of three bonds. A line with a constant slope would depict a steady rate of change in bond prices as yields change. In fact, none of the lines has a constant slope, and each flattens considerably as market yields rise above 12 percent, indicating a decreasing rate of price changes.

THEOREM V. *Holding* N *constant and starting from the same market yield, the higher the coupon rate, the smaller the percentage change in price for a given change in yield.*[8] This principle is illustrated in Figure

---

[8]Theorem V holds for all bonds except perpetuities and bonds with one period to maturity.

FIGURE 8.6	**Bond Theorem V: As Coupon Rate Increases, Percentage Price Changes Decrease as Yields Change**

With term to maturity held constant, the higher the coupon rates, the lower the percentage price changes on bonds as market yields change.

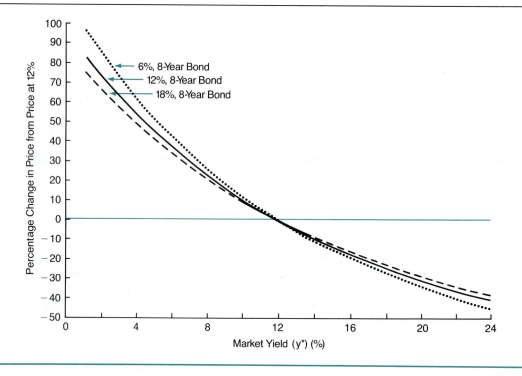

8.6, in which the percentage price changes of three 8-year bonds are plotted against changes in yields, starting from a 12 percent base. As yields drop from a 12 percent level, percentage changes in the price of a 6 percent, 8-year bond are greater than the percentage price changes for a 12 percent or 18 percent bond of comparable maturity. When yields rise from a 12 percent level, the percentage price decreases for the 6 percent bond are greater than for the other two bonds. Percentage price changes for the 18 percent coupon bond are the smallest of the three. This general behavior holds for any base yield from which change occurs.

A comparison of the lines in Figures 8.5 and 8.6 reveals that the coupon effect described in Theorem V has much less impact than does the maturity effect described in Theorem II. Comparison of the interest rate risk of securities considering both coupon and maturity differences is discussed in Chapter 9.

IMPLICATIONS FOR FINANCIAL INSTITUTIONS

The bond theorems show that changes in market rates will not affect all bond portfolios in the same way. In periods of volatile market rates, portfolios heavily invested in long-term securities have greater price fluctuations than portfolios concentrated in money market securities. The value of portfolios heavily invested in low-coupon instruments is more changeable than portfolios of high-coupon bonds. If (a big *if*) managers forecast market changes correctly and understand the bond theorems, they can position their institutions to profit from anticipated rate movements.

Throughout the rest of the book, the bond theorems enhance an understanding of the problems and opportunities confronting specific institutions. Furthermore, knowledge of the bond theorems and the related concept of "duration" enables a manager to develop a measure of interest rate risk. The development and application of such a measure are the subjects of Chapter 9.

EFFECT OF INTEREST RATE CHANGES ON COMMON STOCK

"Fed Move Ignites Explosive Stock, Bond Rallies" read a *Wall Street Journal* headline on Friday, April 10, 1992.[9] The story centered on the behavior of common stock prices after the Fed's April 9, 1992, cut in the discount rate. Analysts attributed the 43.6-point rise in the Dow Jones Industrial Average to the Fed's announcement. Because common stocks are financial assets, their prices behave similarly to those of bonds. As market yields fall, yields on common stock also fall and their prices rise. As market yields rise for other financial assets, the yields on common stock rise and their prices fall.

The relationship between common stock prices and changes in market yields is less clear-cut than the bond theorems imply for bond prices, however. One simply needs to recall the major way in which the cash flows from stocks differ from those of bonds: The timing and amount of expected cash benefits from stock are not fixed but are a function of the earnings of the stock issuer. Although a change in market yields seldom changes the cash flows expected by a bondholder, underlying economic events that change market yields may lead to a reassessment of the cash benefits expected by stockholders. Because the bond theorems assume fixed cash inflows, they cannot be applied to stocks.

Nonetheless, based on empirical evidence, some generalizations can be made. On an *ex post* basis, recent research indicates an inverse relationship between changes in several interest rate indexes and the market values of portfolios of common stock. This relation-

ship, however, seems to be stronger for some firms than for others.[10]

Also, the sensitivity of a firm's stock price to unexpected changes in interest rates is related to the amount of fixed-rate assets and liabilities held by the firm. The more fixed-rate assets (especially fixed-rate financial assets) and the longer the maturity of those assets, the greater the sensitivity of a firm's common stock to unexpected changes in interest rates.[11] In view of the bond theorems, this latter finding is not surprising. If a firm holds a large proportion of fixed-rate, long-term assets as interest rates change, the market value of the firm's assets will change more than if assets are mostly short-term. Because the market value of a firm's common stock is tied to the value of its assets, the more volatile its asset values, the more volatile the market value of its stock.

IMPLICATIONS FOR FINANCIAL INSTITUTIONS

The relationship between interest rates and stock prices is important to financial institutions for two reasons. Managers of institutions with large portfolios of common stock must understand factors that affect changes in stock value to manage these portfolios. Managers of pension funds, insurance companies, brokerage firms, and mutual funds fall into this group. But managers of all stockholder-owned institutions must be concerned with the connection between interest rates and stock prices. For example, although banks and savings and loan associations (S&Ls) cannot currently own common stock as part of their asset portfolios, their own shareholders are affected by interest rate changes, based on the choices managers make within the range of available assets. For firms such as insurance companies with common-stock asset holdings and for their own shareholders, the lesson is doubly important.

[9] Randall Smith and Robert Steiner, "Fed Move Ignites Explosive Stock, Bond Rallies," *The Wall Street Journal,* April 10, 1992, C1. The Dow's reaction to discount rates over a 20-year period is discussed and illustrated in Douglas R. Sease, "Are Five Fed Rate Cuts Enough?" *The Wall Street Journal,* December 2, 1991, C1, C2.

[10] Fogler, John, and Tipton 1981; Christie 1981; Flannery and James 1984; and Sweeney and Warga 1986.

[11] Flannery and James 1984. Actually, Flannery and James found that the interest sensitivity of a firm's common stock is related to the *net* fixed-rate asset position of the firm, or the amount by which long-term, fixed-rate assets exceed long-term, fixed-rate liabilities. The effect was confirmed in Scott and Peterson 1986 and Bae 1990. Neuberger 1992 found that commercial real estate loans have a strong effect on bank stock returns.

SUMMARY

This chapter examined interest rate risk, the dominant risk faced by financial institutions. The degree of interest rate risk an institution faces is affected by a number of factors, such as asset and liability maturities, cash flow characteristics, and the magnitude and direction of changes in interest rates.

The relationship between prices and yields on financial assets is the foundation for understanding interest rate risk. Asset prices and market yields are inversely related. When the supply/demand relationship for loanable funds changes and market yields change, the prices of financial assets also change, but in the opposite direction.

Interest rate risk can be divided into two components: reinvestment risk and market value (or price) risk. Reinvestment risk is most serious when an investor plans to hold an asset to maturity. Market value risk can be severe when an investor plans to sell an asset before maturity. Changes in market yields cause changes in market value in the opposite direction.

The bond theorems further define the impact of interest rate changes on market value. The magnitude of fluctuations in value for a given change in market yields varies with the term to maturity, the size of the security's coupon rate, and the direction of the change in yields. The theorems hold important implications for financial institutions; the management of a given asset/liability mix must recognize varying degrees of sensitivity to shifts in market yields.

Equity securities are also sensitive to changes in interest rates, but the nature of the relationship is more difficult to identify. Recent research indicates an inverse relationship between shifts in interest rates and prices of common stock, so even institutions primarily involved with the management of equity portfolios are susceptible to interest rate risk.

QUESTIONS

1. Explain economic factors that cause the market prices of financial assets to change.

2. Graphically show the relationship between an increase in the supply of securities, the change in the equilibrium rate of interest, and the change in the demand for loanable funds. Repeat the analysis for an increase in the demand for securities. Explain these relationships in your own words.

3. Explain the relationship between changes in market yields and changes in prices of financial assets.

4. What is interest rate risk? Describe the two types of interest rate risk and the relationship of each to changes in market conditions. How does interest rate risk affect *ex post* returns?

5. A portfolio manager has invested in 5-year bonds to be held until maturity. At that time, total proceeds from the bond investment will be needed for a new corporate venture. Explain how this position is exposed to interest rate risk and how returns on the investment may be affected.

6. A small insurance company's board of directors has asked for an explanation of the effect of interest rate changes on bond values and on the choices between high- and low-coupon bonds or between long and short maturities. Based on the bond theorems, what should the directors be told about the ideal composition of a bond portfolio when market yields are rising? When they are falling?

7. Using the bond theorems, but without doing calculations, explain which bond price would fluctuate more, given an increase in market yields from 10 percent to 18 percent:
    a. a 10 percent bond, 10 years to maturity;
    b. a 10 percent bond, 20 years to maturity.

8. Using the bond theorems, but without doing calculations, explain which bond would experience the largest price change, given a decline in market yields from 9 percent to 7 percent:
    a. a 5-year, 10 percent bond;
    b. a 5-year, 8 percent bond;
    c. a 5-year, 15 percent bond.

9. For two bonds maturing on the same date and with equal yields to maturity, will a change in market yields of 2 percent up or down *always* result in equal percentage price changes for both bonds and in both directions? Why or why not?

10. A bond portfolio manager who expects interest rates to fall in the near future asks for advice on which of the following investments should be chosen today to benefit most from the decline in rates. What recommendation would you offer? Why?
    a. 5 percent, 15-year bonds;
    b. 8 percent, 15-year bonds;
    c. 11 percent, 15-year bonds.

11. Briefly summarize the results of empirical studies on the relationship between common stock prices and changes in market yields. Why do the bond theorems not provide a sufficient explanation of this relationship? In what ways are the bond theorems helpful in interpreting stock return/interest rate relationship?

YTM = market rate = market yield.
prevailing rate = coupon rate.

PROBLEMS

1. Reexamine the two bonds described in Question 7. Calculate the market values of both bonds at the 10 percent prevailing rate, as well as the percentage price change resulting if market rates increase from 10 percent to 15 percent. Also calculate the bonds' market values and percentage price changes if YTM falls from 10 percent to 7 percent. To what do you attribute the difference in the size of the price changes? Assume that the bonds have a par value of $1,000 with semiannual interest payments.

2. Your broker has brought three bond portfolios to your attention:
    a. a portfolio of 9 percent, 10-year bonds;
    b. a portfolio of 9 percent, 20-year bonds;
    c. a portfolio of 9 percent, 30-year bonds.

Calculate and compare the change in values of a representative bond from portfolios a and c and from portfolios b and c if market rates drop from 9 percent to 6 percent. Which bond theorem is illustrated by these comparisons? Assume that each bond has a par value of $1,000 with annual interest payments.

3. At the beginning of 1989, Hostess International Corporation issued zero-coupon bonds with an initial time to maturity of 25 years and a par value of $1,000. At the beginning of 1999, you buy one of these bonds for 23.455.
    a. What yield to maturity was the market requiring on the Hostess International bond in 1999?
    b. What will be the percentage change in price if market yields rise to 14 percent immediately after you buy the bond?
    c. Using the bond theorems, comment on the magnitude of the price change.

4. On April 8, 1992, the 13½ RJR Nabisco bond, introduced in Figure 8.3, had a market value of $1,170.00 and a yield to maturity of 10.49 percent. Suppose that an investor purchased the bond on April 8 and planned to hold it until it matured in 2001. If market yields change immediately after the investment, and the yield on this RJR bond drops to 8 percent, what will be the investor's realized annual yield on the 9-year investment? (Hint: Refer to Table 8.1.) Assume annual interest payments.

5. Your father is preparing for your parents' 25th anniversary celebration. He wants to have $5,000 on July 1, 1999, and has set up an annuity to reach that goal. He will invest $869.46 on July 1 of each year from 1995 through 1999 and estimates that he will earn an average annual yield of 7 percent.
    a. Show that if market yields of 7 percent prevail, your father will reach his investment goal of $5,000 by July 1, 1999.
    b. Suppose that market yields drop to 5 percent immediately after the first $869.46 investment, and they remain there until July 1, 1996. Calculate the accumulated funds under these market conditions. What type of risk does this problem demonstrate?

6. Graph the relationship between the percentage price changes on a 7 percent, 5-year bond as market yields change from 1 percent to 25 percent. On the same axes, graph the relationship between the percentage price changes on a 17 percent, 5-year bond and the same range of market yields. Which bond theorem does this graph illustrate? Assume that the bonds have a par value of $1,000 with annual interest payments. Use 10 percent as the base market yield. (Hint: Refer to Figure 8.6 and use the "What-if" feature of your spreadsheet.)

7. Graph the relationship between the price of a 3-year, 10 percent bond and market yields ranging from 1 percent to 25 percent. On the same axes, graph the relationship between the price of 25-year, 10 percent bonds and the same range of market yields. Which bond theorem does this graph illustrate? Assume that the bonds have a par value of $1,000 with annual interest payments. (Hint: Use the "What-if" feature of your spreadsheet.)

SELECTED REFERENCES

Bae, Sung C. "Interest Rate Changes and Common Stock Returns of Financial Institutions: Revisited." *Journal of Financial Research* 13 (Spring 1990): 71–79.

Christie, Andrew A. "The Stochastic Behavior of Common Stock Variances: Value, Leverage, and Interest Rate Effects." *Journal of Financial Economics* 5 (December 1981): 407–432.

Flannery, Mark J., and Christopher M. James. "The Effect of Interest Rate Changes on the Common Stock Returns of Financial Institutions." *Journal of Finance* 39 (September 1984): 1141–1153.

Fogler, Russell H., Kose, John, and James Tipton. "Three Factors, Interest Rate Differentials and Stock Groups." *Journal of Finance* 36 (May 1981): 323–335.

Ibbotson Associates. *Stocks, Bonds, Bills, and Inflation: 1993 Yearbook.* Chicago: Ibbotson Associates, 1993.

Malkiel, Burton G. "Expectations, Bond Prices, and the Term Structure of Interest Rates," *Quarterly Journal of Economics* 76 (May 1962): 197–218.

Neuberger, Jonathan A. "Bank Holding Company Stock Risk and the Composition of Bank Asset Portfolios." *Economic Review* (Federal Reserve Bank of San Francisco) (Number 3, 1992): 53–62.

Scott, William L., and Richard L. Peterson. "Interest Rate Risk and Equity Values of Hedged and Unhedged Financial Intermediaries." *Journal of Financial Research* 9 (Winter 1986): 325–329.

Sweeney, Richard J., and Arthur D. Warga. "The Pricing of Interest Rate Risk: Evidence from the Stock Market." *Journal of Finance* 41 (June 1986): 393–410.

*A 30-year zero is probably three times as volatile as a common stock.
It's like a roller coaster. You'll finish the ride with a dizzy head
and woozy walk and wonder what hit you.*

William H. Gross
Managing Director, Pacific Management Investment Company (1985)

State officials anxious to lower borrowing costs in tight times are always looking for new twists that might catch potential investors' fancy. Usually, bonds issued by state governments appeal primarily to affluent investors because the interest on such bonds is exempt from federal taxes. But in a recession—the time most state governments are short of cash—there may be fewer wealthy investors on whom to draw. Fortunately, during the recession of the early 1990s, Illinois administrators devised a bond that was so popular with middle-income families that the state easily sold all it needed to issue. The secret lay not in hiring a top financial wizard to invent an exotic new breed of municipal bond, but in marketing. The 1991 State of Illinois College Savings Bond program might just as easily, and truthfully, have been called State of Illinois Zero-Coupon, Tax-Exempt Bond program. But because hardworking parents, worried about how they would send their children to college in 20 years, saw the bond issue as the solution to their financial problems, the issue was wildly popular. For every $1,279.35 invested in 1991, a parent could have purchased a bond maturing in 2012 at a face value of $5,000—just in time to pay tuition for his or her child's senior year in college. And in the process, the parent would have virtually eliminated one of the crucial worries of any bond investor—interest rate risk.[1]

Understanding price/yield relationships and the effect of reinvestment rates on portfolio return provides a necessary but insufficient foundation for analyzing interest rate risk in financial institutions. Principles in Chapter 8 were often accompanied by such caveats as "all else equal . . . this will happen," or "given equal coupon rates (or equal terms to maturity) . . . this will occur." In reality, managers analyzing interest rate risk seldom compare financial assets or liabilities with the same coupon rates, maturities, or initial yields. Thus, it is difficult to assess the impact of unexpected economic events on an institution's total asset/liability mix without a tool that cuts across financial instruments with all types of characteristics. Fortunately, although it is not perfect, a measure

[1] John Schmeltzer, "State to Again Offer College Savings Bonds for Sale," *Chicago Tribune,* September 9, 1991, Section 4, 5.

of **interest rate elasticity**—the percentage change in the value of a financial instrument for a 1 percent change in market yields—can be estimated for almost every asset or liability. To calculate and use interest rate elasticities, however, one must first understand the concept of duration.

DURATION: AN IDEA AHEAD OF ITS TIME

It is difficult to find a recent scholarly article on financial institution management that does not mention duration. It would be easy to conclude that duration is a new idea, but, in fact, it was first developed more than 50 years ago by Frederick Macaulay. Similar concepts were developed shortly thereafter, but Macaulay's duration has only recently been widely appreciated for the power it brings to the management of interest rate risk.[2]

DURATION DEFINED

Duration is the weighted average time over which the cash flows from an investment are expected, where the weights are the relative present values of the cash flows. It is an alternative to maturity for expressing the time dimension of an investment. Focusing on maturity ignores the fact that, for most securities, some cash benefits are received *before* the maturity date. Benefits received before maturity are often substantial, especially for bonds with relatively high coupon rates or annuities. It can be argued, therefore, that ignoring the time dimension of cash benefits before maturity is unwise.

The importance of the time dimension is evident in the basic expression for the market value of an investment:

[5.7]

$$P_0 = \sum_{t=1}^{N} \frac{C_t}{(1 + y^*)^t}$$

Because the market value of an investment equals the present value of expected benefits and because discount factors, $(1 + y^*)^t$, are exponential functions of time, early payments are discounted less than those received later. Differences in discounted value become more pronounced as t increases. In essence, the *effec-*

tive maturity—that is, the time period over which the investor receives cash flows with relatively high present values—may differ from the *contractual,* or legally specified, maturity. Duration is a measure of this effective maturity.

DURATION CALCULATED: BONDS

Duration is perhaps best understood through examples. Illustrations in this chapter are based not only on the two RJR Nabisco bonds maturing in 2001 (introduced in the previous chapter in Figure 8.3 on page 220) but also on two ATT bonds maturing that same year and also shown in Figure 8.3. Comparing these four bonds' price behavior after the Federal Reserve System's (Fed's) April 8, 1992, cut in the discount rate is useful in analyzing the relationship between duration and other important factors, including changes in interest rates.

First, consider the two ATT bonds maturing in 2001. As Figure 8.3 shows, one had a coupon rate of 5⅛ percent and was selling for $825.00 on April 8, 1992; the other had a coupon rate of 7 percent and was selling for $948.75. Although both bonds matured in the same year, their coupon rates differed, and investors expected a relatively larger *proportion* of the cash flows from the 7 percent bond earlier than from the 5⅛ percent bond. Stated differently, the *effective maturity* of the 7 percent bond was less than the *effective maturity* of the 5⅛ percent bond. Duration is a measure of this effective maturity which captures the difference.

Table 9.1 illustrates the calculation of these bonds' durations (as well as the durations of the two RJR Nabisco bonds). The market prices on April 8 were equal to the present value of investors' expected cash benefits, discounted at each bond's yield to maturity. (Recall that the calculation of yield to maturity was illustrated in Chapter 5.) Column 4 of the table shows the relative weight of each cash flow—that is, the percentage of the bonds' total present value contributed by each flow. Although the par values and maturities of the ATT bonds were equal, par was only 57.30 percent of the total value of the 7 percent bond, but it was 64.19 percent on the total present value of the 5⅛ percent bond. The reason for the difference is the higher coupon payments on the 7 percent bond.

The final column shows the calculation of duration. First, the time period in which each cash flow is

[2]Macaulay 1938. (References are listed in full at the end of this chapter.)

One early work based on a property similar to duration was Samuelson 1945. Also, several scholars have attributed an idea virtually identical to duration to J. R. Hicks in his *Value and Capital* (1939). For a review of the intellectual history of duration, see Weil 1973.

TABLE 9.1   **Duration of Bonds with Equal Contractual Maturities**

The duration of a financial instrument is based on its maturity, its expected cash flows, and the current market yield. This example illustrates that bonds with the same maturity can have different durations.

ATT, 5⅛ coupon, due in 2001

(1) End of Year	(2) Cash Flows	(3) Present Value in 1992 @ 7.92%	(4) Relative Weight (% of Total Present Value)	(5) Weighted Time Period (years) (1) × (4)
1	$51.25 /(1.0792) = $47.49		5.76%	0.0576
2	51.25 /(1.0792)² = 44.01		5.33	0.1067
3	51.25	40.78	4.94	0.1483
4	51.25	37.79	4.58	0.1832
5	51.25	35.01	4.24	0.2122
6	51.25	32.45	3.93	0.2360
7	51.25	30.07	3.64	0.2551
8	51.25 /(1.0792)⁸ = 27.86		3.38	0.2702
9	1,051.25	529.55	64.19	5.7769
		$825.00	100.00%	7.2461 years (Duration)

(handwritten annotation: 5.125% × 1000)

ATT, 7 coupon, due in 2001

(1) End of Year	(2) Cash Flows	(3) Present Value in 1992 @ 7.81%	(4) Relative Weight (% of Total Present Value)	(5) Weighted Time Period (years) (1) × (4)
1	$70.00	$64.93	6.84%	0.0684
2	70.00	60.22	6.35	0.1269
3	70.00	55.86	5.89	0.1766
4	70.00	51.81	5.46	0.2184
5	70.00	48.05	5.06	0.2532
6	70.00	44.57	4.70	0.2819
7	70.00	41.34	4.36	0.3050
8	70.00	38.34	4.04	0.3233
9	1,070.00	543.63	57.30	5.1570
		$948.75	100.00%	6.9108 years (Duration)

RJR, 13⅛ coupon, due in 2001

(1) End of Year	(2) Cash Flows	(3) Present Value in 1992 @ 12.79%	(4) Relative Weight (% of Total Present Value)	(5) Weighted Time Period (years) (1) × (4)
1	$131.25	$116.37	11.44%	0.1144
2	131.25	103.18	10.14	0.2028
3	131.25	91.48	8.99	0.2697
4	131.25	81.11	7.97	0.3189
5	131.25	71.91	7.07	0.3534
6	131.25	63.76	6.27	0.3760
7	131.25	56.53	5.56	0.3889
8	131.25	50.12	4.93	0.3941
9	1,131.25	383.03	37.64	3.3880
		$1,017.50	100.00%	5.8061 years (Duration)

TABLE 9.1 CONTINUED

RJR, 13½ coupon, due in 2001

(1) End of Year	(2) Cash Flows	(3) Present Value in 1992 @ 10.49%	(4) Relative Weight (% of Total Present Value)	(5) Weighted Time Period (years) (1) × (4)
1	$135.00	$122.18	10.44%	0.1044
2	135.00	110.58	9.45	0.1890
3	135.00	100.08	8.55	0.2566
4	135.00	90.58	7.74	0.3097
5	135.00	81.98	7.01	0.3503
6	135.00	74.20	6.34	0.3805
7	135.00	67.15	5.74	0.4018
8	135.00	60.78	5.19	0.4156
9	1,135.00	462.46	39.53	3.5574
		$1,170.00	100.00%	5.9654 years (Duration)

Note: Some columns may not sum to total because of rounding.

to be received is multiplied by the cash flow's relative weight. The weighted time periods are summed at the bottom of the column for each bond, resulting in a duration estimate of 7.2461 years for the 5⅛ percent ATT bond and 6.9108 for the 7 percent ATT bond. The durations of the RJR Nabisco bonds are discussed later in this chapter.

THE DURATION EQUATION

Although the duration of a financial asset can always be calculated in a tabular fashion, duration is usually expressed as an equation.[3]

[9.1]

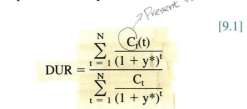

$$\text{DUR} = \frac{\displaystyle\sum_{t=1}^{N} \frac{C_t(t)}{(1+y^*)^t}}{\displaystyle\sum_{t=1}^{N} \frac{C_t}{(1+y^*)^t}}$$

→ Present Value

---

[3] Alternative formulas have been presented for the duration of investments with at least some expected cash benefits in the form of annuity payments. These formulas are especially useful when the contractual maturity of the investment is lengthy, as is the case in calculating the duration of a 25-year, fixed-rate bond with semiannual interest payments. See Benesh and Celec 1984. Other simplified formulas are presented in Chua 1984; Bierwag 1987; and Smith 1988. In practice, most professional analysts have access to microcomputers or to bond duration tables, which present durations for many combinations of yield, coupon rate, and maturity.

Examining this formula reveals that it is familiar. The denominator is Equation 5.7, the financial instrument's total present value using a discount rate (y*) equal to the current effective annual yield on the instrument. The numerator sums the present value of each cash flow, $C_t/(1+y^*)^t$, times the year in which it is received, t. For example, in the case of a 9-year bond, the numerator of the duration equation is the *sum* of the present value of the first year's cash flow times 1, the present value of the second year's cash flow times 2, and so on. The duration statement in Equation 9.1 expresses the procedure followed in Table 9.1 in a compact form and a slightly different order. When data from Table 9.1 are used in Equation 9.1, the result is the same duration estimate, except for rounding differences, for the 5⅛ bond:

$$\Sigma\,(1)\times(3)$$

$$
\begin{aligned}
\text{DUR} = \ &\$47.49(1) + \$44.01(2) + \$40.78(3) + \\
&\$37.79(4) + \$35.01(5) + \$32.45(6) + \$30.07(7) + \\
&\$27.86(8) + \$529.55(9)
\end{aligned}
$$
$$\overline{\$825.00\,\Sigma\,(3)}$$

$$= \frac{\$5,978.08}{\$825.00} = 7.2462$$

Equation 9.1 shows that the duration of a financial instrument is based on a complex interaction of factors—cash flows, their timing, and the current market yield. If any of these changes, the duration of the instrument will change. However, because durations are denominated in numbers of periods (years in the case of Table 9.1), one can compare the durations of several investments even if they have different yields, cash flows, or contractual maturities. It is also possible for two or more assets with very different characteristics to have the same durations.

SIMPLIFYING THE FORMULA

Although Equation 9.1 and its tabular equivalent are easy to apply when one is using a microcomputer, they are rather tedious when one has only a calculator. Fortunately, through mathematical analysis of Macaulay's original work, researchers have derived a simplified formula for calculating bond duration:

$$\text{DUR} = N - \left\{ \left(\frac{C}{P_0 \times y^*} \right) \times \left[N - (1 + y^*) \left(\frac{1 - \frac{1}{(1 + y^*)^N}}{y^*} \right) \right] \right\} \qquad [9.2]$$

Using the data for the 5⅛ ATT bond, Equation 9.2 yields

$$\text{DUR} = 9 - \left\{ \left(\frac{\$51.25}{\$825.00 \times 0.0792} \right) \times \left[9 - \left((1.0792) \left(\frac{1 - \frac{1}{(1.0792)^9}}{0.0792} \right) \right) \right] \right\}$$

$$= 9 - [(0.7844) \times (9 - 6.7641)]$$

$$= 7.2462$$

Except for rounding, this duration estimate is equal to that shown in Table 9.1 and that calculated using Equation 9.1.[4]

---

[4]Equation 9.2 was developed by Caks et al. 1985 and is designed for bonds paying interest annually. It is possible to modify the equation for bonds paying interest more than once a year; see Moser and Lindley 1989.

DURATION CALCULATED: COMMON STOCKS

Although Macaulay originally proposed duration for bonds, others have applied the concept to common stocks. An analyst must make critical assumptions to calculate a stock's duration, but that requirement is not unique to duration. The expected cash flows from the stock, including their growth rate and timing, must be estimated. Because stocks have no maturity date, the relevant holding period must also be estimated. Finally, a method for estimating the expected annual yield must be chosen. These decisions are illustrated in Chapter 5. Once they are made, a stock's duration can be calculated.

Table 9.2 contains duration estimates for two hypothetical stocks with different anticipated cash flows. Assuming that both stocks have an expected rate of return of 10 percent, the duration estimates are computed as in Table 9.1, although Equation 9.1 could also be used. Because the anticipated price of the second stock at the end of 10 years is much higher than that of the first, its relative weight is higher. Therefore, the duration of the stock with low initial dividends but anticipated growth is greater than the duration of the stock with no anticipated dividend growth.

If a stock is a good candidate for the constant growth model and if the planned holding period is essentially perpetual, a simplified formula for calculating duration is[5]

$$\text{DUR}_g = \frac{1 + y^*}{y^* - g} \quad \rightarrow \text{growth rate}$$

$$[9.3]$$

Once again, Equation 9.3 indicates that, given an expected rate of return, y^*, the higher the anticipated

---

[5]A history of the application of duration to common stock is traced in Reilly and Sidhu 1980. The simplified model for common stock duration was presented in Boquist, Racette, and Schlarbaum 1975.

Recently, Martin Leibowitz observed that the actual sensitivity of common stock to interest rate changes is considerably lower than might be predicted from Equation 9.3. He formulated a model of equity duration that results in substantially lower duration estimates than obtained from traditional models. Although Leibowitz's work is controversial, it is sure to attract increased attention in the future. For more discussion, see Johnson 1989; Leibowitz et al. 1989; and Stowe 1991.

TABLE 9.2   **Calculating the Duration of Two Hypothetical Stocks with Equal Expected Holding Periods**

Duration can be estimated for common stocks as well as for bonds. Given equal expected rates of return, the duration of a stock with favorable growth prospects is higher than that of a stock with a lower expected growth rate.

No Growth in Dividends

(1) End of Year	(2) Cash Flows	(3) End of Year 0: Present Value @ 10.00%	(4) Relative Weight (% of Total Present Value)	(5) Weighted Time Period (years) (1) × (4)
1	$ 2.00	$ 1.82	5.76%	0.0576
2	2.00	1.65	5.24	0.1047
3	2.00	1.50	4.76	0.1428
4	2.00	1.37	4.33	0.1731
5	2.00	1.24	3.93	0.1967
6	2.00	1.13	3.58	0.2146
7	2.00	1.03	3.25	0.2276
8	2.00	0.93	2.96	0.2365
9	2.00	0.85	2.69	0.2418
10	52.00	20.05	63.51	6.3512
		$31.57	100.00%	7.9466 years

Dividend Growth Expected

(1) End of Year	(2) Cash Flows	(3) End of Year 0: Present Value @ 10.00%	(4) Relative Weight (% of Total Present Value)	(5) Weighted Time Period (years) (1) × (4)
1	$ 1.00	$ 0.91	2.15%	0.0215
2	1.00	0.83	1.96	0.0392
3	1.40	1.05	2.49	0.0748
4	1.40	0.96	2.27	0.0907
5	1.80	1.12	2.65	0.1325
6	1.80	1.02	2.41	0.1445
7	2.40	1.23	2.92	0.2044
8	3.00	1.40	3.32	0.2654
9	3.50	1.48	3.52	0.3167
10	83.50	32.19	76.31	7.6312
		$42.19	100.00%	8.9209 years

growth in dividends, the greater the stock's estimated duration.

the same way that the bond theorems follow from the formula for the market value of a bond.

SOME GENERAL PROPERTIES OF DURATION

It is helpful to understand the ways duration is related to its three determinants—contractual maturity, existing market yields, and cash flow patterns. The generalizations follow from the duration equation in much

DURATION AND CONTRACTUAL MATURITY

Duration is shorter than contractual maturity for all except one type of investment, a discount security or zero-coupon bond. Because a discount or zero-coupon instrument has but one cash inflow with a present value equal to the asset's market value, the summation operator drops out of the formula:

FIGURE 9.1   **Duration versus Maturity of an 8 Percent Bond**

Holding coupon rate constant, the longer the maturity of a bond, the longer its duration, whether market yields are above or below 8 percent.

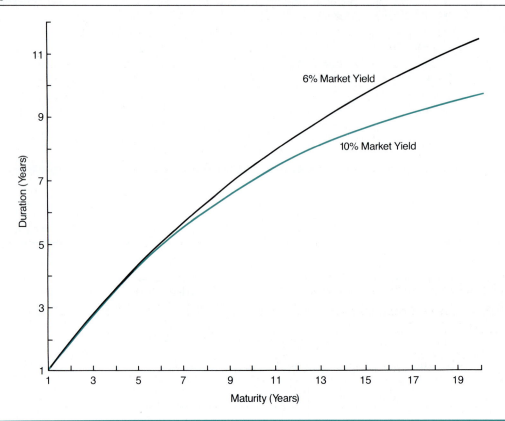

$$DUR_z = \frac{\dfrac{C_N(N)}{(1 + y^*)^N}}{\dfrac{C_N}{(1 + y^*)^N}} = N \qquad [9.4]$$

The duration of any instrument is positively related to maturity, except for maturities in excess of 50 years.[6] Figure 9.1 plots the duration of an 8 percent bond at current market yields (y^*) of 6 percent and 10 percent against maturities of 1 to 20 years. Although the relationship is not linear, because the slopes of the lines are not constant, the duration of the bond at each market yield increases with maturity.

DURATION AND CURRENT MARKET YIELDS

The relative positions of the two lines in Figure 9.1 suggest an inverse relationship between duration and current market yield, the discount rate in the du-

---

[6]The behavior of duration for bonds with very long maturities is discussed and illustrated in Fisher and Weil 1971. They note that for bonds selling at or above par, duration is bounded by $(y^* + m)/(m \times y^*)$, so the maximum duration for a bond paying interest twice a year ($m = 2$) with a yield of 10 percent, regardless of coupon or maturity, would be $(0.10 + 2)/(2 \times 0.10) = 2.10/0.20 = 10.5$ years. For bonds selling at a discount, duration actually decreases for ma-

turities of more than about 50 years. The mathematical expression of the maximum duration for a discount bond is more complex and is presented in Hopewell and Kaufman 1973. Because, as a practical matter, few institutions have investment planning periods exceeding 50 years and because few, if any, bonds with contractual maturities of more than 50 years are available, the limitations of this property are not considered further.

FIGURE 9.2   **Duration versus Yield**

Holding coupon rate and maturity constant, the higher a bond's current market yield, the shorter its duration.

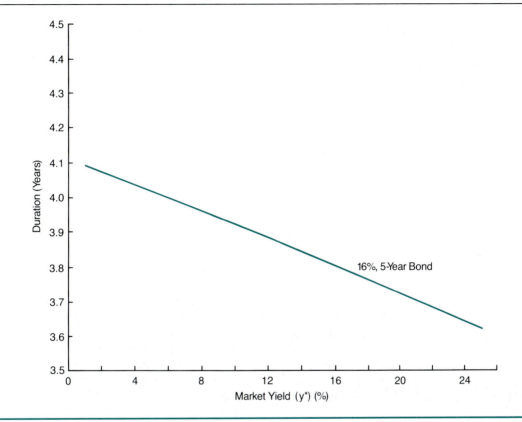

ration equation. For an 8 percent coupon bond, durations at a 10 percent market yield are lower than durations at a 6 percent yield.

As $y*$ increases, the present value of distant cash flows gets exponentially smaller. Thus, the weight given to distant time periods in the numerator of the duration equation also gets smaller, lowering duration. Figure 9.2 shows this relationship directly by plotting the duration of a 16 percent coupon, 5-year bond against market yields ranging from 0 to 25 percent.

Another specific example of the yield/duration relationship is provided by the two RJR Nabisco bonds shown in the latter portion of Table 9.1. Notice that the coupon rates of the two bonds, although not identical, are quite similar and recall that both bonds mature in 2001. Yet their market yields as of April 8, 1992, were more than 2 full percentage points different—12.79 percent for the 13⅛ bond but only 10.49 percent for

the 13½ bond. Recall that the two ATT bonds discussed earlier had coupon rates that differed by more than 2 percent but very similar market yields, so the one with the higher coupon rate had a lower duration. In the case of the RJR Nabisco bonds, however, the difference in yields is much greater than the difference in their coupon rates. Consequently, given the inverse relationship between duration and yield, the bond with the lower yield (10.49 percent) has the higher duration (5.9654 years) even though it has a slightly higher coupon rate than the other RJR Nabisco bond (13½ percent compared with 13⅛ percent).

DURATION AND COUPON RATE

Finally, all else equal or very similar, duration is inversely related to coupon rate, because high-coupon bonds provide a greater proportion of their cash flows

FIGURE 9.3 **Duration versus Coupon Rate**

Holding maturity and yield constant, the higher a bond's coupon rate, the shorter its duration.

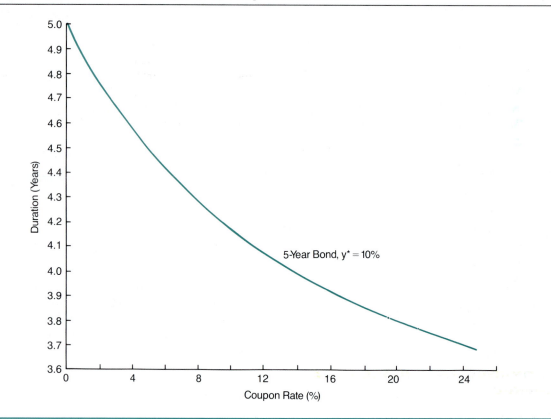

earlier than low-coupon bonds. The effect of coupon rate on duration was shown in Table 9.1 with the two ATT bonds. Figure 9.3 illustrates the relationship over a range of coupons for a 5-year bond at a market yield of 10 percent. As shown by Equation 9.4, the duration of a zero-coupon bond is equal to its maturity.

DURATIONS ARE ADDITIVE

With limitations, a fourth property of duration makes it useful for portfolio management: For assets (or liabilities) with equal market yields, the duration of a portfolio is the weighted sum of the durations of the assets (or liabilities) in the portfolio, where the weights are the proportions invested in each. In financial institutions with a variety of assets and liabilities, the ad-

ditivity of duration permits managers to measure the collective effect of a large number of maturities and coupon rates.[7] In practice, managers often estimate portfolio durations as weighted averages, even when there are small differences among market yields on individual portfolio components.

COMMON STOCK DURATIONS

These properties also apply in general to stocks. The duration of a stock paying no dividends is equal to the planned holding period, because the cash inflow from the sale is the only one anticipated. Also, the

---

[7] For development and proof of the additive property of duration, see Bierwag 1987, 84–86, 109–110.

longer the planned holding period, the longer a stock's duration. Further, the duration of a stock increases with decreases in the current expected yield. Finally, as was suggested in Table 9.2, the higher the interim cash dividends, the lower a stock's duration.

MEASURING INTEREST RATE RISK: THE RELATIONSHIP BETWEEN DURATION AND PRICE CHANGES

Why is duration important in assessing an institution's interest rate risk? The answer is direct: For a given change in market yields, percentage changes in asset prices are proportional to the asset's duration.[8] This is a powerful statement, because duration is a complex variable that considers relationships among the size of cash flows, their timing, and current market expectations. Although the bond theorems allow an analyst to anticipate price changes based on one characteristic at a time, the relationship between duration and price changes considers all characteristics simultaneously.

ESTIMATING PERCENTAGE PRICE CHANGES

The relationship between duration and the percentage price change expected from a change in market yield is closely approximated by

$$\%\Delta P_0 = \frac{\Delta P_0}{P_0} \cong -DUR \frac{\Delta y^*}{1 + y^*} \qquad [9.5]$$

where Δy^* is expressed in **basis points** divided by 100. A basis point is 1/100 of a percent. For example, a positive change in market yields of 53 basis points, from 8.53 percent to 9.06 percent, would appear in Equation 9.5 as 53/100 = +0.53; a decline of 53 basis

points would appear as −0.53. As the following example shows, the percentage price changes estimated by Equation 9.5 are very close to the true changes.

To illustrate, consider the yields and durations of the four ATT and RJR Nabisco bonds as market conditions changed between April 8, 1992, and April 9, 1992. (Figure 8.3 shows prices and other information for those 2 days.) Table 9.3 summarizes relevant data for analyzing the relationship between duration and price changes. By substituting data from Table 9.3 into Equation 9.5, percentage price changes accompanying the change in market yields between April 8 and April 9 can be estimated for the ATT bonds:

$$\%\Delta P_{5\ 1/8} = -7.2461 \times \frac{-0.05}{1.0792} = +0.34\%$$

$$\%\Delta P_7 = -6.9108 \times \frac{-0.04}{1.0781} = +0.26\%$$

As Table 9.3 shows, actual price changes for the two bonds were +0.30 percent for the 5⅛ bond and +0.26 percent for the 7 percent bond. Considering that supply and demand for individual bonds, as well as overall market conditions, play a role in prices, the changes calculated from Equation 9.5 are good estimates, as are the percentage price change estimates for the RJR Nabisco bonds.[9]

ESTIMATING INTEREST RATE ELASTICITY

It is only a short step from Equation 9.5 to a measure of interest rate elasticity for a financial asset, which may serve as a reasonable proxy for the interest rate risk of holding the asset. Earlier, the interest rate elasticity of a financial asset was defined as the

---

[8]Hopewell and Kaufman 1973. This insight and the formula presented as Equation 9.5 are often traced to these authors, although they acknowledge a similar derivation several years earlier in Fisher 1966. A very useful discussion of duration and interest rate risk measurement is provided in Chapter 3 of Bierwag 1987.

[9]The percentage price change estimates shown in Table 9.3 would not be the same if interest rates changed after April 9, even if rates changed by the same amount as they did between April 8 and April 9. Instead, investors would need to calculate *new* durations and elasticities at April 9 YTMs and then estimate future bond prices based on these new figures. In other words, a bond's duration and elasticity apply to only one set of market conditions and must be recalculated each time market conditions change. The availability of computers makes this need to recalculate frequently a manageable problem for financial institutions.

TABLE 9.3   Duration and Bond Price Changes

An asset's duration is a good basis for estimating anticipated price changes if market yields change. In these examples, actual bond price changes from April 8 to April 9, 1992, are almost identical to those estimated from the bonds' durations.

	ATT 5⅛		ATT 7		RJR 13⅛		RJR 13½	
	April 8	April 9	April 8	April 9	April 8	April 9	April 8	April 9
Yield (%)	7.92%	7.87%	7.81%	7.77%	12.79%	12.76%	10.49%	10.43%
Yield (basis points)	792	787	781	777	1,279	1,276	1,049	1,043
Price	$825.00	$827.50	$948.75	$951.25	$1,017.50	$1,018.75	$1,170.00	$1,173.75
Duration	7.2461	NA	6.9108	NA	5.8061	NA	5.9654	NA
Change in yield (basis points, April 8 to April 9)	−5		−4		−3		−6	
Δy^* in Equation 9.4 (basis point change/100)	−0.05		−0.04		−0.03		−0.06	
Change in yield (%, April 8 to April 9)	−0.63%		−0.51%		−0.23%		−0.57%	
Estimated price change (%, April 8 to April 9, using Equation 9.4)	0.34%		0.26%		0.15%		0.32%	
Actual price change (April 8 to April 9)	$2.50		$2.50		$1.25		$3.75	
Actual price change (%, April 8 to April 9)	0.30%		0.26%		0.12%		0.32%	

NA = not applicable

percentage price change expected for a 1 percent change in market yields. Thus,[10]

$$E = -DUR \frac{y^*}{1 + y^*}$$ [9.6]

---

[10] Equation 9.6 can be derived from Equation 9.5 as follows. First, note that the mathematical definition of interest rate elasticity is

$$E = \frac{\%\Delta P_0}{\%\Delta y^*} = \frac{\Delta P_0/P_0}{\Delta y^*/y^*}$$

Therefore, Equation 9.5 can be divided by $\Delta y^*/y^*$ to obtain an expression for E:

$$\frac{\Delta P_0/P_0}{\Delta y^*/y^*} = \frac{- DUR \times [\Delta y^*/(1 + y^*)]}{\Delta y^*/y^*}$$ [9.5A]

After the right side of Equation 9.5A is simplified and E is substituted for the left side, Equation 9.6 results.

To interpret the results of Equation 9.6, it is important to know what is meant by a "1 percent change." A 1 percent change in yields is a change equal to 1 percent of the existing yield; that is, if the present yield is 7.85 percent, a 1 percent change is an increase or decrease of 0.0785 percent (7.85 basis points), *not* an increase to 8.85 percent or a decrease to 6.85 percent (that is, *not* a 100-basis-point change). Using Equation 9.6 on data from April 8, for example, the elasticity of the 5⅛ ATT bond was

$$E = -7.2461 \frac{0.0792}{1.0792} = -0.53177$$

At that time, for every 1 percent change in the bond's yield of 7.92 percent, the bondholder could have expected a price change of 0.53177 percent but in the opposite direction of the yield change. Similarly, the elasticity of the ATT 7 bond on April 8 was

$$E = -6.9108 \frac{0.0781}{1.0781} = -0.50063$$

If the bonds' interest rate elasticities are used as measures of interest rate risk, the 5⅛ bond was riskier than the 7 percent bond as of April 8. Because yields subsequently decreased, percentage price changes for both bonds were positive but were greater for the 5⅛ bond than for the 7 percent bond. The percentage price change in the 5⅛ bond was more favorable to the holder in this case, but it would have been more detrimental had yields increased.[11]

COMPARISON OF EQUATIONS

Is Equation 9.5 or Equation 9.6 more helpful? Either can be used to estimate the percentage price change for an investment if a specific change in yields is anticipated. Equation 9.5 does not, however, provide a relative measure of expected price changes that can be compared across the spectrum of financial assets. Both relationships are important, but Equation 9.6 is of more general assistance to decision making.

LIMITATIONS OF A DURATION-BASED MEASURE OF INTEREST RATE RISK

As with all tools to help manage an unknown future, a duration-based risk measure has imperfections. Perhaps the most important is an assumption underlying both Equations 9.5 and 9.6: When interest rates change, there will be a parallel shift in the yield curve so that for a given level of default risk, yields across the entire structure change equally. Only if this

assumption holds can the interest rate elasticities of two investments be compared without some distortion. Some research indicates that parallel shifts in the yield curve are unusual and that relative volatility in yields, as well as duration, affect price changes. Because the formula for interest rate elasticity involves both yield and duration, this conclusion is not surprising.

Other research on the historical relationship between duration and rates of return on Treasury securities indicates that factors besides duration are needed to explain variation in returns. In addition, the return/duration relationship is not always linear, as Equations 9.5 and 9.6 imply. Nonetheless, many experts view the benefits of duration-based interest rate risk measures to be far greater than their shortcomings.[12] Most successful managers find it essential to understand duration.

APPLICATIONS OF DURATION TO ASSET/LIABILITY MANAGEMENT

Duration and related measures of interest rate risk are relevant for almost every financial institution. The most common applications are discussed here, and others are mentioned in later chapters on specific institutions.

DURATION AND THE TERM STRUCTURE

Some analysts argue that the term structure of interest rates is best viewed as the relationship between yield and duration, not yield and maturity. Forward rates could be calculated from the duration-based curve for use in forecasting future yields. For example, Figure 9.4 shows two sets of yield curves for Treasury securities. The top panel plots yield against maturity, and the bottom plots yield against duration. Although the curves have similar shapes, as is expected from the general duration/maturity relationship, the appropriate managerial response might be quite different.[13]

---

[11] Although in practice one rarely, if ever, sees yields change at one time by a full percentage point (for example, from 9 percent to 10 percent), there is a simple formula for estimating the percentage change in an asset's price should such an unusual shift in yields (of 100 basis points) occur:

$$E = \frac{-\text{DUR}}{(1 + y^*)} \qquad [9.6A]$$

For example, if the yield on the ATT 5⅛ bond had changed from 7.92 percent to 6.92 percent in a single shift, the percentage by which the bond's price would have changed could be estimated as

$$\frac{-7.2461}{(1.0792)} = -6.7143 \text{ percent}$$

[12] Yawitz 1977; Reilly and Sidhu 1980; Kaufman 1984; Leibowitz 1983; and Hess 1982.

[13] These insights are provided in Bisignano and Dvorak 1981, from which the yield curves presented in Figure 9.4 are taken.

FIGURE 9.4   **The Yield Curve: Duration versus Maturity as a Measure of Time**

These duration-based yield curves are more gently sloped than maturity-based curves plotted at the same time, suggesting that investors faced less interest rate risk than they might have thought.

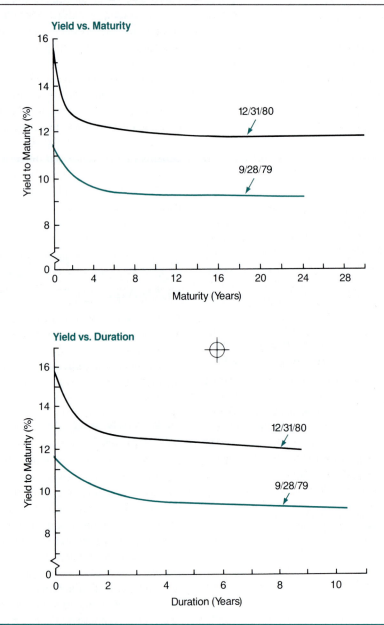

Source: Joseph Bisignano and Brian Dvorak, "Risk and Duration," *Weekly Letter* (Federal Reserve Bank of San Francisco), April 3, 1981.

The yield/maturity panel indicates that the maximum maturity of Treasury securities increased between the two dates. Instead, the duration/yield relationship shows that the maximum duration of Treasury securities *decreased.* Because of the high general level of interest rates in 1980, new Treasury issues had high coupons and relatively short durations, even though the contractual maturities of new issues were not shortened. Using a duration measure, investors in long-term Treasury bonds (T-bonds) were exposed to less, not more, interest rate risk in 1980 than they were in 1979; the traditional yield/maturity relationship would have suggested otherwise. Major investors in the Treasury market may have had lower exposure to interest rate risk in 1980 than many realized.

PORTFOLIO IMMUNIZATION

Interest rate risk, both with respect to changing market values and reinvestment rates, means that the realized yield on an investment will often differ from the expected yield at the time of investment. For some investors, accepting this risk may be extremely unappealing if they have financial goals or obligations that depend on attaining a certain amount of cash at the end of a holding period. For example, a pension fund may have known obligations to retirees, and cash must be accumulated by the due date. Or an individual may retain the services of a bank trust department, and require that his or her funds increase enough by a given date that they will cover the cost of a child's Harvard education.

In the 1970s, a duration-based strategy for portfolio management was introduced and has since been widely adopted by financial institutions.[14] The strategy is known as **immunization** because it makes a portfolio "immune" to the "disease" of interest rate

risk over a given holding period. Immunization is a portfolio management strategy to achieve a realized annual rate of return at the end of a holding period that is no less than the expected annual yield at the beginning of the period. Within constraints addressed later in the chapter, a portfolio is immunized if its duration is equal to the holding period.

IMMUNIZATION ILLUSTRATED. Suppose that an individual wishes to invest over the period January 1, 1994, to October 4, 2000, at which time a loan obligation incurred some time ago must be repaid. An annual return of at least 10 percent (the market yield at the beginning of 1994) must be earned over the period. In other words, during the holding period of 6.759 years (6 years, 277 days), each $1,000 invested must grow to at least $1,000 \times (1.10)^{6.759} = \$1,904.47$. The investor asks a bank trust department to help in evaluating three alternatives, described in Table 9.4.

The first alternative is to buy a 10 percent coupon, 3-year bond in January 1994, followed by the purchase of a bond with 3.759 years to maturity in January 1997 with a coupon rate equal to the market rate at that time. Under this strategy, the investor avoids incurring market value risk because both bonds are to be redeemed at their par values. However, reinvestment risk is involved because the rate at which coupon payments can be reinvested is unknown, and the coupon rate on the 3.759-year bond to be purchased in January 1997 is also unknown. Another possibility is to buy a bond with a term to maturity exactly equal to the holding period—6.759 years. The investor would still incur reinvestment risk but would know the coupon payments over the entire period and would incur no price risk. Finally, a long-term bond with a 10-year maturity as of January 1994 could be chosen. This strategy is subject to both price and reinvestment risk.

Assuming a flat yield curve at 10 percent in January 1994, any one of the bonds could be purchased at its par value of $1,000. No rate changes would be anticipated from the yield curve, but unexpected rate changes could go in either direction. A trust department officer with knowledge of duration should have no trouble recommending one of the alternatives—the 10 percent coupon, 10-year bond.

Data in Table 9.4 demonstrate why this bond is the best choice. If market yields remain at 10 percent throughout the holding period, none of the bonds will

---

[14] Fisher and Weil 1971. The authors acknowledge their indebtedness to the ideas of writers dating back to the 1940s (p. 409). In an interesting history of the use of immunization by institutional portfolio managers, Leibowitz notes that, regardless of its rich and lengthy academic heritage, immunization was put into practice only when the financial markets faced unprecedented events in the late 1970s. At that time, the models still widely followed were developed by practitioners. Leibowitz argues strongly, however, that theoretical interest in immunization by the academic community has immensely benefited those using the technique in the "real world." See Leibowitz 1983. Advanced applications are further discussed in Leibowitz 1981; and Bierwag 1987.

TABLE 9.4	**Duration and Portfolio Immunization**

With immunization, the expected return on a portfolio is protected from both reinvestment and market value risk. In this example, holding bonds with a duration of 6.759 years will lock in an annual rate of return of 10 percent over a holding period of 6.759 years.

Beginning of holding period: January 1, 1994
$y^* = 10\%$ on January 1, 1994; yield curve flat
End of holding period: October 4, 2000
Length of holding period: 6.759 years

Market Yield in 1997 and Beyond (%)	Value (October 4, 2000)	Total Coupons Received During Holding Period[a]	Interest on Coupons[b]	Total Cash (October 4, 2000)	Realized Annual Return (%)
Strategy 1. Buy 10% Bond, with 3-Year Maturity as of January 1, 1994;					
Then Buy 3.759-Year Bond on January 1, 1997					
12.00%	$1,000.00	$751.08	$288.10	$2,039.18	11.12%
10.00	$1,000.00	$675.90	$229.44	$1,905.34	10.01
8.00	$1,000.00	$600.72	$177.38	$1,778.10	8.89
Strategy 2. Buy 10% Bond, with 6.759-Year Maturity as of January 1, 1994;					
Bond Matures at End of Holding Period					
12.00%	$1,000.00	$675.90	$274.55	$1,950.45	10.39%
10.00	$1,000.00	$675.90	$229.44	$1,905.34	10.01
8.00	$1,000.00	$675.90	$186.21	$1,862.11	9.63
Strategy 3. Buy 10% Bond, with 10-Year Maturity as of January 1, 1994; Sell on October 4, 2000					
12.00%	$ 949.77	$675.90	$274.55	$1,900.22	9.96%
10.00	$1,000.56	$675.90	$229.44	$1,905.90	10.01
8.00	$1,055.88	$675.90	$186.21	$1,917.99	10.12

[a] Assumes receipt of 75.9% of the coupon in 2000, because bond will be held for 75.9% of that year.
[b] Assumes reinvestment of coupons at 10% until 1997, then reinvestment at prevailing market yield until October 4, 2000.

be subject to either price or reinvestment risk. If rates rise unexpectedly in 1997 to 12 percent, the first strategy will provide higher coupon payments ($120 per year) for the remaining 3.759 years, plus an opportunity to reinvest them *and* the ones received before 1997 at 12 percent. If rates fall to 8 percent, the coupon rate on the 3.759-year bond will fall to 8 percent, as will the reinvestment rate. In neither case is the investor's ability to earn the required 10 percent return assured.

For the other alternatives, coupon payments will remain at $100 per year for the entire holding period, but the rate at which they can be reinvested could rise to 12 percent or fall to 8 percent. In the third strategy, the price of the bond at the end of the holding period is also uncertain. The 10 percent, 10-year bond will have 3.241 years until maturity in 2000. If it is sold when the market yield is 12 percent, it will bring a price of $949.77, the present value of its remaining cash flows as of October 4, 2000. If rates fall to 8 percent, the bond can be sold for $1,055.88, its remaining present value at 8 percent.

An examination of the total cash accumulated shows that only the 10 percent, 10-year bond will consistently meet the investor's needs. If rates rise, the additional interest on reinvested coupons almost exactly offsets the drop in the bond's price. If rates fall, the increase in the bond's price at the time of sale almost exactly offsets the lower reinvestment opportunities. Either way, the investor's desire for each $1,000 to accumulate to $1,904.47 by October 4, 2000, is more closely realized with the third alternative than the others. At worst, if rates rise unexpectedly to 12 percent and the bond must be sold at a discount, Equation 5A.3 can be used to find the implicit annual rate of return over the holding period:

$$y_H = \sqrt[6.759]{\frac{\$1,900.22}{\$1,000.00}} - 1 = 9.96\%$$

It is no coincidence that the duration of the 10 percent, 10-year bond as of January 1, 1994, is 6.759 years. When the duration of an investment is equal to the desired holding period, the two facets of interest rate risk almost exactly offset one another, enabling the investor to lock in an annual yield at least equal to the original expected annual yield. The investor is immunized against interest rate risk, and potential variation in returns is reduced almost to zero.

IMMUNIZATION: ASSUMPTIONS AND LIMITATIONS. Under certain assumptions, a bond with a duration equal to the desired holding period results in exactly offsetting market value and reinvestment risks. With a flat initial yield curve, and with only *one* unexpected parallel shift in the curve immediately after the beginning of the period, the realized annual return over the holding period will *exactly* equal the expected annual yield.

The example in Table 9.4 does not conform to one of these assumptions; the market yield changes in the middle of the investment period, so the investor is less than perfectly immunized. Also, although not considered in the example, interest rate changes are so common and so unpredictable that single parallel shifts in the yield curve are the exception rather than the rule.[15] Still, empirical tests of duration and maturity strategies over 44 years suggest that the dispersion of realized returns is consistently smaller when durations rather than maturities are matched with holding periods.

Another limitation of immunization is that it is difficult to find an investment with a duration exceeding 10 years.[16] Thus, investors with lengthy desired holding periods may be unable to use the strategy. The recent advent of stripped securities, discussed in a later section, has alleviated this limitation somewhat.

FINANCIAL INSTITUTIONS AND IMMUNIZATION

As the previous example illustrates, one way in which financial institutions use immunization is to offer it as part of an array of portfolio management services to customers. Commercial bank trust departments, securities firms, and investment companies are among those institutions for which knowledge of immunization is important. Yet even institutions that do not sell portfolio management services can benefit from understanding immunization. If an institution has promised to make cash payments to others at specified dates in the future, as is the case with pension funds and life insurance companies, a way to enhance the probability that cash will be available to meet those payments is to invest in assets with a weighted average duration equal to that of future cash obligations. Asset portfolios selected for their durations and designed to help meet future cash outflows are called **dedicated portfolios.**

Despite its usefulness, immunization presents difficulties for institutions. Ideally, immunization locks in a yield for a desired holding period by protecting against both sides of interest rate risk. But immunized portfolios are not protected from default risk, nor is there a guarantee against changes in anticipated yields as a result of unanticipated changes in tax laws. Finally, immunization eliminates the possibility of unexpected gains when interest rates change. In other words, it is a *hedging,* or risk-minimization, strategy, not a profit-maximization strategy. If rates rise to 12 percent in the example in Table 9.4, the first strategy is the most desirable, but an immunizer forgoes that opportunity. Thus, immunization is appropriate for portfolio managers who wish to avoid rate forecasting or who are willing to trade potential unexpected gains for protection from potential unexpected losses.

STRIPPED SECURITIES

It follows from a discussion of the limitations of immunization that perhaps the best way to lock in a desired rate of return without reinvestment or price risk is to invest only in zero-coupon investments, whose maturities are equal to their durations. Until recently, however, it was difficult to find zero-coupon

---

[15] See Yawitz 1977, Bierwag, Kaufman, and Toevs 1983, and Ott 1988.

[16] Details are provided in Footnote 6.

instruments with durations corresponding to a wide range of investment horizons. Furthermore, the total volume of zero-coupon issues of any duration was small, because only a few corporations had issued them.

In 1982, divisions of two major securities firms, Merrill Lynch and Salomon Brothers, introduced a new security designed to meet the potential demand for zero-coupon bonds of all durations. The generic term for these new financial assets is **stripped securities.** The name arose because they were created when the originators "stripped" ordinary T-bonds of their coupon payments, then sold one or more coupon payments or the par value separately to investors wanting single cash inflows at specified dates. The acronyms given to these securities provoked amusement as well as interest. CATS (Certificates of Accrual on Treasury Securities) was the name for the Salomon Brothers version of a strip, while Merrill Lynch's Treasury Investment Growth Receipts were called TIGRs. Other securities firms soon entered the field.[17]

In 1985, to facilitate the issuance of strips, the Treasury Department decided that each coupon payment on specified Treasury issues may be registered in a separate name. The program is called Separate Trading of Registered Interest and Principal of Securities (STRIPS). Treasury issues eligible for the program may be presented to the Treasury for stripping; subsequently, each expected cash flow may be sold as if it were a separate security. This broadening and deepening of the market reduced the liquidity risk of owning strips for investors forced to sell before maturity. As expected, STRIPS have been exceptionally popular, with outstanding volume exceeding $113 billion by the end of 1990.[18] The popularity and availability of STRIPS effectively ended the need for stripped Treasury securities created by securities firms.

FINANCIAL INSTITUTIONS AND STRIPPED SECURITIES. If a pension fund needs a specified amount of cash in 12 years and wishes to lock in existing yields over that time, its managers can purchase a stripped security in the face amount desired to be paid in a single sum in 12 years. The purchase price is a discount

from the face amount; the cash payment to be received in 12 years will be coupon payments on a pool of Treasury securities. The pension fund manager considers the stripped security a 12-year maturity/duration, zero-coupon Treasury instrument, even though the Treasury has never issued such a bond. Because many T-bonds have long contractual maturities, promising the availability of coupon payments for many years, stripped securities enable the creation of "synthetic" zero-coupon investments of long duration.

The Tax Reform Act of 1986 allowed the stripping of municipal bonds for the first time, and large securities firms began doing so within minutes of the signing of the law. Mortgage lenders have fashioned stripped securities based on cash flows from expected mortgage payments. Each new type of strip has addressed a market need, such as the desire to minimize taxes or to immunize particular kinds of cash flow obligations.[19]

The introduction of stripped securities provides an excellent example of financial innovation and the intermediation process at work. For example, creators of stripped securities, by issuing their own secondary securities such as CATS or TIGRs, transformed one financial asset, the T-bond, into another with different risk and expected return characteristics. In so doing, they reduced the transaction costs for owners of stripped securities. In exchange, the creators of stripped securities earned fees that enhanced their own profits.

SUMMARY

Duration is the foundation for analyzing an investor's exposure to interest rate risk. It is a measure superior to contractual maturity for comparing the riskiness of debt instruments because it also captures the effects of differing coupon rates and market yields. Duration can also be calculated for common stocks under certain assumptions. An important property of duration is that it is directly proportional to percentage changes in asset prices that result from a change in market yields. Thus,

---

[17] See Becketti 1988.

[18] See Livingston and Gregory 1989 and Gregory and Livingston 1992.

[19] Ann Monroe, "Goldman Sachs and Salomon Brothers Scramble for Sales of Stripped Municipal Bonds," *The Wall Street Journal,* October 23, 1986, 50; and Sherlock and Chen 1987.

duration can be used to calculate an investment's interest rate elasticity.

Several applications of duration-based measures to financial institution management have been recognized. One of these is analysis of yield curves. Portfolio immunization is a strategy that balances reinvestment risk and market risk to protect a portfolio from the effects of an unexpected shift in interest rates. An immunized portfolio is one with a duration equal to the planned holding period for the investment. Finally, the demand for immunization through longer-duration assets has led to development of a new type of financial asset—the stripped Treasury security.

QUESTIONS

1. In your own words, explain what duration measures.

2. Why is duration more useful than contractual maturity for evaluating the interest rate risk of an investment?

3. Given the yield to maturity for a bond, explain the similarities and differences between calculating its market price and calculating its duration.

4. Under what circumstances are the duration of a bond and its contractual maturity the same? Why?

5. Explain interest rate elasticity and why it is used as a measure of interest rate risk.

6. Explain how a bond's duration is related to its price changes as market yields change.

7. Suppose you are using duration to estimate and compare the interest rate elasticities of two bonds. One has a maturity of 6 years and the other, 14 years. Explain why the assumption of a parallel shift in the yield curve is needed to assure a valid comparison.

8. What important characteristic must an investment portfolio possess to be immunized? What is the interest rate risk exposure on an immunized portfolio? Why? For how long does this condition prevail?

9. The bond portfolio manager of a small life insurance company emphasizes immunization as a primary goal. Is the manager following a hedging or a profit-maximizing approach? Explain.

10. Identify the limitations that prevent immunization from providing total protection against interest rate risk.

11. What are STRIPS? Why are STRIPS and zero-coupon bonds popular choices for immunized portfolios?

12. What is a dedicated portfolio? Under what circumstances is this portfolio management technique useful?

PROBLEMS

1. Calculate the duration of the following bonds, assuming a par value of $1,000, annual interest payments, and a prevailing yield to maturity of 8 percent:
   a. 6 percent coupon rate, 3 years to maturity, market price = 94.846
   b. 10 percent coupon rate, 2 years to maturity, market price = 103.567
   c. 14 percent coupon rate, 5 years to maturity, market price = 123.956

2. Using the format presented in Table 9.1, and data from April 8, 1992, for the two ATT bonds discussed in the chapter, set up a Lotus 1-2-3 duration worksheet. Assume a yield to maturity of 7.9167 percent for the 5⅛ percent bond and a yield to maturity of 7.8141 percent for the 7 percent bond. Check your worksheet against Table 9.1. (Slight differences may occur because of rounding.)

3. A bond mutual fund manager is considering adding two bonds to the portfolio: a 4 percent bond trading at 85 and a 5 percent bond trading for 94. Both bonds have 9 years remaining until maturity. Using your duration worksheet from Problem 2, calculate the duration of each bond. Assume annual interest payments and a par value of $1,000 for each bond. (Hint: Use the @ IRR function to calculate the yield to maturity for each bond.)

4. Using Equation 9.2, calculate the duration of the following bonds, each of which pays interest annually on a par value of $1,000:
   a. 8 percent coupon, 3 years to maturity, yield to maturity = 7 percent
   b. 11 percent coupon, 6 years to maturity, yield to maturity = 9 percent
   c. 10 percent coupon, 12 years to maturity, yield to maturity = 8 percent

5. Evaluate investments in two bonds: an 8 percent bond currently trading at 90 and a 6 percent bond trading at 70. Both bonds have 8 years remaining until maturity. To estimate the interest rate risk, calculate the duration of each bond. Assume annual interest payments and a $1,000 par value. At current market prices, the annual yield to maturity (YTM) of the 8 percent bond is 9.87 percent; for the 6 percent bond, the annual YTM is 12.05 percent.

6. Janice Daley, the manager of an equity portfolio, has asked you to calculate the durations for two stocks she is considering. Both stocks now have an expected return of 14 percent. Ms. Daley plans to sell the stock at the end of 5 years. She has estimated the cash flows for the two stocks over the planned holding period to be as follows:

Year	Stock X	Stock Y
1	$ 4.00	$ 1.05
2	4.00	1.25
3	4.00	1.50
4	4.00	1.75
5	55.00	85.50

Using this information, calculate the requested durations. Explain any difference you find.

7. Refer again to the information provided for the two stocks in Table 9.2. Using Equation 9.1, recalculate the duration of each stock and reconcile your answers with the results in Table 9.2.

8. A stock that currently sells for $20.00 just paid a dividend of $1.50. The dividends are expected to grow at a constant rate of 10 percent indefinitely. If you purchase the stock, you have no plans to sell it in the near future. Calculate the duration for this stock. (Hint: Use Equation 5A.11 to find the expected rate of return on the stock.)

9. As a new analyst for a large insurance firm's investment division, you have been assigned to assist the firm's asset/liability management committee. Durations are calculated for all assets to evaluate risk.
   a. As your first assignment, estimate duration for the following corporate real estate loans, which will be repaid in five equal annual installments:
      1) $10,000 principal, $2,504.56 payment per year
      2) $10,000 principal, $2,705.70 payment per year
      The firm's current required return (y*) for loans of this type is 9 percent. (You may use Equation 9.2 instead of a spreadsheet.)
   b. Recalculate the durations at y* = 14 percent.
   c. Compare the durations for the two loans at each discount rate. Do you find the results surprising? What explanation can you offer for your findings?

10. Compare the interest rate risk for two bonds, one of which has a duration of 6.25 years at its current YTM of 8 percent. The second bond has a duration of 7.3 years at its YTM of 10 percent.
   a. Calculate the elasticity of each bond.
   b. If experts forecast a parallel shift in the term structure of interest rates that will decrease all yields by 2 percent (200 basis points), what percentage price change would you estimate for each bond?
   c. What percentage price change do you estimate if, instead, the forecast is for a 150-basis-point increase in yields?

11. Use your calculations for Problem 5 and assume that the yields for the two bonds increase by 50 basis points and 75 basis points, respectively. Estimate the percentage price changes expected for the two bonds.

12. Using your calculations for Problem 3, assume that the prices of the bonds change by +1.8 percent and +1.50 percent, respectively. What would be the corresponding change in yields for the two bonds, expressed in basis points?

13. A bond with a yield to maturity of 9.75 percent and a coupon rate of 10 percent has 10 years remaining until maturity. Calculate the duration and the interest rate elasticity for this bond, assuming annual interest payments and a par value of $1,000. If you think that the required market yield on this bond will increase to 10.55 percent, what change in the bond price (in dollars) would you expect?

14. A bank manager is comparing two bonds for possible addition to her bond portfolio. Bond A has a yield to maturity of 15 percent, a coupon rate of 17 percent, and 7 years remaining until maturity. Bond B has a yield to maturity of 15 percent, a coupon rate of 3 percent, and 5 years remaining until maturity. Both bonds have a $1,000 par value and annual interest payments. She wishes to invest in the bond that is the least risky. Which bond should she choose? Show all calculations to support your answer.

15. A bond with a yield to maturity of 11.50 percent and a coupon rate of 8 percent has 15 years remaining until maturity. Assume a par value of $1,000 and annual interest payments. You expect the required market yield on this bond to decrease by 37 basis points. Use the price elasticity measure to estimate the percentage change in the bond's price.

16. One of your trust department's clients has asked for assistance in immunizing her yields over a 4-year period. She wants to earn a rate of 8 percent on the $1,270 principal amount she has to invest. You suggest that she purchase a 5-year bond, carrying a 14¾ percent coupon rate. The bond has a $1,000 par value and pays interest annually. The client would sell the bond at the end of 4 years. If market yields remain stable, the selling price would be $1,062.50. The bond's yield to maturity at the current market price is 8 percent.

  a.   If the client reinvests all interim cash flows at 8 percent and does sell the bond for $1,062.50 at the end of Year 4, how much will she accumulate by the end of her investment period? What will be her holding-period yield?

  b.   If the yield to maturity on the bond drops to 6 percent as soon as the client purchases it but remains stable thereafter, she would sell the bond at the end of Year 4 for $1,082.55. If interim cash flows are reinvested at 6 percent, how much would the client have accumulated at the end of 4 years? What is her holding-period yield?

  c.   Based on your answers to Parts a and b, what can you conclude about the duration of the bond? Why?

17. You have been interviewed for an investment counselor position. The hiring decision depends on your recommendation on the following problem that a client has brought to the firm. The client, Mr. Majors, wants to invest in bonds. He must choose between the following, both of which are selling at 118.9:

1)   A bond with a 12 percent coupon and 5 years to maturity (interest paid semiannually)
2)   One with a 14 percent coupon and 6 years to maturity (interest paid semiannually)

Mr. Majors' goal is to earn a 7.4 percent return on his investment annually so that by the end of 4 years he will have accumulated $1,590 for each bond he buys. Earning that amount is crucial, because he must repay a large loan with the proceeds at the end of his 4-year investment horizon. He will sell the bonds at that time.

  a.   Evaluate the two bonds' interest rate risk exposure and decide which issue Mr. Majors should choose.

  b.   Because Mr. Majors may be skeptical, you need supporting data. Show that Mr. Majors will reach his $1,590 goal if he follows your recommendation, even if market yields drop to 6 percent immediately after he buys the bond and do not change for the next 4 years.

SELECTED REFERENCES

Becketti, Sean. "The Role of Stripped Securities in Portfolio Management." *Economic Review* (Federal Reserve Bank of Kansas City) 73 (May 1988): 20–31.

Benesh, Gary A., and Stephen E. Celec. "A Simplified Approach for Calculating Bond Duration." *Financial Review* 19 (November 1984): 394–396.

Bierwag, Gerald O. *Duration Analysis.* Cambridge, MA: Ballinger Publishing Co., 1987.

Bierwag, Gerald O., George G. Kaufman, and Alden Toevs. "Bond Portfolio Immunization and Stochastic Process Risk." *Journal of Bank Research* 13 (Winter 1983): 282–291.

Bisignano, Joseph, and Brian Dvorak. "Risk and Duration." *Weekly Letter* (Federal Reserve Bank of San Francisco), April 3, 1981.

Boquist, John A., George A. Racette, and Gary A. Schlarbaum. "Duration and Risk Assessment for Bonds and Common Stocks." *Journal of Finance* 30 (December 1975): 1360–1365.

Caks, John, et al. "A Simple Formula for Duration." *Journal of Financial Research* 8 (Fall 1985): 245–249.

Chua, Jess B. "A Closed-Form Formula for Calculating Bond Duration." *Financial Analysts Journal* 40 (May–June 1984): 76–78.

Dietz, Peter O., H. Russell Fogler, and Anthony U. Rivers. "Duration, Non-Linearity, and Bond-Portfolio Performance." *Journal of Portfolio Management* 7 (Spring 1981): 37–41.

Fisher, Lawrence. "An Algorithm for Finding Exact Rates of Return." *Journal of Business* 39 (January 1966): 111–118.

Fisher, Lawrence, and Roman Weil. "Coping with the Risk of Interest Rate Fluctuation: Returns to Bondholders from Naive and Optimal Strategies." *Journal of Business* 44 (October 1971): 408–431.

Fogler, Russell H. "Bond Portfolio Immunization, Inflation, and the Fisher Equation." *Journal of Risk and Insurance* 51 (June 1984): 244–264.

Gregory, Deborah W., and Miles Livingston." Development of the Market for U.S. Treasury Strips." *Financial Analysts Journal* 48 (March–April 1992): 68–74.

Hess, Alan C. "Duration Analysis for Savings and Loan Associations." *Federal Home Loan Bank Board Journal* 15 (October 1982): 12–14.

Hicks, J. R. *Value and Capital.* Oxford: Clarendon Press, 1939.

Hopewell, Michael C., and George G. Kaufman. "Bond Price Volatility and Term to Maturity: A Generalized Respecification." *American Economic Review* 63 (September 1973): 749–753.

Johnson, Lewis D. "Equity Duration: Another Look." *Financial Analysts Journal* 45 (March/April 1989): 73–75.

Kaufman, George G. "Measuring and Managing Interest Rate Risk: A Primer." *Economic Perspectives* (Federal Reserve Bank of Chicago) 8 (January/February 1984): 16–29.

Kaufman, George G., G. O. Bierwag, and Alden Toevs, eds. *Innovations in Bond Portfolio Management: Duration Analysis and Immunization.* Greenwich, CT: JAI Press, 1983.

Leibowitz, Martin L. "Bond Immunization: A Procedure for Realizing Target Levels of Return." In *Financial Markets: Instruments and Concepts,* edited by John R. Brick, 443–454. Richmond, VA: Robert F. Dame, 1981.

———. "Financial Theory Evolves into the Real World—or Not: The Case of Duration and Immunization." *Financial Review* 18 (November 1983): 271–280.

Leibowitz, Martin, et al. "A Total Differential Approach to Equity Duration." *Financial Analysts Journal* 45 (September/October 1989): 30–37.

Livingston, Miles, and Deborah Wright Gregory. *The Stripping of U.S. Treasury Securities.* New York: Salomon Brothers Center for the Study of Financial Institutions, 1989.

Macaulay, Frederick R. *Some Theoretical Problems Suggested by the Movements of Interest Rates, Bond Yields, and Stock Prices in the U.S. since 1856.* New York: National Bureau of Economic Research, 1938.

Moser, James T., and James T. Lindley. "A Simple Formula for Duration: An Extension." *Financial Review* 24 (November 1989): 611–615.

Ott, Robert A., Jr. "Duration Analysis and Minimizing Interest Rate Risk." In *Managing Interest Rate Risk: Selected Readings,* 31–34. Atlanta: Federal Home Loan Bank of Atlanta, 1988.

Reilly, Frank K., and Rupinder S. Sidhu. "The Many Uses of Bond Duration." *Financial Analysts Journal* 36 (July–August 1980): 58–72.

Rosenberg, Joel L. "The Joys of Duration." *Bankers Magazine* 169 (March–April 1986): 62–67.

Samuelson, Paul. "The Effects of Interest Rate Increases on the Banking System." *American Economic Review* 35 (March 1945): 16–27.

Sherlock, Patricia M., and Le In Chen. "Stripped Mortgage Backed Securities: The Sum Is Greater than the Parts." *Mortgage Banking* 47 (June 1987): 61–68.

Smith, Donald J. "The Duration of a Bond as a Price Elasticity and as a Fulcrum." *Journal of Financial Education* 17 (Fall 1988): 26–38.

Stowe, David W. "FYI: The Interest Rate Sensitivity of Common Stock," *Economic Review* (Federal Reserve Bank of Atlanta) 76 (May/June 1991): 21–29.

Weil, Roman L. "Macaulay's Duration: An Appreciation." *Journal of Business* 46 (October 1973): 589–592.

Yawitz, Jess B. "The Relative Importance of Duration and Yield Volatility on Bond Price Volatility." *Journal of Money, Credit, and Banking* 9 (February 1977): 97–102.

The creation of futures and options in Chicago created a legion of people who have learned to manage risk in ways they never before could have dreamed of.
William J. Brodsky
President, Chicago Mercantile Exchange (1992)

—————

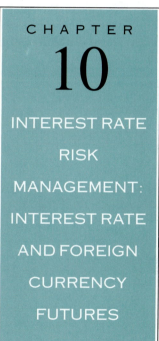

CHAPTER

10

INTEREST RATE

RISK

MANAGEMENT:

INTEREST RATE

AND FOREIGN

CURRENCY

FUTURES

Professor Merton Miller, winner of the Nobel Prize for financial economics and recognized for his contributions to the development of financial futures, recently commented to a *Chicago Tribune* reporter on the innovations in the financial markets. Miller believes that the wonderment of Rip Van Winkle as he awoke after 20 years would pale in comparison with the astonishment felt by a banker or financial services professional who fell asleep in 1970 and awoke in the 1990s to the radically changed financial environment. In fact, the rapidity with which new markets and instruments are introduced is challenging even to those who are wide awake!

In 1992, the futures markets embraced another innovation and took a step toward the video game environment. In a joint venture, the **Chicago Board of Trade (CBOT)** and the **Chicago Mercantile Exchange (CME)** inaugurated **Globex,** a computerized futures trading system designed to link futures markets around the world. On opening day, trading was limited to 16 hours, but when Asian markets sign on, it is intended to offer 24-hour trading. As the first bid and offer popped onto his screen, a trader in New York described the system as similar to a video game, except with real money involved. But Globex is very different from the chaos of the "live" trading pits, and some participants found it challenging to remain alert all night. Experts predicted the environment will become more exciting as new participants join and volume grows, but some European traders were less than excited about the prospect of being asked to work the "graveyard shift."[1]

Although 24-hour markets may require some schedule adjustments for traders, no one doubts that automation and globalization will continue to bring changes to the financial markets and will make the futures markets an ever more integral part of every financial manager's daily environment. In fact, in a complex economic environment, financial institutions and their managers need complex strategies, and duration,

—————

[1] William B. Crawford, Jr., "Still the Wave of the Futures," *Chicago Tribune,* January 20, 1992, Section 4, 1, 2; William B. Crawford, Jr., "Globex Takes Off," *Chicago Tribune,* June 26, 1992, Section 3, 1, 3.

discussed in the previous chapter, is only one of many essential risk management techniques.

Others are explored in this and the next chapter, including financial futures contracts and options on financial futures. All are relatively new; for example, the interest rate futures contract was created in 1975 at the CBOT, and stock index futures began trading in 1982. Since the introduction of futures and options, financial institutions have recognized their potential for improving asset/liability management. This chapter focuses on interest rate and foreign currency futures.

Futures are not without their own risks. The inherent dangers have attracted the attention of regulators and legislators and in some cases have resulted in restrictions on their use by financial institutions. Futures have also presented some new financial reporting problems. Thus, the integration of futures into asset/liability management has, by necessity, moved somewhat slowly, with the largest institutions often serving as the trend setters.

FINANCIAL INSTITUTIONS AND FINANCIAL FUTURES

Although financial futures have received a great deal of attention, in 1987 only about 400 U.S. commercial banks of more than 13,000 actually held a position in the interest rate futures market. The relatively low level of participation can be traced to unfavorable regulatory and accounting rules for futures. Despite these rules, however, all of the ten largest banks were using financial futures to hedge one or more aspects of their operations. Altogether, more than 99 percent of banks participating in the futures markets had assets in excess of $500 million.[2]

Data on financial futures usage by nonbank financial institutions are sparser. Research from the 1980s suggests that some members of the thrift, life insurance, and pension fund industries were participating in the futures markets. As is true in the commercial banking industry, the evidence indicates that large institutions are the major players.[3]

FUTURES CONTRACTS

Futures contracts on agricultural products have existed for more than a century; the first organized market for them was the CBOT, also the birthplace of the interest rate futures contract in October 1975. The International Monetary Market (IMM), a branch of the CME, introduced the first financial futures contracts on foreign currencies in 1972.[4]

FUTURES CONTRACTS DEFINED

A futures contract is a commitment to buy or sell a specific commodity of designated quality at a specified price and at a specified date in the future (the **delivery date**). The specified price is an estimate of the commodity price that is *expected* to prevail at that future time. A distinguishing feature of futures trading is that the two sides of a futures contract do not trade directly with one another but, rather, with a clearinghouse. This feature of futures markets is explained in more detail later in the chapter.

A commodity may fall into one of many categories; the number continues to expand in these innovative markets. However, five categories, three of which are financial, include the vast majority of commodities on which contracts are traded: agricultural products, metallurgical products, interest-bearing assets, stock indexes and other market indexes, or foreign currencies. The last two, although not specifically focused on interest rate risk, have emerged as tools of asset/liability management for some institutions. Foreign currency futures are discussed later in this chapter, and stock index futures are described in Chapter 11.

HEDGING VERSUS SPECULATION

One reason for the development of futures contracts is avoidance of risk. Wheat or soybean farmers can use futures agreements to reduce uncertainty about the prices they will receive for their products. A grower, by agreeing through a futures contract to deliver a certain amount of wheat at a specified future date and price, avoids exposure to unfavorable price movements during the intervening period. Thus, futures contracts, like immunization in the previous chapter, can be used to hedge, or minimize, risk.

On the other side of the farmer's contract may be a **speculator,** someone willing to accept the risk of price fluctuations with the intention of profiting from them. The counterparty to the farmer could also be a hedger who needs the farmer's wheat at the designated time and is minimizing the risk that wheat will be in short suppply at the time. Or both parties in a futures contract could be speculators, each hoping to profit from price fluctuations.

Thus, the distinction between hedging and speculation comes not from which side of a futures contract one takes but from the motivation for entering into the contract. With few exceptions, because of regulatory limitations, financial institutions use the financial futures markets only for hedging.

FINANCIAL FUTURES CONTRACTS

In a financial futures contract, the underlying commodity promised for future delivery is one of three financial commodities—an interest-bearing asset, a

---

[2] See Koppenhaver 1990. (References are listed in full at the end of this chapter.)

[3] See Booth, Smith, and Stolz 1984; Hurtz and Gardner 1984; Lamm-Tennant 1989; Hoyt 1992.

[4] For details on the birth of the first financial futures contract at the IMM, see Miller 1986.

stock or bond index, or a foreign currency. Since 1972, contracts on many financial assets have been introduced with varying levels of success. For example, contracts on Treasury bills (T-bills) have been widely accepted, but futures contracts on commercial paper were tried without success. As of 1993, interest-bearing or discount securities on which contracts were written included T-bills, Treasury notes (T-notes), Treasury bonds (T-bonds), and Eurodollar deposits, among others. The instruments span the entire yield curve, giving managers important flexibility.

ROLE OF THE CLEARINGHOUSE. All trading is conducted through the **clearinghouse** of each exchange. In effect, the clearinghouse acts as a buyer to every seller and a seller to every buyer; it does not simply match buy and sell orders. This procedure eliminates the need for direct contact between traders. The clearinghouse guarantees the performance of the contract and, instead of the seller, assumes responsibility for the creditworthiness of buyers. The willingness of participants to rely on the financial stability of the clearinghouse is an important characteristic of the futures markets, and the fact that the clearinghouses have so far consistently performed as promised testifies to the validity of their role. At the end of each trading day, the clearinghouse settles all accounts, paying profits earned by some traders and collecting payments due from others.

Because the contracts are standardized and default risk is assumed by the clearinghouse, the original owner of a futures contract can easily offset or cancel the contract before its delivery date. Few financial futures contracts (less than 2 percent) are carried to an actual physical transfer of assets, and traders make an offsetting trade to close out their positions rather than delivering or accepting the commodity.[5] The bookkeeping and associated transactions are handled by the exchange clearinghouse.

If the commodity is an agricultural product, movements in the market price of the product affect the contract value. If the commodity is a T-bill, a change in short-term interest rates affects the price of bills in the spot market and also affects the value of a T-bill contract. Similarly, the value of bond futures contracts is tied to changes in long-term yields.

The standardization of futures contracts allows the market to function efficiently. For interest rate futures, the contract size, maturity, and (except for discount securities) coupon rate are predetermined to facilitate efficient trading. For example, a T-bill contract is traded in a standard size of $1 million, based only on a 90-day maturity. T-bond futures contracts are standardized at $100,000 with an 8 percent coupon. The contract size is the face value of the underlying securities.

THE DEVELOPING GLOBAL MARKETPLACE

The rapid growth in the volume of futures contract trading on the exchanges in Chicago has not gone unnoticed in other countries. In the 1980s, in fact, international markets for the trading of futures and other risk management securities opened in strategic locations around the world; at least 18 have originated since 1985. These new exchanges include the **London International Financial Futures Exchange (LIFFE),** the **Marché a Terme International de France (MATIF),** the **Tokyo International Financial Futures Exchange (TIFFE),** and the **Sydney Futures Exchange (SFE).** The **Deutsche Terminbourse (DTB),** which opened in Frankfurt in 1990, is one of the newest entrants, along with futures exchanges in Austria, Belgium, and Italy.

Several of the international exchanges offer more automated trading methods than do the U.S. exchanges. Also, some of the new markets offer greater flexibility. For example, the LIFFE allows traders to settle their positions in a variety of currencies, whereas the Chicago markets are almost entirely dollar-based. Market participants responded favorably to this flexibility, and by 1992, the volume of financial futures trading in Europe was beginning to challenge the dominance of the Chicago markets.

For the most part, expert observers view the emergence of these new markets as a positive development for market participants. The increased competition across international borders has brought the exchanges under pressure to control transactions costs, making futures trading more efficient for participants. Traders can now participate in more than one market

---

[5] *A Guide to Financial Futures at the Chicago Board of Trade,* The Chicago Board of Trade, undated, 29.

simultaneously and enjoy greater liquidity and longer trading hours. In addition, the new exchanges are highly automated and are setting new standards for the use of technology in futures trading.

The growth of these international markets was one of the motivating factors behind the creation of Globex by the CBOT and the CME. As noted in the opening paragraphs to this chapter, Globex is to be a 24-hour, computerized trading network. Traders in London, Paris, New York, and Chicago can transmit buy and sell orders for most of the popular interest rate and foreign currency futures contracts to each other in seconds. The favorable reaction to the announcement of Globex's creation led to predictions that the network would expand rapidly.

However, despite the fact that many futures market professionals view Globex as a system with great potential, they acknowledge that its debut has been disappointing. The average daily volume of trading on the system during its first 6 months was less than 1 percent of the average daily volume on the CBOT or CME. Activity was so low, in fact, that some brokerage firms discontinued their involvement, citing the high cost of 24-hour trading and low customer interest. Globex suffered further from technical problems that halted trading entirely several times in its early months.

Nevertheless, some firms remained loyal and indicated a commitment to stay involved and to help build business. CME officials hope that introducing late afternoon trading will increase volume, but that plan has been slowed by neogtiations with CBOT officials. Still, hopes remain that Globex will eventually constitute a truly global, 24-hour market.

Besides advantages noted above, futures market expansion carries increased risks. Most notable among these is the potential for problems in the clearing process. Although all international futures exchanges have clearinghouses, the settlement of claims may involve counterparties operating under different legal and payments systems. In the view of most experts, however, the increased opportunities clearly outweigh the additional risk exposure.[6]

CHARACTERISTICS OF FINANCIAL FUTURES TRANSACTIONS

Financial futures markets have several unique features.

THE MARGIN. Futures traders are required to post an initial **margin** to support their positions. The margin serves as a deposit in good faith. It may be in the form of cash, a bank letter of credit, or short-term Treasury securities. The margin required is quite small in comparison with the face value of the securities underlying the financial futures contract; the initial deposit is often no more than 5 percent of the contract face value. The margin is set by the exchange; it depends on the type of contract and whether the trader is a hedger or speculator. The price volatility of the underlying instrument is an influencing factor on the margin: the higher the volatility in the underlying instrument, the higher the margin.[7]

At the end of each day, the clearinghouse rquires a trader to settle the account; if there are losses on a given day, they are charged against the trader's margin account. If the charges reduce the account to a balance below the required minimum, the trader must immediately produce additional cash. Futures trading involves some cash flow on every trading day, and many observers believe that the daily resettlement makes the futures markets much safer than they would be otherwise. It also is viewed as a justification for the relatively small initial cash required to trade contracts with a much higher face value. Nevertheless, managers of institutions trading futures contracts must manage cash carefully, because they must be ready each day to make deposits into their margin accounts.

LIMITS ON PRICE CHANGES. A convention of the futures market that controls traders' exposure is the limit on daily price changes. The exchanges set a maximum amount by which the price of a contract is allowed to

---

[6] For more information on the development of international markets, see Remolona 1992–93; Napoli 1992; Scarlata 1992; Abken 1991; David Greising, "Has Chicago Lost Its Edge?" *Business Week,* March 9, 1992, 76–78; William B. Crawford, Jr., "London's Ex-

change to Sign On to Globex," *Chicago Tribune,* September 28, 1992, Section 4, 1, 2; Jeffery Taylor, "Globex System Is Vexed by Low Trading Volume, Overseas Competition, and Technology Glitches," *The Wall Street Journal,* December 14, 1992, C1; Peter J. W. Elstrom, "Sleepy Globex May Start Trading Earlier," *Crain's Chicago Business,* January 18, 1993, 3.

[7] Legislation pending in Congress in late 1992 would transfer to the Federal Reserve Board the authority to set margins for some types of futures contracts. The CBOT and CME opposed the legislation containing this provision.

change. When that limit is reached on a given day, the price cannot move farther, and subsequent trades will take place only if they are within the limits. Risk exposure still exists, however. For example, the maximum price fluctuation allowed by the CBOT on T-bond and T-note contracts is 3 percent of par value, so the price can move by as much as $3,000 on any one day. Several days of "limit moves" in a row could add up to substantial losses.

INTEREST RATE FUTURES

Most **interest rate futures contracts** have interest-bearing or discount securities as the underlying commodity. Recently, contracts based on movements in an interest rate such as the fed funds rate have been developed. Should a trader hold such contracts to maturity, they would be settled in cash rather than by delivery of an underlying security. Because they are an important component of asset/liability management, techniques involving interest rate futures trading will be examined in detail. First, however, it is important to introduce the characteristics of contracts commonly traded by financial institutions.

TERMS OF SELECTED INTEREST RATE FUTURES CONTRACTS

As in any field in which change is the rule rather than the exception, a comprehensive list of interest rate futures contracts is virtually impossible. Undoubtedly, contracts that were unheard of—perhaps even unimagined—at the time this book was written may be traded regularly by the time it is read. Nonetheless, it is clear that certain interest rate futures contracts, such as those for Treasury securities, have had staying power over the years, and it seems reasonable to assume that they will continue to be popular. Table 10.1 summarizes features of these popular contracts as well as three of the new cash-based instruments.

Although the importance of individual features will become clear as applications of futures in asset/liability management are presented, the table shows that interest rate futures contracts are available in a wide range of face values on underlying instruments or indexes with a variety of maturities. The table also indicates that futures contracts have standardized delivery dates in the rare event that delivery is actually

made or taken. By convention, then, a contract with a delivery date of the last trading day in June is known as a "June contract." The varied features provide important flexibility for interest rate risk management in financial institutions.

INTEREST RATE FUTURES AS A HEDGING DEVICE

By definition, a hedge is a position taken in the futures market to offset risk in the cash or spot market position. The preceding chapters stressed the inverse relationship between changes in market values of interest-earning assets and changes in market yields. Because the value of a futures contract depends on the market value of its underlying commodity, the prices of interest rate futures contracts also change inversely with interest rates. Thus, a financial institution can use futures to reduce its exposure to adverse rate changes.

For example, a decline in interest rates, lowering the reinvestment rate on an insurance company's bond portfolio, increases the price of interest rate futures contracts. Profits from the futures transactions could reduce the negative effect of the interest rate reduction on the bond portfolio. Futures can provide similar protection in times of interest rate increases.

FUTURES PRICES AND MARKET YIELDS: AN ILLUSTRATION

When interest rates fell in April 1992 after the Federal Reserve System (Fed) decided to lower the discount rate, the spot prices on bonds rose, as discussed and illustrated in Chapters 8 and 9. The prices of outstanding futures contracts rose as well. Portions of *The Wall Street Journal* quotations of futures prices for Wednesday, April 8, 1992, and Thursday, April 9, 1992, are shown in Figure 10.1 on page 260. The reduction in the discount rate was announced early on April 9. The day before the announcement, a T-bond futures contract for June delivery had a settlement price, listed under the column heading "Settle," of 99-07.

Futures contracts on T-bonds and T-notes, like the prices of their underlying instruments, are quoted in 32nds of a percent, so 99-07 means 99-7/32 percent of the face value of a contract, or $99,218.75 on a $100,000 contract. (Recall that Table 10.1 indicates the face value of T-bond and T-note contracts as

TABLE 10.1	**Features of Selected Interest Rate Futures Contracts**

Interest rate futures are available on a variety of underlying instruments. Face values and other specifications differ, and the choice of contract depends on the cash instrument to be hedged.

Name of Contract	Underlying Instrument	Face Value of Contract	Daily Price Limits	Standard Delivery Months
T-bill futures	13-week T-bills	$1 million	None	March, June, September, December
3-month Euro-dollar futures	None; settled in cash based on prevailing rate on 3-month Eurodollar time deposits	$1 million	None	March, June, September, December
T-note futures	2-year, 5-year, or 10-year T-notes	$100,000 or $200,000	Varies: 1 to 3 points	March, June, September, December
T-bond futures	8% T-bonds, minimum maturity of 15 years	$100,000	3 points ($3,000 per contract)	March, June, September, December
Municipal bond index	None; settled in cash based on Bond Buyer Municipal Bond Index	$1,000 times value of index	$3,000	March, June, September, December
30-day interest rate futures	None; settled in cash based on monthly average of daily fed funds rate	$5 million	150 basis points from previous settlement price	Every month
LIBOR[a]	None; settled in cash based on prevailing LIBOR rate on 1-month Eurodollar time deposits	$3 million	None	First 6 consecutive months, beginning with current month

Source: Adapted from Patrick J. Catania, ed., *Commodity Trading Manual* (Chicago: Chicago Board of Trade, 1989), updated by authors; Chicago Board of Trade, "30-Day Interest Rate Futures," 1992; Chicago Mercantile Exchange, "CME Interest Rate Futures," 1991.

[a]LIBOR is an acronym for the London Interbank Offered Rate, a short-term European interest rate. It is discussed in more detail in Chapter 14.

$100,000.) Each 1/32 change is a dollar change of $31.25 [$100,000 × (1/32 × 0.01)]. At the close of trading April 9, the day of the discount rate change, the June contract price was 100-07, an increase of thirty-two 32nds, or 1 percent of face value. The dollar change was $1,000—up to $100,218.75. Price changes for other futures contracts in Figure 10.1 were also positive, so traders who owned contracts for future delivery gained on their positions. Those who lost on their positions were required to settle with the clearinghouse, including the possibility of adding cash to their margin accounts if the loss eroded their balances below acceptable levels.

Figure 10.1 also shows other data commonly associated with futures trading. The "Yield" column expresses the closing figures for a contract in terms of rates of return instead of price. Recall the inverse relationship between prices and yields, so that rising prices between April 8 and 9 naturally meant decreasing yields between the two dates. The "Open Interest" column reveals the total number of outstanding contracts on an instrument at the close of trading for that day.

LONG VERSUS SHORT HEDGES

A financial institution using futures to hedge can choose either a **long hedge** or a **short hedge**. A long hedge means that the trader *buys* a futures contract. The position obligates the holder either to take delivery of securities at the pre-established price on some future date or to sell the contract, closing out the position through the clearinghouse before the delivery date. When interest rates decline, as they did in April 1992, the value of both interest-earning assets and outstanding futures contracts rises. A trader who actually takes delivery on securities can sell them at an immediate profit over the purchase price written into the

FIGURE 10.1   Interest Rate Futures Prices: April 8 and April 9, 1992

Information on interest rate and other futures contracts is reported daily in the financial pages of major newspapers. The most recent prices and the total volume of contracts outstanding (open interest) are included.

Wednesday, April 8, 1992
INTEREST RATE

TREASURY BONDS (CBT) – $100,000; pts. 32nds of 100%

	Open	High	Low	Settle	Chg	Yield Settle	Yield Chg	Open Interest
June	99-25	100-01	99-05	99-07	– 16	8.079	+ .051	283,445
Sept	98-25	98-30	98-03	98-05	– 16	8.189	+ .052	19,021
Dec	97-23	97-28	97-04	97-04	– 16	8.297	+ .053	5,774
Mr93	96-22	96-30	96-06	96-06	– 16	8.397	+ .054	1,943
June	96-02	96-02	95-11	95-11	– 16	8.488	+ .054	722
Sp94	92-26	92-26	92-05	92-05	– 21	8.843	+ .075	100

Est vol 335,000; vol Tues 205,259; op int 311,186, –200.

TREASURY BONDS (MCE) – $50,000; pts. 32nds of 100%

	Open	High	Low	Settle	Chg	Yield Settle	Yield Chg	Open Interest
June	99-26	100-01	99-05	99-12	– 14	8.063	+ .044	10,720

Est vol 6,800; vol Tues 4,796; open int 10,736, –49.

T–BONDS (LIFFE) $100,000; pts of 100%
Not Available

GERMAN GOV'T. BOND (LIFFE)
250,000 marks; $ per mark (.01)
Not Available

TREASURY NOTES (CBT) – $100,000; pts. 32nds of 100%

	Open	High	Low	Settle	Chg	Yield Settle	Yield Chg	Open Interest
June	102-25	103-01	102-13	102-14	– 9	7.647	+ .040	102,049
Sept	101-28	101-29	101-12	101-12	– 9	7.799	+ .040	800

Est vol 40,000; vol Tues 22,274; open int 102,875, –325.

5 YR TREAS NOTES (CBT) – $100,000; pts. 32nds of 100%

	Open	High	Low	Settle	Chg	Yield Settle	Yield Chg	Open Interest
June	104-14	04-225	104-07	104-08	– 3	6.979	+ .022	127,940
Sept	103-19	103-22	103-10	103-10	– 3	7.199	+ .022	300

Est vol 21,900; vol Tues 15,553; open int 128,241, –15.

2 YR TREAS NOTES (CBT) – $200,000; pts. 32nds of 100%

	Open	High	Low	Settle	Chg	Yield Settle	Yield Chg	Open Interest
June	04-015	104-04	103-30	103-31	+ 1¼	5.868	– .020	14,735

Est vol 1,500; vol Tues 1,947; open int 14,776, +768.

30-DAY INTEREST RATE (CBT)-$5 million; pts. of 100%

	Open	High	Low	Settle	Chg		Chg	Open Interest
Apr	96.01	96.01	96.00	96.00	....	4.00	....	2,446
May	96.03	96.03	96.02	96.02	+ .01	3.98	– .01	2,035
June	96.02	96.03	96.01	96.01	+ .01	3.99	– .01	2,120
July	95.95	95.98	95.95	95.95	+ .03	4.05	– .03	797
Aug	95.93	95.93	95.91	95.92	+ .03	4.08	– .03	423
Sept	95.82	95.85	95.82	95.82	+ .03	4.18	– .03	366
Oct	95.70	95.75	95.70	95.74	+ .05	4.26	– .05	318
Nov	95.60	95.65	95.60	95.62	+ .05	4.38	– .05	400

Est vol 750; vol Tues 550; open int 8,915, +224.

TREASURY BILLS (IMM) – $1 mil.; pts. of 100%

	Open	High	Low	Settle	Chg	Discount Settle	Discount Chg	Open Interest
June	96.15	96.18	96.12	96.12	....	3.88	....	30,385
Sept	95.92	95.98	95.90	95.90	+ .01	4.10	– .01	7,821
Dec	95.47	95.50	95.40	95.41	+ .02	4.59	– .02	4,350
Mr93	95.24	95.26	95.17	95.17	– .01	4.83	+ .01	270

Est vol 11,913; vol Tues 7,289; open int 42,826, +2,066.

LIBOR-1 MO. (IMM) –$3,000,000; points of 100%

	Open	High	Low	Settle	Chg			Open Interest
Apr	95.86	95.87	95.84	95.84	....	4.16	....	9,487
May	95.83	95.85	95.81	95.80	– .01	4.20	+ .01	10,397
June	95.78	95.79	95.75	95.75	....	4.25	....	3,919
July	95.72	95.74	95.71	95.70	....	4.30	....	755
Aug	....	....	....	95.64	....	4.36	....	229
Sept	....	....	....	95.56	+ .01	4.46	– .01	253

Est vol 4,934; vol Tues 4,698; open int 25,040, +124.

Thursday, April 9, 1992
INTEREST RATE

TREASURY BONDS (CBT) – $100,000; pts. 32nds of 100%

	Open	High	Low	Settle	Chg	Yield Settle	Yield Chg	Open Interest
June	99-13	100-13	99-04	100-07	+ 32	7.978	– .101	292,635
Sept	98-11	99-09	98-02	99-03	+ 30	8.092	– .097	19,659
Dec	97-10	98-05	97-05	98-01	+ 29	8.202	– .095	5,964
Mr93	96-24	97-06	96-24	97-02	+ 28	8.304	– .093	1,944
June	95-17	96-09	95-14	96-05	+ 26	8.400	– .088	820
Sp94	....	....	....	92-26	+ 21	8.768	– .075	100

Est vol 380,000; vol Wed 331,900; op int 321,214, +10,028.

TREASURY BONDS (MCE) – $50,000; pts. 32nds of 100%

	Open	High	Low	Settle	Chg	Yield Settle	Yield Chg	Open Interest
June	99-10	100-13	99-04	100-04	+ 24	7.987	– .076	11,614

Est vol 7,800; vol Wed 6,796; open int 11,632, +896.

T–BONDS (LIFFE) U.S. $100,000; pts of 100%

	Open	High	Low	Settle	Chg	Yield Settle	Yield Chg	Open Interest
June	99-12	99-17	99-07	99-11	– 0-16	100-09	96-30	n.a.

Est vol 992; vol Wed 1,257; open int n.a., n.a..

GERMAN GOV'T. BOND (LIFFE)
250,000 marks; $ per mark (.01)

	Open	High	Low	Settle	Chg	Yield Settle	Yield Chg	Open Interest
June	n.a.	n.a.	n.a.	n.a.	....	89.15	85.45	n.a.
Sept	88.38	88.40	88.38	88.38	....	89.46	87.42	n.a.

Est vol 56,362; vol Wed 61,656; open int n.a., n.a..

TREASURY NOTES (CBT) – $100,000; pts. 32nds of 100%

	Open	High	Low	Settle	Chg	Yield Settle	Yield Chg	Open Interest
June	102-19	103-11	102-13	103-09	+ 27	7.527	– .120	103,307
Sept	101-21	102-07	101-21	102-06	+ 26	7.683	– .116	756

Est vol 40,000; vol Wed 28,143; open int 104,090, +1,215.

5 YR TREAS NOTES (CBT) – $100,000; pts. 32nds of 100%

	Open	High	Low	Settle	Chg	Yield Settle	Yield Chg	Open Interest
June	04-095	105-00	104-06	04-305	+22.5	6.815	– .164	130,440
Sept	03-295	03-315	103-29	103-31	+21.0	7.045	– .154	301

Est vol 30,001; vol Wed 27,432; open int 130,742, +2,501.

2 YR TREAS NOTES (CBT) – $200,000; pts. 32nds of 100%

	Open	High	Low	Settle	Chg	Yield Settle	Yield Chg	Open Interest
June	104-00	104-15	103-30	04-132	+14¼	5.635	– .233	15,985

Est vol 1,000; vol Wed 1,903; open int 15,986, +1,210.

30-DAY INTEREST RATE (CBT)-$5 million; pts. of 100%

	Open	High	Low	Settle	Chg		Chg	Open Interest
Apr	96.00	96.17	96.00	96.17	+ .17	3.83	– .17	2,442
May	96.02	96.24	96.01	96.23	+ .21	3.77	– .21	1,994
June	96.02	96.22	96.01	96.22	+ .21	3.78	– .21	2,135
July	95.97	96.20	95.96	96.20	+ .25	3.80	– .25	730
Aug	95.93	96.19	95.92	96.19	+ .27	3.81	– .27	422
Sept	95.82	96.14	95.82	96.13	+ .31	3.87	– .31	346
Oct	95.95	96.03	95.95	96.03	+ .29	3.97	– .29	294
Nov	95.63	95.95	95.63	95.94	+ .32	4.06	– .32	401

Est vol 2,700; vol Wed 917; open int 8,780, –135.

TREASURY BILLS (IMM) – $1 mil.; pts. of 100%

	Open	High	Low	Settle	Chg	Discount Settle	Discount Chg	Open Interest
June	96.14	96.35	96.10	96.33	+ .21	3.67	– .21	31,470
Sept	95.91	96.20	95.90	96.17	+ .27	3.83	– .27	8,090
Dec	95.40	95.73	95.38	95.72	+ .31	4.28	– .31	4,469
Mr93	....	....	....	95.44	+ .27	4.56	– .27	345

Est vol 12,342; vol Wed 10,361; open int 44,374, +1,548.

LIBOR-1 MO. (IMM) –$3,000,000; points of 100%

	Open	High	Low	Settle	Chg		Chg	Open Interest
Apr	95.85	96.06	95.83	96.05	+ .21	3.95	– .21	8,227
May	95.81	96.04	95.80	96.03	+ .23	3.97	– .23	10,685
June	95.76	96.00	95.75	95.99	+ .24	4.01	– .24	4,797
July	95.71	95.95	95.69	95.94	+ .24	4.06	– .24	832
Aug	95.86	95.90	95.86	95.90	+ .26	4.10	– .26	229
Sept	95.77	95.82	95.77	95.84	+ .28	4.16	– .28	253

Est vol 8,533; vol Wed 5,818; open int 25,073, +33.

Source: The Wall Street Journal, April 9, 1992; April 10, 1992.

futures contract. If, instead, the futures contract is sold before the delivery date, the contract selling price will be higher than the purchase price. Either way, the trader benefits from a long position if interest rates decline.

A short hedge, in contrast, means that the trader *sells* a futures contract, incurring an obligation either to deliver the underlying securities at some future point or to close out the position before the delivery date by buying an offsetting contract. If interest rates increase in the intervening period, either obligation can be met at a profit. Suppose an institutional trader chooses to make delivery. The trader will be able to purchase securities at a lower price than would have initially been available, because market prices will decline with an increase in interest rates. It is more likely, however, that the trader will close out the position. In that case, the price of the contract purchased to close out the short position will be lower than the price received on the initial sale of a contract. The difference is the profit on the hedge.

It is important to emphasize that neither the long nor the short position is a hedge unless the futures transaction is undertaken to offset interest rate risk in an existing portfolio. Traders also should know that transactions costs and brokers' commissions reduce the proceeds of both long and short hedges.

THE LONG HEDGE ILLUSTRATED

Suppose that, in June 1995, the manager of a money market portfolio expects interest rates to decline. New funds, to be received and invested in 90 days (September 1995), will suffer from the drop in yields, and the manager would like to reduce the impact on portfolio returns. The appropriate strategy under this forecast is a long hedge, because long futures positions profit from falling rates.

Gains and losses on cash and futures market transactions are summarized in Table 10.2 on page 262. The money manager expects an inflow of $10 million in September. The discount yield currently available on 91-day T-bills is 10 percent, and the goal is to establish a yield of 10 percent on the anticipated funds. Because contracts on 90-day T-bills have face values of $1 million, ten contracts are needed to hedge the cash position. Assuming that the initial margin requirement is 2 percent of the contract price, the cash required in June will be slightly less than $20,000. The market value of the contracts purchased for delivery in September is $9.75 million. If the funds were available now for the T-bill investment at a discount yield of 10 percent, the cost would be $9,747,222.

By the time the new funds arrive in September, suppose interest rates have fallen; the 91-day T-bill yield is down to 8 percent, and it now costs $9,797,778 to purchase bills with a face value of $10 million. The higher price results in an "opportunity loss" to the portfolio manager of $50,556, but the long futures hedge offsets most of that loss. With the decline in market yields, the September contracts have risen in value from $9.75 million to $9.8 million. Their sale

provides a gain of $50,000, almost equaling the loss in the cash market. The effective discount yield on T-bills purchased, including the effect of the hedge, is 9.978 percent, very close to the desired 10 percent.

By definition, a hedge is undertaken to offset potential losses in the institution's existing or planned portfolio of financial assets. Buying long futures contracts when no future investment in T-bills was planned would be speculation, not hedging, because the contract purchase would be an attempt to earn a pure profit on futures.

THE SHORT HEDGE ILLUSTRATED

If a financial institution stands to lose under forecasts of rising rates, it can undertake a short hedge. For depository institutions, many liability costs are tied to yields on short-term Treasury securities, and an increase in interest rates can raise the cost of funds significantly. Profits on a short hedge may be used to lock in a lower cost of funds.

For deposit costs pegged to the T-bill rate, T-bill futures provide a good vehicle for the short hedge. Suppose that a savings institution in September 1996 wants to hedge $5 million in short-term certificates of deposit (CDs) whose owners are expected to roll them over in 90 days. If market yields go up, the thrift must offer a higher rate on its CDs to remain competitive, reducing the net interest margin (NIM). The asset/liability manager can reduce these losses by the sale of T-bill futures contracts. With a subsequent increase in rates, the value of contracts declines, and when the position is closed out through the clearinghouse, a profit will be realized.[8]

The short hedge illustrated in Table 10.3 is designed to offset the increase in CD rates from 7 percent to 9 percent; the interest paid on the CDs will increase by $25,000 for the 3-month period. In September, the savings and loan association (S&L) sells five December contracts at a discount yield of 7 percent. To close out the position in December, after rates have risen to 9 percent, the hedger buys five T-bill contracts from the clearinghouse. They have declined in value, resulting in a $25,000 profit on the futures position. In the

---

[8] This example assumes that the S&L has at least $5 million more short-term liabilities than short-term assets and thus meets regulatory requirements for hedges. The importance of evaluating asset and liability positions simultaneously is explained in later chapters.

TABLE 10.2 The Long Hedge (Forecast: Falling Interest Rates)

A long hedge is chosen in anticipation of interest rate declines and requires the purchase of interest rate futures contracts. If the forecast is correct, the profit on the hedge helps to offset losses in the cash market.

I.

Cash Market	Futures Market
June	
T-bill discount yield at 10%	Buy 10 T-bill contracts for September delivery at 10% discount yield
Price of 91-day T-bills, $10 million par:	Value of contracts:
$9,747,222[a]	$9,750,000[b] $= P_0 = Par \times \left[1 - \frac{dn}{360}\right]$
interest rates fall	$= 10,000,000\left[1 - \frac{(0.1)(90)}{360}\right]$
September	
T-bill discount yield at 8%	Sell 10 September T-bill contracts at 8% discount yield
Price of 91-day T-bills, $10 million par:	Value of contracts:
$9,797,778 $= 10,000,000\left[1 - \frac{(0.08)(91)}{360}\right]$	$9,800,000 $= \$10,000,000\left[1 - \frac{(0.08)(90)}{360}\right]$

II.

Cash Market Loss		Futures Market Gain	
June cost	$9,747,222	September sale	$9,800,000
September cost	(9,797,778)	June purchase	(9,750,000)
Loss *"opportunity loss"*	($ 50,556)	Gain	$ 50,000
	Net Loss: ($556) $= Loss + Gain$		

III.

Effective Discount Yield with the Hedge (using Equation 5.3)

$$\frac{\$10,000,000 - (\$9,797,778 - \$50,000)}{\$10,000,000} \times \frac{360}{91} = 9.978\% = d = \frac{Par - P_0}{Par} \times \frac{360}{n}$$

[a]At a discount yield of 10%, the price of a 91-day T-bill (from Equation 5.5) is *discount yield*, *no. of period*

$$Par \times \left[1 - \frac{dn}{360}\right] = P_0 = \$10,000,000\left[1 - \frac{0.1(91)}{360}\right] = \$9,747,222$$

[b]T-bill futures contracts are standardized at 90-day maturities, resulting in a price different from the one calculated in the cash market.

simplified world of this example, the institution's returns are protected from interest rate fluctuations, because the dollar interest cost for the quarter, netted against the gain on the hedge, is the desired $87,500. Again, transactions costs, brokers' fees, and the opportunity cost of the margin deposit are not included.

As with the long hedge, the short hedge is undertaken only to protect an existing financial position. Attempting to gain a pure profit from rising rates would be speculation.

RISK AND THE FINANCIAL FUTURES MARKETS

The preceding scenarios are extremely simplified. For example, they assume that the changes in spot and futures yields are identical. They also do not address several decisions that investors must make before entering the market, such as the type and number of contracts to be purchased or sold and the length of the hedge. The examples also assume that the interest rate forecasts are accurate and timely. These more complex aspects of hedging and the risks they introduce are discussed in this section.

INCORRECT RATE FORECASTS

The preceding examples illustrate that rate forecasts are an integral part of every hedge but that their accuracy determines management's satisfaction with the results. The assumption made in Table 10.2 was that interest rates would fall and that funds received and invested after 3 months would earn a lower yield.

| **TABLE 10.3** | **The Short Hedge (Forecast: Rising Interest Rates)** |

A short hedge is chosen in anticipation of interest rate increases and requires the sale of interest rate futures contracts. If the forecast is correct, the profit on the hedge helps to offset losses in the cash market.

I.

Cash Market	**Futures Market**
September	Sell 5 T-bill contracts for December delivery at 7%
CD rate: 7%	discount yield
Interest cost on $5 million in deposits (3 months):	Value of contracts:
$87,500 $= 5,000,000 \times (0.07) \times (\frac{3}{12})$	$4,912,500 $= 5,000,000 \times [1 - \frac{(0.07)(90)}{360}]$
December *interest rates rise*	
CD rate: 9%	Buy 5 December T-bill contracts at 9% discount yield
Interest cost on $5 million in deposits (3 months):	Value of contracts:
$112,500 $= 5,000,000 \times (0.09) \times (\frac{3}{12})$	$4,887,500 $= 5,000,000 \times [1 - \frac{(0.09)(90)}{360}]$

II.

Cash Market Loss		**Futures Market Gain**	
September interest	$ 87,500	September sale	$4,912,500
December interest	(112,500)	December purchase	(4,887,500)
Loss	($ 25,000)	Gain	$ 25,000

Net Result of Hedge: $0

III.

Net Interest Cost and Effective CD Rate

$112,500 − $25,000 = $87,500

$$\frac{\$87,500}{\$5,000,000} \times \frac{360}{90} = 0.07 = 7.0\%$$

If interest rates had not fallen, the portfolio manager could have maintained or even increased returns through the cash market position alone. The long hedge would result in a loss, because the contracts owned would decline in value. The loss on the futures hedge would reduce the otherwise favorable returns on the securities investment. The protective hedge not only limits the institution's loss from an *unfavorable* interest rate change, it also limits the potential gains from a *favorable* movement in rates. Thus, hedging is indeed a risk-minimization strategy, intended to reduce potential variation in the NIM.

BASIS RISK

An influence on both the type and number of contracts to be traded is the **basis.** Basis is the difference between the spot price of the underlying financial asset and the price of a futures contract at time t:

[10.1]

$$\text{Basis} = P_{St} - P_{Ft}$$

To execute a perfect hedge, one in which the cash market loss is *exactly* offset by the futures market profit, the hedger must predict the basis accurately and adjust the size of the hedge accordingly. In the simplified world of Table 10.2, the discount yield on the T-bills equaled the effective discount yield at which the T-bill contract traded. The difference in the cash and futures market results arose from the futures market convention of pricing T-bill contracts based on 90 rather than 91 days. In reality, however, although cash yields and futures market yields are closely related, they are not perfectly correlated because each market has its own supply/demand interactions. The possibility of unexpected changes in the relationship between spot and futures market prices introduces another element of risk, known as **basis risk.**

BASIS RISK ILLUSTRATED.[9] When a hedger closes out cash and futures positions, the gains and losses

---

[9] The following section draws on Van Horne 1990, 160–161.

from each are netted. These calculations are shown at the end of Tables 10.2 and 10.3. Presenting them in a different format clarifies the importance of the basis.

At the close of a hedge, the results from the cash market transactions are determined by the number of securities bought or sold and their cost, $Q(P_{St})$. In Table 10.2, ten bills with a par value of $1 million were bought.

$$Q(P_{S1}) = 10 \times \$979,777.80 = \$9,797,778$$

The result of the futures transaction alone is the proceeds from the sale (at t = 1) minus the cost of the purchase (at t = 0):

$$Q(P_{F1}) - Q(P_{F0}) = Q(P_{F1} - P_{F0})$$

For the long hedge:

$$
\begin{aligned}
Q(P_{F1} - P_{F0}) &= 10 \times (\$980,000 - \$975,000) \\
&= 10 \times \$5,000 \\
&= \$50,000
\end{aligned}
$$

The *net cost* of the bills purchased can be expressed as the difference between their spot price in September—the amount the institution would actually pay for the bills—and the profits from the futures trade:

[10.2]

$$
\begin{aligned}
\text{Net Cost} &= Q(P_{S1}) - Q(P_{F1} - P_{F0}) \\
&= 10(\$979,777.80) - 10(\$980,000.00 \\
&\qquad - \$975,000.00) \\
&= \$9,797,778 - \$50,000 \\
&= \$9,747,778
\end{aligned}
$$

Rearranging, the net cost is also

$$
\begin{aligned}
\text{Net Cost} &= Q(P_{S1} - P_{F1}) + Q(P_{F0}) \\
&= 10(\$979,777.80 - \$980,000.00) \\
&\qquad + (10 \times \$975,000.00) \\
&= -\$2,222 + \$9,750,000 \\
&= \$9,747,778
\end{aligned}
$$

In other words, the basis at the time the position is closed out—the quantity $(P_{S1} - P_{F1})$—determines the success or failure of the hedge. If there were no uncertainty about the basis, a hedge in the futures market would involve much less risk. In reality, at the time

the hedge is undertaken the trader does not know P_{S1} or P_{F1} or the difference between the two that will prevail in the future. As basis fluctuates, so does the potential gain or loss on the hedge.

The top panel of Figure 10.2 shows prices on a popular futures instrument, T-bond contracts, as well as prices on T-bonds during the period 1978–1988. The high positive correlation in price movements is evident from the bottom line, which is the basis over that period. Although the basis does not fluctuate greatly, it is not stable. Traders who hedge positions in the cash markets with futures incur basis risk, a fact that must be considered in the hedging decision. As the top of Figure 10.2 illustrates, however, basis risk exposure on the futures position may be lower than price risk exposure in the cash market, especially when the cash and futures instruments are identical or very closely related. The variability in the basis in the top panel is clearly much smaller than the variability in prices on 30-year T-bonds.

THE CROSS HEDGE AND BASIS RISK

In Table 10.2, the money market portfolio manager was protecting yields on an anticipated T-bill investment with a T-bill futures contract. In many hedging decisions, however, the limited variety of futures contracts available makes it impossible to hedge a cash instrument with a contract for future delivery of the same security. Whenever a futures hedge is constructed on an instrument other than the cash market security, as would be the case when hedging a corporate bond portfolio, the hedge is a **cross hedge**. The basis risk for these positions is even greater than when the same security is involved in both sides of the transaction, as the bottom panel of Figure 10.2 demonstrates.

Figure 10.2 shows that from 1979 through 1988, the prices of T-bond futures contracts and the prices of a typical high-grade corporate bond differed more than the prices of T-bond futures and T-bonds. If a portfolio manager had hedged a corporate bond portfolio with T-bond futures during this period, the basis risk would have been higher than if the manager were hedging a T-bond portfolio. The basis in the cross hedge, however, would still have been less variable over the period than the price of the unhedged corporate bond.

If a short-term instrument was hedged with a futures contract on a long-term security, or vice versa,

FIGURE 10.2   ### Prices of 30-Year Bonds and T-Bond Futures Contracts

The basis is the difference between the current price of a hedged asset and the current price of a futures contract. The more nearly identical the characteristics of the hedged asset and the futures contract, the more stable the basis.

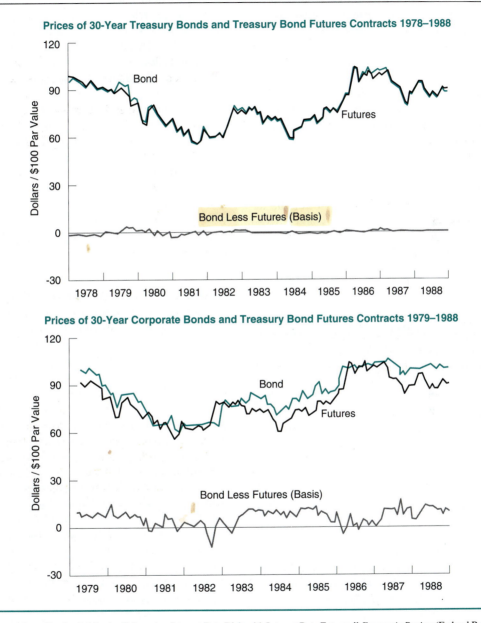

Prices of 30-Year Treasury Bonds and Treasury Bond Futures Contracts 1978–1988

Prices of 30-Year Corporate Bonds and Treasury Bond Futures Contracts 1979–1988

Source: Adapted from Charles S. Morris, "Managing Interest Rate Risk with Interest Rate Futures," *Economic Review* (Federal Reserve Bank of Kansas City) 74 (March 1989): 13.

the basis risk would be even greater. A change in the slope of the yield curve would produce changes of differing magnitudes for long- and short-term yields. In that case, the changes in spot and futures values would certainly diverge, and, consequently, the effectiveness of the hedge would be more uncertain.

The cross hedge exposes the hedger to basis risk for another important reason. Even if the changes in *yields* were the same on two securities, the resulting *price* changes could very well differ. The bond theorems and duration discussions in Chapters 8 and 9 demonstrate that a given basis-point change in yields will not affect the prices of securities in the same way if they have different coupon rates or terms to maturity, differences likely to occur in a cross hedge. As market interest rates fluctuate, the goal of a hedge—minimizing NIM fluctuations by realizing a profit on the futures trade that exactly offsets the cash market loss—is difficult to achieve with a cross hedge.

CHOOSING THE OPTIMAL NUMBER OF CONTRACTS

An asset/liability manager faces additional uncertainties in determining the size of the futures position. The objective of hedging is to offset as closely as possible potential losses on a cash instrument with gains on futures, but price changes on the two types of instruments are seldom exactly proportional to one another. Therefore, simply dividing the total value of the cash portfolio to be hedged by the face value of a single futures contract on an appropriate instrument would give a misleading signal about the number of futures contracts a hedger should buy or sell. Selecting the number of contracts to trade is particularly difficult in a cross hedge, because face value, coupon, and maturity characteristics may all differ between cash and futures instruments.

The first step in structuring the hedge is to identify the assets or liabilities (or both) to be protected. The volume and interest rate characteristics of the instrument to be hedged are the foundation for the futures decision.[10]

THE HEDGE RATIO. Before the optimal position in the futures market can be determined, a **hedge ratio** must be estimated. Although there are other ways of defining a hedge ratio, many experts prefer a definition that focuses on the relative variability of the prices of the cash and futures instrument involved in a contemplated hedge. This definition assumes that the objective of the hedge is to minimize the variability in price/yield changes to which the hedger is exposed:[11]

$$HR = \frac{\text{cov}(\Delta P_S, \Delta P_F)}{\sigma^2_{\Delta P_F}} \qquad [10.3]$$

where

$$HR = \text{hedge ratio}$$
$$\text{cov}(\Delta P_S, \Delta P_F) = \text{covariance between changes in spot prices and changes in futures prices}$$
$$\sigma^2_{\Delta P_F} = \text{variance in changes in futures prices}$$

The covariance is a statistic measuring the extent to which two variables move together. Students of regression analysis may also realize that the covariance between two variables, divided by the variance of one of the variables, is the beta coefficient in a simple regression model between the two variables. Thus, the hedge ratio as defined previously can be estimated by regressing past price changes in the cash instrument to be hedged against past price changes in a futures instrument. The beta of such a regression is the hedge ratio for the proposed hedge.[12]

Suppose that a securities portfolio manager, anticipating a decline in interest rates over the next 3 months, wishes to protect the yield on an investment of $15 million in T-bills and that a T-bill futures contract is now selling for $989,500. If the hedge ratio between price changes in T-bills and T-bill futures contracts has been estimated through regression to be 0.93, the number of contracts to be used in the hedge can be determined by

---

[10] The development of an institutional hedging strategy is a major aspect of asset/liability management. The futures position may revolve around either a macro or micro hedge, terms that refer to the magnitude of the futures position in relation to the institution's balance sheet. This aspect of hedging is explored in Chapter 19.

[11] For further discussion of hedge ratios, including alternative definitions, see Kolb 1988; Schwarz, Hill, and Schneeweis 1986; and Chance 1989.

[12] Note the similarity between this process and estimating the beta coefficient on common stock, illustrated in more detail in Chapter 5.

$$N_F = \frac{V}{F} \times HR \qquad [10.4]$$

where

N_F = number of futures contracts to be purchased or sold

V = total market value of securities to be hedged

F = market value of a single futures contract

In this example, the number of contracts to be purchased (a long position is needed because the forecast is for falling rates) is

$$\frac{\$15,000,000}{\$989,500} \times 0.93 = 14.098$$

Several factors will affect the outcome of the hedge. If the *past* covariance between changes in T-bill prices and changes in T-bill futures prices is not the same as the covariance between those price changes *during* the hedge, the number of contracts calculated using Equation 10.4 will not result in a position that minimizes the hedger's risk exposure. Also, it is not possible to trade fractional amounts of futures contracts, so the hedger in this instance would need to purchase 14 contracts. Thus, even if past and future covariances between price changes were equal, the manager would still expect a less-than-perfect hedge. This inability to trade fractional futures units or, for that matter, fractions of a T-bill explains why the hedge results in Table 10.2 are imperfect. Although many financial theories assume perfect divisibility of financial assets, it seldom exists in practice.

A more complex, duration-based model for estimating hedge ratios is illustrated in the appendix to this chapter.

INTEREST RATE FUTURES: REGULATORY RESTRICTIONS AND FINANCIAL REPORTING

The risks accompanying the futures markets have led regulators to focus attention on policies governing institutional involvement. For state-regulated institutions, there may be as many different policies as there are state regulators. In contrast, federally chartered or federally insured institutions in each industry do have uniform regulations. In general, regulators disapprove of futures transactions that increase the institution's risk exposure. Instead, they expect an institution to assume a futures position that will desensitize the balance sheet to interest rate changes. Because commercial bank balance sheets are less homogeneous than thrift balance sheets, thrift regulators have set more specific rules on the use of futures. Bank regulators have followed a model similar to that used by securities industry regulators by emphasizing a self-policing approach.

In any case, depositories cannot use futures as income generating investments for speculative purposes. Regulators also expect a high-level management committee, often including members of the board of directors, to establish a hedging policy for the institution, including a set of guidelines for establishing hedges and monitoring the results.[13]

ACCOUNTING RULES. Guidelines for reporting futures transactions have also received much attention. The accounting profession has addressed two areas of controversy: what distinguishes a hedge from a speculative trade, and how to report a futures position. Rules of the Financial Accounting Standards Board (FASB) designate a futures transaction as a hedge when two conditions are met[14]

1. The asset or liability to be hedged exposes the institution to interest rate risk.

2. The futures contract chosen reduces interest rate risk, is designated as a hedge, and has price movements highly correlated with the instrument being hedged.

For reporting the results of hedges, institutions prefer to wait until a futures position is closed, and the FASB permits transactions meeting its definition to be reported at that time, after the results are known. Some regulators prefer contemporaneous reporting and

---

[13] For more details on the guidelines established for commercial banks and bank holding companies, see Chicago Board of Trade 1990, 94–95; Parkinson and Spindt 1985, 469–474; and Koppenhaver 1984.

[14] See Drabenstott and McDonley 1984, 24–25; and Chicago Board of Trade 1990, 100–101. The FASB rules became effective December 31, 1984.

FIGURE 10.3   **Exchange Rates and Foreign Currency Futures Prices: August 13 and September 14, 1992**

Prices and other information on foreign currency futures contracts and exchange rates are reported daily in major newspapers.

Thursday, August 13, 1992
CURRENCY FUTURES

```
                                          Lifetime      Open
          Open  High  Low Settle Change  High  Low   Interest
JAPAN YEN (IMM)–12.5 million yen; $ per yen (.00)
Sept     .7856 .7910 .7835 .7909 + .0055 .8090 .7265 52,616
Dec      .7840 .7902 .7827 .7901 + .0055 .8070 .7410  4,480
Mr93     .7848 .7850 .7848 .7904 + .0056 .8050 .7445    984
 Est vol 18,612; vol Wed 13,685; open int 58,081, −199.
DEUTSCHEMARK (IMM)–125,000 marks; $ per mark
Sept     .6792 .6840 .6772 .6835 + .0040 .6843 .5685 78,831
Dec      .6688 .6730 .6668 .6728 + .0040 .6737 .5645  7,847
Mr93     .6580 .6620 .6580 .6630 + .0040 .6625 .5724  1,236
 Est vol 36,238; vol Wed 30,976; open int 87,944, −1,784.

CANADIAN DOLLAR (IMM)–100,000 dlrs.; $ per Can $
Sept     .8373 .8393 .8358 .8362 − .0007 .8774 .8191 25,058
Dec      .8349 .8354 .8326 .8332 − .0007 .8740 .8130  1,676
Mr93     ....  ....  ....  .8309 − .0007 .8712 .8115    282
June     ....  ....  ....  .8281 − .0007 .8355 .8060    875
 Est vol 7,307; vol Wed 8,106; open int 27,950, −1,586.

BRITISH POUND (IMM)–62,500 pds.; $ per pound
Sept    1.9190 1.9250 1.9120 1.9242 + .0046 1.9390 1.6490 24,941
Dec     1.8870 1.8936 1.8800 1.8918 + .0042 1.9040 1.6280  1,169
Mr93    1.8580 1.8610 1.8560 1.8614 + .0034 1.8760 1.7620    194
 Est vol 9,119; vol Wed 5,775; open int 26,304, −352.

SWISS FRANC (IMM)–125,000 francs; $ per franc
Sept     .7540 .7620 .7503 .7617 + .0077 .7778 .6335 29,623
Dec      .7443 .7526 .7410 .7521 + .0075 .7673 .6280    992
 Est vol 20,321; vol Wed 13,274; open int 30,708, −86.

AUSTRALIAN DOLLAR (IMM)–100,000 dlrs.; $ per A.S
Sept     .7165 .7182 .7161 .7161 + .0017 .7610 .7131  3,180
 Est vol 205; vol Wed 952; open int 3,294, +485.

U.S. DOLLAR INDEX (FINEX)–1,000 times USDX
Sept    82.09 82.35 81.70 81.72 − .36 94.20 81.70 4,669
Dec     83.46 83.59 83.10 83.12 − .36 94.93 83.10   541
 Est vol 2,795; vol Wed 2,334; open int 5,216, +191.
 The index: High 81.91; Low 81.29; Close 81.30 −.31
```

Monday, September 14, 1992
CURRENCY FUTURES

```
                                          Lifetime      Open
          Open  High  Low Settle Change  High  Low   Interest
JAPAN YEN (IMM)–12.5 million yen; $ per yen (.00)
Sept     .8026 .8027 .8006 .8020 − .0026 .8177 .7265 22,670
Dec      .7960 .8052 .7960 .8020 − .0012 .8143 .7410 39,578
Mr93     .8005 .8040 .8000 .8013 − .0014 .8135 .7445  1,499
 Est vol 14,861; vol Fri 31,839; open int 63,753, +964.
DEUTSCHEMARK (IMM)–125,000 marks; $ per mark
Sept     .6708 .6827 .6670 .6730 − .0178 .7196 .5685 53,496
Dec      .6605 .6700 .6575 .6620 − .0175 .7083 .5645 49,536
Mr93     .6562 .6562 .6420 .6525 − .0167 .6968 .5724  2,161
June     .6449 .6455 .6415 .6438 − .0161 .6850 .6280    680
Sept     ....  ....  ....  .6360 − .0156 .6720 .6720    500
 Est vol 80,024; vol Fri 93,102; open int 106,398, −1,716.
CANADIAN DOLLAR (IMM)–100,000 dlrs.; $ per Can $
Sept     .8245 .8260 .8240 .8250 + .0024 .8774 .8159  6,234
Dec      .8192 .8226 .8192 .8202 + .0020 .8740 .8112 25,087
Mr93     .8172 .8185 .8170 .8165 + .0022 .8712 .8073    258
June     .8150 .8150 .8135 .8128 + .0024 .8360 .8038    929
 Est vol 5,622; vol Fri 10,023; open int 32,589, −400.
BRITISH POUND (IMM)–62,500 pds.; $ per pound
Sept    1.8860 1.8890 1.8750 1.8886 − .0332 2.0088 1.6490 11,805
Dec     1.8500 1.8694 1.8420 1.8558 − .0308 1.9746 1.6280 21,101
Mr93    1.8150 1.8330 1.8100 1.8240 − .0280 1.9400 1.7620    262
 Est vol 19,212; vol Fri 24,978; open int 33,173, −1,527.
SWISS FRANC (IMM)–125,000 francs; $ per franc
Sept     .7545 .7620 .7545 .7609 − .0161 .8126 .6335 16,187
Dec      .7555 .7594 .7460 .7509 − .0174 .8023 .6280 20,454
Mr93     .7449 .7485 .7370 .7436 − .0163 .7930 .6790    216
 Est vol 25,366; vol Fri 35,336; open int 36,891, −3,703.
AUSTRALIAN DOLLAR (IMM)–100,000 dlrs.; $ per A.S
Sept     .7345 .7345 .7332 .7332 + .0058 .7610 .7053  2,643
Dec      .7272 .7294 .7272 .7291 + .0066 .7462 .7058  2,880
 Est vol 613; vol Fri 2,836; open int 5,538, −73.
U.S. DOLLAR INDEX (FINEX)–1,000 times USDX
Sept    83.16 83.85 82.10 82.95 + 1.79 94.20 78.42  1,143
```

Source: The Wall Street Journal, August 14, 1992, C12, C13; September 15, 1992, C14, C15.

require institutions to use a mark-to-market approach. For example, the Comptroller of the Currency requires national banks to report the market value of their futures positions before closure and thus before any gains or losses are realized. During the course of a hedge, the value of a futures contract may fluctuate substantially as financial market conditions change, although the institution's financial position is not actually affected until a contract is closed out. Thus, many bank managers believe that mark-to-market futures reporting may provide misleading information.

Thrift regulators have allowed savings institutions to use a deferral rather than a mark-to-market approach for several years. Any transactions that do not meet the FASB criteria are considered speculative and must be reported by mark-to-market. Banks, however, must use different methods to report futures transactions to two different audiences.

The risks inherent in the interest rate futures markets, as well as additional regulatory and accounting standards, mean that futures strategies require careful planning and monitoring after they are implemented. Most financial institutions that are successful hedgers have established objectives and safeguards to control the additional risk exposure.

FOREIGN CURRENCY FUTURES

As discussed in detail in Chapter 6, financial institutions active in international markets face exchange rate

FIGURE 10.3 *CONTINUED*   **Foreign Exchange Rates**

Spot and forward exchange rates between the U.S. dollar and other currencies are reported daily in the financial pages. Both direct (U.S. $ equiv.) and indirect (currency per U.S. $) rates are listed.

EXCHANGE RATES

Thursday, August 13, 1992
The New York foreign exchange selling rates below apply to trading among banks in amounts of $1 million and more, as quoted at 3 p.m. Eastern time by Bankers Trust Co., Telerate and other sources. Retail transactions provide fewer units of foreign currency per dollar.

Country	U.S. $ equiv. Thurs.	U.S. $ equiv. Wed.	Currency per U.S. $ Thurs.	Currency per U.S. $ Wed.
Argentina (Peso)	1.01	1.01	.99	.99
Australia (Dollar)	.7180	.7170	1.3928	1.3947
Austria (Schilling)	.09712	.09709	10.30	10.30
Bahrain (Dinar)	2.6522	2.6522	.3771	.3771
Belgium (Franc)	.03341	.03317	29.93	30.15
Brazil (Cruzeiro)	.00023	.00023	4397.00	4356.00
Britain (Pound)	1.9345	1.9300	.5169	.5181
30-Day Forward	1.9238	1.9192	.5198	.5211
90-Day Forward	1.9019	1.8970	.5258	.5271
180-Day Forward	1.8705	1.8657	.5346	.5360
Canada (Dollar)	.8375	.8388	1.1940	1.1922
France (Franc)	.20212	.20161	4.9475	4.9600
30-Day Forward	.20094	.20045	4.9767	4.9887
90-Day Forward	.19859	.19806	5.0355	5.0490
180-Day Forward	.19524	.19478	5.1220	5.1340
Germany (Mark)	.6873	.6832	1.4550	1.4637
30-Day Forward	.6835	.6794	1.4630	1.4719
90-Day Forward	.6763	.6722	1.4787	1.4877
180-Day Forward	.6659	.6619	1.5017	1.5107
Greece (Drachma)	.005556	.005540	180.00	180.50
Hong Kong (Dollar)	.12931	.12953	7.7335	7.7200
South Korea (Won)	.0012703	.0012703	787.20	787.20
Spain (Peseta)	.010715	.010685	93.32	93.59
Sweden (Krona)	.1881	.1881	5.3175	5.3175
Switzerland (Franc) ...	.7645	.7567	1.3080	1.3215
30-Day Forward	.7613	.7536	1.3135	1.3270
90-Day Forward	.7547	.7470	1.3250	1.3386
180-Day Forward	.7454	.7381	1.3415	1.3548
Taiwan (Dollar)	.040193	.040209	24.88	24.87
Thailand (Baht)	.03951	.03951	25.31	25.31
Turkey (Lira)	.0001438	.0001439	6952.00	6951.00
United Arab (Dirham)	.2723	.2723	3.6725	3.6725
Uruguay (New Peso)				
Financial	.000315	.000315	3175.01	3175.01
Venezuela (Bolivar)				
Floating rate	.01508	.01507	66.32	66.34
SDR	1.44862	1.44633	.69031	.69141
ECU	1.39750	1.39120	....	....

Special Drawing Rights (SDR) are based on exchange rates for the U.S., German, British, French and Japanese currencies. Source: International Monetary Fund.
European Currency Unit (ECU) is based on a basket of community currencies.

EXCHANGE RATES

Monday, September 14, 1992
The New York foreign exchange selling rates below apply to trading among banks in amounts of $1 million and more, as quoted at 3 p.m. Eastern time by Bankers Trust Co., Telerate and other sources. Retail transactions provide fewer units of foreign currency per dollar.

Country	U.S. $ equiv. Mon.	U.S. $ equiv. Fri.	Currency per U.S. $ Mon.	Currency per U.S. $ Fri.
Argentina (Peso)	1.01	1.01	.99	.99
Australia (Dollar)	.7337	.7263	1.3630	1.3768
Austria (Schilling)	.09558	.09823	10.46	10.18
Bahrain (Dinar)	2.6522	2.6522	.3771	.3771
Belgium (Franc)	.03265	.03351	30.63	29.84
Brazil (Cruzeiro)	.00018	.00019	5411.00	5354.00
Britain (Pound)	1.8900	1.9250	.5291	.5195
30-Day Forward	1.8790	1.9136	.5322	.5226
90-Day Forward	1.8574	1.8900	.5384	.5291
180-Day Forward	1.8263	1.8557	.5476	.5389
Canada (Dollar)	.8241	.8224	1.2135	1.2160
France (Franc)	.19845	.20331	5.0390	4.9185
30-Day Forward	.19732	.19181	5.0680	5.2135
90-Day Forward	.19505	.19963	5.1270	5.0092
180-Day Forward	.19196	.19617	5.2095	5.0975
Germany (Mark)	.6725	.6916	1.4870	1.4460
30-Day Forward	.6689	.6877	1.4949	1.4541
90-Day Forward	.6622	.6803	1.5101	1.4699
180-Day Forward	.6530	.6700	1.5315	1.4926
Greece (Drachma)	.005397	.005556	185.30	180.00
Hong Kong (Dollar)	.12932	.12937	7.7330	7.7300
South Korea (Won)	.0012723	.0012749	785.95	784.40
Spain (Peseta)	.010386	.010639	96.28	93.99
Sweden (Krona)	.1837	.1891	5.4435	5.2895
Switzerland (Franc) ...	.7596	.7782	1.3165	1.2850
30-Day Forward	.7568	.7753	1.3213	1.2898
90-Day Forward	.7519	.7696	1.3300	1.2994
180-Day Forward	.7447	.7614	1.3428	1.3133
Taiwan (Dollar)	.039984	.040096	25.01	24.94
Thailand (Baht)	.03959	.03981	25.26	25.12
Turkey (Lira)	.0001366	.0001414	7319.00	7070.00
United Arab (Dirham)	.2723	.2723	3.6725	3.6725
Uruguay (New Peso)				
Financial	.000307	.000306	3254.00	3265.01
Venezuela (Bolivar)				
Floating rate	.01476	.01477	67.75	67.72
SDR	1.44847	1.46759	.69038	.68139
ECU	1.35710	1.39800	....	....

Special Drawing Rights (SDR) are based on exchange rates for the U.S., German, British, French and Japanese currencies. Source: International Monetary Fund.
European Currency Unit (ECU) is based on a basket of community currencies.

Source: The Wall Street Journal, August 14, 1992, C13; September 15, 1992, C15.

risk, or variability in NIM caused by fluctutations in currency exchange rates. Foreign currency futures are instruments used to hedge exchange rate risk, just as interest rate futures are used to hedge interest rate risk. Hedging strategies useful to institutions financing international transactions are similar to the choices available for hedging against interest rate fluctuations.

As of mid-1992, futures contracts were available on exchange rates between the U.S. dollar and the Ger-man mark, the Japanese yen, the Swiss franc, the British pound, the French franc, the Australian dollar, and the Canadian dollar. As seen in Figure 10.3, these contract prices are quoted as direct rates, or dollars per unit of the foreign currency. Thus, when the value of the dollar declines, the values of a foreign currency and futures contracts on that currency rise.

In early 1992, the CME introduced futures contracts on currency **cross rates**. (Cross rates are rates of exchange between two nondollar currencies.) The first contract of this type approved for trading was the mark/yen futures contract. The contract price is quoted as yen per mark; contracts are settled in yen. As the value of the mark increases against the yen, the mark/yen contract price rises; when the yen appreciates against the mark, the price of the contract falls.

COMPARISON OF FORWARD AND FUTURES MARKETS

As illustrated in Chapter 6, the forward markets provide a mechanism for avoiding the uncertainty of exchange rate fluctuations over a given planning period, as do foreign currency futures. Before illustrating the use of foreign currency futures to hedge exchange rate risk, it is useful to distinguish between futures and forward contracts.

Forward contracts are not standardized and can be customized to the needs of each trader. For example, they can be negotiated in any currency, in any denomination, and for any maturity. Currency futures contracts, like interest rate futures contracts, are available only in standard denominations and maturities. Forward contracts are arranged electronically by means of a foreign currency dealer or through large financial institutions, especially money center banks. Currency futures contracts are traded on the futures exchanges. As a result, the holder of a forward contract faces default risk, whereas the clearinghouse assumes that risk in the futures markets. Because there is no secondary market for forward contracts, they are less liquid than currency futures, a position that can be offset before maturity. However, as with interest rate futures, currency futures contracts require that a trader's margin account be marked to market daily. Nonetheless, because of the default and liquidity risks faced in the forward markets, usually only very large traders participate.

CURRENCY FUTURES ILLUSTRATED

Suppose a U.S. bank has made a formal commitment in August 1992 to loan a German customer 1 million marks in 30 days. At that time, the bank plans to convert dollars into marks, but management recognizes the risk of exchange rate fluctuations over the period. As Figure 10.3 shows, on August 13, 1992, the

direct exchange rate between marks and dollars was 0.6873; the indirect rate was 1.4550 marks per dollar. In other words, one mark cost $0.6873, and one U.S. dollar would buy 1.455 marks.

Instead of negotiating a forward contract to permit the exchange at a known rate 30 days hence, suppose the bank decides to use futures contracts to hedge against the risk of appreciation in the value of the mark. Because the hedge is undertaken to protect against the appreciation of the mark (that is, against a decline in the value of the dollar), a long futures position is indicated. Figure 10.3 also shows that on August 13, 1992, the settlement price for a September futures contract for German marks was 0.6835. Each mark futures contract has a face value of 125,000, so $1,000,000/125,000 = 8$ contracts will be required to hedge against the entire 1,000,000 mark transaction. Table 10.4 presents the details of the hedge.

As shown in Figure 10.3, the actual spot exchange rate on September 14, 1992, was 0.6725 dollars per mark (or 1.4870 marks per dollar). The mark had actually *depreciated* relative to the dollar, countering the bank's fears. The value of the September mark contract, also shown in Figure 10.3, had fallen to 0.6730. If bank management had chosen not to hedge, the institution would have enjoyed a potential gain of $14,800 from converting dollars to marks in September instead of August. With a hedge, however, this gain was partially offset by the loss on the mark futures contracts, which declined in price as the dollar's value rose. The net result of the hedge in this example was a gain to the bank of $4,300, much smaller than the unhedged gain. Transactions costs, which are ignored here, would actually result in a somewhat lower gain. Although in retrospect this example may seem to suggest that the hedge was a bad decision, it is important to remember that in August, no one knew whether the mark would appreciate or depreciate relative to the dollar. This uncertainty is precisely the reason for a hedge. If the mark had *appreciated* by September 14, the loan to the German customer would have been more costly to the bank than when it was agreed upon in August, but that loss would have been offset by a gain on a long futures position.[15]

---

[15] For more information on currency futures, see Kolb 1988 and Fieleke 1985.

TABLE 10.4   **Hedging with Currency Futures Contracts (Forecast: Falling Dollar)**

Currency futures contracts may be used to protect against a decline in the value of the dollar. A long hedge, requiring the purchase of currency futures, results in a gain if the value of the dollar falls against the currency on which the futures contract is written, but results in a loss when the value of the dollar strengthens.

I.

Cash Market	Futures Market
August 13	
Dollars required to purchase 1 million marks at $0.6873	Buy 8 September contracts at $0.6835
$687,300	Value of contracts:
	125,000 × 8 × $0.6835 =
	$683,500
September 14	
Dollars required to purchase 1 million marks at $0.6725	Sell 8 September contracts at $0.6730
$672,500	Value of contracts:
	125,000 × 8 × $0.6730 =
	$673,000

II.

Cash Market Gain		Futures Market Loss	
August "cost"	$687,300	August purchase	$673,000
September cost	672,500	September sale	683,500
Gain	$ 14,800	Loss	($ 10,500)

Net Gain: $4,300

SUMMARY

Tools for managing interest rate risk include two types of financial futures—interest rate and foreign currency futures. They allow managers to adopt a hedging strategy, through which expected profits on the institution's existing financial position are protected against unfavorable changes in interest rates or foreign exchange rates. Hedging is a risk-minimization approach; it does not allow an institution to profit from unexpected favorable changes. Futures are traded on organized exchanges, facilitating their liquidity, and the clearinghouse plays an important role in transactions.

An interest rate futures contract is an agreement between a buyer and seller to exchange a fixed quantity of a financial asset at a specified price on a specified date. The buyer has a long futures position and purchases a contract when interest rates are expected to fall. The seller of a futures contract takes a short position in anticipation of rising rates. Because the prices of futures contracts move in the same direction as prices on underlying financial assets, falling interest rates coincide with rising prices for futures contracts, and rising rates coincide with falling futures prices.

The hedger uses profits earned on futures transactions to offset losses incurred on other financial assets. Additional markets permit institutions to hedge against the risk of changes in currency exchange rates.

The most compelling reasons to use futures contracts are the low transactions costs of initiating and closing out a hedge, the flexibility to take either a long or short position, and the minimal default risk exposure because of the clearinghouse. Problems faced in futures hedging include the cash-flow requirements from daily margin calls, basis risk, and the difficulty of determining the best hedge ratio. Financial institutions must also be careful to follow regulatory and accounting rules governing the use of futures contracts.

QUESTIONS

1. Describe the characteristics of an interest rate futures contract. Consult a current issue of *The Wall Street Journal* or other major newspaper to find price quotations on interest rate futures contracts. Are contracts written on any financial instruments not shown in Figure 10.1?

2. What features of futures contracts distinguish them from other financial instruments?

3. Explain the difference between using financial futures in a hedging strategy and using futures to speculate.

4. What are the important differences between cash markets and futures markets?

5. Identify interest rate forecasts or investment situations in which each of the following would be appropriate:
 a.   Short hedge
 b.   Long hedge
 c.   Cross hedge

6. Explain the role of clearinghouses in the trading of financial futures. Why do clearinghouses set margin requirements?

7. Find a current article on one or more of the futures exchanges located outside the United States. What is the rate of growth in trading volume? How do policies and trading mechanisms compare with those in U.S. markets such as the CBOT or CME? How much closer are we to a truly global futures market?

8. Suppose that you had perfect foresight and were able to predict accurately the change in interest rates between April 8 and 9, 1992, shown in Figure 10.1 Given your forecasts, would you have taken a long or a short position in Treasury futures on April 8? Why?

9. What is meant by the terms *basis* and *basis risk?* What types of hedges have the greatest exposure to basis risk?

10. What does the hedge ratio measure? Why is the hedge ratio needed to determine the number of contracts to trade?

11. What difficulties arise in accurately estimating the number of contracts for a hedge? What other factors also make it difficult to construct a perfect hedge?

12. What types of restrictions have regulators and accountants developed to control the risk exposure of financial institutions participating in futures markets?

13. If you were charged with managing exchange rate risk for a U.S. commercial bank operating in international markets, in which types of situations might you prefer to enter into a forward contract? To trade foreign currency futures contracts?

14. Consult the financial pages of *The Wall Street Journal* or another major newspaper. Find the price quotations for foreign currency futures contracts. Have any new currencies been added to those shown in Figure 10.3? Based on the current settlement prices you find, is the value of the dollar higher or lower against foreign currencies than it was in late 1992?

15. Suppose it is your responsibility to manage exchange rate risk for a large German bank with activities in the European Community, the United States, and Asia. How does the development of cross rate futures contracts facilitate the bank's exchange rate risk management?

PROBLEMS

1. A portfolio manager will trade futures contracts to protect the value of a $150 million portfolio invested in short-term securities. Calculate the number of contracts that should be traded for the following instruments and hedge ratio estimates. Refer to Table 10.1 to determine the face value of each contract.
 a.   T-bond contracts; hedge ratio = 0.85
 b.   T-bill contracts; hedge ratio = 0.82
 c.   30-day interest rate futures contracts; hedge ratio = 0.91

2. A money market portfolio manager needs to hedge against an expected drop in interest rates that could occur before a large inflow of funds is received and invested. The manager plans to buy 10 T-bill futures contracts at a price of 97. If the contracts are sold 3 months later at 96.25, what will be the gain or loss on the futures position? What if the contracts are sold at 97.625?

3. The manager of a large thrift forecasts an increase in interest rates over the next 2 months. The thrift currently has $20 million in certificates of deposit costing 6 percent. The manager hedges against the expected increase in interest rates by trading twenty 90-day T-bill futures contracts.
 a.   Should a long or short hedge be used? Why?
 b.   Based on the following information, calculate the gain or loss on the hedge.

	CD Cost	T-Bill Futures Settlement Price
Current	6.0%	98.375
Future (2 months)	7.5%	97.995

4. The Executive Vice President of a large bank believes that a forecasted increase in T-bill rates will occur, forcing the bank to pay higher interest on its MMDAs. She decides to hedge $20 million of its deposit accounts by trading T-bill futures contracts.

    a. Should the manager assume a long or short futures position?

    b. If she estimates a hedge ratio of 0.97, how many contracts should be bought or sold?

    c. Suppose the T-bill futures contracts are trading at 98.13 today, but are priced at 98.01 one month from today when the position is closed out. What will be the profit or loss on the futures transactions?

    d. Suppose the bank's MMDA costs rise from 6½ percent to 8 percent between the beginning and end of the 1-month period. What will be the net impact on the monthly interest costs for the institution resulting from the hedge and the change in interest rates?

5. After studying market forecasts, the investment manager of a P/L insurer anticipates an interest rate decline over the next 3 months. He expects to receive $100 million in new funds in 90 days, which he will invest in T-bills. In an effort to avoid the adverse effect of the interest rate decline on expected yield, he hedges in the futures market.

    a. Should he assume a short or a long position?

    b. Based on the following information, calculate the resulting gain or loss on the hedge.

	T-Bill Discount Yield	T-Bill Futures Settlement Price
January	9.85%	97.92
April	8.80%	98.20

    c. Suppose the manager's interest rate forecast is incorrect and interest rates increase instead. By April the discount yield on T-bills is 10.50 percent, and the settlement price on the contracts held is 97.75. What is the resulting gain or loss on the hedge?

6. A finance company is planning to issue $50 million in commercial paper in 4 months. Forecasts of interest rate movements over the intervening period are contradictory, so the firm's manager decides a T-bill futures hedge should be assumed. Fifty T-bill futures contracts are sold at 98.94. The firm estimates that the rate currently required on its commercial paper is 7 percent. Four months later, when the finance company closes out its futures position, the contracts are trading at 98.80 and the company issues commercial paper at a rate of 8.45 percent. Calculate the net interest cost to the firm on its 30-day paper, and the effective interest rate it is paying on this short-term debt.

7. Metropolitan National Bank regularly extends loans to importer/exporter customers. In March, management agrees to finance a shipment of cameras for an importer who does not have to pay for the merchandise until it arrives in June. The current cost of the cameras in Japanese yen is 200 million. The prevailing exchange rate is $/yen = 0.008639 and yen/$ = 115.75. The bank's economists anticipate that the value of the dollar will fall over the next 3 months and recommend a hedge with foreign currency futures. Using the following information, calculate the gain or loss on the hedge.

    a. The most recent settlement price on a June yen futures contract was 0.008642, and the standard size of a Japanese yen futures contract is 12.5 million. Given the economists' forecasts, what position should management assume in the futures market to hedge its foreign currency risk? How many contracts will be traded?

    b. In June, the bank closes out its position. The spot rate ($/yen) is 0.008333, and June yen futures are trading at 0.008345. Calculate the gain or loss on the hedge. Did the hedge work as expected?

    c. Suppose instead that the June spot rate is 0.008929 $/yen and yen futures trade at 0.008928. Calculate the results of the hedge. Comment.

8. A German exporter will receive payment in U.S. dollars for a candle shipment made to an American firm. The current spot rate between marks and dollars is DM/$ = 1.718 or $/DM = $0.5820. The exporter will receive $5 million in exactly 2 months (July). Given the uncertainty about the deutsche mark/$ exchange rate that will be prevailing in July, the German firm decides to hedge with foreign currency futures.

    a. Anticipating a decline in the value of the dollar, will the German firm buy or sell DM futures? The prevailing price on DM futures is 0.5810. How many contracts will be traded? DM futures contracts are written for 125,000 DM.

    b. In July the spot rate is 0.6011 $/DM, and DM futures trade at 0.5995. Calculate the gain or loss on the hedge.

9. An American importer buys French wine. The wine shipment will arrive in 30 days, at which time payment is due. If the payment due is 4 million francs, and the value of the dollar is expected to fall, how could the importer use the forward currency market to hedge? What cost, in U.S. dollars, would the firm be obligated to pay if the current 30-day forward rate is 0.1942 $/franc? What risks is the firm assuming by using the forward market? If the spot rate between dollars and francs at the time payment is due is 0.1875 $/franc, would the forward agreement achieve its purpose? Explain.

10. Turn to the duration-based hedging example in the appendix to this chapter. Suppose that the initial price of the instrument to be hedged is $955. The expected position of the cash instrument is a YTM of 10.14% and a price of $1,008.76, the same as in Table 10A.1. The expected duration of T-bond futures in May 1997 is 10.06, and the expected yield on futures in May 1997 is 8.50 percent. The expected futures price is 96-24. Calculate the number of futures contracts needed, as well as the results of the new hedge.

SELECTED REFERENCES

Abken, Peter A. "Globalization of Stock, Futures, and Options Markets." *Economic Review* (Federal Reserve Bank of Atlanta) 76 (July/August 1991): 1–22.

Booth, James R., Richard L. Smith, and Richard W. Stolz, "Use of Interest Rate Futures by Financial Institutions." *Journal of Bank Research* 14 (Spring 1984): 15–20.

Chance, Don M. *An Introduction to Options and Futures,* 2d. ed. Chicago: The Dryden Press, 1992.

Chicago Board of Trade. *Treasury Futures for Institutional Investors.* Chicago: Board of Trade of the City of Chicago, 1990.

Chicago Mercantile Exchange. *Trading and Hedging with Currency Futures and Options,* Chicago: Chicago Mercantile Exchange, 1985.

Drabenstott, Mark, and Anne O'Mara McDonley. "Futures Markets: A Primer for Financial Institutions." *Economic Review* (Federal Reserve Bank of Kansas City) 69 (November 1984): 17–33.

Federal Reserve Bank of New York. *Clearing and Settlement Through the Board of Trade Clearing Corporation,* 1990.

Fieleke, Norman S. "The Rise of the Foreign Currency Futures Markets." *New England Economic Review* (Federal Reserve Bank of Boston) (March/April 1985): 38–47.

Goldstein, Henry S. "Foreign Currency Futures: Some Further Aspects." *Economic Perspectives* (Federal Reserve Bank of Chicago) 7 (November/December 1983): 3–13.

Hansell, Saul. "The Computer that Ate Chicago." *Institutional Investor* 23 (February 1989): 181–188.

Hieronymous, Thomas A. *Economics of Futures Trading.* New York: Commodity Research Bureau, Inc., 1971.

Howard, Charles T., and Louis J. D'Antonio. "Treasury Bill Futures as a Hedging Tool: A Risk-Return Approach." *Journal of Financial Research* 9 (Spring 1986): 25–39.

Hoyt, Robert E. "Use of Financial Futures by Life Insurers." *Journal of Risk and Insurance* 56 (December 1992): 740–748.

Hurtz, Rebecca M., and Mona J. Gardner. "Surviving in a New Environment." *Best's Review* (Life/Health Edition) 85 (September 1984).

Kolb, Robert W. *Understanding Futures Markets.* Glenview, IL: Scott, Foresman and Co., 1988.

Kolb, Robert W., and Raymond Chiang. "Improving Hedging Performance Using Interest Rate Futures." *Financial Management* 10 (Autumn 1981): 72–79.

———. "Duration, Immunization and Hedging with Interest Rate Futures." *Journal of Financial Research* 5 (Summer 1982): 161–170.

Koppenhaver, Gary D. "An Empirical Analysis of Bank Hedging in Futures Markets." *Journal of Futures Markets* 10 (February 1990): 1–12.

———. "Futures Market Regulation." *Economic Perspectives* (Federal Reserve Bank of Chicago) 11 (January/February 1987): 3–15.

———. "Trimming the Hedges: Regulators, Banks and Financial Futures." *Economic Perspectives* (Federal Reserve Bank of Chicago) 8 (November/December 1984): 3–12.

Lamm-Tennant, Joan. "Asset/Liability Management for the Life Insurer: Situation Analysis and Strategy Formulation." *Journal of Risk and Insurance* (September 1989): 501–517.

Miller, Merton H. "Financial Innovation: The Last Twenty Years and the Next." *Journal of Financial and Quantitative Analysis* 21 (December 1986): 459–471.

Morris, Charles S. "Managing Interest Rate Risk with Interest Rate Futures." *Economic Review* (Federal Reserve Bank of Kansas City) 74 (March 1989): 3–20.

Napoli, Janet A. "Derivative Markets and Competitiveness." *Economic Perspectives* (Federal Reserve Bank of Chicago) 16 (July/August 1992): 13–24.

Parkinson, Patrick, and Paul Spindt. "The Use of Interest Rate Futures by Commercial Banks." In *Proceedings of a Conference on Bank Structure and Competition,* 457–489. Chicago: Federal Reserve Bank of Chicago, 1985.

Remolona, Eli M. "The Recent Growth of Financial Derivative Markets." *Quarterly Review* (Federal Reserve Bank of New York) 17 (Winter 1992–93): 28–43.

Scarlata, Jodi G. "Institutionalization Developments in the Globalization of Securities and Futures Markets." *Economic Review* (Federal Reserve Bank of St. Louis) 74 (January/February 1992): 17–30.

Schwarz, Edward D., Joanne M. Hill, and Thomas Schneeweis. *Financial Futures: Fundamentals, Strategies, and Applications.* Homewood, IL: Dow Jones-Irwin, 1986.

Smirlock, Michael C. "Hedging Bank Borrowing Costs with Financial Futures" *Business Review* (Federal Reserve Bank of Philadelphia) (May-June 1986): 13–23.

Van Horne, James. *Financial Market Rates and Flows,* 3d ed. Englewood Cliffs, NJ: Prentice-Hall, 1990.

APPENDIX

10A

A DURATION-BASED FUTURES HEDGE

In a cross hedge, Equations 10.3 and 10.4 could suggest an inappropriate number of contracts to trade because of the unequal price reactions in instruments with different coupons and maturities, even if yields are perfectly correlated. Including the duration of the cash and futures instruments provides a better estimate of the required number of contracts[1]:

$$N_{DUR} = \frac{R_F\,P_C\,D_C}{R_C\,FP_F\,D_F} \quad [10A.1]$$

where

N_{DUR} = the number of contracts to be traded for *each* cash market instrument being hedged

R_F = 1 + the rate expected to prevail on the instrument underlying the futures contract

R_C = 1 + the expected yield to maturity on the asset to be hedged

FP_F = the price agreed on in the futures contract

P_C = the expected spot price of the asset to be hedged as of the hedge termination date

D_C = the expected duration of the asset to be hedged as of the termination date

D_F = the expected duration of the instrument underlying the futures contract as of the termination date

---

[1] This approach to estimating *N* was developed in Kolb and Chiang 1981, and Kolb and Chiang 1982. For additional discussion, see Chance 1992.

The duration-based equation adjusts the size of the futures position for potential differences in the maturity and coupon rates of the cash and futures securities. For example, consider the decision facing a bond portfolio manager in February 1997 anticipating an $8 million cash inflow in May 1997 and forecasting a decline in corporate bond yields over the intervening period. The manager is watching a bond issue maturing in 2002 and expects the yield on these bonds to be 10.14 percent in May, down from the February level of 11.14 percent. At that yield, their duration in May would be 4.148 years. If funds were available in February, 8,231 bonds ($8 million ÷ $971.83 per bond) could be purchased at the current market price. By May, however, the price is expected to have risen to $1,008.76, and $8 million will buy only 7,930 bonds.

Table 10A.1 shows the calculation of a duration-based hedge position to fit this situation. Because there are no futures contracts on corporate bonds, a cross hedge is required. T-bond futures are a reasonable choice. However, because they are standardized at 8 percent coupon, with at least 15-year maturities, the duration of the cash and futures securities will differ. Constructing a hedge by simply comparing the market values of the cash and futures instruments would lead to a less than optimal hedge. The appropriate long position for this hedge is to buy 41 T-bond contracts, which can later be sold at a profit if rates fall.

TABLE 10A.1	**Duration-Based Estimation of the Futures Position**

Expected Cash Inflow (May 1997)	$8,000,000
Cash Instrument to be Hedged	Corporate bonds: $10\frac{3}{8}$ of 02
	Current YTM (February 1997): 11.14%
	Current price: $971.83
Number of Bonds if Purchased at Current Price	8,231
Expected Position of Cash Instrument in May 1997	Expected YTM: 10.14% ($R_C = 1 + 0.1014$)
	Expected market price: $1,008.76 ($P_c$)
	Duration at expected YTM: 4.148 (D_c)
February 1997 Price on T-Bond Futures (10.12% Yield)	83-24 = 83.75% of par = $83,750 ($FP_F$)
Expected Position of T-Bond Futures in May 1997	Price: 91-16 = 91.5% of par = $91,500
	Yield: 9.12% ($R_F = 1 + 0.0912$)
	Duration: 9.871 (D_F)
Duration-Based Number of Contracts	

[10A.1]

$$N_{DUR} = \frac{R_F P_C D_C}{R_C F P_F D_F}$$

$$N_{DUR} = \frac{(1.0912)(\$1,008.76)(4.148)}{(1.1014)(\$83,750)(9.871)} = 0.005015 \text{ per cash instrument}$$

Total Number of Contracts = 0.005015(8,231) = 41.28 = 41 contracts

Table 10A.2 shows the results of a long hedge with 41 T-bond contracts. Assuming the manager's expectations are perfectly fulfilled, the net gain on the hedge is $13,779, more than offsetting the opportunity loss from the decline in market yields during the period in which investment must be delayed. Nothing guarantees a perfect hedge, but performance is improved if the coupon and maturity of the instrument to be hedged are matched closely to the security underlying the futures contract. As with any duration measure, the hedge protects against only one interest rate movement, so it must be adjusted frequently as market conditions change.

TABLE 10A.2	**Results of the Duration-Based Hedge**

I.

Cash Market	**Futures Market**
February	
Corporate bond yield: 11.14%	Buy 41 T-bond contracts for September delivery
Price: $971.83	at 83-24
Total available if purchased in February 1997	Yield: 10.12%
8,231 bonds	Cost: $3,433,750
May	
Funds received and invested: $8,000,000	Sell 41 September T-bond contracts at 91-16
Corporate bond yield: 10.14%	Yield: 9.12%
Price: $1,008.76	Price: $3,751,500
Total purchase: 7,930 bonds	

II.

Cash Market Loss		**Futures Market Gain**	
February cost (8,231 bonds)	$7,999,133	May sale	$3,751,500
May cost (8,231 bonds)	8,303,104	February purchase	3,433,750
Loss	($ 303,971)	Gain	$ 317,750

Net Gain: $13,779

In financial markets, risk is neither created nor destroyed.
It is simply repackaged—shifted from one form to another so as to change
the profile of an instrument's risk and return.

Steven Bloom
Member, New Products Team
American Stock Exchange (1992)

___

In the early 1990s, members of the financial press anointed a small group of securities experts as Wall Street "Rocket Scientists." These experts—most of whom work for securities exchanges or securities firms—are a new breed of inventors who study financial markets, sources of risk, and the needs of market participants. These "scientists" then devote their creative energy to developing financial instruments capable of satisfying these needs.

For the most part, the rocket scientists are working with **derivatives,** the name given to instruments whose value is derived from prices and price fluctuations in some underlying asset. Financial futures contracts on Treasury bills (T-bills) and bonds (T-bonds), introduced in the previous chapter, are just one category of derivative securities, and futures contracts and options are now available on many other instruments. As the rocket scientists have continued their inventive work into the early 1990s, new derivatives are introduced almost daily.

What continues to drive these innovations? The most important factor is risk. Uncertainty about interest rates, exchange rates, price fluctuations in stock and bond markets around the world, even air pollution—all are categories of risk that market participants want to escape. The rocket scientists are constantly searching for a better means of allowing them to do so. This chapter continues the discussion of hedging techniques begun in Chapter 10 by introducing a variety of new derivative instruments and compares and contrasts several strategies used for managing risk by financial institutions.[1]

CHAPTER

11

INTEREST RATE
RISK
MANAGEMENT:
INDEX FUTURES,
OPTIONS,
SWAPS, AND
OTHER
DERIVATIVES

___

[1] Donald Katz, "Wall Street Rocket Scientists," *Worth,* February/March 1992, 68–74; "Derivatives Sprout Bells and Whistles," *Euromoney,* August 1992, 29–39.

STOCK INDEX FUTURES

Like interest rate and currency futures, **stock index futures** are instruments for hedging exposure to changes in market values, specifically exposure to the change of values in equity portfolios. Participants in the stock index futures markets include commercial bank trust departments, insurance companies, pension funds, equity mutual funds, and securities firms. In contrast to the contracts discussed in Chapter 10, stock index futures do not protect against changes in interest rates, but instead their value is pegged to movements in one of several aggregate measures of stock market performance. Their origins in the wild and woolly commodities markets coupled with their appeal to conservative financial institutions led to an early nickname of "pin-striped pork bellies."[2]

As of 1993, futures contracts were traded regularly on groups of domestic stocks such as the Standard and Poor's (S&P) 500; the New York Stock Exchange (NYSE) Index; the Value Line Composite Index; the Mini Value Line Index; and the Major Market Index (MMI) of 20 large firms, designed to emulate the Dow Jones Industrial Average (DJIA). (An attempt by the Chicago Board of Trade (CBOT) to offer a contract based on the Dow was met by a lawsuit from the Dow Jones Company, thwarting introduction of that futures contract. Indexes tracking the performance of non-U.S. equities have also been introduced—most notably the Nikkei 225.

As is true of interest rate futures, developments in the stock index futures market are rapid. New contracts come into the market and old ones leave relatively often, and the array of available contracts is likely to change with time.

THEORETICAL BASIS OF STOCK INDEX FUTURES

Stock index futures are based on capital market theory as reflected in the Capital Asset Pricing Model (CAPM) and the **efficient markets hypothesis (EMH)**. As explained in Chapter 5, CAPM models the price of an individual asset or portfolio as a function of its beta coefficient, which, in turn, is a function of the covariance between the asset's expected returns and the expected returns on the market portfolio. The market portfolio, with a beta of 1, is a fully diversified combination of assets that represents the standard of comparison for all others. EMH argues that, given the wide availability of information to market participants and the speed with which prices react to it, investors with well-diversified portfolios cannot consistently earn returns higher than those on the market portfolio. Investors who choose portfolios with more or less risk than the market portfolio, as measured by beta, should expect to earn a return commensurate with the risk of the portfolio they choose.

Although not perfect, some stock indexes are used as surrogates for the stock market as a whole; the portfolio of stocks underlying such an index is assumed to have a beta of 1. The performance of many professional portfolio managers is evaluated through comparison to a market index, and those who earn lower returns are soundly criticized. Other indexes may reflect a segment of the market. For example, the Chicago Mercantile Exchange (CME) introduced the S&P MidCap 400 Index in 1992, tracking the performance of a portfolio of firms with market values between $300 million and $5 billion. Smaller investors, who may be prevented by brokerage fees, commissions, or funds limitations from holding a well-diversified portfolio, often use "the market" or a market segment as a standard of comparison for interpreting their own results. Later examples indicate why using a stock index as a benchmark of performance is useful to managers hedging equity portfolios.

HISTORY AND CHARACTERISTICS OF STOCK INDEX FUTURES

The first stock index futures contract, based on the Value Line Composite Index, was traded on the Kansas City Board of Trade in February 1982. Within 3 months, an S&P 500 contract was trading at the CME, and an NYSE contract was trading on the New York Futures Exchange. The indexes are similar, in that they are composite measures of the prices of several stocks, but there are also important differences. Table 11.1 compares the composition and calculation of several indexes, including some developed expressly for use in the index futures and options markets. Because the indexes are not identical, they do not

---

[2] Kathleen Kerwin, "Pin-Striped Pork Bellies: Why Stock Index Futures Are Red Hot," *Barron's*, February 14, 1983, 14, 32–34.

TABLE 11.1	**Composition of Selected Stock Market Indexes**

Some popular futures contracts and options are based on commonly watched indicators of general stock market activity. A wide variety of market indexes is regularly published in the financial pages. Each index is based on a different group of securities. There are many ways of calculating index values.

Index	Composition
S&P 500 Index	Measures value of 500 representative stocks listed on national and regional exchanges. The index is a weighted average; the weights reflect the total market value of all outstanding shares.
NYSE Composite Index	Measures the value of all common stocks listed on the NYSE (more than 1,500 stocks). The index is a weighted average; the weights reflect the total market value of all outstanding shares.
Value Line Composite Index	Measures the value of most stocks listed on the NYSE and some traded on other regional exchanges or the over-the-counter markets. The index is a geometric average; all values are equally weighted.
Dow Jones Industrial Average	Measures the value of 30 blue-chip industrial stocks. The index is a simple average; all prices are equally weighted, with the divisor adjusted for stock splits and stock dividends.
Major Market Index	Measures the price of 20 blue-chip stocks traded on the NYSE, 17 of which are in the DJIA. The index is a simple average.
AMEX Market Value Index	Measures value of all stocks traded on the American Stock Exchange (approximately 850).
S&P 100 Index	Measures value of 100 stocks, selected from and designed to mirror the S&P 500. The index is value-weighted.
Wilshire Index	Measures the value of all NYSE and AMEX stocks plus the most actively traded over-the-counter stocks. The index is a weighted average; the weights reflect the total market value of all outstanding shares.
NASDAQ 100 Index	Measures the value of the 100 largest nonfinancial firms traded over the counter.
S&P MidCap 400 Index	Measures value of 400 stocks—none of which is included in the S&P 500—with firm market values between $300 million and $5 billion. The index includes firms in four main industrial groups. The index is a weighted average like the S&P 500 but is quoted as a percentage of its base value on December 31, 1990.
Nikkei 225 Index	Measures the value of 225 large publicly traded Japanese firms. Historically the index was price-weighted, but it was recently revised to reflect market value weights.
Dow Jones World Stock Index	Measures value of 2,200 stocks traded in 10 countries. The index is calculated in four major currencies: dollar, mark, pound, and yen. It is value-weighted and quoted as a percentage of its base value on December 31, 1991.

behave identically, although their movements are similar. For example, during the period 1987 through 1991, the MMI had a 0.99 correlation with the DJIA.[3]

IMPOSSIBILITY OF DELIVERY. In comparison with almost all other futures contracts, stock index futures have a distinguishing characteristic: It is not possible to make or take physical delivery of an index. If closure does not occur before the delivery month, the contract's settlement level is the same as the level of the index on a given date in either March, June, September, or December, the 4 months during the year when index futures contracts expire. As with other futures

contracts, a trader's account is marked to market daily and cash settlement is required.

VALUE OF A CONTRACT. The value of a stock index contract is calculated as the level of the index multiplied by an established amount, usually $500. The dollar multiplier for each index is given in daily price quotations in major newspapers. For example, Figure 11.1, showing November 4, 1992, data for index futures from *The Wall Street Journal* of the next day, indicates that the settlement price on an S&P 500 Index contract scheduled to expire in June 1993 was

$$417.15 \times \$500 = \$208,575$$

The reported market indexes themselves are also shown in Figure 11.1. Because November 4, 1992, was

[3] Chicago Board of Trade, *MMI Futures and Options,* 1991. (References are listed in full at the end of this chapter.)

FIGURE 11.1 Stock Index Futures and Stock Market Indexes

Data on index futures contracts and on the indexes underlying popular futures contracts are found daily in the financial pages of major newspapers.

FUTURES PRICES

Wednesday, November 4, 1992

Open Interest Reflects Previous Trading Day.

INDEX

	Open	High	Low	Settle	Chg	High	Low	Open Interest

S&P 500 INDEX (CME) 500 times index

Dec	418.50	420.90	416.10	416.20	– 3.65	427.25	390.00	160,843
Mr93	418.95	421.25	416.40	416.65	– 3.65	426.20	390.50	8,223
June	418.40	421.70	417.30	417.15	– 3.65	417.10	391.00	1,466
Sept	422.00	422.00	417.40	417.80	– 3.65	424.50	391.00	161

Est vol 51,879; vol Tues 43,856; open int 170,693, –1,204.
Indx prelim High 421.07; Low 416.63; Close 417.11 –2.81

NIKKEI 225 Stock Average (CME)—$5 times index

Dec	17090.	17130.	17050.	17055.	+ 135.0	21100.	14270.	14,067

Est vol 1,024; vol Tues 493; open int 14,152, +87.
The index: High 17065.20; open int 14,152, +87.
Close 17065.20 +211.84

NYSE COMPOSITE INDEX (NYFE) 500 times index

Dec	230.40	231.85	229.15	229.30	– 1.90	234.05	214.70	5,132
Mr93	230.65	231.55	229.40	229.40	– 1.90	233.70	221.60	784
June	230.85	230.85	229.50	229.50	– 1.90	232.40	223.10	266

Est vol 4,696; vol Tues 4,156; open int 6,185, –390.
The index: High 231.75; Low 229.58; Close 229.79 –1.45

MAJOR MKT INDEX (CBT) $500 times index

Nov	343.50	345.10	339.20	339.40	– 4.45	356.00	326.20	3,075
Dec	343.00	345.00	339.30	339.30	– 4.45	358.90	326.15	455
Mr93				339.20	– 4.45	359.50	340.75	137

Est vol 700; vol Tues 923; open int 3,695, +519.
The index: High 345.76; Low 340.19; Close 340.51 –3.06

OTHER FUTURES

Settlement prices of selected contracts. Actual volume (from previous session) and open interest of all contract months.

	Net			Lifetime	Open
	Vol.	High	Low	Close	Change	High Low	Interest

KC MINI VALUE LINE (KC)—100 times index

	118	358.70	356.20	356.85	– 1.15	361.50	336.20	383

KC VALUE LINE INDEX (KC)—500 times index

Dec	182	358.60	356.20	356.80	– 1.05	366.00	336.20	1,179

The index: High 358.93; Low 357.40; Close 357.77 –.75

S&P MIDCAP 400 (CME)—$500 x S&P 400 Stock Index

Dec	193	148.45	147.35	147.70	– .40	154.20	136.60	4,342

The index: High 148.20; Low 147.59; Close 147.82 –.20

STOCK MARKET DATA BANK   11/4/92

MAJOR INDEXES

HIGH	LOW (†365 DAY)		CLOSE	NET CHG	% CHG	†365 DAY CHG	% CHG	FROM 12/31	% CHG
DOW JONES AVERAGES									
3413.21	2863.82	30 Industrials	x3223.04	– 29.44	– 0.91	+ 184.58	+ 6.07	+ 54.21	+ 1.71
1467.68	1160.50	20 Transportation	x1360.37	+ 3.02	+ 0.22	+ 88.70	+ 6.98	+ 2.37	+ 0.17
226.15	200.74	15 Utilities	x217.89	– 1.06	– 0.48	+ 1.44	+ 0.67	– 8.26	– 3.65
1205.95	1040.27	65 Composite	x1163.60	– 5.82	– 0.50	+ 62.20	+ 5.65	+ 6.78	+ 0.59
400.79	352.36	Equity Mkt. Index	394.69	– 2.36	– 0.59	+ 28.88	+ 7.89	+ 2.79	+ 0.71
NEW YORK STOCK EXCHANGE									
233.73	207.57	Composite	229.79	– 1.45	– 0.63	+ 14.49	+ 6.73	+ 0.35	+ 0.15
291.32	257.77	Industrials	283.20	– 2.21	– 0.77	+ 15.63	+ 5.84	+ 2.62	+ 0.92
104.21	91.57	Utilities	101.60	– 0.18	– 0.18	+ 4.42	+ 4.55	+ 0.53	+ 0.52
212.83	175.86	Transportation	201.90	– 0.90	– 0.44	+ 7.24	+ 3.72	+ 0.03	+ 0.01
185.64	154.11	Finance	184.84	– 0.60	– 0.32	+ 23.58	+ 14.62	+ 12.16	+ 7.04
STANDARD & POOR'S INDEXES									
425.27	375.22	500 Index	417.11	– 2.81	– 0.67	+ 27.14	+ 6.96	+ 0.02	– 0.00
503.30	442.42	Industrials	488.81	– 3.87	– 0.79	+ 29.10	+ 6.33	+ 3.91	+ 0.79
366.54	294.90	Transportation	346.20	– 1.70	– 0.49	+ 19.89	+ 6.10	+ 4.74	+ 1.39
159.03	135.59	Utilities	153.38	– 0.22	– 0.14	+ 5.68	+ 3.85	– 1.78	– 1.15
37.13	29.77	Financials	36.91	– 0.14	– 0.38	+ 5.35	+ 16.95	+ 2.81	+ 8.24
154.74	130.95	400 MidCap	147.82	– 0.21	– 0.14	+ 12.56	+ 9.29	+ 1.23	+ 0.84
NASDAQ									
644.92	522.23	Composite	605.52	+ 0.94	+ 0.16	+ 66.04	+ 12.24	+ 19.18	+ 3.27
741.92	581.60	Industrials	650.30	– 0.24	– 0.04	+ 42.87	+ 7.06	+ 18.65	+ 2.79
731.05	546.90	Insurance	728.50	+ 3.76	+ 0.52	+ 178.01	+ 32.34	+ 127.41	+ 21.20
478.06	318.54	Banks	475.94	– 0.01	– 0.00	+ 145.28	+ 43.94	+ 125.38	+ 35.77
285.08	230.20	Nat. Mkt. Comp.	268.59	+ 0.41	+ 0.15	+ 30.58	+ 12.85	+ 8.85	+ 3.41
296.32	232.48	Nat. Mkt. Indus.	261.09	– 0.11	– 0.04	+ 19.31	+ 7.99	+ 6.70	+ 2.50
OTHERS									
418.99	364.85	Amex	381.94	– 0.89	– 0.23	– 4.71	– 1.22	– 13.11	– 3.32
266.85	228.21	Value-Line (geom.)	249.93	– 0.60	– 0.24	+ 8.37	+ 3.46	+ 0.59	+ 0.24
212.61	174.71	Russell 2000	199.55	– 0.08	– 0.04	+ 15.19	+ 8.24	+ 9.62	+ 5.07
4121.28	3645.57	Wilshire 5000	4057.92	– 21.04	– 0.52	+ 274.15	+ 7.25	+ 16.82	+ 0.42

†–Based on comparable trading day in preceding year.

Source: *The Wall Street Journal*, November 5, 1992, C2, C14.

not a contract expiration date, the closing settlement level on the S&P contract (417.15) was not the same as the closing level of the S&P 500 Index (417.11).

LIMITS ON PRICE MOVEMENTS. Until after the stock market crash of 1987, stock index futures contracts had no limits on daily price movements. Since the crash, however, most index futures contracts have been subject to daily trading limits. Each exchange has handled the limits somewhat differently. The limits on S&P 500 futures contracts, for example, are pegged to price movements on the underlying stocks. In contrast, daily limits for the MMI are based in part on movements away from the previous day's contract settlement price and in part on movements in the DJIA. Limits on other stock index futures contracts are different still.

Besides overall price movement limits, most contracts also require minimum price movements from trade to trade. In general, the limit is 0.05 times the dollar multiplier on the contract. For example, the minimum movement on the MMI contract is $25, because, as shown in Figure 11.1, the dollar multiplier is $500 (0.05 × $500 = $25).[4]

GREATER PRICE VOLATILITY. Observers of stock index futures have identified another distinguishing characteristic. The price volatility of each index futures contract, measured by the standard deviation of daily percentage price changes, is greater than the volatility of the underlying index. Such a relationship suggests that basis risk exposure can be significant for institutions using index futures to hedge their equity portfolios.[5] These early findings, however, have not dampened investor interest in these markets.

FINANCIAL INSTITUTIONS AND STOCK INDEX FUTURES

Because of regulatory restrictions and unfamiliarity with index futures, institutions at first engaged in only limited trading. As risk management strategies used by financial institutions have become increasingly sophis-

ticated, their involvement in the index futures markets has accelerated.

HEDGING AGAINST A DECLINE IN THE MARKET

A direct use of stock index futures is as a hedge for an equity portfolio, designed to protect against swings in the market that could reduce returns. The most obvious need for a hedge occurs when a market downturn is anticipated. The manager of a large equity position naturally wants to avoid a substantial decline in portfolio value if a **bear market** is forecast—one in which prices in general are expected to fall.

One way to avoid losses is to sell large portions of the portfolio before the decline, but transactions costs could be considerable. Another drawback is the time required to choose the stocks to be sold. As an alternative, the manager could hedge against market price declines with a short hedge by selling stock index futures. If the market indexes do indeed fall, so will the value of the contracts, resulting in a profit when the position is closed out and offsetting losses in the stock portfolio.

Again, as with interest rate futures, an increase in expected market yields (decline in prices) suggests a short hedge. The small margin requirements on index futures contracts allow an institution to assume a significant position with a small amount of cash.

IMPORTANCE OF THE NUMBER OF CONTRACTS

A main determinant of the effectiveness of the hedge, as in any other futures position, is the number of futures contracts used. Besides the size of the portfolio, the number of contracts is affected by the volatility of returns on the portfolio relative to the market indexes on which futures contracts are available. Beta is a relative measure of volatility. Because the portfolio of stocks underlying a market index is assumed to have a beta of 1, if the portfolio to be hedged has a beta greater or less than 1, changes in the value of the hedged portfolio will be more or less than changes in the index underlying the futures contract. Thus, the number of contracts must be adjusted to structure an effective hedge.

---

[4] Chicago Board of Trade, *MMI Futures and Options.*

[5] See Hill, Jain, and Ward 1987, 10–11.

TABLE 11.2   The Short Hedge: Portfolio Beta of 1.0 (Forecast: Bear Market)

A short hedge with index futures is used when falling securities prices are forecast. The profit on the short futures position can be used to offset losses in a portfolio of stocks.

Cash Market	Futures Market
May ~Stock's portfolio~	~The number of contracts~
NYSE Index: 190.15	NYSE Index settlement level: 192.75
Stock portfolio value:	Sell 4,669 contracts:
$450,000,000	192.75 × $500 × 4,669 = $449,974,875
June	
Market decline = 2.5% ~(190.15)(97.5%)~	NYSE Index settlement level:
NYSE Index: 185.40	192.75 (1 − 0.025) = 187.93
Stock portfolio value:	Close out position by buying 4,669 contracts:
$450,000,000 (1 − 0.025) = $438,750,000	187.93 × $500 × 4,669 = $438,722,585

~Price loss~

Cash Market Loss		Futures Market Gain	
June value	$438,750,000	May sale	$449,974,875
May value	(450,000,000)	June purchase	(438,722,585)
Loss	($ 11,250,000)	Gain	$ 11,252,290

Net Gain $2,290

THE NUMBER OF CONTRACTS WHEN PORTFOLIO BETA IS 1. Suppose that a pension fund manager holds a stock portfolio of $450 million in May; the NYSE index is at 190.15. The equity market has been on the upswing, but the surge is expected to end soon. Rather than liquidating portions of the portfolio, the manager chooses to sell NYSE stock index futures. The previous day's index settlement level on June futures was 192.75. Assuming that the portfolio beta is 1, the number of contracts to sell is

$$[11.1]$$

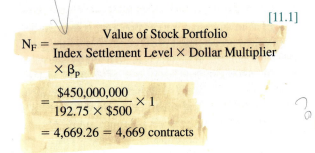

$$N_F = \frac{\text{Value of Stock Portfolio}}{\text{Index Settlement Level} \times \text{Dollar Multiplier}} \times \beta_p$$

$$= \frac{\$450,000,000}{192.75 \times \$500} \times 1$$

$$= 4,669.26 = 4,669 \text{ contracts}$$

Equation 11.1 divides the value of the portfolio the manager is attempting to hedge by the value of one index futures contract at the current settlement level. It then adjusts for the relative riskiness of the cash port-folio as compared to the risk of the market index. In this case, the cash portfolio has a beta of 1, as does the NYSE index.

Now suppose that by June, the market index falls, as anticipated, to 185.40, a decline of 2.5 percent. Results of the hedge are summarized in Table 11.2. The value of the futures contracts, with a settlement level now also down by 2.5 percent to 187.93, falls to

$$187.93 \times \$500 \times 4,669 \text{ contracts}$$
$$= \$438,722,585$$

When the position is closed out, the profits before transactions costs are $11,252,290. Because the original portfolio beta is 1, its value declines by 2.5 percent to $438,750,000, a loss of $11,250,000. The hedge is not perfect because the manager cannot trade fractional contracts; the custom of rounding index values to two decimal places also affects results.

THE NUMBER OF CONTRACTS WHEN BETA IS NOT 1. What are the consequences of the hedge if the price volatility of the portfolio exceeds that of the market index? Suppose that the portfolio beta is 1.3. When the

TABLE 11.3   The Short Hedge: Portfolio Beta of 1.3 (Forecast: Bear Market)

Short hedges with index futures must take into account the market risk (as measured by beta) of the hedged portfolio. Portfolios with high betas must be hedged with a larger number of index futures contracts than portfolios with lower betas.

Cash Market	Futures Market
May	
NYSE Index: 190.15	NYSE Index settlement level: 192.75
Stock portfolio value:	Sell 6,070 contracts:
$450,000,000	192.75 × $500 × 6,070 = $584,996,250
June	
Market decline = 2.5%	NYSE Index settlement level:
Stock portfolio value change:	192.75 (1 − 0.025) = 187.93
−2.5% × 1.3 = −3.25%	
Stock portfolio value:	Close out position by buying 6,070 contracts:
$450,000,000 (1 − 0.0325) = $435,375,000	187.93 × $500 × 6,070 = $570,367,550

Cash Market Loss		Futures Market Gain	
June value	$435,375,000	May sale	$584,996,250
May value	(450,000,000)	June purchase	(570,367,550)
Loss	($ 14,625,000)	Gain	$ 14,628,700

Net Gain $3,700

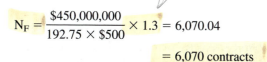

market index declines by 2.5 percent, the portfolio value declines by 1.3 × 2.5% = 3.25%, a dollar decline of $450,000,000 × 0.0325 = $14,625,000. A hedge with only 4,669 NYSE Index contracts would be insufficient protection, because the gain on a hedge using that number of contracts is only $11,252,290. The net result of the hedge would be a loss of more than $3 million.

A better hedge position would adjust for the beta coefficient:

$$N_F = \frac{\$450,000,000}{192.75 \times \$500} \times 1.3 = 6,070.04$$

$$= 6,070 \text{ contracts}$$

As shown in Table 11.3, with a short hedge of 6,070 contracts, the decline in the NYSE settlement price to 187.93 produces a gain of $14,628,700 and a net gain on the hedge of $3,700. Both short hedge examples assume that price movements in the hedged portfolio and the futures contract are perfectly correlated; in practice, the correlation would not be perfect, introducing basis risk exposure.

HEDGING WHEN AN UPTURN IS ANTICIPATED

A stock index futures hedge in anticipation of a stronger equity market would be more unusual but still possible. For example, a long hedge may be undertaken when a trust department has good reason to expect a large inflow of funds at some future point, funds that can be invested only after an expected upswing. The invested funds will miss the benefits of the **bull market,** one in which price increases are anticipated. If the manager buys stock index futures contracts, they will increase in value during the bull market. When the position is later closed out by selling the contracts, the increase in value produces a profit that compensates for the higher prices at which new stock must be purchased. Once again, the effectiveness of the hedge is based on the price volatility of the stock purchased relative to the price volatility of the futures contract.

PROGRAM TRADING: INDEX ARBITRAGE

The term **program trading** encompasses several modern investment strategies. The narrowest definition is the simultaneous placement of buy and sell

| **TABLE 11.4** | **Index Arbitrage** |

Index arbitrage is the simultaneous trading of index futures and stocks composing the underlying index. Computer programs are used to determine when stocks and futures should be bought or sold to profit from temporary price discrepancies in the two markets.

Cash Market	**Futures Market**
February 26	
MMI:	MMI settlement level: 313.55
311.74	Sell 18 contracts:
Buy 2,000 shares of each MMI stock:	$313.55 \times \$500 \times 18 = \$2,821,950$
Value = $2,749,000	
(Sell) *If Prices Increase by March 21*	(Buy)
MMI increase = 5.238%	MMI settlement level:
MMI:	328.07, an increase of 4.631%
$328.07 = (311.74)(1.05238)$	Close out position by buying 18 contracts:
Stock portfolio value:	$328.07 \times \$500 \times 18 = \$2,952,630$
$2,893,000	

Cash Market Gain			**Futures Market Loss**	
3/21 value		$2,893,000	2/26 sale	$2,821,950
2/26 value		(2,749,000)	3/21 purchase	(2,952,630)
Gain		$ 144,000	Loss	($ 130,680)

Net Gain $13,320

Cash Market	**Futures Market**
(Sell) *If Prices Decrease by March 21*	(Buy)
MMI decrease = 5.238%	MMI settlement level: 295.41, a decrease of 5.785%
MMI: $295.41 = (311.74)(1-0.05238)$	Close out position by buying 18 contracts:
Stock portfolio value:	$295.41 \times \$500 \times 18 = \$2,658,690$
$2,605,000	

Cash Market Loss			**Futures Market Gain**	
3/21 value		$2,605,000	2/26 sale	$2,821,950
2/26 value		(2,749,000)	3/21 purchase	(2,658,690)
Loss		($ 144,000)	Gain	$ 163,260

Net Gain $19,260

orders for groups of stocks totaling $1 million or more. A common and controversial form of program trading is the simultaneous trading of stock and stock index futures to profit from changes in the spread between the two, sometimes called **index arbitrage.**[6]

Table 11.4 illustrates a simple example of index arbitrage using the MMI. Suppose that on February 26, a manager buys 2,000 shares of each stock in the MMI, simultaneously selling 18 MMI futures contracts. The MMI is at 311.74, and the futures settlement level is 313.55 on that date. The contracts expire on March 21, and the manager knows, as is true of all index futures, that the contract settlement level and the MMI itself will converge by the expiration date, even though they differ on February 26.

On March 21, the stock portfolio will be liquidated and the short futures position closed out. Regardless of the actual level of stock prices on that day,

[6] These and other definitions can be found in "The Realities of Program Trading," *Market Perspectives* (Chicago Mercantile Exchange) (January/February 1990). The example in Table 11.4 is similar to one in Jeffrey Laderman, "Those Big Swings on Wall Street," *Business Week,* April 7, 1986, 32–36.

the manager profits. If prices rise, the value of the stock will increase more than the loss on the futures contract, resulting in a net profit. If prices fall, the value of the stock will fall less than the value of the futures contracts. This is true because both the index and the contract settlement value must be the same on March 21, but the contract settlement value is higher on February 26. The gain on the futures contracts will exceed losses on the stock portfolio, again resulting in a net profit.

Index arbitrage and other forms of program trading differ from hedging because hedgers use futures to offset adverse changes in a portfolio held in the normal course of operations. Index arbitragers, however, choose and manage portfolios based solely on the characteristics of available futures contracts, with the intention of profiting from fluctuations in the basis.

PROGRAM TRADING AND THE CRASH OF 1987. Because program trading involves buying and selling large quantities of stocks, it has been blamed for wide fluctuations in stock prices in recent years. In the early days of index arbitrage, price swings were particularly noticeable on the four trading days each year in which stock index futures contracts expired, as large numbers of traders closed out positions in stocks, index futures, or both. A widely quoted study in 1986 concluded, however, that small investors could potentially benefit from institutions' use of program trading because they would know in advance when price volatility would be high and could avoid the market on those days.[7]

When the DJIA fell by 508 points to 1,738.74 (a 22.6 percent drop) on October 19, 1987, the debate over program trading's effect on stock price volatility escalated to new heights. The **Brady Commission,** a blue-ribbon panel appointed by President Reagan to investigate causes of the crash, concluded in 1988 that computerized trading by large institutions played a major role in the downward spiral of the market. The commission recommended that the stock and futures markets be brought under a single regulator (the Federal Reserve System [the Fed]) and that the two markets institute coordinated "circuit-breaker" programs to halt trading in both markets when price movements exceeded specified limits. Other observers suggested that the Securities and Exchange Commission (SEC) be given oversight authority for both stock and stock index futures markets. Some critics even called for a complete regulatory ban on computerized trading.

Other experts have come to very different conclusions. They believe that computerized trading of stocks and stock index futures improves the liquidity of the markets and contend that the 1987 crash was actually caused by the NYSE's antiquated system of trading. As stock prices fell during the day on October 19, traders who wished to purchase stock at "cheap" prices were unable to do so because their orders could not be executed. Had the NYSE's computers been more up-to-date, these observers argue, the market decline would have slowed considerably.[8]

Since 1987, the debate over program trading has continued. In fact, it escalated in 1990 when Japanese investors and officials blamed U.S. securities firms for contributing to the steep decline in the Tokyo stock market by using index arbitrage. Some large securities firms, although not condemning the practice, succumbed to pressure from politicians and regulators and curtailed—or even abandoned—index arbitrage for their own accounts. (Many will still engage in it on behalf of clients.) Still, by 1993, no formal ban on program trading was contemplated. Most experts recognize that financial and technological innovation, and the regulatory avoidance they spawn, virtually ensure that no amount of regulation will eliminate institutions' efforts to profit from market opportunities. Instead, it is likely that regulators' efforts will focus on potential abuse of innovation rather than its elimination. In fact, as technology and innovation have increased market efficiency, potential profits from program trading have declined, and the volume of activity has declined as well.

OTHER INDEX FUTURES

An institution's ability to hedge against portfolio declines through index futures is not limited to stock index futures. For example, the CBOT introduced the Bond Buyer Municipal Bond Index futures contracts

---

[7] See Stoll and Whaley 1986. Other studies have questioned the conclusion that program trading increases price volatility. See James T. Moser, "Trading Activity, Program Trading, and the Volatility of Stock Returns." Unpublished Working Paper, Research Department, Federal Reserve Bank of Chicago, September 1992.

[8] Excerpts from the Brady Commission Report, as well as analyses by the commission's critics, can be found in Barro et al. 1989.

in 1985. This contract was motivated by the relatively poor historical results for cross hedges of municipal bond portfolios using T-bond futures. Using a recently created index of 40 municipal bonds, daily settlement prices are calculated as $1,000 times the index level. Institutions with diversified holdings of municipals, such as commercial banks, mutual funds, securities firms, and property/liability insurers, view the contracts as holding much promise for protecting against broad-based declines in the bond markets.

Other index futures contracts have been developed to protect investors against exchange rate risk in general, for those not wishing to hedge against a particular currency (U.S. Dollar Index and European Currency Unit Index), as well as against changes in the value of precious metals (Commodity Research Bureau Index). Stock index futures for stocks traded on the London, Sydney, Tokyo, Singapore, and Hong Kong exchanges have also been developed; most are traded only on foreign stock exchanges, but several have been approved on U.S. exchanges. The popularity of these new index contracts has yet to be determined.

OPTIONS ON FINANCIAL ASSETS

Another financial innovation is enjoying greater acceptance as a hedging instrument for financial institutions—options on stock indexes and stock index futures, T-bonds and T-bond futures, and foreign currencies, among others. Although options are similar to futures contracts, important differences separate the two types of hedging mechanisms. Like futures, options can be used for speculation, but this discussion emphasizes hedging.

Options on individual stocks have existed for some time. When they were concentrated in the over-the-counter (OTC) markets, trading was relatively infrequent. The move in 1973 to offer standardized instruments on the organized exchanges has improved liquidity, and newer types of options have attracted a wider group of market participants.

OPTIONS DEFINED

An option is an agreement giving its holder the right to buy or sell a specified asset, over a limited time period, at a specified price. The option itself is created by an **option writer,** someone who stands ready to buy or sell the asset when the holder wishes to make a transaction. The price written into the option agreement is the **exercise (or strike) price.** Because options are traded on organized exchanges, they may also be sold to other investors before they expire.

Although options are similar to futures agreements, there are differences. As the name suggests, an option does not obligate the holder to undertake the purchase or sale. Depending on movements in the value of the underlying asset, the holder may choose not to exercise the option to buy or sell. If so, the option expires at maturity and becomes worthless. Another difference is that most options (those called **American options**) can be exercised at any point during their lives; with futures contracts, in contrast, an exchange of securities takes place only on the specified delivery date. (A few options, including options on the S&P 500 Index, are **European options,** which can be exercised only at expiration.)

CALL OPTIONS. There are two types of options. A **call option** is an agreement in which the option writer sells the holder the right to buy a specified asset on or before a future date. The buyer of a call option expects the price of the asset to increase over the life of the option, eventually exceeding the exercise price. If the asset price rises, the value of the option also rises, and the option holder has the additional opportunity to sell it at a profit before it expires.

PUT OPTIONS. A **put option** is the opposite of a call. Puts give the holder the right to sell an asset at the strike price, and the option writer is obligated to buy it if the holder desires to sell. The buyer of a put option expects the asset's price to fall below the strike price. If the price falls, the put option becomes increasingly valuable.

PREMIUMS. If market prices do not move as the option buyer forecasts, the option is allowed to expire. There is no obligation to exercise it if market conditions make it unprofitable to do so. The cost, however, is the original price (the **premium**) of the option. If the option is not exercised, that cost cannot be recovered; the writer or seller of the option realizes a gain.

OPTION VALUES ILLUSTRATED

Over the life of an option, its value is influenced by the difference between the market and exercise prices of the underlying asset. Other influences are the time to expiration of the option and the volatility in the price of the underlying asset.

Figure 11.2 shows the value of several index options at the close of trading on November 4, 1992, including options on the S&P 100 Index. As with futures contracts on indexes, it is not possible for investors to take physical delivery of the index when an option is exercised; therefore, index options are settled with cash. The holder of a call option on a stock index is really purchasing the right to "buy" cash, based on the difference between the strike price (in this case a designated value for the S&P 100 Index) and the actual value of the index at the end of trading on the expiration date. The amount the holder receives in cash is determined by the difference between the actual index value and the strike price, times the dollar multiplier assigned to that index. For options on indexes, by far the most common dollar multiplier is $100.

In Figure 11.2, call options on the S&P 100 Index are shown with strike prices ranging from 345 to 420. On November 4, 1992, the call option with a strike price of 380 and an expiration date of January 1993 traded at $10\frac{1}{4}$, or 10.25 × $100 = $1,025. As shown immediately below the S&P 100 option quotations, the index itself closed at 380.48 on November 4, 1992. If the index were still at that level at expiration (an unlikely event), the holder of the option would receive (380.48 − 380) × $100 = $48. This call option, with a strike price below the market index value, is said to be **in the money;** when the strike price of a call option is greater than the index value, the call is **out of the money.**[9] In Figure 11.2, even call options that are out of the money have a positive value, indicating the possibility that by the expiration date the index value could rise above the strike price.

CALL OPTION VALUES, STRIKE PRICES, AND EXPIRATION DATES. Given an underlying asset or index

---

[9] Because put holders benefit when underlying asset or index values fall, put options are in the money when their strike prices exceed the market value of the underlying asset or index; puts are out of the money when the value of the asset or index exceeds the put strike price.

FIGURE 11.2	**Index Options Price Quotations**

Information on index options is found daily in the financial pages of major newspapers.

Wednesday, November 4, 1992

OPTIONS
CHICAGO BOARD

S&P 100 INDEX (OEX)-$100 times index

Strike Price	Calls–Last			Puts–Last		
	Nov	Dec	Jan	Nov	Dec	Jan
345	....	....	....	1/4	1 3/16	2 1/16
350	....	....	....	7/16	1 9/16	2 1/2
355	28 5/8	....	....	1/2	1 15/16	3 1/8
360	22 1/8	24 3/4	....	3/4	2 9/16	4 1/8
365	18	20	....	1 3/16	3 3/8	5 1/8
370	11 5/8	14 1/2	18	1 13/16	4 1/2	6 1/2
375	7 5/8	10 7/8	....	3	6	8
380	4 5/8	7 3/4	10 1/4	5	7 7/8	10 3/4
385	2 1/4	5 1/8	7 1/2	7 5/8	10 3/4	12
390	1	3 1/4	5 1/4	11 3/4	13 1/2	14
395	3/8	1 7/8	3 1/2	14 1/2	17 1/2	17 1/4
400	3/16	1	2 1/2	....	....	22 1/2
405	1/16	1/2	1 1/2	....	24 1/8	....
410	1/16	5/16	1 1/16	....	....	29 1/4
415	1/16	3/16	9/16	....	....	....
420	....	1/8	3/4	....	....	....

Total call volume 134,078   Total call open int. 417,650
Total put volume 118,463   Total put open int. 484,467
The Index: High 384.73; Low 380.07; Close 380.48, −2.93

S&P 500 INDEX (NSX)-$100 times index

Strike Price	Calls–Last			Puts–Last		
	Nov	Dec	Jan	Nov	Dec	Jan
365	....	....	....	5/8	....	....
375	....	....	....	1	4 3/8	....
380	....	....	....	1 5/16	....	....
385	....	....	....	1 5/8	....	....
390	....	....	....	2	....	....
395	....	....	....	2 5/8	....	....
400	....	....	....	3 5/8	8 3/4	13 1/2
405	....	....	....	4 1/4	....	....
410	12 1/8	....	....	5 3/4	....	....
415	9	....	....	7 1/2	....	....

Total call volume 5,445   Total call open int. 248,900
Total put volume 29,457   Total put open int. 469,190
The Index: High 421.07; Low 416.61; Close 417.11, −2.81

AMERICAN

S&P MIDCAP INDEX

Strike Price	Calls–Last			Puts–Last		
	Nov	Dec	Jan	Nov	Dec	Jan
140	....	....	....	....	....	1 3/4
142 1/2	....	....	....	1/2	....	....
145	4 1/8	....	6 1/8	15/16	....	....
147 1/2	1 15/16	....	....	1 13/16	....	....
150	1 1/8	....	....	3 1/4	....	....

Total call volume 726   Total call open int. 22,124
Total put volume 678   Total put open int. 36,627
The Index: High 148.20; Low 147.59; Close 147.82, −0.20

MAJOR MARKET INDEX

Strike Price	Calls–Last			Puts–Last		
	Nov	Dec	Jan	Nov	Dec	Jan
150	....	191 1/4	....	....	1/8	....
300	....	....	....	....	9/16	1 1/4
310	....	....	....	3/16	1	....
315	....	....	....	3/8	....	....
320	....	....	7/16	....	....	....
325	18 1/4	....	....	11/16	2 3/4	....
330	11 3/4	....	....	1 7/16	....	....
335	6 7/8	....	....	2 5/8	5 1/2	....
340	3 7/8	6 5/8	....	4 3/8	6	....
345	1 3/4	5	6 1/4	7 1/4	....	....
350	3/4	2 1/2	....	8 7/8	....	....

Total call volume 5,090   Total call open int. 63,617
Total put volume 3,256   Total put open int. 81,426
The Index: High 345.76; Low 340.19; Close 340.51, −3.66

Source: The Wall Street Journal, November 5, 1992, C18.

and holding the expiration date constant, call options with higher strike prices have lower values. For example, for strike prices ranging from 360 to 420, call options expiring in December 1992 ranged in value from 24¾ to ⅛. The higher the strike price, the less likely the index value will rise above the strike price, so the less valuable the option.

Holding strike price constant, call options with more distant expiration dates are more valuable. For the single strike price of 370, the call option value ranged from 11⅝ to 18 as the expiration date moved from November 1992 to January 1993. The longer time to maturity increases the chances that the actual index value will eventually exceed the strike price.[10]

A final factor influencing option prices in general is unobservable in the data for S&P 100 options in Figure 11.2. All else equal, the greater the price volatility of an underlying asset, the greater the value of an option on that asset. For a call option, for example, the greater the asset price volatility, the greater the probability that the price will eventually exceed the strike price; and the higher the asset's price, the higher the value of the option. Yet the minimum value to which an option can fall, no matter how volatile the price of the underlying asset, is zero. If an option's value falls to zero, the holder will simply not exercise it, losing the premium but nothing else. The fact that losses to option holders are limited but gains are not is illustrated in more detail later in the chapter.

PUT OPTION VALUES, STRIKE PRICES, AND EXPIRATION DATES. In contrast to call options, holding the expiration date constant, the higher the strike price, the higher the value of a put option. Puts on physical assets give the holder the right to sell an asset at the option strike price if its market value falls below the strike price. Because one cannot sell an index, the holder of a put option on an index buys the right to receive cash if the index value falls *below* the strike price by the expiration date.

In Figure 11.2, the value of a put on the S&P 100 Index with a December 1992 expiration date ranged from 1³⁄₁₆ to 24⅛ at strike prices ranging from 345 to 405. The higher the exercise price, the more likely it

will be above the actual index value at the expiration date. As with call options, however, holding strike price constant, put values are higher for more distant expiration dates. Again, the chance that the option will eventually be profitable for the holder is greater the longer the time to maturity. The value of put options is also positively related to volatility in the price of the underlying asset.

OPTIONS AND FINANCIAL INSTITUTIONS

Options on assets other than common stock originated in 1982. Table 11.5 lists the nonstock options traded as of 1993. Options are written both on various financial assets (such as bonds or stock) and on a variety of futures contracts. The list of options on financial instruments is in a state of flux. Based on trading volume, stock index options continued to attract the largest group of traders as of 1993, but this, too, may well change as the markets mature.

REGULATION OF OPTIONS TRADING

As suggested by the earlier discussion of options, writers and holders both can use them for speculative purposes. Either party can profit by correctly forecasting price movements on the underlying asset. Some financial institutions, however, may use options only to hedge against adverse movements in the prices of existing assets. As with futures, federal bank regulators disapprove of options trading that increases risk exposure. For example, buying stock options without owning stock would increase risk and thus be disallowed. Also, regulators may question banks that write, rather than buy, options.

Thrifts are permitted broader authority both to write and to purchase options, as long as they report their positions to regulators and as long as the positions are related to financial instruments in which an institution can legally invest. Federal credit union (CU) regulations permit purchase of put options written on several categories of secondary mortgage market securities. Thus CUs making mortgage loans are able to hedge against increases in market rates.[11]

---

[10] The increase in value with more distant expiration dates holds for most options, with exceptions. For more details, see Chance 1992, Chapter 3.

[11] See Koppenhaver 1986 and Christopher 1989.

TABLE 11.5   **Option Instruments and Markets**

Options are available on financial assets *and* on futures contracts. New options come and go according to the needs of the marketplace. The table lists a representative group of options traded in 1993.

Options on Financial Assets	Options on Financial Futures Contracts
Interest Rate Options	*Options on Interest Rate Futures*
Chicago Board Options Exchange	CBOT
Short-term Interest Rates	T-bonds
Long-term Interest Rates	Municipal Bond Index
Stock Index Options	2-year T-notes
American Stock Exchange	5-year T-notes
LEAPS MMI	CME
Computer Technology Index	Eurodollar
Eurotop 100 Index	LIBOR
Institutional Index	T-bills
S&P MidCap Index	London International Financial Futures Exchange
Japan Index	Eurodollar
Chicago Board Options Exchange	Long Gilt
Russell 2000	
S&P 100 Index	*Options on Stock Index Futures*
S&P 500 Index	CBOT
LEAPS—S&P 500 Index	MMI
LEAPS—S&P 100 Index	CME
CAPS—S&P 500 Index	S&P 500 Index
CAPS—S&P 100 Index	Nikkei 225 Stock Average
NYSE	S&P MidCap 400
NYSE Index	New York Futures Exchange
Philadelphia Exchange	NYSE Composite Index
Gold/Silver Index	
Value Line Index	*Options on Foreign Currency Futures*
O-T-C Index	CME
Pacific Exchange	Australian dollars
Financial News Index	British pounds
Wilshire Index	Deutschemarks
	Swiss francs
Foreign Currency Options	Japanese yen
Philadelphia Exchange	Canadian dollars
Australian dollars	Mark/Yen Cross Rate
British pounds	FINEX
British pound/German mark cross rate	U.S. Dollar Index
Canadian dollars	
French francs	
German marks	
German mark/Japanese yen cross rate	
Japanese yen	
Swiss francs	
European Currency Units	

Source: The Wall Street Journal, various issues.

HEDGING WITH OPTIONS

The choice of options depends on the portfolio to be hedged. The manager of an equity mutual fund might hedge with options on stock indexes or stock index futures. For managers protecting the value of interest-bearing assets, options on debt instruments or interest rate futures are a logical choice.

WHEN OPTIONS MAKE A GOOD HEDGE. Options are a particularly good hedging choice when a financial institution faces potential declines in profitability at the discretion of its customers. In other words, an institution may enter the organized options markets to hedge against the effects of the options it has made available to its customers. For example, a commercial bank may make a commitment to lend in the future at a fixed rate negotiated today. Falling rates can cause the borrower to ignore the commitment; but if interest rates rise, the borrower is almost certain to complete the transaction, and the bank's net interest margin (NIM) will decline when its deposit costs increase. Or, if mortgage rates are expected to decline, existing customers may choose to prepay their mortgages, borrowing at new lower rates and lowering a thrift's interest revenues.

A bank can hedge its commitment to lend in the future by buying a put option on a T-bond. If rates go up, bond values will fall, and the bank can exercise its right to sell bonds at the strike price. The profit on the hedge can be used to offset liability costs that will increase as market rates increase. However, if rates decline, the value of T-bonds will rise, and the bank will not exercise the put. The option premium is the price the lender pays for protecting the spread against rising rates.

A thrift can protect itself against potential mortgage prepayments in the face of falling rates by purchasing a call option on T-bonds. As rates fall and the value of bonds rises, the call option will also rise in value. Profits from selling the option can be used to offset a decline in interest revenues as mortgages are prepaid. If rates rise instead, the option premium is the price paid for attempting to protect the spread.

A PUT OR A CALL? As suggested by the preceding examples, the decision to use options for hedging depends on the choices that customers have been offered by the institution. Once the decision to use options has been made, however, managers still must decide whether to use calls or puts. This choice depends on the anticipated direction of market changes. For example, consider the alternatives faced by an equity fund manager who expects a reversal in the market. With a bear market forecast, a stock index *put* option is indicated. If the market index does, in fact, decline, the option value will increase as the index falls below the strike price. A put option is also the proper choice for hedging an existing portfolio of interest-bearing assets if rates are expected to rise. If the forecast is accurate, the put's value will increase, offsetting the existing portfolio's decline in value.

OR A LEAP? Options on equity securities are a relatively short-term hedge; most expire within 90 days. Some institutional investors, however, have desired an alternative offering longer-term protection. In the early 1990s, a new instrument was introduced to meet that need. These options—called long-term equity anticipation securities, or LEAPS—are traded on approximately 100 stocks and several stock indexes. LEAPS have expiration dates several years into the future and have less price volatility than traditional options. The longer maturity also gives investors more time to determine the best course of action for managing an options hedge (i.e., selling or exercising the option). As of early 1993, LEAPS were still a novelty, and their market was not yet sufficiently developed to assess the role they would play in institutional hedging strategies.[12]

AN OPTION ON AN ASSET OR ON A FUTURES CONTRACT? The choice between an option on a financial asset itself or an option on a financial futures contract is influenced by several factors. One of the most important is that not all option markets are equally liquid. For example, although options on T-bonds are available, the market is small compared with the market for options on T-bond futures contracts. Thus, many managers using options to hedge bond portfolios will prefer options on T-bond futures.

---

[12]Stanley W. Angrist, "Taking Leaps with Treasuries to Buffer Sell-Off," *The Wall Street Journal,* June 5, 1992, C1, C14; Joan Warner, "A Different Kind of Hedge," *Business Week,* September 7, 1992, 94–95.

TABLE 11.6	Market Forecasts and Options Hedges

Managers hedging with options choose calls (giving them the right to buy assets or futures contracts) or puts (giving them the right to sell assets or futures contracts), depending on their forecasts for the financial markets. Falling stock prices or rising interest rates suggest the use of puts. Rising stock prices or falling interest rates suggest the use of calls.

	Hedge			
	Option on Index or Index Futures		Option on T-Bonds or Interest Rate Futures	
Forecast	Call	Put	Call	Put
Increase				
Stock prices	X			
Interest rates				X
Decrease				
Stock prices		X		
Interest rates			X	

If option markets for an underlying asset and a futures contract on the same asset are equally liquid, the option choice is influenced by whether the manager intends to exercise the option. To exercise an option on T-bonds, for example, funds must be available to purchase securities at the strike price. To exercise an option on a futures contract, however, only a relatively small margin requirement is needed to buy the contract.[13] In general, the appropriate hedge strategies, under various market forecasts, are summarized in Table 11.6.

HEDGING WITH OPTIONS: AN ILLUSTRATION

Suppose that in June 1996 the bond portfolio manager for a large insurance firm forecasts a sharp decline in interest rates over the next 3 months. Because of several new products developed by the company, a large inflow from sales of insurance policies in

August also is expected. The manager wants to hedge the opportunity loss on the investment of those premiums.

On the other side of town, however, is the manager of a money market fund who holds the opposite expectation for interest rate movements and who is willing to write a call option on T-bond futures contracts. T-bond futures for September delivery ($100,000 face value) are currently trading at 75.5 (75.5 percent of face value). The call option has a strike price of 76, a premium of $1,187.50, and an expiration date of August 1996. Table 11.7 summarizes the effect of the hedge on the position of the insurance company under three different interest rate scenarios.[14]

First, if interest rates go up instead of down, the bond manager will not exercise the option because the market value of the futures contract will be less than the strike price. The company will lose the $1,187.50 option premium. Second, if interest rates do fall but not by a significant amount, the value of the T-bond futures and the T-bond futures option will increase. But the rise in value—for example, to 77—will be insufficient to recover the entire purchase premium.

---

[13] Another reason for preferring one type of option over another is the difficulty of determining the appropriate size of the hedge. Because T-bond futures contracts are standardized with an 8 percent coupon, they sometimes trade at deep discounts, and the number of contracts (or options on contracts) must be adjusted to reflect that discount. For options on the T-bonds themselves, however, the difference between coupon and current market rates is seldom as large, because T-bond and T-note options are traded on issues with many different coupons.

[14] Specifications on options vary considerably. Options on T-bond futures contracts expire in the month before the futures contract delivery month. See Chicago Board of Trade 1986b.

TABLE 11.7	**Hedging with Options on T-Bond Futures Contracts**

An option provides the opportunity to limit losses to the amount of the option premium if forecasts are incorrect. If forecasts are correct, gains on a hedge can be used to offset losses in cash markets.

Treasury Bond Call Option
Premium: $1,187.50
Strike price: 76
Expiration date: August 1996
Security: Treasury bond futures contract for September delivery
                 $100,000 face value
                 Current market value: 75.5

Scenario 1: Interest Rates Rise
T-bond futures contract market value: <76
Call option not exercised
Results of hedge: −$1,187.50 (premium)

Scenario 2: Interest Rates Fall Slightly
T-bond futures contract market value: 77
Call option exercised: Contract purchased at 76 and sold at 77
Results of hedge:

$1,000.00	Profit on futures trade
− 1,187.50	Premium
($187.50)	Loss

Scenario 3: Interest Rates Fall Significantly
T-bond futures contract market value: 81
Call option exercised: Contract purchased at 76 and sold at 81
Results of hedge:

$5,000.00	Profit on futures trade
− 1,187.50	Premium
$3,812.50	Gain

The bond manager will suffer an opportunity cost on the investment of the new funds received in August, and this cost will be increased by the additional loss of $187.50 on the options transactions.

Finally, suppose interest rates drop sharply. The value of the T-bond futures contract rises sharply to 81. The bond portfolio manager exercises the call at 76 and immediately resells the futures contracts at 81, for a $5,000 profit. That profit is still offset somewhat by the cost of the option, but the hedge has now provided a net gain of $3,812.50, compensating for the lower return on the newly invested funds. The larger the drop in interest rates, the higher the profits earned. The bond manager could also choose to sell the option before its expiration date, also at a profit, although that hedge would require the purchase of a larger number of options. Finally, the manager could retain ownership of the futures contracts and take delivery on the T-bonds at a yield reflecting the higher levels that were available in June.

OPTIONS AND FUTURES HEDGING: A COMPARISON

A financial institution manager needing to hedge unfavorable market movements must evaluate the relative advantages and disadvantages offered by options and futures. The most important differences are the size and nature of the investment required and the potential size of losses and gains on the two instruments.

INVESTMENT REQUIRED

The margin requirements on positions in the futures market are discussed in Chapter 10. They are established by the clearinghouse as a percentage of the contract value and must be maintained on a daily basis. For purchasers of options, however, the investment required is the price of the option. It must be paid when the option is purchased, and no further payments are required unless the option is exercised. Option writers must post margin and mark their positions to market daily.

POTENTIAL RISK AND RETURN

A more important distinction between options and futures is the different risk exposures for an option purchaser and a futures hedger. The potential profits or losses on futures transactions are virtually unlimited, but the loss on the purchase of an option is limited to the option price, and profits are offset by the option premium.[15] A comparison of a long hedge with T-bond futures contracts and the T-bond futures call option just illustrated should clarify the differences in risk/return exposure.

The insurance company manager with a forecast of falling rates could have assumed a long hedge in T-bond futures, buying at a price of 75.5. The results of the futures hedge are summarized in Table 11.8. If interest rates move against the manager's forecasts, his or her losses have no ceiling except for those imposed by the movement of interest rates. If interest rates rise sharply and the contract value falls to, for example, 70, there will be a significant loss when the position is closed out. The greater the increase in interest rates, the greater the loss on the long hedge. Losses on the hedge will offset the returns gained from investing the new funds at the higher market rates.

However, if the manager's forecasts for lower interest rates are correct, there is no purchase premium to reduce the profits from the hedge. If the value of the T-bond futures contract rises to 81, there will be a profit of $5,500 per contract, instead of the gain of $3,812.50 shown in Table 11.7.

Figure 11.3 summarizes graphically the differences in risk exposure between futures and options hedges. The top of the figure assumes a forecast of falling rates. With a call option (shown in Panel A), until the underlying asset price reaches the strike price (S), the loss is equal to the option premium (Pr). As the asset price increases, returns on the option increase, eventually becoming positive after the premium is recovered. With a long futures contract hedge, shown in Panel B, a change in the price of the contract after pur-

TABLE 11.8	**Hedging with T-Bond Futures Contracts**

Futures hedges also provide opportunities to gain if forecasts are correct. If forecasts are incorrect, however, losses on a futures position can be larger than losses on comparable options hedging strategies.

The Long Hedge
T-bond futures contract
$100,000 face value
Current market value: 75.5

Scenario 1: Interest Rates Rise
T-bond futures contract market value: 70
Position closed at loss of 5.5 per contract
Results of hedge: −$5,500

Scenario 2: Interest Rates Fall Slightly
T-bond futures contract market value: 77
Position closed at profit of 1.5 per contract
Results of hedge: $1,500 profit

Scenario 3: Interest Rates Fall Significantly
T-bond futures contract market value: 81
Position closed at profit of 5.5 per contract
Results of hedge: $5,500 profit

chase at P_0 is translated into a gain or loss, because no premium must be recovered. Thus, hedging with futures is riskier than hedging with options.

The lower half of the figure compares a put option and the sale of futures contracts under a forecast of rising rates. Panel C shows that the purchaser of a put suffers a loss equal to the premium until the market price of the underlying asset falls below the strike price. As the asset's price continues to fall, the option holder's position improves and becomes profitable once the cost of the premium has been earned. In contrast, any change in the price of a futures contract translates directly into a profit or loss for the contract holder, as shown in Panel D.

INTEREST RATE SWAPS

Investors' thirst for new risk management strategies may be unquenchable. Despite the wide range of alternatives offered by futures, options, and options on futures, new hedging techniques are constantly under development and finding a place in the financial

---

[15] Theoretically, losses on futures contracts are halted when the value of the contract falls to $0.

FIGURE 11.3   **Comparison of Risk Exposure in Futures and Options Hedges**

The two left panels show that the losses to option holders are limited to the option premium, whereas profits are limited only by movements in the underlying asset's price. In contrast, the right panels illustrate that losses, as well as profits, on futures contracts depend on the price behavior of the underlying asset.

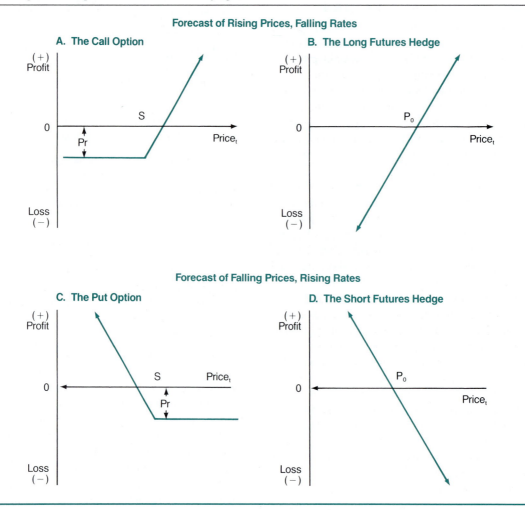

management policies of financial institutions. One of these—**interest rate swaps**—had become a mainstay of risk management by the early 1990s.

A swap agreement, in its basic form, is an exchange of cash flows between two parties (or **counterparties,** in the standard terminology of swaps). An interest rate swap is a transaction in which each of two parties agrees to pay the interest obligations on a specified debt obligation of the other party. In the simplest type of interest rate swap, one counterparty exchanges a fixed-rate payment obligation for a floating-rate one,

while the other counterparty exchanges floating for fixed.[16]

---

[16] Further discussions on the development and purposes of swaps are provided in Brown and Smith 1993; Abken 1991(a and b); Smith, Smithson, and Wakeman 1991; Litzenberger 1992; Marshall 1990/ 1991; Wall, Pringle, and McNulty 1990; Wall and Pringle 1988; Wall and Pringle 1989; Smith, Smithson, and Wakeman 1988; Roy C. Smith, "Swaps and Synthetic Securities," Working Paper Series Number 489, Salomon Brothers Center for the Study of Financial Institutions, New York University, September 1988; Felgran 1987; Whittaker 1987; Bicksler and Chen 1986; Loeys 1985; Hutchinson 1985; and Baldoni and Isele 1986.

MOTIVATIONS FOR SWAPS

A government agency introduced interest rate swaps to the United States, although currency swaps had previously been introduced in international markets. The Student Loan Marketing Association, known as Sallie Mae, pioneered swap programs in the United States in 1982 because of an asset structure heavily dominated by floating-rate student loans and advances. Investors supplying funds to Sallie Mae preferred to lock in the high rates prevailing at that time. The agency preferred to fund its rate-sensitive assets with sources of funds of a similar nature. Hence, Sallie Mae sought a swap to meet both its and its investors' needs. In the intervening years, the popularity of interest rate swaps has increased at a phenomenal rate. By 1992, the interest rate swap market, including financial and nonfinancial institutions, was estimated to involve liabilities with principal values of almost $3 trillion. The market for all swaps and swap-related products increased by 50 percent between 1989 and 1991, and no evidence suggests that the growth will moderate in the near future.[17]

For a financial institution, the objective of an interest rate swap is to trade one form of rate sensitivity on liabilities for another that better matches its asset structure. Federal S&Ls, for example, are permitted by regulation to seek swaps only to trade rate-sensitive deposit costs for fixed costs, and not the reverse. A swap allows a thrift to reduce its rate-sensitivity and to lock in a spread on long-term, fixed-rate assets. Conversely, a multinational commercial bank that borrows in the long-term Eurodollar market may, if most of its assets are rate-sensitive, prefer to swap fixed-rate interest obligations on Eurodollar deposits for floating-rate payments.

Nonfinancial firms also participate in the interest rate swaps market, benefiting from the ability to tailor interest obligations to suit their cash-flow patterns without having to restructure existing balance sheets. This flexibility may save substantial transactions costs. Also, nonfinancial firms, if they find a substantial rate differential between short-term and long-term interest rates, often engage in interest rate swaps to reduce the effective cost of borrowing. By swapping interest payments with a counterparty experiencing similar but opposite rate differentials, a firm can lower the costs of its liabilities.

SWAPS AS A HEDGING TOOL

Many financial institutions use swaps to hedge their interest rate risk exposure.

PLAIN VANILLA SWAP

The most basic type of interest rate swap is known as a **plain vanilla swap.** The mechanics of a swap of this type are shown in the diagram in Figure 11.4. The example involves a savings institution, with interest rate risk from a large proportion of fixed-rate mortgages on its balance sheet. The S&L needs a source of funds with similar interest rate characteristics, but its liabilities are primarily short-term with floating rates. The S&L finds a large commercial bank counterparty with the ability to borrow at fixed rates. The S&L and bank agree to swap interest rate obligations on $50 million of liabilities, called the **notional principal** of a swap.

EXCHANGING INTEREST OBLIGATIONS. The flow of funds is evident in Figure 11.4. The S&L agrees to pay interest on the notional principal at a rate of 8.5 percent; it will receive cash flows from the bank at the London Interbank Offered Rate (LIBOR) plus 25 basis points. Probably, this floating rate will initially be lower than the fixed rate of 8.5 percent. That relationship could change over the life of the swap as interest rate levels fluctuate. The swap allows the S&L to lock in its cost of liabilities, resulting in a more stable net interest margin on its fixed-rate mortgage portfolio.

COSTS AND BENEFITS OF A SWAP AGREEMENT. As with any hedging tool, interest rate shifts can make a swap agreement costly or beneficial. Also, as noted above, it is quite common for the fixed rate agreed on when the swap is initiated to be higher than the floating rate. In the context of this example, that differential is the "insurance premium" paid by the thrift to transfer interest rate risk exposure to its commercial bank counterparty.

---

[17] Remolona 1992–93; Pat Widder, "Trillions at Stake in the Swaps Market," *Chicago Tribune,* June 22, 1992, Section 4, 1, 2; and William Glasgall, "Swap Fever: Big Money, Big Risks," *Business Week,* June 1, 1992, 102–106.

FIGURE 11.4   Exchange of Obligations in an Interest Rate Swap

This swap involves an S&L that exchanges its variable-rate interest obligations for the fixed-rate interest obligations of a counterparty commercial bank. The cost of the swap is the initially higher interest payments the S&L must make.

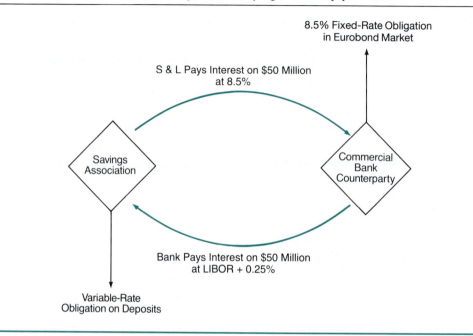

IMPORTANT FACTORS IN A SWAP

Managers face many decisions in a swap agreement.

MATURITY. The maturity of an interest rate exchange can vary from a relatively short period to as long as 20 years. The longer maturities available in the swap market make swaps suitable hedges when futures or options contracts are not. If interest rate forecasts underlying the swap prove to be incorrect, however, 5 or 10 years is a long time to pay for one's mistakes. For this reason, shorter swaps are more popular, and termination clauses are usually included in the original agreement. The party that "unwinds" (the swap market term for ending a swap early) must pay a penalty, but that may be cheaper than the consequences of continuing the swap under an unfavorable interest rate scenario. Many participants in the swap market make arrangements to reverse a swap, in the event of unfavorable rate movements, by agreeing to a swap that offsets the original one. The growing market for options on swaps, discussed later in this chapter, presents an increasingly popular alternative for early termination. A secondary market in swap agreements has also developed.

INTEREST RATE INDEX. Another important issue for negotiation is the index by which floating-rate interest payments will be adjusted. In the example, the S&L would prefer a payment stream positively correlated with the rate on its short-term deposits and at least equal to the average deposit cost. There is no guarantee that the anticipated relationship will materialize.

The LIBOR rate is the predominant index, but the T-bill rate and the prime rate, among others, are also used. Increased competition for deposits may change the effectiveness of a given index.

THE ROLE OF BROKERS AND DEALERS. Interest rate swaps are often arranged through brokers or dealers. Although it is possible for a small depository to find a swap partner on its own, the process is time-consuming and may be expensive. Most market participants prefer to use an intermediary.

In 1984, the Federal Home Loan Bank Board (FHLBB) formally recognized the potential benefits of swaps for thrift institutions and allowed the district FHLBs to serve as brokers and counterparties to member institutions. Thus, member associations can take advantage of reduced transactions costs if they work through the FHLB system.

Many large banks in the United States and Great Britain, as well as large Japanese securities firms, act as brokers and dealers in the swap markets, earning substantial fees for arranging and servicing swaps. As brokers, institutions bring two parties together, but as dealers they may even take the position of counterparty in a swap agreement. In many dealer arrangements, the intermediary guarantees the continuation of the cash flows for the swap, even if one counterparty defaults on the agreement. Thus, the dealer may be exposed to considerable credit risk, while the individual counterparties benefit from greater confidence that their cash flows will be uninterrupted.

CREDIT RISK. A financial institution must evaluate the counterparty's credit position, because some confidence is needed that there will be no default. When a dealer actually becomes a principal in an agreement or guarantees the payment streams, the financial position of the dealer is the most important issue.

Concern about controlling credit risk escalated when Beverly Hills Savings and Loan failed in 1985. It had previously made a swap with one of the subsidiaries of Renault, the French automaker. When the thrift failed, the Federal Savings and Loan Insurance Corporation (FSLIC) and Renault disagreed about who had claim to the $2 million in collateral pledged by Beverly Hills to secure the swap. Although counterparties with weak financial positions had become accustomed to pledging collateral to improve their chances of finding swap partners, the Beverly Hills incident provoked concern from stronger market participants and regulators about access to assets pledged. In the early 1990s, regulators' apprehensions about the swap market were rekindled in the aftermath of the failures of the Bank of New England and Drexel Burnham Lambert, Inc. These two failures alone left behind swaps with more than $30 billion in notional value,

and one European official claimed that the entire global payments system was almost upset.[18]

Although debate continues about the legal and systemic exposure in swap agreements, credit risk does appear to be limited. If a counterparty defaults on an agreement, the other party has responsibility only for its own debt obligations, not for the counterparty's. If the default occurs in an unfavorable interest rate environment, however, the loss of the protective hedge could be expensive.

REGULATORY AND ACCOUNTING ISSUES. As swaps have grown in popularity, regulators and accountants have focused attention on appropriate means for controlling and reporting the potential risk to which swap counterparties are exposed. Regulatory controls on depositories' swap activities have been imposed in the form of the risk-based capital standards discussed in Chapter 17. The Financial Accounting Standards Board now requires that firms involved in financial agreements with off–balance-sheet risk, including interest rate swaps, disclose details about these agreements and the potential loss that could occur should a counterparty fail to perform. Since 1993, firms have been required to disclose unrealized gains and losses from swap agreements.

MORE EXOTIC SWAPS

Market participants have recognized the swap concept as one of the most flexible and effective tools for managing many types of financial risks. As a result, many innovations have appeared. A representative (but not exhaustive) sample of those available in the early 1990s is presented in Table 11.9. The variety and complexity of the swap market are apparent.

Two emerging categories of swaps not shown in the table are **commodity swaps** and **equity swaps.** Commodity swaps allow exchange of risks due to price fluctuations of raw materials or other production inputs. One or both counterparties may lock in a price on future commodity purchases, depending on the terms with the swap dealer. The equity swap allows a portfolio manager to convert interest flows on a debt

---

[18] For more discussion of the risks in the swap market, see Hansell and Muering 1992; Glasgall, "Swap Fever"; Jonathan R. Laing, "The Next Meltdown?" *Barron's,* June 7, 1993, 10–11, 30–34.

TABLE 11.9   **Varieties of Interest Rate and Currency Swaps**

By the early 1990s, swap dealers and brokers were offering a vast array of agreements, all much more complex than the original plain vanilla swap.

Type of Swap	Description
Interest rate swaps	
Amortizing swap	Used to hedge interest rate risk on mortgages or other amortized loans; the notional principal diminishes over the life of the swap
Accreting swap	Used to hedge interest rate risk on agreements with a rising principal value, such as construction loans; notional principal increases over the life of the swap
Seasonal swap	Notional principal may vary up or down over the life of the swap. Also known as roller coaster swap
Basis swap	Exchange of floating rate payments between counterparties, but with interest rates based on different indexes
Zero-coupon swap	All cash flows of the swap occur at the end of the life of the agreement; payment obligations are compounded to future maturity
Yield curve swap	A subset of the basis swap; involves exchange of interest payments indexed to a short-term rate for payments indexed to a long-term rate
Participating swap	Allows the fixed rate to be adjusted downward during the life of the swap, depending on the level of the floating-rate index. Allows counterparty paying fixed to participate in benefit of declining rates
Reversible swap	Allows counterparty to change status from floating-rate payer to fixed-rate payer, and vice versa
Asset swap	Effectively transforms an asset into an asset of another type, such as converting a fixed-rate bond into a floating-rate bond. Results in what is known as a "synthetic security"
Forward swap	Used when new debt is to be issued at a future date; allows issuer to hedge against an undesirable increase in rates before the securities are issued
Forward rate swap	Reduces default risk by establishing, at the time the swap is executed, a schedule for adjusting the fixed rate over the life of the swap
Mark-to-market swap	Reduces default risk by allowing the fixed rate to be reset when fixed and floating rates diverge substantially after the beginning of the swap
Currency swaps	
Currency-coupon swap	Used to hedge currency and interest rate risk; a fixed rate is paid in one currency while a floating rate is paid in another
ECU swap	Used to transform principal and coupon payments denominated in European Currency Units into another currency, and vice versa

Source: Adapted from Abken 1991(a and b); Litzenberger 1992; Brown and Smith 1993.

portfolio to cash flows linked to an equity index, such as the S&P 500. Thus managers can realize the benefit of returns on different asset categories without paying transactions costs.

SWAPS VERSUS FUTURES HEDGING

Table 11.10 summarizes important differences between hedging with futures and hedging with interest rate swaps. In general, the swap market is less complex, and agreements do not require the daily monitoring necessary in futures trading. Swaps allow management more flexibility in negotiating the initial size and maturity of a hedge, but futures hedges are easier and less costly to reverse once in place. Currently, the futures markets are larger, more liquid, and more competitive, although growth in dealer activity and development of a secondary market are facilitating the use of swaps. Thus, the choice between futures and swaps depends on the expertise of managers and the regularity with which hedges will be managed.

SWAP OPTIONS AND FUTURES

Despite the fact that swaps are used as a hedging tool by many market participants, swap dealers and some

TABLE 11.10	Comparing Interest Rate Futures and Interest Rate Swaps	

These comparisons show that swaps are more flexible hedging tools than futures, but futures markets are larger, more well-developed, and more standardized.

Feature	Futures	Swaps
Maturities available	1½ to 2 years	1 month to 20 years
Costs	Margins and commissions	Brokers' or dealers' fees
Size of hedges available	Standardized contract values	Any amount over $1 million
Contract expiration dates	Fixed quarterly cycle	Any dates
Difficulty of management	Complex	Simple
Termination of positions	Closed out with opposite contract	Unwound or reversed
Transactions completed through	Organized exchanges	Commercial or investment banks

Source: Adapted from Robert Baldoni and Gerhard Isele, "A Simple Guide to Choosing between Futures and Swaps," *Intermarket* 3 (October 1986): 16; and Vivian Lewis, "Stop and Swap," *Bankers Monthly* 106 (October 1989): 82–84.

counterparties continue to feel the effect of interest rate risk exposure. Consequently, mechanisms in the form of swap options and futures are now available to assist in more precise management of those risks.

SWAP OPTIONS OR SWAPTIONS

Options on swaps are commonly known as **swaptions.** As is true of other options, swaptions provide the buyer with the right to exercise some choice during the life of the option. In the early 1990s, options on plain vanilla swaps were most common, and the swaptions market had reached a volume of almost $100 billion by 1990.

A call swaption gives the buyer an opportunity to enter into a swap agreement in the future to receive a fixed rate and pay a floating rate. A put swaption gives the buyer the right to make a future swap agreement to receive a floating rate of interest while paying a fixed rate. If a swaption is exercised, the swap will begin at a stipulated future date with a predetermined rate of interest. Most swaptions are of the European variety, meaning that they can only be exercised at the option's expiration date.

A put swaption would be exercised if the option would allow the buyer to pay a rate of interest lower than the level of interest rates prevailing on similar swaps at the swaption's maturity. If the buyer does not really need the swap agreement, the low fixed-rate swap could be sold at a gain to another counterparty.

The swaption market also effectively gives counterparties the opportunity to cancel or otherwise alter a swap agreement before maturity, if interest rate movements are unfavorable. This method of cancellation can be less costly than unwinding a swap before the end of the agreement. A swap can be bundled together with a swaption to allow the holder to terminate the agreement. For example, a counterparty paying the fixed rate can bundle the swap with a call swaption; if interest rates have declined by the time the swaption matures, the swaption can be exercised and the agreement cancelled. Such a combination is known as a **callable swap.** Other types of swaptions allow the holder to exercise the right to extend a swap agreement **(extendable swaps)** or reverse the obligation to pay floating and fixed rates (another way to achieve a reversible swap).

SWAP FUTURES

The CBOT introduced a swap futures contract in mid-1991. The "cash instruments" on which such futures contracts are based are generic, plain vanilla swaps with 3- or 5-year lives, with a variable rate indexed to LIBOR. The price of the futures contract reflects expectations about the fixed rate required for such a swap. At maturity, the price of a swap futures contract is determined by the prevailing fixed rate on swap agreements at that point in time.

Swap futures were primarily designed to offer protection to swap dealers, who face risk exposure in many swap agreements. Dealers, besides assisting in structuring agreements, often serve as counterparties. As such, they face risk from unfavorable fluctuations in interest rates, as well as credit risk from potential nonperformance of counterparties. The swap futures contracts provide a mechanism for managing the interest rate risk exposure of the counterparty paying the fixed rate.[19]

INTEREST RATE CAPS, FLOORS, AND COLLARS

The final interest rate risk management tool introduced in this chapter is a group of relatively new products called **interest rate caps, floors, and collars.** These are designed to limit exposure to interest rate fluctuations on existing assets, liabilities, or payment obligations in a swap agreement. For example, institutions can purchase interest rate caps to limit increases in their cost of funds in a volatile rate environment. Likewise, a cap could serve as an effective ceiling to limit potential increases in floating rate payments required by an existing swap agreement.

Interest rate caps are similar to call options. The purchaser pays a premium for the right to limit the cost of its liabilities to a specified rate (the strike level), just as purchasers of call options pay a premium for the right to buy an asset at the strike price. If the current rate on the index underlying the cap (usually the LIBOR rate, the prime, the T-bill rate, the prime commercial paper rate, or a certificate of deposit index) rises above the strike level, it will be profitable to exercise the cap. If interest rates remain below the strike level, the cap expires unused, and its price serves as an insurance premium.

Alternatively, interest rate floors can be purchased to protect against the possibility that returns on variable-rate instruments will fall so low that they no longer exceed the cost of funding sources. Floors could also be used to protect against the possibility that floating payments received from a swap agreement fall below the existing fixed obligations. Floors are similar to put options. For a premium, institutions that purchase floors own the right to receive interest payments at the strike level, just as put buyers own the right to receive a specified sales price for an underlying asset. If interest rates fall below the strike level, it becomes profitable for the floor owner to exercise the option. If interest rates remain above the strike level, the floor expires unused.

For example, consider a swap agreement with a fixed rate of 7.5 percent. As interest rates rise, the floating rate could easily reach a level several hundred basis points above the fixed rate. By purchasing a cap, the floating-rate counterparty could effectively limit the rate paid to, say, 9 percent. If the indexed rate rises above 9 percent, the cap is exercised and the party who sold it is obligated to pay the difference between the cap rate and the actual rate.

An interest rate floor can protect the recipient of the floating-rate payments. The floor would be exercised if the index rate falls below the strike rate, and the writer of the interest rate floor would again be obligated to pay an amount sufficient to cover the shortfall. Buyers of caps and floors pay a premium, just as is true in the purchase of options.

Finally, some market participants may purchase both caps *and* floors or may purchase a cap and sell a floor. These strategies hedge against both increases and decreases in interest rates or provide some premium income to offset the cost of purchasing the cap. Such arrangements, known as **interest rate collars,** attempt to stabilize the NIM within a defined range.

RISKS IN THE MARKET FOR CAPS AND FLOORS

The market for interest rate caps and floors is similar to the interest rate swap market, in that it is over-the-counter and dominated by large commercial and investment banks acting as dealers or brokers. Many of these dealer/broker institutions purchase caps and floors as part of their own interest rate risk management plans and also write caps and floors for others. Like swaps, caps and floors are tailored to individual user needs. For every cap or floor purchaser entitled to receive payments if the cap or floor goes in the money, there is a cap or floor writer (seller) who is obligated to make those payments. Thus, the purchaser faces the possibility that the writer may default on the

---

[19] Unfortunately, because swaptions are so new, terminology is not yet standardized. Readers may even find conflicting definitions in different sources. For more information on these emerging markets, see Beidleman 1991; Chicago Board of Trade, *CBOT Swap Futures: The Reference Guide.* Chicago: Chicago Board of Trade, 1991; William B. Crawford, Jr., ''CBOT's Planting a New Hedge,'' *Chicago Tribune,* June 18, 1991, Section 4, 1, 4; Abken 1991(a and b); and Brown and Smith 1991.

promised obligations. Furthermore, the purchaser also faces basis risk when attempting to hedge assets or liabilities whose returns or costs are not perfectly correlated with an index on which caps or floors are available.

Data on the volume of caps and floors outstanding are sparse, but most purchasers appear to be banks and other financial institutions, as well as nonfinancial firms using caps to hedge against increases in short-term borrowing costs. Transactions are large, with a typical minimum notional principal amount of $5,000,000. Thus, many purchasers are highly sophisticated businesses whose managers are aware of the risks inherent in the market. Interestingly, however, caps can also be attractive hedging vehicles for weaker institutions with poor credit ratings who are unable to find a willing counterparty in the interest rate swap market. Because the writer of a cap bears no default risk, the credit standing of the purchaser is of no consequence.

Given their relatively low risk levels, caps and floors are enjoying increasing acceptance among financial institution managers. The market has been strengthened by their association with swap agreements. Along with swaptions and swap futures contracts, caps, floors, and collars are the most recent examples of financial innovation and engineering. Fed estimates suggest their collective volume exceeded half a trillion dollars by 1991, with even greater growth predicted in the future.[20]

SUMMARY

This chapter concludes the material on tools for managing interest rate risk by discussing index futures; options; interest rate and other swaps; swaptions; swap futures; and interest rate caps, floors, and collars. Like other financial futures, stock index futures are used to hedge against declines in existing financial positions, especially in equity portfolios. Procedures governing their use are similar to those for all futures contracts.

Futures contracts have also been developed for market indexes on other financial instruments.

Options are also available for hedging. An option enables the holder to purchase or sell a financial asset or a futures contract at the strike price. A call option is purchased in anticipation of rising asset prices or falling interest rates. If the forecast is incorrect, losses are limited to the option premium. In contrast to the call option, the holder purchases a put in anticipation of falling asset prices or rising interest rates.

Hedging with futures and hedging with options are popular risk management tools. In general, financial futures present more risk to the hedger but can be more profitable.

Interest rate swaps allow two parties to exchange cash flows on debt obligations. The most common form of such agreements involves an exchange of fixed-rate payment obligations for floating-rate payments. Swaps allow market participants to manage exposure to interest rate uncertainties. Many forms of interest rate swaps have been developed; currency, commodity, and equity swaps are also increasingly popular risk management tools. Although the futures markets continue to have a higher volume of participation, swap market volume grew exponentially in the late 1980s and early 1990s.

Two very new risk management tools complement the swaps market: swaptions and swap futures contracts. Swaptions are a form of option agreement; when exercised, the holder has the right to enter into a swap with a predetermined fixed rate. Depending on interest rate changes after the option is written, swaptions may provide beneficial interest rate terms for the holder. The swaps futures contract, introduced in 1991, has a value determined by expectations about the fixed rate available on a hypothetical 3- or 5-year swap agreement.

Finally, interest rate caps, collars, and floors allow risk managers to limit their exposure to interest rate fluctuations. Caps can be used to create a ceiling for the costs of deposits or other liabilities of financial institutions. They can also be used to limit increases in floating-rate obligations of a rate swap. An interest rate floor serves the opposite function, limiting potential decreases in returns on variable-rate assets or in the floating-rate payments to be received in a swap agreement.

---

[20] For more information on caps, floors, and collars, see Remolona 1992–93; Abken 1991(a and b); Abken 1989; and Spahr, Luytjes, and Edwards 1988.

QUESTIONS

1. Give an example of a stock index and another market index. Why are these indexes computed and what benefits do they offer to financial market participants?

2. What are stock index futures contracts? Compare and contrast their use by financial institutions for interest rate risk management with the use of interest rate futures contracts.

3. Explain the importance of the correlation between movements in an institution's stock portfolio and movements in the stock index used for hedging. How are the risks posed by this relationship similar to the risks posed by a cross hedge in the interest rate futures market?

4. Given a forecast of a bear market, why might the manager of an equity portfolio hedge with stock index futures rather than adjusting the cash portfolio? What are the advantages and disadvantages of each strategy?

5. Compare and contrast the delivery terms of stock index and interest rate futures contracts. How do the delivery characteristics of stock index futures affect hedging positions in those markets?

6. Suppose that a portfolio manager structures a stock index futures hedge based on an estimated portfolio beta equal to 1. What is the implicit assumption about the volatility of the returns on the portfolio?

7. A stock index futures hedge involved a trade of 1,500 contracts and assumed a portfolio beta of 1. If the portfolio manager reestimates the beta at 1.25, would the number of contracts traded rise, fall, or remain the same? Why?

8. What is meant by the term *index arbitrage*? Could this trading technique work in the T-bill or T-bond futures market? Why or why not?

9. What conclusion did the Brady Commission draw about the relationship between program trading and the stock market crash in 1987? What alternative explanation has been offered by proponents of program trading?

10. Describe the characteristics of an option. Compare a call option and a put option. Under what equity market forecast would a hedger buy a call option? A put option? Why?

11. What is the difference between American and European options?

12. Two call options have equal strike prices, but one has a more distant expiration date. Which option would trade at a higher value? Why?

13. For many investment alternatives, a high degree of price volatility is considered undesirable. Is price volatility of the underlying asset positively or negatively related to option values? Why?

14. Under what interest rate forecast would a hedger buy a call option on debt instruments such as T-bonds? A put option? Why?

15. Explain why an asset/liability manager might choose a financial futures hedge rather than an options hedge. When is the options hedge preferred? Compare the risk exposure of the two alternatives.

16. What is the maximum loss exposure to the *purchaser* of a call option? To the *writer* of a call option?

17. Do you believe that trading of stocks and stock index futures should be regulated by the same government agency? Explain. If so, would you favor the Fed, the Securities and Exchange Commission, the Commodity Futures Trading Commission, or a new agency as the chief regulator of both markets? Why?

18. Describe in your own words a plain vanilla interest rate swap. Draw a simple diagram of a typical swap agreement. Explain the terms notional principal and counterparty.

19. Examine recent forecasts of interest rates for the coming year. How might the manager of a large savings institution heavily invested in fixed-rate mortgages use a swap agreement to hedge interest rate risk? What additional risks may be encountered?

20. Compare and contrast the credit risk exposure in swap agreements and futures contracts.

21. Explain how the market for interest rate swaps is organized, and describe the roles of brokers and dealers.

22. Suppose you were charged with managing interest rate risk exposure for a large commercial bank that is heavily invested in intermediate term securities and loans (i.e., those with maturities of approximately 5 years). Evaluate the relative advantages and disadvantages of hedging with futures versus swaps.

23. Explain a basic call swaption. Does the holder of a call swaption benefit from an interest rate increase or decrease? Give an example.

24. Explain how a swaption and a swap can be combined to give a market participant flexibility in terminating a swap obligation.

25. Describe the interest rate forecast under which it would be beneficial to buy a call option on an interest rate futures contract. Is this the same forecast under which you would buy a call swaption? Why or why not?

26. What is a swap futures contract? What determines the changes in value of swap futures?

27. What are caps and floors? Discuss the similarities be- tween these instruments and options. Give an example of a scenario in which a financial institution manager might buy an interest rate cap.

28. What is an interest rate collar? What is its role in risk management? Could a similar hedge be structured using swaps and swaptions? Explain.

PROBLEMS

1. Mr. Chapman, of Boston Property/Liability Insurance Company, manages a $700 million stock portfolio. In June, he is watching the stock market carefully and anticipates a downturn in the next 2 months. He knows that liquidating part of the portfolio will involve transactions costs, so he instead chooses a hedge with stock index futures. The S&P stock index is currently at 417.40. Yesterday's settlement level for September S&P index futures was 423.75. Mr. Chapman expects the market index and futures prices to fall by 6.5 percent over the next 2 months. He has estimated that the company's portfolio has a beta of 1.25.

    a.   Calculate the number of contracts required and the resulting gain or loss on the hedge, assuming that the market index and futures prices fall by 6.5 percent as predicted.

    b.   Suppose futures prices and cash prices are not perfectly correlated so that futures prices fall by 6.2 percent when the market falls by 6.5 percent. Recalculate the gain or loss on the hedge.

    c.   Now suppose that Mr. Chapman's forecast is incorrect and that stock prices rise by 2 percent after he places the hedge. Assuming a 2 percent rise in futures prices as well, calculate the gain or loss on the hedge. What potential disadvantages of hedging are revealed by this situation?

    d.   Now suppose again that cash and futures positions are not perfectly correlated and that futures rise by 3 percent when stock prices rise by 2 percent. Recalculate the net results of the hedge. If Mr. Chapman anticipated this possibility, what might he do at the time the hedge is placed?

2. Pam Lowry, Titan Corporation's pension fund manager, is expecting a $50 million cash inflow 3 months from now, which she must invest in the equity market. Economists forecast an upswing in the stock market over the next 3 months. Knowing that the expected funds will miss the upswing and resulting benefits, Ms. Lowry has decided to hedge using stock index futures. The Value Line index currently stands at 290.69. Yesterday's settlement level for the Value Line futures index was 297.40. Economists predict an increase of 4.5 percent in the index over the next 3 months. The average beta of the stocks in which the incoming funds will be invested is 0.87.

    a.   Recommend the number of futures contracts to be traded.

    b.   Calculate the gain or loss on the hedge if the economists' forecasts are correct.

    c.   Calculate the gain or loss if the market falls by 4 percent and futures fall by 5 percent.

3. Lisa Brown, a commercial loan officer, has made a commitment to one of her best clients to provide a fixed-rate loan for $100,000 in 3 months at the rate prevailing today. However, she forecasts rising rates in the interim. She recommends to the bank's portfolio manager that the position be hedged by buying a put option on T-bond futures contracts. Assume Ms. Brown's bank will exercise the put if it is profitable to do so. The following information is available:

T-bond futures	Face value: $100,000
	Current price: 97-16
Put option	Strike price: 97-12
	Premium: $2,000

Calculate the gain or loss on the hedge under the following conditions:

    a.   Interest rates decrease; T-bond futures rise to 99.

    b.   Interest rates increase; T-bond futures fall to 95-28.

    c.   Interest rates increase; T-bond futures fall to 94.

4. Suppose Mr. Chapman, whose situation is described in Problem 1, can buy a stock index futures put option for a premium of $1,000, with a strike price of 420. Assume the number of options purchased is equal to the number of contracts that would be involved in a futures hedge.

    a.   Calculate the gain or loss on the options transaction under each of the following conditions that could prevail when options expire:

1) S&P index futures continue to trade at 423.75.

2) S&P index futures settlement level drops to 400.

3) S&P index futures settlement level rises to 440.

b. Calculate the gain or loss on the futures hedge described in Part A of Problem 1 under each of the three scenarios in Part A of this problem.

c. Compare the futures results to the gains or losses on the options hedge and assess the risk exposure of the two alternatives.

Note: This problem does not require you to calculate the *net* result of the options or futures hedges; that is, no calculations are required for the stock portfolio results.

5. Return to the index arbitrage example in Table 11.4. Show that the portfolio manager will gain on the transaction even if the market falls by 20 percent before the expiration date. (Hint: Remember that the futures settlement level and the index must be equal at expiration.)

SELECTED REFERENCES

Abken, Peter. "Interest-Rate Caps, Collars, and Floors." CME Financial Strategy Paper, Chicago Mercantile Exchange, 1991a.

———. "Beyond Plain Vanilla: A Taxonomy of Swaps." *Economic Review* (Federal Reserve Bank of Atlanta) 76 (March/April 1991b): 12–29.

———. "Interest-Rate Caps, Collars, and Floors." *Economic Review* (Federal Reserve Bank of Atlanta) 74 (November/December 1989): 2–24.

Baldoni, Robert, and Gerhard Isele. "A Simple Guide to Choosing between Futures and Swaps." *Intermarket* 3 (October 1986): 15–22.

Barro, Robert J., et al. *Black Monday and the Future of Financial Markets.* Homewood, IL: Richard D. Irwin, 1989.

Beidleman, Carl R., Ed. *Interest Rate Swaps.* Homewood, IL: Business One Irwin, 1991.

Bicksler, James, and Andrew H. Chen. "An Economic Analysis of Interest Rate Swaps." *Journal of Finance* 41 (July 1986): 645–655.

Brown, Keith C., and Donald J. Smith. "Default Risk and Innovations in the Design of Interest Rate Swaps." *Financial Management* 22 (Summer 1993): 94–105.

———. "Forward Swaps, Swap Options, and the Management of Callable Debt." In *New Developments in Commercial Banking,* edited by Donald Chew. Cambridge, MA: Blackwell Publishers, 1991.

Chance, Don M. *An Introduction to Options and Futures.* 2d ed. Chicago: The Dryden Press, 1992.

Chicago Board of Trade. *Commodity Trading Manual.* Chicago: Board of Trade of the City of Chicago, 1989.

———. *MMI Futures and Options.* Chicago: Board of Trade of the City of Chicago, 1991.

———. *Stock Index Futures.* Chicago: Board of Trade of the City of Chicago, 1987.

———. *NASDAQ-100 Index Futures.* Chicago: Board of Trade of the City of Chicago, 1986a.

———. *An Introduction to Options on Treasury Bond Futures.* Chicago: Board of Trade of the City of Chicago, 1986b.

———. *Options on U.S. Treasury Bond Futures for Institutional Investors.* Chicago: Board of Trade of the City of Chicago, 1985.

Chicago Mercantile Exchange. *Using S&P Index Futures and Options.* Chicago: Chicago Mercantile Exchange, 1985.

Christopher, Benjamin B. "Recent Developments Affecting Depository Institutions." *FDIC Banking Review* 2 (Spring/Summer 1989): 37.

Felgran, Steven D. "Interest Rate Swaps: Use, Risk, and Prices." *New England Economic Review* (Federal Reserve Bank of Boston) (November/December 1987): 22–32.

Goodman, Laurie. "New Options Markets." *Quarterly Review* (Federal Reserve Bank of New York) 8 (Autumn 1983): 35–47.

Hansell, Saul, and Kevin Muehring. "Why Derivatives Rattle the Regulators." *Institutional Investor,* September 1992.

Hill, Joanne M., Anshuman Jain, and Robert A. Ward, Jr. *Portfolio Insurance: Volatility Risk and Futures Mispricing.* New York: Kidder Peabody and Co., 1987.

Hutchinson, Michael M. "Swaps." *Weekly Letter* (Federal Reserve Bank of San Francisco), May 3, 1985.

Koppenhaver, G. D. "Futures Options and Their Use by Financial Intermediaries." *Economic Perspectives* (Federal Reserve Bank of Chicago) 10 (January/February 1986): 18–31.

Litzenberger, Robert. "Swaps: Plain and Fanciful." *Journal of Finance* 47 (July 1992): 831–850.

Loeys, Jan G. "Interest Rate Swaps: A New Tool for Managing Risk." *Business Review* (Federal Reserve Bank of Philadelphia) (May/June 1985): 17–25.

Marshall, John F. "Futures Versus Swaps: Some Considerations for the Thrift Industry." *Review of Business* 12 (Winter 1990/1991): 15–22, 44.

Merrick, John J., Jr. "Fact and Fantasy about Stock Index Futures Program Trading." *Business Review* (Federal Reserve Bank of Philadelphia) (September/October 1987): 13–25.

Napoli, Janet A. "Derivative Markets and Competitiveness." *Economic Perspectives* (Federal Reserve Bank of Chicago) 16 (July/August 1992): 13–24.

Remolona, Eli M. "The Recent Growth of Financial Derivative Markets." *Quarterly Review* (Federal Reserve Bank of New York) 17 (Winter 1992–93): 28–43.

Smith, Clifford W., Jr., Charles W. Smithson, and Lee Macdonald Wakeman. "The Market for Interest Rate Swaps." *Financial Management* 18 (Winter 1988): 34–44.

———. "The Evolving Market for Swaps." In *New Developments in Commercial Banking,* edited by Donald Chew. Cambridge, MA: Blackwell Publishers, 1991.

Spahr, Ronald W., Jan E. Luytjes, and Donald G. Edwards. "The Use of Caps as Deposit Hedges for Financial Institutions." *Issues in Bank Regulation* 12 (Summer 1988): 17–23.

Stoll, Hans R., and Robert E. Whaley. *Expiration Day Effects of Index Futures and Options.* New York: Salomon Brothers Center for the Study of Financial Institutions, 1986.

Wall, Larry D., and John J. Pringle. "Interest Rate Swaps: A Review of the Issues." *Economic Review* (Federal Reserve Bank of Atlanta) 73 (November/December 1988): 22–40.

———. "Alternative Explanations of Interest Rate Swaps: A Theoretical and Empirical Analysis." *Financial Management* 18 (Summer 1989): 59–73.

Wall, Larry D., John J. Pringle, and James E. McNulty. "Capital Requirements for Interest Rate and Foreign-Exchange Hedges." *Economic Review* (Federal Reserve Bank of Atlanta) 75 (May/June 1990): 14–29.

Whittaker, J. Gregg. "Interest Rate Swaps: Risk and Regulation." *Economic Review* (Federal Reserve Bank of Kansas City) 72 (March 1987): 3–13.

American financial institutions have been through a drying out after a night of too much revelry.

Roy C. Smith
Finance Professor, New York University (1991)

———————————

The American Bankers Association is the largest trade organization of the richest and most powerful group of depository institutions. Its annual convention, usually held in October in Honolulu, San Francisco, or another vacation paradise, has long been characterized—even through banking's tumultuous 1980s—as a series of "bland presentations in which nary a discouraging word was spoken." In 1992, however, reflecting the new mood in banking, the meeting was moved to Boston, in the heart of economically battered New England, and featured serious sessions on such topics as asset/liability management, community reinvestment, and fee-based income strategies. One highlight was a speech by former Senator Paul Tsongas on his personal struggle to overcome cancer. Said one observer, "Bankers could use a little advice on overcoming adversity."[1]

The study of depository institutions begins with this chapter. Defined earlier, they are firms for which deposits are the largest sources of funds. They include commercial banks, savings and loan associations (S&Ls), savings banks, and credit unions (CUs). The purpose of this chapter is to describe their assets, liabilities, and industry structures. Also, their operations and performance in recent years are compared, including a review of the thrift industry crisis of the late 1980s. Managerial decisions in depositories are the subjects of the ten chapters that follow.

CHAPTER

12

DEPOSITORY

INSTITUTIONS:

OVERVIEW AND

COMPARISON

———————————

[1] Robert M. Garsson, "New Site, New Image for ABA Convention," *American Banker,* October 13, 1992, 1, 9.

COMMERCIAL BANKS: INDUSTRY STRUCTURE

As of mid-1991, there were 12,090 insured commercial banks in the United States.[2] Although the question, "What is a bank?" has no easy answer, this figure refers to institutions for which business loans are a regular and important portion of operations and that collect deposits subsequently redeemable on demand.[3] It excludes thrifts, particularly savings banks, which perform both functions but for which commercial business is not significant.

Commercial banks are not the most numerous depositories—that distinction belongs to CUs—but they hold by far the most assets. Historically, banks have played a dominant role not only in business lending but also in payments transfers and money creation. Although they now share these functions with other depositories, and even some nondepositories, commercial banks remain at the heart of the financial system. But the 1980s were not an easy decade for banks, and some experts question whether they will retain their central role into the next century. Further discussion of this potentially changing role is found later in this chapter.

SIZE DIFFERENCES

Commercial banks are not homogeneous. They differ in how they are chartered, examined, and insured, as well as in their asset and liability choices. They also differ in size. Charters and organizational structures of commercial banks were discussed in Chapters 2 and 4. In this chapter, asset and liability structures of banks of different sizes are addressed.

---

[2] Board of Governors of the Federal Reserve System, *78th Annual Report,* 1991, 267.

[3] For a thorough analysis of distinctions that prevailed between banks and other financial institutions before 1987, see DiClemente 1983. (References are listed in full at the end of this chapter.) In 1987, the Competitive Equality Banking Act (CEBA) changed the legal definition of a bank to include any institution insured by the Federal Deposit Insurance Corporation (FDIC). The Financial Institutions Reform, Recovery and Enforcement Act's (FIRREA) division of the FDIC into the Bank Insurance Fund (BIF) and the Savings Association Insurance Fund (SAIF) then limited the definition to institutions insured by BIF. The discussion in this chapter emphasizes the functional characteristics of commercial banks, not their deposit insurance status, and thus focuses on traditional commercial lending and deposit-taking activities in distinguishing commercial banks from other depositories.

TABLE 12.1 | **Size Distribution of Insured Commercial Banks by Total Assets, Year-End 1991**

The commercial banking industry is highly concentrated; only about 8 percent of the firms in the industry have more than $300 million in total assets.

Size Category	Category Total	% of Total
Less than $10 million	513	4.31%
$10 million to less than $25 million	2,407	20.21
$25 million to less than $50 million	3,206	26.92
$50 million to less than $300 million	4,791	40.23
$300 million and more	992	8.33
Total, all sizes	11,909	100.00%

Source: Prepared by the authors with data from the Board of Governors of the Federal Reserve System.

Table 12.1 divides the banking industry into groups based on total assets. It includes only domestically chartered, insured commercial banks. Although Citicorp, the largest bank holding company in 1991, had assets in excess of $216 billion, less than 9 percent of all insured banks had more than $300 million in assets in 1991. About 4 percent were in the smallest group. Almost 52 percent held less than $50 million in assets. In recent years, the percentage of banks in the smallest size group has been shrinking as a result of mergers and changing economic conditions.

ASSETS OF COMMERCIAL BANKS

Table 12.2 on pages 312 and 313 presents the asset composition of three categories of commercial banks in 1991. Included are data on typical members of the smallest and largest groups of domestically chartered commercial banks.[4] As noted in earlier chapters, foreign banks have established a significant presence in the United States in recent years, reflecting the glob-

---

[4] Tables 12.2 and 12.3 were prepared from data on domestic banks that are more than 3 years old, because young banks tend to differ from their more established counterparts.

alization of financial markets. Accordingly, Table 12.2 also includes data on foreign banks operating in the United States. A comparison of the balance sheets of domestic banks and foreign banks follows the discussion of small versus large banks' financial structure.

Federal regulators require banks to submit financial statements, known in the industry as **call reports,** that provide extensive detail on the institutions' assets, liabilities, income, and expenses. The tables in this chapter include only the major categories. Depositories must also submit financial statements to the Internal Revenue Service, prepared using rules in the tax code. They prepare yet another set of financial reports, using generally accepted accounting principles, for distribution to shareholders. This chapter uses data from regulators' call reports.

CASH AND DUE FROM DEPOSITORIES

The **cash and due** account includes coin and currency in vaults on the premises; reserves on deposit with the Federal Reserve System (Fed); deposits with other banks; and checks deposited by customers on which funds have not yet been collected from the paying bank, the "due" part of the category. The volume of due balances in the banking system as a whole is called the **float.** Although necessary for business, the cash and due account is a nonearning asset because vault cash is idle, and the Fed pays no interest on reserves.[5]

Cash and due is about the same percentage of assets for small and large banks. Banks with deposits of less than 46.8 million must keep only 3 percent of their transactions accounts on reserve with the Fed, but the requirement for larger institutions is 10 percent.[6] Small banks, however, have a relatively large proportion of total liabilities in the form of transactions accounts, whereas large banks incur more liabilities on which reserves need not be held. Reserve account management, part of a bank's liquidity management strategy, is discussed in Chapter 13.

SECURITIES HELD

Securities held consist chiefly of Treasury securities; federal agency securities; and the debt obligations of states, counties, and municipalities, which are included as part of "other securities" in Table 12.2. Securities are held primarily for investment purposes, although some must be held as collateral by institutions with government deposits. Default risk is ordinarily not a serious concern in a bank's securities portfolio, because regulations limit insured banks' investment in corporate bonds and prohibit investment in stock.[7] Management of the bank's securities portfolio is tied to liquidity, and it, too, is discussed in Chapter 13. Securities held do not include customers' portfolios managed by the trust department, for which a bank receives fee income. These securities are the assets of the customers, not the bank.

FEDERAL FUNDS SOLD

By reporting custom, the asset category "federal (fed) funds sold" includes reverse repurchase agreements with other financial institutions, discussed in detail in Chapter 5. More important, however, is the asset for which the category is named. Excess reserves lent to other institutions are fed funds "sold" and are the assets of the lending institution; they earn interest at the fed funds rate, illustrated in Chapter 5. Because these transactions are short-term, they are an important part of an institution's liquidity planning. As a proportion of total assets, small banks sell more fed funds than do large banks. In fact, cash, securities, and fed funds are about half of the typical small bank's assets but less than one-third of a large bank's.

LOANS

Loans are the single largest asset category for banks of all sizes, although large banks typically have a much higher proportion of assets invested in loans than do smaller institutions. Also, small and large banks differ markedly in loan portfolio composition. Real estate loans are loans secured by real property and consist primarily of commercial and residential

---

[5] As noted in Chapter 2, the Fed must pay interest on supplemental reserves that may, at some point in its judgment, be necessary.

[6] Reserve requirements must be held against transactions accounts. The formula is modified annually according to the growth in total system deposits over the previous year. As of 1993, the cutoff point between 3 percent and 10 percent marginal reserve requirements was $46.8 million in transactions accounts. Small institutions are exempt from these requirements.

[7] In the 1970s, some concern for default risk was expressed by institutions with investments in the bonds issued by New York City and Cleveland.

TABLE 12.2 Distribution of Assets: Domestic Banks More Than 3 Years Old and Foreign Banks, Year-End 1991

Asset and liability categories as a proportion of total assets differ considerably between the smallest and largest domestically chartered banks. Foreign banks operating in the United States also have different financial structures, although they compete directly with large domestic banks.

	Average Domestic Bank Less Than $10 Million (469 Banks)		Average Domestic Bank More Than $300 Million (987 Banks)		Foreign Bank Offices in the United States (581 Offices)	
	Thousands	% of Total	Thousands	% of Total	Millions	% of Total
Assets						
Cash and due	$755	10.79%	$260,663	9.63%	$159,637	22.66%
Securities held						
United States Treasury and federal agency	$1,884	26.92%	$344,304	12.73%	$31,030	4.40%
Other securities	251	3.59	124,355	4.60	35,982	5.11
Total securities	2,135	30.50	468,659	17.32	67,012	9.51
Federal funds sold	629	8.99	110,182	4.07	23,914	3.39
Loans						
Real estate	1,199	17.13	641,856	23.72	54,264	7.70
Commercial and industrial	429	6.13	488,405	18.05	167,608	23.79
Consumer	689	9.84	310,583	11.48	NA^a	NA^a
All other	930	13.29	223,421	8.26	88,474	12.56
Less unearned income and allowance for loan losses	(101)	-1.44	(56,174)	-2.08	(158)	-0.02
Total loans	3,146	44.95	1,608,091	59.44	310,188	44.03
Other assets	334	4.77	257,947	9.53	143,756	20.41
Total Assets	$6,999	100.00%	$2,705,542	100.00%	$704,507	100.00%
Liabilities and Equity						
Liabilities						
Deposits						
Domestic IPC	$5,351		$1,610,328		$84,373	
Domestic non-IPC	637		130,281		91,930	
Foreign	0		307,061		159,583	
Total deposits	$5,988	85.56%	$2,047,670	75.68%	$335,886	47.68%
Federal funds purchased	23	0.33	221,106	8.17	81,527	11.57
Other liabilities for borrowed money	12	0.17	140,895	5.21	132,475	18.80
Other liabilities	90	1.29	101,789	3.76	54,311	7.71
Total liabilities	$6,113	87.34%	$2,511,460	92.83%	$604,199	85.76%

TABLE 12.2 *CONTINUED* | **Distribution of Assets: Domestic Banks More Than 3 Years Old and Foreign Banks, Year-End 1991**

Asset and liability categories as a proportion of total assets differ considerably between the smallest and largest domestically chartered banks. Foreign banks operating in the United States also have different financial structures, although they compete directly with large domestic banks.

	Average Domestic Bank Less Than $10 Million (469 Banks)		Average Domestic Bank More Than $300 Million (987 Banks)		Foreign Bank Offices in the United States (581 Offices)	
	Thousands	% of Total	Thousands	% of Total	Millions	% of Total
Subordinated notes and debentures and limited-life preferred stock	1	0.00	24,779	0.92		
Equity capital					NA[a]	
Perpetual preferred and common stock	206	2.94	22,360	0.83		
Surplus	438	6.26	76,627	2.83	NA[a]	
Undivided profits and reserves	241	3.44	71,009	2.62		
Foreign currency translation adjustment	0	0.00	(693)	−0.03		
Total equity capital	885	12.64	169,303	6.26		
Liabilities to related institutions	NA[a]		NA[a]		100,308	14.24
Total Liabilities and Equity	$6,999	100.00%	$2,705,542	100.00%	$704,507	100.00%

[a]NA, Not applicable.

Source: Prepared by the authors with data from the Board of Governors of the Federal Reserve System, Division of Research and Statistics, unpublished; "Assets and Liabilities of U.S. Branches and Agencies of Foreign Banks," *Federal Reserve Bulletin* 78 (May 1992): A76–78.

mortgages. Historically, they had been less important to banks than to other depository institutions, although recently banks have made substantial inroads into the mortgage markets as a result of the thrift crisis. In fact, for banks in general, real estate loans (primarily residential mortgages) are the largest loan category.

Commercial and industrial (C&I) loans are a different story. They are made to corporations, partnerships, and proprietorships for all purposes other than personal, family or household, or charitable uses. They are usually short-term, ranging in maturity from a few months to 5 or more years. Included are not only individually negotiated loans between a bank and a borrower but also assets such as the bankers' acceptances of other banks. As a proportion of total assets, they are much more important for large banks than for small banks.

Traditionally, C&I loans have been the specialty of commercial banks. In recent years, banks have faced increasing competition from other commercial lenders, especially finance companies, insurance companies, mutual funds, and securities firms. They also face *de jure* (legally authorized) but not substantial *de facto* (actual) competition from other depositories, as shown later in this chapter.

Consumer loans are primarily installment loans to individuals for all purposes other than residential mortgages or mobile homes. Included are loans for automobiles and other vehicles, education, and travel, as well as credit extended through credit cards. Most financial institutions have entered the consumer credit market in recent years, escalating competition. Large banks invest a slightly higher percentage of assets in consumer loans than do small banks.

"Other loans" include a wide variety of credit-granting activities such as loans of nonfed funds to other financial institutions; loans for the purchase of securities (made to brokers, dealers, and individuals); loans to not-for-profit organizations; loans to governments; and loans not clearly falling into any of the other categories.

The category "unearned income and allowance for possible loan losses" is a deduction arising from two sources. Unearned income is interest paid in advance on discounted loans and is deducted because, as discussed in Chapter 5, it is actually income to the bank and not principal extended to the borrower. The allowance for possible loan losses is an estimate of the

dollar amount of uncollectible loans. For banks with assets of more than $500 million, this account is used only for financial and regulatory reporting. For tax purposes, it is being phased out in accordance with the Tax Reform Act of 1986. More information on loan loss accounting is given in later chapters.

Perhaps the central asset management problem in a depository institution is managing the loan portfolio, including credit analysis of individual borrowers and decisions about the appropriate mix among different categories of loans. Unlike bonds and stocks, some of these financial assets may not be marketable if the original lender needs cash unexpectedly. Furthermore, information available to the lender before a credit-granting decision is always less than perfect. Although present in any investment decision, the problem is more significant in small, local financial markets compared with, for example, the Treasury security markets. In the late 1980s, large banks began to explore opportunities for packaging and selling parts of their commercial loan portfolios (securitization) to an extent not possible in earlier decades. But the time when banks merely originate loans with no intention of holding them to maturity is still several years away. Thus, credit analysis and management remain an important activity for banks of all sizes. These problems and others in managing the loan portfolio are discussed in Chapters 14 and 15.

OTHER ASSETS

The final asset category in Table 12.2 is a catch-all. Its main component is bank premises and equipment, such as computers and electronic banking machinery, although assets acquired by repossessing the property of borrowers in default also is included. Because large institutions are more likely to have corporate headquarters buildings and extensive branch networks, this category comprises a substantially higher proportion of their assets than it does for the smallest banks. A long-term commitment of funds is clearly required for these activities.

Historically, bank premises and equipment have been considered nonearning because they do not bear an explicit rate of return as securities and loans do. But because they provide necessary services for customers and may increase employee productivity, they are important to the success of financial institutions. Long-term asset decisions for depository institutions are discussed in Chapter 20.

LIABILITIES OF COMMERCIAL BANKS

By definition, the main liabilities of depository institutions are deposits. The generic term *deposits* includes many types of accounts, all of which are financial liabilities of the institution and financial assets of depositors. Also, depositories have various nondeposit liabilities. Chapter 16 is devoted to liability management in depositories, and the following discussion is intended only as a brief overview.

DEPOSITS IN GENERAL

Table 12.2 divides deposits according to type of depositor. Although not reported separately, within each of the three categories are accounts with varying interest rate, transactions, and maturity characteristics. Some of these account categories are discussed in this section.

Domestic individual, partnership, and corporate **(IPC)** accounts are a large majority of deposits for banks of all sizes. Domestic non-IPC deposits are mostly those of financial institutions and governmental units; few are held by smaller institutions. Small banks seldom have offices overseas, but for large banks, deposits in foreign offices can be important sources of funds. Among the most notable types of foreign deposits is the **Eurodollar deposit,** a deposit account denominated in dollars but held outside the United States. At the time of their origination, most of these deposits were in Europe—hence the name *Eurodollars*. Today, dollar-denominated deposits are held all over the world, but the term *Eurodollar* continues to be used. Eurodollar deposits are an important tool of liability management in large banks and are discussed in more detail in Chapter 16.

DEPOSITS: TRANSACTIONS ACCOUNTS

Transactions accounts—those on which checks can be written—include demand deposits and negotiable orders of withdrawal (NOWs). Reserve require-

ments are highest on these deposits. Some transactions accounts are interest-bearing and some are not.

DEMAND DEPOSITS. Demand deposits are noninterest-bearing accounts from which the institution must provide cash on the request of the account holder; that is, demand deposits are traditional checking accounts. No other transactions accounts carry this immediate legal obligation. Demand deposits are eligible for federal deposit insurance up to $100,000. Although savings banks and S&Ls are permitted to issue demand deposits, neither has given commercial banks much competition in this market.

NOWs. First defined in Chapter 2, a NOW account is an interest-bearing checking account. It differs from a demand deposit in that, technically, an institution is not required to honor NOW checks immediately but may withhold payment for 7 days or more. NOWs have no legal maturity nor any limitations on the number of checks that may be written per month. Not-for-profit organizations may have them, but businesses do not qualify for NOWs.

TIME AND SAVINGS DEPOSITS

Time and savings deposits include interest-bearing deposits that customers hold for both transactions and investment purposes and those held for investment purposes alone. **Savings deposits** have no specified period for which funds must be left on deposit to avoid an early-withdrawal penalty. **Time deposits** have a specified maturity date. Withdrawal before maturity results in the forfeiture of some interest earned before withdrawal. In some cases, even part of the principal may be forfeited. Fed regulations may require depositories to hold reserves against all *nonpersonal* time and savings deposits—that is, accounts "in which a beneficial interest is held by a depositor that is not a natural person"—but in recent years, the Fed has required no reserves against these accounts.[8]

MONEY MARKET DEPOSIT ACCOUNTS. First discussed in Chapter 2, money market deposit accounts

---

[8] Board of Governors of the Federal Reserve System, "Regulation D Reserve Requirements of Depository Institutions," Section 204.2, as amended effective June 20, 1983. As of April 1, 1986, rules for withdrawal penalties were transferred from Reg Q to Reg D.

(MMDAs) are a relatively new form of hybrid transactions/savings instrument. The depositor may write a limited number of checks per month on an MMDA, but when the Fed assesses reserve requirements, it does not consider MMDAs to be transactions accounts. The institution may require a 7-day notice for withdrawal, but few do. The yield on MMDAs exceeds that on NOWs because the depositor gives up the unlimited transactions feature. Interest rates are variable and may be adjusted once a month or even more often. Introduced in December 1982, they became, for depository institutions as a whole, the fastest growing accounts in history.

PASSBOOK SAVINGS ACCOUNTS. Passbook savings accounts are nontransactions accounts without a maturity date. "Nontransactions" means that the account owner may not transfer funds from a savings account directly to a third party—someone besides the depositor or the depository institution. Still, passbook savings deposits (so-called because ownership is evidenced by a small account book) are quite liquid because an individual may withdraw funds on very short notice. In exchange for the liquidity, depositors accept a relatively low interest rate. Historically, however, most of these deposits have involved very few transactions per month, requiring little administrative cost to the institution. For many years, they were one of the most stable sources of funds to which a depository had access.

Until 1986, the maximum rate that could be paid on passbooks was fixed well below market levels, making them among the lowest cost of all sources of funds. However, because of the advent of MMDAs and other liquid accounts paying market rates of interest, the passbook account is a diminishing source of funds to depositories. Although not shown in Table 12.2, small banks have proportionately more passbook deposits than do large banks whose customers are primarily large corporations.

CERTIFICATES OF DEPOSIT. The most important type of time deposit is the certificate of deposit (CD), an interest-bearing account with a specified maturity date. CDs are available in all denominations, with variable and fixed rates across the entire spectrum of maturities. Most involve penalties to the depositor for early withdrawal. For this reason, a secondary market for negotiable CDs, previously discussed in Chapter 5, was de-

veloped to allow large depositors to sell their deposits to other investors if they need cash before the maturity date. CDs with denominations less than $100,000 are nonnegotiable, and depositors wishing to avoid penalties must hold their CDs until maturity.

INDIVIDUAL RETIREMENT ACCOUNTS. Individual retirement accounts (IRAs) are time deposits with special tax benefits for consumer depositors. Although annual dollar deposits are limited by federal law, federal tax on contributions by eligible depositors is deferred until withdrawal of funds after age 59½. All taxpayers not covered by an employer-sponsored pension plan are eligible for the tax deferment on contributions, as are taxpayers covered by employer-sponsored pensions but with income below a specified level. All taxpayers, regardless of income or coverage by other pension plans, are eligible for deferment of interest earned on IRA accounts.

BORROWINGS

Besides deposits, banks have nondeposit liabilities. Sources of nondeposit borrowing vary according to bank size.

FEDERAL FUNDS PURCHASED. Federal funds purchased are reserves borrowed from other depositories and are a substantially larger obligation for large banks than for small ones. Repurchase agreements that are liabilities of a bank are also included in this category. The role of these nondeposit obligations in liability management is discussed in Chapter 16.

OTHER LIABILITIES FOR BORROWED MONEY. Other liabilities for borrowed money include miscellaneous debt obligations of the bank, some of which are loans from the Fed's discount window. Use of the discount window is a tool of bank liquidity management and is discussed in Chapter 13. In addition, bankers' acceptances to which the bank is obligated are included in this category. Because only large banks are involved in international finance, this liability category is considerably larger for the average bank with more than $300 million in assets than for other banks.

OTHER LIABILITIES. The "other liabilities" category is comparable to accounts payable and accrued expenses for nonfinancial corporations.

**SUBORDINATED NOTES AND DEBENTURES. Subor-
dinated notes** and **debentures** are long-term, unsecured debt obligations, analogous to the unsecured
bonds of other corporations. Although they are legal
liabilities of the institution, under certain circumstances regulators count them when deciding whether
the depository has adequate capital to protect
depositors.

Subordinated notes and debentures are a relatively small proportion of even the largest banks' total
obligations. They can usually be marketed only by institutions with a presence beyond their local communities. These instruments have an important role explored in Chapter 17.

EQUITY CAPITAL (NET WORTH) OF COMMERCIAL BANKS

As they do for all corporations, the preferred
stock and common stock accounts reflect the par value
of the bank's equity securities. Some net worth accounts, however, are peculiar to bank accounting. A
bank's **surplus** account is the total of proceeds from
the sale of equity securities in excess of their par value,
plus earnings retained until the surplus account equals
the common stock account. **Undivided profits** are
earnings retained in excess of those included in the
surplus account. **Reserves** are portions of retained
earnings set aside to provide a cushion against losses
on securities or other contingencies, such as lawsuits
in which the bank is involved. For reasons apparent in
Chapter 17, equity capital as a percentage of total assets is almost twice as high for small banks as it is for
large ones. Regulations in force since the early 1990s,
however, have already resulted in increased levels of
capital for large banks. Details are provided in Chapter
17.

Reserves in this section of the balance sheet
should not be confused with the reserves of an institution held to comply with Fed reserve requirement regulations. The latter are noninterest-bearing *assets,* accounted for in the cash and due account.

OFF−BALANCE SHEET ACTIVITIES

A category of growing importance in commercial bank asset/liability management is not reflected in
Table 12.2 because in 1991 it was not yet subject to
standard financial reporting procedures. These activi-

ties, traditionally called off−balance sheet items, include positions in financial futures contracts, interest
rate swap agreements, and standby letters by credit,
among others. As first mentioned in Chapter 2, the
Federal Deposit Insurance Corporation Improvement
Act (FDICIA) requires regulators and managers to
focus a great deal of attention on these emerging areas,
including new financial reporting methods. Their impact on asset/liability management and financial institution performance is explored in more detail in Chapters 17, 19, and 22.

INCOME AND EXPENSES OF COMMERCIAL BANKS

It follows logically from a balance sheet analysis that
the income and expenses of small and large banks differ. Table 12.3 presents the percentage distribution of
income and expenses for typical small and large banks
in 1991.

INCOME OF COMMERCIAL BANKS

Commercial banks derive income primarily
from lending and the securities portfolio.

INTEREST INCOME. The categories of interest income
in Table 12.3 correspond in general to the categories
of interest-earning assets on the balance sheets in
Table 12.2. Because loans are a larger proportion of
assets at large banks, interest and fees on loans are a
more important source of their income than for smaller
banks. Small banks are more dependent on income
from securities and fed funds sold, as expected from
the relative size of their securities and fed funds
portfolios.

SERVICE CHARGES ON DEPOSITS. Service charges
are a small proportion of operating income for banks
of all sizes, but they are more important for small
banks. Deposits are more than 85 percent of the funds
sources of small banks but only about 75 percent for
large banks.

ALL OTHER OPERATING INCOME. Because of their
role as **correspondent banks,** large banks derive income from nondeposit activities. In exchange for a fee,
correspondent banks assist smaller institutions with

TABLE 12.3   **Distribution of Income and Expenses: Banks More Than 3 Years Old, 1991**

Income and expense profiles of large and small banks differ. Large banks were less profitable in 1991, although that relationship does not always hold.

	Average Bank Less Than $10 Million (469 Banks)		Average Bank More Than $300 Million (987 Banks)	
	Thousands	% of Total	Thousands	% of Total
Operating Income				
Interest income				
Interest and fees on loans	$406		$171,401	
Interest on balances at depository institutions	26		8,303	
Income on federal funds sold	36		6,647	
Income on securities	173		40,601	
Total interest income	$641	81.35%	$226,952	81.26%
Service charges on deposits	37	4.70	9,769	3.50
Other operating income	110	13.96	42,562	15.24
Total operating income	$788	100.00%	$279,283	100.00%
Operating Expenses				
Interest expense				
Interest on deposits	$318		$105,694	
Expense of federal funds purchased	1		13,851	
Interest on other borrowed money	4		11,947	
Interest on subordinated notes and debentures	0		2,191	
Total interest expense	$323	44.99%	$133,683	50.66%
Provision for loan losses	23	3.20	30,499	11.56
Salaries and employee benefits	173	24.09	41,797	15.84
Other noninterest operating expense	199	27.72	57,922	21.95
Total operating expenses	$718	100.00%	$263,901	100.00%
Net Operating Income	$70	8.88%[a]	$15,382	5.51%
Less taxes	(24)		(5,891)	
Extraordinary items (including net security gains and losses)	3		3,156	
Net Income	$49	6.22%[a]	$12,647	4.53%

[a] Percentage of total operating income.
Source: Prepared by the authors with data from the Board of Governors of the Federal Reserve System, Division of Research and Statistics, unpublished, 1991.

check clearing, cash and portfolio management, and reserve account management, to name but a few services. Also, large banks have led in developing new fee-based services (such as discount brokerage operations and cash management advice), from which they earn noninterest income. Noninterest income also includes profits from trading foreign currencies. Because small banks are seldom involved in these activities, a smaller portion of their operating income arises from these sources.

It is clear why attention to the net interest margin (NIM) is a chief objective of financial institution management. Recall that the NIM is calculated as (Interest Income − Interest Expense)/Total Assets and is a key measure of success for financial institutions. Interest income, one of the key components of NIM, is the overriding source of profits. The next section reveals the role of another key component—interest expense.

EXPENSES OF COMMERCIAL BANKS

Small and large banks also have different expenses.

INTEREST EXPENSE. Interest expenses, especially interest on deposits, dominate total expenses. Although small banks have proportionately more deposit liabilities, their interest expenses are lower as a proportion of total expenses. This difference often arises because larger banks tend to participate in more competitive markets, vying for customers within an entire geographic region or even nationally and internationally. They also have a smaller proportion of traditional savings accounts, which cost less than sources of funds such as negotiable CDs. Because small banks issue almost no subordinated notes and debentures and purchase only minimal amounts of fed funds, other categories of interest expense are also less important to them.

investor, governor, institution

PROVISION FOR LOAN LOSSES. The provision for loan losses is analogous to the "bad debt expense" on the income statements of nonfinancial firms. It is an *estimate* of uncollectible loans, not a report of actual losses during the period. In 1991, loan loss provisions were much higher for large banks than for small ones. Large banks' losses reflect problems in the commercial real estate sector. Recently, however, neither small nor large banks consistently reported higher loan losses.

The Tax Reform Act of 1986 revised the method used by large banks—those with assets in excess of $500 million—to report loan losses for tax purposes. (All banks controlled by a single holding company are grouped together when the $500 million asset test is applied.) Since 1987, large banks or bank holding company subsidiaries have been able to deduct only *actual* losses on loans made after 1986 from taxable income. They may continue to report *estimates* of losses on loans made before January 1, 1987. On their financial statements, however, large banks continue to estimate *potential* losses and deduct this provision from operating income.

SALARIES AND EMPLOYEE BENEFITS. The smallest banks have a higher percentage of expenses in salaries and wages, demonstrating the traditional labor-intensive nature of banking. Although larger banks have widely adopted electronic banking, the high cost of automation has slowed smaller banks' adoption of technology-driven approaches to delivering services. Hence, their employee expenses remain higher.

OTHER NONINTEREST OPERATING EXPENSE. Other noninterest operating expense includes expenses incurred for bank premises, such as depreciation. Supplies and advertising expenses are also included.

PROFITS IN COMMERCIAL BANKING

Several measures of performance are customarily computed and analyzed for commercial banks. As noted in earlier chapters, the NIM is an important indicator of the quality of asset/liability management. Using data from Table 12.3, in 1991, the NIM for the average small bank was [($641 − $323)/$6,999] = 0.0454 = 4.54 percent. The average large bank earned [($226,952 − $133,683)/$2,705,542] = 0.0345 = 3.45 percent. The more competitive markets in which large banks must attract funds and make investments contributed to their lower NIM compared with smaller banks. In fact, small banks' NIMs have been improving steadily since 1987, whereas large banks' performance has been much less consistent.[9]

A second profit measure quoted for commercial banks is **net operating income,** or the difference between total operating income and total operating expense. Table 12.3 shows this amount as a dollar figure and as a percentage of total operating income. Financial institutions typically report capital gains and losses separately, because securities transactions are a substantial portion of their operations but involve management strategies different from those of the loan portfolio. The **net income** of banks reflects the effect of all managerial activities on profits for the reporting period. For the average large bank, net income was between 4 percent and 5 percent of each dollar of operating income in 1991. The smallest banks were more

[9] See Goudreau, 1992; Brunner, Hancock, and McLaughlin 1992; and Goudreau and King 1991.

profitable, primarily because they had lower loan loss provisions.

FOREIGN VERSUS DOMESTICALLY CHARTERED BANKS IN THE UNITED STATES

As noted earlier, the right panel of Table 12.2 shows 1991 balance sheet data on 581 branches and agencies of foreign banks operating in the United States. About 80 percent (458) of these banking offices are in just three states—New York, California, and Illinois. The data are not strictly comparable with those for domestically chartered banks in the same table. First, the data on domestically chartered institutions are presented for the average, or typical, institution in a size group, whereas the foreign branch and agency data are aggregate. Also, the data on foreign branches and agencies do not reflect the operations of the *total* organizations of which the branches and agencies are but subsidiaries. Thus, the foreign entities on which data are reported in the table are not corporations for which equity capital accounts are meaningful. Still, the percentage data on assets and liabilities are useful for making broad comparisons about the activities of international banks in the United States.

ASSETS OF FOREIGN BRANCHES AND AGENCIES

At the end of 1991, foreign banks' branches and agencies had a much larger proportion of assets in the "cash and due" account than did the average large, domestically chartered bank. A large proportion of the "cash and due" account for foreign banks, however, is in the form of interest-earning deposits at other banks, including banks outside the United States. In contrast, domestic banks, as one might expect, hold larger proportions of U.S. government securities than do foreign branches and agencies.

The loan portfolios of foreign subsidiaries are markedly different from those of large, domestically chartered commercial banks. Foreign banks have thus far shown little interest in consumer lending in the United States, choosing to avoid the relatively large degree to which that activity is regulated. They have also shown little interest in real estate lending in the United States. Compared with domestic institutions, however, a larger proportion of the loan portfolio of foreign branches and agencies is invested in commer-

cial loans. Although not shown in the table, these loans are primarily those to U.S. businesses. Thus, these institutions successfully compete toe-to-toe with domestically chartered banks in the latter's home territory. Indeed, data from the Federal Reserve Bank of Chicago show that the share of C&I loans granted by U.S. branches of foreign banks rose from 8.6 percent in 1980 to 14.4 percent in 1988, an increase entirely attributable to the success of Japanese banks in the United States. Ironically, by selling C&I loans to their foreign competitors, domestic banks have themselves further contributed to the growing presence of non-U.S. banks in commercial lending markets.

The "all other" loan category is also larger for foreign organizations. This account includes loans to foreign governments and to other subsidiaries within the foreign entities' parent organization.

LIABILITIES OF FOREIGN BRANCHES AND AGENCIES

The liabilities of foreign branches and agencies show their heavy reliance on foreign deposits. This is an important observation, because, along with the data on commercial lending, it indicates that at the time these data were prepared, foreign organizations were not siphoning funds from the United States for lending abroad. Rather, they were aiding the flow of capital to the United States.

The "other liabilities" account is relatively large for foreign branches and agencies; most of these liabilities are owed to U.S. commercial banks. The final item, "liabilities to related institutions," primarily reflects the investment of parent companies in their U.S. subsidiaries. To the extent that this account is roughly comparable with the net worth of these entities, they have relatively higher capital than the typical large, domestically chartered bank. Although not shown in Table 12.2, data indicate that foreign institutions have a head start compared with U.S. banks in complying with the stricter capital requirements of the Basle Accord. Therefore, foreign banks may be able to grow more rapidly over the next decade.

FOREIGN BANKS IN THE 1990s

In sum, Table 12.2 shows that foreign organizations lend to U.S. firms, borrow from U.S. banks, and use less leverage than many large domestic banks. These data suggest that foreign branches and agencies are unlikely to have a detrimental effect in U.S. markets. In fact, some analysts attribute the modest growth in commercial lending in the early 1990s solely to the willingness of foreign banks in the United States to lend. Although domestic banks seemed crippled by weak balance sheets and fearful of the increased regulatory scrutiny under FIRREA and FDICIA, many foreign banks, bolstered by their relatively strong capital positions, actively sought new U.S. business customers. Although recent economic setbacks in both Germany and Japan may slow the growth of their banks outside the home countries, most observers continue to predict that these and other foreign banks will be formidable competitors for domestic banks for many years to come.[10]

SAVINGS INSTITUTIONS: INDUSTRY STRUCTURE

The second largest group of depositories, measured by total assets, are the savings institutions. As noted earlier, savings institutions are divided into two subgroups: S&Ls and savings banks. Both types of institutions were founded to promote thrift among customers.[11]

DIFFERENCES BETWEEN SAVINGS BANKS AND S&Ls

Savings banks arose in the 1700s because no existing institutions were willing to accept savings deposits from a growing population of workers. By the time the population moved west, commercial banks had turned their attention to individual as well as business customers, so the savings bank movement was never established outside the Northeast. Furthermore, a new type of institution with a dual interest in promoting thrift and home ownership emerged by the 1800s, the forerunner of the modern S&L. S&Ls spread nationwide with the population.

Important regulatory and operating differences separated S&Ls and savings banks for most of their

history. Savings banks could issue demand deposits and make commercial loans in limited amounts. Unlike other depositories, they could also invest in corporate stock. S&Ls' asset choices were greatly restricted until 1980 because a combination of regulations and tax laws virtually assured that more than 80 percent of their assets were mortgage-related. Today, both types of thrifts may invest a small percentage of their assets in commercial loans and may issue traditional demand deposits. With minor exceptions, however, S&Ls are prohibited from investing in corporate stock. FIRREA reinstated provisions limiting investment alternatives for thrifts.

In the past, chartering and insurance regulations differed markedly for the two types of thrifts. In 1989, FIRREA's overhaul of the regulatory structure produced further changes. With the abolition of the Federal Home Loan Bank Board (FHLBB), chartering for all federal thrifts, whether savings banks or S&Ls, is handled by the Office of Thrift Supervision (OTS). States may still charter thrifts of both types, although the activities in which states allow thrifts to engage may be no more permissive than those allowed to comparable federally chartered thrifts.

All federally chartered thrifts *and* state-chartered S&Ls are insured by SAIF, but state-chartered savings banks are insured by BIF. This is more than a cosmetic difference. Until 1998, deposit insurance premiums may be higher under SAIF than under BIF, because Congress mandated in FIRREA that institutions formerly insured by the Federal Savings and Loan Insurance Corporation (FSLIC) (and now insured by SAIF) must partially pay the cost of cleaning up the industry. Thus, new federal thrift charters have seemed particularly undesirable in recent years. Indeed, to prevent existing federal thrifts from switching *en masse* to become state-chartered savings banks, FIRREA also imposed a 5-year moratorium on switching insurance funds, except in special circumstances specifically approved by FDIC officials.

SIZE OF SAVINGS INSTITUTIONS

Like commercial banking, the thrift industry is not homogeneous. Table 12.4 presents the size distribution of all federally insured thrift institutions as of early 1991. The largest firms in the table, less than 10 percent of the industry, held more than 65 percent of the assets. Even the largest thrifts, however, are much

---

[10]For more information on foreign banks in the United States, see Misback 1993; Kraus 1993; Joseph 1992; Baer 1990; and Cohen 1989.

[11]For more details on the history of savings institutions, see Blyn 1981; Kulczycky 1981; and Linnen 1983.

TABLE 12.4   Size Distribution of All Federally Insured Thrift Institutions by Total Assets, March 31, 1991

Like commercial banking, the thrift industry is also concentrated, with about 15 percent of all firms holding more than 75 percent of the industry's assets.

Size Category	Firms in Category	% of Total Firms	% of Industry Assets
Less than $100 million	1,387	46.95%	5.20%
$100 million to less than $500 million	1,111	37.61	18.61
$500 million to less than $1 billion	206	6.97	11.02
$1 billion and over	250	8.46	65.17
Total, all sizes	2,954	100.00%	100.00%

Source: National Council of Savings Institutions, *Economic Commentary,* August 1991.

smaller than the largest commercial banks. The largest savings institution in 1991, Home Savings of America, had total assets of just over $50 billion compared with Citicorp's nearly $217 billion.

THE BALANCE SHEET OF SAVINGS INSTITUTIONS

After the Depository Institutions Deregulation and Monetary Control Act (DIDMCA), it became common for savings institutions to be viewed as quite similar to commercial banks. In fact, both types of depositories are legally permitted to engage in many of the same activities, and many of the assets and liabilities described earlier are found in thrifts. Furthermore, managerial issues in the two types of depositories are similar, because all managers must be concerned with liquidity and capital, credit analysis, and interest rate risk. In the 1990s, however, substantial differences remain in the balance sheets of banks and thrifts. Reasons for these persistent differences and their impact on the recent performance of the two types of institutions are explored in the latter part of this chapter.

Table 12.5 presents the distribution of assets and liabilities for all federally insured savings institutions as of early 1991. Information is divided into that for institutions insured by SAIF and that for institutions insured by BIF. As noted earlier, the SAIF group is S&Ls (including 204 failed thrifts then consigned to the Resolution Trust Corporation [RTC]) and federally chartered savings banks, and the BIF group primarily includes state-chartered savings banks. These data are not strictly comparable with those for domestically

chartered banks in Table 12.2, because the bank data are institutional averages and the thrift data are industry totals. Still, general assessments are possible.

ASSETS OF SAVINGS INSTITUTIONS

BIF-insured institutions had a higher proportion of assets invested in cash and securities than did SAIF-insured institutions. Savings banks have for many years had broader authority to invest in securities than S&Ls, and the BIF group includes no S&Ls.

For the thrift industry as a whole, cash and securities were a much smaller percentage of total assets than for the average commercial bank, reflecting the fact that, because they have fewer transactions accounts, thrifts' liquidity needs are lower.

LOANS. A comparison of the loan portfolios of SAIF- and BIF-insured institutions shows that mortgages and related assets are slightly more important for SAIF-insured thrifts than for those insured by BIF. Commercial loans are included in the "other loans" category in the table. Despite authority to make commercial loans since Garn-St Germain, the SAIF-insured group had few by 1991. BIF-insured thrifts, with the freedom to make C&I loans for a much longer period, also had very few. Consequently, although they were about 30 percent of the loan portfolio of the average large commercial bank and about 20 percent of total assets, C&I loans were less than 3 percent of thrift industry assets in 1991. Even nonmortgage consumer loans, which thrifts made to a much greater extent than commercial loans, were about 4.5 percent of thrift assets, compared with more than 10 percent for the average large

TABLE 12.5 Distribution of Assets: All Federally Insured Savings Institutions, March 31, 1991

The balance sheets of savings institutions differ between the industry's two major branches. The SAIF-insured group, primarily S&Ls, has much lower net worth as a result of recent profitability problems.

	SAIF-Insured (2,487 Institutions)		BIF-Insured (467 Institutions)		All Federally Insured (2,954 Institutions)	
	Millions	% of Total	Millions	% of Total	Millions	% of Total
Assets						
Cash and securities	$ 116,485	11.18%	$ 38,790	14.91%	$ 155,276	11.92%
Loans						
Mortgages and related assets	$788,292	75.64%	$185,756	71.39%	$ 974,048	74.79%
Consumer	47,636	4.57	9,902	3.81	57,538	4.42
Other loans (includes commercial loans)	23,004	2.21	11,194	4.30	34,198	2.63
Total loans	858,932	82.42	206,852	79.50	1,065,784	81.83
Other assets	66,766	6.41	14,542	5.59	81,308	6.24
Total assets	$1,042,183	100.00%	$260,184	100.00%	$1,302,368	100.00%
Liabilities and Net Worth						
Liabilities						
Deposits						
Savings	$156,710		$ 68,193		$224,903	
Time	604,653		130,669		735,322	
Other	55,647		15,424		71,071	
Total deposits	$817,010	78.39%	$214,286	82.36%	$1,031,297	79.19%
Other liabilities for borrowed money	165,868	15.92	24,940	9.59	190,808	14.65
Other liabilities	23,797	2.28	3,484	1.34	27,281	2.09
Total liabilities	$1,006,675	96.59%	$242,710	93.28%	$1,249,386	95.93%
Net worth	35,508	3.41	17,474	6.72	52,982	4.07
Total liabilities and net worth	$1,042,183	100.00%	$260,184	100.00%	$1,302,368	100.00%

Source: National Council of Savings Institutions, *Economic Update*, August 1991.

commercial bank. FIRREA and FDICIA provisions placed limits on commercial and consumer loans permissible for thrifts, restricting them to 10 percent and 35 percent, respectively, of total assets. Other categories of nonmortgage lending were also limited.

ASSET DIFFERENCES BETWEEN BANKS AND THRIFTS. Several differences between depositories emerge from the tables. One of the most important is that asset maturity for the average commercial bank is shorter than for savings institutions. From the lessons of the bond theorems and duration, it follows that thrifts' exposure to interest rate risk is greater than that of commercial banks.

In addition, commercial banks have more diversified portfolios than thrifts, especially those insured by SAIF, despite broadened investment powers for thrifts since 1980. The main implication of this lack of diversification is that thrifts are more vulnerable to performance declines because of developments in a single financial market.

Research indicates that traditional mortgage-dominated portfolios are not simply a function of the recency with which federally chartered thrifts have been given expanded powers. Studies of S&L diversification by economists at the Federal Reserve Bank of Atlanta have indicated that, even in state-chartered institutions with expanded powers for more than a decade, few nontraditional assets are held, primarily because many managers consider the cost of developing expertise in those areas to be prohibitive. Even more recently, researchers from the Board of Governors of the Fed found similar results, using a national sample of thrifts. They predicted that, with the exception of several large mutual savings banks in the Northeast, most thrifts would continue to favor their traditional lines of business well into the future. Besides a lack of expertise in exercising their expanded powers, the Fed researchers based their prediction on constraints on thrift expansion posed by the severe net worth shortage in the industry, increased demand for mortgage loans from potential homebuyers, more attractive mortgage loan terms for thrifts than those available to them in the early 1980s, and favorable tax benefits associated with mortgage lending. This study was conducted before the passage of FIRREA, and data in Table 12.5 bear out the prediction. However, because many customers have recently abandoned thrifts in favor of other depositories, the thrift industry's share of the total mortgage loan market is likely to decline.[12]

DEPOSITS OF SAVINGS INSTITUTIONS

Like commercial banks, savings institutions raise funds primarily from customer deposits. Also like banks, they are authorized to issue traditional demand deposits (called **noninterest NOWs** or **NINOWs**), as well as NOWs, MMDAs, passbook accounts, and CDs of all types. NINOWs are of virtually no importance to thrifts. NOWs, however, have become more significant for thrifts since their nationwide authorization in 1980. MMDAs have also greatly increased in importance since 1982, and passbook accounts have correspondingly declined with the rise in new transactions and market-rate savings vehicles. Because depositors abandoned passbook savings in favor of market-sensitive deposits, the cost of funds to thrifts skyrocketed during the 1980s, when market interest rates were relatively high compared with previous decades.

As noted earlier, thrift assets changed very little during the period when deposit structures were undergoing the most change. Thus, thrift assets remain heavily tied to long-term investments on which yields, even if variable over the life of the loan, change less often than the costs of liabilities. Also, in the eyes of depositors, a thrift's liabilities are highly liquid, whereas its assets, in the eyes of homeowners whose mortgages are those assets, are quite illiquid. Managing the net interest margin of a savings institution is clearly a challenge in a deregulated environment.

OTHER LIABILITIES OF SAVINGS INSTITUTIONS

In Table 12.5, the major component of liabilities for borrowed money in SAIF-insured institutions is advances from the regulators, especially the Federal Home Loan Banks, used to meet liquidity and other

---

[12]Goudreau 1984a and b; Goudreau and Ford 1986; Burke, Rhoades, and Wolken 1987; and Michael L. Wilson, "Differences Among Depositories Aren't Disappearing Yet." *Savings Institutions* 113 (April 1992): 14–15.

operating needs. Because BIF-insured institutions lack access to this source of funding, other liabilities for borrowed money are less important for them.

Further items included in the category of other liabilities for borrowed money are subordinated notes and debentures issued by stockholder-owned thrifts. Mutually owned thrifts are permitted to issue long-term debt securities called **mutual capital certificates,** quite similar to subordinated notes and debentures and described in more detail in Chapter 17. As with commercial banks, only the largest thrifts find a market for these securities, and they are a relatively small proportion of the liabilities of the industry as a whole. The last category of thrift liabilities, "other liabilities," includes items comparable with accounts payable and accrued expenses on a nonfinancial balance sheet.

NET WORTH OF SAVINGS INSTITUTIONS

A final element of the savings industry balance sheet is its net worth, a term that encompasses the reserves and retained earnings accounts of all institutions, as well as the common stock, preferred stock, and paid-in capital accounts of stockholder-owned institutions. Also included in the net worth of thrifts are unique regulatory sources of capital, such as net worth certificates. These items are accounting entries that under specified conditions were counted as net worth for regulatory purposes during the 1980s. Their use is being phased out under FIRREA, as is explained in Chapter 17.

For the industry as a whole, regulatory net worth was about 4 percent of total sources of funds in 1991. This figure is economically deceptive, however, because most experts agree that regulatory accounting practices lingering at that time significantly overstated the extent to which thrifts', and especially S&Ls', asset values exceeded their liabilities. The high economic concentration in the industry, illustrated previously in Table 12.4, accounts for this relatively low figure. Although most thrifts were solvent, some large institutions had such huge net worth deficits—some with ratios of net worth to assets lower than −20 percent—that the industry average was severely depressed. In fact, industry experts claim that if RTC-controlled institutions were excluded, SAIF-insured thrifts would have had net worth equal to 4.5 percent

of industry average assets in 1991. Still, the net worth cushion for thrifts was, and remains, significantly lower than for the banking industry. As discussed earlier in the book and later in this chapter, an unhappy combination of negative interest rate spreads (in which the cost of deposits exceeded the return on earning assets), sectoral economic difficulties, poor lending practices, lax regulation, and mismanagement led to the dismal state of the industry in recent years.

INCOME AND EXPENSES OF SAVINGS INSTITUTIONS

Table 12.6 presents income and expense data for savings institutions, with and without those consigned to the RTC, at the end of the first quarter of 1991.

INCOME OF SAVINGS INSTITUTIONS

As with commercial banks, the asset composition of the industry is the main determinant of income. Interest and fees (mostly mortgage points) on mortgages are by far the largest source of operating income. Noninterest income, including service charges on deposits, accounted for less operating income for thrifts than for large banks.

EXPENSES OF SAVINGS INSTITUTIONS

Interest expense is a larger portion of total operating expenses for thrifts than for commercial banks, because thrifts have almost no noninterest-bearing deposits. Their noninterest operating expenses, such as salaries, wages, and occupancy expenses, are relatively low compared with commercial banks. In recent years, thrifts have been streamlining operations to cut costs. Because interest costs cannot be cut substantially if a thrift is to remain competitive with other depositories, noninterest operating expenses have been the place to start.

PROFITS OF SAVINGS INSTITUTIONS

Given the potential problems in managing a thrift institution suggested by its asset and liability structure, it is not surprising that thrift institutions had very low net operating income compared with

TABLE 12.6	Income and Expenses: Savings Institutions, First Quarter, 1991

After its weakest members were seized by the RTC, the rest of the industry, helped by falling interest costs on deposits, returned to profitability in 1991. Although this table shows first quarter results only, the entire year was a relatively good one for most thrifts.

	All Savings Institutions (2,954 Firms)		All Except RTC-Held Institutions (2,750 Firms)	
	Millions	**% of Total Income**	**Millions**	**% of Total Income**
Income				
Total interest income	$28,738	93.27%	$27,327	93.09%
Other income (except security gains and losses)	2,075	6.73	2,029	6.91
Total income	$30,813	100.00%	$29,357	100.00%
		% of Total Expense		**% of Total Expense**
Expenses				
Total interest expense	$22,262	71.39%	$20,646	72.29%
Noninterest expenses (except loan losses)	7,212	23.13	6,509	22.79
Provision for loan losses	1,709	5.48	1,406	4.92
Total expenses	$31,183	100.00%	$28,561	100.00%
		% of Total Income		**% of Total Income**
Net Income before Loan Losses and Security Gains and Losses	($371)	−1.20%	$796	2.58%
Security gains (losses)	297	0.96	356	1.16
Extraordinary gains (losses)	(19)	−0.06	(1)	−0.00
Less taxes	714	2.32	712	2.31
Net Income	($807)	−2.62%	$439	1.43%

Source: National Council of Savings Institutions, *Economic Insight,* August 1991.

commercial banks. Expenses, including items such as charge-offs of bad loans, losses on foreclosed real estate, and legal expenses, were so high that the SAIF-insured segment drowned in a sea of red ink in 1991, when RTC institutions are included. As mentioned earlier, a relatively small proportion of the thrift industry accounted for most of these losses; when RTC-held thrifts are excluded, the industry was actually profitable for the year. Nonetheless, the magnitude of the industry's problems cannot be dismissed for that reason. Healthy thrifts were tainted in customers' minds by association with their so-called "zombie" counterparts. Net withdrawals from thrifts continued into the 1990s, despite the federal rescue plan mounted with the passage of FIRREA.

CREDIT UNIONS: INDUSTRY STRUCTURE

The third type of depository is the credit union. CUs are the most numerous of depositories, totaling 13,989 institutions in 1991, most of which are federally insured. As discussed in Chapter 4, CUs are not-for-profit organizations, with members associated through a common bond. Technically, the investments of members are called shares, not deposits, but CUs are viewed as depositories despite this difference in nomenclature.

Like other depositories, CUs may choose either state or federal charters. Federally chartered CUs are regulated by the National Credit Union Administration

(NCUA) and insured by the National Credit Union Share Insurance Fund (NCUSIF), a fund similar to the FDIC. State-chartered CUs may choose to obtain share insurance through NCUSIF, and most do. The ability of CUs to offer federal share insurance is, in fact, a main reason why they are considered depository institutions.

As is true of other depositories, the CU industry is not homogeneous. Differences between small and large CUs are highlighted by Tables 12.7 and 12.8. Table 12.7 presents the percentage distribution of CUs by asset size at year-end 1991. The table shows that most CUs are quite small; almost 70 percent have less than $5 million in total assets. Many small CUs depend heavily on volunteer labor and donated facilities. Other CUs are relatively large, although small in comparison with other depositories. For example, Navy Federal Credit Union, the nation's largest, had only $6.3 billion in assets in mid-1992, making it only a ninth as large as the largest thrift. Nonetheless, large CUs offer services that rival those at many large banks, as shown in Table 12.8.

TABLE 12.7	Size Distribution of CUs by Total Assets, Year-End 1991

CUs, although much smaller than other depositories, are also a concentrated group, with more than 65 percent of CUs having total assets less than $5 million.

Size Category	Category Total	% of Total
$500,000 or less	2,259	20.60%
More than $500,000 to $2 million	3,342	26.50
More than $2 million to $5 million	2,680	19.30
More than $5 million to $50 million	4,729	28.50
More than $50 million	979	5.10
Total reporting CUs, all sizes	13,989	100.00%

Source: Credit Union National Association, *1991 Credit Union Report.*

TABLE 12.8	Services Offered by CUs by Size, 1991

CUs' activities differ considerably according to the size of the CU, with larger CUs offering more diversified products and services.

Service	Percentage Offering Service by Size (Millions)				
	$0–$0.2	$1–$2	$10–$20	$100+	Total CUs
Discount brokerage	0.0%	1.6%	8.9%	26.9%	5.4%
Auto leasing	0.5	0.8	3.3	11.6	2.5
Preauthorized payments	2.6	15.6	54.5	72.4	31.9
Direct deposit					
Federal recurring payments	7.9	32.6	88.0	96.5	54.2
Net pay	15.8	30.7	79.7	95.4	51.2
Money orders	4.4	22.7	63.4	80.3	39.1
Safe deposit boxes	0.5	1.4	10.8	56.3	8.4
Remedial financial counseling	9.6	17.4	40.8	53.0	26.5
Formal financial planning	2.3	2.6	7.1	29.0	5.8
Automatic teller machine cards	0.5	2.2	47.9	95.4	23.7
Debit cards	0.2	1.6	15.0	38.2	8.0
Credit cards	0.8	3.2	64.1	93.0	29.3
Share drafts	1.8	14.8	83.6	97.0	44.2
IRAs	2.0	28.2	84.7	98.1	50.1
Traveler's checks	2.6	29.4	83.0	95.7	49.4
Money market accounts	0.8	5.0	40.1	75.5	21.2
Business checking	2.6	20.4	45.2	42.6	23.6
Wire transfer	1.3	16.3	77.1	94.6	44.1

Source: Adapted from Credit Union National Association, Inc., *1991 Credit Union Report.*

SUPPORT SYSTEMS FOR CREDIT UNIONS

CUs enjoy the benefits of strong trade organizations. Because so many CUs are small, they often need facilities and managerial expertise that larger depositories develop in-house. The largest of the trade organizations is the **Credit Union National Association (CUNA)** and its affiliates. Among the most important affiliates is the **Corporate Credit Union (CCU) Network,** a group of credit unions for credit unions. Individual CUs own interest-earning shares in CCUs; the latter pool the funds of small CUs and invest in money and capital market instruments. CCUs also function similarly to correspondent banks, offering advice, cash management, check processing, and assistance necessary for the operations of individual CUs. Further up the support ladder is the **U.S. Central Credit Union,** of which CCUs are themselves members. This large institution, with assets of $28 billion at year-end 1991, manages investments and provides a wide array of other services for CCUs, including product research and development.[13]

The credit union industry also enjoys the benefits of popular support. At year-end 1991, estimated total membership in CUs in the United States exceeded 62 million. Although more citizens probably have a commercial banking relationship, banks do not share the cooperative image of CUs. A recent survey cited in a leading banking publication indicated that CUs' customers are generally more satisfied than are those of banks and thrifts. What CUs lack in size, they make up for in customer loyalty.[14]

BALANCE SHEET OF CREDIT UNIONS

Table 12.9 presents the balance sheet of the CU industry as of year-end 1991. Included are data for all federally chartered CUs as well as for a larger group voluntarily reporting financial information to CUNA.

ASSETS OF CREDIT UNIONS

Compared with other depositories, the asset structure of credit unions is simple. They are permitted to make loans only to members, many of which are for automobile financing. Since 1979, federal CUs have been able to offer home mortgages, and they remain a relatively small but growing portion of the industry's total portfolio. Given the experience of thrifts after 1979, CUs have benefited from slow progress into mortgage lending. Additional consumer credit is extended for educational purposes and through credit cards, especially by larger CUs. Some state-chartered CUs are permitted to make commercial loans, but few have chosen to do so.

The remainder of CU assets is concentrated in cash, investments in the Corporate Credit Union Network, Treasury and federal agency securities, and deposits in commercial banks and savings institutions. Because most CUs are too small to fall under the Fed's reserve requirements and because they offer no traditional demand deposits, CUs' cash balances are modest. Because many CUs operate in headquarters donated by an employer whose workers are credit union members, fixed assets are an even smaller proportion of assets for CUs than for other depositories.

LIABILITIES OF CREDIT UNIONS

Members' savings were more than 90 percent of the total sources of funds for CUs in 1991. Savings consist of **share drafts,** the CU equivalent of NOW accounts; IRAs; **share certificates,** the equivalent of CDs; **money market accounts,** the equivalent of MMDAs; and regular savings, the equivalent of passbook accounts. As indicated in Table 12.8, less than 45 percent of all CUs offered share drafts in 1991, led by those in asset size categories exceeding $2 million.

Like savings institutions, CUs have seen a decline in the proportion of total savings held in regular

---

[13] The role and functions of trade organizations is discussed in Pearce 1984; and CUNA *Annual Reports,* various years.

[14] See Robert M. Garsson, "Credit Unions Outshine Banks on Service," *American Banker,* September 29, 1992. In fact, "grass roots" support of CUs is so strong that some observers attribute the passage

of DIDMCA to the efforts of CU members to ensure the continued existence of interest-bearing checking accounts. CUs' authority to offer them was scheduled to expire on March 31, 1980, the day DIDMCA was passed, unless Congress had acted. CU members launched an "S.O.S." ("Save Our Sharedrafts") campaign, during which more than 150,000 letters were written to members of Congress, urging passage of the act. See "A Blitz on Behalf of Credit Unions," *Business Week,* July 16, 1979, 39–40.

TABLE 12.9 **Distribution of Assets: Federally Chartered and Other Reporting Credit Unions, 1991**

The CU industry's financial structure is less complex than that of banks or thrifts, with most assets concentrated in securities and consumer loans.

	Federally Chartered CUs (8,229 Institutions)		All Reporting CUs (13,989 Institutions)[a]	
	Millions	% of Total	Millions	% of Total
Assets				
Cash	$ 3,268	2.27%		
Securities	53,414	37.11		
Other assets	4,159	2.89		
Cash and securities			$100,223	41.33%
Loans				
Mortgages and related assets			$ 28,661	11.82%
Automobile loans			46,600	19.22
Other loans			66,997	27.63
Total loans	83,075	57.72	$142,258	58.67%
Total assets	$143,916	100.00%	$242,481	100.00%
Liabilities and Capital				
Shares				
Share drafts	$13,182		$ 20,757	
Share certificates	24,496		39,916	
Individual retirement accounts	19,619		31,639	
Regular and other share accounts	72,844		127,322	
Total shares	$130,141	90.43%	$219,635	90.65%
Other liabilities	2,899	2.01	4,233	1.75
Total liabilities	$133,041	92.44%	$223,868	92.40%
Capital				
Reserves	$ 5,538			
Undivided earnings	5,337			
Total capital	$ 10,875	7.56%	$ 18,613	7.60%
Total liabilities and capital	$143,916	100.00%	$242,481	100.00%

[a] Reporting CUs are all institutions voluntarily reporting financial information to CUNA.
Sources: NCUA, *1991 Annual Report;* CUNA, *1991 Credit Union Report.*

savings accounts, with the percentage falling from almost 100 percent in the late 1970s to about 60 percent of total savings as of year-end 1991. Also, the industry has liabilities to other creditors, including borrowings from the **Central Liquidity Fund (CLF),** an agency of the NCUA providing funds to meet CUs' needs for liquidity and other operating funds.

CAPITAL OF CREDIT UNIONS

Because of their not-for-profit form of organization and the common bond requirement, CUs have limited access to funds except through the savings of members or retained earnings. Like other depositories, the balance sheets of CUs contain reserve accounts, or portions of retained earnings designated to serve as cushions against which future loan and investment losses can be charged. Earnings retained in excess of those officially designated as reserves are called undivided earnings, similar to undivided profits in commercial banks. The total of reserves and undivided earnings is equal to the capital or net worth of the CU. For the industry as a whole in 1991, capital exceeded 7 percent of assets, higher than the ratio of net worth to assets for all other depositories except very small banks.

INCOME, EXPENSES, AND EARNINGS OF CREDIT UNIONS

Although CUs are not-for-profit organizations, both CU trade organizations and regulators stress earnings as the most important measure of CU performance. Table 12.10 shows 1991 income and expense data for federally chartered credit unions.

Like other depositories, CUs obtain most of their operating income from interest. The item "refund of interest" reflects a long-standing tradition of some CUs to refund interest to borrowing members if a year's operations are successful. Although larger CUs offer services that generate fee income, most do not, so other sources of operating income are insignificant for the industry as a whole. Interest expenses for CUs are the largest single expense, emphasizing the need for managing interest rate risk in these institutions.

Despite differences in the services offered by small and large credit unions, some research indicates

TABLE 12.10 | **Distribution of Income and Expenses: Federal CUs, 1991**

Although CUs' stated objective is not profitability, the industry's income almost always exceeds its expenses by several percentage points. CUs' tax-exempt status is controversial with other depositories for this reason.

	8,229 Institutions	
	Millions	**% of Total**
Operating Income		
Interest income		
Interest and fees on loans	$9,350	
Interest on investments	3,308	
Less refund on interest	(9)	
Total interest income	$12,649	93.31%
Other operating income	907	6.69%
Total operating income	$13,556	100.00%
Operating Expenses		
Interest expense		
Interest on savings deposits	$7,183	
Interest on borrowed money	70	
Total interest expense	$7,253	58.87%
Noninterest operating expenses	5,067	41.13%
Total operating expenses	$12,319	100.00%
Net Operating Income	$1,237	9.12%[a]
Net nonoperating income (expense)	20	
Less transfer to reserve accounts	170	
Net Income	$ 1,087	8.02%[a]

[a]Percentage of total operating income.
Source: NCUA, *1991 Annual Report,* 22.

relatively few income/expense differences. A study of Georgia CUs conducted at the Federal Reserve Bank of Atlanta noted that the largest CUs in that state were no more efficient, as measured by the average ratio of operating expenses to total assets, than were smaller

TABLE 12.11   **Compound Annual Growth Rates in Assets of Depositories, 1960–1991**

Because they started from such a small base, the compound annual asset growth rate for foreign banks operating in the United States has greatly exceeded that for other depositories during the past three decades. The relatively rapid growth of CUs is evident, as are the ravages of the late 1980s on the thrift industry.

	1960–1991	1960–1965	1965–1975	1975–1980	1980–1985	1985–1990
Commercial banks (domestically chartered)	8.33%	8.36%	8.91%	10.02%	9.47%	5.85%
Commercial banks (foreign operating in the United States)	16.88	4.68	7.77	61.13	7.80	20.40
S&Ls	8.59	12.25	10.09	13.32	11.20	0.72
Savings banks	6.01	7.57	7.44	7.48	4.55	3.98
CUs	12.69	11.88	12.87	12.87	14.75	10.04

Source: Prepared by the authors with data from Board of Governors of the Federal Reserve System, *Flow of Funds Accounts, 1949–1978, 1961–1984, Q-I/92.*

CUs. Other work suggests, in fact, that among occupationally based CUs (the vast majority of the industry), the stability of the employer is the most important factor in explaining performance differences. The more stable the employer, the better CUs seem to fare.[15]

In 1991, credit unions outperformed thrifts and banks by a wide margin, as measured by the ratio of net income to total operating income. CUs' tax exemption was no small factor in that comparison.

FINANCIAL STRUCTURE AND PERFORMANCE OF DEPOSITORIES: A COMPARISON

Recent balance sheets and income statements of depository institutions suggest both similarities and differences among them. Further understanding is gained from comparing the recent performance of these institutions along several dimensions.

ASSET GROWTH

Commercial banks are, on average, the largest depositories by far. In 1991, for example, the largest commercial bank holding company had assets of about $217 billion; the largest S&L had total assets of about

$51 billion; and the largest CU had only about $6 billion in total assets. In fact, the entire CU industry held less than 19 percent of total thrift assets and less than 8 percent of total commercial bank assets as of year-end 1991.

The three types of depositories have also experienced different rates of asset growth during the recent past. Table 12.11 presents compound annual growth rates in total financial assets held by depositories from 1960 through 1991. Savings banks showed the lowest growth rates over the 31-year period. In contrast, the growth of CUs outstripped that of other domestic depositories over the entire period, but not in all subperiods. The biggest gainers were foreign banks operating in the United States. Most recently, the distance between CU and foreign bank growth and that of competitors has widened dramatically. Of course, CUs are also the smallest depositories, so CU growth expressed in dollars has not exceeded dollar asset increases at other depositories.

Another lesson from the table is that, since 1975, the growth rate for commercial banks has declined steadily. In the mid- to late 1980s, a rash of bank failures led to a decline in the industry's growth. Bank failures were particularly dramatic among big Texas and New England banks, which, at the time they failed, were also among the largest banks in the nation. Many experts predict, however, that rapid growth among banks will resume in the mid-1990s, especially as they expand by purchasing thrifts under FIRREA's liberalized acquisition rules.

Finally, the table points out that annual asset growth among S&Ls during recent decades has been

---

[15] See Cox and Whigham 1984. This study somewhat contradicts the economies-of-scale study cited in Footnote 18, although the two studies are not directly comparable. The findings on occupational CUs are provided in Kohers and Mullis 1986.

| FIGURE 12.1 | **Balance Sheets of Depository Institutions, 1991** |

A visual comparison of banks, thrifts, and CUs shows that commercial banks have more diversified assets and that the thrift industry is more highly leveraged than other depositories.

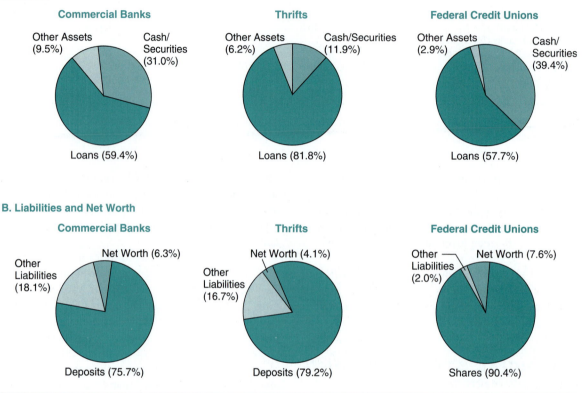

A. Assets

Commercial Banks — Other Assets (9.5%); Cash/Securities (31.0%); Loans (59.4%)

Thrifts — Other Assets (6.2%); Cash/Securities (11.9%); Loans (81.8%)

Federal Credit Unions — Other Assets (2.9%); Cash/Securities (39.4%); Loans (57.7%)

B. Liabilities and Net Worth

Commercial Banks — Net Worth (6.3%); Other Liabilities (18.1%); Deposits (75.7%)

Thrifts — Net Worth (4.1%); Other Liabilities (16.7%); Deposits (79.2%)

Federal Credit Unions — Other Liabilities (2.0%); Net Worth (7.6%); Shares (90.4%)

Source: Prepared by the authors with data from Board of Governors of the Federal Reserve System, unpublished, 1992; National Credit Union Administration, *1991 Annual Report;* and National Council of Savings Institutions, *Economic Insight,* August 1991.

extremely variable, ranging from a high of 13.3 percent in the late 1970s to a low of only 0.72 percent in the late 1980s. The "go-go" days for S&Ls are clearly over, and most observers believe that the industry will continue to shrink throughout the 1990s. For savings banks, the picture has been a bit brighter in recent years. Rebounding from sluggish growth in the early 1980s, they benefited considerably from the mid-1980s boom in housing in the northeastern United States, where most savings banks are located. Although they are unlikely to become the fastest growing depositories, they may hold their own in the next decade.

BALANCE SHEETS COMPARED

Figure 12.1 compares the balance sheets of the three types of depositories as of year-end 1991. In all depositories, loans make up more than half of total assets—and as high as 81 percent for thrifts. A different type of loan dominates the portfolio for each industry, however, with banks focusing on commercial loans, thrifts on mortgages, and CUs on nonmortgage consumer credit.

The graphs also highlight the importance of deposit taking and emphasize the high degree of financial leverage used by all institutions. In fact, all except the relatively small "slices" of net worth in the bottom

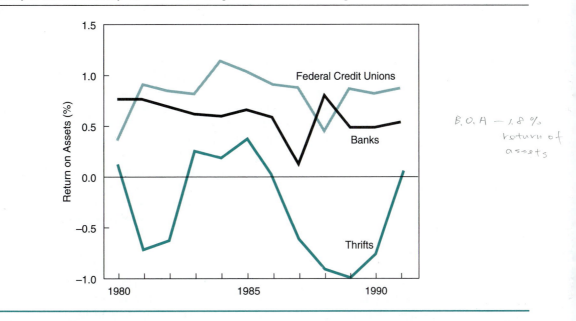

FIGURE 12.2   **Profitability of Depository Institutions**

The profitability of the thrift industry has been dismal compared with that of other depositories.

B.O.A — 1.8% return of assets

Source: Prepared by the authors with data from National Credit Union Administration, *1991 Annual Report;* Martin H. Wolfson and Mary M. McLaughlin, "Recent Developments in the Profitability and Lending Practices of Commercial Banks," *Federal Reserve Bulletin* 75 (July 1989): 469; and Federal Reserve Bank of Kansas City, *Financial Industry Trends,* 1992.

panels represent debt obligations of depositories. Thrifts make the most use of financial leverage. This pattern will change in the 1990s, however, as capital requirements for the industry become stricter. CUs rely heavily on members' shares, lacking access to external sources of funds available to many banks and thrifts.

PROFITABILITY

Profitability is the greatest difference among depositories.

THRIFTS DECLINE. Figure 12.2 illustrates the return on assets (net income ÷ total assets) for commercial banks, S&Ls, and federal CUs during the period 1980 through 1991. Several points are clear from the graph. The profitability of S&Ls was low at best and negative at worst. In contrast, by the time savings institutions hit the bottom of the earnings charts in 1989, banks had rebounded from their earlier low. For most of the

period, in fact, bank profitability was much more stable than were thrift earnings. The exception was 1987, when the problems among large Texas banks, as well as among large New York City banks with significant losses on loans to Latin American nations, depressed earnings for the entire industry. Finally, federal CUs prospered for most of the decade after regulatory ceilings on loan rates were lifted in 1980, freeing them to charge market rates. They experienced a downturn in 1988, however, as some institutions grew more rapidly than their relatively unsophisticated managers could handle. CU regulators immediately increased their examination forces to forestall even a microcosm of the thrift debacle.

Several additional reasons can be offered for these trends. Changes in the regulatory and economic environment for depositories have not affected the NIM of all institutions equally. Institutions with asset maturities substantially longer than liability maturities always have difficulty if market interest rates rise rapidly and liability costs go with them, while asset returns remain unchanged. Savings institutions found themselves in that unenviable position by late 1980. Banks and CUs, with much shorter asset maturities, did not.

Coupled with deposit rate deregulation was the severe downturn in business activity in the early 1980s, producing the highest unemployment rate since the Great Depression. Delinquencies on residential mortgages reached unprecedented levels in the 1980s, further adding to earnings difficulties at savings institutions. Loan losses for commercial banks during this period were also high relative to historical levels, but the portfolio of the industry as a whole is more diversified than that of thrifts. So, while some industries struggled to repay bank debt, others were thriving, especially as economic recovery began.

Figure 12.2 helps to explain why the net worth of savings institutions is lower as a percentage of total assets than it is for the other depositories. The losses of the 1980s eroded reserves and retained earnings from profitable years, leaving the industry in a comparatively weak capital position. The managerial and regulatory implications of a weakened capital position are explored more fully in Chapter 17.

Despite the overall difficulties in the industry, prospects for some individual savings institutions seemed brighter during the 1980s because they were able to replace maturing fixed-rate mortgages with new mortgages on which yields are more closely tied to market yields. For most of 1988, **adjustable-rate mortgages (ARMs)** were about 50 percent of new mortgage loans. By 1992, however, the proportion of new mortgage loans with adjustable rates had fallen to 25 percent.[16] Although few ARMs can be repriced as often as MMDAs, for example, on which costs can change once a month or more often, the ability to shorten asset maturities is an important tool for improving the profitability of thrifts.

FDICIA, FIRREA, AND THRIFT PROFITABILITY. Since 1990, many experts have argued that the potential benefits to thrifts of financial innovations such as ARMs were offset by several provisions in FIRREA. In particular, observers' attention focused on the law's imposition of higher costs for deposit insurance and higher capital requirements, as well as its mandate that thrifts hold at least 70 percent of their assets in mortgage-related assets. In fact, less than a year after FIRREA was passed, it was already clear that the cost of the thrift bailout—intended to be financed in large part by the healthy segment of the industry—would exact such a toll on that group that their survival would be in jeopardy. Regulators' predictions of the number of thrifts needing "assistance" (read "closure") from the RTC exceeded 1,000, fully one-third of the remaining institutions. Yet the RTC's ability to liquidate even the pre-FIRREA "zombies" was proceeding at a snail's pace, fraught by bureaucratic and political snags. The industry's 1989 loss of $19.3 billion was actually 43 percent *worse* than the $13.4 billion loss in 1988. Legislators seemed to recognize the difficulties and relaxed the QTL test in FDICIA. Thrifts were also aided by dramatically lower interest rates in 1991 and 1992. Although the future is, of course, unpredictable, few observers are optimistic that the industry will ever return to its glory days.[17]

SOME BANKS SUFFER, TOO. Figure 12.2 makes another point: The profitability of the banking industry declined throughout most of the 1980s. Several researchers have concluded that the decline in the mid-1980s was largely attributable to the difficulties of the 17 largest banks and of banks with assets of less than $100 million. The largest banks, controlling almost 40 percent of the industry's assets, faced increasing competition for business customers from nondepository lenders. However, noninterest expenses increased more for small banks than for large banks during the period 1980–1985. The decline in the industry's per-

---

[16] The Primary Mortgage Market," *Freddie Mac Reports,* various issues; and Vanessa Bush, "Low Rates Limit Lending Routes," *Savings Institutions* 113 (January 1992): 18–23. The percentage of ARMs originated has varied considerably over the past several years. In fact, there appears to be a relationship between the general level of interest rates and ARM originations. When the general level is high, ARM originations have increased, perhaps because borrowers are reluctant during those times to lock themselves into fixed rates.

---

[17] Robert M. Garsson, "Brady: S&Ls Can't Pay More of Bailout Tab," *American Banker,* May 24, 1990, 1, 14; Bill Atkinson, "Thrifts Lose $19 Billion in Worst Year Ever," *American Banker,* March 27, 1990, 1, 6; and Phil Roosevelt, "Thrift Law, Restricting S&L Loans to Low Margins, Impedes Rescue," *American Banker,* May 1, 1990, 1, 13–14.

formance did not necessarily reflect deregulation, because loan losses from small business and agriculture hit smaller banks hard. Because banks in the smallest and largest groups have a large share of the industry's resources, the profitability of banks as a whole declined. Some banks, however, especially midsized regionals, did relatively well.

By the end of 1988, industry analysts were more optimistic. As is evident in Figure 12.2, the banking industry reported its strongest performance of the decade that year. Large banks led the recovery, primarily because loan loss provisions declined substantially from previous levels. Smaller banks benefited from improvements in the agricultural sector. Efforts to increase noninterest income and to control operating expenses also contributed to the positive earnings report in 1988.

Large loan losses did continue in some regions of the country, however. New England banks in particular suffered from a decline in regional real estate values after several years of increases. These losses, along with further deterioration in the value of loans to Mexico and other less developed countries (LDCs) resulted in disappointing earnings for the banking industry in 1989. As profits improved from 1990 through 1992, however, observers adopted an almost bouyant outlook. Headlines such as "Banking Industry Basks in the Glow of Strong Profits" were common, and many bankers predicted that the worst was behind them.[18]

CREDIT UNIONS. Except for 1988, CUs' earnings have been consistently higher than the 1980 level. Like thrifts, CUs were less diversified than commercial banks before deregulation, although their assets were of considerably shorter maturity than those of savings institutions. Nonetheless, high interest rates drove up their deposit costs and dampened members' loan demand. During the 1981–1982 recession, occupationally based CUs were hit hard by unemployment and experienced savings outflows and increasing delinquencies on loans. By 1984, however, loans were again on the increase.

Furthermore, the industry has successfully argued for changes in the definition of *common bond* so that greater diversification of borrowers and savers is now possible. For example, in 1988, the American Association of Retired Persons (AARP) founded a federal CU intended to serve its 29 *million* members. The common bond for membership in the CU? That a person be 50 years old or older. Given the rapid approach of the baby boom generation to that milestone age, CU competitors cried "Foul!" to what they perceived to be unreasonable permissiveness on the part of regulators in interpreting the common bond requirement. They demanded that the tax-exempt status of CUs be reconsidered. In 1990, the AARP bowed to pressure from fellow CUs and closed its credit union to avoid further assaults on the industry. Although banks continue to rail against the alleged advantages of the CU charter, regulators and Congress have thus far been unmoved, and CUs' tax exemption remains a key operating feature of the industry.

Industry observers suggest CUs should capitalize on high satisfaction levels and attempt to become their customers' primary financial institution by offering electronic and other more sophisticated banking services in the 1990s. Following this advice, CUs in California are engaged in an innovation that may assist them in becoming the primary financial institution for more of their members, although it may once again raise the ire of the banking industry. The experiment is shared branching. Because CUs do not compete for customers, large CUs with widely dispersed memberships have realized that they can share branching facilities and thus serve their customers more conveniently. If this practice becomes more widespread, large CUs will be able to compete geographically with banks and thrifts without incurring excessive costs.[19]

---

[18] See Fortier and Phillis 1985; Nejezchleb 1986; Federal Reserve Bank of New York 1986; Wolfson and McLaughlin 1989, 469–472; John Meehan, David Woodruff, and Chuck Hawkins, "For Most Banks, There Was Nowhere to Hide," *Business Week,* April 2, 1990, 94–95; Meehan et al. 1990; Brunner, Hancock, and McLaughlin, 1992; Brunner and English 1993. Articles on bank profitability in the previous year are published annually in the *Federal Reserve Bulletin.*

[19] Jim McTague, "In the Capital, It's Motherhood, Apple Pie, and Credit Unions," *American Banker,* March 29, 1993, 4. Greg Crandell, "The Outlook for Credit Unions in a Restructured U.S. Financial System," *The Southern Business and Economic Journal* 15 (January 1992): 69–72; Lynn Asinov, "Looking for Better Rates and Lower Fees? Credit Unions Are Favorites These Days," *The Wall Street Journal,* September 2, 1992, C1, C14; Robert E. Taylor, "Retired Persons Association Launches Credit Union for Its 29 Million Members," *The Wall Street Journal,* May 11, 1988, 4; and Bill Atkinson, "AARP's Retreat: Credit Unions Breathe Easier," *American Banker,* April 3, 1990, 1, 6.

DEPOSITORY INSTITUTIONS: MERGERS AND FAILURES

In the 1980s, profitability patterns in depositories affected the number of firms in each industry, as distressed institutions sought merger partners or were consolidated into other institutions at the direction of regulators. Other depositories merged to meet deregulation's challenges as part of larger organizations. Still other institutions ceased to exist because their net worth shrank to the point of insolvency (the value of their liabilities exceeded that of their assets). Commercial banks, although not unscathed, experienced less consolidation than other depositories. But even they experienced greater rates of merger and failure in the 1980s and early 1990s than at any point in recent history.

ECONOMIES OF SCALE REVISITED

Interestingly, the number of thrifts and CUs began to decrease not in the 1980s but almost a decade before that. CUs reached their peak at more than 23,500 organizations in 1970 and have declined in number every year since then. The total number of thrifts has decreased steadily since 1960. Declines in the number of thrifts and CUs before 1980 have been linked to economies of scale in those institutions. As discussed in Chapter 4, economies of scale occur when the unit cost of producing a service—for example, making a mortgage loan or opening a savings account—declines with the volume of business. Research indicates that S&Ls and CUs are both subject to economies of scale; therefore, the shrinking number of savings institutions before 1980 can be explained in part by their managers' desire to achieve cost savings and improve performance.[20]

In contrast, commercial banks have decreased only slightly in number since 1960, when there were 13,484 chartered altogether, compared with their 1991 level of 12,090. Although recent research is beginning to challenge this conclusion, economies of scale in the commercial banking industry have been assumed not to be as great as those for thrifts and CUs, and smaller banks have had less incentive to combine for cost-sav-

ing reasons alone. New banks continue to be chartered, so the overall number of commercial banks has not declined substantially, despite the increased pace of mergers in the 1980s and early 1990s.

MERGER ACTIVITY IN THE BANKING AND THRIFT INDUSTRIES

Data on the number of voluntary bank mergers between 1960 and 1990 reveal that fewer than 100 mergers occurred in 1960. By 1980, the number of mergers approved had grown to 188, and a record 710 bank mergers occurred in 1987. Although the figures moderated slightly in subsequent years, the number of mergers involving very large bank holding companies has increased. Between 1985 and 1990, 13 mergers occurred each year in which both parties involved held more than $1 billion in total deposits.

Research suggests that most mergers were undertaken to enable banking organizations to expand geographically or to withstand takeovers by large out-of-state organizations. The expansion motive is supported by the fact that, despite the increasing number of mergers and decreasing number of banks, the number of *banking offices* in the United States rose almost 25 percent between 1980 and 1990. The merger trend is also explained by the fact that regulators have recently taken a more permissive attitude toward bank mergers and especially toward acquisition of financially troubled banks, leading to predictions that consolidation in the industry will continue.[21]

Since 1980, in contrast, many thrifts merged not by choice but out of necessity, because their net worth eroded. The two recessionary years, 1981 and 1982, were those in which the thrift merger rate—voluntary or directed by regulators—soared. Data from later in the decade, which appeared to show a decline in thrift consolidations, were deceptive without proper interpretation. In fact, the years 1984–1988 were ones in which thrift regulators made every effort to avoid adding to the FSLIC's deficit. Because the condition of so many S&Ls was so bad during that period, supervisory-assisted mergers could seldom have been consummated without financial assistance from the de-

---

[20] As examples of this literature, see Wolken and Navratil 1980; McNulty 1981; Dowling, Philippatos, and Choi 1984; and Mester 1987. Further studies are cited in Chapter 4.

[21] "Statement by John P. LaWare before the House Committee on Banking, Finance, and Urban Affairs, September 24, 1991," *Federal Reserve Bulletin* 77 (November 1991): 932–941; and Rhoades 1985.

posit insurance funds. Thus, most bleeding institutions were simply kept alive with loans from the regulators rather than merged or liquidated.

With the passage of FIRREA, Congress mandated that these "band-aid" practices be discontinued and that the FDIC move expeditiously to resolve problems among S&Ls. These resolution plans, along with FIRREA's and FDICIA's provisions liberalizing cross-industry mergers, lead many experts to predict that in the future, mergers of thrifts with commercial banks or other financial services firms are more likely than mergers within the thrift industry.

DEPOSITORY INSTITUTION FAILURES

Figure 12.3 tracks the number of failures among insured depositories between 1934, when the insurance funds were instituted, and 1991. (It is important to note that, in the years immediately preceding 1934, the number of bank failures exceeded those shown in the figure, leading to the creation of the FDIC.) In the context of Figure 12.3, bank failures are defined as those instances in which institutions were closed or forcibly merged by the FDIC. Because of the previously described forbearance policies followed by the FSLIC in the 1980s, under which few sick institutions were closed or merged, it would be inappropriate to define thrift "failures" only as closures or forced mergers. Instead, the failures depicted in the top panel of Figure 12.3 are all thrifts that were insolvent (liabilities > assets) at the end of the year. Under ordinary circumstances, an insolvent institution would be considered a failed institution, so this definition is consistent with economic, if not political, reality. Note, however, that before FIRREA, thrift regulators kept many insolvent institutions open to avoid a drain on the FSLIC; thus the bars in the graph before 1989 do not depict discrete groups of failed thrifts; that is, some institutions that became insolvent in 1986, for example, were still operating in 1987 and would also be considered "failed" at the end of that year as well.[22] From 1989 forward, the bars in the graph represent thrifts actually closed by the RTC. Despite these defi-

nitional difficulties, the patterns displayed in the graph are revealing.

By historical standards since the institution of deposit insurance, the failure rate for banks and thrifts in the 1980s and early 1990s was nothing short of phenomenal. Because mortgages were formerly among the safest financial assets, thrift failure rates were lower than those for commercial banks until deregulation. In the early 1980s, however, thrift failures not only merely exceeded commercial bank failures, they were more than four times as great in some years. Considering that the number of thrifts was between 20 and 25 percent of the number of commercial banks during that time, the early period of deregulation exacted quite a toll on thrifts.

It is important to note that not all thrift failures can be blamed on bad management; in many cases, particularly in the 1980–1982 period, the managers of thrifts were simply unable to adjust strategies as fast as events developed. In other cases, managers failed to prepare their institutions' asset and liability portfolios to cope with unexpected, or even expected, changes in the environment. After 1985, because of regulators' concern that the FSLIC had insufficient funds to handle as many thrift failures as had occurred in the early 1980s, special programs were instituted to enable otherwise insolvent thrifts to stay in business.

At the same time, economic problems in industries such as oil and farming led to an escalating number of problem banks, many of which banking regulators allowed to fail. In 1989, the number of bank failures reached a postwar high of 206 institutions with total assets of $29 billion. Although the number declined to 124 in 1991, the total assets of failed banks soared to more than $63 billion, putting considerable pressure on BIF's resources. This turnabout illustrates that the future of the industry cannot be evaluated by focusing on the number of failures alone, but rather on the size of the failing institutions.

ARE DEPOSITORY INSTITUTION FAILURES CONTAGIOUS? Apart from their effect on the managers, customers, and shareholders of individual institutions, failures, especially of commercial banks, are often considered undesirable for the financial system as a whole. This view arises from fears of a public run on other depository institutions when one fails, forcing solvent institutions to close, not because their net worth has vanished but because they lack the cash to

---

[22] Indeed, the reluctance of regulators to close insolvent institutions has spawned a new direction in research on depository institution failures. One study (Demirgüç-Kunt 1989) concluded that in some cases regulators' decisions are a significant determinant of failure rates, regardless of financial realities. Additional criticism of regulators' actions in the thrift crisis is discussed in Cole 1990.

FIGURE 12.3 **Bank and Thrift Failures**

The failure rate among banks and thrifts soared after 1980. As a percentage of total firms in the industry, the thrift industry failure rate was especially large.

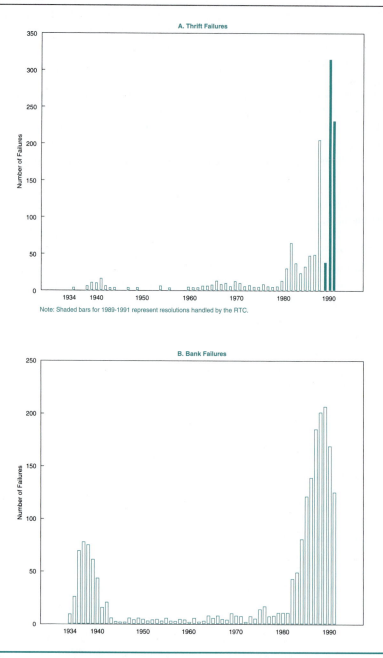

Source: FDIC *Annual Reports;* James R. Barth, R. Dan Brumbaugh, Jr., Daniel Sauerhaft, and George H. K. Wang, "Thrift Institution Failures: Causes and Policy Issues," in *Proceedings of a Conference on Bank Structure and Competition* (Chicago: Federal Reserve Bank of Chicago, 1985), 186; James R. Barth, Philip F. Bartholomew, and Carol J. Labich, "Causes of Thrift Failures: An Analysis of 1988 Resolutions," paper presented at the 25th Annual Conference on Bank Structure and Competition, Federal Reserve Bank of Chicago, 1989; and *RTC Review,* various issues.

pay off all depositors on demand. Fear of this **contagion effect** has been especially high in the case of large bank failures.

In 1984, Continental Illinois National Bank, at that time one of the ten largest banks in the United States with assets exceeding $40 billion, teetered on the brink of failure. Rather than closing the bank, federal regulators kept it afloat by the FDIC purchase of $1 billion of Continental preferred stock to shore up the bank's net worth position. The insurance agency also purchased several billion in problem loans from Continental, enabling it to strengthen its balance sheet. This type of regulatory assistance was almost unprecedented and was interpreted to mean that large banks would not be allowed to fail, although the same treatment would probably not have been accorded to small depositories. Also, the federal assistance was given despite widespread belief that the bank's top management, all of whom were later removed from office, were responsible for the bank's precarious financial condition.

In 1988, the FDIC actions to resolve the financial deterioration of First Republic Bank Corporation of Dallas, Texas, revealed its continuing reluctance to allow outright failures of large banks. First Republic had 41 subsidiary banks and assets of $32.5 billion, making it the largest bank holding company in Texas and the fourteenth largest in the United States. In March 1988, the FDIC provided an interim financial assistance package of $1 billion to First Republic's two largest banks and, as it had done in the Continental case, provided assurances of protection to all bank depositors and creditors.

When it became clear that the bank could not recover on its own, the FDIC entered into an agreement with NCNB Corporation (now NationsBank) of Charlotte, North Carolina, to create NCNB Texas National Bank. This **bridge bank** was to be managed by NCNB. New equity capital of $1.05 billion was invested, with 80 percent provided by the FDIC and 20 percent by NCNB. The North Carolina bank was given an exclusive 5-year option to buy out the FDIC's 80 percent share.[23]

In the Continental and First Republic cases, among others, the regulators seemed to endorse the position that the failure of large institutions is more detrimental to the financial system than the failure of small ones, a belief some researchers suggest is supported by an analysis of financial market data. Other experts argue, however, that federal deposit insurance, nonexistent during the bank runs of the 1930s, simply causes funds withdrawn from one institution to be redeposited in another that is perceived by the market to be safer. According to this line of reasoning, the actions of regulators in the Continental case were "incorrect and dangerous." The contagion effect of depository institution failure is another unresolved issue in depository institutions regulation. However, Congress seemed to acknowledge its belief in the contagion effect by allowing regulators to consider what FDICIA calls systemic risk in their handling of large bank failures.[24]

MERGERS AND CONTRACTION IN THE CREDIT UNION INDUSTRY

Because most CUs are small and members must have a common bond, financial problems in a single CU rarely evoke concern about spillover to other institutions. Still, the industry has contracted in recent years because deregulation and changes in the economic environment have affected CUs across the nation. Figure 12.4 shows the annual net changes in the number of federal CUs since 1960. The figures result from subtracting charter cancellations for the year from new charters granted. Years in which cancellations exceed new charters appear as negative changes in Figure 12.4. Although the cancellation of a charter is not synonymous with failure, many recent charter cancellations involved mergers to avoid the collapse of an individual CU. Other charter cancellations result from liquidation of troubled CUs. Figure 12.4 clearly shows that cancelled charters have greatly outnumbered new ones in recent years.

---

[23] Comptroller of the Currency C. Todd Conover stated in Congressional testimony on September 9, 1984, that none of the 11 largest banks would be allowed to fail. (See Tim Carrington, "U.S. Won't Let 11 Biggest Banks in Nation Fail," *The Wall Street Journal,* September 20, 1984, 2.) As the First Republic case suggests, Conover's

prediction has thus far proved to be accurate, even beyond the largest 11. Further details on the FDIC's handling of the First Republic case are available in the *1988 FDIC Annual Report.*

[24] Contrasting views of the contagion effect and the validity of recent FDIC actions are presented in Swary 1985; Aharony and Swary 1983; Cobos 1989; and Kaufman 1988.

FIGURE 12.4   **Net Changes in Number of Federal Credit Unions**

The number of CUs declined each year throughout the 1980s and into the 1990s, continuing a trend that began a decade earlier.

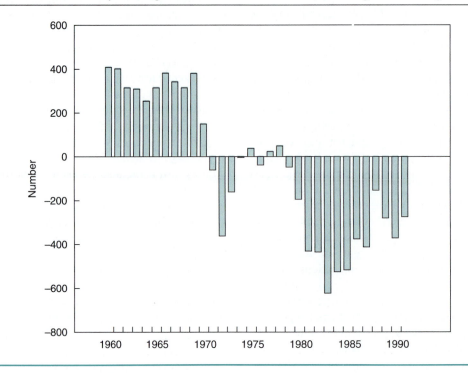

Source: National Credit Union Administration, *Annual Reports.*

PROSPECTS FOR THE FUTURE

What will the future hold for the number of depository institutions? Many experts expect continued consolidation for the remainder of the twentieth century. Shrinkage is expected from continued financial problems, through voluntary mergers for economies of scale, and because the inevitable spread of interstate deposit taking encourages large institutions to purchase smaller ones to gain a foothold in a market.

Still, few observers expect that only a few large depositories will dominate the nation. The classic cases used to support this point of view are California and New York State, both of which house some of the nation's largest depositories next door to some of its smallest, all with their own satisfied customers.

In fact, many experienced bankers agree that customers' demand for personalized services and a community orientation from their financial institutions will continue. A recent study by Fed economists con-

firmed that, while corporate customers may venture nationally or even internationally to conduct their banking business, households continue to prefer local depositories.[25] In recent years, many new banks have been chartered under the leadership of CEOs convinced that they can operate profitably with a small asset base and in a relatively small geographic market.

Perhaps the extreme in personalized service is exemplified by the **private banking** operations being established by a growing number of commercial banks in the United States. The American Bankers Association (ABA) defines private banking as a "deliberate program to attract and serve the affluent individual market." In contrast to traditional private banking operations in international institutions, many domestic operations cater to entrepreneurs as well as to more

---

[25] Elliehausen and Wolken 1992.

conservative wealthy clients, emphasizing discreet and efficient responses to their financial needs. By early 1989, the ABA estimated that more than 75 percent of U.S. banks with assets in excess of $500 million offered private banking programs or had plans to implement them. Eventually, many of these banks hope to use their private banking offices to cross-market a variety of financial services offered in other departments or subsidiaries.[26]

Yet an emphasis on personal service is not the path chosen by all banks. Some large money-center banks have, in fact, decided to focus entirely on large corporate or institutional clients and have discontinued all services to individual customers. Such a strategy is known as **wholesale banking,** in contrast to **retail banking,** the term describing institutions serving a wider variety of businesses and individuals. Bankers Trust and, more recently, Continental Illinois are firms that have chosen to concentrate their efforts entirely in the wholesale banking market. In contrast, small banks and thrifts are joining forces to promote community banking and have even formed consolidated professional organizations to fight for their mutual interests. Still other depositories are concentrating on diversifying into lines of business, especially insurance and securities, that have traditionally been outside their domain. This development is so important that it is the subject of Chapter 21.

DEPOSITORY INSTITUTIONS: DIFFERENT, YET ALIKE

Undoubtedly, deregulation of depositories in the 1980s led to increasing similarity among formerly distinct types of institutions. Even so, it is incorrect to say that all depositories are alike. Indeed, it is not clear that, even after the substantial passage of time, all depositories will *become* alike. Differences among depositories will persist because of the size, location, financial status, historical tradition, and strategic planning decisions of individual institutions and because the current regulatory system virtually ensures that some traditional characteristics will remain.

Even more fundamental questions than whether depositories are different from one another loom on the horizon as the twenty-first century approaches. Historically, the question "Are banks special?" was asked by observers seeking to determine whether banks were different from thrifts or CUs. Today, the query might well be phrased, "Are depositories special?" Such a question is asked increasingly by those who wonder whether depositories continue to perform unique intermediation roles or whether other types of financial institutions, such as securities firms, can perform traditional depository functions more efficiently, and as effectively, as depositories. As first explained in Chapter 1, depositories can reduce the monitoring costs of financial contracts by specializing in the collection, analysis, and evaluation of information so that most lenders need not monitor individual borrowers in detail. But not everyone agrees that only depositories can perform this function, and rival institutions seem determined to prove that depositories are not deserving of the special status and protection that many believe regulators give them.

For now, however, opportunities exist for management to shape the asset and liability structure of individual depository institutions and to influence income and expenses in ways that were unimaginable a decade ago. Successful managers now must set risk/ return objectives, balancing their own interests and those with whom they have an agency relationship; evaluate the advantages and disadvantages of organizational and chartering alternatives; and understand and manage interest rate risk. The skills and knowledge needed to accomplish these goals are common to all depository institutions; difference in their usage in a bank, savings institution, or CU is really one of degree, not kind.

Recognition of these needs is so strong that regulators now require thrifts to issue policy statements on interest rate risk management and to report on the potential effect of changing interest rates on asset values and income. Commercial banks must report asset and liability maturities, contingent liabilities, yields, costs, and net interest income to their regulators on an ongoing basis. Credit unions are increasingly turning to professional management and focusing as much on earnings performance as on service to members. The following chapters examine many of the required management skills in more detail.

---

[26] Further information on these topics is available in Andrews 1988; Makin 1989; and Peter Pae, "Private Bankers Court Merely Affluent," *The Wall Street Journal,* May 12, 1992, B1, B7.

SUMMARY

This chapter analyzes the asset/liability structures, income, and expenses of commercial banks, thrifts, and credit unions. Examination of the financial structures of depositories reveals some similarities but also continuing differences in the types of assets in which each category of institution specializes. Deregulation has produced greater similarity in their sources of funds, although the assets of depositories are much less similar, despite broader powers granted to thrifts in the early 1980s.

Comparison of asset growth rates and financial performance across industries also reveals interesting differences. The commercial banking industry has enjoyed the most stable rate of asset growth and return on assets. The CU industry and foreign banks have enjoyed the highest rate of asset growth. Profitability in the thrift industry has suffered the most since 1980, when deposit rate deregulation and high interest rates combined to produce several consecutive years of losses. This period was followed by even greater losses in the industry as a result of poor lending practices. Provisions of FDICIA and FIRREA further slowed the industry's recovery.

Finally, the chapter examines changes in the number of institutions in each industry. Failures, mergers forced by regulators, and voluntary combinations in pursuit of economies of scale have reduced the number of thrifts and CUs. In the commercial banking industry, although the number of failures has accelerated rapidly since 1980, new charters granted have prevented a material decline in the total number of banking firms. Nevertheless, continued consolidation of depositories is expected to continue, and more competition from nondepository institutions is inevitable.

QUESTIONS

1. Review current publications, including those of federal regulators, for reports on recent commercial bank performance. What trends can you identify over the last 5 years? What explanations are offered? How has the performance of small and large banks compared, and to what do you attribute any significant differences?

2. Identify the most important distinctions in the asset and liability choices of banks, thrifts, and credit unions. What similarities do you note in small banks and thrifts?

3. Compare and contrast asset and liability categories among small and large U.S. banks and foreign banks operating in the United States. Explain how different balance sheet choices affect sources of income and expenses for these three bank categories.

4. What are the most important types of short-term deposit accounts offered by banks and thrifts? Compare their liquidity and interest rate characteristics.

5. Do important differences exist in the loan portfolios of large and small commercial banks? If so, what explanations can you offer for these differences?

6. Why do smaller banks use the services of correspondent banks? How are the services provided and the fees charged to correspondents reflected in the financial statements of larger banks?

7. Several measures of commercial bank profitability are frequently calculated: NIM, net operating income, and net income. Compare these three measures, and explain why each provides important information about financial management decisions not reflected in the others.

8. Review the data on foreign banks operating in the United States presented in Table 12.2. Explain how these data suggest the degree to which foreign banks compete with small and midsized U.S. banks. What has been the effect of recent regulation on the competitive position of foreign banks?

9. What are the important differences between savings associations and savings banks?

10. Explain why the thrift industry's heavy investment in fixed-rate mortgage loans exposed the industry to greater interest rate risk than commercial banks face. How have FIRREA and FDICIA requirements changed this risk exposure?

11. Compare and contrast the functions of the Credit Union National Association and the National Credit Union Administration.

12. How does the not-for-profit status of credit unions affect their performance in comparison to that of commercial banks and thrifts? Do you expect this status to become less controversial in the future?

13. What explanations could be offered for thrifts' slow diversification into commercial lending?

14. Compare S&L profitability during the 1980s and early 1990s to the financial performance of banks and credit unions. What factors contributed to the differences in profitability? Do you expect the trends to continue or change in the near future?

15. Review recent journals to find an analysis of the performance of the thrift industry over the last 4–5 years. Are the remaining institutions reporting stronger performance compared to the late 1980s? Why or why not? What has been the effect of FIRREA's portfolio restrictions on the returns in the thrift industry?

16. Review the data on asset growth rates in Table 12.11. Explain why S&L growth slowed in the late 1980s and why credit union growth was highest. Given the provisions of FIRREA, FDICIA, and subsequent regulatory developments, what predictions would you make about the future growth across the industries?

17. What factors contributed to the growth in thrift and bank mergers in the last 10 years? Compare and contrast the causes of consolidation in the two industries.

18. Using information from newspapers and periodicals, compare the decisions made by banking regulators in handling the financial crises of Penn Square Bank in 1982, Continental Illinois in 1984, and First Republic Bank in 1988. How has the "contagion effect" influenced regulators' decisions? What are other motivations for treating large and small banks differently?

19. What is private banking? Why do many firms consider this to be a growth area? How do such services allow banks to compete with nondepository financial institutions?

20. Do you expect to see more or fewer differences between banks and thrifts as the 1990s progress? Between banks and nondepository institutions? What factors influence changes in similarities and differences? Do you think banks are sufficiently special to deserve their current level of attention from regulators? Why or why not?

SELECTED REFERENCES

Aharony, Joseph, and Itzhak Swary. "Contagion Effects of Bank Failures: Evidence from Capital Markets." *Journal of Business* 56 (1983): 305–321.

Andrews, Suzanna. "The Banker as Entrepreneur." *Institutional Investor* 22 (October 1988): 185–187.

Baer, Herbert. "Foreign Competition in U.S. Banking Markets." *Economic Perspectives* (Federal Reserve Bank of Chicago) 14 (May/June 1990): 22–29.

Barth, James, Philip F. Bartholomew, and Carol J. Labich. "Causes of Thrift Failures: An Analysis of 1988 Resolutions." In *Proceedings of a Conference on Bank Structure and Competition.* Chicago: Federal Reserve Bank of Chicago, 1989.

Benston, George J. *An Analysis of the Causes of Savings and Loan Failures.* New York: Salomon Brothers Center for the Study of Financial Institutions, 1985.

Benston, George J., Gerald A. Hanweck, and David B. Humphrey. "Scale Economies in Banking: A Restructuring and Reassessment." *Journal of Money, Credit, and Banking* 14 (November 1982): 435–456.

Blyn, Martin R. "The Evolution of Money and Capital Markets and Financial Institutions." In *Financial Institutions and Markets,* 2d ed., edited by Murray E. Polakoff and Thomas A. Durkin, 33–54. Boston: Houghton Mifflin, 1981.

Brunner, Allan D., and William B. English. "Profits and Balance Sheet Developments at U.S. Commercial Banks in 1992." *Federal Reserve Bulletin* 79 (July 1993): 649–673.

Brunner, Allan D., Diana Hancock, and Mary M. McLaughlin. "Recent Developments Affecting the Profitability and Practices of Commercial Banks." *Federal Reserve Bulletin* 78 (July 1992): 459–483.

Burke, Jim, Stephen A. Rhoades, and John Wolken. "Thrift Institutions and Their New Powers." *Journal of Commercial Bank Lending* 69 (June 1987): 43–54.

Cobos, Dean Forrester. "Forbearance: Practices and Proposed Standards." *FDIC Banking Review* 2 (Spring/Summer 1989): 20–28.

Cohen, Robert B. "The Foreign Challenge to U.S. Commercial Banks." In *New York's Financial Markets: The Challenges of Globalization,* edited by Thierry Noyelle. Boulder, CO: The Westview Press, 1989.

Cole, Rebel A. "Thrift Resolution Activity: Historical Overview and Implications." *Financial Industry Studies* (Federal Reserve Bank of Dallas) (May 1990): 1–12.

Cox, William N., and Pamela V. Whigham. "What Distinguishes Larger and More Efficient Credit Unions?" *Economic Review* (Federal Reserve Bank of Atlanta) 69 (October 1984): 34–41.

Demirgüç-Kunt, Asli. "Deposit-Institution Failures: A Review of Empirical Literature." *Economic Review* (Federal Reserve Bank of Cleveland) 25 (Quarter IV 1989): 2–18.

DiClemente, John J. "What Is a Bank?" *Economic Perspectives* (Federal Reserve Bank of Chicago) 7 (January/February 1983): 20–31.

Dowling, William A., George Philippatos, and Dosoung Choi. "Economies of Scale through Mergers in the S&L Industry." In *Proceedings of a Conference on Bank Structure and Competition,* 480–497. Chicago: Federal Reserve Bank of Chicago, 1984.

Duca, John V., and Mary M. McLaughlin. "Developments Affecting the Profitability of Commercial Banks." *Federal Reserve Bulletin* 76 (July 1990): 477–500.

Elliehausen, Gregory E., and John D. Wolken. "Banking Markets and the Use of Financial Services by Households." *Federal Reserve Bulletin* 78 (March 1992): 169–181.

Federal Reserve Bank of New York. *Recent Trends in Commercial Bank Profitability: A Staff Study.* New York: Federal Reserve Bank of New York, 1986.

Fortier, Diana, and David Phillis. "Bank and Thrift Performance Since DIDMCA." *Economic Perspectives.* (Federal Reserve Bank of Chicago) 9 (September/October 1985): 58–68.

Goudreau, Robert E. "S&L Use of New Powers: A Comparative Study of State- and Federal-Chartered Associations." *Economic Review* (Federal Reserve Bank of Atlanta) 69 (October 1984a): 18–33.

———. "S&L Use of New Powers: Consumer and Commercial Loan Expansion." *Economic Review* (Federal Reserve Bank of Atlanta) 69 (December 1984b): 15–35.

———. "Commercial Bank Profitability Rises as Interest Margins and Securities Sales Increase." *Economic Review* (Federal Reserve Bank of Atlanta) 77 (May/June 1992): 33–52.

Goudreau, Robert E., and Harold E. Ford. "Changing Thrifts: What Makes Them Choose Commercial Lending?" *Economic Review* (Federal Reserve Bank of Atlanta) 71 (June/July 1986): 24–39.

Goudreau, Robert E., and B. Frank King. "Commercial Bank Profitability: Hampered Again by Large Banks' Loan Problems." *Economic Review* (Federal Reserve Bank of Atlanta) 76 (July/August 1991): 39–54.

Joseph, Milton. "International Banking in the U.S." *Southern Business and Economic Journal* 15 (January 1992): 112–117.

Kaufman, George G. "Bank Runs: Causes, Benefits, and Costs." *The Cato Journal* 7 (Winter 1988): 559–587.

Kohers, Theodore, and David Mullis. "The Effect of Parent Company Business on Occupational Credit Union Behavior." *Applied Economics* 18 (December 1986): 1311–1321.

Krause, James R. "Foreign Banks Face Hurdles." *American Banker,* April 19, 1993, 2A.

Kulczycky, Maria. "The History of Associations: From a Homebuyers Club to a $600-Billion Business." *Savings and Loan News* 101 (December 1981): 70–73.

Linnen, Beth M. "Sister Businesses Grow Together." *Savings Institutions* 104 (July 1983): 42–46.

Mahoney, Patrick I., and Alice P. White. "The Thrift Industry in Transition." *Federal Reserve Bulletin* 71 (March 1985): 137–156.

Makin, Claire. "Cultivating the New Rich." *Institutional Investor* 23 (April 1989): 130–139.

McNulty, James E. "Economies of Scale in the S&L Industry: New Evidence and Implications for Profitability." *Federal Home Loan Bank Board Journal* 14 (February 1981): 2–8.

Meehan, John, et al. "Banks: Is Big Trouble Brewing?" *Business Week,* July 16, 1990, 146–152.

Mester, Loretta. "A Multiproduct Cost Study of Savings and Loans." *Journal of Finance* 42 (June 1987): 423–445.

Misback, Ann E. "The Foreign Bank Supervision Enhancement Act of 1991." *Federal Reserve Bulletin* 79 (January 1993): 1–10.

Moody, J. Carroll, and Gilbert C. Fite. *The Credit Union Movement.* Lincoln: University of Nebraska Press, 1971.

Nejezchleb, Lynn A. "Declining Profitability at Small Commercial Banks: A Temporary Development or a Secular Trend?" *Banking and Economic Review,* FDIC 4 (June 1986): 9–21.

Pearce, Douglas K. "Recent Developments in the Credit Union Industry." *Economic Review* (Federal Reserve Bank of Kansas City) 69 (June 1984): 3–19.

Rhoades, Stephen A. "Mergers and Acquisitions by Commercial Banks, 1960–1983." Board of Governors of the Federal Reserve System, Staff Study Number 142, January 1985.

Swary, Itzhak. "Continental Illinois Crisis: An Empirical Analysis of Regulatory Behavior." Salomon Brothers Center for the Study of Financial Institutions, Working Paper Number 335, January 1985.

Wolfson, Martin H., and Mary M. McLaughlin. "Recent Developments in the Profitability and Lending Practices of Commercial Banks." *Federal Reserve Bulletin* 75 (July 1989): 461–484.

Wolken, John D., and Frank J. Navratil. "Economies of Scale in Credit Unions." *Journal of Finance* 35 (June 1980): 769–777.

Reserves are a deadweight loss and a drag on banks' ability to compete.
Anonymous Fed Official (1992)

The first edition of this book contained the story of Thomas Spiegel, who by 1985 had built his Beverly Hills, California, savings and loan (S&L) into one of the largest and most profitable in the industry. Mr. Spiegel—who at one time drew a $9 million annual salary from the S&L and built not one, but two, gymnasiums for the thrift's employees—accomplished this feat by investing a substantial portion of Columbia Savings' assets in high-yielding (junk) bonds. Although investing in these higher risk assets was controversial from the beginning, Columbia, a state-chartered institution, was taking dual advantage of California's relatively permissive regulations and Mr. Spiegel's friendship with junk bond king Michael Milken of Drexel Burnham Lambert, the so-called guru of high-yield bond investments. At its zenith, Columbia's junk bond portfolio was valued at $4 billion, fully 40 percent of the thrift's assets.

By 1990, as the second edition of this book was in preparation, how the mighty had fallen. Milken had pled guilty to charges of securities fraud and violation of insider trading rules; the market value of Columbia's junk bonds had fallen by almost $1 billion; Congress had outlawed junk bonds as thrift investments; and Spiegel had left Columbia in disgrace.

Although in 1993, Mr. Spiegel's ultimate fate remained uncertain, U.S. taxpayers knew this much: Columbia's closure in 1991 had cost $2 billion, one of the largest failures in the entire thrift debacle. Spiegel awaited trial after his 55-count indictment on charges of misappropriation, fraud, and lying to federal regulators. His story had come to symbolize to many the dark side of deregulation.[1]

Earlier chapters have indicated that efforts to reduce regulation and to encourage competition have broadened market opportunities for depositories. How managers respond to these opportunities is determined by the institution's long-term goals and is influenced by the preferences of shareholders, regulators, customers, and managers themselves. In this

CHAPTER

13

ASSET
MANAGEMENT:
LIQUIDITY
RESERVES AND
THE SECURITIES
PORTFOLIO

---

[1] Kathleen Kerwin, "He Who Lives by the Junk Bond . . . ," *Business Week,* December 25, 1989, 46–47; Richard B. Schmitt, "Spiegel Indicted in Case Stemming from S&L Failure," *The Wall Street Journal,* June 25, 1992, B4.

chapter and those to follow, major areas of decision making in depository institutions—liquidity, portfolio analysis, lending, and liability and capital management—are examined. The final challenge is to coordinate decisions in separate areas into an overall asset/liability management strategy for the institution, addressing the risk and return preferences of all parties. This chapter focuses on managing liquidity and the securities portfolio, in which departure from tradition was the hallmark of the 1980s. Unfortunately, as in Thomas Spiegel's case, results were not always successful, and most institutions entered the 1990s with sobering lessons from the previous decade in mind. But managers continue to adapt and to innovate in an effort to outperform the competition and stay ahead of regulators.

IMPORTANCE OF LIQUIDITY IN DEPOSITORY INSTITUTIONS

As defined in Chapter 5, liquidity is the ease with which an individual, business, or financial institution can obtain cash by selling noncash assets without loss in value. In this chapter, the concept of liquidity is broadened to include the ease with which financial institutions (or others) can obtain cash by borrowing from external sources. As one expert explained it, depository institution liquidity is "the ability . . . to raise a certain amount of funds at a certain cost within a certain amount of time."[2] Access to cash is important in the financial management of all businesses, but because providing liquidity for customers is an intermediation function, a depository institution's own liquidity is even more important. Institutions obtain many deposits under promise of immediate or almost immediate repayment on demand, so the investment and financing decisions for a depository are inseparable.[3] In other words, obtaining deposits and deciding how to invest them are closely intertwined.

REGULATORS REQUIRE LIQUIDITY

Because deposits—especially some transactions accounts—can be volatile, government regulatory agencies emphasize depository institution liquidity. Most depositories operate under a set of liquidity requirements established at either the state or the federal level. Also, after the Depository Institutions Deregulation and Monetary Control Act (DIDMCA) extended Federal Reserve System (Fed) reserve requirements to all depository institutions, all but the smallest institutions must meet standards set by more than one regulator—the Fed's and those of their chartering or insuring agency.

DEPOSITORS REQUIRE LIQUIDITY

Besides the requirements of regulators, liquidity needs are affected by the expectations of depositors. The nation's largest depositories explicitly recognize this fact. A recent annual report of the First Chicago Corporation states, "The Corporation has traditionally viewed liquidity quite simply as the ability to meet all present and future financial obligations in a timely manner."[4] One of Citicorp's annual reports presents a similar view: "Citicorp defines adequate liquidity as having funds available at all times to repay fully and promptly all maturing liabilities in accordance with their terms, including customer demand deposits."[5]

BORROWERS REQUIRE LIQUIDITY

Depository institutions generate most of their interest income from loans and strive to develop a strong base of loan customers. To retain the loyalty of customers, a lender must be able to provide funds for all loan applications that meet its credit standards. Thus, an institution needs to maintain liquidity to support expected loan demand in addition to meeting obligations arising from its liabilities.

LIQUIDITY: THE RISK/RETURN TRADE-OFF

With many compelling reasons to maintain liquidity, one might think that liquidity can be easily managed by keeping a large quantity of cash or marketable securities in the asset portfolio. However, a well-recognized trade-off is that liquid assets contribute relatively little to the firm's net interest margin (NIM), because they ordinarily offer a low rate of return. Cash and most reserve deposits earn no return at all. Under an upward-sloping yield curve, short-term, marketable securities earn a lower yield than assets with longer maturities, and in the early 1990s, the difference between short- and long-term rates has been unusually high. The conflict between the risk of illiquidity and a desire to maintain a high NIM is the heart of liquidity management. The challenge is to maintain enough liquidity to avoid a crisis but to sacrifice no more earnings than absolutely necessary. Although the need for liquid assets arises for a variety of reasons, and all demands must be met simultaneously, each need presents a separate problem. The discussion that follows addresses the components of liquidity management individually.

---

[2] See Burns 1971, 1. (References are listed in full at the end of this chapter.)

[3] See Sealey 1983. See Chapter 1 for further discussion of these concepts.

[4] First Chicago Corporation, *1982 Annual Report,* 25.

[5] Citicorp, *Citicorp Worldwide: 1988 Report,* 34.

ESTIMATING LIQUIDITY NEEDS: FEDERAL RESERVE BOARD REQUIREMENTS

The first reserve requirements for depository institutions were established on deposits of commercial banks with national charters in the National Currency and National Banking Acts of 1863 and 1864.[6] These reserves, established as a percentage of deposits and other liabilities, were required as either cash or interbank deposits, depending on the location of the bank. The rationale for reserve requirements was to protect the liquidity of the banking system to promote public confidence. The Federal Reserve Act of 1913 revised but continued reserve requirements. At the time of its passage, the motivation for the reserve provisions remained prevention of liquidity crises in individual institutions or geographical regions.

NEW RATIONALE

The establishment of the Fed discount window in 1913, through which member banks had access to short-term borrowed funds, provided a source of liquidity that had previously been lacking. With the discount window to protect liquidity, the Fed revised its view of the purpose of reserve requirements. By 1931, they were recognized as a tool for controlling the amount of credit extended by banks, and by the 1950s, they had become an important element of monetary policy. As discussed in Chapter 2, in the 1970s, the Fed argued that existing reserve requirements, applying only to Fed-member commercial banks, limited the Board's ability to achieve monetary policy goals. That view finally prevailed in the passage of DIDMCA, and reserve requirements were extended to all depositories, both state and federally chartered. While the Fed sought greater control over reserve requirements in DIDMCA, many observers (including the anonymous official quoted at the beginning of this chapter) have lamented the fact that the requirements are an unpro-

ductive regulatory tax that either reduces funds available for lending and investing or is passed along to customers in the form of higher loan rates and fees. In the 1990s, the Federal Reserve Board itself has seemed to agree with its critics: Reserve requirements have been lowered several times, to 0 percent in some cases. Details on recent requirements are presented in the next section.

RESERVE REQUIREMENTS SINCE 1980

Although the rationale for imposing reserve requirements on depository institutions is no longer solely to protect the liquidity position of the financial system, meeting the requirements continues to be a key issue in individual institutions. Table 13.1 contains Fed reserve requirements since 1980; for large Fed-member commercial banks, the reserve burden has decreased considerably since that time, and the maximum percentage has been lowered from $16\frac{1}{4}$ to 10. For smaller member banks and for all other depositories brought under the reserve ruling in 1980, the reserve burden has increased slightly. Table 13.1 points out that in 1993, the 10 percent requirement applied to total transactions accounts in excess of $46.8 million.

At the recommendation of the Fed, a reprieve was granted to the smallest depository institutions in the Garn-St Germain Act of 1982. That law contained a provision that the first $2 million of reservable deposits were subject to a 0 percent reserve requirement. The amount of deposits to which this provision applies is adjusted annually, based on the total growth of bank deposits during the year. By 1993, the 0 percent bracket was $3.8 million, as stated in footnote a of Table 13.1.

MANAGING THE RESERVE POSITION

Required reserves must be held as vault cash or as deposits at a district Federal Reserve Bank. The Fed requires weekly reports from large depositories; a quarterly schedule applies to institutions with total deposits below an amount specified in Federal Reserve **Regulation D** (Reg D). If an institution's reserves are below the minimum required, it is subject to a penalty imposed by the Fed. The Fed does not pay interest on

---

[6] For a discussion of the history of reserve requirements, on which the historical information in this chapter is based, see Feinman 1993 and Goodfriend and Hargraves 1983. An earlier survey treatment of this topic is Knight 1974. A good recent article arguing that **no** rationale for reserve requirements is convincing enough to justify them is Stevens 1991.

TABLE 13.1   **Reserve Requirements of the Federal Reserve System**

Reserve requirements vary according to the amount of deposits held by institutions and are set at different levels for different categories of deposits. Requirements have been altered several times in the 1990s and are less burdensome for depositories than in past decades.

Type of Deposit and Deposit Interval	Requirements	
	% of Deposits	Effective Date
Net transactions accounts[a]		
$0 million–$46.8 million	3	12/15/92
More than $46.8 million	10	12/15/92
Nonpersonal time deposits by original maturity		
Less than 1½ years	0	12/27/90
1½ years or more	0	10/6/83
Eurocurrency liabilities, all types	0	12/27/90

[a]0% bracket as of 1993 was $3.8 million.
Source: Federal Reserve Bulletin, March 1993.

reserve deposits, so reserve balances are nonearning assets for depositories.[7] Because of the penalty exacted for having too few reserves and the loss of income from having too many, depositories must estimate their reserve requirements as accurately as possible.

CONTEMPORANEOUS RESERVE ACCOUNTING. From 1968 until early 1984, calculating reserve requirements was relatively straightforward. An institution knew a week in advance the amount of reserves needed, because they were based on average deposits for the week ending 7 days earlier, a system called **lagged reserve accounting (LRA).** The chief problem for management was deciding the most efficient way to obtain this known quantity of funds.

The Fed, however, viewed the lagged system as an impediment to effective monetary control. In October 1979, the Fed revised its monetary control procedures, placing greater emphasis on depository reserves as a way of achieving monetary growth targets. Subsequently, on February 2, 1984, the Board of Gover-

nors instituted a procedure known as **contemporaneous reserve accounting (CRA).** The new system has complicated reserve management. CRA applies only to institutions reporting weekly; others continue to compute required reserves under a lagged system.

CRA RULES. Under CRA, an institution's required reserves on transactions deposits are determined by deposit levels in the same period, rather than in a previous period as is the case under the lagged system. Reserves on nontransactions liabilities are still computed on a lagged basis. The **maintenance period** is the time during which reserve balances must be on deposit. It lasts 2 weeks, extending from a Thursday to a Wednesday 14 days later. The reserve **computation period** is also 2 weeks, beginning on Tuesday in the same week that the maintenance period begins and ending on the Monday 14 days later. The average daily level of reserves during the maintenance period must meet the required percentages on the average level of deposits during the computation period.[8]

---

[7]In one DIDMCA provision, Congress established a range of 8 to 14 percent for the marginal reserve requirements on transactions accounts. It gave the Fed the authority to set a higher percentage for monetary policy reasons but stipulated that the Fed must pay interest on those reserves. The authority has never been exercised. For further details, see "The Depository Institutions Deregulation and Monetary Control Act of 1980," 1980; and Cacy and Winningham 1980.

[8]More details on the comparison between lagged reserve accounting and contemporaneous reserve accounting may be found in the following articles, some of which also serve as the sources for the description of CRA in the paragraphs that follow: Rosenbaum 1984; Hamdani 1984; and Tarhan 1984. Also, major portions of the December 1983 and January 1984 issues of *Roundup,* Federal Reserve Bank of Dallas, were devoted to the change in reserve accounting procedures. See also Stevens 1991.

FIGURE 13.1 Reserve Requirement Computation: Contemporaneous Reserve Accounting

Under contemporaneous reserve requirements, the reserve computation period for transactions accounts and the reserve maintenance period overlap substantially, increasing the difficulty of managing reserves.

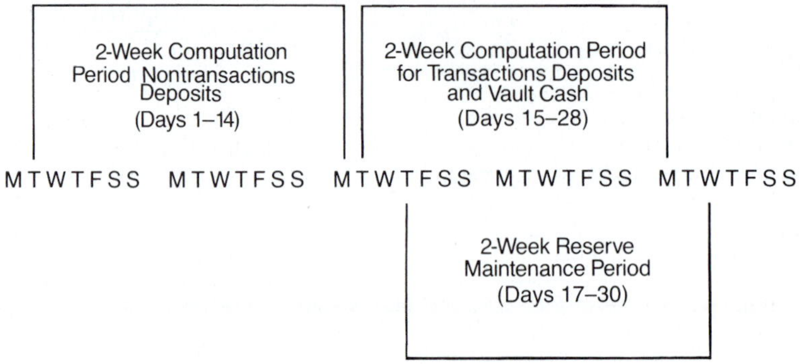

Reserve Management Calendar

M	T 1	W 2	T 3	F 4	S 5	S 6
M 7	T 8	W 9	T 10	F 11	S 12	S 13
M 14	T 15	W 16	T 17	F 18	S 19	S 20
M 21	T 22	W 23	T 24	F 25	S 26	S 27
M 28	T 29	W 30	T 31	F 32	S 33	S 34
M 35	T 36	W 37	T 38	F 39	S 40	S 41
M 42	T 43	W 44				

Lagged Computation Period (Days 1–14)

Contemporaneous Computation Period (Days 15–28)

Maintenance Period (Days 17–30)

(Maintenance Period Is Shaded.)

Source: Adapted from Mary Susan Rosenbaum, "Contemporaneous Reserve Accounting: The New System and its Implications for Monetary Policy," *Economic Review* (Federal Reserve Bank of Atlanta), 69 (April 1984): 47; and "Contemporaneous Reserves Change Accounting Procedures," *Roundup* (Federal Reserve Bank of Dallas), December 1983. Updated by the authors.

These rules, which sound (and are) confusing, are illustrated in Figure 13.1. The computation and maintenance periods are not strictly contemporaneous, although they overlap. On the calendar at the bottom of Figure 13.1, the computation period on transactions deposits extends from day 15 to day 28, and the maintenance period covers days 17 to 30. As deposits fluctuate, reserve balances must be adjusted almost simultaneously. For example, suppose that deposits increase on day 28, at the end of the computation period. The depository must adjust its reserves quickly to meet the minimum required during the maintenance period ending 2 days later. The institution has only 2 days, 29 and 30, to hold higher reserve balances to increase the overall maintenance period average to the required level.

Figure 13.1 also illustrates that if the Fed decides to reimpose them in the future, reserve balances on nontransactions liabilities are to be computed on a lagged schedule. These liabilities include nonpersonal time deposits, such as large negotiable certificates of deposit (CDs) with initial maturities less than $1\frac{1}{2}$ years, and all Eurocurrency liabilities. Since late 1990, however, the reserve requirement on such deposits has been 0 percent.

FORMS IN WHICH RESERVES ARE HELD. Further complicating reserve management is the variety of acceptable forms of reserves. First, an institution may hold deposits at Federal Reserve Banks during the 14-day maintenance period. For nonmember institutions, reserve balances may be deposited at designated institutions; these balances are called pass-through balances. Correspondent banks often serve as holders of reserve deposits for their institutional customers. Also, an institution may count average daily vault cash held during the computation period.[9]

Knowing the exact amount of cash and reserves available to meet reserve requirements is complicated by the check-clearing process. As checks are cleared through the district Fed banks, the Fed transfers funds from the account of one bank to the account of another. At any time, then, an institution's total reserves contain **clearing balances,** which may be subsequently transferred as a result of customers' transactions. Conversely, reserves from other institutions may be transferred in. The Fed recognizes the difficulty of forecasting deposit balances accurately and permits a **carry-over privilege.**

The carryover allows a depository to get credit in one maintenance period for excess reserves in the previous maintenance period. The amount carried over may not exceed the greater of either 4 percent of the average daily minimum reserve balance in the current period or $50,000. (The size of the privilege was doubled in 1992, again suggesting that the Fed is increasingly sensitive to the "taxing" effect of reserve requirements.) An institution also may carry a negative

reserve position for one period without penalty, if reserves in the next period offset the shortcoming.[10]

CALCULATING REQUIRED RESERVES

Table 13.2 provides an example of calculating required reserves under CRA. The institution is a hypothetical commercial bank, but the process would be similar for any institution subject to the CRA rules. The days correspond to the reserve management calendar in Figure 13.1, and all dollar amounts are in millions. The lagged computation period is a 2-week span (days 1–14) that ends 1 day before the contemporaneous computation period (days 15–28) begins.

THE LAGGED COMPUTATION PERIOD. Based on the 0 percent requirement in effect after 1990, no reserves need be maintained against the average level of nontransactions liabilities held during days 1–14 ($456,786,000). Should the Fed choose to reimpose a nonzero requirement on these liabilities, management could determine this component of required reserves before the actual maintenance period begins.

THE CONTEMPORANEOUS COMPUTATION PERIOD. Suppose the average daily level of vault cash for this bank is $9,671,000 during days 15–28. This average can be counted as part of required reserves. Reserves

---

[9] Average cash balances counted toward reserve requirements had been based on the same computation period as that used for reserves against nontransactions balances. See Rosenbaum 1984. For cash balances, the computation period was altered from days 1–14 to days 15–28 in 1992.

[10] Most institutions do, in fact, hold excess reserves most of the time. Research indicates that the quantity of excess reserves held under LRA varied inversely with the size of the depository institution. Research under CRA, published by the Federal Reserve Bank of New York, detected no change in the pattern. The largest commercial banks tend to have the lowest levels of excess reserves, and small banks and thrifts hold higher levels. A common explanation for this pattern has been suggested. If an institution wants to keep reserves at the lowest possible level, the attention of a full-time manager is usually required. For some institutions, these costs may exceed the opportunity cost of holding the extra nonearning reserves.

Difficulty in forecasting the deposit levels against which reserves must be held was considered a particularly serious component of CRA. Research conducted at the Federal Reserve Bank of St. Louis concluded that forecasting errors could be large enough to justify an increase in the positive/negative carryover privilege to 5 percent from the 2 percent used initially. As noted, the carryover privilege *was* increased in 1992. See Gilbert 1980; and Hamdani 1984.

Still, research on actual bank behavior several years after CRA indicates that, on balance, institutions adjusted well to the system. See Saunders and Urich 1988 and Evanoff 1989.

TABLE 13.2   **Reserve Balance Computation (millions)**

Under contemporaneous reserve accounting, management of reserve balances involves complex relationships. The last two days of the maintenance period are particularly important for assuring that the average required minimum balance is achieved.

Lagged Computation Period			Contemporaneous Computation Period				Maintenance Period		
Day #	Day	Non-Transactions Liabilities	Day #	Day	Vault Cash	Transactions Deposits	Day #	Day	Reserve Balances
1	T	$450	15	T	$9.5	$1,082			
2	W	485	16	W	9.3	1,090			
3	T	460	17	T	9.6	1,055	17	T	$93
4	F	445	18	F	9.8	1,085	18	F	99
5	S	445	19	S	9.8	1,108	19	S	104
6	S	445	20	S	9.8	1,115	20	S	101
7	M	440	21	M	9.1	1,100	21	M	97
8	T	425	22	T	9.5	1,110	22	T	103
9	W	465	23	W	9.2	1,112	23	W	105
10	T	450	24	T	9.8	1,150	24	T	96
11	F	475	25	F	9.9	1,155	25	F	98
12	S	475	26	S	9.9	1,138	26	S	94
13	S	475	27	S	9.9	1,256	27	S	102
14	M	460	28	M	10.3	1,338	28	M	99
							29	T	
							30	W	
Average:		$456.786			$9.671	$1,135.286	12-day total:		$1,191.000
							12-day average:		$99.250

A 10% requirement applies to all transactions deposits of over $46.8 million.

Required average daily reserve balance:

0% of nontransactions liabilities (lagged)	$0.000
+ 3% of first $46.8 in transactions deposits (contemporaneous)	$1.404
+ 10% of remaining transactions deposits (contemporaneous)	$108.849
− Average vault cash	($9.671)
Average daily balance required	$100.581[a]

Reserve adjustment required:

Cumulative total reserves required (daily average × 14):	$1,408.136
Less cumulative total achieved in first 12 days:	$1,191.000
Total amount required for last two days	$217.136
Average balance required last two days ($217.136/2):	$108.568

Maximum negative carryover allowed:

Daily requirement × 0.04	$4.023

[a]Does not add because of rounding; slight rounding differences may also affect other calculations.

to be held against transactions deposits subject to reserve requirements will depend on average account levels during the same period (days 15–28). As a part of the planning process, management can forecast transactions deposit levels for the computation and maintenance periods, incorporating information about past deposits, seasonal trends, and other factors relevant for the period. Suppose these forecasts suggest that average reserves on transactions deposits will be $98 million. After adjusting for vault cash, the target daily reserve balance during the maintenance period is $88,329,000.

$$\text{Target Balance} = TR + NTR - VC \qquad [13.1]$$
$$= \$98,000,000 + \$0$$
$$- \$9,671,000$$
$$= \$88,329,000$$

where

TR = transactions deposit reserves
NTR = nontransactions liabilities reserves
VC = average vault cash during computation period

Suppose that deposits rise unexpectedly on the last 2 days of the computation period (days 27–28). For this bank, as shown in Table 13.2, the unanticipated deposit changes result in an actual required average daily reserve balance of $100,581,000. For the first 12 days of the maintenance period, the bank has held an average balance of only $99,250,000—enough to meet the estimated target balance but below the actual minimum requirement. To meet the Fed's standards, the bank must significantly increase reserve holdings for the last 2 days.

The calculations for the additional amount needed are shown at the bottom of Table 13.2. At the average requirement of $100,581,000, cumulative total reserves over the period must be $1,408,136,000, but the total held for the previous 12-day period is only $1,191,000,000. The average balance for the last 2 days of the maintenance period, then, must be $108,568,000.

If the bank has held excess reserves in the previous maintenance period, management would use the positive carryover privilege to cover some of the current required balances. Also, the bank may take advantage of the negative carryover privilege and end the maintenance period with slightly less than the total required ($4,023,000 would be allowed in this case). Still, the bank's managers must make some quick decisions if they want to avoid a Fed-imposed penalty. Alternative actions are discussed later in the chapter.

RESERVE REQUIREMENTS OF OTHER REGULATORS

Many depositories are affected by the reserve requirements of other regulators. Because state rules vary considerably, the following discussion encompasses only federal regulations.

FEDERAL THRIFT REGULATORS

The Federal Home Loan Bank Board (FHLBB) first established liquidity requirements for federal S&Ls in 1950 and revised them relatively often between 1968 and 1989. Instead of setting minimum cash levels or requiring reserve deposits, however, the FHLBB defined liquidity much more broadly than the Fed had defined it for banks. Thus, federal S&Ls were able to count a variety of investments, such as federal funds sold and even municipal bonds, as liquid assets, in addition to cash and short-term government securities. The Office of Thrift Supervision (OTS), replacing the Bank Board as the chief policy-making body for federal S&Ls, was directed by Congress to continue the tradition of defining liquid assets rather broadly, but it was also directed to ensure that savings associations maintain appropriate liquidity levels.

In the Financial Institutions Reform, Recovery, and Enforcement Act (FIRREA), Congress actually expanded the definition of liquid assets for savings associations by adding selected mutual fund holdings, short-term mortgage-backed securities, and even certain types of home mortgage loans to the list of assets that may be considered by the regulators in evaluating liquidity. Minimum liquidity requirements are set as a percentage of a thrift's withdrawable accounts (i.e., transactions accounts, money market deposit accounts [MMDAs], passbook accounts, and short-term CDs), plus borrowings repayable on demand or within 1 year.

The director of the OTS was given the authority to establish minimum liquidity requirements, but Congress mandated that they be between 4 percent and 10 percent of an association's total short-term liabilities, as defined in the previous paragraph. Since FIRREA, different liquidity requirements may be set for different categories of savings associations, depending on size, location, type, or other institutional characteristics. Also, FIRREA allows the OTS to penalize institutions not complying with prescribed liquidity standards.

Congress also noted that the purpose of the new liquidity requirements in FIRREA was to support the supply of mortgage credit. The act states, in fact, that effective and flexible liquidity requirements are necessary so that savings associations can respond to varying levels of funds availability and demand for credit in the mortgage markets.[11]

NATIONAL CREDIT UNION ADMINISTRATION

The National Credit Union Administration (NCUA) has the authority to impose liquidity requirements but does not always exercise it. Between 1979 and 1982, federal credit unions (CUs) offering share drafts or those with assets in excess of $2 million were required to hold liquid assets equal to 5 percent of member accounts plus notes payable. The additional liquidity standards were discontinued after the extension of Fed reserve requirements to these institutions.[12] Nevertheless, the lack of specific regulatory requirements does not eliminate concern for liquidity. Several decisions involved in CU liquidity management are addressed in later sections.

ESTIMATING NONRESERVE LIQUIDITY NEEDS

Besides meeting standards set by government regulators, depository institutions need liquid funds to meet customer loan demand and deposit withdrawals. Commercial banks, having offered transactions accounts and short-term commercial loans longer than other depositories, have traditionally been more concerned with liquidity needs arising from operations, but nonbank depositories now pay increased attention to liquidity because they, too, now offer transactions accounts.

DISCRETIONARY AND NONDISCRETIONARY FACTORS

The balance sheet of a depository can be divided into discretionary and nondiscretionary items.[13] Discretionary items include those over which management can exert considerable influence, such as the use of repurchase agreements. Nondiscretionary items are those beyond the short-run control of an institution, such as deposit fluctuations, loan demand, and reserve requirements. Some nondiscretionary items—such as deposit increases or maturing loans—are sources of liquidity, but others are drains on liquidity.

Managers must understand the implications of nondiscretionary items for their institutions. A depository that derives most of its revenues from loans does not really wish to deny loans to good customers based on liquidity shortages. Such actions would undermine customer relationships built over long years of service and damage profit potential. Refusing to honor customer requests for deposit withdrawals would surely have even more severe consequences. These operations-based liquidity demands are an important part of the planning process.

ESTIMATING LIQUIDITY NEEDS FOR OPERATIONS: AN EXAMPLE

The estimation of liquidity needs arising from anticipated volatility in deposits and expected loan demand involves several techniques, ranging from managerial judgment to quantitative models. Table 13.3 presents a simplified example of estimating a liquidity surplus or deficit over a single planning period.[14] The first step is to estimate total balances in each main asset and funding source category.

LIQUID AND ILLIQUID ASSETS. Asset categories are then divided into liquid or illiquid components; liquid assets in this context are those available to meet operational needs. For example, at the top of Table 13.3, the institution's total cash balances during the next

---

[11] "Conference Report on H.R. 1278," 1989.

[12] See Pearce 1984.

[13] This dichotomy was proposed in Luckett 1980, 12–13.

[14] This example is similar to one in Kaufman and Lee 1977.

TABLE 13.3	**Estimating Liquidity Needs for Operations**				

Institutions need to forecast potential liquidity positions and plan to avoid deficits. The approach illustrated identifies the volatility of funds sources and estimates whether liquid assets could cover large outflows and meet additional loan demand.

	Total (Millions)	Liquid (%)	Liquid	Illiquid
I. Original Assumptions				
Assets				
Cash	$ 209.7	10%	$ 21.0	$ 188.7
Investments	1,037.6	59	609.4	428.2
Loans	1,214.4	0	0.0	1,214.4
Other assets	171.0	9	15.0	156.0
Total	$2,632.7		$645.4	$1,987.3

		Volatile (%)	Volatile	Nonvolatile
Funds sources				
Deposits	$1,755.0	7%	$130.0	$1,625.0
Other liabilities	674.0	82	549.7	124.3
Equity	203.7	0	0.0	203.7
Total	$2,632.7		$679.7	$1,953.0

Liquidity deficit (liquid assets − volatile funds):
$645.4 − $679.7 = ($34.3)

	Total (Millions)	Liquid (%)	Liquid	Illiquid
II. Additional Loan Demand				
Assets				
Cash	$ 209.7	10%	$ 21.0	$ 188.7
Investments	1,037.6	59	609.4	428.2
Loans	1,214.4	−1	(12.1)	1,226.5
Other assets	171.0	9	15.0	156.0
Total	$2,632.7		$633.3	$1,999.4

Liquidity deficit (liquid assets − volatile funds):
$633.3 − $679.7 = ($46.4)

period are estimated to be almost $210 million. But because of reserve requirements and daily transactions, total cash balances are never entirely available to meet deposit withdrawals or increased loan demand. In fact, management has estimated that only $21 million could be used to fulfill these needs. Within the investments category, liquid investments are those that can be sold easily without great loss of value during the planning period. More about managing the securities portfolio to allow for operational liquidity appears later in the chapter.

VOLATILE AND NONVOLATILE SOURCES OF FUNDS. Drains on liquidity can be estimated by examining funds sources. In this institution, most deposits are considered relatively stable, so only $130 million are judged to be volatile. In contrast, other liabilities for borrowed money, including negotiable CDs, repurchase agreements, and federal funds purchased, are quite volatile. Management assumes that most could be withdrawn or become unavailable on short notice. The equity of the institution is entirely nonvolatile in the short run.

A liquidity deficit is projected for the upcoming period because liquid assets are less than volatile funds sources by $34.3 million. If management's estimates are correct, the institution must somehow generate additional cash in that amount.

ADDITIONAL DRAINS ON LIQUIDITY. The top of Table 13.3 assumes that next period's loan demand can be completely met by maturing loans or stable deposits; that is, the loan portfolio is viewed neither as a source of liquidity nor as a drain on liquidity. A more conservative approach would build in coverage for unexpected loan demand by assigning a *negative* balance to the liquid loan category, reflecting the drain on liquidity from increased loan demand. Suppose that management wishes to allow for additional loan demand equal to 1 percent of that already forecast, or a total of $12.1 million. The liquidity deficit from operations would rise to $46.4 million in that case, shown in the bottom panel of Table 13.3.

INCORPORATING QUANTITATIVE MODELS. A more quantitative method of estimating liquidity needs is to forecast from a regression analysis of past data. For example, in the analysis of expected loan demand, management could use a model relating past loan demand, D, to time, t: $D = f(t)$. The resulting regression equation can serve as a basis for projecting a range of future demand, incorporating past volatility and knowledge of other economic or seasonal factors that may cause a change from past trends. An even better forecast might be generated with multiple regression, because loan demand is also affected by factors such as economic conditions, interest rates, and competition from other institutions, to name just a few, and each institution must identify its relevant set of variables. Similar analyses can be performed for all nondiscretionary items affecting liquidity.

Sophistication in forecasting techniques is positively related to the size of depository institutions; this is not surprising because it is expensive to employ forecasting specialists.[15] Regardless of how forecasts

are generated, they are an important part of the liquidity management solution. These estimates combine with estimates of required reserves to represent a target level of liquid funds for the planning period.

MANAGING THE LIQUIDITY POSITION

Table 13.2 presents a bank's reserve dilemma; the bank has a potential reserve deficiency and needs immediate access to liquid funds to bring the 2-week daily average balance in line with the Fed requirements.[16] The institution in Table 13.3 needs liquidity as a result of operational factors. Whatever the reason, managers must act.

BORROWING VERSUS SELLING SECURITIES

Two general liquidity management strategies are available. First, management can borrow funds, either from the regulators or from nondeposit creditors in the financial markets. Obtaining nondeposit sources of cash, a technique used more often by large commercial banks than by other depositories, is called **liability management.** Because the use of nondeposit funds, such as federal funds and Euromarket borrowing, has implications far beyond liquidity management, full discussion of liability management is deferred until Chapter 16. This chapter discusses borrowing from regulators as a source of liquidity.

A second strategy is to use asset management, and liquidate assets from the securities portfolio. High market interest rates can make this approach undesirable. Also, depositories hold securities for purposes other than liquidity, so trade-offs are involved in this approach to liquidity management. Some of them are discussed later in the chapter.

---

[15] A survey of forecasting techniques revealed that the percentage of large banks (deposits in excess of $400 million) using sophisticated forecasting techniques such as multiple regression, time series forecasting, and simulation was higher than among smaller banks. A large number of institutions of all sizes, however, relied on managerial judgment—either alone or in combination with quantitative

methods—for estimating future deposit levels and loan demand. See Giroux 1980.

[16] Management of the reserve position is not limited to the problem of covering reserve deficiencies. Depositories may also find themselves with *excess* reserves toward the end of the maintenance period. When the institution has excess reserves, management may choose to lend them in the federal funds market. The asset thus created is defined in Chapter 12 as "federal funds sold." Calculating the effective yield on federal funds sold is illustrated in Chapter 5.

FACTORS INFLUENCING LIQUIDITY MANAGEMENT

The choice between borrowing or selling securities (i.e., between liability management and asset management) is influenced by several factors, including the size of the institution, its financial stability, its industry, and the risk/return preferences of managers and owners.

SIZE AND FINANCIAL STABILITY. Small or financially weak institutions are especially likely to look to the securities portfolio, not to liability management, for generating liquidity. Within the asset portfolio, too, liquidity is influenced by institutional size. As discussed more fully later, active portfolio management is expensive; thus, a smaller institution is likely to keep larger proportions of readily marketable short-term securities and higher excess reserve balances.

INDUSTRY MEMBERSHIP. Another influence over which a depository institution usually has little control is its industry. Regulatory policies governing an industry limit its operations—including the composition of its securities portfolio, the proportion of liquid assets held, and the sources of short-term loans for liquidity purposes. Recently, however, regulators have provided depository institutions with more freedom to change from one industry to another by simplifying the process of applying for new charters.

RISK/RETURN PREFERENCES. Managers' and owners' risk preferences also influence liquidity management. For a variety of reasons explored in Chapter 16, liability management exposes an institution to greater risks than does a strategy of selling securities when cash is needed. Furthermore, some strategies for managing the securities portfolio are riskier than others, as discussed later in this chapter.

BORROWING FROM REGULATORS AS A SOURCE OF LIQUIDITY

The carryover privilege on Fed reserve requirements is useful in meeting small deficiencies in liquid assets. For example, if deposits fluctuate unexpectedly toward the end of the maintenance period, an institution can postpone major reserve adjustments until the next period as long as the fluctuations are not too large.

However, if deficiencies are large or frequent, the institution can turn to federal regulators for other sources of cash for liquidity management.

THE DISCOUNT WINDOW. The Fed discount window was originally available only to member commercial banks, but DIDMCA opened it to all depositories subject to Fed reserve requirements. Commercial banks remain by far the largest users, because Fed policy requires other depositories to exhaust traditional sources of regulatory borrowing before turning to the discount window.

The Fed administers discount window borrowing under its **Regulation A,** which permits institutions to borrow under three conditions: to meet temporary liquidity needs, such as those illustrated in Table 13.2; to meet seasonal credit demands, such as those arising around Christmas or, for many rural banks, during planting season; and for special "extended credit" purposes, often after disasters such as Hurricane Andrew or the Los Angeles riots, both in 1992, which make unforeseeable demands on institutions. The Fed may also provide extended credit if an institution experiences unusually heavy withdrawals and regulators fear a "run," such as occurred with the near-failure of Continental National Bank in 1984.

The interest cost and availability of these borrowings are major factors in the decision to use the window. Ordinarily, discount-window borrowings are very short-term, used only to meet genuine liquidity emergencies and not as additional funds for expanding the loan portfolio. Officials at the Fed monitor an institution's use of the window and may ask management to discontinue borrowing should norms for the amount and frequency of borrowing be exceeded. Thus, frequent borrowing at the window has negative connotations that managers are careful to avoid.[17]

FHLB ADVANCES. Before FIRREA, federal savings institutions facing a shortage of qualifying liquid assets could apply for advances from the Federal Home Loan Banks (FHLBs). This FHLB lending program was originated in the Federal Home Loan Bank Act of 1932 and modeled after that of the Fed. Advances

---

[17] Details on the administration of the window can be found in Mengle 1986a and Sprong 1990.

from the FHLBs tended to be longer term than the Fed's discount-window loans, and the interest rate was sometimes adjusted by the Bank System in an effort to alter the volume of mortgage lending that thrifts were undertaking.

FIRREA made important changes to the FHLB advance program. Under certain circumstances, commercial banks and CUs are now eligible for advances from the FHLBs. In general, however, longer-term advances are made only to enable an institution to meet unmet demand for mortgage loans and not to provide a more-or-less permanent source of cash. Advances must be collateralized by low-risk assets, and the volume of advances is limited by an institution's level of net worth. Furthermore, the FHLBs must consider an institution's reinvestment in the community and its willingness to lend to first-time homebuyers in deciding whether to grant a requested advance.

FIRREA also specified conditions under which institutions with emergency cash shortages can obtain short-term advances from the FHLBs. Eligible institutions must be solvent and must present substantial evidence that they can repay the debt.[18] With these guidelines, Congress hoped to prevent a recurrence of the situation prevailing immediately before FIRREA, in which the insolvent portion of the industry owed regulators millions of dollars borrowed during the period of extreme forbearance, which it could never realistically repay.

SOURCES OF BORROWING FOR CREDIT UNIONS.

For CUs, three sources of short-term funds are available, two of these from regulatory sources. One source of liquidity was authorized by Congress in 1978, when it approved the creation of the Central Liquidity Facility (CLF), mentioned in Chapter 12 as an arm of the NCUA. The CLF functions as the lender of last resort for CUs voluntarily choosing to join it. In contrast to FHLB advances, CLF loans are made for liquidity purposes only.

Besides interest, the CLF requires borrowing CUs to pay a commitment fee of ¼ of 1 percent. Fed discount-window loans are also available to CUs offering transactions deposits or nonpersonal time de-

posits. Finally, a CU that is a member of a Corporate Credit Union (CCU) may borrow from the CCU.[19]

THE SECURITIES PORTFOLIO AS A SOURCE OF LIQUIDITY

Managing the securities portfolio—in particular, choosing an optimal combination of liquid versus higher-yielding assets—is an integral part of liquidity management for depository institutions. Because commercial banks have carried the highest reserve requirements and the shortest-term liabilities, most research on liquidity management has focused on banks. With the acceleration of deregulation, these issues are of increasing concern to all depositories.

THE RELATIVE LIQUIDITY OF SECURITIES.

Assets central to liquidity planning are often categorized according to their relative liquidity. Cash balances held over and above required reserves are known as **primary reserves.** Securities held to protect short-term liquidity are called **secondary reserves** and consist of short-term marketable securities, such as Treasury bills (T-bills), that can be readily sold without extreme exposure to market-value risk.

Not all highly marketable securities are considered secondary reserves. Some must be held as collateral for repurchase agreements or borrowings from regulators and others as pledges against government deposits. These requirements restrict the securities portfolio as a source of liquidity. For example, institutions receiving deposits from the U.S. government in excess of the Federal Deposit Insurance Corporation (FDIC) insurance ceiling are required to pledge collateral against these deposits. Only certain assets, such as U.S. government, state, or local securities, qualify as collateral. Most states also have laws requiring backing for public deposits. In addition, institutions serving as major dealers in money market assets must keep an inventory of **trading account securities** from which to make trades with customers.

Finally, other investments providing potential liquidity over a longer-term planning horizon are designated as **tertiary reserves.** These securities have longer maturities and are ordinarily held to produce investment income, but they are still marketable if cash

---

[18] See McKenna, Conner, and Cuneo 1989, 49–50.

[19] See Pearce 1984; and *NCUSIF Annual Report* 1991.

is needed to meet unexpected changes in deposit withdrawals or loan demand. Beyond these three categories are securities viewed entirely as investment assets, which may fulfill different objectives, such as the generation of income. A key problem in management of liquidity through the securities portfolio is determining the proportionate investment across these categories.

MATCHING CASH FLOWS. One school of thought for protecting liquidity argues that a depository institution should carefully analyze its deposit structure and loan demand to forecast the timing and quantity of cash needs. Maturities of the investment portfolio should then be chosen to coincide with those forecasts. In other words, investments should mature, providing a cash inflow, at just the time an institution needs liquid funds. The relative proportion of primary, secondary, and tertiary sources of asset liquidity would be determined by cash-flow forecasts. A problem with this policy is that forecasts contain errors, so there could still be a liquidity crisis.

LADDER OF MATURITIES. An alternative investment strategy is the **ladder of maturities,** which spreads the maturity of securities held for liquidity purposes evenly throughout a given period. For example, suppose that a savings bank decided the maximum maturity of its tertiary reserves should be 5 years. In the ladder-of-maturities strategy, an equal proportion of the portfolio would mature each planning period. Cash received at maturity would be reinvested in assets with a 5-year term to maturity. One way of conceptualizing the ladder of maturities is as a conveyor belt. Assets move along the belt for 5 years toward their maturity date; when they reach the end of the line (maturity), the funds are placed back at the beginning through reinvestment if they are not immediately needed for liquidity purposes.

Perhaps the most serious criticism of the ladder portfolio is that it does not attempt to optimize investment returns for the institution. It is a relatively passive approach to investment management; no real effort is made to distinguish between secondary and tertiary reserves. Consequently, the institution may forgo investments that could increase returns without also incurring unacceptable liquidity risks. But for institutions without personnel to manage the securities portfolio, it may be a viable strategy.

BARBELL STRATEGY. An alternative to the ladder-of-maturities strategy is to invest funds at either end of the yield curve but not in the middle, a strategy called the **barbell** or **split-maturity** portfolio. This approach retains some very liquid assets as secondary reserves but (assuming an upward-sloping yield curve) allows a larger investment in higher-return, long-term securities. To manage a barbell portfolio efficiently, however, the institution must devote resources to interest rate forecasting, because the anticipated direction of rate movements plays an important role in the proportionate investments at either end of the yield curve.

For example, under expectations of falling rates, the portfolio manager would want to increase the investment at the long-term end of the portfolio. The manager would be locking in current high rates, and the market value of the securities would benefit from the declining rates if long-term tertiary reserves had to be liquidated. With the opposite interest rate scenario, more funds would be invested in short-term assets. Consequently, knowledge of interest rate theories, the bond theorems, and duration, discussed in Chapters 6 through 9, would play an integral role in the management of liquidity reserves.

BUFFER PORTFOLIO. A third alternative is the **buffer portfolio strategy,** under which most of the investment in securities is concentrated in the short-term end of the maturity schedule, allowing the portfolio to serve as a buffer against even the slightest risk of cash shortages. With this approach, most secondary reserves and even some tertiary reserves would be invested in short-maturity assets. The average maturity under this strategy is considerably lower than under either the ladder-of-maturities or barbell strategies.

CHOOSING A STRATEGY. The ladder-of-maturity, barbell, and buffer portfolio strategies are illustrated side by side in Figure 13.2 for a hypothetical $100 million securities portfolio. The choice of a strategy depends on the institution's risk/expected return objectives. Risk arises from several sources. The risk of illiquidity is obviously the primary concern. But exposure to interest rate risk under a ladder-of-maturities or buffer portfolio is quite different from that of the barbell. A ladder-of-maturities or buffer portfolio, with a regular reinvestment schedule, poses extreme exposure to reinvestment risk but little or no risk from fluctuations in

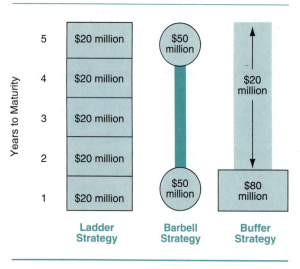

FIGURE 13.2 **The Ladder-of-Maturities, Barbell, and Buffer Portfolio Strategies**

Depending on their risk/return objectives, depository institutions managers may choose either the ladder-of-maturities, barbell, or buffer portfolio strategies as part of liquidity management. The figure shows how a $100 million portfolio might be allocated across maturities under the three strategies.

market value, because securities are held to maturity. In the barbell portfolio, the exposure to market-value risk could be severe, especially if the portfolio is heavily invested at the long end of the term structure. As interest rates change, returns could fluctuate significantly if it becomes necessary to liquidate securities. Yet if managers correctly anticipate interest rate movements, adjusting portfolio maturities in advance of rate changes can allow them to take advantage of favorable price changes. Such regular monitoring of the portfolio and interest rate forecasts requires a larger commitment of resources.[20]

---

[20] An early discussion of the split-maturity portfolio (but called spaced maturity) was included in Robinson 1962, 370–375. Another good source on alternatives for managing liquidity through the investment portfolio is Watson 1972. The descriptions of the ladder-of-maturities and barbell portfolios also draw on Watson. A recent discussion geared to thrift managers is Tom Parliment, "Barbell Strategy Helps to Manage the Yield Curve," *Savings Institutions* 113 (May 1992): 38–39.

IMPACT OF REGULATION ON PORTFOLIO MANAGEMENT

Historically, the focus of asset management in depository institutions has been the loan portfolio, but the importance of the securities portfolio is gaining recognition. Besides liquidity, institutions hope to gain other benefits from their investment in securities. In pursuing these objectives, management's policies must conform to federal and state regulations governing more than just liquidity planning. These regulations, and nonliquidity objectives discussed in subsequent sections of the chapter, have resulted in somewhat different portfolio characteristics among depositories.

DEPOSITORY INSTITUTIONS COMPARED

Figure 13.3 presents recent data on the cash and securities portfolios of depository institutions. A significant feature of the pie chart for commercial banks is the importance of Treasury, federal agency, and tax-exempt securities. The latter group consists of debt issues of state, municipal, and county governments. "Other" securities, primarily foreign and corporate bonds, are a small portion of commercial banks' portfolios.

In the 1990s, the proportion of banks' portfolios held in Treasury and federal agency securities has increased considerably for two reasons. First, loan demand in the early part of the decade was sluggish, and the difference between short-term and long-term rates was unusually high. Many banks invested low-cost short-term deposits in relatively high-yielding intermediate- to long-term government securities to take advantage of this spread. Second, new capital rules (discussed in detail in Chapter 17) are more favorable to institutions with lower-risk assets, such as Treasury securities. Some banks have chosen to reduce the capital pressures they face by dramatically increasing their holdings of government securities relative to traditional commercial loans.[21]

---

[21] These trends are discussed in Rodrigues 1993 and Steven Lipin, "Are Banks Playing a Dangerous Game?" *The Wall Street Journal,* June 30, 1992, C1, C9. Fred R. Bleakley, "Banks Turn to Government Securities in Basic Reassessment of Profitability," *The Wall Street Journal,* October 1, 1991, A2.

FIGURE 13.3   **Cash and Securities Portfolios of Depository Institutions, 1991[a]**

The portfolio choices of depository institutions differ by industry. For example, commercial banks invest a larger proportion of their portfolios in Treasury securities than do other depositories, thrifts favor federal agency securities, and CUs maintain liquidity through their deposits in other depositories.

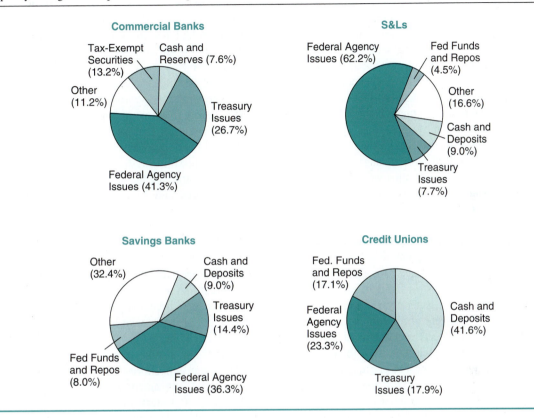

[a] Percent totals in each pie may not add to 100 percent because of rounding.
Source: Prepared by the authors with data from the Board of Governors of the Federal Reserve System, *Flow of Funds,* QI/1992.

The portfolio of S&Ls is quite different. Federal agency securities are most prominent, especially securities issued by government agencies involved in housing finance, such as the Government National Mortgage Association (GNMA). Also key are "other" securities, which in the S&L graph are mortgage-related securities, such as mortgage-backed bonds, discussed in more detail in later chapters. Portfolios of savings banks are similar. The main difference is the large chunk of "other" securities, which for savings banks include corporate stocks and bonds as well as mortgage-related securities. Finally, the cash and securities portfolio of federal CUs is heavily invested in other depositories, especially in commercial banks and S&Ls. Because of their concentration in insured deposits, CU's direct holdings of Treasury securities are smaller than those of commercial banks.

REGULATORY RESTRICTIONS ON THE INVESTMENT PORTFOLIO

Regulators have established specific categories of assets in which investment by federally chartered or federally insured institutions is either limited or prohibited entirely. Although they vary across industries, promoting the safety and soundness of depositories is the stated rationale for all these policies. To that end, investment in Treasury and federal agency securities is unrestricted. Portfolio managers are expected to act prudently in their selection of other securities, carefully weighing risk exposure against potentially higher yields.

The following paragraphs cover specific regulations regarding what can and cannot be held in the securities portfolios of depositories. Although these rules are important to managers, regulations focusing directly on other parts of the balance sheet will exert increasing indirect influence on securities portfolio management in the next decade. As noted earlier, of particular importance are depositories' capital requirements, discussed in detail in Chapter 17. For banks and thrifts, regulators now set minimum net worth requirements based in part on the riskiness of an institution's assets; depositories with riskier assets are required to have a greater net worth cushion. Managers wishing to minimize their firms' capital ratios will hold proportionately more short-term Treasury securities, for example, than higher-risk securities.

RESTRICTIONS ON COMMERCIAL BANKS. With a few minor exceptions, national banks may not invest in corporate equity securities. Banks are also limited in the amount they may invest in the debt securities of any single private issuer; generally, the maximum in any one issuer is 10 percent of the bank's capital and surplus. No limits are placed on the amount that may be invested in municipal securities, even though concentration in the debt of a single issuer may pose considerable threat to individual institutions, as holders of Cleveland and New York City bonds learned in the 1970s. The lack of limitation on municipals is considered by some to be a major oversight in bank portfolio regulation.

In the 1980s, Fed officials urged that restrictions be placed on the ability of federally insured banks to invest in junk bonds. These bonds carry ratings of BB or lower, because they are judged to be of above-average default risk. During the 1980s, they were issued by many companies to finance corporate acquisitions or to repay previous debt obligations. However, in FIRREA Congress chose not to exclude junk bonds from banks' portfolios.

RESTRICTIONS ON THRIFTS. Savings associations generally may not invest in equity securities at all, except in limited quantities through service corporations, but the tale of thrift investments in corporate debt is a bit more complicated. DIDMCA first permitted federally chartered S&Ls to invest in corporate bonds, al-

though important limitations were imposed. (Since the Federal Deposit Insurance Corporation Improvement Act [FDICIA], total investment in bonds, commercial paper, and consumer loans cannot exceed 35 percent of a thrift's assets.) Also, the average maturity of the bond portfolio is limited. Finally, and most important, DIDMCA limited *federal* thrifts' investment in bonds to investment grade issues—those with ratings of BBB or higher.

As the opening paragraphs to the chapter suggest, however, some *state-chartered* institutions gained authority to invest in junk bonds in the 1980s. When the market for junk securities weakened in the latter part of the decade, several thrifts, including Mr. Spiegel's Columbia Savings, sustained substantial losses, further straining the already critically wounded Federal Savings and Loan Insurance Corporation (FSLIC). As a result, FIRREA required that all state-chartered thrifts divest themselves of junk bonds by July 1, 1994, at the latest. FIRREA also emphasized that, in the future, the investment portfolios of thrifts—whether federally or state-chartered—will be closely monitored by the OTS and the FDIC and that restrictions deemed necessary by the regulators to protect the safety of the deposit insurance system can be imposed at any time.[22]

From time to time, regulators have expressed concerns about depositories' investments in reverse repos issued by government securities dealers. In 1984 and 1985, several dealers collapsed. No one could find the securities that had supposedly been pledged as collateral. As a result, many institutions suffered severe losses, and in 1985, Home State Savings in Ohio failed, destroying the system of private deposit insurance in that state. Shortly thereafter, a similar crisis occurred in Maryland. Although no formal restrictions have been established on investment in reverse repos, the Treasury is responsible for standards to which securities dealers are expected to adhere in arranging repos/reverse repos with customers. Depositories, in turn, are urged by regulators to monitor the capital of any party whose reverse repo they hold, to take possession of the securities involved, and to monitor the value of the collateral as market conditions change.[23]

---

[22] See McKenna, Conner, and Cuneo 1989, 20–21.

[23] See Stigum 1990; Tschinkel 1985, 5–9; Haberman and Piche 1985; and "Fed Loses Oversight of Securities Dealers to Treasury," *Savings Institutions* 107 (November 1986): 161–163.

RESTRICTIONS ON CREDIT UNIONS. Federal CUs may make unlimited investment in Treasury and agency securities as well as in insured accounts at other depositories. In 1984, additional authority was granted for investment in Eurodollar deposits and bankers acceptances. Federal CUs may also invest in municipal securities, although holdings from any one issuer may not exceed 10 percent of capital plus surplus. Beyond this, federal CUs may invest only in the securities of organizations providing services "associated with the routine operations of credit unions"; even then, the amount invested may not exceed 1 percent of capital plus surplus. In 1991, further restrictions were placed on CUs when they were prohibited from holding several types of complex mortgage-backed securities.[24]

CONTROVERSY OVER NEW ACCOUNTING RULES. Federal banking, thrift, and securities regulators have been increasingly concerned with accounting rules for securities. A major issue has been whether depositories should more clearly distinguish between "investment" securities, presumably to be held until maturity, and "sale" securities, held to earn potential profits if their prices increase. Investment securities can be shown on the balance sheet at historical cost, but securities held for sale are supposed to be shown at the lower of cost or market value. In the past, many institutions showed most of their securities, including those that had declined in price since originally acquired, at historical cost, implying they were held for investment purposes, and therefore were not to be reported at their market value. Yet these same institutions may have at other times reported big profits on securities sales, implying that most of their securities were, in fact, held for sale, not investment, and thus should have been previously reported on the balance sheet at current value.

Some experts believed that by failing to identify *in advance* which securities are held for investment and which are held for sale, managers may have overstated their institutions' asset values and deceived regulators, depositors, and investors. Managers argued that market values fluctuate so much that reporting current values on the balance sheet would be even more misleading. Furthermore, they said, rigid classifications would reduce managers' abilities to respond intelligently and prudently to changing market conditions.

Regulators, while all expressing interest, took different approaches to the question. The OTS issued rules requiring thrifts to segment their securities portfolios into investment or sale assets and to report values accordingly. The Financial Accounting Standards Board (FASB) studied the question for banks, and banking regulators, generally sympathetic with banks on the matter, awaited the accounting profession's decision. After considerable controversy over its initial proposals, the FASB made a final ruling in 1993, effective with 1994 financial statements. As critics had hoped, the new rules require institutions to report the market value of securities held for sale, preserving historical cost accounting only for those securities being held to maturity. Even before the FASB ruling the Securities and Exchange Commission (SEC), as one of bank accounting's biggest critics, required several banks, including NationsBank, with the largest Treasury securities portfolio in the industry, to revise their financial reports to show more of their securities as being held for sale. Other big banks have decided not to fight the issue and voluntarily changed the way they account for their securities portfolios. As assessing the risk of individual institutions continues to gain importance, the issue is sure to remain in the limelight.[25]

PORTFOLIO MANAGEMENT STRATEGIES

Once liquidity and other regulatory concerns have been addressed, managers must turn their attention to additional objectives for the securities portfolio. Increasingly, managers view securities as income-producing investments, so their potential contribution to the NIM is a consideration in portfolio management.

[24] The Federal Credit Union Act," 1983, 5–6; and National Credit Union Administration, *1984* and *1991 Annual Reports.*

[25] Tom Parliment, "Overall, TB 52 Is a Welcome Tool for Portfolio Managers," *Savings Institutions* 113 (April 1992): 38–39; Lee Berton, "SEC Pushes Market-Value Accounting on Banks Reaping Big Investment Gains," *The Wall Street Journal,* April 29, 1992, A2, A3; Martha Brannigan, "NationsBank Is Reclassifying Part of Portfolio," *The Wall Street Journal,* June 9, 1992, A2; Lee Berton, "Accounting Body Backs Modified Rules on the Valuation of Securities by Banks," *The Wall Street Journal,* July 16, 1992, A2, A6; David Siegel, "FASB Votes to Adopt Mark-to-Market Rule," *American Banker,* April 14, 1993, 1, 20.

For example, special tax provisions apply to certain types of securities. Bond-trading strategies to increase yields in periods of market disequilibrium are also popular.

In addition, the securities portfolio can be managed to reduce exposure to interest rate risk. Although it is difficult to immunize the loan portfolio, some of the securities portfolio can be immunized to shelter part of the institution's balance sheet from reinvestment and market-value risk. Finally, securities are vehicles for diversifying the total portfolio. Each of these objectives and strategies is discussed in this section.

MANAGING FOR INCOME: INFLUENCE OF TAX POLICIES

As mentioned earlier, federal tax policies are a major influence on portfolio management in depository institutions.

DEDUCTIONS FOR HOUSING-RELATED ACTIVITIES. Federal law allows a tax deduction for additions to bad-debt reserves, for which an institution can qualify only if it meets certain asset composition standards. To be eligible for the deduction, for example, a thrift must invest 65 percent of assets in housing-related investments or Treasury securities. This "qualified thrift lender" (QTL) provision is a strong incentive against large holdings of other securities. FIRREA raised the QTL test from 60 to 70 percent, causing experts to question whether thrifts' future dependence on the performance of the housing market would subject them to greater risk for which the tax benefits are inadequate compensation. Congress seemed to agree that the 70 percent requirement was onerous and lowered it to a still high 65 percent in FDICIA.

TAX-EXEMPT SECURITIES. Other federal tax codes address interest income from investment in state, municipal, and county government securities. This income is not taxed at the federal level, and some states also do not tax interest income earned from investments in securities issued by governmental units within the state. There are trade-offs, of course. The interest costs of funds raised to purchase most tax-exempt securities are not tax-deductible at the federal level. Also, as discussed in Chapter 5, stated yields on tax-exempt securities are lower than those on taxable securities, although they are competitive on a tax-ad-

justed basis. Finally, even some portions of normally tax-exempt income may be taxed to ensure that each business pays at least a minimum level of federal tax.

Interest rate and default risk also must be considered. Most municipals are long-term and expose an institution to considerable interest rate risk. Furthermore, Moody's bond rating service reduced the credit ratings of more issues between 1978 and 1983 than it increased, and fear of greater default risk on municipals has discouraged institutional investment since then.[26]

Among depositories, commercial banks hold by far the largest proportion of tax-exempt securities. Nonetheless, because the Tax Reform Act of 1986 eliminated many benefits to banks holding municipals, most banks cut back on their investments in tax-exempt securities during the last part of the 1980s and the early 1990s. Savings institutions, with the special tax benefits offered for mortgages, have not needed the municipal-bond tax exemption as much and have not been major participants in the market. CUs, with their tax-exempt status, have no reason at all to invest in municipals.

MANAGING FOR INCOME: BOND PORTFOLIO SWAPS

A bond swap is the sale of one bond and the purchase of another to increase portfolio yield in the short run. Several types of swaps have been devised to take advantage of temporary market disequilibriums.[27] Swaps require a willingness to engage in active management of the bond portfolio.

SUBSTITUTION SWAP. Suppose that a manager observes a bond with coupon rate, maturity, quality, and other features identical to one already in the institution's portfolio, but selling at a lower price/higher yield. This disequilibrium cannot persist indefinitely,

---

[26] See Proctor and Donahoo 1983–1984, 35. To address the increased concern for default risk, some insurance companies have been willing to insure municipals. In 1991, in fact, about 30 percent of all newly issued long-term municipals were insured, compared with only 3 percent in 1980. See Lynn Asinof, "Bond Insurance Offers Layer of Protection," *The Wall Street Journal,* May 8, 1991, C1, C15.

[27] The classic discussion of bond swaps is found in Homer and Leibowitz 1972, 79–108. Other discussions are found in Dietz, Fogler, and Hardy 1980 and Boardman and Celec 1980.

because demand for the higher-yielding bond will eventually increase its price. But an immediate sale of the higher-priced bond and purchase of the other—a **substitution swap**—may enable a manager to increase portfolio yield in the short run by taking advantage of the expected capital gain on the lower-priced bond.

INTERMARKET SPREAD SWAP. An **intermarket spread swap** involves two bonds similar in all respects but one (such as maturity, quality, coupon). Some price/yield differences between bonds differing according to a single feature are expected, and the portfolio manager must track the difference over time and execute a swap if it seems larger than "normal." As in the substitution swap, the manager sells a bond with a relatively high price and buys one with a relatively low price. Presumably, profits will result when the price of the latter increases as the spread returns to its normal level.

RATE ANTICIPATION SWAP. As discussed in Chapters 8 and 9, bond prices change with interest rate changes, but bonds with different characteristics respond differently to the same rate change. A **rate anticipation swap** is designed to earn short-run profits by altering the portfolio to take advantage of anticipated changes in interest rates. For example, if rates are expected to decrease, shorter-maturity bonds can be swapped for longer-maturity bonds with the same coupon. If interest rate expectations are correct, portfolio value will increase beyond its preswap level. Naturally, because of the hazards of interest rate forecasting, this swap is riskier than swaps that rely only on the assumption that markets are in temporary disequilibrium.

PURE YIELD PICKUP SWAP. The **pure yield pickup swap** is designed solely to earn a short-term increase in income. A lower-yielding bond is sold and a higher-yielding bond purchased. No attempt is made to forecast interest rates or to track spreads between bond prices/yields in different segments of the market. Instead, this swap implies a willingness to change the fundamental characteristics of the portfolio and to accept the additional risk associated with the higher-yielding bond.

TAX SWAP. A **tax swap** is executed if securities can be traded to provide a tax advantage to the institution.

For example, a bond that has declined in value since it was purchased can be sold at a loss. The loss is used to offset profits on other securities in the portfolio, thus reducing taxes; the tax savings and proceeds from the sale are then invested in another bond. In a second type of tax swap, a portfolio manager might identify a bond with the same duration and default risk as a bond currently held, but with a lower coupon rate. To reduce taxes on the coupon payments, the manager might then trade the higher-coupon bond for the lower-coupon security.

SWAPS: SOME ILLUSTRATIONS. Table 13.4 illustrates how and why several of these swaps might be executed. Suppose that a commercial bank's securities portfolio currently contains a 10-year Treasury bond (T-bond) with a coupon rate of 8 percent, a current price of 100.04 (recall that T-bond prices are quoted in 32nds, so the price is 100 and 4/32nds percent of par), and a yield to maturity (YTM) of 7.98 percent. A substitution swap would involve trading this bond for an identical bond selling at a lower price or higher yield—in this case a 10-year, 8 percent coupon T-bond with a price of 99.16 and a YTM of 8.07 percent. As noted earlier, because two identical assets cannot sell at different prices or yields for long, a manager executing this swap would expect the price of the new bond to rise (its yield to fall), providing the bank with additional income on its securities portfolio.

If an intermarket swap were desired instead, the original bond could be traded for a federal agency bond selling at a yield 21 basis points higher (8.19% − 7.98% = 0.21%). Assuming that the normal yield spread between the two bonds is 15 basis points, a manager engaging in the swap would expect the price of the agency bond to rise (its yield to fall), again offering the potential for extra income.

A rate anticipation swap could be undertaken by a manager who understood the principles of the bond theorems and duration. Because the prices of lower coupon or longer maturity bonds change by a greater percentage for a given change in YTM, the portfolio manager anticipating a decline in rates might be willing to swap the current bond for others with greater potential for price appreciation. Accordingly, two possible swaps are suggested in the table.

Finally, a pure yield pickup swap would be conducted by a manager who has decided that obtaining the higher yields generally available on AAA

TABLE 13.4	Bond Swaps

Bond swaps are often a part of bond portfolio management. Swaps involve trading one bond for another and are intended to increase portfolio returns.

Security currently held:	8%, 10-year T-bond Current price: 100.04 Yield to Maturity (YTM): 7.98%

Type of Swap	Expectation/Disequilibrium Condition	Potential Security Swap
Substitution	Temporary supply/demand imbalance; yields must soon be the same	8%, 10-year T-bond Price: 99.16 Yield: 8.07%
Intermarket	Normal spread is 15 basis points	8.20%, 10-year federal agency Price: 100.02 YTM: 8.19% (Spread = 21 basis points)
Rate anticipation	General level of rates will fall; prices of low-coupon or long-maturity bonds will rise more than price of bond now held	6%, 10-year T-bond Price: 86.22 YTM: 7.98% or 8%, 15-year T-bond Price: 100.05 YTM: 7.98%
Pure yield pickup	Corporate AAA bonds are an acceptable risk	9%, 10-year AAA corporate bond Price: 101 YTM: 8.85%

corporate bonds is preferable to continuing to invest in the 8 percent T-bond; no rate forecasting or assumed disequilibrium conditions would be involved in this swap. Managers engaging in bond swaps such as those illustrated in the table must be mindful of the risks discussed earlier and must be prepared to accept the consequences if their market analyses go awry.

MANAGING FOR INCOME: "RIDING THE YIELD CURVE"

A final bond portfolio management strategy designed to increase income is called **riding the yield curve.** To be successful, managers using this approach must be willing to make several rather strong assumptions about the future course of interest rates. To illustrate, suppose that a manager would ordinarily hold 1-year Treasury securities as part of an institution's secondary reserves but now sees an upward-sloping yield curve. The yield on 1-year Treasuries is 7.5 percent and the yield on 2-year Treasuries is 8.1 percent. *If the manager assumes that the shape and level of the yield curve will remain the same,* the price of 2-year Treasuries must rise so that their yield next year (when they will be 1-year Treasuries) will be 7.5 percent. A

manager willing to ride the yield curve would hold 2-year Treasuries this year, then sell them at the end of the year after their price rose to provide additional income on the portfolio. Assuming that the level and shape of the yield curve has, in fact, remained unchanged, the manager would then reinvest the proceeds in 2-year Treasuries and begin the ride again.

If the yield curve does change, the actual return will differ from the manager's expected return. Thus, riding the yield curve is riskier than simply buying and holding 1-year Treasuries, then reinvesting the proceeds on maturity in 1-year securities. Riding the yield curve is also based on the assumption that the pure expectations theory is incorrect. In this example, a manager who believes the expectations hypothesis would expect short-term rates to rise, not remain the same.

REDUCING EXPOSURE TO INTEREST RATE RISK

Financial managers have become increasingly concerned about exposure to interest rate risk, and the securities portfolio is now viewed as a vehicle through which that exposure can be reduced. Two strategies to achieve this objective are matching the maturity of securities with that of selected liabilities and immunizing part of the securities portfolio.

MATCHING MATURITIES. Although they may seem restrictive, many of the federal regulations outlined earlier have been designed to increase the flexibility with which securities portfolios can be managed. Thrift institutions have gained access to many shorter-term loan markets, but the transition to different forms of lending takes time. Thus, through the investment portfolio, they can find a more immediate ability to bring asset maturities in line with their deposit structures. Credit Unions, too, have benefited from increased flexibility. Techniques for managing mismatched asset and liability structures, including the role the securities portfolio can play, are discussed extensively in Chapter 18.

IMMUNIZATION. The benefits of using duration to immunize returns against unexpected changes in interest rates have already been introduced. Recall that an immunized investment protects the investor from both reinvestment and market risk arising from an unexpected change in interest rates. Immunization is achieved by setting the duration of the investment equal to the desired holding period. For a depository institution with many sources of funds, immunization involves matching the weighted average duration of assets with the weighted average duration of funds sources.

Parts of the asset portfolio, including securities held as investments, are especially helpful in achieving the institution's desired asset duration. Investment securities offer a wider selection of maturities and yields than are ordinarily available from originating new loans. This is particularly true for thrifts, where long-term mortgages continue to dominate the asset side of many balance sheets. An example of using duration to immunize a balance sheet is presented in Chapter 19.

FINANCIAL FUTURES AND OPTIONS. As illustrated extensively in Chapters 10 and 11, the financial futures and options markets provide excellent vehicles through which knowledgeable managers can hedge against the risk of changing interest rates. Particularly in institutions with large tertiary reserves or with longer-term securities holdings, the T-bond futures and options markets may be useful. For example, managers expecting an increase in interest rates can protect against significant declines in the value of the securi-

ties portfolio through either short futures positions or put options on T-bonds or T-bond futures contracts.

The futures and options markets can complicate liquidity management as well. If rate movements do not occur as expected, the institution must be prepared to handle the daily cash settlements required in its margin account. Furthermore, the futures or options positions must be monitored carefully to ensure compliance with regulations.

DIVERSIFYING THE PORTFOLIO TO REDUCE RISK

Students of financial management and investments are familiar with the term **diversification,** or reducing variability in returns on a portfolio by selecting a variety of assets rather than concentrating on investments with similar characteristics. Over several decades, in fact, finance theorists have developed a quantitative approach to measuring the benefits of diversification. A major conclusion of the theory of diversification is that the risk of a portfolio is reduced by choosing assets whose returns are not highly correlated with returns on the existing portfolio. Students wishing to review the statistics used to measure and manage portfolio risk through diversification are encouraged to read the appendix to this chapter.

Depository institutions can diversify in many ways—by changing the maturity, the geographic orientation, or simply the types of assets held. These changes can often be made through the securities portfolio. As a depository institution adds securities with expected returns that are less than perfectly correlated with expected returns on existing assets, it reduces its overall exposure to risk. The lower the correlation, the greater the risk reduction.

For example, many small and medium-sized institutions concentrate their lending in a relatively narrow geographic region. As the local economy prospers or declines, so does the performance of the loan portfolio. Among its assets, an institution can easily include securities from issuers in many locations, offsetting the default risk of the locally concentrated loan portfolio. Similarly, the institution can use securities to lengthen or shorten the average maturity of the total asset portfolio, depending on its lending orientation. As long as expected returns on added securities are not perfectly correlated with expected returns on other assets, the overall variability of asset returns should be reduced.

SUMMARY

Liquidity, or the ability to obtain cash with little risk of financial loss, is one of the most important concerns of depository institutions. Sufficient liquidity is necessary for two reasons: to meet regulatory requirements, and to ensure uninterrupted operations in the face of unexpected loan demand or deposit withdrawals.

The Federal Reserve Board influences institutional liquidity through reserve requirements on transactions accounts and time deposits. Because deposit levels fluctuate constantly, estimating liquidity needs is a challenge for management. Recently, large institutions have been required to use contemporaneous reserve accounting, accelerating the need for forecasting tools in depository institutions management. Besides meeting Federal Reserve specifications, some depositories must comply with liquidity requirements set by states or other federal regulators.

Depositories also require liquidity to meet unexpected loan demand or deposit withdrawals. To avoid selling assets at a loss when these needs arise, management should maintain liquid assets in excess of those required by regulators. Because liquid assets are often low-yielding, however, liquidity needs must be balanced against profitability. Several strategies are available, varying according to risk/return characteristics and appropriateness for large versus small institutions.

The securities portfolio also fulfills other institutional objectives. Income generation and risk management are examples of objectives that can be achieved in part through the securities portfolio. Techniques include selecting securities with particular tax features, executing bond swaps, riding the yield curve, matching maturities, hedging with futures or options, immunizing, and diversifying.

QUESTIONS

1. Providing liquidity is one of the functions of a financial intermediary. How does the intermediation role of depository institutions affect their liquidity needs?

2. Explain the historical rationale for the reserve requirements first imposed on national banks in the 1860s and continued after the creation of the Federal Reserve. Since that time, how has the Fed's monetary policy role affected the breadth and management of reserve requirements for all depository institutions?

3. Explain the most important differences between contemporaneous reserve accounting (CRA) and lagged reserve accounting. Does the new CRA system require contemporaneous management of all deposit levels and reserve balances? If not, explain which aspects are lagged.

4. How do the contemporaneous reserve accounting CRA provisions affect liquidity management in depository institutions? How does the carryover privilege assist in reserve management? What policy objectives provided the motivation for implementing CRA?

5. Compare and contrast the categories of assets defined by federal thrift regulators as liquid and those allowed by the Fed for meeting liquidity requirements. What changes did FIRREA introduce to thrift liquidity management? What objective was Congress addressing through its revisions of liquidity standards in FIRREA?

6. A key problem for depository managers is accurately estimating their liquidity needs for operations. How is this effort affected by the relative proportion of volatile and nonvolatile funds? By changes in economic conditions and return to depositors on alternative investments?

7. Depository institution managers may rely on both sides of the balance sheet to ensure adequate liquidity. Compare and contrast the potential effect on risk and return resulting from asset sources of liquidity as compared to that from liability sources. How does an institution's size and financial soundness affect its liquidity management options?

8. Explain the functions of the Federal Reserve discount window. Contrast the Reg A provisions governing use of the window to FHLB advances and to sources of credit union liquidity.

9. The cash and securities portfolios of depository institutions are often characterized by their relative liquidity. Explain the four categories usually used and the types of assets included in each. How does this categorization assist depositories in managing for liquidity and earnings?

10. Evaluate the differences in interest rate risk exposure from the ladder-of-maturities, the buffer, and the barbell portfolio investment strategies. Compare the relative rates of return that managers might expect from the three strategies under upward-sloping, flat, and downward-sloping yield curves.

11. Examine the information on depository institutions' securities portfolios presented in Figure 13.3. What are the most important distinctions between bank and thrift portfolios? Explain how differences in regulations, tax policies, and financial objectives have influenced asset holdings in banks and thrifts.

12. Do you consider the restrictions on bank and thrift investment in equity securities and junk bonds justified? What rationale would you offer for retaining or revising these regulations?

13. Explain the rationale for requiring firms—including depository institutions—to report the market value of financial assets on the balance sheet. Describe the different accounting procedures allowed by the FASB for securities held for sale and for investment. What might be the potential effect on bank portfolio management?

14. Consult recent bank and thrift publications to find discussions of the market value reporting rules implemented in 1994. Is there evidence of any effects on the level or volatility of bank earnings? On securities portfolio management strategies?

15. What is the purpose of a bond swap? Explain the differences in the objectives for executing a substitution swap and an intermarket swap.

16. Suppose that you are managing a bond portfolio heavily invested in Treasury bonds. Your long-term rate forecast is that interest rates will fall. If you attempt to manage your portfolio yield through a rate anticipation swap, would you trade for bonds with shorter or longer maturities? With higher or lower interest rates? Would you consider any other type of bond swap under such a forecast? Why or why not?

17. How may a portfolio manager take advantage of yield differentials on securities of varying maturities to increase portfolio returns? What implicit assumptions would this trading strategy make about the pure expectations theory, and why?

18. What is meant by portfolio diversification and what is its purpose in portfolio management? Explain the relationship between the correlation in expected returns on pairs of assets in a portfolio and the portfolio's total risk.

PROBLEMS

1. You have just been placed in charge of managing your bank's reserve position. It is now the morning of day 29 of the maintenance period. Your immediate responsibility is to set reserve deposit levels for days 29 and 30. You have been given the following information:

Days 15–28	Average vault cash	$ 4,000,000
Days 1–14	Average nontransactions liabilities	220,000,000
Days 15–28	Average transactions balances	625,000,000
Days 17–28	Average reserve balances	61,000,000

a. Compute the average reserve balances required for the maintenance period (days 17–30). Assume a 3 percent reserve bracket of $46.8 million for transactions balances.
b. Compute average balances required for the last two days if the carryover privilege is **not** used.
c. Compute the average balance needed for the final two days of the maintenance period, assuming the bank uses its carryover privilege.

2. Using the data from Problem 1, suppose that in the next reserve maintenance period, average transactions balances during days 15–28 fall to $475 million, and average reserve balances during days 17–28 fall to $66 million. Other balances remain the same. Compute the average reserve balances needed for the maintenance period and the total needed for the last two days. What alternatives are available to the bank in this situation?

One of your major responsibilities at the Algonquin National Bank is calculating Fed reserve requirements. Your supervisor has provided the following data for your bank and for another subsidiary of the holding company. Calculate the average daily reserve target balance and the minimum reserve balances required for the final two days of the maintenance period. Assume a 3 percent reserve bracket of $46.8 million for transactions balances.

Algonguin National: Forecast for average reserves on transactions deposits—$97,000,000.

Day #	Day	Nontransactions Liabilities (in millions)
1	T	$440
2	W	460
3	Th	460
4	F	435
5	Sat	450
6	S	445
7	M	445
8	T	445
9	W	480
10	Th	475
11	F	490
12	Sat	490
13	S	450
14	M	440

Contemporaneous Computation Period				Maintenance Period		
Day #	Day	Vault Cash (in millions)	Transactions Deposits (in millions)	Day #	Day	Reserve Balances (in millions)
15	T	$7.5	$860			
16	W	7.4	864			
17	Th	7.6	875	17	Th	$90
18	F	7.6	880	18	F	84
19	Sat	7.7	880	19	Sat	82
20	S	7.7	880	20	S	82
21	M	7.2	850	21	M	88
22	T	7.4	850	22	T	90
23	W	7.3	862	23	W	92
24	Th	7.6	865	24	Th	88
25	F	7.2	920	25	F	85
26	Sat	7.1	940	26	Sat	84
27	S	7.1	940	27	S	84
28	M	7.7	980	28	M	88
				29	T	
				30	W	

Bayou National: Forecast for average reserves on transactions deposits—$39,450,000

Day #	Day	Nontransactions Liabilities (in millions)
1	T	$150
2	W	140
3	Th	135
4	F	160
5	Sat	155
6	S	155
7	M	130
8	T	135
9	W	150
10	Th	145
11	F	160
12	Sat	135
13	S	135
14	M	140

Contemporaneous Computation Period				Maintenance Period		
Day #	Day	Vault Cash (in millions)	Transactions Deposits (in millions)	Day #	Day	Reserve Balances (in millions)
15	T	$2.10	$350			
16	W	2.00	355			
17	Th	2.40	370	17	Th	$43
18	F	2.30	364	18	F	38
19	Sat	2.50	340	19	Sat	40
20	S	2.50	340	20	S	40
21	M	2.60	370	21	M	48
22	T	2.80	380	22	T	45
23	W	2.30	320	23	W	43
24	Th	2.30	322	24	Th	39
25	F	2.60	335	25	F	39
26	Sat	2.75	345	26	Sat	43
27	S	2.10	345	27	S	43
28	M	2.10	390	28	M	48
				29	T	
				30	W	

4.   a.   West Coast Bank must estimate its liquidity needs over the next 2 months. Using the following information given for that period, estimate the bank's liquidity surplus or deficit:

Assets	Millions	% Liquid
Cash	$ 266.25	12%
Commercial loans	1,002.27	0
Consumer loans	539.68	0
Investments	1,317.45	45
Other assets	217.15	17
Total	$3,342.80	

Sources of Funds	Millions	% Volatile
Deposits	$2,228.38	10%
Other liabilities	885.79	75
Equity	258.63	0
Total	$3,342.80	

b. Assume instead that 65 percent of West Coast's investments are liquid and that 65 percent of nondeposit liabilities are volatile. Recalculate the liquidity surplus or deficit. Compare the advantages and disadvantages of this situation to that in part a.

c. Assume that West Coast Bank wants to be prepared for an increase in commercial loan demand of 1 percent and an increase in consumer loan demand of 2 percent during the next 2 months. Using the data in part a, recalculate the bank's liquidity surplus or deficit under these assumptions.

5. A bond portfolio's manager is interested in active portfolio management techniques and is studying bond swaps. She now holds a 12-year, 10 percent T bond with a current price of $990 and a pre-tax YTM of 10.15 percent. She expects interest rates to fall over the next month or so. The following alternative investments are available. For each alternative, identify the type of swap(s) for which it could be an appropriate candidate. Justify your answers by explaining how and why each swap could be executed.

Alternative	Coupon Rate,%	Maturity, Years	Price	Pre-tax YTM, %
A: T bond	7.00%	12	$ 787	10.15%
B: Municipal	10.15	12	1,000	10.15
C: T bond	10.00	16	988	10.15
D: Agency	10.50	12	990	10.65
E: T bond	10.00	12	985	10.22
F: Corporate AAA	11.00	12	990	11.16

The following problems are based on material presented in Appendix 13A.

6.

	Investment A			Investment B	
Probability	**Possible Outcome**		**Probability**	**Possible Outcome**	
.15	10%		.10	6%	
.20	12		.20	10	
.25	16		.30	15	
.40	20		.40	22	

a. Calculate the expected return and standard deviation for each investment. Which investment is riskier? Why?
b. Calculate the expected return and standard deviation for a two-security portfolio composed of 60 percent investment A and 40 percent investment B. Use correlation coefficients of:

1) $\rho_{ab} = 1.0$
2) $\rho_{ab} = 0.6$
3) $\rho_{ab} = -0.2$

How does the correlation between the expected returns on the two investments affect the total risk of the portfolio?
c. Assuming a -0.2 correlation between the investments, set up a "what-if" table showing how portfolio risk varies as the percentages invested in investments A and B vary. (Suggestion: Vary the proportion invested in investment A in increments of 5 percent—for example, 5 percent in A, 95 percent in B; 10 percent in A, 90 percent in B, and so forth.) Repeat the analysis, assuming a correlation of 0.6. In each situation, which proportions result in the lowest-risk portfolios?

7.

	Asset X			Asset Y	
Probability	**Possible Outcome**		**Probability**	**Possible Outcome**	
.1	0%		.2	0%	
.3	3		.6	3	
.4	8		.1	10	
.2	12		.1	12	

a. Calculate the expected value and standard deviation for asset X and asset Y. Which asset is riskier?

b. Calculate the expected value and the standard deviation for an investment plan in which half of the allocated funds are invested in asset X and half of the funds are invested in asset Y. Assume a correlation coefficient between the expected returns on the two assets of 0.45.

c. Suppose an investor adds a third security with an expected return of 11 percent and a standard deviation of 7.5 percent. Assume that the third security has a correlation of 0.30 with asset X and 0.70 with asset Y. If equal amounts are invested in each security, what is the resulting portfolio standard deviation?

SELECTED REFERENCES

Boardman, Calvin M., and Steven E. Celec. "Bond Swaps and the Application of Duration." *Business Economics* 15 (September 1980): 49–54.

Burns, Joseph E. "Bank Liquidity—A Straightforward Concept but Hard to Measure." *Business Review* (Federal Reserve Bank of Dallas) (May 1971).

Cacy, J. A., and Scott Winningham. "Reserve Requirements under the Depository Institutions Deregulation and Monetary Control Act of 1980." *Economic Review* (Federal Reserve Bank of Kansas City) 65 (September/October 1980): 3–16.

"Conference Report on H.R. 1278, Financial Institutions Reform, Recovery, and Enforcement Act, 1989." *Congressional Record—House of Representatives,* August 4, 1989.

"The Depository Institutions Deregulation and Monetary Control Act of 1980." *Economic Perspectives* (Federal Reserve Bank of Chicago) 4 (September/October 1980): 3–23.

Dietz, Peter O., H. Russell Fogler, and Donald J. Hardy. "The Challenge of Analyzing Bond Portfolio Returns." *Journal of Portfolio Management* 6 (Spring 1980): 53–58.

Evanoff, Douglas D. "Reserve Account Management Behavior: Impact of the Reserve Accounting Scheme and Carry Forward Provision." Federal Reserve Bank of Chicago, WP-89-12, 1989.

The Federal Credit Union Act as Amended January 12, 1983. Washington, DC: National Credit Union Administration, 1983.

Feinnan, Joshua N. "Reserve Requirements: History, Current Practice, and Potential Reform." *Federal Reserve Bulletin* 79 (June 1993): 569–589.

Gilbert, R. Alton. "Lagged Reserve Requirements: Implications for Monetary Control and Bank Reserve Management." *Review* (Federal Reserve Bank of St. Louis) 62 (May 1980): 7–20.

Giroux, Gary. "A Survey of Forecasting Techniques Used by Commercial Banks." *Journal of Bank Research* 11 (Spring 1980): 51–53.

Goodfriend, Marvin, and Monica Hargraves. "A Historic Assessment of the Rationales and Functions of Reserve Requirements." *Economic Review* (Federal Reserve Bank of Richmond) 69 (March/April 1983): 3–21.

Haberman, Gary, and Catherine Piche. "Controlling Credit Risk Associated with Repos: Know Your Counterparty." *Economic Review* (Federal Reserve Bank of Atlanta) 70 (September 1985): 28–34.

Hamdani, Kausar. "CRR and Excess Reserves: An Early Appraisal." *Quarterly Review* (Federal Reserve Bank of New York) 9 (Autumn 1984): 16–23.

Homer, Sidney, and Martin Leibowitz. *Inside the Yield Book.* New York: Prentice-Hall and the New York Institute of Finance, 1972.

Kaufman, Daniel J., Jr., and David R. Lee. "Planning Liquidity: A Practical Approach." *Magazine of Bank Administration* 53 (November 1977): 55–63.

Knight, Robert E. "Reserve Requirements, Part I: Comparative Reserve Requirements at Member and Nonmember Banks." *Monthly Review* (Federal Reserve Bank of Kansas City) 59 (April 1974): 3–20.

Luckett, Dudley G. "Approaches to Bank Liquidity Management." *Economic Review* (Federal Reserve Bank of Kansas City) 65 (March 1980): 11–27.

McKenna, Conner, and Cuneo. *An Analysis of the Financial Institutions Reform, Recovery, and Enforcement Act of 1989.* New York: McKenna, Conner, and Cuneo, 1989.

Mengle, David. "The Discount Window." *Economic Review* (Federal Reserve Bank of Richmond) 72 (May/June 1986a): 2–10.

———. "The Discount Window." In *Instruments of the Money Market.* 6th ed., edited by Timothy Q. Cook and Timothy D. Rowe. Richmond, VA: Federal Reserve Bank of Richmond, 1986b.

Pearce, Douglas K. "Recent Developments in the Credit Union Industry." *Economic Review* (Federal Reserve Bank of Kansas City) 69 (June 1984): 10–12.

Proctor, Allen J., and Kathleen K. Donahoo. "Commercial Bank Investment in Municipal Securities." *Quarterly Review* (Federal Reserve Bank of New York) 8 (Winter 1983–1984): 26–37.

Robinson, Roland I. *The Management of Bank Funds.* New York: McGraw-Hill, 1962.

Rodrigues, Anthony P. "Government Investments of Commercial Banks." *Quarterly Review* (Federal Reserve Bank of New York) 18 (Summer 1993): 39–53.

Rosenbaum, Mary Susan. "Contemporaneous Reserve Accounting: The New System and Its Implications for Monetary Policy." *Economic Review* (Federal Reserve Bank of Atlanta) 69 (April 1984): 46–57.

Saunders, Anthony, and Thomas Urich. "The Effects of Shifts in Monetary Policy and Reserve Accounting Regimes on Bank Reserve Management Behavior in the Federal Funds Market." *Journal of Banking and Finance* 12 (December 1988): 523–535.

Sealey, C. W., Jr. "Valuation, Capital Structure, and Shareholder Unanimity for Depository Financial Intermediaries." *Journal of Finance* 38 (June 1983): 857–871.

Sprong, Kenneth. *Banking Regulation.* Kansas City: Federal Reserve Bank of Kansas City, 1990.

Stevens, E. J. "Is There Any Rationale for Reserve Requirements?" *Economic Review* (Federal Reserve Bank of Cleveland) 27 (Quarter 3 1991): 2–17.

Stigum, Marcia. *The Money Market,* 3d ed. Homewood, IL: Dow Jones-Irwin, 1990.

Tarhan, Vefa. "Individual Bank Reserve Management." *Economic Perspectives* (Federal Reserve Bank of Chicago) 8 (July/August 1984): 17–23.

Tschinkel, Sheila S. "Overview." *Economic Review* (Federal Reserve Bank of Atlanta) 70 (September 1985): 5–9.

Watson, Ronald D. "Bank Bond Management: The Maturity Dilemma." *Business Review* (Federal Reserve Bank of Philadelphia) (March 1972): 23–29.

APPENDIX 13A

REDUCING PORTFOLIO RISK THROUGH DIVERSIFICATION

Standard tools of investment management are the statistical measures of **expected value** and **standard deviation.** To calculate the expected value of an investment, one begins with an estimate of the distribution of potential outcomes—the rates of return possible and the probability of occurrence for each. Although realistically such a distribution is continuous, a reasonable approximation results from a finite number of possible outcomes.

In this example, suppose that a portfolio manager estimates the set of potential outcomes shown in Table 13A.1 and, for each one-period yield, r_i, the probability Pr_i, that it will occur.

The expected value, $E(r)$, is the average of the potential outcomes weighted by their probability of occurrence. Stated formally, the expected value of a series of possible outcomes is

$$E(r) = \sum_{i=1}^{n} r_i\, Pr_i \qquad [13A.1]$$

$$= r_1\, Pr_1 + r_2\, Pr_2 + \cdots + r_n\, Pr_n$$

As shown in Table 13A.1, for this asset, $E(r) = 8.8$ percent.

The investment's risk is the potential variability of its returns. The same data used in measuring expected return are needed to calculate the variance and the standard deviation, which serve as measures of risk because they are statistical measures of variation. The variance is the sum of the squared deviations from the expected value, found as follows:

$$[13A.2]$$

$$\sigma_A^2 = \sum_{i=1}^{n} [r_i - E(r)]^2 \, Pr_i$$

$$= [r_1 - E(r)]^2 \, (Pr_1) + \cdots +$$

$$[r_n - E(r)]^2 \, (Pr_n)$$

The standard deviation is the square root of the variance.

$$\sigma_A = \sqrt{\sigma_A^2}$$

In the example, the variance and standard deviation are 2.126 percent squared and 14.579 percent, respectively. The standard deviation is more frequently used because it is measured in percentages.

PORTFOLIO RISK, RETURN, AND DIVERSIFICATION

In addition to risk/return measures for a single asset, similar estimates are needed for the portfolio as a whole. The expected return of a portfolio of securities is the weighted average of the expected rates of return of its components:

$$[13A.3]$$

$$E(r_p) = \sum_{i=1}^{n} W_i \, E(r_i)$$

where

W$_i$ = the proportion of total funds invested in asset i

E(r$_i$) = the expected return on asset i

Suppose the portfolio manager evaluating the asset in Table 13A.1 (designated asset A) has selected another investment (asset B) with an estimated one-period return and risk of $E(r_B) = 8.8\%$ and $\sigma_B = 14.579\%$, the same as for asset A. If funds are to be split equally between these two securities, $W_A = W_B = .5$. The expected return on the portfolio, shown in Table 13A.2, is also 8.8 percent.

TABLE 13A.1	Measuring Risk and Return for a Single Asset (A)

Estimates of risk and expected return for financial assets are based on a range of expected outcomes and the probability that each outcome will occur. The standard deviation of expected outcomes is a generally accepted measure of an asset's total risk.

Proposed Investment Asset	
Possible Outcomes (r$_i$)	**Probability of Occurrence (Pr$_i$)**
−25%	.1
1	.2
10	.4
18	.2
35	.1

Expected Return

$$[13A.1]$$

$$E(r) = \sum_{i=1}^{n} r_i \, Pr_i$$

$$= -25(.1) + 1(.2) + 10(.4) + 18(.2) + 35(.1)$$

$$= 8.8\%$$

Variance

$$[13A.2]$$

$$\sigma_A^2 = \sum_{i=1}^{n} [r_i - E(r)]^2 Pr_i$$

$$= (-25 - 8.8)^2 \, (.1) + (1 - 8.8)^2 \, (.2)$$

$$+ (10 - 8.8)^2 \, (.4) + (18 - 8.8)^2 \, (.2)$$

$$+ (35 - 8.8)^2 \, (.1)$$

$$= 2.126 \text{ (measured in percent squared)}$$

Standard Deviation (Square Root of Variance)

$$\sigma_A = \sqrt{\sigma_A^2}$$

$$= 14.579\%$$

In addition to the risk of the individual assets, portfolio risk is affected by the correlation, or by the way in which the potential outcomes of the two investments are expected to change in response to similar sources of risk. Portfolio variability is determined partly by the weighted standard deviations of its components, and partly by the correlation of expected returns on each pair of assets in the portfolio. The equation for the variance of a two-asset portfolio is

$$\sigma_p^2 = W_A^2\,\sigma_A^2 + W_B^2\,\sigma_B^2 \quad\quad [13A.4]$$
$$+ 2W_A\,W_B\,(\rho_{AB}\,\sigma_A\,\sigma_B)$$

where

ρ_{AB} = correlation coefficient

The quantity $(\rho_{AB}\,\sigma_A\,\sigma_B)$ is the covariance between assets A and B.

The formula for the variance of an n-asset portfolio is

$$\sigma_p^2 = \sum_{i=1}^{n}\sum_{j=1}^{n} W_i\,W_j\,\rho_{ij}\,\sigma_i\,\sigma_j \quad\quad [13A.5]$$

EFFECT OF THE CORRELATION BETWEEN ASSETS

The correlation coefficient is a statistical measure with a range of -1 to $+1$. If estimated returns on two assets are uncorrelated, they have a correlation coefficient close to 0 and are expected to exhibit little similarity in response to similar sources of risk. However, if ρ_{AB} is close to $+1$, expected returns are positively correlated and expected movements are in the same direction and of similar proportions. With ρ_{AB} close to -1, expected movements are in the opposite direction but of similar proportions.

To examine the effect of correlation on portfolio risk, assume initially that $\rho_{AB} = .35$. The variance of the portfolio, using Equation 13A.4 and the data in Table 13A.2, is 143.47 percent squared, and σ_p is 11.978 percent. It is possible to combine two equally

---

TABLE 13A.2 **Measuring Risk and Return for a Two-Asset Portfolio**

The return on a two-asset portfolio is the weighted average of the returns on the individual assets. The standard deviation of the portfolio reflects the correlation between the returns on the two assets, in addition to their individual standard deviations.

The portfolio is composed of two assets, equally weighted, with expected returns and standard deviations as follows:

$$E(r_A) = 8.8\% \quad\quad \sigma_A = 14.579\%$$
$$E(r_B) = 8.8\% \qu\quad \sigma_B = 14.579\%$$
$$W_A = W_B = .5$$

Expected Return

$$E(r_p) = \sum_{i=1}^{n} W_i\,E(r_i) \quad\quad [13A.3]$$
$$= (8.8\%)(.5) + (8.8\%)(.5)$$
$$= 8.8\%$$

Variance

$$\sigma_p^2 = W_A^2\,\sigma_A^2 + W_B^2\,\sigma_B^2 + 2\,W_A\,W_B\,\sigma_A\,\sigma_B\,\rho_{AB} \quad\quad [13A.4]$$
$$= (.5)^2\,(14.579)^2 + (.5)^2\,(14.579)^2 + 2(.5)(.5)(14.579)(14.579)(.35)$$
$$= 143.47 \text{ (measured in percent squared)}$$

Standard Deviation (Square Root of Variance)

$$\sigma_p = 11.978\%$$

risky assets ($\sigma_A = \sigma_B = 14.579$ percent) into a portfolio that has *lower* risk. Thus, diversification can reduce variability in expected return without sacrificing the level.

Portfolio risk is positively related to the correlation coefficient. If the expected returns of assets A and B had an even lower correlation, the portfolio standard deviation would also be lower. If it were possible to find two assets that were perfectly negatively correlated ($\rho_{AB} = -1$), they could be combined with a particular weighting in a two-asset portfolio that would produce a variance of 0. Table 13A.3 demonstrates changes in portfolio risk as the correlation coefficient for assets A and B varies. Unless they are perfectly positively correlated, in fact, portfolio variance and standard deviation are always less than the risk of the individual assets.

ENLARGING THE PORTFOLIO: THE THREE-ASSET CASE

Few institutions hold only two-asset portfolios, so it is important for managers to understand the effects of additional securities on portfolio risk. This section illustrates the use of Equation 13A.5 for a three-asset portfolio. Assume the addition of a third security, Asset C, with $E(r_C) = 7.5$ percent, and a standard deviation (σ_C) of 12 percent. The correlation between Asset C's returns and those on Asset A is .5; the correlation between Asset C's returns and those on Asset B is $-.25$. For purposes of Equation 13A.5, Assets A, B, and C are considered Assets 1, 2, and 3, respectively; n is equal to 3. Recall, too, that the correlation between the returns on any asset and its own returns is $+1$. Finally, assume that investment is weighted equally among the three assets.

Equation 13A.5 contains two summation signs, requiring the user to proceed as follows in calculating the portfolio variance. Initially, the value of i in the equation is set equal to 1; then, the value of j is allowed to vary between 1 and n, holding i equal to 1. Thus, the first three terms in the portfolio variance formula for a three-asset portfolio are

$$W_1 W_1 \rho_{11} \sigma_1 \sigma_1 + W_1 W_2 \rho_{12} \sigma_1 \sigma_2 + W_1 W_3 \rho_{13} \sigma_1 \sigma_3$$

Substituting and recognizing that the first term is equivalent to $W_1^2 \sigma_1^2$ (because $\rho_{11} = +1$)

$$(.33)^2 (14.579\%)^2 + (.33)(.33)(.35)(14.579\%)$$
$$(14.579\%)$$
$$+ (.33)(.33)(.5)(14.579\%)(12.000\%)$$

The next stage is to set the value of i equal to 2, to allow j to vary between 1 and n, and to add the three resulting terms to the three terms determined initially. In general, regardless of the number of securities in a portfolio, the process of increasing the value of i, varying j between 1 and n, and adding terms continues until the value of i has reached n. Thus, the total number of terms summed to calculate the variance of an n-security portfolio is n^2.

Table 13A.4 presents the details of the calculation for a portfolio consisting of equal investment in Assets A, B, and C. In practice, large institutional investors use sophisticated computer programs to identify optimal multiasset portfolios that minimize risk for a given level of return. In this case, the portfolio standard deviation is considerably lower than the standard deviation of any single asset because expected returns on two of the assets are negatively correlated.

TABLE 13A.3	**Effect of the Correlation Coefficient on Portfolio Risk**

The risk of a portfolio is directly related to the correlation in returns between pairs of assets in the portfolio. The lower the correlation between asset returns, the lower the standard deviation of the portfolio. If the returns on two assets are perfectly negatively correlated, it is theoretically possible to reduce the risk of a two-asset portfolio to 0 percent.

Standard deviations for an equally weighted two-asset portfolio, assuming different correlation coefficients:

ρ_{AB}	σ_p
1.0	14.579%
.6	13.040
.3	11.754
0	10.309
$-.3$	8.625
$-.6$	6.520
-1.0	0.000

TABLE 13A.4 **Measuring Risk and Return for a Three-Asset Portfolio**

The expected return and standard deviation of a portfolio invested in three assets are illustrated. The portfolio standard deviation is based on the correlation between each pair of securities, as well as the variability of expected returns for each asset.

The portfolio is composed of three assets, equally weighted, with expected returns, standard deviations, and correlations as follows:

$$E(r_1) = 8.8\% \qquad \sigma_1 = 14.579\% \qquad \rho_{12} = .35$$

$$E(r_2) = 8.8\% \qquad \sigma_2 = 14.579\% \qquad \rho_{13} = .50$$

$$E(r_3) = 7.5\% \qquad \sigma_3 = 12.000\% \qquad \rho_{23} = -.25$$

Expected Return

$$E(r_p) = \sum_{i=1}^{n} W_i \, E(r_i)$$

$$= (.33)\,(8.8\%) + (.33)\,(8.8\%) + (.33)\,(7.5\%)$$

$$= 8.283\%$$

Variance

$$\sigma_p^2 = W_1 W_1 \rho_{11} \sigma_1 \sigma_1 + W_1 W_2 \rho_{12} \sigma_1 \sigma_2 + W_1 W_3 \rho_{13} \sigma_1 \sigma_3 +$$

$$W_2 W_1 \rho_{21} \sigma_2 \sigma_1 + W_2 W_2 \rho_{22} \sigma_2 \sigma_2 + W_2 W_3 \rho_{23} \sigma_2 \sigma_3 +$$

$$W_3 W_1 \rho_{31} \sigma_3 \sigma_1 + W_3 W_2 \rho_{32} \sigma_3 \sigma_2 + W_3 W_3 \rho_{33} \sigma_3 \sigma_3$$

$$= (.33)^2 (14.579\%)^2 + (.33)(.33)(.35)(14.579\%)(14.579\%) +$$

$$(.33)(.33)(.5)(14.579\%)(12.000\%) +$$

$$(.33)(.33)(.35)(14.579\%)(14.579\%) + (.33)^2 (14.579\%)^2 +$$

$$(.33)(.33)(-.25)(14.579\%)(12.000\%) +$$

$$(.33)(.33)(.5)(14.579\%)(12.000\%) + (.33)(.33)(-.25)(14.579\%)(12.000\%) + (.33)^2 (12.000\%)^2$$

$$= 87.702 \text{ (measured in percent squared)}$$

Standard Deviation (Square Root of Variance)

$$\sigma_p = 9.365\%$$

What's happening is a major turning back of the clock to the standard of conservatism and prudence of a generation ago. Once you turn that clock back, you would expect to operate on 1965 time for a while.

Lyle Gramley
Former Federal Reserve Board Member (1991)

———————————

Charles Dickens' famous *A Tale of Two Cities* was set in the European capitals of London and Paris during revolutionary political times. A modern tale of two cities in revolutionary banking times could perhaps be written of booming Boston and plodding Detroit. In the high-flying 1980s, few cities had image problems as severe as those of Detroit, while Boston was at the heart of an economic renaissance, dubbed the "Massachusetts miracle." Located in the "Rust Belt," and economically crippled by troubles in the U.S. automobile industry, Motown could surely have been considered the Rodney Dangerfield of urban America.

Detroit's banks, too, were labeled stodgy and unimaginative, slow to adopt the more free-wheeling approaches of their counterparts in New England and the Sunbelt. They were vilified throughout the city when they refused to help finance a major commercial center designed to revitalize downtown Detroit; the banks' managers said they did not believe the project was economically viable. Figuratively arriving on white horses, Bank of Boston's managers heroically stepped in to provide the needed funds.

By the early 1990s, the 25-story building was open, but it was also almost empty. Bank of Boston was forced to declare its $96 million loan to the developer in default, one of the many New England banks that almost collapsed under the weight of bad commercial loans, driving the region into a prolonged economic slump. Meanwhile, National Bank of Detroit's holding company, NBD Corp, was known as "No Bad Debt" Corp and was being touted as a model of good management in national newspapers and magazines. Other Michigan banks, similarly conservative, were among the most profitable and best capitalized in the nation.[1]

As the contrasting approaches of National Bank of Detroit and Bank of Boston suggest, lending decisions are among the most important that financial institutions, especially commercial banks, make. Indeed, the loan portfolio continues to comprise over half the assets of

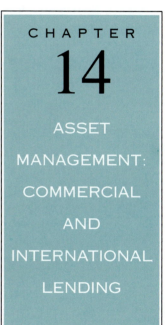

CHAPTER

14

ASSET
MANAGEMENT:
COMMERCIAL
AND
INTERNATIONAL
LENDING

———————————

[1] Bradley L. Sterz, "In Great Lakes Region, Many Bankers Prove Caution Can Pay Off," *The Wall Street Journal,* April 11, 1991, A1; Marcia Berss, "Bank by Fisher," *Forbes,* April 13, 1992, 52.

depositories in general, despite the myriad changes in financial institution management since 1980. Consistently good lending decisions lead not only to institutional success but also to the growth and development of the loan recipients' enterprises. Poor decisions—those that are either too generous *or* that deny credit to worthy borrowers—affect not only lenders but also the broader economic environment.

This chapter initially considers important policy issues in loan portfolio management and continues with applications to commercial and international lending. The next chapter considers consumer and residential mortgage lending.

LOAN PORTFOLIOS OF DEPOSITORY INSTITUTIONS

Depositories offer loans for many purposes and to many types of borrowers. The loans in which each industry specializes have similarities and differences. Figure 14.1 provides information on the loan portfolios of all depository institutions as of year-end 1991.

COMMERCIAL BANKS

Of the total loans outstanding at commercial banks (a volume of more than $2 trillion), the largest category was real estate, followed by commercial and industrial (C&I) and consumer loans. Historically, C&I loans were the largest single category, especially

for the biggest commercial banks, but since 1988 this has not been the case. (Recall from Chapter 12 that real estate lending has always been popular with small banks.) The change for the industry as a whole is attributed to several factors, all of which are discussed later in this or the next chapter: sales of commercial loans by originators; the preference of some borrowers for commercial paper instead of bank loans; and the growth of home equity lending, a relatively new type of real estate credit.

The "other" loan category in the figure includes agricultural lending; loans to foreign, state, and local governments; and loans to other financial institutions. None of these categories is more than 3 percent of the loan portfolio for the banking industry as a whole, although some are more important for individual banks.

FIGURE 14.1   **Loan Portfolios of Depository Institutions, Year-End 1991**

Depositories' loan portfolios differ considerably. Commercial banks have the most diversified lending activities, savings institutions' portfolios are heavily concentrated in real estate-related loans, and credit unions emphasize consumer credit.

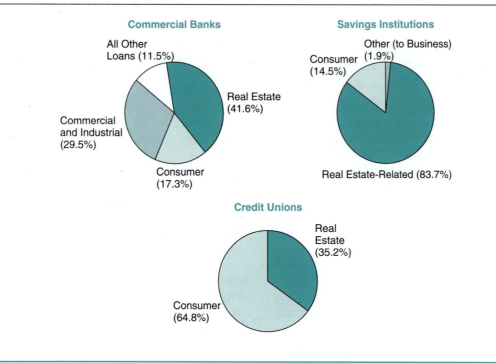

Commercial Banks

All Other Loans (11.5%)
Real Estate (41.6%)
Consumer (17.3%)
Commercial and Industrial (29.5%)

Savings Institutions

Other (to Business) (1.9%)
Consumer (14.5%)
Real Estate-Related (83.7%)

Credit Unions

Real Estate (35.2%)
Consumer (64.8%)

Source: Prepared by the authors with data from Board of Governors of the Federal Reserve System, *Flow of Funds,* QI, 1992; and *Federal Reserve Bulletin,* November 1992, A17.

SAVINGS INSTITUTIONS

For thrifts, most lending is real estate related. Although not shown in the figure, commercial real estate loans are less than 10 percent of real estate lending. Other commercial lending is less than 2 percent of the total portfolio. Consumer loans made by savings institutions include those to finance educational expenditures, automobiles, and other borrowings repaid on an installment basis.

CREDIT UNIONS

Little detail is available about credit union (CU) loan portfolios. Data from the Federal Reserve (Fed) indicate that consumer loans equaled almost 65 percent of CUs' portfolios. Just under half of these loans were for automobiles. As shown in Figure 14.1, more than 30 percent of loan funds were invested in real estate credit.

Figure 14.1 shows the continuation of traditional areas of concentration by depositories, but thrifts and CUs have taken advantage of expanded powers in recent years. Thus, issues in establishing loan policies and procedures span industry lines.

THE "SPECIAL" ROLE OF THE DEPOSITORY LENDERS

As suggested toward the end of Chapter 12, in recent years financial economists have devoted increasing attention to the question of whether depositories, and commercial banks in particular, are "special" intermediaries, requiring unique regulatory treatment. In the past, the special role depositories were said to play in the financial system was often linked to their providing transactions accounts for customers. In the past decade, however, some experts have argued that the special role of depositories is related as much, if not more, to their lending activities as it is to their deposit-taking activities.

Understanding this argument requires one to recall the discussion of financial contracts, monitoring, and asymmetric information in Chapter 1. As noted there, depositors entrusting funds to depositories could, as an alternative use of funds, lend directly to borrowers by purchasing a firm's bonds, for example.

The cost of monitoring individual borrowers' behavior, however, could be substantial. Depositories reduce monitoring costs by entering into financial contracts with (lending to) many borrowers on similar contract terms, then using specialized personnel and resources that can be devoted entirely to enforcing the contracts. Depositories can, in the context of a lending relationship, exert direct influence on a borrower's financial conduct and decisions.

Many of the cost reductions that depositories achieve are based on the ideas of **information reusability** and information asymmetry. Information reusability refers to the fact that once relevant data on a borrower have been collected and an initial loan application processed, cost economies are associated with the next application from that borrower. Not only is it unnecessary to collect some data (such as past financial history) again, but information asymmetry is reduced because the lender knows more about the borrower's ability and intention to pay than at the time of the first application. The more often the borrower and lender make financial contracts, the more often information can be reused, and the more the information asymmetry is reduced; thus, cost reductions can be significant for depositories that cultivate a strong clientele of regular borrowers. These depositories can, in turn, pass the cost savings to their depositors and shareholders.

Borrowers, too, benefit from information reusability and reduction of information asymmetry. For example, applying for a loan becomes less arduous as more financial contracts are made with the same lender. Further, research shows that a corporate borrower's shareholders bid up the firm's stock price after the firm announces it is undertaking new bank borrowing. If a commercial bank, with its "inside" knowledge, is willing to give a firm its "seal of approval," the securities markets appear to interpret that fact as reducing their need to monitor that same firm.

This and other evidence has led some observers to note that if depository lenders were to voluntarily discontinue their current lending practices, or if massive depository failures were to disrupt the flow of credit to customers, the stability of the entire financial infrastructure would be threatened. Under this view of the world, depositories are indeed still special. The issue took on added significance in the early 1990s when many would-be borrowers accused banks of creating a "credit crunch" in response to tightening regulation and supervision. Some applicants, especially small and medium-sized businesses, claimed they could not get loans because banks' credit standards had become so unreasonable that no one could qualify. To the extent that a bank's unwillingness to lend served as a signal to other potential investors in a business, some borrowers believed they were being shut out of the credit markets altogether. One study conducted at the Kansas City Fed during this period concluded that, although bank lending relationships are less important for many large businesses than they were in past decades, they are still "special" for many small and midsized firms, implying that if banks cut off funds to this group, few alternative funding sources would arise. As the opening quotation to this chapter suggests, banks have argued that they are merely exercising prudence in the wake of both the S&L debacle and more stringent supervisory policies introduced in the Federal Deposit Insurance Corporation Improvement Act (FDICIA) and that truly worthy borrowers will always be accommodated.[2]

Although most of this chapter and the next address the effect of lending on individual institutions, it is important to remember the broader significance of this asset management decision.

INSTITUTIONAL POLICIES AND OBJECTIVES: SIZE, COMPOSITION, MATURITY, AND DEFAULT RISK

In administering the loan portfolio, lenders must address several areas, either regularly or infrequently. Although the formality may vary according to the size of the institution and the scope of its operations, every lender establishes lending objectives, reflecting the risk/return preferences of managers and owners through the target net interest margin (NIM) and its expected variability. Institutional objectives must also

meet regulatory requirements. These objectives set the guidelines for evaluating every loan application and identify the lines of authority used in the loan approval process.

Credit policies reflect long-term strategic planning for the overall asset portfolio and set general guidelines for the size of the loan portfolio, its composition, and the maximum acceptable level of default risk. For example, in a commercial bank, decisions must be made about the proportion of loan funds to be invested in C&I loans and the proportions earmarked for other purposes. A thrift institution must decide whether to confine itself to the mortgage markets or to enter the commercial and consumer markets. These decisions influence the way a depository advertises its services, the customers whose loan applications will be given preference, and many other aspects of lending. Major credit policy issues are outlined and discussed in this section.

SIZE

The first decision to be made is the size of the loan portfolio as a proportion of total assets. It influences the quantity of loan funds available and the emphasis placed on lending in comparison with other investments. For most depository institutions, the standard practice is to view lending as the primary function, although the size of the loan portfolio is not entirely under the institution's control. Demand for loans may decrease under poor economic conditions. Even when demand is strong, the institution may lack funds to lend in a rapidly growing economy in which competition for funds is keen. Also, regulators look closely at the size of the loan portfolio relative to an institution's net worth, so regulatory standards may restrict expansion of the loan portfolio. Tighter capital regulations recently adopted will magnify the impact of regulations on lending decisions.

COMPOSITION

Another strategic decision is how funds will be allocated across many potential loan categories. One consideration is the institution's deposit structure and its other sources of funds because their maturities may affect management's loan maturity preferences and

---

[2] For more discussion of the special nature of depository lending, see Becketti and Morris 1992; Greenbaum, Kanatas, and Venezia 1989; James 1987; Berlin 1987; and Fama 1985. (References are listed in full at the end of this chapter.)

thus the types of loans granted. The choices an institution makes also reflect its operating environment. A farm community may have few nonfarm business applicants. In a suburb, demand is high for consumer loans and home mortgages. Banks must also decide whether to confine lending to a local geographic area or to enter new markets, including global ones.

For savings institutions and CUs, the composition of the loan portfolio is a major decision as well, because diversification beyond traditional lending areas requires a significant commitment of resources. Each type of lending requires different areas of expertise, so the movement into new arenas must be preceded by careful planning. The large losses incurred by many thrifts on commercial real estate investments during the 1980s serve as a vivid reminder of the potential problems facing lenders as they move into new territory. These recent experiences and some Financial Institutions Reform, Recovery, and Enforcement Act (FIRREA) provisions (such as the stricter qualified thrift lender [QTL] test) lead many experts to predict that thrifts, in particular, will continue to focus on traditional, housing-related investments.

MATURITY

Closely tied to the types of loans in the portfolio is the decision about average loan maturity. If mortgages are most of an institution's loans, the portfolio maturity will be relatively long. Most nonmortgage commercial loans have initial maturities of 5 years or less, so an institution heavily oriented toward business lending will have a portfolio with a shorter average maturity. Within those general guidelines, however, managers can exercise much discretion, with important ramifications for overall asset/liability performance.

The relative maturities of an institution's assets and sources of funds influence the stability of the NIM. Interest rate volatility is not equal for short- and long-term securities, and, except under a flat yield curve, neither are rates. In fact, the need to shorten average asset maturities to bring them closer to liability maturities was an argument used to support Depository Institutions Deregulation and Monetary Control Act (DIDMCA) provisions allowing broader lending powers for savings institutions.[3]

MANAGING DEFAULT RISK

Every lender faces the possibility that a borrower will default. The degree of default risk faced, however, is influenced by the thoroughness with which the financial position of a borrower is analyzed and by the standards set for accepting or rejecting loan applicants based on the analysis.

ESTIMATING AN APPLICANT'S DEFAULT RISK.
Standards for evaluating the financial stability of a prospective borrower are reflected in information collected at the time of application and in the subsequent analysis. Credit analysis varies according to the type of loan and the type of borrower. In commercial lending, loan officers and credit analysts must be proficient in interpreting financial statements. For consumer loans, credit bureau reports provide a guide to the likelihood of default.

The complexity of risk assessment varies with the size of the institution, the risk aversion of its owners or managers, and their willingness to devote resources to preliminary screening of applicants. Many institutions establish a risk-rating system, which is used by loan officers to assign each application to a risk category reflecting the probability of default. Such a classification scheme is seldom purely quantitative. In commercial banking, for example, a subjective assessment of an applicant's attitude toward financial obligations is widely recognized as an element in the lending decision.

ESTABLISHING CREDIT STANDARDS.
Regardless of how credit risk is estimated, established standards for maximum risk exposure guide the recommendations of loan officers and the subsequent actions of senior officers. These standards affect both the volume of lending and the variability in earnings. A depository deciding to accept borrowers with relatively poor financial ratings will have more qualified applicants and greater opportunities for growth in earnings. Yet lower-quality loans have a higher probability of default. If a lender adopts a policy of greater selectivity, it may lose customers to competing lenders but also may avoid high losses. The risk/return trade-off is once again evident.

---

[3] See West 1982.

TABLE 14.1 The Base Lending Rate Required to Meet Target Rates of Return

A base lending rate is established after considering an institution's target NIM, its target RONW, and its asset mix. The base rate is the starting point from which loan terms for individual borrowers are established.

I. Balance Sheet and Planning Assumptions

Assets		Liabilities and Net Worth	
Securities	$ 30	Liabilities	$ 92
Loans	60		
Nonearning assets	10	Net worth	8
Total	$100	Total	$100

Return on securities: 10.5%
Return on nonearning assets: 0%
Target NIM: 3.2%
t = 34%
Base loan rate: 13.88% (as calculated in text)

Average cost of liabilities: 9%
Net worth multiplier: 12.5
Target RONW: 18%

II. Pro Forma Income Statement

Interest revenues:
   10.50% × $30 = $3.150
   13.88% × $60 = 8.328
   0.00% × $10 = 0.000

Total	$11.478

Interest expense:
   9.00% × $92 = (8.280)

Spread $ 3.198

Less net noninterest expenses:
   1.00% × $100 = (1.000)

Income before taxes $ 2.198
Less income taxes (0.34) (0.747)

Net income $ 1.451
NIM = $3.2/$100 = 3.2%
RONW = $1.451/$8 = 18%

INSTITUTIONAL POLICIES AND OBJECTIVES: ESTABLISHING LOAN TERMS

Equally important to a lender's financial performance are guidelines governing the terms of individual loans.

CALCULATING A BASE LENDING RATE

The dominance of loans in institutions' asset portfolios suggests that keeping loan rates at appropriate levels is a prerequisite to earning the target NIM and target rate of return on net worth (RONW). **Base lending rates** are established at the institutional level and used as benchmarks for determining specific loan rates. Very good customers may be offered a lower

rate, and higher-risk customers are charged a higher rate. But the base sets the boundaries within which the loan officer can exercise discretion.[4]

Chapter 4 introduced the relationship between the target RONW and the target NIM. Although interest revenues earned on the loan portfolio are an important influence on the NIM, other assets also must be considered in the base loan-rate calculation. For example, suppose that the hypothetical institution discussed in Chapter 4 (see pages 89–91) and reintroduced in Table 14.1 has nonearning assets equal to 10

[4]Historically, the base rate at commercial banks was known as the "prime" lending rate. For reasons explained later in the chapter, the terms base rate and prime rate are no longer always synonymous.

percent of total assets. Also, suppose that 30 percent of the institution's total assets are invested in securities on which the before-tax average rate of return is 10.5 percent. The remaining 60 percent of total assets are invested in loans. The mix of assets and rates of return, as well as the fact that some assets are nonearning, must be considered in planning for the total spread:

$$IR - IE = \left[\sum_{i=1}^{n} r_i \times A_i \right] - (c \times TL) \qquad [14.1]$$

where

r_i = the interest rate earned on asset category i
A_i = total dollar investment in asset category i
c = average interest cost of financial liabilities
TL = total liabilities

Note that $\sum_{i=1}^{n} r_i \times A_i$ equals total interest revenues (IR) and that $c \times TL$ equals total interest expense (IE). Equation 14.1 can be used to solve for the base loan rate, r_L.

Table 14.1 notes that the average cost of liabilities is 9 percent and that liabilities total $92 million. If the target NIM—a calculation based on *total* assets—is 3.2 percent, the necessary spread between interest revenues and the interest cost of liabilities is $3.2 million. Using Equation 14.1, the target spread is expressed in millions as follows:

$$\text{Spread} = [(0\% \times \$10) + (10.5\% \times \$30)$$
$$+ (r_L \times \$60)] - (9\% \times \$92)$$
$$\$3.2 = [\$0 + \$3.15 + (r_L \times \$60)] - \$8.28$$
$$r_L \times \$60 = \$8.33$$
$$r_L = \$8.33/\$60 = 13.88\%$$

Because nonearning assets and securities both contribute to the target NIM at a lower rate than do loans, interest earned on loans must provide a higher-than-average return for the institution's financial objectives to be achieved. The **pro forma** (projected) income statement at the bottom of Table 14.1 illustrates

this point. The base rate of 13.88 percent is appropriate only for customers of average cost and average risk; it is a starting point for loan officers in setting loan rates for individual customers.

LOAN PRICING AND INFORMATION ASYMMETRY

Some financial economists studying issues of information asymmetry and reusability in bank lending have come to what may seem at first to be a curious conclusion about lending-rate decisions for individual customers. One might assume that established customers would always get lower rates. But some experts argue that the longer a bank's relationship with a borrower—and therefore the less information asymmetry and the more information reusability—the *higher* the lending rate to that customer. As noted earlier, as a result of reduced information asymmetry and increased reusability, banks' costs should go down with each loan to the same borrower. Because they save the cost of searching for loans elsewhere and enjoy the enhanced reputation being granted a loan gives them, however, borrowers tend to value an existing lending relationship and are reluctant to change banks. The bank might then be able to take financial advantage of this situation by increasing loan rates for well-established customers, thus increasing profits. Eventually, the loan rate may become sufficiently higher than those offered by competing banks that the borrower may switch institutions. But as long as the customer delays a search for a new bank, the original bank should benefit considerably.[5]

FIXED-RATE VERSUS VARIABLE-RATE LENDING

Finally, uncertainty about future interest rates causes lenders to consider whether loan rates should be fixed or variable. Adjustable-rate lending passes the lender's exposure to interest rate risk to the borrower; as the cost of raising funds changes, so does the lender's rate of return. In periods of rising interest

---

[5] Greenbaum, Kanatas, and Venezia 1989; Fred Furlong, "Is the Prime Rate Too High?" *Weekly Letter* (Federal Reserve Bank of San Francisco), July 5, 1991.

rates, depository institutions may emphasize variable-rate loans to protect the level and stability of the NIM. In that case, the base rate is used only to establish the initial interest rate. As with many risk-reduction strategies, however, variable-rate lending limits growth in the NIM, because when interest expense decreases, so do interest revenues. These advantages and disadvantages are explored in detail as specific categories of lending are discussed in this and the next chapter.

INSTITUTIONAL POLICIES AND OBJECTIVES: LOAN AUTHORIZATION, MONITORING AND COMPETITIVE STRATEGY

A successful lending operation also incorporates procedural controls, monitoring of outstanding loans, and competitive strategies.

PROCEDURES FOR LOAN AUTHORIZATION

Loan approval becomes more formal as the size of an institution and its staff grow. If loan officers are also executives of a depository institution, they are directly responsible to the board of directors, owners, and regulators for their decisions. In larger organizations, however, the personnel having direct contact with loan applicants are usually not the executives, so a review procedure by those who will bear ultimate responsibility must be established. Often there is a dollar amount below which a loan officer may grant a loan without prior approval from higher authorities. The maximum amount is positively related to the loan officer's experience and qualifications.

For loans exceeding the maximum amount, the officer must present all relevant data, along with a recommendation for loan terms, to a higher-ranking loan officer or to a loan committee consisting of the executives of the loan department. Final decisions are reviewed by the board of directors to guard against mismanagement of loan funds and to ensure that management's and/or owners' risk preferences are applied. Because of time constraints, however, the loan officer's analysis and recommendations are given great weight.

MONITORING LOANS AFTER APPROVAL

Once a loan is granted, its quality relies on the borrower's continued financial stability; if the borrower's financial position deteriorates, the lender needs to know before the maturity date. In an installment loan, when a regular payment plan is set in advance, the borrower's financial problems are evident as soon as an installment payment is missed, and the lender can contact the borrower.

In a **term loan,** where interest and principal are repaid at maturity, the lender must take a more active role in checking the borrower's compliance. For a commercial loan, for example, the account officer may require that interim financial statements be provided. Loans assigned a relatively high risk rating at the time of their approval need to be reviewed more frequently than less risky agreements. Early detection of problems may enable the lender to intervene and prevent further deterioration, reducing potential variability in the NIM.

LOAN MONITORING, REGULATION, AND FINANCIAL REPORTING. Loan monitoring also has important ramifications for financial reporting to the public and to regulatory agencies. As explained in Chapter 12, institutions estimate problem loans and report them in the Allowance for Possible Loan Losses account on their balance sheets. (Large banks may not use estimates to determine the tax deduction but are permitted to use them for financial and regulatory reports.)

Table 14.2 shows a typical report of a small bank's loss allowance for consumer loans. From the ending balance for the previous year, actual loan losses, called **loan chargeoffs,** are deducted. If any loans previously written off as losses were subsequently collected, they are added back to the allowance. Finally, the allowance is increased by current estimates of anticipated loan losses (the provision for loan losses). Thus, the allowance account is always an estimate of future loan losses, not a record of past losses.[6]

---

[6] For more details, see Walter 1991.

| TABLE 14.2 | Calculating the Loan Loss Allowance |

Loan loss accounting is intended to provide users of depositories' financial statements with an estimate of future defaults; it is not a record of the institution's past loan losses.

	1996 (Dollars in Thousands)	1995 (Dollars in Thousands)
Balance at beginning of year	$226	$190
Deductions		
Loan chargeoffs	$386	$283
Less loan recoveries	(100)	(87)
Net loan chargeoffs	$286	$196
Additions		
Credit loss provision	$346	$227
Other additions	34	5
	$380	$232
Balance at end of year	$320	$226

Estimating future loan losses for planning purposes is of considerable concern to depositories. To estimate losses with a reasonable degree of accuracy, lenders develop procedures to identify when a borrower moves into the "questionable" category. Regulators expect these policies to accomplish their purpose; when they do not, disciplinary actions may be taken. Monitoring and documenting loans took on added importance after FDICIA. As noted in Chapter 2, FDICIA required all depository institution regulators to develop formal "tripwire" systems intended to alert both managers and regulators if an institution's risk is increasing. Congress specified that these tripwires must include consideration of a depository's credit-granting and documentation methods as well as the proportion of outstanding loans that are **classified assets.** Classified loans are those posing significant default risk to the institution and for which loan loss provisions must account. Institutions that fail to meet minimum standards in these areas are subject to severe operating restrictions.

DELINQUENT LOANS. Despite careful scrutiny of loan applications, some borrowers inevitably will be unable or unwilling to meet their repayment schedules. When a borrower is seriously delinquent, management of the loan moves from the loan officer to those responsible for collection. In all cases, collection personnel want to avoid legal action, because it consumes resources and time. For example, a savings institution does not really want to foreclose on a mortgage loan; the legal expenses are large, and the institution must sell or maintain the repossessed property. Lenders will usually work closely with borrowers to set up revised repayment plans, suggest general financial counseling, or provide advice on financial management. Such efforts are often termed **workouts.**

Monitoring collateral can be difficult in some cases. When vehicle loans become delinquent, the lender must move quickly—because the collateral is mobile! As with other aspects of loan management, the more resources committed to the collection effort, the greater the protection against instability in the NIM but also the greater the additions to net noninterest expenses.

COMPETITIVE LENDING STRATEGIES

The competitive strategy that an institution chooses is reflected in many aspects of its lending policy, including the types of customers served, the interest rates charged, other loan terms offered, and the riskiness of approved borrowers. But the competitive strategy affects other activities as well. Depository institutions are increasingly undertaking formal marketing campaigns preceded by extensive research to identify potentially profitable market segments. In the early 1990s, for example, many banks identified midsized firms as a promising market niche for commercial lending. The result was a substantial increase in the competition to attract such customers and the introduction of aggressive strategies to win new borrowers. In the New York area, the competition was particularly strong, because many midsized firms are headquartered there. Chemical Bank chose to send out 800 loan officers to visit approximately 3,000 companies; the visits were preceded by the distribution of Nestle Crunch candy bars to send the message that Chemical was a willing lender and not a party to the much-publicized "credit crunch" of the early 1990s.[7] Banks throughout the United States are using mail solicitations and other offers in attempts to penetrate the midsized firm lending market or to expand the geographic regions they serve.

Requiring lenders to undertake "selling" activities, as Chemical Bank did, is a major change from historical practice. These selling programs contrast with the traditional idea of waiting for loan customers to come to the institution. Today, loan officers may research potential customers, visit prospects to explain how the institution's services can meet their needs, and report the results in regular meetings. More aggressive competitive strategies, however, may involve higher expenses and greater risk exposure as the institution moves into markets where it lacks historical experience to serve as a guide.

RECENT TRENDS IN COMMERCIAL LENDING

The remainder of this chapter and the next apply general principles of lending to several types of loans, beginning with commercial loans, a category that actually includes quite a variety of investments. The definition of a commercial loan has important implications for regulatory decisions, as discussed in Chapter 4, because the Bank Holding Company Act defined a commercial bank as one that both accepts demand deposits and makes commercial loans. In applying the law to bank holding companies (BHCs), the Fed traditionally defined commercial loans broadly as "all loans to a company or individual, secured or unsecured, other than a loan the proceeds of which are used

to acquire property or services used by the borrower for his own personal, family or household purposes, or for charitable purposes." The Board later expanded this definition to include indirect lending through the purchase of commercial paper, bankers' acceptances, certificates of deposit (CDs), and the sale of federal funds.[8] The discussion in this chapter is confined to direct lending.

As Figure 14.1 reveals, C&I loans are heavily concentrated in the commercial banking industry. Periodic surveys of commercial lending practices at commercial banks conducted by the Fed indicate that short-term loans represent most business lending agreements.[9] In 1992, for example, the average maturity of short-term loans averaged just under 2 months, with maturities of long-term agreements averaging 45 months.

Despite more than a decade of regulatory authority to serve commercial customers, thrifts do not have a high profile in the market for commercial loans. Nonreal estate commercial loans were less than 2 percent of thrift loan portfolios at year-end 1991. Not even New England savings banks, the largest commercial lenders among thrifts, devote large proportions of their portfolios to business loans.[10]

Studies of savings banks and S&Ls have offered insights into factors influencing their loan portfolio decisions. Researchers have examined how commercial lending strategies are affected by institutional size, market conditions, and experience with commercial customers and nonmortgage consumer lending. Larger thrifts are more likely to move into the business loan markets as are those whose employees have expertise in serving commercial customers, evidenced by commercial real estate lending or nonmortgage consumer lending. To avoid the costly errors of learning the hard way, some thrifts have even hired experienced personnel from the banking industry, although some errors from inexperience are unavoidable. Researchers have

---

[7] See Steven Lipin, "With Big Loans Slow, Major Banks Romance Local Midsized Firms," *The Wall Street Journal,* February 26, 1991, A1, A5.

[8] See Gagnon 1983, 37.

[9] Surveys are conducted and published several times a year by the Fed, including the Survey of Terms of Bank Lending and the Senior Loan Officer Opinion Survey of Bank Lending Practices. For a discussion of survey methods and results, see Wolfson and McLaughlin 1989 and Brady 1985.

[10] See Brantley 1987; Goudreau 1984; Moulton 1984; and Dunham 1985.

also found support for the hypothesis that thrifts are more likely to serve the small business market. Finally, if commercial bank services in the community are highly concentrated in a few banks, with the attendant possibility of higher loan rates, thrifts may have an opportunity to capture a competitive edge.[11]

COMMERCIAL LOAN CREDIT ANALYSIS

Assessing the credit worthiness of a commercial loan applicant involves collecting, analyzing, and interpreting financial and personal data.

THE CS OF CREDIT

Over the years, a framework called the **Cs of credit** has become common for describing the lending decisions. At first only three Cs were used: **character, capacity, and capital.** Then two more were added: **conditions** and **collateral.** This framework helps the decision maker group information into a small number of categories to assess borrower risk.[12]

Perhaps the most difficult C to evaluate is the applicant's character, because the term is supposed to capture many personal qualities, such as integrity—in short, it indicates the intention to repay any financial obligations. Information about the individual's involvement in the business community or charitable efforts is used, and particular weight is given to previous credit records. The character rating is certainly the most subjective part of the credit analysis and the C that exposes the lender to perhaps the most information asymmetry.

Determining capacity relies on financial statements to assess the borrower's ability to repay the loan through income generated by the business.

Capital also refers to the ability to repay, but it focuses more on the soundness of financial position and whether the borrower has nonborrowed sources of funds sufficient to withstand a temporary setback.

The effect of potential changes in the level of economic activity—national, local, or both—is the purpose of the conditions category. A business may be doing well at the time of the loan application, but the analyst must consider what could happen to the borrower's financial position as conditions change. This factor is especially important under certain loan terms, such as a variable interest rate. The borrower may be able to service the loan at prevailing interest rates but might not be able to do so at higher rates, as became painfully evident under the extremely high lending rates in 1980–1982.

The final C, collateral, is self-explanatory; it involves the availability of collateral and the quality of the assets involved. Commercial lenders have traditionally disliked collateralized lending, now often called **asset-based lending.** Recent research suggests, in fact, that some borrowers may view asset-based loans as signals. If one lender is willing to accept the firm's assets as collateral, other potential creditors or investors may recognize the high quality of the borrower's assets.

Although quality of collateral is important, the real hope is that the lender never needs to take possession of the collateral. The old saying, "Never take collateral that eats" is a reminder that the costs of acquiring assets as a result of defaulted loans can be substantial.

TYPES OF INFORMATION REQUIRED

The evaluation of a loan application is based on information from a number of sources. If the applicant is not a new customer, the loan officer already has much reusable information, including the borrower's previous payment record, past financial statements, and personal contacts. For new applicants, the credit analyst-loan officer will need some of or all the following:

- Past financial statements for the firm
- Personal financial information from the owner if the firm is not large, with diversified ownership
- Projections of the future financial position, defined previously as *pro forma* statements
- A credit report
- Financial performance measures for similar firms as a basis of comparison

---

[11] See Dunham and Guerin-Calvert 1985; Pavel and Phillis 1985; and Goudreau and Ford 1986.

[12] The three or five or more Cs of credit are discussed in many sources; three of these sources are Gill 1983, 203–214; Crigger 1975; and Compton 1985.

■ Personal contact with the potential borrower and a personal visit to the business
■ Economic projections.

FINANCIAL ANALYSIS

Analysis of the applicant's financial position begins with calculating and interpreting standard balance sheet and income statement ratios, but it may go beyond that, depending on the size of the loan and the size of the lending institution.

INFORMATION PROVIDED BY THE BORROWER. There are hundreds of financial ratios, but not all are necessary for credit analysis. The more ratios, the more difficult it is to interpret them and to draw conclusions about the borrower's financial standing. In fact, a sizable body of research suggests that it is possible to capture all dimensions of financial performance with a

relatively small number of measures. The research also indicates that the same ratios should not be used for all industries, because certain ratios provide more accurate signals for some types of firms than for others.[13]

One survey of loan officers at the nation's 100 largest commercial banks attempted to identify the financial ratios considered most useful in analyzing the credit risk of borrowers.[14] Respondents were asked to rank the usefulness of 59 ratios, then to identify which aspect of financial performance they believed each measured best. The three ratios on which there was greatest agreement were the debt/equity and current ratios and the ratio of cash flow to current maturities of long-term debt. Table 14.3 lists the 15 most important ratios and the primary area of performance they are used to measure.

Two of the important ratios involve cash flow. The borrower's cash position and its importance in evaluating loan quality are gaining more attention

---

TABLE 14.3   **Financial Ratios Perceived as Important by Loan Officers**

Although many financial ratios can be calculated, loan officers believe that some are better than others. One survey showed that a firm's debt/equity ratio was viewed as the most useful ratio, followed by the current ratio.

Ratio	Significance Rating	Primary Measure
Debt/equity	8.71	Debt
Current ratio	8.25	Liquidity
Cash flow/current maturities of long-term debt	8.08	Debt
Fixed charge coverage	7.58	Debt
Net profit margin after tax	7.56	Profitability
Times interest earned	7.50	Debt
Net profit margin before tax	7.43	Profitability
Degree of financial leverage	7.33	Debt
Inventory turnover (days)	7.25	Liquidity
Accounts receivable turnover (days)	7.08	Liquidity
Quick ratio	6.79	Liquidity
Cash flow/total debt	6.71	Debt
Return on assets after tax	6.69	Profitability
Accounts receivable turnover (times)	6.58	Liquidity
Return on equity after tax	6.30	Profitability

Significance:
   0–2 Low Importance
   7–9 High Importance
Source: Charles Gibson, "Financial Ratios as Perceived by Commercial Loan Officers," *Akron Business & Economic Review,* Vol. 14, No. 2, Summer, 1983, pp. 23–27. Reprinted with permission.

---

[13] A good summary of this research is available in Chen and Shimerda 1981. Subsequent support is offered in Gombola and Ketz 1983.

[14] See Gibson 1983.

among analysts. Although cash-flow projections are not part of standard financial statements, a lender can request them as part of the loan application. A growing number of analysts believe that cash position provides more insight into the borrower's ability to repay than traditional accounting earnings measures. The accounting profession itself has emphasized cash-flow reporting recently, at least on a historical basis. Generally accepted accounting principles now require firms to produce a Statement of Cash Flows annually.

EXTERNAL SOURCES OF INFORMATION. Several other sources of information supplement that provided by the applicant. For example, other creditors of the firm, such as suppliers, may be willing to discuss the firm's payment record. The lender can also purchase a Dun and Bradstreet (D&B) Business Information Report, which includes D&B's own assessment of a firm's creditworthiness and other details about its operations, owners, and management.

If the firm has a credit relationship with another commercial lender, information can be requested from that institution. Robert Morris Associates (RMA), the national trade organization for commercial loan officers, has developed a code of ethics to guide the exchange of information among lenders.[15] RMA also publishes *Annual Statement Studies,* containing standard performance measures for more than 300 lines of business. Other industry average ratios are found in D&B's *Key Business Ratios,* the *Quarterly Financial Report for U.S. Manufacturing Corporations* (Federal Trade Commission [FTC] and Securities and Exchange Commission [SEC]), *Financial Studies of Small Business* (Financial Research Associates), and the *Almanac of Business and Industrial Ratios* (Prentice-Hall). In all cases, industry averages must be interpreted with care, because an individual loan applicant is likely to have unique characteristics requiring the lending officer's judgment.[16]

EVALUATING RISK

Evaluating creditworthiness requires more than financial analysis. Commercial loan officers should learn as much as possible about a business and the way it is managed. Some experts suggest that good risk analysis asks, "What could go wrong?" and investigates all aspects of the business in an attempt to find out. Careful investigation serves another purpose as well. The more complete and accurate the information collected on a loan, the better the lender's position when regulatory examiners review the institution's loan portfolio. As noted earlier, maintaining accurate records, known as **loan documentation,** is important when examiners are assessing the quality of outstanding loans, especially under FDICIA's tripwire provisions.

After a lending officer has tapped available information sources, the hardest task is ahead—organizing the data, rating the applicant on each dimension of the institution's risk-rating system, and recommending approval or denial. Some lenders use quantitative credit-scoring models to integrate information from a variety of sources. Data on an applicant are weighted according to predetermined standards, and a score for creditworthiness is calculated. Applicants falling below a predetermined minimum acceptable score are rejected.[17] A credit-scoring model is illustrated in Chapter 15.

If the loan is approved, the risk category to which the borrower is assigned has important ramifications for other aspects of the lending decision, including the interest rate, whether collateral is required, and whether financial standards such as minimum working capital ratios are imposed on the firm over the life of the loan.

FINANCIAL AND TECHNOLOGICAL INNOVATION AT WORK: EXPERT SYSTEMS FOR CREDIT ANALYSIS

As the preceding discussion indicates, a commercial loan application requires a complex series of

---

[15] The Code of Ethics is available from Robert Morris Associates, RMA National Office, 1616 Philadelphia National Bank Building, Philadelphia, PA 19107.

[16] There are literally hundreds of sources of information on interpreting and using financial ratios and industry averages. Two comprehensive treatments are Foster 1986 and Higgins 1989.

---

[17] Most credit-scoring models used in commercial lending stem from the work of Altman 1968. Some new applications of credit scoring to commercial lending decisions are discussed in Alan Radding, "Credit Scoring's New Frontier," *Magazine of Bank Management* (September 1992): 57.

evaluations by the loan officer. In fact, so complex—and presumably so intuitive—is the credit-granting decision that, until quite recently, few lenders would have entertained the idea that it could be largely divorced from human judgment. Yet financial and technological innovation have invaded even this sacrosanct arena, in the guise of the **expert systems** approach to commercial loan analysis.

Expert systems are computerized approaches, not just to data processing but to actual decision making. They are founded on a step-by-step charting of the stages in a decision, as illustrated in Figure 14.2 for the commercial lending decision. (Note that the figure includes all relevant stages of credit analysis, as discussed earlier in the chapter.) Once the decision-making process is clearly understood, a computer program is developed that mimics, as closely as possible, the thinking process of decision makers recognized for their expertise in applying judgment at each stage of the flowchart. Expert systems incorporate the ability to perform calculations necessary to evaluate a credit application (such as financial ratios, which enter the model in Stage D in Figure 14.2). They also incorporate the capacity to *interpret* the results of those calculations as seasoned loan officers would, then to make decisions (Stage F in the figure) based on interpretation of results from previous stages. At appropriate stages in the decision, users of expert systems technology can interact with the computer to provide additional data or to perform supplementary calculations that may improve the system's ability to make the "right" decision.[18]

Supporters of expert systems point to their tremendous cost-saving potential. Once they are on-line, they never take paid vacations, never enter the hospital (although they may be subject to viruses), and are never lured away from the institution for higher-paying jobs. Cautious observers note, however, that the true test of expert systems will be their success in making lending decisions that are as profitable, at a comparable level of risk, as those made by human loan officers. It is much too early to know the results of that

test. Research suggests, however, that although expert systems cannot replace loan officers, they can substantially improve productivity and effectively supplement the efforts of lenders.

INTEREST RATES ON COMMERCIAL LOANS

Commercial loan officers tailor the terms of a loan to fit the customer's needs and those of the lending institution. Among the most important is the interest rate. When the general level of interest rates is high, public attention focuses on these rates—particularly the **prime rate.** For reasons explained later, it is now virtually impossible to provide a precise definition of the term *prime rate.* Historically, it was used to identify the interest rate charged on short-term loans to a bank's most creditworthy commercial customers. All other borrowers, businesses or individuals, could expect to pay more. These simple rules no longer apply.

A HISTORICAL LOOK AT THE PRIME

The idea of the prime was born in the depressed economy of the 1930s, when loan demand was so low that commercial lending rates approached 0 percent. The prime was introduced to establish a floor below which rates would not be allowed to fall. Although the prime was an administered, not a market-determined, rate until the early 1970s, regulators and legislators viewed it as an economic indicator of business activity.

As financial managers in large corporations became more sophisticated, however, they found other sources of short-term credit. Many turned to the commercial paper market or even to overseas sources of funds. Figure 14.3 suggests why: Before 1970, the commercial paper rate was usually lower than the prime. Also, the commercial paper rate—which is market-determined, not administered—rose and fell with economic conditions, whereas the prime remained unchanged for long periods. The flight of large business borrowers from commercial banks to money markets had begun.

In response, most **money-center banks** (large banks located in metropolitan financial centers such as New York, Chicago, Los Angeles, and San Francisco)

---

[18] An expert system is sometimes called a "knowledge-based system." Recent discussions of specific expert systems software for use in commercial lending include Duchessi and Belardo 1987; Shaw and Gentry 1988; Duchessi, Shawky, and Seagle 1988; Plath and Kloppenborg 1989; McGinn 1990; and Arend 1992.

FIGURE 14.2   Model of the Commercial Lending Decision-Making Process

Expert systems for loan analysis begin with a detailed diagram of the stages in the lending decision. Then a computer program that emulates the thinking of a skilled loan officer is developed.

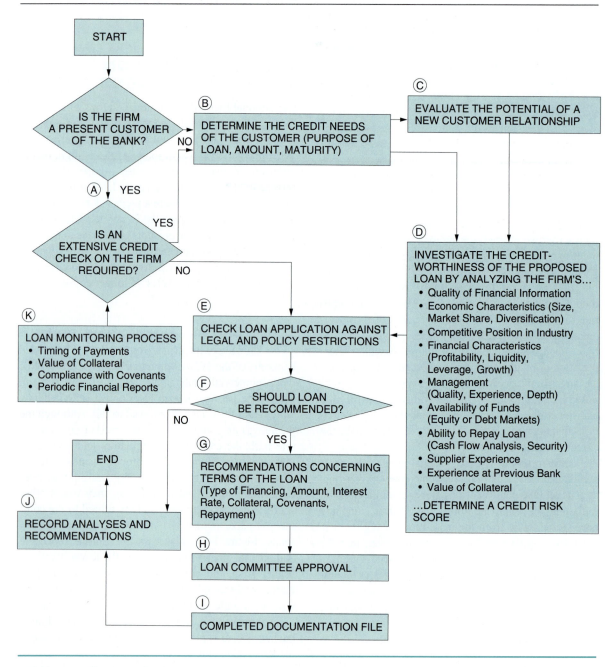

Source: Michael J. Shaw and James A. Gentry, "Using an Expert System with Inductive Learning to Evaluate Business Loans," *Financial Management* 17 (Autumn 1988): 47.

FIGURE 14.3   The Prime Rate and the Commercial Paper Rate

The prime rate is an administered interest rate that often differs from the commercial paper rate, which is market determined. In recent years, the prime has consistently exceeded the commercial paper rate.

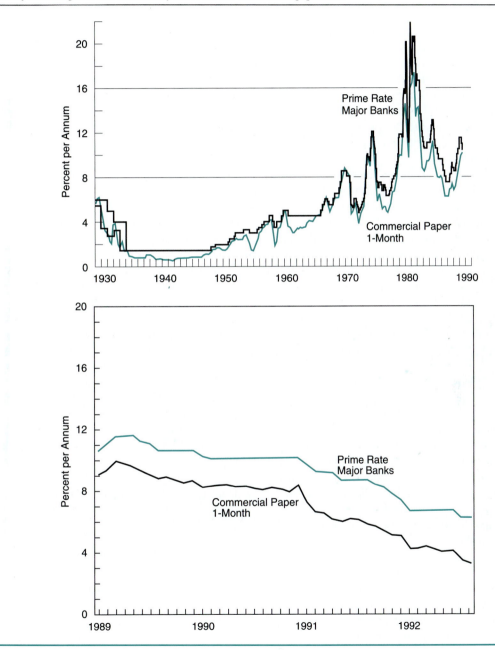

Source: Board of Governors of the Federal Reserve System, *1989 Historical Chart Book,* 99; *Federal Reserve Bulletin,* various issues.

formally began to link their prime rates to the commercial paper rate. This linkage is evident in Panel A of Figure 14.3 by the early 1970s. But the flight by large borrowers to other credit markets accelerated, spurred by the convenience, flexibility, and lower administrative costs in those markets. Because linking the prime to money market rates had failed to serve its purpose, most large banks had discontinued this practice by 1980, returning the prime to its administered status. As Panel B of the figure clearly demonstrates, the prime has consistently exceeded the 1-month commercial paper rate in the early 1990s, resulting in continued popularity of commercial paper financing among eligible borrowers.

Today, money center banks tend to keep their prime rates closely in line with one another. The prime at smaller regional and community banks may differ considerably, because their access to money markets is limited and their operating characteristics are different. The prime is, therefore, an administered rate that is also sensitive to market conditions. As Panel B of Figure 14.3 shows, the prime moves in the same direction as the commercial paper rate but tends not to change as quickly or as much.

DEVELOPMENT OF THE TWO-TIERED MARKET

Many banks use the practice of *below-prime pricing* or lending at rates below the announced prime rate to preferred customers. These loan rates are tied to federal funds or negotiable CD rates—that is, to a bank's *marginal* cost of funds. Data from the Fed's quarterly surveys on bank lending indicate that below-prime pricing has become quite common at large banks, exceeding 75 percent of the dollar volume of all short-term loans in 1992.

Smaller banks use this pricing approach for a lower proportion of loans (just under 50 percent in late 1992). Therefore, below-prime loans are often concentrated in a few banks and are available primarily to large borrowers whose credit ratings are strong enough to give them access to the commercial paper market. Loans to those in poorer financial condition or to smaller businesses (concentrated at smaller institutions) are still more likely to be priced at or above the prime rate. Thus, two distinct pricing strategies are used for two distinct markets.

WHAT, THEN, *IS* THE PRIME?

The practice of below-prime pricing initially provoked a strong reaction from borrowers who were not getting preferred treatment, beginning in 1980 when a suit was filed against the First National Bank of Atlanta by a small business customer.[19] Litigation against many other banks followed. As a result, institutions have redefined the prime or, perhaps more accurately, have given it a "nondefinition." For example, Morgan Guaranty Trust announced, "The bank's prime shall mean the rate of interest publicly announced by the bank in New York from time to time as the prime rate," a definition described by *Time* magazine as "sounding as if it were drafted by committee."

At many institutions, the terms *base rate* or *reference rate* are replacing the phrase *prime rate* as the basis for commercial loan pricing. In a single institution, there may be a reference rate for one category of customer and another reference rate for another category. As noted earlier, for below-prime loans, the reference rate is often tied to the bank's marginal cost of funds. As an alternative, below-prime loans may have rates tied to **LIBOR,** an acronym for the London Interbank Offered Rate. LIBOR is a European market rate, used when European banks negotiate loan agreements. Large borrowers, with access to funds in the

---

[19] The customer had borrowed from the bank at a rate 1 percent over prime. But the "prime" was identified in the loan contract as the "rate available to the bank's best commercial customers." When the news media reported that the bank routinely offered large commercial customers loans at rates below prime, the eventual litigant, Jackie Kleiner, requested that his rate be lowered also. When First Atlanta refused, he sued. In the years that followed, more than 40 suits were filed against other commercial banks, and the definition of the prime has been carefully re-evaluated. In March 1984, First Atlanta proposed a settlement to avoid the cost of further litigation. Under that settlement, all plaintiffs were given the opportunity to negotiate loans at preferable rates.

For more discussion, see "The Prime Is Anything but Prime," *Time,* May 18, 1981, 165; Tom Birsky, "A Look at Lessons in 'Kleiner v. First Atlanta,'" *ABA Banking Journal* 76 (June 1984): 59–62; and Gerald D. Fischer, "The Prime Rate Controversy: There Is Light at the End of the Tunnel," *Journal of Commercial Bank Lending* 67 (November 1984): 13–22.

international as well as domestic markets, at times may prefer to have the market-determined LIBOR as the reference rate for their loans rather than the administered prime or a domestic market rate.

The reference rate for smaller customers may be the bank's announced prime plus a risk premium. Although researchers disagree about exactly how prime rates are set today, many experts believe that rates designated as "prime" reflect the *average* cost of funds to the lender. By reflecting an average, not marginal, cost of funds, the prime is relatively stable. This characteristic benefits small borrowers, who may be unable to bear the risk associated with highly volatile interest costs. It also benefits lenders, who avoid the administrative costs of frequent rate changes and can maintain higher loan yields for a longer period of time when market rates begin to fall.[20]

VARIABLE-RATE COMMERCIAL LENDING

Another recent trend in C&I lending is variable- or **floating-rate loans.** The choice of a floating rate is influenced by the maturity of the loan and expectations about interest rate movements until maturity. Growth in variable-rate lending also reflects deregulation of interest rates on deposits and subsequent attempts by lenders to protect their spread. The Fed's surveys of bank lending practices in 1989 showed that about 80 percent of long-term C&I loans were made at floating rates.

Given the uncertainty about changes in interest rates over a loan period, many borrowers prefer fixed-rate loans. In fact, financial futures and options provide an opportunity for lenders to avoid adverse customer reaction by hedging in the futures market rather than transferring interest rate risk to borrowers. If, for example, deposit costs are expected to rise, lenders can make variable-rate loans, or they can offer fixed-rate loans and hedge their interest costs by selling futures or options contracts. As an alternative, a commercial lender could offer a floating-rate loan indexed to a market rate on which interest rate futures were traded; the ability to trade in futures contracts would allow the borrower to hedge the uncertainty of future interest costs. By using an index such as the Treasury bill (T-bill) rate, the lender would not be forcing the borrower to use a cross-hedge; in return, the depository institution would avoid the costs and regulatory restrictions associated with the futures markets. The resulting arrangement has been called a **"synthetic" fixed-rate loan.**[21]

FORWARD COMMITMENTS

Banks do take advantage of futures and options hedges to manage interest rate risk for another type of lending agreement. Borrowers who plan their financing needs well in advance may negotiate with a lender weeks or months before they actually plan to borrow. Those negotiations often include the interest rate to be charged, a fact borrowers need to know to complete other financial planning. For the lender, committing to an interest rate before knowing the cost of funds is risky. For competitive reasons, however, most large banks have been willing to make **forward commitments,** and many of them hedge their resulting interest rate risk in the futures and options markets.[22]

SETTING THE STATED RATE ON A COMMERCIAL LOAN

For loan rates tied to an institution's base rate, the starting point on an individual loan is the calculation of the base rate from Equation 14.1. Adjustments are made to that base rate to reflect each borrower's condition. A borrower with higher-than-average default risk would have a premium added. This system is commonly known as "base plus" pricing, or "prime plus" pricing when the institution's prime is the base. Some institutions use "prime times" pricing, determining the loan rate as the product, rather than the

---

[20] Research on determinants and use of the prime includes Slovin and Sushka 1983; Goldberg 1984; Benston 1984; Thomas F. Brady, "The Role of the Prime Rate in the Pricing of Business Loans by Commercial Banks, 1977–1984," Board of Governors of the Federal Reserve System, Staff Study No. 146, November 1985; Elizabeth Laderman, "The Changing Role of the Prime Rate," *Weekly Letter* (Federal Reserve Bank of San Francisco), July 13, 1990; Furlong, "Is the Prime Rate Too High?"; and Forbes and Mayne 1989.

[21] See Abel 1983.

[22] See Brady 1985, 12–13.

sum, of the base or prime rate and a risk adjustment. For example, a risky borrower might be quoted a rate of 1½ times prime.

COMMERCIAL LENDING: NONINTEREST TERMS AND CONDITIONS

Commercial lenders use more than the interest rate to determine the effective yield on loans. A term commonly used to describe the evaluation of the total institutional relationship with a loan customer is **customer profitability analysis.** It involves examining the funds received from and the nonlending services provided to a customer, as well as a specific loan application. For example, a customer voluntarily keeping large demand deposit balances is a valuable one, because no explicit interest is paid on those balances. Customers using the institution's cash management services or those whose pension fund balances are managed by the bank's trust department are also valuable. These factors can affect noninterest loan terms and conditions, the most common of which are compensating balances, commitments and commitment fees, discounting, and collateral.

COMPENSATING BALANCES

A **compensating-balance requirement** obligates a borrower to maintain a stated minimum deposit at the lending institution, normally a demand deposit account. Because the borrower earns nothing on such compensating balances, the effective cost of the loan and the effective return to the lender are increased. The lender reduces the variability of the institution's deposits and has guaranteed access to inexpensive funds. Compensating balances also reduce the lender's risk exposure, because the funds on deposit guarantee a certain degree of borrower liquidity. Usually, compensating balances are set at 10–20 percent of the credit agreement and held in demand deposit accounts. Some institutions permit the use of low-interest time deposits for some of these balances to avoid reserve requirements against demand deposits and to increase the profitability of the total loan agreement.

Recent analyses suggest that the compensating-balance requirement is becoming less widespread. Although a 1985 survey of lending officers at the 400 largest U.S. banks indicated that 97.3 percent of the respondents imposed compensating balances on some borrowers, a Fed survey of 60 large banks in late 1987 found a shift from compensating balances to explicit loan fees at almost 75 percent of participating banks. Experts also believe that compensating balances weaken the ability of U.S. banks to compete with foreign lenders, and corporate cash management experts are increasingly vocal proponents of paying explicit fees rather than holding compensating balances. Therefore, many banks now maintain two pricing schedules—one for borrowers who prefer the traditional compensating balance agreement, and one for those who prefer to pay separately for loan and deposit services.[23]

LINES OF CREDIT AND COMMITMENTS

Lines of credit and **commitments** are agreements by the lender to extend funds to the borrower over some prearranged time period. Because lines and commitments give valuable flexibility to the borrower, they are very popular. The difference between the two is based on the formality of the agreement. In a line of credit, a lender agrees to stand ready to quote a price for a fixed-rate loan in an amount and maturity requested by the borrower. Neither the loan rate nor the amount is agreed on in advance, and if a loan request is made, the rate is influenced by current market conditions. Should loan demand be high at the time of a request, the lender can ration credit by quoting a high rate to less-valued customers.

A commitment is more formal, because the maximum loan amount and the spread over the reference or base rate are agreed on in advance. The customer can, over the credit period, choose to borrow all, some, or none of the authorized funds. When funds are borrowed, they are said to be "taken down." The terms of a commitment usually require the borrower to pay a **commitment fee** based on any amount of unused credit over the life of the agreement and to pay interest

---

[23] See Ulrich 1985; Nadler 1989; Mahoney 1988; and Stigum 1990.

on funds actually taken down. The fee compensates the lender for the additional complications in liquidity management produced by the agreement and is analogous to an insurance premium for the borrower. Recent Fed data indicate that large borrowers are quite willing to pay the premium; nearly 70 percent of long-term commercial loans at large banks in 1992 were made with a prior commitment by the lender. At small banks, customers favored short-term commitments; more than 70 percent of short-term loans were made under these prearranged agreements.

The most common type of commitment is a **revolving commitment,** guaranteeing that funds can be borrowed, repaid, and borrowed again over an extended period, perhaps as long as 3 years. The interest rate negotiated in advance may be fixed, or it may be pegged to a reference rate such as the prime or a market rate. The lender assumes considerable risk in a guarantee of this type because of the potential financial deterioration of the borrower during the period, so the commitment fee will be higher than arrangements giving the lender more flexibility. Some banks protect themselves by including clauses in the agreements that allow them to void a commitment if a material adverse change in the borrower's condition occurs.[24]

It is not uncommon for commitments to require a compensating balance in addition to the commitment fee. Both conditions increase the lender's returns and the borrower's costs—the fee income supplements interest revenues, and the guaranteed deposit funds reduce the amount the lender must raise from other sources.

Effect of Commitment Fees Illustrated. An example of the combined effect of interest and noninterest terms on the lender's total return from a loan commitment is provided in Table 14.4.[25] The base rate plus the appropriate risk premium is 11.5 percent. A commitment fee of 0.25 percent of the credit agreement is imposed, along with compensating balances of 8 percent on the entire commitment and an additional 4 percent on funds actually borrowed. To estimate the

effective rate of return on this agreement, the lending institution must project what portion of the line will actually be taken down, on average, over the commitment period. The assumption here is that the borrower will use only 60 percent of the $2 million commitment during the next 1-year period.

The commitment fee of 0.25 percent will be paid on $800,000 (the 40 percent of the commitment expected to be unused), and the interest rate of 11.5 percent will be paid on the portion taken down, or $1,200,000. The lender earns total interest and fee revenues of $140,000. Net funds extended, however, are less than $1,200,000, because of compensating balances in demand deposit accounts. After adjusting for a 10 percent marginal reserve requirement, the borrower is providing $187,200 for use by the lender, funds that do not have to be raised from other sources. The depository institution is investing only $1,012,800, and the expected yield is 13.82 percent. The lending institution also incurs implicit costs not included here, such as additional uncertainty about the timing and quantity of funds demanded. No one knows when, or in what quantity, the borrower will actually request the committed funds.

DISCOUNTING

A lending practice that also increases the return to the lender beyond the stated interest rate is discounting. A discounted loan, illustrated in Chapter 5, is one in which interest is paid at the beginning of the loan period; that is, interest is deducted before loan funds are made available to the borrower. Because the lender never commits funds equal to the face amount of the loan, discounting increases the lender's yield and the borrower's cost.

REQUIRING COLLATERAL

Traditionally, commercial lenders in depository institutions have preferred unsecured lending. Asset-based lending was left to commercial finance companies. As many large commercial borrowers turned to other sources of credit, more depositories began to offer secured financing to their commercial customers. By requiring collateral, a lender can service customers who would be too risky for an unsecured loan. But

[24] See Wolfson and McLaughlin 1989, 465. For an analysis of lending under commitment, see Berlin 1986.

[25] This example draws on a presentation in Brick 1984.

TABLE 14.4	**Effect of Noninterest Terms on the Lender's Expected Return**

The cost to a borrower and the yield to the lender can be significantly affected by noninterest loan terms. The table illustrates how a commitment fee on a line of credit can increase an institution's rate of return.

Stated interest rate	11.5% (base rate plus risk premium)
Commitment fee	0.25% on unused portion of the commitment
Term	1 year
Compensating balances	8% of commitment plus 4% of borrowed funds
Estimated average loan balance	60% of commitment
Maximum line of credit	$2,000,000
Loan Interest and Noninterest Revenues	
Interest [$2,000,000(0.6)(0.115)]	$138,000
Fees [$2,000,000(0.4)(0.0025)]	2,000
Total revenues	$140,000
Net Funds Invested	
Average loan balance	$1,200,000
Portion offset by compensating demand deposit balances	
$2,000,000(0.08)	$ (160,000)
$1,200,000(0.04)	(48,000)
Deduct reserve requirements [10% × ($160,000 + $48,000)]	20,800
Total offsetting funds	(187,200)
Net invested funds	$1,012,800

Total Expected Return

$$\frac{\text{Interest and Noninterest Revenues}}{\text{Net Invested Funds}} = \frac{\$140,000}{\$1,012,800} = 13.82\%$$

because lenders do not want to be forced to take possession of the borrower's assets, credit analysis is just as important (if not more so) for a secured loan agreement as for an unsecured one. Recent data on commercial lending show that in 1992 more than 60 percent of long-term loans involved collateral. Small banks are more likely to make collateralized loans than their larger counterparts.

Asset-based lending adds several important dimensions to loan analysis:

1. Determining the value of the assets to be pledged as collateral

2. Meeting all legal requirements for securing those assets

3. Monitoring the condition of the collateral during the loan period.

Assets pledged in C&I loan agreements are usually tangible inventory or financial assets such as accounts receivable. The legal agreement assigning the assets as collateral is called the **security agreement.** The Uniform Commercial Code, a body of law adopted individually by states but containing many common provisions across states, establishes guidelines under which these agreements are drawn.

A **floating lien** is the most general type of security agreement; it gives the lender recourse to the borrower's entire inventory, even those portions acquired after the loan is made. **Warehouse receipts** place specific inventory items assigned as collateral under the control of a third party, and the goods are often physically transferred to a bonded public warehouse for safekeeping. **Floor planning** allows the borrower to retain possession of the collateral; it is an agreement often used to finance expensive retail items such as major appliances or heavy equipment that can be distinguished by serial number or description.[26]

In the case of accounts receivable financing, the collateral may be either pledged or actually sold to the lender. The latter arrangement is called **factoring** and means the bank assumes default risk and responsibility for collection. Whether pledged or factored, the loan amount is always less than the face value of the receivables to allow for potential default.

LOAN PARTICIPATIONS AND SYNDICATIONS

A **loan participation** is an arrangement by two or more lenders to share a loan in some agreed on proportion. A lead institution initiates the loan and usually has all of the contacts with the borrower. Closely related to participations are loan syndications, in which several lenders simultaneously lend to a single borrower and all lenders have a direct relationship with that borrower. Participations and syndications are often necessary in large loans because of the limitations placed on the amount a commercial bank may loan to a single borrower, limitations established as a percentage of the depository's capital. Both types of agreements allow institutions to share the risk.[27]

Loan participations and syndications allow smaller institutions to enlarge their loan portfolios, especially if they lack ready access to a business community large enough to support a direct lending program. Such agreements also allow lenders to diversify geographically. But they can lead to severe problems, especially if the participants do not perform their own credit analysis. Publicity surrounded the heavy losses incurred by Continental Illinois, Chase Manhattan, and other commercial lenders on loan participations with Penn Square Bank of Oklahoma City, which failed in 1982 when most of its loans to energy-related companies went into default. Fed data suggest that fewer than 15 percent of commercial loans result from participation agreements.

LOAN MONITORING AND REVIEW

Despite even the best credit analysis and loan policies, problems occur. Monitoring procedures are designed to identify problems early enough to circumvent a need for legal action later. A comprehensive loan review system also serves to monitor the effectiveness of an institution's loan officers by providing incentives for them to make good decisions initially and then periodically to assess the borrower's subsequent financial position. Recent data suggest that banks have significant investments in loan monitoring and that the investment is positively related to the riskiness of the loan portfolio.[28]

As previously noted, many lending institutions assign a special group of personnel to workouts in an effort to avoid default. Workout specialists know that most of the financial problems of borrowers are traced to mismanagement arising from inadequate training and experience or perhaps even fraud.

Problems are accelerated by the state of the local or national economy or by the condition of a particular industry. Consider, for example, the effect of declining oil prices on energy-related industries throughout the 1980s. Similarly, overbuilding of commercial properties in many of the nation's largest cities posed severe problems for thrifts that invested directly in these properties or lent to the developers. As banks increased their commercial real estate lending, some were faced with similar prospects of problem loans. Unfortunately for lenders, even secured loans provide little protection under those conditions, because the

---

[26] A more detailed discussion of terms used in asset-based lending is provided in Gill 1983, 58–62. The Fed's surveys of commercial lending periodically report the percentage of total loans that involve collateral.

[27] For commercial banks with federal charters, these limitations were revised in the Garn-St Germain Act of 1982. A bank may lend to one borrower an unsecured amount not to exceed 15 percent of capital and surplus. If "readily marketable collateral" is pledged as security, the limit rises to 25 percent of capital and surplus. FIRREA imposed the same limitations on savings associations but allowed loans up to $500,000, regardless of the percentage of capital. For more information, see Garcia et al. 1983; Bush and Morrall 1989; "Conference Report on H.R. 1278" 1989; and Simons 1993.

---

[28] Gregory F. Udell, "Loan Quality, Commercial Loan Review, and Loan Officer Contracting," Salomon Brothers Center for the Study of Financial Institutions, Working Paper No. 459, March 1988.

property obtained on default has usually declined in value.[29]

CURRENT ISSUES IN COMMERCIAL LENDING

As with most topics in this book, developments in commercial lending occur too frequently for coverage in the text to be completely up-to-the-minute. Several issues, however, are likely to become more important as the decade progresses.

LENDER LIABILITY

A growing problem for commercial lenders is the threat of suit by a borrower if the borrower is in financial difficulty. A recent study of **lender liability** showed that most suits arise because an institution has refused to advance funds or has attempted to take possession of collateral. Although the number of lawsuits against depositories has grown rapidly in recent years, many cases have yet to find their way through all levels of the court system. Thus, it is too early to determine whether plaintiffs or depositories will win most cases. Most experts caution lenders that the best way to prevent lawsuits is to follow institutional monitoring and foreclosure procedures scrupulously, to give ample notice to borrowers if credit is not to be extended, and to keep excellent records.

But even careful record keeping may not be enough. Courts have interpreted lending contracts in inconsistent, even contradictory, ways. For example, some lenders have been fined for failing to provide advance notice that a line of credit will not be renewed, whereas others have been sued for "threatening" borrowers by providing just such notice! Consequently, some financial economists have concluded that the spectre of being held liable for monitoring borrowers' actions may eventually result in credit rationing against borrowers whom lenders believe are most likely to need monitoring. At best, such high-risk borrowers may pay even higher interest rates to compensate lenders for the extra cost of being sued. Although acknowledging that borrowers are entitled to protection from the capricious acts of lenders, these experts conclude that lending markets are sufficiently competitive and the permissible construction of financial contracts is sufficiently flexible that borrowers already enjoy adequate protection without having to sue banks. Thus, the lender liability battleground is likely to be a lively one for the rest of this decade.[30]

COMMUNITY REINVESTMENT

The Community Reinvestment Act (CRA) of 1977, first introduced in Chapter 2, requires regulators to encourage depositories to meet the credit needs of their local communities, including low- and moderate-income neighborhoods. The act is enforced primarily through regulators' examinations of credit policies and practices. Examinations have become increasingly rigorous in recent years. Institutions may be required to provide evidence that personnel have met with community leaders to determine credit needs, that they have taken an active role in economic development, and that they have responded to past complaints about credit allocation in the community. Since July 1990, institutions have been required to disclose the CRA ratings they receive from examiners. One of four ratings is possible, ranging from "outstanding" to "substantial noncompliance." Since 1992, lenders have been required to analyze their lending on a detailed geographic basis, correlating the location of borrowers to whom they give loans against demographic data for that location, such as income, percent of minority population, and so forth. The new rules came in the wake of a Fed study arguing that in 1990, minority mortgage applicants were rejected four times more often than nonminority applicants. Although lenders responded that the study failed to control for applicants' credit histories and existing debt, many institutions have subsequently re-examined their loan approval practices to

---

[29] For some examples of experiences with problem loans, see John Meehan, "America's Bumbling Bankers: Ripe for a New Fiasco," *Business Week,* March 2, 1992, 86–87; Neil Barsky, "Tired of Endless Talk with Big Developers, Banks Try Foreclosure," *The Wall Street Journal,* May 8, 1991, A1, A8; John Meehan, "Suddenly, All This Terra Doesn't Feel So Firma," *Business Week,* October 23, 1989, 64.

[30] For more information, see Benjamin E. Hermalin, "The Negative Effects of Lender Liability," *Weekly Letter* (Federal Reserve Bank of San Francisco), September 20, 1991; Fischel 1989; Glancz, Freer, and Melton 1989; and Elyse Tanouye, "Investors Burned in Commodities Deals Sue Lenders That Supplied the Money," *The Wall Street Journal,* January 24, 1992, C1, C17.

eliminate policies that may have resulted in discrimination, even if inadvertent.

Although the historical focus of CRA enforcement has been mortgage lending, commercial lending to small businesses is increasingly under scrutiny. Institutions failing to demonstrate community reinvestment can face denial when they seek regulators' permission to branch, merge, or acquire another institution.[31]

GREATER RISK-TAKING

Concern about risk-taking in the thrift industry has overshadowed—but not eclipsed—concern about increased risk-taking among other depositories. Commercial banks, in particular, have faced criticism for the willingness of some members of the industry to make riskier loans than in the past.

HIGHLY LEVERAGED TRANSACTIONS. Especially harsh criticisms have been leveled at bank lenders in **leveraged buyouts (LBOs).** Leveraged buyouts are transactions in which a group of investors, often including a firm's managers, buys a firm by using huge amounts of debt capital and relatively little net worth. At year-end 1988, LBO and related loans accounted for over 10 percent of the commercial loan portfolio at 60 of the largest commercial banks.[32] Although few LBOs occurred before the mid-1980s, when the economy was comparatively robust, weakening economic indicators in the late 1980s and early 1990s caused many observers to be concerned that LBO borrowers would not be able to meet their debt obligations in the future, thereby putting their lenders substantially at risk. Although most observers believe that additional regulation against bank and thrift involvement in LBOs is not needed, most also believe that the practice should be confined to lenders with high levels of capital.[33]

MEZZANINE LENDING. Some commercial banks have approached participation in highly leveraged transactions through the practice of **mezzanine lending.** Mezzanine loans are longer-term, unsecured loans in which a firm's cash flow is the major source of repayment; in addition, the financial contract contains an option through which the lender can share in the increased value of the business if the venture is particularly successful. The potentially high return on the option is designed to compensate for the relatively high risk of the loan. The option is used in place of a higher interest rate, which might increase the probability of borrower default in the short run. Because mezzanine loans are new, their effects on parties to these financial contracts cannot yet be determined, but they serve as a good example of financial innovation at work.[34]

SALES OF COMMERCIAL LOANS

As noted early in the chapter, in 1988, for the first time, commercial loans were no longer the largest category of loans for the commercial banking industry. Besides the flight of some borrowers to the commercial paper market, a main reason for this change is that large commercial banks are increasingly turning from so-called **portfolio lending**—in which financial contracts are written with the intent that the lender will hold the loan until maturity—to the origination and subsequent sale of loans in the capital markets. This trend has important implications for the future of the banking industry. Although purchasers of loans, including small nonmoney-center banks, can benefit from the resulting diversification, issues of information reusability and asymmetry become somewhat more complicated. For example, if the original lender has no intention of holding a loan to maturity, will credit analysis be as rigorous as before? Will originating lenders conclude that it is in their best interests to sell weaker credits and to retain only the less risky loans for themselves? If so, are purchasers—especially less sophisticated banks or even thrifts—equipped to evaluate the risk exposure they assume, particularly when the information required to make proper evaluations in one instance may not be reusable in another? Although sales of loans of all types will

---

[31] See Barefoot 1989; Paulette Thomas, "Mortgage Rejection Rate for Minorities Is Quadruple that of Whites, Study Finds," *The Wall Street Journal,* October 21, 1991, A2; "CRA Policy Released," *Fedwire* (Federal Reserve Bank of Chicago), January 1992; and Garwood and Smith 1993.

[32] See Wolfson and McLaughlin 1989, 464.

[33] See Pozdena 1989; Kenneth H. Bacon, "Indebted Firms to Get Relief on Bank Loans," *The Wall Street Journal,* January 22, 1992, A2; Osterberg 1993.

[34] For more details, see Stacy 1988.

undoubtedly be among the most important asset/liability management tools of the 1990s, they present a whole new set of unanswered questions. These issues are explored more fully in Chapter 19.

MANAGEMENT OF INTERNATIONAL LOANS

International lending, a special category of commercial loans, is confined to large commercial banks for several reasons. Gaining access to international markets is difficult and usually requires special facilities. Also, lenders bear added regulatory burdens because of separate provisions applying to international loans. Finally, the additional risk that accompanies international lending acts as a deterrent. Nevertheless, the volume of international loans, even in the more risky categories, has increased dramatically in the past two decades.

Banks gain access to international markets in several ways. The simplest is through loan participations in which another bank acts as the lead institution. A bank just beginning to expand beyond the domestic market might choose this route while developing the necessary expertise. Just as in the domestic markets, however, loan participations expose banks to significant risks, so even nonlead banks must proceed carefully and perform conscientious credit analysis.

A more extensive commitment to foreign lending involves a larger investment and greater risk exposure. As first discussed in Chapter 3, banks have been allowed, since 1981, to establish international banking facilities (IBFs), which are located in the United States but serve international customers exclusively. Another alternative for originating international loans is through Edge Act subsidiaries, defined in Chapter 3 as branches of the parent institution serving international customers. Unlike IBFs, Edge Act offices operate as full-service branches and are subject to regulation.

GROWTH AND REGULATION OF INTERNATIONAL LENDING: THE CASE OF LDCS

One category of foreign lending has received special attention in recent years as regulators have become painfully aware of the potentially serious level of risk exposure. Loans to borrowers in less-developed countries (LDCs) are seriously affected by changes in world economic conditions and the price level of energy products. The volume of loans from large U.S. banks to countries in this category grew rapidly after the mid-1970s. The debt is highly concentrated among the largest commercial banks. For example, in 1987, two-thirds of the almost $90 billion in loans to the 15 most heavily indebted nations was held by just nine money-center banks; this amount of indebtedness was 113 percent of the total capital of those banks, putting them substantially at risk. Although the Office of the Comptroller of the Currency reported that risk exposure in the LDC market declined in 1988, significant risks remained. The extent of the continuing risk became clear in 1989 when LDC loan losses at major banks were blamed for a sharp decline in the industry's profitability.[35]

PROBLEMS AND PROPOSED SOLUTIONS IN THE 1980s. Unfortunately, 32 foreign governments were in arrears on international payments as early as 1981. Worse fears were realized in 1982, when Mexico and other LDC borrowers announced that they were unable to service their debt agreements. Observers generally attribute this crisis to three factors: overly aggressive lending efforts by U.S. banks, who sought to compensate for declining loan demand at home during the 1981–1982 recession by greatly increasing the volume of foreign lending; rising interest rates, which caused cash-flow problems for borrowing nations attempting to make payments; and poor use of the borrowed funds by debtor countries, resulting in returns on invested capital that were inadequate to service their debt.[36]

Congress responded to the crisis in 1983 by passing the **International Lending Supervision Act (ILSA)** in an attempt to control the magnitude of fu-

[35] These and other statistics on LDC debt are found in Todd 1988; "Statement of Robert J. Herrmann, Senior Deputy Comptroller for Bank Supervision Policy, before the House Subcommittee on International Development, Finance, Trade and Monetary Policy of the Committee on Banking, Finance, and Urban Affairs," *Quarterly Journal,* 8 (September 1989): 47–52; John Meehan, David Woodruff, and Chuck Hawkins, "For Most Banks, There Was Nowhere To Hide," *Business Week,* April 2, 1990, 94–95; and Duca and McLaughlin 1990.

[36] Extensive details on the 1982 crisis and related trends in LDC lending are provided in Young 1985; Fieleke 1983; Terrell 1984; Corrigan 1988; and Truman 1989.

ture problems. The act established special examination procedures for international loan portfolios, granted power to supervisory agencies to set minimum capital guidelines to ensure adequate support in the case of loan losses, and required a special allocation to loan loss reserves by institutions engaged in foreign lending. A final deterrent to excessive international exposure came in the form of a requirement that income from loan origination fees be amortized over the life of the loan rather than recognized as income in the year negotiated, greatly diluting the importance of these fees to bank earnings.

Since 1982, the ratio of bank capital to international loans has increased. Federal banking regulators carefully monitor the financial position of foreign governments that borrow heavily from U.S. banks, and they have at times issued special directives for reporting interest income and reserves for loans to specific countries deemed highly risky.[37]

LDC DEBT IN THE 1990S AND BEYOND. Despite the hopes of Congress and regulators after the 1983 legislation, concern about LDC loans again escalated in 1987 when Brazil, then the largest debtor nation in the world, announced that it was suspending payment on its loans to foreign banks. Although Brazil's action could hardly be termed good news, it did cause many large banks to develop specific plans for solving their LDC dilemmas. One of the first to act was Citicorp, whose Chairman announced in mid-1987 that the bank was adding *$3 billion* to its loan loss reserves. Other large banks followed, and the financial markets interpreted these moves as a necessary fresh breath of realism. Similar large write-offs continued in 1988 and 1989.[38]

Fortunately, as a result of the 1982 and 1987 crises, as well as subsequent actions by Congress, regulators, and the banking industry itself, problems in LDC lending are moving closer to a solution than they were a decade ago. Recognizing the growing interdependence of world markets, most experts believe that continued foreign investment in LDCs is necessary if both developing and developed nations are to prosper.

Most also believe that private sector lenders must continue to play an important role; that is, commercial banks cannot expect governments of developed nations to be the sole, or even the main, suppliers of capital to LDCs, nor can U.S. banks expect that the federal government will step in to guarantee LDC loans if borrowers default.

Instead, bank managers are engaging in better and more realistic risk assessment of LDC loans. Also, new techniques for managing LDC debt exposure have developed, including secondary markets for these loans; debt-for-equity swaps, in which a lender converts a debt contract to equity investment in the debtor nation; and the restructuring of existing debt agreements to ease cash-flow burdens on LDCs. Particularly noteworthy are 1992 agreements between several large U.S. banks with the largest risk exposures and the governments of Argentina and Brazil. The arrangements call for banks to swap nonperforming loans to these governments for long-term bonds. The bonds are collateralized by Argentina's and Brazil's holdings of U.S. Treasury securities. As a result of this agreement, banks that once thought their loans to these countries might bring as little as 35 percent of book value expect to be repaid more than 65 percent of the loans' original value. To strengthen their own financial positions, weakened as a result of high LDC loan losses, several large banks have raised additional equity capital in recent years.

LDCs, too, have made strides to put their financial "houses" in order. Many are attempting to stem the flight of capital from within by encouraging citizens to invest in domestic industry rather than investing abroad. Some are seeking to sell bonds in the global securities markets, thus reducing reliance on foreign bank debt. Many are also striving to make better use of borrowed funds so that the return on the investment will be sufficient to repay obligations incurred. Although few experts have been lulled into believing that LDC debt problems have been eliminated, most are more optimistic than they were a few years ago.[39]

[37] For more details on examination and supervision of international lending, see Martinson and Houpt 1989.

[38] Sarah Bartlett et al., "A Stunner from the Citi," *Business Week,* June 1, 1987, 42–43; Fissel 1991.

[39] The steps taken by both borrowers and lenders to solve LDC debt problems are discussed in most of the sources cited in Footnotes 35 and 36, as well as in Lane 1987; Garg 1989; Fissel 1991; John Meehan, "Now the Third World May Do Banks a World of Good," *Business Week,* June 8, 1992, 94–96.

RISK ANALYSIS IN INTERNATIONAL LENDING

Along with the usual concerns about the financial stability of a borrower, institutions competing in the international markets face other sources of risk. One of these, exchange rate risk, arises from floating currency exchange rates and is explained in Chapter 6. Others are addressed in this section.

COUNTRY RISK. Several related sources of variability are grouped together under the term *country risk,* also known as **transfer risk** or **sovereign risk.** Country risk includes any political, economic, social, cultural, or legal circumstances in the home country of the borrower that could prevent the timely fulfillment of debt obligations. This uncertainty can arise from many sources, such as social unrest, civil or international wars, economic decline, or a change in political ideology, and is clearly illustrated by the rapid, global economic changes that followed Iraq's unexpected invasion of Kuwait in 1990. A slightly different problem is one that occurs when a country's economic condition weakens and a foreign borrower's government prohibits a currency exchange for repayment of debts (hence the term *transfer risk*). Even cultural attitudes toward indebtedness can affect borrowers' timely repayment of obligations.[40] In short, country risk includes any source of uncertainty specific to international rather than domestic lending.

As a result of the proliferation of problem foreign loans, regulators have struggled with methods of measuring and predicting country risk. The ILSA requires special procedures for rating the country risk of a bank's international loan portfolio. These ratings are *ex post* assessments that reflect the repayment record of a borrower once a loan has been granted. Finding reliable signals for *ex ante* risk is difficult, because it depends on a country's future economic and political stability. Measuring that with any degree of confidence is indeed difficult, yet it is necessary if the institution expects to earn a rate of return sufficient to compensate for the additional risk. The overthrow of communist governments in the Soviet Union and Eastern Europe at the beginning of this decade and the subsequent opportunities—*and* uncertainties—that it poses for U.S. banks are vivid illustrations of the difficulty of assessing *ex ante* lending risk.

DIVERSIFICATION. Although exchange rate and country risk can increase variability in an institution's NIM, international loans also provide an avenue for diversification. International lending offers access to different geographical regions and economic climates. If expected returns on international loans have low correlations with expected returns on domestic loans, the overall riskiness of the institution's loan portfolio can be reduced.

INSTITUTIONAL RESPONSES. Banks have responded to risks in international lending in a variety of ways. For example, in the early 1980s, Citicorp negotiated a controversial insurance policy with Cigna Corporation for the bank's foreign loans, but the policy was subsequently canceled. Concerns expressed by regulators over the effect of such agreements on the financial stability of the insurance industry suggest that insurance may not be a viable risk-reduction strategy for international lenders.

Smaller institutions have become considerably more reluctant to enter the foreign loan market. Regional banks wanting to pursue the diversification potential of foreign markets are turning to trade financing through **letters of credit**—financial instruments through which a bank guarantees payment on imported goods, substituting its financial strength for that of the importing firm. Although less risky than direct loans to LDCs, letters of credit expose the lender to default risk if the client firm cannot make payments. Regulators' concern over risk exposure from letters of credit is discussed in Chapter 17. Finally, some institutions use overseas offices to pursue Western European markets, where country risk is much lower than in LDC lending. But even this market poses new risks for U.S. institutions, depending on the progress of financial system integration in those countries.

---

[40] An interesting example of country risk occurred after the price of crude oil fell dramatically in 1986. Many Islamic borrowers with significant indebtedness to U.S. banks invoked the doctrine of *sharia,* which holds that the payment of interest is against the teachings of the Koran. Although they had avoided earlier conflict with the doctrine by encouraging banks to call interest charges "administrative fees," when oil prices fell, some borrowers again began viewing the so-called fees as interest and decided it was against their religion to pay charges previously incurred. See Bill Powell, "The Sheiks Rediscover Religion," *Newsweek,* May 12, 1986, 62–63.

SUMMARY

Loans are the largest category of assets of depository institutions. Although commercial banks, thrifts, and CUs tend to specialize in different types of loans, important elements of successful lending are shared by all depositories. In fact, lending is one of the functions that makes depositories "special" financial institutions in regulators' eyes. Lending policies must incorporate specific objectives for the size, composition, maturity, interest rate characteristics, and default risk of the loan portfolio.

Procedures for evaluating and approving loan applications must then be devised to achieve those objectives. A major step is to establish a base lending rate from which individual loan-pricing decisions follow. The process of evaluating and approving a loan includes decisions regarding what rate to charge a given customer, how often the rate will change, and whether special terms and conditions should be attached. Finally, procedures must be developed to monitor the loan's performance to avoid borrower default.

Loans to businesses are of particular interest to commercial banks, although thrifts have begun to enter the market in small numbers in recent years. Of special importance in commercial lending is an analysis of the borrower's financial condition. Applicants must be categorized according to the level of default risk to which the institution is exposed. Technology, in the form of expert systems, is expected to play a larger role in credit granting in the future.

After analysis of an applicant's financial condition, specific loan terms must be determined. In the past, the standard pricing practice was to charge the institution's best customers the prime rate and to scale other loan rates upward from there. Recently, a two-tiered pricing system has emerged for large and small borrowers. Further decisions involve compensating balances, commitments, discounting, and collateral. The expected yield to the depository will reflect all these decisions. Some institutions choose loan participation or syndication agreements originated by a lead bank instead of, or in addition to, direct lending.

International loans, a special type of commercial lending, pose unique risks and are centered only in relatively small segments of the banking industry. International lending, especially to developing countries, has been common among very large commercial banks since the 1970s. It exposes the institution to country risk. Because of the large risk exposure presented by such loans, special regulations apply to international lenders.

QUESTIONS

1. Compare and contrast the loan portfolio composition of commercial banks, thrifts, and credit unions and explain recent trends.

2. Explain the terms *information asymmetry* and *information reusability.* How are these concepts used to support the argument that depository institution lenders play a "special" economic role?

3. Discuss the importance of loan portfolio policy decisions concerning size, composition, and maturity. What financial objectives influence these policy decisions?

4. Explain the important elements of policies concerning default risk in the loan portfolio. How are credit risk policies affected by regulatory standards and conditions such as the "credit crunch" of the early 1990s?

5. What is a base lending rate? How is it related to an institution's target NIM? How is it affected by other assets held by an institution?

6. Are a bank's annual provision for loan losses and its net loan charge-offs for a given year expected to be equal? Why?

7. In FDICIA, Congress identified tripwire measures that are monitored to determine the need for regulatory intervention. Explain how the quality of the loan portfolio may become a tripwire.

8. Review current trade publications for thrifts. What recent progress, if any, have thrifts made toward establishing a presence in the commercial lending markets? What factors are influencing the loan portfolios of savings institutions in the mid-1990s?

9. What is an "expert system" approach to lending decisions? What are some of the potential benefits of replacing (or supplementing) loan officers with expert systems? What potential difficulties can you foresee?

10. Review the expert system lending decision described in Figure 14.2. Identify two or three points in the process at which qualitative judgment would ordinarily be exercised. In your opinion, for which decisions would it be most difficult to replace personal decisions with a computerized "expert"?

11. What are the five Cs of credit? How many of them can be measured objectively? Explain how expert systems for loan decision making are related to the traditional analysis using the Cs of credit.

12. What has been the historical definition of the term *prime rate?* How has the interpretation changed since the early 1980s?

13. Why do many lending institutions offer below-prime rates to some loan customers? How is this practice related to the emergence of a two-tier loan market?

14. What are the substantive risk/return considerations in an institution's choice between fixed or variable loan rates?

15. What is a forward commitment? How does such an agreement influence a lender's interest rate risk exposure?

16. Suppose that you are a corporate financial manager faced with a choice between one bank requiring a compensating balance on a loan and another charging a higher interest rate but no noninterest charges. What factors would you consider in choosing betwen the two lenders?

17. Compare a line of credit and a loan commitment. Evaluate the differences in the lender's exposure to interest rate, liquidity, and default risk under the two types of agreements. What is a revolving commitment, and to what additional risk does it expose the lender?

18. What additional costs are incurred by a lending institution under asset-based loan agreements? What types of agreements are traditionally used to protect the value of the collateral pledged to secure this type of loan?

19. What are the main benefits of loan participations and syndications to the lenders involved?

20. What is your opinion of litigation alleging lender liability? Under what circumstances would you consider a lender substantially responsible for the financial problems of a customer? How might the trend toward lender liability cases affect loan applicants in general?

21. Consult a recent issue of the *Federal Reserve Bulletin* and review the actions of the Board of Governors on the merger and acquisition applications of commercial banks. What consideration does the Board give to each institution's compliance with the Community Reinvestment Act, and how does such compliance influence the Board's decisions?

22. What is mezzanine lending? Does the option contained in these agreements reduce the risk exposure of a lender in a highly leveraged transaction? Why or why not? What is the effect on expected returns?

23. Depository institutions are reducing their portfolio lending and increasing the proportion of loans sold in the secondary markets. How does this transition affect the role of these institutions as financial intermediaries? In what ways does this management practice resemble a brokerage role?

24. Explain the access to international loan markets provided through Edge Act subsidiaries and international banking facilities.

25. What was Congressional intent in the passage of the International Lending Supervision Act? What provisions were included to control the risk exposure of financial institutions lending in international markets?

26. What risks are especially prevalent in LDC lending? Consult current banking literature to identify strategies used by U.S. banks to reduce their risk exposure in the LDC markets.

27. Explain the dimensions of country risk exposure in international lending. Find a recent example of a large commercial lender that has faced unexpected losses or gains resulting from political or economic changes in the loan recipient's home country.

PROBLEMS

1. Hartford Savings Bank is considering a loan application from Dottie Bushnell, who wants to purchase a video store and needs $50,000. The bank considers the loan to be of above-average risk and will add a 2 percent premium to the base rate. The bank's total assets are $200 million, interest expense is $14 million, net noninterest expense is $2 million, and the marginal tax rate is 35 percent. The target NIM is 3.8 percent, and the bank's asset structure is as follows:

- Securities: $35 million; average yield, 9.45 percent
- Loans: $120 million
- Nonearning assets: $15 million

a. What rate will Dottie be offered?

b. Prepare a *pro forma* income statement, assuming that the bank earns, on average, the base loan rate on its loan portfolio. Calculate the NIM under this assumption.

c. What RONW is expected if the net worth multiplier is 12?

d. Using a "what if" table, show how the base lending rate would change as the yield on securities varies between 8.5 percent and 10 percent. Also show how the base rate would change as the target NIM varies between 3.0 percent and 4.0 percent. To which of these variables does the base rate seem to be more sensitive? (Suggestion: In your tables, vary the yield or the NIM in 0.1 percent intervals.)

2. First National Emporia has total assets of $140 million, a net worth multiplier of 12.5, and net noninterest expense of $1,500,000. Its target NIM is 2.9 percent, and liability costs average 8 percent annually. Assets are distributed as follows:

- Securities: $25 million; average yield, 8.25 percent
- Mortgages and consumer loans: $110 million
- Nonearning assets: $5 million

a. What is the base lending rate First National must earn to achieve its target NIM?

b. Prepare a pro forma income statement, assuming that First National earns the base rate on its loans. Show that this rate will allow the bank to earn its desired NIM.

c. What RONW is expected if the marginal tax rate is 35 percent?

3. a. Suppose that the management of First National in Problem 2 decreases the target NIM to 2.5 percent. What base rate must be earned to achieve this target?

b. Suppose interest costs rise to 9 percent. What base rate is required to achieve a 2.5 percent target NIM?

c. Using "what-if" analysis, examine the sensitivity of the base rate to variation in average liability costs between 8 percent and 11 percent.

What is the significance of this type of analysis for an institution with short-term liabilities and long-term assets? (Suggestion: Use liability cost increases of 0.1 percent in your table.)

4. a. Bob Jefferson is negotiating a $4 million line of credit with State Bank of New Mexico. The 1-year agreement requires a 0.20 percent commitment fee, with a 12 percent compensating balance on the entire commitment and an additional 5 percent on funds actually borrowed. The stated rate of interest is 11 percent, and the loan officer estimates that Bob will use, on average, 85 percent of the line. Calculate the total expected dollar return and rate of return for the bank, assuming a 10 percent marginal reserve requirement.

b. Using "what-if" analysis, how would the bank's expected rate of return change as the average amount Bob borrowed varied from 70 percent to 90 percent? (Suggestion: Vary the average percentage borrowed in 2 percent increments in your table.) How can you explain the pattern revealed in your analysis?

5. Suppose that Bob Jefferson in Problem 4 is offered a $4 million line of credit from First National Bank, with a stated rate of 11.9 percent. The compensating balance requirement is 6 percent on the total line, with an additional 4 percent on the amount borrowed. If other terms remain the same, does First National expect to earn more or less on the agreement than State Bank of New Mexico?

6. Your bank is willing to offer a $1 million line of credit for 1 year to help you establish your own consulting firm. The agreement requires a 0.15 percent commitment fee, a 10 percent compensating balance on the entire commitment, and 4 percent more on funds actually borrowed. The stated rate of interest is 12 percent, and you have told the bank that you probably will not need more than an average of 60 percent of the line.

a. Calculate the total expected dollar return and rate of return for the bank, assuming a 10 percent marginal reserve requirement.

b. Using "what-if" analysis, show how the lender's return would change if you drew down amounts of your line ranging from 50 to 80 percent. (Use 5 percent increments in your table.) Under these loan terms, is the bank better off if you borrow relatively more or less of your line? Why?

7. What is the annual yield on a 1-year loan if interest is discounted and the stated rate is 10 percent? If it is 13 percent? If it is 9.6 percent? (Discounted loan yields are calculated in Chapter 5.)

SELECTED REFERENCES

Abel, Oliver IV. "Fixed-Rate Loans Using Variable-Rate Funds—A New Lending Instrument." *Journal of Commercial Bank Lending* 65 (August 1983): 36–43.

Altman, Edward I. "Financial Ratios, Discriminant Analysis, and the Prediction of Corporate Bankruptcy." *Journal of Finance* 23 (September 1968): 589–609.

Arend, Mark. "New Automated 'Experts' Ready for Lenders." *ABA Banking Journal* (January 1992): 61.

Barefoot, Jo Ann S. "Take Time for a CRA Inventory—or Else." *ABA Banking Journal* 81 (January 1989): 22–23.

Becketti, Sean, and Charles Morris. "Are Bank Loans Still Special?" *Economic Review* (Federal Reserve Bank of Kansas City) 77 (Third Quarter 1992): 71–84.

Benston, George. "Interest on Deposits and Survival of Chartered Depository Institutions." *Economic Review* (Federal Reserve Bank of Atlanta) 69 (October 1984): 42–56.

Berlin, Mitchell. "Loan Commitments: Insurance Contracts in a Risky World." *Business Review* (Federal Reserve Bank of Philadelphia) (May/June 1986): 3–12.

————. "Bank Loans and Marketable Securities: How Do Financial Contracts Control Borrowing Firms?" *Business Review* (Federal Reserve Bank of Philadelphia) (July/August 1987): 9–18.

Brady, Thomas F. "Changes in Loan Pricing and Business Lending at Commercial Banks." *Federal Reserve Bulletin* 71 (January 1985): 1–13.

Brantley, R. Lamar. "Portions of the Business Sample Diversification." *Savings Institutions* 108 (February 1987): 131, 133.

Brick, John R. "Pricing Commercial Loans." *Journal of Commercial Bank Lending* 66 (January 1984): 49–52.

Bush, Vanessa, and Katherine Morrall. "The Business Reviews a New Script." *Savings Institutions* 110 (October 1989): 30–35.

Chen, Kung H., and Thomas A. Shimerda. "An Empirical Analysis of Useful Financial Ratios." *Financial Management* 10 (Spring 1981): 51–60.

Compton, Eric N. "Credit Analysis *Is* Risk Analysis." *The Bankers Magazine* 168 (March/April 1985): 49–54.

"Conference Report on H.R. 1278, Financial Institutions Reform, Recovery and Enforcement Act, 1989." *Congressional Record—House of Representatives,* August 4, 1989.

Corrigan, E. Gerald. "A Balanced Approach to the LDC Debt Problem." *Quarterly Review* (Federal Reserve Bank of New York) 13 (Spring 1988): 1–6.

Crigger, Jack R. "An Ocean of C's." *Journal of Commercial Bank Lending* 58 (December 1975): 2–8.

Duca, John V., and Mary M. McLaughlin. "Developments Affecting the Profitability of Commercial Banks." *Federal Reserve Bulletin* 76 (July 1990): 477–499.

Duchessi, Peter, and Salvatore Belardo, "Lending Analysis Support System (LASS): An Application of a Knowledge-Based System to Support Commercial Loan Analysis." *IEEE Transactions on Systems, Man, and Cybernetics* SMC-17 (July-August 1987): 608–616.

Duchessi, Peter, Hany Shawky, and John P. Seagle. "A Knowledge-Engineered System for Commercial Loan Decisions." *Financial Management* 17 (Autumn 1988): 57–65.

Dunham, Constance. "Recent Developments in Thrift Commercial Lending." *New England Economic Review* (Federal Reserve Bank of Boston) (November/December 1985): 41–48.

Dunham, Constance, and Margaret Guerin-Calvert. "How Quickly Can Thrifts Move into Commercial Lending?" *New England Economic Review* (Federal Reserve Bank of Boston) (November/December 1985): 47–52.

Fama, Eugene. "What's Different about Banks?" *Journal of Monetary Economics* 15 (1985): 29–36.

Fieleke, Norman S. "International Lending on Trial." *New England Economic Review* (Federal Reserve Bank of Boston) (May/June 1983): 5–13.

Fischel, Daniel. "The Economics of Lender Liability." *Yale Law Journal* 99 (1989): 131–154.

Fissel, Gary S. "The Anatomy of the LDC Debt Crisis." *FDIC Banking Review* 4 (Spring/Summer 1991): 1–14.

Forbes, Shawn M., and Lucille S. Mayne. "A Friction Model of the Prime." *Journal of Banking and Finance* 13 (1989): 127–135.

Foster, George. *Financial Statement Analysis,* 2d ed. Englewood Cliffs, NJ: Prentice-Hall, 1986.

Gagnon, Joseph A. "What Is a Commercial Loan?" *New England Economic Review* (Federal Reserve Bank of Boston) (July/August 1983): 36–41.

Garcia, Gillian, et al. "The Garn-St Germain Depository Institutions Act of 1982." *Economic Perspectives* (Federal Reserve Bank of Chicago) 7 (March/April 1983): 3–31.

Garg, Ramesh C. "Exploring Solutions to the LDC Debt Crisis." *The Bankers Magazine* 172 (January-February 1989): 46–51.

Garwood, Griffith L., and Dolores S. Smith. "The Community Reinvestment Act: Evolution and Current Issues." *Federal Reserve Bulletin* 79 (April 1993): 251–267.

Gibson, Charles. "Financial Ratios as Perceived by Commercial Loan Officers." *Akron Business and Economic Review* 14 (Summer 1983): 23–27.

Gill, Edward G. *Commercial Lending Basics.* Reston, VA: Reston Publishing Co., 1983.

Glancz, Ronald R., Kenneth O. Freer, and Tina W. Melton. "Suing the Lender." *Magazine of Bank Administration* 65 (February 1989): 24–32.

Goldberg, Michael A. "The Sensitivity of the Prime Rate to Money Market Conditions." *Journal of Financial Research* 7 (Winter 1984): 269–280.

Gombola, Michael J. and J. Edward Ketz. "Financial Ratio Patterns in Retail and Manufacturing Organizations." *Financial Management* 12 (Summer 1983): 45–56.

Goudreau, Robert E. "S&L Use of New Powers: Consumer and Commercial Loan Expansion." *Economic Review* (Federal Reserve Bank of Atlanta) 69 (December 1984): 15–33.

Goudreau, Robert E., and Harold D. Ford. "Changing Thrifts: What Makes Them Choose Commercial Lending?" *Economic Review* (Federal Reserve Bank of Atlanta) 71 (June/July 1986): 24–39.

Greenbaum, Stuart I., George Kanatas, and Itzhak Venezia. "Equilibrium Loan Pricing Under the Bank–Client Relationship." *Journal of Banking and Finance* 13 (1989): 221–235.

Higgins, Robert C. *Analysis for Financial Management,* 2d ed. Homewood, IL: Richard D. Irwin, 1989.

James, Christopher. "Are Bank Loans Special?" *Weekly Letter* (Federal Reserve Bank of San Francisco) (July 24, 1987).

Lane, Leroy O. "The Secondary Market in Developing Country Debt: Some Observations and Policy Implications." *Economic Review* (Federal Reserve Bank of Dallas) (July 1987): 1–12.

Mahoney, Patrick I. "The Recent Behavior of Demand Deposits." *Federal Reserve Bulletin* 74 (April 1988): 195–208.

Martinson, Michael G., and James V. Houpt. "Transfer Risk in U.S. Banks." *Federal Reserve Bulletin* 75 (April 1989): 255–258.

McGinn, Carol. "Computer Mentors Give Loan Officers a Hand." *ABA Banking Journal* (November 1990): 45.

Moulton, Janice M. "Antitrust Implications of Thrifts' Expanded Commercial Loan Powers." *Business Review* (Federal Reserve Bank of Philadelphia) (September/October 1984): 11–21.

Nadler, Paul. "Balances and Buggy Whips in Loan Pricing." *Journal of Commercial Bank Lending* 72 (February 1989): 4–9.

Osterberg, William P. "Bank Exposure to Highly Leveraged Transactions." *Economic Commentary* (Federal Reserve Bank of Cleveland), January 15, 1993.

Pavel, Christine, and Dave Phillis. "Cautious Play Marks S&L Approach to Commercial Lending." *Economic Perspectives* (Federal Reserve Bank of Chicago) 9 (May/June 1985): 18–27.

Plath, D. Anthony, and Timothy J. Kloppenborg. "Do Expert Systems Help Make Better Lending Decisions?" *Journal of Retail Banking* 11 (Winter 1989): 27–37.

Pozdena, Randall. "Banks and High Leverage Debt." *Weekly Letter* (Federal Reserve Bank of San Francisco) (December 8, 1989).

Shaw, Michael J., and James A. Gentry. "Using an Expert System with Inductive Learning to Evaluate Business Loans." *Financial Management* 17 (Autumn 1988): 45–56.

Simons, Katerina. "Why Do Banks Syndicate Loans?" *New England Economic Review* (Federal Reserve Bank of Boston) (January/February 1993): 45–52.

Slovin, Myron B., and Marie Elizabeth Sushka. "A Model of the Commercial Loan Rate." *Journal of Finance* 38 (December 1983): 1583–1596.

Stacy, Ronald L. "Mezzanine Lending: A Primer for Asset-Based Lenders." *Journal of Commercial Bank Lending* 71 (October 1988): 54–66.

Stigum, Marcia. *The Money Market,* 3d ed. Homewood, IL: Dow Jones-Irwin, 1990.

Terrell, Henry S. "Bank Lending to Developing Countries: Recent Developments and Some Considerations for the Future." *Federal Reserve Bulletin* 70 (October 1984): 755–763.

Todd, Walker F. "Developing Country Lending and Current Banking Conditions." *Economic Review* (Federal Reserve Bank of Cleveland) 24 (Quarter 2, 1988): 27–36.

Truman, Edwin M. "U.S. Policy on the Problems of International Debt." *Federal Reserve Bulletin* 75 (November 1989): 727–735.

Ulrich, Thomas A. "Are Compensating Balance Practices Declining?" *Magazine of Bank Administration* 61 (January 1985): 48–52.

Walter, John R. "Loan Loss Reserves." *Economic Review* (Federal Reserve Bank of Richmond) 77 (July/August 1991): 20–30.

West, Robert Craig. "The Depository Institutions Deregulation Act of 1980: A Historical Perspective." *Economic Review* (Federal Reserve Bank of Kansas City) 67 (February 1982): 10–13.

Wolfson, Martin H., and Mary M. McLaughlin. "Recent Developments in the Profitability and Lending Practices of Commercial Banks." *Federal Reserve Bulletin* 75 (July 1989): 461–484.

Young, John E. "Supervision of Bank Foreign Lending." *Economic Review* (Federal Reserve Bank of Kansas City) 70 (May 1985): 31–39.

*In a recession, consumers are more worried
about having the available credit than getting lower rates.*

Joe Belew
President
Consumer Bankers Association (1991)

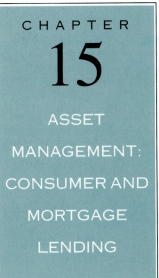

CHAPTER

15

ASSET
MANAGEMENT:
CONSUMER AND
MORTGAGE
LENDING

Individuals borrow money from depository institutions in a wide variety of forms, and this portion of the loan portfolio is an important contributor to returns. But it is also fraught with risks—a fact well know to American institutions, but one being learned the hard way by some of their international competitors, particularly in Japan.

The Japanese, for many years, have been known for their frugality and conservative spending. But with the economic prosperity of the 1980s, some behaviors changed. One Tokyo executive thought he had found a new sense of financial freedom after borrowing to buy a car in 1989. Soon he had negotiated additional loans, acquired several credit cards, and within 2 years owed $167,000 and was in bankruptcy court. Many other Japanese consumers, some of whom grew accustomed to relying on their credit cards while in college, are also finding themselves deep in debt when they accelerate their spending after graduation. Delinquency rates on consumer lending in the country are on the rise.[1]

Although consumer delinquencies such as those described above are not as rare as lenders would like them to be, careful management and evaluation of potential borrowers can keep such losses under control. They are exacerbated during periods of economic recession and may also vary across depository institutions as some lenders choose more aggressive strategies for expanding their consumer loan portfolios. These management issues are explored in some detail in this chapter.

Consumer and residential mortgage loans fit the lending framework in the initial portions of Chapter 14. For example, institutions must decide how much of the loan portfolio to devote to consumer lending, what credit standards to establish, what loan terms to offer, how to calculate appropriate lending rates, how to develop competitive strategies, how to monitor loans after they are made, and what policies to use in handling consumer and mortgage loan delinquencies. But just as there are distinct features of commercial loans, loans to consumers have special characteristics. One distinguishing feature is that many are

---

[1] Ted Holden, "The Japanese Discover the Perils of Plastic," *Business Week,* February 10, 1992, 42.

installment loans on which the borrower repays both principal and interest on a regular schedule. Credit evaluation, loan monitoring, and customer relations differ as well. Consumer credit is heavily regulated, complicating the lending process. And even within the realm of consumer lending, terms and conditions of residential mortgages differ from those of other types of consumer loans.

FIGURE 15.1   **Ratio of Household Debt to Household Income, 1952–1991**

The indebtedness of households has increased dramatically since the end of the second world war. Home mortgage debt accounts for most credit outstanding, but nonmortgage borrowing has increased as well.

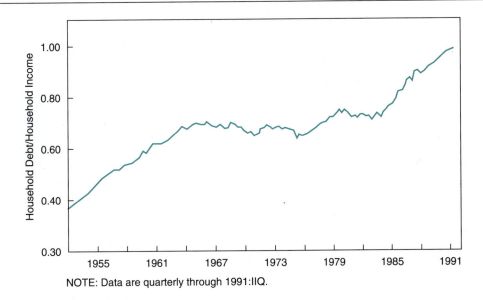

NOTE: Data are quarterly through 1991:IIQ.

Source: Economic Commentary, Federal Reserve Bank of Cleveland, February 1, 1992.

CONSUMER CREDIT: AN OVERVIEW

American households have been increasing their debt since the end of World War II. After the late 1970s, however, the pace of consumer borrowing accelerated. Figure 15.1 shows the volume of consumer credit outstanding as a proportion of disposable personal income from 1952 through mid-1991. Note that by the end of 1990, the ratio of household debt to income in the United States reached a historic high of almost 99 percent.

Although not shown in the figure, most debt is mortgage debt. Installment borrowing is the second largest category, including automobile loans and the use of credit cards. Data gathered in a 1990 survey by federal regulatory agencies indicated that about 85 percent of American families had credit obligations, a larger proportion than ever before.[2]

The growth in consumer credit during the 1980s and early 1990s is attributed to a variety of factors, such as changing societal attitudes toward personal indebtedness; increased willingness of lenders to service consumer credit needs; and increased demands for consumer goods, as items once considered luxuries are now viewed as necessities. Although the Tax Reform Act of 1986, which eliminated the tax deductibility of interest on nonmortgage consumer debt, was expected to dampen demand, other factors point to consumers' continued use of credit. These include easier access to credit through credit cards and other financial innovations, increased need for student loans to finance higher education, growth of home equity loans, and the relatively low proportion of households with existing mortgage debt.

The high proportion of debt to disposable household income evident by the early 1990s has not necessarily been viewed with alarm by experts. The Federal Reserve System (Fed) data gathered in 1990 and 1991, in fact, revealed that 86 percent of indebted households regularly met or exceeded their debt payments. Of the households reporting at least one

---

[2] See Canner and Luckett 1991. (References are listed in full at the end of the chapter.)

delinquency in the previous year, the researchers found a substantial proportion that were not considered serious delinquencies. Thus they concluded that despite the relatively high debt burden, the vast majority of consumers was capable of managing the resulting interest and repayment schedules. Further, the ratio of debt to assets for U.S. households rose no faster in the 1980s than it did in the 1960s. However, one fact that cannot be overlooked is that personal bankruptcies rose rapidly between 1985 and 1990. As is explored in more detail later in the chapter, experts caution that this trend probably reflects the easing of bankruptcy laws as much or more than it reflects increases in the proportion of households with financial difficulties.

By late 1992, researchers were debating whether the growth trend in consumer debt would continue into the mid-1990s. One consumer survey found 68 percent of respondents agreeing that consumers have taken on too much debt; 57 percent indicated they were trying harder to save money than they had in the past.[3] Nevertheless, the provision of credit to consumers continues to be a service with great potential for depositories.

WHO LENDS TO CONSUMERS?

Depository institutions, particularly commercial banks and credit unions (CUs), are already major suppliers of consumer credit. As shown in Figure 15.2, in 1992 banks held almost half of outstanding consumer installment credit, and CUs held more than 10 percent.[4] Although not shown in the chart, automobile loans are the largest category of consumer installment debt (more than 35 percent). Commercial banks lead in the provision of automobile credit, with CUs providing less than finance companies.

[3] Studies and reports include Pearce 1985; Luckett and August 1985; Avery, Elliehausen, and Kennickell 1987; Jeffery Kutler and Judy Ferring, "Consumers Vow Less Debt, More Saving," *American Banker,* September 23, 1992, 1, 6; and John Meehan, "Buddy Can You Borrow A Dime?" *Business Week,* November 11, 1991, 148–149.

[4] Even though some forms of nonmortgage consumer credit are not repaid on an installment basis, the Federal Reserve Board follows the convention of referring to all consumer, nonmortgage debt as installment credit. That convention has been followed in Figure 15.2 and the rest of the chapter.

FIGURE 15.2 **Suppliers of Consumer Credit, 1992**

Commercial banks, finance companies, and CUs are the leaders in providing consumer credit.

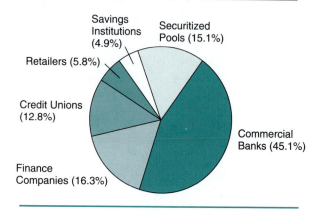

Savings Institutions (4.9%)
Securitized Pools (15.1%)
Retailers (5.8%)
Credit Unions (12.8%)
Finance Companies (16.3%)
Commercial Banks (45.1%)

Source: Federal Reserve Bulletin, November 1992, A37.

In 1989, for the first time, the Fed statistics included "securitized pools" as sources of consumer credit. The 15 percent share for securitized pools in Figure 15.2 indicates the proportion of household debt supplied by investors holding bonds backed by consumer installment loans. The process of securitizing loans and the role of financial institutions in that process are discussed further in Chapter 19.

Fed statistics indicate that the percentage of families with outstanding debt obligations to depository institutions is larger than the percentage having obligations to other lenders. Nonetheless, other suppliers of financial services are strong competitors; in 1992, three of the six largest individual suppliers of consumer installment credit, by dollar volume, were nondepository institutions. In the late 1980s, in fact, finance companies affiliated with automobile manufacturers engaged in aggressive attempts to make car loans, offering interest rates on some loans as low as 0 percent! In 1992, General Motors introduced a new competitive strategy—a GM MasterCard used to promote GM products. Customers are able to earn rebates equal to 5 percent of their charge purchases (up to a specified limit) and then are encouraged to apply those rebates toward the purchase of a new GM car or truck. Thus, policies that depositories develop for managing consumer lending have an important effect on their competitive position and financial performance.[5]

Two studies of consumers in the 1980s indicate that prospective borrowers shop among competing lenders before signing a loan agreement, and the focus of their attention is usually the interest rate. Although finance company customers have often been characterized as being higher-risk, that stereotype was not confirmed; one study found that fewer than 25 percent of a sample of finance company borrowers would not have met typical bank credit standards. Instead, most finance company borrowers had deliberately chosen the finance company over competing depository institutions.

Previous experience or a customer relationship with a lender is important, especially if the association has been positive. Generally, research indicates that depository institutions must convince potential customers that they offer competitive rates and must make the process of applying for a loan relatively easy and fast. They may also find that their current depositors represent an important pool of potential borrowers.

Data collected by the Fed in 1989 suggest that location is also an important factor. A survey of consumers' financial decisions revealed that almost 70 percent of households had borrowed from local institutions; only 15 percent of households had loans or mortgages or other credit from institutions outside their local area. Thus, despite the competition on a national scale, a financial institution should be able to attract borrowers within its market area.

When it comes to credit card borrowing, however, consumers do not seem to be quite so selective. Studies of credit cardholders indicate that they devote little effort to comparing interest rates and fees charged by different issuers of credit cards, which range from depository institutions to diversified financial services firms like American Express to nonfinancial companies such as AT&T.[6] (The credit extended through through General Motors' MasterCard, mentioned ear-

lier, is actually provided by a finance company, not General Motors.)

REGULATION OF CONSUMER CREDIT

Among the most heavily regulated operations in financial institutions are the financial services they offer to consumers.

TRUTH-IN-LENDING, FAIR CREDIT REPORTING, AND EQUAL CREDIT OPPORTUNITY

As noted in Chapter 2, beginning in 1968, a layer of federal consumer protection legislation was added to that already provided at the state level with the passage of the Consumer Credit Protection Act (Truth-in-Lending, or TIL). The goal of that legislation was to ensure that consumers receive accurate information about the cost of credit to facilitate comparison of different lenders' credit terms.

Several other acts have been passed since then. **The Fair Credit Reporting Act of 1970** requires consumer credit reporting agencies to stress accuracy, to correct errors promptly, and to release individual consumers' credit histories only for legitimate purposes. Of particular interest to consumer lenders are the Equal Credit Opportunity Act of 1974, passed to control discrimination in credit evaluation, and the Truth-in-Lending Simplification and Reform Act of 1980, designed to simplify the disclosure of credit terms for the benefit of both lenders and consumers. The Federal Reserve Board enforces the provisions of TIL through **Regulation (Reg) Z** and of the Equal Credit Act through **Regulation (Reg) B.** Institutions must comply with both state and federal legislation; if there are any contradictions between the two, federal statutes prevail.

Reg Z sets standards for disclosing the terms and costs of a consumer credit agreement *before* the borrower becomes obligated. It establishes a period during which a consumer may cancel a transaction, as well as procedures through which a consumer can challenge billing errors on revolving credit agreements. A later section of this chapter illustrates Reg Z's requirements for calculating and disclosing interest rates on consumer loans. Reg B prohibits discrimination based on

---

[5] See Aguilar 1990; *Federal Reserve Bulletin,* various issues; Kathleen Kerwin, "Can GM Sell Cars With a Credit Card?" *Business Week,* September 21, 1992, 78.

[6] See Calem 1992; Elliehausen and Wolken 1992; Peter Pae, "Many Keep On Paying High Rates in Cards, Through Bad Planning," *The Wall Street Journal,* December 26, 1991, A1, A8; Peterson and Black 1982; Johnson and Sullivan 1981.

sex, age, race, marital status, color, religion, and national origin; it establishes the rights of loan applicants, including the right to receive an explanation if a credit request is denied.

EFFECT OF BANKRUPTCY LAWS ON DEFAULT RISK

Another law that has influenced consumer credit analysis is the **Bankruptcy Reform Act,** passed by Congress in November 1978 and effective as of October 1980. The nation's bankruptcy laws had not been revised for 40 years, and the old code allowed most standards for the declaration of personal bankruptcy to be set at the state level. Of particular concern to debtors was the maximum dollar amount of assets that could be protected from liquidation when an individual filed for bankruptcy. Many state codes specified low amounts considered incompatible with current price levels. The revision established federal standards preempting state provisions unless a state revised its code after 1978.

Many lenders consider the 1978 federal guidelines to be overly generous to individuals with credit problems. For example, an individual was allowed to protect from creditors $7,500 in real and/or personal property used as a personal place of residence; up to $1,200 for a motor vehicle; up to $500 for jewelry; and future income from certain sources. For debtors who were not homeowners, the $7,500 housing exemption could be used to protect other assets. Thus, the ability of a lender to foreclose against the property of a borrower in default was limited if the borrower chose to file for personal bankruptcy.[7] In reaction to federal

provisions, most states passed new codes after 1978. Although some new state codes are more restrictive than the federal guidelines, in all cases they are more lenient to debtors than standards in effect before 1978.[8]

The new lenience in bankruptcy provisions led to a surge in personal bankruptcy filings in 1980 and 1981, although a concurrent economic recession certainly contributed. Filings increased by 60 percent in 1980 and by more than 40 percent in 1981, when nearly 600,000 debtors declared bankruptcy.[9] In response to increasing loan losses, consumer lenders set higher standards for loan approvals. Ownership of tangible assets in excess of prevailing exemptions became a key variable, serving as the lender's recourse if the borrower defaulted and then declared bankruptcy. Some consumer lenders argued that the more lenient bankruptcy codes hurt lower- and middle-income families, who no longer qualified for loans under the higher standards.

The protests of lenders were addressed when Congress passed the Bankruptcy Amendments and Federal Judgeship Act of 1984.[10] The amendments were designed to prevent abuses of the bankruptcy provisions that had occurred since 1978. They set lower limits on the amount of property protected from creditors and improved the monitoring system. If a federal bankruptcy judge believes an individual is abusing the law (that is, if someone actually capable of meeting financial obligations attempts to declare bankruptcy), the case can be dismissed. One provision particularly welcomed by consumer lenders requires debtors to be responsible for debts incurred shortly before bankruptcy, discouraging an individual from increasing debt with no intention of repaying it.

---

[7] An individual declaring bankruptcy can seek two forms of protection from creditors. One form, pursuant to Chapter 7 of the bankruptcy code, seeks complete absolution from indebtedness. Another form, through Chapter 13 of the code, seeks protection from creditors while the debtor works under a court-approved plan to repay obligations. Chapter 7 filings present greater potential for loss to creditors than do Chapter 13 filings. Unfortunately for lenders, Chapter 7 filings have increased in recent years. Although legislation designed to further reform bankruptcy codes and discourage Chapter 7 filings was considered in Congress in 1992, the legislative session ended with no changes enacted.

Research has identified borrower characteristics most often associated with the inability to repay debts versus those associated with the possibility of making at least partial repayment over time. Results of the research can provide judges with information in determining whether Chapter 7 or Chapter 13 proceedings are more appropriate for a given debtor. See, for example, Peterson and Woo 1984.

[8] See Gatty 1982 and Shuchman and Rhorer 1982.

[9] The research staff at the Federal Reserve Bank of Atlanta estimated that from 72 percent to 82 percent of the 1980 and 1981 increases was attributable to the bankruptcy code revisions rather than to economic conditions. For further discussion, see Carter 1982. Subsequent researchers concurred that the increase in personal bankruptcies could not be attributed to changed economic conditions alone and concluded that their findings were "consistent with the notion that the federal law increased bankruptcy filing rates." See Peterson and Aoki 1984.

[10] Congress took action only after the labor movement joined the protests against the bankruptcy reforms. For a discussion of the provisions of the new amendments, see Chatz and Schumm 1984 and "Reform Strengthens Creditors' Rights" 1984.

**BANKRUPTCY FILINGS AFTER THE 1984 AMEND-
MENTS.** Creditors' hopes that the 1984 amendments would decrease the rate of personal bankruptcies were dashed in the last part of the decade. As Figure 15.3 illustrates vividly, the rate of filings soared after 1984. Furthermore, unlike previous upsurges, the rate of increase in the late 1980s was not related to recessionary economic conditions as reflected in the shaded areas of the figure. (The recessionary conditions of 1991 and 1992 were, however, given some credit for the growth in bankruptcy filings in the early part of that decade. Filings exceeded 900,000 in 1992 alone.) A major study conducted at the Fed attempted to resolve the anomaly with only partial success. For example, the study found that, although bankruptcies were more frequent in states with sectoral economic difficulties (e.g., the Southwest), regional problems could not explain the rapid increase in other states. The author suggested several hypotheses that will undoubtedly be the focus of additional research in the 1990s: a lessening of the stigma of bankruptcy, increased advertising by attorneys, more marital problems, and growth in consumer debt among families least likely to be able to service it.[11] Investigation of these hypotheses is of great interest to depository lenders.

USURY CEILINGS

Besides disclosure and bankruptcy laws, some states restrict the rate of interest that may be charged on certain categories of loans—primarily consumer loans, but also some agricultural and small business loans. First mentioned in Chapter 2, usury laws establish rate ceilings that a lender may not exceed, regardless of the lender's costs. Usury ceilings apply to lenders of all types, not just to depository institutions.

RATIONALE FOR USURY CEILINGS. Usury laws have a long history. They developed from a perceived need to protect individual borrowers, presumably less sophisticated than business borrowers, from unscrupulous lenders. During periods of low market interest rates, when the usury ceilings are above lenders' base lending rates, usury laws are not controversial. When economic conditions change, however, as they did in the late 1970s, usury laws attract attention. Congress included a provision in the Depository Institutions Deregulation and Monetary Control Act (DIDMCA) suspending state usury ceilings on some categories of loans at banks and thrifts—they included residential mortgages and business and agricultural loans but not nonmortgage consumer debt. This provision preempted state regulations unless a state passed revised legislation before April 1, 1983. A separate provision of DIDMCA covered loan rate ceilings at federally chartered CUs.[12]

DO USURY CEILINGS ACCOMPLISH THEIR OBJECTIVES? Although usury laws were designed to benefit consumers, a substantial body of research questions their benefits. Regulatory ceilings requiring loan rates below those dictated by market conditions ("binding" ceilings) lead lenders to reduce the quantity of credit they supply. The credit-reduction effect of binding ceilings can be shown in the framework of the loanable funds theory. In Figure 15.4, the market determined rate is y*, and the quantity of credit supplied is Q*. If the usury ceiling is binding ($y_U < y*$), supply of and demand for credit will be out of balance. Lenders will divert loan funds to other investments. The amount of credit available will fall to Q_s significantly below Q_d, the quantity demanded.[13]

When credit is restricted, the burden of reduced funds does not fall equally on all consumers. Instead, only the least risky applicants are approved. Consequently, although some consumers may receive loans at below-market rates, others are denied credit, an inequity difficult to justify. Furthermore, if retailers raise prices to compensate for low interest on credit sales, even cash customers bear the burden of usury ceilings.[14]

---

[11] See Stahl 1993; Canner and Luckett 1992; Luckett 1988; Johnson 1989; and Mike Dorning, "Bankruptcy Filings Gaining with the Public," *Chicago Tribune*, January 5, 1992, Section 7, 1, 10.

[12] Details on DIDMCA usury provisions, including the responses of state legislatures, are discussed in Vandenbrink 1985. Federal CUs are governed by the Federal Credit Union Act of 1934, as amended by a portion of DIDMCA. The statutory ceiling rate on loans of all types at federal CUs is 15 percent; however, the National Credit Union Administration (NCUA) has the authority to change the ceiling if economic conditions warrant it. In recent years, the NCUA has imposed a limit of 21 percent.

[13] Some researchers argue that only installment loans are restricted. Credit offered by retailers continues to be available, because merchants tend to increase the price of the merchandise to offset the loss in interest income on credit sales. Thus consumers who are denied credit by installment lenders may be able to obtain it elsewhere. See Peterson 1983.

[14] Several articles document such inequities, including Wolken and Navratil 1981 and Vandenbrink 1982.

FIGURE 15.3 **Personal Bankruptcy Filings, 1960–1990**

The soaring rate of personal bankruptcies in the 1980s is attributed in part to changes in federal bankruptcy law.

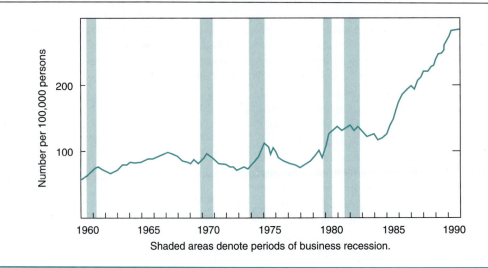

Shaded areas denote periods of business recession.

Source: Federal Reserve Bulletin 77 (November 1992): 219.

FIGURE 15.4 **Impact of Binding Usury Ceilings**

Usury ceilings cause the demand for credit to exceed the supply; thus, the quantity of credit available is less than the equilibrium quantity.

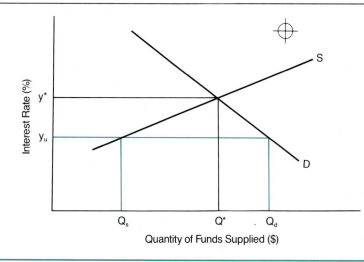

Source: Adapted from Donna M. Vandenbrink, "The Effects of Usury Ceilings," *Economic Perspectives* (Federal Reserve Bank of Chicago) 6 (Midyear 1982): 44.

A second negative result of binding usury ceilings is an increase in noninterest costs to borrowers. Lenders will do whatever they can to reduce loan-processing costs and protect available profits. They may shorten loan maturities, forcing borrowers to repay funds more quickly, or they may increase the minimum loan size to reduce administrative costs per dollar invested. They may also charge higher fees for transactions deposits and related services in an effort to substitute noninterest income for loan revenues.

INSTITUTIONAL RESPONSE TO USURY CEILINGS. In the early 1980s, some depository institutions took an innovative approach to binding ceilings on consumer loans. Historically, large discrepancies have existed in the maximum allowable interest rates in different states. On credit granted through credit cards, the U.S. Supreme Court ruled that a bank may charge customers the rate allowed by the *bank's* home state, regardless of the *customer's* state of residence. As a result, consumers in the same state could pay different borrowing rates for the same type of credit, depending on the legal domicile of their creditors. The ruling also opened up unimagined possibilities for innovative creditors.

In 1980, Citicorp announced it would move its credit card operations from New York to South Dakota, a state that had removed all ceilings from credit card interest rates. Other lenders announced similar plans. Citicorp's strategy stimulated reform activity in many state legislatures, including New York's, but Citicorp and others enacted their plans.

Also, many lenders announced new pricing strategies in response to binding usury ceilings. They increased noninterest fees for bank credit cards, imposing an annual fee for the privilege of receiving a card, whether it was used or not. Before that time, the only cost on most credit cards was interest on the unpaid monthly balance.

RENEWED LEGISLATIVE ACTION. In response to the actions of consumer lenders and at the urging of federal regulators, most states have revised their consumer protection legislation since 1981. In 1983, the American Bankers Association (ABA) surveyed lending institutions in states that had previously had binding usury ceilings. Results indicated that several of the ceiling's undesirable effects had been reversed. Lend-

ers stated that more credit was available, credit standards had been relaxed, and procedures were more flexible. The rates charged on personal loans were higher than in the past, but according to the ABA, were never out of line with the prime rate.[15]

In the revisions, some states removed ceilings altogether for consumer and credit card lending, and some adopted a sliding scale dependent on the size or type of loan. Other states set an adjustable ceiling pegged to a market interest rate, such as Treasury bill (T-bill) yields. Still others retain a fixed usury ceiling, higher than before DIDMCA. Thus, usury regulations remain an important influence on depository lending decisions.

THE REGULATORY DIALECTIC REVISITED. The effects of changes in usury laws are not limited to financial institutions. A study at the Federal Reserve Bank of Chicago showed that during the period 1980–1987, credit card lending grew 243 percent in the United States as a whole. Although that may seem impressive, the research also revealed growth of 24,375 percent in Delaware (a state that acted to liberalize consumer credit legislation in 1981) and growth of an incredible *207,876 percent* in South Dakota. Even considering the relatively small base from which credit card lending in South Dakota began in 1980, the growth rate is astonishing. During the same period, employment in and tax revenues from the Delaware and South Dakota banking industries skyrocketed, whereas they declined in many other states. These statistics show the regulatory dialectic at work.[16] The thesis of former usury laws was met with antithetical behavior from major consumer lenders, which in turn led to a synthesis represented by the current array of state consumer-lending laws.

But by definition, a dialectic is never finished. In late 1991, the possibility of interest rate ceilings was again in the headlines. The issue arose after then-President Bush made an extemporaneous comment indicating his desire to see banks lower interest rates on

---

[15] The ABA survey was reported in Stanley 1983.

[16] Results of the Fed study are reported in Erdevig 1988. For a summary of some of the new state laws, see Reichenstein and Bonello 1984 and Kramer and Canner 1982. An analysis of the complexity of balancing federal and state statutes for lenders operating in more than one state is provided in Lobell and Finkelstein 1984.

credit cards. The next day, Senator D'Amato of New York introduced a measure to limit credit card rates to a level no higher than 4 percent (400 basis points) above the rate charged by the Internal Revenue Service on unpaid taxes. As of December 1991, that would have forced credit card issuers to lower rates by almost 5 percent. Although the Senate hurriedly passed the bill, the House did not. The ceiling was not enacted, despite the consumer support it generated. The furor, however, did force many issuers to re-evaluate their credit card pricing systems.[17] As a result of this continuing process of change and innovation, most financial economists believe the public (whom laws and regulations are presumably designed to protect) *and* the regulated benefit.

CONSUMER CREDIT ANALYSIS

Depository institutions offer loans to consumers for a wide variety of purposes. Loans to purchase automobiles, to finance education, or to support other personal needs are usually on installment terms. Noninstallment credit is available, too, in the form of short-term personal loans and credit cards such as MasterCard or Visa. As with commercial lending, the credit decision requires estimating an applicant's default risk category and setting appropriate loan terms for approved applications.

PERSONAL FINANCIAL DATA

Evaluating the financial position of an applicant for a consumer loan requires information similar to that needed in commercial lending, but the form in which it is received is usually quite different. Individuals do not have financial statements prepared periodically, but lenders request detailed information on the assets, liabilities, and net worth of a household. Current and anticipated income are also important. In collecting the information, the institution must comply with Reg B. For example, for certain types of non-

mortgage loans, an applicant may not be required to provide information on marital status, race, or religion.[18]

To verify information provided and to obtain further data, consumer lenders use the services of credit bureaus, which collect information on the credit history and financial position of individuals and are subject to the Fair Credit Reporting Act. The credit report indicates whether the applicant has been delinquent on previous repayment obligations, what other debts are outstanding; where checking and savings accounts are kept and their average balances; and employment information.

Recently, however, the accuracy of credit bureau data has been called into serious question. The uproar began in 1991 when the clerk of a small Vermont town discovered that every person on the town's tax rolls had been entered as a delinquent taxpayer in the records of TRW, one of the three largest credit reporting bureaus. Soon, hundreds of similar incidents came to light, and the Federal Trade Commission (FTC) confirmed that credit reports had become the largest source of consumer complaints in the United States. To improve its very tarnished image, TRW offered to provide credit reports to consumers free of charge, rather than demanding the usual fee of $15 or $20. The firm also agreed to pay compensating fines to its Vermont victims. The TRW incident and violations by other firms have focused new attention on enforcement of the Fair Credit Reporting Act in the 1990s.[19]

ASSESSING INFORMATION: CREDIT SCORING

The main problems in credit analysis include assessing all important factors about an applicant simultaneously and evaluating all applicants objectively and by the same standards. **Credit-scoring models** are quantitative efforts to ensure that both these problems are addressed. As noted in Chapter 14, credit-scoring

[17] See Kenneth H. Bacon and David Wessel, "Credit Card Cap Furor Will Have Big Effect, Economic and Political," *The Wall Street Journal,* November 18, 1991, A1, A6; and Kenneth H. Bacon, "Senate Votes to Cap Credit Card Rates, Tying Charges to IRS's Interest Rate," *The Wall Street Journal,* November 14, 1991, A3.

[18] Not surprisingly, Reg B is complicated. For a good summary, see Smith 1985.

[19] John Schwartz, "Consumer Enemy No. 1," *Newsweek,* October 28, 1991, 42–43; and Michael W. Miller, "TRW to Give Credit Reports Free of Charge," *The Wall Street Journal,* October 15, 1991, B1, B2; Nancy Ryan "FTC Cites Trans Union Over Credit Data," *Chicago Tribune,* January 13, 1993, Section 3, 1, 3.

TABLE 15.1	Hypothetical Credit-Scoring System

Credit scoring models are designed to allow lenders to classify credit applicants into "good" or "bad" risks based on past credit history, employment history, and other variables. The table illustrates a typical scoring system.

Applicant Characteristics	Allotted Points	Applicant Characteristics	Allotted Points
Own or rent		Checking or savings account	
Own	41	Neither	0
Rent	0	Either	13
Other finance company		Both	19
Yes	−12	Applicant age	
No	0	30 years or less	6
Bank credit card		30+ to 40 years	11
Yes	29	40+ to 50 years	8
No	0	Older than 50 years	16
Applicant occupation		Years on job	
Professional and officials	27	5 or less	0
Technical and managers	5	5+ to 15	6
Proprietor	−3	More than 15	18
Clerical and sales	12		
Craftsman and nonfarm-laborer	0		
Foreman and operative	26		
Service worker	14		
Farm worker	3		

Source: Adapted from Gilbert A. Churchill, Jr., et al., "The Role of Credit Scoring in the Loan Decision," *The Credit World* 65 (March 1977): 7. *The Credit World* is the official publication of the International Credit Association, headquartered in St. Louis, MO. Reprinted with permission.

models are available for analyzing commercial loan applications, but they are more widely used by consumer lenders.

CALCULATING A SCORE FOR EACH APPLICANT. The first step in developing a model is to determine, from past data, borrower characteristics most often associated with bad and good loans, where "bad" is defined as slow-paying, delinquent, or in default. Typical characteristics include how long the applicant has been employed at his or her current job, whether the credit history is good, number of dependents, whether the applicant rents or owns a home, and his or her income and occupation. Points are assigned to new applicants based on these characteristics. For example, a borrower with a higher income would be assigned more points on that characteristic than one with a lower income.

Table 15.1 illustrates a typical scoring system. In the table, some characteristics are assigned negative points because they are so often associated with default risk. Some characteristics have higher points and thus count more heavily in an applicant's final score.

The relative importance of each characteristic in overall loan quality is determined by statistical analysis of historical data, most often using a technique called discriminant analysis.[20]

ACCEPT/REJECT DECISION. Once all characteristics have been assigned points, a total score for the applicant is determined. Suppose, for example, that an applicant under the scoring system illustrated in Table 15.1 owns a home (41); has a loan from another finance company (−12) and a bank credit card (29); owns a business (−3); has both a checking and savings account (19); is 37 years old (11); and has been on the job for 10 years (6). The total score is 91. This total is compared with a predetermined minimum acceptable score. The lower the minimum, the larger the number of acceptable applicants and the greater the default risk exposure; the higher the minimum, the larger the

---

[20] A thorough review of the theory, history, and statistical properties of credit-scoring models can be found in Altman 1981, Chapter 4, 167–198. Another good source is Capon 1982.

FIGURE 15.5   **Evaluating Credit Scores**

Difficulty arises when an applicant's score does not fall clearly into either group. Lenders must then decide between the opportunity cost of not giving credit to a potentially "good" customer and the risk of loaning to a "bad" one.

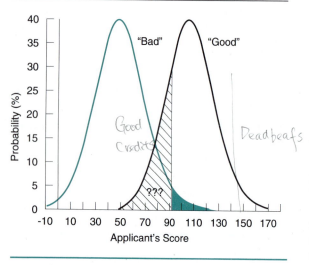

number of rejected applicants and the greater the potential loss of revenue. Ideally, the minimum should be established in an attempt to balance these costs.

Figure 15.5 illustrates the accept/reject decision and associated risks. Suppose that information from past customers indicates a mean score for "good" applicants is 110, with a standard deviation of 20, and a mean score for "bad" applicants is 50, with a standard deviation of 20. The probability that a given score will fall in the "good" or "bad" range can be estimated from these distributions. Ordinarily, then, new applicants with scores of 110 or more would be granted credit, and applicants with scores of 50 or less would be denied it. The figure shows, however, that the "good" and "bad" distributions overlap; that is, new applicants who score between 50 and 110 could be "good" or "bad," depending on the population of which they actually are members. The example applicant in the previous paragraph, with a score of 91, falls in the overlap range.

Anytime a credit-granting decision is made, the lender is exposed to risk. Applicants scoring as high as 150 in this example could still default on a loan, be-

cause credit-scoring models use historical data and are not perfect guides to the future. Similarly, applicants with scores as low as 60 could be faultless borrowers in the future. But users of credit-scoring systems are willing to "play the odds" that the distributions of past scores are good guides to the creditworthiness of future applicants, and few would agonize over a decision to accept a score of 150 or reject a score of 60.

When an applicant falls in the overlap group, however, uncertainty increases. Suppose the lender hypothesizes that an applicant with a score of 91 is a member of the "good" group. If the distributions in Figure 15.5 hold true, there is a measurable chance (shaded in the graph) that the applicant could actually be drawn from the population of "bad" applicants. However, if the lender assumes that the applicant is part of the population of "bad" risks, there is a somewhat larger chance (hatched in the graph) that a "good" credit risk will be rejected. The closer to the middle of the overlap range a score falls, the fuzzier the decision becomes on purely statistical grounds and the more judgment is required from the loan officer. As indicated, the usual procedure is to establish a minimum acceptable score based on an attempt to balance the costs of rejecting "good" applicants against accepting "bad" ones. Note that the cutoff would seldom be at the point at which the chance of rejecting a "good" applicant and accepting a "bad" one are equal—a score of 80 in this example. For most institutions, the costs (including cash losses and the penalties of possible regulatory displeasure) of accepting a "bad" applicant are higher than the opportunity costs of rejecting a "good" one; thus, in this case, the cutoff score below which applicants would not be accepted might be 90 or higher.

PERFORMANCE OF CREDIT-SCORING MODELS. Perhaps not surprisingly, recent research has indicated that the accuracy of classifying loan applicants correctly *ex ante* as either "good" or "bad" improves when a combination of statistical credit-scoring models and judgmentally determined decision rules are used. The experience of some institutions provides even stronger endorsement for quantitative models. For example, NationsBank uses credit-scoring models for virtually all its consumer loan applications but allows loan officers to override a score with approval from supervisors. A recent comparison showed that the delinquency rate for loans granted on the basis of loan-officer overrides was *seven times* higher than for loans approved solely on the basis of credit scores. Such findings will lead, undoubtedly, to the refinement of expert systems for consumer lending in the next decade.

Given the success of credit-scoring models for consumer loans, lenders have begun investigating ways to use this technique to evaluate many categories of potential borrowers and even to predict the actions of current borrowers whose loan payments are delinquent. The newest application of the credit-scoring concept is **behavior scoring,** which attempts to predict the behavior of borrowers in the future, rather than simply scoring the acceptability of a current loan applicant. Behavior scoring may also draw on the repayment history of the borrower in previous lending agreements, using the lending institution's own records or those of a credit bureau. Finally, credit scoring and behavior scoring are now being used more frequently to evaluate mortgage applicants, in addition to applicants for traditional consumer loans.[21]

LIMITATIONS OF CREDIT-SCORING MODELS. Like all models, credit-scoring schemes have limitations. The statistical complications were illustrated previously. In addition, they focus only on default risk and may ignore such information as deposit or other service relationships with the customer. They also must be carefully structured to comply with Reg B: Applicant characteristics included in a model must be "demonstrably and statistically sound," as defined by the Fed.[22] But despite these limitations, major consumer lenders, especially retailers, regularly use the models, as do many depositories offering credit cards.

---

[21] See Edmister 1988; Alexander 1989; and Alan Radding, "Credit Scoring's New Frontier," *The Magazine of Bank Management* (September 1992): 57. Interesting anecdotes on how some lenders use scoring models can be found in Robert Guenther, "Credit-Card Issuers Ease Their Standards to Get New Accounts," *The Wall Street Journal,* May 22, 1989, A1, A4; and Sanford Rose, "Improving Credit Evaluation," *American Banker,* March 13, 1990, 4.

[22] See Smith 1985, 915; and Board of Governors of the Federal Reserve System, "Revision of Regulation B: Official Staff Commentary," November 13, 1985. (Reg B is frequently amended.)

TERMS ON CONSUMER INSTALLMENT LOANS

Because consumer loans are made on an installment basis, borrowers and lenders both must understand installment terms. In fact, it was the variety and complexity of terms on consumer loans that led to the enactment of the truth in lending provisions. The intent of Congress was to enable consumers to compare accurately the cost of different types of loans.

ADD-ON LOANS

Chapter 5 introduced the differences between installment loan terms and those of other loans. In an installment agreement, the borrower makes equal periodic payments. In addition, many automobile and other consumer loans use the add-on interest method: The interest on the full amount borrowed must be paid for each year of the loan term, even though the entire balance is not outstanding for the full term.

CALCULATING THE ANNUAL PERCENTAGE RATE

Suppose that a couple decides to buy a new car, priced at $12,000. After making a $2,000 down payment, they approach their CU for a $10,000 loan and are quoted an add-on rate of 9 percent for 4 years. They will repay a total of

$$\$10,000(0.09)(4) + \$10,000 = \$13,600$$

The repayment schedule will be $13,600/48 = $283.33 per month, resulting in a monthly interest rate of 1.3322 percent and an **annual percentage rate (APR)** of just under 16 percent, based on Equation 5.7:

$$\$10,000 = \sum_{t=1}^{48} \frac{\$283.33}{(1 + y_p)^t}$$

$$y_p = 0.013322 = 1.3322\%$$

$$APR = 1.3322\% \times 12 = 15.9864\%$$

Reg Z requires lenders to disclose the APR to borrowers. The Fed defines the APR as the periodic rate multiplied by, not compounded by, the number of periods in a year. Thus, the APR is a legal definition of an interest rate and is not the effective annual yield to

TABLE 15.2   Installment Loan Amortization Schedule: Add-on Loan

The amortization schedule for a typical installment loan shows how interest (calculated at the APR) and principal are allocated for each payment during the life of the loan. This schedule shows how an add-on loan with a stated rate of 10 percent and an APR of 15.9864 percent would be amortized.

Monthly Payments: Initial Balance: Initial Maturity: APR:
$283.33 $10,000   4 years   15.9864% /₁₂ —>1.3322%

Month	(1) Payment	(2) Beginning Balance	(3) Interest 0.159864/12 × (2)	(4) Principal Paid (1) − (3)	(5) End-of-Month Balance (2) − (4)
1	$283.33	$10,000.00	$133.22	$150.11	$9,849.89
2	283.33	9,849.89	131.22	152.11	9,697.77
3	283.33	9,697.77	129.19	154.14	9,543.63
4	283.33	9,543.63	127.14	156.19	9,387.44
5	283.33	9,387.44	125.06	158.27	9,229.17
6	283.33	9,229.17	122.95	160.38	9,068.79
7	283.33	9,068.79	120.81	162.52	8,906.27
8	283.33	8,906.27	118.65	164.68	8,741.58
9	283.33	8,741.58	116.46	166.88	8,574.71
10	283.33	8,574.71	114.23	169.10	8,405.60
11	283.33	8,405.60	111.98	171.35	8,234.25
12	283.33	8,234.25	109.70	173.64	8,060.61
20	283.33	6,778.63	90.30	193.03	6,585.61
21	283.33	6,585.61	87.73	195.60	6,390.01
22	283.33	6,390.01	85.13	198.21	6,191.80
23	283.33	6,191.80	82.49	200.85	5,990.96
24	283.33	5,990.96	79.81	203.52	5,787.43
25	283.33	5,787.43	77.10	206.23	5,581.20
26	283.33	5,581.20	74.35	208.98	5,372.22
27	283.33	5,372.22	71.57	211.76	5,160.46
28	283.33	5,160.46	68.75	214.59	4,945.87
29	283.33	4,945.87	65.89	217.44	4,728.43
30	283.33	4,728.43	62.99	220.34	4,508.09
40	283.33	2,388.12	31.81	251.52	2,136.60
41	283.33	2,136.60	28.46	254.87	1,881.73
42	283.33	1,881.73	25.07	258.26	1,623.47
43	283.33	1,623.47	21.63	261.71	1,361.76
44	283.33	1,361.76	18.14	265.19	1,096.57
45	283.33	1,096.57	14.61	268.72	827.85
46	283.33	827.85	11.03	272.30	555.54
47	283.33	555.54	7.40	275.93	279.61
48	283.33	279.61	3.72	279.61	0.00

the lender, an economic concept based on the mathematics of interest rates. Specific limitations are permitted for rounding, and the rate disclosed can vary from the exact APR by a maximum of ⅛ of 1 percent.[23]

[23] Board of Governors of the Federal Reserve System, "Official Staff Commentary on Regulation Z Truth-in-Lending as Amended April 1, 1990," June 1990.

An amortization schedule demonstrating the meaning of the APR is provided in Table 15.2. The lender earns 15.9864 percent on the outstanding principal over the life of the loan, but monthly payments are not allocated to principal and interest equally each month. Early in the loan term, a higher proportion is interest because the principal balance is large. In the last payment, only $3.72 is interest. The monthly allocation to interest is always 15.9864% ÷ 12 of the outstanding loan balance.

THE RULE OF 78S

When a borrower repays an installment loan before the original maturity date, lenders often apply the **rule of 78s** to calculate the remaining principal balance. This approach, also called the **sum-of-digits method** involves adding together the digits for the number of payments to be made. The *78* in the name is derived from the sum of digits for a 12-month loan:

$$12 + 11 + 10 + 9 + 8 + 7 + 6 + 5$$
$$+ 4 + 3 + 2 + 1 = 78$$

For the example of a 4-year (48-month) automobile loan, the sum of digits is 1,176.[24] According to the rule of 78s, were the borrowers to pay the loan off early, they would receive credit for 48/1,176 of their total interest obligation in the first month, 47/1,176 in the second month, and so on.

Suppose that the borrowers repay the loan after 1 year. After 12 payments of $283.33, they have paid a total of $3,999.96. Under the rule of 78s, they would be credited with (510/1,176) × $3,600 = $1,561.22 in interest. The numerator, 510, is the sum of 48, 47, 46, and so on, through 37. Thus, $1,838.74 of the principal balance ($3,399.96 − $1,561.22) would be considered repaid. To discharge their obligation, the borrowers would have to pay the credit union $10,000 − $1,838.74, or $8,161.26.

THE RULE AS A PREPAYMENT PENALTY. The rule of 78s is controversial because it specifies a balance for repayment higher than the balance indicated by an amortization schedule based on the APR, shown in Table 15.2. After 12 payments at an APR of 15.9864 percent, the borrowers owe $8,060.61. In most states, however, lenders are permitted to use the rule of 78s, although a few states have adopted laws specifically prohibiting it. The discrepancy is more notable for loans with higher initial balances, longer initial maturities, and higher APRs. It is essentially a prepayment penalty.

Lenders argue that it is justified because it helps them recover fixed lending costs, although consumer advocates argue that the rule of 78s is unfair to borrowers.[25]

LOAN MATURITIES

An important factor contributing to growth in consumer debt in the past decade is the trend toward loans with longer maturities. As prices of consumer goods purchased on credit have increased, loan terms have been adjusted so that goods will still be affordable. For example, the principal amount of a new-car loan increased more than 50 percent between 1983 and 1992, to $13,570. At commercial banks in 1983, the standard maturity on a loan for a new car was 36 months, but since 1984, 48-month loans have predominated. For finance company lenders, the average maturity on auto loans issued in July 1992 was 54.4 months; some loans had maturities as long as 72 months.[26]

VARIABLE-RATE INSTALLMENT LOANS

Variable interest rates are a relatively new development in consumer installment lending. In some states, usury laws still prevent variable-rate consumer loans, but where permitted to do so, some lenders are using them. The use of variable-rate consumer loans differs by institutional size. A 1985 nationwide survey revealed that 45 percent of large banks and thrifts were offering them; a similar survey a year earlier showed that only 25 percent of smaller institutions were involved in this market.[27]

When the interest rate on a consumer loan changes, lenders may offer borrowers two options:

1. An adjustment in the monthly payment so that the loan is still amortized over the initial loan period; or

---

[24] A shortcut for calculating the sum of the digits is (N/2) × (N + 1), where N is the number of payments.

[25] An examination of the size of the prepayment penalty in relationship to maturity, loan size, and APR is provided in Kramer 1981. The Rule of 78s came under Congressional attack in 1992, when a provision prohibiting its use in consumer loan agreements was introduced in legislation under consideration by the House Banking Committee. The amendment was later withdrawn but is likely to resurface.

[26] "Terms of Consumer Installment Credit," *Federal Reserve Bulletin* 78 (November 1992): A38; and Melinda Grenier Guiles, "Hidden Perils of Longer-term Car Loans," *The Wall Street Journal,* August 10, 1988, 17.

[27] See Goodman and Luckett 1985.

TABLE 15.3   Installment Loan Amortization Schedule: Adjustable Rate, Adjustable Payment

When the interest rate changes on some installment loans, the payment is changed to amortize the loan at the new interest rate. In this case, a higher interest rate results in a higher payment.

| Initial Monthly Payment: $214.62 | Initial Balance: $8,000 | Initial Maturity: 4 years |
| Initial Rate: 13.00% | Adjusted Rate: 14% after month 12 | Payment after Rate Adjustment: $217.70 |

Month	(1) Payment	(2) Beginning Balance	(3) Interest 0.13/12 × (2) or 0.14/12 × (2)	(4) Principal Paid (1) − (3)	(5) End-of-Month Balance (2) − (4)
1	$214.62	$8,000.00	$86.67	$127.95	$7,872.05
2	214.62	7,872.05	85.28	129.34	7,742.71
3	214.62	7,742.71	83.88	130.74	7,611.97
4	214.62	7,611.97	82.46	132.16	7,479.81
5	214.62	7,479.81	81.03	133.59	7,346.22
6	214.62	7,346.22	79.58	135.04	7,211.19
7	214.62	7,211.19	78.12	136.50	7,074.69
8	214.62	7,074.69	76.64	137.98	6,936.71
9	214.62	6,936.71	75.15	139.47	6,797.24
10	214.62	6,797.24	73.64	140.98	6,656.25
11	214.62	6,656.25	72.11	142.51	6,513.74
12	214.62	6,513.74	70.57	144.05	6,369.69
13	217.70	6,369.69	74.31	143.39	6,226.30
14	217.70	6,226.30	72.64	145.06	6,081.24
15	217.70	6,081.24	70.95	146.75	5,934.49
40	217.70	1,849.74	21.58	196.12	1,653.62
41	217.70	1,653.62	19.29	198.41	1,455.21
42	217.70	1,455.21	16.98	200.72	1,254.48
43	217.70	1,254.48	14.64	203.07	1,051.42
44	217.70	1,051.42	12.27	205.43	845.98
45	217.70	845.98	9.87	207.83	638.15
46	217.70	638.15	7.45	210.26	427.90
47	217.70	427.90	4.99	212.71	215.19
48	217.70	215.19	2.51	215.19	0.00

2. An adjustment in the loan maturity without changing the monthly payment.

Under the second option, the loan period is extended if interest rates increase or shortened if rates decline. In 1985, almost 80 percent of institutions with variable-rate consumer loans offered the maturity-change option, whereas less than 35 percent offered the payment-change option. As the percentages suggest, some institutions offer both.

CHANGING THE MONTHLY PAYMENT. Table 15.3 provides a standard amortization schedule for a 4-year,

$8,000 loan with an initial annual interest rate of 13 percent, or a monthly rate of $13\% \div 12 = 1.083$ percent. Using Equation 5A.7 for the present value of an annuity, the monthly payment (C_1) is $214.62 in each of the 48 months if the interest rate does not change:

$$C_0 = C_1 \left[\frac{1 - (1 + k)^{-n}}{k} \right]$$

$$\$8,000 = C_1 \times 37.275$$

$$C_1 = \$214.62$$

TABLE 15.4 **Installment Loan Amortization Schedule: Adjustable Rate, Fixed Payment**

When the interest rate changes on some installment loans, the periodic payment remains the same but the maturity is changed. In this example, a higher interest rate results in a longer maturity.

| Initial Monthly Payment: $214.62 | Initial Balance: $8,000 | Initial Maturity: 48 months |
| Initial Rate: 13.00% | Adjusted Rate: 14% after month 12 | Maturity after Rate Adjustment: 36.64 months |

	(1)	(2)	(3)	(4)	(5)
Month	Payment	Beginning Balance	Interest 0.13/12 × (2) or 0.14/12 × (2)	Principal Paid (1) − (3)	End-of-Month Balance (2) − (4)
1	$214.62	$8,000.00	$86.67	$127.95	$7,872.05
2	214.62	7,872.05	85.28	129.34	7,742.71
3	214.62	7,742.71	83.88	130.74	7,611.97
4	214.62	7,611.97	82.46	132.16	7,479.81
5	214.62	7,479.81	81.03	133.59	7,346.22
6	214.62	7,346.22	79.58	135.04	7,211.19
7	214.62	7,211.19	78.12	136.50	7,074.69
8	214.62	7,074.69	76.64	137.98	6,936.71
9	214.62	6,936.71	75.15	139.47	6,797.24
10	214.62	6,797.24	73.64	140.98	6,656.25
11	214.62	6,656.25	72.11	142.51	6,513.74
12	214.62	6,513.74	70.57	144.05	6,369.69
13	214.62	6,369.69	74.31	140.31	6,229.38
14	214.62	6,229.38	72.68	141.94	6,087.44
15	214.62	6,087.44	71.02	143.60	5,943.84
40	214.62	1,946.85	22.71	191.91	1,754.95
41	214.62	1,754.95	20.47	194.15	1,560.80
42	214.62	1,560.80	18.21	196.41	1,364.39
43	214.62	1,364.39	15.92	198.70	1,165.69
44	214.62	1,165.69	13.60	201.02	964.67
45	214.62	964.67	11.25	203.37	761.30
46	214.62	761.30	8.88	205.74	555.57
47	214.62	555.57	6.48	208.14	347.43
48	214.62	347.43	4.05	210.57	136.86
49	138.46	136.86	1.60	136.86	0.00

Table 15.3 shows the effect of an increase in the interest rate, from 13 percent to 14 percent, after the twelfth payment has been made. The monthly payment rises to $217.70 for the last 36 months, and the amortization schedule reflects the change as of payment 13.

CHANGING THE LOAN TERM. The other alternative is to keep the monthly payment constant but to adjust the loan maturity. The effect is demonstrated in Table 15.4. After 12 payments, the interest rate again increases to 14 percent; if the monthly payment remains at $214.62, a partial payment of $138.46 is owed in the forty-ninth month. When a borrower believes a

payment increase would unacceptably strain the monthly budget, this option may be desirable. Under neither option, however, does a 100-basis-point increase in the interest rate greatly change the borrower's obligations. If a variable-rate loan also carries a lower initial interest rate than a comparable fixed-rate loan—and most do—the impact of a payment increase may seem even less severe.

Lenders pioneering in variable-rate loans believe that transferring interest rate risk to borrowers ensures that consumer credit will continue to be available, regardless of the interest rate environment. Because such loans are relatively new, there is little evidence about consumer response to them. One study of consumers with automobile loans from a commercial bank found that the choice between fixed and variable rates was affected by borrowers' expectations about future interest rates and inflation. Borrowers taking adjustable rates were more optimistic about economic trends and more confident that their incomes would increase, enabling them to meet potentially higher payments.[28]

CONSUMER CREDIT THROUGH CREDIT CARDS

Credit cards allow consumer credit to be extended on a prearranged basis, similar to formal commercial loan commitments discussed in the previous chapter. Credit issued through cards is **revolving credit,** on which the lender designates a prearranged interest rate and maximum line of credit. The cardholder chooses when and whether to borrow, repaying the lender partially or in full on receipt of a monthly statement. The annual fee most borrowers pay for the privilege of carrying a card is analogous to a commitment fee in commercial lending.

BRIEF HISTORY

Retailers were the first firms to offer credit cards. In 1951, however, Franklin National Bank of New York recognized untapped profit potential, and the bank card was born. ("Bank card" is used in this chapter to refer to cards issued by all depositories.) In the late 1950s, larger banks began to participate. The depository most closely identified with bank cards is BankAmerica, which promoted its card nationwide starting in 1966; this was the origin of the current Visa system. By 1968, because of prohibitive marketing expenses, many banks dropped their private cards and joined cooperative marketing organizations, the largest of which are Visa and MasterCard.[29]

Because of regulation, thrifts and CUs entered the credit card business later than banks. In 1977, fed-

eral CUs were permitted to offer lines of credit for the first time. This authority paved the way for their entry into the bank card business, although by 1991, fewer than 30 percent of all CUs had done so. Still, more than 90 percent of the largest CUs were involved. DIDMCA gave federal thrifts authority to issue cards, and many have done so. Data from the U.S. League of Savings Institutions show that 47 percent of federally insured thrifts were issuing credit cards by the end of 1989.[30]

The cards are widely dispersed among the population. A 1989 survey by the Fed and other regulators found that 54 percent of all American families had bank cards. Almost 70 percent of families have at least one type of credit card, and many households have more than one card. These cards do not sit idly in purse or pocket; in 1990, consumers used credit cards to purchase more than $400 billion of goods and services, and these charges accounted for about 13 percent of consumer expenditures.[31]

RISKS AND RETURNS FROM CREDIT CARDS

Like other financial products, credit cards offer their issuers both benefits and risks.

SOURCES OF PROFIT. Annual fees, originated when many state usury ceilings were binding, are standard practice among depositories issuing credit cards. Now that usury ceilings are less burdensome, the fees are a welcome source of income not really dependent on economic conditions. Because many current usury ceilings were set in the early 1980s, in a period of extremely high interest rates, depositories have been able to charge very profitable rates of interest on credit cards throughout most of the decade. For example, in 1992, interest rates on bank cards continued to be in the 18–19 percent range nationwide, while the prime rate at major banks averaged between 7.25 and 8.5 percent. This situation has been common for many years.[32]

[28] A. Charlene Sullivan, "Consumers' Choice of Consumer Loan Contract Terms," Working Paper No. 51, Credit Research Center, Purdue University, 1985.

[29] Details on the early history of bank credit cards are provided in Russell 1975.

[30] CUNA, *1991 Credit Union Report;* and Price 1989.

[31] See Canner and Luckett 1992.

[32] See Calem 1992; and John Meehan, "Pushing Plastic Is Still One Juicy Game," *Business Week,* September 21, 1992, 76–78.

Institutions that process credit transactions and bill customers for other depositories are able to earn additional revenues. Finally, the issuing bank charges merchants accepting bank cards fees usually ranging from 2 percent to 5 percent of a transaction.

In the late 1980s, consumer groups and regulators took increasing notice of the variety of lenders' income sources. Of particular concern were the activities of some lenders that many observers termed deceptive. For example, some institutions lowered the interest rate on bank cards with great fanfare but at the same time raised annual fees or eliminated the "grace period" during which interest is not charged. Thus, the effective cost to cardholders was not reduced as the interest rate was lowered, and in some cases it was actually increased. Other lenders failed to disclose the full cost of credit until after a customer was approved for credit, rather than at the time of application.

Congress responded to these concerns by passing the **Fair Credit and Charge Disclosure Act of 1988,** directing the Fed to amend Reg Z, effective August 31, 1989. The amended regulations require card issuers to disclose interest rates, fees, grace periods, and other terms and conditions at the time of application. The disclosure must be in the form of a chart so that comparison among lenders is facilitated. Interestingly, banks supported the legislation. The industry had strongly objected to previous disclosure bills, which had also included federal usury ceilings on credit card rates. When the usury provisions were dropped, the banking industry lobbied to speed the disclosure law through Congress.[33]

SOURCES OF RISK. Because credit cards carry pre-established lines of credit, consumers may accumulate substantial borrowings before the card issuer knows financial problems have developed. The problem is compounded because many consumers carry more than one bank card, a situation perpetuated when institutions conduct mass mailings to solicit new cardholders. The mass-mailing strategy has hit some snags. For example, the Bank of New Orleans sent unsolicited credit cards to a group identified by the bank's computers as having steady employment and noteworthy credit records. The mailing list consisted of inmates at a state prison.[34]

Also, credit card issuance may lead to heavy reliance on credit-scoring models. Card applications lend themselves to use in statistical models, but the borrower's condition may change so rapidly that the results of the model do not reflect the risk to which the lender is exposed when the card is issued. Because the lender may have had no personal contact with the borrower, credit decisions are often made on no other basis.

As is discussed in Chapter 22 on financial performance, the rate of return on total assets for depository institutions is low compared with other industries, often 1 percent or less. The difficult banking environment in the late 1980s and early 1990s caused many institutions to view the 2–3 percent net return on credit card assets (after deducting administrative costs, loan losses, and the interest cost of money raised to fund credit card loans) as extremely attractive. Unfortunately, some ignored the higher risk that comes with potentially higher returns. Lenders conducted mass mailings so indiscriminately, and loosened credit standards to such an extent, that loan losses skyrocketed. Many institutions targeted the United States's 12 million college students. The Young Americans Bank of Denver, Colorado, went a step further (enraging many parents and educators in the process) by conducting a nationwide campaign to issue credit cards to children 12 years and older.

In the early 1990s, some banks introduced an innovative approach to limiting risk while expanding market share. The concept involves a **secured card,** which requires a customer who is deemed a poor credit risk to leave a security deposit at a bank to become a cardholder. The bank issuer also charges higher interest rates and fees. Customers with no other access to credit are more than willing to accept these terms. In early 1992, for example, more than 400,000 secured cards were outstanding. Although issuers reported

---

[33]"Credit Card Rules Take Effect," *Chicago Tribune,* August 31, 1989; Robert Guenther, "Lower Rates on Bank Credit Cards Can Mask Some Costly New Twists," *The Wall Street Journal,* June 6, 1987; and "Get Ready for New Card Disclosure Rules," *ABA Banking Journal* 80 (December 1988): 20.

[34]Charles F. McCoy, "Losses on Credit Cards, Other Consumer Debts Are Climbing Rapidly," *The Wall Street Journal,* December 2, 1985, 1, 12.

higher losses on secured cards than on regular bank credit cards, the higher revenue potential is attractive to a growing number of issuers.[35]

INCREASING COMPETITION AND NARROWING MARGINS. As the U.S. market has become more saturated, competition among depository institution issuers of credit cards has become keener. In the late 1980s, the competition became global as MasterCard and Visa expanded their Japanese markets (noted in the opening story) and later began to penetrate Eastern European markets. Competition from nondepository credit card issuers has also grown rapidly, as firms such as AT&T, American Express, General Electric, and General Motors have enthusiastically entered the credit card market. These new entrants have vied for customers with innovative pricing schemes and promotions. As a result, bank issuers are being forced to respond with similar offers, such as lower fees or tiered pricing programs, in which customers with good payment records are offered lower rates.

Some issuers introduced a controversial marketing strategy known as **affinity cards.** Affinity cards are issued to members of special interest groups, with which issuing banks share profits based on cardholders' purchases. At first these groups were formal organizations, such as university alumni associations or the Sierra Club. Later, the groups became more loosely defined, and in some cases issuers offered to contribute to specific charitable causes based on the cardholders' purchases. The affinity cards are controversial because they often include higher interest rates or annual fees, leading many observers to note that cardholders would be wiser to donate money directly to the preferred charitable organization. Also, politicians and consumer groups argue that profits on the affinity cards (and other credit cards, for that matter) must be excessive, or the issuer would be unable to afford the contributions. That argument strengthens the case for limitations on card interest rates and fees.[36]

Adding to the competitive pressure, customers have become more aggressive in the demands they place on issuers. Suits were filed in 1991 to limit or even prevent issuers from charging penalties for late payment on credit card accounts. Although the first defendants were nonbank issuers, challengers against bank cards followed.

By the early 1990s, the effect of these pressures on returns was evident. Studies indicated that, while return on assets in the card business averaged about 5 percent in the late 1980s, the return was almost 25 percent less than that in 1992. Most observers expected an increasingly competitive environment and narrowing profit margins throughout the 1990s.[37]

MORTGAGE LENDING: AN OVERVIEW

Because home ownership is such an important goal in the United States, the demand for mortgage loans is expected to continue unabated. Volume, however, is seasonal and strongly affected by the economy and interest rates. As inflation drove up housing prices in the late 1970s, accompanied by interest rate increases, home ownership seemed out of reach for many. Since that time, in fact, the percentage of U.S. families owning their homes has declined slightly. But financial innovations, such as the many new mortgages analyzed in this chapter, and legislative initiatives have been at work to ensure the viability of the housing market into the twenty-first century.

For example, the Tax Reform Act of 1986 retained the tax deduction for mortgage interest, continuing the national commitment to home ownership. That law also paved the way for growth in home equity loans, discussed in detail later in the chapter, in which homeowners can borrow against the accumulated net worth in their property. The Financial Institutions Reform, Recovery, and Enforcement Act (FIRREA) again

---

[35] Suzanne Woolley, "Plastic for a Pretty Penny," *Business Week,* May 18, 1992, 118.

[36] Troy Segal, "Charging for Charity Isn't All That Simple," *Business Week,* February 1, 1988, 95.

[37] "Plastic Profits Go Pop," *Economist,* September 12, 1992, 92; Yvette Kantrow, "Retailers' Cards Show Unexpected Strength," *American Banker,* September 30, 1992, 1, 2; Tim Smart, "Mad As Hell About Late Fees," *Business Week,* February 24, 1992, 32; Bruce W. Morgan, "Credit Card Interest Rates: Perceptions, Politics, and Realities," *Banking Policy Report* 11 (January 20, 1992): 1; "The Nonbanks Muscle In," *Economist,* May 25, 1991, 84, 89; and Leah N. Spiro, "More Cards in the Deck," *Business Week,* December 16, 1991, 100–104.

reaffirmed that affordable housing is a national economic policy objective. The revamped Federal Home Loan Bank (FHLB) System has as one of its main functions the promotion of programs to make home ownership available to low- and moderate-income families. Thus, mortgage lending is certain to be an important use of funds for depositories into the foreseeable future.[38]

A mortgage is a legal agreement assigning property as collateral on a loan. Although the home buyer technically holds the title to the property, the lender may take action to obtain it if the borrower defaults. When a home purchase is financed, the buyer signs a note stipulating the interest rate and repayment schedule for a loan to purchase the home, as well as a mortgage agreement designating the property as collateral on the loan.

LENDERS' MARKET SHARES

As noted, home financing accounts for most consumer debt. Figure 15.6 provides recent data on the share of funds provided by depository institutions and other lenders to finance residential real estate. Although the proportion of mortgage debt held by thrifts declined in the 1980s and early 1990s, they continue to hold a slightly larger share than commercial banks. CUs included in the "Other" slice of the pie, have relatively small, but growing, amounts. For reasons discussed in later chapters, federal agencies and institutions such as pension funds and insurance companies play increasingly large roles in the mortgage market.

THE MORTGAGE MENU

The most publicized features of housing finance in recent years are the new types of mortgages offered to consumers. In fact, so many different features have been introduced, collectively called the "mortgage menu," that some experts believe even financially sophisticated homebuyers are unable to evaluate them adequately.[39] Buyers are offered mortgages with vari-

| FIGURE 15.6 | **Holders of Home Mortgage Debt, Year-End 1991** |

Commercial banks, savings institutions, and securities pools are the largest suppliers of mortgage credit.

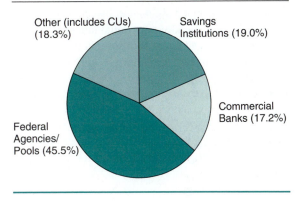

Source: Federal Reserve Bulletin, November 1992, A36.

able interest rates and loan maturities; plans with lower payments in the early years of the loan; agreements refinanced periodically, with renegotiated interest rates; and many more arrangements. For many reasons, consumer acceptance of **adjustable-rate mortgages (ARMs)** grew in the 1980s. In recent years, the proportion of home loans originated with variable rates has ranged from about 25 percent to more than 70 percent, depending on interest rate levels and other factors.[40]

LENDERS WANT FLEXIBILITY. Mortgage lenders have good reason to offer variable-rate instruments. With the increased level and volatility of deposit interest costs, lenders are less willing to offer long-term loans carrying a fixed rate of interest. Furthermore, regulatory changes since 1981 have given mortgage lenders more flexibility to develop new mortgage instruments.

---

[38] These issues are discussed in Gabriel 1987; Obrinsky 1988; and "Conference Report on H.R. 1278" 1989.

[39] For an interesting discussion of the dilemma facing homebuyers, see Guttentag 1983.

---

[40] *Freddie Mac Reports,* various issues; and Vanessa Bush, "Low Rates Limit Lending Routes," *Savings Institutions* 113 (January 1992): 18–23.

BORROWERS WANT CHOICE. High interest rates made consumers willing to accept the uncertainty of a variable-rate mortgage (VRM). For example, the average interest rate charged on a new mortgage in December 1978 was less than 10 percent. It had risen to more than 15 percent by the end of 1981, exceeded 13 percent in 1984, and had fallen to just over 8 percent by 1992. Lenders usually offer initial interest rate discounts on VRMs, so many borrowers find them more affordable than fixed-rate mortgages, and particularly desirable in times of high interest rates. Research indicates, in fact, that the initial rate discount is the most important factor in a borrower's decision to choose a VRM. It also shows that borrowers like a variety of home financing alternatives, because choice tends to make home ownership more affordable for many types of homebuyers.[41]

GOVERNMENT REGULATIONS AND MORTGAGE LENDING

The attention of regulators and legislatures to consumer credit protection has extended to the mortgage markets. Besides the Truth-in-Lending and Equal Credit acts, mortgage lenders must comply with the Fair Housing Act of 1968, the Home Mortgage Disclosure Act of 1975, and the Community Reinvestment Act of 1977. The last two acts were strengthened further in provisions of FIRREA. These laws are designed to prevent discrimination on the basis of a borrower's race or neighborhood location and to ensure that credit is available in all communities.

Federal regulations also control specific loan terms. Until 1981, federal thrifts' ability to offer VRMs was severely limited. In April of that year, the FHLB Board (FHLBB) approved regulations for a very flexible instrument, originally called the "adjustable mortgage loan" but now more frequently known as an ARM. These federal regulations overrode state laws that were more restrictive. Regulations for national banks, set by the Comptroller of the Currency,

give bankers less freedom in developing new mortgage plans. Federal credit union mortgage regulations were revised in 1982, also allowing terms more attractive to lenders. These regulations are discussed more fully later in the chapter.

EVIDENCE ON MORTGAGE LENDERS' COMPLIANCE WITH REGULATIONS. The provisions of the Home Mortgage Disclosure Act, as amended in 1989, greatly expanded the quantity of data available to assess the fairness and equity of mortgage lenders' credit decisions and thus their compliance with federal regulations. The data evaluated for 1991 lending reflected statements from more than 9,000 depository institutions and mortgage companies and almost 30,000 loan decisions. Although interpretations of recent research vary somewhat, many experts believe the evidence presents a disturbing picture of widespread discrimination in mortgage lending.

For example, the data indicate that, after controlling for income levels and other demographic differences, African-American and Hispanic loan applicants faced a substantially higher probability of being rejected than did white applicants. Further, the data indicate that many mortgage lenders have not been complying with mandates in the Community Reinvestment Act to respond to credit needs of the entire community from which they accept deposits, including the less affluent areas. Many lenders were found to be making mortgage loans much more readily available in white neighborhoods than in those with higher proportions of nonwhites. (This practice has traditionally been known as **redlining.**)

Although this evidence is disturbing, the publicity surrounding these revelations has already led to some reforms in lending practices. Also, the American Bankers Association has created a Center for Community Development to train lenders and to facilitate the exchange of information about successful efforts of institutions complying with the Community Reinvestment Act. The Mortgage Bankers Association prepared a task force report on the issue and created programs to ensure that mortgage bankers are aware of innovative lending programs that improve borrowing opportunities for those who have had difficulty receiving a fair evaluation of their applications. These efforts, along with the continuing involvement of regu-

---

[41] These and other conclusions were drawn by authors of the following studies: Colton, et al.; Albaum and Kaufman 1977; *Buying a Home in the 1980s* 1982; Mills and Gardner 1986; Yohannes 1991; and Nothaft and Wang 1992.

latory agencies, suggest that the future may offer a new degree of equity in the availability of mortgage loans.[42]

CREDIT RISK AND MORTGAGE LENDING

When evaluating the credit risk of a mortgage loan application, lenders rely on much of the same information used for other consumer loans, but they must consider additional factors.

IMPORTANT VARIABLES IN ASSESSING CREDIT RISK

A sizable amount of research has been conducted to identify factors related to mortgage delinquency of default.[43] Even though the loans are secured, foreclosure is a lengthy and expensive procedure. Furthermore, the property may be in poor condition by the time the lender takes possession of it, and its resale value may be less than the outstanding loan balance.

LOAN-TO-VALUE RATIO. One form of self-protection for lenders is to make sure that the value of the property at the time of application exceeds the loan amount by enough to protect them in case of default. Research indicates that the initial **loan-to-value ratio** is positively related to both delinquency and default. The difference between the outstanding loan balance and the value of the property is the borrower's equity in the home. When the loan-to-value ratio is high (the maximum allowed initially by most lenders is 95 percent), the borrower has a small personal investment. If the

borrower encounters financial trouble early in the loan term, defaulting on the agreement may be the least painful course of action. If the market value of the home declines as a result of economic conditions or neighborhood deterioration, the reduction in the borrower's equity may contribute to default even several years after the loan agreement is made.

To estimate property values, lenders hire trained real estate appraisers and base the loan amount on the appraisal report. Recently, concern has been expressed about the quality of appraisals. In an environment of relatively low inflation, lenders must be confident that the initial appraisal does not exaggerate the value of the property. One study in 1985 attributed 10 percent of the financial problems at federally insured savings and loan associations (S&Ls) to faulty or fraudulent appraisals.

As the thrift industry's problems worsened in 1987 and 1988, regulators found that in some "zombie" thrifts, more than 80 percent of loans were made on the basis of wildly inflated appraisals. Congress reflected public outrage in FIRREA, when it mandated that the appraisal industry be more strictly regulated. Among FIRREA's provisions are those requiring each state to establish criteria for appraiser licensing and certification (attesting to a higher level of competency than mere licensing) and those stipulating that only certified appraisers may be employed for certain types of tasks. Congress's intent was to promote standards of competence and conduct similar to those for the licensure and certification of accountants and comparable professionals.[44]

BORROWER INCOME. Another key variable is the expected growth and stability of the borrower's future income. The more fluctuations in income, the more difficult it may be to meet monthly payments, because a mortgage payment is usually the largest single debt obligation for a household. Again, with an adjustable-rate loan, potential income variability may be even more problematic.

[42] See Canner and Smith 1992; Paulette Thomas, "Blacks Can Face a Host of Trying Conditions in Getting Mortgages," *The Wall Street Journal,* November 30, 1992, A1, A4; Paulette Thomas, "Boston Fed Finds Racial Discrimination in Mortgage Lending is Still Widespread," *The Wall Street Journal,* October 9, 1992, A3, A4; "U.S. Probes Bank Records for Race Bias," *The Wall Street Journal,* May 10, 1992, A2; Robert B. Avery, Patricia E. Beeson, and Mark S. Sniderman, "Home Mortgage Lending by the Numbers," *Economic Commentary* (Federal Reserve Bank of Cleveland) (February 15, 1993).

[43] Among the many studies on this topic are Herzog and Earley 1970; von Furstenberg and Green 1974; Campbell and Dietrich 1983; and Gardner and Mills 1989.

[44] For more details, see "Conference Report on HR 1278" 1989; "Appraising the Appraiser," *Freddie Mac Reports,* July 1989; and Michael Allen, "Appraisers, Culprits in S&L Crisis, Are Now Key to S&L Recovery," *The Wall Street Journal,* January 24, 1990, 1, 11.

The **payment-to-income ratio,** comparing the borrower's gross monthly income with the monthly loan payment, is widely used to assess the burden on the borrower. The payment is sometimes adjusted to include homeowners' insurance and property taxes. Because the *future* debt burden is of interest, however, research indicates that the initial payment-to-income ratio is not as good a predictor of delinquency or default as one might expect.

ECONOMIC CONDITIONS

Another important influence on credit risk is outside the lender's control. The economy's general strength is negatively correlated with loan default. In a recession, for example, the unemployment rate rises. At the same time, property values may level off or even decline, putting pressure on the payment-to-income and the loan-to-value ratios. A borrower may lack the incentive to sell the home to discharge the loan and may choose to simply walk away, leaving the lender with financial losses.

Recent delinquency and default rates illustrate the impact of economic conditions. During the double-digit inflation years of the late 1970s, homebuyers expected the value of their houses to rise rapidly. When inflation was brought under control, followed by an economic recession, those expectations were not fulfilled. Mortgage delinquencies soared and, by the first quarter of 1985, exceeded all previous levels. As unemployment fell in the last part of the decade, delinquencies returned to more normal levels, although they rose again slightly in the recession of 1991–92.

ADJUSTABLE-RATE LENDING AND CREDIT RISK

Because ARMs have been widely issued only since the 1980s, little is known about whether adjustable-rate loans increase the lender's exposure to default risk. Lacking empirical data, researchers have simulated the potential for borrower default under a variety of assumptions about interest rates and borrower income. Although ARMs permit a lender to transfer interest rate risk to the borrower, financial institutions may be more able to bear the uncertainty of rate changes than are individuals. The question is

whether or when too much risk is shifted. Unfortunately, research is as yet inconclusive and the findings are often contradictory. Many agree that upwardly mobile borrowers are not high default risks, but beyond that there is little consensus.[45] Resolution of the issue awaits collection and analysis of data on the incidence of default under ARMs.

MORTGAGE INSURANCE

Offsetting some of the default risk faced by lenders is mortgage insurance. Lenders may require borrowers to pay the premiums for insurance policies, naming the lender as the beneficiary in case of borrower default. Insurance is offered by federal agencies such as the **Federal Housing Administration (FHA)** and by private mortgage insurance companies. FHA insurance was mandated by the National Housing Act of 1934 as an encouragement to lenders to make housing loans in an unfavorable economic environment. Since that time, other federal mortgage-guarantee programs have been introduced, including those offered by the Veterans Administration (VA).[46] FHA and VA programs have restrictions on interest rates and other terms that make them relatively unattractive to depository institution lenders. They also may require several weeks for approval or denial. As a result, most FHA- and VA-insured mortgages are originated by **mortgage bankers,** specialized financial institutions that originate mortgages, then sell them to other investors.

Mortgages not VA-guaranteed or FHA-insured are known as **conventional mortgages.** The unattractive features of government programs left an opening for private insurers, who insure conventional mortgages with a loan-to-value ratio as high as 95 percent.

---

[45] A representative sampling of this research including Boehm and McKenzie 1983; Buckley and Villani 1983; Crawford and Harper 1983; Vandell 1978; and Webb 1982.

[46] Technically, FHA mortgages are *insured* against default; the borrower pays a modest insurance premium for protection up to a specified maximum amount. In contrast, VA mortgages are *guaranteed.* The VA establishes a maximum dollar amount the lender is guaranteed to receive at no cost to the borrower. This guarantee may allow a borrower to obtain a loan without a down payment, because it reduces the amount the lender has at risk. Congress mandated changes in the FHA pricing structure in the National Affordable Housing Act of 1990. See Weicher 1992 for details.

Their coverage is widely used by depository institutions. Borrowers with down payments below a specified amount may be required to apply for insurance, paying an annual premium based on the principal balance. The insurance does not remove all of the lender's credit risk, however, because it protects only a portion (usually up to 25 percent) of the funds invested in the loan.

ADJUSTABLE-RATE MORTGAGE TERMS

As discussed later in the chapter, mortgage innovations are not limited to interest rate characteristics, although these have been the focus of consumers and regulators. Major issues in ARM lending are presented in this section.

TABLE 15.5   Major Characteristics of Federal Regulations Governing Adjustable-Rate Home Mortgage Lending

Federal regulations governing ARMs differ for banks and for thrifts. Thrift regulations allow more flexible terms.

Major Characteristics	Federal S&Ls and Mutual Savings Banks	National Banks
Requirement to offer fixed-rate mortgage instrument to borrower	None	None
Limit on amount of ARMs that may be held	None	None
Indexes governing mortgage rate adjustments	Any interest rate index that is readily verifiable by the borrower and not under the control of the lender, including national or regional cost-of-funds indexes for S&Ls	1 of 3 national rate indexes—a long-term mortgage rate, a T-bill rate, or a 3-year T-bond rate
Limit on frequency of rate adjustments	None	Not more often than every 6 months
Limit on size of periodic rate adjustments	None	1 percentage point for each 6-month period between rate adjustments, and no single rate adjustment may exceed 5 percentage points
Limit on size of total rate adjustment over life of mortgage	Must be disclosed[a]	Must be disclosed[a]
Allowable methods of adjustment to rate changes	Any combination of changes in monthly payment, loan term, or principal balance	Changes in monthly payment or rate of amortization
Limit on amount of negative amortization	No limit, but monthly payments must be adjusted periodically to fully amortize the loan over the remaining term	Limits are set, and monthly payments must be adjusted periodically to fully amortize the loan over the remaining term
Advance notice of rate adjustments	30 to 45 days before scheduled adjustment	30 to 45 days before scheduled adjustments
Prepayment restrictions or charges	None	Prepayment without penalty permitted after notification of first scheduled rate adjustment
Disclosure requirements	Subject to Reg Z rules: full disclosure of ARM characteristics no later than time borrower receives application form	Subject to Reg Z rules: full disclosure of ARM characteristics no later than time borrower receives application form

[a]The Competitive Equality Banking Act of 1987 required an overall rate cap but did not specify what the cap must be.
Source: Adapted from David F. Seiders, "Changing Patterns of Housing Finance," *Federal Reserve Bulletin* 67 (June 1981): 468; updated to conform to subsequent changes in federal law.

REGULATION OF ARMS

The greatest step forward in VRM lending occurred in 1981, when regulations for national banks and federally chartered thrifts were revised. Both types of lenders gained more freedom to tailor mortgages to fit their own asset/liability management targets. The federal regulations give thrifts more flexibility than banks, as Table 15.5 shows.

INTEREST RATE INDEX. A widely debated issue in ARM lending is the choice of the index on which interest rate adjustments are based. National banks have only three choices: indexes of long-term mortgage rates, T-bill rates, or Treasury bond (T-bond) rates. Thrifts may use any interest rate series that is widely published, verifiable by the borrower, and not in the direct control of an individual lender. The lender must explain to the borrower exactly how the loan interest rate is related to the index and how it will be adjusted as the index changes. A 15-year history of the index used must be provided. Recent data indicate that the 1-year Treasury rate is by far the most common index.[47]

The index choice is a central part of an institution's asset/liability management strategy because of its influence on the size and stability of the net interest margin (NIM). ARMs provide opportunities to protect the spread between interest costs and interest revenues. Ideally, the choice of an index should depend on the marginal cost of funds used to finance mortgage loans. Figure 15.7 shows why the 1-year Treasury index is more popular with lenders in achieving that purpose than a typical average cost of funds index. Although the data plotted are for 1981–1987, the relationship between movements in the two indexes is typical of other periods as well. The average cost index is more stable because it reflects historical as well as current rates, whereas the Treasury index reflects only current market conditions.

INTEREST RATE AND PAYMENT ADJUSTMENTS. Federal regulations allow thrift institutions to offer ARM plans with any frequency of rate adjustments,

FIGURE 15.7 | **Cost of Funds versus 1-Year Treasury Indexes, April 1981–August 1987**

The choice of index for an ARM affects how the interest rate on the loan changes. For example, cost-of-funds indexes are less variable than T-bill indexes.

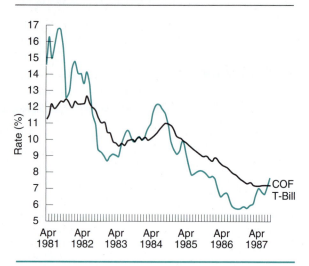

Source: Prepared by the authors with data from *Mortgage Borrowers: Adjusting to Changing Times* (Chicago: U.S. League of Savings Institutions, 1987), 40.

but national banks may not change the mortgage interest rate more than once every 6 months. Banks also have limits, called **caps,** on the size of the periodic rate adjustment. An overall rate cap is required by federal law, and many lenders have attempted to overcome borrower resistance to ARMs by offering a cap on each periodic interest rate adjustment, which limits the borrower's interest rate risk. Recent data indicate that more than 95 percent of all ARMs originated have either rate or payment caps or both. In fact, research indicates that some type of interest rate cap is a very influential factor in gaining borrower acceptance of ARMs.[48]

LOAN TERM EXTENSION AND NEGATIVE AMORTIZATION. A lender has several ways of protecting the borrower from "payment shock," a large increase in

---

[47] Survey results are reported in Fahey 1985; Lea 1985; and Mindy Fetterman, "Lenders Link ARMs to Unfamiliar Indexes," *USA Today,* May 16, 1988, 3B.

[48] See Mills and Gardner 1986; Carroll 1989; and Peek 1990.

the monthly payment. Thrifts, but not banks, can extend the loan maturity, illustrated earlier in Table 15.4 for an installment loan. Thrifts are allowed to increase a mortgage loan term up to a maximum of 40 years, keeping the mortgage payment in a more affordable range.

When an ARM has a periodic payment cap but no periodic rate cap, there is potential for **negative amortization.** Negative amortization occurs whenever the interest rate increases but the payment does not increase enough to cover the additional interest charges. In that case, the unpaid interest in any one month is added to the outstanding loan balance. Instead of amortizing, or reducing, the principal, the borrower's obligation increases, and equity in the home is reduced. Plans allowing negative amortization are unpopular with consumers. A good reason for consumer resistance is that under negative amortization, the borrower actually pays compound interest, or interest on interest. A normal amortization schedule involves simple interest only.

Table 15.6 provides an example of negative amortization, using the first 2 years of a $100,000, 30-year mortgage with an initial rate of 13 percent. The monthly payment at that rate is $1,106.20. The example assumes that the payment cannot change during the first 2 years of the loan but that the interest rate can be adjusted annually. If, after the first year, the interest rate is increased to 16 percent, the payment to fully amortize the mortgage over the remaining 29 years would be $1,342.82 per month. After the interest rate rises in period 13, the interest due is higher than the payment. The difference is added to the outstanding balance, and from that point, the end-of-month balance rises rather than declines. The borrower begins paying interest on the unpaid interest due in the previous month, as well as the original loan principal. Negative amortization would continue until the payment goes up or the interest rate goes down. Eventually, one or the other must occur to protect both the borrower and the lender. Thus, federal thrift regulations require that at some point the payment must be adjusted to fully amortize the loan.

Negative amortization exposes the lender to additional risk because the borrower's equity position influences the likelihood of default. A mortgage plan that deliberately reduces the homeowner's equity increases the lender's credit risk, a fact to be considered

when offering ARM plans that allow negative amortization.

SETTING THE INITIAL INTEREST RATE

Lenders gain customer acceptance of ARMs by offering an interest rate discount that makes the initial cost of an ARM less than that of a fixed-rate mortgage (FRM). Nevertheless, the lender must proceed cautiously. The importance of identifying a base rate required by the institution was emphasized in the previous chapter. That base rate must be earned, on average, if financial objectives are to be achieved.

With a low initial rate and a periodic rate cap, the lender may not be able to earn a market rate of return if interest rates rise significantly. For example, suppose that a lender offers a loan permitting annual rate adjustments with a periodic rate cap of 200 basis points and an initial rate discount 250 basis points below the rate that would be charged on a fixed-rate loan. Under a rising-rate scenario, it could take more than 2 years for the lender to bring the rate on that loan in line with other assets and liabilities.

CONVERTIBLE ARMS

Among the newest ARM variations is the **convertible ARM,** under which borrowers may switch their ARMs to FRMs during a specified period. The terms under which conversion will occur (FRM rate, associated fees, and so forth) are determined at the time the ARM is originated. To avoid the pitfalls of bad forecasting, the promised FRM rate is usually described in terms of the standard FRM rate *at the time of conversion;* in other words, a specific numerical interest rate is not promised to the borrower in advance. Conversion is usually permitted at specified times through the fifth year of the loan, and the conversion privilege is often reserved for borrowers with excellent payment records.

Because convertibles provide an attractive option to the borrower, it should not be surprising that lenders typically levy higher points, charge a higher interest rate, or build in higher spreads over the index than they would with comparable nonconvertibles. As with any financial innovation, lenders face new rewards and new risks with convertibles. A major risk is

| TABLE 15.6 | Mortgage Loan with Negative Amortization: Adjustable Rate, Fixed Payments |

The principal balance of loans with a negative amortization feature can increase if interest rates increase more often than payments can be changed. For this reason, they are not popular with borrowers.

Initial Monthly Payment:	Initial Balance:	Initial Maturity:	Initial Rate:	Adjusted Rate:
$1,106.20	$100,000	30 years	13.00%	16% after month 12

Month	(1) Payment to Fully Amortize at Prevailing Rate	(2) Fixed Payment	(3) Beginning Balance	(4) Interest 0.13/12 × (3) or 0.16/12 × (3)	(5) Principal Paid (2) − (4)	(6) End-of-Month Balance (3) − (5)
1	$1,106.20	$1,106.20	$100,000.00	$1,083.33	$22.87	$ 99,977.13
2	1,106.20	1,106.20	99,977.13	1,083.09	23.11	99,954.02
3	1,106.20	1,106.20	99,954.02	1,082.84	23.36	99,930.66
4	1,106.20	1,106.20	99,930.66	1,082.58	23.62	99,907.04
5	1,106.20	1,106.20	99,907.04	1,082.33	23.87	99,883.16
6	1,106.20	1,106.20	99,883.16	1,082.07	24.13	99,859.03
7	1,106.20	1,106.20	99,859.03	1,081.81	24.39	99,834.64
8	1,106.20	1,106.20	99,834.64	1,081.54	24.66	99,809.98
9	1,106.20	1,106.20	99,809.98	1,081.27	24.92	99,785.06
10	1,106.20	1,106.20	99,785.06	1,081.00	25.19	99,759.86
11	1,106.20	1,106.20	99,759.86	1,080.73	25.47	99,734.39
12	1,106.20	1,106.20	99,734.39	1,080.46	25.74	99,708.65
13	1,342.82	1,106.20	99,708.65	1,329.45	(223.25)	99,931.90
14	1,342.82	1,106.20	99,931.90	1,332.43	(226.23)	100,158.13
15	1,342.82	1,106.20	100,158.13	1,335.44	(229.24)	100,387.37
16	1,342.82	1,106.20	100,387.37	1,338.50	(232.30)	100,619.67
17	1,342.82	1,106.20	100,619.67	1,341.60	(235.40)	100,855.06
18	1,342.82	1,106.20	100,855.06	1,344.73	(238.53)	101,093.60
19	1,342.82	1,106.20	101,093.60	1,347.91	(241.72)	101,335.31
20	1,342.82	1,106.20	101,335.31	1,351.14	(244.94)	101,580.25
21	1,342.82	1,106.20	101,580.25	1,354.40	(248.20)	101,828.45
22	1,342.82	1,106.20	101,828.45	1,357.71	(251.51)	102,079.97
23	1,342.82	1,106.20	102,079.97	1,361.07	(254.87)	102,334.83
24	1,342.82	1,106.20	102,334.83	1,364.46	(258.26)	102,593.10

that if most borrowers convert after the first few years of the loan, the lender could hold a mortgage portfolio dominated by FRMs—the very situation that most lenders are tying to avoid by offering ARMs in the first place. However, if interest rates fall substantially after a convertible is issued, the borrower will no doubt convert to lock in a lower fixed rate, but at least will remain a customer, providing fee income to the institution. In contrast, ARM borrowers without convertible privileges may prepay their loans and take their business elsewhere. Further, some experts believe that the convertible option gives borrowers greater incentive to keep their mortgage payments current, thus lowering default risk for the institution. A recent study found that the availability of convertible ARMs was a main determinant of the growth in ARM lending, suggesting

that convertibles are likely to be a permanent item on the mortgage menu.[49]

MORTGAGES WITHOUT ADJUSTABLE RATES

Innovations in mortgage finance are not limited to variable-rate plans. Loans with nontraditional features have been designed to meet the needs of many differ-

---

[49]For more information, see Nothaft and Wang 1992; Peek 1990; Josie McElhone, "Convertibles Cruise to New Popularity," *Freddie Mac Reports,* November 1987; and James P. Miller, "Interest-Rate Swings Spawn New Breed of More Flexible Convertible Mortgages," *The Wall Street Journal,* July 2, 1987, 21.

ent categories of borrowers. It is not hard to see why modern mortgage finance has been compared to alphabet soup.

GRADUATED PAYMENT MORTGAGES

One of the earliest alternatives to the standard FRM was designed to make housing more affordable for first-time homebuyers. As inflated home prices and high interest rates drove up mortgage payments, many who dreamed of owning a home were priced out of the market. The **graduated payment mortgage (GPM)** was designed to enable those who anticipated higher future incomes to buy a home earlier than the FRM would allow.

Under a GPM, monthly payments are set at an artificially low level in the earliest years—that is, a level below the payment required to amortize the mortgage. Thus, in the first few years, the GPM relies on negative amortization. In each of the first 3 to 5 years, monthly payments are increased, according to a schedule known in advance, until they finally become stable at a level above the payment required had the borrowers originally had an FRM. If a borrower's income keeps pace, the higher GPM payments will not be unbearable. There is also no uncertainty, because borrowers know in advance exactly what the payments will be over the life of the mortgage. For lenders, however, the low initial payments mean lower cash flows in the early years, making them less desirable than an FRM. Thus, depositories have had little incentive to encourage borrowers to choose GPMs.

REVERSE ANNUITY MORTGAGES

Another program for a specialized clientele—the elderly who own their homes but face cash shortages—is the **reverse annuity mortgage (RAM).** Rather than a homeowner paying the institution, the opposite occurs: The lender makes regular payments to the homeowner over a contracted annuity period. The homeowner borrows on the basis of the value of the home and receives the borrowed funds periodically, to meet living expenses, instead of in a lump sum. At a specified maturity date, or when the homeowner with a RAM moves or dies, the property is sold, and the lender is repaid, with interest, from the proceeds.

Reverse annuity mortgages have been offered sporadically since the mid-1970s and were authorized nationwide in the Garn-St Germain Act unless states passed legislation after 1982 prohibiting them. In 1989, the FHA began a pilot program to insure RAMs, and their market began to expand in the years following. In 1992, the Department of Housing and Urban Development approved assistance for a limited number of loans in that year only but was expected to renew and perhaps expand the program. Thus, the predictions are that RAMs will be more common in the coming years.

Reverse annuity agreements may take one of several forms. One type of agreement guarantees the homeowner a flat dollar amount as long as he or she occupies the home. Another type guarantees the dollar amount for a specified period and identifies a repayment date; presumably the homeowner will be ready to sell the home by that time, using some of the proceeds to repay the lender. A third variation offers terms similar to a line of credit, with the home as collateral. As their popularity grows, new twists on reverse annuity agreements will undoubtedly appear as lenders better understand the needs of this segment of the market.

However, some generalizations are already appropriate. For example, lenders are unlikely to prefer lifetime agreements because no one can predict with accuracy how long the annuitant will live. The homeowner, in contrast, has good reason to prefer a lifetime contract, because at the end of the reverse annuity agreement, the settlement would be made with the estate rather than the individual. Either way, as is true with GPM plans, a lender offering a RAM must be willing to wait several years before realizing its investment returns.[50]

QUICK-PAY MORTGAGES

A trend in the 1980s was borrower preference for shorter mortgage maturities. One type of instrument, sometimes called a **quick-pay mortgage,** allows borrowers to build equity more quickly and to reduce total interest payments. The monthly payment for a 15-year plan is higher than for its 30-year counterpart, although the difference is less than one might

---

[50] See Chen 1983; "Reverse Mortgages Unlock Home Equity for Senior Citizens," *Savings Institutions* 110 (December 1989): 20–21; and Michael Leonetti, "Beefing Up Retirement Income With a Reverse Annuity Mortgage," *AAII Journal,* July 1992, 20–21.

expect. For example, on a $100,000 mortgage with an 11 percent interest rate, the monthly payment is $952 over a 30-year amortization period and $1,137 for a 15-year period, an increase of less than 20 percent.

GROWING EQUITY MORTGAGES

The **growing equity mortgage (GEM)** offers a fixed interest rate and a relatively short amortization period. The GEM, however, does not have fixed payments over the entire term but, rather, has a predetermined schedule of payment increases over the life of the mortgage. Initial payments are set at the level that would amortize the mortgage over 30 years, but scheduled increases result in a shorter actual maturity.

The popularity of shorter-term mortgages is traced to several factors. Lending institutions, especially thrifts, are anxious to shorten the average maturities of their loan portfolios. Thus, lenders have offered interest rate discounts to borrowers who agree to the shorter mortgages, making them more appealing. Homeowners also see increased opportunities to borrow against the equity value of their homes, loans traditionally known as **second mortgages.** Home equity loans, yet another means by which borrowers can benefit from accumulated net worth, are very popular as well. If homebuyers wish to take advantage of these opportunities, it is in their best interests to build the equity position as rapidly as possible. Quick-pay mortgages and GEMs offer an effective way for doing so.

PRICE-LEVEL-ADJUSTED MORTGAGES

A mortgage plan highly touted but not widely implemented is the **price-level-adjusted mortgage (PLAM).** The PLAM has an adjustable interest rate tied to an inflation index rather than an interest rate index. The theoretical foundation for the PLAM is Fisher's theory on inflationary expectations and interest rates, introduced in Chapter 6. Fisher argued that the nominal rate of interest is composed of two factors: the real rate and a premium for expected inflation. In the PLAM, the initial interest rate is the real rate; the lender does not charge the borrower the inflationary premium in advance because inflationary expectations may be incorrect.

The traditional FRM has been criticized because borrowers pay in advance for anticipated future inflation, incorporated in the nominal rate quoted by the lender, whereas only after inflation occurs does borrower income rise to reduce the mortgage burden. This imbalance is known as **tilt.** Under the PLAM, a borrower pays for *actual* inflation (an adjustment made after the fact), avoids tilt, and benefits from lower initial interest costs.

For example, if the real rate is estimated to be 4 percent at the time of the loan, the amortization schedule is based on that rate. If inflation is 6 percent during the first year, the unpaid balance is increased by 6 percent, and new monthly payments based on amortizing the new balance at 4 percent are required. In the following year, if inflation is 3 percent, the unpaid balance is increased by 3 percent, and so forth. An illustration of a PLAM under these conditions is presented in Table 15.7. Ideally, cost-of-living wage increases would keep real income in a stable ratio to housing payments. The lender, meanwhile, is theoretically protected from inflation-induced interest rate shocks. PLAMs offer no protection, however, from unexpected rate increases caused by other economic factors.

Despite the theoretical benefits, implementation of the PLAM has moved slowly. Several operational factors have interfered, including the problem of estimating the real rate of interest. Furthermore, the PLAM is an FRM, created under the assumption that the real rate is stable. However, some economists believe that real rates are volatile; thus a PLAM would not protect a lender against interest rate risk. Moderation in the inflation rate after 1981 also reduced the attention paid to the PLAM. In addition, the borrower's income may not keep pace with inflation, increasing the lender's exposure to default risk. But perhaps the greatest drawback is the imbalance between the lender's cost of funds and the rate charged on the PLAM. Depository institutions must pay the nominal, not the real, rate to obtain funds and could face liquidity and profitability problems in the early portion of the mortgage term if they earned only the real rate on their mortgage assets. In effect, the PLAM transfers the tilt from borrowers to lenders, who must raise funds by paying in advance for expected inflation.[51]

---

[51] Good discussions and illustrations of the PLAM and its advantages and disadvantages are found in Erdevig and Kaufman 1981; Ronald Bailey, "PLAM!" *Forbes,* January 23, 1989, 38–39; Rogers 1989; Leeds 1989; and Peek and Wilcox 1991.

TABLE 15.7	Price Level-Adjusted Mortgage

PLAMs are based on a fixed real interest rate, plus adjustment of principal and reamortization to reflect the *ex post* rate of inflation. Ideally, the borrower's real payment burden stays constant.

	Initial Monthly Payments: $477.42	Initial Balance: $100,000	Initial Maturity: 30 years	Initial Rate (Real Rate): 4.00%	Inflation Rates: Year 1: 6% Year 2: 3% 0% thereafter
	(1)	**(2)**	**(3)**	**(4)**	**(5)**
Month	**Monthly Payment**	**Beginning Balance**	**Interest** $0.04/12 \times (2)$	**Principal Paid** $(1) - (3)$	**End-of-Month Balance** $(2) - (4)$
1	$477.42	$100,000.00	$333.33	$144.08	$ 99,855.92
2	477.42	99,855.92	332.85	144.56	99,711.36
3	477.42	99,711.36	332.37	145.04	99,566.31
4	477.42	99,566.31	331.89	145.53	99,420.78
5	477.42	99,420.78	331.40	146.01	99,274.77
6	477.42	99,274.77	330.92	146.50	99,128.27
7	477.42	99,128.27	330.43	146.99	98,981.28
8	477.42	98,981.28	329.94	147.48	98,833.81
9	477.42	98,833.81	329.45	147.97	98,685.84
10	477.42	98,685.84	328.95	148.46	98,537.37
11	477.42	98,537.37	328.46	148.96	98,388.42
12	477.42	98,388.42	327.96	149.45	98,238.96
13	506.06	**104,133.30**	347.11	158.95	103,974.35
14	506.06	103,974.35	346.58	159.48	103,814.87
15	506.06	103,814.87	346.05	160.01	103,654.86
16	506.06	103,654.86	345.52	160.54	103,494.32
17	506.06	103,494.32	344.98	161.08	103,333.24
18	506.06	103,333.24	344.44	161.62	103,171.62
19	506.06	103,171.62	343.91	162.15	103,009.47
20	506.06	103,009.47	343.36	162.70	102,846.77
21	506.06	102,846.77	342.82	163.24	102,683.54
22	506.06	102,683.54	342.28	163.78	102,519.75
23	506.06	102,519.75	341.73	164.33	102,355.43
24	506.06	102,355.43	341.18	164.88	102,190.55
25	521.24	**105,256.27**	350.85	170.39	105,085.88
26	521.24	105,085.88	350.29	170.96	104,914.92
27	521.24	104,914.92	349.72	171.53	104,743.40
28	521.24	104,743.40	349.14	172.10	104,571.30
29	521.24	104,571.30	348.57	172.67	104,398.63
30	521.24	104,398.63	348.00	173.25	104,225.38
31	521.24	104,225.38	347.42	173.82	104,051.56
32	521.24	104,051.56	346.84	174.40	103,877.16
33	521.24	103,877.16	346.26	174.98	103,702.17
34	521.24	103,702.17	345.67	175.57	103,526.60
35	521.24	103,526.60	345.09	176.15	103,350.45
36	521.24	103,350.45	344.50	176.74	103,173.71

OTHER TERMS OF MORTGAGE LOANS

Several other characteristics are common to both FRM and ARM loans.

POINTS

Mortgage lenders customarily charge initial service fees, known as points, at the time of the loan origination. First discussed in Chapter 5, a point is 1 percent of the principal of the loan. Points increase the effective cost for the borrower and the effective return to the lender. Under binding usury ceilings, lenders used these service charges to compensate for a below-market rate of interest. Although mortgage usury ceilings were eliminated in most states after DIDMCA, points still influence the pricing of mortgages of all types.

PREPAYMENT PENALTIES

Prepayment penalties, designed to compensate lenders for the uncertainty in asset management caused by a prepayment, are used less and less. Lenders face potentially large volumes of prepayments if market yields fall and borrowers with fixed mortgage rates refinance their homes at lower rates. In the early 1980s, as market rates rose and most lenders were locked into low yields on outstanding mortgages, many began to waive existing prepayment penalties, hoping to remove old loans from their portfolios. To attract new borrowers at the higher rates, however, lenders had to make loans without prepayment penalties. When rates fell substantially in 1985 and 1986 and again in 1991–1992, borrowers with mortgages originated a few years earlier refinanced in droves, but there were no prepayment penalties for lenders to enforce.

Also leading to the virtual demise of the prepayment penalty is the fact that, as compensation to borrowers for additional risk exposure, federal regulations prohibit prepayment penalties on ARMs. Innovations such as convertibles, too, are incompatible with penalties for prepayments.

ASSUMPTIONS

Increasingly common is the **due-on-sale clause,** in which the lender can require the borrower to repay the outstanding loan balance when the mortgaged property is sold. Mortgages without due-on-sale clauses are **assumable** by the new homeowner.[52]

---

[52] Federal agency policies require that VA and FHA mortgages be assumable; conventional mortgages usually have a due-on-sale clause. Federal regulations carefully define sale for purposes of enforcement of due-on-sale clauses. For a review of the technicalities, see Priess 1983.

Due-on-sale clauses protect the lender in two ways:

1. The lender may evaluate the financial position of the new owner and choose whether to continue the loan.
2. When the new owner applies for a loan, the lender can increase the interest rate, if necessary.

The Garn-St Germain Act of 1982 established the ability of lenders to enforce due-on-sale clauses in all mortgage agreements originated thereafter.

SECONDARY MARKET PURCHASES AND SALES

The sale or purchase of mortgages, two important alternatives to originating and holding them, deserves brief mention.

INFLUENCE OF SECONDARY MARKETS

Although secondary markets exist for other loans, the **secondary mortgage market** is the largest and most active one. Detailed discussion of market participants and use of the markets is deferred until Chapter 19, however, because of the importance of these markets to a depository's overall asset/liability management strategy. The relevant point now is that secondary market investors exert influence on loans made in the primary market. If management wants to have the option to sell portions of the portfolio to other investors, it must be sensitive to the types of instruments that are saleable in the secondary markets.

In fact, government or quasi-governmental agencies operating in the secondary mortgage markets have led the way toward standardization of mortgage terms. As suggested by the abundance of mortgage alternatives, investors as well as borrowers find it difficult to evaluate all possibilities. When large secondary investors publicly announce that they will buy only mortgages with certain characteristics, depository institutions must respond if they plan to deal with those investors. Secondary market participants have been quite willing to accept financial innovations thus far. Indeed, the secondary mortgage market itself reflects the staying power of well-designed financial innovations, and is a forerunner of asset securitization in the consumer and commercial loan markets. Securitization is discussed and illustrated in detail in Chapter 19.

EXPANDING THE PORTFOLIO THROUGH PURCHASES

Depository institutions can purchase loans originated elsewhere. For example, mortgage bankers frequently sell loans to other lenders. Usually, the originator attempts to ensure that the borrower meets the credit standards of the depository institution purchasing the loan. By acquiring loans originated elsewhere, a depository institution may geographically diversify its portfolio, an especially important benefit because of the sensitivity of mortgage delinquency and default rates to local economic conditions. Purchases also allow diversification in the types of mortgages held in the portfolio, enabling a depository to alter its cash inflow patterns.

THE FUTURE OF THRIFTS IN MORTGAGE LENDING: TROUBLE AHEAD?

Despite innovations in the primary and secondary mortgage markets, several prominent researchers have concluded that portfolio lenders concentrating on mortgages are not likely to enjoy consistent rates of return adequate to compensate for the level of risk assumed. The research indicates that mortgage lending was a losing proposition for most of the 1980s, subject to large swings in profitability. To capitalize on the benefits available from mortgage loans, lenders need substantial flexibility to move in and out of the mortgage markets as conditions dictate.[53]

Unfortunately for thrifts, Congress has reduced, rather than increased, lending flexibility; now, thrifts must hold 65 percent or more of their assets in mortgage-related investments (up from 60 percent before FIRREA and the Federal Deposit Insurance Corporation Improvement Act [FDICIA]). Further, mortgage portfolios themselves are subject to added restrictions

related to the goal of affordable housing. Although Congress undoubtedly had laudable intentions (preventing managers from taking excessive speculative risks and promoting availability of funds to prospective homebuyers at most income levels), many observers believe that the effects of its actions are actually likely to be detrimental to society by further weakening thrifts' ability to diversify.

Finally, as is evident from the data displayed in Figure 15.6, thrifts no longer dominate the mortgage lending of depository institutions. By the end of 1991, the dollar volume of mortgages originated by commercial banks was almost equal to that of thrifts. As a result, thrifts are facing greater competition in local and regional markets as they attempt to attract potential homebuyers.

HOME EQUITY LOANS

The Tax Reform Act of 1986 spurred intense interest in **home equity loans,** a type of credit with characteristics of both mortgage and nonmortgage consumer lending (and with the irreverent, but generally accepted, acronym of **HELs**). The Tax Reform Act phased out the tax deductibility of interest expenses for consumer borrowers, with two main exceptions—interest on mortgage loans and HELs. Almost immediately, depositories recognized HELs' potential appeal to consumers who might be reluctant to use credit cards under the new tax law.[54]

HELs versus Second Mortgages. HELs are different from second mortgages, which are additional loans backed by the property on which a first mortgage has been issued. Like first mortgages, second mortgages are ordinarily made for fixed dollar amounts with specified maturity dates, requiring regular monthly payments of interest and principal. Because

---

[53] See, for example, Carron and Brumbaugh 1989.

[54] Information in this section was drawn from several excellent articles on HELs, including Thomas A. Durkin, "Home Equity Credit Lines in Perspective," *Finance Facts,* June–July 1987; "Home Equity Lines of Credit Revisited," *Finance Facts,* August 1987; Canner, Fergus, and Luckett 1988; Canner and Fergus 1988; Canner and Luckett 1989; Canner, Durkin, and Luckett 1989; DeMong and Lindgren 1989; John Meehan, "It's Like Being on the Edge of a Precipice," *Business Week,* July 6, 1992, 56–58; and Steve Rodgers, "CUs Gain Home Equity Market Share," *Credit Union Magazine,* June 1992, 20–24; Eugeni 1993.

the lien is junior to the first mortgage, the interest rate on second mortgages is higher than on first mortgages. The amount that homeowners can borrow is limited by the amount of equity they have accumulated in their homes.

In contrast, a HEL is a revolving line of credit against which a homeowner can borrow. As the name suggests, the maximum line that a lender will grant is tied to the borrower's equity accumulation (usually 70 to 85 percent of it). Because the lender has the security of a junior lien on the borrower's home in case of default, HELs are offered at lower interest rates than credit cards or unsecured consumer loans. Interest rates on HELs are variable, sometimes changing monthly and often tied to movements in a prime rate (although not the lender's own) or a T-bill index. Repayment schedules are more flexible than with second mortgages, and the borrower often may draw on unused but approved credit simply by writing a check. Both thrifts and banks have moved into HELs in a big way; CUs increased their volume of home equity lines in the early 1990s.

REGULATION OF HELs. HELs actually became feasible in their current form after the Fed changed Reg Z in 1980, specifying the terms under which revolving credit could be issued against residential property. Not until after the 1986 tax act, however, were these loans marketed aggressively by institutions. Despite the popularity of HELs, consumer-advocate groups greeted them coolly at best and with hostility at worst. They argued that unsuspecting borrowers were risking their homes by using the proceeds of HELs for frivolous purposes, such as vacations, recreational vehicles, or swimming pools. Several consumer organizations called for strict regulation of the product, including rate caps and maturity limits.

Several studies conducted by Fed economists and others showed that the typical HEL borrower was better-educated, older, and wealthier than homeowners in general and that most used HELs to make home improvements or to repay other debts. Most HEL borrowers interviewed by Fed researchers believed that they were adequately informed about loan terms, and few abuses of HELs by lenders were documented. Nevertheless, Congress responded to pressure from consumer groups. In 1987, the Competitive Equality

Banking Act (CEBA) mandated that HELs must have lifetime interest rate caps. In 1988, Congress passed the **Home Equity Loan Consumer Protection Act;** it specifies rigid disclosure rules and restricts the right of creditors to change loan terms after a HEL has been approved. Thus, the flexibility in HEL terms was reduced.

"A GLOWING" FUTURE FOR HELs. Although many experts regret what they view as unneeded scrutiny of HELs, few observers expect current regulation to kill these popular products. Fed research showed that only 5.6 percent of homeowners had HELs by 1988, indicating a huge untapped market. Aggregate balances of HEL lending reached over $125 billion in 1991, reflecting a growth rate of 55 percent annually. HELs' relatively low default risk compared with unsecured consumer credit, as well as the fact that they carry variable rates, will continue to appeal to lenders. The recession of the early 1990s, however, accompanied by declining real estate values in many parts of the United States, resulted in a rising rate of HEL delinquencies in 1992. But the tax deductibility of interest, the relatively low interest rates compared with credit cards, and the flexibility will continue to appeal to borrowers. Thus, despite repeated assertions by consumer groups that HELs encourage people to borrow unwisely, they are financial innovations with staying power.

SUMMARY

This chapter continued the discussion of lending with emphasis on consumer installment and mortgage loans. Traditionally, CUs and thrifts, respectively, have been main lenders in these markets, although commercial banks also are active participants. One of the major differences between consumer and commercial lending is the degree of legal and regulatory protection afforded to consumer borrowers.

As with commercial lending, analysis of financial statements and credit bureau reports is important when granting consumer installment loans and issuing credit cards. Credit-scoring models assist in this task. The lender must also be alert to applicable bankruptcy laws and the influence of usury laws. Also, creditors must decide what loan terms are appropriate, how payments will be calculated, whether the rate will be variable or fixed, and whether prepayment penalties will be attached. Credit card lending has become more competitive in recent years, as nondepositories have entered the credit card market.

Many similar decisions must be made in the granting of mortgage loans, although special emphasis is placed on the value of the mortgaged property and on the expected pattern of the borrower's income. These considerations are especially important in variable-rate lending or when economic conditions are uncertain.

ARMs are increasingly popular with lenders because of the protection they offer in stabilizing the NIM. Borrowers are willing to accept them if lenders share the interest rate risk by including rate/payment caps and offering initial rate discounts. Other important issues include how often rates or payments can be adjusted, to what index rate changes will be tied, whether the maturity of the mortgage contract can be extended, and whether negative amortization will be permitted. Some ARMs permit conversion to a fixed rate after several years.

Lenders and borrowers who want other special features may prefer any one of several alternatives, such as the GPM, the RAM, the quick-pay, the GEM, or the PLAM. Each of these instruments is designed either to appeal to a special demographic segment of borrowers or to meet special economic needs of borrowers and lenders. Loan portfolio managers may sell and purchase loans in secondary markets, permitting additional flexibility for achieving institutional objectives. Finally, HELs provide a promising new market for consumer lenders.

QUESTIONS

1. Describe the trends in the rate of consumer borrowing in the United States during the 1990s. Find current information that indicates whether the growth in consumer credit is accelerating. Why were economists not alarmed by the growth of consumer credit in the 1980s and 1990s? Explain whether you agree with their interpretations.

2. Many consumer loans are made on an installment basis. Explain how terms on such loans differ from terms on typical commercial loans. What types of financial institutions provide the most credit to consumers?

3. Explain the intentions of Congress in the passage of the Truth-in-Lending Act. What has been the law's effect on consumer lending through the implementation of Regulation Z? Do you agree that close regulation of consumer lending is justified? Why or why not?

4. What protections are consumers afforded under the Fair Credit Reporting Act? How does the proliferation of information technology affect the need for enforcement of the act's provisions?

5. What protections for borrowers were introduced in the Bankruptcy Reform Act of 1978? What was the effect on lenders, and what changes in bankruptcy laws were subsequently made in the mid-1980s? What explanations, other than economic conditions, have been offered for the relatively high rate of bankruptcy filings since the mid-1980s?

6. What are usury laws, and why do they exist? Under what circumstances do consumers benefit from usury laws, and when do they not benefit? Does the growth in the consumer credit card market in South Dakota and Delaware reflect an antithesis or a synthesis? In the context of the regulatory dialectic, how would you expect financial institutions to respond if usury ceilings are placed on bank credit cards?

7. What types of information about loan applicants do financial institutions use in consumer credit analysis (excluding mortgage loans)? What factors are present in the evaluation of consumer borrowers that are not introduced in the evaluation of commercial loan applicants?

8. What are credit-scoring models? Explain the advantages and disadvantages of using credit-scoring models, including behavior scoring, for loan evaluation. If you were in the consumer lending business, would you rely heavily on credit-scoring systems? Why or why not?

9. In the early 1990s, some employers began using an applicant's personal credit history as a factor in personnel hiring decisions. Do you believe that credit records are an appropriate factor in personnel procedures? Explain.

10. What is an add-on loan? With an add-on provision, what is the relationship between the stated interest rate and the APR?

11. What are the sources of revenues and risks to financial institutions from credit card lending? What advantages are offered by a secured card? What protections were provided to consumers in the Fair Credit and Charge Disclosure Act of 1988?

12. What is an affinity card? Would you recommend that a friend or family member use an affinity card in support of a charitable cause? Why or why not?

13. Explain the controversy of the early 1990s concerning discriminatory practices in mortgage lending. Consult recent periodicals to determine current assessments of the extent to which such practices have persisted, and whether there has been a legislative or regulatory response.

14. What two ratios are relied on most heavily in assessing the credit risk of a mortgage loan? How has ARM lending made it more difficult to evaluate credit risk over the life of a mortgage loan?

15. Discuss the factors that a lending institution must evaluate before setting ARM terms, including rate/payment caps and adjustment periods. What factors should a lender consider when selecting an index for rate adjustments on its ARMs?

16. What is negative amortization? Explain the mortgage terms that can lead to negative amortization when interest rates rise. What are the advantages and disadvantages to borrowers? To lenders?

17. What is a convertible ARM? What are the advantages offered to consumers by this type of ARM? What additional risk exposure must a lender accept compared to nonconvertible ARMs?

18. Compare and contrast graduated payment and growing equity mortgages. What type of borrower would prefer each one? Explain.

19. What is a reverse annuity mortgage (RAM)? What type of borrower would prefer a RAM? What characteristics of RAMs tend to reduce their popularity with lenders? Why?

20. Explain the theoretical foundation for the price–level–adjusted mortgage (PLAM). Despite supporting arguments, why has the PLAM not been widely accepted among mortgage lenders?

21. What benefits do lenders receive from including a due-on-sale clause in the mortgage agreement?

22. Explain how the existence of the secondary mortgage markets provide flexibility to financial institutions in the management of their mortgage loan portfolios?

23. What are the most common features of a home equity loan (HEL)? How does a HEL differ from the traditional second mortgage? What factors have contributed to the rising demand for home equity loans?

24. Review current issues of trade publications or other sources covering the mortgage markets. Have new mortgage instruments been introduced recently? What is the current assessment of the future of HELs? How have tax laws, economic conditions, or regulatory decisions contributed to recent mortgage innovations?

PROBLEMS

1. You are purchasing a new van priced at $24,000 and have saved enough money to make a 20 percent down payment. Your credit union will finance the remaining balance at an 11 percent add-on rate for 4 years (48 months).
   a. Calculate the annual percentage rate.
   b. Would you be better off borrowing from your bank at a 12 percent add-on rate for only 36 months?

2. Mr. and Mrs. Wilson have decided to purchase a recreational vehicle to use for family vacations and weekend trips. The RV costs $30,000, and the Wilsons are able to make an $8,000 down payment. Their bank has quoted an add-on rate of 14 percent, with 60 months to finance the remaining balance.
   a. Based on this information, calculate the Wilsons' monthly payments.
   b. Suppose that after 15 months, the Wilsons win $25,000 in the state lottery. Using the rule of 78s, would their winnings allow them to pay off the loan?
   c. If, instead, the Wilsons could negotiate a 14 percent, 60-month loan *without* add-on interest, how much would each monthly payment be? If the rule of 78s does *not* apply to this new loan, how much principal would remain after 15 months? (Hint: To find the remaining principal without preparing an amortization schedule, compute the present value of the remaining 45 payments.) Compare your answers to those in parts a and b.
   d. If the rule of 78s *does* apply to the loan in part c, how much would the Wilsons owe after 15 months? Based on your comparisons, does the rule of 78s or the add-on interest provision make a greater difference in the Wilsons' rate of principal repayment?

3. Jeannie Scott is buying her first car. After extensive negotiations, she has agreed on a price of $12,000. She can afford a $2,000 down payment and will finance the remaining balance over a 48-month period. The bank has offered an add-on rate of 6 percent, which sounds reasonable to Jeannie. The car manufacturer's subsidiary, however, is offering 4-year loans at an annual percentage rate of 6¾ percent. Compare the APRs on the two loans and decide which one Jeannie should accept.

4. Your credit union offers you a 6-year, $10,000 loan with an annual interest rate of 10 percent. The loan has an adjustable rate on which monthly payments are changed to reflect changes in the interest rate. After you make six payments, rates rise and yours is adjusted to 11.5 percent. Prepare an amortization schedule reflecting the required monthly payments for the first 2 years of the loan.

5. First Federal Savings and Loan is offering an 18-month loan with an annual interest rate of 10 percent. The loan has an adjustable rate with fixed payments; the loan term is changed to reflect changes in the interest rate. You borrow $8,000, and 6 months later the interest rate on the loan is adjusted to 12 percent.
   a. Prepare an amortization schedule that reflects the change in the loan term. The new interest rate goes into effect with the seventh payment.
   b. Suppose, instead, that the loan rate falls to 8 percent after 6 months. Prepare a new amortization schedule.

6. You have found a nice starter home for $75,000. You plan to borrow $60,000 from your credit union at a 10.5 percent interest rate. The CU offers a choice of a standard, 30-year, fixed-rate loan or a 15-year, fixed-rate, quick-pay loan.
   a. Calculate the monthly payments under each loan.
   b. How much total interest do you pay under each loan?
   c. Assuming that you can comfortably meet either monthly payment, which loan would you choose? Why?

7. Suppose that the $60,000 mortgage in Problem 6 is a 30-year adjustable-rate mortgage on which the interest rate can change every 6 months but on which the payment cannot change for 1 year. After six months, the interest rate rises to 13 percent. Prepare an amortization schedule for the first year of the loan. What feature of ARMs is illustrated by this mortgage?

8. Jerry Olson is negotiating a $100,000 mortgage loan. He is offered a price–level–adjusted mortgage. The loan has an initial maturity of 25 years, and the real rate is estimated to be 4.0 percent. Assume that during the first year, inflation is 8 percent. Calculate the principal balance for Jerry's loan at the beginning of year 2.

SELECTED REFERENCES

Aguilar, Linda. "Still Toe-to-Toe: Banks and Nonbanks at the End of the 80s." *Economic Perspectives* (Federal Reserve Bank of Chicago) 14 (January/February 1990): 12–23.

Albaum, Gerald, and George Kaufman. "The Variable Rate Residential Mortgage: Implications for Borrowers." In *Alternative Mortgage Instruments Research Study,* Volume I. Washington, DC: Federal Home Loan Bank Board, November 1977.

Alexander, Walter. "What's the Score?" *ABA Banking Journal* 81 (August 1989): 58–63.

Altman, Edward I., et al. *Application of Classification Techniques in Business, Banking, and Finance.* Greenwich, CT: JAI Press, 1981.

Avery, Robert B., et al. "Survey of Consumer Finances, 1983: A Second Report." *Federal Reserve Bulletin* 70 (December 1984): 857–868.

Avery, Robert B., Gregory E. Elliehausen, and Arthur B. Kennickell. "Changes in Consumer Installment Debt: Evidence from the 1983 and 1986 Surveys of Consumer Finances." *Federal Reserve Bulletin* 73 (October 1987): 761–778.

Boehm, Thomas P., and Joseph McKenzie. "The Affordability of Alternative Mortgage Instruments: A Household Analysis." *Housing Finance Review* 2 (October 1983): 287–294.

Buckley, Robert M., and Kevin Villani. "Problems with the Adjustable-Rate Mortgage Regulations." *Housing Finance Review* 2 (July 1983): 183–190.

Buying a Home in the 1980s: A Poll of American Attitudes. Washington, DC: Federal National Mortgage Association, September 14, 1982.

Calem, Paul S. "The Strange Behavior of the Credit Card Market." *Business Review* (Federal Reserve Bank of Philadelphia) (January–February 1992): 3–14.

Campbell, Tim S., and J. Kimball Dietrich. "Determinants of Default on Insured Conventional Residential Mortgage Loans." *Journal of Finance* 38 (December 1983): 1569–1581.

Canner, Glenn B. "Changes in Consumer Holding and Use of Credit Cards." *Journal of Retail Banking* 10 (Spring 1988): 13–24.

Canner, Glenn B., Thomas A. Durkin, and Charles A. Luckett. "Recent Developments in the Home Equity Loan Market." *Journal of Retail Banking* 11 (Summer 1989): 35–47.

Canner, Glenn B., and James T. Fergus. "Home Equity Lines of Credit—How Well Do They Fit the Needs of Consumers and Creditors?'' *Journal of Retail Banking* 10 (Summer 1988): 19–32.

Canner, Glenn B., James T. Fergus, and Charles A. Luckett. "Home Equity Lines of Credit." *Federal Reserve Bulletin* 74 (June 1988): 361–373.

Canner, Glenn B., and Charles A. Luckett. "Home Equity Lending." *Federal Reserve Bulletin* 75 (May 1989): 333–344.

———. "Payment of Household Debts." *Federal Reserve Bulletin* 77 (April 1991): 218–229.

———. "Developments in the Pricing of Credit Card Services." *Federal Reserve Bulletin* 78 (September 1992): 652–666.

Canner, Glenn B., and Delores S. Smith. "Expanded HMDA Data on Residential Lending: One Year Later." *Federal Reserve Bulletin* 78 (November 1992): 801–824.

Capon, Noel. "Credit Scoring Systems: A Critical Analysis." *Journal of Marketing* 46 (Spring 1982): 82–91.

Carroll, David. "Benchmark Pricing Enhances ARM Design." *Savings Institutions* 110 (February 1989): 69–74.

Carron, Andrew S., and R. Dan Brumbaugh, Jr. "The Future of Thrifts in the Mortgage Market." In *Proceedings of a Conference on Bank Structure and Competition,* 385–395. Chicago: Federal Reserve Bank of Chicago, 1989.

Carter, Charlie. "The Surge in Bankruptcies: Is the New Law Responsible?" *Economic Review* (Federal Reserve Bank of Atlanta) 67 (January 1982): 20–30.

Chatz, James A., and Brooke Schumm II. "Bankruptcy Changes Bode Well for Banks." *ABA Banking Journal* 76 (September 1984): 85–90.

Chen, Alexander. "Alternative Reverse Mortgages: A Simulation Analysis of Initial Benefits in Baltimore." *Housing Finance Review* 2 (October 1983): 295–308.

Colton, Kent W., Donald R. Lessard, David Modest, and Arthur P. Solomon. "National Survey of Borrowers' Housing Characteristics, Attitudes, and Preferences." In *Alternative Mortgage Instruments Research Study,* Volume I. Washington, DC: Federal Home Loan Bank Board, November 1977.

"Conference Report on H.R. 1278, Financial Institutions Reform, Recovery, and Enforcement Act, 1989." *Congressional Record—House of Representatives,* August 4, 1989.

Crawford, Peggy, and Charles P. Harper. "The Effect of the

AML Index on the Borrower." *Housing Finance Review* 2 (October 1983): 309–320.

DeMong, Richard F., and John H. Lindgren, Jr. "Home Equity Lending in 1988: Market Trends and Analysis." *Journal of Retail Banking* 11 (Fall 1989): 23–34.

Edmister, Robert O. "Combining Human Credit Analysis and Numerical Credit Scoring for Business Failure Prediction." *Akron Business and Economic Review* 19 (Fall 1988): 6–14.

Elliehausen, Gregory E., and John D. Wolken. "Banking Markets and the Use of Financial Services by Households." *Federal Reserve Bulletin* 78 (March 1992) 169–181.

Erdevig, Eleanor R. "Small States Teach a Big Banking Lesson." *Chicago Fed Letter,* June 1988.

Erdevig, Eleanor, and George Kaufman. "Improving Housing Finance in an Inflationary Environment: Alternative Residential Mortgage Instruments." *Economic Perspectives* (Federal Reserve Bank of Chicago) 5 (July/August 1981): 3–23.

Eugeni, Francesca. "Consumer Debt and Home Equity Borrowing." *Economic Perspectives* (Federal Reserve Bank of Chicago) 17 (March/April 1993): 2–14.

Fahey, Noel. "Consumers and Lenders Blend Needs to Shape Sound ARMs." *Savings Institutions* 106 (August 1985): 49–55.

Furstenberg, George von, and R. Jeffrey Green. "Estimation of Delinquency Risk for Home Mortgage Portfolios." *AREUEA Journal* 2 (Fall 1974): 101–112.

Gabriel, Stuart A. "Housing and Mortgage Markets: The Post-1982 Expansion." *Federal Reserve Bulletin* 73 (December 1987): 893–903.

Gardner, Mona J., and Dixie L. Mills. "Evaluating the Likelihood of Default on Delinquent Loans." *Financial Management* 18 (Winter 1989): 55–63.

Gatty, Bob. "Failings of Our Bankruptcy Law." *Nation's Business* 70 (May 1982): 44–46.

Goodman, John L., Jr., and Charles A. Luckett. "Adjustable Rate Financing in Mortgage and Consumer Credit Markets." *Federal Reserve Bulletin* 71 (November 1985): 823–835.

Guttentag, Jack. "Solving the Mortgage Menu Problem." *Housing Finance Review* 3 (July 1983): 227–252.

Herzog, John P., and James B. Earley. *Home Mortgage Delinquency and Foreclosures.* New York: National Bureau of Economics and Research, 1970.

Johnson, Robert W. "The Consumer Banking Problem: Causes and Cures." *Journal of Retail Banking* 11 (Winter 1989): 39–44.

Johnson, Robert W., and A. Charlene Sullivan. "Segmentation of the Consumer Loan Market." *Journal of Retail Banking* 3 (September 1981): 1–7.

Kerr, Donald E., and Seamus McMahon. "Competing in the Maturing Bankcard Industry." *The Bankers Magazine* 171 (September–October 1988): 25–28.

Kramer, Susan. "An Analysis of the Rule of 78s." *Journal of Retail Banking* 3 (September 1981): 46–55.

Kramer, Susan B., and Glenn B. Canner. "The Current Status of Usury Legislation in the United States." *Issues in Bank Regulation* 6 (Summer 1982): 11–23.

Lea, Michael. "ARM Pricing Reflects Cap and Discount Costs." *Savings Institutions* 106 (February 1985): 60–65.

Leeds, Eva Marikova. "Interest Rate Risk with Price-Level Adjusted Mortgages." *Housing Finance Review* 8 (1989): 107–116.

Lobell, Carl D., and Howard J. Finkelstein. "Bank Interest Rate Ceilings: 'Borrowing,' 'Exporting,' and 'Importing' Rates." *Journal of Retail Banking* 6 (Winter 1984): 45–49.

Luckett, Charles A. "Personal Bankruptcies." *Federal Reserve Bulletin* 74 (September 1988): 591–603.

Luckett, Charles A., and James D. August. "The Growth of Consumer Debt." *Federal Reserve Bulletin* 71 (June 1985): 389–402.

Mills, Dixie L., and Mona J. Gardner. "Consumer Response to Adjustable Rate Mortgages: Implications of the Evidence from Illinois and Wisconsin." *Journal of Consumer Affairs* (Summer 1986): 77–105.

Nothaft, Frank E., and George H. K. Wang. "Determinants of ARM Share of National and Regional Lending." *Journal of Real Estate Finance and Economics* 5 (June 1992): 219–234.

Obrinsky, Mark. "Young, First-Time Home Buyers Face Financial Hurdles." *Savings Institutions* 109 (November 1988): 32–33.

Pavel, Christine, and Paula Binkley. "Costs and Competition in Bank Credit Cards." *Economic Perspectives* (Federal Reserve Bank of Chicago) 11 (March/April 1987): 3–13.

Pearce, Douglas K. "Rising Household Debt in Perspective." *Economic Review* (Federal Reserve Bank of Kansas City) 70 (July/August 1985): 3–17.

Peek, Joe. "A Call to ARMs: Adjustable Rate Mortgages in the 1980s." *New England Economic Review* (Federal Reserve Bank of Boston) (March/April 1990): 47–61.

Peek, Joe, and James A. Wilcox. "A Real Affordable Mortgage." *New England Economic Review* (Federal Reserve Bank of Boston) (January/February 1991): 51–66.

Peterson, Richard L. "Usury Laws and Consumer Credit: A Note." *Journal of Finance* 33 (September 1983): 1299–1304.

Peterson, Richard L., and Kiyomi Aoki. "Bankruptcy Filings before and after Implementation of the Bankruptcy Reform Act." *Journal of Economics and Business* 36 (February 1984): 95–105.

Peterson, Richard L., and Dan A. Black. "Consumer Credit Shopping." *Journal of Retail Banking* 4 (Fall 1982): 50–61.

Peterson, Richard L., and Margaret Woo. "Bankrupt Debtors: Who Can Repay?" *Journal of Retail Banking* 6 (Fall 1984): 42–51.

Price, Joan. "Consumer Lending in the 1990s Faces Pluses and Pitfalls." *Savings Institutions* 110 (July/August 1989): 36–39.

Priess, Beth. "The Garn-St Germain Act and Due-on-Sale-Clause Enforcement." *Housing Finance Review* 2 (October 1983): 369–377.

"Reform Strengthens Creditors' Rights." *Credit Union Magazine* 50 (September 1984): 10–16.

Reichenstein, William R., and Frank J. Bonello. "Usury Laws: Today and Tomorrow." *Issues in Bank Regulation* 7 (Winter 1984): 25–31.

Rogers, Paul R. "Inflation-Proof Mortgage Designs: It's Time to Get Real." In *Financial Services Yearbook,* Vol. 2, 1–96. Berkeley: University of California Press, 1989.

Russell, Thomas. *The Economics of Bank Credit Cards.* New York: Praeger Publishers, 1975.

Shuchman, Philip, and Thomas L. Rhorer. "Personal Bankruptcy Data for Opt-Out Hearings and Other Purposes." *American Bankruptcy Law Journal* 56 (Winter 1982): 1–28.

Smith, Dolores S. "Revision of the Board's Equal Credit Regulation: An Overview." *Federal Reserve Bulletin* 71 (December 1985): 913–923.

Stahl, David. "The Rising Tide of Bankruptcy." *Savings and Community Banker* 2 (May 1993): 14–20.

Stanley, William J., Jr. "Far from Doomsday, State Usury Relief Really Helps Consumers." *ABA Banking Journal* 75 (April 1983): 75–76.

Vandell, Kerry D. "Default Risk under Alternative Mortgage Instruments." *Journal of Finance* 33 (December 1978): 1279–1296.

Vandenbrink, Donna C. "The Effects of Usury Ceilings." *Economic Perspectives* (Federal Reserve Bank of Chicago) 6 (Midyear 1982): 44–55.

———. "Usury Ceilings and DIDMCA." *Economic Perspectives* (Federal Reserve Bank of Chicago) 9 (September/October 1985): 25–30.

Watro, Paul R. "The Bank Credit-Card Boom: Some Explanations and Consequences." *Economic Commentary* (Federal Reserve Bank of Cleveland), March 1, 1988.

Webb, Bruce. "Borrower Risk under Alternative Mortgage Instruments." *Journal of Finance* 37 (March 1982): 169–183.

Weicher, John C. "FHA Reform: Balancing Public Purpose and Financial Soundness." *Journal of Real Estate Finance and Economics* 5 (June 1992): 133–150.

Wolken, John D., and Frank J. Navratil. "The Economic Impact of the Federal Credit Union Usury Ceiling." *Journal of Finance* 36 (December 1981): 1157–1168.

Yohannes, Arefaine G. "FRM or ARM: Simplifying the Choice." *Real Estate Appraiser* (August 1991): 21–24.

I think the CD will be extinct in the next few years.
Charles Clough,
Chief Investment Strategist, Merrill Lynch & Co. (1992)

———————

Ah, the 1950s—a decade of middle-class prosperity in the United States, and the heyday of the Chevy convertible, the drive-in hamburger stand, the hula hoop, and Elvis Presley, considered the undisputed King of Rock 'n' Roll by the infamous baby boom generation (including the authors). When the King's famous hit "Heartbreak Hotel" was riding high in the charts in 1956, the rate most banks and savings and loan associations (S&Ls) were paying on passbook savings accounts was 3.15 percent, so low a figure that few savers in the 1970s and 1980s (when short-term Treasury bill (T-bill) rates topped 16 percent for a brief time) believed they would ever see it again.

Ah, the 1990s—a decade about as different from the 1950s as one can imagine, with fears of federal budget deficits, unemployment, and a declining standard of living for the middle class frequently in the headlines. City dwellers now fax hamburger orders for subsequent delivery to their offices, and virtual reality video games have replaced the hula hoop. Popular music is so diverse that no single act could possibly claim to be on top. And, as this book is written, rates on passbook accounts at banks and thrifts are . . . *lower than 3.15 percent.*[1]

Say it isn't so, given the massive changes in depository institution management since 1956! Interestingly enough, the passbook rate in the early 1990s was what it was because institutions are now free to pay a rate that moves with the market, whereas in 1956, they were not. The three previous chapters have examined uses of funds in depository institutions, but managers must also make important decisions about sources of funds, many of which are influenced by the availability of federal insurance. In this and the next chapter, those decisions are in the spotlight, beginning with a history lesson about two restrictions on managing the deposit-taking function: 1) the prohibition of interest on demand deposits; and 2) Regulation Q (Reg Q), the Federal Reserve (Fed) rule that for half a century determined the maximum interest rates that could be paid on deposits.

Because regulation breeds innovation by the regulated (remember the regulatory dialectic introduced in Chapter 2?), these restrictions led

CHAPTER

16

DEPOSIT AND

LIABILITY

MANAGEMENT

———————

[1] Mike Dorning, "3.15% Passbook Rate a 'Heartbreak' for Depositors," *Chicago Tribune,* November 11, 1991, 1, 10.

to responses from depository institutions that shape the environment of today: liability management, noninterest competition, and new deposit instruments. These innovations, in turn, have led to concern about institutional safety and soundness under deregulated deposit and liability structures and to questions about the current and future roles of federal deposit insurance.

INTEREST RATE RESTRICTIONS: A HISTORY

The number of bank runs in the early 1930s convinced the federal government that the financial system would best be served by a federal deposit insurance program.[2] After January 1, 1934, banks could advertise their membership in the Federal Deposit Insurance Corporation (FDIC) by paying a set percentage, originally ½ of 1 percent of *total* deposits, as an annual fee to the FDIC. Thus, most FDIC financing was initially provided by large institutions, whose managers objected because a substantial portion of their banks' deposits exceeded the initial insurance limit of $2,500 per account. To obtain large banks' support of the FDIC, and because some politicians believed paying interest on demand deposits drained funds from rural areas to cities where rates were higher, the Banking Act of 1933 (the Glass-Steagall Act [G-S]) prohibited that practice. Because banks were the only financial institutions permitted to offer demand deposits, they enjoyed lower interest costs without losing checking account customers.[3]

Congress believed that competition among commercial banks should be limited in exchange for the benefits of federal deposit insurance, so G-S also gave the Fed authority to control maximum interest rates on time and savings deposits at national banks. Similar authority was granted to the FDIC over nonmember commercial banks in the Banking Act of 1935. In 1966, at the urging of the thrift industry, the FDIC and the Federal Home Loan Bank Board (FHLBB) were instructed to control deposit interest rates at thrifts as part of the Interest Rate Adjustment Act. Congress required all regulators to coordinate their efforts. As a result, Reg Q, although technically a Fed policy, became a generic term for all regulations on deposit rate ceilings.

REG Q AND MARKET RATES: THE EARLY YEARS

Figure 16.1 traces the history of deposit interest rates from 1927 to 1986, when Reg Q ended. The top panel shows that from 1933 until 1954, the Reg Q ceiling rate on time and savings deposits was well above yields on 3-month T-bills. Thus, risk-averse depositors were unlikely to find other short-term investments more attractive. Because all banks faced the same rate ceilings, price competition was virtually nonexistent. Banks tended to focus on nonprice factors, such as customer service. Thrifts could, and usually did, offer higher rates on savings deposits than did banks, but they were prohibited from offering transactions accounts and nonmortgage loans. Thus, banks were able to obtain customers by requiring them to maintain deposit accounts to receive the services they desired.

As market rates rose, regulators gradually increased Reg Q ceilings so that by 1962 they were again above prevailing market yields. Shortly thereafter, Congress sought to encourage home ownership by extending interest rate ceilings to thrifts, presumably permitting them to offer lower mortgage rates. To prevent banks from competing with thrifts, slightly higher ceilings (¼ percent to ½ percent) were permitted for thrifts. The ceiling structure also became more complicated after 1965, with separate ceilings for different types and sizes of deposits.[4]

THE LATER YEARS

The extension of Reg Q to thrifts coincided with other important economic and political events, such as escalated spending for domestic social programs and increased involvement in the Vietnam War. These developments led to greater government borrowing, which accelerated expectations of inflation and drove market rates higher. The relationship between market yields and the Reg Q ceiling on passbook savings deposits from 1955 to 1986 is depicted at the bottom of Figure 16.1. After 1966, the ceiling seldom equaled, much less exceeded, yields on T-bills.

Figure 16.2 plots T-bill yields along with average yields on bank and thrift deposits from 1965 until 1989. The deposit yields are averages and thus do not

---

[2] As noted in earlier chapters, some experts have concluded that bank failures during 1929–1933 were so atypical that it is inappropriate to base public policy on that period. Nevertheless, those years have been the predominant influence on depository institution regulation for more than 60 years. See George J. Benston and George G. Kaufman, "Risks and Failures in Banking: Overview, History, and Evaluation," Staff Memorandum 86-1, Federal Reserve Bank of Chicago, 1986.

[3] Analyses of the reasons for and effects of interest rate restrictions are given in Benston 1984 and Higgins 1977. (References are listed in full at the end of this chapter.)

[4] For more details on the history of Reg Q, see Winningham and Hagan 1980 and Gilbert 1986.

FIGURE 16.1 **Regulation Q and Market Interest Rates**

In the early years of Reg Q, the ceiling on deposit rates was consistently higher than market interest rates. After 1957, however, market rates frequently exceeded Reg Q ceilings, resulting in disintermediation or cross-intermediation.

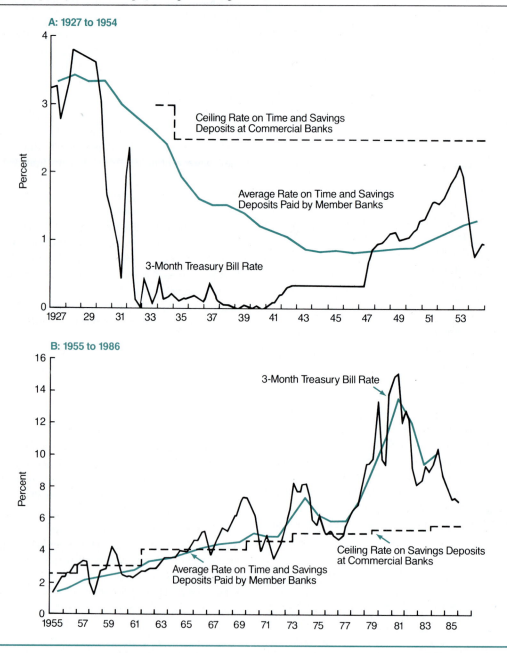

Source: R. Alton Gilbert, "Requiem for Regulation Q: What It Did and Why It Passed Away," *Review* (Federal Reserve Bank of St. Louis) 68 (February 1986): 25, 29.

FIGURE 16.2 **Three-month T-bill versus Deposit Yields**

Between 1965 and 1980, T-bill yields frequently exceeded average yields available at depositories. Disintermediation occurred, causing regulators and legislators to study the problem and to experiment with solutions. After the Depository Institutions Deregulation and Monetary Control Act, depositories offered more competitive rates, and thrifts consistently offered higher yields than banks.

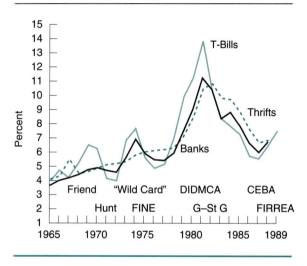

Source: Average yield data are from various issues of U.S. League of Savings and Loans, *Savings and Loan Fact Book;* U.S. League of Savings Institutions, *Savings Institutions Source Book;* and Board of Governors of the Federal Reserve System, *Federal Reserve Bulletin.*

coincide with the ceiling on any one instrument. In the periods 1965–1966, 1968–1970, 1973–1974, and 1979–1981, risk-averse depositors could have earned more by investing in T-bills than by holding deposits at banks and thrifts. Credit unions (CUs) enjoyed higher Reg Q ceilings than other depositories—a 6 percent limit on regular share account dividends at federal CUs, increased to 7 percent in 1973. The common-bond requirement was presumed to prevent adverse competition within the industry and with other depositories, and the CU goal of providing low loan rates to members was thought to inhibit the payment of excessively high rates on shares. Still, even this higher ceiling was not competitive with market rates as the 1970s progressed.

DEPOSITORS RESPOND. These facts did not go unnoticed by depositors, regulators, or politicians. During each of the periods in which T-bill rates exceeded deposit yields, banks and thrifts experienced disintermediation, cross-intermediation, or both. As discussed in Chapter 2, disintermediation is the switch by investors from indirect investment via intermediaries to direct investment in money and capital market instruments. Cross-intermediation occurs when investors switch from one financial institution to another. When either occurs, banks and thrifts can have liquidity problems if they are unable to convert their assets to cash or to attract enough new funds to pay off departing depositors. At these times, regulators and legislators are reminded that regulations have both intended and unintended consequences.

The authorities sought to counteract the unintended consequences of Reg Q through a series of actions ultimately leading to its elimination. These actions are noted in Figure 16.2. For example, in 1965–1966 and 1968–1970, disintermediation hit all depositories, and none appeared to gain or lose at the others' expense. Furthermore, housing starts declined by more than 25 percent in each period, events that were blamed on the unavailability of funds at thrifts. The official response to these problems was to appoint national commissions to study, among other things, the effect of Reg Q. One was the Friend Study on the S&L industry, and the other was the Commission on Financial Structure and Regulation, also known as the Hunt Commission. The Hunt Commission recommended that Reg Q be eliminated but that the prohibition of interest on demand deposits be retained.[5] By the time each study was made public, market yields were below Reg Q ceilings, and the need to remove it seemed less pressing.

NEW FINANCIAL INSTRUMENTS. The 1973–1974 period, which began with disintermediation and ended with cross-intermediation, too, elicited a different response. In 1973, federal regulators permitted banks and thrifts to offer "Wild Card" certificates—4-year, $1,000-minimum certificates of deposit (CDs) with no rate ceilings. The experiment lasted only 4 months, because commercial banks immediately offered rates that

[5]The report of the Hunt Commission, in particular, is one of the most important on the financial system before 1980. For more details, see Luttrell 1972.

were higher than thrifts, which were locked into fixed-rate mortgages, could offer.[6]

Elimination of the "Wild Card" did not prevent the outflow of funds from thrifts, however, because of the concurrent development of money market mutual funds (MMMFs). As noted in earlier chapters, MMMFs are nondepository financial intermediaries that invest their shareholders' funds in money market instruments. With no regulatory ceilings on returns to their shareholders, MMMFs have been able to offer yields that consistently match or exceed those on short-term Treasury securities and have provided substantial competition for savings.[7]

ARRIVAL OF INTEREST-BEARING CHECKING. The interest-bearing transactions account also arose during this period. Led by savings banks in Massachusetts, the negotiable order of withdrawal (NOW) account was introduced in 1972. To distinguish these accounts from demand deposits, institutions offering NOWs held to the technicality that they could refuse to honor transactions for 14 days, although few did so. NOWs quickly proved to be popular in New England, but Congress was reluctant to allow them nationwide and passed a law in 1976 restricting NOWs to banks and thrifts in New England, New York, and New Jersey.

THE FINAL CHAPTERS

The tradition of a national commission on the problem of disintermediation continued with the Financial Institutions and the Nation's Economy (FINE) report, submitted to a Congressional committee in 1975.[8] It recommended that Reg Q be eliminated and that interest be paid on demand deposits. Also in keeping with tradition, Congress took no action because market yields fell below Reg Q ceilings soon after the report. In 1978, however, interest rates began to climb,

fueled by unprecedented inflation. For once, disintermediation did not go away, and market yields remained above their pre-1978 level until 1985.

SHARE DRAFTS. In 1978, federal regulators took two significant actions. The National Credit Union Administration (NCUA) authorized CUs to offer share drafts nationwide. Although experimental use of share drafts by some CUs had been permitted since 1974, the 1978 rule was the first allowing an entire class of depositories to have interest-bearing checking. A federal judge later ruled that regulators had exceeded their bounds because only Congress had the authority to permit interest on transactions accounts. As noted in Chapter 12, however, the popularity of share drafts was enormous, leading to a national letter-writing campaign by CU members to retain them. Congress responded by including permanent authority for share drafts *and* NOW accounts in the Depository Institutions Deregulation and Monetary Control Act (DIDMCA).

THE MONEY MARKET CERTIFICATE. In 1978, federal regulators also created the money market certificate (MMC), called the money market share certificate at CUs. The MMC was a 6-month, $10,000-minimum CD with a rate ceiling tied to the 6-month T-bill rate. The floating ceiling, with a ¼ percentage advantage given to thrifts and CUs over commercial banks was designed to stem disintermediation while protecting thrifts from a recurrence of the "Wild Card" experience.[9] The MMC was extremely popular with depositors. But again, the regulations creating it had unintended consequences. The short maturity and floating ceiling of the MMC greatly increased the cost of funds for depositories. Thrifts, with their long-term, fixed-rate mortgage portfolios, were hit especially hard. As discussed in Chapter 12, the collision of short-term, market-rate sources of funds and long-term, fixed-rate uses of funds set in motion by the introduction of the MMC produced severe earnings problems for thrifts. Some observers argue, in fact, that the MMC may have been the beginning of the end for the thrift industry.

---

[6] For more information and an evaluation of the "Wild Card" experiment, see Kane 1976.

[7] During the 1973–1974 period, MMMF managers invested a substantial portion of their funds in the negotiable CDs of large banks, thus returning some of the cross-intermediated funds to the banking system. Of course large banks benefited more than small banks or thrifts. For more information, see Dunham 1980.

[8] U.S. Congress 1975.

---

[9] Regulations governing the MMC were actually much more complex than this by the time they were fully in place. For further details and an interesting chronology of the deregulation of deposit accounts, see Mahoney et al., 1987, pp. 25–29.

IMPACT OF THE NEW INSTRUMENTS. Even the MMC could not prevent the flow of funds from depository financial institutions. The 6-month maturity of the MMC seemed too long to some depositors, given the rapid increase in market rates through early 1980. MMFs continued to grow, financed by depositors who abandoned their banks, thrifts, and CUs for yields that could increase daily. Thrifts' profitability problems were compounded by liquidity problems resulting from cross-intermediation. By March 1980, Congress concluded that a permanent solution to disintermediation and cross-intermediation was essential, and the phase-out of Reg Q was mandated as part of DIDMCA.

The 6-year phase-out was to ease the way for small banks and thrifts, which argued that they would be unable to compete for deposits in a deregulated environment. Administration of the phase-out was assigned to the **Depository Institutions Deregulation Committee (DIDC),** composed of the heads of six federal regulatory agencies. Because members could not agree on steps for the removal of Reg Q, the committee did little during its first 2 years.

CUs were the only beneficiaries of this arrangement. Although the chairman of the NCUA sat on the DIDC, CU rate ceilings were not under the DIDC's jurisdiction. In 1981, the NCUA increased the maximum rate on share accounts to 12 percent, well above savings rates at banks and thrifts. No ceiling at all was imposed after 1982.

THE MONEY MARKET DEPOSIT ACCOUNT. The promise of Reg Q's elimination did not keep depositors from defecting from banks and thrifts after the passage of DIDMCA. Depositories continued to lose market share to MMMFs, forcing Congressional action to permit a deposit account competitive with MMMFs. In October 1982, the Garn-St Germain Act (G-St G) effectively ended the reign of Reg Q as a factor in depository institutions management by creating the money market deposit account (MMDA). As explained in Chapter 12, the MMDA is a short-term deposit with a variable interest rate on which a limited number of third-party transactions is permitted. G-St G also authorized an account called the **Super NOW,** which was an interest-bearing, unlimited transactions account with a high minimum balance and no interest ceilings.

The effect of the MMDA on depositories was immediate and astounding, as the left panel of Figure 16.3 illustrates. The volume of MMDAs grew from $0 in December 1982 to nearly $400 billion only a few months later. The dollar volume of MMMF shares, labeled MMF in the figure, dropped markedly at the same time. The right panel of the figure shows that the effect of MMDAs was not temporary, as they have continued to dominate MMMFs since their introduction. (Dollar volumes are shown on the right axis of Panel B, whereas the left axis shows the level of short-term interest rates during the period.) Experts believe that the attraction of FDIC or National Credit Union Share Insurance Fund (NCUSIF) insurance explains investors' preference for MMDAs over MMMFs in virtually all interest rate environments, from the historic highs of the 1980s to the unexpected lows of the early 1990s. Note also that both banks and MMMFs have gained at the expense of thrifts since Financial Institutions Reform, Recovery, and Enforcement Act (FIRREA) provisions forcing closure of many of that industry's weakest members.

CURRENT SITUATION

Table 16.1 shows characteristics of deposit accounts, which vary according to maturity, interest rate sensitivity, liquidity, and other features. The relatively simple deposit structure of the 1930s has been transformed into an array of choices, and each institution theoretically can offer as many unique accounts as it has customers. The table does not include Super NOWs, because after April 1, 1986, *regulatory* distinctions between NOWs and Super NOWs disappeared (although some institutions continue to offer preferential account features to NOW depositors with large balances). An ironic footnote to Reg Q history is that the first major change in the passbook rate after complete deregulation was a decrease, from 5½ percent to 5 percent, by Security Pacific National Bank of Los Angeles in August 1986. By 1992, in fact, rates on both MMDAs and savings accounts were less than 3 percent at many depositories, a development that could never have been anticipated when DIDMCA and G-St G were passed only a relatively short time before. One of the few remaining regulatory issues is whether to allow interest on demand deposits, giving businesses access to interest-bearing checking.

FIGURE 16.3   **Money Market Funds versus Various Deposit Accounts**

Until MMDAs were approved, depositories lost funds to other markets, particularly MMMFs. After 1982, deposits flowed back into MMDAs at banks and thrifts.

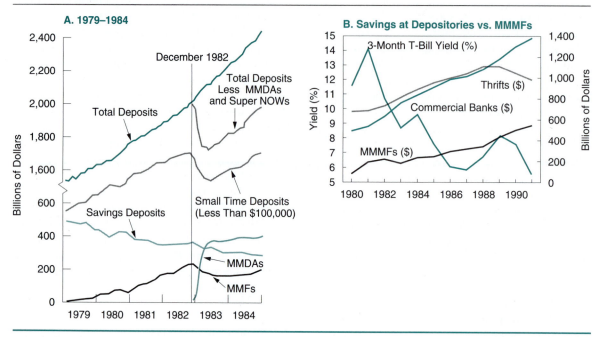

Source: Panel A adapted from Michael C. Keeley and Gary C. Zimmerman, "Competition for Money Market Deposit Accounts," in *Proceedings of a Conference on Bank Structure and Competition* (Chicago: Federal Reserve Bank of Chicago, 1985), 615; Panel B prepared by the authors with data from *Federal Reserve Bulletin* (various issues) and *Flow of Funds,* 1992, Q1.

DEPOSITORS LIKE COMPETITION. What managerial lessons arise from this history of interest rate restrictions? Perhaps one of the most important is that depositors like competition for their business and are willing to switch institutional relationships for a better deal. They also like the safety of deposit insurance and are eager to do business with institutions that offer it. Third, deposit taking is not a passive activity for any depository. Fourth, each deposit category and its relative proportion in an institution's financial structure affect interest and noninterest costs, as well as the expected level and variation in the net interest margin (NIM). The target mix and pricing structure for these accounts are explored later in the chapter.

CHANGE IS PERMANENT. It is also clear that regulators and legislators are willing to alter major policies, so planning for change has become a necessity. Further, management must anticipate the unintended as well as the intended consequences of regulations. As long as managers and investors are creative, they will find a way to circumvent regulatory controls. The dialectic will continue.

LIABILITY MANAGEMENT

As managers of depositories have watched regulators and Congress respond to a changing economy, few have sat idly by awaiting the final removal of competitive restrictions. As early as 1961, in fact, money-center banks began to develop alternatives to traditional deposits. The active search for nondeposit funds to meet liquidity needs, enhance profits, or achieve growth is defined in Chapter 13 as liability management. Although liability management arose primarily because large institutions wished to grow more quickly than traditional strategies allowed, it accelerated in the late 1960s because of constraints imposed

TABLE 16.1   Characteristics of Deposit Accounts

Depository institutions offer accounts with a wide variety of interest rates and other characteristics. Few regulatory restrictions remain.

Account	Minimum Maturity	Interest Rate Characteristics	Reserve Requirements	Special Features
Demand deposits (noninterest negotiable orders of withdrawal at thrifts)	None; payable on demand of the depositor	No explicit interest permitted	3% on first ≈ $46.8 million total of demand deposits and NOW accounts; 10% on total thereafter	May not be offered by federal CUs
NOW accounts (share drafts at CUs)	Institution *may* reserve the right to require 7 days' advance notice before withdrawal	Fixed or variable; no restrictions at banks and thrifts[a]	Same as demand deposits	Unlimited number of transactions; may not be offered to businesses
Money market deposit accounts (MMDAs)	Institution *must* reserve the right to require 7 days' advance notice before withdrawal	Fixed or variable; no restrictions	None	Preauthorized transfers to and from account limited to 6 per month, including 3 by check; unlimited in-person, mail, or automatic teller transactions
Passbook savings (savings shares at CUs)	Same as MMDAs	Same as MMDAs	Same as MMDAs	No check-writing privileges
Non-negotiable certificates of deposit, or share certificates at CUs	7 days	Same as MMDAs	Same as MMDAs	Forfeiture penalties imposed on withdrawals within the first 6 days; additional penalties may be imposed on nonpersonal accounts with original maturities of 18 months or more
Individual retirement accounts (IRAs)	Depends on type of plan; MMDA-type plan has no legal minimum; CD-type plan has minimum based on maturity	Depends on plan selected	None	Depositors with income below specified levels may make tax-deferred additions to these accounts up to a maximum of $2,000 per year per individual; interest earned on accounts is tax-deferred, regardless of depositor income; penalties for withdrawal before age 59½
Negotiable CDs (Jumbos)	7 days	Same as MMDAs	Same as MMDAs	$100,000 minimum denomination; depositor can sell the deposit to a buyer before maturity, price is market-determined; no federal insurance on amount over $100,000

[a] Federal law sets a 6% ceiling for CU interest on deposits, but the NCUA may override it. As of 1992, the NCUA had imposed no interest ceiling for CU deposits.
Source: Prepared by the authors from information in Board of Governors of the Federal Reserve System, "Regulation Q: Interest on Deposits," as amended effective January 1, 1984; "Insured Accounts for Savers," pamphlet, Federal Reserve Bank of Richmond, April 1988; and *Federal Reserve Bulletin,* various issues.

by Regulation Q and the absence of interest-bearing demand deposits. Even without Reg Q, liability management is a vital part of the strategies of many institutions.[10]

HISTORY OF LIABILITY MANAGEMENT

Commercial banks ended World War II with about 75 percent of their assets in cash and T-bills; thus, it took considerable time—in fact, until the late 1950s—for them to run out of assets to liquidate to meet postwar loan demand. By the early 1960s, however, money-center banks needed additional loanable funds. The shortage of funds was exacerbated by improvements in corporate cash management that caused large firms to reduce demand deposit balances to the bare minimum, investing surplus cash in T-bills and commercial paper.

PRECIPITATING EVENTS. As explained in Chapter 5, First National City Bank of New York (now Citibank) developed the negotiable CD in response to changed customer preferences. Although large CDs had been sold by major banks before this time, the key to First National City's success was an agreement by securities dealers to create a secondary market, permitting corporations to invest in the CDs and yet maintain liquidity. The negotiable CD became a tool for keeping current depositors as well as attracting new ones, allowing a bank's loan portfolio to grow. Soon, other nondeposit funds were used for the same purposes. Large banks so actively sought cash in the financial markets, rather than by liquidating assets, that managed liabilities went from 0 percent of new funds at large banks in 1960 to almost 30 percent by 1974. In the 1970s, a few large savings institutions also began to use the technique.

EXPANDED OBJECTIVES. Today liability management serves several purposes. It plays a role in managing the reserve position and in meeting loan demand.[11] It is also used by institutions to balance the maturity and interest rate sensitivity of liabilities with those of the asset portfolio. The first two motivations for liability management, the tools used to achieve them, and the risks and rewards are discussed in this section. Chapters 18 and 19 address further the third use of liability management.

USING LIABILITIES TO COVER RESERVE DEFICIENCIES

One of the motivations for liability management is to maintain liquidity, an issue explored in Chapter 13 from the asset side of the balance sheet. As explained in that chapter, for many years depository institutions looked for liquidity solely in their asset portfolios. But that approach to liquidity management may not coincide with the risk/expected return preference of managers and owners, so institutions have increasingly turned to nontraditional deposits and other liabilities as sources of liquidity.[12] If one categorizes funds as either discretionary or nondiscretionary, nontraditional deposits and other liabilities (along with short-term investment securities) are discretionary items. They can be actively used to adjust a depository's liquidity position.

The main categories of discretionary liabilities are the Fed's discount window and borrowings from other regulators; the Fed funds market; and the issuance of repurchase agreements, large CDs, liabilities collateralized by the institution's assets, and Eurodollar deposits. Borrowing from regulators is ordinarily used only to cover reserve deficiencies and not to expand assets; it is discussed in the sections on reserve position management in Chapter 13. Remaining tools of liability management are discussed in the following paragraphs.[13]   *(Seasonal needs*
emergency.)

FEDERAL FUNDS PURCHASED. Unlike the discount window, regular use of which is discouraged by the Fed, the fed funds market, first discussed in Chapter 5, is used by many depositories, some on a daily basis. Fed funds play a main role in reserve requirement

---

[10]For an early discussion of liability management, see Schweitzer 1974.

[11]See Kane, 1979. Note that these are the same reasons for liquidity identified in Chapter 13.

[12]For more discussion of the choice between asset liquidity and liability liquidity, see McKinney 1980.

[13]The following discussion relies on Stigum 1990; Brewer 1980; and Goodfriend and Whelpley 1986.

management.[14] As early as 1970, more than 60 percent of all member banks were reportedly involved.

Like discount-window borrowings, fed funds are not considered deposits, so no reserves must be held against them. The lending institution instructs the Fed or its correspondent bank to transfer agreed-upon balances to the borrower instantaneously through Fedwire, the Fed's communication system. Because most fed funds transactions are **overnight loans,** the transaction is usually reversed the next day, including 1 day's interest calculated at the fed funds rate. The yield on these transactions was illustrated in Chapter 5.

Because the fed funds rate changes daily, a major problem with fed funds as a regular source of financing is estimating the cost. This problem has escalated since late 1979, when the Federal Reserve Board began placing less emphasis on the fed funds rate as a target of monetary policy. (Recall the discussion in Chapter 3 of the effect of this policy change on financial institutions management.) As seen in Panel A of Figure 16.4 on page 464, fluctuations in the fed funds rate increased after 1979, and fed funds have usually been more expensive than discount-window borrowings, although the spread between the two is not constant. When the differential becomes too great, institutions sometimes try to substitute one source of funds for the other, complicating the Fed's efforts to manage the discount window.

Fed funds are readily available, but the cost is difficult to forecast, as suggested by both panels of Figure 16.4. An institution borrowing fed funds and investing them in assets on which yields do not change daily increases potential variability in its net interest margin. For this reason, a relatively small market exists for **"term" fed funds** transactions, with maturities of 1 week to 6 months, or sometimes even longer.

USING LIABILITIES TO MEET LOAN DEMAND OR PURSUE GROWTH

Institutions can also use liability management to obtain cash when a valued customer has an unplanned need to borrow or when a customer withdraws a large

deposit unexpectedly. Customers who might disintermediate may be persuaded not to if the institution can offer an attractive alternative. An institution can also bid aggressively for funds in the financial markets to expand its size and customer base, even when disintermediation of existing customers is not a problem. The characteristics of discount-window borrowing and fed funds make them inappropriate for these purposes, so alternative ways of raising funds have been developed.

NEGOTIABLE CERTIFICATES OF DEPOSIT. Negotiable CDs, called **jumbos** by thrifts, are large-denomination ($100,000 or greater) time deposits with a minimum maturity of 7 days, for which there is a secondary market. They can be marketed aggressively when an institution needs cash. As noted, when first created, they helped stem the flow of corporate deposits from large banks and enabled the banks to meet new loan demand. But after the mid-1960s, because Reg Q ceilings were below market rates more often than not, negotiable CDs were not competitive with T-bills, and the loss of these deposits contributed to disintermediation at money-center banks. In a move sympathetic to large institutions, the Fed temporarily suspended ceilings on negotiable CDs in 1970 and finally removed them altogether in 1973. Thus, for many years, they have been a tool for aggressive liability managers.

Most negotiable CDs are issued directly to customers, although some large institutions issue them to dealers, who then sell them to other investors. Dealer participation allows institutions to obtain funds with fewer delays. The high face value of the CDs means that the portion in excess of $100,000 is not federally insured. Consequently, institutions in financial difficulty find that this source of funds may increase in cost or even evaporate, a particular problem if CDs are habitually used to fund reserve deficiencies or are invested in long-term loans to customers.

Continental Illinois, in 1984 among the ten largest banks in the country, serves as an extreme example. In the spring of that year, the bank's financial problems surfaced as a result of large loan losses. Large CDs were almost 75 percent of its deposits worldwide, and depositors reacted quickly by withdrawing large volumes of these uninsured deposits. Only an unprecedented pledge by the FDIC to guarantee all deposits, regardless of size, stemmed the outflow. Continental was able to meet its daily liquidity requirements only through loans from the Fed and other large commercial

[14]Research on reserve position management has suggested that managers are risk-averse and borrow fed funds early in a maintenance period to avoid emergency borrowing at the end. Thus, excess supplies may be accumulated by the end of a period, and the funds rate may be lower than at earlier points. For a review of this literature, see Wood and Wood 1985, Chapter 9.

FIGURE 16.4   **The Federal Funds Rate versus the Discount Rate, 1930–1992**

The fed funds rate is usually higher than the Federal Reserve discount rate, although the spread fluctuates. The fed funds rate became more volatile after 1979, increasing the complexity and riskiness of liability management.

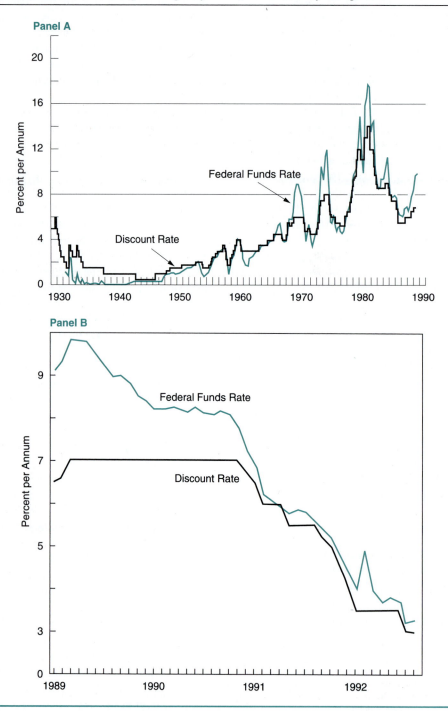

Source: Board of Governors of the Federal Reserve System, *1989 Historical Chart Book,* 98; *Federal Reserve Bulletin,* various issues.

banks. Although this experience is the exception, not the rule, it demonstrates that acquisition of liquidity or the pursuit of growth through liability management is riskier than storing liquidity in the asset portfolio or tailoring growth to traditional deposit flows.

In the 1990s, large corporate customers have been especially vigilant in their decisions about whether to purchase negotiable CDs from banks with high loan losses or weak capital positions, and some money-center banks have had to pay interest costs as much as a full percentage point higher than their stronger competitors. The Federal Deposit Insurance Corporation Improvement Act (FDICIA) provisions mandating regulators to take prompt corrective action if a bank appears weak and to avoid following the severely criticized "too big to fail" policies of the 1980s leads many observers (including customers) to predict that some large banks may, in fact, be forced to close in the 1990s, potentially leaving uninsured deposits unprotected, unlike the Continental case. Thus, savvy corporate treasurers are sure to avoid the negotiable CDs of banks they believe are at risk.[15]

EURODOLLAR DEPOSITS. Eurodollar deposits (**Eurodeposits**) are time deposits denominated in dollars but held in banks outside the United States, including foreign branches of U.S. banks. Eurodeposits are created in several ways, but the most straightforward is when a domestic customer transfers funds on deposit in the United States to a foreign bank or branch. The motivation is usually to obtain a higher rate of interest, and the depositor faces no currency exchange risk because the deposits remain in dollars. For many years, in fact, Eurodeposits were the only time deposits on which Reg Q ceilings were not binding, because they did not apply to funds held outside the United States. Therefore, when Reg Q became binding at home, domestic banks encouraged their customers to transfer funds to foreign branches where they could pay a competitive rate to prevent disintermediation.

Eurodeposits become a source of funds to domestic institutions when they borrow from foreign banks or branches, creating a liability reported on the domestic bank's balance sheet as "Due to Foreign Banks or Branches." Eurodeposits may range in maturity from as short as overnight to as long as 5 years, but most have maturities of 6 months or less. They are non-negotiable, and all funds obtained through Eurodeposits are not currently subject to Fed reserve requirements.[16]

HOW EURODOLLAR DEPOSITS ARE CREATED. Figure 16.5 traces the creation of a typical Eurodeposit. If a large corporation such as General Motors (GM) wishes to withdraw funds from its domestic demand deposit account to earn interest, it may notify one of its New York banks—Citibank, for example. To avoid losing the funds, Citibank can encourage GM to make a Eurodollar deposit at a London branch, where the going rate of interest may be higher than on deposits of similar maturity in the United States (Panels A, B, and D). Citibank's London branch will then deposit the funds received in an account at its parent bank in New York (Panel C). The New York branch now has a "due to" liability on its books, and the London branch has a "due from" asset. By tradition, all transactions are carried out electronically over the **Clearing House Interbank Payments System (CHIPS),** a privately owned funds transfer system in New York. GM keeps $10 million on deposit with Citibank (Panel A) and earns a competitive rate of return. Citibank not only retains the deposit but gains loanable funds, because there are no reserve requirements on "due to" liabilities.

Citibank could use the same approach to obtain GM's business from a competing bank. If GM had demand deposits in Chemical Bank, for example, Citibank might offer to pay a relatively high rate of return on Eurodollar deposits in its London branch. If GM withdrew its funds from Chemical to hold a Eurodeposit in Citibank's London office, the London branch would again show a "due from" asset in the amount of the deposit, while Citibank New York would show a "due to" liability.

An important point about both examples is that *at no time does a Eurodeposit actually leave the home*

[15] See Willemse 1986; Furlong 1984; Jeff Bailey and G. Christian Hill, "Continental Illinois Gets Full U.S. Support," *The Wall Street Journal,* May 18, 1984, 3; Larry Light et al., "Taking from Weak Banks and Giving to the Rich," *Business Week,* February 4, 1991, 76–77; and Wall 1993.

[16] As noted in Chapter 5, there are also *negotiable* Eurodollar CDs, for which there is a secondary market centered in London. This market is relatively small, however, and few institutions are able to raise funds by issuing them. Non-negotiable Eurodeposits, the subject of the current discussion, are much more common sources of funds to U.S. banks.

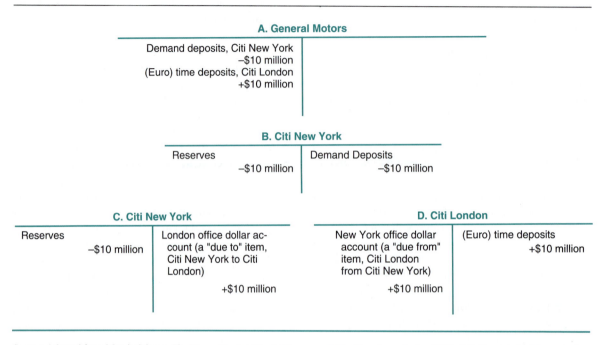

FIGURE 16.5 **Creation of a Eurodollar Deposit**

A Eurodollar deposit is created as a customer moves an account from a U.S. bank to a dollar-denominated deposit in a foreign branch of the bank. The bank exchanges a deposit account for a "due to" liability to its foreign branch. Required reserves are not affected.

A. General Motors

Demand deposits, Citi New York
−$10 million
(Euro) time deposits, Citi London
+$10 million

B. Citi New York

Reserves	Demand Deposits
−$10 million	−$10 million

C. Citi New York

Reserves	London office dollar account (a "due to" item, Citi New York to Citi London)
−$10 million	+$10 million

D. Citi London

New York office dollar account (a "due from" item, Citi London from Citi New York)	(Euro) time deposits
+$10 million	+$10 million

Source: Adapted from Marcia Stigum, *The Money Market,* 3d ed. (Homewood, Ill.; Dow Jones-Irwin, 1990), 201. Reprinted with permission.

country. Funds that start out in the United States end up there as well. Eurodeposits are really nothing more than a series of accounting entries, resulting in the customer's holding a time deposit and the domestic bank's incurring a liability.

COST OF EURODEPOSITS. The costs of Eurodollar liabilities and alternative sources of funds are very closely related. For example, overnight Eurodollars often (but not always) cost slightly more than fed funds. A larger difference exists between 3-month Eurodollar deposits and domestic CDs with similar maturities. Because most Eurodeposits are held by U.S. investors, a premium is demanded as protection against the lack of deposit insurance and against country risk, or potential loss caused by unanticipated problems in a foreign country. A depository must weigh the additional costs of Eurodollars against the benefits, such as the potential for growth, the absence of reserve requirements, and the fact that no deposit insurance premiums are paid on them.[17]

REPURCHASE AGREEMENTS. Repurchase agreements (repos), explained and illustrated in Chapter 5, are another tool of liability management. Repos are the "sale" of marketable securities by an institution, with an agreement to repurchase at a specified future date. The seller obtains use of cash for other purposes. Buyers are seeking liquid, short-term investments as an alternative to nonearning demand deposits; they consider the transactions "reverse repos."

---

[17] It is difficult to assess the riskiness of Eurodeposits versus domestic deposits accurately. The elements of risk previously discussed are given from the viewpoint of an American deposit holder. An Iranian, in contrast, might consider Eurodeposits less risky than dollar-denominated deposits in a bank in the United States. For more discussion of the problems involved in evaluating Eurodollar risk, see Goodfriend 1986.

The depository institution secures the funds obtained by pledging some of its own investment securities as collateral. As long as securities pledged against repos are U.S. government or government agency securities, repos are not subject to reserve requirements. The cost of issuing repos is ordinarily lower than the rate paid on similar maturities in the fed funds or negotiable CD markets. Because repos are backed by high-quality securities, default risk is lower. If the investor insists that the institution transfer the collateral elsewhere for safe-keeping, the rate paid on the repo may be even lower, because of the increased cost to the depository and lower risk to the investor.

Repo maturities range from overnight to 30 days or longer. Transactions can occur between institutions and individuals, in which case they are called "retail repos," or between financial institutions. Because they involve collateral, they are not considered deposits and are therefore ineligible for deposit insurance. This further lowers the cost to the institution issuing them.

MORTGAGE-BACKED SECURITIES.[18] The growth of the repo market in recent years has encouraged depository institutions to envision other ways to use existing assets as collateral to obtain new funds. For mortgage lenders, using mortgages to back new securities is a logical step, and in the 1980s, several types of mortgage-backed securities were developed. They enable an institution to raise funds for new mortgage loans at current rates without having to sell existing mortgages, which may have declined in value. Among the most popular of the securities are **mortgage-backed bonds** and **collateralized mortgage obligations (CMOs).** As their names suggest, they are long-term nondeposit liabilities. A mortgage-backed bond is the debt obligation of an institution backed by expected cash flows from its general mortgage portfolio. A CMO is a special kind of **pay-through bond.** A pay-through bond

is one for which cash flows from specific existing mortgages are designated to repay bond principal and interest. CMOs can be tailored to provide a variety of cash flow streams to investors. For example, some are issued with a staggered maturity schedule, allowing an institution to attract buyers with different investment criteria to a single issue. Each maturity class is paid off sequentially; all obligations from one class are paid before any payment is made on the next class.

Because mortgages are high-quality collateral, institutions issuing mortgage-backed securities often do so at only a slight premium over the Treasury bond (T-bond) rate. Initially, only fixed-rate mortgages were believed to be suitable collateral. The variety of adjustable-rate mortgage (ARM) plans discussed in the preceding chapter made it difficult to assemble a pool of similar loans, and uncertainty about their future cash flows exposed the purchaser of an ARM-backed bond to additional risk. By 1985, however, standardization of ARMs and increasing familiarity with mortgage-backed securities encouraged issuance of ARM-backed securities. This development is important to mortgage lenders, who can use ARMs to shorten the interest sensitivity of asset portfolios while retaining access to the mortgage-backed bond market as a source of nondeposit funds.

Because of administrative and flotation costs, mortgage-backed bonds are usually issued with minimum face values of $100 million. To make it easier for small depositories to use mortgage-backed securities, methods have been developed by which several firms working together can pool collateral and issue bonds. Pooling has increased the participation of small thrift institutions in this form of liability management.[19]

BROKERED DEPOSITS. Brokered deposits are obtained when a depository engages a broker to raise funds. The broker receives a commission and may solicit money on a national or even international basis, usually assigning the total funds raised to individual

[18]Information in this section was obtained from *Freddie Mac Reports,* various issues; Barbara Donnelly, "CMOs May Promise Big Fat Yields But Investors Should Know the Risks," *The Wall Street Journal,* November 12, 1991, C1, C11; and Golly 1992. The focus here is on the use of CMOs by issuers, but much has been written about the risks of these securities to their purchasers. The primary risk is that of early prepayment of underlying mortgages if interest rates fall after the CMOs are issued. The prices of CMOs also fluctuate as interest rates change, exposing investors to market value risk as well.

[19]Another type of mortgage-backed security, the pass-through, is also one on which borrowers' monthly payments on a package of mortgages are passed directly each month to the mortgage-backed security holder. They are discussed in more detail in Chapter 19. A pay-through bond is similar, although there are differences in the tax treatment of returns on the two types of bonds. Pay-throughs are designed to appeal to tax-exempt investors. See Puglisi and McKenzie 1983. Further information on CMOs is found in Allen 1986.

accounts in fully insured portions of up to $100,000 each. Institutions raising funds in this way may be small and unable to sell uninsured negotiable CDs because they lack the necessary financial reputation. But larger institutions that find it difficult to raise uninsured funds, perhaps because they are perceived by investors as relatively risky, have also been prominent in this market. Through the use of brokered deposits, depositories can attract funds from a wide geographic area and expose depositors to no default risk. In the 1980s, some institutions using brokered deposits achieved much greater than normal growth, paying yields higher than the going rate and advertising features seldom offered on deposits. As the decade progressed, the practice was especially common among savings associations, and many experts attribute the premium on average deposit yields at thrifts over average yields at banks (see Figure 16.2) to the aggressive buying of deposits by weak S&Ls, especially those in the Southwest.

There are several motivations for such a strategy. A financially weak institution may view insured brokered deposits as a good source of liquidity if it faces a potential drain of funds from uninsured sources. Institutions in low-growth areas may be unable to diversify or restructure their assets if they depend solely on local deposit growth for new cash. Nevertheless, an institution using brokered deposits is faced with the task of finding investment outlets for the funds raised. Ordinarily, it would be difficult to quadruple a firm's assets quickly without a substantial increase in riskiness. If management is unskilled in risk assessment or if it is venturing into uncharted territory, it is unlikely to succeed. Failure of an institution heavily dependent on brokered deposits could require substantial assistance from the federal insurance funds. As a consequence, in 1985 the FHLBB restricted the percentage of brokered deposits used by Federal Savings and Loan Insurance Corporation (FSLIC)-insured savings institutions with weak net worth positions.

Despite these restrictions, however, brokered deposits continued to be popular; one Fed official estimated their volume at thrifts alone to be $59 billion in early 1989. And although regulators opposed the provision, arguing that restrictions were already sufficiently stringent, Title II of FIRREA included a provision that prohibits a "troubled" depository—defined in the law as one that does not meet minimum net worth requirements—from accepting brokered deposits, including reinvestment of maturing ones. In its discussion of FIRREA, Congress recognized the appropriateness of brokered deposits in some circumstances and stressed that it did not intend to prohibit them altogether. The law even allowed regulators to make exceptions to the rule for troubled institutions, *if* brokered deposits are deemed not to pose unacceptable risks to the insurance system. Lawmakers emphasized, however, that all banks and thrifts—whether adequately capitalized or not—are subject to FDIC scrutiny of fund-raising practices, including the use of brokered deposits.

By the time FDICIA was passed, concerns about the health of the FDIC were great enough that Congress went much further toward curbing the use of brokered deposits. Not only was the prohibition against them reinforced for institutions with especially weak capital positions, but even firms deemed to have "adequate" capital are required to obtain permission from regulators before seeking brokered funds. Regulators are also authorized to impose interest rate ceilings on brokered deposits to prevent a reoccurrence of the excessive and risky growth strategies used by some thrifts in the 1980s. Well-capitalized depositories, however, may continue to seek brokered deposits on which interest rates are unrestricted as part of an overall liability management strategy.[20]

DEPOSIT NOTES AND BANK NOTES. Two of the newer instruments of liability management appeared in the mid-1980s, when several large depositories began issuing **deposit notes** and **bank notes.** Both these instruments are medium-term sources of funds (maturities ranging from 2 to 5 years) and are designed to appeal to investors with particular risk/return preferences. Deposit notes are similar to negotiable CDs, in that an investor receives deposit insurance protection up to $100,000. Unlike CDs, however, deposit notes are evaluated by rating agencies and are often accompanied by a brief circular describing the financial condition of the issuing institution. Although they are not negotiable, the existence of a formal rating for

[20] See Harless 1984; "Statement of Robert L. Clarke, Comptroller of the Currency, Before the House Subcommittee on General Oversight and Investigations of the Committee on Banking, Finance, and Urban Affairs," *Quarterly Journal,* Office of the Comptroller of the Currency 8 (September 1989): 32–36; "Conference Report on HR 1278," 1989; Moore 1991; and *FDIC Annual Report,* 1991.

the notes makes them attractive to some investors, such as insurance companies, which ordinarily do not (or cannot in some states) own unrated securities. As a result of costs associated with the rating process, deposit notes carry lower interest rates than negotiable CDs issued by the same institution.

Bank notes are similar to deposit notes, in that they carry agency ratings, but they differ in that they are completely uninsured and can be traded in secondary markets. The lack of insurance means that they pay a higher interest rate than deposit notes issued by the same institution. The additional interest cost is offset, however, by the fact that the issuer need not pay deposit insurance premiums on its notes. Bank notes came into the spotlight in 1988 when the FDIC briefly considered extending deposit insurance to them; the proposal was criticized by bankers as being solely motivated by the agency's need to raise new resources. Bank notes, particularly those issued by thrifts, have also been controversial in that some critics fear that unwitting investors may purchase them under the assumption that they are covered by deposit insurance. Issuing institutions counter the criticism by pointing out that the notes are marketed primarily to large, sophisticated investors.[21]

USING CONTINGENT LIABILITIES TO MEET LOAN DEMAND AND PURSUE GROWTH

Another funding source of growing importance to depository institutions is contingent liabilities, such as fees received for guaranteeing letters of credit on a standby basis. These arrangements obligate an institution to assume a customer's debts in the event the customer is unable to repay them; thus, they are an institution's potential liabilities and are discussed in further detail in Chapters 17 and 22. They are relevant in the present context of liability management, however, because they provide a way for depositories to gain access to funds without either selling assets or incurring deposit insurance premiums or reserve requirements. Thus, as are other liability management instruments, the fees generated from contingent liabilities are discretionary funds that allow depositories to fulfill demand for new loans or to take advantage of other investment opportunities.

Recent research has addressed another important function of contingent liabilities in depositories. Because many of these fee sources are subject to fewer regulatory restrictions than are traditional activities, they allow institutions to avoid the additional costs imposed by regulations such as deposit insurance premiums or reserve requirements. This lower cost allows institutions to take advantage of investment opportunities that would otherwise be forgone because they failed to provide adequate benefits to shareholders—a condition termed the **underinvestment problem** in the research literature. Although the effects of contingent activities on the risk and return of depositories are numerous and complex, their potential to reduce the underinvestment problem in commercial banks is gaining increased attention.[22]

FACTORS INFLUENCING THE USE OF LIABILITY MANAGEMENT

Confidence-sensitive money is any source of funds sensitive to a loss of confidence either in a particular institution or in the banking system in general. Many tools of liability management are confidence-sensitive. Further, even when an institution is not the object of a loss of confidence, major investors in the instruments of liability management are willing to move funds from one institution to another to gain a few basis points. Funds that move quickly in response to yield differences are often called **hot money** or **money at a price.**[23]

Institutions relying heavily on either confidence-sensitive or hot money adopt an aggressive strategy; as financial conditions change, they can lose access to those funds. In contrast, managers who prefer to rely on their own resources for immediate liquidity needs and "store" those resources in the asset portfolio are adopting a more conservative stance, as are those institutions that plan their asset growth at the same pace as expected growth in deposits and net worth. Several

---

[21] See Stigum 1990, Chapter 24.

[22] See James 1989. Recall from Chapter 2 that contingent liabilities are often referred to as "off–balance sheet" items because, before FDICIA, they were not required to be reported in an institution's financial statements.

[23] The term *confidence-sensitive* was introduced in Luckett 1980. Other references to these issues include Crosse 1975; Burns 1971; and "Statement of Robert L. Clarke," 1989, 32–33.

factors are associated with a depository's choice between these management styles.

SIZE AND INDUSTRY MEMBERSHIP. The smaller an institution, the less likely that it will issue large CDs, repurchase agreements, or Eurodollar liabilities, simply because it lacks a large enough capital base or securities portfolio to support those operations. Also, the customers may be individuals or small local businesses lacking the funds to make these investments. Further, access to the Eurodollar markets is difficult for nonmoney-center banks or for those without foreign branches. Thus, liability management continues to remain in the realm of very large commercial banks and a few savings institutions.

In the past, thrifts using liability management have issued large-denomination CDs through New York dealers, but the volume is small. Recently, thrifts have also increased their use of mortgage-backed bonds, CMOs, and brokered deposits. CUs, with the common-bond requirement, are greatly restricted in the use of liability management tools such as brokered deposits. They can use repurchase agreements, fed funds, or borrowings from federal regulators, and some have done so. But because one of their objectives is to offer relatively low loan rates to members, CUs' aggressive use of high-cost nonshare sources of funds is not great.

FINANCIAL STRENGTH. The firm's financial position affects its access to uninsured liabilities. When an institution issues liabilities beyond the protective umbrella of federal insurance, all funds suppliers assess their exposure to default risk. Increasing depository failure rates have made prospective investors and uninsured depositors more cautious. When an institution's financial performance deteriorates, investors require a larger risk premium, and they may eventually withdraw all funds regardless of the premium the institution is willing to pay. In 1984, the nation's largest thrift institution, American Savings, faced just such a scenario; uninsured depositors withdrew substantial sums when its financial condition worsened. The chief executive officer, architect of American's aggressive liability management strategy, was forced to resign. American eventually became hopelessly insolvent and was the object of a controversial bailout in December 1988. American is one of many such stories in the past decade.

NONINTEREST COMPETITION AMONG DEPOSITORIES

New deposit instruments and liability management are not the only consequences of historical restrictions on deposit taking. Both Reg Q and the prohibition of interest on demand deposits led to the use of **implicit interest payments,** or services provided to depositors in lieu of explicit interest. Implicit interest permits depository institutions to compete when explicit interest competition is prohibited or when managers believe that implicit interest competition is less costly or more desirable to customers than increasing explicit interest. Over the years, implicit interest has taken many forms, ranging from pots and pans for new account holders to opening branch offices or drive-through windows to increase convenience. Depositories also offer a wide range of account-related services such as free checking, automatic transfer of funds from savings to checking, preauthorized bill payments, automatic payroll deposits, or preferential treatment on loans.

ECONOMIC EFFICIENCY OF NONINTEREST COMPETITION

An important question for individual institutions and for the financial system as a whole is whether implicit interest payments benefit financial market participants. Most experts conclude that they do not.

THE INSTITUTION'S POINT OF VIEW. Before the removal of Reg Q, small depositories, in particular, argued that they could not afford to pay market rates on so-called **core deposits**—transactions accounts, passbook savings, and small consumer CDs. Research indicates, however, that savings in explicit interest costs under Reg Q did not result in increased profits; rather, they were redirected toward increased operating expenses. Estimates of implicit annual interest rates paid to demand depositors through the provision of services range from less than 1 percent in 1954 to nearly 5 percent in the late 1960s.[24]

It is easy to see how these costs arise. Suppose a bank offers "free" checking to demand deposit customers, who then have no economic incentive to restrict the number of checks they write. To the extent that the institution's resources are tied to check processing rather than to income-producing activities, the

---

[24] White 1976; Taggart 1978; and Dotsey 1983.

cost of providing services to depositors may equal or even exceed what the bank saves by not paying interest on the deposits. Of course, if profits are significantly less variable as a result of implicit rather than explicit interest, institutions and their owners may not be harmed even if operating expenses increase. Evidence indicates, however, that explicit interest costs are unrelated to systematic risk and negatively related to total risk for banks. This evidence implies that institutions would not be more risky, and might even be less risky, if explicit interest payments *increased* as a percentage of total expenses.[25]

Some implicit interest payments, such as building additional branches or hiring additional staff, are analogous to fixed costs in industrial firms. Although the analogy is not perfect, it is useful for examining why implicit interest payments may be financially undesirable for a depository. The costs of operating a branch or employing a new staff member are harder to adjust downward with revenue decreases than are explicit interest payments. As students of corporate financial management know, a high level of fixed costs in a firm means a high **degree of operating leverage (DOL).** The DOL is defined as the percentage change in operating profits resulting from a 1 percent change in total revenues (TR):

$$DOL_{TR} = \frac{\%\Delta \text{ Operating Income}}{\%\Delta \text{ Revenues}}$$

A degree of operating leverage of 3, for example, means that each 1 percent change in revenues, up or down, is expected to result in a 3 percent change in operating income in the same direction.

DOL is a function of the variable-cost versus fixed-cost structure of a firm at its current level of revenue, calculated as[26]

[16.1]

$$DOL_{TR} = \frac{TR - VC}{TR - VC - FC}$$

where
VC = total variable costs
FC = total fixed costs

The higher the level of fixed costs, the higher the degree of operating leverage. The higher the degree of operating leverage, the greater the variation in operating income as revenue varies. In a depository institution, total revenues vary as the general level of interest rates or the term structure changes. It follows that a higher level of implicit interest payments, which are usually fixed costs, results in greater variation in the operating income of a depository than if the institution paid more in explicit interest, a variable cost.

THE CUSTOMER'S POINT OF VIEW. The use of implicit rather than explicit interest may not benefit depositors either, although the issue is less clear-cut than it is for financial institutions. On the one hand, an individual may not want a new toaster from a bank, preferring to earn the equivalent amount in cash. Regulations permitting the toaster but not the cash are not to the customer's benefit. Some economists also argue that interest rate controls, forcing implicit interest competition, increase loan rates at depositories. Without rate controls, the quantity of deposits should increase, increasing the availability of loanable funds and simultaneously reducing wasteful implicit interest costs. The result should be lower, not higher, lending rates.[27]

There are reasons, however, why some customers prefer implicit to explicit interest. Implicit interest is not taxed, whereas for most recipients, explicit interest is. To the extent that a customer actually desires the "free" services provided by the depository, implicit interest, or at least some combination of explicit and implicit interest, is preferable. The higher the personal tax bracket, the more likely this is to be true. This argument suggests that even if interest were paid on demand deposits, some forms of implicit interest would remain.

IMPLICIT INTEREST AFTER THE REMOVAL OF REG Q

Based on this analysis, one would expect to find changes in the behavior of depositories after the removal of Reg Q. The evidence so far is consistent with expectations.

[25] This research is examined in Benston 1984.

[26] The derivation and assumptions underlying Equation 16.1 are given in many good financial management texts. One example can be found in Eugene F. Brigham, *Fundamentals of Financial Management,* 6th ed. (Ft. Worth: Dryden Press, 1992), Chapter 11.

[27] For arguments supporting the benefits of explicit interest to customers, see Friedman 1970 and Keeley 1984.

By late 1986, 70 percent of transactions balances were held in interest-bearing checking accounts, suggesting that many customers prefer explicit to implicit interest. Fed statistics also showed that at the end of 1987, just over 25 percent of all demand deposits were held by households, down substantially from the percentage in 1980; researchers attributed the decline in consumers' demand deposit holdings to the availability of explicit interest on checking accounts.[28]

In early 1989, conditions returned that were reminiscent of those before deposit interest-rate ceilings were lifted, as the yield curve inverted and T-bill yields exceeded yields on 6-month bank CDs. This situation provided the first real test of depositories' response to explicit interest rate deregulation. Although the removal of Reg Q ceilings left banks free to fight disintermediation by upping explicit yields on deposits, evidence suggests that they used a wide variety of approaches to keep depositors' dollars. For example, one Boulder, Colorado, bank offered costly implicit interest benefits, including hunting rifles, VCRs, and Rolex watches, to customers opening new CDs, but customers were told that they would forgo higher explicit interest if they selected the "gifts." Some banks used a combination of explicit interest at the market rate *and* premiums such as jewelry and rare coins. Several banks have recently offered their premiums through a marketing technique rarely used in depository institutions—coupon offers. Prospective customers receive coupon booklets in the mail; they redeem the coupons when opening a new deposit account, and the free gifts are sent directly to their homes.

Despite this array of creative implicit interest schemes, other institutions compete solely with explicit interest, offering above-market rates to keep depositors from disintermediating. For example, in times of extremely low interest rates, such as the early 1990s, some institutions have offered multiple-year CDs on which yields are guaranteed to increase every 3 or 6 months. Managers point out to customers that T-bill yields *might* increase over the same period, but there is no guarantee that they will. (Recall from Chapter 7, however, that when the general level of interest rates is low, the yield curve is upward-sloping, a relationship that held true in the early 1990s. These CDs are, therefore, based on a belief in the pure expecta-

tions theory.) And even more innovative possibilities for offering competitive explicit returns are becoming common. For example, as interest rates plunged in the early 1990s, many customers withdrew funds from depositories to invest directly in stocks, which seemed to offer the only hope for higher returns. In response, some banks began to tempt customers with CDs on which yields are tied to the performance of the stock market. A typical **linked CD** offers a guaranteed return of principal (and, of course, FDIC insurance on the first $100,000 of that principal), plus the possibility of appreciation based on the increase in the value of the S&P 500 during the term of the deposit. Institutions offering these CDs protect themselves against the potentially higher costs of these products by hedging in the index options market. The wide variety of competitive strategies illustrated in this section is likely to continue, as there appear to be clienteles for many explicit–implicit interest combinations.[29]

INCREASED USE OF DEPOSIT SERVICE CHARGES

Another recent development is the imposition of deposit service charges where none existed or the increase in charges at institutions that had previously had them. At many institutions, customers with high balances are given "free" checking and other implicit interest benefits. Less affluent customers are charged explicitly for each deposit or withdrawal and in some cases for simply using a teller. A study conducted for the House Banking Committee estimated that the average U.S. household faced an increase of 104 percent in the cost of basic banking services from 1979 to 1983—from $91.94 per year to $187.59. A study by economists at the Federal Reserve Board concluded that the overall profitability of personal checking accounts did not increase, however, and that banks were simply charging fees necessary to cover their costs.[30]

---

[28] See Zimmerman and Keeley 1986 and Mahoney 1988.

[29] Georgette Jasen, "This Bank Uses Hunting Rifles, Shotguns as It Targets Depositors," *The Wall Street Journal,* February 15, 1989, C1, C10; Zimmerman and Neuberger 1990; William Glasgall, "Souped-up Certificates of Deposit," *Business Week,* August 3, 1992, 55; Cohn and Edleson 1993.

[30] Daniel Hertzberg, "Smaller Customers Get Less Service at Banks and Pay More Charges," *The Wall Street Journal,* October 18, 1984, 16; and Glenn B. Canner and Robert D. Kurtz, "Service Charges as a Source of Bank Income and Their Impact on Consumers," Federal Reserve Board Staff Study No. 145, August 1985.

Nonetheless, because new pricing systems permit those with high balances to receive free or low-cost banking services, they are consistent with the idea that wealthy customers benefit from the nontaxable implicit interest. Concern has been raised about the ability of low-income households to afford services formerly offered as a substitute for market interest rates. Many consumer groups have called for **basic** (or **lifeline**) **banking** legislation at the federal level, requiring that depositories offer a minimum level of financial services to households at low or even no cost. "Basic banking" is generally considered to include the right to a checking account with a low minimum balance requirement and a limited number of free checks per month. Regulators have successfully opposed such legislation, preferring instead to encourage institutions to provide low-cost banking services voluntarily; recent data from the Fed suggest that almost 50 percent of financial institutions had no-frills service packages in 1988 and that the proportion of households without checking accounts has not increased despite deregulation. Regulators continued to stress that depositories should not offer basic banking (or any other service, for that matter) if it cannot be offered on at least a break-even basis. Despite stepped-up lobbying by consumer groups in the early 1990s, in Title II of FDICIA Congress stopped short of making lifeline accounts mandatory and instead endorsed regulators' position. FDICIA required the Federal Reserve Board and the FDIC to define the characteristics necessary for a product to be officially deemed a lifeline account and directed the FDIC to charge institutions only one-half the usual deposit insurance premium on accounts that meet the definition.[31]

ACQUISITION OF FUNDS IN A DEREGULATED ENVIRONMENT

The managers of depository institutions are faced with a complex set of decisions when planning how to raise and retain funds. Although no single, comprehensive model is available for a mechanical analysis of these

[31] See Canner and Maland 1987; Board of Governors 1988, 157; Scott 1988; Robert Trigaux, "Right or Wrong, 'Lifeline' Battle Looms for Banks," *American Banker,* February 1, 1990, 1, 8; and *FDICIA,* December 19, 1991, Title II, Subtitle C.

problems, certain issues must be considered systematically. They can be classified into three categories:

1. The broad choice between wholesale and retail funds sources
2. The balance between deposit and nondeposit liabilities and the mix of deposit sources
3. The costs and pricing of accounts and services

WHOLESALE VERSUS RETAIL FUNDS

expensive; if maintain less expensive

The first major decision is whether to seek wholesale or retail funds. **Wholesale funds** are those provided by nonfinancial businesses and other financial institutions; **retail funds** are provided by households. This decision is part of strategic planning, because it determines many operating policies thereafter. Managers must evaluate several points in making the decision.

cheap; if maintain more expensive.

AVAILABILITY. Chapter 6 notes that only the household sector is a net supplier of funds and that businesses and governments are net borrowers. Thus, in the financial system as a whole, more retail funds are available than wholesale funds, and few depository institutions can afford to ignore the retail market altogether. Still, in some areas—midtown Manhattan, for example—wholesale funds may be more plentiful. In 1980, Bankers Trust of New York, one of the nation's ten largest banks, abandoned retail business completely by selling the few branches it operated. The bank already had a solid base of corporate customers, and its prime New York location positioned it well to pursue additional wholesale funds. Continental Illinois embarked on a similar strategy in 1988; more than $600 million in retail accounts were sold to the First National Bank of Chicago. These strategic steps away from retail banking reflected the conclusion that the long-run benefits were greater in the wholesale markets.

The discussion of liability management noted other factors that influence an institution's decision to use nontraditional funds sources: size, industry membership, and financial condition. Because the tools of liability management are largely wholesale, those characteristics also play a role in a depository's strategic choice between wholesale and retail funds. Yet even large banks on solid financial ground do not always depend solely on wholesale funds just because they can get them. Citibank, for example, with its extensive branch network, continues its commitment to retail banking by expanding credit card operations and other consumer services. The choice between wholesale and retail funds affects the entire range of products and services offered.

FUNDS VOLATILITY. Retail and wholesale funds can both be volatile, but wholesale funds ineligible for deposit insurance are especially rate- and confidence-sensitive, as the cases of Continental Illinois and American Savings indicate. Institutions relying heavily on wholesale funds must be prepared to bid aggressively to keep them when rates increase and to have alternative funds sources in case of emergencies.

In contrast, retail deposits may involve commitments to depositories on the part of the consumer. Households choose institutions based not only on their rates and reputations but also their locations and convenience. Although consumers did not hesitate to switch to other forms of investment in the mid- to late 1970s, they returned to depositories quickly when given a reasonable opportunity to do so in 1982. MMDAs gained market share quickly, even though MMDA yields were below money fund rates from 1983 through early 1985. Fed surveys of households' financial preferences continue to substantiate the significance of convenience and physical proximity to consumers when they establish their banking relationships. Once they choose, consumers are also reasonably loyal. For example, one survey reported that more than 40 percent of households with interest-bearing checking accounts said they would not move an account to an equally convenient depository on the basis of interest rate differentials. Another 30 percent said that only a rate differential of at least 2 percent would induce them to move.[32]

COST. Many managers argue that the cost of retail funds is higher because retail banking requires a branch network and/or a large staff, but the pursuit of wholesale funds is also costly. For small institutions, or for thrifts only recently involved with commercial customers, the cost of locating sources of corporate and institutional money can be substantial. Some depositories have turned to brokers, but they lack loyalty to individual institutions and are willing to move funds to capture small interest rate differentials.

ANTICIPATED USES OF FUNDS. For many institutions, the decision to pursue particular types of liabilities depends on planned uses of the funds. The relationship between asset and liability strategies is the subject of Chapters 18 and 19 and is not discussed in detail here, but it is risky, for example, to make 10-year mortgage loans if they are funded by hot money in times of rising rates. Conversely, if funds are needed temporarily to meet a shortfall of required reserves, raising the money through retail CDs would be inappropriate. Further, if the planned use of funds is commercial loans, management may wish to develop a customer base by first obtaining wholesale deposits. If consumer credit is the desired investment, it may be appropriate to seek retail deposits.

MIX OF FUNDS SOURCES

Beyond the choice between deposit and nondeposit liabilities, which has been explored in earlier sections, many decisions remain regarding the mix of deposit accounts. In the past, the rule of thumb for choosing the deposit mix was relatively simple: Attract as many core (checking) deposits as possible, because they were relatively cheap, plentiful, and uncomplicated. Competition was limited by Reg Q and restrictions on geographic expansion, and core deposit inflows were based on convenience and location. The environment has changed significantly, however, and now the cost of core deposits and the sensitivity of their costs in a changing interest rate environment must be compared with other sources of funds. For example, when the cost of reserve requirements is considered, an MMDA paying higher explicit interest may actually be less costly than a demand deposit or a NOW account.

Further, the variety of deposit types available to institutions continues to grow. For example, in 1990, the Federal Reserve Board began allowing U.S. banks to accept deposits denominated in foreign currencies, opening the door to a new category of customers in-

---

[32] Mark Flannery has argued that retail deposits can be considered quasi-fixed sources of funds, because the depositor is required to incur both search and set-up costs when choosing an individual institution. Still, there is likely to be some threshold yield on alternate investments that will cause the depositor to switch to another institution, even though additional costs will be incurred. See Flannery 1982b. See also Elliehausen and Wolken 1992 on the importance of local deposit relationships to households.

volved in international transactions and investments. Several banks have since offered new types of foreign currency–denominated CDs. Institutions must also evaluate the maturity and stability of different deposit categories, and the choice among account alternatives may reflect an institution's strategy for marketing other financial services to depositors as well.

PRICING

Pricing deposit accounts involves four separate but related analyses: the explicit interest rate to be offered, the costs incurred in servicing each account, the division of costs between explicit and implicit interest, and the effect of one deposit account's price on customer acceptance of other accounts and services. After the pricing decision is made, institutions must provide clear explanations to customers. Target levels for different sources of funds are unlikely to be realized unless effective pricing strategies are used to achieve them.

SETTING EXPLICIT INTEREST RATES. Most depository institution managers had little experience in setting rates to attract funds before 1980. The negotiable CD, fed funds, and Eurodollar markets are national or international in scope, so even managers practicing liability management faced limited discretion in rate setting. Today, managers of all depositories are required to use judgment. One course of action is simply to follow the crowd—to establish interest rates similar to those offered by key competitors, especially ones viewed as market leaders. For many years, some depositories have used this strategy to establish loan rates.

Many institutions appear to take more control over the explicit prices paid for deposits. A study of retail deposit pricing between 1983 and 1985, conducted by researchers at the Board of Governors, found a number of differences in account pricing patterns among depositories. At that time, thrifts tended to pay higher prices than banks for every category of deposits (although the difference declined markedly by the end of the decade). But within each industry, banks and thrifts seldom followed the crowd all the time. An individual institution would often raise or lower rates relative to its market competitors. Further, as market rates rose or fell, not all institutions adjusted rates equally quickly or in the same magnitude.

Further study substantiates that depository institutions' pricing decisions are more than imitation. Researchers at the New York Fed interviewed bankers in that Federal Reserve District in 1986 and 1987 and found that they took an aggressive approach to pricing consumer deposits. An important factor the bankers considered was the cost of alternative sources of wholesale funds; the rates set by competitors were less influential. Managers were also concerned about the degree to which customers would respond to changes in interest rates, and they gathered data to estimate depositors' sensitivity to pricing decisions. For example, by collecting data on account balances over time, managers can use statistical techniques such as regression analysis to study the relationship of deposits to many factors, including past interest rates, rates paid by competitors, or rates available on alternative investments. With the increasing accessibility of microcomputers and statistical software, all depositories can use quantitative models to improve deposit pricing, and many do.[33]

COSTS INCURRED FOR SPECIFIC ACCOUNT-RELATED SERVICES. Fee-based services, whether specifically related to deposits or offered as supplements to traditional depository services, have become so important that Chapter 21 is entirely devoted to them. Deposit account pricing now also involves identifying prices for each type of service formerly included in a deposit-related package. Pricing theorists refer to this development as the **unbundling** of services.

Ideally, prices should be related to the costs incurred by the institution, so cost analysis has begun to attract more attention. The Fed provides a functional cost analysis (FCA) service, through which it calculates the unit costs of key services for institutions providing the necessary data. Some depositories also seek other sources of cost data. Many have recently instituted cost accounting systems and use the data to price products. Trade groups in each industry have been

---

[33] See Mahoney et al. 1987. The bankers' survey is reported in Davis, Korobow, and Wenninger 1986–87. Quantitative analyses of the interest rate sensitivity of deposits are illustrated by Murphy and Kraas (1984), who used weekly deposit data from a small bank. Two researchers at the Federal Reserve Bank of Atlanta used a similar approach to assess the rate sensitivity of MMDA balances and concluded that longer-term rather than weekly data were more useful. See Wall and Ford 1984.

active in assisting small institutions with cost accounting problems.

Besides estimating the cost of providing a service, some institutions estimate the value of that service to customers. If the cost of providing it exceeds the value to the recipient, the service is eliminated. For example, preauthorized bill payment services are offered by some depositories as part of a transactions account package. Through this service, a depository automatically transfers funds from a customer's account to pay regular household expenditures such as insurance and utilities. The value of this service to a customer is unlikely to exceed the sum of the costs of a stamp, an envelope, and the time necessary to write and record a check, probably no more than $0.40 to $0.50 for most persons. If the institution can provide the service and make a profit for less than that, both parties will benefit. If not, the service is not worth its cost.[34]

ESTIMATING THE MARGINAL COST OF A DEPOSIT ACCOUNT. After determining the interest and servicing costs of each type of deposit account, managers must consider additional costs imposed by regulation. One model widely cited in the academic and practitioner literature estimates the marginal interest and noninterest costs of an additional deposit dollar (MC_D) as follows[35]:

[16.2]

$$MC_D = \frac{i_D + s_D + DI}{(1 - RR)}$$

where

i_D = current market interest rate on type of deposit

s_D = servicing costs of deposit (expressed as percentage of each dollar acquired)

DI = deposit insurance premium (expressed as percentage of each insured dollar)

RR = Fed reserve requirement on type of deposit

Suppose an institution's managers have decided to pursue a retail banking strategy. They have determined that the current market interest rate on NOW accounts is 6.5 percent and the cost of servicing a basic NOW

account is 3.4 percent (including unlimited transactions and the use of a teller window). Also, Fed reserve requirements on transactions accounts are 10 percent, and the deposit insurance premium is 0.254 percent. Using Equation 16.2, the marginal cost of offering a NOW account in this interest rate and regulatory environment is

$$MC_{NOW} = \frac{0.06500 + 0.03400 + 0.00254}{(1 - 0.10000)}$$

$$= 0.1128 = 11.28\%$$

A similar analysis can be performed for each funds source customarily used by the institution, and an average of these costs can also be estimated. The average cost of deposits and other liabilities is one of the main determinants of required lending rates, discussed and illustrated in Chapter 14. As shown in later sections, some of these data are also used in deciding how to price accounts to attract the quantity of desired deposits from target customer segments.

EXPLICIT VERSUS IMPLICIT PRICING. As noted earlier, some depositors prefer to be compensated entirely with explicit interest, whereas others prefer implicit interest to avoid taxation. Thus, setting an explicit rate is not enough to ensure that the desired deposit structure will be attained. Because some customers may prefer one combination while others prefer another, a pricing approach that allows consumer choice is likely to be most satisfactory.

Two general explicit–implicit pricing strategies have been suggested. One is based on the New England experience with NOW accounts in the 1970s. A **conditionally free account** is, as the name implies, one for which no service charges are imposed under certain conditions—usually, that the depositor keeps a specified minimum balance in the account. If the balance falls below the minimum, a service charge is imposed as a flat fee, a price per service rendered, or both. The customer determines the mix of implicit and explicit interest by the way the account is managed.

An alternative to the conditionally free account is the **interest buydown account.** With this approach, each service associated with an account is priced on a markdown basis from the explicit interest rate. Table 16.2 illustrates such a strategy. Suppose that using data from the previous section, management sets the explicit interest rate on a NOW account at 6.5 percent.

[34] See Gardner and Lammers 1988 and Logue 1983.

[35] See Watson 1977 and Watson 1978.

Reserve
Requirement

TABLE 16.2 The Interest Buydown Pricing Strategy

As institutions emphasize explicit pricing strategies, customers may be offered the opportunity to exchange explicit interest on deposit accounts for "free" services that would otherwise carry an explicit fee.

Service	Cost (%)	Desired by Customer
Unlimited transactions	2.90%	Included
Use of automatic teller machines	0.50	Yes
Use of teller window	0.50	Included
Free travelers checks	0.50	No
Free safe deposit box	0.50	No
Preauthorized bill payments for:		
Mortgage	0.50	Yes
Car	0.50	No
Insurance	0.50	No
Credit life insurance for:		
Mortgage	1.00	Yes
Car	1.00	No
Personal computer linkage with:		
Stock market data	1.50	No
Bond market data	1.50	Yes

Base explicit interest rate: 6.5%
Total cost of "bought" services: 3.5%
Explicit interest rate: 3%

Source: Adapted from Elmer 1985.

Also, suppose that the services listed in Table 16.2 are available to account holders, although the basic NOW account includes only two: unlimited transactions, and the use of a teller window. With the interest buydown pricing strategy, the customer selects the desired additional services in exchange for a lower explicit rate of interest. Should the customers wish to use services not initially "bought," fees can be charged as services are used. In this example, the explicit interest is bought down to 3 percent, because the account holder has selected services considered equivalent to a 3.5 percent annual return.[36]

PRICING AND CUSTOMER RELATIONSHIPS. A final consideration in deposit pricing is the potential effect of one pricing decision on a customer's acceptance of other services or accounts. Many institutions now consider their total relationship with a customer when setting prices on accounts customers view as important in the selection of a primary financial institution. For example, some banks have recognized that higher fee structures for demand deposits alienated many younger customers, who turned to CUs or thrifts for their transactions account services. Because this customer group also comprises an important segment of the demand for other financial services, such as consumer loans, that demand also moved to CUs and thrifts.

Some institutions have revised pricing structures for basic checking account services to re-establish relationships with an important market segment. Some depositories have introduced **tiered pricing systems,** recognizing that wealthier customers may be more rate-sensitive than customers with lower incomes. Tiered systems offer higher explicit rates as a customer's balance increases beyond a threshold level. For example, one rate may be paid on NOW balances less than $500, and successively higher rates may be offered as the account balance exceeds $1,000, $5,000, and so forth. Alternatively, using the example in Table 16.2, a high-balance customer might be given access to free travelers checks and personal computer linkage to stock market data with no reduction in the base explicit interest rate of 6.5 percent. The institution would set this price assuming the customer might use other income generating services, such as borrowing money or trust department services.

Other strategies include packaging financial accounts, or cross-selling different financial services. For example, when a customer accepts a core service such as a checking account or a loan, he or she is also offered access to another group of financial services, such as preapproved credit cards or an MMDA. A third tier of value-added services, such as credit card protection, free checks, or combined monthly statements, can also be made available to the new customer. Presumably, the value of the available services will be recognized even if they are never actually used.[37] The challenge for financial institution managers is to evaluate the costs of each service individually (as with

---

[36] Further discussion of pricing strategies is provided in Rogowski 1984; Elmer 1985; and Parliment 1985.

[37] For further discussion, see Terrence P. Paré, "Banks Discover the Consumer," *Fortune,* February 12, 1990, 96–104; Cook 1989; "Checking Accounts Build the Base for Retail Banking," *Savings Institutions* 109 (June 1988): 118–119; and "Financial Service Packages Continue to Draw Interest," *Savings Institutions* 108 (December 1987): 142–143.

unbundled strategies) so that appropriate and profitable terms can be offered when the financial services are packaged and offered to customers.

DISCLOSURE REQUIREMENTS: TRUTH IN SAVINGS

After managers have reviewed the issues addressed in the preceding sections and have determined a pricing structure, they must carefully communicate the results of those decisions to customers. This truth-in-savings requirement, introduced in Title II of FDICIA, became effective in 1993. Administered under the Fed's **Regulation DD,** truth-in-savings rules stipulate that depositories must uniformly publish the fees, service charges, and annual yields associated with each account. As with truth-in-lending regulations, the purpose of Reg DD is to promote intelligent shopping for financial services among consumers. As one might expect, the actual rules are lengthy (initially 267 pages) and cover a multitude of detailed situations. Key provisions include a prohibition against advertising accounts as "free" if they contain any conditions, such as a minimum account balance, that might cost the customer if the conditions were violated. The **annual percentage yield (APY)** on accounts must be disclosed, including the effect of service charges and fees that may reduce that yield below the stated interest rate; the Fed has established the formula institutions must use. Specific applications of the formula to the myriad of account types, maturities, and conditions are extremely complex—indeed, some managers say they are the most onerous banking regulations ever written. But in its simplest form, the APY on deposits is calculated as follows:

$$APY = [(1 + I/P_0)^{365/n}] - 1, \qquad [16.3]$$

where

I = net dollars of interest during a period (interest less service charges)

P_0 = principal balance at beginning of period

n = number of days during over which interest is earned

Notice that Equation 16.3 compounds a periodic yield [as reflected in $(1 + I/P_0)$] for the number of com-

pounding periods (365/n) in a year. Thus, it is closely related to the intrayear compounding formula, Equation 5A.2, presented earlier in the book.

Suppose a customer purchases a one-quarter (defined in this example as 91-days), $10,000 share certificate on which her credit union offers a stated annual rate of 3 percent. Interest will be paid at the end of the 91 days, with no service charges on the account. At the end of the quarter, the customer will receive $(0.03/4) = 0.0075$ percent interest, for a total of $10,000 \times 0.0075 = $75. The APY, using Equation 16.3, will be:

$$APY = [(1 + \$75/\$10,000)^{365/91}] - 1 = 0.030424 = 3.0424\%$$

If service charges would in any way reduce the *net* interest on the account, these charges must be considered when the dollars of interest are calculated. Thus, if there were a $2.00 quarterly service charge on a similar account, making the net interest to the customer only $73, the APY would be:

$$APY = [(1 + \$73/\$10,000)^{365/91}] - 1 = 0.029603 = 2.9603\%, \textit{less} \text{ than the stated 3 percent rate.}$$

If an institution offers tiered pricing for a particular account, the APY must be disclosed for all tiers. Generally, the longer the maturity of the deposit, and the more complex its features, the greater the required information for consumers.[38]

PRICING STRATEGIES IN PRACTICE

As expected in a deregulated environment, depository managers have approached pricing problems in a variety of ways in recent years.

USE OF CONDITIONALLY FREE ACCOUNTS. A 1983 survey of banks and thrifts indicated that conditionally free pricing strategies dominated both MMDAs and Super NOWs; within states, thrifts imposed fewer fees

---

[38] See Brian P. Smith, "Adding Up Truth in Savings," *Savings and Community Banker* 2 (August 1993): 46–48; "Truth in Savings," *Banking Legislation and Policy* (Federal Reserve Bank of Philadelphia), September/October 1992, 3; Phil Roosevelt, "Banks Race Truth-in-Savings Deadline," *American Banker,* January 7, 1993, 1, 10; Francis A. Grady, "Innocent Errors Create Liability Under the Truth-in-Savings Act," *American Banker,* March 23, 1993, 4, 17.

than banks and offered slightly higher explicit rates on both accounts. By 1985, the use of conditionally free accounts was common, with minimums to avoid service charges ranging from more than $1,000 to more than $3,300.

In response to proponents of basic banking and to the incentives offered in FDICIA, both regulators and trade organizations have urged depositories to develop "no frills" accounts on which fees are minimized. The American Bankers Association reported in 1993 that 95 percent of banks and thrifts offered such accounts. A Federal Reserve Board poll of 81 banks in all 50 states found that 84 percent charged a fixed monthly fee for a package of basic banking services; the fee averaged $2.58. These basic banking accounts usually limit the number of transactions and pay no explicit interest on deposited funds.[39]

OTHER PRICING STRATEGIES. A 1983 survey at the Federal Reserve Bank of Cleveland provided additional evidence of depositories' account pricing and served as an indicator of strategies in subsequent years. Some institutions were using a tiered system for setting explicit interest rates, although tiering was more common for CDs than for more liquid accounts. On interest-bearing accounts, required minimum balances varied negatively with the liquidity of the account. A study reported by the New York Fed in 1987 indicated that most banks required customers to maintain a minimum balance in order to earn interest on accounts such as NOWs and MMDAs. In most cases, monthly fees were waived if the account balance exceeded an established level—an example of the conditionally free pricing system combined with other terms. These data suggest that minimum balance requirements will remain an important pricing strategy. Experts praise the economic efficiency of new pricing strategies allowing customers to choose the accounts they want while bearing the costs of their choices. Ideally, cost-based pricing strategies should allow customers to pay no more, but no less, than their fair share of the cost of receiving deposit services.[40]

DEREGULATION AND FEDERAL DEPOSIT INSURANCE

A discussion of deposit taking and liability management in a deregulated world is incomplete without examining the relationship between depository institution management and the federal deposit and share insurance funds.

MORAL HAZARD

Financial economists argue that liability management increases the efficiency with which scarce capital is allocated. If institutions with profitable investment opportunities obtain funds by bidding in a competitive marketplace, the potential for funds to flow to the most efficient users is enhanced. Deposit deregulation, and the resulting competition for funds among intermediaries, should have a similar effect on economic efficiency. Unfortunately, most experts also believe that until quite recently these benefits were reduced considerably, and perhaps even outweighed, by allocational inefficiencies caused by the federal deposit and share insurance programs.

The basis for this conclusion is that the historical deposit insurance pricing system produced a **moral hazard** for the insurers; that is, it increased the likelihood that institution managers would take excessive risks with depositors' funds and, therefore, that the insurer would be required to pay claims. President Franklin D. Roosevelt foresaw this hazard at the time the deposit insurance system was inaugurated and stated, "As to guaranteeing bank deposits, the minute the government starts to do that . . . the government runs into a probable loss." To address the concerns raised by Roosevelt and others, the Banking Act of 1933 limited competition and prohibited depositories from engaging in certain risky activities. These checks on the problem of moral hazard, however, were largely eliminated after 1980.[41] To understand the grave risks

---

[39] See Staten 1989; and Robyn Meredith, "95% of Banks Offer Basic Checking, Study Finds," *American Banker,* August 5, 1993, 8. Supporters of basic banking legislation cited research findings that only 14 percent of banks surveyed by the U.S. Public Interest Research Group offered low-cost accounts. The group of researchers with the most representative sample is unknown, but the Federal Reserve Board could be considered the most objective source. For other discussions of deposit pricing, see Rogowski 1984 and Zimmerman 1985.

[40] See Davis and Korobow 1987; and Watro 1984.

[41] A history of the deposit insurance system is found in "A Case for Reforming Federal Deposit Insurance," *1988 Annual Report,* Federal Reserve Bank of Minneapolis.

to the system that arose, one must first understand how it operated.

FINANCING THE INSURANCE FUNDS

To advertise themselves as federally insured, depository institutions must pay premiums to the federal agencies providing the guarantee. The premium structure differs by type of institution, but all had one thing in common before FDICIA: Unlike other insurance policies, the insured was *not* charged a premium based on the estimated risk posed for the insurer. No matter how risky the assets of a depository, its insurance premium was no more per insured dollar of deposits than a fellow institution whose only assets were T-bills. This flat premium was the primary source of moral hazard.

BANK PREMIUMS BEFORE FIRREA. Until 1989, commercial and savings banks insured by the FDIC were assessed a premium of 1/12 of 1 percent (8.3 basis points) per year on average total *domestic* deposits, payable in advance, on a semiannual basis. By law, the FDIC was required to rebate premiums to member banks in July following an assessed calendar year. The last pre-FIRREA rebate formula was established in DIDMCA and was designed to maintain the fund's level at between 1.25 percent and 1.40 percent of insured deposits. In 1986, as a sign of the massive problems that eventually led to FIRREA, the FDIC had no excess premiums to rebate for the first time in nearly 40 years; no rebates could be issued in either 1987 or 1988 as well.[42]

THRIFT PREMIUMS BEFORE FIRREA. Until its last 4 years, the FSLIC assessed premiums the same way. Both the FSLIC and the FDIC were authorized to make special assessments if necessary, however, and the FSLIC did so for the first time in 1985. Between 1985 and mid-1989, an additional 1/32 of 1 percent per quarter (or 12.5 basis points per year) was imposed on federally insured S&Ls and FSLIC-insured savings banks to help pay for the escalating thrift crisis. In 1987, Congress directed a phase-out of the special assessment in the Competitive Equality Banking Act's ill-conceived refinancing plan for the FSLIC, but the

condition of the insurer deteriorated to such a degree that the FHLBB was subsequently forced to maintain the special assessment for the next 2 years. Healthy thrifts labored under a premium burden that severely weakened their profitability and, thus, the industry's hopes for recovery. Many federally chartered S&Ls sought to become state-chartered savings banks, thus gaining eligibility for lower-cost FDIC insurance. Relationships between these institutions and the FHLBB were increasingly contentious, and the Bank Board eventually instituted a policy prohibiting switches between insurance funds.

BANK AND THRIFT PREMIUMS BETWEEN FIRREA AND FDICIA. Among the most controversial features of FIRREA was a change in the deposit premium structure. As noted earlier, FIRREA abolished the FSLIC and provided for two separately administered deposit insurance funds under the aegis of the FDIC—the Bank Insurance Fund (BIF), which covers depositories previously insured by the FDIC, and the Savings Association Insurance Fund (SAIF), which serves institutions previously covered by the FSLIC. For both funds, a phased-in premium schedule was intended to be used. Banks' premiums were scheduled to almost double, from their original 8.3 basis points per year (i.e., 8.3 cents per $100 of insured deposits) to 15 basis points per year. Premiums of SAIF-insured institutions skyrocketed to 23 basis points by early 1991, but they were slated to decline during the middle and last part of the decade. Also, the FDIC was given authority to increase BIF and SAIF premiums to a maximum of 32.5 basis points per year if its managers believed the funds were seriously imperiled. In August 1990, amid reports of the fund's rapidly weakening condition, the FDIC stunned commercial banks by exercising its discretionary authority and raising BIF premiums for 1991 to 19.5 basis points, exceeding the 15 basis points anticipated when FIRREA was passed. In 1992, they increased even further, to 23 basis points.[43]

The FIRREA-imposed financing structure for the insurance system was criticized for several reasons. Managers of thrifts that were alive after the slaughter of the 1980s believed it was wrong to make

---

[42] Details on the operations of the FDIC before FIRREA can be found in that agency's annual reports.

[43] "Conference Report on H.R. 1278," 1989; and Bill Atkinson, "FDIC Premiums to Skyrocket 63%," *American Banker*, August 15, 1990, 1, 12.

their institutions pay for their counterparts' bad decisions. Many bank managers argued that they had been unfairly made to shoulder the burdens of the thrift industry. Financial economists believed the new premium structure failed because it was little more than a regulatory tax on existing institutions to pay for *past* losses, not an attempt to garner funds to pay for anticipated *future* losses—the role insurance premiums ought to serve.

But even if assessing the future to pay for the past were a sound policy, the amount collected under the new structure would have been woefully short of the funds required to clean up after the FSLIC. The assumptions on which politicians based the premium schedule included predictions of no economic recession for 10 years; an inflation rate close to 0 percent; and rapid growth in thrift deposits (thus a higher base on which premiums could be assessed). Most analysts know, however, that thrifts had been losing, not gaining, deposits for several years before FIRREA. Most also believe that recessions are inevitable phases of the business cycle and that 0 percent inflation is an impossibility. Finally, and perhaps most important, the premium structure established in FIRREA did nothing to address the problem of moral hazard, because it failed to account for the individual riskiness of insured institutions.[44]

THE POST-FDICIA STRUCTURE. As one might have predicted, given these problems and the continuing weakness of the banking and thrift industries, which were exacerbated by a worldwide economic downturn, it was not long before additional legislation addressing the deposit insurance system was necessary. Fearing a funding crisis at the FDIC large enough to rival the FSLIC bailout, Congress at last insisted in Title III of FDICIA that deposit insurance be assessed on a risk-adjusted basis. Although not legally required to do so until January 1, 1994, regulators began using the new system on an experimental basis in 1993. Risk-adjusted premiums had been discussed for many years before FDICIA, and many questions about the appropriate risk measurement had surfaced. Should it be based on the interest rate risk exposure of the institution, the potential default risk on assets, the level of capital (and thus the risk to the insurance fund and to uninsured creditors and shareholders), the extent to which the depository has diversified investments, or a combination of these factors? Should an institution's contingent liabilities be considered? How often should risk be measured? And what is the proper price for each "unit" of risk?

The FDIC's initial scheme was, in fact, a relatively simple one, based on a matrix of capital ratios and supervisory evaluations, especially its CAMEL (for banks) or MACRO (for thrifts) ratings. The latter are themselves based on detailed analyses of different aspects of the institution's management and overall financial health, including its liquidity, asset quality, and earnings potential. Because it was the subject of considerable debate and became the foundation for subsequent plans, the top panel of Table 16.3 shows this first risk-adjusted matrix, used to assess premiums in 1993. The columns into which an institution could be placed reflect three possible supervisory "grades," from A (best) to C (worst). The rows of the matrix reflect the institution's capital adequacy category, as prescribed in FDICIA. (Details on the classification of institutions' capital are provided in Chapter 17.) Each cell shows the insurance premium assessed per $100 of insured deposits (for example, an adequately capitalized bank with a C grade from supervisors would have paid $0.30 per $100 in 1993). Another way of thinking of this premium is that it amounts to 30 basis points (0.30 percent, or 0.0030) times the institution's total insured deposits. For comparative purposes, each cell also shows the number and percentage of banks and thrifts that fell into each cell during that experimental year. Noteworthy is the 7 percent of thrifts falling into the worst cell, at the bottom right of the matrix. This situation reflects the continuing weakness of some segments of the industry. Still, most institutions were both well capitalized and received favorable supervisory ratings. Because the flat insurance premium for both banks and thrifts in 1992 had been $0.23 per $100, those falling into the top left cell of the matrix in 1993 experienced no increase in premiums.

Interestingly, it was precisely this point that caused the most controversy. As critics saw it, the problem was not that so many institutions received no *increase* under the FDIC's initial scheme, it was that no *decrease* was available to even the most stellar

---

[44] These points are discussed further in Paulette Thomas, "As S&L Bailout Plan Draws Nearer Passage, Flaws Become Clearer," *The Wall Street Journal,* July 21, 1989, A1, A16; and G. Thomas Woodward, "The Economics of Deposit Insurance," Congressional Research Service Report for Congress, January 4, 1989.

TABLE 16.3   **Assessing Risk-Adjusted Deposit Insurance Premiums**

FDICIA required a move away from flat deposit insurance premiums to those charged according to an institution's risk. The FDIC used a much-criticized experimental system in 1993 before turning to one proposed for 1994 that provides greater incentives for improvement. The risk-adjusted premiums are based on a combined rating of an institution's capital position and its ongoing management as evaluated by supervisors.

A. Experimental System (1993)

	Supervisory Rating					
	A		B		C	
Well capitalized	$0.23		$0.26		$0.29	
Banks (% of total banks)	9,115	(75.7%)	1,766	(14.7%)	363	(3.0%)
Thrifts (% of total thrifts)	1,428	(61.9%)	266	(11.5%)	33	(1.4%)
Adequately capitalized	$0.26		$0.29		$0.30	
Banks (% of total banks)	192	(1.6%)	164	(1.4%)	174	(1.4%)
Thrifts (% of total thrifts)	136	(5.9%)	157	(6.8%)	79	(3.4%)
Undercapitalized	$0.29		$0.30		$0.31	
Banks (% of total banks)	18	(0.1%)	26	(0.2%)	222	(1.8%)
Thrifts (% of total thrifts)	7	(0.3%)	38	(1.6%)	162	(7.0%)

B. Proposed Revised System (1994)

	Supervisory Rating			
	A	B	C	D
Very well capitalized	$0.200	$0.220	$0.240	$0.255
Well capitalized	0.220	0.235	0.250	0.275
Adequately capitalized	0.250	0.235	0.290	0.320
Less than adequately capitalized	0.260	0.300	0.320	0.340
Bridge bank or conservatorship	0.250			

Sources: Prepared by the authors with data from Kenneth H. Bacon, "FDIC Approves Lower Fee Rise than Expected," *The Wall Street Journal,* September 16, 1992, A4; Barbara H. Rehm, "FDIC May Widen Premium Range in 1994, Benefiting Healthy Banks," *American Banker,* December 16, 1992, 2.

institutions. Financial economists and management experts alike argued that the system was seriously flawed because it provided no incentive for the best institutions to improve. Further, they held that the spread between the best and worst banks was not large enough to give the worst banks incentives, either. The FDIC argued, in response, that Congress had ordered it in FDICIA to rebuild the insurance fund to 1.25 percent of insured deposits within 15 years and that the only way to do so was to charge risky institutions more than in the past while keeping low-risk depositories' premiums at their 1992 levels. In fact, the FDIC's 1993 proposal had originally called for substantial premium increases for even the best institutions, but it had been scaled back after an outcry from the industry and leading academics.

The 1993 system had barely been in operation when the FDIC announced that it was indeed considering revisions to permit strong institutions to pay re-

duced premiums. The initial proposal for 1994 and beyond is shown in the bottom panel of Table 16.3. Additional categories for both capital and supervisory ratings were added, allowing regulators to make finer gradations among institutions. (The blank cells reflect the fact that institutions that are so-called "bridge banks" or in conservatorship are those temporarily being managed by the FDIC itself pending reorganization or merger with another institution, and, naturally, would not receive anything but the highest supervisory rating!) The premium spread between the best and worst firms is widened, and those in the top group enjoy a considerable reduction over the premiums that they paid in 1993.

Because the risk-adjusted system is still so new, it is likely that further refinements will be made for the rest of this decade. But whatever the ultimate formula, it is already clear that the switch away from the traditional flat premium system is the most significant improvement in the deposit insurance system in its history.[45]

CREDIT UNION INSURANCE. The National Credit Union Share Insurance Fund (NCUSIF), is operated quite differently from SAIF or BIF. Between its founding in 1970 and 1984, NCUSIF used a premium system similar to that of the FDIC and the FSLIC. As a result of funding inadequacies that became apparent in the early 1980s, however, the Deficit Reduction Act of 1984 changed the way NCUSIF was financed. The 1984 law requires federally insured CUs to maintain a deposit in NCUSIF equal to 1 percent of their insured shares. Interest earned on NCUSIF investments made with these deposits adds to the fund each year, although NCUSIF's assets may not exceed 1.3 percent of total insured shares in any year. Accumulations in excess of that amount are returned to CUs. Special assessments are prohibited, although annual premiums can be charged if regulators deem them necessary. As of 1992, the fund was operating with a balance between 1.25 and 1.3 percent of insured shares. No premiums were levied until 1992, when for the first time since 1984, CUs were charged $\frac{1}{12}$ of 1 percent of insured shares. The premium was necessary to replenish NCUSIF after it handled several large CU failures in the early 1990s.[46]

INSURANCE FUND RESOURCES. None of the three funds has, nor is intended to have, resources equal to the total amount of deposits for which insurance coverage is provided. This point is often misunderstood. The best insurance any depositor has (indeed, any creditor of any business firm has) is the quality of the firm's assets, which is, in turn, based on the present value of the assets' expected cash inflows. The creditors of most depositories have no need of the guarantee, because returns on the firm's assets are used to pay interest and to repay principal to funds suppliers. Even if most depositories were closed today, the liquidation

of assets would provide cash to pay off liabilities in full.

Federal deposit insurance has a great psychological impact, however, because it prevents a recurrence of the debilitating runs on depositories that occurred in the 1930s. Furthermore, the insurers have lines of credit with the Treasury, assuring them of cash should funds be depleted in an emergency. This arrangement further enhances public confidence in the banking system. The public appears to value these lines of credit greatly. In 1985, for example, runs on nonfederally insured thrifts in Ohio and Maryland forced the failure of some and the temporary closure of others, but the runs did not extend to federally insured institutions. A similar occurrence in Rhode Island in 1990, when a private insurer of credit unions failed but federally insured CUs were not affected, reiterated the importance of the federal guarantee. Confidence in federal insurance is more important than the insurance itself.

COVERAGE PROVIDED

Because of insurance coverage rules and because the financial resources of consumers and businesses differ, the effect of federal insurance on depositor behavior varies according to type of depositor.

EFFECT ON CONSUMER DEPOSITORS. A commonly held notion of federal insurance coverage is that depositors are insured up to a maximum of $100,000, exclusive of individual retirement accounts (IRAs), at each depository in which they have funds. Additional coverage of up to $100,000 is provided for IRAs at the same institution. As Table 16.4 demonstrates, however, the possibilities for coverage beyond these amounts are considerable. A family of four could have deposit insurance of up to $1.4 million *at each institution* with which it had a relationship. The key is identifying the ownership of different accounts in such a way that no more than $100,000 is claimed by any one legal owner. In this example, for instance, revocable trust accounts are shown for all family members. These are accounts established for the benefit of one person but administered by another; they are legally separate from other accounts owned by either individual and can be established by a simple deposit signature card.

Although this example is deliberately extreme, it makes an important point: Under the current system,

---

[45] Debates on the initial risk-adjusted premium structure were commonly reported. See, for example, Barbara A. Rehm, "FDIC Fixes Premium at Average of 25.4 Cents," *American Banker,* September 16, 1992, 1, 10; and "FDIC May Widen Premium Range in 1994, Benefiting Healthy Banks," *American Banker,* December 16, 1992, 1, 2, 12.

[46] Details on NCUSIF's operations are reported regularly in its annual reports and in the annual reports of the NCUA.

TABLE 16.4	**Extending Deposit Insurance Coverage**

The maximum amount of federal deposit insurance available is generally believed to be $100,000 per individual per institution. The regulations actually allow a higher level of coverage, however, if trust or joint accounts are established. A family of four could receive full deposit insurance coverage on $1,400,000 at one bank, thrift, or CU.

Husband, Wife, and Two Children: Insured accounts totaling $1,400,000	
Individual Accounts	
Husband	$100,000
Wife	100,000
Child 1	100,000
Child 2	100,000
Joint Accounts[a]	
Husband and wife	$100,000
Husband and child 1	100,000
Wife and child 2	100,000
Child 1 and child 2	100,000
Revocable Trust Accounts	
Husband as trustee for wife	$100,000
Husband as trustee for child 1	100,000
Husband as trustee for child 2	100,000
Wife as trustee for husband	100,000
Wife as trustee for child 1	100,000
Wife as trustee for child 2	100,000

[a] Joint account with right of survivorship.
Source: Adapted from "Insured Accounts for Savers," Federal Reserve Bank of Richmond, September 1989.

most consumers can have full insurance coverage for all their deposits. For this reason, consumer depositors, even though they are creditors, have little reason to examine the creditworthiness of institutions.[47] Thus, insured depositors exert little influence on management's decisions about how deposits will be invested. Some financial economists believe, in fact, that to expect consumer depositors to serve as main sources of monitoring for depositories would destabilize the banking system by making it more prone to panics, including those started from rumors or incomplete infor-

mation. Congress seemed to agree when it made no changes in the insurance limit in FDICIA.[48]

EFFECT ON BUSINESS DEPOSITORS. Commercial and institutional investors are different. Establishing insured accounts in many different names would usually be legally impossible and, in any case, too costly. Consequently, many corporate and institutional deposits exceed the federally insurable limit. In theory, these large depositors should be prime sources of **market discipline,** which is the possibility that creditors, owners, or both will react negatively to management's decisions and subsequently refuse to entrust funds to the institution. Confronted by market discipline, bank, thrift, or CU managers facing the loss of confidence-sensitive money should think twice before investing funds in excessively risky loans or securities.

IMPACT OF INSURANCE ON MARKET DISCIPLINE. In the past, large depositors had little reason to exercise market discipline. Except for the failure of Penn Square Bank in 1982, it had been the apparent, if not stated, policy of federal insurers to prevent even uninsured depositors from losing money when an institution fails. The insurers' approach to institutional failures was almost always to merge a failed depository into a healthy one so that creditors, insured and uninsured, simply became creditors of another, healthier firm. This approach reduced the incentive of uninsured creditors to monitor the risk-taking activities of the depositories with which they do business.

In the Penn Square case, the bank had a high proportion of energy-related loans and was poorly diversified. Its credit-granting standards were extremely low, and many of the loans were in default. After the bank was closed on July 5, 1982, the deposits of fully insured depositors were assumed by an FDIC-created bank, which opened for business the next morning. More than half of Penn Square's deposit accounts exceeded the insurance limit, however, and the FDIC gave unprecedented notice that it did not intend to guarantee them. This action was widely interpreted to mean that federal insurers were embarking on a new

---

[47] An interesting exception to this rule occurred in 1989 during the darkest days of the thrift crisis. Depositors became increasingly wary of the FSLIC guarantee and began to show a marked preference for FDIC insurance, to the glee of commercial banks. One of the stickiest political issues in FIRREA was whether thrifts would subsequently be able to use the same FDIC insurance logo as commercial banks. In a compromise that allowed the bill to move through Congress, a "separate but equal" logo was designed for SAIF institutions.

[48] These arguments are summarized in Mack E. Levonian and Paul P. Cheng, "Changing the $100,000 Deposit Insurance Limit," *Weekly Letter* (Federal Reserve Bank of San Francisco), May 10, 1991; Evanoff 1992; and Kenneth H. Bacon and Steven Lipin, "Under New Bank Law, More Large Depositors Face Losses in Failures," *The Wall Street Journal,* October 22, 1992, A1, A8.

approach to handling failures, invoking market discipline as a substitute for federal bailouts. Shortly thereafter, in fact, the FDIC announced a "modified payout" plan under which it would cover deposits over the insured limit only when there was a high probability that a liquidated bank's assets would provide the cash to do so.

Only months later, the course was diverted by FDIC actions in the crisis at Continental Illinois, a $40 billion institution. All creditors were notified that FDIC guarantees were completely in force, regardless of the size or nature of Continental's liabilities. When the FDIC was unable to find a suitable merger partner for Continental, it arranged for the bank to remain open under new management. Not a penny was lost by any creditor. Similar approaches were used to avert a systemic crisis that regulators feared might result from the failure of several large Texas banks in 1987 and 1988. The so-called too-big-to-fail doctrine, although inequitable, unpopular even with large institutions, and economically unsound, loomed large in the problems of the deposit insurance system in the past decade because it eroded incentives for market discipline.

As first mentioned in Chapter 2, continuing anxiety about the effects of the too-big-to-fail policy caused Congress to address the issue, at least partially, in FDICIA. Regulators are now required to act as soon as a depository's condition begins to weaken, including closing it immediately if it becomes insolvent. Officials must use the most economical method of handling failures and are prohibited from protecting uninsured depositors if doing so would increase costs to the deposit insurance funds. To the dismay of many critics, however, Congress also included a "systemic risk" exception to these rules. If the Secretary of the Treasury, two-thirds of the FDIC and Fed Boards, and the President agree, regulators may keep an institution open if its failure is thought to be a danger to the financial system. Some experts believe, therefore, that the institutions formerly considered too big to fail will automatically be considered eligible for the "systemic risk" exception. Fortunately, as of this writing, the new policy has yet to be tested, as none of the nation's largest banks have become insolvent since FDICIA.[49]

CONTINUED NEED FOR REFORM

The current federal deposit insurance system promotes greater internal managerial discipline than in the past (to avoid higher insurance premiums) but relatively little market discipline. When asset choices and deposit interest rates were constrained by regulation, moral hazard existed, but consequences for the insurance funds were not as great. The benefits of holding a depository charter—especially the shelter from competition and the low-cost funding available under Reg Q—prevented most managers and owners from seeking assets so risky that the institution risked failure and loss of the lucrative charter. Now that managerial discretion is much broader, however, and the regulatory "subsidy" of Reg Q has been eliminated, the moral hazard built into the system must be continually evaluated and policies implemented to minimize it. Considerable progress has been made with the risk-adjusted premiums and stronger capital requirements. But many experts argue that additional changes are needed. Some of the thorniest issues remaining are outlined in the following paragraphs.[50]

AMOUNT OF COVERAGE. Some argue that the financial system is weakened by less than 100 percent insurance coverage on all depository liabilities, particularly those of short maturity. Pointing to Continental Illinois, they note that the crisis occurred because uninsured creditors fled the bank, precipitating a liquidity crisis.

Others argue that protecting the small depositor is the objective of the system and that large depositors, presumably more sophisticated, are better able to protect themselves. This argument implies that the $100,000 limit is too high, not too low, and that lower limits would encourage vigilance and expose the

---

[49] FDIC policies in the Penn Square case are described in FDIC *Annual Reports* for 1982 and 1984. The "too big to fail" doctrine is discussed in Kuprianov and Mengle 1989; Hetzel 1991; and Jed Horowitz, "Banks in NY Clearing House Vote to Oppose 'Too Big to

Fail' Credo," *American Banker,* January 26, 1990, 1, 13. FDICIA rules are discussed in the Fed's 1991 *Annual Report,* p. 199; and Wall 1993.

[50] The literature on insurance reform is fascinating and would fill several books. Students are encouraged to consult some of the many good sources, including Flannery 1982a; "Research on Federal Deposit Insurance," a series of ten articles in Section II of *Proceedings of a Conference on Bank Structure and Competition,* 1983; Kane 1985; Kane 1989; and other articles cited throughout this section of the chapter.

Also of interest are regulators' position papers prepared to comply with Garn-St Germain: FDIC, *Deposit Insurance in a Changing Environment,* 1983; FHLBB, *Agenda for Reform,* 1983; and NCUA, *Credit Union Share Insurance,* 1983.

insurers to fewer losses. If federal insurance has dual objectives, however—protecting the financial system from runs as well as protecting small depositors—then lower coverage will not prevent runs. Thus, some reform proposals that lower insurance coverage limits also include a feature by which depositors themselves pay for additional insurance above the minimum if they desire it.[51] Related proposals suggest that deposit insurance should operate with a **coinsurance clause,** similar to many health insurance policies. Under coinsurance, the amount of insurance coverage might be quite large, but the depositor would bear a certain portion (10 percent is often mentioned) of any loss.

A different approach to lowering the amount of insured deposits is the idea of **narrow** or **safe banks** (called monetary service companies in some sources). Under such a proposal, these institutions alone would be allowed to offer deposit insurance; in exchange for the privilege, they would be authorized to invest exclusively in assets with very little or no risk.[52] Institutions holding riskier assets—*wide* banks—would not be able to purchase deposit insurance. Investors would then choose the type of firm in which to deposit their money and would be required to exert market discipline if they opted for other than narrow banks. If narrow banks were formed in large numbers, however, one might ask why an insurance system would be necessary at all, except in the instance of management fraud or theft. Some observers are also concerned that, considering the popularity of deposit insurance, a narrow banking system might result in insufficient funds directed to wide banks; thus, the flow of capital to new or expanding enterprises might be inefficient. Also, the higher cost of funds at wide banks could potentially increase the underinvestment problem discussed earlier in the chapter.

PRIVATE VERSUS GOVERNMENTAL PROVIDERS. Another issue in the reform of deposit insurance is who

should provide the insurance. Some experts advocate private-sector solutions for almost all economic problems, and deposit insurance is no exception. They argue that competition among potential providers of insurance will encourage efficiency and effectiveness, removing institutions from the tangles of the federal bureaucracy. Interestingly, FDICIA-based reforms of the deposit insurance system have in no way quieted proponents of privatizing. They argue, in fact, that the elaborate supervision requirements almost guarantee even greater inefficiency than in the past and continue to substitute the judgment of bureaucrats for that of the private sector. Furthermore, the FDIC's risk-sensitive premiums are based on historical information, whereas private insurers would evaluate expectations of an institution's future condition.

Opponents question the ability of the private sector to protect both individual depositors and the financial system as a whole. For example, are private firms large enough? Would they act in the public interest, or would they simply cancel the insurance of an institution they believe is too risky? If federal monitoring and intervention are needed, is it better simply to keep the federal insurance agencies? Finally, would the public trust private insurance? Some observers, including depository institution managers, doubt that it would. As the President of the Federal Reserve Bank of Cleveland stated of the bank runs in Ohio in 1985, "My most lasting impression of the crisis is how quickly depositors' confidence plummeted at the privately insured institutions. . . . Without depositors' confidence, even the best capitalized financial institution can be severely affected."[53]

NECESSARY REGULATION AND SUPERVISION. Federal deposit insurance raises questions about the need to regulate and/or supervise depository institutions. Many argue that the tools needed to prevent excessive risk taking were already in place before FDICIA but that regulators should have enforced them more zealously. To this end, considerable attention in recent years has been given to public disclosure of so-called enforcement actions—that is, regulators' orders to managers to cease undesirable practices. Public disclo-

---

[51] The public's outrage at the Bush administration's pre-FIRREA "trial balloon" proposal to charge user fees for deposit insurance (25 cents per $1,000) suggests that assessing depositors may be politically unpalatable. Apparently, depositors prefer to pay for insurance coverage through budget deficits.

[52] An often-cited narrow bank proposal is in Litan 1987 and was officially recommended by a recent national commission. See "Regulators, Congress Are Cited by Panel for Thrift Debacle," *The Wall Street Journal,* July 28, 1993, C 20. See also Randall J. Pozdena, "The False Hope of Narrow Banking," *Weekly Letter* (Federal Reserve Bank of San Francisco), November 8, 1991.

[53] The quotation is from Karen N. Horn, *1985 Annual Report,* Federal Reserve Bank of Cleveland, 3. Proposals for "privatizing" the deposit insurance system are discussed in Colwell and Trefzger 1989 and Petri and Ely 1992.

sure was to have begun in 1986, but it was postponed when depositories howled in protest. Fortunately, Title IX of FIRREA recognized the essential link between market discipline and disclosure by requiring publication of enforcement actions unless regulators believe that an institution's safety and soundness are threatened.[54] Even so, Congress eventually grew tired of regulators' excessive forbearance policies and passed rules in FDICIA that many believe result in extreme and unnecessary interference in the ongoing management of institutions. If neither pre-FDICIA laxity nor post-FDICIA micromanagement is ideal, where is the proper balance?

A SET OF COMPLEX TRADE-OFFS

Whatever the outcome over the next decade, Congress, depository institutions, and regulators know that any solution to the remaining problems of the deposit insurance system involves a complex set of trade-offs; as economists say, there is no "first-best" solution to this problem. For example, a trade-off exists between moral hazard and instability in the financial system. If full insurance coverage is provided, instability from bank runs is minimized, but moral hazard is increased. With no deposit insurance, moral hazard is minimized, but instability is maximized.

Another potential trade-off involves equity and efficiency. An equitable deposit insurance system would treat all depositors and depositories in the same way. If regulators believe that some institutions are too important to fail, for example, all would be protected from failure. Foreign and domestic depositors would be treated equally; the current system does not assess premiums on foreign deposits. Thus, although large banks do not pay insurance premiums on their foreign deposits, under the "too-big-to-fail" doctrine they effectively got billions of dollars of coverage ($16.6 billion in the Continental Illinois case, for example) for which they were not paying.[55] In contrast, an economically efficient deposit insurance system would allow poorly managed institutions, regardless of size, location, or type of business, to suffer the consequences of their errors.

Finally come the trade-offs between economic and political realities. The most economically advisable solution may be politically unthinkable. Because politicians must ultimately decide the fate of the system, this final trade-off will undoubtedly be the most influential of all.

SUMMARY

Deposit and nondeposit liabilities for depository institutions and regulations governing their management were the subjects of this chapter. The phase-out of Reg Q gave institutions new freedom to offer a wide variety of accounts with different maturities and interest rate characteristics. Larger and more aggressive institutions also rely heavily on managed liabilities, including negotiable CDs, Eurodollar deposits, repurchase agreements, mortgage-backed securities, brokered deposits, deposit notes, and bank notes. Even contingent liabilities serve as sources of discretionary funds for some institutions.

The elimination of restrictions on institutions' access to funds has given managers new challenges. Institutions formerly relying on implicit interest payments as the only allowable form of competition now develop pricing strategies, and the choice between explicit and implicit interest affects the volatility of returns. Many firms offer flexible pricing mechanisms that provide more choices to customers and to management. New Fed rules require uniform disclosure of an institution's fee structure and yields on deposits. In conjunction with pricing decisions, management must evaluate wholesale and retail market strategies and choose the mix of funds that firms will seek.

Federal deposit insurance continues to influence management decisions. Insurance reduces the risk borne by depositors and therefore reduces the potential instability of funds to insured institutions. Because insurance premiums have only recently been adjusted to reflect the relative riskiness of an institution, it is too early to know whether the substantial moral hazard, which contributed to many depository failures over the past decade, has been brought under control. Several recommendations for additional reform have been considered, but there is no doubt that some form of deposit insurance will continue to provide a buffer against loss of confidence in the financial system.

[54] FDIC, *Annual Reports;* "Conference Report on HR 1278," 1989.

[55] Insurance for foreign deposits is discussed further in Cumming 1985 and Lawrence and Arshadi 1988. Until a large U.S. bank fails in the post-FDICIA era, whether uninsured foreign depositors will continue to receive protection is unknown.

QUESTIONS

1. What was the rationale for including ceilings on deposit interest rates (Regulation Q) in the Glass-Steagall Act of 1933? Contrast Reg Q's impact on depository institutions before 1966 and between 1966 and 1980. Why was Reg Q finally abolished?

2. When William Isaac, former Chairman of the FDIC, was asked in 1990 to name the most important banking event of the 1980s, he chose the removal of Reg Q rather than the Garn-St Germain Act, FIRREA, the growth of interstate banking, and other major economic occurrences. Why do you think he did so? Do you agree with his choice? Why or why not?

3. What was the "Wild Card" certificate? What changes have occurred in regulations and economic conditions that give deposits like Wild Card certificates, considered unacceptable in the 1970s, a major role in today's financial system?

4. What is liability management? Explain its purposes and the types of funds used for each purpose. Compare and contrast the risks of each liability source with those of traditional deposit sources of funds.

5. Do you view the recent decline in the negotiable CD market (recall the discussion of this market in Chapter 5) as a setback to institutions wishing to pursue liability management? Why or why not? How do deposit notes and bank notes compare to negotiable CDs as tools of liability management? How do market perceptions of a bank's riskiness affect its ability to pursue successful liability management strategies?

6. TRX Incorporated is a large corporate customer of First City Bank. TRX's cash managers have just contacted the bank to arrange a withdrawal of $50 million from the corporate checking account for reinvestment in interest-bearing marketable securities. Bank management suggests, as an alternative, that the corporation consider a Eurodollar deposit in its branch in Zurich. Illustrate with T-accounts the creation of the Eurodollar deposit and its effect on the assets and liabilities of both the domestic and foreign branches of the bank.

7. Explain how mortgage lenders use mortgage-backed bonds and collateralized mortgage obligations to obtain new funds.

8. Explain how contingent liabilities are used as a part of a liability management strategy. Describe the relationship between an institution's access to contingent liabilities and its avoidance of the underinvestment problem.

9. What are brokered deposits and what advantages do they offer to financial institutions? What are the risks involved? What stance did Congress take toward brokered deposits in FIRREA and FDICIA? Do you agree with the provisions on brokered deposits? Why or why not?

10. Explain the difference between confidence-sensitive money and hot money. What factors influence a depository institution manager's choice between aggressive and conservative approaches to funds management?

11. What are implicit interest payments? Why have depositories used them, and why do some depositors prefer them even after the removal of interest rate ceilings? How can implicit-interest pricing strategies affect the stability of earnings as interest revenues change?

12. Compare the cost and volatility of retail and wholesale funds. What additional factors affect a depository's decision to specialize in one source of funds or the other? From banking publications, find examples of one successful wholesale and one successful retail depository. What are the keys to the success of each?

13. Review bank and thrift advertisements in current newspapers and periodicals. What strategies are institutions using to attract retail deposits? What implicit pricing strategies can you identify? How would you measure their potential cost?

14. Do you agree with FDICIA provisions, or do you believe basic banking services are an essential entitlement for U.S. citizens? Why? What alternatives do you suggest for consumers who believe that they cannot afford banking services offered at private-sector prices?

15. Setting deposit account prices is a complex process. What types of analyses are required? Find an example of an innovative pricing strategy used by a depository in your area. To what type of customer does this strategy seem designed to appeal?

16. What factors determine the marginal cost of a deposit account? Why is knowledge of this marginal cost important to managers?

17. What motivates a depository to offer conditionally free accounts? Are such accounts really "free" to the customer? Why or why not?

18. Explain the intention of Congress in establishing truth-in-savings requirements in FDICIA. How might these regulations benefit consumers? In what ways do you think they will affect institutions' deposit pricing strategies?

19. Discuss the concept of moral hazard and its impact on the effectiveness of federal deposit and share insurance programs. From recent publications, find an example of a depository failure in which moral hazard played a role.

20. What changes did FDICIA make in the premium structure for deposit insurance; and what was the basis of Congress's decisions? Does the post-FDICIA structure address the moral hazard problem? Explain.

21. Consult recent bank and regulatory publications for information on risk-adjusted deposit insurance premiums. Are current rates higher or lower than the proposed system shown in Table 16.3? Has the system succeeded in restoring the resources of the FDIC? In strengthening the solvency of U.S. banks?

22. Is the failure of large institutions more dangerous to the financial system than the failure of small ones? Why or why not? What inequities are inherent in the "too-big-to-fail" doctrine? Are there benefits to this doctrine that outweigh the inequities? Explain.

23. In 1990, officials at the Federal Reserve Bank of Minneapolis proposed a reform of the deposit insurance system that included the following provisions: only one fully insured account per person; full insurance on only $10,000; 90 percent insurance on all other deposits. From the perspectives of reducing moral hazard and promoting economic stability, what are the advantages and disadvantages of such a plan?

24. Do you think that a private deposit insurance system is a viable alternative for some institutions? Why or why not?

25. Could the financial system survive without federal deposit insurance? Why or why not? Would your answer change if you were retired and living on Social Security? If you were on *Forbes* magazine's annual list of the 400 richest Americans? In your opinion, whom should the ideal federal insurance program protect? How much protection should be available? Who should pay the cost? What responsibilities should be placed on depository institution managers under the ideal system?

PROBLEMS

1. Community State Bank has agreed to sell Commercial National Bank $6 million in federal funds for 2 days at a quoted rate of 8.5 percent. How much must Commercial National repay to Community? What is the effective annual yield to Community? (Fed funds yields are illustrated in Chapter 5.)

2. Singapore Suburban Bank is purchasing $300 million in fed funds at a rate of 7.85 percent. How much must the bank repay in 3 days? What is the effective annual cost of the transaction?

3. Yosemite Savings sells a jumbo CD to Alta Vista Corporation in a face amount of $1.75 million. The stated annual rate is 8.00 percent, and the maturity is 180 days. How much must Yosemite provide to Alta Vista upon maturity? What is the effective annual cost of the CD? Carry your percentage to three decimal places—for example, 0.08002 = 8.002 percent. (Yields on negotiable CDs are illustrated in Chapter 5.)

4. Suppose, instead, that the maturity of the CD in Problem 3 was 182 days. How much must Yosemite repay, and what is the effective annual cost? Compare your results to those in Problem 3 and explain the similarities and differences.

5. a. Calculate the degree of operating leverage (DOL) for First National Bank if total revenues are $1.3 billion, variable costs are $850 million, and fixed costs are $350 million. If revenues increase by 15 percent, by how much will operating income increase?
b. Assume that total revenues increase to $1.5 billion and that fixed costs do not change. Also assume that variable costs increase to $980 million. Recompute the DOL. Why is your answer different from that in part a? What are the implications for management?

6. The management of Lincoln Bank and Trust is analyzing the bank's cost structure. You have been asked to evaluate the effect of implicit interest payments on operating income; approximately 25 percent of fixed costs is traced to implicit interest. The following information is provided:
- Total revenues: $65 million
- Total variable costs: 80 percent of total revenues
- Total fixed costs: $8.0 million
a. If explicit interest were substituted for implicit interest, what percentage of total revenues would variable costs be? What would total fixed costs be?
b. Calculate the degree of operating leverage with and without implicit interest payments (that is, under the current structure *and* under the one described in part a).
c. If revenues increase by 10 percent, by how much would you expect operating income to change under the current cost structure? Under the alternative structure?

d. If revenues decrease by 10 percent, what would operating income be under the current and alternative cost structures?

e. What risk/return trade-off is involved with implicit versus explicit interest?

7. a. The manager of Great Smoky Mountains Savings and Loan wishes to estimate the total marginal cost of retail MMDAs. Reserve requirements are 0 percent, and the cost of deposit insurance is 0.23 percent. Competing institutions are paying 8 percent on MMDAs, and the manager estimates that servicing costs are 2.5 percent.

b. The manager is considering a marketing campaign to attract more NOW account customers because the explicit interest rate on NOWs is only 5.5 percent, compared to 8.0 percent on MMDAs. The unlimited transactions feature of NOWs increases reserve requirements to 10 percent and servicing costs to 4 percent. Will the institution enjoy cost reductions if customers switch from MMDAs to NOWs? Explain why or why not.

8. A large superregional bank is estimating the average marginal cost of its retail deposit accounts. The finance department has collected the following data on each type of account:

	Explicit Effective Interest Rate	Servicing Cost	Insurance Premium	Reserve Requirement	Expected Total Balances (billions)
Demand deposits	0.0%	6.50%	0.23%	10%	$1.77
NOWs	5.0	4.00	0.23	10	1.27
MMDAs	8.0	1.50	0.23	0	1.92
Passbook savings	4.5	0.50	0.23	0	0.64
CDs*	8.9	0.25	0.23	0	1.03

*(<$100,000 per account).

a. What is the average marginal total cost? (Hint: Weight the total cost of each deposit by its proportion of total deposits.)

b. From the perspective of cost, should the bank seek additional dollars through the federal funds market or should it attempt to attract more MMDA accounts? Fed funds are customarily purchased with 3-day maturities, and the current rate is 7.75 percent. What other factors besides cost should management consider in making this decision?

9. In the following situations, would the depositor have any uninsured deposits? If so, explain how much and why.

a. Mary Edwards has a NOW account with a $10,000 balance and an MMDA with a $45,000 balance. She and her husband Phil have two joint accounts, one for $70,000 and the other for $35,000. Mary also has an individual retirement account in which she has accumulated $35,000. All accounts are held at the same bank.

b. Mike Seeborg purchased a $90,000 CD at the beginning of the year on which he has earned one year's interest at 12 percent. The interest was reinvested in the account. He also has a joint savings account for $20,000 with his son Kevin. All accounts are at the same savings bank.

c. Bill and Emily Fisher have two joint accounts for $60,000 each. The accounts are at two different S&Ls. Bill has also recently opened a $50,000 account for Emily at one of the S&Ls, for which he serves as trustee.

Using the proposed risk-adjusted premium schedule for 1994 and beyond, shown at the bottom of Table 16.3, rank the following institutions (1 = lowest premium) according to the annual dollar insurance premium each would pay. Assume each institution has $100,000,000 in deposits eligible for federal insurance coverage.

Name	Supervisory Rating	Capital Adequacy
Biloxi National Bank and Trust	B	Less than adequate
Westoff National Bank	C	Adequate
Minot State Bank	A	Very well capitalized
Biltmore Federal Savings	D	Well capitalized
Groton Savings Bank	B	Very well capitalized

11. Suppose you deposit $20,000 at the beginning of the year in Summersville National Bank. The bank offers a stated annual interest rate of 8 percent.

    a. Show that if interest is paid annually and there are no service charges, the annual percentage yield (APY) equals the stated annual rate.

    b. Now suppose that interest is paid monthly and that service charges are $1.50 per month. The bank defines a month as 30 days. Calculate the APY.

    c. Calculate the APY if, instead, interest is paid quarterly and service charges are $3.00 per quarter. The bank considers a quarter to be 90 days.

    d. Finally, suppose interest is paid semi-annually and that each semi-annual period is defined as 182 days. If service charges are $5.00 every six months, what is the APY?

SELECTED REFERENCES

Allen, Pat. "CMO Conduit Participants Use Proceeds to Boost Profits." *Savings Institutions* 106 (October 1986): 76–79.

Avery, Robert B., Gerald A. Hanweck, and Myron L. Kwast. "An Analysis of Risk-Based Deposit Insurance for Commercial Banks." In *Proceedings of the Conference on Bank Structure and Competition,* 217–250. Chicago: Federal Reserve Bank of Chicago, 1985.

Baer, Herbert. "Private Prices, Public Insurance: The Pricing of Federal Deposit Insurance." *Economic Perspectives* (Federal Reserve Bank of Chicago) 9 (September/October 1985): 45–57.

Baer, Herbert, and Elijah Brewer. "Uninsured Deposits as a Source of Market Discipline." *Economic Perspectives* (Federal Reserve Bank of Chicago) 10 (September/October 1986): 23–31.

Benston, George. "Interest on Deposits and the Survival of Chartered Depository Institutions." *Economic Review* (Federal Reserve Bank of Atlanta) 69 (October 1984): 42–56.

Board of Governors of the Federal Reserve System. *1988 Annual Report.* Washington, DC: Board of Governors, 1988.

Brewer, Elijah. "Bank Funds Management Comes of Age—A Balance Sheet Analysis." *Economic Perspectives* (Federal Reserve Bank of Chicago) 4 (May/June 1980): 13–18.

Burns, Joseph E. "Bank Liquidity—A Straightforward Concept but Hard to Measure." *Business Review* (Federal Reserve Bank of Dallas) (May 1971): 1–4.

Campbell, Tim S., and David Glenn. "Deposit Insurance in a Deregulated Environment." *Journal of Finance* 39 (July 1984): 775–787.

Canner, Glenn B., and Ellen Maland. "Basic Banking." *Federal Reserve Bulletin* 73 (April 1987): 255–269.

Carraro, Kenneth C., and Daniel L. Thornton. "The Cost of

Checkable Deposits in the United States." *Economic Review* (Federal Reserve Bank of St. Louis) 68 (April 1986): 19–27.

Cohn, Jeffrey, and Michael E. Edleson. "Banking on the Market: Equity-Linked CDs." *AAII Journal* 15 (March 1993): 11–15.

Colwell, Peter F., and Joseph W. Trefzger. "A New Look at Deposit Insurance Reform." *ORER Letter* (University of Illinois) (Fall 1989): 1–3.

"Conference Report on H.R. 1278, Financial Institutions Reform, Recovery and Enforcement Act, 1989." *Congressional Record—House of Representatives,* August 4, 1989.

Cook, Richard W. "A Low Cost/Price Checking Account that Works." *Bank Marketing* 21 (August 1989): 46–47.

Crosse, Howard D. "Bank Liquidity Revisited." *The Bankers Magazine* 158 (Spring 1975): 37–41.

Cumming, Christine M. "Federal Deposit Insurance and Deposits at Foreign Branches of U.S. Banks." *Quarterly Review* (Federal Reserve Bank of New York) 10 (Autumn 1985): 30–38.

Davis, Richard G., and Leon Korobow. "The Pricing of Consumer Deposit Products—The Non-Rate Dimensions." *Quarterly Review* (Federal Reserve Bank of New York) 11 (Winter 1986–87): 14–18.

Davis, Richard G., Leon Korobow, and John Wenninger. "Bankers on Pricing Consumer Deposits." *Quarterly Review* (Federal Reserve Bank of New York) 11 (Winter 1986–87): 6–13.

Dotsey, Michael. "An Examination of Implicit Interest Rates on Demand Deposits." *Economic Review* (Federal Reserve Bank of Richmond) 69 (September/October 1983): 3–11.

Dotsey, Michael, and Anatoli Kuprianov. "Reforming Deposit Insurance: Lessons from the Savings and Loan Crisis."

Economic Review (Federal Reserve Bank of Richmond) (March/April 1990): 3–28.

Dunham, Constance. "The Growth of Money Market Funds." *New England Economic Review* (Federal Reserve Bank of Boston) (September/October 1980): 20–34.

Elliehausen, Gregory E., and John D. Wolken. "Banking Markets and the Use of Financial Services by Households." *Federal Reserve Bulletin* 78 (March 1992): 169–184.

Elmer, Peter J. "Developing Service-Oriented Deposit Accounts." *Bankers Magazine* 168 (March/April 1985): 60–63.

Evanoff, Douglas D. "Preferred Sources of Market Discipline: Depositors vs Subordinated Debt Holders." Federal Reserve Bank of Chicago, Working Paper #92–21, 1992.

Flannery, Mark. "Deposit Insurance Creates a Need for Bank Regulation." *Business Review* (Federal Reserve Bank of Philadelphia) (January/February 1982a): 17–24.

————. "Retail Bank Deposits as Quasi-Fixed Factors of Production." *American Economic Review* 72 (June 1982b): 527–536.

Flood, Mark D. "The Great Deposit Insurance Debate," *Review* (Federal Reserve Bank of St. Louis) 74 (July/August 1992): 51–77.

Friedman, Milton. "Controls on Interest Rates Paid by Banks." *Journal of Money, Credit, and Banking* 2 (February 1970): 15–32.

Furlong, Frederick. "A View on Deposit Insurance Coverage." *Economic Review,* Federal Reserve Bank of San Francisco (Spring 1984): 31–38.

Gardner, Mona J., and Lucille E. Lammers. "Cost Accounting in Large Banks." *Management Accounting* 69 (April 1988): 34–39.

Gilbert, R. Alton. "Requiem for Regulation Q: What It Did and Why It Passed Away." *Review,* Federal Reserve Bank of St. Louis 68 (February 1986): 22–37.

Golly, Jr., Albert J. "An Individual Investor's Guide to the Complex World of CMOs." *AAII Journal,* July 1992, 7–10.

Goodfriend, Marvin. "Eurodollars." In *Instruments of the Money Market,* 6th ed., 53–64. Richmond, VA: Federal Reserve Bank of Richmond, 1986.

Goodfriend, Marvin, and William Whelpley. "Federal Funds." In *Instruments of the Money Market,* 6th ed., 8–22. Richmond, VA: Federal Reserve Bank of Richmond, 1986.

Hanweck, Gerald A. "Federal Deposit Insurance: A Critical Review of Some Proposals for Reform." *Issues in Bank Regulation* 9 (Winter 1986): 25–29.

Harless, Caroline T. "Brokered Deposits." *Economic Review* (Federal Reserve Bank of Atlanta) 69 (March 1984): 14–25.

Hetzel, Robert L. "Too Big to Fail: Origins, Consequences, and Outlook." *Economic Review* (Federal Reserve Bank of Richmond) 77 (November/December 1991): 3–15.

Higgins, Byron. "Interest Payments on Demand Deposits: Historical Evolution and the Current Controversy." *Monthly Review* (Federal Reserve Bank of Kansas City) 62 (July-August 1977): 3–11.

Hirschhorn, Eric. "Developing a Proposal for Risk-Related Deposit Insurance." *Banking and Economic Review* (Federal Deposit Insurance Corporation) 4 (September/October 1986): 3–10.

James, Christopher. "Off-Balance Sheet Activities and the Underinvestment Problem in Banking." *Journal of Accounting, Auditing, and Finance* 4 (Spring 1989): 111–124.

Kane, Edward J. "All for the Best: The Federal Reserve Board's 60th Annual Report." In *Current Perspectives in Banking,* edited by Thomas Havrilesky and John T. Boorman, 523–532. Arlington Heights, IL: AHM Publishing Corp., 1976.

————. "The Three Faces of Commercial Bank Liability Management." In *The Political Economy of Policy-Making,* edited by M. J. Dooley. Beverly Hills, CA: Sage Publications, 1979.

————. "A Six-Point Program for Deposit Insurance Reform." *Housing Finance Review* 2 (July 1983): 269–278.

————. *The Gathering Crisis in Federal Deposit Insurance.* Cambridge, MA: The MIT Press, 1985.

————. *The S&L Insurance Mess: How Did It Happen?* Washington, DC: The Urban Institute Press, 1989.

Keeley, Michael C. "Interest-Rate Deregulation." *Weekly Letter* (Federal Reserve Bank of San Francisco), January 13, 1984.

Keeley, Michael C., and Gary C. Zimmerman. "Competition for Money Market Deposit Accounts." *Economic Review* (Federal Reserve Bank of San Francisco) (Spring 1985): 5–27.

Kuprianov, Anatoli, and David L. Mengle. "The Future of Deposit Insurance: An Analysis of the Alternatives." *Eco-*

nomic Review (Federal Reserve Bank of Richmond) 75 (May/June 1989): 3–15.

Lawrence, Edward C., and Nasser Arshadt. "The Distributional Impact of Foreign Deposits on Federal Insurance Premia." *Journal of Banking and Finance* 12 (March 1988): 105–115.

Litan, Robert. *What Should Banks Do?* Washington, DC: Brookings Institution, 1987.

Logue, James A. "Pricing Strategies for the 1980s." *Magazine of Bank Administration* 59 (September 1983): 28–34.

Luckett, Dudley. "Approaches to Bank Liquidity Management." *Economic Review* (Federal Reserve Bank of Kansas City) 65 (March 1980): 11–27.

Luttrell, Clifford B. "The Hunt Commission Report—An Economic View." *Review* (Federal Reserve Bank of St. Louis) 54 (June 1972): 8–12.

Mahoney, Patrick I. "The Recent Behavior of Demand Deposits." *Federal Reserve Bulletin* 74 (April 1988): 195–208.

Mahoney, Patrick I., et al. "Responses to Deregulation: Retail Deposit Pricing from 1983 through 1985." Board of Governors of the Federal Reserve System, Staff Study Number 151, January 1987.

McKinney, George W. "Liability Management: Its Costs and Uses." In *Financial Institutions and Markets in a Changing World,* edited by Donald R. Fraser and Peter S. Rose, 90–104. Dallas: Business Publications, 1980.

Moore, Robert R. "Brokered Deposits: Determinants and Implications for Thrift Distributions." *Financial Industry Studies* (Federal Reserve Bank of Dallas) December 1991, 15–27.

Murphy, Neil B., and Richard H. Kraas. "Measuring the Interest Sensitivity of Money Markets Accounts." *Magazine of Bank Administration* 60 (May 1984): 70–74.

Murton, Arthur J. "A Survey of the Issues and the Literature Concerning Risk-Related Deposit Insurance." *Banking and Economic Review* (Federal Deposit Insurance Corporation) 4 (September/October 1986): 11–20.

Parliment, Tom. "Not Paying Market Is an Option." *Savings Institutions* 106 (April 1985): S12–S17.

Petri, Thomas E., and Bert Ely, "Real Taxpayer Protection." *Policy Review* (Spring 1992): 25–29.

Puglisi, Donald J., and Joseph A. McKenzie. "Capital Mar-

ket Strategies for Thrift Institutions." *Federal Home Loan Bank Board Journal* 16 (November 1983): 2–8.

"Research on Federal Deposit Insurance." In *Proceedings of a Conference on Bank Structure and Competition,* 196–298. Chicago: Federal Reserve Bank of Chicago, 1983.

Rogowski, Robert J. Pricing the Money Market Deposit and Super-NOW Accounts in 1983." *Journal of Bank Research* 15 (Summer 1984): 72–81.

Schweitzer, Stuart A. "Bank Liability Management: For Better or for Worse?" *Business Review* (Federal Reserve Bank of Philadelphia) (December 1974): 3–16.

Scott, Charlotte H. "Low-Income Banking Needs and Services." *Journal of Retail Banking* 10 (Fall 1988): 32–40.

Simons, Katerina, and Stephen Cross. "Do Capital Markets Predict Problems in Large Commercial Banks?" *New England Economic Review* (Federal Reserve Bank of Boston) (May/June 1991): 51–56.

Staten, Michael. "Retail Banker's Review of Laws and Regulations—Winter 1989." *Journal of Retail Banking* 11 (Winter 1989): 62–63.

Stigum, Marcia. *The Money Market.* 3d ed. Homewood, IL: Dow Jones-Irwin, 1990.

Taggart, Robert A., Jr. "Effects of Deposit Rate Ceilings: The Evidence from Massachusetts Savings Banks." *Journal of Money, Banking, and Credit* 10 (May 1978): 139–157.

U.S. Congress, House Committee on Banking, Currency, and Housing. *Financial Institutions and the Nation's Economy (FINE): Discussion Principles.* Washington, DC: 94th Congress, November 1975.

Wall, Larry D. "Too-Big-To-Fail After FDICIA." *Economic Review* (Federal Reserve Bank of Atlanta) 78 (January/February 1993): 1–14.

Wall, Larry D., and Harold D. Ford. "Money Market Account Competition." *Economic Review* (Federal Reserve Bank of Atlanta) 69 (December 1984): 4–14.

Watro, Paul R. "Deregulation and Deposit Pricing." *Economic Commentary* (Federal Reserve Bank of Cleveland), April 23, 1984.

Watson, Ronald D. "Estimating the Cost of Your Bank's Funds." *Business Review* (Federal Reserve Bank of Philadelphia) (May/June 1978): 3–11.

———. "The Marginal Cost of Funds Concept in Banking." *Journal of Bank Research* 8 (Autumn 1977): 136–147.

White, Lawrence J. "Price Regulation and Quality Rivalry in a Profit Maximizing Model: The Case of Bank Branching." *Journal of Money, Credit, and Banking* 8 (February 1976): 97–106.

Willemse, Rob J. M. "Large Certificates of Deposit." In *Instruments of the Money Market.* 6th ed., 36–52. Richmond, VA: Federal Reserve Bank of Richmond, 1986.

Winningham, Scott, and Donald G. Hagan. "Regulation Q: An Historical Perspective." *Economic Review* (Federal Reserve Bank of Kansas City) 65 (April 1980): 3–17.

Wood, John H., and Norma L. Wood. *Financial Markets.* Chapter 9. San Diego: Harcourt Brace Jovanovich, 1985.

Zimmerman, Gary C. "Shopping Pays." *Weekly Letter* (Federal Reserve Bank of San Francisco), November 8, 1985.

Zimmerman, Gary C., and Michael Keeley. "Interest Checking." *Weekly Letter* (Federal Reserve Bank of San Francisco), November 14, 1986.

Zimmerman, Gary C., and Jonathan A. Neuberger. "Interest Rate Competition." *Weekly Letter* (Federal Reserve Bank of San Francisco), July 27, 1990.

*. . . it is increasingly obvious that thrifts will find raising capital
about as easy as raising the dead.*
Charles McCoy
Staff Reporter, *The Wall Street Journal* (1989)

———————————————————

Ralph Esposito is President of Gilman & Ciocia, a financial planning firm with almost 30 offices on the East Coast. His firm has a long
history of profitable operations. But when he applied to his New York
bank to increase his line of credit to finance the establishment of 10
new West Coast offices, the bank refused the loan. Mr. Esposito told
The Wall Street Journal, "I can run through hoops, collateralize the loan
six times over, but the bank does not want to help us expand our
business."[1]

In 1992, scarcely a week went by without a similar story in the
financial press describing the difficulties faced by many small- and
medium-sized firms as their owners and managers tried to obtain loans
from commercial banks. Politicians and regulators debated whether it
really was more difficult for business firms to obtain commercial
loans—generally known as a "credit crunch"—or whether bankers
were just exercising appropriate caution in their lending decisions by
rejecting questionable borrowers. As this debate continued, many firms
realized that commercial banks were not particularly interested in their
business, and the economic slump persisted.

While they argued over the existence of a credit crunch in the
early 1990s, bankers and federal officials found one point on which they
could agree: The new capital standards imposed on depository institutions in 1991 and 1992 were definitely affecting commercial lending
decisions. These risk-based capital standards require banks and thrifts to
hold more capital as the riskiness of assets increases. Because smaller
companies usually are assigned lower credit ratings by the rating agencies and have limited access to the capital markets, federal regulations
place loans to such borrowers in the higher risk categories. Banks with
capital at or near minimum required levels cannot afford to approve
additional loans falling into these categories. The plight of Mr. Esposito
and the owners of many other small business firms led to a renewed
appreciation for the importance of capital in the management of financial institutions.

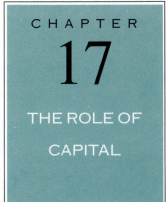

CHAPTER

17

THE ROLE OF

CAPITAL

———————————

[1] Fred R. Bleakley, "Many Midsized Firms Still Find That Insurers and Banks Deny Loans,"
The Wall Street Journal, November 16, 1992, A1, A4.

In fact, although depository institutions rely heavily on deposits and other liabilities, they could not operate without **capital.** Capital consists of all long-term, nondeposit funds subordinate to deposits in claims on the firm's income and assets. Major sources of capital are long-term debt, common and preferred stock, and retained earnings. All businesses need capital, but only financial institutions have minimum capital requirements specifically identified by regulators. That fact indicates the significant role of capital in the financial management of depositories.

The initial question addressed in this chapter is, Why is capital so important? Next, more precise definitions of capital than the one in the preceding paragraph are examined. Regulators' **capital adequacy** standards are also discussed. The standards are their attempts to answer the question, How much capital is enough? Finally, problems in determining and attaining the desired level of capital in an individual depository are outlined.

WHY CAPITAL?

Capital fulfills several functions, but their relative importance is a subject of debate.

CAPITAL PROVIDES SUPPORT FOR FIXED INVESTMENT

Everyone agrees on one reason for capital. The long-term commitment of funds by investors willing to put money at risk enables a business to begin operations. Initial capital is used to purchase or rent premises, to hire employees, and to obtain other assets necessary to begin taking deposits and making loans. In the early stages, cash contributed by initial capital suppliers may be critically important until a profitable operating plan can be developed. Once a depository is firmly established, expansions requiring additional fixed assets are usually financed with capital rather than deposits. Because these assets are permanent additions to the institution's operations, paying for them with short-term liabilities would be unwise.

CAPITAL PROMOTES CONFIDENCE

The preceding chapter emphasized the significance of depositor confidence in an institution. Federal deposit insurance plays a major role in transmitting that confidence and reducing the probability of bank runs, but uninsured depositors and other short-term creditors require additional evidence to justify placing confidence-sensitive money in an institution. Because capital suppliers have a subordinate claim on the depository's income and assets, their investment helps to reassure uninsured creditors. Even if the institution has financial difficulty, uninsured depositors know the extent to which the value of assets can shrink before they are in danger of not recovering all their funds; that amount is equal to the total capital of the institution. The more capital, the more protection is afforded to uninsured depositors and other short-term creditors, making a run on the institution less likely.

THE ROLE OF CAPITAL ILLUSTRATED. Suppose that a savings bank has assets with a market value of $100 million and deposits of $92 million, of which $80 million qualify for full federal insurance. Total capital in the institution is $8 million:

Majestic Savings Bank
Balance Sheet

Assets		Deposits and Capital	
$ 30,000,000	Treasury bills	$ 92,000,000	Deposits ($80,000,000 insured)
70,000,000	Loans (including $55,000,000 in mortgages)	8,000,000	Capital
$100,000,000	Total	$100,000,000	Total

Suppose a major employer in town announces that it is transferring its headquarters out of state. Many of the firm's employees are to lose their jobs, and Majestic has made mortgage loans to some of them. If delinquent payments reduce mortgage income, Majestic's uninsured depositors may begin to evaluate whether the institution could fail. Any mortgages on which payments are not being made will decline in value, determined as the present value of the remaining cash flows expected from the loans.

The $8 million in capital, however, means that the value of the firm's assets must decline by $8 million before uninsured deposits are endangered. Because that amount would represent an immediate deterioration of about 14.5 percent ($8/$55) in the mortgage portfolio, many uninsured depositors may conclude that such a sharp decline is unlikely and leave their money on deposit. Obviously, that decision will greatly assist Majestic as it copes with the delinquencies, because a liquidity crisis may be averted. Were capital low—for example, only $2 million—the decline in the mortgage portfolio would have to be only 3.6 percent ($2/$55) for capital to be exhausted, a much more probable occurrence. Large depositors would be more likely to withdraw funds, impeding the institution's ability to resolve its financial problems in time to avoid failure.

CAPITAL SUPPORTS GROWTH

Capital also assists depositories in achieving growth objectives. Although an institution may actively seek a deposit volume and mix based on a strategic plan, it faces unknown responses from customers and competitors. If specific investment goals are to be attained, they must wait if deposit growth takes longer to materialize than anticipated. Capital is an alternative source of funding. If an institution sells new stock or bonds or retains profits from previous periods, it can acquire new assets. It can also pursue opportunities without delays that may result from sluggish deposit growth or the risks that may be incurred from using confidence-sensitive money.

This does not imply that depository institution managers are eager to use capital. Suppliers of capital must be compensated for their investment, so managers must make a convincing case for the funds, and investors must have prospects for earning an expected return commensurate with the risk they take. If capital is raised by issuing common stock, existing shareholders may be concerned that additional shares will dilute their claims to residual income and assets. Nonetheless, capital may sometimes be the most appropriate source of funds for achieving growth.

CAPITAL REDUCES MORAL HAZARD

The previous chapter discussed the moral hazard produced by the federal deposit insurance system. The scope of coverage and regulators' handling of past failures may encourage depository managers to take excessive risks. Economists also argue that the amount of capital an institution maintains is related to moral hazard. The less capital, the greater the moral hazard and, conversely, the more capital, the greater the protection for the deposit insurance funds.[2]

Consider an institution that begins with assets of $5 million in cash; the source of the cash is $5 million of capital. The cash can be used to make loans with a 50 percent probability of default (that is, the entire initial $5 million will be lost) and a 50 percent probability of producing a $5 million profit after all expenses are paid. The expected dollar return on the investment is:

$$0.5(-\$5,000,000) + 0.5(\$5,000,000) = \$0$$

The expected rate of return to capital suppliers is 0 percent, and they would probably encourage management to seek better investments.

In contrast, suppose that the institution is funded by $4 million in insured deposits at a cost of 10 percent ($400,000 interest expense) and $1 million in capital. The most that capital suppliers can lose is $1 million, and *their* expected dollar profit if the depository makes the loans is now

$$0.5(-\$1,000,000) +$$
$$0.5(\$5,000,000 - \$400,000) = \$1,800,000$$

Their expected rate of return is 180 percent, not 0 percent, even though the firm's potential investments are the same. The lower the amount of capital, the less incentive capital suppliers have to monitor the actions of management to prevent excessive risk taking. They have less to lose if things go poorly and more to gain if things go well.

This example recalls a principle discussed in Chapter 4—the impact of leverage on expected return to the residual claimants. In most businesses, creditors would step in to prevent a firm from using so much leverage that their own funds were in jeopardy. But when the creditors are insured by an outside agency, as is the case of federally insured depositors, their monitoring incentive is removed. All things equal, then, a federally insured depository with more capital will have fewer reasons to take excessive risks than one with less.[3]

COMPONENTS OF CAPITAL

Because capital serves different purposes and because the relative importance of those purposes may differ among customers, managers, owners, and regulators, complete agreement is lacking on exactly how capital should be defined. The arguments are not simply hair splitting. The reasons for capital suggest that regulators are likely to favor more capital for an institution

---

[2] The following example is similar to one used by Furlong and Keran 1984. (References are listed in full at the end of this chapter.)

[3] Assumptions about the actions of uninsured creditors derive from the agency theory literature in corporate finance, introduced in Chapter 1. Deposit insurance, however, undermines creditors' incentive to monitor. Capital regulations are, in fact, often viewed as a regulatory tool to offset the moral hazard problem introduced by the deposit insurance system. Analyses of this relationship are provided in Furlong and Keeley 1987a, Kim and Santomero 1988, Osterberg and Thompson 1989, and Furlong 1991.

than its managers and capital suppliers might like. Viewed in this context, exactly what should be considered capital takes on added importance. The discussion is furthered by partitioning capital into two broad categories—net worth and debt capital.

NET WORTH: TRADITIONAL SOURCES

As discussed in Chapter 4, net worth is the amount by which the value of the institution's assets exceeds the value of its liabilities, whether short- or long-term, insured or uninsured. Controversy exists over whether net worth should be measured in market values or accounting (book) values, a controversy explored in more detail later. Here, book-value definitions are assumed.

COMMON EQUITY. In shareholder-owned institutions, "net worth" and "equity capital" are synonymous, where equity capital is the claim on the business by common and preferred shareholders. Common equity—the sum of funds initially contributed by common shareholders plus retained earnings—is the owners' claim on shareholder-owned financial institutions. Owners are entitled to all residual profits but also must absorb losses. Thus, common equity fulfills all the purposes capital is intended to have: It is a long-term source of funds with a claim on the institution's income and assets subordinate to deposits. It provides the initial funding by which a shareholder-owned depository begins operations, promotes confidence on the part of uninsured depositors, supports growth, and reduces moral hazard. It is one component of all capital on which everyone can agree.

Of course, not all depositories are shareholder-owned. In mutually owned or not-for-profit depositories, the only permanently invested funds are earnings retained from profitable operations. As noted in Chapter 4, however, retained earnings (or undivided profits or reserves, as they are sometimes called) in a mutual or not-for-profit institution serve a function identical to common equity in a shareholder-owned firm. Thus, everyone agrees that they also fulfill the purposes of capital.

PREFERRED STOCK. The classification of preferred stock, another long-term source of funds for depositories, is less clear-cut. Some preferred stock is issued with a maturity date; most is not. Some is convertible into common stock at the option of the preferred stockholder; some is not. Thus, the permanence with which preferred stockholders view their holdings may differ, depending on the specific issue of stock they have purchased. Yet preferred stock has a claim on income and assets subordinate to the claims of depositors and other creditors. So, with some exceptions, preferred stock fulfills the purposes of capital. In shareholder-owned institutions, the sum of common equity and perpetual preferred stock is the firm's total equity capital, or its net worth.

Although preferred stock issues have historically been more popular for banks than for thrifts, in 1984, the Federal Home Loan Bank Board (FHLBB) enabled mutual as well as stockholder-owned savings and loan associations (S&Ls) to sell preferred stock through affiliated service corporations. Many have done so. Also, to meet regulators' increasingly stringent capital requirements discussed later in the chapter, many bank holding companies (BHCs) have issued preferred stock.[4]

MUTUAL CAPITAL CERTIFICATES. Similar to preferred stock but designed for direct issuance by mutual institutions are **mutual capital certificates (MCCs),** first authorized in the Depository Institutions Deregulation and Monetary Control Act (DIDMCA). MCCs are securities with a minimum denomination of $100,000 and a minimum maturity of at least 10 years. Their claim on income and assets is subordinate to that of depositors and other creditors. MCCs are intended to supplement undivided profits and reserves as a source of net worth for a mutually owned institution. As shown later, MCCs are one of several types of capital that regulators have deemed to be less effective than common stock or retained earnings in protecting the interests of the insurance funds. Thus, they serve a relatively minor role in institutional management.

NET WORTH: REGULATORY SOURCES

In the 1980s, federal regulators created nontraditional sources of net worth to support institutions with earnings or liquidity problems. These sources have been controversial, for many financial market

---

[4] "Finance Subsidiary Rule" 1984 and Wolfson 1985.

participants do not believe that they fulfill the intended purposes of capital. For the most part, federal regulators intended them to be temporary solutions to the problems of the thrift industry. Their use, with limitations, has persisted into the 1990s, however. In a few important instances, regulatory net worth sources have been used in the banking industry, too.

NET WORTH CERTIFICATES. Authorized in the Garn-St Germain Act and first defined in Chapter 2, net worth certificates (NWCs) are a form of capital assistance. They were originally offered by the Federal Savings and Loan Insurance Corporation (FSLIC) or the Federal Deposit Insurance Corporation (FDIC) to thrifts considered viable in the long run but with earnings squeezes that endangered traditional net worth in the short run. Although the program was intended to expire after 3 years, it received an extension until 1991 in the Competitive Equality Banking Act (CEBA); under the Financial Institutions Reform, Recovery, and Enforcement Act (FIRREA), administration was entirely assumed by the FDIC pending phase-out of the program.

Figure 17.1 illustrates the mechanics of NWCs for First Federal S&L. As shown, no cash changed hands in an NWC issue, so a participating institution received no additional funds. Nonetheless, capital (as defined by regulators) was increased. An institution meeting established guidelines was permitted to issue certificates in exchange for a promissory note from the insurer. The NWC then counted as capital, and the promissory note from the insurer served as the offsetting increase in assets. The insurer paid cash interest on the note to the thrift. The thrift was obligated on paper to pay the insurer dividends on the NWCs, but none was actually paid until and unless the thrift returned to profitability.

In Panel A of the figure, the institution has net worth equal to 0.5 percent of total assets. After issuing NWCs, as shown in Panel B, it now has more capital, even though it has received no real injection of funds. Presumably, the additional "paper" net worth enables the S&L to avoid insolvency—that is, to avoid being forced to close because the value of its assets no longer equals or exceeds the value of legal claims against them. If the institution recovers, it must remove the certificates from its books as income permits, offsetting any decrease in NWCs by writing down the value

of the promissory note. This effect is shown in Panel C. Suppose that the institution is able to add $100,000 to retained earnings and expects a profitable future. It decides to "repay" $50,000 in NWCs, writing down the promissory note by an equivalent amount. If, instead, the thrift fails, the promissory note from the insurer is considered an asset to be liquidated to meet liabilities.[5]

Initial supporters argued that the NWC program would make it possible for many thrifts to remain open while confining actual cash outlays by the insurance agencies to only the most severe cases. In fact, the effect of the NWC program was far smaller and the capital problems of the industry much greater than many anticipated. In the late 1980s, thrifts in need of assistance had so little possibility of returning to health that they did not qualify for assistance under the NWC program. Also, accountants (among others) compared the NWC method of creating net worth to the "smoke and mirrors" tricks of magicians. Eventually, Congress, bank regulators, economists, and the public became disgusted with so-called **regulatory accounting principles (RAP)** that allowed phony net worth to justify continued forbearance by the FHLBB and the FSLIC.[6] As a result, CEBA required banks and thrifts to use generally accepted accounting principles (GAAP) instead of RAP in all financial reports except those submitted to regulators; it also required them to reconcile RAP and GAAP net worth measurements in the footnotes to these statements. Under FDICIA provisions, insured depository institutions are now required to use GAAP in the preparation of all reports and statements, even those they must file with federal regulatory agencies.

OPEN BANK ASSISTANCE. Although the use of RAP instead of GAAP in the NWC program was severely criticized by accountants and officials of other depository institutions, it was not the only nontraditional source of net worth in the 1980s. In 1984, the FDIC purchased, for cash, $1 billion of preferred stock from

---

[5] The accounting provisions for NWCs were actually much more complicated than Figure 17.1 indicates. For more information, see Baer 1983 and Vartanian 1983.

[6] See Bennett 1984; Lee Berton, "Accounting at Thrifts Provokes Controversy as Gimmickry Mounts," *The Wall Street Journal,* March 29, 1985, 1, 13; and Auerbach and McCall 1985.

| FIGURE 17.1 | **Capital Injection through Net Worth Certificates** |

NWCs were regulatory capital instruments that allowed struggling but promising institutions to operate until they could return to profitability. They increased capital "on paper" without requiring cash outlays from the regulators.

First Federal Savings and Loan Balance Sheet

A. Before the Issuance of Net Worth Certificates:

Assets		Liabilities and Net Worth	
$ 9,900,000	Securities	$ 99,500,000	Liabilities
90,000,000	Loans	500,000	Net Worth
100,000	Premises		
$100,000,000	Total	$100,000,000	Total

Net Worth/Total Assets = 0.50%

B. After the Issuance of Net Worth Certificates:

Assets		Liabilities and Net Worth	
$ 9,900,000	Securities	$ 99,500,000	Liabilities
90,000,000	Loans	500,000	Net Worth
100,000	Premises		
1,500,000	Insurer Note	1,500,000	Net Worth Certificate
$101,500,000	Total	$101,500,000	Total

Net Worth/Total Assets = 1.97%

C. After a Profitable Period:

Assets		Liabilities and Net Worth	
$ 10,000,000	Securities	$ 99,500,000	Liabilities
90,000,000	Loans	600,000	Net Worth
100,000	Premises		
1,450,000	Insurer Note	1,450,000	Net Worth Certificate
$101,550,000	Total	$101,550,000	Total

Net Worth/Total Assets = 2.02%

Continental Illinois Corporation, the holding company for Continental Illinois National Bank and Trust. Some of the preferred stock was convertible into common stock; according to the FDIC's own estimate, if converted, its initial investment would have equaled 80 percent ownership of the holding company. This financing plan was undertaken to avoid the closure of Continental Illinois Bank and its default on nearly $30 billion in uninsured deposits. At the time, 2,300 small banks had uninsured deposits at Continental, many with amounts equal to 50 percent or more of their own total capital.

To be sure, the parallels between the FDIC action in the case of Continental and the FHLBB's use of RAP instead of GAAP to solve the net worth crisis of thrifts in the 1980s are imperfect. The FDIC actually paid cash in the Continental rescue, whereas insurers promised to pay cash only if necessary under the NWC program. Continental needed immediate cash to stay in business, whereas the thrifts using NWCs, though technically insolvent, did not have liquidity crises. Also, the FDIC plan for Continental, which was termed **open bank assistance** and was used again during the wave of banking failures in the Southwest, provided the potential for the FDIC to recover its funds when a bank's financial condition improved. In fact, in 1988, the insurer sold some of its stock in Continental to the public, and in May 1991 sold all remaining shares, returning Continental to private ownership.

Still, there are conceptual similarities between the forms of regulatory assistance. In particular, the programs were developed to prevent the potential insolvency of a large number of depositories in a short period and to minimize the cash outflow required by the federal insurers to maintain the stability of the financial system. Each program has also brought new meaning to the term *net worth*. Despite the controversy surrounding the use of open bank assistance, the FDIC continued to rely on it to delay or to prevent the outright failure of troubled institutions. In 1991, for example, three insured banks received open bank assistance. All were relatively small, however; none had total assets of more than $32 million.[7]

DEBT CAPITAL

In addition to net worth, depositories have access to long-term debt as a source of capital. Because all debt has a maturity date, whether it really fulfills the role of capital can be questioned. On the one hand, long-term debt carries a repayment obligation that is just as real as an uninsured deposit, so it is not actually a permanent source of funds. On the other hand, long-term debt, when legally subordinate to deposits, is a source of funds that does not place an immediate repayment burden on the institution and offers some protection to depositors; thus, it offers a quasi-permanence similar to equity capital.

Besides focusing on its technical priority of claims against assets, arguments on the appropriateness of subordinated debt as capital focus on its potential as a source of market discipline. Supporters note that subordinated debtholders serve as important monitors of an institution, because they stand to lose if a depository's management takes excessive risks. For this reason, some financial economists argue that subordinated debt is even better than equity capital as a source of protection for the deposit insurance system and that all depositories should be *required* to issue subordinated debt. Under these proposals, increasing yields would signal the market's assessment of an institution's increased riskiness. Presumably, managers so signaled would reduce risk taking and thus also reduce the risk exposure of the deposit insurers.

Other experts note that recent regulatory policies—notably the too-big-to-fail doctrine, which protected not only uninsured depositors but also subordinated debtholders—eroded monitoring incentives to such an extent that market discipline is now almost totally absent. Furthermore, this argument goes, even if abandoning the too-big-to-fail doctrine restores the monitoring incentives of subordinated debtholders, the continuing existence of deposit insurance can still create a substantial moral hazard. Thus, allowing subordinated debt to count as capital serves no real purpose.[8]

The consensus on long-term debt is a compromise position. Most observers, including federal regulators, consider subordinated notes and debentures with carefully specified characteristics to be part of a depository's capital. Subordinated notes and debentures qualify as capital under three conditions:

1. They must have an original maturity of 5 years or more.
2. They must be clearly identified at the time of issuance as subordinate to deposits.
3. They must be uninsured.

Debt securities with those features satisfy arguments on both sides of the priority-of-claims debate.

HOW IS CAPITAL MEASURED?

It should not be surprising that no consensus exists on how capital, once defined, should be measured. Issues

---

[7] FDIC, *1984 Annual Report,* 4–5; *1988 Annual Report,* xv; *1991 Annual Report,* 13, 22.

[8] For more on these arguments, see Watson 1975; Furlong and Keeley 1987b; Wall 1989b; and Osterberg and Thomson 1992.

relating to the appropriate measurement of capital revolve around the book-value versus market-value approach, the relative importance of specific capital components, and the other firm-specific financial variables to which capital should be related.

BOOK VERSUS MARKET VALUES

Finance and accounting theorists have debated for years whether the periodic results of the financial activities of a business should be reported at book or market value. Although most experts acknowledge the distortions produced by book-value measures, which are based on historical events, many also believe that reporting the value of balance sheet items at estimated current market value is too imprecise to be justified. They reason that unless something is sold, its potential market value is subject to rapid change. Indeed, for some financial assets and liabilities, there is no secondary market in which value can be determined. Supporters of market-value measurements argue, however, that market values are the only relevant ones if a firm is forced to liquidate its assets, and any measure of capital that does not consider market values is severely distorted.

This debate is important for the measurement of capital because of capital's role as a cushion between the value of the firm's assets and the value of its outstanding liabilities. While the book versus market question is relevant for all businesses, it is especially significant to depository institutions because of their high degree of financial leverage. The greater the proportion of financing from debt obligations, the less the value of assets can shrink before insolvency.

MARKET-VALUE CAPITAL AND INTEREST RATES. In a financial institution, the difference between book and market values is primarily related to changes in interest rates occurring between the time an asset is acquired and a subsequent period. The difference between using book and market values to measure an institution's capital is illustrated in Figure 17.2. For simplicity, this generic depository institution is assumed to have only three assets: cash and due from other depositories, 3-month Treasury bills (T-bills), and 10 percent automobile loans with a 4-year remaining maturity. All deposits are assumed to be variable rate so that depositors always earn current market

rates. (If some deposits were fixed-rate, long-term certificates of deposit (CDs), their value to depositors would change with market conditions.)

In Panel A of the figure, capital is measured as the difference between the book value of assets and the book value of liabilities. Alternately, the book value of capital could be obtained by simply adding the book values of all the capital components on an institution's balance sheet, such as the common stock, preferred stock, and retained earnings accounts.

Suppose that after the loans were made, the market rate for auto loans rises to 13 percent. The market value of the 10 percent loans will no longer be as high as the book value should the institution wish to sell them. The current value of the deposit liabilities will not drop, however, because the institution is obligated to repay them at their full face value. As shown in Panel B of Figure 17.2, the capital of the institution, calculated by subtracting the current value of liabilities from the current value of assets, is considerably lower than its book value.

Of course, changes in interest rates can increase as well as decrease market values. In Panel C, market rates for automobile loans are assumed to fall to 7.5 percent. Measuring net worth at market instead of book value improves the institution's capital position.

The divergence between book and market values is shown in Figure 17.3, which plots the ratio of the market value of equity to the book value of equity for 80 large BHCs from 1975 through 1990. A ratio of 1 implies that book and market values are equal, a condition only remotely close to reality for a brief period in the mid-1970s. Most of the time, market and book values diverge. In the 1980s, market values were less than book values much of the time, but the market value of the holding companies' equity rebounded in the last half of the decade. Although not shown in the figure, a similar analysis of nonfinancial firms during the same period revealed that their market-to-book value ratios were never below 1.

CALCULATING MARKET-VALUE CAPITAL. Measures of capital now used by regulators are based on book values. Because of the problems of identifying current values for marketable assets and because there are no markets for some assets, difficulties in calculating market-value measures are seen by many as outweighing their benefits. For a stockholder-owned institution

---

FIGURE 17.2   **Book Value versus the Market Value of Capital**

The market value of assets (and, therefore, of net worth) reflects changing economic conditions. In this example, changing interest rates cause the market value of loans to fall (Panel B) or to rise (Panel C) when compared with their book value. Net worth falls or rises correspondingly.

A. Book-Value Accounting:

Assets		Liabilities and Net Worth	
$ 1,000,000	Cash	$ 65,800,000	Deposits
19,000,000	T-Bills	4,200,000	Net Worth
50,000,000	10% Loans[a]		
$ 70,000,000	Total	$ 70,000,000	Total

Net Worth/Total Assets = 6.00%

[a]Amortizing these loans over 48 months at a monthly rate of 10%/12 = 0.833% results in expected monthly payments of $1,268,129.20. That is, the present value of $1,268,129.20, discounted at 0.833% for 48 months, is $50,000,000.

B. Market-Value Accounting (loan rates rise to 13%):

Assets		Liabilities and Net Worth	
$ 1,000,000	Cash	$ 65,800,000	Deposits
19,000,000	T-Bills	1,469,757	Net Worth
47,269,757	10% Loans[b]		
$ 67,269,757	Total	$ 67,269,757	Total

Net Worth/Total Assets = 2.18%

[b]The present value of the monthly payments discounted at 13%/12 = 1.0833.

C. Market-Value Accounting (loan rates fall to 7.5%):

Assets		Liabilities and Net Worth	
$ 1,000,000	Cash	$ 65,800,000	Deposits
19,000,000	T-Bills	6,647,757	Net Worth
52,447,757	10% Loans[c]		
$72,447,757	Total	$ 72,447,757	Total

Net Worth/Total Assets = 9.18%

[c]The present value of the monthly payments discounted at 7.5%/12 = 0.625%.

---

with publicly traded stock, however, the difference between the market value of its assets and liabilities can be estimated by calculating the total market value of common and preferred stock. This simply requires multiplying the number of shares of each type of stock outstanding by the current price. Theoretically, the financial markets evaluate the shares based on participants' estimate of the value of the shareholders' residual claims on the institution's assets. This total market value will be either less than or greater than the book

FIGURE 17.3   **Relationship between Market Value and Book Value of Equity for 80 Large Bank Holding Companies, 1975–1990**

During the past several decades, the market value of large banks' common equity has seldom equaled its book value. When market values are lower than book values, capital provides less protection for the deposit insurance funds.

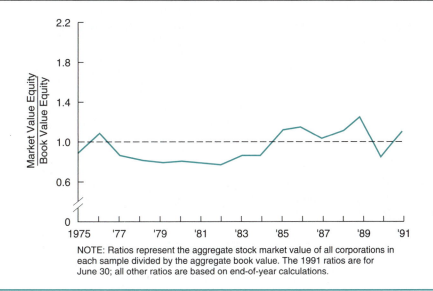

NOTE: Ratios represent the aggregate stock market value of all corporations in each sample divided by the aggregate book value. The 1991 ratios are for June 30; all other ratios are based on end-of-year calculations.

Source: Mondschean 1992, 18.

value of net worth, depending on the markets' assessment of the value of the firm's assets, a comparison shown in Figure 17.3.

In many depository institutions, however, either no stock is outstanding or the stock is not publicly traded, so market/book-value assessments of the type shown in Figure 17.3 are unavailable. Thrift regulators proposed plans for measuring the market value of assets on several occasions, but Congress declined in FIRREA to require so-called mark-to-market accounting for depositories. Congress revised its position, however, and included provisions in the Federal Deposit Insurance Corporation Improvement Act (FDI-CIA) requiring regulatory agencies to develop policies for market value disclosures in the quarterly reports institutions file with their regulators. At about the same time, the Chairman of the Securities and Exchange Commission began to advocate more extensive market-value reporting for depository institutions.

As noted in earlier chapters, the Financial Accounting Standards Board (FASB) had begun to study this issue long before Congress and the regulators became involved. The FASB embarked on its study of market-value accounting in 1986; the first result of its efforts was FASB Rule 107, issued in 1991 and effective for financial statements prepared by large firms on or after December 15, 1992. The new rule set banks, other financial institutions, and nonfinancial firms on the road toward market-value accounting by requiring firms with assets of $150 million or more to disclose in footnotes to their financial statements the fair market value of all financial instruments on their balance sheets—assets as well as liabilities. Smaller firms had 3 extra years before complying with the new rules. In early 1993, the FASB issued another final rule on market value accounting, this time requiring firms to report—on the balance sheet—the market value of securities in the investment portfolio likely to be sold before maturity. Only securities being held to maturity can be reported under historical cost accounting rules.

Although the new FASB rules affect all firms, they are particularly challenging for banks and other financial institutions because of the large proportion of financial securities they hold. The FASB did not, however, specify the method firms must use to arrive at their market-value estimates, so experts predict large variations in the calculations used. Many observers also believe that it will not be long before market values become a more important part of capital standards enforced by regulators. The FASB proposed in late 1992, for example, that banks be required to include some problem loans on their balance sheets at market rather than book value, a rule which would affect banks' provisions for loan losses and, consequently, their reported earnings.[9]

RELATIVE IMPORTANCE OF CAPITAL COMPONENTS

Capital measurement problems are not confined to book versus market values; also at issue is whether the various components are equally important. Because specific numerical standards for depository capital are set by federal regulators, the relative significance of each component plays a role in determining how well an institution meets its capital standards.

VIEW OF FEDERAL BANKING REGULATORS. Federal banking regulators categorize components as core or supplementary capital. **Core (Tier 1) capital** consists of items that the regulators believe truly serve as a cushion against unexpected or abnormally large losses—capital components with no maturity or redemption dates. These sources include common stock, retained earnings, and perpetual preferred stock. **Supplementary (Tier 2) capital** includes other items, such as redeemable preferred stock or subordinated notes and debentures, that have some of the characteristics of a cushion but not all. Details on this division are given in Table 17.1. Most of the table is self-explanatory, based on earlier discussions and the descriptions in the table, although a few clarifications are in order.

Primarily, only traditional sources of equity capital are considered core capital with no strings attached. An item that is at any time something other than equity, such as convertible debt, is counted partially as supplementary capital.

Also, from the sum of core capital components, deductions are made for the book value of some intangible assets. By far the largest intangible asset in most financial institutions is **goodwill.** Goodwill, illustrated in Figure 17.4, arises when one institution purchases another. It represents dollar values that may not be realized should the combined institution be forced to liquidate, so federal banking regulators deduct goodwill from capital calculations.

In Figure 17.4, the depository institution in Figure 17.2 is purchased by another depository when market rates on auto loans are 13 percent. The market value of the acquired firm's loans is less than book value, and the combined balance sheet reflects that market value as part of the Loans account for the combined firm. The difference between market and book value is goodwill. In the eyes of bank regulators, the capital of the combined institution would not include goodwill, because it could not be liquidated to pay off liabilities. The net worth remaining after deduction of goodwill is **tangible net worth.**

Capital components as defined in Table 17.1 are products of the Basle Accord of 1988, in which banking regulators in the G-10 nations, plus Switzerland and Luxembourg, agreed to enforce uniform capital standards, effective December 31, 1992. As first discussed in Chapters 2 and 3, the accord came about after regulators realized that commercial banks are inevitably going to interact globally. Therefore, unless important banking rules are uniform, the flow of funds will be inefficient as regulated institutions and their customers seek the most favorable regulatory climate available.

VIEW OF FEDERAL THRIFT REGULATORS. Before FIRREA, thrift regulators had permitted considerably less stringent definitions of capital, including not only NWCs but other forms of regulatory net worth with questionable value in fulfilling the functions of capital. Title III of FIRREA, however, mandated that thrift capital regulations be "no less stringent" than those for national banks. Accordingly, in October 1989, the Office of Thrift Supervision announced capital defini-

---

[9] See Mondschean 1992; Moore 1992; David Siegel, "FASB Votes to Adopt Mark-to-Market Rule," *American Banker,* April 14, 1993, 1, 20; David Siegel, "Fair Value Rule Being Extended to Bad Loans," *American Banker,* December 10, 1992, 1, 10; David Siegel, "Disclosures to Herald Accounting's New Age," *American Banker,* September 21, 1992, 1, 18; Ford S. Worthy, "The Battle of the Bean Counters," *Fortune,* June 1, 1992, 117–126; Lee Berton, "FASB Adopts Rule Requiring Updated Values," *The Wall Street Journal,* December 17, 1991, A3, A4; Mengle and Walter 1991; Kane and Unal 1990; Berger, Kuester, and O'Brien 1989; and Benston 1989.

TABLE 17.1   **Components of Bank Capital as Measured by the Federal Bank Regulatory Agencies**

U.S. banking regulators, along with regulators in 11 other nations, have recently agreed on the definitions of core and supplementary items used to determine institutions' capital adequacy.

Item	Description
Core (Tier 1) Capital	
Common stock	Aggregate par or stated value of outstanding common stock
Perpetual preferred stock	Aggregate par or stated value of outstanding perpetual preferred stock. Preferred stock is a form of ownership interest in a bank or other company that entitles its holders to some preference or priority over the owners of common stock, usually with respect to dividends or asset distributions in a liquidation. Perpetual preferred stock does not have a stated maturity date and cannot be redeemed at the option of the holder. It includes those issues that are automatically converted into common stock at a stated date
Surplus	Amount received from the sale of common or perpetual preferred stock in excess of its par or stated value
Undivided profits	Accumulated dollar value of profits after taxes that have not been distributed to shareholders of common and preferred stock as dividends
Capital reserves	Contingency and other capital reserves. Reserves for contingencies include amounts set aside for possible unforeseen or indeterminate liabilities not otherwise reflected on the bank's books and not covered by insurance. Capital reserves include amounts set aside for cash dividends on common and preferred stock not yet declared and amounts allocated for retirement of limited-life preferred stock and debentures subordinated to deposits
Minority interest in consolidated subsidiaries	Sum of the equity of the subsidiaries in which the bank has minority interest multiplied by the percentage ownership of the bank in the subsidiaries
Intangible assets[a]	Purchased credit card relationships and purchased mortgage servicing rights
Minus:	
All other intangible assets (primarily goodwill)	Generally these other intangible assets represent the difference between the purchase price and the book value of acquired institutions
Supplementary (Tier 2) Capital[b]	
Limited-life preferred stock	Preferred stock with an original maturity of 5 years or more
Subordinated notes and debentures[c]	Debt obligations of issuer, with original maturities of 5 years or more, that are subordinated to depositors in case of insolvency. Subordinated notes and debentures issued by depository institutions are not insured by the federal deposit insurance agencies
Reserves for loan and lease losses	Amount set aside to absorb anticipated losses. All charge-offs of loans and leases are charged to this capital account, and recoveries on loans and leases previously charged off are credited to this capital account
Mandatory convertible subordinated debt	Debt issues that mandate conversion to common or perpetual preferred stock at some future date
Other items accepted as capital in international banking	Items such as "undisclosed reserves" that are similar to retained earnings but are not revealed on the balance sheet using accounting practices accepted in some nations

[a]The intangible assets regulators allow banks to include cannot total more than 50 percent of an institution's Tier 1 capital.
[b]Total supplementary capital cannot exceed the total of Tier 1 items.
[c]Subordinated debt may not exceed 50 percent of supplementary capital.

tions that are largely identical to those in Table 17.1. A few exceptions should be noted, though.

Besides the components of core capital accepted by bank regulators, thrift regulators include certain nonwithdrawable customer deposits that are really more like perpetual preferred stock; that is, they have no maturity and the institution's obligation to pay interest can be suspended. Furthermore, thrifts' goodwill

FIGURE 17.4 **The Effect of Goodwill on Capital Measurement**

Goodwill arises in mergers and acquisitions when the market value of acquired assets is different from their book value. Regulators have determined that banks must deduct goodwill when calculating net worth; thrifts can count some forms of goodwill until 1995.

Book Value before Purchase (Acquired Firm):

Assets		Liabilities and Net Worth	
$ 1,000,000	Cash	$ 65,800,000	Deposits
19,000,000	T-Bills	4,200,000	Net Worth
50,000,000	10% Loans[a]		
$ 70,000,000	Total	$ 70,000,000	Total

[a]The current market rate is 13%, giving these loans a market value of $47,269,757 ($2,730,243 less than the book value).

Book Value Accounting (Acquiring Firm):

Assets		Liabilities and Net Worth	
$ 25,000,000	Cash	$211,500,000	Deposits
		13,500,000	Net Worth
200,000,000	Loans		
$ 225,000,000	Total	$225,000,000	Total

Net Worth/Total Assets = 6.00%

Book Value Accounting (Combined Firm):

Assets		Liabilities and Net Worth	
$ 26,000,000	Cash	$277,300,000	Deposits
19,000,000	T-Bills	17,700,000	Net Worth
247,269,757	Loans		
2,730,243	Goodwill		
$295,000,000	Total	$295,000,000	Total

Tangible Net Worth: $17,700,000 – $2,730,243 = $14,969,757
Tangible Net Worth/Total Assets = 5.07%

acquired in supervisory mergers during the 1980s can count as part of core capital, in limited declining amounts, until December 31, 1994. Like commercial banks, thrifts may also count selected intangible assets arising from the sale of mortgages.

Although the exact regulations are too complicated to be summarized here, supplementary capital for thrifts includes mutual capital certificates (MCC) as well as items identified for banks in Table 17.1. Also, thrifts must deduct from total capital the value of

certain investments—such as direct holdings of real estate—that are not permitted to national banks.[10]

---

[10] Office of Thrift Supervision, "Regulatory Capital: Interim Final Rule," 12 CFR Parts 561, 563, and 576, October 27, 1989; Robert M. Garsson, "Government Loses Case on Goodwill Writedowns," *American Banker,* August 9, 1990, 1, 18; and Mike McNamee, "Nobody Is Laughing About This Funny Money Now." *Business Week,* May 4, 1992, 168.

VIEW OF FEDERAL CREDIT UNION REGULATORS. In the credit union (CU) industry, measuring capital is considerably simpler than for other depositories, because CUs have not-for-profit status. Because they may not sell securities to the general public, CU capital consists entirely of undivided earnings and reserves from past operations. Reserves are amounts set aside from earnings each year to cover future losses on investments or loans; undivided earnings are those retained in excess of reserves.

CAPITAL COMPARED WITH WHAT?

A final problem in capital measurement is deciding what comparisons should be made to determine how an institution's capital stacks up against its own internal standards or those of regulators. Like all financial data, dollar figures alone are not sufficient for decision making. It would mean very little, for example, to say that a bank had $1 million in capital. Unless the value of its assets, its uninsured deposits, or its loans is also known, the raw figure has no significance.

BALANCE SHEET MEASURES

Federal regulators have a long history of comparing an institution's capital with balance sheet items, although specific measures have varied.

TRADITIONAL BASES OF COMPARISON. In 1914, the Comptroller of the Currency decided that commercial banks should have equity capital equal to 10 percent of deposits. In the 1930s, the FDIC emphasized a capital/assets ratio instead. However, when banks' assets were dominated by risk-free Treasury securities purchased to help finance World War II, that measure became less useful, and the ratio of capital to **risk assets** (then defined as total assets minus cash and Treasury securities) emerged.[11]

GOING OFF THE BALANCE SHEET

In 1986, the Federal Reserve Board (Fed) proposed a new basis against which capital could be compared. Although controversial, by 1988 the proposal

had been refined and adopted formally not only by all three U.S. banking regulators but also by other nations as part of the Basle Accord. The new comparison reflects two important points absent in previous capital regulations:

1. It recognizes that the traditional definition of risk assets fails to consider degrees of risk among those assets.
2. It recognizes that some risks against which capital must protect depositors are not on the balance sheet at all.

ASSESSING THE RISK OF ITEMS ON THE BALANCE SHEET. The new rules require managers and regulators to divide an institution's assets into four risk categories, each assigned a weight that increases with higher credit risk. Risk weights begin at 0 percent for vault cash, balances due from the Fed, and investments in U.S. government and agency securities. A 20 percent weight applies to assets with limited credit risk such as balances due from other depositories, federal funds (fed funds) sold, investments collateralized by government securities (for example, repos), and state and municipal general obligation bonds. A 50 percent weight is used for state and municipal revenue bonds and residential mortgage loans, which are viewed by regulators as having moderate risk. Finally, a 100 percent weight represents standard or normal risk, such as commercial loans, corporate bonds, commercial paper, and all assets not included in other categories.

Certain assets, such as mortgage-backed securities, can fall into any one of the four risk categories, depending on the specific terms of their issue. Furthermore, assets with no default risk but with substantial interest rate risk can be assigned a weight of 20 percent at the discretion of regulators.[12]

ASSESSING THE RISK OF ITEMS OFF THE BALANCE SHEET. The second important feature of the new capital comparisons considers contingent liabilities, or off–balance sheet obligations of an institution. First introduced in Chapter 2, contingent liabilities include obligations, such as loan commitments and lines of credit, arising in the ordinary course of business but

---

[11] More information on the history and use of specific capital measures in banking before 1985 is found in Mitchell 1984.

[12] Wall 1989a; and Ernst and Young, *Risk-Based Capital: Developing a Strategy and Implementation Plan,* October 1989.

TABLE 17.2   **Calculating a Risk-Based Capital Ratio**

Capital standards are based in part on the riskiness of an institution's assets and on the degree of its off–balance sheet involvement. Depositories with lower-risk assets and lower-risk off–balance sheet activities will have more favorable capital ratios than higher-risk institutions.

(1) Risk Category	(2) Amount (in thousands)	(3) Risk Weight	(2) × (3) Risk-Weighted Value
On–Balance Sheet Assets			
Cash and Treasury securities	$ 20,000	0.00	$ 0
Repos and fed funds	30,000	0.20	6,000
Mortgages	10,000	0.50	5,000
Commercial loans and fixed assets	40,000	1.00	40,000
Total on–balance sheet items	$100,000		$51,000
Contingent Liabilities (Off–Balance Sheet Items)			
Cancellable short-term loan commitments	$ 5,000	0.00	$ 0
Commercial letters of credit	20,000	0.20	4,000
Long-term loan commitments	10,000	0.50	5,000
Selected forward agreements	15,000	1.00	15,000
Total off–balance sheet items	$ 50,000		$24,000
Total risk-weighted value			$75,000
Core (Tier 1) capital	$5,000		
Core capital/Risk-weighted total value: ($5,000/$75,000)	6.67%		

not reflected in traditional financial statements. Also included are **standby letters of credit,** which are fee-based agreements obligating the institution to pay some of a customer's debts if the customer defaults. (Recall that standby letters were introduced in the previous chapter in connection with the underinvestment problem.) Because of their potential to expose a bank to additional credit risk, bank regulators also view some tools of interest rate risk management and exchange rate risk management—such as forward currency agreements, some options contracts, and some swap agreements (discussed in detail in Chapter 19)—as relevant for determining capital adequacy. In the Basle Accord, regulators agreed that an institution's risk exposure differs according to the types of contingent liabilities its managers have accepted. Therefore, off–balance sheet items are also divided into four categories for the purpose of comparing them with capital.[13]

The risk categories and their application to a hypothetical institution are shown in Table 17.2. The institution is assumed to have total assets of $100 million, with $50 million in off–balance sheet items, divided into the appropriate groups. Table 17.2 shows that this institution benefits substantially by having a relatively large investment in low-risk assets and by making comparatively low-risk contingent liability agreements. If its core capital of $5 million were compared with unadjusted on– and off–balance sheet values, the ratio would be only 3.33 percent; but the risk-based ratio shown in the table is twice as large.

FEDERAL THRIFT REGULATIONS

Although FIRREA mandated thrift capital standards that are "no less stringent" than those for commercial banks, it did not preclude even more stringent regulations for savings associations. The Office of Thrift Supervision (OTS) accepts the on– and off–balance sheet risk categories defined in the Basle Accord and adds a high-risk category of its own. Thrifts must assign a 200 percent risk weight both to real estate on which they have foreclosed and to delinquent loans.

[13]Calculating the credit-equivalent dollar amount of off–balance sheet items to be added to risk weighted assets is complex and is not detailed in this discussion. See Wall, Pringle, and McNulty 1990.

INCOME MEASURES

Not everyone agrees that on–balance sheet or off–balance sheet ratios are the best way to evaluate capital, and some argue that measuring capital against expected earnings is better. They reason that the main purpose of capital is to absorb temporary losses, and capital ratios are useful only if they compare an institution's capital with anticipated profits or losses. Losses from many sources can be estimated—because of default, changes in interest rates, fluctuating exchange rates, even fraud.[14] Although this argument is conceptually appealing, it suffers from many of the same implementation difficulties as market-value accounting. Thus, regulators have not yet adopted anticipated earnings tests as official capital measures, although estimates of earnings quality are used by examiners in developing (CAMEL) ratings.

HOW MUCH CAPITAL IS ENOUGH?

Assuming that ratios of capital to balance sheet or off–balance sheet accounts, despite measurement flaws, remain the most carefully watched indicators of capital adequacy, how high should those ratios be? This question raises another one: Who should decide?

SHOULD THE MARKET DECIDE?

Some economists advocate complete deregulation of depositories' capital ratios, or at least those of large institutions. They argue that the financial markets are equipped to evaluate whether existing capital provides a sufficient cushion. Institutions with too little capital will be unable to attract funds from uninsured depositors and will be forced to rein in their risk-taking activities. Shareholders, too, will put pressure on managers if they take too many risks; excessive riskiness will be reflected in a lowered price for the institution's stock. Conversely, managers of institutions with too much capital will be pressured to use more leverage to increase investors' expected returns. A costly layer of bureaucracy will be removed if markets, not regulators, determine capital standards.

ARE MARKET SOLUTIONS FEASIBLE? Opponents of this view argue that many institutions are not exposed to market discipline. The stock of most small banks and thrifts is not traded publicly, and most mutual institutions have no public securities of any kind. Also, as discussions of the federal deposit insurance system in Chapter 16 suggest, the financial markets may lack sufficient incentives to exert the discipline required.[15]

If market solutions are used, more public disclosure of the activities of depository institutions is required. Currently, much of the information that regulators collect on individual firms is unavailable to the public. Limited steps were taken in FIRREA, however, to promote disclosure of regulators' enforcement actions. The FDIC has instituted a system encouraging voluntary disclosures by the institutions it regulates. The evidence on whether the markets would assess new information correctly is mixed. Generally, the equity and subordinated debt markets appear to monitor and respond to changes in an institution's financial condition more rapidly than do uninsured depositors, but even this conclusion is controversial.[16]

ARE MARKET SOLUTIONS OPTIMAL? Some experts note that the appropriate capital/assets ratio depends on for whose benefit the standard is—individual institution or the financial system as a whole.[17] Too little capital in a depository can result in its failure; too little capital in the banking system as a whole could result in a chain of failures, with disruptive social consequences. Too much capital also has negative consequences. For individual institutions, excess capital reduces the expected return to capital suppliers. For society as a whole, too much capital in depository institutions means less available for industries in which it might be invested more profitably.

For an individual institution, the ideal amount of capital is the level at which the marginal costs and marginal benefits to its capital suppliers are equal. For society as a whole, the ideal level of capital is the

---

[14] This approach is outlined and illustrated in detail in Vojta 1973.

[15] The argument is further developed in Heggestad and King 1982, Mitchell 1984, and Forrestal 1985.

[16] For a review and analysis of the literature on disclosure and market discipline, see Gilbert 1983; Brewer and Lee 1986; Avery, Belton, and Goldberg 1988; Gilbert 1990; Koppenhaver and Stover 1991; Berger 1991; and Osterberg and Thomson 1992.

[17] Santomero and Watson 1977; Wall 1985; and Wall 1989a.

FIGURE 17.5   The Socially Optimal Capital Ratio

At low levels of capital/assets, the marginal benefit of increasing the ratio is high and the marginal cost of increasing the ratio is low. At high capital/assets ratios, the marginal cost of more capital in depositories is high and the marginal benefit of more capital is low. The ideal capital/assets ratio is the one at which marginal costs and benefits are equal.

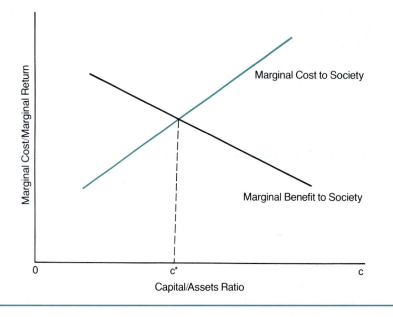

Source: Adapted from Anthony M. Santomero and Ronald J. Watson, "Determining an Optimal Capital Standard for the Banking Industry," *Journal of Finance* 32 (September 1977): 1278. Reprinted with permission.

amount at which the marginal cost of reduced investment in other industries is balanced against the marginal return from preventing the failure of additional depositories, a relationship demonstrated in Figure 17.5. The optimum capital/assets ratio (c*) for the system as a whole is determined at the intersection of the social marginal cost and marginal return functions.

There is no guarantee, however, that the optimal capital ratio of an individual institution will be the same as c*. It may or may not be, depending on the relationship between the specific marginal costs and benefits of more capital in an institution compared to their relationship for society as a whole.

SHOULD THE REGULATORS DECIDE?

If public costs are to be explicitly considered in all cases, capital ratios must be regulated. Although some experts have argued that regulators will err on the high side of optimum, because they tend to weigh the social costs of undercapitalization more heavily

than the costs of overcapitalization, some research suggests that regulators' capital standards in recent years may actually have been less than optimal from a societal viewpoint. The evidence is mixed, however, because other research indicates that capital rules in effect in the late 1980s imposed significant costs on banks that market discipline would not have imposed.[18]

Empirical research also indicates that when no specific capital requirements exist, capital/assets ratios in commercial banks vary inversely with interest rates. Because periods of high rates are those in which bank capital may be most needed, this evidence suggests a need for required minimum capital ratios.[19] Thus, federal regulators have been charged with the responsibility for determining capital adequacy standards.

---

[18] Santomero and Watson 1977; Shome, Smith, and Heggestad 1986; Wall 1989a; and Furlong 1991.

[19] See Marcus 1983.

CAPITAL REGULATIONS IN COMMERCIAL BANKS BEFORE 1985. Historically, the three federal bank regulators avoided setting specific required ratios of capital to assets. Each agency reserved the right to analyze capital adequacy on a case-by-case basis. In fact, many experts argue that scrutiny of capital ratios, and accompanying pressure to increase them if examiners found them deficient, served as an important risk adjustment in the absence of risk-based deposit insurance.[20]

Under this flexible system, an institution was evaluated primarily in relation to its peers. Thus, if an entire group of banks were undercapitalized according to some optimal standard, regulators took no action against any one of them. Similarly, an entire group of banks could be overcapitalized. The result of this system was that large banks operated with much less capital than small banks, and large banks' capital/assets ratio fell dramatically until the early 1980s, as illustrated in Figure 17.6.

CAPITAL REGULATIONS IN COMMERCIAL BANKS FROM 1985 TO 1990. Congressional concern about the decline became so great that in the International Lending Supervision Act of 1983, Congress required federal banking regulators to enforce minimum capital ratios. All three agencies established specific standards in 1985. All insured commercial banks and their holding companies became subject to the same minimum capital/assets ratios. Total capital was required to be at least 6 percent of total assets. As Figure 17.6 shows, the ratio of capital/assets for large banks did, in fact, rise substantially in the late 1980s. Many experts concluded that the new regulations had the desired effect in increasing banks' net worth cushion, at least as measured by book-value accounting rules. As noted earlier, however, some researchers suggested that the regulations resulted in the accumulation of more capital than was necessarily optimal and may have even caused banks to shift to off–balance sheet activities that, at the time, did not affect their capital requirements.[21]

---

[20] Buser, Chen, and Kane 1981; and Furlong and Keeley 1987a.

[21] See Baer and Pavel 1988.

FIGURE 17.6 **Capital/Assets Ratio for Large Banks, 1964–1988**

As regulators became more lenient in enforcing capital requirements for large banks, the ratio of capital to assets declined substantially, exposing the deposit insurance funds to greater risk. Recent attention to capital adequacy has resulted in increased ratios.

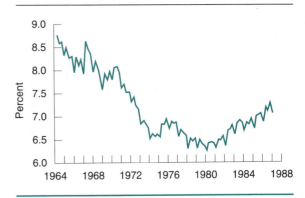

Source: Michael C. Keeley, "Bank Capital Regulation in the 1980s: Effective or Ineffective?" *Economic Review* (Federal Reserve Bank of San Francisco) (Winter 1988), 6.

BANK CAPITAL REGULATIONS SINCE 1990: RISK-BASED STANDARDS AND PROMPT CORRECTIVE ACTION. In addition to specifying risk categories for on– and off–balance sheet items against which commercial banks' capital is measured, the Basle Accord established quantitative standards for both core and supplementary capital. As of January 1, 1993, banks were required to have *core capital equal to 4 percent of risk-weighted on– and off–balance sheet items* (as illustrated in Table 17.2) and *total (Tier 1 + Tier 2) capital equal to 8 percent of risk-weighted items.*

Regulators in individual countries may set higher, but not lower, standards. For example, in addition to the risk-based standard, U.S. banking regulators have imposed a leverage standard, which establishes a minimum level of capital in proportion to a bank's total (unadjusted) assets. The minimum leverage ratio allowed is 3 percent. In other words, for banks with the best CAMEL ratings, Tier 1 capital must be at least 3 percent of *total* assets; banks with lower CAMEL ratings must have higher capital/assets ratios. If, however, 3 percent of a bank's total assets were less than 4 percent of the total of its risk-weighted assets and off–balance sheet items, the more stringent

TABLE 17.3	Definitions of Capital Adequacy

Regulators have identified levels of capital characterizing well-capitalized and undercapitalized banks. Banks in any of the three undercapitalized categories face severe penalties and regulatory intervention.

Category	Total Capital Ratio[a]		Tier 1 Capital Ratio[b]		Leverage Ratio[c]
Well Capitalized	10% or higher	*and*	6% or higher	*and*	5% or higher
Adequately Capitalized	8% - less than 10%	*and*	4% - less than 6%	*and*	3% - less than 5%
Undercapitalized	6% - less than 8%	*or*	3% - less than 4%	*or*	Less than 3%
Significantly Undercapitalized	Less than 6%	*or*	Less than 3%	*or*	More than 2% but less than 3%
Critically Undercapitalized					2% or less

[a]Tier 1 capital + Tier 2 capital/risk-adjusted assets.
[b]Tier 1 capital/risk-adjusted assets.
[c]Tier 1 capital/average total assets. Institutions with poor CAMEL ratings must have higher leverage ratios.
Source: Richard Cantor and Ronald Johnson, "Bank Capital Ratios, Asset Growth, and the Stock Market," *Quarterly Review* (Federal Reserve Bank of New York) 17 (Autumn 1992): 11–12; Kenneth H. Bacon, "FDIC Proposed Curbs on Banks' Loans for Real Estate, Seeks 5 Capital Levels," *The Wall Street Journal,* June 24, 1992, A5; and Catherine Lemieux, "FDICIA Mandated Capital Zones and the Banking Industry," *Financial Industry Trends* (Federal Reserve Bank of Kansas City) (1993): 11–14.

4 percent requirement would apply. Likewise, if a bank were involved in very low risk activities so that 3 percent of total assets were greater than 4 percent of risk-weighted items, the more rigorous rule (3 percent of total assets in this case) would be enforced. The regulation, therefore, ensures that the highest dollar amount of capital will always be required.[22]

In addition to establishing minimum capital standards, Congress, in FDICIA, gave regulators further responsibility to increase scrutiny of insured institutions. The law required regulators to intervene more quickly or to otherwise restrict managerial discretion in high-risk institutions, such as limiting access to brokered deposits as described in Chapter 16. To facilitate that process, regulators have issued their definition of well-capitalized and undercapitalized institutions. Banks just meeting minimum standards are considered adequately capitalized. To be classified as well capitalized—which qualifies banks for less regulatory scrutiny, lower deposit premiums, and other benefits—institutions must have substantially higher capital. The institution's CAMEL rating, reflecting examiners' evaluation of other characteristics, also affects regulatory actions. Finally, the rate of growth in a bank's assets is a factor in determining its capital adequacy. A summary of these criteria for classifying institutions into capitalization categories is provided in Table 17.3.

Institutions in the three undercapitalized categories find themselves subject to intense scrutiny by regulators. Undercapitalized banks must restrict growth, prepare plans to restore capital, and receive approval from regulators before expanding operations, making acquisitions, or opening new branches. Significantly undercapitalized banks face more strict limitations, including prohibitions on increases in compensation to senior executives. Finally, Congress required regulators to take prompt corrective action against critically undercapitalized banks. They are likely to be placed in receivership (FDIC control) within 90 days if their managers cannot correct the deficiencies. These policies reflect the view that severely undercapitalized institutions have little incentive to control risk, and thus expose the deposit insurance system to substantial moral hazard.

INTEREST RATE RISK AND CAPITAL STANDARDS.
Also in FDICIA, Congress pushed bank regulators to broaden the definition of risk considered in capital standards. FDICIA mandated that, by mid-1993, regulators incorporate interest rate risk into bank capital requirements. As of this writing, standards jointly proposed in July 1992 by the Federal Reserve Board, the FDIC, and the Comptroller of Currency had not been formally adopted. The proposed standards, however, focus on the range of maturities of a bank's assets and liabilities and their cash flow characteristics. Assets and liabilities with longer maturities (or longer time to

---

[22]See Cantor and Johnson 1992; Baer and McElravey 1992; and Neuberger 1992.

interest rate adjustments) and those with delayed cash flows (such as discounted securities or nonamortizing loans) would be viewed as carrying higher levels of interest rate risk. Groups of assets and liabilities would be assigned risk weights reflecting their interest rate risk and used to estimate the potential change in market value as interest rates change. By comparing the potential change in value of assets and liabilities, regulators can estimate the potential change in the value of a bank's net worth as market conditions change. The proposed standards rely on duration measures and their ability to estimate interest rate elasticity—concepts explained in detail in Chapter 9.

The Fed's proposed standards recognize that a certain amount of interest rate risk is inherent in any bank. Thus they attempt to identify banks with a level of exposure that is greater than the norm in the industry. Banks with "excessive" interest rate risk would be required to hold more capital. Not surprisingly, the definition of "excessive" is a subject of much debate. The Fed has proposed—rather arbitrarily in the view of some bankers—that any bank whose net worth value could change by more than 1 percent with a 100-basis-point change in interest rates be placed in the excessive risk category. The regulators have indicated, however, that they may lighten or eliminate the leverage standard once the new interest rate risk standards are implemented.

The discussion and evaluation of the proposed standards have emphasized the importance of balancing the need for a reliable measure of interest rate risk with the need to limit the costs imposed on banks by the accompanying reporting requirements. The initial reactions to the proposals indicated that this will not be an easy task.[23]

THRIFT INSTITUTIONS: DOES "CAPITAL" PUNISHMENT SERVE AS A DETERRENT? Capital requirements for thrifts are much stricter now than in the 1980s. FIRREA established the following minimum guidelines: core capital can be no less than 3 percent of a thrift's total assets; and tangible capital (recall that core capital for thrifts can include goodwill at least

until 1995) must be no less than 1.5 percent of total tangible assets. But FIRREA also said that thrifts' standards were to be "no less stringent" than commercial banks. Thus, in addition to the amounts specified in FIRREA, the Office of Thrift Supervision decided to adopt the risk-based capital rules in effect for the banking industry—that is, core capital of at least 4 percent of risk-weighted on– and off–balance sheet items. Even before the FDICIA mandates, the OTS proposed capital standards that consider interest rate risk and impose additional requirements on thrifts with assets of long duration. For example, thrift capital must be proportionate to the change in the market value of capital that would result from a 200-basis-point change in interest rates.

Like banks, savings associations face multiple standards, all of which must be met to avoid censure (or even seizure) by regulators. Because higher-risk assets greatly increase required capital under risk-based guidelines, the new rules are expected to serve as a strong check on managers tempted to expose the deposit insurance funds to senseless risk.

CAPITAL STANDARDS FOR CREDIT UNIONS. Because credit unions are not-for-profit institutions and issue no subordinated debt, their capital consists only of reserves and undivided (retained) earnings. Figure 17.7 shows that in the late 1970s, federal credit unions experienced a deterioration in the ratio of capital to total assets. At that time, a 12 percent usury ceiling on loans, in effect since the 1930s, as well as rapidly escalating interest costs on CU shares made it difficult for CU income to exceed expenses. In addition, as noted in Chapter 15, revisions in federal bankruptcy law escalated default rates on consumer loans, the major assets of CUs. By 1987, the decline in capital ratios for the industry as a whole had been reversed. Helping this were improved economic conditions, an increase in the loan rate ceiling to 21 percent, and a tightening of bankruptcy laws. No special capital regulations, other than those historically in effect, have been imposed on the industry.

The National Credit Union Administration (NCUA) approach differs from the plans of both banking and thrift regulators because it is based on size and age, and does not identify risk weights for different categories of assets. In general, federal CUs are expected to focus on the ratio of reserves to total risk

---

[23] For further discussion of the prompt corrective action (PCA) criteria and the proposed interest rate risk standards, see Cantor and Johnson 1992; Gilbert 1992; Neuberger 1992b; Riley 1992; and Houpt and Embersit 1991.

FIGURE 17.7   **Capital/Assets at Federal Credit Unions**

CU regulators also became lax in monitoring capital in the 1970s, but their renewed vigor in the past decade has resulted in higher ratios.

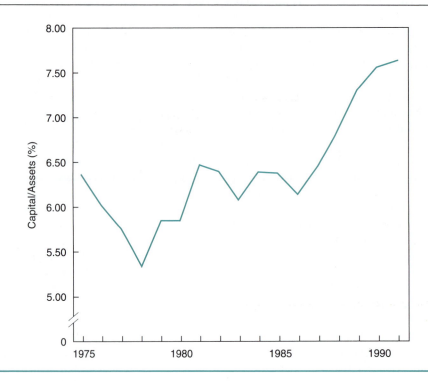

Source: Prepared by the authors with data from National Credit Union Administration, *1991 Annual Report* and earlier issues.

assets. Risk assets are defined by the NCUA to be total assets minus cash, Treasury securities, and loans not considered subject to default risk, such as federally guaranteed student loans and loans to members backed by their personal share accounts. Institutions 4 years old or older with more than $500,000 in total assets are required to have reserves/risk assets ratios equal to 6 percent. CUs with less than $500,000 in assets or those less than 4 years old must have a ratio of 10 percent. Special restrictions are placed on very small CUs not meeting the 10 percent requirement.

THE ROAD AHEAD: UNRESOLVED ISSUES IN CAPITAL REGULATION

As different as 1990s capital regulations are from their historical roots, several important unresolved issues remain. Two of these relate to how capital standards are currently defined. First, as discussed earlier, current rules continue to focus on book-value, not market-value, measures. Thus regulators still cannot use capital ratios to determine whether the deposit insurance funds are exposed to the risk of an institution failing because it can no longer meet its obligations in the marketplace. Second, current rules emphasize credit and interest rate risk but give little weight to other sources of risk. Poor portfolio diversification, for example, might result in the deterioration of an institution that exclusively holds securities issued by a single state and home mortgages issued within that state. Because these assets are ordinarily defined as low to moderate risk, the institution could be allowed to maintain relatively small amounts of capital, and regulators might not see a problem caused by a failing regional economy soon enough to intervene.

Other unresolved issues are more general. Clearly, any new set of rules (a synthesis of sorts) causes the antithesis stage of the regulatory dialectic to "heat up." Risk weights assigned in the Basle Accord create incentives for institutions to innovate with new assets and off–balance sheet items that *look* as if they are low to moderate risk but that may actually be higher risk (and thus potentially more profitable) than, for example, municipal bonds. Then, as regulations become more technical to prevent regulatory avoidance, the system becomes more cumbersome and more costly to enforce.

The new standards also raise questions of competitive fairness and economic efficiency. Some observers believe their basing banks' capital rules in part on their contingent liabilities places them at an unfair disadvantage compared with securities firms, insurance companies, and finance companies, which are not subject to the same rules. Finally, researchers have yet to determine whether the new rules impose costly regulatory taxes on banks and thrifts by forcing them to raise excessive amounts of equity. To the extent that a greater-than-optimal level of capital is directed to the banking system and away from more productive uses, economic efficiency is thwarted.

MANAGEMENT OF CAPITAL: GROWTH

For operational as well as for regulatory reasons, no manager can ignore capital requirements. The rest of the chapter discusses several specific management problems. They include estimating the rate at which capital can be generated from operations without need of external sources; estimating the cost of capital in long-term planning; and, for stockholder-owned firms, evaluating the impact of dividend policy.

ESTIMATING THE RATE OF CAPITAL GROWTH FROM OPERATIONS

It may be difficult to generate capital externally because the financial markets' reception may be uncertain (or even nonexistent in the case of CUs) and existing shareholders may object to a dilution of their claims on the institution. To be sure of meeting capital requirements, managers often prefer to generate capital by increasing net worth through retained earnings. That requires an understanding of some fundamental financial relationships between growth, the net interest margin (NIM), and the return on net worth (RONW).

WHAT IS GROWTH IN NET WORTH? Assuming the use of book values, the rate of growth in net worth

(g_{NW}) from one period to the next can be defined as $\Delta NW/NW$. (NW represents net worth.) If no funds are raised externally, any additions (ΔNW) must come from net income for the period, minus any dividends (DIV) that are paid:

$$\Delta NW = NI - DIV \qquad [17.1]$$

Thus, the rate of growth in net worth is tied to dividend policy in shareholder-owned firms, a topic considered later.

From the definition of return on net worth (RONW), calculated as NI/NW, another relationship emerges:

$$NW = NI/RONW \qquad [17.2]$$

Substituting Equations 17.1 and 17.2 in the definition of g_{NW} ($\Delta NW/NW$) and simplifying results in the following:

$$g_{NW} = \Delta NW/NW \qquad [17.3]$$
$$= RONW \times (NI - DIV)/NI$$

The ratio $(NI - DIV)/NI$ is the percentage of net income retained in the institution, or the **retention rate.** Internally generated growth in net worth is a function of the expected RONW and the expected retention rate. The higher the expected return, or the greater the proportion of earnings retained, the greater the growth of internally generated capital. If return on net worth is expected to be 16 percent and if 60 percent of net earnings will be retained, growth in net worth will be 16 percent $\times$ 0.60 = 9.6 percent. A more difficult task is setting and achieving targets for the two decision variables—RONW and the rate of retention.

GROWTH AND THE NET INTEREST MARGIN. In Chapter 4, it is shown that a depository's target NIM is a function of its target RONW, its capital position (as measured by the reciprocal of the equity multiplier), and net noninterest expenses:

$$\frac{IR - IE}{TA} = \left(\frac{NI}{NW} \times \frac{NW}{TA} \times \frac{1}{1 - t} \right) + \frac{NIE}{TA} \qquad [4.4]$$

Although Equation 4.4 was used as a planning tool to set *ex ante* targets, the relationships also hold *ex post;* if the target NIM is not achieved, neither RONW nor capital adequacy targets will be achieved. And because growth in net worth is related to RONW (Equation 17.3), if NIM is not managed skillfully, the institution's net worth position may fail to grow as planned.

IMPORTANCE OF THE RATE OF INTERNAL CAPITAL GROWTH

Issue Common Stock.
Pay less RE

Planning for growth in net worth is important because if external sources of capital are unavailable or undesirable, the rate of growth in net worth determines how much the depository's liabilities and assets can grow without violating capital adequacy standards. It does little good to plan an ambitious campaign to increase deposits or loans by 25 percent if the expected rate of capital growth is too low to support such a program. In fact, if existing capital ratios are exactly equal to required ratios, asset and liability growth must be no greater than the expected rate of capital growth. Otherwise, capital standards will be violated. If existing ratios exceed requirements, the institution can support a higher level of asset and liability growth. If the institution is approaching required capital standards from a deficient position, asset and liability growth must be lower than growth in net worth.

Limitations placed on institutions by the expected rate of growth in net worth are especially important in depositories because these institutions have less control over growth in their liabilities, and thus the offsetting growth in assets, than many other businesses. The interest that institutions pay on many deposit accounts is automatically reinvested by account holders. Thus, if an S&L paid an average of 10.5 percent annually on deposits and if all depositors reinvested their interest, deposits would grow by 10.5 percent even if the institution made no effort to attract new funds. Assets would automatically grow by a slightly lower percentage, depending on the total assets/deposits ratio. Unless net worth is expected to grow by at least 10.5 percent, the capital ratios of the S&L would deteriorate over time. Because growth in net worth depends on the rate that the institution earns

on existing net worth, which depends on the net interest margin, managing the NIM is the key.

GROWTH AND CAPITAL ADEQUACY: AN EXAMPLE

Table 17.4 presents a condensed balance sheet and income statement for Giantcorp; data are simplified from a recent annual report of one of the largest BHCs. Table 17.5 uses data from Table 17.4 and the growth relationships discussed earlier. All calculations assume that the RONW and dividend payout of the institution will remain unchanged from current levels, so these data are used to estimate growth for the next year. At the beginning of the planning period, Giantcorp just meets the minimum standard for Tier 1 capital as a percentage of risk-weighted assets.

Because the institution has issued redeemable preferred stock, which is not considered a permanent source of net worth, the numerator of RONW is earnings available to common shareholders, measured as net income minus preferred dividends ($890 million − $56 million), not net income. Of that amount, $263 million was paid to common shareholders, for a retention rate of 68.47 percent. Assuming that those rates will continue, growth in net worth can be projected (using Equation 17.3) to be 9.87 percent.

Before the dollar growth rate in assets can be calculated, a growth rate in liabilities (g_L) is estimated. Suppose that it is 10.25 percent for Giantcorp, resulting in projected growth in liabilities of $14,842 million. The total dollar growth in assets is $15,413 million—the sum of expected increases in liabilities and net worth. Because the g_A, growth rate in assets (10.24 percent), exceeds the expected growth rate in net worth, the capital position of Giantcorp would decline to a level that no longer meets regulators' standards. The reason is that the growth in liabilities is expected to exceed the growth in net worth. Because the institution is highly leveraged, the growth rate in assets is greatly influenced by the expected growth in liabilities.

The asset growth rate could also be calculated directly as a weighted average of the growth rates of liabilities and net worth:

$$g_A = w_L g_L + w_{NW} g_{NW} \qquad [17.4]$$

where

TABLE 17.4	**Selected Financial Information for Giantcorp (in Millions)[a]**

Hypothetical data used in planning for growth while maintaining minimum capital requirements.

Assets		Risk Weight	Liabilities and Equity	
Cash and deposits at the Fed	$ 14,285	0.0	Deposits	$ 90,349
Repos and fed funds sold	16,808	0.2	Other liabilities and long-term debt	52,110
Loans and leases	102,707	1.0	Convertible notes	12
Other assets	14,646	1.0	Subordinated debt	1,649
Premises	2,140	1.0	Redeemable preferred stock	680
			Total liabilities	$144,800
			Common stock (par and surplus)	$ 1,514
			Retained earnings	4,637
			Less Treasury stock	(365)
			Total equity (core capital)	$ 5,786
Total assets	$150,586		Total liabilities and equity	$150,586

Income and Dividends

Interest revenue	$18,194
Interest expense	(13,875)
Spread (IR − IE)	$ 4,319
Loan loss expense	(619)
Income after loan losses	$ 3,700
Net nonoperating income and expense	(2,156)
Income before taxes	$ 1,544
Taxes	(654)
Net income	$ 890
Preferred stock dividends	(56)
Earnings available to common shareholders	$ 834
Common stock dividends	$ 263

[a] Risk-weighted off–balance sheet items total $21,500.

w_L = percentage of assets financed by liabilities
w_{NW} = percentage of assets financed by net worth.

In this example,

$$g_A = 0.9616(10.25\%) + 0.0384(9.87\%)$$
$$= 10.24\%$$

PLANNING FOR GROWTH

The expected decrease in the core capital/risk-weighted items ratio can be prevented in several ways if it is anticipated.

INCREASE THE RETENTION RATE. Managers can try to increase the rate of internal growth. Because growth in net worth is determined by RONW and by the rate of retention, the firm could retain a greater proportion of earnings. This may displease shareholders, who may have come to expect a certain level of dividends, but it may be less painful than other alternatives.

INCREASE EARNINGS OR DECREASE DEPOSIT AND LOAN GROWTH. Managers can try to increase RONW. Increased asset yields, reduced interest expense, or better control of noninterest costs could result in a higher RONW. These strategies carry risks. Pursuing higher asset yields usually means accepting greater risk. Reducing interest costs may be a more promising strategy. A decision to pay lower rates on deposits might lead some depositors to defect to competitors; if so, not only will interest costs be reduced, but the rate of growth in assets and liabilities will be slowed as funds are withdrawn. Together, these developments could result in improved capital ratios by the end of the next year.

TABLE 17.5	Expected Growth in Net Worth and Capital Adequacy (in Millions)

Unless managers pay careful attention to the relationship between growth in assets and growth in net worth, an institution may not meet minimum capital standards at the end of a planning period.

Return on net worth:	
($890 − $56)/$5,786	14.41%
Retention rate:	
($834 − $263)/$834	68.47%
Net worth/total assets ratio:	
$5,786/$150,586	3.84%
Net worth/risk-weighted items ratio[a]:	
$5,786/$144,355	4.01%
Liabilities/total assets ratio:	
$144,800/$150,586	96.16%
Projections for Next Year:	
Expected rate of growth in net worth:	
(g_{NW} = RONW × retention rate)	9.87%
Expected dollar growth in net worth:	
0.0987 × $5,786	$571
Total net worth, year-end	$6,357
Growth in liabilities (assumed at a rate of 10.25%):	
Expected dollar growth in liabilities:	
0.1025 × $144,800	$ 14,842
Total liabilities, year-end	$159,642
Growth in assets:	
Expected dollar growth in total assets:	
$571 + $14,842	$ 15,413
Expected growth rate in total assets:	
$15,413/$150,586	10.24%
Total assets, year-end	$165,999
Expected net worth/total assets ratio	3.83%
Expected net worth/risk-weighted items ratio[b]	
$6,357/($144,355 + $15,413)	3.98%
Expected liabilities/total assets ratio	96.17%

[a] Total risk-weighted items ($144,355) include risk-weighted assets (using weights and categories in Table 17.4) of $122,855, plus $21,500 in risk-weighted off–balance sheet items.
[b] Total new risk-weighted items assumes investment of $15,413 in new assets in the 100 percent risk-weighted category, plus no change in off–balance sheet, risk-weighted items.

The risk with this strategy would be to force such a high proportion of withdrawals that a liquidity crisis is provoked, although lowering rates on only the least interest-sensitive accounts probably would prevent this. Further, if the institution does not actively plan for growth, some borrowers may be denied loan funds. To avoid the potential clash between capital adequacy and growth, some institutions have used fees generated by contingent liabilities to increase income without increasing liabilities and assets, a strategy addressed by the Basle Accord.

SELECTING LOWER-RISK ASSETS. The Basle Accord with its risk-weighted plan for determining capital ratios provides incentives for managers to use a strategy in this situation that they probably would not have considered earlier. In Table 17.5, it was assumed that all new funds would be invested in assets, such as commercial loans, that carry a 100 percent risk weight. If, instead, management chose lower-risk assets as the locus for investment of new funds, the dollar amount of capital needed to meet minimum standards would be lower than in Table 17.5. Clearly, regulators hope that the risk-based standards will influence many depository managers to make such choices and, in the process, to reduce moral hazard.

The regulation-induced incentive for managers to reduce the riskiness of assets played a prominent role in the debate over the "credit crunch" in the early 1990s, introduced in the opening paragraphs to this chapter. Some experts criticized the new capital standards as too severe, arguing that they forced bankers to refuse legitimate requests for new commercial loans and instead increase investments in lower risk assets, such as government securities. Other experts, however, said the risk-based standards were just encouraging banks to manage risk wisely and to reduce moral hazard to the deposit insurance fund by denying requests for credit in marginal cases.

Preliminary research indicates that the new capital standards are, in fact, influencing the asset choices of banks. Banks in the United States falling in the undercapitalized category have experienced a lower rate of growth in total assets, as well as in loans and other assets carrying high-risk weights. Well-capitalized banks, in contrast, are experiencing strong growth potential. In Europe and Japan, experts have also noted the tendency for banks to reduce holdings in higher risk securities and to substitute assets with lower-risk designations.[24] Thus, although the debate over

[24] See Cantor and Johnson 1992; Baer and McElravey 1992; and Michael S. Sesit, "New Bank Rules Are Expected to Spur Volume on Global Securities Markets," *The Wall Street Journal*, July 7, 1991, C1, C13.

whether the risk-based standards are having unwanted effects on the availability of capital to deserving business borrowers awaits resolution, the ability of the new standards to reduce risk in the banking system is seldom questioned.

RAISE EXTERNAL CAPITAL. Finally, capital could be raised externally to supplement the expected $571 million increase in retained earnings during the next year. This approach has its risks, too, because market reception is uncertain. Existing shareholders might object to the sale of additional stock especially in small, closely held institutions. Despite these risks, banks have relied heavily on new external capital to assure compliance with the new capital standards. In 1992, U.S. banks issued a record volume of new stocks and bonds to bolster their levels of both Tier 1 and Tier 2 capital.[25]

For mutual institutions, MCCs or subordinated notes and debentures are the only types of securities available. Some mutual organizations, concerned about their limited access to external capital, have converted to stock ownership. As discussed in Chapter 4, however, conversion is part of a long-run strategic plan, not a short-run adjustment, as is needed in the Giantcorp example.

GROWTH AND CAPITAL ADEQUACY: A REVISED PLAN

Specific actions would be based on the risk/return preferences of managers and owners; in cases such as Giantcorp, when capital ratios are relatively low already, the regulators might have a suggestion or two. In any case, a range of options is available to managers who understand the relationship between growth and capital adequacy.

To illustrate, suppose that managers invested all new funds ($15,413 million) in T-bills, with a 0 percent risk weight. Although total assets would increase by the same amount as in Table 17.5 (to $165,999 million), risk-weighted items would continue to equal $144,355 million. Table 17.6 presents estimates of expected capital ratios under this new assumption.

TABLE 17.6 Capital Adequacy under Revised Investment Plan (in Millions)

Under capital rules established in the Basle Accord, managers can maintain minimum capital standards by lowering the risk-weight category in which they invest newly generated funds.

Expected net worth/total assets ratio	3.83%
Expected net worth/risk-weighted items ratio[a]	4.40%
$6,357/($144,355 + $0)	
Expected liabilities/total assets ratio	96.17%

[a] Total new risk-weighted items assumes investment of $15,413 in new assets in the 0 percent risk-weight category, plus no change in off–balance sheet, risk-weighted items.

The revised plan would result in a higher ratio of net worth (core capital) to risk-weighted items. In this example, the ratio would increase from the bare minimum to 4.4 percent. It is unlikely that such an extreme investment decision would be made. Instead, managers would no doubt select some assets with low or no risk weights but would also make additional investments with greater risk and higher expected return. If management did decide to invest the full $15,413 million in assets with a 100 percent risk weight, other approaches to meeting the capital requirements, including selling additional stock or cutting dividends, would have to be considered.

MANAGEMENT OF CAPITAL: COST OF CAPITAL

Another capital-related concept of concern to many managers is the **cost of capital,** or the weighted average rate of return expected by suppliers of new long-term funds. Because their expected return is a cost to the institution, the phrase *cost of capital* connotes an insider's look at the issue. As the phrase is defined here, it is distinguished from the **cost of funds,** or the weighted average cost of *all* sources of funds in a depository, including deposits, nondeposit liabilities, and capital. (Recall that the *marginal* cost of an individual deposit or nondeposit liability was illustrated in the previous chapter.)

COST OF CAPITAL VERSUS COST OF FUNDS

For an institution to operate successfully in the long run, the average yield on its total asset portfolio must equal or exceed the average cost of all funds. Some theorists, therefore, do not distinguish between the cost of capital and the overall cost of funds, arguing that the latter is the only relevant cost. It is certainly true that overall funds costs are important, and discussions of the NIM throughout the book emphasize that asset returns must exceed the cost of deposits and liabilities *and* provide a target return on net worth.

Nonetheless, many argue for the need to identify the cost of long-term funds, or capital, separately. In some institutions, the cost of capital is an important consideration in decisions concerning long-term nonfinancial assets, such as new office buildings, computer hardware, or electronic funds transfer equipment—decisions that are the subject of Chapter 20. According to this belief, the need to identify a cost of capital is based on the first function of capital: to serve as the source of funds for fixed, noninterest-bearing assets required to operate and expand over time.[26] The depository must therefore estimate the yield that current investors require to justify continued investment and that new investors require to supply additional funds. Although its use is controversial, managers should understand how the cost of capital is calculated and applied in some institutions.

CONCEPTUAL ISSUES

Calculating the cost of capital requires assimilating concepts already discussed at several points in the book.

EXPECTED YIELDS. The first is the concept of expected annual yields, illustrated at length in Chapter 5. Because there are several sources of capital, each with different characteristics, it would be wrong to use the expected annual yield of preferred shareholders, for example, as *the* cost of capital to the institution. In-

stead, a weighted average annual yield expected by all sources of capital is more appropriate. Management can estimate the yields that current bondholders, preferred stockholders, and common stockholders expect, using the same data investors themselves use. Suppliers of new capital will certainly be unwilling to accept yields lower than those on existing capital, so existing yields are good starting points for estimating the marginal cost of new long-term funds.

EFFECT OF TAXES. Taxation must also be considered. Banks and S&Ls can deduct interest paid to bondholders from income *before* taxes, effectively reducing the required cash outflow. As a result, the cost of long-term borrowed funds is lower than the expected yield to bondholders, a fact to be considered in estimating the weighted average cost of capital. The issue is irrelevant for CUs, because they pay no taxes. Also, CUs do not consider long-term borrowings as capital.

CAPITAL STRUCTURE IN THEORY

A third factor in the cost of capital is the institution's **capital structure,** the proportions of debt and equity that compose a firm's total sources of funds. The existence of an **optimal capital structure**—one that maximizes the value of the institution—is a controversial idea among finance theorists and practitioners.[27] The line labeled V_0 in Figure 17.8 illustrates the concept as typically portrayed for a nonfinancial firm. The left section of line V_0 slopes upward, reflecting an increase in the value of a firm as managers move from using no leverage (a 0 percent ratio of debt/total assets) to the use of some debt financing. According to the optimal capital structure argument, the tax deductibility of interest payments on debt makes it cheap com-

---

[26] For a practitioner's discussion of the importance of identifying the cost of capital, see Perry 1982. For a theoretical treatment of the cost of capital versus the overall cost of funds, see Mason 1979, 228–232.

[27] A substantial portion of many corporate finance courses is spent on capital structure analysis, including conflicting theories on the existence of an optimal capital structure. Not only is the conflict unresolved after several decades, but there is additional controversy about the applicability of these theories to regulated financial institutions. This material will not be reviewed here. Three good treatments of the capital structure decision in nonfinancial corporations can be found in Brealey and Myers 1991, Chapters 17 and 18; Brigham and Gapenski 1991, Chapters 12 and 13, and Van Horne 1989, Chapters 9 and 10. Each of these texts provides many references to original research. The discussion of capital structure in depositories relies on Buser, Chen, and Kane 1981.

pared with preferred or common stock financing. Shareholders benefit from the cash saved as a result of lower taxes and may value the firm's stock more highly. If the continued use of debt were to produce additional tax reductions with no offsetting costs, the value of the firm would continue to increase without limit, as illustrated by line V_L in the figure.

Of course, the unlimited use of debt is *not* costless. The right section of line V_0, with its negative slope, illustrates the point that using too much debt exposes the firm to potential insolvency. Both shareholders and bondholders may consider their securities less valuable as the risk of insolvency increases. Thus, the concept of an optimal capital structure implies that there is a judicious mix of debt and equity capital that allows a firm to avoid the hazards associated with either extreme. The total value of the firm is lower when the ratio of debt to total assets is either "too low" (and tax benefits are forgone) or "too high" (and the risk of insolvency increases). At a particular proportion of debt financing, however—D_0 in Figure 17.8—the value of the firm can be maximized.

ENTER THE REGULATORS. As the earlier discussion of minimum capital standards suggests, the concept of an optimal capital structure for depositories is complicated by regulation. In a well-known article, Professors Buser, Chen, and Kane integrate depositories' capital structure decisions with the existence of deposit insurance and regulators' capital requirements. To understand their argument, recall that a depository's debt includes both deposit and nondeposit liabilities and assume, for simplicity, that all deposits are fully insured. In the absence of deposit insurance, line V_0 in Figure 17.8 would apply to depositories as well as to other firms, and D_0 would be the ideal amount of debt financing. In contrast, if deposit insurance were free, line V_L would apply. There would be no penalty for using too much debt because all deposits would be insured. Thus managers would have an incentive to use an unlimited amount of leverage in the form of deposits, gaining more tax benefits with each dollar of deductible interest charges incurred. Under such a system, institutions would have virtually no reason to have core (Tier 1) capital, the type that provides the most protection for the deposit insurance funds. The potential added value to the firm from these costless tax benefits is shown as the shaded area of the graph.

FIGURE 17.8   Relationship between Capital Structure and Value

Many finance theorists believe that there is an optimal capital structure. Too little or too much debt capital can result in a lower value for the firm than if managers find the ideal range. The optimal capital structure in depositories is also influenced by the deposit insurance system and capital regulations.

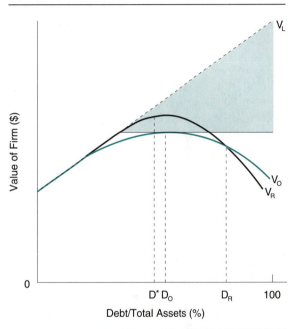

Source: Adapted from Buser, Chen, and Kane 1981.

Regulators could completely dampen this incentive by charging explicit premiums such that an institution's insurance costs for a desired quantity of deposits *exactly* offset the tax benefits added by those deposits. But with no potential gain from deposit insurance, Buser, Chen, and Kane argue that managers would have no incentive to purchase it, given that an insured institution must incur the burdens of greater regulation and examination. Therefore, to provide incentives for most institutions to choose deposit insurance despite the added regulation it entails, regulators allow depositories to capture some of the value in the shaded area. They accomplish this objective by underpricing deposit insurance, at least as measured by *explicit* premiums. Under such a system, minimum capital requirements (limiting the maximum debt/total assets ratio to, say, D_R on the graph) then become *implicit* deposit insurance premiums.

According to Buser, Chen, and Kane, the theoretical relationship between the value of a depository and its use of leverage can be depicted as line V_R, located between the curve that would apply without either insurance or regulation (V_0) and the line that would apply with free insurance (V_L). Considering the added costs of regulation and examination and the desire of most managers to avoid extra scrutiny of their operations when Tier 1 capital approaches the minimum acceptable level, Buser, Chen, and Kane argue that the optimal capital structure for a depository may imply a lower level of leverage (say, $D*$) than would be implied without regulation (D_0). Yet there is always an incentive for managers to choose deposit insurance (and thus to subject themselves to regulation) because firm value will be higher with it than without it.

THE OPTIMAL STRUCTURE IS ELUSIVE. In theory, if an optimal capital structure exists, managers should attempt to find it by changing the capital structure and observing market and regulatory response to incremental changes. In practice, capital structure decisions in many depositories are decided on less theoretical grounds. Lack of access to financial markets renders market-directed attempts to find an optimal capital structure impossible for many depositories. Preferences of managers, owners, and regulators are likely to be the deciding factors. Thus, an institution may achieve a **target capital structure** (one that is an established managerial objective) but not a theoretically optimal capital structure (one that maximizes the value of the firm's capital).

Even so, whether an optimal capital structure exists for depositories is not an irrelevant question. The search for an answer may lead regulators to make better decisions about capital adequacy and deposit insurance pricing and may lead managers to make better operating decisions. Given current knowledge and regulatory policies, however, the search for an optimal capital structure in many depositories may not be fruitful.

EFFECT OF MUTUAL OWNERSHIP. Finally, a question arises about the relevance of calculating a "cost" of capital in mutually owned or not-for-profit depositories. Because new capital arises primarily from additions to retained earnings, it is tempting to think that retaining earnings are costless. In a deregulated environment, however, it is a mistake to consider earnings retained as having no marginal cost to the institution's owners-depositors or members. Every dollar retained in the institution is a dollar unavailable to depositors or members, on which they could earn at least the going rate on money market deposit accounts (MMDAs) or CDs. Thus, raising new funds by retaining earnings has an opportunity cost that management cannot ignore.

CALCULATING THE COST OF CAPITAL

The definition of the cost of capital implicitly contains its formula. Because the cost of capital is the weighted average cost of long-term sources of funds, its calculation is a weighted average of the yields expected by suppliers of capital, adjusted for tax differences between the institution and investors. The weights assigned to each yield are the proportions of the target capital structure that are devoted to a particular source of funds. Thus K_A, the weighted average cost of capital, is calculated as:

[17.5]

$$k_A = \sum_{i=1}^{n} w_1 k_i$$

The w_i are the weights of each source of capital, and the k_i are the costs. Because of tax-deductible interest costs in banks and thrifts, the expected return to investors (y_D^*) must be reduced to estimate k_D, the marginal after-tax cost of debt capital:

[17.6]

$$k_D = y_D^*(1 - t)$$

Table 17.7 contains a sample calculation for Giantcorp, for which financial data are given in Table 17.4. It is assumed that effective annual yields on each source of capital (y^*) have been determined using formulas from Chapter 5. Also, the institution's existing capital structure is assumed to be its target capital

| TABLE 17.7 | Calculating the Weighted Average Marginal Cost of Capital for Giantcorp | | | | |

An institution's cost of capital is the weighted average of the costs of individual sources of capital.

Source of Capital	Amount (Millions $)	w_i (%)	y_i^* (%)	K_i (%)	Weighted Cost
Convertible notes	$ 12	0.15%	11.50%	7.59%	0.01%
Subordinated debt	1,649	20.29	12.50	8.25	1.67
Redeemable preferred stock	680	8.37	14.00	14.00	1.17
Common equity	5,786	71.19	18.50	18.50	13.17
Total capital	$8,127	100.00%			16.02% → K_A

Notes:
1. The current capital structure is the target capital structure.
2. Giantcorp's marginal tax rate is 34 percent; thus, the after-tax annual cost of debt is $y^* \times (1 - t)$, where t is the institution's marginal tax rate. For example:

$$k_D = y_D^*(1 - t) = 11.50\%(1 - 0.34) = 7.59\%.$$

3. $k_A = \sum_{i=1}^{n} w_i k_i.$

structure. If the mix of capital changes, future weights should be used to calculate the marginal cost of capital.

The first step is to identify the institution's sources of capital and to determine their weight in the total capital structure. Expected annual yields (y_i^*) for the different sources of funds are then estimated; the input data are not shown here. Next, factors causing the depository's costs to differ from investors' expected yields, such as the tax deductibility of interest on debt, must be considered. Finally, the costs are weighted and summed to obtain the weighted average marginal cost of capital, or the expected annual cost to the firm of raising new capital. If, in the future, investors' expected yields change because the riskiness of the institution changes or if the target capital structure changes, k_A must be re-estimated.

In mutual or not-for-profit firms, the main cost to be considered is the cost of net worth. As suggested earlier, the opportunity cost (analogous to y*) of the institution's decision to retain earnings would be, at a minimum, the market rate on long-term, risk-free investments such as Treasury bonds (T-bonds) or CDs. The appropriate weight would be the weight of reserves and undivided earnings in the institution's total capital structure. To estimate k_A, that weighted cost would then be summed along with the cost of mutual capital certificates, preferred stock, subordinated notes and debentures, and other sources of capital in the target capital structure.

MANAGEMENT OF CAPITAL: DIVIDEND POLICY

The final issues addressed in this chapter are those surrounding the payment of dividends by stockholder-owned depositories. No policy decision is required for preferred stock dividends. For most types of preferred stock, these dividends must be paid as scheduled, or no dividends can be declared for common shareholders. Dividend policy decisions, then, really revolve around what proportion of earnings available to common shareholders should be retained rather than paid in dividends.

DIVIDEND DECISIONS AS FINANCING DECISIONS

A full examination of the controversy on common stock dividend policy is beyond the scope of this text. The academic literature is full of theoretical and empirical analyses, although no consensus has been reached on the optimal policy. At issue is whether some dividend policies are favored by the financial markets, leading to increases in the value of the firm's stock. One theory holds that investors prefer cash dividends to capital gains after a firm reinvests earnings. An opposing view holds that investors are concerned with returns on the firm's assets and are indifferent between receiving benefits from these earnings as current cash dividends or future capital gains.[28]

Regardless of the controversy's resolution, an important point holds. Every dollar paid in dividends is a dollar unavailable to meet capital requirements and support growth. The division of net income between dividends and retained earnings is really a decision about how to finance the institution.

DIVIDENDS AS RESIDUALS

Because paying dividends reduces cash available for investment in additional assets, one principle managers sometimes use in setting dividend policy is whether the institution has reinvestment opportunities superior to those available to individual shareholders. If so, earnings should be retained; if not, cash dividends should be paid. This principle implies that dividends are a residual of asset portfolio decisions. If strictly followed, a **residual dividend policy** could result in an erratic stream of dividends over time, depending on the firm's investment opportunities from year to year. The concept of dividends as a residual must be balanced against other factors.

INFORMATION CONTENT OF DIVIDENDS

In recommending a dividend policy to the board of directors, which legally authorizes dividend payments, managers must understand another key point. Current dividends have **information content** (that is, changes in dividends often signal changes in the firm's future earnings prospects). Unexpected dividend changes from quarter to quarter and year to year, the likely result of following a residual dividend policy exclusively, are undesirable.

To avoid conveying unintended messages to shareholders, many managers prefer to compromise between paying out cash only if there are no investments to be made and paying out so much cash that future earnings of the firm are impaired. The results of the compromise are seen in **increasing-stream dividend policies.** Under these policies, stable or gently rising dividends per share are observed over time. The pattern is interrupted only if long-term changes in the firm's prospects are anticipated.

REGULATION AND DIVIDEND POLICY

Besides considering the institution's investment opportunities and the information content of dividends, managers of depository institutions know that the payment of cash dividends is constrained by capital adequacy requirements and other regulatory pressures. In 1985, for example, federal banking regulators publicly warned against the payment of high cash dividends in certain economic environments and threatened enforcement actions against institutions defying their advice. In 1990, regulators repeated their warnings in light of deteriorating loan quality and the onset of higher capital requirements.[29] It is likely that statements such as these influence some banks to retain earnings even if they cannot be invested to earn a marginal return as high as shareholders could earn by investing cash dividends. Also, management's ability to use dividends as a signal about a firm's future prospects is impaired. These examples indicate that some policies regulators believe are socially optimal may not be optimal for an individual depository and its shareholders.

DIVIDEND POLICIES IN COMMERCIAL BANKS

From 1980 until 1990, despite fluctuations in earnings, many commercial banks increased dividend distributions. A study of federally insured banks revealed that, on average, banks raised both the dollar

[28] Discussions of the dividend policy controversy can be found in Brealey and Myers 1991, Chapter 16; Brigham and Gapenski 1991, Chapter 14, and Van Horne 1989, Chapter 11. Again, many references to original research are provided.

[29] Leon E. Wynter, "Regulators Warn Banks on Dividends, Urge Use of Profits to Shore Up Capital," *The Wall Street Journal,* November 4, 1985, 8; and Kenneth H. Bacon, "Regulators Press Weak Banks to Reduce Dividends to Shore Up Equity Capital," *The Wall Street Journal,* December 18, 1990, A3.

FIGURE 17.9   **Earnings and Common Stock Dividends in Insured Commercial Banks: 1980–1990**

The dollar amount of dividends paid by insured commercial banks, and their ratio of dividends to earnings, increased steadily throughout the 1980s, despite fluctuating profits.

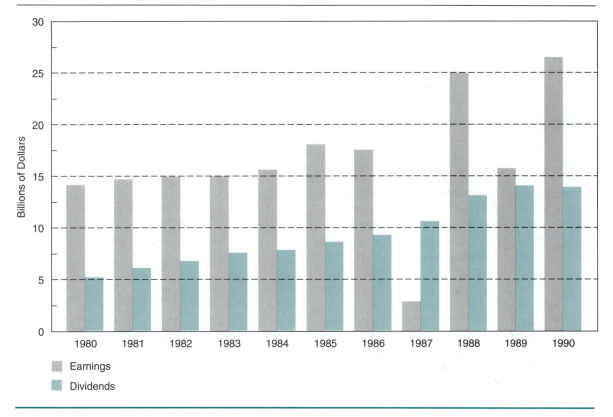

Source: David K. Horne, "Bank Dividend Patterns," *FDIC Banking Review* 4 (Fall 1991): 13.

amount of common dividends paid and the proportion of earnings paid as dividends, a pattern charted in Figure 17.9. As revealed in the figure, dividends in 1987 actually exceeded earnings of insured banks, and in 1989, dividends came close to equaling earnings.

In 1991, however, with the new capital standards on the horizon, many banks lowered their dividends. Of the approximately 150 largest banks, 50 either reduced or eliminated their dividends; for this group, common dividends averaged only 1 percent of earnings. But the picture began to change in 1992. With profits rebounding and capital positions strengthened from the issuance of new securities, many large banks

were once again announcing substantial dividend increases.[30]

Several studies of the determinants dividend policies of commercial banks have been published. According to one survey, the most important influence on bank managers was the desire to maintain stable or

---

[30] See Horne 1991; Richard Layne, "Wave of Banks Hike Dividends; Many Others Expected to Follow," *American Banker,* October 26, 1992, 1, 32; and David Siegel, "Banks Pay More in Dividends As Earnings Keep Rolling In," *American Banker,* December 17, 1992, 1, 16.

increasing dividend streams. The idea that dividends are residuals was not supported by respondents' statements. Researchers noted, however, that dividends were lower in regions with high economic growth rates, suggesting that the residual principle was implicitly influencing dividend decisions. No evidence is available on the dividend policies of stockholder-owned thrifts.[31]

SUMMARY

Capital is the permanent financing of a depository. Controversies exist about what should be considered capital, how much a depository should have, and its role in asset/liability management. Most experts agree, however, that capital promotes confidence in the financial stability of a business organization, supports growth, and reduces moral hazard.

Sources of capital to depository institutions include traditional ones such as common or preferred stock, retained earnings, and long-term debt. In the 1980s, regulatory policies introduced nontraditional sources such as mutual capital certificates and net worth certificates. Controversy continues over whether capital should be measured at book or market value. Since the Basle Accord and FIRREA, regulators have set more uniform standards for banks and thrifts that reflect varying risk levels in on– and off–balance sheet items. But few would view current policies as perfect.

There is no question, however, that managers must meet the standards explicitly imposed by regulators and implicitly influenced by owners. Managing the net worth position is closely tied to other targets, such as the NIM. In addition, as managers plan for growth in assets and liabilities, they must also plan for growth in net worth. Finally, managing capital involves understanding its cost as well as its relationship to the firm's dividend policy.

---

[31] Van Horne and Helwig 1967; Gupta and Walker 1975; and Kennedy and Scott 1983.

QUESTIONS

1. In your own words, provide a definition of capital for depository institutions. Explain the role of capital in support of growth and public confidence for an institution.

2. Explain why capital in depository institutions serves to reduce moral hazard and to provide protection for deposit or share insurance systems.

3. What is a mutual capital certificate? What rights do holders of MCCs have on an institution's earnings or assets? Do you consider them an effective tool for strengthening the capital position of a mutual institution? Why?

4. Under what circumstances did the FDIC offer net worth certificates to thrifts? Explain the mechanics of a net worth certificate. Do you think regulators and Congress were correct to permit this form of net worth assistance? Why or why not?

5. Explain your views on the appropriateness of the regulatory accounting techniques for thrifts that were widely used in the 1980s.

6. What is open bank assistance? Do you approve of this form of regulatory action? Why? In your opinion, does it expose the deposit insurer to more or less risk than is presented by the net worth certificate program?

7. Using your library resources, find the most recent annual report of the FDIC. Was open bank assistance provided to any institutions that year? If so, how many, and what total asset volume did they hold? What rationale is provided for taking this action rather than closing or merging the banks?

8. Explain why market value capital is theoretically better than book value for measuring the ability of capital to perform its functions of providing protection and supporting growth. Why do you think that, despite its theoretical importance, market-value accounting was not implemented until the mid-1990s?

9. Under what conditions does a depository institution's long-term debt qualify as capital? What are the advantages and disadvantages of using such debt to fulfill the functions of capital?

In what manner might the use of subordinated debt by a depository institution introduce its managers to market discipline and reduce the risk to the deposit insurance system? In the views of some experts, how does the "too–big–to–fail" doctrine offset the potential for subordinated debt to impose market discipline on the managers of some institutions?

11. Explain the difference between core capital and supplementary capital as defined by federal bank regulators. How do federal bank regulators treat goodwill in the definition of capital? What is the rationale for this treatment?

12. How have the Basle Accord of 1988 and the capital provisions in FIRREA and FDICIA contributed to standardization of capital regulations across industries and across national borders?

13. Explain the potential advantages to regulators and to depository institution managers of the new risk-adjusted capital measures. How do they differ from more traditional measures of capital adequacy?

14. Risk-weighted capital guidelines have introduced capital requirements for contingent liabilities (off–balance–sheet commitments). Explain why these items, such as standby letters of credit, are important considerations in the evaluation of capital adequacy.

15. Responding to mandates in FDICIA, regulators in 1993 introduced a new method for evaluating capital adequacy and financial strength. Explain the measures now used to measure capital adequacy. How will CAMEL ratings be combined with these to determine when regulatory action is needed?

16. FDICIA required regulators to respond more quickly to the deterioration in an institution's financial position. Give examples of the types of prompt corrective actions regulators may take, and explain the conditions that may trigger these actions.

17. Interest rate risk has recently been targeted as a factor to be included in determinations of capital adequacy. Explain the challenges faced in measuring and tying together these two concepts. Do you agree that interest rate risk exposure affects the adequacy of an institution's capital position? Why?

18. Discuss advantages and disadvantages of allowing the financial markets to determine adequate capital for an institution. Is it a feasible process? An optimal one? Why do you think many managers of depository institutions have opposed additional disclosure of information, especially information discussed in routine regulatory examinations?

19. In the late 1980s and again in the "credit crunch" of the early 1990s, many reports indicated that some commercial banks were responding to increased capital requirements by reducing asset size rather than increasing capital. As a result, higher-risk borrowers were denied loans. Are higher capital standards for all institutions unfair to some segments of society? Why or why not?

20. Review the trends in federal bank capital adequacy requirements during the 1980s and early 1990s. In your opinion, do the provisions introduced in the Basle Accord, FIRREA, and FDICIA promote financial soundness in the banking industry better than previous capital standards did?

21. Compare and contrast sources of capital and capital regulations for credit unions with those for banks and thrifts.

22. How may capital adequacy requirements affect an institution's dividend payout ratios and growth potential? If a depository institution anticipates a decrease in its capital adequacy, what options are available to prevent the decline? What risks, if any, are present in each strategy?

23. Distinguish between the terms *cost of capital* and *cost of funds*. Why must financial managers understand both terms? Do mutually owned and not-for-profit institutions have a cost of capital? Explain.

24. Some experts argue that the optimal capital structure for financial institutions is affected by regulatory policies. Explain how the availability of fixed-premium deposit insurance influences the optimal use of leverage. Under this model of optimal capital structure, how are capital adequacy requirements related to deposit insurance premiums? What is the ultimate effect of regulation on the capital structure chosen by most institutions?

25. Why is the dividend policy decision of a financial institution often viewed as a financing decision? What is a residual dividend policy? If dividends are treated as a pure residual, what other dividend considerations are ignored?

PROBLEMS

1. Based on the following information, measure the capital adequacy of Cosmopolitan Bank using risk-adjusted capital standards. Tier 1 capital is $60 million. Tier 2 capital is $15 million.
  a. Does the institution meet minimum standards? (Hint: Be sure to consider not only the Basle Accord requirements but also the Fed's minimum core capital to total asset requirement of 4 percent.)
  b. Using the definitions of capital adequacy in Table 17.3, determine into which category Cosmopolitan would fall.
  c. What suggestions do you have for the bank's managers?

Assets (Thousands)	
Cash	$ 10,000
Short-term Treasury securities	28,000
Long-term Treasury securities	243,500
Municipal bonds (GOs)	150,000
Other long-term securities	50,000
Residential mortgages	400,000
Consumer loans	200,000
Commercial loans	520,000

Risk Category	Off–Balance Sheet Items in Category
Cancellable loan commitments	$ 30,000
Standby letters of credit	100,000
Forward agreements	200,000

2. Citizens Savings and Loan has the following balance sheet (in millions):

Assets		Liabilities and Equity	
Cash and reserves	$ 20	Deposits	$850
Treasury securities	75	Subordinated debt	15
Mortgages	740	Common stock	10
Fixed assets	70	Retained earnings	30
Total	$905	Total	$905

Because of severe economic difficulties in Citizen's region, $50 million of the mortgages are in default.

Off–balance sheet items:
Long-term loan commitments $200 million
Interest rate swap agreements $ 30 million

a.   Calculate Citizen's risk-adjusted capital ratios. Comment on the extent to which it is adequately capitalized.
b.   Suppose that the institution decides to examine the effect that varying the quantity of its long-term loan commitments would have on its capital ratios. Use a "what-if" table to determine the point, as loan commitments increase in increments of $20 million, at which Citizen's would fail to meet the minimum required ratio of total capital to risk-weighted items.

3. The following book-value balance sheet is available for Metropolitan Credit Union:

Assets		Liabilities and Net Worth	
$ 300,000	Cash	$40,500,000	Deposits
7,000,000	T-Bills	1,800,000	Net Worth
35,000,000	12% Loans		
$42,300,000	Total	$42,300,000	Total

All loans are consumer installment agreements, with an average maturity of 36 months; the credit union receives monthly payments on all of them.
a.   If the current market rate on consumer loans is 8 percent, illustrate Metropolitan's balance sheet on a market-value basis. Compare the book-value ratio of capital/risk-adjusted assets to the market-value ratio of capital/risk-adjusted assets. Does the CU meet minimum standards for the industry?

b.   Suppose, instead, that current market rates on consumer loans average 15 percent. Show the market-value balance sheet and the market-value capital/risk-adjusted assets ratio under this situation.

4.   It is the year 2000, and new regulations using market value accounting for banks have just been imposed. Robert Leekley, President of Valley State Bank, is aware that recent decreases in market interest rates have lowered the bank's interest income. The bank has a large portfolio of very-short-term T-bills on which yields have fallen dramatically (from 7.5 percent to 6 percent) in recent weeks. Mr. Leekley is worried that the lower interest revenues will reduce the amount of earnings that management had planned to retain this year to remove the bank from regulators' "undercapitalized" list.

The institution also holds a substantial portfolio of long-term municipal revenue bonds with an average maturity of 12 years. The bonds have par values of $1,000 and an average annual coupon rate of 10 percent. Recently, yields on these bonds have fallen from 10 to 9 percent. You believe you can show Mr. Leekley that the decline in rates has actually improved the capital adequacy of the bank on a market-value basis. The bank's market-value balance sheet immediately before the rate decline is as follows:

Assets		Liabilities and Net Worth	
$ 2,000,000	Cash	$311,000,000	Deposits
75,000,000	T-Bills		(variable rate)
80,000,000	Municipal Bonds	16,000,000	Common Equity
170,000,000	Commercial Loans (variable rates)		
$327,000,000	Total	$327,000,000	Total

a.   Calculate the bank's ratio of capital to risk-weighted assets (on a market-value basis) before the interest rate decline.
b.   Calculate the ratio of capital to risk-weighted assets after the rate decline. Assuming a market value for T-bills of $82,000,000 after the rate decline, calculate the ratio of capital to total assets (on a market value basis).
c.   Show how the capital to risk-weighted assets ratio would change as the yield on municipals varies between 6 percent and 15 percent (use 1 percent increments). Based on your results, how might market value accounting complicate regulators' decisions about the extent to which an institution has adequate capital or is solvent?

5.   University Savings and Loan is being purchased by an out-of-state bank. The balance sheets of University and the acquiring bank are presented here:

Book Value before Purchase:
University Savings and Loan

Assets		Liabilities and Net Worth	
$ 5,000,000	Cash	$ 87,000,000	Deposits
21,000,000	Treasury Securities		
65,000,000	Mortgage Loans	4,000,000	Net Worth
$ 91,000,000	Total	$ 91,000,000	Total

Acquiring S&L

Assets		Liabilities and Net Worth	
$ 15,000,000	Cash	$275,000,000	Deposits
50,000,000	Treasury Securities		
225,000,000	Mortgage Loans	15,000,000	Net Worth
$290,000,000	Total	$290,000,000	Total

University's loans now have a market value of $54,000,000 because of an increase in the general level of interest rates. Prepare a balance sheet for the combined firm, showing the effect of goodwill. What is the ratio of net worth to risk-adjusted assets? What is the ratio of tangible net worth to risk-adjusted assets?

6. Flower Mound National Bank, with total assets of $850 million and a net worth multiplier of 11.5, expects to earn an RONW of 15 percent. Dividends will be 40 percent of net income, which is projected at $9 million. Risk-weighted off–balance sheet items total $200 million. The bank has $150 million in cash and Treasury securities. All other assets are commercial loans and fixed assets.

    a. What is the present ratio of net worth to risk-weighted items? Is the bank adequately capitalized?

    b. What growth rate in net worth is expected?

    c. If deposits increase by 7 percent, what asset growth rate is expected?

    d. If these projections materialize, will the net worth multiplier be higher or lower than 11.5 at the end of next year? Explain without calculations. Then check your explanation by calculating next year's anticipated net worth multiplier.

    e. Using "what if" analysis, show how the anticipated net worth multiplier would increase as the dividend payout ratio increased from 0 percent to 100 percent. How does this exercise explain why regulators monitor an institution's dividends carefully?

    f. Assuming a payout ratio of 40 percent, what will be the ratio of net worth to risk-adjusted items if all additions to assets are invested in commercial loans? If they are invested in Treasury securities? Assume no change in risk-weighted off–balance sheet items. Compare your answers to the current situation (part a) and explain the changes.

7. The management of First Federal Savings and Loan forecasts a 5 percent growth in assets for the coming year and a 5.5 percent growth in liabilities.

    a. If the net worth/total assets ratio is now 8 percent, what rate of growth in net worth is anticipated for next year? At this rate, will the net worth multiplier increase, decrease, or remain the same? Do these plans make sense?

    b. Now suppose planned asset growth for next year is 7.5 percent. Using "what if" analysis, show, for liability growth rates ranging between 2 percent and 10 percent, how the growth in net worth must change if the 7.5 percent planned asset growth is to be achieved. (Suggestion: Vary the liability growth rate in 1 percent increments.) Do you see any parallels between the results of this analysis and the financial condition of some thrifts in the late 1980s? Explain.

8. The management of American Bank & Trust is very pleased about the bank's capital adequacy. Therefore, management has decided to increase the rate of growth in assets for the coming year by pursuing a more aggressive liability management approach. A 15 percent growth in liabilities is projected, and the bank plans to maintain a stable dividend payout ratio.

    Last year, the firm earned net income of $18 million and paid dividends of $12 million. It expects the same RONW and payout ratio to prevail this year as well. The bank has no off–balance sheet items. Assets not invested in Treasury securities are invested in consumer loans. Management will invest all new funds in consumer loans during the coming year.

    The following additional information is available:

- Total assets: $1,500,000,000 ($350,000,000 in cash and Treasury securities)
- Total liabilities: $1,400,000,000
- Core capital (net worth): $100,000,000

    a. What is the current ratio of capital to risk-adjusted assets?

    b. Calculate the expected growth (in percentages and in dollars) in net worth and assets.

    c. What ratio of capital to risk-adjusted assets is expected by the end of the next year?

    d. If this ratio is unacceptably low to management, suggest ways to improve it.

9. The partial market-value balance sheet of Scottsdale Bank follows (in thousands). Scottsdale is in the 35 percent marginal tax bracket. Deposit insurance is not free.

Liabilities and Equity		Before-Tax Cost
Deposits	$1,670,000	9.8%
Fed funds purchased	164,000	8.2
Long-term debt	50,000	10.2
Common equity	155,000	16.8
Total	$2,039,000	

    a. What is the bank's weighted cost of funds? How does this differ conceptually from its cost of capital?

    b. If the current capital structure is optimal, calculate Scottsdale's marginal cost of capital.

    c. Suppose instead that management decides to alter the capital structure so that the market value of long-term debt equals $70,000,000 and the market value of common equity equals $135,000,000. Recompute the cost of capital, assuming no change in before-tax costs. Why does your answer differ from that in part b?

d. Now suppose that management decides to change again so that long-term debt equals $90,000,000 and common equity equals $115,555,000. The before-tax cost of debt increases to 12 percent and the cost of equity rises to 18 percent. Refigure the cost of capital. Explain the difference in your answers to this part and your answers to parts b and c.

e. Suppose deposit insurance were free. What kind of capital structure would you recommend to management in the absence of minimum capital requirements? Why?

SELECTED REFERENCES

Auerbach, Ronald P., and Alan S. McCall. "Permissive Accounting Practices Inflate Savings and Loan Industry Earnings and Net Worth." *Issues in Bank Regulation* 9 (Summer 1985): 17–21.

Avery, Robert B., Terrence M. Belton, and Michael A. Goldberg. "Market Discipline in Regulating Bank Risk: New Evidence from the Capital Markets." *Journal of Money, Credit, and Banking* 20 (November 1988): 597–610.

Baer, Herbert. "The Garn-St Germain Depository Institutions Act of 1982: The Act's Impact on S&Ls." *Economic Perspectives* 7 (March/April 1983): 10.

Baer, Herbert, and John McElravey. "Capital Adequacy and the Growth of U.S. Banks." Working Paper 92-11, Federal Reserve Bank of Chicago, June 1992.

Baer, Herbert, and Christine A. Pavel. "Does Regulation Drive Innovation?" *Economic Perspectives* (Federal Reserve Bank of Chicago) 12 (March/April 1988): 3–15.

Bennett, Barbara. "S&L Accounting." *Weekly Letter* (Federal Reserve Bank of San Francisco), December 21, 1984.

Benston, George J. "Market-Value Accounting: Benefits, Costs and Incentives." In *Proceedings of a Conference on Bank Structure and Competition,* 547–563. Chicago: Federal Reserve Bank of Chicago, 1989.

Berger, Allen N. "Market Discipline in Banking." In *Proceedings of a Conference on Bank Structure and Competition,* 419–437. Chicago: Federal Reserve Bank of Chicago, 1991.

Berger, Allen N., Kathleen A. Kuester, and James M. O'Brien. "Some Red Flags Concerning Market Value Accounting." In *Proceedings of a Conference on Bank Structure and Competition,* 515–546. Chicago: Federal Reserve Bank of Chicago, 1989.

Brealey, Richard, and Stewart Myers. *Principles of Corporate Finance.* 4th ed. New York: McGraw-Hill, 1991.

Brewer, Elijah, and Cheng Few Lee. "How the Market Judges Bank Risk." *Economic Perspectives* (Federal Reserve Bank of Chicago) 10 (November/December 1986): 25–31.

Brewer, Elijah III. "Full Blown Crisis, Half-Measure Cure." *Economic Perspectives* (Federal Reserve Bank of Chicago) 13 (November/December 1989): 2–17.

Brigham, Eugene F., and Louis C. Gapenski. *Financial Management: Theory and Practice.* 6th ed. Hinsdale, IL: The Dryden Press, 1991.

Buser, Stephen A., Andrew H. Chen, and Edward J. Kane. "Federal Deposit Insurance, Regulatory Policy, and Optimal Bank Capital." *Journal of Finance* 36 (March 1981): 51–60.

Cantor, Richard, and Ronald Johnson. "Bank Capital Ratios, Asset Growth, and the Stock Market." *Quarterly Review* (Federal Reserve Bank of New York) 17 (Autumn 1992): 10–24.

"Conference Report on H.R. 1278, Financial Institutions Reform, Recovery, and Enforcement Act, 1989." *Congressional Record—House of Representatives,* August 4, 1989.

"Finance Subsidiary Rule Boosts Use of Preferred Stock." *Savings Institutions* 105 (October 1984): 135–137.

Forrestal, Robert P. "Bank Safety: Risks and Responsibilities." *Economic Review* (Federal Reserve Bank of Atlanta) 70 (August 1985): 4–12.

Furlong, Frederick, and Michael C. Keeley. "Bank Capital Regulation and Asset Risk." *Economic Review* (Federal Reserve Bank of San Francisco) (Spring 1987a): 20–40.

———. "Subordinated Debt as Bank Capital." *Weekly Letter* (Federal Reserve Bank of San Francisco), October 23, 1987b.

Furlong, Frederick T. "Can Bank Capital Regulation Work? Research Revisited." *Economic Review* (Federal Reserve Bank of San Francisco) (Summer 1991): 32–48.

Furlong, Frederick T., and Michael W. Keran. "The Federal Safety Net for Commercial Banks: Part II." *Weekly Letter* (Federal Reserve Bank of San Francisco), August 3, 1984.

Gilbert, Gary G. "Disclosures and Market Discipline: Issues and Evidence." *Economic Review* 68 (Federal Reserve Bank of Atlanta) (November 1983): 70–76.

Gilbert, R. Alton. "Market Discipline of Bank Risk: Theory and Evidence." *Economic Review* (Federal Reserve Bank of St. Louis) 72 (January/February 1990): 3–18.

Gilbert, R. Alton. "The Effects of Legislating Prompt Corrective Action on the Bank Insurance Fund." *Economic Review* (Federal Reserve Bank of St. Louis) 74 (July/August 1992): 3–22.

Gupta, Manak C., and David A. Walker. "Dividend Dispersal Practices in Commercial Banking." *Journal of Financial and Quantitative Analysis* 10 (September 1975): 515–529.

Heggestad, Arnold A., and B. Frank King. "Regulation of Bank Capital: An Evaluation." *Economic Review* (Federal Reserve Bank of Atlanta) 67 (March 1982): 35–43.

Horne, David K. "Bank Dividend Patterns." *FDIC Banking Review* 4 (Fall 1991): 13–24.

Houpt, James V., and James A. Embersit. "A Method for Evaluating Interest Rate Risk in U.S. Commercial Banks." *Federal Reserve Bulletin* 77 (August 1991): 625–640.

Kane, Edward J., and Haluk Unal. "Modeling Structural and Temporal Variation in the Market's Valuation of Banking Firms." *Journal of Finance* 45 (March 1990): 113–136.

Kennedy, William F., and David F. Scott, Jr. "Some Observations on the Dividend Policies of Large Commercial Banks." *Journal of Bank Research* 13 (Winter 1983): 292–296.

Kim, Daesik, and Anthony M. Santomero. "Risk in Banking and Capital Regulation." *Journal of Finance* 43 (December 1988): 1219–1233.

Koppenhaver, Gary D., and Roger D. Stover. "Standby Letters of Credit and Bank Capital: Evidence of Market Discipline." In *Proceedings of a Conference on Bank Structure and Competition,* 373–394. Chicago: Federal Reserve Bank of Chicago, 1991.

Marcus, Alan J. "The Bank Capital Decision: A Time Series-Cross Section Analysis." *Journal of Finance* 38 (September 1983): 1217–1232.

Mason, John M. *Financial Management of Commercial Banks.* Boston: Warren, Gorham, and Lamont, 1979.

Mengle, David L., and John R. Walter." How Market Value Accounting Would Affect Banks." In *Proceedings of the Conference on Bank Structure and Competition,* 511–533. Chicago: Federal Reserve Bank of Chicago, 1991.

Mitchell, Karlyn, "Capital Adequacy at Commercial Banks." *Economic Review* (Federal Reserve Bank of Kansas City) 69 (September/October 1984): 17–30.

Mondschean, Thomas. "Market Value Accounting for Commercial Banks." *Economic Perspectives* (Federal Reserve Bank of Chicago) 16 (January/February 1992): 16–31.

Moore, Robert R. "The Role of Bank Capital in Bank Loan Growth: Can the Market Tell Us Anything That Accountants Don't?" *Financial Industry Studies* (Federal Reserve Bank of Dallas) (December 1992): 11–18.

Neuberger, Jonathon A. "Risk-Based Capital Standards and Bank Portfolios." *Weekly Letter* (Federal Reserve Bank of San Francisco) January 10, 1992a.

———. "Interest Rate Risk and Bank Capital Standards." *Weekly Letter* (Federal Reserve Bank of San Francisco) November 6, 1992b.

Osterberg, William P., and James B. Thompson. "Bank Capital Requirements and the Riskiness of Banks." *Economic Review* (Federal Reserve Bank of Cleveland) 25 (1989, Quarter 1): 10–17.

———. "Forbearance, Subordinated Debt, and the Cost of Capital for Insured Depository Institutions." *Economic Review* (Federal Reserve Bank of Cleveland) 28 (Quarter 3 1992): 16–26.

Perry, Robert D. "The Cost of Capital." *Magazine of Bank Administration* 58 (February 1982): 26–31.

Riley, Kevin P. "Will Rate-Risk Regs be 'No Big Deal'?" *ABA Banking Journal 83* (November 1992).

Santomero, Anthony M., and Ronald D. Watson. "Determining an Optimal Capital Standard for the Banking Industry." *Journal of Finance* 32 (September 1977): 1267–1282.

Shome, Dilip K., Stephen D. Smith, and Arnold A. Heggestad. "Capital Adequacy and the Valuation of Large Commercial Banking Organizations." *Journal of Financial Research* 9 (Winter 1986): 331–341.

Van Horne, James C. *Financial Management and Policy,* 8th ed. Englewood Cliffs, NJ: Prentice-Hall, 1989.

Van Horne, James C., and Raymond C. Helwig. "Patterns in Bank Dividend Policy." *Bankers Magazine* 150 (Spring 1967): 61–65.

Vartanian, Thomas P. "The Garn-St Germain Depository Institutions Act of 1982: The Impact on Thrifts." *Housing Finance Review* 2 (April 1983): 169–171.

Vojta, George J. *Bank Capital Adequacy.* New York: Citicorp, 1973.

Wall, Larry D. "Regulation of Banks' Equity Capital." *Economic Review* (Federal Reserve Bank of Atlanta) 70 (November 1985): 4–18.

———. "Capital Requirements for Banks: A Look at the 1981 and 1988 Standards." *Economic Review* (Federal Reserve Bank of Atlanta) 74 (March 1989): 14–29.

———. "A Plan for Reducing Future Deposit Insurance Losses: Puttable Subordinated Debt." *Economic Review* (Federal Reserve Bank of Atlanta) 74 (July/August 1989): 2–17.

Wall, Larry D., and Pamela P. Peterson. "The Choice of Capital Instruments by Banking Organizations." Working Paper 92-3, Federal Reserve Bank of Atlanta, April 1992.

Wall, Larry D., John J. Pringle, and James E. McNulty. "Capital Requirements for Interest Rate and Foreign Exchange Hedges." *Economic Review* (Federal Reserve Bank of Atlanta) 75 (May/June 1990): 14–28.

Watson, Ronald D. "Banking's Capital Shortage: The Malaise and the Myth." *Business Review* (Federal Reserve Bank of Philadelphia) (September 1975): 3–13.

Wolfson, Martin H. "Financial Developments of Bank Holding Companies in 1984." *Federal Reserve Bulletin* 71 (December 1985): 924–932.

ASSET/ LIABILITY MANAGEMENT IN DEPOSITORY INSTITUTIONS

PART FOUR

- ASSET/LIABILITY MANAGEMENT: GAP ANALYSIS

- ASSET/LIABILITY MANAGEMENT: BEYOND GAP ANALYSIS

- LONG-TERM ASSET/ LIABILITY MANAGEMENT DECISIONS: EFT AND MERGERS

- FEE-BASED SERVICES

- PERFORMANCE EVALUATION

*It's not the bank's strategy to bet on interest rates,
but rather to control interest rate risk.*
Arjun Mathrani
Executive Vice President and Treasurer
Chase Manhattan Corporation (1992)

CHAPTER

18

ASSET/LIABILITY

MANAGEMENT:

GAP ANALYSIS

In 1991 and 1992, interest rates fell to their lowest levels in decades. Some might expect bankers to be discouraged by a prime rate in the range of 6 to 7 percent and expect banks' profits to show the strain as well. That was not the case, however, for many banks. Andrew Craig, Chairman of Boatmen's Bancshares, Inc., in St. Louis said, for example, "We structured our balance sheet in anticipation of a downturn in rates." The result? Boatmen's net income rose 11 percent in 1991, despite an economic recession.

What was the secret? Boatmen's increased its holdings in longer-term securities and loans—the portion of the yield curve where rates were the highest. At the same time, the bank shortened maturities on deposits and other liabilities, where costs were the lowest. This active asset and liability management strategy allowed the bank to increase the spread between interest income and interest costs.

The strategy followed by Boatmen's and many other commercial banks in the early 1990s improved profitability in the industry in the short run. But because it also widened the gap between the maturities of banks' assets and liabilities, it raised concern about their long-term profitability. Experts noted that it was a similar strategy (a large GAP, or imbalances in the maturities of assets and liabilities) that brought financial disaster to many thrifts in the 1980s. What is a GAP? That is the main question addressed in this chapter.[1]

Preceding chapters have established that individual decisions about investment in assets, types of funds sought, and capital position clearly affect a depository's performance. What has not yet been considered, however, is how asset and liability decisions combine to affect financial objectives.

---

[1] Fred R. Bleakley, "Banks, Thrifts Scored As Interest Rates Fell, but Difficulties Loom," *The Wall Street Journal,* February 12, 1992, A1, A6.

THE NEED FOR AN INTEGRATED POLICY

The net interest margin (NIM) reflects the joint effect of asset and liability decisions because its numerator, the spread (IR − IE), is affected by both sides of the balance sheet. The targeted level for NIM and the return on net worth (RONW) cannot be achieved if management makes investment decisions without being sensitive to the nature of funds sources or if deposits and other liabilities are acquired without some assurance that they can be invested profitably. Managers must simultaneously consider credit risk, which affects asset yields and liability costs, and interest rate risk, which is related to the relative maturities of assets and liabilities and affects the variability of returns.

HIGH-COST FUNDS AND CREDIT RISK

Suppose an institution adopts a growth strategy based on an aggressive liability management policy of raising funds in the negotiable certificate of deposit (CD) market. If the institution is smaller than its competitors, uninsured depositors may perceive it as riskier and require it to offer a higher rate of interest. Recognizing this, managers face a major difficulty: Investment choices must reflect an acceptable level of risk exposure but must contribute enough to the spread to enable the institution to achieve its NIM and RONW targets. Obviously, then, a liability management policy must be consistent with the firm's investment policies.

Unfortunately, recent financial history is littered with stories of depositories whose managers ignored the relationships between institutional risk, yields on assets, and liability costs. The failure of Oklahoma City's Penn Square Bank in 1982 provides an excellent example of the perils involved. In an effort to increase its asset size rapidly, the bank's chief lending officers garnered funds at increasingly higher costs in the negotiable CD market. These funds were then placed almost entirely in supposedly high-yielding energy-related loans—loans on which high rates were charged because, in many cases, the borrowers' capacities to repay were questionable. As the institution's loan losses mounted, wary depositors withdrew funds from Penn Square in numbers sufficient to create a liquidity crisis for the bank. The Federal Deposit Insurance Corporation (FDIC) closed the bank, and uninsured depositors faced substantial losses.[2]

A similar example in the thrift industry is the failure of Lincoln Savings and Loan of Irvine, California, in 1988. The savings and loan association (S&L), after its acquisition by Charles Keating, undertook an aggressive growth strategy financed by a variety of sources, including high-cost brokered funds and high-yielding, uninsured liabilities issued to many unsuspecting customers. Some of the funds raised by the thrift were invested in risky assets such as real estate syndications and other ventures, which lost value rapidly after an economic downturn in the Southwest. Regulators finally forced the institution to close.[3]

RELATIVE ASSET AND LIABILITY MATURITIES

Severe maturity mismatches can undermine NIM and RONW performance just as readily as mismanaging default risk in the asset/liability portfolio, as many S&Ls discovered in the 1980s, during periods of high interest rates and high volatility. Although successful for many years, the traditional S&L practice of holding long-term mortgages financed by short-term funds was not viable as short-term rates increased in the late 1970s. S&Ls, protected by government regulations, had ignored a long-standing tenet of financial management, the **hedging principle.**

The hedging principle suggests that a firm should finance long-term or permanent assets with long-term sources of funds and short-term or temporary assets with short-term sources of funds. With the advent of variable-rate financial instruments, hedging can also be achieved with assets and liabilities that

---

[2] The causes of the Penn Square failure should not be oversimplified; after its failure, Penn Square's executives were accused of questionable practices that extended beyond their poor asset/liability management decisions. An assessment of the costs of the Penn Square failure was presented in G. Christian Hill, "Losses from Penn Square Bank's Failure Total $1.22 Billion and Are Still Growing," *The Wall Street Journal,* April 12, 1984.

[3] Lincoln S&L's financial troubles were widely documented in the media. For one example of Lincoln's investment and financing strategies, see Paulette Thomas, "Keating Defends Thrift's Accounting, but Admits Obscure Records in One Deal," *The Wall Street Journal,* January 8, 1990, A14.

may be **repriced** (that is, have interest rate adjustments) at similar points in time, even though the contractual maturities are different. One objective of this principle is to protect against illiquidity by ensuring that a firm invests in assets that will provide cash when it is needed to retire liabilities. Another objective, particularly applicable to financial institutions, is to protect against insolvency, which occurs when the value of assets falls below the value of liabilities.

In the early 1980s, savings institutions, relying on passbook or other short-term deposits to finance investments in long-term mortgages, fell victim to negative spreads when liability costs increased much more rapidly than asset returns. Of course, at the time, many thrifts operated under such inflexible portfolio regulations that it would have been virtually impossible to match maturities. Under regulations permitting greater use of short-term assets and with greater customer acceptance of adjustable-rate mortgages (ARMs), savings institutions have restructured their balance sheets. By late 1992, for example, fixed-rate mortgages were less than 25 percent of assets in the thrift industry, compared with almost 45 percent in 1984. Nevertheless, experts noted that thrifts continued to be exposed to the risks of interest rate changes as a result of maturity mismatches.[4]

Commercial banks and credit unions (CUs), in contrast, have traditionally had more closely matched asset/liability portfolio maturities. Their emphasis on shorter-term commercial and consumer loans limited their exposure to interest rate risk arising from maturity mismatches. Still, as noted in the opening story, the balance sheets of banks and CUs are by no means perfectly matched and became less so in the early 1990s. Thus their managers, too, must understand the consequences of mismatching on risk and financial performance. In fact, Congress and federal regulators have a continuing concern about interest rate risk in depository institutions. That concern was an incentive for the Federal Deposit Insurance Corporation Improvement Act (FDICIA) requirements, discussed in Chapter 17, that regulators develop and enforce an in-

terest rate risk provision to supplement the new risk-based capital standards.

ALTERNATIVES FOR ASSET/LIABILITY MANAGEMENT

What strategies do depository institutions have to control their exposure to these dangers? Would it be feasible, for example, for an S&L to find enough long-term funds to support all its mortgage investments? Could a CU always sell 3-month CDs to support its 3-month loans, or 4-year CDs to fund all its 4-year automobile loans?

It is unlikely that funds with the preferred maturity will always be available on acceptable terms. Adjusting the loan portfolio to match the maturity of available funds sources may not be wise either, because such adjustments might result in the acquisition of assets that are unacceptably risky. For example, a mortgage lender with most of its deposits in negotiable orders of withdrawal (NOWs) and money market deposit accounts (MMDAs) would not find many borrowers if it offered only short-term mortgages. Even if it did, requiring all borrowers to repay mortgages rapidly might subject the institution to excessive loan losses. Although management can exercise some discretion in adjusting the composition of assets and liabilities, there are limits to the degree to which the hedging principle can serve as an absolute guide to asset/liability concerns.

Fortunately, in recent years several complementary strategies for addressing the problems of asset/liability management have been developed. One of these strategies requires actively managing the composition of both asset and liability portfolios. Following this approach, managers adjust portfolios in response to economic conditions and interest rate forecasts to prevent undesirable imbalances between asset and liability maturities. Other strategies rely on tools for managing interest rate risk (introduced in earlier chapters), such as duration analysis, financial futures, options, interest rate swaps, and caps, collars, and floors, as alternatives to balance sheet restructuring. In fact, many managers use all these strategies at one time or another. The remainder of this chapter focuses on principles of balance sheet restructuring.

---

[4]Phil Roosevelt, "S&Ls Fear A Rate Shock Despite Gains," *American Banker,* December 22, 1992, 6.

TABLE 18.1   ABC Bank Balance Sheet

GAP management begins with a balance sheet analysis. This table shows data on assets, rates of return, liabilities, and costs for a hypothetical institution.

	Average Balances (Millions $)	Average Annual Rate of Return[a] (%)
Assets		
Cash and due (floating rate)	$ 4,743	11.500%
Cash and due (fixed rate)	2,554	10.850
Total cash and due (interest bearing)	$ 7,297	
Short-term Treasury securities	1,105	8.900
Other Treasury and agency securities	248	9.750
State and municipal securities	514	7.500
Other securities:		
Floating rate	798	10.950
Fixed rate	638	12.000
Matched with liabilities	160	12.700
Total securities	3,463	
Commercial loans:		
Floating rate	11,500	12.000
Short term (more than 3 months)	4,040	12.750
Long term (more than 1 year)	4,300	13.240
Consumer loans:		
Fixed rate	2,360	14.700
Floating rate	690	14.150
Other loans:		
Fixed rate	476	14.200
Floating rate	3,213	14.000
Lease financing	359	14.960
Gross loans and leases	26,938	
Total earning assets	37,698	
Cash and due (noninterest bearing)	1,640	
Credit loss provision	(202)	
Other assets	1,497	
Total assets	$40,633	

[a]The average rate of return is interest income on an asset category divided by the average asset balance in that category.

Chapter 19 considers risk management tools to supplement that restructuring.

MONITORING THE BALANCE SHEET: GAP ANALYSIS

The first step in restructuring the balance sheet to manage interest rate risk is to focus attention on the *interest rate characteristics* of an institution's sources and uses of funds. If a depository selects assets and liabilities that are repriced on a similar schedule, even if their contractual maturities differ, it should be possible to earn a positive spread and maintain a reasonably stable NIM and RONW despite interest rate variability. For example, variable-rate mortgages (VRMs) are designed to keep asset returns in line with the cost of funds, even though the mortgages themselves have long-term contractual maturities. Monitoring the interest rate sensitivities and maturities of an institution's

TABLE 18.1 *CONTINUED*

	Average Balances (Millions $)		Average Total Cost (%)	Interest Expense (%)
Liabilities and Equity				
Domestic demand deposits		$ 4,008	7.550%	0.000%
NOW balances		1,789	10.550	5.250
Other transactions balances		811	11.100	10.550
Time deposits:				
Savings	$1,320		8.550	5.500
Consumer time (fixed rate)	1,339		12.350	11.950
Consumer time (floating rate)	236		11.750	11.550
Other time (fixed rate)	2,844		13.400	12.500
Other time (floating rate)	4,809		11.600	11.150
Other time (matched)	1,336		10.200	9.850
Total domestic time deposits		11,884		
Foreign deposits:				
Fixed rate	3,800		13.050	12.340
Floating rate	6,806		11.970	11.150
Total foreign deposits		10,606		
Total deposits		29,098		
Borrowed funds		6,215	11.500	11.400
Long-term debt		1,230	11.000	11.000
Other liabilities (accrued expenses, etc.)		2,248	7.150	0.000
Total deposits and liabilities		38,791		
Capital stock and paid-in capital	899			
Retained earnings	943			
Total equity capital		1,842	25.000	
Total liabilities and equity		$40,633		

assets and liabilities is called **GAP management,** a technique defined and examined in the sections to follow.[5]

THE CONCEPT OF INTEREST RATE SENSITIVITY

GAP management begins with analysis of the interest rate characteristics of the earning assets and the liabilities on the existing balance sheet. That evaluation reveals relative interest rate sensitivities and, in turn, the extent of current exposure to risks arising from changing interest rates.

Table 18.1 shows the average asset and liability balances and average returns and costs of a large commercial bank. All costs and yields are adjusted to reflect noninterest expenses and revenues, such as check-processing costs or loan origination fees. For example, demand deposits with no explicit interest expense have an average total cost of 7.55 percent. Also, all yields and costs, including the target RONW, are

---

[5] The professional literature includes many articles on GAP management. Examples are a series of five articles in *Banking* (now the *ABA Banking Journal*) by James V. Baker, monthly from June through October 1978; a series of three articles by Barrett F. Binder in the *Magazine of Bank Administration* (now the *Magazine of Bank Management*) from November 1980 through January 1981; Gardner and Mills 1981; and French 1988. The example in this chapter incorporates many of the approaches suggested in these and other articles. (References are listed in full at the end of this chapter.)

TABLE 18.2	Balance Sheet Sensitivity Analysis

Data from Table 18.1 are reorganized according to the rate-sensitivity of each balance sheet account using a 3-month definition of sensitivity. A GAP (RSA − RSL) of $1,996 million ($17,306 − $15,310) emerges. The GAP, which can also be thought of as the amount of RSAs financed by FRLs, has a rate differential equal to 1.754 percent (12.210% − 10.456%).

Rate-Sensitive Assets	Average Balances (Millions $)	Rate of Return (%)	Rate-Sensitive Liabilities	Average Balances (Millions $)	Cost (%)	
Short-term Treasury securities	$ 1,105	8.900%	Other transactions balances	$ 811	11.100%	
Floating-rate commercial loans	11,500	12.000	Consumer time deposits (floating)	236	11.750	
Other securities (floating rate)	798	10.950	Other time deposits (floating)	4,809	11.600	
Consumer loans (floating rate)	690	14.150	Foreign (floating rate)	4,306	11.970	
Other loans (floating rate)	3,213	14.000	Borrowed funds	5,148	11.500	
Total rate-sensitive assets	$17,306		Total rate-sensitive liabilities	$15,310		Rate Differential
Average return on rate-sensitive assets		12.210%	Average cost of rate-sensitive liabilities		11.646%	(12.210 − 11.646) = 0.564%

Matched-Rate Assets	Average Balances (Millions $)	Rate of Return (%)	Matched-Rate Liabilities	Average Balances (Millions $)	Cost (%)	
Cash and due (floating)	$ 4,743	11.500%	Other time deposits (matched)	$ 1,336	10.200%	
Other securities (matched)	160	12.700	Foreign (floating but matched)	2,500	11.970	
			Borrowed funds (matched)	1,067	11.500	
Total matched-rate assets	$ 4,903		Total matched-rate liabilities	$ 4,903		Rate Differential
Average return on matched-rate assets		11.539%	Average cost of matched-rate liabilities		11.385%	(11.539 − 11.385) = 0.154%

expressed on a *pretax* basis. The balance sheet is representative of the asset/liability mix of many of the nation's largest banks in recent years. Although the example is complex, it is used to illustrate asset/liability management realistically.

From the data in the table, the degree of interest rate sensitivity on both sides of the balance sheet can be determined. A **rate-sensitive asset or liability** is one on which the interest rate can change with market conditions during the institution's planning period. The definition of rate sensitivity varies from institution to institution depending on the planning horizon,

which is heavily influenced by sources of funds. A small savings institution or CU that extensively relies on nonnegotiable CDs may view a rate-sensitive asset or liability as one that can be repriced at least once a year. Many larger institutions reduce the rate-sensitive time horizon over which they make strategic plans to a much shorter period—perhaps even a day—because they rely more heavily on negotiable CDs, repurchase agreements, or federal funds (fed funds) purchased. Some institutions have a series of planning periods over which they monitor the interest rate sensitivity of their assets and liabilities.

TABLE 18.2 *CONTINUED*

Fixed-Rate Earning Assets	Average Balances (Millions $)	Rate of Return (%)	Fixed-Rate Liabilities	Average Balances (Millions $)	Cost (%)
Cash and due (fixed rate)	$ 2,554	10.850%	Domestic demand deposits	$ 4,008	7.550%
Other Treasury and agency securities	248	9.750	NOW balances	1,789	10.550
State and municipal securities	514	7.500	Savings deposits	1,320	8.550
Other securities (fixed rate)	638	12.000	Consumer time deposits (fixed rate)	1,339	12.350
Short-term commercial loans (3 months–1 year)	4,040	12.750	Other time deposits (fixed rate)	2,844	13.400
Long-term commercial loans (more than 1 year)	4,300	13.240	Foreign (fixed rate and noninterest bearing)	3,800	13.050
Consumer loans (fixed rate)	2,360	14.700	Long-term debt	1,230	11.000
Other loans (fixed rate)	476	14.200	Other liabilities	2,248	7.150
Lease financing	359	14.960			
Total fixed-rate earning assets	$15,489		Total fixed-rate liabilities	$18,578	**Rate Differential** (12.712 − 10.456) = 2.256%
Average return on fixed-rate assets		12.712%	Average cost of fixed-rate liabilities		10.456%
Nonearning assets (including nonearning cash and due)	$ 2,935		Equity capital	$ 1,842	
			Total liabilities and equity		
Total assets	$40,633		equity	$40,633	

IDENTIFYING INTEREST RATE SENSITIVITY

Assume that ABC Bank uses a 3-month definition of sensitivity. Given that definition, what is its profile of rate-sensitive assets and liabilities? The results of an analysis are shown in Table 18.2.

RATE-SENSITIVE ASSETS. The asset portfolio contains several items that are rate-sensitive:

Securities (including fed funds) with remaining maturities of less than 3 months or with floating rates

Fixed-rate loans with remaining maturities of less than 3 months

Floating-rate loans that can be repriced within 3 months, regardless of contractual maturity

The total dollar volume of rate-sensitive assets (**RSAs**)—assets that can be repriced during the planning period—is $17.306 billion.

RATE-SENSITIVE LIABILITIES. On the liability side are the following rate-sensitive balances:

Transactions balances such as MMDAs

Consumer time deposits with remaining maturities of less than 3 months or with floating rates

Other time deposits with remaining maturities of less than 3 months

Foreign deposits that can be repriced within 3 months

Borrowed funds, including some fed funds purchased and repurchase agreements

The volume of rate-sensitive liabilities (**RSLs**) is $15.310 billion.

FIXED-RATE ASSETS AND LIABILITIES. The returns or costs of **fixed-rate assets (FRAs)** and **fixed-rate liabilities (FRLs)** will remain constant over the 3-month period. Assets that do not earn an explicit rate of return are not considered in analyzing interest rate sensitivity, but the cost of funding them must be considered when estimating profits. Nonearning asset totals are shown at the bottom of Table 18.2.[6]

IDENTIFYING AND MEASURING THE GAP

Segregating balance sheet items by interest rate sensitivity rather than by traditional accounting categories permits managers to examine several distinct asset/liability groupings:

The dollar volume of RSAs financed by RSLs. Because RSAs exceed RSLs, this figure is $15.310 billion, equal to the total amount of RSLs.

The dollar volume of FRAs financed by FRLs. This amount is $15.489 billion, the full amount of FRAs.

Matched assets and liabilities including sources and uses of funds with a predetermined rate spread and identical maturities. For example, a repurchase agreement with a 3-month maturity may be issued to a customer and the proceeds invested in a reverse repo of the same maturity and dollar volume. The matched category totals $4.903 billion for ABC.

The dollar volume of nonearning assets financed by FRLs (that is, the amount by which nonearning assets exceed total equity capital).

The dollar volume of RSAs financed with FRLs. This category is known in asset/liability management parlance as **the GAP:**

$$\text{GAP} = \text{RSAs} - \text{RSLs} \qquad [18.1]$$

ABC's GAP is $1.996 billion, calculated as $17.306 − $15.310. In other words, $1.996 billion of the bank's rate-sensitive investments are not financed with rate-sensitive or matched funds sources; consequently, they are financed with fixed-rate funds.

Another way of comparing RSAs and RSLs is the **GAP ratio,** defined as

$$\text{GAP Ratio} = \frac{\text{RSAs}}{\text{RSLs}} \qquad [18.2]$$

For ABC Bank, the GAP ratio is

$$\frac{\$17.306}{\$15.310} = 1.13$$

In other words, ABC Bank has $1.13 of RSAs for every $1 of rate-sensitive funds during the next 90-day period.

Like other ratios, the GAP ratio permits comparison of the relative interest rate sensitivity of an institution to other depositories or to the institution's previous positions, allowing for differences in institutional size. The GAP expressed as a dollar amount, although used in estimating expected profits, is not useful for making comparisons.

POSITIVE AND NEGATIVE GAPs. A GAP ratio of 1 (or a $0 GAP) means that the rate sensitivity of earning assets and liabilities is perfectly matched; as interest rates rise, returns on assets should rise to protect the margin over funding costs. Although the perfect match is unobtainable, many risk-averse managers using GAP management strive to achieve as small a GAP as possible—or a GAP ratio close to 1—over the planning horizon.

A positive GAP, such as ABC Bank's, means that there are more rate-sensitive assets than there are rate-sensitive liabilities. If interest rates increase, insti-

---

[6] In practice, costs are associated with nonearning assets (such as facilities maintenance and repair) that must be considered in profitability analyses. Because these costs are relatively small for the average depository institution, only the costs of funding these assets are considered here. The impact of other costs is discussed in other chapters.

tutions with large positive GAPs should find their asset returns increasing faster than their liability costs. Negative GAPs are also possible, indicating that the amount of RSLs exceeds the volume of RSAs. If interest rates fall, liability costs for firms with large negative GAPs should fall faster than asset yields. Few institutions are so confident of their interest rate forecasts, however, that they are willing to risk the potentially dangerous consequences of a large GAP, either positive or negative.[7] Among S&Ls, in fact, minimizing the GAP has become a common objective as federal regulators have increasingly emphasized GAP management in the industry.

THE GAP AND THE PLANNING HORIZON

It is important to emphasize that evaluation and management of the GAP and the GAP ratio depend on the planning period. For example, a savings institution with ARMs may have a positive GAP if measured over a 5-year horizon but a negative GAP in the short run if it has substantial funding in the form of MMDAs. Both GAP measurements are important for long-range planning and for regulatory assessments of an institution's viability. In the short run, a substantial rate increase could produce a liquidity crisis for the institution, although in the long run, its chances of insolvency might be small.

Recognizing the difficulties in identifying a single planning period for GAP analysis, most depositories calculate several periodic GAPs and a **cumulative GAP** which is the algebraic sum of the periodic GAPs. An example of such a GAP analysis, similar to one in the annual report of a large, regional bank holding company (BHC), is shown in Table 18.3.

The first column of numbers in the table shows total interest-earning assets and liabilities for the bank, as of the end of the year. The second column reveals that within 90 days, $2,733 million in assets will be

maturing and must be renewed at prevailing market rates. The volume of deposits and purchased funds maturing within the 90-day period is almost as large, resulting in a GAP of $142 million. For the second 3-month period, however, the bank actually has a negative GAP of $168 million, and a negative cumulative GAP as well. In other words, for that period, the dollar amount of RSLs exceeds the amount of RSAs. During the entire 365-day planning period, the bank's GAP is positive, as is its cumulative GAP for the whole balance sheet.

Even though savings and NOW accounts are subject to immediate withdrawal, note that the bank's asset/liability managers decided to place them in the "Over 1 Year" category. The explanation is that these balances are considered core deposits, and thus are sometimes viewed as long-term sources of funds. Other institutions, however, recognizing that these accounts may be subject to intermediate repricing, might place them in a shorter maturity category.

IMPACT OF THE GAP ON RONW

Rate-sensitivity analysis is important for evaluating the effect of an institution's current position on RONW. Table 18.4 shows an estimate of pretax profits and RONW for ABC Bank at the interest rate and cost levels identified in Tables 18.1 and 18.2.

CALCULATING RATE DIFFERENTIALS

The first step in developing a GAP profitability analysis is identifying the **rate differentials** on each of the asset/liability groupings from data in Table 18.2. These differentials are simply the weighted average expected return on the assets in a particular category minus the weighted average cost of their funding sources. To calculate the weighted average return or cost of a category, each account must be expressed as a percentage of the total in that category and multiplied by the account's rate of return or cost. For example, the average return on matched assets is 11.539 percent:

Table 18.2 (matched-rate Asset)

$$[(\$4{,}743/\$4{,}903) \times 11.50\%]$$
$$+ [(\$160/\$4{,}903) \times 12.70\%]$$
$$= 11.539\%$$

---

[7]Recent summary statistics on the GAP positions of depository institutions are difficult to find, primarily because regulatory reporting requirements do not include sufficient data to calculate GAPs. In late 1992, however, thrift industry experts estimated persistent GAPs large enough to cut the industry's profit by one-quarter to one-half should rates fall substantially. Similar but less severe forecasts were made for commercial banks. See Roosevelt, "S&Ls Fear a Rate Shock Despite Gains."

TABLE 18.3	Rate-sensitivity Analysis during Multiple Periods

Most depository institutions realize that measuring the GAP for only one planning period is not sufficient for managing interest rate risk. Several periodic and cumulative GAPs are usually calculated.

	Total	0–90 Days	91–180 Days	181–270 Days	271–365 Days	Over 1 Year
Interest-Earning Assets (millions $)						
Loans	$4,858	$2,279	$ 208	$222	$177	$1,972
Investment securities	959	157	138	123	117	424
Funds sold	296	296	—	—	—	—
Interest-bearing deposits in banks	1	1	—	—	—	—
Total	$6,114	$2,733	$ 346	$345	$294	$2,396
Interest-Bearing Liabilities (millions $)						
Deposits:						
Savings and NOW	$ 913	—	—	—	—	$ 913
Other interest-bearing deposits	3,580	2,095	510	300	196	479
Funds purchased	498	496	1	—	—	1
Long-term debt	63	—	3	3	—	57
Total	$5,054	$2,591	$ 514	$303	$196	$1,450
Total GAP	$1,060	$ 142	$(168)	$ 42	$ 98	$ 946
Cumulative GAP	—	142	(26)	16	114	1,060

TABLE 18.4	Profitability Analysis

Estimated annual profits for the institution, shown according to the amount contributed by each rate-sensitivity grouping, are expected to result in a pretax RONW of 19.77 percent.

$$GAP = RSAs - RSLs = \$1,996 \text{ million}$$

Rate Differentials (Annual)

On RSAs and RSLs	0.564%
On matched assets and liabilities	0.154
On FRAs and FRLs	2.256
On nonearning assets financed by FRLs	(10.456)
On the GAP:	
Return on RSAs − Cost of FRLs	1.754

Sensitivity Category	Amount (Millions $)	Rate Differential (%)	Expected Profit (Millions $)
Matched assets and liabilities	$ 4,903	0.154%	$ 7.538
FRAs financed by FRLs	15,489	2.256	349.439
RSAs financed by RSLs	15,310	0.564	86.412
Nonearning assets financed by FRLs	1,093	(10.456)	(114.289)
The GAP	1,996	1.754	35.016
Total pretax profits			$364.116
Pretax RONW (annualized)			19.77%

The average cost of matched liabilities is 11.385 percent, so the rate differential for the matched category is 0.154 percent. On average, the return on a dollar of matched assets exceeds the cost of matched liabilities by just over 15 basis points. This differential, calculated net of noninterest expenses, is smaller than the net difference in interest rates alone. In other words, the differential, expressed in dollars, is smaller than the spread, IR−IE, expressed in dollars.

In Table 18.4, all average costs and rate differentials are rounded to three decimal places, causing small rounding differences among some of the subsequent calculations.

ESTIMATING PRETAX PROFITS

The dollar amount in each category of rate sensitivity is identified in Table 18.2. As shown in Table 18.4, anticipated annual pretax profits for ABC Bank are estimated by multiplying the rate differential for each category by the corresponding dollar amount of assets. Note that the rate differentials between rate-sensitive, matched-rate, and fixed-rate assets and liabilities are calculated in Table 18.2. The rate differential for nonearning assets financed by fixed-rate liabilities is the actual cost of FRLs (10.456%), also shown in Table 18.2.

Total pretax profits, projecting the quarterly performance to an annual basis without compounding, are estimated to be approximately $364 million, giving a pretax RONW of $364/$1,842 = 19.77 percent. Assuming management's target pretax RONW is 18 percent, the current GAP should allow that goal to be achieved if interest rates remain the same during the year *and* if maturing assets and liabilities are replaced with similar ones. If the bank pays an average of 40 percent of its pretax income in state and federal taxes, the target pretax RONW translates into an after-tax RONW of 18 percent × (1 − 0.4) = 10.8 percent. The profitability analysis projects an after-tax RONW of 11.86 percent.

MANAGING THE GAP IN RESPONSE TO INTEREST RATE FORECASTS

As students of interest rates recognize, the assumption that rates will remain unchanged is seldom appropri-

ate. Suppose the bank's economists forecast declining rates over the next 90 to 180 days. The preceding GAP analysis allows managers to re-estimate annual pretax RONW if they make no attempt to "manage the GAP" in light of this forecast.

RESULTS OF NOT MANAGING THE GAP

If returns and costs for rate-sensitive assets and rate-sensitive liabilities decline to the levels shown in Table 18.5, and managers have chosen not to adjust (or manage) the size of the GAP, the bank's returns on short-term investments and floating-rate loans will fall. The interest expense and total cost of short-term deposits and liabilities will also go down. For example, note in Table 18.5 that the rate on short-term Treasury securities drops from 8.9 percent to 7.6 percent, and on floating-rate commercial loans, it drops from 12.0 percent to 11.2 percent. The total cost of short-term consumer time deposits falls from 11.75 percent to 11.05 percent.

Although rate-sensitive accounts move in the same direction, it is usually impossible to hold the rate differential between RSAs and RSLs constant. A major reason, introduced in Chapter 16 in the discussion of operating leverage, is that implicit interest expenses will probably not change as the general level of interest rates falls. Consequently, the total cost of liabilities will change less than the expected return on assets.

A revised profitability analysis shown in Table 18.6 indicates that the differential on rate-sensitive categories declines from 0.564 percent to 0.263 percent. The key figure that has affected profit estimates, however, is the differential on the GAP, down from 1.754 percent to 0.910 percent. Average returns on RSAs drop with the general decline in interest rates, but the cost of funding those assets remains the same because they are financed through FRLs. The estimate of the annualized pretax profit falls to $300.27 million. The pretax RONW of 16.30 percent and the after-tax RONW projection of only 9.78 percent [16.30 percent × (1 − 0.4)] are below management's targets.

ACTIVE GAP MANAGEMENT

In an active GAP management strategy managers attempt to change the size of the GAP to mitigate some of the negative impact of changing rates. Active

TABLE 18.5	Balance Sheet Sensitivity Analysis under Lower Interest Rates with No Balance Sheet Revisions

If interest rates fall from previous levels but managers make no balance sheet changes, a new set of rate differentials will emerge as the returns and costs on RSAs and RSLs fall but returns and costs on FRAs and FRLs do not.

Rate-Sensitive Assets	Average Balances (Millions $)	Rate of Return (%)	Rate-Sensitive Liabilities	Average Balances (Millions $)	Cost (%)	
Short-term Treasury securities	$ 1,105	7.600%	Other transactions balances	$ 811	10.850%	
Floating-rate commercial loans	11,500	11.200	Consumer time deposits (floating)	236	11.050	
Other securities (floating rate)	798	9.950	Other time deposits (floating)	4,809	10.950	
Consumer loans (floating rate)	690	13.750	Foreign (floating rate)	4,306	11.450	
Other loans (floating rate)	3,213	13.100	Borrowed funds	5,148	11.000	
Total rate-sensitive assets	$17,306		Total rate-sensitive liabilities	$15,310		**Rate Differential**
Average return on rate-sensitive assets		11.367%	Average cost of rate-sensitive liabilities		11.104%	11.367 − 11.104 = 0.263%

Matched-Rate Assets	Average Balances (Millions $)	Rate of Return (%)	Matched-Rate Liabilities	Average Balances (Millions $)	Cost (%)	
Cash and due (floating)	$ 4,743	10.770%	Other time deposits (matched)	$ 1,336	9.700%	
Other securities (matched)	160	11.900	Foreign (floating but matched)	2,500	11.050	
			Borrowed funds (matched)	1,067	11.000	
Total matched-rate assets	$ 4,903		Total matched-rate liabilities	$ 4,903		**Rate Differential**
Average return on matched-rate assets		10.807%	Average cost of matched-rate liabilities		10.671%	10.807 − 10.671 = 0.136%

GAP management requires managers to monitor all the markets in which the institution customarily operates. It also requires a willingness to use interest rate forecasts as the basis for restructuring the institution's balance sheet. These requirements mean that active GAP management has its drawbacks, discussed later in the chapter. The illustrations in Tables 18.7 and 18.8 on the following pages demonstrate the effects of active GAP management in an institution with a *positive* GAP. *Negative* GAP examples appear later in the chapter.

Under ABC's forecast of declining rates, an active GAP manager would attempt to narrow the GAP

before rates fell so that the proportion of RSAs supported by FRLs would be reduced. Personnel throughout the bank would become involved, because both the loan and the securities portfolios would be affected by this GAP management goal.

ASSET RESTRUCTURING. Initially, the bank's managers could attempt to reduce the total volume of RSAs. As commercial or individual customers come to discuss new loans or to renegotiate maturing loans, they could be encouraged to accept fixed-rate rather than floating-rate alternatives. In that way, the bank could lock in existing higher returns and reduce expo-

TABLE 18.5 *CONTINUED*

Fixed-Rate Earning Assets	Average Balances (Millions $)	Rate of Return (%)	Fixed-Rate Liabilities	Average Balances (Millions $)	Cost (%)	
Cash and due (fixed rate)	$ 2,554	10.850%	Domestic demand deposits	$ 4,008	7.550%	
Other Treasury and agency securities	248	9.750	NOW balances	1,789	10.550	
State and municipal securities	514	7.500	Savings deposits	1,320	8.550	
Other securities (fixed rate)	638	12.000	Consumer time deposits (fixed)	1,339	12.350	
Short-term commercial loans (3 months–1 year)	4,040	12.750	Other time deposits (fixed)	2,844	13.400	
Long-term commercial loans (more than 1 year)	4,300	13.240	Foreign (fixed rate and noninterest bearing)	3,800	13.050	
Consumer loans (fixed rate)	2,360	14.700	Long-term debt	1,230	11.000	
Other loans (fixed rate)	476	14.200	Other liabilities	2,248	7.150	
Lease financing	359	14.960				
Total fixed-rate earning assets	$15,489		Total fixed-rate liabilities	$18,578		**Rate Differential**
Average return on fixed-rate assets		12.712%	Average cost of fixed-rate liabilities		10.456%	12.712 – 10.456 = 2.256%
Nonearning assets (including nonearning cash and due)	$ 2,935		Equity capital	$ 1,842		
Total assets	$40,633		Total liabilities and equity	$40,633		

sure to the impact of falling rates. Most fixed-rate loans would also have to include prepayment penalties to discourage borrowers from taking advantage of future rate declines. As discussed in more detail later in the chapter, however, these strategies will be met with resistance if customers have the same interest-rate expectations. Also, the securities portfolio could be reallocated, within liquidity constraints limiting transfers of funds, from short-term to longer-term securities.

LIABILITY RESTRUCTURING. On the liability side, little restructuring could occur without new deposit inflows. Ideally, managers would prefer to increase the bank's rate-sensitive sources of funds to take advantage of anticipated declining costs, but customers with long-term CDs could not be forced to transfer funds to floating-rate deposits. Only if total deposits or other liabilities increased could active liability restructuring be practiced. If new funds materialized, the liability maturity mix could be adjusted in the direction opposite from that of asset restructuring. This, too, would narrow the GAP. Competitive pricing strategies might be necessary to convince customers to make the desired selections.

RESULTS OF ACTIVE GAP MANAGEMENT

An example of a rate-sensitivity analysis after asset restructuring, but assuming no immediate increase in deposits and thus no change in liability

TABLE 18.6	Profitability Analysis with Lower Rates, No Balance Sheet Revisions

Because the rate of return on RSAs falls but the cost of FRLs does not, the rate differential on the GAP declines, lowering expected profitability.

GAP = RSAs − RSLs = $1,996 million

Rate Differentials (Annual)

On RSAs and RSLs	0.263%
On matched assets and liabilities	0.136
On FRAs and FRLs	2.256
On nonearning assets financed by FRLs	(10.456)
On the GAP:	
Return on RSAs − Cost of FRLs	0.910

Sensitivity Category	Amount (Millions $)	Rate Differential (%)	Expected Profit (Millions $)
Matched assets and liabilities	$ 4,903	0.136%	$ 6.649
FRAs financed by FRLs	15,489	2.256	349.439
RSAs financed by RSLs	15,310	0.263	40.301
Nonearning assets financed by FRLs	1,093	(10.456)	(114.289)
The GAP	1,996	0.910	18.174
Total pretax profits			$300.273
Pretax RONW (Annualized)			16.30%

structure, is shown in Table 18.7. The total dollar volume of floating-rate loans has been reduced by about $1.75 billion, and the securities portfolio has also been adjusted to lower the proportion of short-term securities.

Figure 18.1 presents a graphic comparison of the rate sensitivity of ABC's balance sheet before and after the restructuring. Management's efforts have almost eliminated the GAP, which falls from $1.996 billion to $53 million. As shown in Table 18.8, expected profits under an active asset/liability policy are better than they would be without one. The amount of FRAs financed by FRLs has been increased to take advantage of the higher differential, and the GAP has been reduced to lessen the effect of its lower return. The pretax performance is better than under a passive strategy: Profits are $344.099 million, and pretax RONW is 18.68 percent. Although returns are still lower than expected before the decline in interest rates and the projected RONW is slightly lower than management's target return, the forecast in Table 18.8 is much better than the estimates in Table 18.6. The after-tax RONW is held above 11 percent by restructuring the balance sheet.

PRINCIPLES OF GAP MANAGEMENT

Although most institutions cannot eliminate the GAP, those that choose to keep the GAP as close to $0 as possible in all interest rate environments emphasize stability of returns. Those that are willing to adjust the GAP in anticipation of interest rate changes, as ABC Bank did, are willing to risk potential variability in exchange for higher expected rates of return. The risk preferences of managers and owners, as well as the resources available for balance sheet adjustments, often are a function of the size of the institution and affect the choice of a GAP strategy. If an active approach is chosen, several important principles apply.

GAP MANAGEMENT AND INTEREST RATE FORECASTS

The ABC Bank example illustrated a narrowing of the GAP in anticipation of rate declines. With a forecast of rising rates, the appropriate strategy under active GAP management would be to increase the size of the GAP, because the spread on the GAP would widen as the returns on RSAs rose while fixed-rate funding costs remained stable. In fact, a general principle of GAP management is to increase positive GAPs under forecasts of rising rates and to narrow positive GAPs under forecasts of falling interest rates. Figure 18.2 shows appropriate management goals for a positive GAP in relation to changing interest rate expectations.

The GAP management strategies chosen will depend not only on the direction of but also on the degree of uncertainty about future interest rates. In periods of high interest rate volatility, confidence in interest rate forecasts may be low, and managers may choose to adopt a more closely matched position.

If managers revise a balance sheet based on a forecast that proves to be incorrect, the result will be poorer financial performance than if no active GAP management were undertaken. This point is vividly illustrated by the unfortunate results of active GAP management at NationsBank, a major superregional

---

TABLE 18.7   **Balance Sheet Sensitivity Analysis under Lower Interest Rates after Balance Sheet Revisions**

Anticipating interest rate changes, management can attempt to restructure the balance sheet. In this illustration, the GAP is narrowed so that under a falling rate forecast, the institution is less dependent on RSAs.

Rate-Sensitive Assets	Average Balances (Millions $)	Rate of Return (%)	Rate-Sensitive Liabilities	Average Balances (Millions $)	Cost (%)	
Short-term Treasury securities	$ 915	7.600%	Other transactions balances	$ 811	10.850%	
Floating-rate commercial loans	10,200	11.200	Consumer time deposits (floating)	236	11.050	
Other securities (floating rate)	798	9.950	Other time deposits (floating)	4,809	10.950	
Consumer loans (floating rate)	690	13.750	Foreign (floating rate)	4,306	11.450	
Other loans (floating rate)	2,760	13.100	Borrowed funds	5,148	11.000	
Total rate-sensitive assets	$15,363		Total rate-sensitive liabilities	$15,310		**Rate Differential**
Average return on rate-sensitive assets		11.377%	Average cost of rate-sensitive liabilities		11.104%	11.377 − 11.104 = 0.273%

Matched-Rate Assets	Average Balances (Millions $)	Rate of Return (%)	Matched-Rate Liabilities	Average Balances (Millions $)	Cost (%)	
Cash and due (floating)	$ 4,743	10.770%	Other time deposits (matched)	$ 1,336	9.700%	
Other securities (matched)	160	11.900	Foreign (floating but matched)	2,500	11.050	
			Borrowed funds (matched)	1,067	11.000	
Total matched-rate assets	$ 4,903		Total matched-rate liabilities	$ 4,903		**Rate Differential**
Average return on matched-rate assets		10.807%	Average cost of matched-rate liabilities		10.671%	10.807 − 10.671 = 0.136%

TABLE 18.7 CONTINUED

Fixed-Rate Earning Assets	Average Balances (Millions $)	Rate of Return (%)	Fixed-Rate Liabilities	Average Balances (Millions $)	Cost (%)	
			Domestic demand			
Cash and due (fixed rate)	$ 2,554	10.850%	deposits	$ 4,008	7.550%	
Other Treasury and agency securities	263	9.750	NOW balances	1,789	10.550	
State and municipal securities	514	7.500	Savings deposits	1,320	8.550	
Other securities (fixed rate)	663	12.000	Consumer time deposits (fixed)	1,339	12.350	
Short-term commercial loans (3 months–1 year)	4,440	12.750	Other time deposits (fixed)	2,844	13.400	
Long-term commercial loans (more than 1 year)	5,100	13.240	Foreign (fixed rate and noninterest bearing)	3,800	13.050	
Consumer loans (fixed rate)	2,760	14.700	Long-term debt	1,230	11.000	
Other loans (fixed rate)	779	14.200	Other liabilities	2,248	7.150	
Lease financing	359	14.960				
Total fixed-rate earning assets	$17,432		Total fixed-rate liabilities	$18,578		**Rate Differential**
Average return on fixed-rate assets		12.805%	Average cost of fixed-rate liabilities		10.456%	12.805 − 10.456 = 2.349%
Nonearning assets (including nonearning cash and due)	$ 2,935		Total equity capital	$ 1,842		
Total assets	$40,633		Total liabilities and equity	$40,633		

TABLE 18.8   Profitability Analysis after Balance Sheet Revisions

A smaller GAP in anticipation of falling rates results in a greater estimated RONW than in Table 18.6.

GAP = RSAs − RSLs = $53 million

Rate Differentials (Annual)

On RSAs and RSLs	0.273%
On matched assets and liabilities	0.136
On FRAs and FRLs	2.349
On nonearning assets financed by FRLs	(10.456)
On the GAP:	
Return on RSAs − Cost of FRLs	0.920

Sensitivity Category	Amount (Millions $)	Rate Differential (%)	Expected Profit (Millions $)
Matched assets and liabilities	$ 4,903	0.136%	$ 6.649
FRAs financed by FRLs	17,432	2.349	409.479
RSAs financed by RSLs	15,310	0.273	41.772
Nonearning assets financed by FRLs	1,093	(10.456)	(114.289)
GAP	53	0.920	0.488
Total pretax profits			$344.099
Pretax RONW (Annualized)			18.68%

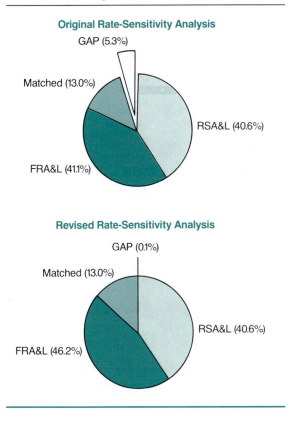

FIGURE 18.1 **Results of Active GAP Management**

Active GAP management in anticipation of falling rates produces a GAP that is a smaller proportion of assets than before balance sheet adjustments are made.

Original Rate-Sensitivity Analysis

GAP (5.3%)
Matched (13.0%)
RSA&L (40.6%)
FRA&L (41.1%)

Revised Rate-Sensitivity Analysis

GAP (0.1%)
Matched (13.0%)
RSA&L (40.6%)
FRA&L (46.2%)

The investment decisions of Boatmen's Bancshares, introduced in the opening paragraphs to this chapter, reflect a more successful adjustment to interest rate changes. But not all institutions are willing to adopt such a risky profile. The manager of a New Jersey savings bank in 1992 described his more conservative strategy and uncertainty about interest rates: "If we do invest, it's short-term until we get a better feel for where interest rates are going."[9]

As the previous examples illustrate, GAP management decisions are increasingly complex and are always accompanied by uncertainty about the direction in which interest rates will actually move. These conditions have led to the development of sophisticated computer models for simulating the effects of alternate courses of action available to asset/liability managers. Simulation software allows depository institution managers to measure the effects of rate changes in different directions and with varying magnitudes. This information assists in evaluating the potential positive and negative results of GAP management. Federal regulators increasingly encourage this type of "what if" analysis.

GAP MANAGEMENT AND THE PROPORTION OF RATE-SENSITIVE ASSETS

The success of a GAP management strategy is affected by a number of institutional as well as market factors, one of which is the proportion of rate-sensitive assets and rate-sensitive liabilities to total earning assets. For the ABC Bank in Table 18.1, RSAs made up more than 40 percent of the institution's total asset portfolio. Thus, a fairly large proportion of total assets was available for repricing during the next planning period, enhancing the restructuring of the balance sheet. If this proportion had been smaller, however, even an active GAP management effort would have offered less potential to protect profits than the bank achieved in this example.

bank, in 1989 and 1990. Forecasting a sharp drop in interest rates in 1990, managers in 1989 deliberately narrowed the GAP by lengthening the average maturity of the bank's securities portfolio. When interest rates rose in the first quarter of 1990, returns on these long-term assets were locked in while the bank's short-term liability costs soared. Analysts estimated that overall losses on the "bet" were $180 million.[8]

---

[8]For a theoretical discussion of matching and interest rate uncertainty, see Deshmukh, Greenbaum, and Kanatas 1983. The authors characterize the well-matched portfolio as a managerial decision to perform brokerage functions instead of intermediation. The brokerage strategy is more conservative than engaging in asset transfor-

mations, which necessarily require more significant and deliberate mismatching. For an analysis of the size of the GAP resulting in the least risk exposure, see McNulty, Morgan, and Smith 1991. The NationsBank example is discussed in Kelley Holland, "NCNB Loses Big Bet on Long-term Rates," *American Banker*, March 20, 1990.

[9]Fred Bleakley, "Banks, Thrifts, Scored As Interest Rates Fell," A6.

FIGURE 18.2	**GAP Management and Rate Cycles**

Assuming a positive GAP, rising rates call for increasing the size of the GAP and falling rates suggest decreasing the GAP. At the peak of a rate cycle, the GAP should be at its largest.

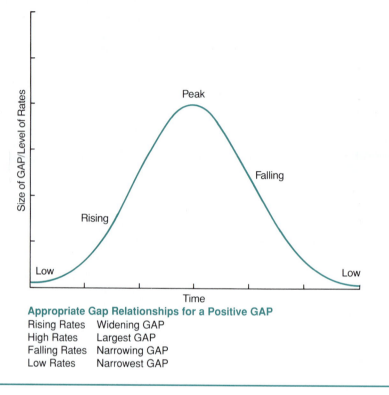

Appropriate Gap Relationships for a Positive GAP

Rising Rates	Widening GAP
High Rates	Largest GAP
Falling Rates	Narrowing GAP
Low Rates	Narrowest GAP

MANAGING A NEGATIVE GAP

For depository institutions with a high proportion of RSAs, including most commercial banks and many CUs, the GAP calculated from Equation 18.1 will be a positive number. The ABC Bank is a typical example of such an institution. Yet for some depositories—and for thrift institutions in particular—the GAP, when calculated from Equation 18.1, will be a *negative* number. In other words, during most reasonable planning periods, the volume of RSLs will exceed the volume of RSAs. It is important to recognize how to incorporate this fact into estimating pretax profits. It is also important to understand how principles of GAP management differ in negative GAP institutions compared with institutions such as ABC Bank.

INTERPRETING NEGATIVE GAPS AND ESTIMATING PRETAX PROFITS

Table 18.9 shows a simplified rate-sensitivity analysis and an estimate of pretax profits for a hypothetical negative GAP depository.

The negative GAP (RSAs < RSLs) means that $400 million of rate-sensitive liabilities are *not* financing rate-sensitive assets. Therefore, they must be financing fixed-rate assets, and the rate differential on the negative GAP is the difference between the yield on FRAs and the cost of RSLs, or (10 percent − 7 percent) = 3 percent in this case. Given these yields and costs, it is clear that expected profits on the GAP are *not* negative. In fact, a rate differential of 3 percent on each dollar of FRAs financed by RSLs means that

| **TABLE 18.9** | **Estimating Pretax Profits in a Negative-GAP Depository** |

Because this institution has more RSLs than RSAs, it has a negative GAP; $400 million of FRAs are financed by RSLs. When short-term rates are lower than long-term rates, the rate differential on the GAP is positive, and a negative GAP can be the source of substantial profits.

A. Rate-Sensitivity Analysis

Assets			Liabilities and Net Worth		
	Amount (Millions $)	**Yield (%)**		**Amount (Millions $)**	**Cost (%)**
RSAs	$ 250	8%	RSLs	$ 650	7%
FRAs	750	10	FRLs	350	9
Nonearning assets	100	0	Net worth	100	
Total	$1,100		Total	$1,100	

B. Profitability Analysis

Category	Amount (Millions $)	Rate Differential (%)	Profits (Millions $)
RSAs financed by RSLs	$250	1%	$ 2.5
FRAs financed by FRLs	350	1	3.5
GAP (RSAs − RSLs)	(400)	3	12.0
Nonearning assets	100	0	0.0
		Total	$17.0

Expected RONW = $17/$100 = 17%

---

a positive $12 million profit is expected on the GAP during the next period. Expressing the GAP as a negative number is just a notational convention followed when RSLs exceed RSAs. Although the notation is mathematically a bit confusing, managers in institutions with negative GAPs are aware of the convention and know how to work with it.

So why is a negative GAP considered so risky, and why have many thrift institutions worked so hard to close their negative GAPs in the last decade? The answer is that profits on a negative GAP *can* turn negative if the term structure of interest rates is inverted or if the cost of RSLs rises faster than the institution can adjust the average returns on its asset portfolio. Table 18.10 shows a rate-sensitivity analysis and profitability estimate for the same institution in an environment in which the yield curve is downward-sloping. The rate differential on the GAP is now negative; RSLs cost 2 percent *more* than FRAs are yielding. Expected profits on the GAP are negative, and the GAP is large enough that the overall profit estimate is negative, too. Many institutions with a high proportion of fixed-rate assets such as home mortgages found themselves in this situation in the early 1980s, as the yield curve inverted and the cost of short-term liabilities rose above asset returns.

ACTIVE MANAGEMENT OF A NEGATIVE GAP

As the previous discussion suggests, managers of institutions with large negative GAPs will be particularly concerned when interest rates are expected to increase. An active manager would attempt to close the negative GAP by encouraging new loan customers to choose variable rate loans and new depositors to select fixed-rate deposits. As securities mature, proceeds would be invested in short-term or variable-rate instruments.

As Table 18.9 shows, negative GAPs can be profitable if interest rates are expected to rise but short-term rates are expected to be lower than long-term rates. If such a scenario were forecast, an active GAP manager would attempt to increase the size of the negative GAP by making mostly fixed-rate loans and issuing mostly variable-rate deposits. Table 18.11

TABLE 18.10	**A Negative GAP in an Inverted Term Structure Environment**

If variable-rate liability costs increase while asset returns remain fixed, the rate differential on the GAP becomes negative, and a large negative GAP can be detrimental to profitability.

A. Rate-Sensitivity Analysis

	Assets			Liabilities and Net Worth	
	Amount (Millions $)	Yield (%)		Amount (Millions $)	Cost
RSAs	$ 250	13%	RSLs	$ 650	12%
FRAs	750	10	FRLs	350	9
Nonearning assets	100	0	Net worth	100	
Total	$1,100		Total	$1,100	

B. Profitability Analysis

Category	Amount (Millions $)	Rate Differential (%)	Profits (Millions $)
RSAs financed by RSLs	$250	1%	$ 2.5
FRAs financed by FRLs	350	1	3.5
GAP (RSAs − RSLs)	(400)	−2	(8.0)
Nonearning assets	100	0	0.0
		Total	$(1.0)

Expected RONW $= -\$1/\$100 = -1\%$

summarizes the effects of active GAP management on profitability for both positive GAP and negative GAP depositories. Just as institutions with positive GAPs can benefit when rates rise, institutions with negative GAPs can increase profits when interest rates fall and RSL costs decrease.

LIMITATIONS OF GAP MANAGEMENT

Unfortunately, it is probably impossible to achieve all the desired outcomes of GAP management. Many market and institutional factors interfere with adjustments of the asset/liability mix and an institution's ability to achieve profitability targets.

GAP MANAGEMENT AND CUSTOMERS

One of the strongest obstacles to desired GAP adjustments can be the institution's customers. The objectives of those customers, in the light of generally held interest rate expectations, would be the opposite of the institution's objectives. If interest rates were ex-

pected to fall, a depositor would want to move funds quickly into a fixed-rate certificate so that today's higher rate could be locked in. At the same time, the institution would be trying to move funds *out* of fixed-rate and into floating-rate deposits to narrow the GAP. If the forecast were for rising interest rates, a depository would be urging borrowers to take floating-rate loans. But prospective borrowers approach variable-rate loans warily if interest rate increases are expected, so a manager might find GAP adjustment strategies thwarted by customer resistance. Of course, it is possible for managers to attempt to persuade customers to select deposits or loans whose terms are more desirable to the institution, as long as the expected benefits of those incentives exceed their costs. But because of potential differences between preferences of institutions and their customers, supplements to GAP management, such as those presented in the next chapter, have been developed.

BALANCING INTEREST RATE RISK AND DEFAULT RISK

Also, managers' efforts to reduce the institution's exposure to interest rate risk simultaneously

TABLE 18.11	GAP Management and Profitability

Active GAP management *and* correct interest rate forecasts can improve profitability. When rates rise, a positive GAP can increase profits. Losses will occur, however, if a positive GAP is held in the face of rate decreases. Institutions with negative GAPs benefit if they correctly anticipate declines in interest rates. Profits at depositories with negative GAPs suffer, however, when interest rates rise.

	GAP > $0 (RSA > RSL)	GAP < $0 (RSA < RSL)
Rates increase	Profits increase	Profits decrease
Rates decrease	Profits decrease	Profits increase

pass that exposure on to customers. If rates rise after borrowers have been induced to take variable-rate loans, loan losses may increase if some borrowers cannot make their higher interest payments. Similarly, if rates are expected to fall and customers have been encouraged to borrow at high fixed rates, the potential for default risk is increased if borrowers have difficulty meeting the higher required loan payments. During the 1980s, as deregulation allowed new flexibility in S&L asset management, many thrifts assumed extensive credit risk exposure in the form of shorter-term construction and real estate development loans. Many profitability problems in the industry resulted from defaults on these instruments that were intended to reduce the institution's interest rate risk. Thus, GAP management requires a recognition that a lower exposure to interest rate risk may increase default risk, a concept first introduced in Chapters 14 and 15.

GAP MANAGEMENT USES RESOURCES

GAP management may also lead to higher costs, even if it does not increase the institution's exposure to default risk. To obtain the desired interest-sensitivity profile, a bank may have to offer premium rates on deposits with the interest rate characteristics it wishes to attract, or it may need to offer discounts on the loan categories into which it wants to direct borrowers. These costs may reduce the profitability of active GAP management.

INTEREST RATE FLUCTUATIONS AND NONOPERATING INCOME

As financial institutions have become more adept at GAP management, their managers have discovered circumstances in which even a perfectly

matched institution can find its profitability endangered by interest rate fluctuations. The reason? Many institutions rely heavily on nonoperating sources of income—such as loan origination fees—to supplement income from earning assets. Unfortunately, many of these supplemental sources are also affected by changes in the interest rate environment. For example, as interest rates rise, prospective homebuyers become more scarce, and the housing market suffers. So a savings institution with a zero GAP (and theoretically no interest rate risk exposure) could still experience a decline in profitability as the number of mortgage loan originations decreases, causing a drop in nonoperating income.[10]

TWO SIDES OF INTEREST RATE RISK REVISITED

Finally, GAP management as illustrated in this chapter concentrates only on funds flows—that is, variability in revenues and costs and, subsequently, in the NIM and RONW. No attention has yet been given to the effect of interest rate movements on the *value* of an institution's assets and liabilities over the longer term.[11] Earlier discussions, which began in Chapters 8 and 9, emphasize that interest rate risk has two sides—the risks of changing reinvestment rates and of changing market values. Although GAP management is important, supplemental risk management techniques must be part of every manager's plans if the goals of asset/liability management are to be achieved. The additional tools are used when active GAP management

---

[10] For further explanation and illustrations, see Parliment 1987 and Kulczycky 1988.

[11] This point is argued and amplified in Simonson and Hempel 1982.

is infeasible or undesirable or when it fails to provide enough protection from earnings variability.

OTHER TOOLS SUPPLEMENT GAP MANAGEMENT

Because managers recognize the limitations of GAP management, they do not rely solely on rate-sensitivity analysis to control an institution's exposure to interest rate risk. In fact, managers have an increasingly wide array of alternatives for supplementing GAP management. These involve many of the techniques and financial instruments introduced in Chapters 9–11, such as duration analysis, interest rate futures, interest rate swaps, and caps and collars. These and other more sophisticated interest rate risk management tools are discussed in Chapter 19.

SUMMARY

Techniques for managing individual assets and liabilities are of limited usefulness unless they are part of an integrated strategy for achieving a target net interest margin and return on net worth. This chapter explored one of the most commonly used integrated financial management strategies: GAP management.

GAP management involves frequently monitoring the interest rate characteristics of a depository institution's assets and liabilities. Managers must identify the volume and mix of rate-sensitive, matched, and fixed-rate assets and liabilities. Once assets and liabilities have been classified, the GAP—the difference between the amount of RSAs and the amount of FRLs—can be identified.

Maintaining a GAP as close to $0 as possible is a risk-minimization strategy. In contrast, active GAP management adjusts the size of the GAP to achieve desired financial goals in anticipation of changes in interest rates. If rates are expected to rise, a positive GAP can be widened to take advantage of anticipated increases in asset yields. If rates are expected to fall, a positive GAP can be narrowed to take advantage of anticipated lower liability costs. Adjustments of the GAP in opposite directions are appropriate for negative GAP institutions. Successful GAP management allows an institution to attain the targeted NIM and RONW.

GAP management has limitations as a tool for protecting a depository against adverse developments in the financial markets. The institution's desires may conflict with the desires and needs of customers, complicating GAP adjustments. Furthermore, if interest rate forecasts prove to be inaccurate, adjusting the GAP may harm, rather than enhance, financial performance. Nonoperating income may also be affected by changing interest rates. Finally, GAP management is designed to assist in managing only one facet of interest rate risk, the risk of changing reinvestment rates and funding costs. Most institutions need other integrated risk management tools as well.

QUESTIONS

1. What is meant by an "integrated" asset/liability management strategy, and what is the effect of such a strategy on interest rate risk? How is the hedging principle related?

2. Explain what is meant by rate-sensitive assets and liabilities, and give an example of each. Would you classify a variable-rate mortgage with a 30-year maturity as rate sensitive? Why or why not?

3. Explain why the definition of rate sensitivity may vary across financial institutions of different sizes and in different industries.

4. Define the GAP and the GAP ratio. What are the objectives of GAP management? Discuss the risks that a positive GAP presents to a financial institution when interest rates rise and when interest rates fall.

5. What is a cumulative GAP? Why do many depositories measure the GAP over multiple planning periods? How might this complicate GAP management?

6. Discuss the difference between an active GAP management strategy and a risk-minimization strategy. What factors influence an institution's choice between the two? Compare and contrast the asset/liability strategies of now NCNB(NationsBank) in 1989 and Boatmen's Bancshares in 1991–92. How do their experiences illustrate the difficult choices among GAP management strategies?

7. Explain the options available to managers for restructuring the balance sheet under active GAP management. What are the advantages and disadvantages of each? As interest rates change, why is it difficult to maintain a stable rate differential between rate-sensitive assets and rate-sensitive liabilities?

8. For an institution with a positive GAP using active GAP management, what adjustments should managers make under expectations of declining interest rates? Under expectations of rising rates?

9. How are the preferences of customers for rate-sensitive and fixed-rate deposits (or loans) affected by their expectations about future interest rates? How do those preferences influence a depository institution's ability to manage its GAP? What strategies might a bank or thrift use to achieve its optimal GAP?

10. Define *negative GAP*. For an institution with a negative GAP, which direction in interest rate movements has an adverse effect on earnings? Why? Explain how the asset and liability structure of the thrift industry before the passage of DIDMCA in 1980 contributed to its interest rate risk exposure.

11. For an institution with a negative GAP whose managers practice active GAP management, what adjustments in the size of the GAP are appropriate under expectations of rising rates? Under expectations of falling rates?

12. FIRREA included some provisions affecting thrift asset structure (for example, the new QTL requirement), and FDICIA also addressed the QTL. How did these acts affect the ability of thrifts to manage interest rate risk exposure effectively?

13. Explain how a depository institution's efforts to manage interest rate sensitivity through the loan portfolio might also affect its default risk exposure.

14. Discuss the limitations of active GAP management. What supplemental tools might depository institution managers use to overcome these limitations?

15. Consult current financial publications to review recent forecasts for future interest rate levels. Given experts' predictions, what asset and liability adjustments should an institution with a positive GAP be planning? What adjustments should be undertaken by a depository with a negative GAP?

16. If you were a depository institution manager, would you try to achieve a $0 GAP for the institution? Why or why not?

PROBLEMS

1. The managers of a regional bank are conducting an interest-rate sensitivity analysis for the planning period and have prepared the following information.

Assets			Liabilities and Net Worth		
	Amount (Millions)	**Yield (%)**		**Amount (Millions)**	**Cost (%)**
RSAs	$950	3.5%	RSLs	$840	3.0%
FRAs	660	6.5	FRLs	770	5.5
Matched	200	7.0	Matched	200	6.5
Nonearning	160	0.0	Net worth	160	—

The target pretax RONW is 14 percent. Interest rate forecasts suggest that rates will remain steady or fall during the planning period.
    a. Calculate the GAP and the GAP ratio.
    b. Calculate expected pretax RONW. Will the bank meet its target? If not, what changes in the rate-sensitivity structure would you suggest, given its interest rate forecast?

2. Suppose that, with all else remaining the same, management is able to reverse the dollar amounts of RSAs and FRAs in Problem 1.
    a. Calculate the GAP, the GAP ratio, and the expected pretax RONW under this new asset structure.
    b. If rates are expected to remain steady or decline, is the bank better off or worse off than under the asset structure in Problem 1? Explain.

3. The following is a simplified balance sheet for National Bank of Las Colinas. Annual average rates of return or average costs are provided for each asset and liability category.

National Bank of Las Colinas
Balance Sheet
(Millions)

Interest-Bearing Assets			Interest-Bearing Funds Sources		
Matched	$100	(12.0%)	Matched	$100	(11.0%)
Rate-sensitive	450	(12.5%)	Rate-sensitive	400	(11.0%)
Fixed-rate	150	(8.0%)	Fixed-rate	200	(6.0%)
Total earning assets	$700		Total funds sources	$700	

a. Calculate the bank's GAP and its GAP ratio.
b. Estimate the annual pretax profits. (Special note to spreadsheet users: To facilitate answering later parts of this problem, the set-up for part b is important. Express as many of your calculations as possible using functions or formulas.)
c. If interest rates are expected to fall in the near future, should bank management widen or narrow the GAP? Explain without calculations.
d. Using a "what if" table, show how pretax profits would change if the rate of return on RSAs were to rise by as much as 5 percent or decline by as much as 5 percent. Vary the rate on RSAs in 0.5 percent intervals. Assume that the rate differential between RSAs and RSLs remains constant at 1.5 percent. (Hint: Remember that the key variable that determines profitability is the rate differential on the GAP.)
e. Using the current rate on RSAs as the starting point, graph the relationship between pretax profits and changes away from the current rate, given the bank's existing GAP.

4. Suppose instead that National Bank of Las Colinas has $350 million in RSAs and $250 million in FRAs. All other balance sheet data are as presented in Problem 3.
a. What annual pretax profits are expected?
b. How will pretax profits change if the return on RSAs increases or decreases by as much as 5 percent? (Use the same approach as in part d of Problem 3.)
c. Graph the relationship between changes in interest rates and changes in pretax profits. Compare your results to those in part e of Problem 3. What lessons are there for active GAP managers?

5. Consider the financial data for Clayton Savings and Loan:

Clayton Savings and Loan
Balance Sheet
(Millions)

Interest-Bearing Assets			Interest-Bearing Funds Sources		
Matched	$ 5	(8.0%)	Matched	$ 5	(7.0%)
Rate-sensitive	20	(7.0%)	Rate-sensitive	35	(5.5%)
Fixed-rate	40	(9.5%)	Fixed-rate	25	(7.5%)
Total earning assets	$65		Total funds sources	$65	

a. Calculate Clayton's GAP and GAP ratio.
b. Estimate annual pretax profits.
c. Recalculate profits, assuming no GAP management and an upward shift in the yield curve of 200 basis points.
d. What active GAP management strategy would be indicated if the increase in interest rates were anticipated? Explain why Clayton may not be able to stabilize profits even if its managers use an active GAP management strategy.
e. Using "what if" analysis, estimate pretax profits under the current interest rate environment if the size of the GAP were to vary, with total assets remaining the same. That is, show how pretax profits would change if interest-bearing funds sources remained constant but the distribution between RSAs and FRAs were to change. How does the size of the GAP in relation to total assets affect expected profits? (Hints: Vary RSAs between $10 million and $50 million in $5 million increments. This analysis is a bit trickier than it might seem at first. Remember that when the GAP moves from positive to negative, the rate differential on the GAP will change as well. Thus, your spreadsheet formula for the GAP rate differential should be set up as an @IF statement so that the number will change as the sign of the GAP shifts.)
f. Repeat the analysis in part e under the assumption of an inverted yield curve; assume that the return on RSAs is 11.5

percent and the cost of RSLs is 10 percent. Vary the size of the GAP. On the same graph, plot the results of your analysis in parts e (normal yield curve) and f (inverted yield curve), placing the size of the GAP on the horizontal axis and pretax profits on the vertical axis. Explain why the lines intersect at the point they do.

g.   Now assume, more realistically, that the GAP can change not only because asset structure can change but also because liability structure can change. In the inverted-yield-curve environment described in part f, show how pretax profits will change not only when asset proportions vary but also when liability proportions vary. (Hint: This will require a two-way data table. Vary the amount of RSLs from $10 million to $50 million in $5 million increments.) Repeat the analysis for the normal yield curve environment described in part a.

Your completed tables should provide a comprehensive look at expected profits for Clayton Savings under different interest rate scenarios with both positive and negative GAPs of different sizes. Interpret the tables by comparing and contrasting the results in each one.

6.   The year-end 19X3 balance sheet for the St. George National Bank follows. A second table provides the average yields and costs for the bank's assets and liabilities as of January 1, 19X4. Assume that the bank uses a 6-month planning horizon for defining a rate-sensitive asset or liability.

St. George National Bank
Balance Sheet as of Year Ending
December 31, 19X3
(Millions)

Assets		Liabilities and Net Worth	
Cash and due	$ 80	Demand Deposits	$ 270
Interest-bearing deposits	13	MMDAs	325
Fed funds sold	150	Time deposits	591
Investments	519	Fed funds purchased	225
Loans		Long-term debt	48
Commercial	534	Other liabilities	20
Real estate	178	Net worth	80
Other assets	85		
Total assets	$1,559	Total liabilities and net worth	$1,559

St. George National Bank
Asset/Liability Yields and Costs as of January 1, 19X4
(Millions)

Investments		Yield	Deposits		Cost
Short-term Treasury securities*	$ 270	9.60%	Noninterest-bearing	$ 270	7.50%
Fed funds sold	150	10.45	MMDAs	325	8.90
Other Treasury securities	180	11.30	Time (less than 6 months)	210	10.50
State and municipal	69	11.45	Time (1 year)	160	10.85
Interest-bearing deposits	13	7.00	Time (more than 1 year)	221	11.15

Loans		Yield	Purchased Liabilities		Cost
Floating-rate commercial*	$ 175	12.40%	Fed funds purchased	$ 225	9.90%
Short-term commercial*	265	12.95	Long-term debt	48	11.50
Long-term commercial	94	13.21			
Floating-rate real estate*	115	11.50			
Fixed-rate real estate	63	12.15			

Other		Yield	Other		Cost
Cash	$ 80	0.00%	Other liabilities	$ 20	7.05%
Other assets	85	0.00	Core capital	80	
Total assets	$1,559		Total liabilities and equity	$1,559	

*Maturity or interest rate change in 6 months or less.

a. Categorize St. George's balance sheet according to the rate sensitivity of its assets and liabilities. (Note: St. George has no matched assets and liabilities.)

b. Using the results of the balance sheet analysis, calculate the following:
   1) RSAs financed by RSLs;
   2) FRAs financed by FRLs;
   3) the amount of nonearning assets financed by FRLs;
   4) the GAP.

c. Calculate the rate differentials for each of the asset/liability categories in part b, as well as the bank's estimated annual pretax profits at current interest yields/costs.

d. Assume that the economic forecasters whose services are purchased by the bank are predicting an interest rate decline. To help the bank's managers develop some pro forma forecasts, assume that the yield curve will shift downward by 100 basis points. Revise your estimates of the bank's annual pretax profits, assuming that managers are unable to make any balance sheet adjustments before rates fall.

e. If managers are able to restructure the balance sheet before the yields and costs change, what adjustments should they make if they want to stabilize profits? What actions should they take if they wish to maximize potential profit? What risks are associated with a maximization strategy?

7. Centenary Federal Savings and Loan is under new management, after its recent acquisition by a large S&L with nationwide operations. The institution will operate as an autonomous unit, and you have been brought in as a consultant.

The thrift has been managed rather conservatively in the past, and it survived the industry debacle of the late 1980s better than many of its fellow institutions. The future is uncertain, however, because its customers usually resist change, particularly when it is in the form of adjustable-rate mortgages or other variable-rate loans. The management personnel who were retained after the takeover are also rather conservative and have expressed some skepticism toward suggestions that the S&L's asset/liability mix may need adjustment.

Centenary's financial data follow. The balance sheet as of December 31, 19X4, and asset/liability yields and costs as of January 1, 19X5, are also available. The planning period is 6 months.

Centenary Federal Savings and Loan
Balance Sheet as of Year Ending December 31, 19X4
(Millions)

Assets		Liabilities and Net Worth	
Cash	$ 37.4	NOWs and passbook deposits	$ 441.3
Investments	320.2	Time deposits	1,875.7
Loans		Borrowed funds	563.8
Real estate	2,481.4	Other liabilities	146.3
Other loans	220.3	Net worth	245.6
Other assets	213.4		
Total assets	$3,272.7	Total liabilities and net worth	$3,272.7

Centenary Federal Savings and Loan
Asset/Liability Yields and Costs as of January 1, 19X5
(Millions)

Investments		Yield	Deposits		Cost
Less than 6 months	$ 126.8	8.70%	Less than 6 months	$ 499.0	8.80%
6 months–1 year	86.1	8.70	Passbook	441.3	8.80
1–2 years	78.0	10.00	6 months–1 year	807.1	9.00
2–3 years	26.0	10.50	1–2 years	269.6	9.15
3–4 years	3.3	10.75	2–3 years	142.6	9.40
			3–4 years	86.1	10.00
			Over 4 years	71.3	10.25

Loans		Yield	Purchased Liabilities		Cost
Less than 6 months	$ 85.1	8.90%	Less than 6 months	$ 377.2	8.65%
6 months–1 year	88.3	9.00	6 months–1 year	100.5	8.75
1–2 years	162.5	10.15	1–2 years		
2–3 years	170.8	10.50	2–3 years	52.0	10.95
3–4 years	185.4	11.00	3–4 years	34.1	11.05
Over 4 years	$2,009.6	11.25			
Other		**Yield**	**Other**		**Cost**
Cash	$ 37.4	0.00%	Other liabilities	$ 146.3	10.00%
Other assets	193.4	0.00	Net worth	245.6	
Total assets	$3,272.7		Total liabilities and net worth	$3,272.7	

a.   Before you recommend any actions, complete an analysis of balance sheet sensitivity, compute rate differentials for each category, and estimate the thrift's pretax profits and RONW under the current rate levels. (Centenary has no matched assets and liabilities.)

Be careful: Calculating the GAP in this situation is more complicated than at first thought. In negative-GAP institutions, nonearning assets that are *not* financed by net worth are financed by *RSLs*. In the positive-GAP examples in the chapter, nonearning assets not financed by net worth were financed by FRLs. In the negative-GAP examples, it was assumed that nonearning assets were equal to net worth, so Centenary's situation did not arise. After calculating the GAP as (RSAs − RSLs), you must add back the amount of nonearning assets financed by RSLs, as this quantity should *not* be part of Centenary's negative GAP.

b.   To convince both old and new managers of the risks that the thrift is facing under its current balance sheet structure, prepare new estimates of pretax earnings and RONW in the following scenarios:

  1)   a parallel upward shift in the yield curve of 300 basis points
  2)   a parallel downward shift in the yield curve of 300 basis points
  Hint: Be sure to remember that because nonearning assets not financed by net worth are financed by RSLs, the rate differential on that amount will change when interest rates change, just as the rate differential on the GAP will change.

c.   Using this information, prepare recommendations for Centenary managers. Discuss how they should adjust the balance sheet under different interest rate forecasts if they wish to stabilize profits and if they wish to maximize profits.

d.   What problems might the thrift encounter if it implements these strategies?

SELECTED REFERENCES

Baker, James V., Jr. "Why You Need a Formal Asset/Liability Management Policy." *Banking* 70 (June 1978): 33–43. The first of a five-part series. *Banking* is now the *ABA Banking Journal.*

Binder, Barrett S. "Asset/Liability Management: Part 1." *Magazine of Bank Administration* 56 (November 1980): 42–48. The first of a three-part series.

Deshmukh, Sudhakar D., Stuart I. Greenbaum, and George Kanatas. "Interest Rate Uncertainty and the Financial Intermediary's Choice of Exposure." *Journal of Finance* 38 (March 1983): 141–147.

French, George E. "Measuring the Interest-Rate Exposure of

Financial Intermediaries." *FDIC Banking Review* 1 (Fall 1988): 14–27.

Gardner, Mona J., and Dixie L. Mills. "Asset/Liability Management: Current Perspectives for Small Banks." *Journal of Commercial Bank Lending* 64 (December 1981): 14–31.

Graddy, Duane B., and Adi S. Karma. "Net Interest Margin Sensitivity among Banks of Different Sizes." *Journal of Bank Research* 14 (Winter 1984): 283–290.

Kulczycky, Maria. "GAP Management Eases Interest Rate Swings." *Savings Institutions* 109 (November 1988): 44–49.

McNulty, James E., George E. Morgan III, and Stephen D.

Smith, "Estimating the Minimum Risk Maturity GAP." Working Paper 91-7, Federal Reserve Bank of Atlanta, 1991.

Parliment, Tom. "Don't Always Look to Interest Hedges for Protection." *Savings Institutions* 108 (December 1987): 144–145.

Simonson, Donald G., and George H. Hempel. "Improving Gap Management for Controlling Interest Rate Risk." *Journal of Bank Research* 13 (Summer 1982): 109–115.

Troughton, George H., ed. *Asset/Liability Management.* Homewood, IL: Dow Jones-Irwin, 1986.

*You can securitize virtually everything;
the imagination is our only constraint.*

Andrew D. Stone
Senior Managing Director, Daiwa Securities America, Inc. (1992)

In 1992, Bankers Trust New York was the seventh largest bank in the United States. But the institution had little in common with other money-center banks. For example, its nine largest competitors had invested almost 60 percent of assets in the loan portfolio, but Bankers Trust held only 19 percent of assets in loans. Competitors placed less than 20 percent of assets in securities, whereas Bankers Trust invested more than 50 percent of assets in different types of securities.

What management philosophy guided the bank to this position? Bankers had adopted a radical approach to asset/liability management, believing that extensive involvement in derivative securities would lead the bank to the best profit performance. In fact, the Chairman and CEO of Bankers Trust called holding loans on the balance sheet a "discontinued business" and allowed almost no loans to be granted if the bank did not have a plan for selling—or securitizing—the loan. Bankers also was heavily involved in the interest rate swaps market, acting as broker/dealer or counterparty in many agreements. The initial results of this strategy were gratifying, because Bankers Trust reported return on net worth (RONW) figures above 20 percent 2 years in a row![1]

Most depository institutions do not seek to follow a strategy as radical as Bankers Trust has adopted. Their managers do, however, recognize the challenge of managing interest rate risk exposure of a more traditional balance sheet and understand that balancing rate sensitivity through GAP adjustments alone is seldom successful. Thus, many depository institutions supplement GAP management with some of the same techniques used by Bankers Trust, but on a more limited scale. Securitization and interest rate swaps are joined by hedging techniques such as financial futures, duration models, and interest rate caps, collars, and floors as increasingly important aspects of the asset/liability management of depositories.

Yet these tools introduce many new hazards and sometimes result in profits that are no higher (and perhaps even lower) than those achieved through more traditional GAP management alone. Nevertheless, a thoughtful combination of asset/liability techniques provides more flexibility and offers more benefits in the long run than any single tool.

---

[1] Carol J. Loomis, "A Whole New Way to Run a Bank," *Fortune,* September 7, 1992, 76–85.

WHY GAP MANAGEMENT IS INSUFFICIENT

The GAP management efforts of ABC Bank, presented in Chapter 18, were reasonably successful but did not prevent the institution's expected profits from falling. Besides GAP management's less-than-perfect effectiveness, several factors have led institutions to implement other techniques.

LIMITED FLEXIBILITY

The ability of managers to widen or to narrow the GAP depends to a certain extent on the response of depositors and loan customers. For the ABC Bank, the rate sensitivity of deposits could not be "managed" unless new funds flowed into the institution. Thus, the volume of any GAP adjustment is limited, as is the speed with which managers can change the rate-sensitivity balance. Market instruments that allow managers to avoid potentially resistant customers while hedging interest rate risk increase the viability of asset/liability management.

ILLIQUIDITY VERSUS INSOLVENCY

The rate-sensitivity GAP model presented in Chapter 18 focuses on an institution's net interest position. A perfectly matched balance sheet theoretically matches changes in interest revenues and costs so that pretax net interest margins (NIMs) remain stable despite fluctuations in market rates. But for depositories with the long-run goal of protecting owners or members by preserving the value of net worth, stable pretax income is insufficient.

Management of the rate-sensitivity GAP may protect an institution from illiquidity, but it does not necessarily protect against insolvency. Even under matched cash flows, changing interest rate conditions can alter the value of a depository institution's assets and liabilities so that the value of liabilities may exceed the present value of assets.

INSOLVENCY VERSUS ILLIQUIDITY: AN EXAMPLE. Table 19.1 clarifies the distinction between these two financial concerns.[2] Data are provided for a hypothetical savings institution assumed to have nonearning assets of $50 million; net worth of $50 million; a single category of earning assets—3-month variable-rate

loans; and a single category of rate-sensitive liabilities (RSLs)—3-month certificates of deposit (CDs).

The initial stated interest rate on the 3-month loans is 9.645 percent, which translates into an expected annual yield of 10 percent, assuming quarterly reinvestment of principal and interest. The initial stated rate on the CDs is 7.77 percent; thus, a depositor reinvesting principal and interest every 90 days for a year (assuming a 360-day year) expects to earn an effective annual yield of 8 percent. The rate-sensitivity GAP for this institution is $0 (and the GAP ratio is 1) for every 90-day period over the course of a year because the rate sensitivity of assets and liabilities is identical. This example ignores noninterest income, noninterest expenses, and taxes.

The figures in the top panel of Table 19.1 are generated under the assumption that interest rates remain constant over a 1-year period. Loans made on day 0 are repaid, with interest, at the end of each quarter; those inflows are reinvested in new loans. The CDs are also rolled over, with interest reinvested by depositors, every 3 months. The spread (IR − IE) for each quarter is shown in the row labeled "Net interest." Because noninterest expenses and taxes are ignored, this amount each quarter is available to be added to net worth. The total present value of these additions, calculated at a 20 percent annual required RONW (5 percent quarterly), is $8,842,100.

In the lower panel, the assumption is made that expected annual yields increase by 50 basis points at the end of the first quarter. Thus, the stated interest rate on 90-day loans rises to 10.11 percent at the end of the first quarter (an expected annual yield of 10.50 percent), and the CD rate goes to 8.24 percent at the same time (an expected cost to the institution of 8.50 percent annually). Because the GAP ratio is still 1, quarterly net interest is protected from deterioration; in every quarter the spread is equal to or even better than under stable economic conditions.

What has not been protected is the present value of additions to the institution's net worth. As interest rates rise, stockholders will require higher rates of return. Consequently, the required return on net worth increases to 20.50 percent, and the present value of ad-

---

[2] For additional discussion of liquidity versus value hedging, see Belongia and Santoni 1985; and Shaffer 1991. (References are listed in full at end of this chapter.)

TABLE 19.1   **GAP Management: Protecting Present Value versus Matching Rate Sensitivity**

Matching maturities can stabilize profits but does not always protect the value of net worth. In this example, an increase in interest rates lowers net worth, even though the rate-sensitivity GAP is $0.

Interest Rates Stable	Day 0	Day 90	Day 180	Day 270	Day 360
Assets (loans)		$\left(1 + \frac{9.645\%}{4}\right) \times (500\,mil)$			
Cash outflows	($500,000.00)	($512,056.84)	($524,404.42)	($537,049.75)	
Cash receipts (9.645% stated rate, adjusted quarterly)		512,056.84	524,404.42	537,049.75	$550,000.00
Interest revenues		$ 12,056.84	$ 12,347.58	$ 12,645.33	$ 12,950.25
Liabilities (CDs)					
Cash inflows	$500,000.00	$509,713.27	$519,615.24	$529,709.57	
Cash outflows (7.77% stated rate, adjusted quarterly)		(509,713.27)	(519,615.24)	(529,709.57)	(540,000.00)
Interest costs		$ 9,713.27	$ 9,901.97	$ 10,094.33	$ 10,290.43
Net interest (interest revenues − interest expense)		$ 2,343.57	$ 2,445.61	$ 2,551.00	$ 2,659.82
Present value of change in net worth: $\sum_{t=1}^{4} [C_t/(1 + 0.05)^t]$		C_4	C_3	C_2	C_1 $ 8,842.10

Effective Annual Yields Increase by 50 Basis Points	Day 0	Day 90	Day 180	Day 270	Day 360
Assets (loans)					
Cash outflows	($500,000.00)	($512,056.84)	($524,999.33)	($538,268.93)	
Cash receipts (9.645% stated rate, adjusted to 10.11% at day 90)		512,056.84	524,999.33	538,268.93	$551,873.94
Interest revenues		$ 12,056.84	$ 12,942.48	$ 13,269.61	$ 13,605.00
Liabilities (CDs)					
Cash inflows	$500,000.00	$509,713.27	$520,209.61	$530,928.22	
Cash outflows (7.77% stated rate, adjusted to 8.24% at day 90)		(509,713.27)	(520,209.61)	(530,928.22)	(541,867.67)
Interest costs		$ 9,713.27	$ 10,496.34	$ 10,718.60	$ 10,939.46
Net interest		$ 2,343.57	$ 2,446.14	$ 2,551.00	$ 2,665.55
Present value of change in net worth: $\frac{C_1}{1.05} + \sum_{t=2}^{4} \frac{C_t}{1.05125^t}$					$ 8,823.76

Note: Amounts are in thousands. Some do not add because of rounding.

ditions to net worth falls by more than $18,000. If that seems like a minor amount, consider the impact of such changes over long periods of time under interest rate conditions more volatile than those used in the example. Even in the simplified world of Table 19.1, the savings and loan association (S&L) has been protected from reinvestment risk, but it has not been protected from market value risk. Fortunately, however, the concept of duration is useful for managing this risk exposure.

DURATION AS AN ASSET/LIABILITY MANAGEMENT TOOL

Chapter 9 presented the concept and mathematics of duration, its potential as a measure of interest rate risk, and its use in several isolated situations. As defined in that chapter, the duration of an asset or liability is the weighted average time over which cash flows are expected, where the weights are the relative present values of the cash flows. Mathematically, the duration (DUR) of security j is defined as

$$[9.1]$$

$$DUR_j = \frac{\sum_{t=1}^{n} \frac{C_t(t)}{(1 + y^*)^t}}{\sum_{t=1}^{n} \frac{C_t}{(1 + y^*)^t}}$$

where

$$n = \text{maturity of security j}$$

$$C_t = \text{cash flow of security j in period t}$$

$$y^* = \text{current market yield}$$

$$\sum_{t=1}^{n} \frac{C_t}{(1 + y^*)^t} = \text{market value of the security.}$$

Recall also that an alternate formula for calculating duration may be used:

$$[9.2]$$

$$DUR = N - \left[\left(\frac{C}{P_0 \times y^*} \right) \times \left[N - (1 + y^*) \left(\frac{1 - \frac{1}{(1 + y^*)^n}}{y^*} \right) \right] \right]$$

where

P_0 is the market value of the security or financial instrument.

Duration can play a major role in an integrated asset/liability management strategy as an alternative measure of the time dimension of a financial asset or liability. Consequently, matching the durations of assets and liabilities, instead of matching time until repricing, is another way to approach GAP management. In fact, a growing number of experts argue that measuring and managing the duration GAP is a more effective way to protect the value of an institution from interest rate risk than traditional GAP management.[3]

In addition, as discussed in Chapter 17, federal regulators have identified duration as an important component of their measurement of a depository institution's interest rate risk. The merits of those arguments are examined after the mechanics of the duration GAP are illustrated.

THE DURATION GAP: DATA COLLECTION

Measuring the duration GAP is more complex than measuring the rate-sensitivity GAP because the dollar amounts and the timing of cash flows for both assets and liabilities must be identified. For fixed-rate assets and liabilities (FRAs and FRLs), this task is not too difficult, although prepayments on long-term loans must be estimated. For assets and liabilities with variable rates, interest to be received or paid over entire contractual maturities must be projected.[4] Forward rates on Treasury securities, illustrated in Chapter 7, can be used as forecasts of risk-free rates to which appropriate risk premiums can be added. Other data needed to calculate a duration GAP are current market yields on assets and liabilities.

ASSET MATURITIES AND RETURNS. Table 19.2 provides year-end balance sheet data adapted from the financial statements of one of the ten largest credit unions (CUs) in the United States, hypothetically named Heartland Credit Union (HCU). The data are used to illustrate the calculation of a duration GAP.

The first step is to estimate the maturities and yields for assets, shown in Table 19.3. Most consumer loans at CUs are 3- to 5-year personal or automobile installment loans to members, so it is reasonable to assume an average maturity of 3.5 years for HCU's consumer loans. The average rate of return is assumed to be 10 percent. Because most mortgages are prepaid, an *effective* average maturity of 10 years is estimated for the mortgage loan portfolio, even though the initial contractual maturity is 30 years. The mortgages have an estimated average rate of return of 9.6 percent.

---

[3] See, for example, Rosenblum 1981, Kaufman 1984, Toevs 1985, Haley 1982, Simonson and Bennett 1985, Rosenberg 1986, Shaffer 1991, and Houpt and Embersit 1991.

[4] Some argue that variable-rate instruments can be treated as zero-coupon instruments maturing at the time of repricing. In that case, their durations would always be equal to the length of time until repricing. See Rosenberg 1986. Others, such as Kaufman (1984) base duration on expected cash flows until contractual maturity.

TABLE 19.2	**Heartland Credit Union Balance Sheet**

These balance sheet data are used in the duration GAP example in this chapter.

Assets	Amount (Millions $)	%	Liabilities and Ownership	Amount (Millions $)	%
Cash and equivalents	$ 0.5	a	Regular shares	$108.3	39%
CDs owned	27.0	10%	Share drafts	15.8	6
Investments	30.0	11	Share certificates	132.8	47
Consumer loans	162.0	58	Notes payable	9.9	3
Mortgage loans	51.0	18	Other liabilities	2.6	1
Land and buildings	5.8	2	Reserves and undivided earnings	10.4	4
Other assets	3.5	1			
Total assets	$279.8	100%	Total liabilities and members' ownership	$279.8	100%

Lia 96%

ªLess than 1%.

TABLE 19.3	**HCU Assets and Liabilities: Estimated Maturities and Yields/Costs**

These data on asset and liability maturities, yields, and costs are also used in the duration GAP example.

Category	Estimated Average Maturity (Months)	Average Annual Yield/Cost (%)	Current Market Yield/Cost (%)
Cash	0 months	0.00%	0.00%
CDs owned	3	15.75	17.20
Investments	3	13.25	14.80
Consumer loans	42ª (3.5 yrs)	10.00	18.00
Mortgage loans	120ᵇ	9.60	13.50
Land and buildings	—	0.00	0.00
Other assets	—	0.00	0.00
Regular shares	3	6.50	6.50
Share drafts	0.5	6.50	6.50
Share certificates	3	10.05	15.30
Notes payable	6	17.50	17.50
Other liabilities	0	0.00	0.00

ªThe assumption of a 3½-year (42-month) maturity for consumer installment loans and an annual rate of 10 percent (0.833 percent per month) results in estimated monthly cash flow to the CU of $4.587 million, based on amortization of the $162 million in consumer loans outstanding at the end of the year.
ᵇThe assumption of an existing annual mortgage rate of 9.6 percent (0.80 percent per month) results in estimated total monthly mortgage payments to HCU of $433,000 when payments on the $51 million of mortgages outstanding are amortized over a 30-year contractual maturity. Under the assumption that mortgages will be prepaid at the end of the tenth year, a single cash flow of $46.1 million would be received at that time.

The CDs and investments, primarily Treasury securities, owned by the CU are almost entirely short term. The example assumes an average maturity of 3 months for these assets. Because these data were collected when market rates were quite high, the average rate of return was around 15.75 percent for 3-month CDs and 13.25 percent for Treasury securities.

LIABILITY MATURITIES AND COSTS. The maturities of HCU's shares and share drafts are subject to depos-itor wishes and are difficult to determine. Estimating the maturity and/or duration of these accounts is a sub-ject of some debate. Should they be considered to have an instantaneous maturity because they can be with-drawn at will? Depositors certainly can reclaim their funds, but their loyalty, as well as their cash-flow needs, make it highly unlikely that the shortest-case scenario will actually occur. In fact, many institutions count on a core volume of transactions or pass-book deposits that remain relatively stable. Thus, a depository must examine the behavior of its deposits under various interest rate conditions and use that information to estimate deposit maturity.[5] Because share drafts are transactions accounts, their average maturity is estimated to be a relatively short 2 weeks and the average maturity of regular shares to be 3 months. The average interest cost for both those accounts is assumed to be approximately 6.5 percent.

Most share certificates have an original maturity of 6 months. If they mature at an even pace, the average maturity of the total volume of CDs is 3 months, and their average cost is about 10.05 percent. Notes payable are short-term floating-rate loans secured by property and costing 17.5 percent on average. The other liabilities are accruals, which bear no interest cost. The CU follows a policy of adding to reserves and undivided earnings each year at a target rate of 20 percent. At a minimum, management desires to maintain these accounts at their current levels—in other words, avoiding erosion in net worth is a major objective.

MARKET DATA. Additional data needed to calculate the duration GAP for HCU are estimates of current market yields for the different categories of assets and liabilities. It is assumed that market conditions have changed since many of the CU's assets were acquired; the yield to CUs on new consumer loans is now about 18 percent.[6] Conventional mortgages with a 10-year effective maturity are yielding 13.50 percent, and the average yield on new 3-month Treasury securities is about 14.80 percent. The estimated average cost of new short-term CDs tied to Treasury securities is 0.5 percent higher, or 15.30 percent. The cost of shares and share drafts is unchanged from previous levels. These assumptions are summarized in Table 19.3.

---

[5] George Kaufman (1984) concluded that the correct duration for transactions deposits "awaits additional research" and that the price behavior of an individual institution's deposits must guide the duration estimate.

[6] The difference between the relatively low yields to maturity on HCU's existing assets and assumed current market rates may seem large, but it was realistic at some points in the last decade. After interest rates fell, existing asset yields were often higher than prevailing market rates. Unless interest rates remain stable for an extended period, differences of varying magnitudes and directions will occur.

THE DURATION GAP: CALCULATING DURATIONS

Once data are collected, weighted average durations of assets and liabilities are estimated and the duration GAP calculated.

ASSETS AND LIABILITIES. Determining the duration of HCU's assets and liabilities is easier than it may seem in view of the data that must be estimated. A careful examination of the CU's assets and liabilities shows that many are very similar to zero-coupon instruments, for which duration is equal to maturity. Short-term CDs on both sides of the balance sheet, Treasury bills (T-bills), regular shares, and share drafts fall into this group because they do not involve interim cash flows. Although shares and share drafts are interest-bearing, the interest earned during their assumed short maturity would not have a large impact on a duration calculation; in any case, it does not resemble coupon payments. These facts make it possible to estimate the durations of many instruments by using their maturities.

The two largest categories of assets, however, are not similar to zero-coupon securities, and their durations must be calculated using Equation 9.1 or Equation 9.2.

For HCU's 3.5-year (or 42-month) installment loans, using Equation 9.1, duration is:

$$DUR_j = \frac{\displaystyle\sum_{t=1}^{42} \frac{C_t(t)}{(1 + 0.015)^t}}{\displaystyle\sum_{t=1}^{42} \frac{C_t}{(1 + 0.015)^t}}$$

For these loans, each monthly cash flow (C_1 through C_{42}) is equal to $4.587 million. The relevant monthly market rate with which these cash flows are discounted is $18\% \div 12 = 1.5\%$, and the total present value is $142.17 million. This figure is also the estimated current market value of the loans; it is below book value because market rates increased after most of the loans were made. The numerator of Equation 9.1, in which each cash flow is weighted by the time period in which it is to be received, is $2,747.68 million ($2.748 billion). The estimated duration of HCU's installment loans is $2,747.68 \div 142.17 = 19.3$

months, or 1.61 years, lower than their maturity of 42 months.

Alternatively, using Equation 9.2, the duration of these installment loans can be calculated as:

$$DUR = 42 - \left[\left(\frac{\$4.587}{(\$142.17)(0.015)} \right) \times \right.$$

$$\left. \left[42 - (1.015) \left(\frac{1 - \frac{1}{(1.015)^{42}}}{0.015} \right) \right] \right]$$

$$= 42 - \left[(2.152) \times \right.$$

$$\left. \left[42 - (1.015)(30.9941) \right] \right]$$

$$= 42 - 22.674 = 19.3 \text{ months}$$

For mortgage loans, each monthly cash flow (C_1 through C_{119}) is $433,000 ($0.433 million), with a final cash flow (C_{120}) of $46.1 million. Using Equation 9.1 the duration is $2,781.1 ÷ $40.3 = 68.9 months, or 5.74 years, almost half the estimated effective maturity, and less than one-fourth of their contractual maturity of 30 years.

DURATION GAP. The last step is to estimate the weighted average duration of the CU assets and liabilities. This calculation is shown in Table 19.4. Each asset and liability is expressed as a percentage of total assets or liabilities, the duration of each account is weighted by its percentage, and weighted durations are summed to obtain the weighted average asset and liability durations. For HCU, the weighted average asset duration is 24.23 months, or 2.02 years; the weighted average liability duration is 2.94 months, or 0.25 years. Managers must remember that when assets or liabilities have different market yields, these weighted average durations are only approximations. Nonetheless such models, although imperfect, are often used in practice.

The duration GAP can be calculated after the weighted average liability duration is adjusted to reflect the percentage of liabilities to total assets on the balance sheet. Reserves and undivided earnings are 4 percent of the CU's sources of funds, so liabilities are 96 percent. The duration GAP is

$$DUR_{GAP} = DUR_A - w_L DUR_L \quad [19.1]$$

where w_L is the percentage of assets financed by liabilities.

For HCU,

$$DUR_{GAP} = 2.02 - (0.96)(0.25) = 1.78 \text{ years.}$$

Because duration is a measure of time, the duration GAP has a time dimension and is not a dollar figure like the rate-sensitivity GAP.

INTERPRETING THE DURATION GAP

In view of the extensive calculations necessary to measure a duration GAP, why would depository institutions and federal regulators wish to do so? The answer lies in the property of duration introduced in Chapter 9. The duration of an asset or liability is directly related to the change in its market value as interest rates change. Recall that Δy^* in Equation 9.5 is the change expressed in basis points and divided by 100:

$$\%\Delta P_0 = \frac{\Delta P_0}{P_0} = -DUR \frac{\Delta y^*}{1 + y^*} \quad [9.5]$$

Suppose there is an immediate 50-basis-point increase in market interest rates. What would be the expected percentage change in the market value of HCU's mortgage loans, currently at $40.3 million? Using Equation 9.5,

$$\%\Delta P_0 = -5.74 \frac{0.50}{1 + 0.135} = -2.53\%$$

The new market value of the mortgages is estimated to be $40.3 - (0.0253 × $40.3) = $39.2 million after the increase in interest rates. For consumer loans, the estimated percentage change in value is $-1.61 × (0.50/1.18) = -0.68\%$. Their market value, previously $140 million, would decline to $139.05 million.

Duration directly measures the potential variation in the value of assets because of interest rate changes. If interest rates rise substantially, asset values could decline enough to threaten capital adequacy or

| TABLE 19.4 | Heartland Credit Union: Duration and Weighted Average Duration of Assets and Liabilities |

An institution's weighted average asset duration is the sum of each asset category's duration times that asset category's proportion of total assets. Weighted average liability duration is the sum of each liability category's duration times the category's proportion of total liabilities.

Assets	Duration (Months)	%	Weighted Duration (Months)
Cash	0 months	a	a
CDs owned	3	10%[b]	0.30 months
Investments	3	11	0.33
Consumer loans	19.3	58	11.19
Mortgage loans	68.9	18	12.41
Land and buildings	NA[c]	2	—
Other assets	NA[c]	1	—
		Weighted average duration[d]:	24.23 months (2.02 years)

Total value of assets = $279.8 million

Liabilities and Ownership	Duration (Months)	% of Total Liabilities	Weighted Duration (Months)
Regular shares	3 months	40%	1.20 months
Share drafts	0.5	6	0.03
Share certificates	3	49	1.47
Notes payable	6	4	0.24
Other liabilities	0	1	0.00
Reserves and undivided earnings	NA[c]	NA[c]	—
		Weighted average duration[d]:	2.94 months (0.25 years)

Total value of liabilities = $269.4 million
Total value of liabilities and members' ownership = $279.8 million

[a] Less than 1 percent.
[b] Technically, the weights applied to individual durations to determine the weighted average duration of assets should be market value weights. In this case, however, the difference between book-value and market value weights would be quite small, so the recalculation is ignored.
[c] Not applicable.
[d] The weighted average duration is calculated by summing the weighted durations of the assets or liabilities.

even endanger solvency. Financial institution managers aware of this risk exposure could try to reduce it before interest rates change. The new Financial Accounting Standards Board (FASB) market value reporting requirements add to the importance of monitoring the potential fluctuations in value arising from interest rate changes.

DURATION GAP AND CHANGES IN THE MARKET VALUE OF NET WORTH. The duration GAP directly indicates the exposure of the market value of the institution's net worth to a change in interest rates. As noted, the management of Heartland Credit Union, like managers of most depositories, desires at a minimum to protect reserves and undivided earnings at their current levels. By modifying Equation 9.5 to include the ratio of total assets to net worth, the duration GAP can be used to estimate the percentage change in the institution's net worth that would occur if interest rates change and assets and liabilities are restated at

| FIGURE 19.1 | **Trends in Thrift Institutions' Duration GAPs** |

In the late 1980s, the duration GAP for thrifts narrowed significantly following regulators' emphasis on controlling interest rate risk.

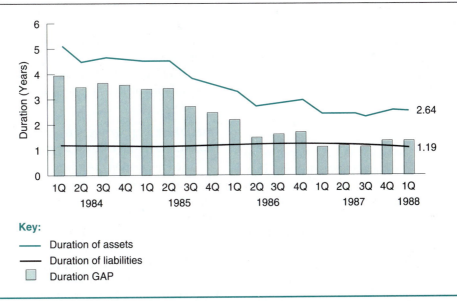

Key:

─── Duration of assets

─── Duration of liabilities

▦ Duration GAP

Source: Maria Kulczycky, "Gap Management Eases Interest Rate Swings," *Savings Institutions* 109 (November 1988): 49.

their new market values. Again, suppose that yields increase by 0.5 percent[7]:

$$\frac{\Delta NW_j}{NW_j} = -DUR_{GAP}\left(\frac{\Delta y^*}{1 + y^*}\right)\left(\frac{TA}{NW}\right) \quad [19.2]$$

$$\frac{\Delta NW_j}{NW_j} = -1.78 \times \frac{0.5}{1 + 0.20} \times \frac{\$279.8}{\$10.4}$$

$$= -19.95\%$$

This calculation uses book values of total assets and net worth; ideally, market values would be used. Even so, the projected increase in interest rates, al-though seemingly small, would result in a little less than a 20 percent decline in the value of capital. The greater the increase in interest rates, the larger the decline in the value of reserves and undivided earnings. In addition, the larger the duration GAP and the higher the ratio of total assets to net worth, the greater the potential erosion of net worth, given an increase in interest rates.

But if an institution's managers know the duration GAP, they can take steps to manage it actively. For HCU, managing the duration GAP would involve lengthening liability durations, shortening asset durations, or both—strategies similar to those undertaken in managing the rate-sensitivity GAP. Characteristics of securities that would reduce the duration GAP, however, are not necessarily the same as those that would reduce maturity GAP, because durations are affected not only by maturity but also by an asset or liability's interest rate characteristics (such as coupon-bearing versus discount) and by the existing level of market rates.

---

[7] This equation shows the impact of the duration GAP assuming that management's goal is to preserve the level of net worth. If the focus is the capital/assets ratio, the duration GAP is measured as $DUR_A - DUR_L$. Toevs also presents a use of duration GAP to protect net income. These alternatives are discussed in Kaufman 1984; Toevs 1983; and Brewer 1985.

Active duration GAP management might result in the development of a different mix of products than under active maturity GAP management, and these products might be more appealing to customers than those involving maturity adjustments alone. Still, active duration GAP management as a strategy for integrated asset/liability management is likely to encounter some of the same hurdles that active rate-sensitivity GAP management encounters. However, duration more accurately estimates the effect of rate changes on the institution.[8]

Depository institution managers, with the encouragement of regulators, have increased their emphasis on monitoring the duration GAP as part of an integrated asset/liability management strategy. Data collected by the Federal Home Loan Bank of San Francisco suggest that regulatory pronouncements are having an important effect. Trends in the duration GAP for thrifts in that Federal Home Loan Bank (FHLB) district are shown in Figure 19.1. The duration of liabilities has been relatively stable, but asset duration dropped from 5 years in early 1984 to 2.64 years in early 1988. The duration GAP, consequently, declined from about 4 years to about 1.5 years during the period.

Although the data reflect a marked decline in interest rate risk, the average duration GAP of almost 1.5 years in 1988 still constituted significant exposure to the effects of changes in interest rates. By the early 1990s, thrift regulators were requiring savings institutions to report sufficient data so that it was possible to monitor market value net worth exposure to interest rate changes. Regulators estimated in late 1991 that approximately 73 percent of thrifts were exposed to rising interest rates; that means the value of their assets would decline more rapidly than the value of liabilities when interest rates rose. In other words, these institu-

tions had positive duration GAPs, just as did HCU, and faced the risk of a substantial reduction in net worth. This exposure is presented graphically in Panel A of Figure 19.2. (Note that the difference between the value of assets and the value of liabilities is the thrifts' net worth.) At the same time (late 1991), about 22 percent of thrifts faced danger from *falling* interest rates, and the potential effect on their net worth is shown in Panel B of Figure 19.2.[9] Data were not available to allow a similar analysis for the banking industry.

IMMUNIZATION: A PARTIAL DURATION GAP STRATEGY

Active duration GAP management presents another complication: The duration GAP is subject to frequent changes, because durations change with each interest rate change. For this reason, and to avoid the marketing problems introduced by active GAP management, some institutions choose to use a limited duration-based management strategy. Matching the duration of designated deposits and assets causes the duration GAP on a portion of the balance sheet to be zero. That part of the balance sheet is then immunized against unexpected changes in interest rates. Immunization was introduced in Chapter 9 to illustrate how an investor could select a security of a specified duration to lock in a current market yield during a predetermined holding period. A depository can use the same strategy to lock in a specific asset/liability spread. Enhancing the potential use of this strategy is the removal of most restrictions on the types of accounts that institutions can offer.

Suppose that because of the current interest rate environment, managers of an S&L believe it is desirable to offer fixed-rate mortgages with a contractual maturity of 15 years and a duration of 4 years. A partial duration GAP strategy would fund those mortgages only with deposits of equal duration, possibly 4-year CDs sold at a discount with no intervening interest payments. No mortgages with a 4-year duration would be issued unless matched deposits were available to fund them. This is a very different strategy from matching maturities, and a 4-year deposit is

---

[8] Despite the difficulties of active duration GAP management, there is strong support for its use. Haley concludes, for example, that "value immunization is sufficient to protect financial intermediaries from failure." See Haley 1982, 317.

As noted in footnote 5 of Chapter 9, some experts have argued recently that the actual sensitivity of net worth to interest rate changes is considerably lower than traditional duration models suggest. The implication is that Equation 19.2 may overstate the degree to which net worth will change as interest rates change. See Leibowitz 1986 and Leibowitz et al. 1989.

---

[9] See Kulczycky 1988 and Mays 1992.

| FIGURE 19.2 | **Effect of Changing Interest Rates on the Net Worth of Thrifts, 1991** |

In late 1991, Panel A shows that almost 75 percent of thrift institutions had positive duration GAPs, exposing their net worth position to serious declines should interest rates rise. Other institutions faced negative effects from falling rates as shown in Panel B.

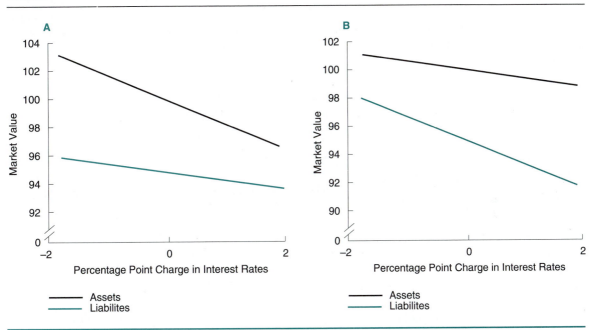

Source: Elizabeth Mays, "Assessing Rate Risks Eases Exposure Shock," *Savings Institutions* 113 (February 1992): 25.

likely to be much more palatable to depositors than a 15-year CD. Although the duration of the liabilities cannot be guaranteed, because customers are free to withdraw before maturity, the institution can reduce that likelihood by imposing withdrawal penalties. Thus, a particular part of the balance sheet would be immunized against interest rate changes, and the interest rate risk to which the institution is exposed would be limited to that of the remaining asset/liability mix.

This strategy has one further advantage. If the institution is uncomfortable with making interest rate forecasts on which its entire profitability depends, immunization provides relief from that problem. Once the spread between particular assets and liabilities has been immunized, it is essentially fixed, regardless of the next rate change. Although the chance to profit unexpectedly is minimized, so is the chance for unanticipated losses. All or parts of the remaining asset/liability mix can then be managed using techniques requiring active rate forecasting. Nevertheless, man-

agers using immunization must remember the assumptions on which the technique is based, discussed in Chapter 9.

VIEWS OF FEDERAL REGULATORS

The importance of protecting the value of an institution's net worth from interest rate risk has been emphasized by federal regulators since 1989. The Office of the Comptroller of the Currency issued new examination guidelines focusing on the duration of a bank's assets and liabilities and on the exposure of a bank's equity to changes in interest rates.

Federal thrift regulators issued Thrift Bulletin 13 (known in the industry as TB-13), "Responsibilities of the Board of Directors and Management with Regard to Interest Rate Risk." In TB-13, insured thrifts were required to develop formal interest rate risk management policies specifically designed to monitor and protect against potential changes in the present value of assets, liabilities, and off–balance sheet instruments. (TB-13, in effect, addresses the value of net worth—the difference between the present value of assets and the present value of liabilities.) Interest rate risk management policies of individual thrifts must establish the maximum percentage change in net interest income and value that an institution's directors are willing to accept. Thrift regulators indicated that they expect directors to take corrective action if unacceptably high interest rate risk exposure is present.

Most recently, as noted earlier, Congress in the Federal Deposit Insurance Corporation Improvement Act (FDICIA) mandated that federal banking regulators develop a measure of interest rate risk that could be incorporated in the evaluation of capital adequacy and assessment of minimum capital requirements. The interest rate risk measures were to become a part of the risk-based capital standards in 1993. The approach proposed by regulators focuses on the value of net worth. At the time of this writing, interest rate risk was to be measured as the potential change in value of net worth resulting from a 100-basis-point change in interest rates, although some depositories were arguing to have their risk exposure calculated using a 200-basis-point or greater potential swing in interest rates. Regulators had even decided to allow large banks to use their own formulas for measuring interest rate risk, as long as they are approved by regulators and results are reported on schedule. Institutions with excessive interest rate risk will be required to hold more capital to offset the higher level of risk.[10]

OPTION-ADJUSTED SPREAD MODELS

Given the importance regulators place on managing interest rate risk in depositories, it is not surprising that managers pay continuing attention to improving the reliability of measuring potential fluctuations in value caused by interest rate changes. One of the newest approaches, usually **called option-adjusted spread (OAS) modeling**, estimates potential changes in asset and liability values using **option-adjusted spreads**.

The OAS approach differs in several important ways from the rate-sensitivity and duration methodologies discussed in this and earlier chapters. Perhaps the most substantive difference is the emphasis on the effect of interest rate changes on customers' tendency to exercise the options embedded in the assets and liabilities of depository institutions. For example, fixed-rate mortgages allow borrowers to prepay the outstanding principal balance, and they are more likely to do so if interest rates on new mortgages fall below their existing fixed rate. Customers also have the right to withdraw their deposits if interest rates on other investment alternatives are more attractive. Also, most adjustable-rate mortgages (ARMs) have options that are automatically exercised—for example, the rate caps limiting the amount by which interest rates can be changed in a given period or over the life of the mortgage. Even duration analysis, with all its complexity, relies on cash flow estimates that do not incorporate the probability that any of these options will be exercised. Consequently, proponents of OAS modeling argue that standard duration analysis cannot provide a true measure of value.

OAS models rely on extensive simulations to measure the fair value of assets and liabilities. They begin with estimation of thousands of future interest rate scenarios; these scenarios are based on the slope of the yield curve and implied forward rates, as discussed in Chapter 7. Next is added the behavioral component—models of the probable reactions of borrowers and depositors to various interest rate scenarios, resulting in thousands of estimates of cash flows over the life of an asset or liability. A simplified diagram of the OAS modeling process is shown in Figure 19.3.

As indicated in the figure, the end results are OAS values and option adjusted spreads. OAS *values* (expressed in dollars) reflect the average of the discounted values of all these simulated cash flows. The result is quite different from the duration approach presented earlier, which calculates a change in the value of net worth resulting from a single estimated interest rate change.

The total return on an asset can be projected by comparing the future cash flows estimated through a simulation to its current market price. The option ad-

---

[10] For more information on regulatory developments see James Brewer, "Regulatory Redirection," *ABA Banking Journal* 82 (February 1990): 82, 86; Office of Regulatory Activities, Federal Home Loan Bank System, "Responsibilities of the Board of Directors and Management with Regard to Interest Rate Risk," Section 420, TB-13, January 26, 1989; Parliment 1989; Ernst and Young, *Current Issues in the Financial Services Industries,* 1989; Lam 1989; and Neuberger 1992.

FIGURE 19.3   **Option Adjusted Spread Models**

OAS models use simulations to evaluate the effect of embedded options and potential interest rate changes on the value of a depository's assets and liabilities.

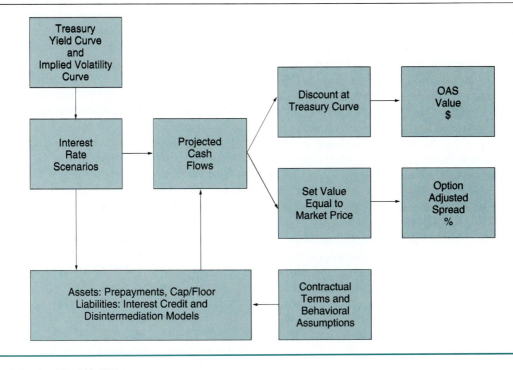

Source: Fabozzi and Konishi, 1991.

justed *spread* (expressed as a percentage) is the average difference between the total return on a particular asset or liability and the return on T-bills resulting over all simulations. Another way of interpreting the OAS is that it measures the average spread over Treasury yields needed to compensate the holder for the risk of the embedded options. Consequently, depositories would want to hold assets with a positive OAS and, if possible, to hold liabilities with a negative OAS.[11]

Besides calculating the OAS value and the option adjusted spread, the simulation results can be used to estimate an "effective" duration based on option-adjusted cash flows. The effective durations of assets and liabilities would yield a more reliable measure of

the duration GAP. Beyond being used to estimated effective durations, the simulated cash flows are dynamic estimates of value that are superior to other, static measures, and can be used in conjunction with futures, swaps, and other hedging techniques.

FINANCIAL FUTURES AS AN ASSET/LIABILITY TOOL

It is clearly impossible to achieve a desired level of exposure to interest rate risk as measured by either the rate-sensitivity or duration GAP. Something other than balance sheet restructuring is needed. One effective and popular supplement to GAP management is futures hedging. As the discussion in Chapter 10 emphasizes, futures provide a powerful method for managing exposure to interest rate risk. Managing a futures position is a challenging task, however.

---

[11] For further discussion and applications, see Fabozzi and Konishi 1991 and Smith 1991.

FUTURES INCREASE FLEXIBILITY

One benefit of the futures hedge as an asset/liability management tool is that it allows a depository institution to offer a wide range of financial products and services to attract as broad a customer base as its objectives dictate. The potential costs of an interest rate sensitivity mismatch are avoided by taking the appropriate position in the futures market rather than by forcing customers to choose deposit accounts or loans that may displease them or even cause them to patronize a competitor.

Perhaps a more important advantage of the futures markets is that they allow management to "unbundle" asset and liability decision making. A bank or thrift can pursue investment choices that management hopes will provide the highest rates of return in a particular interest rate environment. At the same time, it can pursue sources of funds that carry the lowest costs, even if the asset/liability mix produces a rate-sensitivity mismatch. Hedging in the futures market offers managers enough flexibility to fulfill one of the intermediation functions—offering loans and deposits tailored to individual maturity preferences—without exposing their institutions to excessive interest rate risk.[12]

FUTURES AS A SUPPLEMENT TO GAP MANAGEMENT

An example will clarify the benefits contributed by futures instruments. The top panel of Table 19.5 presents a rate-sensitivity and duration analysis for a hypothetical bank. The bank has a rate-sensitivity GAP ratio of 1.06 and a duration GAP of 0.95 years. The target return on net worth is 11.5 percent. The profitability analysis at the bottom of the table indicates expected profits of $4.87 million and an expected return on net worth of more than 12 percent, in excess of the target.

ACTIVE GAP MANAGEMENT. If the bank's managers expect a 75-basis-point increase in interest rates, they may want to maintain or even increase the positive rate-sensitivity GAP before rates rise. In managing the

GAP, the emphasis would be on increasing rate-sensitive assets (RSAs) whose returns will rise with market rates as the cost of fixed-rate funding sources remains unchanged. Table 19.6 analyzes the results of bank management's efforts. The GAP ratio has been increased to 1.1, and the duration GAP is shortened to 0.80 years. Earnings are down slightly, although results are still above the target RONW.

Potential damage remains, however, from the bank's positive duration GAP. Despite the balance sheet restructuring, which reduced the weighted average duration of assets, the DUR_{GAP} is still a positive 0.80 years. If interest rates increase, the present value of the bank's assets will fall more than the value of its liabilities, eroding the present value of net worth. A 75-basis-point increase will reduce the value of the bank's net worth by more than 7 percent, from $40 million to $37.07 million:

$$\frac{\Delta NW_j}{NW_j} = -0.80 \times \frac{0.75}{1 + 0.115}$$
$$\times \frac{\$545}{\$40} = -7.33\%$$

USING FUTURES TO OFFSET THE GAP. To overcome some of the difficulties in bringing the duration GAP to its optimal level, the bank's managers could use futures to protect the value of the firm. For this bank, the need to increase the variable-rate portion of the loan portfolio would be reduced if GAP strategies were augmented by futures trading. In this case, the bank managers should sell futures contracts (assume a short position). The institution does not receive cash initially, but each day cash will be deposited to or deducted from the institution's margin account, consistent with the daily settlement practices of futures trading.

If interest rates increase, the value of the contracts sold will decline and the value of the margin account will increase. If the proper number of contracts is sold, the increase in cash will offset the decline in the value of other assets when the short position is closed out. Ideally, the net change in asset value will equal the change in the value of liabilities, and net worth value will remain stable.

This situation is illustrated in Table 19.7. Suppose that the bank's managers decide to hedge against

[12]This point is made in Jaffee 1981. Other support is offered in Nagle 1981 and Shaffer 1991.

TABLE 19.5   **Rate Sensitivity, Duration, and GAP Analysis (Millions of $)**

Hypothetical institution's rate-sensitivity and duration GAPs before active management under expectations of rising interest rates.

Rate-sensitive assets (RSAs)	$275	Rate-sensitive liabilities (RSLs)	$260
Fixed-rate earning assets (FRAs)	205	Fixed-rate liabilities (FRLs)	245
Nonearning assets	65	Net worth	40
Weighted average duration of assets	1.56 years	Weighted average duration of liabilities	0.66 years
Interest-sensitivity (maturity) GAP			
($275 − $260)	$15		
GAP ratio ($275/$260)	1.06		
Duration GAP [1.56 − (0.927)(0.66)]	0.95 years		

(handwritten margin notes: 545; 505) 505) 545; =0.927)

Profitability Analysis
(Maturity GAP)

Sensitivity Category	Amount (Millions $)	Rate Differential (%)	Expected Annual Profit (Millions $)
FRAs funded by FRLs	$205.00	2.05%	$4.20
RSAs funded by RSLs	260.00	0.95	2.47
Nonearning assets funded by FRLs	25.00	−8.00	(2.00)
GAP	15.00	1.30	0.19
			Total $4.87
Expected RONW ($4.87/$40.00)	12.17%		
Target RONW	11.50%		

TABLE 19.6   **Rate Sensitivity, Duration, and GAP Analysis: Revised (Millions)**

Following balance sheet restructuring, the duration GAP is reduced, but the rate-sensitivity GAP increases. In general, it is impossible to hedge both GAPs with the same management action.

Rate-sensitive assets (RSAs)	$285	Rate-sensitive liabilities (RSLs)	$260
Fixed-rate earning assets (FRAs)	195	Fixed-rate liabilities (FRLs)	245
Nonearning assets	65	Net worth	40
Weighted average duration of assets	1.41 years	Weighted average duration of liabilities	0.66 years
Interest-sensitivity (maturity) GAP			
($285 − $260)	$25		
GAP ratio ($285/$260)	1.10		
Duration GAP [1.41 − (0.927)(0.66)]	0.80 years		

(handwritten margin note: 545)

Profitability Analysis
(Maturity GAP)

Sensitivity Category	Amount (Millions $)	Rate Differential (%)	Expected Annual Profit (Millions $)
FRAs funded by FRLs	$195.00	2.05%	$4.00
RSAs funded by RSLs	260.00	0.91	2.37
Nonearning assets funded by FRLs	25.00	−8.00	(2.00)
GAP	25.00	1.45	0.36
			Total $4.73
Expected RONW ($4.73/$40.00)	11.82%		

TABLE 19.7	Hedging the Duration GAP

With the proper number of contracts and a correct forecast for interest rate increases, managers can use gains on a short futures position to offset the potential decline in net worth resulting from a positive duration GAP.

Initial Position	
Sell 1,600 Eurodollar futures contracts	
Yield: 8.55%	
Price: 91.45 × 100 × $25 × 1,600 =	$365,800,000
$(100 - 8.55)$	
Two Months Later	
Buy 1,600 Eurodollar futures contracts	
Yield: 9.30%	
Cost: 90.70 × 100 × $25 × 1,600 =	362,800,000
$(100 - 9.30)$	
Gain on hedge	$ 3,000,000

the feared $3 million potential decline in net worth by selling Eurodollar futures contracts. The London Interbank Offered Rate (LIBOR) rate, against which Eurodollar futures are priced, is now at 8.25 percent but is expected to increase by 75 basis points, to 9 percent, within the next 2 months; the yield on 3-month Eurodollar futures is now 8.55 percent and is expected to be 9.30 percent in 2 months.

To understand the results of the hedge shown in the table, it is necessary to know how Eurodollar futures contracts are priced. Each contract is quoted at a price of 100 minus the yield, or $(100 - 8.55) = 91.45$ when the hedge is initiated. Because there is no underlying instrument for Eurodollar futures (that is, because they are settled in cash, similar to stock index futures), the 91.45 price is first converted to basis points, then converted to a dollar figure by multiplying by $25, the dollar multiplier for the contract:

$$91.45 \times 100 \times \$25 = \$228,625$$

If interest rates increase by the 75-basis-point forecast, the price of a single Eurodollar futures contract will be $(100 - 9.30) = 90.70$ in 2 months, for a dollar value of

$$90.70 \times 100 \times \$25 = \$226,750$$

In other words, managers forecast a gain of $(\$228,625 - \$226,750) = \$1,875$ on each contract sold today. To hedge against the entire $3 million potential decline in

net worth as a result of the existing duration GAP, $\$3,000,000/\$1,875 = 1,600$ contracts must be sold. If the interest rate forecast is correct, the gain on such a hedge should provide substantial protection against the projected loss of value on the rest of the bank's assets, preserving the value of net worth.[13]

It is important to recognize that the bank managers in this example were faced with a choice between managing the rate-sensitivity GAP and managing the duration GAP. By assuming a short position, the positive duration GAP was reduced. Yet, by selling futures, management has added to the bank's RSAs (through the margin account) and thus has actually enlarged the rate-sensitivity GAP. The potential earnings variability resulting from changes in interest rates has been increased through a strategy designed to minimize a potential decline in the value of net worth.

MACRO HEDGES VERSUS MICRO HEDGES

The hedging strategy just described is a **macro hedge** because it is designed to hedge the bank's *net* duration position to bring the entire asset/liability portfolio into balance so that the interest-rate sensitivity of assets and liabilities is matched. The macro hedge requires detailed knowledge of the bank's total exposure to interest rate risk. It requires a relatively large transaction in the futures market because it is designed to protect the value of or the earnings generated by the

---

[13] A model for estimating the number of futures contracts necessary to offset a forecast decline in existing asset values involves solving for N_f in the following equation:

$$[19.3]$$

$$DUR_p = DUR_a + DUR_f \frac{N_f \times FP_f}{P_a}$$

where
DUR_p = the desired duration of a combined asset/futures portfolio
DUR_a = the duration of existing assets
DUR_f = the duration of the security underlying the futures contract
FP_f = the price agreed on in the futures contract
N_f = the number of futures contracts to be bought or sold
P_a = the market value of existing assets.

If N_f is negative, contracts should be sold; if it is positive, a long futures position is indicated. See Toevs 1983, 28; and Brewer 1985, 19.

entire asset portfolio. The institution makes a significant commitment to its interest rate forecast.

In contrast, a **micro hedge** ties the futures position to a specific category of assets or liabilities rather than to the institution's net interest rate exposure. Although macro hedges are theoretically more effective, micro hedges are a more realistic alternative for several reasons.[14]

INFORMATION REQUIREMENTS. First, the amount of information required to monitor the depository institution's total GAP position continuously may be prohibitive. Managers often find it more feasible to select a group of assets or liabilities, such as fixed-rate loans or CDs of a given dollar volume and average maturity, that will be adversely affected by changes in interest rates. A futures trade is then chosen to hedge that specific category of accounts. Under both micro and macro strategies, the futures position must be closely monitored and adjusted as interest rate expectations change.

ACCOUNTING STANDARDS. The FASB recommends more favorable accounting methods for futures hedges linked to an identifiable cash market instrument (micro hedges) than for more general hedges (macro hedges). In other words, hedging a portfolio of 6-month ARMs with T-bill futures contracts (a micro hedge) qualifies for more favorable reporting than a macro hedge that lowers the rate-sensitivity GAP but cannot be linked to a specific asset category.

Unless an institution can identify a specific asset or liability for which a hedge has been selected, accounting rules require the results of the hedge to be reported as gains or losses on the income statement *before* the final futures position is closed out. Because changes in interest rates during the course of a hedge may produce temporary losses that are ultimately recovered, reporting hedging results before the position is closed can increase variability in reported earnings. The results of micro hedges, in contrast, must be reported only when closed out, and they can be amortized over the remaining life of a hedged asset or lia-

bility. Not surprisingly, then, managers often favor micro hedges for accounting reasons alone.[15]

MANAGERIAL FLEXIBILITY. The micro hedge is also espoused by some managers who think that it gives them flexibility to structure bank or thrift services to meet the needs of particularly desirable customers. For example, a bank may have a large commercial borrower who expects to borrow at fixed rates and whose business the bank wants to keep. The lender can accommodate the wishes of the borrower and at the same time limit its own exposure to interest rate risk by structuring a futures position properly. Because the lender's profits will be hurt if rates rise, a short position in the futures market can be used to hedge against this possibility.[16]

Some institutions have devised a twist on this strategy, offering customers variable-rate loans indexed to an instrument on which futures contracts are traded. They then assist the borrower in structuring a futures position that hedges against changes in the loan rate. As first discussed in Chapter 14, such an arrangement is called a synthetic fixed-rate loan. It gives both the borrower and lender the advantages of reduced risk exposure while avoiding potentially undesirable futures accounting treatment for the depository.[17]

LIMITATIONS OF FUTURES IN ASSET/LIABILITY MANAGEMENT

As discussed in Chapter 10, setting the appropriate hedge ratio and selecting the most effective futures instrument are difficult problems for any type of hedge. For many assets held by depositories, no futures contracts exist, forcing institutions to cross hedge and increasing basis risk. These decisions are less complex for a micro hedge, however, because only one instrument and one maturity are involved. Monitoring

---

[14] More detailed analysis of the choice between macro and micro hedging strategies is provided in Kolb, Timme, and Gay 1984; McCabe and McLeod 1983; and Chance 1992, Chapter 10.

[15] A good explanation of the effect of accounting standards on the macro and micro strategies is provided in Brewer 1985, 21; further discussion is contained in Koppenhaver 1984.

[16] Several articles advocate hedging to allow more flexibility in lending terms to meet the needs of individual customers. See, for example, Laudeman 1983; Walters 1985; Jacobs 1983; and Gau and Goldberg 1983.

[17] See Wurman 1988 and Abel 1983.

the institution's futures position is also time-consuming, especially in a micro strategy that may involve many individual hedges. Finally, the daily cash settlements required for futures trading place additional liquidity demands on the institution, especially if rate forecasts prove to be incorrect. The disadvantages must be weighed against the additional flexibility that futures provide.

INTEREST RATE SWAPS

Interest rate swaps, introduced in Chapter 11, are increasingly popular additions to the asset/liability management "tool box." Bankers Trust, for example, profiled in the opening paragraphs to this chapter, was estimated in 1992 to be a party in swap agreements with more than $25 billion in notional principal. (Recall from Chapter 11 that a SWAP's notional principal is the dollar amount of liabilities on which interest payments to be swapped are calculated.) Swaps are important hedging strategies for depositories because

they allow institutions to manage the rate sensitivity of liabilities and better match their interest rate characteristics with those of the asset portfolio.

SWAPS AND ASSET/LIABILITY MANAGEMENT

A simple example of the use of the simplest type of swap (a plain vanilla swap) to manage interest costs and earnings is presented in Tables 19.8 through 19.11. The example involves both a savings institution, with interest rate risk exposure from substantial long-term mortgage commitments, and a large bank, with more ready access to the Eurobond and other long-term fixed-rate funding markets.

Southwest Savings and Loan has a negative GAP when estimated over the next 2-year planning period; that is, a large portion of its fixed-rate mortgages is funded by rate-sensitive liabilities to be repriced within 2 years. Under a forecast of rising rates, sufficient GAP adjustments are not feasible, and the thrift's asset/liability committee is considering an interest rate

---

TABLE 19.8   Southwest Savings Association Financial Data (Millions $)

These balance sheet and earnings data are used in the interest rate swap example in this chapter.

Assets		Liabilities and Net Worth	

Short-term securities and adjustable-rate loans
  Average return: 10.50%
	$25.5	Short-term and floating-rate funds
		  Average cost: 9.80%
			$62.5

Fixed-rate loans
  Average return: 13.50%
	65.8	Fixed-rate funds
		  Average cost: 11.85%
			28.8

Nonearning assets	4.5	Net worth	4.5
Total assets	$95.8	Total liabilities and net worth	$95.8

$$GAP = \$25.5 - \$62.5 = -\$37.0$$

Projected Pretax Earnings

Revenues:		
Rate-sensitive assets (RSAs)	$2.678	$(25.5 \times 10.50\%)$
Fixed-rate assets (FRAs)	8.883	$(65.8 \times 13.50\%)$
	$11.561	
Interest expense:		
Rate-sensitive liabilities (RSLs)	($6.125)	$(62.5 \times 9.8\%)$
Fixed-rate liabilities (FRLs)	(3.413)	$(28.8 \times 11.85\%)$
	($9.538)	
Pretax earnings	$2.023	

TABLE 19.9   **Southwest Savings Association Projected Pretax Earnings with Swap and No Interest Rate Change (Millions $)**

Before any interest rate changes, the cost of the swap is apparent: Projected pretax profits are lower than without the swap.

Revenues:		
Rate-sensitive assets (RSAs)	$2.678	
Fixed-rate assets (FRAs)	8.883	
Swap interest income ($15 at 10.60%)	1.590	
		$13.151
Interest expense:		
Rate-sensitive liabilities (RSLs)	($6.125)	
Fixed-rate liabilities (FRLs)	(3.413)	
Swap payments ($15 at 11.50%)	(1.725)	
		(11.263)
Pretax earnings		$ 1.888

Handwritten annotations near "Swap interest income": 10.35 + .25 / LIBOR

TABLE 19.10   **Southwest Savings Association Projected Pretax Earnings after Interest Rate Increase (Millions of $)**

If interest rates increase as forecast, expected profits will be higher with the swap than without it.

Without Swap

Revenues:		
Rate-sensitive assets (at 12.30%)	$3.137	(25.5 × 12.390)
Fixed-rate assets (at 13.50%)	8.883	
	$12.020	
Interest expense:		(62.5 × 11.10%)
Rate-sensitive liabilities (at 11.10%)	($6.938)	
Fixed-rate liabilities (at 11.85%)	(3.413)	
	($10.351)	
Pretax earnings	$ 1.669	

With Swap

Revenues:		
Rate-sensitive assets (at 12.30%)	$3.137	
Fixed-rate assets (at 13.50%)	8.883	
Swap interest income ($15 at 12.20%)	1.830	
		$13.850
Interest expense:		
Rate-sensitive liabilities (at 11.10%)	($6.938)	
Fixed-rate liabilities (at 11.85%)	(3.413)	
Swap payments ($15 at 11.50%)	(1.725)	
		($12.076)
Pretax earnings		$ 1.774

Handwritten annotations near "Swap interest income": 11.95 + .25 / LIBOR

TABLE 19.11   **Southwest Savings Association Projected Pretax Earnings after Interest Rate Decrease (Millions of $)**

A swap that would be beneficial if interest rates increase will reduce profitability if interest rates decrease instead. Although this institution will enjoy higher profits if rates fall, the cost of the swap offsets some of the benefits of the decline.

Without Swap		
Revenues:		
Rate-sensitive assets (at 9.50%)	$2.423	
Fixed-rate assets (at 13.50%)	8.883	
		$11.306
Interest expense:		
Rate-sensitive liabilities (at 8.90%)	($5.563)	
Fixed-rate liabilities (at 11.85%)	(3.413)	
		(8.976)
Pretax earnings		$ 2.330
With Swap		
Revenues:		
Rate-sensitive assets (at 9.50%)	$2.423	
Fixed-rate assets (at 13.50%)	8.883	
Swap interest income ($15 at 9.55%)	1.433	
		$12.739
Interest expense:		
Rate-sensitive liabilities (at 8.90%)	($5.563)	
Fixed-rate liabilities (at 11.85%)	(3.413)	
Swap payments ($15 at 11.50%)	(1.725)	
		(10.701)
Pretax earnings		$ 2.038

swap. The first step in structuring an agreement is estimating the average cost of short- and long-term funding sources and the expected yield on long-term fixed-rate assets. Table 19.8 shows the results of this evaluation; the current return on the thrift's RSAs is 10.5 percent, and on FRAs it is 13.5 percent.

The earnings projections for Southwest S&L, also shown in Table 19.8, are positive, but the firm has a negative GAP of $37 million. It is exposed if interest rates increase. The thrift's managers decide to reduce the GAP by finding an interest rate swap partner willing to assume some of the floating-rate liability costs. In exchange, the S&L will accept some of the counterparty's fixed-rate obligations. In effect, the swap reduces the S&L's volume of RSLs and thereby reduces the GAP.

TERMS OF THE INTEREST RATE SWAP

Suppose the association finds a multinational bank willing to negotiate an agreement covering debt with a notional principal value of $15 million. The swap reduces Southwest's GAP to −$22 million. The terms of the agreement require Southwest to pay the interest costs on $15 million of the bank's debt, which carries an interest rate of 11.50 percent. The bank will make payments to the S&L at a floating rate, set at 25 basis points above the LIBOR rate, currently at 10.35 percent. Thus, the S&L will receive payments at a rate of 10.60 percent, 80 basis points higher than its current cost of rate-sensitive liabilities. It will pay interest at a cost that provides a rate differential on fixed-rate assets of 13.50% − 11.50% = 2.00%.

FIGURE 19.4   **Plain Vanilla Swap for Southwest Savings**

Southwest Savings exchanges its variable-rate interest obligations to depositors for a fixed-rate obligation to the commercial bank counterparty. Initially, Southwest pays a higher interest rate.

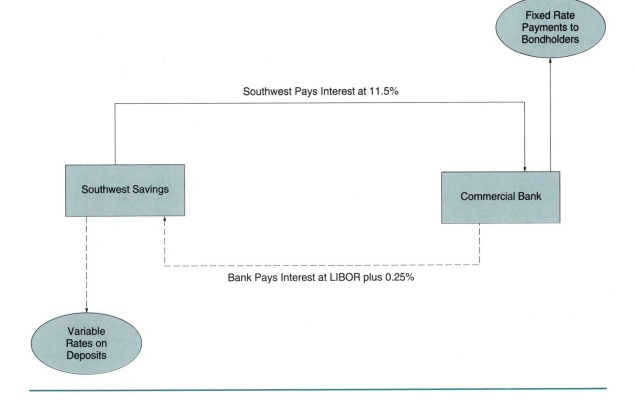

The flow of funds in this agreement is illustrated in Figure 19.4. The S&L initially exchanges lower-cost for higher-cost funds as it switches from floating to fixed rates. The added cost is the price of the "insurance" against interest rate increases. The bank counterparty is exposed to the risk that the floating rank will rise above its current fixed-rate obligation of 11.50 percent.

COSTS AND BENEFITS OF A SWAP AGREEMENT

Before any interest rate shifts, the swap agreement appears costly to the S&L. As shown in Table 19.9, the swap interest inflows initially are less than the S&L's outflows in the agreement. But this is a hedging technique; the agreement was sought to protect against future rate increases.

What happens if rates do increase and the S&L's costs of RSLs rise significantly? Assume that average returns on RSAs rise to 12.30 percent, and RSL costs rise to 11.10 percent. The LIBOR rate goes up to 11.95 percent, increasing the rate at which payments are received from the banking counterparty to 12.20 percent (11.95 percent plus 25 basis points). Without the swap, as shown at the top of Table 19.10, pretax earnings would fall to $1.669 million. But the swap protects returns, and the earnings decline is less with the swap in place than it is in the scenario without the swap—down to $1.774 million, as shown at the bottom of

Table 19.10. The S&L could have increased protection by agreeing to a larger swap, but the "insurance" cost would also have been greater.

As with all hedging tools, if interest rate forecasts are in error, swap agreements prevent an institution from profiting from unexpectedly favorable interest rate movements. The "cost" of the swap insurance is evident in Table 19.11, which illustrates the effects of an interest rate decline. Recall from the discussion in Chapter 18 that institutions with a negative rate-sensitivity GAP (such as Southwest Savings) can benefit from falling rates. The top portion of Table 19.11 shows that if the yield on RSAs falls to 9.50 percent and the cost of RSLs falls to 8.90, Southwest's profits will be higher than they would have been before the interest rate change. The drop in interest rates reduces interest expense to a larger degree than it reduces revenues. The bottom of the table shows, however, that if the swap is executed, a portion of the potential benefits is offset by the fact that, when interest rates decline, the S&L must pay more in interest expense to its swap counterparty than it receives.

As noted in earlier discussions, the markets for interest rate swaps have grown rapidly and now are quite well developed with many participants. Consequently, Southwest Savings would have the ability to reverse this swap agreement, should changes in interest rates make it desirable to do so. As an alternative, the thrift's managers could have chosen to bundle the original swap agreement with a swaption to create a callable swap. Southwest would exercise its swaption to escape an unfavorable interest rate environment. Of course, the thrift would also incur additional transactions costs as a result.

CHOICE BETWEEN THE FUTURES HEDGE AND THE SWAP HEDGE

As the alternatives for hedging interest rate risk multiply, managers of depository institutions face increasingly complex choices. The previous examples illustrate the effects of a futures hedge and a swap hedge on earnings and earnings variability. What are some of the influential factors that must be a part of managers' choice between the two?[18]

One factor would be the characteristics of the assets being hedged. Thrifts, with the need to protect against the risk exposure of long-term, fixed-rate mortgages funded by variable-rate deposits, must use a cross hedge if they take a position in the futures markets, because no contracts are currently written on mortgage-backed securities. As explained in detail in earlier chapters, the cross hedge increases basis risk and the probability that the hedge will not fully offset potential losses. A swap agreement, in contrast, allows a more effective match of interest rate characteristics.

However, as is clearly shown in the Southwest Savings example, a swap can be quite costly. The transfer of interest rate uncertainty to the counterparty results in lower profits, regardless of the movement in interest rates. A futures hedge requires low transactions costs and, if structured wisely, could have a less negative impact on the earnings of a depository.

Another factor to consider is the maturity of the assets being hedged. Technically, a depository might want to structure a swap agreement that hedges interest rate uncertainty for the entire life of the fixed-rate assets. For many commercial banks, that period might be only a year or two, but for major participants in the mortgage markets, the maturities could be quite lengthy. Suppose, for example, an institution agreed to an interest swap of 20 years to cover its exposure on 20-year mortgages. The danger is the possibility of mortgage prepayments, which may accelerate if interest rates decline. Although a lender might attempt to estimate those prepayments in advance, it is impossible to do so with accuracy. Should the mortgages be prepaid before the swap agreement expires, the lender would be paying the "insurance" fee longer than necessary. By building in options for early termination at the time of the initial swap agreement, this problem could be alleviated, but such options also carry a cost.

Futures contracts, on the other hand, have short maturities, and thus there is little danger that the hedge will outlive its usefulness. Also, if a depository's asset portfolio grows or shrinks, managers can adjust the size of a futures hedge to reflect these changes, while the notional principal of the swap is not ordinarily subject to renegotiation. The futures hedge must be monitored closely and renewed many times over the life of the hedged asset, so the futures position requires a great deal more managerial attention than does a swap agreement.

---

[18] For further discussion of these points, see Marshall 1990/1991.

It is important to recognize that asset/liability managers are not forced to choose between swaps and futures. In fact, institutions might use both hedging techniques, as well as others, at any one time. The swaps might be used for longer-term assets or a portion of the mortgage portfolio not subject to prepayment, whereas futures contracts could be used to hedge interest rate exposure from other assets.

THE SECONDARY MORTGAGE MARKET AS AN ASSET/ LIABILITY TOOL

Another asset/liability management alternative is of special interest to mortgage lenders, because it is an opportunity to alter the structure of the asset portfolio by selling mortgages to secondary investors or trading mortgages for securities that can be either held or sold. These transactions are part of the secondary mortgage market, mentioned briefly in Chapter 15. This market has grown rapidly since 1980, a trend attributed to the innovative securities offered and the increasing number of investors responding to interest rate uncertainty.

A detailed description of all participants and instruments in the secondary mortgage markets could fill several chapters. This discussion is a brief overview of the market and the managerial objectives determining an institution's involvement.[19]

DEVELOPMENT OF THE SECONDARY MORTGAGE MARKET

In the 1930s, when Congress authorized the creation of what is now the **Federal National Mortgage Association (Fannie Mae or FNMA),** it envisioned the secondary mortgage market as facilitating the flow of capital to residential housing. Today, a nationwide secondary market continues to fulfill the original purposes: alleviating geographic mismatches in supply and demand for mortgages; smoothing out cyclical fluctuations in the housing market; and providing mortgage lenders with access to liquidity.

In 1968, Congress transformed Fannie Mae into a semiprivate corporation, now stockholder-owned and profit-oriented. It no longer receives direct funding from the U.S. Treasury, but it enjoys the status of a government agency when issuing debt securities in the credit markets, which reduces its borrowing costs.[20] Also in 1968, Congress created the **Government National Mortgage Association (Ginnie Mae or GNMA)** to continue government involvement in the secondary mortgage market.

Finally, in 1970, the **Federal Home Loan Mortgage Corporation (Freddie Mac or FHLMC)** was formed as a subsidiary of the Federal Home Loan Bank System. Freddie Mac was initially intended to serve only FHLB members, but now it services a broader audience. In 1989, Freddie Mac became a publicly held corporation, similar to Fannie Mae. The new Freddie Mac continues to receive the benefits of government agency status when it borrows in the financial markets.

Together, Fannie Mae, Ginnie Mae, and Freddie Mac have accounted for between 40 and 50 percent of the dollar volume of purchases in the secondary mortgage market in recent years, leading many observers to question whether the federal government should be so extensively involved in a private market. The Financial Institutions Reform, Recovery, and Enforcement Act (FIRREA) left no doubt, however, that Congress intends for the federal government to remain a major player. Title X required a Government Accounting Office study of both FNMA and FHLMC, with particular concern for the risks faced by these agencies and for their capital adequacy. The law left open the possibility for further regulation pending the results of the report.

---

[19] For further information on the history and operations of the secondary mortgage market, several references are available. Sources include Bennewitz 1984; Villani 1984; and "The Secondary Mortgage Market Is a Key to the Future," *Savings Institutions* 105 (January 1984): S1-S105. Special alternatives for CUs are discussed in Smuckler 1984.

---

[20] The favored borrowing status of Fannie Mae, leading many investors to believe that the federal government would not allow the corporation to default, has been sharply criticized by some experts. According to this view, the quasi-public status of FNMA produces a moral hazard for the Treasury similar to the one produced for deposit insurers under fixed-rate deposit insurance: FNMA's managers have little reason to avoid excessive risk taking. See Kane and Foster 1986.

Congress acted in a surprisingly rapid fashion, passing additional legislation that was signed into law by President Bush in late October 1992. The bill set minimum capital requirements for Fannie Mae and Freddie Mac, part of which are based on interest rate risk. The agencies also must increase their support of affordable housing, particularly in inner cities. The law also created the **Office of Federal Housing Enterprise Oversight,** a new regulatory body to monitor compliance with congressional mandates.[21] Although other investors such as pension funds, life insurance companies, mortgage bankers, and depositories also purchase mortgages from originators, the dominance of the three government-related organizations requires that managers understand their activities.

RESTRUCTURING ASSETS THROUGH THE SECONDARY MORTGAGE MARKET

Each of the organizations offers a slightly different mix of alternatives to managers of mortgage lending institutions, and the complexity of tools offered is growing at a rapid pace.

SELLING MORTGAGE LOANS. The simplest secondary market transaction is a straightforward sale of mortgage loans, either new or old. Institutions may adopt this strategy to obtain cash to make new loans in times of heavy demand. Until recently, many mortgage lenders had limited ability to sell mortgages, because secondary market investors would not accept adjustable-rate loans. Now, however, all three major participants in the secondary market have adjustable-mortgage programs. In 1988, for example, Freddie Mac had purchase programs for more than 40 distinct types of fixed-rate mortgages (FRMs) and ARMs.

Some mortgage lenders, wary of the risk of holding long-term assets, adopt a regular policy of selling mortgages as soon as they are originated. For a fee, these institutions continue to collect monthly payments from borrowers, passing them along to new mortgage investors. Fee income generated from

servicing mortgages can be substantial. Servicing has taken on added importance, in fact, since FIRREA. Using a specified formula, Congress allows thrifts to count as capital part of the value of their future mortgage servicing rights. Thus, thrifts can benefit from the management flexibility available from the secondary mortgage markets without sacrificing the income and capital benefits of servicing the mortgages they originate.[22]

Sometimes the sale of old mortgages is designed to increase the average rate of return on the entire portfolio in an environment of rising interest rates. If the lender wishes to continue to hold mortgages, proceeds from a sale can be reinvested in higher-yielding assets. The drawback, however, is that the market value of the older loans sold will be below their book value, requiring the institution to recognize a loss on its financial statements that might be postponed otherwise. Lenders may believe this is an acceptable price to pay, especially because the loss is a tax-deductible expense that may be used to shelter future earnings or recover taxes paid previously. Management must also consider transactions costs involved in secondary market sales.

Fannie Mae, Ginnie Mae, and Freddie Mac are all engaged in the purchase of mortgages from originating institutions, as are private investors such as pension funds. But private investors often buy only in large volumes, so small lenders, such as CUs, usually sell only to agencies such as Ginnie Mae and Freddie Mac.

MORTGAGE SWAPS. Freddie Mac and Fannie Mae have programs that allow a mortgage lender to alter its asset composition by exchanging mortgage loans for securities issued by the secondary market agency. The objective of the lending institution is to change the liquidity and expected return on its existing investments by swapping conventional, fixed-rate mortgages for securities that can then be resold to investors, used as collateral for borrowing, or held for repurchase agreements. In contrast to an outright sale, a swap of mortgages for other securities allows the lender to avoid reporting a loss of value on the mortgages if rates have risen since their issue.

The first program of this type, called the **Guarantor Program,** was introduced by Freddie Mac in

---

[21] For more information, see Snigdha Prakash, "Regulator of Fannie, Freddie Counts on Political Clout," *American Banker,* September 8, 1993, 8–9; Bush 1990; and Kenneth Bacon, "Congress Passes Housing Bill, Imposing New Rules on Fannie Mae, Freddie Mac," *The Wall Street Journal,* October 9, 1992, A4.

[22] "Conference Report on H.R. 1278" 1989.

1981. In exchange for mortgages, lenders receive a security issued by FHLMC called a **participation certificate (PC),** which can be used to change the rate sensitivity or duration of the asset portfolio. Details on PCs are given later; for accounting and tax purposes, they are considered real estate investments, just like mortgages, but are much more liquid. FNMA instituted a similar program after FHLMC's.[23]

If mortgage rates and loan demand are high, the lender might sell the PCs obtained through the mortgage swap to other investors, thereby raising cash that can be reinvested in new variable-rate mortgages (VRM) or shorter-term mortgages. If a firm wants to attract new liabilities, it might use the securities in repurchase agreements. Thrifts, the FHLMC, and the FNMA continue to experiment with a variety of alternative uses for mortgage swaps.

A typical series of transactions involving a mortgage swap is illustrated in Figure 19.5. In step 1, the lender designates a package of mortgages to be assigned to FHLMC. In exchange, FHLMC issues PCs to the lender. Step 2 illustrates the choices now available to the lender. On the one hand, the PCs can be sold to other investors for cash. As an alternative, the PCs can be used as collateral for repurchase agreements or mortgage-backed bonds, enabling the lender to obtain cash for new investments.

CHARACTERISTICS OF GUARANTEED MORTGAGE SECURITIES

The two choices available in the secondary mortgage market—sell or swap—are better appreciated after examining characteristics of secondary market securities.

GNMA PASS-THROUGH PROGRAM. One security arising from secondary mortgage market transactions is called a **pass-through (PT).** PTs are guaranteed by GNMA but are actually issued by mortgage lenders. If the issuer defaults, there are back-up guarantees.

Figure 19.6 illustrates the process by which GNMA pass throughs are created. In step 1, a lender

deposits a pool of Federal Housing Administration (FHA)-insured or Veteran's Administration (VA)-guaranteed mortgages with a trustee, usually a commercial bank commissioned by GNMA; no conventional mortgages may be used in the GNMA program. Both the trustee and GNMA examine the designated pool, and, if it is satisfactory, GNMA agrees to provide subsequent guarantees against default on these mortgages.

With the benefit of the GNMA guarantee, the original lender sells securities to investors for cash. This cash can then be used to make additional investments, a process not shown in Figure 19.6. The GNMA securities have maturities equal to the remaining maturity of the mortgage pool. Unlike ordinary bonds, on which no principal is due until maturity, GNMA securities are amortized like mortgages; that is, monthly payments include both principal and interest. Furthermore, as mortgages in the pool are prepaid, investors in GNMAs receive these prepayments.

In step 2 of the figure, borrowers continue to make payments on the pool of FHA or VA mortgages as usual. As lenders receive these cash payments, they pass them through to GNMA investors. Should any borrower default, GNMA guarantees assure investors that they will continue to receive their promised payments.

PARTICIPATION CERTIFICATES. A participation certificate is a security issued and guaranteed against default by FHLMC. As illustrated earlier in Figure 19.5, PCs are collateralized by mortgages that FHLMC has received from mortgage lenders in a purchase or swap. FNMA issues similar securities called "mortgage-backed securities" (MBS). Subsequent discussions use PC to refer to both FHLMC and FNMA issues.

Like PTs, PCs pass returns through to investors in the form of monthly principal and interest payments from a specified pool of mortgage loans. Unlike PTs, however, the mortgage pool backing PCs is owned by the secondary market agency, rather than the original lender. FNMA and FHLMC reduce the risk to the security holder by promising to continue payments even if the borrower defaults on an underlying mortgage. This guarantee makes the securities more marketable than the mortgages themselves. This factor explains why, in Figure 19.5, the mortgage originator can use PCs as collateral against a repo or mortgage-backed

[23] Further discussion on mortgage swap programs is available in "Rate Volatility Points to Increase in Mortgage Swaps," *Freddie Mac Reports* 2 (August 1984): 1–2; and Villani 1985.

| FIGURE 19.5 | **Results of a Mortgage Swap** |

Mortgage swaps allow originators to exchange mortgage assets for mortgage-backed securities (PCs in this example) with different cash-flow and liquidity characteristics. PCs can then be used to generate additional cash.

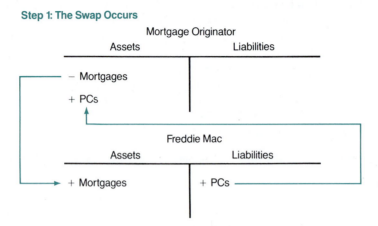

bond issue when the mortgages themselves might not have qualified.

PTS AND PCS AS INVESTMENTS. PCs and PTs are not used by depositories solely as ways of raising new funds. They also serve as investments for mortgage lenders with excess funds. When mortgage demand in a market is low, holding PCs or PTs allows the lender to continue the desired level of involvement in the real estate market, but as a secondary rather than a primary market investor. The willingness of traditional mortgage lenders to buy PCs and PTs allows mortgage funds to be efficiently redistributed among geographic regions. In fact, savings institutions are the largest cat-egory of investors in the PC market, holding almost half of the PCs outstanding in recent years.

A major drawback of PTs and PCs to the secondary market investor is the uncertainty of cash flows, because there are no assurances that the underlying mortgage will not be prepaid. This possibility exposes the security holder to reinvestment risk. To address this problem, Fannie Mae began selling stripped PTs in 1986, similar to the stripped Treasury securities discussed in Chapter 9.

CMOS. Another security that attempts to circumvent the reinvestment problem is the collateralized mortgage obligation (CMO), first described in the section

FIGURE 19.6   **GNMA Pass-Through Program**

GNMA pass throughs permit FHA and VA mortgage originators to sell pools of these assets to obtain additional cash. Interest and principal repayments on the mortgage pools are passed through to investors, who also receive the security of GNMA guarantees if borrowers default.

Step 1: GNMAs Are Issued

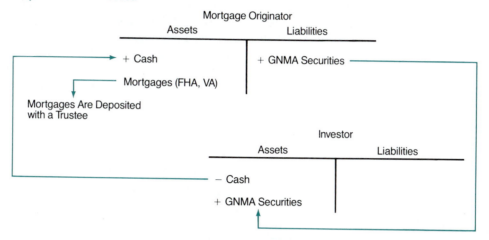

Step 2: Mortgage Payments Are Passed through to Investors

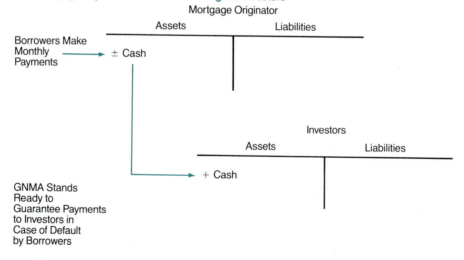

on liability management in Chapter 16. CMOs are issued by Freddie Mac as well as primary mortgage lenders. Because CMOs are issued with several different classes of cash-flow characteristics and are accompanied by greater assurances to investors that returns will follow a desired pattern, some thrifts buy them to adjust their asset portfolios. CMOs can be purchased with short, intermediate, or long maturities, depending on the desired change in the weighted average duration of assets.

REMICs. As part of the Tax Reform Act of 1986, Congress authorized a new type of mortgage-backed instrument, bearing the cumbersome name of **Real**

Estate Mortgage Investment Conduit (REMIC). As with CMOs, REMICs can be structured with a variety of cash-flow characteristics. Issuing institutions, however, avoid tax and other disadvantages associated with CMOs. Although private institutions are authorized to issue REMICs, so are Freddie Mac and FNMA. Freddie Mac immediately created REMIC issues by repackaging its own previously issued PCs; by 1989, Freddie Mac's REMIC volume had soared to $28 billion. In the 1990s, experts predict that Freddie Mac–issued REMICs will be *the* preferred secondary mortgage market asset for depositories, because risk-based capital rules require that a risk weight of only 20 percent be attached to them. REMICs issued by private institutions require a 50 percent risk weight. REMICs also qualify as housing-related investments for thrifts, giving them important tax advantages not offered when CMOs are held as assets.[24]

RESTRUCTURING LIABILITIES THROUGH THE SECONDARY MARKET

Although the greatest attraction of the secondary mortgage market is to reposition the asset portfolio, there are a few avenues for restructuring liabilities as well. One alternative illustrated earlier is to use the PCs obtained through mortgage sales or swaps to obtain new funds through mortgage-backed bonds. In fact, if the goal is to better match longer-term assets with longer-term liabilities, this could be an attractive strategy. Although investors would require a risk premium for buying uninsured debt from depositories, those pledging PCs as collateral could find interested buyers at affordable rates.

Some lending institutions have begun to set aside portions of their mortgage portfolio to secure long-term debt, a strategy that can reduce both the rate-sensitivity and duration GAP. Mortgage-backed bonds also provide cash-flow flexibility, because the interest and principal payments on the collateral are received monthly but returns are paid only semiannually to investors in the bonds backed by the mortgages.

Although increasing liability duration is desirable to most mortgage lenders, accomplishing that adjustment through mortgage-backed bonds has drawbacks. The most serious is the volume of loans that must be pledged as collateral. In an environment of rising interest rates, the market value of loans will decline, and the principal value of mortgages required to collateralize the debt can exceed the bond principal significantly. A related problem is that mortgage loans are repaid on an amortized basis, but bonds are not. The bond principal is outstanding for the entire time, and a very large volume of mortgages is required to produce full collateral over their entire maturity. Finally, issuing bonds involves transaction costs, which reduce profits.

SECURITIZATION: DEVELOPMENT OF OTHER SECONDARY LOAN MARKETS

Also increasing the flexibility of depositories' asset portfolios is the development of secondary markets for loans other than mortgages. First defined in Chapter 2, the process of converting nonmarketable assets into forms acceptable to secondary market purchasers is called securitization. Securitization has economic characteristics of both intermediation and disintermediation. As in intermediation, a financial institution must first transform claims on itself (secondary securities) into its own claims on borrowers (primary securities). As in disintermediation, however, securitization changes the distribution of asset holdings among investors. After a package of loans is securitized, it is held by an investor other than the original intermediary. Some investors who may at one time have preferred to hold deposits as investments may now be willing to purchase securitized loans as substitute investments.[25]

An early effort was the creation of a security backed by automobile loans, marketed in 1985 by Marine Midland Bank of New York with help from Salomon Brothers investment bankers. The securities were aptly named Certificates for Automobile Receivables (CARs). These securities were followed by oth-

---

[24] See Pozdena 1987; Greg Guillaime, "Happy Birthday, REMICs," *Freddie Mac Reports,* March 1988; Paul Allen, "Freddie Mac after FIRREA," *Freddie Mac Reports,* January 1990; and Bush 1991.

[25] For a more detailed comparison of securitization, intermediation, and disintermediation, see Carlstrom and Samolyk 1993 and Cumming 1987.

ers backed by loans on cars, trucks, and computers. As of 1993, almost every type of credit offered by depository institutions had become a candidate for securitization, including credit card debt. Many other types of securities, such as commercial paper, are also being securitized. The volume of nonmortgage asset-backed securities has grown at an astronomical rate—from $0 in 1985 to more than $300 billion by year-end 1992. Some experts estimated the potential size of the market at $6 trillion.[26]

STEPS IN SECURITIZATION

The new secondary market instruments, generically called **asset-backed securities,** are similar to mortgage pass throughs—a financial institution passes through monthly loan payments to security holders. In some cases, a third party, such as an insurance company or a large bank, promises to continue payment on the loans should original borrowers default. In other cases, the issuer provides its own limited guarantee or pledges collateral in excess of the security principal. These **credit enhancement features** of securitized assets provide for an acceptable level of risk sharing among financial institutions with expertise in risk bearing and financial market investors who may be willing to bear some, but not all, of the risk of consumer and commercial lending. Figure 19.7 illustrates the steps in securitization and highlights the roles of multiple financial institutions, including the originating lender, the insurer, and the underwriting securities firm. Although not every asset-backed security is created precisely as illustrated in the figure, the processes of origination, credit enhancement, and marketing to the public are inherent in securitization.

RISKS AND REWARDS

Asset-backed securities promise improvements in asset management and GAP management as well. They offer ways for commercial banks and CUs, for example, to sell loans to increase liquidity. Thrifts with difficulty building a clientele of consumer borrowers may be able to diversify asset portfolios more quickly by investing in asset-backed securities than by originating loans themselves. Also, institutions with loan demand but without sufficient capital to support growth can benefit from selling their loans to other investors. The desire for liquidity and diversification have, in fact, been found by researchers to be motivations behind the growth of commercial bank loan sales and the resulting increase in securitization in recent years.[27]

Some observers have also noted that the decline in the value of ongoing relationships between institutions and their traditional customers has fostered the rapid growth of securitization. Traditional depositors, for example, now have close substitutes for deposits, causing them to be less dependent on depositories. Potential borrowers find many nondepository competitors eager to offer credit. Some lenders, too, no longer find it profitable to operate as portfolio lenders to a familiar group of customers, given the risks posed by financial market volatility.

Technological innovation has also made securitization possible for institutions that could not have dreamed of packaging and selling loans in decades past. The ability to assemble and analyze simultaneously a large volume of information on a large quantity of loans at relatively low cost, which is essential in the process of securitization, is now widespread.

However, regulators and investors have expressed concern about securitization. A market for asset-backed securities with low-quality loans as collateral is not likely to arise. Consequently, institutions desiring to issue asset-backed securities may be pressured to pledge their highest-quality loans, exposing existing creditors to increased risk. The new risk-based capital rules, which permit institutions with less risky assets to operate with less capital, will undoubtedly constrain a single institution from selling all its high-quality loans and retaining only its higher-risk investments. Yet few observers expect the capital rules to slow the trend toward securitization. Most, in fact, expect securitization to increase as a result of the new

---

[26] See Cantor and Demsetz 1993; Caouette 1992; Richard L. Stern and Jason Zweig, "Bank Reform Wall Street Style," *Forbes* (March 30, 1992): 62–67; "All the World's a Security," *The Economist* (August 29, 1992): 69; "CARs Program Leads the Way to New Types of Securities," *Savings Institutions* 106 (June 1985): 109, 111; Olson 1986; Shapiro 1985; Pozdena 1986; and Booth 1989.

---

[27] See Pavel 1988.

FIGURE 19.7   **Typical Structure of an Asset-Backed Security Issue**

Asset-backed securities are created when an originating lender packages loans for resale in the secondary market. Guarantees against default provided by institutions such as insurance companies add to the marketability of the issue.

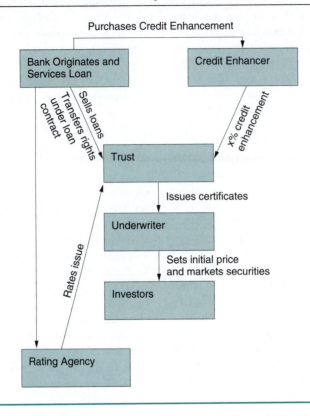

Source: Christine Pavel, "Would You Buy a Car Loan from This Bank?" *Chicago Fed Letter* (Federal Reserve Bank of Chicago), No. 21, May 1989.

---

regulations: After all, a depository needs *no* capital against a loan it has sold. Thus, the successful origination, packaging, and resale of loans has the potential to generate considerable fee income to a depository without adding to its capital requirements. Also, as mentioned in the section on secondary mortgage markets, securitization offers the possibility for depositories with higher-risk assets to lower their capital requirements by purchasing high-quality securitized assets from other depositories.[28]

Furthermore, securitization is not inconsistent with depositories' abilities to take advantage of economies of scale. Institutions specializing in loan originations, even if they do not hold the loans to maturity, should enjoy economic efficiencies from both the human and physical assets involved in credit analysis.

Despite the promise of securitization, regulators will continue to scrutinize the process. Particular concern surrounds securitization *with recourse,* in which the investor in a securitized asset receives a guarantee from the original depository lender in case the borrower defaults. Recourse agreements pose special dangers when lower-quality assets are securitized. Yet these are the very assets for which investors are most likely to seek recourse. For this reason, regulators re-

---

[28] For further discussion, see Cantor and Demsetz 1993; Carlstrom and Samolyk 1993; Kavanagh, Boemio, and Edwards 1992; Aber 1988; Ellspermann 1988; and Silver and Axilrod 1989.

quire institutions that securitize assets with recourse to report them on the balance sheet and to hold capital against them. Institutions that purchase securitized assets also face potential liquidity risks. Although many assets are now being securitized, some markets remain quite thin, with few participants and relatively low trading volume. In an emergency, it is possible that some securitized assets would have to be sold at "fire sale" prices.

Finally, as with all complex asset/liability tools, accounting problems exist. Regulators, institutions, and accountants may—and often do—differ in how they believe the financial results of securitization should be presented, and consistent regulatory accounting and GAP rules have yet to be worked out. These difficulties, however, are unlikely to diminish the importance of securitization as a financial innovation.[29]

NEW DIRECTIONS: INTEREST RATE CAPS, FLOORS, AND COLLARS

As should be evident from discussions of financial and technological change throughout the book, one innovation often breeds others. Certainly that pattern is evident among hedging tools for interest rate risk management. Caps and floors, introduced in Chapter 11, are recent derivatives of earlier hedging instruments. As lenders have embraced adjustable-rate loans and interest rate swaps in efforts to manage the rate-sensitivity GAP or the duration GAP, they have found themselves exposed to additional risks. For example, a depository may need to confine rate increases on adjustable-rate loans to prespecified limits to make them attractive to customers; at the same time, lenders also usually promise borrowers that rates on their variable-rate loans can *decrease* without limit. As a result, the terms offered on many adjustable-rate assets erode some of the interest rate risk protection the instruments were designed to offer for the lender. Interest rate caps and interest rate floors are designed to hedge against that erosion.

HEDGING WITH CAPS AND FLOORS

Simple examples of a cap and a floor demonstrate their use as supplements to active GAP management.

USING A CAP TO HEDGE CD COSTS. Suppose an institution has issued $10 million of ARMs with an initial rate of 10.5 percent and a lifetime maximum rate of 12.5 percent. The index to which these mortgage rates are linked is the 1-year T-bill index, currently at 8.5 percent. Interest rates on these ARMs can change every 6 months; they are funded by 6-month CDs on which the institution pays an interest rate also tied to the 1-year T-bill index. Although these ARMs are considerably more useful in protecting the institution against interest rate risk than FRMs would be, the lender is still exposed to the risk that, over the life of the mortgage, the index may rise more than the 2 percent limit on the ARMs. If that happens, the cost of CDs will continue to increase, but the ARM returns will not.

By purchasing an interest rate cap with a 10.5 percent strike level, linked to the 1-year T-bill index, and covering $10 million of notional principal (the same term used in the interest rate swap market), the lender will be protected if the T-bill index rises above 10.5 percent. At that point, the cap will be "in the money" (the same term used in the options market). The cap can be purchased to cover various time periods, ranging from 3 months to 10 or more years, depending on the buyer's desired protection horizon. The points at which comparisons are made between the T-bill index and the strike level on the cap (called **determination dates**) can also vary; typical periods are 1-month, 3-month, or 6-month intervals. If the cap is "in the money" on the comparison dates, the owner is entitled to receive payment from the writer (seller) of the cap.

Suppose the institution learns on a given determination date that the T-bill index is at 11 percent. The cap holder will be entitled to receive the difference between the current market rate and the strike level, times the notional principal value covered by the cap, times the fraction of a year between determination dates (assumed to be semiannual in this example): $(11\% - 10.5\%) \times \$10,000,000 \times 0.5 = \$25,000$. This payment can then be used by the cap owner to offset the increased interest costs of the CDs when they

---

[29] See Dreyer 1991; Wall 1991; Boemio and Edwards 1989; Swegle 1989; and Morrison 1988.

rise above returns on the ARMs. Whenever the cap is in the money on determination dates, the cap holder will receive payments.

Cap prices (called premiums) behave much like call option prices. All else equal, the greater the time to maturity and the greater the volatility in the underlying index, the higher the cap price; all else equal, the higher the strike level on the cap, the lower its price. Cap premiums are quoted in percentages and are converted to dollar figures by multiplying by the notional principal covered. In this example, if the price for a 5-year cap with a strike level of 10.5 percent tied to the T-bill index were 3.75 percent, its initial cost to the purchaser would be $0.0375 \times \$10,000,000 = \$37,500$. Presumably, the cap purchaser expects to receive payments whose present value over the life of the cap will exceed this cost, plus provide protection against interest rate increases. If the T-bill index in this example never rises above 10.5 percent, the cap will expire unused. The $37,500 premium would be viewed as insurance against increases in the T-bill rate greater than 2 percent.

USING A FLOOR TO PROTECT ARM RETURNS. Suppose that the ARMs in the previous example are instead funded by CDs with an initial cost of 9.5 percent, on which the interest rate can change every 2 years. If interest rates fall, the returns on the ARMs may decline below the interest cost on the CDs. To protect against this possibility, the lender can purchase an interest rate floor linked to the T-bill index with a strike level of 7.5 percent. Now suppose that interest rates fall 1.5 percent in 6 months; the index falls from 8.5 percent (its original level) to 7 percent, and the interest rate on the ARMs also falls by 1.5 percent. The cost of the 2-year CDs, however, does not fall. In this situation, the floor holder would receive an amount equal to the strike level minus the current level of the index, times the notional principal, times the fraction of a year between determination dates: $(7.5\% - 7\%) \times \$10,000,000 \times 0.5 = \$25,000$. This amount, and others received whenever the floor is in the money on a determination date, could be used to offset the loss that arises when the return on ARMs falls below the cost of the CDs. Like prices on interest rate caps, floor prices are quoted in percentages and are translated to dollars by multiplying by the notional principal amount being protected. If the T-bill index never falls below 7.5 percent

in this example, the price (premium) would be viewed by the lender as an insurance cost.

Finally, some market participants purchase caps *and* floors, hedging against both increases and decreases in interest rates. These arrangements, which in essence attempt to stabilize the net interest margin (NIM) within a defined band, are known as interest rate collars.[30]

SUMMARY

Traditional GAP management has limitations that have led to the development of supplementary tools for asset/liability management. One is the use of duration-based GAP management. Duration GAP measurements are more closely related to potential changes in the value of net worth than are rate-sensitivity GAP measurements. The disadvantage is the somewhat complex calculations required to manage duration GAPs properly and the fact that estimates of value based on duration reflect a single interest rate shift. Models based on option adjusted spreads (OAS) improve estimates of market value by simulating a large number of interest rate scenarios and by incorporating the potential effects of embedded options in institutions' assets and liabilities.

Additional techniques are available for hedging GAPs rather than restructuring them. Prominent ones are the markets for interest rate futures and interest rate swaps. Their advantage is the avoidance of the active balance sheet restructuring required in GAP management. Their disadvantages are that they require considerable management expertise and, as hedging tools, do not permit an institution to increase profits from unexpected but favorable shifts in interest rates.

Secondary markets exist for some assets, especially mortgages. Securitization of most other types of loans has increased rapidly since the mid-1980s. These markets present substantial opportunities for balance sheet restructuring. Finally, interest rate caps and floors, which are related to both swaps and options, are the most recent innovations for managing interest rate risk. Managers must familiarize themselves with these

---

[30]For more information on caps, floors, and collars, see Abken 1989 and Spahr, Luytjes, and Edwards 1988.

tools to meet their goals for the net interest margin and return on net worth.

QUESTIONS

1. Explain how a depository could become insolvent even with perfectly matched asset and liability maturities. What does this potential occurrence imply about the need for supplements to active management of the rate-sensitivity GAP?

2. Explain how a duration GAP differs from a rate-sensitivity GAP. What advantages does the former hold over the latter?

3. The duration and rate-sensitivity GAPs reflect the potential variability in specific financial measures. Compare and contrast the interest rate risk management capabilities of the two strategies. How is an institution's duration GAP related to regulators' view of its capital adequacy?

4. Why do some financial institutions immunize only portions of the balance sheet when using a duration GAP management strategy? What limitations or difficulties does duration GAP management present?

5. Compare and contrast strategies for managing a positive rate-sensitivity GAP and a positive duration GAP under expectations of rising rates and under expectations of falling rates.

6. How would you interpret a *negative* duration GAP? What type of asset/liability structure would lead to a negative duration GAP? Would a negative duration GAP ever be desirable? If so, under what type of interest rate forecasts?

7. Describe trends in duration GAPs in the thrift industry from the mid-1980s to the early 1990s. What economic and regulatory changes affected these patterns? What conclusions would you draw about interest rate risk exposure in the industry?

8. Given the interest rate risk management requirements included in FDICIA, would you expect to see more or less emphasis on the duration GAP in the near future? Why or why not?

9. Option-adjusted spread models incorporate a large number of factors potentially affecting risk and return of a depository's assets and liabilities. What are the "options" considered in these models? How are they related to future interest rate levels?

10. Explain what an option-adjusted spread actually measures.

11. Compare and contrast the potential effectiveness of du-

ration estimates resulting from OAS-simulated cash flows with a duration GAP approach.

12. What advantages are offered by futures hedges that are not provided by GAP management? Explain the difference between a macro hedge and a micro hedge. Which type is more realistic for most institutions? Why? How do accounting and regulatory standards affect hedging strategies?

13. Explain how futures can be used to create loan terms that meet the interest rate risk preferences of both borrowers and lenders. What problems are faced by depository institution managers who use futures in asset/liability management?

14. Can an institution's managers hedge both its rate-sensitivity GAP and its duration GAP with the same futures position? Why or why not?

15. What is a "plain vanilla" interest rate swap? What are depository institutions' motivations for participating in swaps?

16. Suppose an institution with a negative rate-sensitivity GAP, based on a forecast of rising interest rates, has arranged to swap its own floating-rate interest obligations for payments on another institution's fixed-rate obligations. What are the potential negative consequences of the swap if interest rates fall instead? How can the negative-GAP institution attempt to mitigate these consequences?

17. Managers of a large thrift with an asset portfolio dominated by mortgage loans are evaluating hedging strategies. What issues should they consider in choosing between futures and interest-rate swaps? Which would you recommend? Why?

18. Explain how mortgage lenders can use the secondary mortgage market as an asset/liability management tool. Compare the effects of selling versus swapping mortgages.

19. Explain the federal government's role in developing the secondary mortgage market. Do you believe that the debt of private firms such as Fannie Mae and Freddie Mac should continue to carry government agency status and thereby receive favorable borrowing rates? If so, do you support recent legislation imposing minimum capital requirements on these organizations and establishing a new regulatory agency? Why or why not?

20. What are participation certificates? How do financial institutions use them in asset/liability management? Explain differences in the ownership of the mortgage pool backing pass-throughs and participation certificates.

21. Under what circumstances do mortgage lenders utilize pass-throughs, participation certificates, CMOs, and

REMICs as investments? For secondary market investors, what risks are associated with holding pass-throughs, participation certificates, and REMICs?

22. How can the secondary mortgage markets be used to adjust the liability structure of a depository institution?

23. Explain securitization and its economic characteristics. Briefly outline the securitization process.

24. What are the advantages of securitization to commercial banks? To credit unions? How does securitization change the traditional operating characteristics of lending institutions such as Bankers Trust?

25. Do you think that depositories' participation in emerging secondary asset markets should be regulated? Why or why not? Do you expect the risk-based capital rules to have

a major effect on the growth of securitized asset markets? Why or why not?

26. Do you believe that the growth of securitization will lead to the demise of traditional portfolio lenders? Why or why not?

27. To what types of institutions, with what types of asset/liability structures, are interst rate caps attractive? Interest rate floors? Give an example of a situation in which a cap would be desirable, and one in which a floor would be useful.

28. Explain an interest rate collar. What is its role in managing interest rate risk exposure?

29. Compare and contrast the advantages and disadvantages of interest rate swaps and interest rate caps and floors as risk management tools.

PROBLEMS

1. The following is the *market-value* balance sheet for Republic National Bank of Westwood. The required return on net worth is now 15 percent. All income is received at the end of the year and is reinvested in the bank.

Assets		Liabilities and Equity	
RSAs at 10% yield	$1,000,000	RSLs at 9% cost	$1,000,000
FRAs (Bonds—5 year maturity, 12% coupon)	1,000,000	FRLs (5 year CDs at 10.5% cost)	1,000,000
Nonearning assets	160,000	Common equity	160,000
Total	$2,160,000		$2,160,000

a. Calculate the rate-sensitivity GAP and expected annual pretax profits under current conditions. Also calculate the *present value* of this year's expected additions to net worth.
b. Suppose that the yield curve shifts up by 3 percent. Calculate expected pretax profits and the present value of expected additions to net worth.
c. Now suppose that the bank's managers are forecasting the same level of expected pretax profits and a 15 percent required return on net worth each year for the next 20 years. What is the total present value of expected additions to net worth over the entire period? If interest rates rise unexpectedly by 3 percent, what is the new total expected present value?
d. Is this institution free from interest rate risk? Explain.

2. Return to the Heartland Credit Union (HCU) example in the chapter. Assume that the consumer loans (10 percent annual rate) have an average maturity of 60 months and that mortgages (9.6 percent annual rate) are expected to be prepaid in 12 years. Current market yields/costs are as shown in Table 19.3.
a. Under these new assumptions, calculate the duration GAP. (Hints: Use the simplified formula to calculate asset durations. The amount to be received in 12 years when the mortgages are prepaid is the remaining principal balance at that time. To find it easily, calculate the present value 12 years from now of the remaining payments at that time. In calculating the mortgage duration using Equation 9.2, $N = 144$ months.)
b. Estimate the percentage by which net worth would change, given the following changes in market rates. Recall that management targets a 20 percent return on net worth.
  1) an increase of 100 basis points
  2) a decrease of 75 basis points
c. Based on the duration GAP you calculated in part a, use a "what if" analysis to show by what percentage net worth would change if interest rates increased or decreased by as much as 200 basis points. To illustrate the relationship more clearly, graph your results. (Suggestion: Vary your rate changes in 10 basis-point intervals.)

d.   In the early 1980s, at the time the data on HCU were collected, market interest rates were quite high relative to their historic levels. Prepare a "what if" analysis showing how the duration GAP would change if market interest rates on installment loans decreased by as much as 8 percent from their assumed level of 18 percent. Use 0.5 percent intervals. Assume that the duration of mortgages remains as you calculated it in part a. In general, what impact would such rate declines have on the CU's capital?

3.   The balance sheet of Landmark Savings Bank follows, along with the average duration of each account.

Landmark Savings Bank
Balance Sheet Analysis
(Millions)

Assets		Liabilities and Net Worth	
Short-term securities and adjustable-rate loans	$210	Short-term and floating-rate funds	$580
Duration: 3 months		Duration: 1 month	
Fixed-rate loans	650	Fixed-rate funds	280
Duration: 8 years		Duration: 35 months	
Nonearning assets	80	Core capital (net worth)	80
Total assets	$940	Total liabilities and net worth	$940

a.   Calculate Landmark's duration GAP.
b.   If return on net worth is now 16 percent, and if the general level of interest rates increases by 60 basis points, by how much will Landmark's net worth change?
c.   Suppose that the expected change in net worth is unacceptable to management. Suggest several actions that could be taken to counteract it. What are the advantages and disadvantages of each action?
d.   Suppose that interest rates fall, instead, by 100 basis points. Show the effect on Landmark's capital.

4.   The Sofia National Bank has the following balance sheet:

Sofia National Bank
Balance Sheet Analysis
(Millions)

Assets		Liabilities and Net Worth	
Short-term securities and adjustable-rate loans	$660	Short-term and floating-rate funds	$210
Duration: 3 months		Duration: 1 month	
Fixed-rate loans	200	Fixed-rate funds	650
Duration: 8 years		Duration: 35 months	
Nonearning assets	80	Core capital (net worth)	80
Total assets	$940	Total liabilities and net worth	$940

a.   Calculate Sofia's duration GAP.
b.   If return on net worth is now 16 percent, and if the general level of interest rates increases by 60 basis points, by how much will Sofia's net worth change? If you were the bank manager, would you be pleased with this result? Why or why not?
c.   Now suppose that interest rates fall sharply, by 300 basis points. By how much will Sofia's net worth change? If you were Sofia's manager, would you be pleased with this result? Why or why not?
d.   Notice that Sofia National's assets and net worth are identical to the assets and net worth of Landmark Savings in Problem 3, as are the durations of both institutions' assets and liabilities. If you have also answered Problem 3, compare and contrast your results for that problem with those for Sofia National. Do you understand why managing institutions with large positive duration GAPs has been stressful in recent years?

5. Return to the example of the Southwest Savings and Loan Association interest rate swap in the chapter. Suppose that Southwest agrees to swap interest on $30 million notional principal value under the same terms as those described in the chapter—paying interest of 11.50 percent on the bank's debt while receiving 25 basis points above the LIBOR rate, currently at 10.35 percent.

   a.   What is the dollar cost of the "insurance" that the swap provides if there is no rate increase after the swap?

   b.   What would pretax earnings be if rates increase after the $30 million swap, as described in the chapter—that is, if the yield on rate-sensitive assets increases to 12.30 percent, the cost of rate-sensitive liabilities increases to 11.10 percent, and the LIBOR rate increases to 11.95 percent?

   c.   Again assuming a $30 million notional principal, what would pretax earnings be if interest rates decline as described in the chapter—that is, if the yield on rate-sensitive assets declines to 9.5 percent, the cost of rate-sensitive liabilities falls to 8.9 percent, and the LIBOR rate falls to 9.3 percent?

   d.   Summarize your results by completing the following matrix.

Pretax Earnings

	No swap	$15 million swap	$30 million swap
No rate change			
Rates increase			
Rates decrease			

Based on this summary, what factors should management consider in determining whether or not to enter into a swap and, if so, for how much notional principal?

6. The management of Hathaway Bank and Trust has conducted an interest-rate sensitivity analysis of the bank's balance sheet. The result is given below:

Hathaway Bank and Trust
Balance Sheet Analysis
(Millions)

Assets		Liabilities and Net Worth	
Short-term securities and floating-rate loans	$ 75.0	Short-term and floating-rate funds	$ 40.0
Average return: 8.5%		Average cost: 7.2%	
Fixed-rate loans	20.0	Fixed-rate funds	55.0
Average return: 10.0%		Average cost: 9.0%	
Cash and nonearning assets	8.0	Equity	8.0
Total assets	$103.0	Total liabilities and equity	$103.0

Management expects interest rates to decline but is reluctant to force customers into fixed-rate loans or to encourage depositors into floating-rate deposits for fear of alienating them. A broker has found an S&L forecasting higher interest rates that is willing to serve as a counterparty to an interest rate swap. The S&L will assume interest payments on $35 million of fixed-rate deposits at an average rate of 8.8 percent. Hathaway agrees to pay interest on $35 million at a floating rate 1 percent higher than the 1-year T-bill index. The initial rate that Hathaway will pay is 7.5 percent.

   a.   Calculate Hathaway's expected pretax profits before the swap.

   b.   Calculate Hathaway's expected pretax profits after the swap but before any interest rate change. Is the swap a "free lunch"?

c. Suppose the bank's managers are right and rates begin to fall. The T-bill index drops to 6 percent, the return on rate-sensitive assets falls to 8.0 percent, and the cost of rate-sensitive liabilities falls to 6.5 percent. Recompute Hathaway's expected pretax profits after the swap.

d. Suppose the S&L is right and rates increase. The T-bill index rises to 8.0 percent, the return on rate-sensitive assets rises to 9.0 percent, and the cost of rate-sensitive liabilities rises to 8.5 percent. Calculate Hathaway's expected profits under this scenario.

e. Besides the risk of incorrect interest rate forecasts, to what other risks does the swap expose Hathaway?

7. Consider the following information on LIBOR caps. The current 3-month LIBOR rate is 7.5 percent.

Cap Prices as Percentage of Notional Amount									
Maturity (Year)					**LIBOR Cap Strike Level**				
	8%	**8.5%**	**9%**	**9.5%**	**10%**	**10.5%**	**11%**	**12%**	**13%**
2	1.91	1.53	1.20	0.93	0.76	0.58	0.47	0.29	0.19
3	3.79	3.10	2.47	2.03	1.77	1.46	1.20	0.83	0.57
4	4.62	4.78	4.05	3.40	2.99	2.51	2.09	1.56	1.14
5	7.45	6.38	5.48	4.75	4.10	3.10	3.10	2.35	1.78
7	—	—	8.30	—	6.30	—	4.80	3.95	3.10
10	—	—	—	—	—	—	—	—	—

a. Across the 3-year row, why do cap prices decline as strike levels increase?

b. Down the 12 percent strike level column, why do prices increase as the maturity of the cap increases?

c. Suppose that a manager purchased a 10 percent, 4-year LIBOR cap with quarterly determination dates, covering $70,000,000 of notional principal. What would be the cost of such a cap? If the LIBOR rate rose to 11 percent, how much would the cap owner receive after the determination date?

8. Russell Savings has issued $40 million in ARMs on which the rate cannot increase more than 3 percent over the life of the loan. However, the rate on the ARMs can decrease without limit. Adjustments in the rate can occur once a year. The mortgages are indexed to the rate on T-bills, which currently stands at 8.0 percent. The current rate on the mortgages is 11 percent. They are funded by 3-year CDs linked to the T-bill rate; the current CD cost is 9.5 percent.

The following caps and floors are available on the T-bill index. All have quarterly determination dates:

Type of Instrument	Strike Level, Percent	Price
Cap	7.5	4.10
Cap	9.0	3.60
Cap	10.0	2.70
Cap	11.0	2.35
Cap	12.0	1.50
Floor	9.0	4.20
Floor	8.0	3.80
Floor	7.0	3.20
Floor	6.5	2.50
Floor	6.0	1.80

a. What is the current price (in dollars) of the following instruments:
  i) 7.5 percent cap, $20,000,000 notional principal
  ii) 7.0 percent floor, $40,000,000 notional principal

b. Which caps are in the money? Which floors are in the money? Explain.

c. Suppose that interest rates are expected to increase dramatically in the next year. Of the available choices, which cap or floor would you recommend to management? Why? What is the dollar cost of your choice, based on $40 million notional principal?

d. Assume that Russell's management purchases the instrument you recommend in part c. If the T-bill rate rises to 9 percent by the next determination date, how much would the institution receive? How much would it receive if the T-bill rate rises to 12 percent?

e. Suppose instead that interest rates are forecast to fall drastically. What cap or floor would you recommend to management? Why? What is the dollar cost of your choice, based on $40 million notional principal?

f. Now assume that Russell's management purchases the instrument you recommend in part e and that the T-bill index falls to 6.0 percent by the next determination date. How much would Russell receive? How much would it receive if the T-bill index falls to 7.5 percent?

SELECTED REFERENCES

Abel, Oliver, IV. "Fixed Rate Loans Using Variable Rate Funds—A New Lending Instrument." *Journal of Commercial Bank Lending* 65 (August 1983): 36–43.

Aber, Jack W. "Securitization in the Retail Banking World." *Journal of Retail Banking* 10 (Spring 1988): 5–12.

Abken, Peter A. "Interest-Rate Caps, Collars, and Floors," *Economic Review* (Federal Reserve Bank of Atlanta) 74 (November/December 1989): 2–24.

Baldoni, Robert, and Gerhard Isele. "A Simple Guide to Choosing between Futures and Swaps." *Intermarket* 3 (October 1986): 15–22.

Beidleman, Carl R., Ed. *Interest Rate Swaps.* Homewood, IL: Business One Irwin, 1991.

Belongia, Michael T., and G. J. Santoni. "Cash Flow or Present Value: What's Lurking Behind the Hedge?" *Review* (Federal Reserve Bank of St. Louis) 67 (January 1985): 5–13.

Bennewitz, Dall. *Introduction to the Secondary Mortgage Market: A Primer,* revised ed. Chicago: U.S. League of Savings Institutions, 1984.

Bicksler, James, and Andrew H. Chen. "An Economic Analysis of Interest Rate Swaps." *Journal of Finance* 41 (July 1986): 645–655.

Boemio, Thomas R., and Gerald A. Edwards, Jr. "Asset Securitization: A Supervisory Perspective." *Federal Reserve Bulletin* 75 (October 1989): 659–669.

Booth, James R. "The Securitization of Lending Markets." *Weekly Letter* (Federal Reserve Bank of San Francisco), September 29, 1989.

Brewer, Elijah. "Bank Gap Management and the Use of Financial Futures." *Economic Perspectives* (Federal Reserve Bank of Chicago) 9 (March/April 1985): 12–22.

Bush, Vanessa. "FHLMC and FNMA: Adequate Capital Guarantees Their Future." *Savings Institutions* 111 (January 1990): 38–43.

————. "MBS: Different Players Give the Market a New Look." *Savings Institutions* 112 (October 1991): 18–23.

Cantor, Richard and Rebecca Demsetz. "Securitizaton, Loan Sales, and the Credit Slowdown." *Quarterly Review* (Federal Reserve Bank of New York) 18 (Summer 1993): 27–38.

Caouette, John B. "Securitization: What's Next?" In *Proceedings of a Conference on Bank Structure and Competition,* 304–309. Chicago: Federal Reserve Bank of Chicago, 1992.

Carlstrom, Charles T. and Katherine A. Samolyk. "Examining the Microfoundations of Market Incentives for Asset-Backed Lending." *Economic Review* (Federal Reserve Bank of Cleveland) 29 (Quarter 1 1993): 27–38.

————. "Securitization: More Than Just a Regulatory Artifact." *Economic Commentary* (Federal Reserve Bank of Cleveland) (May 1, 1992).

Chance, Don M. *An Introduction to Options and Futures.* Fort Worth: Dryden Press, 1992.

Chicago Board of Trade. *Interest Rate Futures for Institutional Investors.* Chicago: Board of Trade of the City of Chicago, 1985.

"Conference Report on H.R. 1278, Financial Institutions Reform, Recovery, and Enforcement Act, 1989." *Congressional Record—House of Representatives,* August 4, 1989.

Cumming, Christine. "The Economics of Securitization." *Quarterly Review* (Federal Reserve Bank of New York) 12 (Autumn 1987): 11–23.

Dreyer, Franklin D. "Statement before the Subcommittee on Policy Research and Insurance." *Federal Reserve Bulletin* 77 (September 1991): 726–731.

Ellspermann, W. R. "Supporting Growth through Securitization." *Magazine of Bank Administration* 64 (October 1988): 22–27.

Fabozzi, Frank J., and Atsuo Konishi, Eds. *Asset/Liability Management.* Chicago: Probus Publishing, 1991.

Felgran, Steven D. "Interest Rate Swaps: Use, Risk, and Prices." *New England Economic Review* (Federal Reserve Bank of Boston) (November/December 1987): 22–32.

Gau, George W., and Michael A. Goldberg. "Interest Rate Risk, Residential Mortgages, and Financial Futures Markets." *AREUEA Journal* 11 (1983): 445–461.

Haley, Charles W. "Interest Rate Risk in Financial Intermediaries: Prospects for Immunization." In *Proceedings of a Conference on Bank Structure and Competition,* 309–317. Chicago: Federal Reserve Bank of Chicago, 1982.

Houpt, James V., and James A. Embersit. "A Method for Evaluating Interest Rate Risk in U.S. Commercial Banks." *Federal Reserve Bulletin* 77 (August 1991): 625–637.

Hutchinson, Michael M. "Swaps." *Weekly Letter* (Federal Reserve Bank of San Francisco), May 3, 1985.

Jacobs, Rodney L. "Fixed-Rate Lending and Interest Rate Futures Hedging." *Journal of Bank Research* 13 (Autumn 1983): 193–202.

Jaffee, Dwight. "Interest Rate Hedging Strategies for Savings and Loan Associations." In *Managing Interest Rate Risk in the Thrift Industry,* 83–108. San Francisco: Federal Home Loan Bank of San Francisco, 1981.

Kane, Edward J., and Chester Foster. "Valuing Conjectural Government Guarantees of FNMA Liabilities." In *Proceedings of a Conference on Bank Structure and Competition,* 347–368. Chicago: Federal Reserve Bank of Chicago, 1986.

Kaufman, George. "Measuring and Managing Interest Rate Risk: A Primer." *Economic Perspectives* (Federal Reserve Bank of Chicago) 8 (January/February 1984): 16–29.

Kavanagh, Barbara, Thomas R. Boemio, and Gerald A. Edwards, Jr. "Asset-Backed Commercial Paper Programs." *Federal Reserve Bulletin* 78 (February 1992): 107–116.

Kolb, Robert W., Stephen G. Timme, and Gerald D. Gay. "Macro versus Micro Futures Hedges at Commercial Banks." *Journal of the Futures Markets* 4 (1984): 47–54.

Koppenhaver, Gary. "Trimming the Hedges: Regulators, Banks, and Financial Futures." *Economic Perspectives* (Federal Reserve Bank of Chicago) 8 (November/December 1984): 3–12.

Kulczycky, Maria. "GAP Management Eases Interest Rate Swings." *Savings Institutions* 109 (November 1988): 44–49.

Lam, James C. "A Management Framework for Hedging Thrift Risk." *Bankers Magazine* 172 (November/December 1989): 10–17.

Laudeman, Mark L. "An Application of Financial Futures to Fixed Rate Lending." *Journal of Commercial Bank Lending* 65 (August 1983): 23–35.

Leibowitz, Martin L. "Total Portfolio Duration: A New Perspective on Asset Allocation." *Financial Analysts Journal* 42 (September/October 1986): 18–29, 77.

Leibowitz, Martin L., et al. "A Total Differential Approach to Equity Duration." *Financial Analysts Journal* 45 (September/October 1989): 30–37.

Lewis, Vivian. "Stop and Swap." *Bankers Monthly* 106 (October 1989): 82–84.

Loeys, Jan G. "Interest Rate Swaps: A New Tool for Managing Risk." *Business Review* (Federal Reserve Bank of Philadelphia) (May/June 1985): 17–25.

Marshall, John F. "Futures Versus Swaps: Some Considerations for the Thrift Industry." *Review of Business* 12 (Winter 1990/1991): 15–22, 44.

Mays, Elizabeth. "Assessing Rate Risk Eases Exposure Shock." *Savings Institutions* 113 (February 1992): 24–28.

McCabe, George M., and Robert W. McLeod. "The Use of Financial Futures in Banking." *Journal of Commercial Bank Lending* 65 (August 1983): 6–22.

Morrison, Randall Clark. "Regulatory Problems in the Securitization of Bank Assets." *Financial Services Yearbook* 1 (1988): 147–212.

Nagle, Reid. "The Use of Financial Futures in Asset/Liability Management." In *Managing Interest Rate Risk in the Thrift Industry,* 109–132. San Francisco: Federal Home Loan Bank of San Francisco, 1981.

Neuberger, Jonathon A. "Interest Rate Risk and Capital Standards." *Weekly Letter* (Federal Reserve Bank of San Francisco) November 6, 1992.

Olson, Wayne. "Securitization Comes to Other Assets." *Savings Institutions* 107 (May 1986): 81–85.

Parliment, Tom. "Accurate Valuation of Deposits Aids in TB-13 Compliance." *Savings Institutions* 110 (May 1989): 80–81.

Pavel, Christine A. "Loan Sales Have Little Effect on Bank Risk." *Economic Perspectives* (Federal Reserve Bank of Chicago) 12 (March/April 1988): 23–31.

Pozdena, Randall Johnston. "Mortgage Securitization and REMICs." *Weekly Letter* (Federal Reserve Bank of San Francisco), May 8, 1987.

_____. "Securitization and Banking." *Weekly Letter* (Federal Reserve Bank of San Francisco), July 4, 1986.

Rosenberg, Joel L. "The Joys of Duration." *Bankers Magazine* 169 (March-April 1986): 62–67.

Rosenblum, Harvey. "Liability Strategies for Minimizing Interest Rate Risk." In *Managing Interest Rate Risk in the Thrift Industry,* 157–180. San Francisco: Federal Home Loan Bank of San Francisco, 1981.

"The Secondary Mortgage Market Is a Key to the Future." *Savings Institutions* 105 (January 1984): S1–S105.

Shaffer, Sherrill. "Interest Rate Risk: What's A Bank to Do?" *Business Review* (Federal Reserve Bank of Philadelphia) (May/June 1991): 17–27.

Shapiro, Harvey D. "The Securitization of Practically Everything." *Institutional Investor* 19 (May 1985): 196–202.

Silver, Daniel B., and Peter J. Axilrod. "Pushing Technology to Its Limits: Securitizing C&I Loans." *The Bankers Magazine* 172 (May-June 1989): 16–21.

Simonson, Donald G., and Dennis E. Bennett. "How Much Is Your Balance Sheet Worth?" *Trends and Topics* (Federal Home Loan Bank of Chicago) 4 (Winter 1985): 9–11.

Smith, Clifford W., Jr., and Charles W. Smithson, and Lee Macdonald Wakeman. "The Market for Interest Rate Swaps" *Financial Management* 18 (Winter 1988): 34–44.

Smith, Clifford W., Jr., Charles W. Smithson, and D. Sykes Wilford. *Managing Financial Risk.* New York: Harper and Row, 1990.

Smith, Stephen D. "Analyzing Risk and Return for Mortgage-Backed Securities." *Economic Review* (Federal Reserve Bank of Atlanta) 76 (January/February 1991): 2–11.

Smuckler, Gary. "The Secondary Mortgage Market." *Credit Union Executive* (Winter 1984): 12–19.

Spahr, Ronald W., Jan E. Luytjes, and Donald G. Edwards, "The Use of Caps as Deposit Hedges for Financial Institu-tions," *Issues in Bank Regulation* 12 (Summer 1988): 17–23.

Stigum, Marcia. *The Money Market.* 3d ed. Homewood, IL: Dow Jones-Irwin, 1990.

"Survey of World Banking." *The Economist* (May 2, 1992).

Swegle, Robert W., Jr. "Accounting for Asset Securitiza-tion." *The Bankers Magazine* 172 (May-June 1989): 22–24.

Toevs, Alden L. "Gap Management: Managing Interest Rate Risk in Banks and Thrifts." *Economic Review* (Federal Reserve Bank of San Francisco) (Spring 1983): 20–35.

_____. "Proper Tools Are Needed to Build a Good Risk Shelter." *Savings Institutions* 106 (April 1985): S75–S78.

Villani, Kevin. "Liquidity, Flexibility Spur the Market." *Savings Institutions* 106 (January 1985): S33–S36.

_____. "The Secondary Mortgage Markets: What They Are, What They Do, and How to Measure Them." *Secondary Mortgage Markets* 1 (February 1984): 24–44.

Wall, Larry D. "Recourse Risk in Asset Sales." *Economic Review* (Federal Reserve Bank of Atlanta) 76 (September/October 1991): 1–13.

Wall, Larry D., and John J. Pringle. "Interest Rate Swaps: A Review of the Issues." *Economic Review* (Federal Reserve Bank of Atlanta) 73 (November/December 1988): 22–40.

_____. "Alternative Explanations of Interest Rate Swaps: A Theoretical and Empirical Analysis." *Financial Management* 18 (Summer 1989): 59–73.

Wall, Larry D., John J. Pringle, and James E. McNulty, "Capital Requirements for Interest Rate and Foreign-Exchange Hedges." *Economic Review* (Federal Reserve Bank of Atlanta) 75 (May/June 1990): 14–29.

Walters, Jeffrey M. "The Futures Alternative to Fixed-Rate Financing." *Journal of Commercial Bank Lending* 67 (February 1985): 39–46.

Whittaker, J. Gregg. "Interest Rate Swaps: Risk and Regulation." *Economic Review* (Federal Reserve Bank of Kansas City) 72 (March 1987): 3–13.

Wurman, Leslie K. "The Synthetic Fixed Rate Loan: An Illustration." *Market Perspectives* (Chicago Mercantile Exchange) 6 (September 1988): 1–3.

*Manny Hanny's people are wedded to their system,
and Chemical's are wedded to theirs. It's a religious issue.*
Edward D. Miller,
Vice Chairman, Manufacturer's Hanover (now Chemical) (1991)

"Don't leave home without them." For many years, American Express used this advertisement to urge travelers to buy its well-known traveler's checks. By the early 1990s, most international travelers would not have considered boarding an international flight without a stack of traveler's checks in a pocket or purse. But by the mid-to-late 1990s, things may be different. Why? Because some of the largest **automated teller machine (ATM)** networks in the United States have already expanded their market to Europe, and further expansion is on the horizon. These ATMs give international travelers the opportunity to obtain cash in a foreign currency, either by withdrawing it from their accounts in U.S. banks or through a cash advance on a MasterCard, Visa, or other credit card.

Obtaining cash from an ATM rather than writing a traveler's check offers several advantages. One is a preferential exchange rate, because machine transactions are processed at a wholesale rate applying to exchanges of $1 million or more. That rate may be as much as 5 to 10 percent better than one offered to travelers at hotels or banks. Another advantage is a universal benefit of ATMs—24-hour access. These benefits led *The Wall Street Journal* to note that visitors to the American Express office in Rome or Prague would benefit by leaving their traveler's checks at home and visiting the ATMs outside those offices instead.[1]

By 1993, the two largest ATM networks had more than 40,000 ATMs abroad. The number of cash dispensing machines in international locations is expected to multiply rapidly in the next 5 to 10 years, but so is the number of ATMs in the United States. In fact, many banks are increasingly relying on ATMs rather than bank branches to expand their operating regions. But the equipment is expensive, and investment decisions must be analyzed carefully; once undertaken, they must be managed properly to increase the probability that expected benefits will materialize. The investment in international locations requires even greater attention to the evaluation of risk and expected benefits. Long-term asset/liability management, such as an investment in ATMs, is explored in this chapter.

C H A P T E R

20

LONG-TERM

ASSET/LIABILITY

MANAGEMENT

DECISIONS: EFT

AND MERGERS

---

[1] One important benefit of traveler's checks, of course, is the safety they offer through issuers' replacement guarantees. See Kenneth H. Bacon, "For Trips Abroad, Technology Offers New Alternative to Traveler's Checks," *The Wall Street Journal,* July 7, 1992, C1, C17.

SHORT-RUN VERSUS LONG-RUN DECISIONS

A main portion of the material in Chapters 13 through 19 focuses on decisions that restructure a depository's balance sheet in response to expected changes in interest rates or to actions of competitors and regulators. Many of those decisions are intended to be relatively short-term adjustments. Even if they are not, they can usually be reversed, should conditions dictate, through the natural passage of time. For example, the periodic maturing of loans and deposits provides managers with opportunities to alter the asset and liability mix, undoing past decisions if necessary. Thus, even though costs are associated with making the wrong portfolio decisions, few such decisions are irreversible.

Other decisions that restructure the balance sheet may be harder to undo. Implementing a plan to computerize lending and deposit taking, which substantially increases investment in fixed assets, may take months or even years. Once the equipment is in place, only as it wears out or becomes technologically obsolete are there automatic opportunities to reverse the course, so management must be prepared to monitor decisions and to take action necessary to secure their success. If not, the consequences of a bad decision may be costly. Frequently, as in this example, decisions that are difficult to undo involve investment in real, instead of financial, assets.

This chapter examines long-term asset/liability planning in depository institutions, beginning with a decision framework for long-term investments. The framework is applied to two of the most important types of long-term decisions made by depositories: 1) whether to invest in electronic funds transfer equipment; and 2) whether to merge by acquiring another financial institution. Although the information in this chapter is limited to those two issues, the process illustrated applies to any long-term commitment of funds by the institution, such as opening a new branch office or remodeling headquarters.

THE MODEL FOR LONG-TERM INVESTMENT DECISIONS

Students of corporate finance need not look far for a model of long-term investment in depositories, because **net present value (NPV)** is relevant for both nonfinancial and financial firms.

GENERAL FORMULA

The net present value of a decision is the present value of the after-tax cash inflows expected during a planning period (N) netted against the present value of the expected after-tax cash outflows required. This concept is reflected in the formula below, in which i is used in a general sense to reflect the interest rate, discount rate, or required rate of return. This is the same sense in which i is used to reflect the general level of market yields in earlier chapters.

[20.1]

$$NPV = \sum_{t=0}^{N} \frac{C_t}{(1 + i)^t}$$

Periodic cash flows (C_t) can be positive or negative, depending on whether they are inflows or outflows. The only relevant after-tax cash benefits and costs are *incremental* ones—those cash flows specifically resulting from the proposed decision, *not* those expected whether or not the decision is made.

MODIFICATIONS TO THE GENERAL FORMULA

Of course, no single interest or discount rate applies to all present value decisions. The discount rate used to calculate an NPV should reflect the riskiness of the decision. For long-term decisions considered to be of average risk compared with the ongoing operations of the business, the weighted average cost of capital (k_A) is often suggested as the appropriate discount rate. Introduced in Chapter 17, k_A represents the average yield expected by the institution's suppliers of long-term funds. Thus, the NPV model for projects of average risk is

[20.2]

$$NPV = \sum_{t=0}^{N} \frac{C_t}{(1 + k_A)^t}$$

Investments of above- or below-average risk should be discounted at a rate lower or higher than the cost of capital.[2]

---

[2] Selecting the proper discount rate for decisions that are not of average risk is not a cut-and-dried matter. Some scholars advocate using a Capital Asset Pricing Model (CAPM)-determined rate re-

If cash outflows are expected only when the decision is made, the NPV equation is often written as

$$\text{NPV} = \sum_{t=1}^{N} \frac{C_t}{(1 + k_A)^t} - C_0 \qquad [20.3]$$

In Equation 20.3, C_0 is the after-tax cash cost of a project.

OBJECTIVE OF NPV ANALYSIS

Once cash flows have been estimated, calculating the NPV is a mechanical task that acquires meaning only with proper interpretation. Fortunately, interpretation is straightforward: If the NPV of a decision is positive, the institution expects to earn more than its minimum required rate of return; the present value (PV) of benefits outweighs the PV of costs, including the opportunity cost reflected in the discount rate. If the NPV is negative, the opposite is true. If the NPV is $0, the decision is expected to have a neutral long-term financial effect on the institution.

A positive NPV is economically desirable; value will be added to the existing value of the institution. A negative NPV decision will decrease the value of the institution, and a $0 NPV decision will leave value unchanged. Thus, institutions avoid negative NPV decisions unless required for legal or regulatory reasons.

NPV analysis has another desirable characteristic from a decision-making standpoint. The NPVs of investments can be compared directly with one another because each NPV calculation implicitly considers the size and riskiness of the project involved. Thus,

if one decision has an NPV of $50,000 while another has an NPV of only $40,000, a manager knows that the higher NPV project is expected to add more value to the institution, even if it costs more initially and is riskier. Although both projects are acceptable, the $50,000 NPV project is better.

NPV ANALYSIS AND THE NET INTEREST MARGIN

An institution's long-term investment decisions can affect interest revenues and expenses, noninterest revenues and expenses, or both. Thus, on a year-by-year basis, they affect the net interest margin (NIM) and return on net worth (RONW), just as other management decisions do. But because projects most suitable for NPV analysis are often relatively small compared with the institution's overall portfolio, their impact on the firm from start to finish can get lost in the short run. NPV analysis attempts to isolate the effect of a single decision on the long-run value of the depository. Thus, it is complementary to, not in conflict with, strategies for short-run asset/liability management.

ELECTRONIC FUNDS TRANSFER SYSTEMS

Analyzing potential investments in electronic funds transfer (EFT) systems is an important application of NPV models. First defined in Chapter 2, EFTs are methods of transmitting funds from one party to another by electronically encoded impulses rather than by paper check, money order, currency and coin, or other physical means. Although nonphysical methods of transferring funds date at least to the establishment of the Federal Reserve System's (Fed's) wire transfer system in 1915, emphasis on EFTs has grown in recent years.

For example, the federal government promotes direct deposit of Social Security payments to individuals and, in 1987, began to pay many of its own suppliers electronically. Originally, direct deposit or payment transactions involved magnetic tapes electronically encoded with instructions, which were delivered to regional Federal Reserve Banks for processing. The Fed would increase the account of the recipient's institution and, in turn, notify the institution

---

flecting the yield the financial markets require on financial assets that are equivalent in risk to the project at hand. This approach requires estimating the β coefficient of the project, a difficult process for investments without a large body of data. Others suggest selecting the discount rate based on different measures of risk, such as the standard deviation or coefficient of variation of the investment's cash flows. Practitioners often suggest a subjective assessment, adjusting the discount rate up or down from the cost of capital, depending on management's personal assessment of project risk.

There are many discussions of these alternatives and other NPV issues, among which are Richard Brealey and Stuart Myers, *Principles of Corporate Finance* (New York: McGraw-Hill, 1991), Chapters 5, 6, and 9; Haim Levy and Marshall Sarnatt, *Capital Investment and Financial Decisions,* 3d ed. (Englewood Cliffs, NJ: Prentice-Hall, 1986); and Seed 1982. (References are listed in full at the end of this chapter.)

to increase the recipient's account. Recently, many direct deposit transactions have become truly electronic, with instructions sent by computers and telephone lines and involving no physical transfers of computer tapes or paper.

ADVANTAGES AND DISADVANTAGES OF EFT

The advantages of direct deposit and electronic payment—two applications of EFT—are numerous. Many transactions can be completed almost instantaneously. Record keeping is streamlined, enabling large users to reduce personnel costs. Checks cannot get lost in the mail, destroyed, or stolen. Funds are deposited even when the recipient is hospitalized or immobile. Finally, the mountain of paper processed by the government, the depository institution, and the recipient is reduced.

There are disadvantages, too. The equipment for processing transactions electronically is expensive. Transactions can be executed incorrectly, creating difficulty in tracing the source of the error once funds have been transferred. Further, there is a small risk of loss through fraud or damaged equipment.

Many institutions and individuals have concluded in recent years that the benefits of EFTs far outweigh their disadvantages. A staff study for the Board of Governors of the Fed found, in fact, that as early as 1981, the present value of the savings to the federal government and financial institutions from direct deposit of Social Security benefits in lieu of paper checks ranged from $4.11 to $51.62 *per account,* depending on how a recipient actually deposited his or her check. Considering the millions of Social Security accounts, the potential savings are substantial, and direct deposit is only one of many possible ways EFT can replace checks. At the time the federal government implemented its electronic payment program, the estimated cost of writing and mailing a check to a supplier was 26 cents. An electronic payment was expected to cost only 3 cents, promising sizable cost reductions for the federal Treasury.[3]

Depository institutions also recognize the potential savings available through increased customer usage of EFTs. By 1990, in fact, the estimated cost of a check transaction had reached 79 cents, compared with electronic transfer costs in the range of 29 to 47 cents per transaction.[4] Thus, banks, thrifts, and credit unions (CUs) have offered a variety of promotions to encourage customer use and acceptance of electronic systems. Institutions face a wide range of EFT applications, and the options continue to increase rapidly. A brief overview of EFT systems available to institutions is useful before examining an application of the NPV framework to an EFT decision.

AUTOMATED CLEARINGHOUSES

A clearinghouse is a system through which a depository institution receives information about payments to and from its customers' accounts. Since its creation, the Fed has played a major role in clearing services as part of its mandate to provide the nation with a stable payments system. Typically, regional Federal Reserve Banks serve as clearing locations where institutions' accounts are debited or credited as necessary, and checks are sorted, bundled, and returned to participating depositories. Often the Fed's clearing services are supplemented by privately operated systems, such as the New York Clearing House Association, which arose to assist institutions with large numbers of daily transactions drawn on one another.

By the 1970s, population growth and prosperity had pushed estimates of the annual volume of paper checks in the 1980s to astronomical levels, beyond the capabilities of existing processing systems.[5] This con-

clude estimates of the relative costs and benefits of both systems to the payment recipients.

The transition to electronic transfers can be slow. By the early 1990s, the federal government was still disbursing almost 60 percent of its payments by paper check. See Wood and Smith 1991.

[4] These cost estimates are cited in Humphrey and Berger 1990.

[5] Based on the annual growth rate in check volume from 1960 to 1973, an estimate of 1985 check volume was 54 billion items, made in the 1970s in Knight 1974. Actually, by 1988, annual check volume had reached only 51 billion items: experts expected the volume to peak in the early 1990s. See Benjamin Christopher, "Recent Developments Affecting Depository Institutions," *FDIC Banking Review* 2 (Spring/Summer 1989): 43.

[3] William Dudley, "A Comparison of Direct Deposit and Check Payment Costs," Board of Governors of the Fed, Staff Study No. 141, November 1984. Dudley's estimates do not include the costs of fraud with either check or direct deposit payments, nor do they in-

cern led to the formation of **automated clearing-houses (ACHs),** processing systems established by private institutions agreeing to exchange information by magnetic tape. The Fed and four private processing organizations handle transactions, with the Fed processing by far the largest volume. In 1990, the New York ACH, the third largest processor, converted its operations to a totally electronic system, eliminating reliance on magnetic tapes. In 1991, the Fed announced that it would accept only electronic transmissions of commercial ACH transactions as of July 1993.

The role of the Fed in ACH operations has been controversial. On the one hand, some argue that the cost of establishing an ACH is so great that only the Fed can afford it. If promoting EFTs is in the nation's best interests, Fed involvement is indicated. On the other hand, it can be argued that federal presence in the development of ACHs prevents private initiative and innovation. Congress was influenced by the latter view in 1980, when the Depository Institutions Deregulation and Monetary Control Act (DIDMCA) included a requirement that the Fed price its own clearing services so as not to stifle private entry into the market. In 1990, the Fed announced its intention to turn over many of its funds-transfer functions to the private sector. Predictably, this announcement too was controversial. Large institutions welcomed what they believe is an opportunity to compete without regulatory interference, but small institutions fear their costs will increase without government involvement.[6]

The federal government is also the largest user of ACHs. Not only does it encourage Social Security recipients to use direct deposit, but it also encourages federal employees and federal suppliers to accept salaries, wages, and payments that way. Other major users include life insurance companies, many of which encourage customers to preauthorize electronic transfer of premium payments from their accounts to the insurers'. In 1991, the Fed alone processed more than 1 billion commercial ACH transactions, an increase of almost 25 percent over the previous year.[7]

ACHs in the Future. Resistance to EFT from large corporations has been perhaps the single biggest reason why ACH usage has not yet reached the level forecast by early proponents. The traditional method of meeting a payroll allows corporations to use the float. If payday is on a Friday and an employee cashes or deposits his or her check on the way home from work, the corporation has the use of the funds at least until Monday when the check is physically cleared at the nearest Fed or other clearinghouse. Float is also available on other types of corporate funds transfers, such as the payment of accounts payable.[8]

Historical opposition to EFT from large corporations is declining, however. DIDMCA's mandate to the Fed to reduce or eliminate the float has resulted in attempts to speed check processing of all types and to charge the users of any remaining float. The **Expedited Funds Availability Act** (Title VI of the Competitive Equality Banking Act [CEBA]) also mandated faster processing of checks to make funds accessible to customers more quickly. In some cases, depositories have responded by charging customers higher fees for paper transactions. As corporations automate routine functions to increase productivity of computer systems, EFT usage has also benefited. Between 1986 and 1989, the number of private-sector funds transfers through ACHs more than doubled, a fact which observers attributed to the increased popularity of direct payroll deposits and electronic settlement of accounts payable.

The decreasing cost of electronic equipment and changing customer attitudes increase the likelihood that ACH volume will grow in the 1990s. The transformation of the New York Clearing House and the Fed's ACH to all-electronic processing was accompanied by a significant growth in transactions, attributed by managers to customer recognition of the improved effectiveness and efficiency of services.

Yet some uncertainty remains in the outlook for automated transfers. By 1992, for example, only 10

---

[6] For further discussion, see Shull 1981, 696; Stone 1986b,c; Duprey 1986; and Jeanne Ida, "Fed Plan to Cut Payments Role Divides Bankers," *American Banker,* May 9, 1990, 1, 3.

[7] Board of Governors of the Federal Reserve System, *1991 Annual Report,* 228.

[8] In 1983, for example, the Westinghouse Electric Corporation estimated that it would have a net loss of approximately $2.7 million per year if it used EFT rather than checks for accounts payable; although substantial savings in banking fees and administrative costs could be achieved, the loss of the float pushed the overall result into the red. See Robert L. Caruso, "New Look at ACH Cost/Benefit Details," *ABA Banking Journal* 75 (April 1983): 44–45. For other sources of corporate resistance, see Stone 1986a.

percent of private sector employees in the United States received salaries through ACH transfers compared with 67 percent of government employees. Federal Reserve float in 1991 was still almost $350 billion, although that figure represented a substantial reduction from previous years. The existence of float continues to be an influential factor in the use of paper checks. Many experts believe check writers are not yet charged the full costs of using the float, and the legal status of policies to charge them for access to the float also remains unclear. Finally, consumer habits continue to favor checks for many transactions.[9]

AUTOMATED TELLER MACHINES

As their name suggests, ATMs are machines that perform the functions of tellers using electronic instructions from a customer. ATMs verify account balances, dispense cash, accept deposits, receive bill payments, and even make loans. They are available 24 hours a day. Of all the EFT applications, ATMs are by far the most commonly used by consumers. By 1992, over 85,000 ATMs had been installed in the United States; during one month in late 1992, just over 600 million consumer ATM transactions were recorded.[10]

CUSTOMER ATTITUDES TOWARD ATMs. Because of their dominant role, ATMs provide the basis for most research into consumer attitudes toward EFT. Early surveys indicated that consumers did not like the substitution of machines for human beings and that they were apprehensive about the safety and security of ATM transactions. In recent years, however, data on transactions volumes suggest increasing approval of ATMs. From 1978 to 1988 usage per ATM per month increased at a compound annual rate of almost 25 percent. The number of ATMs increased at an annual rate of 22 percent during the same period. This growth in total transactions and in average number of transac-

tions per machine is impressive evidence that customers will accept substitutes for paper checks. By 1991, researchers estimated that 68 percent of all Americans owned an ATM card, and that 53 percent of these cardholders used ATM services regularly. ATMs are generally found to be most popular with younger people, those with higher educational levels, and city dwellers who are frequent users of credit cards.[11]

Customer acceptance of EFT has been modeled according to the theory of **innovation adoption.** According to this theory, the proportion of individuals accepting a particular innovation follows an S-curve, such as the one projected for ATMs by researchers at the Federal Reserve Bank of Atlanta, shown in Figure 20.1. When an innovation appears, the proportion of people willing to try it grows slowly, as occurred with the ATM from 1977 to 1980. Then a point is reached at which popularity increases rapidly, and the slope of the adoption curve becomes much steeper, as depicted for the period 1980–1984. Finally, the rate of adoption slows, because most people willing to try the innovation have already done so. That phase is illustrated by the 1984–1986 period in Figure 20.1. In 1983, the time of the Atlanta Fed study, the ATM was expected to plateau at an adoption level of 65 percent by 1987. Interestingly, the researchers' projections were optimistic. ATM market penetration did not rise above the 60 percent level until 1991. Some researchers believe the adoption of other EFT systems will follow a similar pattern.[12]

ATMs IN THE FUTURE. Although market penetration has not grown at the predicted rates, the number of ATMs has continued to increase. The U.S. Postal Service announced in early 1990 that banks would even be invited to place ATMs in post office lobbies. But as the number of installed machines has grown, institutions have been increasingly concerned about the rate of usage of those machines needed to recover the high costs of purchases, installation, and maintenance.

[9] See Laderman 1992; Board of Governors, *Annual Report 1991,* 230; and Summers 1988.

[10] See Matt Barthel, "ATM Growth Puts a Lid on Branch Costs," *American Banker,* December 7, 1992, 1, 3; and Barton Crockett, "EDS Plans Its Own Network of 10,000 Teller Machines," *American Banker,* August 20, 1992, 1, 3.

[11] For examples of research on consumer usage of EFT, see Taube 1988; Lederman 1988; and Christine Winter, "ATMs a Perk, Pain and Fact of Life," *Chicago Tribune,* September 9, 1988, Section 4, 1, 5.

[12] Melia 1991 and Cox and Metzker 1983.

FIGURE 20.1   **Innovative Adoption Curve for ATMs**

Theory holds that the percentage of customers adopting an innovation follows an S-shaped pattern. Accordingly, the innovation adoption curve that researchers projected for ATMs shows low growth at first, followed by a period of widespread adoption, followed by a return to low growth.

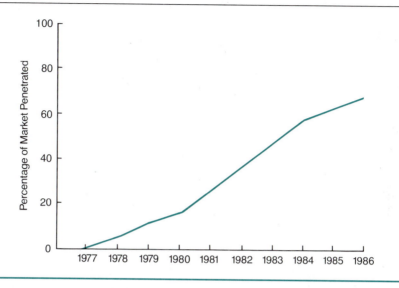

Source: William N. Cox and Paul F. Metzker, "Special Issue: Displacing the Check," *Economic Review* (Federal Reserve Bank of Atlanta) 68 (August 1983): 33.

The differences in ATM's frequency of usage across various customer groups and geographic regions has not gone unnoticed by depository institutions, and ATMs are often placed strategically. As early as 1985, for example, ATMs located on the University of Pennsylvania campus were generating 47,000 to 60,000 transactions per month. Citibank has opened CitiStations that look like gas stations, but with ATMs instead of pumps. The machines adjust to accommodate drivers in all types of vehicles and are located on busy commuting routes between New York City and its suburbs. Some institutions have even developed mobile ATMs that follow customers; when traffic patterns shift, so can ATM locations.

Many institutions are less worried about the number of transactions than about the size of the transaction and its cost-effectiveness. Some institutions have begun to discuss new pricing strategies to impose extra charges for using ATMs. In 1992, for example, Citibank announced plans to charge its customers $1 for every transaction on an ATM outside the Citibank ATM system. These policies signal a new attitude toward ATMs—one that changed the focus from persuading customers to accept ATMs to recognizing that many customers actually prefer ATMs and might pay for the privilege of using them. Uncertainty remains about the potential effect of these new pricing systems on the volume of ATM transactions, although a 1990 survey found that almost half of ATM users said fees would not reduce their usage.[13]

Several other important influences affect the costs to institutions of providing ATMs to customers, and, consequently, influence ATM pricing decisions. One of these is the Americans with Disabilities Act of 1990. This act prohibits discrimination against disabled persons in any publicly available service or location, including ATMs. Institutions must make some

---

[13] See Yvette D. Kantrow, "Citibank Plans to Charge $1 for Use of 'Foreign' ATMs," *American Banker,* December 1, 1992, 5; Lynn Homa, "ATM Fees Are Gaining Acceptance," *American Banker,* October 24, 1990, 6; Lederman 1988; and Linda Fenner Zimmer, "A Time for Opportunity," *Magazine of Bank Administration* 61 (May 1985): 20–32.

changes in existing teller machines, and more extensive adjustments are required in newly installed or renovated ATMs. Issues include assuring that the height of machines makes them accessible to wheelchair customers and that ramps are installed to replace steps. More problematic is service to blind customers. Providing braille keypads is an intermediate step, but it is possible that audio technology will be needed in the future.

Another policy issue of expanding importance is developing methods to ensure customer safety. Although not numerous, several violent incidents at ATM sites were widely publicized in the late 1980s and early 1990s. Institutions recognized that they must take steps to reduce the danger to their customers. Subsequently, several state legislatures adopted laws setting mandatory standards for lighting and visibility at ATMs, besides requiring that customers be given safety literature.[14]

HOME BANKING

Perhaps the most unusual EFT application is **home banking,** in which a customer directs the transfer of funds from his or her checking account using an in-home video terminal. Although the novelty of this application attracted considerable attention in the early 1980s, including predictions that it would be in use by 30 to 40 percent of all American homes by 1990, home banking is not a major force in EFT. Its potential is limited for two reasons: 1) It is costly for customers, who must have a computer terminal or microcomputer and modem at home; and 2) the most popular EFT transactions, withdrawing cash and making deposits, are not possible with home banking.

By 1989, only 36 institutions had home-banking programs, with only 100,000 subscribers nationwide. Few observers predict sizable market penetration in the near future unless improved technology allows the service to be priced more attractively. In the early 1990s, however as nationwide computer information networks gained acceptance by home computer enthusiasts, several large banks reentered the home banking

market. Others increased their investments in technology in hopes of building their customer base.[15]

POINT-OF-SALE TERMINALS AND DEBIT CARDS

An EFT application with more growth potential is the **point-of-sale (POS) terminal** and the accompanying use of **debit cards.** POS terminals are in-store machines to transfer funds from a buyer's to a seller's account when the buyer uses an electronically encoded debit card. The debit card is used with a number known only to the buyer (the **personal identification number,** or **PIN**) and is a substitute for a checkbook. PINs are also used with ATMs, and the plastic cards required to access many ATMs are a type of debit card because they permit the immediate withdrawal of funds from a customer's account.

As is true of other electronic transfers, a customer paying by debit card at a POS terminal loses use of the float. A 1984 survey by the Bank Administration Institute, however, found that consumers objected more to the loss of canceled checks and the possibility of computer error than to the loss of the float.[16] Thus, debit transactions do not automatically appeal to purchasers, unless there are other cost-saving reasons to use them instead of checks or credit cards. With the increasing cost of checking accounts and with recent increases in fees and interest on credit cards, however, the loss of the float may become less costly than other methods of payment.

POS AND DEBIT CARDS IN THE FUTURE. An increasing number of consumers carry debit cards; approximately 2 percent of U.S. households reported holding some type of debit card in 1992. As shown in Figure 20.2, the growth in debit card transactions was rapid between 1987 and 1991, averaging almost 40 percent annually—a growth rate projected to acceler-

---

[14] See Melia 1991; Laura G. Bellet, "Banks Scramble to Make ATMs Accessible to Disabled," *American Banker,* December 7, 1992, 11A; and Matt Barthel, "Banks Under the Gun as ATM Safety Laws Increase," *American Banker,* December 7, 1992, 12A, 13A.

[15] See Jan Jaben, "Can Home Banking Rise from the Ashes?" *Bankers Monthly* 106 (May 1989): 50–55; Laura Zinn, "Electronic Banking May Have to Log Off," *Business Week,* April 10, 1988, 75; Barton Crockett, "Chemical Plans to Again Offer Home Banking via PC," *American Banker,* December 23, 1992, 3.

[16] See Marjolijn van der Velde, "Point of Sale: Attitudes and Perceptions of Financial Institutions, Merchants and Customers," *Magazine of Bank Administration* 60 (April 1985): 42–48.

FIGURE 20.2   Growth in Debit Card Transactions

Although still a small proportion of total financial transactions, debit card and POS transactions have grown rapidly in recent years. Their acceptance by consumers and merchants is expected to accelerate use during the 1990s.

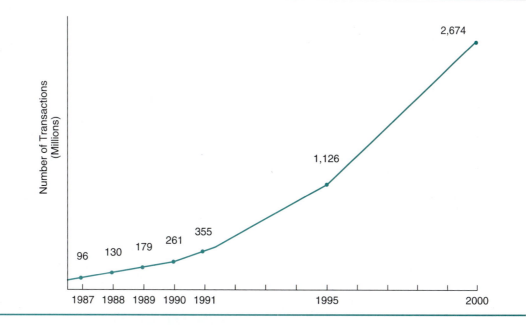

Source: Jeane Ida, "After Series of False Starts, Debit Cards Show Promise," *American Banker,* August 18, 1992, 1.

ate throughout the 1990s. Debit card usage is also likely to benefit from the increased acceptance and use of ATMs, because often the same card and PIN are used for both types of EFT transactions.

The growth in POS transactions using debit cards also depends on the attitudes of merchants and issuing institutions. They must both be linked electronically for a POS transaction to occur. But a system for sharing the costs of the technology considered equitable by both parties has been difficult to develop. Merchants have resisted the cost structure offered by some institutions, and some depositories have had to reduce fees to attract retail outlets. About 60 percent of banks also charge the cardholders an annual fee for debit card privileges.

Another issue affecting debit card use is the choice between an off-line and an on-line system. In an off-line system, all transactions are accumulated during the day and processed as a batch at the same time. An on-line system transmits information imme-

diately to the institution holding a customer's funds on deposit. The on-line system, although more expensive, prevents use of a debit card when a customer's balance is insufficient to cover the purchase. Thus institutions can offer the cards to more customers, rather than reserving them for a small group of high-balance accounts. By increasing volume, institutions choosing higher-cost, on-line systems hope to recover their investment and recognize a profit. By 1992, on-line systems processed about half of all debit card transactions, but many of the institutions involved were still waiting for the projected earnings.[17]

---

[17] See Barton Crockett, "Banks Unlikely to Find a Bonanza in Debit Cards," *American Banker,* September 2, 1992, 1, 10; and Jeanne Iida, "After Series of False Starts, Debit Cards Show Promise," *American Banker,* August 18, 1992, 1, 6.

SHARED EFT SYSTEMS

An important decision that individual institutions must make about EFT is whether to invest in equipment that only their customers can use—**proprietary systems**—or whether to initiate or join **shared systems.** Because of high start-up costs, many small institutions participate in shared ATM and POS systems. Institutions investing in electronic equipment can also benefit from shared systems by earning fee income from participating depositories.

Shared networks are also attractive because they allow customers to use ATMs across a wider geographic area. By 1990, about 85 percent of ATM terminals in the United States were shared with at least one other institution. The growth in shared systems is to a certain extent the result of legal requirements, because many states have enacted laws that require sharing of ATM networks. Yet sharing is also widespread in states without these laws.

As one would expect, however, shared systems also introduce complications. Depositories sharing ATMs must work cooperatively with institutions that would otherwise be competitors, meaning that network policies that benefit one member benefit all. Therefore, incentives exist for institutions to circumvent pricing agreements to profit at the expense of other members without sacrificing the advantages of network participation.

Despite these frictions, the ability of shared systems to offer accessibility and convenience to customers continues to enhance their growth potential. In fact, the wider the geographic range of a network, the more customers are willing to pay to use it. As noted in the opening paragraphs of this chapter, networks are even expanding to international markets, and no decline in this trend is anticipated.[18]

PARTIALLY ELECTRONIC FUNDS TRANSFER

A final application of nontraditional funds transfers for which there is growth potential could be called "PEFT," for partially electronic funds transfers. The best example is **check truncation.** With check trun-

cation, an account holder writes a check, and the payee deposits or cashes it as usual. The check writer, however, never receives a canceled check on completion of the transaction. The "paper trail" may stop at either the clearinghouse or the payee's bank. The check itself may be put into storage or filmed and destroyed. Information on the check is electronically encoded and included as part of the account holder's regular monthly statement.

Credit unions were pioneers in check truncation, and many share drafts are truncated. The motivation for shortening the paper trail is that the issuing institution reduces processing costs. Although early speculation held that customers would oppose truncation, CUs and thrifts, whose customers' checking accounts are relatively new anyway, have not faced great resistance. Banks, which have historically provided full check processing, have had a more difficult time introducing truncation, because their customers have perceived it as a decrease in service. Recently, however, the acceptance of check truncation has increased even among commercial bank customers.[19]

REGULATION OF EFT

As with most operations of depository institutions, EFT is regulated. In the Electronic Funds Transfer Act of 1974, Congress instructed each of the major depository institution regulators to enforce provisions guaranteeing consumers the right of redress in case of electronic errors, the right to receive receipts for EFT transactions, limited liability for fraudulent use of a debit card or PIN, and other protections. These regulations were codified by the Fed in **Regulation E** (Reg E), which serves as a model for other regulators.

Initially, depositories expressed concern about the cost of compliance with Reg E, which first took effect in 1980. In 1985, however, a study for the Board of Governors of the Fed indicated that large institutions enjoy substantial economies of scale in compliance costs. Although small institutions offering a full line of proprietary EFT services may be at a cost disadvantage, those wishing to join shared systems can benefit from scale economies. Further, the Fed has amended Reg E to exempt depositories with less than $25 million in assets. The study also found "negligible" fraud and error with EFT, suggesting that consumers will not be jeopardized as EFT displaces traditional methods of funds delivery.[20]

APPLICATION OF NPV ANALYSIS TO EFT

The analysis to follow focuses on one of the simplest and most common long-term decisions facing depositories: whether to invest in ATMs for dispensing cash, the EFT transaction most popular with customers. A systematic plan should be followed. The first step is to determine the time frame. Then, expected cash inflows and cash outflows—on an incremental, after-tax basis—are estimated. Next, a discount rate is selected, based on the relative riskiness of the decision. Finally, the NPV is calculated. If it is positive, the decision should be undertaken. If the NPV is negative, the plan should be rejected. If it is $0, it is a matter of indifference.

ESTIMATING THE TIME FRAME

There are a few rules for estimating a planning horizon. Sometimes a long-term decision has a known horizon, such as the termination date on a lease. In other situations, the planning period is a matter of judgment. For example, if the decision involves EFT with the possibility of technological obsolescence, the physical life of the equipment may be quite different from its economic life. In any case, the mathematics of present value mean that planning periods of great length are usually unnecessary. The present value of a cash flow expected at a point far in the future is virtually nil anyway.

Suppose that in 1994, a thrift is considering the installation of four cash-dispensing machines at stra-

tegic locations in the community, such as shopping malls and grocery stores. The proposed machines are state of the art and are not anticipated to become obsolete for 10 years; their physical life is likely to be longer. Because the present value of cash flows expected in later years, especially at relatively high discount rates, is quite small, management decides that the period from the beginning of 1994 to the end of the year 2004, an 11-year horizon, is most appropriate.

ESTIMATING THE CASH FLOWS

The next step in the NPV analysis is estimating incremental cash costs and benefits.

NET CASH OUTFLOWS. The thrift currently has several ATMs that it plans to continue operating. Thus, the cost of the four new machines will be entirely incremental; there is no salvage value in 1994 from selling existing machines. Furthermore, no large cash outflows are expected after time 0. The price of a single ATM is estimated at $40,000, but when four are purchased at once, they can be obtained for $35,000 apiece. Installation will add another $35,000 total to the cost in 1994. These figures are certain, because they are based on firm quotations from the ATM vendor. Thus, total cash outflows are $175,000.[21]

NET CASH INFLOWS. The cash benefits expected from the new ATMs are much less certain. Both the per-transaction cash savings to the institution over the next 10 years and the volume of transactions are subject to variation. Based on figures available to

---

[20] Frederick J. Schroeder, "Compliance Costs and Consumer Benefits of the Electronic Funds Transfer Act: Recent Survey Evidence," Board of Governors of the Fed, Staff Study No. 143, April 1985; and Schroeder 1983.

[21] Because long-term investments may change revenues and expenses of the firm, they have tax implications for most institutions. Discussion of specific tax issues is beyond the scope of this text. In practice, managers of banks and thrifts pay careful attention to taxation, because the tax savings involved in an investment, including the depreciation tax shield, may substantially affect the estimate of value.

In this section, most of the estimates of cash flow and volume are based on actual and projected published data. Main sources for these estimates are Cox and Metzker 1983; "Electronic Banking," *Business Week,* January 18, 1982, 80–90; Marjolijn van der Velde, "Two New Models Tell How Much an ATM Transaction *Really* Costs," *Magazine of Bank Administration* 59 (June 1983): 34–40; Judy Wenzel, "Electronic Buying to Come, in TYME," *Milwaukee Journal.* March 6, 1983, Business and Finance Section, 1; and Melia 1991.

management, the per-transaction savings expected when a customer uses an ATM instead of writing a check for cash ranges from $0.15 to $2.50, depending on what happens to a check during processing. The most likely savings is $0.45.

A manager can make a better decision if probabilities are attached to several possible outcomes, and the expected cash savings is based on those probabilities. Suppose there is only a 1 percent chance that the per-transaction savings will be $2.50, a 26 percent chance that the savings will be $0.15, and a 73 percent chance that the cash benefit will be $0.45. The expected per-transaction savings is

$$0.01(\$2.50) + 0.26(\$0.15)$$
$$+ 0.73(\$0.45) = \$0.39.$$

For simplicity, the manager also assumes that the costs of ATM and paper transactions will increase by approximately equal amounts so that year-to-year per-transaction savings will remain the same over the 10-year period. If this were not the case, separate savings could be estimated for each year. All cash savings are also estimated on an after-tax basis.

Estimating volume is a bit trickier, but clues are available. Using 1983 and 18 billion personal payments as base figures, assume that researchers forecast a 4 percent growth in personal funds transfers of all types into the 1990s. Other studies indicate that a relatively stable 12 percent of all personal transactions are for cash. As noted earlier, about 65 percent of all cash transactions are projected to occur through ATM when the market becomes fully saturated. If this point is reached by 1994, it is possible to estimate system-wide ATM transactions volume for the period 1994 to 2004. Based on the 80,000 ATMs assumed to be in operation in 1994, it is then possible to estimate per-machine volume for use in the NPV calculation.

Estimates of per-machine volume for the planning period are shown in Table 20.1. The annual transactions per machine are estimated to be 27,000 in 1994, growing to 40,000 by the end of the planning period.

SELECTING A DISCOUNT RATE

The thrift has used EFT for many years, and nothing about the proposed ATMs makes them either more or less acceptable to customers than other similar machines. Thus, management views the decision to add these cash dispensers as one of average risk to the institution. The weighted average cost of capital (k_A), 18.5 percent, calculated using the model shown in Chapter 17, is selected as the appropriate discount rate.

CALCULATING THE NPV

Using these data, the NPV of the decision is calculated in Table 20.2. The positive NPV of $46,166 indicates that installation of the four ATMs is expected to be economically feasible and will add value to the thrift. The same NPV approach would be used for any other EFT decision or for any potential expenditure for fixed assets, such as the opening of a new branch office. NPV is also appropriate for any decision about a potential reduction in equipment and technology investments, such as those resulting from "outsourcing"—or transferring to an external vendor—functions such as check processing or data processing.[22]

MERGER ANALYSIS: ANOTHER USE OF NPV

The discussion of depository institutions in Chapter 12 includes a look at the increasing number of mergers in recent years. Many mergers have been involuntary, especially among thrifts forced by federal regulators to consolidate. But many have also been voluntary—the result of conscious decisions by managers or owners to join with other institutions. Although NPV analysis is used in involuntary mergers, as regulators and acquiring firms haggle over how much the assets of an insolvent institution are *really* worth, it is essential in analyzing the economic aspects of voluntary mergers.

Merger analysis is an extremely complicated subject, with legal, regulatory, marketing, accounting, and financial dimensions that must be fully explored before a merger is undertaken. Merger analysis also differs depending on whether a depository is the acquired or the acquiring firm, and this chapter cannot treat the subject fully from both sides. The following discussion focuses on the financial implications of a

---

[22] For example, an illustration of NPV analysis applied to POS is presented in Morris 1978.

TABLE 20.1   Volume Estimates for Transactions per ATM, 1994–2004

The table shows one approach to estimating future benefits from an investment in ATMs. These data demonstrate how a manager might project volume per machine by using data on transactions and estimated growth rates.

Assumptions
Base year (1983) volume of personal payments transactions: 18 billion
Estimated annual growth in personal payments: 4%
Percentage of all transactions made to obtain cash: 12%
Percentage of cash transactions made via ATMs: 65%
Total ATMs in operation at saturation point: 80,000
Yearly total personal transactions volume in millions $= 18,000(1.04)^t$, where t = the number of years since 1983 (for example, for 1994, t = 11)

(1)	(2)	(3)	(4)	(5)
	Total Transactions	Total Cash Transactions	Total ATM Cash Transactions	Transactions per ATM (Millions)
Year	(Millions)	$0.12 \times$ (2)	$0.65 \times$ (3)	(4) $\div$ 80,000
1994	27,710.17	3,325.22	2,161.39	0.027
1995	28,818.58	3,458.23	2,247.85	0.028
1996	29,971.32	3,596.56	2,337.76	0.029
1997	31,170.18	3,740.42	2,431.27	0.030
1998	32,416.98	3,890.04	2,528.52	0.032
1999	33,713.66	4,045.64	2,629.67	0.033
2000	35,062.21	4,207.47	2,734.85	0.034
2001	36,464.70	4,375.76	2,844.25	0.036
2002	37,923.29	4,550.79	2,958.02	0.037
2003	39,440.22	4,732.83	3,076.34	0.038
2004	41,017.83	4,922.14	3,199.39	0.040

TABLE 20.2   Calculating the NPV of the ATM Decision

The total value of investing in ATMs is the present value of their expected benefits. The discount rate should reflect the riskiness of the benefits; if benefits are of normal risk, the institution's cost of capital is the appropriate rate. The NPV of the decision nets the benefits against the costs.

Assumptions
Initial cash cost plus installation = $175,000, to be paid at the beginning of 1994
Cash savings realized at the end of each year, including 1994
k_A = 18.5% for a project of average risk
Cash Inflow per Year = Per-ATM Volume $\times$ 4 ATMs $\times$ $0.39

End of Year	Volume per ATM (Thousands)	Total Annual Volume	Cash Inflow	Present Value at 18.5%
1994	27,000	108,000	$42,120	$ 35,544
1995	28,000	112,000	43,680	31,106
1996	29,000	116,000	45,240	27,187
1997	30,000	120,000	46,800	23,734
1998	32,000	128,000	49,920	21,364
1999	33,000	132,000	51,480	18,592
2000	34,000	136,000	53,040	16,165
2001	36,000	144,000	56,160	14,444
2002	37,000	148,000	57,720	12,527
2003	38,000	152,000	59,280	10,857
2004	40,000	160,000	62,400	9,645
				$221,166 Total present value

Net present value = $221,166 − $175,000 = $46,166 (acceptable)

voluntary decision by an institution or a holding company to acquire another institution. Students wishing a more comprehensive treatment of merger analysis should consult sources listed at the end of the chapter.

ECONOMIC OBJECTIVES OF MERGERS

Like the analysis of EFT decisions, the economic objective of a merger is to acquire ownership rights to assets whose future benefits exceed their costs. It is important to understand what an institution is buying when it acquires another. Essentially, the acquiring institution is buying the net worth of the acquired institution—the amount by which the value of the acquired institution's assets exceed its liabilities, the latter of which become the liabilities of the acquiring firm. Thus, in stockholder-owned firms, the acquirer offers to buy the common stock of the acquired firm. For mutual firms, the merger process involves conversion of one or both to the stock form of ownership first, followed by the acquisition of one institution's stock by another. Either way, the objective is for the acquirer to obtain rights to assets whose present value exceeds their cost.

At first, this objective may seem impossible. If the acquired firm's stock is publicly traded, wouldn't the acquiring firm simply pay the market price of the stock? If the price reflects the present value of the benefits of owning the stock, how could the acquiring firm expect to buy the stock in anything other than a $0–NPV transaction? That is, would not the firm expect to pay what the stock is worth, no more and no less? If the acquired firm's stock is not publicly traded, would not the acquiring firm simply pay the book value of net worth plus or minus a discount or premium to reflect current market values for the firm's assets? Should not that price, too, reflect the true value of the acquired firm's net worth, no more and no less?

Research into recent bank mergers provides what may be surprising answers to those questions. Because most acquired banks are small and because stocks of most small banks are not publicly traded, much available data compare merger prices with book, not market, value. According to information collected from 1968 to 1985, most acquiring banks pay *more* than book value for acquired firms' stock—from 110 percent to 280 percent of book value. Even more recent research continues to support the conclusion that

merger premiums are substantial. Economists at the Federal Reserve Bank of Atlanta found that during the period 1981 through 1986, the average purchase price nationally was 167 percent of book value, and it averaged as high as 190 percent in some regions.[23]

Is it possible that most of these mergers were actually negative NPV transactions from the acquirers' points of view? Some observers have, in fact, argued that bank merger prices are often too high, based on the real value of the acquired institution. It is unlikely, however, that all acquiring institutions make bad investment decisions year after year. Some research suggests that economic forces as familiar as supply and demand play a role in mergers; the more bidders in the market, the higher the price and the lower the profits to acquirers. Also, there is more to the economics of mergers than has been seen so far.

MATHEMATICS OF MERGERS: 2 + 2 = 5

Synergy occurs when the combined value of two institutions exceeds their total value as independent entities; it is often expressed more simply as $2 + 2 = 5$. If the acquiring institution expects synergy from a merger, its management believes that the present value of the combined operations of two firms will exceed the cost of executing the merger, including the cost of acquiring the other firm's stock. In other words, the acquiring firm believes that it can increase total cash inflows from the assets of the two firms by managing them as one. There are several major sources of these expectations.

---

[23] Historical information on mergers is provided in Darnell 1973; Bullington and Jensen 1981; Cates 1985; Beatty, Santomero, and Smirlock 1987; Hunter and Wall 1989; James and Wier 1987; and Boyd and Graham 1991.

Rhoades examined 4,383 bank acquisitions from 1960 through 1983. He found that small banks (less than $50 million) accounted for 84 percent of the acquisitions during this period. See Stephen Rhoades, "Mergers and Acquisitions by Commercial Banks," Board of Governors of the Federal Reserve System, Staff Study No. 142 (January 1985), Table 5. Beatty, Santomero, and Smirlock found that acquiring banks have been, on average, seven times larger than acquired institutions.

Voluntary thrift mergers have also historically involved the acquisition of small firms by much larger ones. See Woerheide 1984, Chapter 9; and Neely and Rochester 1987.

ECONOMIES OF SCALE. Some firms acquire others because they believe they can reap the benefits of economies of scale. If a savings and loan association (S&L) doubles the number of negotiable order of withdrawal (NOW) accounts serviced as a result of a merger, its managers may expect check-processing costs to increase by less than 100 percent, reducing the cost per account. Because economies of scale occur when unit costs decline with volume (recall the discussion in Chapter 4), the net cash saved may increase total cash benefits available to owners. When Manufacturers Hanover and Chemical Bank announced their plans to merge in 1991, senior management promised an annual cost savings of $650 million by 1995. Intermediate cost reduction targets were met primarily by decreasing staff. Because these banks were offering duplicate services in many markets, economies of scale through a merger were more easily obtainable. If the institutions had operated in totally separate markets, they would have found it more difficult to achieve cost savings through staff reductions or branch office closures. The terms "in-market" and "out-of-market" are used to distinguish the two types of mergers.

COMBINATIONS OF STRENGTH. Merging firms may also believe that their assets "fit" well together. For example, in 1985, when Wachovia Corporation of North Carolina and First Atlanta Corporation of Georgia announced plans to merge into an institution called First Wachovia, financial analysts pronounced the merger a good fit because it combined First Atlanta's $870 million credit card operations with Wachovia's large consumer lending portfolio. Opportunities for geographic expansion of both operations and the possibility of cross-selling (selling credit cards to consumer borrowers and consumer loans to credit card holders) led to expectations of increases in total cash benefits to the owners of the combined firm.

BETTER MANAGEMENT. Another potential source of synergy is improved management of the acquired bank's existing assets. For example, some small depositories have been founded, owned, and managed by a single family throughout their history. Managers and officers may have been hired more for their family relationships than for their managerial skills. The acquiring depository may believe that under its management,

the assets of the acquired firm can be more profitable. If so, the expected cash inflows of the combined institution will exceed those of the institutions operated separately, thus increasing value. A study conducted at the Federal Reserve Bank of Chicago concluded that the potential to improve income from fee-generating services was a major motivation behind premiums paid in several recent interstate mergers.[24]

GEOGRAPHIC DIVERSIFICATION AND MARKET PENETRATION. A motivation that many observers have recently assigned to depository institution mergers is the acquirer's desire to enter new geographic markets. Penetration of a new market can be potentially beneficial for two reasons: The resulting geographic diversification may reduce earnings variability (that is, reduce risk); and entry into new regions may provide the acquiring organization with opportunities for growth. Many acquiring firms believe that purchasing an existing institution in a target region is a better way to enter that region than starting a competing institution *de novo*. Furthermore, small depositories in a growing region may lack the resources to capitalize substantially on that growth potential. By merging, managers may believe that the resulting organization will have a brighter future than the two firms would have separately and that, through geographic diversification, the benefits of growth can be achieved without substantially increasing risk.

SURVIVAL. Perhaps the reason most often cited recently for depository institution mergers is survival—to avoid either merger partner's being subsequently taken over by one of the nation's financial giants. Said one Missouri banker, "Before being thrown against Citicorp . . . , we should be permitted to reach a certain fighting weight."[25] Although continuity is no

---

[24] See Phillis and Pavel 1986. The authors also found that institutions with high spreads (IR − IE) and low loan charge-offs were especially attractive.

[25] Felix Kessler, "Here Comes the Regional Superbanks," *Fortune*, December 10, 1984, 138. This comment is typical of bankers' sentiments as reported in other sources. See, for example, Scott Scredon, "Bank Mergers Start to Sizzle in the South," *Business Week*, July 1, 1985, 25–26, in which $20 billion in assets was suggested as the minimum necessary fighting weight; and Daniel Hertzberg, "Competition Spurs Mergers of U.S. Banks," *The Wall Street Journal*, October 2, 1984.

TABLE 20.3	**Potential Objectives for Acquisition of Another Financial Institution**

Bank managers identified these motivations for mergers in a survey in the mid-1980s.

To maximize profit
To maximize shareholder wealth
To increase management prestige
To minimize risk (to diversify)
To become the largest holding company in state
To maintain holding company's market position
To achieve profit rate targets
To achieve growth rate targets
To achieve a "critical" mass
To achieve commercial strength
To complement existing subsidiaries
To enter new markets

Source: Jan R. Squires, "An Acquisitions Checklist for Bank Holding Company Managers," *Bankers Magazine* 176 (January/February 1984): 72.

guarantee of increased institutional value, this statement implies at least some belief in synergy. If a combined institution can be operated to maximize value, a financial giant is less likely to find opportunities to improve that value by a takeover attempt and may turn its attention to other targets.

EVIDENCE ON MERGER MOTIVATIONS. These objectives for financial institution mergers were reflected in the responses of bank holding company (BHC) executives to a survey about the process of merger decision making. As shown in Table 20.3, survey participants indicated a variety of possible objectives for an acquisition; although not stated in identical terms, key factors included the concern for enhancing management, diversifying, increasing growth and profitability, and reaching an optimal size.

To gain insight into the relative importance of depository merger motivations, several researchers have examined financial data to learn to what target characteristics acquirers are most attracted and for what features they will pay the highest premiums. Although the evidence is mixed, there is relatively less support for the hypothesis that mergers are undertaken to improve the quality of the target firm's existing management. Relatively more support exists for the idea that mergers are undertaken from a desire to grow, to diversify, or to achieve economies of scale. A 1991

study by researchers at the Federal Reserve Bank of Minneapolis concluded that market economies were not driving factors in bank consolidation. Instead, they identified the desire to dominate market share and become too big to fail as the prevailing motivations.[26] Such motivations may help explain why acquirers often pay more than an institution's book value.

NEW DIRECTIONS. The Financial Institutions Reform, Recovery, and Enforcement Act (FIRREA) and the Federal Deposit Insurance Corporation Improvement Act (FDICIA) provided new opportunities for commercial banks to acquire not only failing thrifts but also profitable and growing savings institutions. Some commercial bank managers now consider the acquisition of an established thrift to be an alternative way to enter a new market. Because the plight of ailing thrifts has affected the reputation of the entire industry, many managers believe that financially strong thrifts can be acquired at lower prices than banks of comparable size in the same market.

Since the passage of FIRREA and FDICIA, some banks have acquired thrifts and converted them to banks, a strategy more attractive since FDICIA eliminated the exit and entry penalties assessed for changing deposit insurance funds. Nonetheless, commercial bank managers must be careful to analyze a potential thrift acquisition thoroughly to avoid unpleasant surprises.[27]

ESTIMATING VALUE IN A MERGER

The most critical estimate required before a merger is the present value of the acquired institution's net worth, and the previous discussion suggests that *current* market or book value may not always reflect that value. In fact, the cash-flow analysis used in all NPV decisions is needed. The present value of estimated

---

[26] Stephen A. Rhoades, "The Operating Performance of Acquired Firms in Banking before and after Acquisition," Board of Governors of the Fed, Staff Study No. 149, April 1986; Fraser and Kolari 1988; Neely and Rochester 1987; Beatty, Santomero, and Smirlock 1987; Hunter and Wall 1989; Benston, Hunter, and Wall 1990 and 1992; and Boyd and Graham 1991.

[27] See Quackenbush and Willkomm 1990; and Vanessa Bush, "Why Are Banks Buying Savings Institutions?" *Savings Institutions* 111 (April 1990): 31–35.

cash flows can then be compared with the price demanded by the acquired institution's current owners, usually a multiple of current book or market value. If the estimated present value exceeds what must be paid to obtain the stock, the merger is economically feasible. If not, the merger should be reconsidered.

ESTIMATING PRESENT VALUE: AN ILLUSTRATION

Suppose a bank is considering acquiring another institution with a book value of $100 per share. Before the acquisition, the candidate's average return on net worth has been 12 percent. For the first 10 years after the merger, RONW is expected to increase to 18 percent because it is believed that management of the acquired firm's assets can be improved substantially without increasing risk. After the initial period, when opportunities for superior profits have dissipated, RONW is expected to fall to 15 percent. For the first 10 years, growth in assets and net worth are expected to be 8 percent, but after that, the growth rate will drop to a more normal 5 percent indefinitely. The acquiring firm's required rate of return on long-term investments is 15 percent.

The acquiring firm's objective is to estimate the cash flows to owners of the acquired firm under these assumptions. Because g_{NW} = RONW × Retention Rate (Equation 17.3), estimates of an 18 percent RONW and a growth of 8 percent annually imply a planned retention rate of 8% ÷ 18% = 44%. Therefore, cash available for dividends to the firm's owners will be 56 percent of earnings each year. Resulting cash flows for the first 10 years are given in Table 20.4. The present value of these cash flows totals $67.15.[28]

The bottom of Table 20.4 shows estimates of the present value of the cash flows from year 11 onward. Because the acquisition is expected to provide annual cash flows growing at a rate of 5 percent from that point, their present value is estimated, using the constant-growth model, at $53.61. Adding $53.61 to the total present value of the first 10 years' cash flows ($67.15) gives an estimate of the stock's per-share value of $120.76, a 21 percent premium over the current $100.00 book value. This analysis follows the pattern used in the earlier EFT decision: identification of the time frame, estimation of the periodic cash flows, selection of a discount rate, and calculation of total present value.

THE MERGER DECISION

Existing owners of the proposed acquisition will have their own ideas about its worth. Because most acquirers of commercial banks have paid a hefty premium over book value to obtain an acquisition candidate, the latter's owners will no doubt attempt to obtain a price considerably higher than $100. Even if the full potential of the institution's assets cannot be realized under current management, selling owners will attempt to capitalize on the desire of the acquiring firm to close the deal. The present value analysis indicates, however, that from an economic standpoint the acquirer should pay no more than $120.76 per share. Otherwise, the NPV of the transaction to the acquirer would be negative, decreasing the long-run value of the institution.[29]

OTHER ESTIMATES OF ACQUISITION VALUE

Because estimating the present value of the benefits from an acquisition is difficult and uncertain, many managers and owners are accustomed to thinking of merger values in other terms. Because these measures are often cited in reports of institutional mergers, a brief review is in order. Each of them, however, has limitations compared with NPV analysis.

MERGER MARKET VALUE (CASH-TO-BOOK RATIO)

The **merger market value,** or cash-to-book ratio, of an institution is simply its value based on cash prices recently paid in merger transactions involving similar institutions:

---

[28] This example is partially based on one in Bullington and Jensen 1981.

[29] In practice, administrative costs of executing the merger must be included in NPV analysis. Because consultation with accountants and attorneys is essential to a successful merger, their fees must also be added to the total price paid to the acquired firm's owners; these total costs would then be compared with the present value of the benefits from the merger.

TABLE 20.4	Estimating the Present Value of an Acquisition Candidate

Acquirers determine the maximum share price they will pay for a merger candidate by calculating the present value of the benefits expected after the merger. In this example, per-share benefits are estimated at $120.76; the price offered should not exceed that figure if the merger is to be beneficial to the acquiring firm:

(1) Year	(2) Book Value ($) at Beginning of Year	(3) Book Value ($) at End of Year $(g = 8\%)$	(4) Net Income Per Share $18\% \times (2)$	(5) Earnings Retained $44\% \times (4)$	(6) Cash Available $(4) - (5)$	(7) Present Value of Cash at 15%
0		$100.00				
1	$100.00	108.00	$18.00	$ 7.92	$10.08	$ 8.77
2	108.00	116.64	19.44	8.55	10.89	8.23
3	116.64	125.97	21.00	9.24	11.76	7.73
4	125.97	136.05	22.67	9.98	12.70	7.26
5	136.05	146.93	24.49	10.78	13.71	6.82
6	146.93	158.69	26.45	11.64	14.81	6.40
7	158.69	171.38	28.56	12.57	16.00	6.01
8	171.38	185.09	30.85	13.57	17.28	5.65
9	185.09	199.90	33.32	14.66	18.66	5.30
10	199.90	215.89	35.98	15.83	20.15	4.98
						$67.15 Total

At the end of year 10, RONW is expected to drop to 15%. This implies a retention rate of $5\% \div 15\% = 33\%$ from year 11 on. Thus, in year 11, earnings will be $15\% \times \$215.89 = \$32.38$, and cash available to owners will be $67\% \times \$32.38 = \$21.69$.

Because the stock is expected to conform to the constant-growth model from that point on, the value of all future cash flows from the end of year 11 on, as of the end of year 10, is

$$V_{10} = \frac{C_{11}}{k - g} = \frac{\$21.69}{0.15 - 0.05} = \$216.90$$

As of year 0, its present value is $\$216.90/1.15^{10} = \$53.61$.

Thus, the total per-share value of the acquisition is estimated as

$ 67.15
+ 53.61
$120.76

[20.4]

Merger Market Value =
  Average Cash-to-Book Ratio
  × Candidate's Book Value

If the average ratio of cash/book value for recent mergers in a state were 1.75, the per-share merger market value of an acquisition with book value of $50 per share would be $1.75 \times \$50 = \$87.50$. Use of this measure to determine the value of an acquisition ignores special institutional circumstances that make its economic value greater or less than average.

BOOK VALUE TO BOOK VALUE

In many mergers, transactions are completed by exchanging stock for stock rather than by paying cash to the acquired firm's current owners. It is possible, therefore, to estimate the value of a potential acquiree's stock by examining the average ratio of book values exchanged in similar mergers. Suppose an acquiring firm knows that recent mergers in the region have resulted in an average book value–to–book value exchange ratio of 1.58. If the book value of a candidate's stock is $95, the book value of shares that might be offered by the acquiring firm is

$$[20.5]$$
$$\text{Merger Book Value} = \text{Average Book-to-Book}$$
$$\text{Ratio} \times \text{Candidate's Book Value}$$
$$\$150 = 1.58 \times \$95$$

If the current book value of the acquiring firm's stock is $75, two shares with a total book value of $150 would be offered for one share of the acquiree's stock. A major problem with evaluating merger terms on this basis is that book values may have little relationship to the economic value exchanged by either party.

VALUE BASED ON EARNINGS

Some analysts argue that assessing the value of an acquisition according to earnings is superior to measuring it based on book value. Thus, examining the ratio of purchase price to earnings per share (EPS) is sometimes suggested. Suppose an S&L knows that the average ratio of price paid to acquiree's EPS has been 11.58 recently. If a candidate's EPS were $9.50 last year, the value of the acquiree's stock could be estimated as

$$[20.6]$$
$$\text{Price/Earnings Value} =$$
$$\text{Average Price/Earnings Ratio}$$
$$\times \text{Candidate's EPS}$$
$$\$110 = 11.58 \times \$9.50$$

The problem with this measure is that the acquiring institution is buying, and the selling owners are giving up, future earnings. Unless future earnings remain similar to current figures (an unlikely expectation if a merger is synergistic), values based on historical earnings ratios are unlikely to equal economic values.

DILUTION: IS NPV BEST IN THE SHORT RUN?

A main concern of owners and managers in an acquiring institution is **dilution,** or a reduction in per-share earnings caused by the issuance of new shares. A well-known bank analyst noted that fear of dilution is one of the two driving forces behind agreed-on bank

merger prices.[30] If he is correct, then in stock-for-stock mergers, acquirers attempt to avoid issuing so many shares to obtain the acquired firm that EPS falls after the merger, regardless of whether the long-run economic value exchanged would justify the decision.

A simplified example of dilution after a merger is illustrated in Table 20.5[31] Suppose, based on NPV analysis, that a large bank acquires a small one and issues 1.08 million new shares, equal in total to 1.62 times the book value of the acquired bank. If the synergistic benefits of increased earnings do not occur immediately, the table shows that from the acquiring shareholders' point of view, EPS will fall from $2.00 to $1.85 the first year after the merger. This is a percentage dilution of 7.5 percent, exceeding the 5 percent level some analysts believe is acceptable.[32]

Should the NPV criterion be ignored if dilution is expected? Not at all. In the short run, decisions based on NPV sometimes conflict with other standards. In this example, the acquired firm has a higher book value ratio of capital to assets than the acquiring firm, so the resulting book value capital/assets ratio in the combined institution will be larger than the acquiring firm's. As explained in Chapter 17, the higher capital ratio means a higher potential growth rate in assets and earnings than would have been possible before the merger. That possibility, joined with synergy expected from combining administrative operations, for example, may result in a long-run earnings stream that exceeds the acquiring firm's earnings before the merger. Also, the acquired firm, even if not more highly capitalized, may have assets with greater growth prospects after the merger than those of the acquiring firm. Any or all these three factors may work to add long-run value that is not instantly captured in short-run accounting earnings figures.

Based on the merger in Table 20.5, Table 20.6 shows future EPS possibilities for 10 years, assuming

---

[30] See Cates 1985, 38; Cates' other driving force was the market value–to–market value ratio, which is relevant only for institutions with frequently traded stock.

[31] This example is based, in part, on one in Eisemann and Budd 1982.

[32] The 5 percent figure is cited by Cates as a rule of thumb of investment bankers and professional investors. See Cates 1985, 37. In other work, he has called larger percentage dilutions "dilutions of grandeur."

TABLE 20.5 **Dilution Resulting from a Merger**

Present value calculations and accounting measures are not always compatible, so a merger with a positive NPV can result in earnings dilution in the short run. In this example, EPS falls from $2.00 per share to $1.85 per share immediately after a merger.

	Acquiring Institution	**Acquired Institution**
Total assets	$800 million	$100 million
Total net worth (book)	$40 million	$8 million
Net worth/total assets	5.0%	8.0%
Net income	$10 million	$1.25 million
Shares outstanding	5 million	
Stock price (per share)	$12	
Earnings per share (EPS)	$2.00	

A purchase price of 1.62 times the book value of the acquired firm is

$$1.62 \times \$8 \text{ million} = \$12.96 \text{ million}$$

That requires the issuance of $12.96 ÷ $12 = 1.08 million new shares.

If earnings do not increase at first, EPS for year 1 will be

$$(\$10 \text{ million} + \$1.25 \text{ million}) \div (5 + 1.08) = \$1.85$$

TABLE 20.6 **Dilution and Growth**

These data show that *after the first year of dilution,* EPS with the merger will exceed EPS without the merger as long as the growth rate projected for the target firm exceeds that estimated for the acquiring firm.

		Without-Merger Growth = 5%	**Acquiree Growth = 3%**	**Acquiree Growth = 10%**	**Acquiree Growth = 15%**	**Acquiree Growth = 20%**
Year 1 EPS		$2.00	$1.85	$1.85	$1.85	$1.85
Combined growth rate (weighted average)		5.00%	4.78%	5.55%	6.10%	6.65%
Future EPS of combined firm						
	Year					
	2[a]	$2.10[b]	$2.09	$2.11	$2.12	$2.13
	3	2.21	2.19	2.23	2.25	2.27
	4	2.32	2.30	2.35	2.39	2.42
	5	2.43	2.41	2.48	2.53	2.58
	6	2.55	2.52	2.62	2.69	2.76
	7	2.68	2.64	2.76	2.85	2.94
	8	2.81	2.77	2.92	3.02	3.14
	9	2.95	2.90	3.08	3.21	3.34
	10	3.10	3.04	3.25	3.40	3.57

[a] In year 2, a one-time earnings increase of 8 percent occurs for the combined firm as a result of synergy. Then the expected growth path resumes.
[b] Reflects only the 5 percent annual growth expected for the original firm without the merger.

no synergy occurs until year 2. The EPS figures for the combined firm in the first year are $1.85, but in the second year earnings are expected to increase an *additional* 8 percent over and above the increase caused by growth without the merger. For the acquiring firm, earnings are expected to increase annually by 5 percent.

The point at which EPS for the combined firm exceeds the EPS the acquiring firm could achieve without the merger depends on three factors: 1) the expected growth rate in EPS of the acquired institution; 2) the synergistic effect, which here is the one-time boost in year 2; and 3) the relative size of the two institutions. In this example, the smaller firm is only one-eighth the size of the larger firm, so it is one-ninth of the combined firm. Its effect is less dramatic than if two firms of relatively equal size but different expected earnings growth were to combine.

The EPS estimates in Table 20.6 are based on growth rates for the smaller firm ranging from 3 to 20 percent. The long-term growth rates for the combined banks are estimated as the weighted average of the two separate institutions and range from 4.78 to 6.65 percent. For example, if the acquired firm's expected growth rate is 10 percent, the estimated growth rate of the combined firms would be $1/9(10\%) + 8/9(5\%) = 5.55\%$. In year 2, recall that synergy makes the growth rate 8 percent higher. For all but one possible growth rate, combined EPS will exceed the nonmerger level by the second year. Only if the acquired firm's postmerger growth prospects are disappointing—3 percent in this case—will postmerger EPS continue to show the effects of dilution after 1 year.

REGULATION OF DEPOSITORY INSTITUTIONS MERGERS

It should come as no surprise that the merger activities of depository institutions are regulated. Regulatory authority over mergers follows the same pattern as regulation of other activities. The Fed is the chief regulator of mergers involving BHCs or state member banks; the Comptroller of the Currency must approve national bank mergers; the Federal Deposit Insurance Corporation (FDIC) oversees state-chartered, insured banks;

the Office of Thrift Supervision (OTS) and the FDIC must approve Savings Association Insurance Fund (SAIF)-insured depository mergers; and the National Credit Union Administration (NCUA) must sanction the mergers of federal CUs. State authorities must also approve the merger of all state-chartered institutions.

Because they may reduce competition, especially if institutions within relative geographic proximity wish to combine, mergers are closely watched by regulators and by the U.S. Department of Justice, which is responsible for antitrust actions against financial as well as nonfinancial firms. The history of merger regulation and legislation in depository institutions is long and rich and is not reviewed in detail here. Rather, the purpose of this discussion is to outline main issues that could affect depository mergers in the future.

Since the inception of federal antitrust legislation, its thrust has been to prevent business combinations that decrease competition. To determine whether a merger will have an adverse competitive effect, the regulators must answer several critical questions. The answers influence whether a merger is approved, and each of the questions involves a gray area. An illustrative example of the Federal Reserve Board's answers to the questions is presented in Figure 20.3, which announces the approval of the 1992 acquisition of Hibernia National Bank in Dallas, Texas, by Comerica, Incorporated, a BHC which is headquartered in Detroit, Michigan. The figure contains excerpts only (the full approval order is lengthy), and key passages are highlighted.

WHAT IS THE RELEVANT MARKET AREA?

One competitive question is how the relevant geographic market for the merger is to be defined. If the only two banks in a small town ask to merge and if neither one serves customers outside the community, identifying the relevant market is easy. But rarely is the question so clear-cut.

Ideally, a market should be defined in economic terms; that is, the geographic area in which deposits will be taken and loans made after the merger should be identified, regardless of whether it conforms to

(text continues on page 630)

FIGURE 20.3	Approval of a Merger Application by Federal Regulators

Comerica Incorporated
Detroit, Michigan

Order Approving Acquisition of a Bank

Comerica Incorporated, Detroit, Michigan ("Comerica"), a bank holding company within the meaning of the Bank Holding Company Act ("BHC Act"), has applied for the Board's approval under section 3(a)(3) of the BHC Act (12 U.S.C. § 1842(a)(3)) to acquire all of the voting shares of Hibernia National Bank in Texas, Dallas, Texas ("Hibernia-Texas"), from Hibernia Corporation, New Orleans, Louisiana ("Hibernia"). Upon consummation of the proposal, Comerica proposes to mere Hibernia-Texas into Comerica's subsidiary bank, Comerica Bank-Texas, Dallas, Texas ("Comerica-Texas"). . . .

Comerica, with approximately $26.8 billion in consolidated assets, controls seven banks and one thrift located in California, Florida, Illinois, Michigan and Texas. Comerica is the 11th largest commercial banking organization in Texas, controlling deposits of $1.2 billion, representing less than 1 percent of total deposits in commercial banks in the state. Hibernia-Texas is the 14th largest commercial banking organization in Texas, controlling deposits of nearly $1 billion, representing less than 1 percent of total deposits in commercial banks in the state. Upon consummation of the proposed transaction, Comerica would become the eighth largest commercial banking organization in Texas, controlling deposits of $2.2 billion, representing 1.5 percent of total deposits in commercial banks in the state.

Competitive, Financial, Managerial and Supervisory Considerations

Comerica and Hibernia compete directly in the Dallas banking market. Upon consummation of this proposal, Comerica would become the fifth largest commercial or thrift organization ("depository institution") in the Dallas banking market, controlling deposits of $1.7 billion, representing approximately 5.6 percent of total deposits in depository institutions in the market ("market deposits"). After considering the number of competitors remaining in the market, the relatively small increase in concentration as measured by the Herfindahl-Hirschman Index ("HHI"), market share, and all other facts of record, the Board concludes that consummation of the proposal would not result in a significantly adverse effect on competition in the Dallas banking market or any other relevant banking market.

The Board also concludes that the financial and managerial resources and future prospects of Comerica and Hibernia, and their respective subsidiaries, and the other supervisory factors that the Board must consider under section 3 of the BHC Act, are consistent with approval.

Convenience and Needs Considerations

In acting on an appliction to acquire a depository institution under the BHC Act, the Board must consider the convenience and needs of the communities to be served, and take into account the records of the relevant depository institutions under the Community Reinvestment Act (12 U.S.C. § 2901 *et seq.*) ("CRA"). The CRA requires the federal financial supervisory agencies to encourage financial institutions to help meet the credit needs of the local communities in which they operate, consistent with the safe and sound operation of such institutions. To accomplish this end, the CRA requires the appropriate federal supervisory authority to "assess the institution's record of meeting the credit needs of its entire community, including low- and moderate-income neighborhoods, consistent with the safe and sound operation of such institution," and to take that record into account in its evaluation of bank holding company applications.

The Board has received comments from two organizations ("Protestants") alleging that Comerica-Texas and Hibernia-Texas have not complied with the CRA and lending laws designed to provide borrowers with equal access to credit. In particular, the Protestants assert that Comerica-Texas and Hibernia-Texas have failed to meet the credit and deposit needs of low- and moderate-income residents of South Dallas. The Protestants also allege that Comerica-Texas illegally discriminates against ethnic minorities in making lending decisions, citing data for 1990 filed under the Home Mortgage Disclosure Act ("HMDA").

The Board has carefully reviewed the CRA performance records of Comerica, its subsidiary banks, and Hibernia-Texas, as well as all comments received regarding this application, Comerica's responses to those comments, and all of the other relevant facts of record in light of the CRA, the Board's regulations, and the Statement of the Federal Financial Supervisory Agencies Regarding the Community Reinvestment Act ("Agency CRA Statement").

Record of Performance Under the CRA

A. CRA Performance Examination

The Agency CRA Statement provides that a CRA examination is an important and often controlling factor in the consideration of an institution's CRA record and that these reports will be given great weight in the applications process. The Board notes that Comerica-Texas received an overall "outstanding" rating in the examination of CRA performance conducted by the Federal Deposit Insurance Corporation ("FDIC") as of October 11, 1991. In this regard, Comerica-Texas's overall CRA performance improved since its "satisfactory" CRA rating in the FDIC's previous examination as of March 29, 1990. In addition, Comerica's other six subsidiary banks have received either "satisfactory" or "outstanding" ratings from their primary supervisors in the most recent examinations of their CRA performance. Hibernia-Texas is currently being examined for CRA performance by its primary regulator, the Office of the Comptroller of the Currency ("OCC"), and has preliminarily been assigned an overall "satisfactory" CRA performance rating.

B. Corporate Policies

Comerica-Texas has in place the type of policies outlined in the Agency CRA Statement that contribute to an effective CRA program. For example, the board of directors of Comerica has adopted a written CRA plan for 1991–1993, which includes goals, objectives, and methodology for self-assessment. . . .

C. Ascertainment and Marketing

Community credit needs are ascertained by Comerica-Texas through a multi-layered approach to community outreach. For example, the bank's management has ongoing, substantive contacts with numerous civic, religious, neighborhood, minority, and small business organizations. Comerica-Texas also has an extensive officer call program at each branch. Approximately 25 percent of all calls are made by the four branches located in low- and moderate-income areas of the bank's delineated market. . . .

D. Lending and Other Activities

Comerica-Texas supports a number of governmental programs designed to help meet the housing-related credit needs of low- and moderate-income borrowers. For example, the bank has provided a $5 million commitment to the Dallas Affordable Housing Partnership ("DAHP") to provide low-interest mortgages to low-income first-time homebuyers. Comerica-Texas has also provided a $100,000 line of credit to DAHP for use in acquiring and rehabilitating homes before permanent financing is obtained. Comerica-Texas was the first bank to participate in DAHP to offer this type of interim financing. Senior bank personnel are members of DAHP's board of directors, and DAHP pamphlets and materials are made available at all branches. . . .

E. HMDA Data and Lending Practices

The Board has reviewed the 1990 and 1991 HMDA data reported by Comerica-Texas and Hibernia-Texas, as well as Protestants' comments regarding this data. The HMDA data shows disparities in the rates for housing-related loan applications, approvals, and denials that vary by racial or ethnic group in certain areas of Dallas. Protestants have alleged illegal discriminatory lending practices on the basis of this data.

The most recent examinations for CRA compliance and performance conducted by bank supervisory agencies found no evidence of illegal discrimination or other illegal credit practices at Comerica-Texas or Hibernia-Texas. In the case of Comerica-Texas, the examination specifically considered the results of the 1990 HMDA data and the loan policies and procedures which governed the loan applications that were the source for the 1991 data. . . .

F. Conclusion Regarding Convenience and Needs Factors

The Board has carefully considered the entire record, including the comments filed in this case, in reviewing the convenience and needs factor under the BHC Act. Based on a review of the entire record of performance, including information provided by Protestants and by the banks' primary regulators, the Board believes that the efforts of Comerica and Hibernia to help meet the credit needs of all segments of the communities served by Comerica-Texas and Hibernia-Texas, including low- and moderate-income neighborhoods, are consistent with approval.

The Board recognizes that the record compiled in this application points to areas for improvement, especially in housing-related lending to minority and low- and moderate-income borrowers. Comerica has initiated steps designed to strengthen the CRA performance of the insured institutions. In this regard, the outstanding CRA performance rating received by Comerica-Texas reflects Comerica's willingness to address promptly areas where the improvements can be made to help meet community credit needs. The Board believes that this record, and the initiatives proposed by Comerica-Texas, will help the resulting organization improve its CRA performance and address weaknesses identified by Protestants.

In this light, and on the basis of all of the facts of record, the Board concludes that the convenience and needs considerations, including the CRA performance records of Comerica-Texas and Hibernia-Texas, are consistent with approval of this application. The Board expects Comerica-Texas to implement fully the CRA initiatives discussed in this Order, and contained in this application. Comerica-Texas's progress in implementing these initiatives will be monitored by the Federal Reserve Bank of Chicago, and in future applications by Comerica to expand its deposit-taking facilities.

Based on the foregoing, including the conditions and commitments described in this Order and those made in this application, and all of the facts of record, the Board has determined that this application should be, and hereby is, approved. The Board's approval is specifically conditioned upon compliance by Comerica with all the commitments made in connection with this application. The commitments and conditions relied on by the Board in reaching this decision are both conditions imposed in writing by the Board in connection with its findings and decision, and as such may be enforced in proceedings under applicable law. This approval is also conditioned upon Comerica receiving all necessary Federal and state approvals. . . .

Source: *Federal Reserve Bulletin* 79 (January 1993: 31–36).

legal boundaries such as city, county, or state lines.[33] In practice, legal boundaries are most often used, but Justice Department guidelines are the final determining factor.[34]

In the Comerica acquisition of Hibernia, the Board briefly examined the Texas banking market and then turned its attention to the Dallas metropolitan area. Regional and national markets evidently were not considered relevant in this case.

HOW SHOULD THE DEGREE OF COMPETITION BE MEASURED?

After the relevant market is defined, regulators must measure competition in that market. Currently, two measures of competition are used. One is a simple market concentration ratio, in which the percentage of total market deposits held by merger candidates before and after the merger is examined. The Fed's recent policy has been to refrain from challenging a merger unless the three largest firms in the market have a combined deposit concentration ratio exceeding 75 percent after the merger.[35]

A more complex measure of competition is the **Herfindahl-Hirschman Index (HHI),** which is the sum of the squares of the market shares of all competitors in a market. It is calculated before and after a potential merger. In 1984, the Justice Department revised its guidelines for merger approvals based on the HHI, which is believed by many economists and legal scholars to be more theoretically sound than simple concentration ratios.[36] The Justice Department defines a mar-

ket as unconcentrated if the HHI is 1,000 or less, moderately concentrated if it is 1,000–1,800, and highly concentrated if it is greater than 1,800. Generally, a merger in a market with an HHI of 1,000 or less will go unchallenged by the Justice Department, but those in markets with higher HHIs may be questioned, depending on the effect of the merger on the market's HHI. For example, the 1984 guidelines indicate that the Justice Department may question a bank merger if the HHI is 1,800 or greater and the merger would increase it by 200 points or more. For clarification, Table 20.7 shows measures of competition for a hypothetical market before and after a merger of the first and fourth largest institutions.[37]

Although it was not shown in Figure 20.3, in the Comerica–Hibernia acquisition, the Fed calculated both the HHI and the deposit concentration measures for the Dallas market, but only deposit concentration ratios for the state of Texas. The Board noted that the HHI would increase by only 11 points, to a level of 1,380, which placed the market in the Justice Department category of "moderately concentrated." Consequently, the Board concluded that the merger would not have a significantly adverse effect on competition in any relevant market.

WITH WHOM ARE THE MERGER CANDIDATES POTENTIALLY COMPETING?

Another issue in depository institution mergers is identifying the institutions with whom the proposed merger candidates are competing. On the one hand, increasing similarity in products offered by depositories suggests that competitive measures such as the deposit concentration ratio or the HHI should be calculated using all depositories in the defined market. On the other hand, evidence in earlier chapters suggests many

---

[33] Economists have made many attempts to define markets in general and banking markets in particular. A review and synthesis of this research is provided in John D. Wolken, "Geographic Market Delineation: A Review of the Literature," Board of Governors of the Fed, Staff Study No. 140, October 1984.

[34] The Justice Department issued new guidelines for analyzing the competitive effects of mergers in 1992. These guidelines are used to review all potential mergers, including those of commercial banks, and sometimes are in disagreement with Fed recommendations. The new policies (horizontal merger guidelines) define product and geographic markets. See Guerin-Calvert and Ordover 1992 for more details.

[35] There are other criteria, primarily related to the size of the banks involved, that also govern whether the Fed will challenge a merger. For more details, see Stutzer 1984.

[36] Rhoades argued, based on a review of recent literature, that the three-firm concentration ratio is as good a measure of banking mar-

ket structure as is the HHI. See Stephen Rhoades, "Structure-Performance Studies in Banking: An Updated Summary and Evaluation," Board of Governors of the Fed, Staff Study No. 119, August 1982.

[37] The *real* concern is the effect of the merger on future competition, something static measures such as the deposit concentration ratio or the HHI do not capture. Will the merger cause the candidates or their remaining competitors to act in ways they would not have acted without the merger? There is obviously no easy answer to that question. For further analysis, see Stutzer 1984; Guerin-Calvert and Ordover 1992; and Rhoades 1993.

areas in which thrifts, CUs, and banks do not yet compete. It is not surprising, therefore, that both state and federal regulators have only recently widened the scope of competitive measures to include other depositories besides those undertaking a merger. For example, some analysts believe that the 1986 merger of two giant California banks, Wells Fargo and Crocker National, was permitted only because thrifts were viewed as "capable competitors" of commercial banks in the state.[38]

In the Comerica–Hibernia combination, the Board considered only bank and thrift institutions to determine relevant competitors. In some cases, however, the Board has included CUs, finance companies, other nondepositories, and even *potential* competitors to the merged organization.

DOES THE INSTITUTION SERVE THE COMMUNITY?

The final question regulators attempt to answer when evaluating a merger request is whether the applicants are "good citizens." In particular, decision makers must consider the extent to which institutions have previously met the credit needs of low- and moderate-income customers, pursuant to the Community Reinvestment Act (CRA) provisions of different federal banking laws. As noted at several points earlier in the book, recent legislation, including FIRREA, has placed increased emphasis on CRA compliance, and ensured the public disclosure of the degree to which institutions serve the needs of their communities. The Home Mortgage Disclosure Act (HMDA), strengthened in FDICIA, results in closer scrutiny of institutions' loan portfolios in the evaluation of merger applications.

As shown in Figure 20.3, the Board noted that Comerica–Texas had received an "Outstanding" rating in the examination of its CRA compliance. Hibernia had received a "Satisfactory" rating. Despite these assessments by regulators, several community organizations had filed protests alleging that the banks had not met the needs of low- and moderate-income citizens in the Dallas area. The Board examined corporate policies, marketing and outreach activities, and lend-

TABLE 20.7	Measures of Competition in a Geographic Market

The Herfindahl-Hirschman Index (HHI) is found by summing the squares of the market shares of all competitors in a market. If Institutions A and D merge, the HHI will rise from just over 1,740 to almost 2,500. HHIs exceeding 1,800 reflect high concentration.

Institution	Total Deposits (Millions $)	Concentration Ratio (% of Total)	% Squared
A	$1,200	26.45%	699.56[a]
B	975	21.49	461.82
C	800	17.63	310.92
D	650	14.33	205.25
E	200	4.41	19.43
F	175	3.86	14.88
G	160	3.53	12.44
H	120	2.64	7.00
I	98	2.16	4.67
J	75	1.65	2.73
K	43	0.95	0.90
L	27	0.60	0.35
M	14	0.31	0.10
Totals	$4,537	100.00%	1,740.04 = HHI

Market Competition Measures Assuming Institutions A and D Merge

Institution	Total Deposits (Millions $)	Concentration Ratio (% of Total)	% Squared
A + D	$1,850	40.78%	1,662.67
B	975	21.49	461.82
C	800	17.63	310.92
E	200	4.41	19.43
F	175	3.86	14.88
G	160	3.53	12.44
H	120	2.64	7.00
I	98	2.16	4.67
J	75	1.65	2.73
K	43	0.95	0.90
L	27	0.60	0.35
M	14	0.31	0.10
Totals	$4,537	100.00%	2,497.89 = HHI

[a] Calculated as 26.45×26.45, not 0.2645×0.2645.

ing policies of the banks, including HMDA disclosures. Based on this review of the entire record, the Board concluded that the banks had indeed attempted to meet the credit needs of all segments of the Dallas community, although it identified areas in need of improvement. As a result, the Board members approved Comerica's application.

SUMMARY

This chapter focused on techniques for analyzing long-term financial decisions. Generally, these decisions require NPV analysis, in which the cost of an investment is compared with the present value of future benefits. Such decisions also require an awareness of special legal and/or regulatory issues that may affect the results of the investment. For each investment, the NPV technique requires: 1) choice of a planning period; 2) estimation of incremental costs and benefits; 3) identification of a risk-adjusted required rate of return; and 4) comparison of the discounted values of costs and benefits.

NPV is presented in the context of two important categories of long-term investments: EFTs and acquisitions of other depository institutions. EFT systems include ATMs, ACHs, POS systems, and home-banking equipment. Cash-flow estimates for any of these investments must consider potential response of individual and institutional customers and costs imposed by regulations. Because customer acceptance of this technology is still in the growth stage, future cash flows are subject to considerable variability.

Whether to acquire another depository institution is a decision faced by many asset/liability managers. Again, the NPV technique provides the best decision about the acquisition. Because acquisitions involve payment to the owners of the target institution, an important aspect of the decision is the offering price. That choice must reflect the potential synergistic effects of the combination over and above the normal profits of the two separate institutions. Although other techniques are sometimes suggested for analyzing mergers, NPV is advocated, even with short-run earnings dilution. Any merger of financial institutions may be prohibited if the resulting combination is anticompetitive or fails to serve community needs.

QUESTIONS

1. What is the net present value of an asset or investment alternative? How is the NPV of an acquired asset related to the value of an institution? Why are expected marginal benefits and costs the only ones appropriate for consideration in an NPV analysis?

2. What discount rate should be used to calculate the NPV of investments of average risk? Should the same rate be used for long-term decisions of above- or below-average risk? Why or why not?

3. What are electronic funds transfer systems? Give examples of three EFT systems and explain how they affect institutions and their customers.

4. Trace the evolution of ATM pricing and incentive policies used by institutions as customer attitudes toward ATMs have changed during the last decade.

5. What are automated clearinghouses, and what role do they play in EFTs? Why did many corporations resist the use of electronic funds transfers in the early stages of EFT implementation, and how has that attitude changed in recent years?

6. Why has the Fed's involvement in development and expansion of automated clearinghouses been controversial? What long-term effects would you expect to result from the Fed's efforts to transfer ACH control to the private sector? Do you think private-sector control will encourage expanded usage of EFT by corporations and other customers? Why or why not?

7. Compare and contrast the rate of customer acceptance of ATM transactions to the rate of growth in usage of ACH direct payroll deposit systems.

8. How does the theory of innovation adoption explain the public's response to ATMs? Does this theory suggest extensive growth in ATM networks in the next decade? Why or why not? Would you expect home banking to follow the same adoption pattern? Why or why not?

9. What do you consider to be the appropriate degree of government involvement in the development and regulation of EFT systems? Why?

10. Review recent periodicals and trade publications for discussions of developments in ATMs. What current trends are apparent? Have the provisions regarding customer access in the Americans with Disabilities Act had noticeable effects on institutions offering ATMs? Explain.

11. Explain a point-of-sale transaction and the role of a debit card in it. Compare the relative advantages and disadvantages of on-line and off-line POS systems for customers, merchants, and depositories.

12. Explain the potential benefits and disadvantages to depository institutions of participating in shared ATM networks. What are the potential advantages from the customer's point of view?

13. What is check truncation? Why may customers of credit unions and thrifts have accepted this form of EFT more readily than bank customers?

14. What are the attractions and disadvantages of home banking systems from the customer's point of view? Consult recent editions of trade publications for the banking industry to evaluate the current status of home banking. What impediments to widespread acceptance remain? What technological innovations have been introduced?

15. What problems was Regulation E designed to prevent? What requirements are placed on depositories as a result of this regulation?

16. Define synergy in the context of financial institution mergers. What are the potential sources of synergy in such combinations? How might potential synergy be affected by in-market versus out-of-market mergers?

17. Review recent information in *The Wall Street Journal,* the *American Banker,* or other industry publications for reports of the acquisition of a thrift institution by a commercial bank. What was the thrift's financial status? How did the purchase price compare to its book value? What motivations for the merger were either identified by the bank's managers, implied by reports covering the acquisition, or both?

18. Other than PV estimates, what alternatives are available for estimating the value of a potential acquisition? What are the advantages and disadvantages of each? What approach best protects the long-term value of the acquiring institution? Explain.

19. Explain why an emphasis on potential short-run dilution following a merger may lead to a decision that conflicts with NPV. What factors affect realized earnings per share for a combined firm after a merger?

20. What questions do regulators consider when evaluating whether a proposed merger will have an adverse effect on competition? In your opinion, how much weight should be placed on the presence of thrifts and credit unions in evaluating the effect of a proposed bank merger in a market area? Why?

21. Discuss the Herfindahl-Hirschman Index (HHI) as a measure of a proposed merger's impact on market competition. What are some of the difficulties that regulators face in applying the HHI measure?

22. Review the explanation of the decision by the Board of Governors concerning Comerica's acquisition of Hibernia National Bank, provided in Figure 20.3. Do you agree with the Board's approach to measuring and interpreting the potential competitive effects of the acquisition? Why or why not?

23. What influences do the provisions of the Community Reinvestment Act (CRA) exert on the Fed's evaluation of a proposed merger or acquisition? Consult a recent edition of the *Federal Reserve Bulletin* and analyze the discussions of the Fed's decisions to approve or deny acquisitions. In your opinion, what relative weight is placed on the applicant's "good citizenship" as reflected in CRA-related activities? Can you find a decision in which the proposed merger passed all market competition tests but was denied based on the applicant's failure to comply with the CRA? If so, what shortcomings did the Fed find particularly objectionable? If not, what conclusions might you draw about the importance of CRA compliance in merger applications?

24. Many depository institutions find that long-term asset/liability strategies lead them into requirements to comply with additional regulations, such as consumer protection and the Americans with Disabilities Act provisions affecting ATM services. Identify other relevant regulatory requirements affecting depositories' long-term strategies. Can the costs of this compliance be quantified? How should such costs be incorporated in NPV analysis?

PROBLEMS

1. The management of Fresno National Bank is contemplating the purchase of a new computer to reduce costs associated with its growing number of transactions accounts. After allowing for trade-in on the current computer, the new computer will cost $102,000 plus $7,500 for installation. Management estimates an after-tax cost savings of $2 per year per account. The current volume of transactions accounts is 15,000, although a 3 percent growth in the number of accounts is expected each year for the next 5 years. Fresno National's required rate of return on long-term investments is 12 percent annually.
  a.   Using projections over the next 5 years, should the computer be purchased?
  b.   What is the maximum amount that Fresno National should invest in a new computer system, considering the expected benefits of such a system?
  c.   Using "what if" analysis, determine the NPV of the computer purchase at discount rates ranging between 10 percent and 20 percent. Summarize your findings.
  d.   Suppose that management's forecasts for the rate of growth in account volume are quite uncertain and that it is even possible that account volume could decline. Through "what if" analysis, determine the NPV of the decision, using a 12 percent discount rate and account growth rates ranging between 5 percent and −2 percent. Summarize your findings.
  e.   Finally, suppose that the estimate of cost savings per account is also uncertain and could actually range between $0.75 and $2.50. Using "what if" analysis, a 12 percent discount rate, and a 3 percent growth in account volume, determine how the NPV would change as cost savings change. (Suggestion: Vary the savings in $0.25 intervals.) Summarize your findings.
  f.   Based on your analyses in parts c through e, to what variable(s) does NPV seem especially sensitive? Explain.

2. The Cranberry Growers and Workers Credit Union is considering whether to open a branch office close to one of the largest cranberry bogs in New Jersey. Cash start-up costs, including architectural and construction expenses, are estimated at $180,000. Because of the convenience of the new location, management expects additional business from workers in the bog who are not currently members. Based on the anticipated volume of consumer lending, interest revenues in each of the next 30 years are expected to be $430,000 higher than the current level. Interest and operating costs as a result of new share accounts are expected to be $410,000 higher each year.

    a. If the credit union requires a 10 percent annual return on all long-term investments, should the new branch be opened?

    b. Suppose that management is uncertain about the proper discount rate and thinks that the branch expansion decision is of higher-than-average risk. If the decision is reevaluated at a risk-adjusted rate, will it be more or less desirable than it is at a 10 percent discount rate? Why?

    c. At what discount rate will the NPV of the branch be equal to $0?

    d. Based on your answer to part c, if management is truly uncertain about the riskiness of the project, would you recommend opening the branch?

3. The Flagstaff National Bank is analyzing the purchase of Chinle State Bank. The acquiree's shares have a current book value of $140, with an average RONW of 10 percent. The management of Flagstaff believes that the merger could increase RONW to 16 percent for 8 years after the acquisition. After that time, RONW is expected to stabilize at 13 percent. During the first eight years, growth in assets and net worth for Chinle is expected to be 5 percent, falling to a constant rate of 3 percent thereafter. Flagstaff's required rate of return on the investment is 12 percent.

    a. Calculate the expected retention rate for Chinle during the first 8 years.

    b. Using the retention rate found in part a, estimate the earnings that will be retained each year for 8 years and the cash available each year.

    c. Calculate the retention rate for the period of constant growth beginning in the ninth year after the merger, and also calculate the cash available at the end of the ninth year.

    d. Calculate the total present value of the cash available to Flagstaff as a result of the merger. What is the most that should be paid for each share of Chinle's stock?

    e. Using "what if" analysis, show how the purchase price would change if Flagstaff National's required rate of return ranged between 10 percent and 20 percent.

    f. Using "what if" analysis, show how the purchase price would change if the anticipated growth rate for Chinle State during the first eight years after the merger ranged between 4 percent and 8 percent. Use 0.5 percent intervals. Assume, as in parts a and b, that the growth rate after this period will be 3 percent and that Flagstaff National's required rate of return is 12 percent.

    g. Based on the results of parts e and f, to estimates of which variable—required return or growth rate—should Flagstaff National's management pay greater attention? Explain.

4. Suppose that the management of Flagstaff National Bank in Problem 3 wants to estimate the value of a share of Chinle's stock using data from other mergers recently completed in the region. Flagstaff's stock currently has a book value of $85.

    a. If recent mergers have resulted in an average cash-to-book value ratio of 1.6, what price is suggested for Chinle?

    b. If recent mergers have resulted in an average book-to-book exchange ratio of 1.3, how many shares of Flagstaff's stock would be exchanged for one share of Chinle's?

    c. If the ratio of price to acquiree's EPS has averaged 14.3 recently, what is your estimate of the per-share price Flagstaff should offer to Chinle's shareholders?

    d. What limitations do these measures have compared to NPV analysis?

5. Using NPV analysis, Jersey State Bank has recently agreed to pay 1.55 times the book value of Northeast Savings' net worth in an upcoming merger. Stock will be sold to obtain the cash to acquire Northeast. Assume no change in net income during the first year. Jersey's growth rate is currently projected at 6 percent without the merger.

	Jersey	Northeast
Total assets	$600 million	$75 million
Net worth (book)	$27 million	$6 million
Net income	$7.5 million	$937,500
Shares outstanding	4 million	
Market price/share	$10.25	

a. Based on the information shown, determine whether EPS will be diluted in the first year as a result of the merger. If so, can you conclude that the merger is a mistake from the point of view of Jersey's shareholders?

b. Suppose that the management of Jersey State Bank anticipates a one-time 9 percent growth in earnings in the second year after the merger. (This estimate includes normal growth plus a synergistic effect.) What EPS can Jersey's shareholders anticipate during that year? Is the merger a mistake?

c. Using "what if" analysis, determine how the *third* year's EPS would change if anticipated growth in Northeast Savings ranges between 2 percent and 20 percent. (Hint: Remember, as part of the set-up, to develop a formula to calculate the weighted growth rate if the merger occurs.) What can you conclude from your analysis?

6. First National Bank has applied to acquire DeSoto National Bank. The regulators require a competitive analysis using both the market concentration ratio and HHI. The relevant market is the southern third of the state, and the following information is available:

Institutions	Deposits (Millions)
First National Bank	$1,050
Kendall State Bank	960
Hampton Bank and Trust	875
United Security S&L	700
DeSoto National Bank	650
King Federal Savings	300
Citizens National Bank	175
Newport State Bank	92
Palm Beach Federal Savings	55
Walnut Grove National Bank	37
Golden East State Bank	22
Logansport Savings Bank	11

a. Measure the degree of competition before and after the merger, using the market concentration ratio. What is the three-firm concentration ratio before and after?

b. Measure the degree of competition before and after the merger, using the HHI. Is the Justice Department likely to challenge the proposed merger? Why or why not?

c. Repeat your analysis after omitting the four thrift institutions. How much difference does this make in your results?

d. What factors besides these might regulators consider?

SELECTED REFERENCES

"The Automated Clearinghouse Alternative: How Do We Get There from Here?" *Economic Review* (Federal Reserve Bank of Atlanta) 71 (April 1986): entire issue.

Beatty, Randolph P., Anthony M. Santomero, and Michael C. Smirlock. *Bank Merger Premiums: Theory and Evidence.* New York: Salomon Brothers Center for the Study of Financial Institutions, 1987.

Benston, George J., William C. Hunter, and Larry D. Wall. "Motivations for Bank Mergers and Acquisitions: Enhancing the Deposit Insurance Put Option versus Increasing Operating Net Cash Flow," Working Paper 92-4, Federal Reserve Bank of Atlanta, 1992.

————. "Potential Diversification and Bank Acquisition Prices." Working Paper 90-11, Federal Reserve Bank of Atlanta, 1990.

Boyd, John, and Stanley L. Graham. "Investigating the Banking Consolidation Trend." *Quarterly Review* (Federal Reserve Bank of Minneapolis) 15 (Spring 1991): 3–15.

Bullington, Robert A., and Arnold E. Jensen. "Pricing a Bank." *Bankers Magazine* 164 (May/June 1981): 94–98.

Cates, David C. "Prices Paid for Banks." *Economic Review* (Federal Reserve Bank of Atlanta) 70 (January 1985): 36–41.

Cox, William N., and Paul F. Metzker, "Special Issue: Displacing the Check." *Economic Review* (Federal Reserve Bank of Atlanta) 68 (August 1983): entire issue.

Darnell, Jerome C. "Bank Mergers: Prices Paid to Marriage Partners," *Business Review* (Federal Reserve Bank of Philadelphia) (July 1973): 16–25.

Duprey, James N. "A Visible Hand: The Fed's Involvement in the Check Payments System." *Quarterly Review* (Federal Reserve Bank of Minneapolis) 10 (Spring 1986): 18–29.

Eisemann, Peter C., and George A. Budd. "Acquisitions and Dilution." *Magazine of Bank Administration* 58 (November 1982): 34–38.

Fraser, Donald P., and James W. Kolari. "Pricing Small Bank Acquisitions." *Journal of Retail Banking* 10 (Winter 1988): 23–28.

Frisbee, Pamela S. "The ACH: An Elusive Dream." *Economic Review* (Federal Reserve Bank of Atlanta) 71 (March 1986): 4–8.

Furlong, Frederick T. "Assessing Bank Antitrust Standards." *Weekly Letter* (Federal Reserve Bank of San Francisco), May 15, 1987.

_____. "The Wells Fargo–Crocker Acquisition." *Weekly Letter* (Federal Reserve Bank of San Francisco), November 29, 1986.

Guerin-Calvert, Margaret E. and Janusz A. Ordover. "The 1992 Agency Horizontal Merger Guidelines and the Department of Justice's Approach to Bank Merger Analysis." In *Proceedings of a Conference on Bank Structure and Competition,* 545–560. Chicago: Federal Reserve Bank of Chicago, 1992.

Hume, D. William, Otto P. Trostel, and Eleanor M. Kruk. "Implementing Check Truncation." *Bankers Magazine* 168 (November/December 1985): 36–42.

Humphrey, David B., and Allen N. Berger. "Market Failure and Resource Use: Economic Incentives to Use Different Payment Instruments." In *The U.S. Payment System: Efficiency, Risk, and the Role of the Federal Reserve.* Boston: Kluwer Academic Publishers, 1990.

Hunter, William C., and Larry D. Wall. "Bank Merger Motivations: A Review of the Evidence and an Examination of Key Target Bank Characteristics." *Economic Review* (Federal Reserve Bank of Atlanta) 74 (September/October 1989): 2–19.

James, Christopher M., and Peggy Wier. "Returns to Acquirers and Competition in the Acquisition Market: The Case of Banking." *Journal of Political Economy* 95 (1987): 355–370.

Knight, Robert E. "The Changing Payments Mechanism: Electronic Funds Transfer Arrangements." *Monthly Review* (Federal Reserve Bank of Kansas City) 60 (July/August 1974).

Laderman, Elizabeth. "Shared ATM Networks: An Uneasy Alliance?" *Weekly Letter* (Federal Reserve Bank of San Francisco), February 23, 1990a.

_____. "The Public Policy Implications of State Laws Pertaining to Automated Teller Machines." *Economic Review* (Federal Reserve Bank of San Francisco) (Winter 1990b): 43–58.

_____. "Progress in Retail Payments." *Weekly Letter* (Federal Reserve Bank of San Francisco), February 7, 1992.

Lederman, Cary Jon. "ATM Strategies: Looking Ahead." *Journal of Retail Banking* 11 (Winter 1988): 17–25.

McAndrews, James J. "The Evolution of Shared ATM Networks." *Business Review* (Federal Reserve Bank of Philadelphia) (May/June 1991): 3–16.

Melia, Marilyn. "The ATM Agenda." *Savings Institutions* 112 (November 1991): 38–42.

Morris, Russell D. "An Empirical Analysis of Costs and Revenue Requirements for Point-of-Sale EFTS." *Journal of Bank Research* 9 (Autumn 1978): 136–145.

Neely, Walter P., and David P. Rochester. "Operating Performance and Merger Benefits: The Savings and Loan Experience." *Financial Review* 22 (February 1987): 111–130.

Osterberg, Ronald. "POS Is on Its Way." *Economic Review* (Federal Reserve Bank of Atlanta) 69 (July/August 1984): 32–35.

Phillis, Dave, and Christine Pavel. "Interstate Banking Game Plans: Implications for the Midwest." *Economic Perspectives* (Federal Reserve Bank of Chicago) 10 (March/April 1986): 23–39.

Quackenbush, Christopher, and Scott E. Willkomm. "New Opportunities in Thrift Acquisitions." *Bankers Magazine* 173 (January/February 1990): 24–29.

Rhoades, Stephen A. "The Herfindahl-Hirschman Index." *Federal Reserve Bulletin* 79 (March 1993): 188–189.

Schroeder, Frederick. "Developments in Consumer Electronic Fund Transfers." *Federal Reserve Bulletin* 69 (June 1983): 395–403.

Seed, Allen H., III. "Structuring Capital Spending Hurdle Rates." *Financial Executive* (February 1982): 20–28.

Shull, Bernard. "Economic Efficiency, Public Regulation, and Financial Reform: Depository Institutions." In *Financial Institutions and Markets.* 2d ed. Edited by Murray E.

Polakoff and Thomas A. Durkin. Boston: Houghton Mifflin, 1981.

Stone, Bernell K. "Corporate Trade Payments: Hard Lessons in Product Design." *Economic Review* (Federal Reserve Bank of Atlanta) 71 (April 1986): 9–21.

————. "Electronic Payment Basics." *Economic Review* (Federal Reserve Bank of Atlanta) 71 (March 1986): 9–18.

————. "Electronic Payments at the Crossroads." *Economic Review* (Federal Reserve Bank of Atlanta) 71 (March 1986): 20–33.

————. "The Revolution in Retail Payments: A Synthesis." *Economic Review* (Federal Reserve Bank of Atlanta) 69 (July/August 1984): 46–55.

Stutzer, Michael J. "Probable Future Competition in Banking Antitrust Determination: Research Findings." *Quarterly Review* (Federal Reserve Bank of Minneapolis) 8 (Summer 1984): 9–17.

Summers, Bruce. "Electronic Payments in Retrospect." *Economic Review* (Federal Reserve Bank of Richmond) 74 (March/April 1988): 16–19.

Taube, Paul M. "The Influence of Selected Factors on the Frequency of ATM Usage." *Journal of Retail Banking* 10 (Spring 1988): 47–52.

Welker, Donald L. "Thrift Competition: Does It Matter?" *Economic Review* (Federal Reserve Bank of Richmond) 72 (January/February 1986): 2–10.

Woerheide, Walter J. *The Savings and Loan Industry.* Westport, CT: Quorum Books, 1984.

Wood, John C., and Dolores S. Smith. "Electronic Transfer of Government Benefits." *Federal Reserve Bulletin* 77 (April 1991): 230–217.

*Personal trust no longer refers to doling out money
by dead employees to dead people.*
Alice Arvin
Bankers Monthly (1989)

C H A P T E R

21

FEE-BASED

SERVICES

C. Robert Brenton is a third-generation Iowa banker and Chairman of Brenton Banks, Des Moines, Iowa. Although some might expect an Iowa banker to hold tightly to past traditions, Mr. Brenton defies generalizations. He has transformed himself and his bankers into a sales force offering a wide array of financial services, including mutual funds, annuities, and other investment products. As Mr. Brenton described it, the transformation from thinking like a banker to thinking like a broker is "like a Christian learning to be a Buddhist. You have to embrace it wholeheartedly." By 1992, his bank boasted 15 experienced brokers, and he planned to double that sales force in 1993. They are serving a group of customers with money to invest, in need of someone they can trust. Mr. Brenton believes Brenton Brokerage will meet that need, and the bank will benefit from the steady stream of fee income generated by the sale of financial products.

Many bankers share his view. An example of a much larger institution acting aggressively to enter the securities business is J. P. Morgan. The bank holding company's (BHC's) subsidiary, J. P. Morgan Securities, Inc., not only offers brokerage services but also began underwriting corporate debt in 1989. Within 2 years, it had exceeded the debt underwriting volume of such well-known Wall Street firms as Paine-Webber and Bear Stearns. Not resting on its laurels, the BHC plans to continue the growth of its securities subsidiary. Executives want to build broad relationships with customers, and brokerage and underwriting will be an important component of J. P. Morgan's full-service approach. These relationships will generate fee income for the bank, supplementing the more traditional interest income.[1]

The transformation of Brenton Banks and J. P. Morgan is being replicated elsewhere in the banking industry. During the late 1980s, banks began actively modernizing and expanding the operations of trust

---

[1] Dale Cheney, "Iowa Banker Adopts the Brokerage Gospel," *American Banker,* January 13, 1993, 1, 10; Fred R. Bleakley, "J. P. Morgan Expands Role in Underwriting, Irking Securities Firms," *The Wall Street Journal,* November 13, 1991, A1, A8; and James R. Norman, "Morgan Makes Its Move," *Forbes,* October 26, 1992, 181–182.

departments, taking advantage of the industry's new powers to offer a variety of financial services to customers. Many firms, like Brenton Banks and J. P. Morgan, have gone much further and developed new services, including brokerage, underwriting, and insurance. The purpose of this chapter is to trace the rise of these phenomena and to outline their relationship to other facets of asset/liability management.

THE ROLE OF FEE-BASED SERVICES

If a growing number of depository institutions are discovering lines of business somewhat removed from deposit taking and lending, there must be reasons. The primary ones are financial.

WHY FEE INCOME?

Most depositories' revenues continue to come from interest-earning assets and most expenses from interest-bearing liabilities. In the increasingly competitive environment, however, rate differentials between various categories of assets and their funding sources are narrower than in the past. This narrowing puts downward pressure on net income, the institution's capital position, internal growth, and possible dividend payments—unless noninterest sources of revenue, such as service fees, can be found.

Fee income is also more stable than other revenue sources because it is less likely to rise and fall with the general level of interest rates or with shifts in the term structure. It also is independent of unpredictable day-to-day deposit inflows and outflows. In other words, fee income rarely is highly positively correlated with other cash flows, so it provides diversification benefits by reducing variability in cash flows.

A third reason why depositories find fee income attractive can be traced to recent international capital rules. Unlike loans, which provide income, but against which institutions must maintain risk-weighted capital standards, fee-based services generate income but do not increase a bank's, thrift's, or CU's capital requirements. Thus, they may be appealing to institutions that see additional revenues but do not wish to incur the risks of increasing the size of the loan portfolio.

GROWTH OF FEE INCOME

As with other changes, the recent emphasis on fee-based services is often traced to money-center banks. As explained in Chapter 14, by the late 1970s, most large banks faced the possibility of losing their best commercial lending customers to the commercial paper market. As a result, some banks, notably Bankers Trust of New York, began replacing lost interest income with fees from offering cash management services to corporate customers.[2]

Nevertheless, evidence from depository institutions of all sizes and types indicates that this view of the rise of fee-based income is too narrow. From 1981 to 1991, for example, noninterest income as a percentage of average assets grew for banks of all sizes, from 0.65 percent to 0.72 percent. In contrast, net interest income fell during the same period, from 5.05 percent to 4.20 percent of average assets.[3]

Statistics from the thrift and credit union (CU) industries also show the growing importance of noninterest income. From 1980 to 1988, fee income unrelated to mortgages (fee income in excess of mortgage points) grew from 6.1 percent to 13.3 percent of operating income at Federal Savings and Loan Insurance Corporation (FSLIC)-insured institutions. By year-end 1991, noninterest income from all sources at federally insured thrifts was almost equal to 12 percent of interest income. Among federal CUs, noninterest income grew more than 40 percent *per year* between 1982 and 1985, the largest single change in any income or expense category during those years. Between 1989 and 1991, noninterest income grew from 5.5 to 6.9 percent of total income for these depositories. Indications are that these trends mark an era in which fee-based activities are assuming a major role in the management of depository institutions.[4]

TRADITIONAL FEE-BASED SERVICES

Some sources of fee income have been available to depositories for many years but only recently have received greater attention as part of an overall financial management strategy. Several traditional sources of fee income, such as deposit service charges, credit card

---

[2] For more details, see "Wholesale Banking's New Hard Sell," *Business Week,* April 13, 1981, 82–86. For a more current view, see Kelley Holland, "Banking On Fees," *Business Week,* January 18, 1993, 72–73.

[3] Federal Financial Institutions Examination Council, *Uniform Bank Performance Report,* 1985, 1992.

[4] *1989 Savings Institutions Source Book* (Chicago: U.S. League of Savings Institutions, 1989), 54; National Credit Union Administration, various annual reports; and Office of Thrift Supervision, "4th Quarter 1991 Financial Developments for Private Sector Savings Associations," March 1992.

fees, and fees associated with electronic funds transfers (EFTs), are discussed in earlier chapters. Credit card fees have grown in recent years to the largest single source of noninterest income for many banks, particularly those with a retail focus; virtually all depositories have increased service charges on some or all of their transactions accounts; and fee income associated with EFTs increases as these services grow more popular with corporations and households. Because these topics are covered in considerable detail elsewhere in the book, they are not addressed further in this chapter.

Two other important traditional services are trust departments and correspondent banking. Although growth in fee income may occur primarily from nontraditional lines of business, the evolving nature of these two traditional services is of interest.

TRUST DEPARTMENT OPERATIONS

Trust departments are responsible for managing the investments of individuals or institutional clients such as pension funds. These monies are the clients' assets, separate from the depository institution's assets, and are managed according to clients' risk/return preferences. Besides investment management, many trust departments offer related services, such as estate planning and tax preparation.

Trust departments have historically been most important in large institutions, although smaller institutions have become more active in recent years. Insured commercial and savings banks must receive the approval both of state regulators and the Federal Deposit Insurance Corporation (FDIC) before engaging in trust management. Approximately 20 percent of commercial banks offer trust services; fewer thrift institutions have trust management. However, thrift publications indicate an increasing interest in trust services. Although CUs seldom offer formal trust departments, by 1991 almost 30 percent of large CUs were providing financial planning services to members.[5]

In the past, trust services were offered to wealthy customers at no explicit charge in exchange for the client's agreement to keep low-cost deposit balances with the institution. As reflected in the opening quotation for this chapter, trust departments were "loss leaders," rarely profitable but operated because they enabled the institution to attract desirable (even if less than lively) customers. Consequently, trust department managers were under minimal pressure to earn high rates of return on trust assets. Many customers viewed the trust department as an added convenience of doing business with a particular institution and not as the source of high investment returns.

These conditions are also reflected in available data on trust operations in the past. In one survey of trust officers in the early 1970s, 60 percent believed that maximizing service was their chief objective. Only 19 percent indicated that maximizing portfolio profitability was the goal, and only 3 percent indicated that fee income generated by the department was an important measure of success. Another study of 300 bank trust departments during 1972–1981 indicated that they provided customers with only a 4 percent average annual return, compared with 4.9 percent for other money managers.[6]

NEW DIRECTIONS

It is understandable that when yields on most investments were relatively low over long periods, the performance of trust departments was not considered important to an institution's success. Customers with conservative investment preferences might not have been able to do much better anywhere else. But higher market rates and deregulation changed that. As market yields rose in the 1980s, few high-balance customers were willing to keep their money in low- or no-interest accounts, and few were willing to settle for lower risk-adjusted rates of return on trust assets than they could receive elsewhere. Also, corporations seeking managers for their employees' pension funds would not settle for below-market returns, because an employer's contributions to the fund depend on how much investment income is earned on existing fund assets.

In response to new pressures to contribute fee income to the depository and to satisfy customers, trust

[5] Credit Union National Association, *1991 Credit Union Report,* 2.

[6] See Smith and Goudzwaard 1972; and Daniel Hertzberg, "In Big Shift, Bankers Start Hiring Outsiders for Money Management," *The Wall Street Journal,* December 6, 1982. (References are listed in full at the end of this chapter.)

departments are changing. Most now charge explicit fees for trust services, often based on the principal value of the client's assets. Marketing strategies are aimed at newly affluent individuals and families instead of traditional "old money" clients. Some depositories continue to offer in-house trust departments, but they assign the management of the portfolio to outside managers. This strategy can result in the hiring of a competitor, such as a mutual fund, to manage clients' money.

Many institutions retain internal management of trust portfolios and place increasing emphasis on portfolio management results. This new focus requires more highly trained personnel who are schooled in the sophisticated investment techniques illustrated in earlier chapters, such as duration, options, and futures. A study of more than 200 trust departments conducted in 1987 and 1988 found that about 11 percent of the total sample used stock index futures and options. However, more than 20 percent of the large institutions (defined as those managing $1 billion or more in assets) regularly participated in the futures and options markets. Respondents used these instruments primarily for hedging, but a few were speculators.[7]

The new emphasis in trust departments on more highly trained personnel is paying off, according to a recent study commissioned by the American Bankers Association. A comparison of rates of return earned by commercial bank trust departments with those achieved by mutual funds from 1978 to 1988 found that the bankers were doing quite well. For example, trust departments had earned a 10-year average return of 15.9 percent on equity investments, compared with 15.1 percent for mutual funds. The banks also performed better on fixed-income investments than did mutual funds; however, insurance companies outperformed trust departments on both measures.[8]

Despite their improving performance, trust departments face growing competition for customers. Bank trust officers must also encounter the skepticism of wealthy customers. A survey conducted by a New York bank in 1992, for example, revealed that wealthy Americans will seek investment advice from many constituencies, including insurance agents and relatives, before they will turn to a commercial or private banker. Banks are likely to persevere in their quest for trust customers, however, because of potential earnings. A 1992 survey of CEOs of large regional banks found that 78 percent ranked trust income among the top three sources of income for their institutions.[9]

A RELATED SERVICE: PERSONAL FINANCIAL PLANNING

New emphasis on fee income has generated interest in another service that is a natural outgrowth of trust departments: personal financial planning. Financial planners assist individuals with decisions on budgeting, taxes, investments, retirement and estate planning, and other financial matters. Institutions emphasizing this service know it can be costly: If truly individualized advice is given, the expense of hiring, training, and maintaining a staff is considerable. Fees must therefore be commensurate with the cost of producing the service. For this reason, some institutions have developed general financial plans that can be quickly generated by computer, using basic information about the client (such as age, income, family size, and assets). Financial planning of this type is a low-fee, low-cost service, dependent on high volume for profitability.[10]

---

[7] A follow-up survey after the stock market crash of 1987 found that the nonusers were even more reluctant to enter the markets for futures and options. For further discussion on these applications, see Block and Gallagher 1988 and Bollenbacher 1984.

[8] Interestingly, neither banks, mutual funds, or insurance companies were able to equal market indices for the 1978–1988 period. See "Trust Bests Mutual Funds," *ABA Banking Journal* 81 (April 1989): 7; Michael C. Baker, "Equity Performance Study Shows Banks Coming on Strong," *Trusts and Estates* 125 (May 1985): 19–20; Donald Korytowski and Carolyn Mainguene, "Banks versus Counselors: The Race Continues," *Trusts and Estates* 124 (Septem-

ber 1985): 45–48; and Dexter Hutchins, "Banks Shine at Managing Money," *Fortune* 112 (1986 Investors Guide), 161. Not all recent performance studies have favored banks, however. For an opposing view, see William B. Madden, "New Figures Show Bank Investing Slips," *Trusts and Estates* 124 (November 1985): 53–55.

[9] Karen Talley, "Wealthy Shun Bankers as Advisers," *American Banker*, January 13, 1993, 11; and Debra Cope, "Profits From Fee Products Coming—But How Soon," *American Banker*, December 23, 1992, 1, 5.

[10] See Webb and Hawk 1988; and Lewis Mandell, Neil B. Murphy, and James Sifridis, "Consumer Demand for Personal Service and Financial Planning in Banking," unpublished paper presented at the Financial Management Association annual meeting, October 19, 1988.

Recent research indicates that depositories are moving into the financial planning arena more rapidly in the 1990s than in previous periods, with savings and loan associations (S&Ls) trailing banks. Wealthier customers may not be the ones willing to pay for such services however, because they may receive them elsewhere or have sufficient expertise to manage their own money. Thus far, personal financial planning services seem of particular interest to institutions that have chosen a retail focus or that have been successful at attracting a large quantity of core deposits.

CORRESPONDENT BANKING

Correspondent banks, first defined in Chapter 12, sell management and administrative services such as check clearing, securities safekeeping, and federal funds (fed funds) trading, to smaller institutions (**respondents).** Like trust operations, correspondent banking is now very different from its earlier days. A particularly interesting change is the unusual competition for fee income between large commercial banks and federal regulators.

MAJOR SERVICES OFFERED

In the past, services were usually offered to respondents at less than full cost in exchange for their keeping relatively high demand deposit balances with the correspondent bank. Like trust customers, respondents were willing to forgo interest income in exchange for convenience and management expertise. Often, correspondents offered a bundle of services for a single fee, a deposit balance requirement, or both. In fact, a complete list of all correspondent services would require several pages and might be misleading.

Although literally dozens of functions could be hired out, the bulk of correspondent banking was centered on just a few activities. More than 80 percent of the correspondents surveyed in the late 1970s considered check collection to be their most important service, followed by securities safekeeping, fed funds trading, wire transfer, and securities transfer and clearance. The importance of a service was based on the volume of respondent balances that the service attracted. More recent surveys support the continued importance of most of these five functions, as well as of loan participations offered to respondents by their correspondents.[11]

DIDMCA AND THE FED'S ENTRY INTO CORRESPONDENT BANKING

Before the Depository Institutions Deregulation and Monetary Control Act (DIDMCA), parties in a correspondent banking relationship had few reasons to complain because each side believed it had something to gain. DIDMCA, however, contained several provisions that "upset the apple cart." The most important were those mandating universal reserve requirements, access to Federal Reserve System (Fed) services for all depositories, the explicit pricing of Fed services, and the authorization of transactions accounts for thrifts and CUs.

PRICING FED SERVICES

Before DIDMCA, the Fed charged member banks no explicit fees for check clearing and other services as compensation for required noninterest-bearing reserves. Because most correspondent banks were large and most large banks were Fed members, they would use the Fed's "free" services and charge their smaller nonmember respondents explicit fees for the same services. Now, however, with universal reserve requirements, access by all to Fed services, and explicit Fed pricing, all institutions are motivated to shop for the services they need.

Now included among the price lists to be checked is the Fed's, and because the Fed publishes an unbundled list in which each service is priced separately, traditional correspondents have also gone to unbundled explicit pricing. Respondents pay only for the services they need and feel less obligation to keep excess low-earning balances with correspondents. One study found, for example, that between 1981 and 1984, percentage declines in correspondent balances at

---

[11] "Correspondent Products: Which Is No. 1?" 1988; Dunham 1981, Table 2, p. 29; Rideout and Seidler 1981; and Steve Cocheo, "Correspondent Banking Isn't Quite Ready for a Glass Case," *ABA Banking Journal* 93 (May 1991): 37–40.

the six largest correspondents ranged from 11 percent to nearly 45 percent.[12]

Data collected by the American Bankers Association indicate that large correspondent commercial banks consider the Fed their strongest competitor. Although smaller correspondent banks consider large banks their most formidable competitors, correspondents of all sizes believe that the Fed's explicit pricing of services has hurt profitability.[13]

COMPETITIVE OUTLOOK FOR THE FED. According to a study of the Fed's impact on correspondent banking during the 5-year period after the passage of DIDMCA, the Fed initially lost customers to private correspondents and clearinghouses. On recognizing the loss of market share, however, the Fed revised services and pricing and began to recapture lost customers. Despite protests that the Fed is an unfair competitor, Congress supports an expanded Fed role in correspondent services. In fact, some observers argue that the Fed's entry into traditional correspondent banking has produced more efficient markets for these services. The conclusion of a 1985 study was that the Fed is committed to the market for correspondent services and that its influence is likely to grow, not diminish.[14]

RELATIVE BENEFITS OF CORRESPONDENT SERVICES

With the trend toward unbundled pricing has come the recognition that not all services are equally profitable. Figure 21.1 shows the correspondent prod-

---

[12] See Burns 1986.

[13] As cited in Merrill 1983, Table 3.

Congress mandated that Fed prices incorporate a private sector markup, reflecting the cost of capital, to allow private correspondents to compete. Determining what that cost should be, however, has been controversial. See Kuprianov 1986.

[14] See Evanoff 1985. Although many bankers argue that the Fed is unfair competition, given its size and the fact that it makes the rules by which banks must abide, not all experts agree. Some argue that the Fed's activities have been procompetitive, not anticompetitive, and that the Fed is not likely to end up a monopolist in the provision of correspondent services. See, for example, Reichert 1981, Merrill 1983, and Frodin 1984.

In its annual report of operations, the Board of Governors identifies the volume of Fed services sold and the income from those services. Recent data indicate that the volume of services continues to grow and that the prices charged actually result in a net profit to the Board of Governors. See Board of Governors of the Federal Reserve System, *1991 Annual Report*, 227–236.

FIGURE 21.1   ## Profitability of Correspondent Services

Correspondent banking services are not equally profitable. Check clearing, a traditional service, continues to lead in profitability, followed by data processing and short-term loans to respondents (overlines).

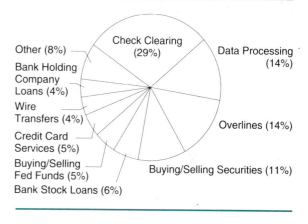

Source: "Correspondent Products: Which Is No. 1?" 1988.

---

ucts and services considered to be the most profitable by more than 300 correspondent banks responding to a survey conducted by the *ABA Banking Journal* in 1988. Check clearing dominated all other services on the profitability measure. Although not shown in the figure, check clearing was also considered to be the service that was most important to the success of a bank's correspondent service operation. Data processing and overlines (short-term loans to respondents) ranked second in profitability. Even though assisting respondents in the fed funds market was less profitable, that service was considered very important for maintaining successful relations with respondents. The study also revealed that despite the increased competition from the Fed, 86 percent of respondents believed that, in the late 1980s, correspondent banking was at least as profitable as in previous years. In fact, almost 50 percent thought profits had improved.[15]

ENTRY OF OTHER COMPETITORS

The entry of thrifts and CUs into the business of providing transactions accounts in the past decade added a layer of complexity to correspondent banking.

---

[15] "Correspondent Products: Which Is No. 1?" 1988.

THE FHLB SYSTEM. Because they are relatively small, few thrifts or CUs have established their own check-clearing systems, but many have sought to speed their entry into the market by offering truncated checks. (Recall that check truncation was first discussed in Chapter 20.) Traditional check clearing by correspondent banks seldom provided a truncation feature, however, encouraging the Federal Home Loan Bank (FHLB) system to offer check-clearing services, including truncation, for interested thrifts. As a consequence, the FHLB system initially captured a greater share of thrifts' check-clearing business than did correspondent commercial banks.[16] Despite changes in the FHLB system, Title VII of the Financial Institutions Reform, Recovery, and Enforcement Act (FIRREA) authorizes FHLBs to continue to offer correspondent services to Savings Association Insurance Fund (SAIF)-insured thrifts or to other system members.

CORPORATE CREDIT UNIONS. Correspondent banking has also been changed by the introduction of transactions accounts in the credit union industry. The changes are welcomed by CUs because most are small enough to escape post-DIDMCA reserve requirements, although they remain eligible to purchase Fed services.

Corporate CUs, defined in Chapter 12 as CUs for CUs, gained access to Fed services under DIDMCA provisions. Using this access, corporate credit unions grew rapidly in the 1980s, offering technology and expertise to small CUs. For example, corporate credit unions provide securities safekeeping for member CUs by establishing a corporate CU account at the Fed. The cost to a small CU of having its securities safeguarded this way is often lower than if it obtained the service from a correspondent bank. In 1985, the estimated savings to CUs from using corporate CUs instead of correspondent banks was $72 million; annual savings by 1990 were projected at $200 million. The volume of correspondent services provided by corporate CUs continued to grow rapidly during the early 1990s.[17]

BANKERS' BANKS. Analogous to corporate CUs are **bankers' banks.** They are what their name suggests: banks for banks. The first was formed in Minnesota in 1975, and by 1990, an estimated 2,834 small banks nationwide were using their services. Like corporate CUs, bankers' banks are formed when small institutions band together to purchase stock in a newly chartered bank; the new institution performs functions for owner banks that would be more costly if performed individually. Included are functions such as check clearing, securities safekeeping, and other correspondent services. Also like corporate CUs, bankers' banks have access to Fed services. Like the FHLB system and corporate CUs, bankers' banks provide increasing competition for the traditional suppliers of correspondent services.[18]

WHAT LIES AHEAD? Services currently provided by correspondent banks are not uniform across the industry but vary depending on the size and location of the correspondent and respondent banks. One opinion that does seem to be uniform, however, is that fee-based pricing is here to stay.

Although smaller institutions may not be able to offer a full range of services, they are able to compete effectively by emphasizing the efficiency of the ones they do offer. Further, many correspondents are recognizing opportunities to offer new services or expand their markets. Bankers expect higher demand in the future for services such as consulting, training, capital markets products, and trust. Finally, banks must recognize that savings institutions and CUs are potentially important markets in which to compete.[19]

RELATED SERVICES: CORPORATE CASH MANAGEMENT AND MANAGEMENT CONSULTING

Several fee-based services closely related to correspondent banking are developing. Of particular im-

---

[16] See Morphew 1981, 243.

[17] Credit Union National Association, *1985 Annual Report,* 20–21; *1988 Annual Report,* 37; *1991 Annual Report.*

[18] For more information on the functions of and laws governing bankers' banks, see Frisbee 1984; and A. Joseph Newman, Jr., "Pennsylvania Bankers' Bank Exemplifies A Vibrant Breed," *American Banker,* August 23, 1990, 2, 5.

[19] "Correspondent Banking's Changing Face" 1988; Merrill and Neely 1983; "Correspondent Banks Set New Courses," *ABA Banking Journal* 77 (March 1985): 48–49; Reichert 1985; and Burns 1986.

TABLE 21.1	**Banker Attitudes toward Sources of Fee Income**

The table reveals attitudes of a sample of bankers toward the attractiveness of offering different fee-based services and toward the probability of entering into those markets. Fees from loan originations and credit life insurance were attractive and feasible; discount brokerage, although an attractive product, was not as likely to be added to these bankers' range of services offered.

Probability of Adding or Expanding	Product Attractiveness[a]		
	High	**Medium**	**Low**
High	Credit life insurance Fee-generating lending services Increased fees on current products	Shared automatic teller machine	Money market funds
Medium	Leasing Life and health insurance brokerage Mortgage banking	Consumer finance Property/liability insurance Real estate development	Card-based services Discount brokerage Financial planning Home banking Point-of-sale systems Proprietary automatic teller machines
Low	Securities brokerage	Property management Real estate brokerage Travel agency (full-service)	Insurance underwriting Real estate appraisals

[a] Product attractiveness is the potential for substantially increasing income.
Source: Bank Administration Institute, *Banking Issues and Innovations,* Sample Issue, 1984, 3. Also from Survey of Texas Bankers conducted by The MAC Group for the Texas Bankers Association, *The Impact of Deregulation on Small and Medium Sized Texas Banks,* 1983. Reprinted with permission of The MAC Group.

portance are cash management services for nonfinancial corporations, offered by commercial banks with which businesses maintain close financial relationships. Cash management services include assisting customers with collecting accounts, disbursing expenditures, forecasting cash balances, and investing temporarily idle cash in money market instruments.

Cash management revenue grew rapidly in the 1980s, and growth continued in the 1990s, but at a slower pace. For example, at the 300 largest U.S. banks, revenues generated by cash management services increased 7.5 percent between 1990 and 1991. A 1992 survey of these large institutions revealed bankers' confidence in the continuing promise of this market. They indicated their intentions to increase investment in technology to provide expanded services with greater efficiency.

Although traditionally the province of large banks, the field is also promising for small institutions. One survey indicated that more than 60 percent of small business managers responding named cash management as their greatest concern. The *American*

Banker reported that medium-sized businesses accounted for 24 percent of banks' cash management revenue in 1991—a 20 percent increase in that sector as a source of cash management revenue.[20]

Some institutions are broadening their range of corporate services to include management consulting, data processing and information systems, or other technological services. Management consulting services allow corporate customers to purchase expert advice to address a variety of management problems. Information systems and software marketed by banks assist clients in collecting, analyzing, and reporting data effectively and efficiently.

Among the most promising new technological services are **electronic data interchange (EDI) systems,** which allow corporations to exchange accounts receivable and accounts payable records electronically, as well as to transfer funds automatically to settle

---

[20] Matt Barthel, "Cash Management Units Expect Larger Budgets," *American Banker,* October 5, 1992, 3. Also see Pastorell 1983 and Brockman 1985.

FIGURE 21.2 Fee-Based Services as Future Sources of Revenue

Executives of the 300 largest U.S. banks expect brokerage and insurance services to be increasingly important as sources of income to their institutions by 1997.

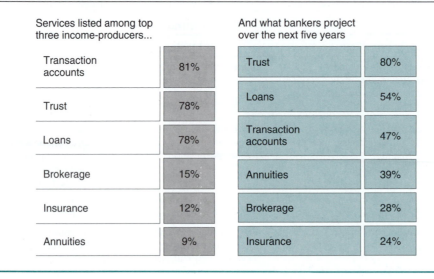

Services listed among top three income-producers...		And what bankers project over the next five years	
Transaction accounts	81%	Trust	80%
Trust	78%	Loans	54%
Loans	78%	Transaction accounts	47%
Brokerage	15%	Annuities	39%
Insurance	12%	Brokerage	28%
Annuities	9%	Insurance	24%

Source: Debra Cope, "Profits from Fee Products Coming—But How Soon," *American Banker,* December 23, 1992, 5.

---

these accounts. Large financial institutions generate fee income by providing the EDI technology to their customers.

EMERGING FEE-BASED SERVICES

Although trust and correspondent services have enjoyed renewed attention recently, depositories have shown even greater interest in expanding the range of fee-based services. The type, legal and regulatory status, and perceived financial benefits of new services vary substantially.

Table 21.1 shows the results of a survey of bankers in the mid-1980s to ascertain their views on two categories of products: those that they believed would enhance income, and those that they would probably offer whether profitable or not. Many of the products and services are discussed at earlier points in this book, including EFT-based products, credit cards, personal financial planning, consumer lending, and money market accounts. The surveyed bankers ranked most of

those low in profitability. Among items of high or medium attractiveness, many relate to two product areas: insurance and securities.

As of late 1992, views on the potential of these nontraditional fee-based services continued to be favorable. Figure 21.2 provides the views of executives of the 300 largest U.S. banks on the top three sources of income expected during 1993–1997. Twenty-eight percent of bankers included brokerage, and 24 percent insurance, in their future top income-producing categories. Unfortunately for survey respondents, direct participation of depositories in some aspects of these businesses is limited, although restrictions are becoming less severe.

As later chapters indicate, recent financial conditions in the insurance and securities industries cause one to wonder whether the survey results in Table 21.1 and Figure 21.2 reflect the "grass is always greener" syndrome. Indeed, many insurers and securities firms seek to enter the areas of deposit taking and lending, while depositories bemoan the profitability of these traditional functions. As barriers to entry on both sides are being eroded rapidly, depository managers must understand the issues and opportunities involved.

SECURITIES ACTIVITIES: BHCs AND MEMBER BANKS

In its broadest form, the phrase *securities activities* means underwriting, distributing, investing in, advising about, and trading government and corporate debt instruments and corporate stock. Restrictions on depository institutions' involvement in these activities are covered at several points earlier in the book, such as the discussion of investment portfolio restrictions in Chapter 13. Most managers view other types of securities regulations, especially those on underwriting and brokerage services, to be more onerous. Like many regulations, specific restrictions depend on an institution's charter type.

SECURITIES UNDERWRITING

Because of their size and influence in the financial system, Fed member banks have been particularly active in attempting to enter the securities business. They have also been subject to the tightest restrictions. Activities of BHCs with member bank subsidiaries are governed by Federal Reserve Regulation Y (Reg Y), discussed in Chapter 4. That regulation is based on the premise that the activities of nonbank affiliates of BHCs must be "closely related" to banking. Separate restraints on Fed member banks, besides their parent holding companies, were imposed by post-Depression legislation.

HISTORICAL PROHIBITIONS ON UNDERWRITING OF CORPORATE SECURITIES. Of particular concern to Fed member banks are prohibitions against underwriting corporate securities. In performing this intermediation activity, which involves assisting in the transfer of securities and cash between a seller and an initial buyer, the underwriter usually assumes temporary ownership of the securities. Although underwriters earn income from fees charged for these transfer services, underwriting profits (or losses) also result from price changes in the securities during the brief time the underwriter owns them.

As noted in Chapters 2 and 4, opposition to securities underwriting originated after the banking crisis of the 1930s. Opposition was based on the belief that underwriting could expose a depository to market, default, and interest rate risk over and above the riski-

ness of the institution's primary assets. At that time, Congress believed that banks involved in underwriting were more likely to fail than others, a belief that led to the passage of the Glass-Steagall Act (G-S). G-S prohibited the affiliation of a Fed member bank with any other firm "engaged principally in the issue, flotation, underwriting, public sale, or distribution" of securities, except those securities specifically exempted in the act.[21] The next section of the law prohibited underwriters from accepting deposits. Henceforth, commercial banking, in theory at least, was legally separated from investment banking. In practice, however, the issues are not at all clear-cut.

RECENT DEVELOPMENTS. G-S exemptions and later legal interpretations have for many years permitted Fed member banks to underwrite Treasury securities, federal agency securities, Eurobonds, and certain types of state and municipal securities. In December 1986, BHCs won a battle ongoing since 1979, when a federal appeals court ruled that their subsidiaries may act as advisors and agents in the sale of commercial paper, although they may not take an independent financial stake in a transaction. This ruling and Fed guidelines issued after the court's decision technically prohibited underwriting, but for the first time since G-S the door was opened for BHC involvement in the sale of corporate securities.

In 1987, the Fed and the Comptroller of the Currency approved proposals to allow BHCs to underwrite municipal revenue bonds and asset-backed securities, such as collateralized mortgage obligations (CMOs). The Fed required these activities to be conducted through nonbank subsidiaries and established limitations on the percentage of the subsidiary's revenues that could be derived from the securities activities. The Comptroller's ruling did not include any of these restrictions on underwriting municipal bonds or securitized consumer receivables. Because most institutions interested in and capable of competing in investment banking are the large holding companies, however, the Fed's regulations tend to be the most binding.

The securities industry immediately took its opposition to the new powers to the courts and succeeded

---

[21] This phrase is from Section 20 of the Act and is cited in many sources, among them Fischer, Gram, Kaufman, and Mote 1984.

in winning temporary restraining orders. Congress cooperated by including a provision in the Competitive Equality Banking Act (CEBA) placing a 1-year moratorium on the granting of new powers by federal banking agencies.

Although Congress evidently intended to act before its moratorium expired, it did not do so. Large banks that had been waiting for clarification of the legal status of the Fed rulings began to initiate limited activities. Then, in January 1989, the Fed announced that five large BHCs could, for the first time, underwrite corporate bonds. The Fed attached some important restrictions, including a requirement that the new underwriting activities had to be carried out in separate, well-capitalized subsidiaries, with strong firewalls to protect the bank subsidiary from risk exposure. Also, the Fed continued to limit the percentage of the subsidiary's revenues that could be generated from underwriting.

The remaining prohibition was against underwriting corporate equities. In February 1990, the Fed set in motion the final steps toward permitting six large BHCs to engage in limited equity underwriting, again in subsidiaries with thick firewalls and with a limited proportion of revenues to be generated from the underwriting activities. At almost the same time, the powers to underwrite securitized assets, first granted in 1987, were finally deemed permanent when the Supreme Court refused to review a lower court's decision upholding the Comptroller's ruling. In September 1990, J. P. Morgan became the first BHC to win Fed approval to underwrite corporate equities through a subsidiary, with the understanding that the proportion of revenues from stock underwriting would be strictly limited.[22]

By the end of 1990, commercial banks had gained a stronger position relative to Wall Street investment banking firms. They increased their proportion of debt and equity securities underwritten to 4.5 percent of all new issues, compared with 2.8 percent in 1989. After the first 10 months of 1991, J. P. Morgan's securities subsidiary was ranked seventh in the volume of corporate debt underwritten. As of year-end 1991, seven BHCs had gained Fed approval to underwrite any debt and equity securities through subsidiaries.[23]

Despite large banks' obvious interest in securities underwriting, some observers are concerned that the Fed's rules may make it difficult for BHCs to generate sufficient profits on these activities. In particular, the limits on revenues that may be generated from underwriting are matters of concern. Investment banking margins are increasingly slim, and firms must rely on a high volume of business to operate profitably. Many experts argue that the firewalls the Fed requires between investment and commercial banking prohibit the most efficient use of resources and that the restrictions under which U.S. banks must operate place them at a disadvantage in competing with banks in international markets. These experts believe that placing risk-adjusted, market value capital requirements on a bank's securities activities would be a more effective way of monitoring risk to the deposit insurance system.[24]

OTHER COMPETITIVE EFFECTS. In their efforts to win the freedom to engage in corporate debt and equity underwriting, banks claimed that they wanted to expand their existing relationships with corporate customers. They also argued that large underwriters had

---

[22] Comprehensive reviews of legal foundations and recent developments are provided in Dale 1988; Kaufman 1988; and George G. Kaufman and Larry R. Mote, "Securities Activities of Commercial Banks: The Current Economic and Legal Environment," Staff Memorandum 88-4, Federal Reserve Bank of Chicago, 1988. See also Bill Atkinson, "Supreme Court Reaffirms Banks' Securitization Power," *American Banker,* February 21, 1990, 1, 16; Robert M. Garsson, "Underwriting Ruling Shifts to Final Step," *American Banker,* February 16, 1990, 2; James O'Shea, "Banks Win New Bond Powers," *The Wall Street Journal,* January 19, 1989, Section 3, 1, 4; and Paul Duke Jr., and Randall Smith, "Fed Allows J. P. Morgan to Underwrite Stocks," *The Wall Street Journal,* September 24, 1990, C1, C13.

[23] William Goodwin, "Commercial Banks Increase Foothold in Underwriting," *American Banker,* January 13, 1991, 1, 10; Fred R. Bleakley, "J. P. Morgan Expands Role in Underwriting, Irking Securities Firms," *The Wall Street Journal,* November 13, 1991, A1, A8; and Board of Governors of the Federal Reserve, *78th Annual Report,* 1991, 210.

[24] By late 1992, banks were increasingly vocal in their pleas to the Fed to raise the proportion of revenues permitted from underwriting. Bankers argued that low interest rates were depressing revenue levels in general, so the existing 10 percent ceiling was growing more restrictive. The Fed was considering allowing a small increase but feared a large adjustment would result in retaliatory actions by Congress and the Securities Industry Association. See Claudia Cummins, "Fed Moving to Ease Cap on Securities Income," *American Banker,* December 23, 1992, 1, 14.

invaded commercial bank territory through their affiliation with brokerage firms offering deposit-type accounts. Some securities firms had even been allowed by the Comptroller of the Currency to establish commercial bank affiliates, although these were mostly structured as nonbank banks.[25]

Besides the arguments raised by banks, many economists believe that allowing banks into corporate underwriting may have positive consequences. Existing underwriters appear to have charged unnecessarily high fees for underwriting the securities of small firms. With competition from commercial banks, some experts argue that underwriting services will be more competitively priced and that the benefits will outweigh the costs of potential abuses by banks. Indirect support for allowing greater competition among underwriters is provided by events following the implementation of **Rule 415** of the Securities and Exchange Commission (SEC). Discussed in more detail in Chapter 26, Rule 415 permits firms to obtain approval to issue securities up to 2 years in advance instead of contracting with an underwriter at the time of a security issue. Firms using Rule 415 have found underwriters competing for their business, often resulting in lower fees than they would have paid otherwise.[26]

Congress continues to see underwriting of corporate stocks and bonds by commercial banks as threatening to the deposit insurance system and as adding to the moral hazard problem introduced in Chapters 16 and 17. Only through a clarification of congressional attitude toward the Glass-Steagall Act will all financial institutions understand the true status of the playing field.

PRIVATE PLACEMENT VERSUS UNDERWRITING. The status of member banks and the private placement of corporate securities is clearer. A financial intermediary's role in private placements is much more limited than in underwriting. Usually, the private placement of new issues involves bringing together the securities issuer and one or several large buyers. The intermediary earns a "finder's fee" of sorts but does not take even brief possession of the securities. Both the Fed and Comptroller have ruled that private placement is not

underwriting under G-S and have permitted commercial banks to earn private placement fees. In 1987, the eight largest commercial banks privately placed securities valued at $34 billion. Although this amount may seem large, it is less than half of the $83 billion placed by the top eight securities firms in the same year.[27]

SECURITIES BROKERAGE SERVICES

Fed member banks also view securities brokerage services as potential sources of lucrative fee income, and they have enjoyed more success in pursuing them than in underwriting. Regulators and the courts have interpreted G-S prohibitions against the "public sale" of securities by banks to mean underwriting, not simply arranging the purchase or sale of securities for members of the public.

Ironically, member banks and BHCs themselves may be responsible for continuing litigation on securities brokerage, even though some experts believe that there was really no serious legal question. In 1982, Security Pacific Bank and the BHC of which BankAmerica is a subsidiary filed applications with their principal regulators to establish discount brokerage services. As noted in Chapter 1, discount brokers arrange the purchase and sale of securities for customers but do not offer investment advice, in contrast to full-service brokers, who do both.

A point made by both Security Pacific and BankAmerica Corporation was that because the services they proposed did not include investment advice, the affiliated banks did not have even a remote interest in the success or failure of any company or security. Consequently, they would be insulated from any alleged increase in riskiness caused by a close relationship between securities activities and commercial banking. Both applications were approved and, after challenge by the securities industry, were upheld in court. In 1987, the Supreme Court ruled that BHCs and national banks may operate discount brokerage offices nationwide without violating interstate banking laws.[28]

[25] See Fischer, Gram, Kaufman, and Mote 1984, 498–502.

[26] See Saunders 1985 and 1989 and Rogowski and Sorenson 1985.

[27] See Dale 1988, 9; and Fischer, Gram, Kaufman, and Mote 1984, 495–498.

[28] See Kaufman and Mote, "Securities Activities of Commercial Banks," 1988.

REGULATORY INTERPRETATION. In 1984, the Fed added discount brokerage to the list of permissible BHC subsidiaries under Reg Y, but it explicitly noted that full-service brokerage services were not permitted. In contrast, the Comptroller's office began permitting national banks to offer both discount brokerage and investment advice as part of their securities activities, stating that it found nothing in G-S to prohibit it. In 1987, the Board of Governors changed its earlier ruling and concurred with the Comptroller's view. In 1992, the Fed further facilitated banks' introduction of full-service brokerage by speeding up the application process and eliminating some restrictive provisions.[29]

THE SEC AND BANK BROKERAGE. As banks moved into the securities brokerage industry, the SEC began to flex its regulatory muscle, and in 1985 it ruled that banks soliciting any kind of brokerage business were required to register with the SEC or transfer all securities operations to a separate subsidiary. Subsequently, the Fed ruled that it had the authority to regulate and supervise all bank-affiliated brokerage activities and that decision has not been overturned by the courts.[30]

BANK AND BROKERAGE FIRM PARTNERSHIPS. In late 1992, NationsBank and Dean Witter Securities announced intention to enter a partnership that presents a new test of regulatory limits. NationsBank, one of the most aggressive of the "superregionals," plans to have Dean Witter brokers in its bank lobbies to provide a vast array of services to the bank's customers. The two organizations agreed to split commissions and other fees on a 50–50 basis.

Both firms will benefit. NationsBank saves the investment in training employees and other start-up costs associated with entering a new line of business. Dean Witter gains access to a new and very large customer base. The regulatory response was pending as this was written, but regulators will not be able to delay their decisions for long. Shortly after this unusual partnership was formed, Comerica announced its plans to *acquire* an entire brokerage firm. Bank executives indicated plans to operate the brokerage as a

separate subsidiary but expect a sharing of customer information between bank and brokerage firm as well as extensive cross-selling.[31]

MUTUAL FUNDS: THE NEWEST FRONTIER?

Combining the quest for fee income with customers' willingness to buy nonbank financial services from their bankers, banking institutions are moving rapidly into the mutual fund business. For the most part, this means selling mutual fund shares on bank premises. A 1992 survey found 69 percent of mid-sized banks selling mutual funds and other investment products. Banks in the South and the Midwest were particularly aggressive in their move toward mutual fund sales. Bankers participating in the survey viewed these new products as one of their best alternatives for increasing profit margins and had high hopes for the product; the median forecast was a 25 percent growth rate in mutual fund sales in the next year. By the end of 1992, banks already accounted for 12.5 percent of mutual fund sales, triple the level of only 4 years earlier.

Smaller banks have also been anxious to join the trend toward mutual fund sales. With their encouragement, the Independent Bankers Association of America (IBAA)—a trade group for community banks—sought interaction with mutual fund managers. The IBAA invited bids from a selected group of mutual funds to enter into an exclusive agreement to sell their products through the association's member banks. Such an arrangement would give the mutual funds ready access to millions of new customers.

WELLS FARGO'S STAGECOACH. Wells Fargo, one of the nation's largest banks, took a different approach. Wells Fargo *created* a new family of mutual funds (called the Stagecoach Funds) to sell through its branches. Introduced in late 1991, fund assets rose quickly to $2.2 billion by the end of 1992. Wells Fargo will reap fee income as both manager and investment adviser to the 11 funds.

[29] Kaufman 1988, 9; and Debra Cope, "Fed Loosens Restrictions on Brokerage Activities," *American Banker,* September 2, 1992, 1, 14.

[30] See Kaufman 1988.

[31] Debra Cope, "NationsBank, Dean Witter Team Up to Sell Securities," *American Banker,* October 27, 1992, 1, 5; and Steve Klinkerman, "Comerica to Pay $45 Million for Detroit Brokerage Firm," *American Banker,* January 12, 1993, 1.

POTENTIAL COSTS. As banks expand the offerings of alternative investments to their customers, several reasons for caution are evident. One emanates from regulators and legislators, who have made it clear they will monitor closely the way the products are promoted. The primary concern is that customers understand that the financial products they are buying are not insured by the FDIC, even though they are sold by an FDIC-member bank.

Other questions have been raised about the potential customer reaction to losses. For example, bond funds were popular products in late 1992 and early 1993, a period of very low interest rates. As market rates begin to rise, customers may very well experience some loss as outstanding bonds decline in market value. Whether customers realizing a loss in principal value will transfer resentment from fund managers to the banks who marketed the funds is unclear.[32]

SECURITIES ACTIVITIES OF OTHER DEPOSITORY INSTITUTIONS

As recently as 1987, CEBA brought the securities activities of nonmember banks under G-S. Thrifts and CUs, however, are not bound by the specific language of the G-S Act. Limits on their securities activities are thus somewhat different from those of banks and BHCs.

BIF-INSURED NONMEMBER INSTITUTIONS

BIF-insured institutions, regardless of charter type, must abide by FDIC regulations. In 1984, the FDIC released an official policy statement that FDIC-insured institutions, both banks and thrifts, were *not* prohibited from engaging in securities activities. The

insurer also noted, however, that "some risk may be associated with those activities" and that restrictions may apply on specific activities or on transactions between nonmember depositories and their securities affiliates.[33]

The securities activities of savings banks are determined by state laws; as a result, some state-chartered institutions can engage in underwriting or full-service brokerage activities. Before CEBA, some states, such as South Dakota and Delaware, used their authority to lure nonresident institutions to establish local state-chartered securities subsidiaries. BHC regulations still applied, however, so money center banks affiliated with BHCs did not succeed in entering corporate underwriting through the back door.

SAIF-INSURED INSTITUTIONS

Although not prohibited from securities activities by Glass-Steagall, SAIF-insured institutions have only recently moved aggressively into the securities business. Because they have few corporate customers, underwriting corporate securities is not a feasible source of fee-based income. Brokerage services are another matter, however, although these activities may be conducted only by service corporations. FIRREA provisions also limited activities of state-chartered institutions to those permitted for federally chartered firms.

In 1986, more than 650 savings institutions were involved in discount or full-service brokerage activities. Many thrifts offering brokerage services have entered by means of collectively owned service corporations. The largest of these organizations is Invest of Tampa, Florida. Invest establishes booths in S&L offices, from which personnel provide advice and execute securities trades for the thrift's customers. Recommendations to clients are not based on original research but are taken from standard sources such as Value Line. As a result, fees charged are between those of discount and full-service brokers. Participating thrifts provide space, salaries, and advertising, and they split commission fees with Invest. Some thrifts not wishing to participate in Invest-type programs have elected to affiliate with discount or full-service brokers or to develop in-house brokerage facilities.

[32] See Debra Cope, "Mutual Funds Now Being Offered by Seven of Ten Middle-Size Banks," *American Banker,* October 28, 1992, 1, 7; Debra Cope, "IBAA Program Will Bring Mutual Funds to Small Banks," *American Banker,* November 13, 1992, 1, 8; Debra Cope, "Banks Making Inroads on Mutual Funds," *American Banker,* December 12, 1992, 1, 12; Claudia Cummins, "Dingell Panel Probing Disclosure of Investment Risks to Consumers," *American Banker,* January 11, 1993, 1, 5; Debra Cope, "Wells Fargo's Mutual Fund Brands Are Riding High," *American Banker,* January 20, 1993, 6; and Barbara A. Rehm, "OCC Issues Guidelines on Selling Investments," *American Banker,* July 20, 1993, 1, 11.

[33] Federal Deposit Insurance Corporation, *1984 Annual Report,* 39.

In 1987, the U.S. League of Savings Institutions (now Savings and Community Bankers of America) introduced another service to assist savings institutions wishing to offer investment services to customers without committing substantial resources. The program allows institutions to sell to customers shares in mutual funds managed by U.S. League Investment Services; the thrifts earn income through sales commissions on the shares.[34]

CREDIT UNIONS

As of year-end 1991, only 5.4 percent of credit unions had moved into the brokerage business, and most had total assets in excess of $20 million.[35] Similar to the thrift industry, brokerage services are offered through credit union service organizations (CUSOs). Credit unions of all sizes are assisted by CUNA Brokerage, a division of the industry's major trade organization, the Credit Union National Association (CUNA). CUNA Brokerage enables participating CUs to offer retail brokerage services to members without employing in-house personnel trained in the securities business. CUNA Brokerage executes trades for individual members of affiliated CUs; because of its not-for-profit status, fees can be lower than those charged by competing brokers.

FINANCIAL IMPLICATIONS OF SECURITIES ACTIVITIES

As with other fee-based services, one motivation for depositories' entry into brokerage services and underwriting activities is increased profitability. Data on the securities industry in general suggest that earnings can be quite volatile. For example, during 1977–1983, the after-tax return on net worth (RONW) of brokerage firms exceeded that for BHCs. Discount brokerage was also lucrative; the profitability of discount brokers exceeded that of full-service brokers each year. Yet by 1990, many large securities firms were in disarray, and competition among brokers was reducing profit margins.

SECURITIES ACTIVITIES AND PORTFOLIO RISK

Although securities activities can increase fee income, they cannot be undertaken without careful analysis of all ramifications. Discount brokerage firms have proportionately more fixed costs than do full-service brokers, because the former have large investments in computers and other electronic equipment and fewer personnel. Because of operating leverage, profits of discount brokers are more volatile as revenues vary than are profits of firms with smaller fixed costs.[36]

There is no reason to assume that the discount brokerage activities of depositories differ. Thus, institutions considering a heavy commitment to discount brokerage must also consider whether the higher potential returns may be accompanied by higher risk. Portfolio theory, discussed in Chapter 13, suggests that before drawing conclusions an institution must also consider the covariability of revenues from securities operations with the institution's other sources of income.

Research on the diversification potential of securities activities for depository institutions has led to mixed conclusions. Some studies have examined correlations between return on assets for commercial banks and rates of return for securities firms or other nonbank industries. The results vary, depending on the time period during which the study was conducted. In most cases, if diversification benefits are identified, they are found to be rather small. From a public policy standpoint, these findings suggest that the repeal of Glass-Steagall will not necessarily result in reduced risk in the banking industry.

However, other economic benefits may emerge. Economies of scale may be realized by large institutions engaging in both commercial and investment banking, particularly because banks already specialize in gathering financial information and monitoring corporate customers. They may benefit from this expertise by extending it to underwriting and other securities activities.[37]

---

[34] See Britt 1993; Frank 1983; Morrall 1986; and Spooner 1987.

[35] CUNA, *1991 Credit Union Report*, 2.

[36] See Felgran 1984, 14.

[37] Representative studies on diversification and other benefits from bank entry into securities activities include Brewer 1989; Rose 1989; Pozdena 1989; Kwast 1988 and 1989; Eisenbeis and Wall 1984; and Kim 1991.

NO GUARANTEES OF SUCCESS

To date, brokerage activities of depositories have yet to provide substantial profits. Although estimates vary, some experts believe that it takes an average of 100 trades a day for a full-service brokerage operation to be profitable for a depository and an average of 35 trades a day for a profitable discount brokerage. In reply to a 1985 survey conducted for the American Bankers Association, most respondents offering brokerage services for more than 6 months stated that few customers actually used the brokerage accounts they had opened. Consequently, brokerage services in the early years were quite costly to administer while providing few revenues, a situation the researchers said could be an "embarrassing flop" for bankers. Others argue, however, that brokerage services kept customers who wanted a full-service financial institution from abandoning their depository in favor of a competitor that offered a greater range of services.

It is interesting that discount brokerage, one of the first securities activities into which banks demanded entry, has been one of the first from which some have retreated. For example, after making history by purchasing the Charles Schwab discount brokerage firm in 1983, BankAmerica also made the news by selling all the Schwab offices in 1987. Security Pacific, now a subsidiary of Bank of America and the bank that initiated the legal battle in 1982 to gain brokerage powers, announced in January 1990 that it would sell most of its discount brokerage offices. Decisions by a number of major banks to leave the discount brokerage business are attributed to the strong competition and lean profit margins in that business.[38]

Thus, although no firm conclusions can be drawn, the assumption of automatic success from depositories' diversification beyond traditional activities is not warranted. Managers considering the potential benefits of securities activities must also recognize the costs, and thorough analysis must replace the "herd instinct" to offer a service just because another institution is doing it. In particular, institutions with low

capital ratios must be cautious in pursuing activities that may expose them to additional risk without additional profits.

INSURANCE ACTIVITIES AS SOURCES OF FEE-BASED INCOME

Insurance is another area of increasing interest to depositories. Like securities activities, insurance activities consist of both underwriting and brokerage.

BASIC PRINCIPLES

Insurance underwriters agree to bear, for a fee, the financial risk against which the insured seeks protection. An automobile insurance underwriter agrees to bear potential costs resulting from a car accident in exchange for a premium paid by the car owner. If no accident occurs, the insurer profits from the premium and from earnings on investment of the premium, minus the administrative costs of providing insurance services. If there is an accident, the insurer suffers a loss in an amount unknown at the time the policy is written. Thus, insurance underwriters act as intermediaries, transforming the unknown financial risk to which the insured is exposed to a fixed dollar amount consisting of the policy premium.

Insurance brokers, in contrast, sell insurance policies for a fee without bearing risks. Insurance brokerage is a marketing function, bringing together underwriters and policy seekers. Local insurance agents are brokers; for a commission, they sell policies underwritten by others. Like other financial institutions, insurance agencies reduce transactions costs for both parties, especially search costs that underwriter and policyholder might otherwise bear.

Until recently, these distinctions were somewhat academic for depository institutions, especially national banks, because most of them acted neither as underwriters nor as brokers. The exceptions to this general rule were the offering of **credit life insurance** to borrowers and the sale (but not underwriting) of annuity policies to customers of all types. In a credit life policy, the insurer, usually also the lender, agrees to pay the borrower's loan in case of death; fees are levied at the time the loan contract is signed. Annuity

[38] See Yvette D. Kantrow, "Security Pacific to Sell Most of Discount Broker Offices," *American Banker,* January 19, 1990, 1, 10; Robert M. Garsson, "Limited Value Seen in Power to Underwrite," *American Banker,* February 20, 1990, 1; and Blount and Glass 1985.

insurance policies are savings vehicles under which the purchaser receives the right to a series of future cash payments guaranteed by an underwriter. Now, however, the legal status of insurance activities in depositories is no longer clearly defined, and changes are occurring as rapidly as they are in securities underwriting and brokerage. The current status of insurance activities depends on the size and type of institution.

INSURANCE ACTIVITIES OF FED MEMBER BANKS AND THEIR BHCs

Federal legislation on national banks, BHCs, and insurance spans the period 1916–1982. In 1916, the National Bank Act permitted national banks in communities with a population of less than 5,000 to act as agents for any insurance firms authorized to do business in that state. For many years, this provision was interpreted as allowing the bank to sell insurance only in its own small community. Because there was virtually no interstate banking at that time, this provision prevented money center banks—those most likely to want to do so—from pursuing insurance. Subsequent BHC laws gave the Fed the right to apply the "closely related" test to potential insurance subsidiaries of BHCs, and the Fed determined that the underwriting and sale of credit life *were* closely related to banking.

In the Garn-St Germain Act (G-St G), Congress decided to limit the scope of large BHCs' insurance activities. That law holds that BHCs with total assets less than $50 million have unlimited rights to engage in insurance activities, but other BHCs are prohibited from acting as underwriters or brokers of all insurance products except credit life, accident, health, or unemployment insurance.[39]

In recent years, banks have followed a circuitous route in their efforts to expand their involvement in insurance activities. Most avenues have been blocked, either by regulators or the courts. Congressional action, which would clarify bank powers, has been delayed; lobbyists for the banking and insurance indus-

tries continue to apply strong pressure, and legislators have not found an acceptable compromise.

For a short period in the late 1980s and early 1990s it appeared banks would prevail in their efforts to market insurance products. The Comptroller of the Currency ruled in 1986 that banks could sell insurance *nationwide* from banking offices located in towns with populations of less than 5,000. Following this ruling, several large institutions began to set up nationwide distribution systems in very small towns.

A test case ruling by a court of appeals in 1992, however, brought these activities to a sudden halt. The court held that national banks did *not* have the authority to sell insurance at all, even from small towns. Since recent legislation, including the Federal Deposit Insurance Corporation Improvement Act (FDICIA), has tied state-chartered bank powers to those permitted for national banks, the ruling erected a major blockade. Although some experts predicted that this unexpected development would finally spur Congress to act, no new legislation was passed. However, in 1993, the U.S. Supreme Court gave banks a long-awaited victory by overturning the Court of Appeals ruling, thus establishing the right of banks to sell insurance nationally from small towns.[40]

INSURANCE ACTIVITIES OF OTHER DEPOSITORY INSTITUTIONS

Like securities activities, the insurance activities of non-Fed member depositories are subject to more varied rules and regulations than those of Fed member institutions or BHCs.[41]

BIF-INSURED NONMEMBER INSTITUTIONS. The insurance activities of state-chartered commercial and savings banks are left to state laws, and many states

---

[39] G-St G also contained a "grandfather clause," permitting large BHCs with any other kind of insurance services allowed by the Fed before May 1, 1982, to retain them. For more details on G-St G insurance provisions, see Felgran 1985.

[40] For discussion of several of these developments, see Barbara A. Rehm, "Banks Win Big Victory in Fight to Sell Insurance," *American Banker,* July 19, 1993, 1, 11; Kenneth H. Bacon, "Court Rejects Banks' Right to Sell Insurance," *The Wall Street Journal,* February 10, 1992, A3; "Recent Developments," *Banking Legislation and Policy* (Federal Reserve Bank of Philadelphia) 11 (January/March 1992): 1; and Barbara H. Rehm, "Court Backs Power to Sell Insurance From Banks," *American Banker,* May 9, 1990, 1, 7.

[41] A good summary and comparison of the regulations governing insurance activities of depositories, by charter type, as of 1986 is Crum 1986.

see no conflict between banking and insurance. In fact, savings banks and some state-chartered commercial banks have engaged in various aspects of the insurance business for several years. Until quite recently, state-chartered commercial banks in states prohibiting bank branching faced fewer restrictions on their insurance activities than those in states permitting geographic expansion of banks. The reason for this difference was that unit banks provide less competition for existing insurers than do banks with extensive branch networks. Thus, state legislators were able to offer something to both types of institutions without alienating either.

In 1988, however, voters in California reversed the traditional pattern. Angry about what they perceived to be the unreasonably high cost of automobile insurance in the state's largest cities, they passed Proposition 103, a significant revision of California law first introduced in Chapter 2 and discussed in more detail in Chapter 24. Among Proposition 103's main provisions was the authority for state-chartered commercial banks to sell insurance. Because California has permissive branching and merger/acquisition laws, as well as some of the nation's largest banks, the door was opened for these banks to sell insurance in the nation's biggest market. By early 1990, Security Pacific, Wells Fargo, First Interstate, and Bank of America either had established insurance operations in their previously owned state-chartered subsidiaries or had acquired state-chartered banks from which to begin marketing a wide range of insurance policies.[42]

Some smaller states have been particularly creative in their banking/insurance laws. For example, in a 1983 law soon nicknamed the **South Dakota loophole,** the state invited out-of-state depository institutions to set up insurance operations by purchasing state-chartered banks in South Dakota. According to the law, insurance could then be marketed by these organizations in every state *but* South Dakota, thus protecting existing insurance agents in the state! The Fed was not amused, however, and, invoking its BHC authority, subsequently refused to permit any non–South

Dakota banks to enter insurance through the loophole route.[43]

Sensing an increasingly accommodating posture on the part of federal regulators by 1990, Delaware, a small-state rival to South Dakota in passing creative banking legislation, enacted a similar law permitting any bank chartered in the state to *underwrite* as well as sell insurance nationwide. The law appeased the potential ire of Delaware insurance agents by stating that banks could sell most insurance products *within* the state only through agents who had Delaware licenses at the time the law was passed; thus, new out-of-state banks could not rush to Delaware with the sole intent of selling insurance there. Most observers—including representatives of large out-of-state banks—noted that the prohibition against selling insurance in the Delaware market was unlikely to be a deterrent to large institutions, which were interested in national markets.

Immediately after passage of the law, Citicorp and Chase Manhattan moved to establish insurance underwriting operations headquartered in Delaware. In a September 1990 ruling that brought the controversy to a boil, the Fed forbade Citicorp from taking advantage of the Delaware law, stating that only Congress had the authority to permit subsidiaries of BHCs to engage in nationwide insurance operations. A federal appeals court overturned the Fed's prohibition the next year, however, and ruled that selling insurance by Delaware-chartered banks was permissible nationwide. Underwriting continues to be inaccessible to most state-chartered banks subsequent to FDICIA provisions.[44]

NONBANK DEPOSITORY INSTITUTIONS. In 1967, federally chartered S&Ls were permitted to broker all types of insurance except private mortgage insurance and to engage in limited underwriting through affiliated service corporations. Provisions governing state-chartered institutions varied widely, including those that were both more and less restrictive than Federal Home Loan Bank Board (FHLBB) rules. Since

---

[42] See Sam Zuckerman, "Banks Gain New Insurance Powers," *American Banker,* February 26, 1990, 1, 13; and Yvette D. Kantrow, "First Interstate Targets Insurance," *American Banker,* April 11, 1990, 21.

[43] William Gruber, "Fed Blocks Citicorp on Insurance," *Chicago Tribune,* August 2, 1985, Sec. 2, 1; and Felgran 1985.

[44] A. Joseph Newman, Jr., "Delaware Widens Entry to Insurance," *American Banker,* May 31, 1990, 2; "Excerpt from Fed Order Barring Citicorp from Insurance," *American Banker,* September 7, 1990, 8; and Wade Lambert and David B. Hilder, "Banks Cleared to Underwrite, Sell Insurance," *The Wall Street Journal,* June 11, 1991.

FIRREA, the permissible insurance activities of all SAIF-insured thrifts are defined by that law's provisions forbidding state-chartered institutions from engaging in activities not also permitted for federally chartered thrifts. The Office of Thrift Supervision (OTS) has not specifically rescinded earlier FHLBB rules on insurance, although the FDIC has been given broad authority to prohibit any activities its officials deem too risky. Thus, many observers believe that the insurance operations of individual thrifts will closely parallel those of national banks to avoid excessive regulatory scrutiny.

Some states restricting commercial bank entry into insurance give savings banks considerable authority to pursue insurance. Savings banks in Massachusetts, Connecticut, and New York have a long and successful involvement in life insurance, rooted in their origin as depositories for the urban working class. By eliminating agent commissions, the nearly 300 savings banks in these states offer customers life insurance at a lower cost than comparable policies marketed by insurance companies.

Many CUs have offered insurance similar to credit life for several years. Unlike banks and thrifts, however, the loan protection insurance offered by CUs was often paid for by CUs, not by members themselves. These programs were offered as part of the service objectives of the CU movement. But CUs have found their net interest margins (NIMs) squeezed and are seeking sources of fee-based income to protect earnings. As a result, many are now selling member-paid credit life insurance, as well as other types of life and property/liability insurance policies.

State-chartered CUs are governed by state laws. Federal CUs are subject to the National Credit Union Administration (NCUA's) regulations, which currently require that insurance be offered through CUSOs, the industry's equivalent of S&L service corporations. CUSOs may offer policies underwritten by other insurance providers. Among the largest underwriters with which CUSOs deal is the CUNA Mutual Insurance Group. CUNA Mutual, founded by CUs for CUs, is a major national provider of credit life insurance, based on dollar volume of coverage in force. It also underwrites a variety of other insurance products for CU members nationwide.[45]

RATIONALE FOR EXCLUDING DEPOSITORIES FROM INSURANCE ACTIVITIES

It is useful to understand the historic rationale for keeping large depositories out of the insurance business. Most objections to mixing banking and insurance fall into two categories: those related to safety and soundness, and those related to potential coercion of borrowers.

SAFETY AND SOUNDNESS. As with securities underwriting, insurance underwriting was viewed as being riskier than normal banking activities by the framers of post-Depression financial legislation. Discussed in more detail in Chapter 24, the risks to which insurers are exposed differ from those faced by depositories in their day-to-day operations. Congress, concerned about the problem of moral hazard, has chosen to view these risks as not necessarily compatible with a depository's ability to offer deposit insurance to customers. Inroads to insurance involvement by depositories have largely come from the actions of state legislators.

COERCION OF BORROWERS. A second argument used by opponents of mixing depositories and insurance is that depositories, if permitted to underwrite and sell insurance, would make lending contingent on the purchase of insurance from the lender. Although few data are available, studies by some consumer interest groups have concluded that fees for credit life insurance "are the nation's worst insurance rip off" and that the number of policies sold exceeds the normal expected level of market penetration. In contrast, Fed studies of the insurance activities of major lenders have found little evidence of coercion. Depositories defend their credit life practices on the basis of the increased convenience offered to consumers who need not shop for what is essentially an inexpensive product anyway. Despite the lack of concrete evidence, the potential for coercion has been argued repeatedly by influential Congressional lobbyists working for the nation's independent insurance agents.[46]

---

[45] For a 50-year history of insurance services in the CU industry, see CUNA Mutual Insurance Group, *1984 Annual Report.*

[46] See Pat Allen, "Treasures in Insurance: Regulators and Market Forces Make the Gold Hard to Get," *Savings Institutions* 105 (November 1984), 99; Shafton and Gabay 1985; and David Isgur, "Credit Life Insurance Curbs Sought," *American Banker,* June 19, 1990, 6.

FINANCIAL IMPLICATIONS OF INSURANCE ACTIVITIES

Because widespread insurance involvement is new, few data about its impact on depositories are available. It is possible, however, to identify the expected financial effect.

INSURANCE ACTIVITIES AND PORTFOLIO RISK

Insurance activities are attractive to depositories because these activities require few fixed costs and have a low degree of operating leverage. Often, no new facilities or personnel are needed, and the opportunities to cross-sell insurance and other depository products are considerable. Riskiness also must be considered. Research has shown that during some periods, variability in profits for life insurers and agents has been less than variability in banking profits. In contrast, property/liability insurance profits are often more variable over time than are those of depositories. In fact, for reasons explained further in Chapter 24, property/liability insurance earnings are especially subject to cyclical economic variations.

Additional research has suggested, however, that property/liability cash flows are negatively correlated with cash flows in banking. Thus, even if some insurance operations are riskier than banking if conducted by themselves, it is possible that a *portfolio* of activities including both banking and insurance could be less risky than either separately. There is even recent evidence to suggest that the diversification potential of insurance activities is becoming influential on the thinking of many regulators. As with securities and banking, further research is needed to determine whether generalizable relationships exist or whether the effects of mixing lending, deposit-taking, and insurance differ over time.[47]

The profitability of insurance also seems alluring—at least at times. During 1970–1980, the average return on assets of insurance underwriters and agencies exceeded that of banks and thrifts. From 1976 through 1983, the return on equity for insurance agencies and brokers, although declining over the period, substantially exceeded that of savings institutions each year. From 1979 through 1983, the returns on equity for life and property/liability underwriters also exceeded those for thrifts.[48] More recently, however, insurers have suffered profitability downturns that make the business seem less than a sure thing.

EXPOSURE TO NEW RISKS. It is also important for banks and thrifts considering underwriting to recognize the differences between assessing credit risk or interest rate risk and assessing underwriting risks. Techniques such as financial statement analysis and GAP management are central to successful depository institutions, but they do not necessarily develop the skills required to evaluate life expectancies or to estimate the probabilities that property damage will occur. For most depositories, especially small ones, entering insurance by the brokerage route is probably more appropriate. Also, institutions with low capital ratios must be especially careful.

EXPECTED VOLUME OF BUSINESS

Depositories have learned from their securities activities that no avenue of fee income is beneficial without sufficient volume. Some evidence suggests greater potential for insurance volume in depositories than for brokerage operations. For example, recent surveys indicate that the public has a more favorable impression of depository institutions than of insurance companies in areas such as quality of service, reliability, and trustworthiness. California's Proposition 103 provided strong evidence of this view. Consequently, many depositories hope to capitalize on this perceived advantage to take insurance business from insurers and insurance agencies.[49]

Besides image, depositories also have an edge in convenience. A 1980 study indicated that the average consumer had 38 contacts per year with a bank and 20 with a thrift, but only six with a property/liability

---

[47] See Rose 1989 and Eisenbeis and Wall 1984.

[48] See Eisenbeis and Wall 1984, 345; Pat Allen, "Treasures in Insurance: Many Paths Lead to Profitability," *Savings Institutions* 105 (October 1984): 81; and Allen, "Treasures in Insurance: Regulators and Market Forces Make the Gold Hard to Get," 100.

[49] These surveys, conducted by insurance industry representatives, private consulting groups, and depository institutions representatives, are cited in Allen, "Treasures in Insurance: Many Paths Lead to Profitability"; Shafton and Gabay 1985; and Howard L. Lax, "Life Insurance Survey Has Some Good News for Banks," *American Banker,* July 26, 1990, 9.

insurer and five with a life insurer.[50] Many purposes for which consumers visit depositories—for example, to obtain financing for a car or a house—also lead to the purchase of insurance. Opportunities for depositories to cross-sell loan and insurance products are especially attractive.

Furthermore, the branch networks established by depositories would allow them to offer insurance at a cost advantage over traditional insurers. Because the average depository already has the necessary personnel, equipment, and facilities through which to sell insurance policies, most institutions would simply be using existing facilities to greater capacity. A recent national survey of bank and thrift executives indicated that 75 percent had formal plans to enter insurance, primarily through establishing agencies in existing facilities.[51] In contrast, most independent insurance agencies do not have data-processing capabilities, so they must hire outsiders to process policies, increasing their costs and the commissions they charge.

OTHER EMERGING FEE-BASED SERVICES

The previous discussions of securities and insurance illustrate some of the reasons why new sources of fee income are both attractive and risky for depositories. They also indicate the controversy arising when one group of financial institutions attempts to enter territory that other firms have previously considered to be theirs alone. Securities and insurance, while getting the most attention recently, are not the only controversial activities. This section briefly describes a few others. Although not all these areas provide income in the form of fees alone, they are all somewhat removed from the traditional lending and deposit-taking functions of banks, thrifts, and CUs.

REAL ESTATE–RELATED ACTIVITIES

All depository institutions can lend money secured by real property, but few can invest in real estate directly. Many managers of depositories believe that the potential profitability of real estate investments is quite high, however, because greater price appreciation is possible on real estate than on typical depository institution assets. In addition, although real estate–related activities such as fee-generating property management, real estate brokerage, and title certification services are attractive to depositories, they are not yet universally available to them. As always, both state and federal regulations apply. Historically, most national banks and their BHCs were prohibited from owning real property either directly or through subsidiaries. In early 1987, the Fed revised Reg Y to permit BHCs to own real estate subsidiaries, with limitations tied to a BHC's capital ratios. National banks and their BHCs are prohibited from operating subsidiaries for either property management or residential real estate brokerage. The laws governing state institutions vary.[52]

Before FIRREA, thrifts, more closely allied to mortgage lending than other depositories, faced fewer restrictions on real estate–related activities than did commercial banks. As a consequence, some S&Ls engaged in property management, appraisal, and even direct real estate development through service corporations. As a result of severe earnings problems among institutions that had engaged relatively heavily in real estate investment in the mid- to late 1980s, Congress, in FIRREA, greatly curtailed the expansion of thrifts' real property investments. Title II specifically prohibits direct equity investment in real estate by state-chartered institutions unless regulators permit similar activities for federally chartered thrifts. The law further requires institutions to divest themselves of real estate acquired before FIRREA. For thrifts' real estate powers to be renewed, the FDIC would now be required to state that such activities pose little threat to the deposit insurance system. Given the events leading to FIRREA, it is unlikely that FDIC officials will do so.

---

[50] See Allen, "Treasures in Insurance: Many Paths Lead to Profitability," 80.

[51] See Randall 1985.

---

[52] Some depositories may own real estate not of their own choosing because mortgage defaults may result in the lenders acquiring the mortgaged property. Real estate owned for this reason does not violate laws prohibiting equity positions in real property, although limits are placed on the length of time the property can be held before sale. For more details on laws and regulations applying to banks, see Felgran 1988.

OFF–BALANCE SHEET ACTIVITIES AS SOURCES OF FEE INCOME. The growing attention to depositories' off–balance sheet activities has been noted at several points earlier in the book. Regulators have recently imposed added capital and financial reporting requirements to improve monitoring of these practices. Despite the added regulatory burdens, however, some institutions continue to show a strong interest in developing off–balance sheet services for an important reason—such activities are major sources of fee income.

Some of the most prominent fee-generating off–balance sheet activities are traditional ones, such as offering customers standby letters of credit and loan commitments. In recent years, however, off–balance sheet innovations—such as swaps, caps, collars, and floors—have also been lucrative fee-generating ventures for money-center banks that arrange these hedging strategies for their customers. Many experts believe that these off–balance sheet services, and others spawned by continuing financial and technological innovation, will be among the most important sources of fee-based income for large institutions in the future.

AND THE LIST GOES ON

Additional areas in which depository institutions have experimented in recent years include services as diverse as travel agencies and **venture capital** subsidiaries. Venture capital operations are those in which an institution takes a temporary equity position in a young or brand new company. This relationship contrasts considerably with traditional commercial relationships in which the depository acts as creditor to a business after careful financial analysis of past performance. Although potential growth in the value of a venture capital investment may be attractive, the risks are high.

Other institutions do not offer nontraditional services themselves but cash in on the trend toward fee-based income by leasing space to direct providers of the services. These depositories benefit from the lease income while offering their customers the on-premises convenience of a wider range of services.

Given the creativity of managers and the pace at which the financial system has changed recently, the list of potential fee-based sources of income is in a constant state of flux, as the regulatory dialectic predicts. Today's list will no doubt be incomplete or obsolete tomorrow. Regardless of the services considered by a depository, however, the need to supplement interest income to remain profitable and competitive will continue, as will the need to assess the risks involved in introducing each new service.

SUMMARY

The focus of this chapter was the increasingly important role of fee-based services in depository institution management. Fee-based products include traditional ones, such as trust departments and correspondent banking, and new ones, such as securities underwriting and brokerage, insurance, and off–balance sheet activities. Experience suggests that some sources of fee income may be less volatile than traditional income sources.

Trust departments are changing in response to customer preferences. An emphasis on improved performance has made such operations more competitive. The services offered by correspondent institutions also face greater competition. With regulatory changes, the Fed, the FHLB system, and corporate CUs all compete in the correspondent services markets.

Some depository institutions are interested in expanding securities activities. Although restrictions against full underwriting powers remain, depositories have made substantial inroads. Banks can now underwrite most types of securities, although there are stringent rules they must follow. Regulators agree that institutions can offer brokerage services and sell mutual funds. In response to these developments, managers must move cautiously; brokerage income tends to be volatile, but may offer a source of diversification. Mutual funds, with their sensitivity to market changes, may require careful communication with bank customers who are used to the safety of insured CDs.

Another new service alternative is insurance. Federal regulators closely watch banks' involvement in insurance brokering, and especially in underwriting, based on concerns that insurance activities may threaten institutional safety or lead to coercion of customers. State regulators, however, have been more permissive, as have the thrift and credit union regulators. Both thrift and credit union service organizations actively broker insurance policies, but underwriting activity is limited.

Additional service areas emerge regularly as depository institutions seek to diversify their sources of funds and to capitalize on opportunities for increasing income and profitability. Each opportunity also poses additional risks.

QUESTIONS

1. Compare and contrast sources of fee income to the more traditional sources of revenue for depository institutions. Why is fee income increasingly important to these institutions?

2. Describe trends in the profitability of trust departments over the last decade. What conditions prompted the shift in emphasis on profitability? What risk management tools are appropriate for use in trust departments?

3. From recent industry sources, determine the extent to which depositories have become involved in personal financial planning. What successes and obstacles are they encountering as they attempt to increase market share? Who are their major competitors in this market?

4. Explain how correspondent banks' pricing techniques have evolved in the past decade. What factors influenced the change?

5. Do you believe that the Fed and other regulators provide unfair competition to privately operated financial institutions in the market for correspondent banking services? Explain. Why do you think economies of scale exist for some correspondent services but not for others?

6. Describe new management services for corporate customers that bankers have begun to offer in recent years. Based on reports in current publications, are traditional correspondent services or newer corporate services growing more rapidly? What explanations can you offer for your findings?

7. What restrictions did the Glass-Steagall Act impose on the securities activities of commercial banks? Why? Briefly trace the loosening of these restrictions in the 1980s and 1900s.

8. Explain the major remaining restrictions on the securities activities of Fed member banks and BHCs. What is the rationale for the restrictions? Considering the operating advantages and disadvantages of being a Fed member bank, do you think current securities regulations are unfair to member banks relative to their domestic and international competitors? Explain.

9. Do you believe that corporations would benefit if commercial banks were allowed to underwrite all corporate securities? Why or why not?

10. Compare the regulation of securities activities of SAIF-insured institutions, BIF-insured nonmember banks, and credit unions. Do they have advantages or disadvantages compared to Fed member banks?

11. According to research, what are the financial implications of securities activities for depository institutions? Are there benefits? Are there additional risks?

12. Using information from recent articles, determine whether depositories are retreating from or actively entering into securities brokerage activities. What reasons can you find for their current level of involvement? Are the bank-brokerage firms partnerships, such as the one between NationsBank and Dean Witter, prospering? Are others emerging? Explain their current status.

13. Describe the strategies used by commercial banks to enter the mutual fund industry. What benefits are these banks seeking? Review recent trade publications to evaluate the current involvement of banks in the mutual fund arena.

14. From the time of the Glass-Steagall Act to the early 1990s, trace federal restrictions against large banks' and BHCs' involvement in selling and underwriting insurance. What is the current status of national banks' involvement in selling and underwriting insurance products?

15. Review recent developments in the regulation by the states of depository institutions' insurance-selling and underwriting activities. What are the primary motivations for new state laws in these areas?

16. In general, how do regulations on the insurance activities of thrifts and CUs compare to restrictions on commercial banks?

17. What objections are raised by opponents of depository institutions' entry into insurance activities? Evaluate the merit of these objections.

18. Discuss the financial implications of insurance activities for depositories. Explain the risks involved.

19. Would you choose a depository institution based on whether it offered brokerage services or could sell insurance? If your current depository began offering these services, would you use them if needed, or would you choose a firm specializing in securities brokerage or insurance? Why?

20. Should depository institutions be prohibited from taking direct ownership positions in real estate, small businesses, and other nontraditional investments? Why or why not? What implications do these activities have for the deposit insurance system? Explain.

21. Do you believe that the fees large institutions generate through off–balance sheet activities justify the additional risks the institutions assume by engaging heavily in those activities? How do you expect new risk-based capital standards to affect institutions' involvement in these services?

SELECTED REFERENCES

Block, Stanley B., and Timothy J. Gallagher. "How Much Do Bank Trust Departments Use Derivatives?" *Journal of Portfolio Management* (Fall 1988): 12–15.

Blount, Edmon W., and Louise Glass. "Will Banks Pass the Brokerage Test?" *ABA Banking Journal* 77 (February 1985): 61–71.

Bollenbacher, George M. "Using Stock Index Products in Trust Banking." *Bankers Magazine 167* (July–August 1984): 57–61.

Brewer, Elijah, III. "The Risk of Existing Nonbank Activities." In *Proceedings of a Conference on Bank Structure and Competition,* 401–423. Chicago: Federal Reserve Bank of Chicago, 1989.

Britt, Phil. "Building Fee Income." *Savings and Community Banker* 2 (March 1993): 22–29.

Brockman, Brett Hart. "Planning and Marketing Cash Management Services." *Magazine of Bank Administration* 61 (May 1985): 74–86.

Burns, Merrill O. "The Future of Correspondent Banking." *Magazine of Bank Administration* 62 (May 1986): 54–64.

"Correspondent Banking's Changing Face." *ABA Banking Journal* 80 (October 1988): 104–113.

"Correspondent Products: Which Is No. 1?" *ABA Banking Journal* 80 (October 1988): 116–122.

Crum, William C. "Banking in Insurance: A Guide to Chaos." *Bankers Magazine* 169 (January/February 1986): 51–58.

Dale, Betsy. "The Grass May Not Be Greener: Commercial Banks and Investment Banking." *Economic Perspectives* (Federal Reserve Bank of Chicago) 12 (November/December 1988): 3–13.

Dunham, Constance. "Commercial Bank Costs and Correspondent Banking." *New England Economic Review* (Federal Reserve Bank of Boston) (September/October 1981): 22–36.

Eisenbeis, Robert A., and Larry D. Wall. "Bank Holding Company Nonbanking Activities and Risk." In *Proceedings of a Conference on Bank Structure and Competition,* 340–357. Chicago: Federal Reserve Bank of Chicago, 1984.

Evanoff, Douglas D. "Priced Services: The Fed's Impact on Correspondent Banking." *Economic Perspectives* (Federal Reserve Bank of Chicago) 9 (September/October 1984): 31–44.

Felgran, Steven D. "Bank Entry into Securities Brokerage: Competitive and Legal Aspects." *New England Economic Review* (Federal Reserve Bank of Boston) (November/December 1984): 12–33.

_____. "Bank Participation in Real Estate: Conduct, Risk, and Regulation." *New England Economic Review* (Federal Reserve Bank of Boston) (November/December 1988): 57–73.

_____. "Banks as Insurance Agencies: Legal Constraints and Competitive Advances." *New England Economic Review* (Federal Reserve Bank of Boston) (September/October 1985): 34–49.

Fischer, Thomas G., William H. Gram, George G. Kaufman, and Larry R. Mote. "The Securities Activities of Commercial Banks: A Legal and Economic Analysis." *Tennessee Law Review* 51 (1984): 467–518.

Frank, John N. "Stock Brokerage Joins the Growing List of Association Offerings." *Savings Institutions* 104 (February 1983): 38–43.

Frisbee, Pamela. "Bankers' Banks: An Institution Whose Time Has Come?" *Economic Review* (Federal Reserve Bank of Atlanta) 69 (April 1984): 31–35.

Frodin, Joanna. "Fed Pricing and the Check Collection Business: The Private Sector Response." *Business Review* (Federal Reserve Bank of Philadelphia) (January/February 1984): 13–21.

Hayes, Samuel H., III. "Commercial Banking Inroads into Investment Banking." *Issues in Bank Regulation* 8 (Autumn 1984): 21–31.

Karkut, Carol T. "The Growing Importance of Fee Income in Strategic Planning." *Magazine of Bank Administration* 59 (January 1983).

Kaufman, George G. "Securities Activities of Commercial Banks: Recent Changes in the Economic and Legal Environments." *Journal of Financial Services Research* 2 (January 1988): 183–199.

Kim, Sun Bae. "The Use of Equity Positions by Banks: The Japanese Evidence." *Economic Review* (Federal Reserve Bank of San Francisco) (Fall 1991): 41–55.

Kuprianov, Anatoli. "An Analysis of Federal Reserve Pricing." *Economic Review* (Federal Reserve Bank of Richmond) 72 (March/April 1986): 3–19.

Kwast, Myron. "Banks' Securities Powers: Are There Diversification Gains?" In *Proceedings of a Conference on Bank Structure and Competition,* 515–532. Chicago: Federal Reserve Bank of Chicago, 1988.

Kwast, Myron L. "The Impact of Underwriting and Dealing on Bank Returns and Risks." *Journal of Banking and Finance* 13 (1989): 101–125.

Merrill, Peter. "Correspondent Banking and the Payments System." *Economic Review* (Federal Reserve Bank of Atlanta) 68 (June 1983): 33–39.

Merrill, Peter, and John H. Neely. "A Shaking Out Is Shaping Up for Correspondents." *ABA Banking Journal* 75 (March 1983): 43–46.

Morphew, Ronald R. "Correspondent Financial Services—The Federal Home Loan Bank System Reacts to Title III Consumer Checking Account Equity Act of 1980." In *Proceedings of a Conference on Bank Structure and Competition.* Chicago: Federal Reserve Bank of Chicago, 1981.

Morrall, Katherine. "New Strategies and Stronger Management Role Trigger Profits." *Savings Institutions* 107 (November 1986): 110–116.

Pastorell, James R. "Cash Management for Community Banks." *Magazine of Bank Administration* 59 (July 1983): 46–48.

Pozdena, Randall J. "Do Banks Need Securities Powers?" *Weekly Letter* (Federal Reserve Bank of San Francisco), December 29, 1989.

Randall, Ronald K. "Insurance: A Survey of Bankers' Plans." *Magazine of Bank Administration* 61 (September 1985): 20–26.

Reichert, Alan K. "Correspondent Banking: Services in Transition." *Magazine of Bank Administration* 61 (August 1985): 16–18.

_____. "The Role of the Federal Reserve in the Provision of Correspondent Financial Services." In *Proceedings of a Conference on Bank Structure and Competition,* 231–240. Chicago: Federal Reserve Bank of Chicago, 1981.

Rideout, Thomas P., and Susan Seidler. "Special Report: Correspondent Banking." *ABA Banking Journal* 73 (November 1981): 67–72.

Rogowski, Robert J., and Eric H. Sorenson. "Deregulation in Investment Banking: Shelf Registrations, Structure, and Performance." *Financial Management* 14 (Spring 1985): 5–15.

Rose, Peter S. "Diversification of the Banking Firm." *Financial Review* 24 (May 1989): 251–280.

Saunders, Anthony. "Banks and Securities Markets." Working Paper No. 509, Salomon Brothers Center for the Study of Financial Institutions, March 1989.

_____. "Securities Activities of Commercial Banks: The Problem of Conflicts of Interest." *Business Review* (Federal Reserve Bank of Philadelphia) (July/August 1985): 17–27.

Shafton, Robert M., and Donald D. Gabay. "The Banking Outlook for Diversification into Insurance." *Bankers Magazine* 168 (January/February 1985): 22–26.

Smith, Keith V., and Maurice B. Goudzwaard. "The Profitability of Commercial Bank Trust Management." *Journal of Bank Research* 3 (Autumn 1972): 166–177.

Spooner, Lisa. "Bottom-Line Concern Puts Fee Income in the Spotlight." *Savings Institutions* 108 (October 1987): 110–114.

Webb, James R., and David N. Hawk. "Personal Financial Planning at Depository Financial Institutions." *Journal of the American Society of CLUs and ChFCs* 42 (September 1988): 80–85.

By the time financial statements are sent to the shareholders, they are a stewardship document, not the relevant current information about the company.

J. Michael Cook
Chairman, Deloitte and Touche (1991)

After several inconclusive rounds, the bout is coming to an end. In one corner, wearing white trunks, are the Securities and Exchange Commission (SEC) Chairman, the Comptroller General of the United States, the head of the General Accounting Office (GAO), leaders of several "Big Six" accounting firms, and influential financial economists. In the opposite corner, wearing red trunks, are the Chairman of the Federal Reserve Board, the Treasury Secretary, the Federal Deposit Insurance Corporation (FDIC) Chairman, and leading financial institutions managers. After several years of trading punches, it appears, however, that the final round will occur no later than in the mid-1990s. The prize to the winning fighters? The right to determine which accounting methods financial institutions will use to present financial performance information to shareholders and other observers into the next century.

That a seemingly arcane subject could provoke such passion is one of the lingering results of the savings and loan (S&L) debacle of the 1980s. Which set of rules prevails—the market-value ones advocated by the fighters in the white trunks, or the historical-cost rules favored by the red team—can make quite a difference in how one views a firm's asset values, earnings, and protection for depositors. For example, SunTrust Banks of Atlanta lists the historical cost value of its Coca-Cola stock, much of which was acquired in 1919 when Coke first went public, at $110,000; yet the market value of the stock in 1992 was more than $1 billion! Alas, differences appear in the opposite direction, too. Roosevelt Financial Group of St. Louis, a believer in market-value accounting and a provider on a voluntary basis, recently disappointed investors by showing that its market value was 9 percent lower than its value at historical cost.[1]

Because financial reports and thus conclusions about the relative success of one firm versus another are so heavily influenced by the accounting rules managers are permitted to use, experienced observers are careful to look at many dimensions and sources of information

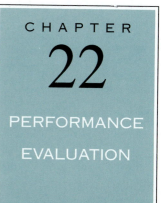

C H A P T E R

22

PERFORMANCE

EVALUATION

---

[1] Ford S. Worthy, "The Battle of the Bean Counters," *Fortune*, June 1, 1992, 117–126.

before drawing conclusions. Good analysts know, too, that small as well as large management decisions influence the relative performance of a bank, thrift, or credit union (CU). Therefore, they consider multiple sources of income, expense, and risk in conducting a financial analysis. This final chapter on depository institution management explores how reported financial data, covering all aspects of management, are used to evaluate institutional performance.

GENERAL OBJECTIVES AND GUIDELINES

The objectives of performance evaluation and the information used in such an analysis vary, depending on the evaluator's perspective. For example, bank, thrift, and CU examiners are concerned about an institution's ability to serve the public without placing the deposit insurance system at unnecessary risk. They have developed special data collection and evaluation procedures, including the CAMEL and MACRO rating systems (introduced in Chapter 2), which serve as indexes of performance based on criteria important to regulators. Although examiners have some concern about a depository's net interest margin (NIM), they may be as concerned about potential loan losses and capital adequacy ratios. In contrast, shareholders are most concerned about after-tax profitability, whereas depositors may focus on the institution's liquidity. In fact, an institution has many stakeholders, encompassing employees, shareholders, competitors, and even potential acquirers. Although they have different motivations, they all have an interest in evaluating performance. Regardless of their specific objectives, however, virtually all performance evaluators use accounting and other data to assess the financial condition of an institution at a point in time, as well as to determine how well it has been managed over a period of time. Results of such analyses are often the basis for judging an institution's performance in the future.

External observers are main users of performance evaluation, but managers of depositories must also know how the results of their activities are interpreted by others. Although managers may find NIM and return on net worth (RONW) the key variables, they understand that many additional measures must be used in the process of integrating the results of various decisions. A thorough performance analysis may assist managers in diagnosing areas of greatest strength and weakness and in formulating plans for improvement of asset/liability decisions.

PERFORMANCE: MORE THAN PROFITABILITY

The organizational scheme for preceding chapters provides a convenient framework for financial analysis: Liquidity management, investment policies, the loan portfolio, liability and capital management, and overall interest rate sensitivity are the decision areas affecting an institution's risk and return. Ratio analysis of each area helps to explain the bottom line.

A PROFIT BY ANOTHER NAME MAY NOT SMELL AS SWEET. Looking beyond (or, more accurately, above) the bottom line is important for other purposes as well. Because of differing regulatory and accounting standards for reporting financial data, managers of banks, thrifts, and CUs may exercise a great deal of discretion in reporting performance. For example, differences still remain in accounting for tax purposes, regulatory accounting, and generally accepted accounting principles (GAAP). Another challenge to performance evaluation has been presented by proliferation of off–balance sheet activities, which have not traditionally been reflected in accounting statements. (Readers may recall that the Federal Deposit Insurance Corporation Improvement Act [FDICIA] mandated better accounting for these activities. Final rules had not been established as of this writing.) Further, a single "snapshot" of 1 year's performance can be deceiving. For example, in 1983, Financial Corporation of America (FCA), at the time one of the nation's largest thrift holding companies, earned an amazing *82 percent* RONW. One year later, its CEO was forced to resign and Wall Street pundits were referring to FCA as "Financial Corpse of America."[2] The moral to the story: One or two reported performance indicators seldom provide a complete picture of an institution's financial position.

COMMON-SIZE STATEMENTS AND TREND ANALYSIS

Besides financial ratios, useful information is gleaned by expressing balance sheet accounts as a percentage of total assets and income statement items as a percentage of total revenues. The resulting **common-size statements** allow comparisons among firms and help managers or external analysts to identify performance areas that are out of line with those of competitors.

---

[2] Jennifer Bingham Hull, "Financial Corp. of America's Auditor Questions Its Future as a Going Concern," *The Wall Street Journal,* January 2, 1985, 2; and Teresa Carson, "FCA Still Has to Live up to Its Stock Price," *Business Week,* March 10, 1986, 34.

In addition, evaluators always find it useful to examine patterns in financial ratios over time. Usually called **trend analysis,** this technique reveals longer-term patterns in financial measures indicating whether a firm's performance is improving or deteriorating in different categories.

FOREIGN CURRENCY TRANSLATION

Financial institutions operating in international markets and engaging in transactions denominated in currencies other than the U.S. dollar must abide by Financial Accounting Standards Board (FASB) Statement No. 52, "Foreign Currency Translation." The objective of the statement is to isolate the effects of gains and losses resulting solely from changes in exchange rates. For example, suppose a U.S. bank operates a branch in Paris that makes loans in French francs. When loans are made, their value may be "booked" at one level, but when the operations of the branch are incorporated into the bank's financial statements (and reported in dollars, of course), the bank may experience a gain or loss on the value of the loan because of movements in exchange rates. FASB No. 52 recognizes that it is important that gains or losses such as these are viewed as being distinct from credit risk. Although the rules are too complex to be illustrated here, FASB No. 52 requires translation gains or losses as a result of the activities of foreign subsidiaries *not* to be shown as increases or decreases in an institution's income in a given year but, rather, to be *cumulatively* reported in a separate section within the institution's capital accounts.

Many large banks also hold inventories of foreign currencies and trade them frequently for the convenience of their customers. Gains and losses on these exchange operations are part of the institution's ongoing risk exposure and are reported as direct increases or decreases in income in the period in which they occur.

RECENT DEVELOPMENTS IN FINANCIAL REPORTING

During the past decade, the FASB has announced several changes in the reporting requirements for depository institutions and other firms. In 1987, the FASB substantially revised the third standard accounting statement, formerly known as the Statement of Changes in Financial Position. The current statement is known as the Statement of Cash Flows, and the initial rules were controversial among financial institution managers, who argued that many aspects of the document would be of questionable value in interpreting performance of their firms. The FASB approved one set of revisions for financial institutions, but continues to require the statement despite additional complaints from institutions.

A second important development that will assist in evaluating performance in the light of risk is the newly required disclosure of information about contingent liabilities and other nontraditional or innovative activities. New rules are intended to provide information about the risk exposure of an institution—such as positions in financial futures and options, forward commitments, and swaps—that has not been evident in standard financial statements. The disclosures are intended to reveal a great deal of information about potential losses to the firm.

Is Market-Value Accounting Close at Hand?

A third and highly controversial rule involving accounting for investment securities was issued by the FASB in early 1993. (It had provoked such heated debate that it had been under consideration for more than 4 years.) As noted in earlier chapters, the new rule supported by many in the accounting profession and some regulators, especially the SEC, requires depositories to classify all debt securities as "investment assets," which will be reported at book value; "trading assets" (those held for potential short-term gain), which will be reported at market value; or "assets held for sale," which will also be reported at market value. (Assets held for sale are those that management may choose to sell within a reasonable time.) Furthermore, the SEC advocates market-value accounting for an even broader range of financial assets and liabilities.

Depository institution managers argue that such rules will make income more volatile, and that short-term market fluctuations will play too large a role in the determination of earnings. Supporters of market-value accounting believe it will prevent managers from selling assets to show a profit on those that have increased in value, while hiding losses on those assets that have decreased in value by retaining them at book value on the balance sheet. The banking industry had favored disclosure of current values in a footnote to the financial statements rather than directly on the balance sheet.[3]

INTERPRETING THE NUMBERS

Performance evaluation is more complicated than simply calculating ratios and common-size statements. The hard part is interpreting the numbers. One calculation, viewed in isolation, means little. It is only informative when compared either with a standard for the industry or industry subgroup or with the firm's recent past performance.

SOURCES OF INDUSTRY INFORMATION. Industry standards providing a perspective for interpreting the performance of an individual firm are available from several sources. A comprehensive source of operating statistics for the banking industry, entitled *Uniform Bank Performance Reports,* is available from the Federal Financial Institutions Examination Council. Average ratios are provided for asset size groups and states in the *Peer Group Report* and the *State Average Report,* respectively. Aggregate data for national banks are published in the Comptroller of the Currency's *Quarterly Journal.* Less detailed annual summaries on the performance of commercial banks and bank holding companies (BHCs) are published in the *Federal Reserve Bulletin* and the FDIC's *Banking Review.* The Federal Reserve Banks also compile statistics on performance within their districts; these reports concentrate on selected size groups or a limited number of performance measures. The U.S. Bureau of the Census publishes time series data, including performance ratios, on all types of depository institutions in its *Statistical Abstract of the United States.* Finally, several private consulting groups, such as Sheshunoff and Company of Austin, Texas, and Veribanc, Inc., of Woburn, Massachusetts, analyze industry performance.

The Economic and Research Division of the Credit Union National Association (CUNA) regularly publishes summaries of CU data, entitled "Credit Union Operating Ratios and Spreads." Selected data are available every month in *Credit Union Magazine.* The complete, detailed reports are available from CUNA. For the thrift industry, the FDIC, the Office of Thrift Supervision (OTS), the district Federal Home Loan Banks (FHLBs), and the Saving and Community Bankers of America are sources of aggregate performance data for comparison purposes.

BEWARE: RATIO DEFINITIONS ARE NOT STANDARD. Before choosing from among many possible ratio or common-size calculations, an analyst is well advised to select the industry standards to be used for comparison. The publishers of aggregate performance data often use different definitions for a given ratio. Unless ratios are calculated in the same way as industry comparison data, conclusions are suspect.

CATEGORIES OF PERFORMANCE EVALUATION

Ratios should be categorized according to the area of performance with which they are most closely connected. For every area of performance evaluation, many ratio measures are available. Each can contribute something, but using too many may cause confusion. Consequently, the following discussion includes only a representative group of ratios. Alternative specifications of these measures, along with additional ratios, are provided in Appendix 22A. Although interpretation of these measures is similar to that of the ratios discussed in the text, data availability, the source of industry data, or a special purpose may cause an analyst to choose one measure over another.

PERFORMANCE EVALUATION ILLUSTRATED

The financial statements of First National Corporation, a regional bank holding company, are used to provide a framework for calculating and interpreting financial ratios and other performance data. A midwestern institution, First National was managed rather conservatively during most of the 1980s. Although some acquisitions were completed, the BHC did not expand as rapidly or widely as some of its nearby

---

[3] Jim McTague, "Wider Reach Feared for Market Value Accounting," *American Banker,* August 27, 1993, 1, 2; Robin Goldwyn Blumenthal, "FASB Moves Closer to Forcing Banks to Value Securities Near Market Prices," *The Wall Street Journal,* September 11, 1992, A2; Worthy, "The Battle of the Bean Counters"; and Mondschean 1992. (References are listed in full at the end of this chapter.)

rivals. As the analysis will reveal, however, management became more aggressive in the 3-year period examined here. In fact, some experts believe the BHC itself might become a target of a larger acquirer. Thus, while many stakeholders have an interest in assessing the institution's performance, this analysis is conducted primarily from the viewpoint of a prospective investor.

The statements of condition and earnings for this unidentified BHC for the years 1989 through 1991 are provided in Tables 22.1 and 22.2. Besides raw data, common-size statements are shown. In Table 22.1, asset, liability, and net worth accounts are expressed as a percentage of total assets; in the second table, income and expense figures are expressed as a percentage of total operating income (that is, the sum of interest and noninterest income).

Useful information is also provided in the notes and tables accompanying the financial statements in the annual reports of publicly held institutions. Examples of these data are shown in Appendix 22B. Obtaining this information enhances the accuracy of performance evaluation.

LIQUIDITY AND PORTFOLIO MANAGEMENT

The first management areas examined for First National are the institution's cash and securities portfolio holdings.

LIQUIDITY POSITION

A depository's liquidity is harder to measure than it might appear at first glance. The objective is to determine the institution's ability to respond to unexpected changes in asset or liability accounts. Difficulty arises because institutions have access to liquidity from two distinct sources: 1) cash and near-cash assets; and 2) funds that can be purchased in the form of short-term liabilities.

On the asset side, it is not readily apparent to an external analyst what portion of liquid assets is held to meet reserve requirements and what portion is available to meet unexpected operating liquidity needs. On the liability side, it is possible to identify the extent to which a firm has already relied on purchased liabilities, but even management cannot be sure of the *additional* liquidity that could be purchased quickly if needed.

ASSET LIQUIDITY. To measure the liquidity of the asset portfolio, the firm's shortest-term assets—cash, deposits at other institutions, short-term securities, and federal funds (fed funds) sold—are compared with other balance sheet accounts. The resulting ratios (Ratios 22.1 and 22.2 in Table 22.3) indicate the proportion of total assets held in cash and securities (Ratio 22.1) and the amount of these assets relative to average deposits (Ratio 22.2). Calculations for Ratios 22.1 and 22.2 rely on the maturity schedule of the investment portfolio, found in the BHC's annual report and shown in Appendix 22B for 1991 only. The source of comparison peer group data is the *Uniform Bank Performance Report.*

A complication in financial analysis should be noted at this point. Annual reports for BHCs aggregate data for all bank subsidiaries, so First National's ratios reflect the operations of the lead bank (with assets of $3.88 billion) and of 11 smaller institutions. In examining a BHC, analysts must sometimes choose which peer group figures to use for comparison—those for banks the size of the lead bank, or those for banks the size of the BHC ($6.6 billion in the case of First National). Because First National's ratios are calculated from the annual report of the BHC, peer group comparisons are based on banks with $3 to $10 billion in assets. If the lead bank were even slightly smaller, some analysts might select a peer group in the range of $1 to $3 billion.

Ratio 22.1 provides a general assessment of the institution's asset maturity mix. Ratio 22.2 compares liquid or near-liquid assets with deposits, many of which are short term. Ideally, analysts and managers would like to know what portion of deposits is expected to turn over in the short run. Unfortunately, account titles on balance sheets do not provide that information. For example, the core level of transactions deposits is obscured. Also, some accounts classified as time deposits may have relatively short maturities.

The ratios in Table 22.3, and those introduced later, use an *average* rather than a *total* balance for most balance sheet accounts. When evaluating performance, an analyst would like to know the ongoing position of the firm rather than the year-end position.

TABLE 22.1 First National Corporation and Subsidiaries, Consolidated Statements of Condition as of December 31, 1989–1991 (Thousands of $)

Three years of balance sheet data for First National Corporation, a large regional bank holding company, are used in the performance analysis illustrated in this chapter.

	1991	% of Total	1990	% of Total	1989	% of Total
Assets						
Cash and due from banks	$ 328,378	4.94%	$ 416,441	6.62%	$ 440,739	7.41%
Investment securities:						
U.S. Treasury and agencies	$ 874,949		$ 716,172		$ 705,420	
States and political subdivisions	72,845		83,445		91,733	
Other securities	10,725		21,724		22,511	
Total investment securities	958,519	14.42	821,341	13.05	819,664	13.78
Fed funds sold and reverse repos	296,150	4.46	316,625	5.03	230,000	3.87
Loans:						
Commercial and agricultural	$1,685,188		$1,798,784		$1,628,424	
Real estate—construction	192,220		211,315		243,007	
Real estate—mortgage	1,708,466		1,359,056		1,134,600	
Installment and credit card	1,326,013		1,255,717		1,214,361	
Other	0		0		124,984	
Total loans	$4,911,887		$4,624,872		$4,345,376	
Less unearned interest	(53,491)		(65,156)		(77,688)	
Less allowance for possible loan losses	(73,805)		(65,938)		(57,433)	
Net loans	4,784,591	71.99	4,493,778	71.38	4,210,255	70.77
Premises and equipment	101,937	1.53	74,421	1.18	73,634	1.24
Acceptances, customers' liability	23,594	0.36	28,439	0.45	35,278	0.59
Other assets	152,736	2.30	144,339	2.29	139,831	2.35
Total assets	$6,645,905	100.00%	$6,295,384	100.00%	$5,949,401	100.00%
Liabilities and Net Worth						
Deposits:						
Noninterest-bearing deposits	$ 935,732		$ 879,735		$ 845,629	
Interest-bearing deposits:						
Savings	912,958		714,034		676,567	
Time	3,579,858		3,535,987		3,450,858	
Total deposits	$5,428,548	81.68%	$5,129,756	81.48%	$4,973,054	83.59%
Short-term borrowings (primarily fed funds purchased and repos)	498,058	7.49	521,834	8.29	338,400	5.69
Long-term debt	62,868	0.95	31,929	0.51	35,431	0.60
Acceptances executed	23,594	0.36	28,439	0.45	35,278	0.59
Other liabilities	77,855	1.17	83,377	1.32	104,749	1.76
Total liabilities	$6,090,923		$5,795,335		$5,486,912	
Preferred stock	$18,004	0.27	$0	0.00	$0	0.00
Common stock	145,520	2.19	145,334	2.31	144,459	2.43
Surplus	69,425	1.04	68,490	1.09	68,007	1.14
Undivided profits	322,033	4.85	286,225	4.55	250,023	4.20
Total net worth	$ 554,982		$ 500,049		$ 462,489	
Total liabilities and net worth	$6,645,905	100.00%	$6,295,384	100.00%	$5,949,401	100.00%
Market value of securities at year-end	$ 982,823		$ 823,927		$ 820,002	

TABLE 22.2   First National Corporation and Subsidiaries, Consolidated Statements of Earnings for Years Ending December 31, 1989–1991 (Thousands of $)

Income statement data for First National are also essential for financial analysis.

	1991	% of Total Operating Income[a]	1990	% of Total Operating Income	1989	% of Total Operating Income
Interest income:						
Interest and fees on loans	$490,865	74.27%	$496,084	74.80%	$465,409	73.26%
Interest on federal funds sold	14,409	2.18	18,827	2.84	29,559	4.65
Interest on investment securities:						
Taxable	65,908	9.97	63,298	9.54	62,764	9.88
Nontaxable	4,636	0.70	5,540	0.84	5,526	0.87
Other interest income	935	0.14	3,080	0.46	680	0.11
Total interest income	$576,753		$586,829		$563,938	
Noninterest income:						
Trust income	$ 31,517	4.77	$ 26,752	4.03	$ 26,510	4.17
Service charges and fees	47,618	7.21	41,011	6.18	41,201	6.49
Other operating income	5,002	0.76	8,625	1.30	3,621	0.57
Total noninterest income	84,137		76,388		71,332	
Interest expense:						
Interest on savings deposits	$ 35,889	5.43	$ 32,927	4.96	$ 32,776	5.16
Interest on time deposits	241,523	36.55	271,953	41.01	269,215	42.38
Interest on short-term borrowings	25,282	3.83	31,481	4.75	30,362	4.78
Interest on long-term debt	4,639	0.70	3,844	0.58	3,946	0.62
Total interest expense	307,333		340,205		336,299	
Provision for possible loan losses	39,913	6.04	40,417	6.09	35,418	5.58
Noninterest expense:						
Salaries	$ 88,416	13.38	$ 80,691	12.17	$ 77,136	12.14
Pension and other employee benefits	15,835	2.40	14,147	2.13	11,960	1.88
Equipment expense	15,704	2.38	15,172	2.29	15,294	2.41
Occupancy expense	12,866	1.95	11,615	1.75	10,873	1.71
Other operating expense	83,125	12.58	68,255	10.29	68,956	10.85
Total noninterest expense	215,946		189,880		184,219	
Net operating income before tax	$ 97,698	14.78	$ 92,715	13.98	$ 79,334	12.49
Taxes	30,128	4.56	27,785	4.19	22,143	3.49
Income before securities gains or losses	$ 67,570	10.22	$ 64,930	9.79	$ 57,191	9.00
Other income (primarily security gains or losses)	(1,738)	-0.26	(41)	-0.01	7	0.00
Net income	$ 65,832	9.96	$ 64,889	9.78	$ 57,198	9.00
Per share:						
Net income	$2.24		$2.23		$2.01	
Dividends on common stock	$1.00		$0.96		$0.88	
Dividends on preferred stock	$3.00		NA		NA	
Total operating income	$660,890		$663,217		$635,270	

[a] Total Operating Income = Total Interest Income + Total Noninterest Income.

That information is usually unavailable externally and may be costly to obtain internally. By averaging beginning and ending balances, an external analyst roughly estimates average levels during the year.

As shown by Ratio 22.1, between 1989 and 1991 the proportion of short-term assets held by First National declined from more than 18 percent of average total assets to 16.75 percent.[4] The reduction in liquid assets is also evident in Ratio 22.2; by 1991, the BHC had about 20½ cents of short-term assets for every dollar of deposits, just over the peer group average. Generally, First National's asset liquidity ratios are quite compatible with industry averages, reflecting slightly more liquidity than peer institutions.

PURCHASED LIQUIDITY. Other liquidity measures indicate an institution's reliance on purchased liabilities. Ratio 22.3 in Table 22.3 reveals the relative sizes of

---

[4]To conserve space, specifics on the calculation of every ratio are not given. For clarification, details on the calculation of Ratio 22.1 for 1991 are as follows:

- Year-end short-term assets, 1991:

Cash and due	$ 328,378	(from Table 22.1)
Short-term securities maturing within 1 year:		
U.S. Treasury and agency	484,779	(from Appendix 22B)
States and political subdivisions	47,201	
Other bonds, notes, debentures	1,006	
Fed funds sold	296,150	(from Table 22.1)
Total	$1,157,514	

- Year-end short-term assets, 1990 (from Table 22.1 and from footnotes of 1990 financial statements, not shown here): $1,010,053
- Average short-term assets, 1991:

$$[\$1,157,514 \text{ (year-end 1991)} + \$1,010,053 \text{ (year-end 1990)}]/2 = \$1,083,783.50$$

- Average total assets:

$$(\$6,645,905 + \$6,295,384)/2 = \$6,470,644.50$$

Ratio 22.1 for 1991 (as shown in Table 22.3):

$$\frac{\text{Average Short-Term Assets}}{\text{Average Total Assets}} = \frac{\$1,083,783.50}{\$6,470,644.50}$$
$$= 0.1675$$
$$= 16.75\%$$

net loan and total deposit accounts; if the ratio is greater than 1, a depository may be using purchased liabilities to support loans. Given the volatility in the liability markets, such an institution will be exposed to more risk than if the ratio is 1 or less. The final liquidity measure (Ratio 22.4) focuses directly on the proportion of assets funded by purchased liabilities. Balance sheets of depository institutions may not identify negotiable certificates of deposit (CDs) as a separate account category, so external analysts may have to obtain the information elsewhere. Appendix 22B presents First National's 1991 deposit mix and maturity of large time deposits, from which some of the data used in Ratio 22.4 are taken.

For First National, Ratio 22.3 indicates that the loan/deposit ratio was less than 88 percent in all 3 years, although it increased each year. Ratio 22.4 shows that the proportion of purchased funds to total assets declined over the same period, however, suggesting that the bank has not relied on potentially volatile funds sources to make new loans. A comparison with its peer group shows that First National manages its purchased liabilities conservatively.

INVESTMENT PERFORMANCE

Because the maturity of the investment portfolio is used to assess liquidity, liquidity ratios also evaluate one aspect of portfolio management. Portfolio composition by type of issuer, such as the U.S. Treasury, government agencies, municipalities, or private corporations, provides additional information on investment management. To external observers, these data may reveal whether liquidity and safety are primary goals or whether expected yields or tax considerations are more influential.

EXAMINING TAX EFFECTS. In the banking industry, income statement details on gains and losses from securities transactions (SGLs) have become obscure, thanks to a change in reporting methods introduced by the SEC in 1984.[5] Before then, commercial banks with

---

[5]The concern over the new SEC rules has been discussed in several forums. See, for example, Daniel Hertzberg, "Bank Profit Reports Are Distorted by New SEC Rules, Other Changes," *The Wall Street Journal,* January 2, 1984.

TABLE 22.3	**Measures of Liquidity and Portfolio Management in Depository Institutions**

Liquidity ratios measure the extent to which short-term assets and purchased liabilities are used by an institution in meeting its needs for cash. The ratio of market-to-book value of securities serves as one indicator of the portfolio's response to changing market conditions.

		First National			Peer Group Averages[a]
Ratio		**1991 (%)**	**1990 (%)**	**1989 (%)**	**1991 (%)**
Liquidity Ratio[b]					
22.1	$\dfrac{\text{Average Cash and Short-Term Securities}^{c}}{\text{Average Total Assets}}$	16.75%	16.86%	18.05%	15.84%
22.2	$\dfrac{\text{Average Cash and Short-Term Securities}}{\text{Average Deposits}}$	20.53	19.55	21.60	19.91
22.3	$\dfrac{\text{Average Net Loans}}{\text{Average Deposits}}$	82.88	86.15	82.96	78.59
22.4	$\dfrac{\text{Average Purchased Liabilities}^{d}}{\text{Average Total Assets}}$	16.40	17.36	17.71	27.04
Portfolio Management Ratio					
22.5	$\dfrac{\text{Market Value of Securities}}{\text{Book Value of Securities}}$	101.51%	100.18%	98.96%	

[a] Source of peer group averages is *Uniform Bank Performance Report,* Peer Group Report, June 30, 1992, published by the Federal Financial Institutions Examination Council.

[b] The average balance for these and all subsequent calculations is defined as

$$(\text{Beginning Balance} + \text{Ending Balance})/2$$

[c] Cash + Short-Term Securities + Due from Depositories + Federal Funds Sold. Data from the Investment Maturity Schedule, shown in Appendix 22B for 1991 only, were used to identify average short-term assets.

[d] Purchased Liabilities = Negotiable Certificates of Deposit + Foreign Deposits + Acceptances Executed + Short-Term Borrowings.

The latter two items are shown on the balance sheet; negotiable Certificates of Deposit are taken from the Maturity of Time Deposits table in Appendix 22B. First National has no foreign deposits.

publicly traded stock were required to report income before and after securities gains and losses, separating the effects of operating and investment decisions. Under the new standards, both need not be directly reported. In Table 22.2, the data for First National have been rearranged somewhat from their original format to isolate net operating income; the tax effect of SGL cannot be isolated, however, because it is aggregated in the "Taxes" data item.

To ensure comparability when evaluating *rates* of return on investments, dollar returns from investment in nontaxable municipal bonds must be evaluated on a tax-equivalent basis, as explained in Chapters 5 and 13. Returns on tax-exempt securities must be multiplied by the factor $1/(1 - t)$, where t is the depository's tax rate, to convert them to a pretax basis.

Such an adjustment is only meaningful, of course, when an institution operates at a profit so that $t > 0$. Some institutions make the adjustment in their financial reports, and external analysts should look for this information.

YIELDS AND RISKINESS. Often, even after adjustments for tax effects, the average yield earned on the investment portfolio is difficult to determine. Many depositories now provide that information in annual reports. In First National's schedule of investment maturities, for example, shown in Appendix 22B, yields are given for different investment categories, and all are provided on a tax-equivalent basis.

Equally important is assessing the risk of the securities. The relative weight given to Treasury and federal agency securities is a clue. But for an external analyst, information on the default risk of nonfederal securities is difficult to obtain, as are estimates of duration and of the correlations between returns on different categories of securities. Because these elements of portfolio analysis are important, the skills of portfolio managers cannot be assessed from financial statements alone.

MARKET VERSUS BOOK VALUES. Finally, a comparison of market and book values of securities owned (Ratio 22.5 in Table 22.3) provides information about the portfolio's response to changing market conditions. Although this will change in the future, in 1991, the market value of the portfolio is found on the report of condition or in an accompanying note. Data for First National for 1991 are given at the bottom of the balance sheet in Table 22.1. The market value of First National's portfolio changed slightly in relation to book value from 1989 to 1991, ranging from 99 percent to more than 101 percent. Despite the fluctuations in market yields, First National maintained a very close relationship between book and market values.

THE LOAN PORTFOLIO

Loan portfolio analysis includes an examination of both returns and credit risk exposure.

ANALYZING LOAN LOSSES

The analyst cannot directly identify the *ex ante* [expected] level of loan portfolio risk. But the provision for loan losses on the income statement and the allowance for loan losses on the balance sheet can be informative. Each institution may identify, based on past experience, an annual provision for loan losses, which is charged against current earnings. Although not equal to actual loan losses for the year, the provision reflects management's estimate of the additions to the allowance for loan losses on the balance sheet necessary to reflect total exposure to credit risk. Thrifts choosing not to use this experience-based method may simply deduct 8 percent of taxable income as a provision for loan losses each year, as long as they have 65 percent or more of assets in mortgage-related investments.

Analysts have recognized that loan loss provisions and allowances may be overstated because of errors in judgment, or deliberately underestimated to disguise risky lending policies. Because these measures may be misleading, the Tax Reform Act of 1986 disallowed them for banks and BHCs with assets exceeding $500 million, beginning in 1987. For tax reporting purposes, these institutions may now deduct only *actual* loan losses from income before calculating taxes. The SEC, too, is concerned about these and other practices that rely heavily on management's judgment and discretion, practices that many cynics refer to as "psychoanalytic" accounting! The SEC is urging the FASB to eliminate financial reporting rules that depend upon management's intent, and depositories may well see further changes in loan loss reporting requirements by the end of this decade.[6]

NET CHARGE-OFFS. *Ex post* credit risk is easier to determine than *ex ante* risk. Analysts can examine net charge-offs, or the difference between loans actually written off as uncollectible and recoveries on loans previously classified as uncollectible. Net charge-offs are reported to regulatory authorities and are available in supplementary data in publicly held institutions' annual reports. As an example, the 1991 charge-off experience of First National is presented in Appendix 22B.

LOSSES ON INTERNATIONAL LENDING. Although First National had no international investments as of 1991, questions have been raised about the default risk exposure of commercial banks heavily invested in loans to foreign borrowers, especially borrowers in developing countries. In recognition of the higher risk, regulators have required banks to set up special "allocated transfer risk reserves"; the amounts required are determined as a percentage of funds invested in certain countries.[7] Charging off these special amounts lowers

[6]Details on the changes are available in Staff of Joint Committee on Taxation, "Title IX. Financial Institutions," *Summary of Conference Agreement on HR 3838 (Tax Reform Act of 1986)* (Washington, DC: U.S. Government Printing Office, August 29, 1986), 31; and Blumenthal, "FASB Moves Closer."

[7]"Statement of Robert J. Herrman, Senior Deputy Comptroller for Bank Supervision," *Quarterly Journal* 8 (September 1989): 47–52; and Andrews 1984. Recall from Chapter 14 that *transfer risk* is a synonym for country risk.

TABLE 22.4	**Measures of Credit Risk in Depository Institutions**

Credit risk measures focus on different indicators of loan quality.

Ratio		First National			Peer Group Averages
		1991 (%)	1990 (%)	1989 (%)	1991 (%)
22.6	$\dfrac{\text{Loan Loss Provision}}{\text{Average Net Loans}}$	0.86%	0.93%	0.88%	1.52%
22.7	$\dfrac{\text{Allowance for Loan Losses}}{\text{Average Net Loans}}$	1.51	1.42	1.36	2.48
22.8	$\dfrac{\text{Net Loan Charge-offs}^a}{\text{Average Net Loans}}$	0.80	0.75	0.74	1.33
22.9	$\dfrac{\text{Net income}^b}{\text{Loan Loss Provision}}$	1.65 times	1.61 times	1.61 times	0.72 times

[a] Net loan charge-off data are given in the Summary of Loan Loss Experience, shown in Appendix 22B.

[b] Income before securities gains or losses may be substituted.

net income for institutions lending heavily to countries on the list. The list is influenced by a desire not to offend close allies of the United States, so the debate continues over adequacy of loss reserves for international lenders. In the 1990s, in fact, political influences on the list are likely to be especially strong as Eastern European nations, many with weak economies, seek to borrow from American banks.

CREDIT RISK RATIOS

Ratios commonly used to measure credit risk are listed in Table 22.4. Ratios 22.6 through 22.8 express the loan loss provision, the allowance for loan losses, and net charge-offs as a percentage of average net loans. A trend analysis of these figures, examining changes over time, is particularly revealing. If the trends reveal a notable change, it is important to determine whether riskier lending policies have been implemented or whether management has changed its opinion on the credit risk of loans made in past years. Finally, a loss coverage ratio (Ratio 22.9) compares net income or income before securities gains and losses (IBSGL) to the loan loss provision or to actual loan losses. The higher this ratio, the more earnings are protected.

First National's credit risk ratios reflect a relatively conservative position compared with its peer group. The loan loss provision as a percentage of av-

erage net loans decreased slightly between 1989 and 1991. The allowance for loan losses and the actual net loan charge-offs, however, increased during the period as a proportion of net loans. The upward trends may indicate an assessment by bank management that the riskiness of the loan portfolio is increasing. The bank's loan loss coverage (Ratio 22.9) changed little over the period. Indeed, although not revealed in Table 22.4, First National's loan loss ratios were much higher in this period than in any time in the previous 15 years, reflecting the deteriorating credit quality of many bank loans nationwide in the late 1980s and early 1990s. Nevertheless, all four risk measures in Table 22.4 indicate that First National's credit risk exposure in 1991 was lower than that of its peer banks.

MANAGEMENT OF LIABILITIES AND CAPITAL

A main concern to all observers of financial institutions is the adequacy of the net worth cushion. Many ratios are available for evaluating the safety of a depository institution; the measurement is complicated by the numerous and contradictory definitions of capital presented in Chapter 17. Ratios discussed here are those typically calculated from publicly available financial statements and do not reflect regulators' capital adequacy rules.

| TABLE 22.5 | Measures of Leverage in Depository Institutions |

Leverage ratios examine the relationship of net worth to other key financial variables.

Ratio		First National			Peer Group Averages
		1991 (%)	1990 (%)	1989 (%)	1991 (%)
22.10	$\dfrac{\text{Average Net Worth}}{\text{Average Total Assets}}$	8.15%	7.86%	7.69%	6.31%
22.11	$\dfrac{\text{Average Net Worth}}{\text{Average Risk Assets}}$	10.10	9.83	9.69	NA[a]
22.12	$\dfrac{\text{Average Net Worth}}{\text{Average Net Loans}}$	11.37	11.06	11.09	10.09
22.13	$\dfrac{\text{Average Net Worth}}{\text{Average Deposits}}$	9.99	9.53	9.20	7.93

[a]NA = Not available

COMPARING NET WORTH WITH ASSETS

Two widely quoted traditional ratios compare an institution's net worth with average total assets (Ratio 22.10 in Table 22.5) or with average risk assets (Ratio 22.11), defined as total assets minus those not subject to default risk. The first comparison indicates the maximum amount by which the book value of the institution's assets can decline before falling below the value of total liabilities. Some analysts prefer the second ratio, because it focuses on assets that are subject to potential default risk. Another ratio, Ratio 22.12, compares net worth with net loans, which for many institutions is the largest and riskiest asset category.

First National had no preferred stock outstanding until 1991. That year, preferred stock is added to common equity (the sum of the common stock, surplus, and undivided profits accounts) to determine total net worth. As explained in Chapter 17, net worth then differs from common equity.

COMPARING NET WORTH WITH LIABILITIES

It is also possible to assess the institution's capital adequacy by comparing net worth with liabilities. For smaller institutions, deposits are the shortest-term liabilities, and the ratio of capital to deposits is an important measure, shown as Ratio 22.13 in Table 22.5. All four leverage ratios shown for First National in the table grew stronger during the 1989–1991 period. The ratios indicate that First National's net worth position increased slightly when compared with other key financial variables. The figures indicate a conservative use of leverage compared with the bank's peer group. First National is well-capitalized according to traditional financial statement measures.

A REMINDER ON DEFINING *CAPITAL* FOR PERFORMANCE ANALYSIS

Chapter 17 indicates that bank and thrift regulators include long-term debt in the regulatory definition of capital. For evaluative purposes, however, some analysts use only net worth to assess solvency. Even then complications remain, such as the treatment of intangible assets. CUs, with no access to external capital, allow a more straightforward analysis, because net worth consists solely of undivided earnings and reserves. These industry differences must be considered in measuring the performance of individual institutions.

EFFICIENCY AND PRODUCTIVITY

Many researchers have identified the ability of managers to control noninterest expenses while generating target levels of interest and noninterest revenues as a

TABLE 22.6 **Measures of Efficiency and Productivity in Depository Institutions**

Efficiency and productivity ratios are among the most important factors determining the prosperity of an institution. Low expenses and high income are hallmarks of success.

	First National			Peer Group Averages
Ratio	**1991 (%)**	**1990 (%)**	**1989 (%)**	**1991 (%)**
Noninterest Expenses				
22.14 $\dfrac{\text{Noninterest Expenses}}{\text{Total Operating Expenses}}$	38.34%	33.28%	33.14%	39.70%
22.15 $\dfrac{\text{Noninterest Expenses}}{\text{Total Operating Income}^a}$	32.68%	28.63%	29.00%	36.53%
Noninterest income				
22.16 $\dfrac{\text{Noninterest Income}}{\text{Total Operating Income}}$	12.73%	11.52%	11.23%	15.60%
22.17 $\dfrac{\text{Loan Fee Income}}{\text{Average Net Loans}}$	NA	NA	NA	NA
22.18 $\dfrac{\text{Noninterest Income}}{\text{Average Total Assets}}$	1.30%	1.25%	1.23%	1.58%
Productivity (Asset Utilization)				
22.19 $\dfrac{\text{Total Operating Income}}{\text{Average Total Assets}}$	10.21%	10.83%	10.95%	10.13%

^{a}Total Operating Income = Interest Income + Noninterest Income.

distinguishing characteristic of outstanding performers among depositories. Thus, no "report card" on asset/liability management would be complete without measures of efficiency and productivity.

NONINTEREST EXPENSES

One way to measure efficiency is to compare noninterest expenses—such as personnel costs, occupancy expense, and equipment expense—to total operating expenses, including interest expense. Noninterest expenses may also be compared with total operating income for the period. These two efficiency ratios are Ratios 22.14 and 22.15 in Table 22.6.

Trend analysis of these ratios gives cautionary signals for First National's efficiency. Ratios 22.14 and 22.15 suggest considerable change from 1989 to 1991, when noninterest expenses increased in relation to other operating figures. Still, First National's noninterest expenses are slightly lower than those of its peer institutions, regardless of the measure used.

NONINTEREST INCOME

As discussed in Chapter 21, to supplement revenues from investments in loans and securities, institutions generate income by charging fees for both traditional and nontraditional products and services. Offering services efficiently so that they can be priced competitively has become increasingly important in the current operating environment.

The contribution of noninterest income to institutional performance can be measured by comparing it with total operating income—Ratio 22.16 in Table 22.6. If a separate figure is available for fee income from originating and servicing loans, it may be compared with total average net loans (Ratio 22.17); this measure is especially important for thrift institutions charging mortgage points. If the institution reports only a combined figure for loan fees and service charges, as is the case for First National, total noninterest income can be compared with total assets, shown as Ratio 22.18. Throughout this period, First National was well below peer group banks when the amount of noninterest income is compared with either operating income or total assets.

PRODUCTIVITY (ASSET UTILIZATION)

Productivity measures focus on the firm's ability to generate revenues compared with the asset base on which revenues can be earned. The most common measure, called **asset turnover** in industrial firms and **asset utilization** in financial institutions, compares total operating income with average total assets (Ratio 22.19 in Table 22.6). First National's asset utilization declined from 1989 to 1991, but remained above its peer group average. Its relatively high investment in loans may explain its higher ratio of income to assets compared with banks of similar size. However, the declining trend would be of concern to the analyst. First National had emerged by 1991 from a period characterized by the acquisition of several small banks, mergers of several subsidiary banks, and the creation of a new subsidiary in a large city in the BHC's home state. Although not shown in Table 22.6, the bank had experienced a decline in productivity during this acquisition and merger wave. By 1991, although the productivity figures exceeded those of the mid-1980s, they continue to suggest "digestion" problems. Good analysts and managers observing First National's asset utilization would bear this point in mind and be on the lookout for potential restructuring to reduce costs and increase income. In 1992, in fact, First National announced a major layoff program to streamline its operations.

PROFITABILITY

Profitability ratios include the figures most often quoted in evaluating asset/liability management. All profitability measures compare income with another financial statement figure. The proper definition of income is subject to debate, however.

MEASURING INCOME

Previous discussion distinguished net income from income before securities gains and losses (IBSGL). When information on IBSGL is available, some analysts believe it best reflects the management of traditional loan and deposit activities. The final net income figure, in contrast, reflects more than the results of an institution's "core" operations. If it is used alone to assess performance, conclusions may be distorted.

For example, an institution anticipating poor IBSGL performance may be able to boost net income by selling parts of the securities portfolio or by liquidating real estate or other assets acquired from borrowers in financial difficulty. In 1985, BankAmerica actually sold its corporate headquarters in what was described as "obviously an earnings-driven deal."[8] The financial giant had experienced highly publicized profitability problems for several years and added $580 million to reported earnings in subsequent years as a result of the sale. Because such transactions are one-time occurrences, however, it would be unwise to use them to judge an institution's past performance or potential. When possible, it is worthwhile to isolate income generated by ongoing operations.

PROFITABILITY RATIOS

Two common profitability ratios compare a measure of income with revenues and average total assets (Ratios 22.20 and 22.21 in Table 22.7). The first measure, the **profit margin,** reflects the percentage of each dollar of revenue remaining after all costs and expenses are paid. An institution with a relatively high cost structure has a lower profit margin than a more efficient institution. The second ratio, known as return on assets (ROA), is viewed as a comprehensive measure of profitability, indicating the dollar return per dollar of assets held by the firm. A third profitability ratio (Ratio 22.22) is the rate of return on net worth (including preferred stock). The ratio compares after-tax income to common and preferred equity.

First National's profitability calculations are based on net income, because in 1 of the 3 years, income from securities trading was quite small. Also, the industry average source that was selected uses net income. Ratio 22.20 increased slightly during the period, and profit margin and ROA are strong in comparison with peer group banks. First National's RONW, Ratio 22.22, was more erratic, explained by the fact that the

[8]Patricia Bellew Gray, "BankAmerica Agrees to Sell Headquarters," *The Wall Street Journal,* September 16, 1985, 8.

TABLE 22.7	**Measures of Profitability in Depository Institutions**

Profitability ratios focus on the overall performance and incorporate the effects on net income of managers' decisions about liquidity, credit risk, leverage, efficiency, and productivity.

Ratio			First National			Peer Group Averages
			1991	1990	1989	1991
22.20	Profit Margin $= \dfrac{\text{Net Income}^a}{\text{Total Operating Income}}$		9.96%	9.78%	9.00%	6.81%
22.21	(ROA) Return on Assets $= \dfrac{\text{Net Income}}{\text{Average Total Assets}}$		1.02%	1.06%	0.99%	0.69%
22.22	$\dfrac{\text{Net Income}}{\text{Average Net Worth}}$		12.48%	13.48%	12.82%	10.43%
22.23	Earnings per Share $= \dfrac{\text{Net Income}}{\text{Number of Common Shares Outstanding}}$		$2.24	$2.23	$2.01	—
22.24	NIM Net Interest Margin $= \dfrac{\text{Interest Revenues} - \text{Interest Expense}}{\text{Average Total Assets}}$		4.16%	4.03%	3.92%	3.94%

^{a}IBSGL could be substituted for net income.

BHC issued preferred stock in 1991 and thus increased its net worth. The rise in First National's RONW, despite the decrease in financial leverage, is explained by an increase in ROA over the period. More is said later about the relationship between asset and equity returns.

Another profitability measure that equity investors watch closely is performance on a *per share* basis. The earnings per share (EPS) ratio is Ratio 22.23 in Table 22.7. As illustrated in Chapter 20, trends in EPS can be used to identify potential earnings dilution on a per-share basis, which may occur even when aggregate earnings increase. In most instances, EPS is included in reported financial data and need not be calculated. First National's EPS increased over the period.

Finally, the NIM (Ratio 22.24) is a comprehensive measure of management's ability to control the spread between interest revenues and interest costs. (This ratio, of course, is identical to Equation 1.1.) The NIM for First National increased during the period, exceeding the comparable peer group average. In general, the bank's profitability ratios are quite favorable compared with institutions of similar size.

AN INTEGRATED MODEL OF PROFITABILITY

A helpful model for measuring, evaluating, and explaining profitability is the **Dupont system.** The Dupont model illustrates the joint effect of efficiency and productivity on ROA and the ability of financial leverage to boost the RONW above ROA.

A MODEL OF RETURN ON ASSETS. The Dupont system recognizes that ROA is determined by asset use and profit margin:

$$\text{ROA} = \frac{\text{Total Revenues}}{\text{Average Total Assets}} \times \frac{\text{Net Income}}{\text{Total Revenues}} \qquad [22.25]$$

This formulation focuses attention on the source of either particularly good or particularly bad performance. For example, a thrift reporting a return on assets above the industry average may have reached that enviable position either by being more cost-efficient (reflected in a high profit margin), by using its assets better (reflected in high asset utilization), or by excelling in both areas. Conversely, relatively poor performance could arise from problems in one of the two areas or both. The areas deserving closer examination by managers or analysts are pinpointed more easily within the Dupont framework.

The Dupont ROA calculation for First National is numerically consistent with the calculation shown in

Table 22.7, because the Dupont method is merely a different way of looking at the same data. For 1991, for example, using Ratio 22.25,

$$ROA = 0.1021 \times 9.96\% = 1.02\%$$

As noted earlier, the ROA exceeds industry averages. Although First National's asset utilization is not much different from the average, its profit margin is quite a bit higher, resulting in a return on average assets that exceeds that of peer institutions. Thus, the BHC's efficiency compensates for the shortfall in productivity. The interaction of these effects is not evident in the simple ROA calculation given in Ratio 22.21. As the bank's managers seek to raise ROA to even higher levels, the Dupont method indicates that asset utilization is an area to examine. Management should also be concerned about the declining *trend* in its efficiency, discussed earlier. Although the bank remained superior to its peers on these measures through 1991, its increasing noninterest expense ratios suggest it could lose its edge over competitors in the future.

A MODEL OF RONW. The second contribution of the Dupont model is to explain the relationship between ROA and RONW. The difference between the two arises from the use of financial leverage. By multiplying ROA by the net worth multiplier—the ratio of total assets to net worth—an analyst can also calculate RONW.[9]

[22.26]

$$RONW = \frac{Total\ Revenues}{Average\ Total\ Assets} \times \frac{Net\ Income}{Total\ Revenues} \times \frac{Average\ Total\ Assets}{Average\ Net\ Worth}$$

The benefit of this formulation is that it better explains performance. If an institution reports RONW

---

[9] Another way of expressing this same relationship is

[22.26a]

$$RONW = \frac{ROA}{1 - (Total\ Liabilities/Total\ Assets)}$$

Note that the denominator of this expression is equal to Ratio 22.10 and is the reciprocal of the net worth multiplier.

either above or below industry standards, it is possible to trace that performance to the ROA, to leverage, or to both. If high financial leverage results in a high RONW, analysts and shareholders recognize the risk incurred in achieving the reported level of performance. If, in contrast, a high RONW is achieved through superior asset management (itself a product of productivity and efficiency as seen in Ratio 22.25), quite a different message is conveyed about managerial practices.

Using Ratio 22.26 for First National in 1991,

$$RONW = 0.1021 \times 9.96\% \times 12.27$$
$$= 12.48\%$$

The Dupont RONW model clarifies the fact that the bank's RONW was greater than that of peer institutions because of its higher profit margin.

In the thrift industry, the Dupont formulation has been particularly informative in explaining RONW. For example, aggregate data for Federal Savings and Loan Insurance Corporation (FSLIC)-insured thrift institutions for 1988 indicate a net worth multiplier of 23.81. That year, the net income for the industry was negative. Average ROA was −0.94 percent, but average RONW was −21.37 percent, providing a striking example of the risk of a highly leveraged balance sheet.[10]

TREND ANALYSIS

This dimension to performance analysis compares an institution with its own past history. An institution may currently look profitable compared with industry averages but still be in the midst of a decline that is revealed only through trend analysis. To illustrate the process, Figures 22.1 through 22.3 depict information on three important ratios for First National during the period from year-end 1976 through year-end 1991.

The figures should be examined together, because they depict a time series of Dupont relationships. Figure 22.1 shows that ROA for First National declined from 1979 through 1983, with an upturn in

---

[10] U.S. League of Savings Institutions 1989, 51. A good article on integrating the Dupont system into asset/liability management in thrifts is Cole 1985.

FIGURE 22.1   **First National Bank: Return on Assets**

First National's ROA declined erratically during 1976–1991.

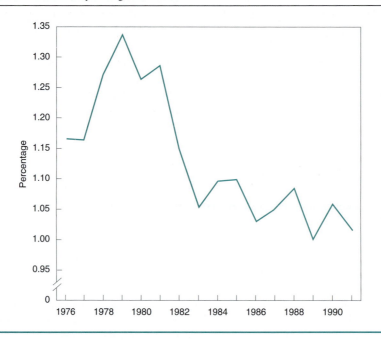

FIGURE 22.2   **First National Bank: Net Worth/Total Assets**

First National's use of leverage increased steadily during the middle period of analysis, as illustrated by the decline in the ratio of net worth to total assets between 1976 and 1986. Toward the end of the 1980s, equity capital as a percentage of assets began to increase.

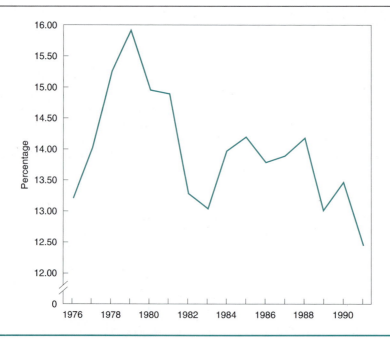

| FIGURE 22.3 | **First National Bank: Return on Net Worth** |

Because of the increased use of leverage, First National's RONW rose in the latter part of the 1970s. It turned downward in the 1980s as ROA declined. In the last few years illustrated, improvements in ROA resulted in improved returns to shareholders.

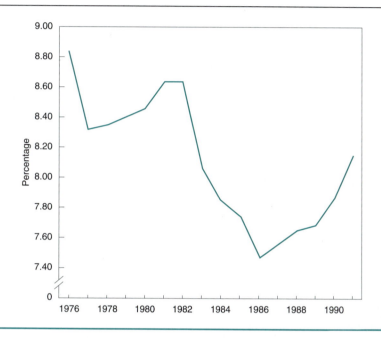

1984. From that point on, ROA was erratic (as was the case for the entire industry, in fact). At the same time, Figure 22.2 shows that the ratio of net worth to total assets increased from 1977 through 1981, then decreased sharply after 1982. The decline was reversed in 1987. Finally, Figure 22.3 shows that RONW followed a trend similar to ROA, declining through 1983 and moving erratically thereafter.

During 1978–1982, the initial years of banking deregulation, First National's managers appear to have taken a relatively low-risk approach by decreasing reliance on borrowed funds even though ROA was declining. They could have attempted to boost RONW through aggressive liability management during this period but did not do so. Because market interest rates were high during this period, that strategy would have been both risky and costly. Only after ROA continued to decline in 1983 does management appear to have responded by increasing leverage. Market interest rates had fallen, so funds costs were relatively lower. By 1984, ROA had also turned upward, and the increase in RONW that year can be attributed both to

liability management strategies and to increased asset returns. Despite a decline in ROA and RONW in 1986, First National reversed a trend and began to increase the net worth/total assets ratio slightly. This appears to have been a wise move in view of regulators' increasing scrutiny of capital adequacy.

The complete analysis of First National reveals an institution managed very conservatively during much of the 1980s but somewhat less so in recent years. The bank, like most depositories, experienced earnings pressures during the early and late 1980s. Although First National had declining capital ratios until 1987, it was more highly capitalized than similar institutions and easily exceeded even the most rigorous regulatory standards for capital. The BHC also maintained reasonable asset liquidity and below-average reliance on purchased liabilities, other indicators of a conservative management philosophy.

The expansion undertaken after 1986, however, accompanied by a willingness to reduce asset utilization figures somewhat may indicate a change toward a more aggressive philosophy. Declining liquidity and changes in the loan loss ratios and other measures of credit risk also indicate that management may have revised its definition of acceptable risk levels. Generally, though, the trends suggest little possibility that First National will soon be operating more aggressively than its typical peer institution. Indeed, in 1992, it became an acquisition target for a more aggressive competitor in its region. The buyout was unsuccessful, and as of this writing, First National remained independent.

DETERMINANTS OF EXCEPTIONAL PERFORMANCE IN DEPOSITORIES

Many studies have attempted to identify performance areas that distinguish exceptional institutions from others. Here, "exceptional" refers both to very good and very bad institutions; failed institutions have received as much attention as profitable firms. This research focuses managers' attention on key operating characteristics. Although some critical factors are qualitative, not quantitative, such as the innovativeness of managers or the ability to assess market needs, many determinants of success are evident in reported financial data.[11]

COMMERCIAL BANKS

More research on performance has been conducted for banks than for other depository institutions. Several representative studies summarize the conclusions of this body of research.

HIGH-PERFORMANCE BANKS IN THE 1970S.
Widely quoted conclusions are based on the results of a multiyear analysis of high-performance banks conducted by William Ford and Dennis Olson during the mid-1970s.[12] Using a sample of high-performance banks (high ROA and RONW) during 1972–1977, they compared key operating statistics for this group with those of other banks. Although the authors found some performance determinants to be outside management's control, such as the level of competition in their markets, they also identified important operating characteristics that reflected managerial decisions. For example, high performers had higher loan revenues relative to total loans, achieved through strategic pricing decisions. Flexibility in the asset portfolio was also a key factor, a characteristic perhaps even more important under deregulation because it allows management to respond to a changing interest rate environment.

Superior performers had lower overhead and occupancy expenses, lower personnel expenses per employee, and lower ratios of fixed assets to total assets. Ford and Olson concluded that although high revenues are important, proper control of noninterest expenses is even more important.

Later, two economists at the Federal Reserve System (Fed) analyzed ROA for banks with more than $500 million in assets during 1970–1977. Their conclusions were somewhat different from those of Ford and Olson. They concluded that pricing policies and cost efficiencies were *not* significantly different between high- and low-performance banks and that regional and local economic conditions, portfolio and risk preferences, and "some aspect of managerial ability not captured here" accounted for profitability differences.[13] Their study called attention to the need for more research into performance differences among depository institutions, a challenge accepted by other researchers in the late 1980s, as noted later in this section.

LESSONS FROM FAILED BANKS.
Other studies have focused on the lowest end of the profitability spectrum. In a comparison of failed and nonfailed banks during 1970–1975, Sinkey concluded that the distinguishing factor was management of costs. Costs that seemed most important were 1) the cost of poor loan quality, measured by the provision for loan losses; 2) the cost of liability management, measured by the expense of federal funds purchased; and 3) the cost of poor expense control, measured by the size of noninterest operating expenses. More recent research, attempting to

---

[11] Many of the important qualitative factors are discussed in Long 1988; and Donnelly, Gibson, and Skinner 1988. As noted later in this section, even the most sophisticated statistical studies of bank performance have concluded that intangible management factors are instrumental in institutional profitability.

[12] See Ford and Olson 1978. Other studies in the series include Ford 1974 and 1978 and Olson 1975.

[13] See Kwast and Rose 1982.

quantify management's role in bank failures, suggests that poor asset allocation decisions and insensitivity to customers and markets contribute to an institution's demise.[14]

BANKING PROFITABILITY IN THE 1980s. Studies by Larry Wall at the Federal Reserve Bank of Atlanta in the early 1980s drew similar conclusions to those of the Ford and Olson studies, despite changes in the regulatory and economic environment since the 1970s.[15] Wall agreed that control of noninterest expenses was a key determinant of profitability. He also found that the most profitable banks held a proportionately larger investment portfolio, earning additional revenues without the high expenses associated with lending. Stronger performers also used lower-cost sources of borrowed funds and relied more heavily on equity capital. He concluded that "the road to consistently high bank profitability (as measured by banks' return on assets) has not changed in recent years." The relatively high profitability of First National during 1976–1991 reflects many of these characteristics.

Evidence published in the late 1980s and early 1990s continues to suggest that relatively more investment securities, fewer loan losses, lower noninterest expenses (especially personnel and premises expenses), and more capital are the keys to successful commercial banking.[16]

This research also indicates that it is becoming increasingly difficult to determine whether banks affiliated with BHCs are less or more profitable than comparable independent banks. In the 1970s, the Ford and Olson studies showed that independent banks had higher earnings ratios, presumably because they were often located in smaller communities where they faced less competition. Recent studies find few, if any, profitability differences between BHC subsidiaries compared with independent banks. Deregulation and the loosening of geographic restrictions on banking appear to have removed any competitive advantage that independent banks may once have had.

An intriguing question is raised by the authors of one recent study. Gup and Walter noted that many of the high-performance banks they studied were *consistently* more profitable than others; in other words, membership in the high-performance "club" was more stable than the researchers had expected. Economic theory would predict, however, that these banks' competitors would begin to emulate their success to increase their own profitability and, consequently, that the differences between a given group of successful banks and others would diminish over time. Undoubtedly, research in the 1990s will seek to determine why abnormally high profits seem to persist among a fortunate group of institutions.

THRIFT INSTITUTIONS

Studies of the performance of thrift institutions are more difficult to interpret in the light of the many changes in the industry in recent years. Two studies were published in the late 1970s. One concluded that competitive and regulatory conditions and institutional size were important influences on performance. Managerial decision making was also crucial, especially efforts to control costs and the choice of loan portfolio composition.[17]

The second study found that high-performance S&Ls relied more heavily on borrowed funds relative to deposits, maintained lower liquidity, and had a stronger net worth position. The more profitable institutions also generated more income from fees and returns on the securities portfolio. Control of noninterest expenses was again a characteristic distinguishing the better performers.[18] Another conclusion drawn by several investigators is that high-performance thrifts follow a strategy of rapid turnover of the mortgage loan portfolio through frequent sales in the secondary mortgage market.[19]

As one might expect, research into the financial characteristics of failed versus healthy thrifts blossomed in the 1980s. In a particularly interesting example, the authors used an expert system to predict failure, based on a set of financial ratios. The ratios the

---

[14] See Sinkey 1979 and Siems 1992.

[15] See Wall 1983. Wall controlled for several factors not considered by Ford and Olson, such as changes in the economic environment. He also found that factors beyond managerial control, such as market concentration (competition), did not appear to have an effect on profitability.

[16] See Watro 1989; Gup and Walter 1988; and Tannenwald 1991.

[17] See Verbrugge, Schick, and Thygerson 1976.

[18] See Smith, Kaplan, and Ford 1977.

[19] An excellent summary and discussion of this body of literature is provided in Woerheide 1984, 28–48.

authors found most useful in predicting whether an institution was likely to fail or succeed included, among others, the ratio of net worth to total assets (measured on a GAAP, not a RAP, or regulatory accounting principles, basis), which was negatively associated with failure; the ratio of real estate owned (REO) as a result of foreclosure to total assets, which was positively associated with failure; the ratio of noninterest expenses to total operating income, which was positively associated with failure; and different liquidity ratios, including those measuring liquid assets (negatively related to failure) and purchased liabilities (positively related to failure) as a percentage of total assets. The researchers based the relative importance of each ratio on the judgment of an experienced group of professional analysts. They found that the expert system was as successful in predicting S&L failure as more traditional statistical methods.[20] These ratios, especially those related to capital and noninterest expenses, are similar to ratios distinguishing between successful and not-so-successful commercial banks.

CREDIT UNIONS

Research on performance in the CU industry is more descriptive than analytical. An obvious explanation is that, in the alleged absence of a profitability goal, it is difficult to define "high performance." Researchers at the Federal Reserve Bank of Atlanta published a study of CUs in 1984; they focused on *efficiency,* trying to identify distinguishing characteristics of the more efficient organizations.[21]

Two definitions of efficiency were applied; each focused on the level of noninterest expenses and were similar to Ratios 22.15 and 22.16 in Table 22.6. Although the study was limited to large CUs in Georgia, so conclusions should be interpreted with care, the findings offer the only available analysis of superior performance. More efficient organizations had significantly fewer loans and emphasized investment in securities, which is cheaper to administer. This manage-

ment strategy may conflict with the service-to-members goal often suggested for CUs. The high-performance group also managed to accumulate a higher proportion of deposits through less expensive regular share and share draft accounts. Again, however, reducing interest expenses is not necessarily consistent with the presumed orientation of CUs. The researchers expected better performers to be more aggressive in generating service charges and fee income as sources of revenue, but they found that less efficient organizations had higher proportions of noninterest income.

Generally, the benefits of more efficient operations were passed on to customers in the form of lower rates on loans and higher rates on some deposits. Thus, although the more efficient institutions made fewer loans, those that were granted were at favorable rates. Also, although the efficient CUs had relatively fewer interest-bearing share accounts, their interest-bearing accounts paid higher rates than those at less efficient CUs. The higher returns were not used to boost net worth to a relatively larger proportion of assets.

OFF–BALANCE SHEET ACTIVITIES AND PERFORMANCE EVALUATION

Several references have been made to data not traditionally included on the balance sheet or income statement. The investment maturity schedule, for example, is used to evaluate the liquidity position. Other off–balance sheet data also deserve analysts' attention, as they have been viewed as increasingly important determinants of financial health in recent years. Regulators have been especially concerned with contingent liabilities or other instruments that might conceivably increase the riskiness of an institution so much that deposit insurance funds could be threatened.

STANDBY LETTERS OF CREDIT

Chapter 17 explains and illustrates the growing importance of off–balance sheet items in determining capital adequacy. One of the items on which attention has been focused is the standby letter of credit. A commercial letter of credit is often used in international trade when a lender agrees to provide a customer financing to purchase specific goods. On documentation of the completion of a transaction between the cus-

---

[20] See Elmer and Borowski 1988.

[21] See Cox and Whigham 1984. A subsequent article provided CU industry aggregate data in a comparison of black-controlled CUs with other organizations, but it did not investigate the sources of performance differences. See Black and Schweitzer 1985.

tomer and a third party, the bank fully expects to advance funds. A standby letter of credit is a similar idea with an important difference: Rather than being a definite commitment to finance a transaction, a standby letter is an obligation of the bank to pay a third party *only if* the bank's customer defaults. Standby letters are used not only in commercial transactions but also to enhance the marketability of municipal bonds or to guarantee performance on construction contracts. They act as insurance for a risk-averse third party in a transaction.

Ideally, banks provide this insurance only for the obligations of customers on which there is little likelihood of nonperformance. The bank charges a fee for the commitment and, most important, assumes that the standby letter will expire unused. Because they require no advance commitment of funds, standby letters have not been included as liabilities on the balance sheets of issuing depository institutions, but they are considered contingent liabilities.

The volume of commitments made with standby letters of credit more than quadrupled in the 1980s to a level of about $300 billion. More than 50 percent of all U.S. banks reported standby letters by 1986, and virtually all the largest banks in the United States issued them. By 1988, banks with assets in excess of $10 billion reported an average volume of standby letters equal to almost 9 percent of assets. During most of the 1980s, the growth in standby letters of credit greatly exceeded the rate of growth of banks' commercial and industrial (C&I) loans.

As noted in the discussion of risk-based capital standards in Chapter 17, regulators observed the trends in standby letters and other off–balance sheet items with some concern. Research results indicated that banks using these instruments were not adjusting capital levels concurrently, and the new capital standards were developed to reverse that condition. Congress underscored its concern in FDICIA by mandating that contingent liabilities be formally incorporated in financial reports. As of this writing, no definitive reporting standards had been developed.[22]

---

[22] Several excellent references evaluating reporting and risk issues in standby letters of credit are available. These include Koppenhaver 1987; James 1987; Goldberg and Lloyd-Davies 1985; Bennett 1986; Andrews and Sender 1986; Chessen 1986; and Benveniste and Berger 1986.

INCORPORATING STANDBY LETTERS INTO FINANCIAL ANALYSIS. The recent actions of Congress, regulators, and the FASB have ensured that information will soon be available to allow analysts to consider the risk exposure of any institution's off–balance sheet activities. Federal regulators already require banks to report standby letters outstanding. First National, for example, identifies its total volume of standby letters in a footnote to its financial statements entitled "Financial Instruments with Off-Balance-Sheet Risk," shown in Appendix 22B. The $137 million volume at year-end 1991 was only about 2 percent of the BHC's total assets. The FASB's statement on financial instruments with off–balance sheet risks requires the bank to report the total potential loss that would be incurred should parties to these commitments fail to perform; this figure allows analysts to interpret an institution's credit risk exposure more accurately.

LOAN COMMITMENTS

Loan commitments—including revolving lines of credit; lines backing the commercial paper of large corporations; and note issuance facilities, in which the bank agrees to buy short-term notes if a borrower is unable to sell them elsewhere—are other off–balance sheet liabilities. In the late 1980s loan commitments at insured commercial banks were almost ten times the estimated volume of standby letters of credit. First National's position, shown in Appendix 22B, is typical: $1.37 billion in loan commitments versus $137 million in standby letters. Like standby letters, loan commitments are often activated only if a borrower's financial condition deteriorates. Ideally, they, too, should be considered by external analysts in assessing the total risk to which an institution is exposed.

HEDGING STRATEGIES: FINANCIAL FUTURES AND SWAPS

Although banks and thrifts are allowed to engage in financial futures transactions for hedging purposes only, hedges are accompanied by exposure to basis risk. It is never easy, and may even be impossible, to assess the degree of a depository's involvement by looking at published financial statements. Ordinarily, it is necessary to consult regulatory sources to get this information. (Appendix 22B contains a sample report on First National's peer group's exposure to off–balance sheet risk including swaps and futures.)

For more than a decade, large commercial banks have been required to report their total obligations for future delivery of securities on quarterly call reports. That information, however, is not yet reported separately on the balance sheet, nor are the results of hedges isolated on the income statement. Although the number of banks and thrifts actively engaged in futures trading is still relatively small, forecasts for growing participation suggest that questions about hedging should be asked as a part of performance assessment. The problem does not arise for federal CUs, of course, which are currently prohibited by regulation from involvement in the futures markets, although they may use options.

Interest rate swaps are also off–balance sheet commitments. Although swap activity is reported to federal regulators, standard financial statement analysis does not reflect the true exposure of institutions with high profiles in the market. Futures and swaps will also be included in the new post-FDICIA reporting guidelines. Thus, more complete information will be available to analysts. First National included information on these items in a footnote to its 1991 annual report (see Appendix 22B).

PERFORMANCE RATING SERVICES

Just as well-known agencies provide risk ratings for debt issues of nonfinancial corporations, risk-rating services for depository institutions are becoming increasingly important to potential investors and depositors—especially to those with accounts in excess of the FDIC-insured maximum. As these rating agencies have become better known, they have generated controversy. Institutions receiving riskier ratings are critical of procedures used to arrive at the rankings.

Most rating agencies sell their analyses on a proprietary basis and are reluctant to reveal the data on which conclusions are based. One rating service for the S&L industry drew the criticism of the U.S. League of Savings Institutions for "nondisclosure of methodology."[23] Other observers have noted, however, that institution executives are often willing to provide these services with data not generally available to other analysts in hopes of maintaining or improving their ratings.[24] Thus, the opinions of professional risk raters may reflect better information than that available to the average analyst.

SUMMARY

Financial performance evaluation of a depository institution is a multifaceted procedure, involving ratio analysis, common-size statements, trend analysis, and consideration of additional data not always found in published financial reports. Analysts look behind the reported numbers because financial statements are prepared using accounting rules that may disguise important developments. Relationships among different financial ratios and between financial and nonfinancial data must also be considered.

It is convenient to analyze the results of a depository institution's operations using several performance dimensions: liquidity, credit risk exposure, financial leverage, efficiency or productivity, and profitability. Many ratios are available to capture each dimension. Integrated models such as the Dupont system show how different dimensions of performance interact to produce a given level of ROA or RONW.

Trend analysis shows whether the depository's performance has changed over time and is as important as knowing the current position of the institution. Finally, the footnotes to financial statements may highlight the presence of off–balance sheet items that may affect projections of future performance. Future regulations to bring exposures formerly off–balance sheet into routine financial reports are planned.

QUESTIONS

1. Objectives for performance evaluation may vary across regulators, shareholders, depositors, and managers. Identify different objectives across these groups. What goals might they share?

---

[23] "Performance Rating Focuses Debate on Use of FHLBB Data," *Savings Institutions* 106 (September 1985): 7–10.

[24] Jeff Bailey and G. Christian Hill, "Bank-Rating Service's Influence Grows," *The Wall Street Journal,* August 6, 1985, 6. The authors reported that First Chicago CEO Barry Sullivan traveled to New York in June 1985 to lobby analysts of the Keefe, Bruyette and Woods agency in an effort to avoid further downgrading of the bank's rating.

2. Describe the different areas of a depository's activities that can be analyzed through financial ratios and common-size statements. What difficulties may be encountered when using financial information to make performance comparisons of different institutions?

3. What sources of industry performance information are available to depository institution analysts?

4. Identify several recent developments in bank and thrift accounting that affect the financial analysis of such firms. From current articles, can you find evidence that market value accounting rules have influenced managers' financial decisions? If so, how?

5. Do you agree with the current emphasis being placed on reporting the market value of the assets of financial institutions? Why or why not? Explain your views on the importance of reporting the market value of liabilities.

6. What problems do analysts face when using financial ratios to assess the liquidity of a depository?

7. In evaluating portfolio management, what financial ratios should be considered? Why? Besides financial ratios, what other data would you find useful to analyze an institution's securities portfolio management?

8. Why is trend analysis especially important in the evaluation of credit risk ratios? What complications in loan portfolio analysis are introduced by international lending?

9. What conclusions have researchers drawn about the importance of efficiency and productivity measures in depository performance? Do you believe that noninterest income and noninterest expenses will become more or less important to institutional performance in the future? Why?

10. Explain the benefits of the Dupont system for analyzing return on assets, RONW, and the management of capital.

11. What important information is typically provided in the notes and tables that accompany financial statements?

12. Why is the examination of off–balance sheet items essential to the financial analysis of depositories? What disclosures of these activities must institutions make? Do you believe that additional disclosures are needed? Why or why not?

13. According to research, what financial attributes distinguish very successful institutions from others? What attributes distinguish failed institutions from others?

PROBLEMS

1. The First National Bank and Trust company has year-end financial data for the most recent period as follows:

ROA	0.99%
RONW	12.57%
Net income	$11,798,000

a. Calculate the bank's net worth multiplier and its ratio of net worth to total assets.
b. Calculate the institution's total assets and net worth.
c. Suppose that the bank increases total liabilities by $10 million and reduces net worth by the same amount. Assuming no change in net income, what will be the new ROA and RONW ratios? What do these changes reveal about the impact of financial leverage?

2. You have been hired by Quincy Bank Corporation, the largest bank holding company in the state. Your first project is to complete an analysis of Quincy's performance over the past year. That analysis involves calculating performance ratios and comparing them to those for similar banks. To assist you in completing the evaluation, your supervisor has provided comparative figures from the 1996 Uniform Bank Performance Reports Peer Group Averages. The balance sheets for 1995 and 1996 and the statement of income for 1996 are also provided.

PROBLEM 22.2	**Quincy Bank Corporation and Subsidiaries, Consolidated Statements of Condition as of December 31, 1995 and 1996 (Thousands)**			
	1996		**1995**	
Assets				
Cash and due from banks		$ 233,685		$ 193,303
Investment securities:				
U.S. Treasury and agencies	$401,500		$341,604	
States and political subdivisions	140,834		142,588	
Other securities	4,102		114,417	
Total investment securities		546,436		598,609
Federal funds sold and reverse repos		547,607		563,610
Loans:				
Commercial and agricultural	$513,408		$415,185	
Real estate—construction	29,320		14,452	
Real estate—mortgage	310,268		253,657	
Installment and credit card	341,728		242,948	
Other	157,251		102,700	
Less unearned interest	(41,765)		(39,099)	
Less allowance for possible loan losses	(14,112)		(12,264)	
Net loans		1,296,098		977,579
Premises and equipment		60,443		57,399
Acceptances, customers' liability		45,267		30,500
Other assets		73,849		60,146
Total assets		$2,803,385		$2,481,086
Liabilities and Net Worth				
Deposits:				
Noninterest-bearing deposits	$567,773		$459,404	
Interest-bearing deposits:				
Savings	582,915		458,394	
Time	800,109		707,743	
Total deposits		$1,950,797		$1,625,541
Short-term borrowings (primarily federal funds purchased and repos)	$460,472		$522,476	
Long-term debt	65,536		43,729	
Acceptances executed	45,267		30,500	
Other liabilities	47,170		38,629	
Total nondeposit liabilities		618,445		635,334
Preferred stock	$ 0		$ 0	
Common stock	35,000		35,000	
Surplus	70,000		70,000	
Undivided profits	129,143		115,211	
Total net worth		234,143		220,211
Total liabilities and net worth		$2,803,385		$2,481,086
Market value of securities at year-end		$ 584,159		$ 625,403

PROBLEM 22.2 *CONTINUED*	**Quincy Bank Corporation and Subsidiaries, Consolidated Statement of Earnings for the Year Ending December 31, 1996 (Thousands)**

Interest income:		
Interest and fees on loans	$136,820	
Interest on federal funds sold	47,065	
Interest on investment securities:		
Taxable	39,211	
Nontaxable	7,909	
Other interest income	3,101	
Total interest income		$234,106
Noninterest income:		
Trust income	$ 10,052	
Service charges and fees	16,496	
Other operating income	6,185	
Total noninterest income		32,733
Interest expense:		
Interest on savings deposits	$ 13,250	
Interest on time deposits	86,357	
Interest on short-term borrowings	42,405	
Interest on long-term debt	4,943	
Total interest expense		146,955
Provision for possible loan losses		8,033
Noninterest expense:		
Salaries	$ 35,869	
Pension and other employee benefits	5,245	
Equipment expense	7,755	
Occupancy expense	6,042	
Supplies	3,793	
Other operating expense	20,308	
Total noninterest expense		79,012
Net operating income before tax		$ 32,839
Taxes		5,826
Income before securities gains or losses (IBSGL)		$ 27,013
Other income (primarily security gains and losses)		104
Net income		$ 27,117
Per share:		
Net income		$6.14
Dividends		$2.95

PROBLEM 22.2 *CONTINUED*	Quincy Bank Corporation, Peer Group Ratios		

Ratio	Peer Group Averages, 1996		

Liquidity

| 22.1 | $\dfrac{\text{Average Cash and Short-Term Securities}}{\text{Average Total Assets}}$ | | 30.99% | |

| 22.2 | $\dfrac{\text{Average Cash and Short-Term Securities}}{\text{Average Deposits}}$ | | 43.41% | |

| 22.3 | $\dfrac{\text{Average Net Loans}}{\text{Average Deposits}}$ | | 58.74% | |

| 22.4 | $\dfrac{\text{Average Purchased Liabilities}}{\text{Average Total Assets}}$ | | 30.43% | |

Portfolio Management

		Taxable		**Nontaxable**
22.5	$\dfrac{\text{Market Value of Securities}}{\text{Book Value of Securities}}$	103.72%		101.64%

Credit Risk

| 22.6 | $\dfrac{\text{Loan Loss Provision}}{\text{Average Net Loans}}$ | | 0.69% | |

| 22.7 | $\dfrac{\text{Allowance for Loan Losses}}{\text{Average Net Loans}}$ | | 1.34% | |

| 22.8 | $\dfrac{\text{Net Loan Charge-offs}}{\text{Average Net Loans}}$ | | 0.58% | |

| 22.9 | $\dfrac{\text{Net Income}}{\text{Loan Loss Provision}}$ | | 2.98 times | |

Leverage

| 22.10 | $\dfrac{\text{Average Net Worth}}{\text{Average Total Assets}}$ | | 8.49% | |

| 22.12 | $\dfrac{\text{Average Net Worth}}{\text{Average Net Loans}}$ | | 21.98% | |

| 22.13 | $\dfrac{\text{Average Net Worth}}{\text{Average Deposits}}$ | | 13.79% | |

Efficiency: Noninterest Expenses

| 22.14 | $\dfrac{\text{Noninterest Expenses}}{\text{Total Operating Expenses}}$ | | 36.57% | |

| 22.15 | $\dfrac{\text{Noninterest Expenses}}{\text{Total Operating Income}}$ | | 32.48% | |

Efficiency: Noninterest Income

| 22.16 | $\dfrac{\text{Noninterest Income}}{\text{Total Operating Income}}$ | | 7.49% | |

| 22.18 | $\dfrac{\text{Noninterest Income}}{\text{Average Total Assets}}$ | | 0.74% | |

PROBLEM 22.2 *CONTINUED*	**Quincy Bank Corporation, Peer Group Ratios**

Ratio	Peer Group Averages, 1996
Productivity (Asset Utilization)	
22.19 $\dfrac{\text{Total Operating Income}}{\text{Average Total Assets}}$	9.88%
Profitability	
22.20 $\dfrac{\text{Net Income}}{\text{Total Operating Income}}$	9.01%
22.21 $\dfrac{\text{Net Income}}{\text{Average Total Assets}}$	0.89%
22.22 $\dfrac{\text{Net Income} - \text{Preferred Dividends}}{\text{Average Net Worth}}$	10.48%
22.24 $\dfrac{\text{Interest Revenues} - \text{Interest Expense}}{\text{Average Total Assets}}$	3.98%

In addition, the following figures from the tables and footnotes in the bank's 1996 annual report may be useful:

	1996	1995
Short-term securities	$195,025	$147,990
Negotiable CDs	171,003	167,318
Net loan charge-offs	5,391	2,383

Prepare a report of Quincy Bank Corporation's performance in 1996. Evaluate the bank holding company's strengths and weaknesses in each of the following areas:

   a.   Liquidity
   b.   Credit risk
   c.   Leverage
   d.   Efficiency
   e.   Productivity
   f.   Profitability

3.   a.   Using the information in Problem 2, recalculate Quincy Bank Corporation's ROA and RONW using the Dupont ratios.
   b.   What information does the Dupont method provide for interpreting the bank's return on assets that is not provided by the ratios used in Problem 2? What recommendation would you give to Quincy's managers for improving performance?
   c.   How has the bank's use of leverage affected its return to shareholders, especially in comparison to peer banks?

4.   The summary of loan loss experience for Second Bank and Trust Company from 1994 through 1996 is provided in the following table. Using that information and appropriate ratios, answer the following questions about the bank's credit risk.

PROBLEM 22.4   **Second Bank & Trust, Summary of Changes in the Allowance for Possible Loan Losses, 1994–1996 (Thousands)**

	1996	1995	1994
1. Balance at beginning of period	$ 1,115	$ 999	$ 950
Deductions:			
2. Loan charge-offs	720	694	729
3. Less loan loss recoveries	180	135	128
4. Net charge-offs [(2) − (3)]	540	559	601
Additions:			
5. Provision for possible loan losses	700	675	650
6. Balance at end of period [(1) − (4) + (5)]	$ 1,275	$ 1,115	$ 999
Net income	$ 1,602	$ 1,548	$ 1,301
Average net loans	$120,619	$115,751	$111,053
Average net worth	$ 14,275	$ 13,191	$ 12,009
Average total assets	$176,286	$163,607	$151,579

Ratios	Peer Group Averages		
22.6	0.67%	0.66%	0.61%
22.7	1.18%	1.16%	1.07%
22.8	0.54%	0.52%	0.52%
22.9	2.13	2.15	2.20 times
22.10	8.00%	8.20%	8.20%

a. What trend is apparent in the bank's *actual* loan loss experience? Which ratios help to assess *ex post* risk?
b. What trend is evident in management's estimate of potential loan losses? On which ratio(s) do you base your response?
c. What is your assessment of the bank's overall ability to handle its current level of credit risk?
d. Using the Dupont ratios for RONW, explain the trend in the bank's RONW. If you were asked to recommend ways in which Second Bank could improve its RONW, what is the first additional item of data you would request? Why?

5. Mary LeGare is a financial analyst for one of the nation's largest banks. Her institution has followed an aggressive growth strategy over the last 4 years, and is now considering acquiring the Champion Federal Savings and Loan, a thrift operating in the same state but in a different metropolitan area. She has Champion's financial statements for the past 2 years and has been asked to provide an opinion of the institution's financial performance.

PROBLEM 22.5	**Champion Federal Savings and Loan Association, Statements of Condition as of December 31, 1995 and 1996 (Millions)**			
	1996		**1995**	
Assets				
Cash		$ 16.677		$ 15.883
Short-term securities		39.579		39,706
Loans:				
Mortgages	$367.205		$348.911	
Home improvement	61.148		58.766	
Education	2.224		1.588	
Other consumer	14.898		9.000	
Total loans		445.475		418.265
Long-term securities		23.903		19.589
Real estate owned		5.559		4.235
Building and equipment		7.227		7.412
Other assets		44.471		36.531
Total assets		582.891		541.621
Liabilities and Net Worth				
Deposits:				
NOWs, passbooks, MMDAs	$110.622		$131.825	
CDs	335.202		302.298	
Total deposits		$445.824		$434.123
FHLB advances	40.580		37.059	
Other borrowed money	37.245		26.471	
All other liabilities	10.562		18.591	
Total nondeposit liabilities		96.387		82.121
Net worth		40.680		25.377
Total liabilities and net worth		$582.891		$541.621
Market value of securities		$ 60.064		$ 59.782

| PROBLEM 22.5 *CONTINUED* | **Champion Federal Savings and Loan Association, Income and Expenses for Year Ending December 31, 1996 (Millions)** |

Interest income:
Interest on loans	$38.545
Interest on investment securities	7.594
Loan fees and discounts	2.999
Other operating income	14.678

| Total operating income | | $63.816 |

Interest expense:
Interest on deposits	$43.009
Interest on borrowed money	7.531
Salaries and employee benefits	3.788
Other expenses	6.965

Total operating expenses		61.293
Net operating income before tax		$ 2.523
Nonoperating income (expense)		(1.001)
Income before taxes		$ 1.522
Taxes		0.500
Net income		$ 1.022
Earnings per share		$ 0.23

| PROBLEM 22.5 *CONTINUED* | **Champion Federal Savings and Loan Association, Peer Group Ratios** |

Ratio	Peer Group Averages, 1996	Champion Federal Performance Ratios	
		1995	1994
Liquidity			
22.1 $\dfrac{\text{Average Cash and Short-Term Securities}}{\text{Average Total Assets}}$	6.95%	7.05%	6.95%
22.2 $\dfrac{\text{Average Cash and Short-Term Securities}}{\text{Average Deposits}}$	8.75%	8.50%	8.10%
22.3 $\dfrac{\text{Average Net Loans}}{\text{Average Deposits}}$	94.88%	92.65%	91.85%
22.4 $\dfrac{\text{Average Purchased Liabilities}}{\text{Average Total Assets}}$	10.95%	12.25%	11.95%
Portfolio Management			
22.5 $\dfrac{\text{Market Value of Securities}}{\text{Book Value of Securities}}$	97.95%	100.80%	99.00%

| PROBLEM 22.5 *CONTINUED* | **Champion Federal Savings and Loan Association, Peer Group Ratios** | | |

Ratio	Peer Group Averages, 1996	Champion Federal Performance Ratios	
		1995	1994
Leverage			
22.10 $\dfrac{\text{Average Net Worth}}{\text{Average Total Assets}}$	7.20%	6.04%	6.59%
22.12 $\dfrac{\text{Average Net Worth}}{\text{Average Net Loans}}$	8.91%	7.45%	8.88%
22.13 $\dfrac{\text{Average Net Worth}}{\text{Average Deposits}}$	8.47%	7.23%	8.02%
Efficiency: Noninterest Expenses			
22.14 $\dfrac{\text{Noninterest Expenses}}{\text{Total Operating Expenses}}$	16.75%	16.99%	16.80%
22.15 $\dfrac{\text{Noninterest Expenses}}{\text{Total Operating Income}}$	14.65%	15.79%	14.95%
Efficiency: Noninterest Income			
22.16 $\dfrac{\text{Noninterest Income}}{\text{Total Operating Income}}$	22.75%	23.80%	22.50%
22.17 $\dfrac{\text{Loan Fee Income}}{\text{Average Net Loans}}$	0.85%	0.84%	0.86%
22.18 $\dfrac{\text{Noninterest Income}}{\text{Average Total Assets}}$	2.25%	2.47%	2.35%
Productivity (Asset Utilization)			
22.19 $\dfrac{\text{Total Operating Income}}{\text{Average Total Assets}}$	11.65%	10.75%	10.95%
Profitability			
22.20 $\dfrac{\text{Net Income}}{\text{Total Operating Income}}$	4.25%	3.19%	3.85%
22.21 $\dfrac{\text{Net Income}}{\text{Average Total Assets}}$	0.55%	0.34%	0.42%
22.22 $\dfrac{\text{Net Income} - \text{Preferred Dividends}}{\text{Average Net Worth}}$	7.63%	5.63%	6.37%
22.23 $\dfrac{\text{Net Income}}{\text{Number of Common Shares Outstanding}}$		$.29	$.32
22.24 $\dfrac{\text{Interest Revenues} - \text{Interest Expense}}{\text{Average Total Assets}}$	1.23%	0.15%	0.18%

a.   Using the balance sheet and income statement data in the table, along with the industry comparative data and ratios for previous years, evaluate Champion's financial strengths and weaknesses.

b.   Based on the analysis in part a, should Mary LaGare recommend proceeding with the acquisition? Why or why not?

6. The LaCrosse Federal Credit Union is one of the state's largest credit unions. The chairperson of the asset/liability management committee is evaluating LaCrosse's financial strength.

Statements of condition and income for the CU are given in the following tables. The institution's net loan losses for the period are: $277,950 (for 1994) and $230,036 (for (1993). Evaluate LaCrosse Federal's financial position.

PROBLEM 22.6 **LaCrosse Federal Credit Union, Statements of Condition as of December 31, 1993 and 1994 (Millions)**

	1994		1993	
Assets				
Cash		$ 2.142		$ 1.646
Short-term securities		3.980		8.789
Loans:				
Consumer	$139.305		$106.798	
Mortgages	38.320		26.082	
Home improvement	2.013		2.300	
Less allowance for loan losses	(0.300)		(0.300)	
Net loans		179.338		134.880
Long-term securities		11.471		15.170
Real estate owned		0.480		0.000
Building and equipment		2.363		2.406
Other assets		1.890		0.847
Total assets		$201.664		$163.738
Liabilities and Net Worth				
Deposits:				
Share accounts and share drafts	$118.813		$107.353	
Share certificates	69.142		44.865	
Total deposits		$187.955		$152.218
All other liabilities		2.374		1.711
Reserves and undivided earnings		11.335		9.809
Total liabilities and net worth		$201.664		$163.738
Market value of securities		$ 14.080		$ 23.446

| PROBLEM 22.6 *CONTINUED* | **LaCrosse Federal Credit Union, Income and Expenses for the Year Ending December 31, 1994 (Millions)** |

Interest income:

Interest on loans	$15.602	
Interest on investment securities	1.851	
Loan fees and discounts	0.290	
Other operating income	0.008	
Total operating income		$17.751

Interest expense:

Interest on shares	$ 8.148	
Interest on borrowed money	2.254	
Salaries and employee benefits	3.332	
Other expenses	2.372	
Total operating expenses		16.106
Net operating income		$ 1.645
Nonoperating income (expense)		(0.086)
Net income		$ 1.559

| PROBLEM 22.6 *CONTINUED* | **LaCrosse Federal Credit Union, Peer Group Ratios** |

Ratio		Peer Group Averages, 1994	94	93
Liquidity				
22.1	Average Cash and Short-Term Securities / Average Total Assets	4.60%	3.04	6.37 %
22.2	Average Cash and Short-Term Securities / Average Deposits	4.90%	3.26	6.8 9%
22.3	Average Net Loans / Average Deposits	79.52%	95	88
Portfolio Management				
22.5	Market Value of Securities / Book Value of Securities	94.89%		
Credit Risk				
22.7	Allowance for Loan Losses / Average Net Loans	3.45%		
22.8	Net Loan Charge-offs / Average Net Loans	0.38%	0.16	.17.

PROBLEM 22.6 CONTINUED	**LaCrosse Federal Credit Union, Peer Group Ratios**		

Ratio	Peer Group Averages, 1994		
Leverage			
22.10 $\dfrac{\text{Average Net Worth}}{\text{Average Total Assets}}$	6.00%	5.6	6.0
22.12 $\dfrac{\text{Average Net Worth}}{\text{Average Net Loans}}$	9.86%	6.7	7.7
22.13 $\dfrac{\text{Average Net Worth}}{\text{Average Deposits}}$	6.45%	6	6.4
Efficiency: Noninterest Expenses			
22.14 $\dfrac{\text{Noninterest Expenses}}{\text{Total Operating Expenses}}$	35.95%		
22.15 $\dfrac{\text{Noninterest Expenses}}{\text{Total Operating Income}}$	24.85%		
Efficiency: Noninterest Income			
22.16 $\dfrac{\text{Noninterest Income}}{\text{Total Operating Income}}$	1.58%		
22.18 $\dfrac{\text{Noninterest Income}}{\text{Average Total Assets}}$	0.17%		
Productivity (Asset Utilization)			
22.19 $\dfrac{\text{Total Operating Income}}{\text{Average Total Assets}}$	9.35%	8.8	
Profitability			
22.20 $\dfrac{\text{Net Income}}{\text{Total Operating Income}}$	6.10%	8.8	
22.21 $\dfrac{\text{Net Income}}{\text{Average Total Assets}}$	0.93%	0.77	
22.24 $\dfrac{\text{Interest Revenues}-\text{Interest Expense}}{\text{Average Total Assets}}$	3.55%	3.5	

SELECTED REFERENCES

Andrews, Suzanna. "Accounting for LDC Debt." *Institutional Investor* 18 (August 1984): 189–194.

Andrews, Suzanna, and Henny Sender. "Off-Balance-Sheet Risk: Where Is It Leading the Banks?" *Institutional Investor* 20 (January 1986): 75–84.

Bennett, Barbara. "Off-Balance-Sheet Risk in Banking: The Case of Standby Letters of Credit." *Economic Review* (Federal Reserve Bank of San Francisco) (Winter 1986): 19–29.

Benveniste, Lawrence M., and Allen N. Berger. "An Empirical Analysis of Standby Letters of Credit." In *Proceedings of a Conference on Bank Structure and Competition,* 387–412. Chicago: Federal Reserve Bank of Chicago, 1986.

Black, Harold A., and Robert L. Schweitzer. "Black-Controlled Credit Unions: A Comparative Analysis." *Journal of Financial Research* 8 (Fall 1985): 193–202.

Chessen, James. "Off-Balance-Sheet Activity: A Growing Concern?" In *Proceedings of a Conference on Bank Structure and Competition,* 369–386. Chicago: Federal Reserve Bank of Chicago, 1986.

Cole, David W. "Profitability: The Key to Success." *Trends and Topics* (Federal Home Loan Bank of Chicago) 2 (Fall 1985): 13–21.

Cox, William N., and Pamela V. Whigham, "What Distinguishes Larger and More Efficient Credit Unions?" *Eco-*

nomic Review (Federal Reserve Bank of Atlanta) 49 (October 1984): 34–41.

Donnelly, James H., Jr., James L. Gibson, and Steven J. Skinner. "The Behaviors of Effective Bank Managers." *Journal of Retail Banking* 10 (Winter 1988): 29–37.

Elmer, Peter J., and David M. Borowski. "An Expert System Approach to Financial Analysis: The Case of S&L Bankruptcy." *Financial Management* 17 (Autumn 1988): 66–76.

Federal Financial Institutions Examination Council. *Uniform Bank Performance Report.* Annual.

Federal Reserve Bank of New York. *Recent Trends in Commercial Bank Profitability.* New York: Federal Reserve Bank of New York, 1986.

Ford, William F. "Profitability: Why Do Some Banks Perform Better than Average?" *Banking* 66 (October 1974): 29–33.

————. "Using High-Performance Data to Plan Your Bank's Future." *Banking* 70 (October 1978): 40–48, 162.

Ford, William F., and Dennis A. Olson. "How 1,000 High-Performance Banks Weathered the Recent Recession." *Banking* 70 (April 1978): 36–48.

Goldberg, Michael A., and Peter R. Lloyd-Davies. "Standby Letters of Credit: Are Banks Overextending Themselves?" *Journal of Bank Research* 16 (Spring 1985): 28–39.

Gup, Benton E., and John R. Walter. "Top Performing Small Banks: Making Money the Old-Fashioned Way." *Economic Review* (Federal Reserve Bank of Richmond) 75/6 (November/December 1988: 23–35.

James, Christopher. "Off-Balance-Sheet Banking." *Economic Review* (Federal Reserve Bank of San Francisco) (Fall 1987): 5–19.

Koppenhaver, Gary D. "Standby Letters of Credit." *Economic Perspectives* (Federal Reserve Bank of Chicago) 11 (July/August 1987): 28–38.

Kulczycky, Maria. "Institutions Trim Costs for Bigger Profits." *Savings Institutions* 106 (September 1985): 47–53.

Kwast, Myron L., and John T. Rose. "Pricing, Operating Efficiency, and Profitability among Large Commercial Banks." *Journal of Banking and Finance* 6 (1982): 233–254.

Long, Robert H. "High Performance Bank Culture." *Journal of Retail Banking* 10 (Fall 1988): 13–22.

Mondschean, Thomas. "Market Value Accounting for Commercial Banks." *Economic Review* (Federal Reserve Bank of Chicago) 16 (January/February 1992): 16–31.

Olson, Dennis A. "How High-Profit Banks Get that Way." *Banking* 67 (May 1975): 46–58.

Siems, Thomas F. "Quantifying Management's Role in Bank Survival." *Economic Review* (Federal Reserve Bank of Dallas) (January 1992): 29–41.

Sinkey, Joseph F., Jr. *Problem and Failed Institutions in the Commercial Banking Industry.* Greenwich, CT: JAI Press, 1979.

Smith, David L., Donald M. Kaplan, and William F. Ford. "Why Some Associations Perform Far above Average." *Federal Home Loan Bank Board Journal* 10 (November 1977): 7–13.

Tannenwald, Robert. "Cyclical Swing or Secular Slide? Why Have New England's Banks Been Losing Money?" *New England Economic Review* (Federal Reserve Bank of Boston) (November/December 1991): 29–43.

U.S. League of Savings Institutions. *Savings Institution Source Book.* Chicago: U.S. League of Savings Institutions. Annual, 1989.

Verbrugge, James A., Richard A. Schick, and Kenneth J. Thygerson. "An Analysis of Savings and Loan Profit Performance." *Journal of Finance* 31 (December 1976): 1427–1442.

Wall, Larry A. "Why Are Some Banks More Profitable?" *Economic Review* (Federal Reserve Bank of Atlanta) 48 (September 1983): 42–47.

Watro, Paul R. "Have the Characteristics of High-Earning Banks Changed? Evidence from Ohio." *Economic Commentary* (Federal Reserve Bank of Cleveland) (September 1, 1989).

Woerheide, Walter J. *The Savings and Loan Industry: Current Problems and Possible Solutions.* Westport, CT: Quorum Press, 1984.

APPENDIX

22A

ALTERNATIVE

RATIOS FOR

EVALUATING

PERFORMANCE

Liquidity
Cash and Due from Depositories/
    Average Demand Deposits
Short-Term Assets/Demand Deposits
Short-Term Securities/Average
    Assets
Short-Term Liabilities/Total
    Liabilities
Average Net Loans/Average Assets
Short-Term Loans/Net Loans
Average Short-Term Assets/Average
    Net Loans

Credit Risk
Loan Recoveries/Average Net Loans
(Loan Recoveries − Loan Charge-offs)/Average Net
    Loans
Loan Loss Provision/Average Assets
Loan Loss Provision/Net Charge-offs
Allowance for Loan Losses/Loan Loss Provision
Net Loan Charge-offs/Net Income

Leverage
Total Liabilities/Net Worth
(Net Worth − Intangible Assets)/
    Average Total Assets
(Net Worth + Long-Term Debt)/
    Average Total Assets
Net Worth/Average Short-Term
    Liabilities

Efficiency
Personnel Expenses/Number of
    Employees
Number of Employees/Average Total Assets
Occupancy Expense/Average Total Assets
Occupancy Expense/Total Revenues
Personnel Expenses/Total Revenues
Noninterest Expenses/Net Income
Loan Fee Income/Net Income
Noninterest Income/Net Income

A P P E N D I X

22B

SUPPLEMENTARY

FINANCIAL

INFORMATION FOR

FNC AND ITS GROUP

First National Corporation
Investment Securities

As of December 31, 1991
(thousands $)

	Carrying Value	Market Value	Average Maturity	Fully Taxable Equivalent Weighted Average Yield
U.S. Treasury and agencies:				
Within 1 year	$484,779	$492,086	0.4 years	7.20%
1–5 years	294,267	304,701	2.0 years	7.37%
5–10 years	38,831	40,835	6.6 years	8.89%
More than 10 years	57,072	60,292	23.0 years	9.28%
Total	$874,949	$897,914	2.5 years	7.47%
Obligations of states and political subdivisions:				
Within 1 year	$ 47,201	$ 47,385	0.5 years	7.41%
1–5 years	19,630	19,984	2.2 years	9.68%
5–10 years	5,218	5,482	6.2 years	10.36%
More than 10 years	796	743	15.3 years	9.95%
Total	$ 72,845	$ 73,594	1.5 years	8.26%
Other debt securities:				
Within 1 year	$ 1,006	$ 1,006	0.7 years	8.82%
1–5 years	1,550	1,557	2.4 years	8.27%
5–10 years	25	25	8.6 years	6.00%
More than 10 years	1,583	1,576	15.7 years	8.41%
Total	$ 4,164	$ 4,164	7.1 years	8.44%
Federal Reserve Bank stock and other equity securities	$ 6,561	$ 7,151		
Total investment securities	$958,519	$982,823		

Note: Information related to mortgage-backed securities included above is presented on the basis of contractual maturities.

First National Corporation Maturity of Time Deposits $100,000 and More

As of December 31, 1991 (thousands $)

3 months or less	$317,230
More than 3 months through 6 months	102,804
More than 6 months through 12 months	84,098
More than 12 months	35,791
Total	$539,923

FIRST NATIONAL CORPORATION: FINANCIAL IN-STRUMENTS WITH OFF–BALANCE SHEET RISK The corporation becomes a party to financial instruments with off–balance sheet risk in the normal course of business to meet the financing needs of its customers. These financial instruments include commitments to extend credit, standby letters of credit, interest rate caps and floors, and commitments to purchase or sell foreign currencies. These instruments involve, to varying degrees, elements of credit and interest rate risk in excess of the amount recognized on the corporation's consolidated balance sheet. The contract or notional amounts of those instruments reflect the extent of involvement the corporation has in particular classes of financial instruments.

The corporation's exposure to credit loss for commitments to extend credit, standby letters of credit, and commercial letters of credit is represented by the contract amount of those instruments. The corporation uses the same credit policies in making commitments and conditional obligations as it does for on–balance sheet instruments. The need for collateral is assessed on a case-by-case basis, based upon management's credit evaluation of the other party. As of December 31, 1991, the total contract amount of commitments to extend credit, standby letters of credit, and commercial letters of credit amounted to $1,374 million, $137 million, and $19 million, respectively.

The corporation utilizes interest rate caps and floors, commitments to purchase or sell foreign currencies, and commitments to sell residential real estate loans to hedge positions taken in transactions with customers. The notional amounts of these instruments do not represent exposure to credit loss. Risks associated with these types of financial instruments arise from the movement of interest rates or foreign exchange rates should the other party to the transaction fail to perform. The corporation controls the risk of such instruments through approvals, limits, and monitoring procedures. As of December 31, 1991, the total notional amount of interest rate caps and floors, foreign currency purchase and sale commitments, and commitments to sell residential real estate loans amounted to $26 million, $6 million, and $58 million, respectively.

First National Corporation: Summary of Loan Loss Experience—

As of December 31 (thousands $)	1991	1990	1989	1988	1987
Average loans—net of unearned interest	$4,718,795	$4,452,993	$4,054,382	$3,689,429	$3,077,382
Allowance for loan losses:					
Balance—beginning of year	$ 65,938	$ 57,433	$ 51,931	$ 43,196	$ 32,957
Charge-offs:					
Commercial	(17,718)	(15,298)	(11,628)	(6,307)	(7,198)
Real estate	(3,064)	(4,091)	(6,083)	(590)	(736)
Retail	(24,265)	(19,946)	(18,240)	(16,628)	(13,857)
Total charge-offs	(45,047)	(39,335)	(35,951)	(23,525)	(21,791)
Recoveries:					
Commercial	1,769	1,126	1,484	2,266	2,563
Real estate	208	67	77	82	128
Retail	6,000	5,462	4,474	3,977	4,134
Total recoveries	7,977	6,655	6,035	6,325	6,825
Net charge-offs	(37,070)	(32,680)	(29,916)	(17,200)	(14,966)
Provision charged to earnings	39,913	40,417	35,418	25,935	25,205
Allowances of banks acquired	5,024	768	—	—	—
Balance—end of year	$ 73,805	$ 65,938	$ 57,433	$ 51,931	$ 43,196
Ratio of net charge-offs to average loans	0.79%	0.73%	0.74%	0.47%	0.49%
Ratio of allowance for loan losses to end-of-year loans, net of unearned interest	1.52	1.45	1.35	1.34	1.27

Uniform Bank Performance Group Peer Group Data
for All Insured Commercial Banks in First National's Peer Group 2

Off–Balance Sheet Items

Percentage of Total Assets	12/31/91	12/31/90
Unused commitments		
Home equity (1–4 family)	1.77%	1.52%
Credit card	3.46%	3.52%
Commercial real estate secured by real estate	1.16%	1.87%
Commercial real estate not secured by real estate	0.05%	NA
All other	13.95%	15.69%
Total loan and lease commitments	24.34%	26.06%
Securities underwriting	0.00%	0.00%
Standby letters of credit	2.61%	3.15%
Amount conveyed to others	0.05%	0.06%
Commercial letters of credit	0.27%	0.39%
Interest rate contracts		
Notional value of interest rate swaps	6.23%	4.62%
Futures and forward contracts	0.50%	0.42%
Option contracts	0.62%	0.36%
Foreign exchange rate contracts		
Notional value of exchange swaps	0.00%	0.00%
Commitments to purchase foreign currency	0.14%	0.24%
Option contracts	0.00%	0.00%
Principal balance of mortgage pools	0.01%	0.00%
Amount of recourse exposure	0.00%	0.00%
All other off–balance sheet items	0.18%	0.23%
Gross off–balance sheet items	44.93%	45.33%

PART FIVE

ASSET/
LIABILITY
MANAGEMENT
IN
NONDEPOSITORY
INSTITUTIONS

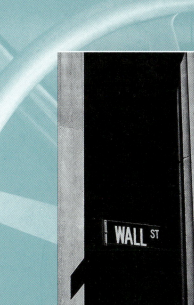

- FINANCE COMPANIES

- INSURANCE COMPANIES

- PENSION FUNDS AND
  INVESTMENT COMPANIES

- SECURITIES FIRMS

- DIVERSIFIED FINANCIAL
  SERVICES FIRMS

Finance companies have gone from competing with the banks to being able to pick and choose among old bank customers.

Richard Schmidt
Analyst, Standard & Poor's (1992)

Some taxpayers grow impatient waiting for their federal tax refunds to arrive. They should visit the nearest Beneficial Finance Corporation office. By taking completed Internal Revenue Service (IRS) tax forms to Beneficial and paying a $29 fee, customers can receive from the finance company an amount equal to the refund claimed, as long as they sign away their rights to the actual refund. In 1991 and 1992, more than 5 million Americans took advantage of this Beneficial service.

The program has also been "beneficial" for the company's financial position; the firm estimated that pretax earnings were about $40 million on its tax refund business. Why so profitable? Beneficial receives electronic transfers from the IRS and also submits customers' tax forms electronically, so the finance company receives the refunds in about 2 weeks. On an advance of $1,500, that means the company earns just over a 50 percent annual rate of return![1]

This innovative approach to financial services and products has characterized the finance company industry in recent decades. Although Beneficial has recently narrowed its scope of activities to concentrate on consumer finance, many other companies are in the process of expanding theirs. Some, like General Electric Capital, have acquired nonbank banks and are strong competitors in the credit card business. Some have bought thrifts, while others, as suggested by the quote at the beginning of the chapter, vie with banks to offer financing alternatives to corporate customers. Finance companies have also assumed a leadership role in asset securitization, a phenomenon that originated in the finance company industry. In short, many finance companies are full-fledged competitors in the consumer and corporate banking markets. The management strategies propelling Beneficial, General Electric Capital, Prudential Capital, and other finance companies into the spotlight are the subject of this chapter.

CHAPTER

23

FINANCE

COMPANIES

---

[1] Howard Rudnitsky, "Tax Play," *Forbes,* May 1, 1992, 48, 50.

NONDEPOSITORY INSTITUTIONS: WHAT ARE THEY?

For the rest of the book, the focus is on nondepository financial institutions: finance companies, insurance companies, investment companies, securities firms, pension funds, and diversified financial services firms.

NONDEPOSITORIES ARE INTERMEDIARIES

These institutions do what depositories do: accept funds on which investors expect a rate of return and reinvest those funds in financial assets—in other words, they are intermediaries. Consequently, many management tools explained earlier are useful in the asset/liability management of nondepository firms. What separates nondepositories from depositories is that the former cannot offer transactions accounts insured by federal agencies. The problem of moral hazard is less likely to arise, and the financial assets in which they can invest are less restricted than the assets of depositories.

Not all nondepositories are alike, however. Laws and regulations dating back decades separate the activities of some nondepositories, such as insurers, from others, such as investment companies. As a result of these legal and regulatory differences, the asset choices, liability preferences, tax considerations, and portfolio management strategies of some nondepositories vary markedly from those of others.

GROWING COMPETITION

Deregulation of depositories has brought increasing competition between them and nondepositories, and changing business and consumer behavior has increased competition among nondepositories. Thus, it is somewhat artificial to make fine distinctions between what a finance company, an insurance company, a securities firm, or even a bank can do that other firms cannot. Nonetheless, enough differences remain that this book's discussion of asset/liability management in nondepositories is divided by type of institution.

FINANCE COMPANIES: WHAT ARE THEY?

The opening vignette suggests that finance companies have undergone a transformation that makes them hard to define. Actually, although finance companies have changed in the past decade, they have always been hard to define. Only two things characterize firms that are traditionally considered finance companies:

1. Their lending practices are regulated almost entirely at the state level.
2. Their funds sources are not deposits.

Their origins help to identify finance companies more clearly.

BRIEF HISTORY

Most finance companies are twentieth-century creations. They arose mainly to serve the unmet credit needs of consumers, although they now serve broader purposes. Traditionally, the industry consisted of three distinct types of companies, based on primary clientele. Although the distinctions are now blurred, this historical material follows the traditional lines.

SALES FINANCE COMPANIES. A **sales finance company** provides credit, usually on an installment basis, to buyers making specific purchases. The first sales finance company was formed in 1904 by a piano manufacturer, which extended installment contracts to consumers who otherwise could not afford such an expensive item. The idea was rapidly adopted by automobile manufacturers rising to prominence at the time. By 1922, more than 1,000 sales finance firms operated in the United States.

Their credit practices were virtually unregulated because a principle of British common law was in effect, holding that the difference between the cash price of a good and the total sum of the installment payments required to purchase it was not defined as ''interest.'' Therefore, installment contracts offered by these firms were exempt from state usury laws.[2] This

---

[2] See Selden 1981, 205–206. (References are listed in full at the end of this chapter.)

legal principle has since fallen from favor, and sales finance companies are now subject to state and federal laws governing the provision of credit, including usury statutes and truth-in-lending regulations.

As sales finance companies grew in number, they were distinguished by whether they were operated as subsidiaries of major manufacturers. Subsidiaries of industrials came to be known as **captive finance companies,** whereas others were termed **independent finance companies.** Automobile and appliance manufacturers led the development of captive finance companies, and General Motors Acceptance Corporation (GMAC) and Ford Motor Credit Corporation are now familiar names to most consumers. The distinction between captive and independent continues to influence the financial strategies of finance companies, discussed in more detail later in the chapter.

CONSUMER FINANCE COMPANIES. About the same time sales finance companies emerged, the Russell Sage Foundation, a not-for-profit philanthropic organization based in New York, became concerned about the scarcity of consumer credit. Commercial banks were interested in business lending, and thrifts were interested in financing homes. Sometimes desperate consumers had few opportunities to obtain emergency cash except through loan sharks, who might demand "an arm and a leg" (literally and figuratively) in interest charges. The Russell Sage Foundation waged a nationwide campaign to reform state laws on consumer credit. The intent was to make consumer lending attractive to legitimate lenders by permitting them to charge relatively high, but state-regulated, interest rates. **Consumer finance companies** arose in this new environment as providers of small, unsecured personal loans.

In recent years, the distinction between sales finance and consumer finance companies has virtually disappeared. Most finance companies, captive or independent, make both unsecured and secured personal loans. Secured lending today includes residential mortgages, second mortgages (sometimes called **junior liens** to indicate their subordinate claim on mortgaged property), and home equity lines (HELs).

COMMERCIAL FINANCE COMPANIES. A third market in which finance companies have become active in re-

cent years is commercial lending. As of mid-1992, business loans accounted for more than 61 percent of the dollar volume of credit outstanding at finance companies.[3] Chapter 14 notes that, until recently, commercial banks shunned asset-based lending, or business loans collateralized by the borrowing firm's inventory or receivables. **Commercial finance companies** arose to fill the need for this type of business credit.

These companies are traced to the incorporation of the Mercantile Credit Company in Chicago in 1905. Its founders were encyclopedia salesmen who had suffered cash shortages but found no lenders interested in borrowers whose only assets were inventory and installment receivables. They left the encyclopedia business to found a specialized financial institution making cash loans collateralized by receivables. After 1954, states' widespread adoption of the Uniform Commercial Code clarified the rights of asset-based lenders and provided strong impetus for growth of commercial finance companies. Today, many such companies continue to provide short-term asset-based loans, but they also offer long-term commercial financing and leasing.[4]

AT LAST, A DEFINITION. The previous discussion explains why Federal Reserve System (Fed) economists define a finance company as follows:

any company (. . . excluding banks, credit unions, savings and loan associations . . . and mutual savings banks) the largest portion of whose assets is in one or more of the following kinds of receivables . . . sales finance receivables, personal cash loans to individuals and families, short- and intermediate-term business credit, junior liens on real estate. . . .[5]

(No one claims that economists are persons of few words.) Firms meeting this definition are profiled in the following paragraphs.

---

[3] "Domestic Finance Companies, Assets and Liabilities," *Federal Reserve Bulletin* 79 (January 1993): A35.

[4] Doreen Wolchik, "History of Asset-Based Lending," unpublished paper, Citicorp Industrial Credit, 1984.

[5] Hurley 1981.

TABLE 23.1 **Distribution of Finance Companies by Size of Loan Portfolio, June 1985**

Like depositories, the finance company industry is concentrated. A few large firms hold almost 90 percent of the industry's assets.

Size Category	No. of Firms in Category	% of Total Firms	Assets of Firms in Category (Millions of $)	% of Total Assets
Less than $5 million	1,287	74.09%	$ 857	0.29%
$5–$24 million	161	9.27	2,028	0.70
$25–$99 million	96	5.53	5,639	1.94
$100–$499 million	115	6.62	25,530	8.78
$500 million and more	78	4.49	256,652	88.29
Total, all sizes	1,737	100.00%	$290,706	100.00%

Source: Board of Governors of the Federal Reserve System, unpublished data, 1987.

CURRENT INDUSTRY STRUCTURE

All finance companies are stockholder-owned, but their ownership structures are not homogeneous. Some, like Household International, are independent, publicly held companies. Some, including (but not limited to) captive finance companies, are owned by nonfinancial firms. For example, ITT, a diversified conglomerate, owns ITT Financial Corporation. Others are operated as subsidiaries of financial institutions. In fact, because the Fed has determined that finance company activities are "closely related" to banking, some bank holding companies (BHCs), especially those of money-center banks, operate finance subsidiaries.

The number of finance companies has declined since the 1970s, down from nearly 3,400 in 1975 to fewer than 1,800 in 1985.[6] Reasons for the decline are familiar: Competition and changing laws and regulations have resulted in merger or failure, as is the case with depository institutions. The financial management problems of finance companies are discussed more fully later.

The finance company industry is similar to depositories in another way, too: It consists of many relatively small firms and a few very large institutions. Table 23.1 provides data on the number and size of finance companies as of 1985. About 75 percent of the firms in the industry had less than $5 million in total loans outstanding; fewer than 5 percent of the firms were in the largest category. In fact, firms with receivables of $25 million or more accounted for more than 99 percent of total finance company assets in the industry, thus signifying a high degree of economic concentration.

As noted in Chapter 2, most states require finance companies to demonstrate to authorities that a new branch office will provide "convenience and advantage" to customers. Unlike depositories, however, finance companies are free from restrictions on interstate expansion. In the past, this relative freedom gave finance companies a competitive edge over depositories in reaching customers, and consequently, the largest finance companies built extensive nationwide branch networks. Recently, the cost of operating "brick and mortar" branches has risen, and finance companies have turned to less expensive ways, such as mail solicitations and credit cards to attract customers and deliver services. The result is that the number of branch offices operated by finance companies declined about 20 percent between 1977 and 1989.[7]

---

[6] These data, and many others cited in the chapter, are drawn from a series of quinquennial (occurring every 5 years) surveys conducted by the staff of the Board of Governors of the Fed. The most recent industry figures were generalized from those obtained from a systematic random sampling of firms in 1985. (The results of the 1990 survey will not be available until the mid-1990s.) The Fed's 1985 sample included all finance companies with assets in excess of $25 million and selected smaller institutions. See Hurley 1981 for methodological details of typical surveys. Between these quinquennial studies, the Fed publishes quarterly updates of certain balance sheet data in the *Federal Reserve Bulletin.*

[7] Isabel B. McAleer, "Finance Companies 1977–1989," *Finance Facts,* (American Financial Services Association), July 1990.

| TABLE 23.2 | **Balance Sheet of Finance Companies, Year-End 1991** |

The assets of finance companies are dominated by loans. Most funds are obtained by issuing commercial paper and long-term debt. Finance companies are highly leveraged, as are most financial institutions.

	Billions of $		% of Total	
Assets				
Consumer receivables	$121.9		21.72%	
Business receivables	292.5		52.12	
Real estate loans	65.8		11.72	
Total receivables, gross	$480.2		85.57	
Less unearned income and allowance for losses	(68.0)		−12.12	
Total receivables, net		$412.2		73.45%
Other assets		149.0		26.55
Total Assets		$561.2		100.00%
Liabilities and Net Worth				
Bank loans	$ 42.3		7.54%	
Commercial paper	159.4		28.40	
Due to parent	34.5		6.14	
Not elsewhere classified	191.3		34.09	
All other liabilities	69.0		12.30	
Total liabilities		$496.5		88.47%
Net worth		64.7		11.53
Total Liabilities and Net Worth		$561.2		100.00%

Source: Prepared by the authors with data from the *Federal Reserve Bulletin* 79 (January 1993), A35.

ASSETS AND LIABILITIES OF FINANCE COMPANIES

The industry's asset and liability structure differs according to firm size. Data on the year-end 1991 balance sheets of finance companies are given in Table 23.2.

ASSETS OF FINANCE COMPANIES

Finance company portfolios, even more than those of depositories, are dominated by loans. The importance of different types of receivables, however, has changed over time.

CONSUMER LENDING. The industry originated to supply consumer loans, and finance companies of all sizes are active in this market. Although not shown in the table, for small firms, consumer lending has traditionally comprised more than 50 percent of total assets. Within consumer lending, personal cash loans are more important for small companies, but automobile

loans are more important for large firms. Sometimes, car loans are made directly by a finance company; at other times, a car dealer originates the transaction and sells the loan contract to a finance company. Finance companies also finance mobile homes and consumer goods as diverse as furniture, appliances, boats, and private planes.

BUSINESS LENDING. Although business receivables are held by most finance companies, large firms hold more. As with depositories, large companies are able to offer a wider variety of services. Small institutions, with fewer personnel and facilities, can often offer only the basics. Large finance companies make larger loans, too, for reasons that become clear as sources of funds are considered. Historically, regardless of size, most finance companies served small and medium-sized businesses.[8]

---

[8] For more information on historical trends in business lending by finance companies, see Harris 1979.

Finance company receivables are often divided into wholesale and retail categories. Wholesale receivables (often called **wholesale paper**) include manufacturers' loans to dealers, later purchased by finance companies. A typical transaction involves a loan by a large manufacturer, such as John Deere, to a rural farm implement dealer. If a finance company later purchases the loan from Deere, it appears as a receivable on the finance company's books. Because the dealer is not the ultimate user of the goods, the financial transaction is termed a wholesale one. In contrast, **retail paper** includes credit arising from the final sale of goods to business firms, such as the purchase by IBM of cars for its executives. Because IBM is the ultimate user of the cars, the transaction is a retail one, although it is business lending because household consumers are not involved.

Business lending by finance companies includes three other categories. Asset-based lending accounts for a large portion of business loans at small finance companies. Another is leasing, which has grown rapidly as a receivables category since 1980. Finally, securitized assets, introduced in earlier chapters and discussed in more detail later in this chapter, is the fastest growing category of business lending.

REAL ESTATE LOANS. Real estate lending is a relatively recent addition for finance companies. In the early 1980s, they showed a decided preference for second mortgages because yields on junior liens are higher than on first mortgages, to compensate for the subordinate claim on the property in case of default. Still, even a secondary claim on real property is less risky for the lender than a personal cash loan to a consumer. For the borrower, the cost of a second mortgage loan may be lower than that of a personal cash loan, because collateral is involved. In the high-interest environment of the early 1980s, finance company customers took note of the lower-cost borrowing opportunity, and second mortgage financing grew.

As interest rates fell in the mid-1980s, borrowers lost interest in second mortgages. Also, high delinquency rates on first mortgages made second mortgages seem even riskier to lenders, so the growth of junior lien financing plummeted. However, tax reform measures passed in 1986 that eliminated interest deductions on many consumer loans but not on second mortgages renewed demand. And, as discussed in detail in Chapter 15, the 1986 tax law also spurred tre-

---

FIGURE 23.1   **Growth in Finance Company Receivables: 1980–1990**

The volume of lending by finance companies grew substantially during the 1980s. Loans and leases to businesses accounted for most of the growth.

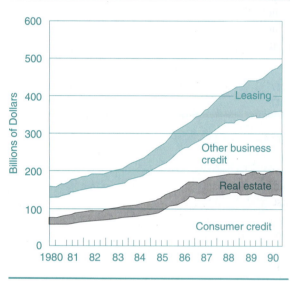

Source: Remolona and Wulfekuhler 1992.

---

mendous consumer interest in home equity lines of credit. From the end of 1988 to the end of 1991, real estate–secured consumer lending at finance companies (including second mortgages and HELs) grew by 36 percent—quite a contrast to the 1.7 percent growth rate in 1986, before the Tax Reform Act was enacted.

Figure 23.1 charts data on the lending and leasing activities of finance companies between 1980 and 1990. During the 10-year period, business lending—particularly leasing—accounted for the highest growth in finance company receivables. Toward the latter part of the decade, real estate loans also grew rapidly.

UNEARNED INCOME AND ALLOWANCE FOR LOSSES. The account called "unearned income and allowance for losses" is the sum of interest on discounted loans and the allowance for expected loan losses. The 1991 figure in Table 23.2 is the total for all loans; amounts for each category are unavailable.

OTHER ASSETS. The miscellaneous category called "other assets" includes premises, cash, investments in subsidiary companies, and securities. The securities holdings of finance companies are conspicuous by their absence, providing one of the main differences between depositories and finance companies. The recent growth of securitization will undoubtedly influence some finance companies, particularly small ones, to purchase asset-backed securities created by large finance companies. Treasury securities, corporate bonds, and stocks, however, will likely remain absent from finance companies' balance sheets.

LIABILITIES AND NET WORTH OF FINANCE COMPANIES

The sources of funds for finance companies differ somewhat from those of depositories.

Bank Loans. Most bank borrowing is by small finance companies. The reason will become clear in the discussion of other funding sources.

Commercial Paper. Almost one-third of the funds of finance companies are raised through commercial paper. Because only large, nationally known firms raise money in this market, commercial paper is inaccessible to the small firms that make up most of the industry. Further, because commercial paper is sold only in large denominations, small firms do not need the quantity of funds that typically must be raised in a commercial paper issue. In 1985, for example, only 78 finance companies accounted for 93 percent of the industry's outstanding commercial paper.[9] As noted, small finance companies rely more heavily on commercial bank financing.

Other Liabilities. The remaining liability categories—"due to parent," not elsewhere classified, and other liabilities—represent a variety of sources.[10] "Other liabilities" includes short- and long-term borrowing. Although not shown directly in the table, large firms have greater access to the bond markets, so they

rely more heavily on long-term borrowings than do small finance companies. Also, large firms are more heavily involved in mortgage lending and leasing, two activities contributing to longer asset portfolio maturities. From a maturity-matching perspective, long-term funds are more attractive to large firms than to small finance companies whose assets are concentrated in relatively short-term consumer cash loans.

"Due to parent" represents funds obtained by captive finance companies from parent organizations. As indicated earlier, many large manufacturing firms have formed captive finance companies to facilitate the sale of the parent's goods by providing financing to potential purchasers. Although most firms in the finance company industry are not captives, the large size of some captives (such as GMAC) is reflected by the fact that, within the industry, debt owed to parent companies equals more than 10 percent of total funding.

Net Worth. For the industry as a whole, net worth is almost 12 percent of total sources of funds. Large firms are more highly leveraged, however, and small finance companies rely on equity for almost half of their financing. Clearly, returns to shareholders of large finance companies are potentially much more variable. The industry profile is consistent with that of depository institutions, because large depositories are more highly leveraged than small ones. The limited access of small institutions to the money and capital markets helps to account for their more conservative financial structures. But even the largest finance companies use less leverage than small depositories, for reasons explained later.

INCOME, EXPENSES, AND PROFITABILITY OF FINANCE COMPANIES

Little information is available on the income, expenses, and profitability of finance companies, because Fed surveys, on which previous asset and liability data are based, do not include income statement

[9]Board of Governors of the Federal Reserve System, unpublished data, 1987.

[10]A small proportion of these liabilities is savings deposits and saving certificates that are deposit-type liabilities of "industrial" or "Morris plan" banks. These financial institutions, of which there were more than 1,000 in 1984, are small state-chartered finance companies authorized to make installment loans to consumers and

small businesses. They are concentrated in only a few states and are not considered commercial banks because they do not accept demand deposits. For more details, see Ysabel M. Burns and Thomas A. Durkin, "Industrial Banking Companies," *Finance Facts,* February 1984.

TABLE 23.3	**Selected Income and Expense Data for Finance Companies: 1977–1989**

Finance companies' profitability has fluctuated in recent years, although the industry has fared better than in the 1970s as managers have become more skillful in managing the spread.

	1977 (%)	1978 (%)	1979 (%)	1980 (%)	1981 (%)	1982 (%)	1983 (%)	1984 (%)	1985 (%)	1986 (%)	1987 (%)	1988 (%)	1989 (%)
Gross income/total assets	11.4	12.0	13.1	15.0	15.4	16.0	14.3	14.2	13.2	13.0	12.2	12.3	13.1
Operating expenses/total assets	4.6	4.5	4.6	5.3	4.5	4.6	4.5	4.6	4.6	5.0	4.4	4.8	4.8
Cost of borrowed funds/total assets	4.7	5.4	6.8	8.0	9.4	8.9	6.8	7.2	6.3	6.0	5.5	5.8	6.6
Net income/total assets (return on assets)	1.3	1.3	1.2	1.2	1.0	1.5	1.9	1.6	1.5	1.5	1.6	1.3	1.3
Net income/net worth (return on net worth)	11.2	11.3	10.6	9.6	8.6	12.2	18.3	15.4	16.2	16.2	17.7	13.7	13.7

Source: Ysabel Burns McAleer, "Finance Companies 1977–1989," *Finance Facts,* July 1990.

information. Until 1989, the American Financial Services Association, a trade organization for finance companies, collected data from voluntarily reporting finance companies, but that data base was discontinued. Table 23.3 contains selected information from a subsample of consistently reporting firms during 1977–1989.

As the table shows, return on assets (ROA) improved, as did return on net worth (RONW), after a periodic low in 1981. Reasons for the trends are seen in the first and third rows of the table. Between 1977 and 1981, interest costs increased more relative to total assets than did gross income or interest revenues. As interest rates began to fall in 1982, interest costs as a percentage of assets declined more than gross income as a percentage of assets. In other words, finance company managers controlled the spread well enough between 1982 and 1989 to earn higher ROA and RONW than in the early part of the period.

A study by economists at the Federal Reserve Bank of New York found that from 1975 to 1984, large finance companies had higher ROAs and RONWs on a pretax basis than did commercial banks, although on an after-tax basis, banks had higher RONWs. During the last part of the period, however, the profitability of large finance companies improved considerably, and their ROA was more than twice as high as the ROA for banks (1.68 percent versus 0.71 percent). The researchers attributed the superior performance of finance companies during this period to managers' ability to manage the spread and to the larger proportion of higher-yielding consumer loans in finance companies' portfolios.[11]

Higher potential yields also connote higher risk. By the late 1980s, the luster of the industry's profits had dimmed somewhat. In particular, the rising tide of personal bankruptcies began to increase loan losses. As the table shows, operating expenses as a percentage of total assets climbed in both 1986 and 1988. As a result, ROA fell to a level not seen since the early part of the decade.

Figure 23.2 compares rates of return on net worth for commercial banks and the two segments of the finance company industry during the 1980s. Consumer finance companies enjoyed the strongest performance, despite the uncertainties introduced by revised bankruptcy laws. After 1982, however, both consumer and diversified finance companies reported higher RONWs than commercial banks. Although not shown in the figure, the finance company industry's increased use of financial leverage explains at least some of this growth in RONW ratios. Finance companies also escaped the default risk exposure banks encountered in agricultural lending, loans to oil producers, and international lending.

As in depositories, then, finance company managers must understand what affects the amount and

---

[11] Federal Reserve Bank of New York 1986, 277–281.

stability of net interest income, or they cannot achieve the target level of RONW. The net interest margin (NIM) is affected by the interest rate sensitivity of the company's assets and liabilities, and managers must pay attention to relative asset/liability maturities and to interest rate forecasts that may dictate a shift in maturity composition. Also, because many large finance companies are highly leveraged but have no insured liabilities, asset quality—especially the default risk exposure of receivables—is an important management concern. Not only does poor asset quality depress earnings in a single period through loan losses charged off, it also affects expected future earnings. If a finance company's investors believe that its assets have deteriorated, they will demand higher yields to compensate for the additional risk, squeezing NIM in later periods. Ultimately, investors may refuse to provide funds at any price. These issues are addressed in the discussion of asset/liability management topics in the next sections.

ASSET MANAGEMENT

Because finance companies do not offer transactions accounts, they are not subject to reserve requirements or to unanticipated withdrawal of funds by investors. Maturity dates on bank notes, commercial paper, and long-term debt are known in advance, so liquidity planning is easier for finance companies than it is for depositories. This explains finance companies' relatively low holdings of cash and securities. Of course, loan demand cannot be completely anticipated, and maturing liabilities must be repaid or rolled over, so cash-flow planning cannot be ignored. Generally, however, default risk and interest sensitivity are more important managerial considerations.

DEFAULT RISK

Like depositories, finance companies must assess the creditworthiness of businesses or consumers. Issues central to credit analysis, presented in Chapters 14 and 15, apply to the management of finance companies. Finance companies also face special credit analysis problems because of the types of loans on which they concentrate.

| **FIGURE 23.2** | **Return on Net Worth for Finance Companies and Commercial Banks in the 1980s** |

Both consumer finance companies and diversified finance companies earned higher rates of return on net worth than did commercial banks during the 1980s.

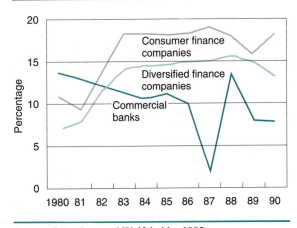

Source: Remolona and Wulfekuhler 1992.

UNSECURED PERSONAL LOANS. For the industry as a whole, and especially for its many small companies, personal cash loans are major assets. These loans are relatively small, and the cost of administering each one is high as a proportion of loan size.[12] Personal cash loans are also unsecured. Together, these factors allow the lender to charge a higher interest rate than on automobile or other collateralized loans.

With the expected higher yield to the lender comes greater default risk. Relatively high interest rates not only dissuade applicants who can get more favorable terms elsewhere, they also increase the borrower's repayment requirements. Thus, assessing the borrower's willingness and ability to repay—or character and capacity, two of the "Cs of credit" mentioned in Chapter 14—is particularly important. Because individuals do not supply audited financial statements, accurate assessment is often more difficult than with business borrowers. Information such as past credit history, occupation, age, income, and existing

---

[12] An analysis of operating costs relative to loan size in finance companies is provided in Benston 1977.

assets and liabilities are critical proxies for character and capacity.

SECOND MORTGAGE LOANS. Second mortgage loans are riskier than first mortgages, because if a borrower defaults, the second mortgage holder's position is subordinate to that of the first mortgage lender. Since 1979, the availability of private mortgage insurance on second mortgages has diminished that risk somewhat. Nonetheless, default risk remains. A study by the National Second Mortgage Association showed that delinquency rates on second mortgages were highest at finance companies and lowest at commercial banks, thrifts, and mortgage banks. Uncertainty in finance company cash flows is further increased by growth in the proportion of second mortgage loans with variable rates.[13]

RISKINESS OF FINANCE COMPANY BORROWERS. Complicating credit analysis is the fact that finance company borrowers often have no previous financial relationship with the lender. In contrast, borrowers from depositories usually have a deposit account. Thus, managers of finance companies cannot directly examine how the potential borrower handles finances. In other words, their access to reusable information may be more limited than is the case for depositories. It is often alleged, in fact, that consumers who borrow from finance companies would not do so if they qualified for loans at depositories. This allegation implies that consumer lending is riskier for finance companies than for other suppliers of consumer credit.

It is interesting to examine the direct and indirect evidence for that contention. One study of borrowers at commercial banks and finance companies found that about 75 percent of the finance company borrowers would also have qualified for loans using typical commercial bank credit standards. Finance company borrowers, however, *perceived themselves* to be less creditworthy than bank borrowers and believed that they were more likely to receive credit at a finance company than at a bank. The authors concluded that the

market for consumer credit was not segmented because of lenders' views of credit risk but because of consumer choice.[14]

The same authors found evidence, however, that some financial characteristics of finance company borrowers differ significantly from those of depository institution borrowers. For example, borrowers from banks had significantly higher average monthly incomes and greater average total assets, conditions confirmed in a later survey by researchers at the Fed. Selected results from the Fed survey are shown in Table 23.4, which compares nonmortgage borrowers from four types of financial institutions.

Much of the financial data are median figures, so 50 percent of the borrowers from a particular lender ranked above the relevant number in the table and 50 percent ranked below. Depository institution borrowers had higher median incomes and accumulated financial assets than finance company borrowers, even though the mean age of borrowers was about the same. The results suggest that most families who used finance company credit had lower incomes and fewer assets on which to draw in case of emergencies than did borrowers from depository institutions. Finance company borrowers, however, had less consumer debt outstanding. They were also less likely to be homeowners or to have credit cards, so they were less able to tap equity accumulated in a home or a line of credit on a bank card than were depository borrowers.

Although these data do not prove that finance company borrowers are greater credit risks than depository institution borrowers, they do show that, on average, finance companies lend to consumers with fewer financial resources. Careful personal credit analysis is an essential element of finance company management, and credit-scoring models have been developed for this purpose. Managers must also establish systems to monitor the payment performance of individual loans, as well as policies for collecting on delinquent receivables.

[13] Dru Johnston Bergman, "Second Mortgages Build Image as First Class Investment," *Freddie Mac Reports* 3 (November 1985): 1–2.

[14] See Johnson and Sullivan 1981. Similar findings were reported using data from 1970 in Boczar 1978. Recent reports suggest the differences between depository institutions' and finance companies' customers persist. See Yvette D. Kantrow, "Finance Companies Are Thriving While Retail Loans Worry Banks," *American Banker,* March 1, 1990, 1, 13.

TABLE 23.4	Comparison of Characteristics among Finance Company and Depository Institution Borrowers, 1983

Survey data from the 1980s show that finance company borrowers are less wealthy and less likely to be homeowners or to have credit cards than depository borrowers. They also have lower incomes and less liquidity.

	Lender			
Borrower Characteristic	**Commercial Bank**	**Thrift**	**Credit Union**	**Finance Company**
Average age of family head (years)	40	41	39	39
Median 1982 family income	$24,200	$26,800	$32,200	$23,080
Median checking account balance	$ 300	$ 300	$ 300	$ 200
Median liquid assets	$ 1,398	$ 3,863	$ 2,453	$ 950
Median financial assets	$ 1,800	$ 4,300	$ 2,815	$ 1,000
Median consumer debt outstanding	$ 4,430	$ 4,365	$ 4,705	$ 4,183
Percentage of homeowners	68	74	74	62
Percentage with bank credit card	54	56	60	44

Source: Prepared by the authors with data from Robert B. Avery et al., "Survey of Consumer Finances, 1983: A Second Report," *Federal Reserve Bulletin* 70 (December 1984): 866–867.

EFFECT OF BANKRUPTCY LEGISLATION ON CONSUMER CREDIT. The impact on depositories of changes in personal bankruptcy laws was discussed in Chapter 15, but no financial institutions have been more affected than finance companies. The first year the 1978 Bankruptcy Reform Act went into effect, making it easier for consumers to declare bankruptcy while retaining many of their assets, loan losses at finance companies more than doubled. In fact, the bankruptcy law changes explain the large increase in finance companies' operating expenses in 1980, shown in Table 23.3. Another bad year was 1981; profits for the industry as a whole fell 20 percent. GE Credit, for example, estimated that by 1982, 3,085 consumer borrowers *per month* were declaring bankruptcy.[15]

Finance companies' responses to these events are a good illustration of the regulatory dialectic. They reacted to soaring bankruptcies in two ways. The first was to diversify away from unsecured consumer lending. Some finance companies virtually shut down traditional personal cash-lending operations. Large firms' move into second mortgage lending, already evident by 1980, accelerated. By 1981, these firms had an estimated 40 percent share of the market for second mortgage loans.

On a second front, the industry worked to change bankruptcy laws at the state level. The 1978 federal bankruptcy law preempted state bankruptcy statutes unless states specifically passed new ones. Armed with an industry-financed study by researchers at Purdue University, demonstrating that almost 30 percent of those declaring bankruptcy under the 1978 law could have repaid their debts from future income, finance companies began lobbying in earnest. By mid-1982, 33 states had enacted new bankruptcy legislation, in most cases less lenient than the 1978 federal law, although still more generous to debtors than before 1978. In June 1984, a new federal bankruptcy law was passed, making it more difficult for debtors to abuse their credit privileges by declaring bankruptcy. The new law encouraged the reentry of finance companies into the market for personal cash loans.

Unfortunately for all consumer lenders, the number of personal bankruptcy filings began another rapid ascent in 1986. The growth in nonbusiness bankruptcies continued to the end of the decade; between

---

[15] Some of the information in this and the following paragraphs is drawn from "A New Source of Mortgage Money," *Business Week,* March 23, 1981, 95; "Finance Companies Show the Strain," *Business Week.* March 22, 1982, 80–81; "The Allure of Second Mortgages," *Business Week,* March 16, 1981, 126; "Turning Back a Tide of Personal Bankruptcy," *Business Week,* June 14, 1982, 32; Johnson 1989; Staten 1989; Stephen Wermiel, "Court Clears Chapter 11 Use By Individuals," *The Wall Street Journal,* June 14, 1991, A2; and Stahl 1993. Additional discussion of bankruptcy and consumer lending is found in Chapter 15.

1985 and 1990, new filings for personal bankruptcy increased at an average annual compound rate of just over 17 percent. In 1992, more than 900,000 new cases were filed.

The new surge in bankruptcies affects the profitability of all aspects of the consumer finance markets, including credit cards, home equity lending, and unsecured personal loans. Economists and other experts continue to search for explanatory factors that might assist in reversing the trend in bankruptcies. Thus far, however, results are not definitive, so they provide little assistance in developing corrective responses. Also, despite extensive lobbying efforts by consumer lenders and the introduction of bankruptcy reform legislation in the early 1990s, Congress had yet to act on the issue as this book went to press.

CREDIT RISK AND BUSINESS LENDING. Finance companies also face special problems in granting business credit, because most of their commercial borrowers are small to medium-sized. The failure rate among small businesses is higher than for large ones, and in times of economic hardship, small businesses' financial difficulties are especially severe. In 1981, for example, when many finance companies were turning away from consumer credit for reasons previously discussed, the business failure rate jumped 45 percent, putting further pressure on finance company earnings during that difficult time.

In addition, the effects of a recession on creditors are often felt long after an economic upturn, as lenders write off loans that went sour during the slump. Commercial loan losses continued to be high for finance companies into the mid-1980s, even though most economists view that period as one of economic expansion. Thus, finance company managers must not only conduct a thorough credit analysis of individual borrowers; they must also keep a watchful eye on the overall level of credit risk to which the company is exposed in case of an economic downturn.

ADDITIONAL INFLUENCES ON THE EXTENSION OF CREDIT

Like other consumer lenders, finance companies are affected by state usury laws. Recall that usury laws restrict the interest rates lenders can charge on specific types of loans. Chapter 15 notes that one impact of binding usury ceilings is to make less credit available to borrowers at depository institutions. The same effect has been observed for finance company borrowers. One study of finance company lending noted that the ratio of consumer installment loans to total loans held by finance companies declined from 50 percent to 39 percent during 1965–1974, a period characterized by increasing interest rates but static usury ceilings in most states.[16] A similar decrease in available credit occurred more recently. For example, as the general level of interest rates reached its historical high in 1981, Beneficial Corporation, at that time the nation's second-largest consumer finance company, closed 400 of its 1,900 offices. The states in which offices were closed were those with the lowest usury ceilings. Because many state usury laws were rewritten in the 1980s to permit higher ceilings, the future problems that they pose for finance companies will be less severe.

Other regulations that affect the consumer-lending operations of finance companies concern the disclosure of terms and equal access to credit. Finance companies are required to comply with federal truth-in-lending legislation and with regulations governing nondiscriminatory credit-granting practices. Although these regulations benefit many borrowers, they add to finance companies' costs of offering consumer loans.

INTEREST SENSITIVITY OF ASSETS

Because finance companies of all sizes rely on short-term sources of funds, their managers must be alert to the relationship between asset and liability maturities. The average maturity of commercial and consumer nonmortgage loans is shorter than for mortgages, so finance companies have never faced the large negative maturity GAP that thrifts face. But large finance companies, which are more dependent on short-term financing than smaller, highly capitalized firms, now offer variable-rate consumer loans pegged to commercial paper or other short-term market rates. As in depositories, the objective of minimizing the GAP by matching maturities is to lock in a spread, reducing potential variability in NIM and RONW.

---

[16] See Benston 1977.

The attention given to rate sensitivity varies, however, depending on whether the finance company is of the captive sales type. Many captive sales companies use credit terms to attract buyers for the parent company's products. This tactic was clearly seen in 1985 and 1986, when the captive finance subsidiaries of General Motors, Ford, and Chrysler offered widely publicized below-market (as low as 0 percent in some cases!), fixed-rate financing to spur flagging automobile sales. The campaigns succeeded in increasing car sales, although they locked the captive finance companies into low returns on a portion of their asset portfolios for several years to come. Despite the pressure on captive finance company profits, some observers believe that the campaigns may have succeeded in permanently attracting many borrowers away from depositories.[17]

NEW DIRECTIONS IN ASSET MANAGEMENT

Like depositories, finance companies are expanding the scope of operations. New directions involve finance companies in financial markets they have previously ignored, creating opportunities and challenges both for them and for their competitors.

HOME EQUITY LINES OF CREDIT. A potentially lucrative market for finance companies is home equity lending. The growth in traditional second mortgages since 1986 was noted earlier in the chapter. Since the Tax Reform Act of 1986 mandated a phase-out of deductions for interest paid on consumer loans, consumers' uses of funds obtained by borrowing against accumulated home equity have expanded. As a result, the proportion of homeowners borrowing against the equity in their homes increased from 5.4 percent in 1977 to 11 percent (or 6.5 million homeowners) in 1988. Of those 6.5 million borrowers, about 45 percent used the traditional fixed-maturity second mortgage, whereas about 55 percent chose the more flexible line of credit. In a 1989 survey of consumer finances, researchers at the Fed found that almost 11 percent of

U.S. households borrowed through a home equity or other line of credit from some type of financial institution.

By the early 1990s, finance companies had not made notable inroads into the newer and growing home equity *line of credit* market. For example, although nearly one-third of second mortgages with traditional installment credit characteristics were provided by finance companies in 1988, less than 4 percent of the home equity lines of credit originated in the industry. Fed researchers concluded that the customers attracted to the two types of loans are distinctly different, with credit-line customers having higher incomes and holding larger amounts of home equity. It would be beneficial for finance companies to attract a larger share of those borrowers. However, the fact that many home equity lines of credit are accessed through checking accounts presents a major hurdle, because few finance companies offer transactions accounts.

Some large finance companies, such as Household Finance, entered the home equity line of credit market, however, often doing so through their non-bank bank subsidiaries. Fed data gathered in 1989 indicated that a larger percent of U.S. households held home equity credit lines with finance companies than with savings institutions, but the percentage using commercial banks was three times as large as the percentage using finance companies.[18]

SECONDARY MORTGAGE MARKETS. As finance companies continue their activity in residential mortgages, they will no doubt become participants in the secondary mortgage markets. As noted in Chapter 19, the secondary markets provide opportunities for mortgage lenders to update yields by selling older mortgages and lending the proceeds at current market rates.

To add to the confusion, there is even a secondary market for second mortgages, which is important for finance companies because of their heavy investment in these loans. The secondary market for second mortgage loans is small but growing; Freddie Mac began purchasing selected types of second mortgages

---

[17] Details on the interest rate reduction programs of auto manufacturers' captive finance companies are discussed in Luckett 1986. For a discussion of longer-term competitive effects, see Aguilar 1990.

[18] See Elliehausen and Wolken 1992; Canner, Durkin, and Luckett 1989; DeMong and Lindgren 1989; and Ysabel Burns McAleer, "Data on Home Equity Borrowers Released," *Finance Facts,* December 1988, 1, 6.

in 1981, and participation by other institutions had broadened substantially by 1985.[19]

The secondary mortgage markets are complex, however, and participants must appreciate the effect of interest rate risk on the market value of financial assets. Because finance company managers are more accustomed to analyzing credit risk, entry into the mortgage markets requires development of new expertise in risk analysis.

The secondary market for finance company loans secured by real estate gained a new dimension in 1989 when Household Finance issued securities backed by HELs. Described in Chapters 15 and 19, organized trading in securities, backed by loans to consumers, is one of the newest of the financial markets. Household's asset-backed security was the first mortgage-related instrument to be issued based on revolving lines of credit. Its development was unexpected because of the uncertainty in the cash flows of the underlying credit lines, given the borrower's ability to exercise discretion over the size and timing of the borrowings. But Household was able to bring the securities to market by obtaining sufficient credit enhancement from other institutions involved in the securitization process.

SECONDARY MARKETS FOR LOANS AND LEASES. Securitization of automobile loans is a development of special interest to finance companies. In fact, although depositories have now entered these markets, it was actually a cooperative effort between finance companies and securities firms that introduced securitization. In February 1985, the Salomon Brothers securities firm bought $10 million in automobile loans from the Lloyd Anderson Group of finance companies. This transaction resulted in the first Certificates for Automobile Receivables, or CARs.

Like Ginnie Mae and Freddie Mac pass-throughs, borrowers' payments of principal and interest on automobile loans are passed through to investors in CARs. Shortly after the Lloyd Anderson Group transaction, Marine Midland Bank joined Salomon Brothers in the program, as did other securities firms

and lenders throughout 1985. The size of the secondary market for automobile loans—and its credibility, according to many observers—was increased dramatically when GMAC packaged almost $1 billion in car and truck loans for sale in late 1985 and early 1986.

From this beginning in 1985, the market for asset-backed securities has mushroomed. In 1991 alone, new issues reached the $50 billion level. Many consumer and corporate assets are being securitized, many of which finance companies hold on their balance sheets. In addition to car loans, credit card receivables, recreational vehicle and boat loans, HELs, leases, and small business loans have all been used to back newly issued securities. In 1992, experts estimated that only about 20 percent of available consumer credit assets held by institutions had been securitized. That leaves room for substantial growth, and large finance companies are expected to be important participants.[20]

ISSUANCE OF CREDIT CARDS. Consumer finance companies have also entered the credit card business as a supplement to personal cash loans. Most have joined the national Visa and MasterCard networks. In late 1992, two of the largest finance companies entered the credit card markets with a different twist: General Electric (GE) and General Motors (GM). Both firms announced plans to offer MasterCards, and their new cards carried features the finance companies hoped would provide a competitive advantage—rebates on consumer products purchased from qualifying companies. For GM, the rebate is earned by purchasing GM cars; for the GE Rewards MasterCard, products from about 24 retail and service firms will qualify.[21] Both cards are issued through banks. GM's is offered by Household Bank, a subsidiary of Household International, while GE's is offered through its own Mono-

---

[19] See Bergman, "Second Mortgages Build Image as First Class Investment," 1985.

[20] Receivables Are Receivables," *Financial World* 154 (March 6–19, 1985): 27; Shapiro 1985; Olson 1986; Suzanne Woolley, "You Can Securitize Virtually Everything," *Business Week,* July 20, 1992, 78–79; "All the World's a Security," *The Economist,* August 29, 1992, 69; Caouette 1992; and Cantor and Demsetz 1993.

[21] Yvette Kantrow, "GE Offers Credit Card with Lure of Rebates," *American Banker,* September 3, 1992, 1, 10; Yvette Kantrow, "GM to Offer Credit Card Priced Lower than GE's," *American Banker,* September 9, 1992, 1, 14; and Leah Nathans Spiro, "More Cards in the Deck," *Business Week,* December 16, 1991, 100–104.

gram Bank, a nonbank bank. As the credit card receivables in the industry grow, firms will have additional impetus to issue new securitized assets.

LOAN PARTICIPATIONS WITH COMMERCIAL BANKS. Now that commercial banks are more interested in asset-based lending, it is not unusual to see cooperative lending agreements between them and commercial finance companies. Because commercial finance companies are leaders in asset-based lending, banks, which are more accustomed to monitoring unsecured loans, depend on the expertise of finance companies for monitoring the receivables and inventory of firms to which credit has been extended.

In a typical deal, a commercial finance company sells participations in an asset-based loan to banks in exchange for cash. Proceeds from the loan are then divided between the finance company and the banks according to their relative shares in the participation. Although some participations are actually arranged by banks, then sold to finance companies, most participations require the finance company to remain active in tracking the performance of the assets pledged as collateral. Often, because bank lending rates are lower than finance company rates, the borrower is given a "blended" rate reflecting the relative shares of the two lenders.[22]

LIABILITY AND CAPITAL MANAGEMENT

Although finance companies lack the benefits of deposit insurance, many finance companies, especially the largest ones, have a degree of flexibility in financing not shared by depositories. Finance companies are not directly subject to capital requirements, nor are they participants in the implicit and explicit interest competition that pervades the consumer deposit market. Thus, the specific liability management issues they face differ from those faced by depositories. Still, managers of finance companies confront the same question facing managers of depository institutions: What financial structure will allow the institution to achieve its risk/expected return objectives?

RAISING FUNDS EXTERNALLY: BOND AND COMMERCIAL PAPER MARKETS

Because of the size of commercial paper issues and the methods of issuance, most commercial paper is held by institutional investors. Certainly, that is true of finance company paper. Many long-term bonds issued by large finance companies are also held by large institutional investors. Through skillful negotiation with funds suppliers, large finance companies with access to both the commercial paper and long-term bond markets have opportunities to tailor the terms of their financing to conform to interest rate forecasts or to match the maturities of their planned asset structures.

MARKET DISCIPLINE. In exercising these opportunities, finance companies are subject to the market discipline from which depositories have thus far been largely exempt. One source of market discipline for finance companies is publicly disclosed risk ratings on their bonds and commercial paper. All the major rating agencies—Standard and Poor's Corporation, Moody's Investors Service, Duff & Phelps, Inc., and Fitch Investors Service, Inc.—focus heavily on asset quality, the primary determinant of future earnings. The views of the rating agencies can profoundly affect finance company performance. During finance companies' peak period of loan losses in the early 1980s, net earnings of the largest companies were further depressed by high interest costs, the result not only of an increase in interest rates but also of lowered bond and commercial paper ratings.

A watchful eye on the ratings keeps many large finance companies from using as much leverage as depositories because financial structure plays a role in the rating agencies' risk assessments. In 1991, for example, GE Capital's net worth was about 12 percent of assets, much higher than the capital position of large commercial banks. Finance company subsidiaries also are affected by the health of their parent companies. Some have faced higher liability costs when the rating agencies lower the risk ratings of the parent firm, even though the risk of the finance subsidiary may not have changed.

---

[22]For more information on participations, see Logan and Dorgan 1984; and Dorgan 1984.

| FIGURE 23.3 | **Finance Company Liabilities in the 1980s** |

During the 1980s, finance companies relied increasingly on commercial paper and long-term debt as sources of funds. This pattern greatly increased their exposure to market discipline.

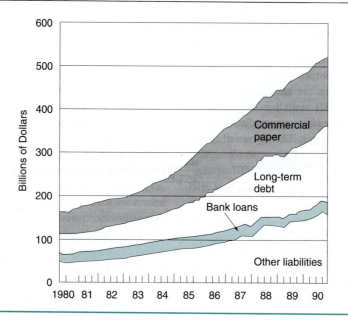

Source: Remolona and Wulfekuhler 1992.

The degree to which finance companies' exposure to market discipline has increased in recent years is apparent in Figure 23.3. Long-term debt and commercial paper as sources of funding have grown at a much higher rate than bank loans and other liabilities. This heavy reliance on funds raised through the debt markets has increased the importance of credit ratings to finance companies.

INDIRECT REGULATION. In some states, regulators indirectly control finance company capital structures through their direct control of institutional investors such as insurance companies. Some regulated institutions can purchase bonds only if the issuing companies maintain minimum capital levels. A finance company needing access to these investors may be forced to limit its use of leverage, even in the absence of specific capital requirements.

RAISING FUNDS EXTERNALLY: ARE BANKS ALLIES OR COMPETITORS?

The discussion of finance company balance sheets indicates that some companies depend on bank financing as a main source of funds. At the same time, finance companies compete with banks for access to business and consumer borrowers. This cooperative/competitive relationship with banks is especially true for small finance companies, which depend much more on commercial bank financing than do large finance companies. Small companies are less likely, therefore, to price their loans aggressively to take business away from their funds suppliers, the banks.

Not so for large finance companies. Their access to the bond and commercial paper markets gives them more freedom to compete with commercial banks. The competitiveness of finance companies in the market for automobile loans during the past two decades is apparent in Figure 23.4, which presents data on the market shares of automobile loans held by these two industries. From 1974 to 1986, finance companies gained market share while commercial banks' proportion of automobile loans declined.

In 1989, the balance appeared to shift, however, but that actually reflects the rapid growth in the securitization of automobile loans rather than declining competitiveness of finance companies. The line labeled "Pools of Securitized Assets" reveals the volume of car loans that has been removed from the balance sheets of the original lenders and sold as asset-backed securities. Because finance companies have been the most enthusiastic about securitizing their automobile loans, the firms in the industry hold a smaller share of outstanding loans on their balance sheets.[23]

Depositories and finance companies continue to compete on other fronts as well, as is reflected in the opening quotation to this chapter. In 1986, Household International launched its nationwide banking operation under the name Household Bank, through its savings banks in Illinois, Maryland, and Ohio. With more than 1,000 finance company offices, the firm has made major inroads into consumer banking on both the lending and deposit sides. Also in 1986, BankAmerica sold its consumer finance subsidiary to Chrysler, giving the automaker's captive finance arm an additional 267 branches. In 1985, Ford Motor Company bought First Nationwide Savings, a pioneer in interstate banking and franchising. Although the two were not formally combined, the president of First Nationwide reports to the president of Ford's finance subsidiary. When it acquired Associates Corporation (a consumer finance company) in 1989, Ford gained a major presence in the credit card industry. GE Capital has its own nonbank subsidiary, as noted earlier. Each of these developments suggests that finance companies intend to be major participants in the deregulated financial markets for years to come.[24]

USE OF OVERALL ASSET/LIABILITY TECHNIQUES

Besides specific management issues, finance company managers must consider integrated asset/liability management strategies. Many techniques discussed earlier in the text, such as the use of secondary asset markets to restructure portfolios and the use of variable-rate lending, are already in place in finance companies. Also, approaches such as GAP management on both a maturity and duration basis and the use of financial futures to lock in borrowing costs in a rising-rate environment are as applicable to finance companies as they are to depositories. The risks and rewards of using these techniques are similar regardless of the type of institution, although finance companies enjoy fewer legal restrictions on their use of futures and options than do depositories. At present, however, there are no data indicating the extent to which finance companies use these tools for asset/liability management.

PERFORMANCE MEASUREMENT IN FINANCE COMPANIES

Potential creditors and stockholders, as well as finance company managers, are interested in assessing the performance of individual firms. The process is similar in most ways to analyzing the performance of an individual depository institution. Financial ratios are calculated, then compared with the firm's history and with financial data for similar firms. Using these comparisons in conjunction with other information about the company, such as off–balance sheet commitments, the analyst draws inferences about the firm's prospects.

---

[23] Credit unions (CUs) are major participants in the automobile loan market, too; their share of the market has declined slightly since 1980. According to Fed statistics, at year-end 1980, CUs held 18 percent of automobile loans outstanding; by the end of 1991, their share had fallen to 17 percent. They have maintained approximately 13 percent of the total volume of consumer loans. Board of Governors of the Federal Reserve, *Federal Reserve Bulletin,* various issues; and Credit Union National Association, *Credit Union National Report* 1991.

[24] See Stephen Kleege, "Household Bank Still Virtually Unknown, but GM Card Issuer Has Insiders' Respect," *American Banker,* August 5, 1993, 15; Aguilar 1990; and Jenster and Lindgren 1988.

FIGURE 23.4   **Percentage of Automobile Loans Held**

During the 1980s, aggressive automobile lending policies, especially among car manufacturers' captive finance companies, helped the industry grab substantial market share from commercial banks. Finance companies' share of auto loans held directly on the balance sheet has declined as securitization of automobile loans has increased.

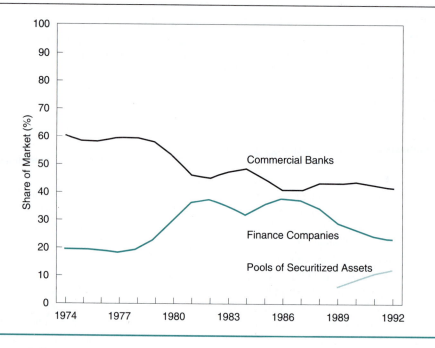

Source: Federal Reserve Bulletin, various issues.

SOURCES OF INDUSTRY FINANCIAL INFORMATION

Because a wide variety of firms are defined as finance companies, it is more difficult to identify a peer group to which to compare an individual company than it is to identify peer group depositories. With the use of careful judgment, however, several sources of financial data on finance companies are available.

One publicly available data base on finance company performance is compiled by the First National Bank of Chicago and summarized annually in the *Journal of Commercial Lending,* a publication of Robert Morris Associates, a trade organization for commercial lenders. Separate data are shown for consumer finance companies and diversified (both commercial and consumer) finance companies. Although the primary purpose of these data is to assist bankers who lend to finance companies, they also contain ratios of interest to shareholders.

The American Financial Services Association (AFSA), formerly a source of performance data on finance companies, no longer conducts research on the industry. The National Commercial Finance Association, a trade organization for asset-based lenders, compiles financial ratios annually; information is available to members only. Finally, economists at the Fed, besides conducting comprehensive studies of finance company balance sheets periodically, provide monthly updates of key balance sheet accounts for the industry in the *Federal Reserve Bulletin.*

All these sources provide only aggregate data for groups of firms; information on the best or worst performing companies is not presented. For information on finance companies given by quartiles, Dun and Bradstreet's (D&B) *Key Business Ratios* is a source. Unfortunately, the ratios given by D&B are not necessarily the areas of greatest interest to the analyst.

TABLE 23.5	**Selected Performance Measures for Finance Companies**

Some performance measures for finance companies differ from those used for depositories. In particular, analysts focus on key financial variables relative to total finance company receivables.

Ratio	Consumer Finance Industry Averages, 1991	Diversified Finance Industry Averages, 1991
Liquidity		
23.1 Cash/Short-Term Debt	NA[a]	NA
23.2 Receivables Maturing in 12 Months/Total Receivables	NA	37.50%
23.3 Unused Credit Lines/Open Market Debt	121.00%	125.50%
Credit Risk		
23.4 Direct Cash Loans/Gross Receivables	42.20%	9.70%
23.5 Net Charge-offs/Average Net Receivables	2.60%	1.70%
Leverage		
23.6 Total Debt/Net Worth	5.70 times	7.90 times
23.7 Interest Expense/Average Net Receivables	7.30%	6.90%
Efficiency/Productivity		
23.8 Operating Expenses (Exclusive of Loan Loss Expense)/Average Net Receivables	7.50%	3.20%
23.9 Average Monthly Principal Collections/Average Net Monthly Receivables	4.20%	NA
28.10 Annual Gross Finance Revenues/Average Net Receivables	19.60%	15.30%
Profitability		
23.11 Net Finance Profit/Average Net Receivables	3.40%	1.40%
23.12 Net Interest Margin = (Gross Finance Revenue − Interest Expense)/Average Net Receivables	12.30%	8.40%
23.13 Return on Net Worth = Net Income/Average Net Worth	18.70%	10.90%

[a]NA = not available.
Source: Mark C. Kramer and Raymond M. Neihengen, Jr., "Analysis of Finance Company Ratios in 1991," *Journal of Commercial Lending* 75 (September 1992): 39–47.

IMPORTANT FINANCIAL RATIOS FOR FINANCE COMPANIES

The important dimensions of finance company performance are similar to those used to assess depository institution performance: liquidity and portfolio management, credit quality, leverage, efficiency and productivity, and profitability. Table 23.5 contains a representative set of ratios for the financial analysis of a finance company, as well as industry averages for two broad subgroups in the industry. Except as noted in the following discussion, data used to construct these ratios, and their interpretation, are similar enough to the presentation in Chapter 22 that they are not repeated here.

LIQUIDITY. Because finance companies have few investments in short-term marketable securities, asset liquidity is best measured by the amount of actual cash on hand relative to the short-term obligations of the firm. (Industry data for cash balances were not available for 1991, although they are sometimes included in the First Chicago analyses from which Table 23.5 is prepared.) Another view of liquidity is the proportion of receivables to be repaid within 1 year. Thus, Ratios 23.1 and 23.2 assist the analyst in estimating how easily the company's assets can be converted to cash.

Like depositories, however, finance companies may also meet liquidity needs through liability management. Comparing the dollar amount of unused credit lines arranged through commercial banks to the amount of open-market debt already outstanding (Ratio 23.3) provides an indication of the company's ability to generate cash from additional borrowing. Information on unused credit lines is found in footnotes to the company's annual report.

CREDIT RISK. Because personal cash loans are among the riskiest made by finance companies, the ratio of those loans to total credit extended by the company (Ratio 23.4) suggests the overall riskiness of the portfolio. In addition, a measure of credit risk using net charge-offs is relevant (Ratio 23.5). As with depository institutions, however, the analyst must recognize that this is an *ex post,* not an *ex ante,* measure of risk.

LEVERAGE. Besides familiar measures of leverage, such as total debt to net worth (Ratio 23.6), it is useful to compare interest expense with receivables (which for most finance companies are approximately equal to total earning assets). Not only when compared with the figure for other firms but also when used as part of a trend analysis of a single company, this ratio (Ratio 23.7) provides a good indication of a firm's debt service burden.

EFFICIENCY/PRODUCTIVITY. As with depositories, how well a finance company controls its nonlending operating expenses affects its performance. Ratio 23.8, which compares these expenses with average net receivables, is one measure of operating efficiency. Additional measures of productivity are Ratios 23.9 and 23.10. Ratio 23.9 is average monthly principal collections to average net monthly receivables. When calculated over a period of time, this ratio may indicate the thoroughness of the firm's collection and loan-monitoring policies. A declining trend indicates either that the firm is increasing the maturity of its loan portfolio and, as a result, a smaller amount of principal is collected on loans made recently, or that efforts to collect are more lax than in the past. Either way, questions should be asked. One cautionary note: The schedule of collections can be difficult to obtain. A firm may include some of this information in footnotes to the financial statements, but if not, unpublished information is necessary.

The last ratio in this category, Ratio 23.10, compares total revenue from finance operations with average receivables and is analogous to asset utilization for depositories. It reveals how much revenue was generated per dollar lent during the period. For example, Table 23.5 shows that for consumer finance companies as a whole in 1991, 19.6 cents of finance revenue was returned to the firm for every dollar of credit extended.

Because some finance companies have nonfinance subsidiaries, the intent of this ratio is to focus only on the firm's financial operations. For finance companies that have not diversified beyond lending, the numerator of Ratio 23.10 would be total revenues.

PROFITABILITY. Ratio 23.11, comparing the net profit on financial operations with average net receivables, is analogous to measuring the net rate of return on earning assets in other firms. Similarly, Ratio 23.12 is a measure of the NIM appropriate for finance companies. Finally, Ratio 23.13 is a standard measure of RONW.

SUMMARY

Finance companies are diverse financial institutions grouped together under one industry classification. They share an emphasis on consumer and business lending, and they differ from depositories in their lack of deposits as a source of funds. The industry was historically grouped into sales, personal, and commercial finance companies, although these distinctions are now blurred.

Most assets in the industry are invested in loans, although proportions invested in different loan categories vary by firm size and type. Large finance companies raise funds in the money and capital markets, and finance companies of all sizes borrow from commercial banks. Finance companies are increasingly involved in securitization.

An important issue in asset management of finance companies is default risk. Unsecured personal loans and second mortgage loans have a great potential for loss. Lending policies are governed by federal and state consumer protection laws. Like depositories, finance companies must consider the maturities of funds sources when selecting asset maturities.

In response to operating difficulties in the late 1970s, finance companies introduced new products and techniques, many of which are part of an integrated asset/liability strategy. Securitization of real estate and automobile loans, issuance of credit cards, entry into the primary mortgage market, and asset-based loan participations all provide managerial flexibility. Entry into these markets makes finance companies more competitive with depositories, and analysis of finance company performance uses ratios similar to those used for depositories.

QUESTIONS

1. How do finance companies' asset and liability structures distinguish them from those of other financial institutions? Into what categories, and on what basis, is the industry traditionally divided?

2. How and why do the financial characteristics of small and large companies differ? In what ways do you expect securitization to affect finance companies of varying sizes?

3. Why have some finance companies invested more heavily in second mortgages than first mortgages? What risks are associated with junior liens? What are home equity lines of credit, and what potential do they hold for finance companies?

4. Trace the relative profitability of banks and finance companies during the 1980s. What competitive strategies and differences in financial structure and leverage are reflected in the comparative performance figures?

5. Based on the results of research comparing finance company and commercial bank borrowers, what characteristics do each possess? Do finance companies face greater credit risks? What are the implications for credit analysis of finance company applicants?

6. What has been the impact of bankruptcy legislation from 1979 to the early 1990s on finance company profitability? Explain the responses of the finance company industry in the context of the regulatory dialectic. What were the results of these actions?

7. Explain the competitive/cooperative relationship between finance companies and commercial banks. How does the size of a finance company affect this relationship?

8. Describe the role of finance companies in developing the securitized asset market. What are the financial benefits and risks to finance company participants in this market?

9. Consult recent trade publications for an update on the success of General Electric and General Motors finance companies' entry into the credit card market. What have been the financial consequences?

10. Do you believe that finance companies are subject to a greater or lesser degree of market discipline than depositories? Explain. How has that exposure changed in recent years?

11. At a speech the authors once attended, the chairman of Chrysler Corporation's captive finance company said he "felt sorry" for banks. What do you think he meant? Do you agree? If you were a banker, what would be your reactions to such a comment?

12. As noted in the chapter, in the 1980s several large auto manufacturers offered low-interest-rate loans through their captive finance companies. Some commercial banks charged that these low rates were deceptive, because the manufacturers compensated for the financing costs by raising prices on the cars. Do you agree with the bankers or with the finance companies? Do such special offers violate the spirit of truth-in-lending legislation if they are accompanied by higher prices? Why or why not?

13. In your opinion, how has the aggressive move toward securitizing loans affected the ability of large finance companies to compete against commercial banks in the automobile lending business?

14. Explain how financial analysis of finance companies resembles that of depository institutions. How is it different? What sources of industry performance information are available for finance companies?

15. In what ways do average financial ratios for consumer and commercial finance companies differ? Explain the origins of the differences.

16. Would you expect a typical large finance company to use each of the following risk management tools to a greater or lesser degree than a typical large commercial bank? Why?
   a.   interest rate futures
   b.   currency futures
   c.   stock index futures
   d.   GAP management (rate-sensitivity, duration)
   e.   immunization
   f.   interest rate swaps
   g.   interest rate caps and floors

17. Using library or other resources, find the most recent financial statement for GE Capital, General Motors Acceptance Corporation (GMAC), or another large finance company. What is the apparent degree of involvement in securitization? in credit cards? in home equity lines of credit? What discussion do you find about use of asset/liability management strategies such as futures, duration, or swaps? Can you identify recent developments in financial management not discussed in the chapter? If so, explain these and their effects on financial performance.

PROBLEM

1. The financial statements for the Manufacturer's Credit Corporation for the year ending December 31, 19XX, are provided in the following tables. Manufacturer's Credit is a commercial finance subsidiary of a large, diversified firm that your company may acquire. As a member of the financial analysis staff, you have been asked to assess the financial position of the finance subsidiary. The notes to Manufacturer's Credit's financial statements indicate that the firm has lines of credit with various financial institutions totaling $5.5 million. Footnotes also indicate that $1.245 million in receivables will be maturing in the next year.

a. Use the ratios and industry average data provided in Table 23.5 to evaluate the liquidity, leverage, and efficiency of Manufacturer's Credit.

b. Is Manufacturer's Credit's profitability above or below industry averages? Its level of risk? Explain your findings.

c. Based on these ratios, would you consider Manufacturer's Credit a desirable acquisition? Why or why not?

d. If Manufacturer's Credit were a consumer finance company, what differences would you expect to find in its financial statements? Why? In your opinion, would those differences be associated with more or less exposure to credit risk? Why?

e. Considering these limited data on Manufacturer's financial characteristics, which of the following risk management tools might be potentially useful to Manufacturer's managers? For each item, explain why it might or might not be useful.

    1)   interest rate futures
    2)   stock index options
    3)   duration GAP analysis
    4)   rate-sensitivity GAP analysis
    5)   interest rate swaps
    6)   interest rate caps and floors
    7)   securitization
    8)   option-adjusted spreads
    9)   currency futures.

PROBLEM 23.1   **Manufacturer's Credit Corporation Statement of Financial Position as of December 31, 19XX (Thousands)**

Assets		
Cash and short-term investments		$ 98.7
Marketable securities		287.7
Financing receivables		
Direct cash lines	$ 137.5	
Other installment credit	745.6	
Retailer financing	898.5	
Commercial loans	635.8	
Equipment sales financing	407.4	
Real estate loans	730.3	
Leases	1,903.9	
Other	320.2	
Total receivables, gross	5,779.2	
Less unearned income and allowance for losses	(553.1)	
Total receivables, net		5,226.1
Buildings and equipment		355.7
Other assets		187.5
Total assets		$6,155.7

PROBLEM 23.1 *CONTINUED* **Manufacturer's Credit Corporation Statement of Financial Position as of December 31, 19XX (Thousands)**

Liabilities and Net Worth

Commercial paper outstanding		$1,530.3	
Bank notes payable within 1 year	$1,277.9		
Bank notes payable after 1 year	1,353.0		
Total notes payable		2,630.9	
Accounts payable		167.1	
Other liabilities		804.9	
Total liabilities			$5,133.2
Preferred stock		$ 30.2	
Common stock		223.7	
Additional paid-in capital		130.4	
Retained earnings		638.2	
Total net worth			1,022.5
Total liabilities and net worth			$6,155.7

Statement of Earnings for Year Ending December 31, 19XX

Income		
Interest income	$507.9	
Lease income	228.2	
Other income	101.3	
Total income		$837.4
Expenses		
Interest expense	$358.6	
Operating and administrative expense	171.1	
Loan losses	37.0	
Other expense	144.6	
Total expenses		711.3
Income before taxes		$126.1
Taxes		19.5
Net income		$106.6
Cash dividends paid		$ 57.0

SELECTED REFERENCES

Aguilar, Linda. "Still Toe-to-Toe: Banks and Nonbanks at the End of the '80s." *Economic Perspectives* (Federal Reserve Bank of Chicago) 14 (January/February 1990): 12–23.

American Financial Services Association. *Finance Facts.* Various issues.

Benston, George J. "Rate Ceiling Implications of the Cost Structure of Consumer Finance Companies." *Journal of Finance* 21 (September 1977): 1169–1194.

Boczar, Gregory E. "Competition between Banks and Finance Companies: A Cross Section Study of Personal Loan Debtors." *Journal of Finance* 33 (March 1978): 245–258.

Canner, Glenn B., Thomas A. Durkin, and Charles A. Luckett. "Recent Developments in the Home Equity Loan Market." *Journal of Retail Banking* 11 (Summer 1989): 35–47.

Cantor, Richard, and Rebecca Demsetz. "Securitization, Loan Sales, and the Credit Slowdown," *Quarterly Review* (Federal Reserve Bank of New York) 18 (Summer 1993): 27–38.

Caouette, John B. "Securitization: What's Next?" In *Proceedings of a Conference on Bank Structure and Competition,* 304–309. Chicago: Federal Reserve Bank of Chicago, 1992.

DeMong, Richard F., and John H. Lindgren, Jr. "Home Equity Lending in 1988: Market Trends and Analysis." *Journal of Retail Banking* 11 (Fall 1989): 23–34.

Dorgan, Richard J. "Banks Keen to Make Asset-Based Loans." *NCFA Journal* 40 (September 1984): 5–14.

Elliehausen, Gregory E., and John D. Wolken. "Banking Markets and the Use of Financial Services by Households." *Federal Reserve Bulletin* 78 (March 1992): 169–181.

Federal Reserve Bank of New York. *Recent Trends in Commercial Bank Profitability.* New York: Federal Reserve Bank of New York, 1986.

Fooladi, Iraj, Gordon Roberts, and Jerry Viscione. "Captive Finance Subsidiaries: Overview and Synthesis." *Financial Review* 21 (May 1986): 259–275.

Harris, Maury. "Finance Companies as Business Lenders." *Quarterly Review* (Federal Reserve Bank of New York) 4 (Summer 1979): 35–39.

Hurley, Evelyn M. "Survey of Finance Companies, 1980." *Federal Reserve Bulletin* 67 (May 1981): 398–409.

Jenster, Per V., and John H. Lindgren, Jr. "The New Game in Retail Auto Financing." *Journal of Retail Banking* 10 (Winter 1988): 39–45.

Johnson, Robert W. "The Consumer Banking Problem: Causes and Cures." *Journal of Retail Banking* 11 (Winter 1989): 39–45.

Johnson, Robert W., and A. Charlene Sullivan. "Segmentation of the Consumer Loan Market." *Journal of Retail Banking* 3 (September 1981): 1–7.

Kramer, Mark C., and Raymond M. Neihengen, Jr. "Analysis of Finance Company Ratios in 1991." *Journal of Commercial Lending* 75 (September 1992): 39–47.

Logan, John, and Richard J. Dorgan. "Asset-Based Lending: You're Doing It, but Are You Doing It Right?" *Journal of Commercial Bank Lending* 67 (June 1984): 9–16.

Luckett, Charles A. "Recent Developments in Automobile Finance." *Federal Reserve Bulletin* 72 (June 1986): 355–365.

McGoldrick, Beth. "The Carmakers that Would Be Bankers." *Institutional Investor* 20 (February 1986): 175–177.

Olson, Wayne. "Securitization Comes to Other Assets." *Savings Institutions* 107 (May 1986): 81–85.

Remolona, Eli M., and Kurt C. Wulfekuhler. "Finance Companies, Bank Competition, and Niche Markets." *Quarterly Review* (Federal Reserve Bank of New York) 17 (Summer 1992): 25–38.

Selden, Richard T. "Consumer-Oriented Intermediaries." In *Financial Institutions and Markets.* 2d ed. Edited by Murray Polakoff and Thomas A. Durkin, 202–215. Boston: Houghton Mifflin, 1981.

Shapiro, Harvey D. "Securitizing Corporate Assets." *Institutional Investor* 19 (December 1985).

Stahl, David. "The Rising Tide of Bankruptcy." *Savings and Community Banker* 2 (May 1993): 14–20.

Staten, Michael. "Statistics: Bankruptcy Watch." *Journal of Retail Banking* 11 (Winter 1989): 65–69.

Swift, John R. "Consumer Finance Companies: A Step Back and a Look Forward." *Journal of Commercial Bank Lending* 65 (January 1982).

Give insurers a free lunch,
and they'll complain that you forgot the champagne.
Jill Andresky,
Writer, *Forbes* Magazine (1987)

———————————

Herbert D. Eagle was a senior vice president of Transamerica Occidental Life Insurance in 1983 when he invested $100,000 in a life insurance annuity product sold by Executive Life Insurance Company. In 1991, Executive Life was seized by regulators. With the benefit of hindsight, many would say that such an experienced professional should have known better. Although he did not lose his entire investment, the limited guarantees provided by regulators mean his returns will definitely be below expectations.

Just 1 year later, the property/liability (P/L) insurance industry was rocked by several natural disasters, including Hurricane Andrew, which resulted in a record dollar volume of loss claims filed. Despite these pressures, major P/L insurers such as State Farm were commended for their ability to weather the year's heavy losses and even increase capital reserves in a most difficult period.

What accounts for the differences in insurer financial strength? The answers are complex, but asset/liability management is one of the keys. Managing risk in a changing interest rate and economic environment is crucial. Executive Life had more than 60 percent of its investment portfolio concentrated in junk bonds. Many P/L firms, in contrast, relied on more stable investment income to offset the losses of Hurricane Andrew, the Los Angeles riots, and the Chicago flood of 1992. For both segments of the insurance industry, however, consumer advocates and politicians immediately began to call for closer regulatory scrutiny. The responses of insurers to economic challenges, competition, and regulatory developments, and the accompanying financial management techniques, are addressed in this chapter.[1]

The financial opportunities and problems that insurers face are both similar to and different from those faced by the institutions discussed in previous chapters. Similarities arise because most assets of insurers are financial and subject to interest rate and other risks in the

CHAPTER

24

INSURANCE

COMPANIES

———————————

[1] Richard S. Teitelbaum, "How Safe Is Your Insurance?" *Fortune,* September 9, 1991, 137–141; Greg Steinmetz et al., "In Wake of Hurricane, Insurers Face Financial and Regulatory Tests," *The Wall Street Journal,* September 2, 1992, A1, A4.

financial markets. Differences occur because most liabilities of insurers are neither deposits, commercial paper, nor bonds but are potential claims against the company by policyholders or their beneficiaries. Another difference between insurers and depositories, mentioned in Chapter 2, is that the McCarran-Ferguson Act of 1945 leaves the regulation of insurers to states. Examination of these similarities and differences is the objective of this chapter.[2]

---

[2] As discussed initially in the context of depositories in Chapter 21, there are two main types of insurance activities: underwriting and brokerage. The management strategies discussed in this chapter are geared to firms acting primarily as underwriters. Firms operating as agencies, selling policies underwritten by others, are not discussed in the text, because their financial management problems are not particularly adaptable to the asset/liability framework.

AN INDUSTRY FOUNDED ON PROBABILITIES

The financial problems against which insurance companies provide risk protection span a broad spectrum, from the traumatic to the merely inconvenient. Most Americans are protected from multiple risks by a variety of insurance policies. For example, as of 1990, 81 percent of American households had some form of life insurance coverage. About 96 percent of American homeowners and 26 percent of renters carried household insurance in 1989, and an even larger proportion of the U.S. population carried automobile insurance.[3] These data do not include the many policies purchased each year by businesses and not-for-profit organizations.

The purchase of insurance also has social welfare implications, because coverage provided by insurance may encourage individuals or businesses to engage in risky, but productive activities. For example, the decision by a physician to practice obstetrics may be influenced by the availability of malpractice insurance, and the decision of a pharmaceuticals company to introduce a new drug may be influenced by the availability of product liability insurance.

POLICYHOLDERS ASSESS PROBABILITIES

The public's ownership of insurance does not necessarily correspond to its estimate of the probability that it will actually need protection. Some people have insurance because an employer provides it or it is required with another financial transaction, such as a mortgage loan. More often, however, people buy insurance because they believe that the risk of loss without the policy is too great. In making a decision, the prospective policyholder considers not only the probability of loss but also the dollar amount of protection required if loss occurs. More formally, a person buys insurance if the expected value of a policy's benefits—emotional and financial—exceeds the present value of premiums required to obtain it.[4] This emotional element reflects risk aversion. A risk-averse individual is willing to pay some amount to avoid risk and can purchase insurance to do so. In return, the insurance company indemnifies the policyholder if a loss occurs. Thus, the purchase of insurance reduces potential variability in a policyholder's wealth by exchanging payment of a claim on an uncertain future financial loss for a known premium.

To see how the purchase of insurance can benefit someone who is risk averse, consider a simple two-state world in which an individual will have wealth equal to W if no loss occurs and wealth equal to W-L if a loss occurs.[5] Also assume the maximum loss is the initial wealth. Point E on curve U_1 in Figure 24.1 shows the initial level of satisfaction (or utility, in economists' terms) an individual would attain in this two-state world. Suppose the individual purchases full insurance coverage of I at an actuarially fair premium P. (An actuarially fair premium reflects only the probability of loss and the amount of loss and includes no profit for the insurer.) With full coverage, I = L, and the individual is fully compensated for the loss. After purchasing insurance, the individual will attain a higher level of utility, represented by point F on curve U_2. At that point, since L and I are equal, the policyholder has wealth of W-P regardless of whether a loss occurs. Movement from the initial position, E, to the point of utility with full insurance coverage, F, benefits the individual.

In this very simplified world, no profit or load was added to the premium charged by the insurer. An individual who is risk averse, however, would be willing to pay some amount above the actuarially fair premium for the desired amount of insurance coverage.

The access to insurance coverage need not involve a financial institution. Individuals could get together (or pool) and agree to share in each other's losses by contributing a premium. The premiums collected would be used to compensate those in the pool who incur losses. However, search and monitoring costs are associated with this pooling process. An insurance company may be able to reduce such transactions costs.[6] Insurance companies may have an

---

[3] American Council of Life Insurance, *1992 Life Insurance Fact Book;* Insurance Information Institute, *1993 Property/Casualty Insurance Facts.*

[4] For an analysis of the problem facing an individual purchasing an insurance policy, see Mehr and Gustavson 1984, Chapter 2, 25–29. (References are listed in full at the end of this chapter.)

[5] Mossin 1968 examined the optimal purchase of insurance by individuals.

[6] Transactions and information costs are discussed in Chapter 1.

FIGURE 24.1   **Individual Demand for Insurance**

An individual who purchases an insurance policy believes with some confidence that unexpected losses will be repaid by the insurer. Insurance, therefore, increases the individual's utility.

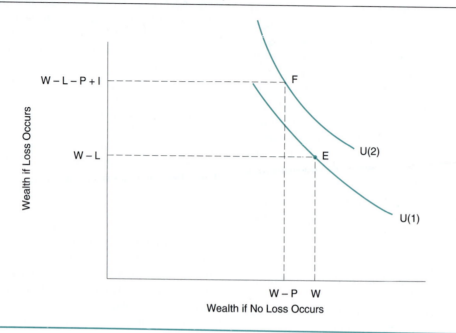

additional advantage through economies of scale in the processing of claims.[7]

Corporations as well as individuals purchase insurance, but this choice cannot be explained by risk aversion. Through holding diversified portfolios, a corporation's shareholders can eliminate insurable risk, so with a load or profit for the insurer included in the insurance premium, a firm's purchase of insurance reduces its shareholder's wealth. Still, corporations *do* purchase insurance, and several possible factors may explain this behavior.[8] First, insurance may be mandatory, as is the case with workers' compensation laws. Because premiums are tax-deductible, the purchase of insurance may also reflect the corporation's desire to minimize tax liabilities. Finally, corporations may purchase insurance because of the costs imposed by employees, creditors, suppliers, and customers in the absence of insurance coverage. For example, employees want to promote job security and customers want companies to be available to fulfill service or warranty obligations. Thus, a corporation's decision not to purchase insurance may affect the wages demanded by employees, the rate of return required by creditors, the price charged by suppliers, or the price paid by customers.

AND SO DO INSURERS, BUT DIFFERENTLY

The insurer also must consider probabilities, but the insurer's task is different from the policyholder's. The policyholder asks, "What is the probability that a given loss will occur to *me*, and how much protection do I need if it does?"; the insurer asks, "Out of all the firm's policyholders, what proportion will make claims during the period, and how much will they cost?" The insurance company also must evaluate the probability of loss, but its real concern is with a statistical principle called the **law of large numbers.** According to this law, one cannot determine the probabil-

---

[7] These efficiencies may include a nationwide network of adjusters or legal representatives.

[8] For further discussion, see Mayers and Smith 1982.

ity that an individual will die (or become disabled, or have an automobile accident, or lose a home in a fire) in a given period. However, the number of persons among a large group who will die or face other losses in a period is more predictable, especially when relevant demographic and other data are available on that group.

The law of large numbers is illustrated with the following example. Consider two groups of insured individuals of different sizes. Group A contains 100 policyholders, and group B contains 10,000 policyholders. For each group, there are only two possible outcomes; loss or no loss. There is a 5 percent probability of loss for each individual in the group. How many losses will be experienced in each group? With this binomial distribution for outcomes, the mean ($\bar{x}$) and standard deviation (σ) of losses can be found as

$$\bar{x} = n(p) \qquad [24.1]$$

$$\sigma = \sqrt{n(p)(1-p)} \qquad [24.2]$$

in which n is the sample size and p is the probability of loss. The mean number of losses for groups A and B is

$$\bar{x}_A = 100(.05) = 5$$

$$\bar{x}_B = 10,000(.05) = 500$$

Insurers must know not only the expected number of losses, but also how predictable that number is. Thus, measures of variability, such as the standard deviation, are essential. Using Equation 24.2, the standard deviation (σ) of losses for the two groups is

$$\sigma_A = \sqrt{100(.05)(.95)} = 2.18$$

$$\sigma_B = \sqrt{10,000(.05)(.95)} = 21.79.$$

To compare the variability of outcomes for groups of different sizes, the coefficient of variation (CV) can be used, calculated as the standard deviation divided by the mean. For groups A and B, the coefficients of variation are

$$CV_A = \frac{2.18}{5} = 0.44$$

$$CV_B = \frac{21.79}{500} = 0.04$$

Note that as the number in the group increases, the dispersion about the expected loss decreases. The reduced dispersion of the losses means that the predictability of outcomes increases as the group size increases. Thus, it is easier for insurers to predict losses among 10,000 policyholders than among 100.

Ex ante loss prediction among a group of policyholders is usually based on analysis of *ex post* data from a similar group of insureds. Estimating the probability of losses of a certain type and size among a group of policyholders during a designated period is the business of **actuaries.** The difficulty of estimating probabilities differs, depending on the event involved. For example, actuarial calculations of the mortality rate among a group of individuals are more reliable than estimates of the probability of property damage to their houses. The difference arises because random factors such as tornadoes, earthquakes, and vandalism play a large role in property damage, whereas a single nonrandom factor, age, is highly correlated with mortality. Liability claims are also difficult to predict because they sometimes include award decisions made by juries.

This actuarial difference explains the traditional division of the insurance industry into the two main subgroups discussed at several points earlier in the book: life insurers and P/L insurers. Underwriters of health insurance policies are usually grouped with life insurers because serious illness is correlated with age, although to a lesser extent than death.

Insurers use actuarial calculations not only to estimate probable cash outflows during a period but also to establish the premium payments necessary for cash inflows to be equal to or greater than expected cash outflows. An example of premium estimation is provided in the appendix to this chapter.

OWNERSHIP STRUCTURE OF THE INSURANCE INDUSTRY

Premiums on the many insurance policies Americans hold add up to big business. In 1991, the more than 6,000 domestically chartered life and P/L insurance companies held more assets in total than any other financial institutions except commercial banks. Insurers are both mutually and stockholder-owned.[9] Table 4.2 on page 101 indicates that in 1991, less than 6 percent of all life insurance companies were mutually owned. These firms, however, accounted for most of the assets in the industry. Although not shown in the table, more than one-half of P/L companies were mutually owned, but most assets were concentrated in a few stock P/L insurers.[10]

The trend is away from mutual ownership, for the same reason as in the thrift industry: difficulty in generating net worth from internal sources alone.[11] Chapter 2 notes that states impose minimum capital requirements on insurers selling policies in the state. Financial problems among both life and P/L companies have increasingly complicated the generation of capital through retained earnings. A solution short of failure is conversion to the stock form of organization. Besides offering access to external sources of capital, conversion provides flexibility for financing future acquisitions and greater potential for diversification into other financial services. Also, federal tax laws favorable to the mutual form of organization were revised in 1984, and the stock form is now financially more attractive than in the past.

Procedures by which mutual insurers may convert and the consequences of doing so are less clear than for mutually owned thrifts, because the absence of federal regulation leaves conversion rules up to individual states. As a result, the number of mutuals actually converting since 1980 has been lower than once anticipated.

DISTRIBUTION OF INSURANCE

Two systems are used to distribute—or sell—insurance. The **direct writer system** involves an agent representing a single insurer, whereas the **independent agent system** involves an agent representing multiple insurers. An independent agent is responsible for running an agency and for the operating costs associated with it. Independent agents are compensated through commissions, but direct writers may receive either commissions or salaries. An important distinction between the two systems is the right to renew business. With the direct writer system, the customer is associated with the company, whereas in the independent agent system, the customer is associated with the agent. The relative efficiency of the two systems for delivering insurance has been the subject of substantial research. Independent agents have the advantage of offering policies from a variety of insurers, but direct writers have the advantage of support from the insurance company.[12]

REGULATION OF INSURERS

Regulation of insurers, first introduced in Chapter 2, covers three primary areas: financial solvency, policy language, and the pricing of coverage.[13] Regulators enforce capital restrictions to encourage insurer financial stability and ensure that companies can fulfill claims when they are made.[14] Because insurance policies are legal contracts, the language can be difficult to interpret, and regulation of contracts is aimed at encouraging intelligible wording in policies. Rate regulation is designed to ensure a pricing structure that provides a reasonable return and is nondiscriminatory. Some concern exists, however, that rate regulation may suppress prices below the costs of providing cov-

---

[9] Several other organizational forms exist besides stock and mutually owned insurers. These include reciprocals, Lloyds Associations, Lloyd's of London, and insurance exchanges.

[10] American Council of Life Insurance, *1992 Life Insurance Fact Book;* Insurance Information Institute, *1993 Property/Casualty Insurance Facts.*

[11] More than 125 mutual insurers converted to stock ownership between 1930 and 1987. Most conversions were in the P/L insurance industry. See David F. Babbel and Random B. Jones, "Not Whether, But When," *Best's Review,* January 1988: 54–60.

---

[12] For the P/L insurance industry, both Joskow 1973 and Cummins and Vanderhei 1979 found empirical support for the direct writer system as the most efficient distribution form.

[13] Joskow 1973 and the American Insurance Association 1988 examine the structure of the insurance industry. Both studies suggest the industry possesses characteristics associated with a competitive market.

[14] The National Association of Insurance Commissioners (NAIC) introduced new financial reporting requirements in 1992 related to asset valuation (see Crosson 1992). New capital requirements based on the riskiness of investments and operations have been approved by the NAIC for life insurers and are discussed in a later section. The NAIC has also formed a property-liability risk-based working group to consider risk-based capital standards for the industry (Lauranzann 1992).

erage and thus may place additional stress on insurer solvency.[15]

Apart from ownership structure, distribution, and some aspects of regulation, life and P/L insurers have so many differences that they are discussed separately.

ASSETS OF LIFE INSURERS

Like those of other financial institutions, the balance sheets of life insurers have changed in recent years. Some changes are responses to the deregulation of competitors, and others reflect changes in the economic environment.

Table 24.1 presents data on the assets of life insurers as of year-end 1991. Although all states permit the general types of investments outlined in this section, many states limit the *percentage* of the total portfolio that can be invested in specific categories, especially common stock and real estate.

GOVERNMENT SECURITIES

Insurers hold substantial amounts of Treasury and federal agency securities but have only small investments in state, local, and foreign government issues. Since 1973, when state, local, and foreign issues were more than 60 percent of all the governmental securities held by life insurers, the relative importance of various types of government securities has changed completely.[16]

Like finance companies, life insurers do not face unexpected deposit withdrawals, so their government securities portfolios are held primarily for purposes of investment, not liquidity. In recent years, however, life insurers have increased their holdings of Treasury bonds (T-bonds) relative to long-term corporate obligations, because T-bonds are much more marketable should cash be required unexpectedly. Later in this chapter, the changing portfolio management strategies of life insurers are discussed further.

CORPORATE SECURITIES

Life insurers are not bound by the same portfolio restrictions as are depositories, so their corporate holdings include common and preferred stock as well as bonds. Because of their low need for liquidity, insurers hold relatively few money market securities such as commercial paper and bankers acceptances, although the percentage has increased slightly in recent years.

IMPORTANCE OF PRIVATE PLACEMENTS. Investment in corporate bonds is not new for life insurers; they have been the largest holders of corporate bonds since the 1930s. As of year-end 1991, in fact, they held about one-third of all corporate and foreign bonds in the United States. Most are obtained through **private** or **direct placement,** involving face-to-face negotiation between a life insurer and a bond issuer. Although private placement has substantial advantages, because issues can be tailored to suit both borrower and lender, it also has risks. Of particular relevance to life insurers in the past was the absence of a secondary market for privately placed bonds. Because private placements are not accompanied by the same financial disclosure required in a public issue, most cannot be resold to the public. Consequently, some privately placed bonds are among the least liquid assets a financial institution can hold. In 1990, however, the liquidity of private placements was improved considerably by the passage of Securities and Exchange Commission (SEC) Rule 144a, which permits large institutional investors to trade certain types of privately placed securities among themselves. Many life insurers welcomed the new rule.[17]

CORPORATE STOCK. Investment in corporate stock has increased in recent years for several reasons:

1. State laws have been liberalized to permit insurers to hold stock.

2. The variable cash flows expected from stock are now more attractive because insurers' financial obligations have become less predictable. More details

---

[15] Harrington 1990 and Grabowski, Viscusi, and Evans 1989 found evidence suggesting that prices in regulated markets are lower than the overall market for automobile insurance.

[16] Unless otherwise noted, the statistics cited here and later in the life insurance section of the chapter are drawn from various issues of the *Life Insurance Fact Book.*

---

[17] See Curry and Warshawsky 1986; Board of Governors of the Federal Reserve System, *Flow of Funds Accounts: Sector Statements of Financial Assets and Liabilities,* June 11, 1992; and Kevin G. Salwen, "SEC Eases Rules on Securities Privately Placed," *The Wall Street Journal,* April 20, 1990, C1, C18.

TABLE 24.1	Assets and Obligations of Life Insurance Companies, 1991 (2,105 Firms)

About 50 percent of the assets of life insurers are invested in corporate securities—predominantly bonds. The vast majority of the industry's liabilities are policy reserves, and firms in the industry are highly leveraged.

		Millions of $		% of Total
Assets				
Government securities (includes Treasury, federal agency, state, local, and foreign governments)		$ 269,490		17.37%
Corporate securities		788,030		50.80
Bonds	$623,515		40.20%	
Stock	164,515		10.61	
Real estate loans		265,258		17.10
Farm mortgages	$ 10,044		0.65%	
Nonfarm (primarily conventional)	255,214		16.45	
Real estate investments		46,711		3.01
Loans to policyholders		66,364		4.28
Other assets		115,348		7.44
Total Assets		$1,551,201		100.00%
Obligations and Net Worth				
Policy reserves		$1,304,778		84.11%
Life insurance	$372,082		23.99%	
Health insurance	38,225		2.46	
Annuities	885,437		57.08	
Other	9,034		0.58	
Policy dividend obligations		31,727		2.05
Accumulations	$ 18,531		1.19%	
Payable during the year	13,196		0.85	
Other obligations		108,658		7.00
Total obligations		$1,445,163		93.16%
Surplus		$ 102,645		6.62%
Common stock		3,393		0.22
Total Net Worth (surplus and common stock)		106,038		6.84
Total Obligations and Net Worth		$1,551,201		100.00%

Source: Prepared by the authors with data from American Council of Life Insurance, *1992 Life Insurance Fact Book.*

are given later about the changing nature of these obligations.

3. Federal law permits corporations holding common and preferred stock in their asset portfolios to exempt a specified percentage of dividend income from taxation. In recent years, the exemption percentage has ranged between 70 and 85 percent. (Because depository institutions are, in general, prohibited from owning stock, they do not enjoy the benefits of this exemption.)

4. The relatively long durations of common and pre-

ferred stock may make those assets good matches for the longer-term obligations of life insurers.

REAL ESTATE LOANS AND INVESTMENTS

Because their liquidity needs are less than those of depositories and because their liabilities are of relatively long duration, life insurers are well suited to make mortgage loans. In fact, mortgages are the third largest category of life insurance assets. In the 1960s, almost 60 percent of the mortgages held by insurers were for one- to four-family homes, but the attractiveness decreased in the 1970s as interest rates rose and residential mortgage rates were held down by state usury laws. Today, most insurers' mortgages are non-farm conventional loans, made primarily to finance commercial properties or apartment buildings.

Unlike some depositories, life insurers are permitted to invest directly in real estate. Most of their real estate holdings are commercial properties such as apartment buildings, shopping centers, and office complexes, on which they receive periodic cash inflows from rental or lease payments.[18] Direct real estate investment has declined slightly as a proportion of assets during the past three decades. This category also includes investment in premises, a small proportion of total assets, as is common in financial institutions.

LOANS TO POLICYHOLDERS

Loans to policyholders are personal cash loans to customers who have borrowed against the **cash values** of certain types of life insurance policies. The accumulated cash value of a policy is the total amount paid in premiums since the inception of the policy, minus the cost of providing insurance protection over that period, plus interest or other benefits accruing on previously paid premiums.[19] Policies that accumulate a cash value permit the insured to borrow against that value on terms specified when the policy is written. The proportion of insurer assets devoted to policy loans was higher in the 1980s and 1990s than at any time since the 1930s. This phenomenon is discussed in greater depth later in the chapter.

OTHER ASSETS

Liquidity differences between depositories and insurers are underscored by the fact that insurers have only 1 percent of their assets in cash. The miscellane-ous category "other assets" also includes premiums due but not yet paid and bond interest accrued but not received.

OBLIGATIONS OF LIFE INSURERS

Life insurers issue a large volume of financial liabilities, but these obligations are unlike those associated with deposits, bonds, or commercial paper.

POLICY RESERVES

By far the largest category of life insurance liabilities is **policy reserves.** Because the word *reserves* is used so often in financial institutions, it is easy to confuse its meaning in a given context. In depositories, cash held to meet regulators' reserve requirements is an asset of the institution. In thrifts and credit unions (CUs), the term *reserves* may be synonymous with capital or net worth. The policy reserves of insurance companies are liabilities, however, not assets or capital. Insurers' reserves are analogous to the deposits of a depository.

ESTIMATION OF RESERVES. The dollar amount of reserves is an estimate of the total present value of future financial obligations—that is, the total present value of expected death, medical, or lifetime income benefits that the company may be required to pay to current policyholders. The amount, determined actuarially, considers the following information:

1. Mortality and morbidity (disease) rates, reflecting the reasons future claims will be made

2. The present value of future premium payments to be received from those currently insured

3. The expected rate of return on the company's investments

In sum, the reserves on a life insurer's balance sheet are the present value of expected claims, *net* of the present value of estimated receipts of premium and investment incomes.

RESERVES FOR ANNUITIES. Table 24.1 indicates that the largest single category of reserves is not for

---

[18] For a discussion of insurer portfolios, including real estate, see Kopcke 1992.

[19] The cash value of a policy is a complicated function of the face value of the policy, the period over which the premiums are to be paid, the interest rate paid on premiums not needed to provide death protection, and something actuaries call "survivorship benefits." There are many good, detailed treatments of the economics of life insurance policies. See, for example, Mehr and Gustavson 1984, Chapter 3.

outstanding life insurance policies but for **annuity policies.** Besides providing death benefits, life insurers sell protection against the risk of outliving one's accumulated financial resources. In exchange for a lump sum payment or a series of smaller payments relatively early in a policyholder's life, insurers provide a predetermined post retirement monthly income, either fixed or variable and usually lasting for the life of the policyholder.

Actuaries project the cash outflows expected under an annuity policy, based on how long the policyholder may live after annuity payments begin. The amount that the customer must pay before receiving the first annuity payment is set equal to the present value of the insurer's anticipated cash outflows. Although individual annuity policies can be purchased, most of the annuity obligations of life insurers are from group pension plans established by employers for employees.

POLICY DIVIDEND OBLIGATIONS

Like *reserves, dividend* has an ambiguous meaning. Typically, a dividend is a benefit paid to common stockholders of a firm after all other operating and financial obligations have been fulfilled. These benefits are taxable to the recipient under current federal tax law.

In the case of mutual insurance companies, however, the meaning of *dividend* is somewhat different, closer to the meaning of *refund*. Policy dividends are features of **participating insurance policies.** A participating policyholder receives a rebate on premiums paid during the year if the loss experience, operating expenses, and investment income of the insurer are better than expected at the beginning of the year. In practice, to maximize the probability that dividends can be paid regularly, premiums on participating policies are higher than premiums on **nonparticipating policies** providing similar coverage. Holders of nonparticipating policies are not entitled to dividends.

In Table 24.1, policy dividend "accumulations" are past dividends that policyholders have reinvested in interest-bearing accounts; dividend obligations "payable" are policy dividends declared during the current year but not yet paid to policyholders. Because policy dividends are considered refunds of previous

payments, they are not taxable to the insured when paid.

OTHER OBLIGATIONS

The miscellaneous category called "other obligations" includes accrued expenses and prepaid premiums.

SURPLUS AND COMMON STOCK

Surplus and common stock are the net worth or capital of the life insurance industry. The surplus account is analogous to retained earnings in other firms. The common stock shown is for shareholder-owned insurers. The book value of an insurer's surplus plus common stock shows how much the book value of assets can shrink before estimated claims on the insurer exceed asset values.

As noted earlier, protecting policyholders from the risk of insurer insolvency is the objective of minimum capital standards set by state insurance commissions. In mutual firms, in particular, capital increases only when premium and investment income exceeds claims and expenses. In attempting to maintain or exceed capital adequacy standards, financial managers of life insurance companies face problems similar to those of depositories.

INCOME AND EXPENSES OF LIFE INSURERS

The income statement for the industry is shown in Table 24.2.

REVENUES

In 1991, almost twice as many dollars were received from premium payments as from investment income. Investment income is stated on a *net* basis, and portfolio management costs are deducted before a total is reported. The proportions of premium and investment income vary with conditions in the financial markets, although premium income is consistently greater. Large firms spend more on portfolio management and rely more heavily on investment income than do small insurers.

TABLE 24.2	Income and Expenses of Life Insurers, 1991 (Millions of $)

Life insurers' revenues are derived primarily from premiums paid by customers, but investment income provides an important supplement. Over one-half of total revenues are expended for benefit payments.

		Millions ($)		Percent of Total Revenues
Revenues				
Premium payments		$263,862		64.20%
Net investment earnings and other income		147,138		35.80
Total revenues			$411,000	100.00%
Expenses				
Benefit payments		$240,846		58.60%
Additions to policy reserves		97,818		23.80
Operating expenses				
Commission to agents	$18,495			
Office expenses	28,770			
Total Operating Expenses		47,265		11.50
Total Expenses			$385,929	93.90%
Taxes			10,275	2.50
Net income			$14,796	3.60%
Dividends to stockholders of shareholder-owned firms			$5,754	1.40%
Additions to surplus			$9,042	2.20%

Source: Adapted from the American Council of Life Insurance, *1992 Life Insurance Fact Book.*

EXPENSES

The two main expense categories are obligations to policyholders or their beneficiaries and operating expenses. As noted, policy obligations include both current disbursements and reserves against expected future claims. Operating expenses include payments to sales agents and costs such as depreciation, rent, and managerial salaries. Altogether, 1991 expenses equaled more than 90 percent of the industry's net revenues. The remaining 6.1 percent of net revenues was consumed by taxes, dividends to stockholders, and additions to surplus.

NET INTEREST MARGIN MODIFIED

The net interest margin (NIM) defined as (interest revenues − interest expense)/total assets, applies to every financial institution discussed thus far. In the insurance industry, however, the basic NIM concept is modified to reflect the nature of the industry's main source of funds and expenses—insurance policies. For all types of insurers, a managerial target analogous to the NIM in other institutions is

$$\text{Net Underwriting Margin} = \frac{\text{Premium Income} - \text{Policy Expenses}}{\text{Total Assets}} \quad [24.3]$$

Despite the different focus, the basic nature of asset/liability management is the same in the insurance industry.[20] Management must earn a sufficient margin

---

[20] This statement is somewhat simplistic. Because policy premiums are actuarially determined based on expected policy expenses, an excess of income over expenses may result from conservative assumptions that set premiums higher than necessary to cover expenses. If all firms in a state make assumptions based on conservative insurance codes in the state, an excess of premium income over expenses may not reflect good management but may simply be a function of assumptions. For an individual firm, however, using more conservative assumptions solely to increase premiums could reduce total income as policyholders choose other firms. The role of assumptions in setting premiums is explained in greater depth later in the chapter.

after all policy-related costs to pay operating expenses and to earn an acceptable return on net worth (RONW). Otherwise, neither policyholders, stockholders, nor regulators will be satisfied, and in extreme situations, the insurer may become insolvent. Important risk/return characteristics of premium income and premium expenses for insurers are discussed later in the chapter.

To achieve financial objectives, insurers usually need additional income from investments. In fact, the difference between an insurer's and a depository's central financial management problem is one of emphasis: Depositories use fee income to supplement interest revenues to attain their financial objectives, and insurers use interest income to supplement fees to achieve theirs. Because insurers' assets and liabilities differ from those of other institutions, they also require different risk management tools, as discussed later.

TYPES OF LIFE INSURANCE POLICIES

Because the unusual nature of life insurers' liabilities influences their financial management strategies, it is important to distinguish among the types of policies from which those obligations arise. Little more than a decade ago, a list of the major life insurance policies would have been as uncomplicated as a list of deposits then available at a savings and loan association (S&L). However, the regulatory and economic changes that caused depositories to broaden their product lines have affected life insurers as well, and the range of insurance products has expanded. Although Table 24.1 shows that annuity policies are an important part of insurers' business, the most significant changes have occurred in life insurance products, the focus of much of the remaining discussion.

WHOLE LIFE

The traditional best-seller in the life insurance industry is the **whole life policy.** A whole life policyholder pays fixed annual premiums in exchange for a known death benefit, the **face amount** of the policy. The annual premium is established when a policy is

written and, for an equivalent face amount and medical history, is inversely related to the policyholder's age. Because the probability of dying increases with age, the policyholder pays more than is actuarially needed to protect his or her beneficiaries during the early years a policy is in force and less than is actuarially needed during the later years.

A whole life policy is so named because it provides death protection for the policyholder's entire life. The insured's beneficiary receives the full face amount, regardless of the date of death. As a consequence of the premium payment system, whole life policies accumulate cash values that the insured may take in lieu of maintaining the full death protection. In any year in which the policyholder does not die, the portion of the premium exceeding the cost of providing death protection adds to the cash value of the policy. A fixed annual rate of return, established at the time the policy is written, is earned on the cash value.

In some states, the minimum yield that insurers must guarantee to policyholders on the cash buildup of their policies is about 4 percent. Because this yield is not taxable to the policyholder unless the policy is surrendered, the tax equivalent of 4 percent to someone in the 28 percent tax bracket is 4% $(1 - 0.28) = 5.56\%$, or about what could be earned on passbook savings accounts when the now-defunct Regulation Q was still in effect. Policyholders with participating policies may also receive dividends if the company's earnings are good.

TERM INSURANCE

Whole life policies have both death protection and savings features, but **term insurance policies** offer only death protection for a specified period.[21] The probability of the insured's dying increases with age. To reflect this fact, the most popular type of term policy involves a premium that increases with age for a constant amount of death benefits. In another common type, sometimes called **decreasing term,** the premium remains constant but the amount of insurance

---

[21] Some term policies contracted for a long period may build up cash value, but these are the exception, not the rule.

coverage decreases with age. Other options are also available, and term policies are frequently offered as part of employee benefits packages. Until the late 1970s, term and whole life were virtually the only types of life insurance policies available.

VARIABLE LIFE

First introduced in 1975, **variable life policies** gained popularity after 1980 as an insurance vehicle providing some protection against inflation. Like whole life policies, variable life policies require level premium payments throughout the policyholder's life, but there are important differences. For example, excess premiums that add to cash value earn variable, not fixed, rates of return, based on the insurer's yield on assets of the *policyholder's* choice. If the selected assets perform well, cash value and death benefits both increase. If not, the cash value may be zero, so the insured bears the entire investment risk. A minimum death benefit is specified in the policy, although there is no maximum. The actual payment to beneficiaries depends on yields earned on excess premiums.

UNIVERSAL LIFE

Another flexible policy, **universal life,** was introduced in 1979. It combines the death protection features of term insurance with the opportunity to earn market rates of return on excess premiums. Unlike variable life, with its level premium structure, premiums on universal life policies can be changed. The policyholder can pay as high a "premium" as desired, instructing the insurer to invest the excess over that required for death protection in the *insurer's* choice of assets. Later, if the policyholder wishes to pay no premium at all, the insurer can deduct the cost of providing death protection for the year from the cash value accumulated in previous years. With other types of policies, skipping a premium would cause the policy to lapse.

Unlike whole or variable life policies, the face amount of guaranteed death protection in a universal life policy can be changed at the policyholder's option. Also, unlike variable life, the cash value has a minimum guaranteed rate of return.

VARIABLE UNIVERSAL LIFE

The newest life insurance product is **variable universal life,** introduced in 1985. So named because it combines the investment flexibility of variable life with the death benefit and premium flexibility of universal life, this new type of policy has gained rapid acceptance among purchasers of life insurance. Variable universal life gives policyholders the greatest freedom to adjust death benefits, premium payments, and investment risk/expected return as their cash-flow and death protection needs change. (Some sources also use the name **flexible premium life** for this new policy.)

Table 24.3 summarizes the characteristics of the five categories of life insurance policies. The table is especially useful for clarifying the similarities and differences among the three newest forms of life insurance products.

COMPARISON OF POLICY CASH FLOWS

The five policy types result in different premiums, and a comparison of the cash flows is important to financial managers. The following examples consider a 35-year-old man seeking a policy in a face amount of $100,000.

ROLE OF MORTALITY TABLES

Regardless of the policy, the insurer begins calculating the premium by examining a mortality table. Table 24.4 presents excerpts from a typical mortality table. This one was published in 1980, based on mortality from 1970 through 1975. It is called the Commissioners Standard Ordinary (CSO) Table because it was recommended as a basis for calculating required insurer reserves by the National Association of Insurance Commissioners (NAIC), an organization of insurance regulators. Death rates per 1,000 are calculated conservatively, according to the number of insured men actually dying during the 1970–1975 period, with an increase to allow for a margin of error. When setting premiums, an insurer uses actuarial estimates reflecting the most recent information available,

| TABLE 24.3 | **Characteristics of Life Insurance Policies** |

Life insurance policies now fall into five broad categories. Much of the demand for traditional term and whole life policies has been supplanted by demand for newer and more flexible products such as variable and universal life. The new policies allow clients to customize their cash flow requirements and death benefits.

	Premiums	**Cash Value**	**Death Benefit**
Term	■ Buy protection in the form of a death benefit ■ Payments increase when the policy is renewed	■ None	■ Amount is fixed
Whole life	■ Buy protection in the form of a death benefit ■ Build a cash value ■ Payments are fixed	■ May be borrowed against by the policyholder ■ Yields a fixed return guaranteed to be more than 4%	■ Amount is fixed
Universal life	■ Buy protection in the form of a death benefit ■ Build a cash value ■ Payments may vary at the discretion of the policyholder	■ May be borrowed against by the policyholder ■ Is invested by the insurer to yield a return that varies but is guaranteed to be more than 4%	■ Amount may vary at the discretion of the policyholder
Variable life	■ Buy protection in the form of a death benefit ■ Build a cash value ■ Payments are fixed	■ May be borrowed against by the policyholder ■ Is invested by the policyholder in a choice of mutual funds ■ No guaranteed minimum rate of return ■ Amount varies with the performance of the mutual fund	■ Guaranteed minimum amount ■ Amount varies with the performance of the mutual fund
Variable universal	■ Buy protection in the form of a death benefit ■ Build a cash value ■ Payments may vary at the discretion of the policyholder	■ May be borrowed against by the policyholder ■ Is invested by the policyholder in a choice of mutual funds ■ No guaranteed minimum rate of return ■ Amount varies with the performance of the mutual fund	■ Guaranteed minimum amount ■ Amount varies with the performance of the mutual fund ■ Amount may also vary at the discretion of the policyholder

Source: Terence Paré, "The New Game in Life Insurance," *Fortune*, March 27, 1989, 142. © 1989 The Time Inc. Magazine Company. All rights reserved.

including new causes of death such as AIDS or new treatments for formerly fatal diseases. For illustrative purposes, however, the 1980 Commissioners Table is used.[22]

According to the conservative estimates in the table, of any 10,000,000 men, 9,491,617 are expected to reach age 35, and 146,720 are expected to reach age 95. Of those reaching 35 years, 20,027 are expected to die before age 36, a rate of 2.11 men per 1,000. The

---

[22] Because mortality rates for men and women differ, life insurers use separate tables to calculate premiums for each sex. Also, P/L companies use separate premium schedules for men and women drivers, for example, because women have had better driving records. Recently, these practices have been challenged in court as being discriminatory against both sexes. Most insurers object vig-

orously to so-called unisex pricing, believing that premium and benefit differences between the sexes are justified. Few states have passed unisex pricing laws; only in Montana does the law mandate unisex life insurance and P/L premiums. The issue has also been raised in Congress. See Dennon 1988.

probability that an individual claim will be made during the year a policyholder is 35 years old can be estimated as

$$20{,}027 \div 9{,}491{,}617 = 0.00211 = 0.211\%$$

OTHER ASSUMPTIONS

To set premiums, an insurer assumes at what point during the year death claims will be made and when premium payments will be received. In this example, the assumption is that claims are not paid until the end of the year for which insurance is purchased, although premium payments are assumed to occur at the beginning of a policy year. The insurer also estimates the rate of return to be earned on premium payments made in advance of claims. Because most states require insurers to use conservative assumptions about the rate they will earn on invested premiums, this example assumes a rate of 4 percent.

PREMIUM ON A 1-YEAR TERM POLICY

Suppose that a 35-year-old man seeks a $100,000 term policy for only 1 year. The expected value of the cash outflow required by the insurer at the *end* of the year is the face amount of the policy times the probability that a claim will be made

[24.4]

$$\text{1-Year Term Premium} = \frac{\text{Face Amount} \times}{\text{Probability of Claim}}$$

$$\$100{,}000 \times 0.00211 = \$211.00$$

The $211 can also be viewed in another way. Suppose that the insurer has 9,491,617 35-year-old male policyholders, each with $100,000 policies. According to the CSO table, 20,027 will die during the year. If they do, the total cost to the insurer would be $2,002,700,000. Because, at the beginning of the year, no one knows which individuals will die, the insurance industry operates on the principle that the cost of providing death protection should be shared by everyone. Each person's equal share is

$$\frac{\$2{,}002{,}700{,}000}{9{,}491{,}617} = \$210.99, \text{ or } \$211$$

TABLE 24.4   **Excerpts from Commissioners 1980 Standard Ordinary Mortality Table (Based on Death Rates of Males, 1970–1975)**

Life insurance premiums are based on actuarial data. This Standard Ordinary Mortality Table indicates the probability of death for males of different ages and allows insurers to estimate the probability of paying cash benefits for a given category of customers.

(1) Age (Years)	(2) Number Living	(3) Number Dying	(4) Deaths per 1,000 [(3)/(2)] × 1,000
0	10,000,000	41,800	4.18
1	9,958,200	10,655	1.07
2	9,947,545	9,848	0.99
3	9,937,697	9,739	0.98
4	9,927,958	9,531	0.96
5	9,918,427	8,927	0.90
6	9,909,500	8,522	0.86
7	9,900,978	7,921	0.80
8	9,893,057	7,519	0.76
9	9,885,539	7,315	0.74
10	9,878,223	7,211	0.73
.	.	.	.
.	.	.	.
.	.	.	.
35	9,491,617	20,027	2.11
36	9,471,590	21,216	2.24
37	9,450,374	22,681	2.40
38	9,427,693	24,323	2.58
39	9,403,369	26,235	2.79
.	.	.	.
.	.	.	.
70	6,274,100	247,890	39.51
71	6,026,210	260,935	43.30
72	5,765,275	274,715	47.65
73	5,490,560	289,023	52.64
74	5,201,537	302,677	58.19
75	4,898,859	314,458	64.19
.	.	.	.
.	.	.	.
95	146,720	48,412	329.96
96	98,308	37,804	384.55
97	60,504	29,054	480.20
98	31,450	20,693	657.97
99	10,756	10,756	1,000.00

The present value of this amount at the *beginning* of the year, when premiums are assumed to be paid, is the required or **pure premium.** It will be increased by a **loading** to cover operating expenses and profit for shareholders. Using a discount rate of 4 percent, the pure premium is

$$\$211.00 \div 1.04 = \$202.88$$

If someone were 70 years old and wished to purchase 1-year term insurance with a face value of $100,000, the cost to the insurer at the end of the year, using Equation 24.4, would be

$$\$100,000 \times (247,890 \div 6,274,100) = \$3,951$$

The pure premium would be $3,951 ÷ 1.04 = $3,799, a charge reflecting the higher expected cost of providing death protection.[23]

ROLE OF THE DISCOUNT RATE. The low 4 percent rate assumed on the insurer's investments produces a higher premium than if a higher discount rate were used. Throughout the 1980s, life insurers' net (after management expenses) return on investments exceeded 8 percent, and from 1984 to 1988, it exceeded 9 percent. Insurers and state regulators justify the continued use of low rates in the interests of conservatism. If a higher discount rate were used in premium calculations and if *ex post* investment income failed to reach that rate, some argue that insurers' solvency would be threatened and that policyholders would face the risk that their claims could not be met. As seen later, policyholders are increasingly reluctant to accept this argument.

ANNUAL PREMIUM ON A WHOLE LIFE POLICY

The calculation of the annual premium on a $100,000 whole life policy for a 35-year-old man is based on the same principles used for term insurance. An adjustment is made, however, because death protection is being purchased for the rest of the insured's life. Although the premium is fixed, the probability of death changes each year, a fact considered at the time the policy is written. An illustration is given in the appendix to the chapter, resulting in an annual pure premium of $1,260.43.

CASH VALUES AND DEATH BENEFITS. The beginning-of-year cost of providing death protection for a man at age 35 years was estimated earlier to be only $202.88, but the pure whole life premium is $1,260.43. If the policyholder does not die, the insurer invests premiums in excess of those actually required to provide death protection. The $1,260.43 would be collected each year, but the cost of death protection would increase as the policyholder ages, with less added to the cash value. Cash value also increases based on the assumed interest rate. Regardless of the insurer's actual investment earnings, nonparticipating whole life policyholders earn a fixed rate, and their beneficiaries receive a fixed death benefit. In contrast, participating policyholders may receive dividends in good years.

UNIVERSAL, VARIABLE, AND VARIABLE UNIVERSAL LIFE PREMIUMS

The basic concepts involved in calculating term and whole life policy premiums hold for variable, universal, and variable universal life policies. For these policies, a 35-year-old man seeking $100,000 of coverage would be quoted a pure annual premium of $1,260.43 plus a markup for operating costs and profit margin. The amount required for death protection each year would be deducted and the remainder invested in market-rate instruments. The interest rate actually earned on the cash value is not determined in advance. As noted, universal and variable universal life policies give the holder great flexibility. The insured may pay

---

[23] Not every insurer would charge the pure premium plus the same loading. Individual insurance underwriters must decide what types of risks they are willing to bear. In some cases, if a company prefers to deal with one type of client (say, nonsmokers), it may undercharge them and overcharge smokers to make up the difference. As a result, policies with identical features may be priced differently, depending on the underwriter's risk preferences. For an example of the range of premiums on a given term policy, see Richard Morais, "Double Indemnity," *Forbes* 136 (November 18, 1985): 280.

more or less than the quoted level premium; the difference between what is paid and the cost of death protection is added to or subtracted from the cash value.

THE EVOLVING LIFE INSURANCE PRODUCT MIX: CAUSES AND RESULTS

When disintermediation and/or cross-intermediation occur, financial institutions face unexpected withdrawals of funds as customers seek more attractive yields from direct investments or from other financial institutions. Consider the situation facing life insurers in the early 1980s. Whole life customers were earning relatively low rates on the cash buildup of their policies. Although not subject to income tax, the tax-equivalent yield simply was intolerably low. Many policyholders dissatisfied with the low return on the "forced" savings in the early years of a whole life policy did one of three things: They switched to term insurance; borrowed against the accumulated cash value of existing whole life policies; or stopped paying premiums, allowing policies to lapse. The collective effects of these actions changed the life insurance business permanently.

THE SWITCH TO TERM INSURANCE

Between 1972 and 1982, the face value of new whole life policies as a percentage of "ordinary" insurance purchased declined steadily from 53 percent to 40 percent, and term insurance rose from 41 percent to 60 percent of new insurance in force. This development was critical to the financial management of life insurance companies. Steady, predictable cash flows declined, and because premiums from most term policies vary from year to year, uncertainty in insurers' cash inflows increased. The increased riskiness affected life insurers' investment choices, as discussed later in the chapter. Although whole life regained market share as interest rates fell in the mid-1980s and as customers adopted variable and universal policies, changes in insurers' investment practices remain.

THE INCREASE IN POLICY LOANS

Figure 24.2 illustrates the second way in which whole life policyholders responded to the changing economic environment. It tracks the dollar volume borrowed against the cash value of whole life policies since 1960. In the past, the rate at which a policyholder could borrow was usually established at a rate prevailing at the time the policy was written. During periods in which market rates remained relatively stable, there was no systematic incentive for a large number of policyholders to borrow against accumulated cash values at one time.

In the late 1970s and early 1980s, however, as market rates reached historical highs, the ability to borrow against one's life insurance policy at, for example, 5 percent and to reinvest loan proceeds in Treasury bills (T-bills) at, say, 16.5 percent proved irresistible to many policyholders.[24] Many insurers lobbied successfully to persuade regulators to increase permissible policy loan rates (up to 8 percent or more in some states) or to permit variable-rate policy loans. The volume of policy loans was stable in the mid-1980s but began to grow again in the latter part of the decade.

Growth in policyholder loans added to the riskiness of insurers' cash flows. Because the insurer is legally obligated to provide policy loans on the terms established in the policy, cash must be obtained somewhere. High demand for policy loans coincided with the switch to term insurance, and some insurers were forced to liquidate assets, sometimes at a loss in value. In 1980, in fact, the industry was forced to use more than 22 percent of total funds available for investment to make new policy loans.[25] Some insurers even had to borrow at rates higher than they earned on the policy loans they made with the borrowed money.

---

[24] For insurers, perhaps the "unkindest cut of all" came in 1982, when a former insurance agent founded a company called Idle Assets. Idle Assets trained bank and S&L employees to call their own customers, encouraging them to bring their life insurance policies into the depository. If a customer complied, the employee would then explain how to borrow against the policy and encourage the policyholders to reinvest the policy loan in a high-yielding bank or S&L certificate of deposit (CD). Idle Assets collected a modest fee from the bank or S&L for services rendered. David P. Garino, "Life Insurers Irked by Reinvestment Plan that Hurts Them but Aids Holders, Banks," *The Wall Street Journal,* March 5, 1982.

[25] See Curry and Warshawsky 1986, 449.

FIGURE 24.2   **Growth of Policy Loans**

As interest rates rose in the late 1970s and early 1980s, many whole life insurance policyholders borrowed against policy cash values at below-market interest rates. This rapid growth in policy loans placed life insurers in a difficult financial position. The volume of policy loans stabilized in the mid-1980s but regained upward momentum in the early 1990s.

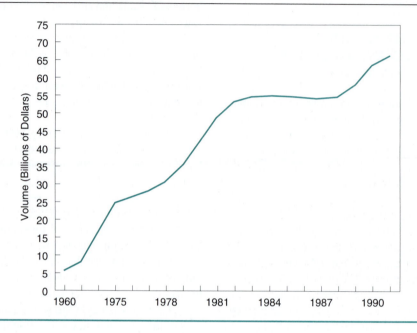

Source: American Council of Life Insurance, *1992 Life Insurance Fact Book.*

POLICY LAPSES

One of the most serious effects on insurer cash flows came from cancellation of life insurance policies as customers relied on "self-insurance" from savings or on term insurance available through employers. Between 1960 and 1985, voluntary policy terminations per year more than doubled, from about 5 percent to more than 12 percent of policies in force. The rate began to decline in 1986, but by 1991 it was still 8.6 percent.

Policy lapses are especially likely to occur among customers with the least need for insurance protection. The result of continued cancellations could be to skew insurers' customer base toward riskier customers rather than those on which mortality tables are based. A declining customer base threatens not only the profitability of insurers in the short run, as shown by a decrease in premium income and the net underwriting margin, but also their long-run solvency.

INTRODUCTION OF VARIABLE, UNIVERSAL, AND VARIABLE UNIVERSAL LIFE

Variable, universal, and variable universal life policies are designed to attract customers who fled whole life policies, but they have also affected the financial management of insurers.

IMPACT ON CASH FLOWS. Because customers' satisfaction with new policies depends on the performance of the insurer's investment portfolio, emphasis on that aspect of management has intensified. Further, servicing the new policies costs more, because market rates are paid on the cash buildup portion of premiums. The increased cost is reflected in the reserves required to provide for future policy obligations, considerably squeezing the net underwriting margin. The cash inflows and outflows for the new policies are also much less predictable than for traditional whole life, creating a need for asset liquidity that had not been significant for insurers. Liquidity pressures made many insurers reluctant to offer the new products at first; they did so only after extensive cancellations taught the bitter lesson that a return to the old days was unlikely.[26]

IMPACT ON OPERATING COSTS. The new policies have also caused the management of operating costs to change. Historically, because the yield paid on whole life policies was so low, insurers could keep a large force of sales agents and pay them huge commissions on the sale of new policies, often up to 100 percent of the first year's premium. With underwriting margins on the more flexible life policies squeezed to a minimum, the compensation system must be overhauled. Some insurers are reducing their sales force and finding new ways to market policies, such as renting space in local depositories or selling through the mail. Remaining agents must be trained in the complex details of the new policies. Furthermore, sophisticated computer systems are needed to maintain necessary records. These expenses put further pressure on insurer earnings as their product mix changes.

IMPACT ON REPORTED REVENUES. In 1989, the Financial Accounting Standards Board (FASB) proposed a new policy that has the potential to reduce significantly the reported premium income for some life insurers. The FASB noted that a sizable portion of the premiums paid for the new variable and universal policies was not for death benefits but rather was for investment income and cash-value accumulation accruing to the policyholder. As a result, the FASB believes that only the part of a premium required to cover death benefits and administrative expenses should be reported by the life insurer as premium income; the remainder is to be credited to the individual policyholder's account. This proposal would affect only stockholder-owned firms, however, because mutuals are not required to issue public annual reports.

NEW POLICIES IN FORCE

The initial popularity of variable, universal, and variable universal life policies exceeded the estimates of even the most optimistic observers, as illustrated in Figure 24.3. Because the growth in the number of these policies has been so rapid, the scale on the graph is not linear but logarithmic. That means that the distances between points on the vertical scale reflect equal rates of change, not equal amounts. In the figure, the equal distances between points labeled 1, 10, 100, 1,000, and 10,000 all represent a tenfold increase in policies from the previous point. Between 1981 and 1983 and again between 1982 and 1985, the amount of universal life in force increased almost tenfold! The same rate of increase is evident for variable universal life between 1985 and 1988. Although the rate of growth in nontraditional policies has slowed somewhat in the 1990s, the days of predictable cash obligations of insurers are gone forever. Financial managers in insurance companies need to understand how asset management is affected.[27]

LIFE INSURERS: ASSET MANAGEMENT

Because the assets of life insurers are mostly stocks and bonds, many management tools described in previous chapters are relevant for insurers. It is important for insurers to analyze carefully the default risk to which bond portfolios are exposed. In fact, because so many of the corporate bonds held by life insurers are privately placed, assessment of default risk is paramount. As noted in the opening paragraphs of this chapter, the financial problems of Executive Life, which was taken over by regulators in 1991, have been traced to the firm's investments in high-risk bonds.

Assessment of interest rate risk is also critical, now more than ever, because increasing needs for liquidity mean insurers may have to sell assets before

---

[26] For example, the second largest life insurer did not introduce universal life policies until 1983. When it did, premiums on universal life policies grew rapidly to 47 percent of all new premiums written. See "Upheaval in Life Insurance" 1984.

[27] The traditional whole life policy continues to provide a package of options for the policyholder provided by no other insurance product, so it is likely to remain a viable product regardless of its interest rate features. For an analysis and empirical support, see Smith 1982 and Walden 1985.

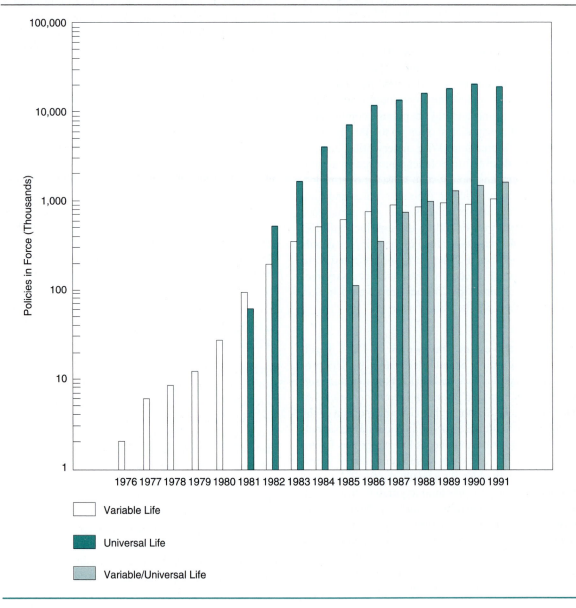

FIGURE 24.3   **Growth of Variable and Universal Life**

Life insurance customers greeted the introduction of new, more flexible whole life policies with enthusiasm. The volume of variable, universal, and variable universal life policies grew rapidly throughout the 1980s.

☐ Variable Life

■ Universal Life

▨ Variable/Universal Life

Source: American Council of Life Insurance, *1992 Life Insurance Fact Book.*

maturity. Insurers must have knowledge of portfolio diversification using correlations between expected returns on individual investments, as well as the ability to assess the market risk of a common stock portfolio. These issues are explored in Chapters 5, 8, 9, and 13.

Investment in a third category of life insurer assets, real estate, requires a somewhat different approach, also discussed earlier in the text. These investments are significant long-term commitments by insurers to the development and management of real property. Thus, they are particularly suited to net present value (NPV) analysis, illustrated in Chapter 20. Recent evidence indicates that life insurers are increasingly using NPV techniques for this purpose. By 1983, about 50 percent of a sample of life insurance executives indicated that their firms used NPV to assess after-tax cash flows from real estate investments, compared with less than 10 percent a decade earlier.[28] The trend toward more sophisticated real estate investment analysis will undoubtedly continue, particularly because the financial problems of several insurers, such as Mutual Benefit, have been linked to investments in commercial real estate.

NEW DIRECTIONS IN ASSET MANAGEMENT

Although basic asset management issues are of continuing importance to life insurers, their greatest challenge is determining the best asset portfolio in a competitive environment in which interest rate risk management has become critical. In the past, a buy-and-hold strategy was common among insurers; yields on assets exceeding the yield paid on whole life policies were "gravy." Now, asset portfolios must be structured to earn competitive yields but must be flexible enough to change as insurers' cash obligations change. One adjustment to new conditions was an increase in short-term U.S. government securities held in case of increased policy loan demand.[29]

Earnings pressures have raised concerns both in and outside the industry. Just as some depositories have been tempted to invest in riskier-than-normal assets to attract depositors to above-average yields, some insurers have been accused of taking excessive risks to attract buyers of variable and universal life policies. The mortality and morbidity risks that actuaries assess are different from risks in the financial markets. Fortunately for insurers, however, most integrated asset/liability management tools available to depositories are suitable for insurers, too.

LIFE INSURERS: RISK-BASED CAPITAL REGULATIONS

In late 1992, the National Association of Insurance Commissioners (NAIC) adopted a model program of risk-based capital standards for the life insurance industry. The standards focus on four types of risk faced by life insurers: asset, insurance, interest rate, and business risks. State regulators will calculate risk-adjusted capital ratios and use the results to evaluate the financial strength of each firm. Regulators will also be expected to intervene if the results suggest a high risk of insolvency. In the absence of uniform federal regulations, the standards can only become official as they are adopted in individual states.[30]

LIFE INSURERS: TECHNIQUES FOR INTEGRATED ASSET/ LIABILITY MANAGEMENT

The following sections illustrate the use of several integrated asset/liability management tools in life insurance firms.

MATURITY AND DURATION MATCHING

Matching is as legitimate a risk management tool for insurers as it is for depositories, and the idea is not a new one. In 1942, an economist at a Philadelphia life insurance company stressed the importance of

---

[28] See Webb 1984, 501, 503.

[29] For more discussion of these points, see Saunders 1984. Other evidence on integrated balance sheet structures is provided in Stowe and Watson 1985.

[30] See Charles Schmidt, "Regulators Adopt RBC Standards for Life/Health Insurers," *Best's Review,* January 1993, 94–95; Greg Steinmetz, "Life Insurers Get New Rules for Capital," *The Wall Street Journal,* December 7, 1992, A2.

matching the cash flows from assets and liabilities to lock in an overall rate of profit. A 1952 article in an actuarial science journal developed a measure of the "mean term" of insurer asset and liability cash flows. The measure was virtually identical to the duration measure Macaulay had developed 15 years earlier. Insurers were encouraged to match the mean term of assets and liabilities to stabilize profits in an environment of changing rates.[31]

Although insurance companies were among the first institutions for which matching maturities or durations were suggested, many small and medium-sized companies have not yet embraced the suggestion. As in small depositories, the main reason is the extensive data collection and analyses required in establishing a GAP management system. Nonetheless, industry insiders increasingly encourage life insurers of all sizes to practice matching to reduce the adverse effect of interest rate risk.

DURATION AND THE IMMUNIZATION OF SEPARATE ACCOUNTS

For duration to be a useful tool, managers of life insurance companies need not manage the overall duration GAP. Segments of the asset portfolio can be immunized to lock in yields, even if the total portfolio is not. Immunization is especially appropriate for insurers with substantial **separate accounts,** defined as groups of assets designated as backing for specific obligations. If an insurer manages pension fund obligations for an employer, separate accounts are often used to support these obligations. Also, reserves for variable and universal life policies are often backed by separate accounts.

To immunize yields on separate accounts, the insurer must estimate the holding period over which a given yield is desired. A logical holding period is the estimated duration of the obligations for which a separate account has been established. The average duration of the designated assets is then set equal to that holding period. As explained in Chapter 9, immunization balances the reinvestment risk of the assets with their exposure to price risk. Whether rates increase or decrease, the initial yield is protected. In attempting to immunize, however, life insurers face the difficulty of finding assets with sufficient duration to match the duration of their liabilities. Immunization strategies for separate accounts are similar to those used in pension fund management, and an example is included in Chapter 25.[32]

FINANCIAL FUTURES AND OPTIONS

The substantial number of bonds owned by life insurers makes these companies ideal candidates for using financial futures for several reasons. First, the value of long-term assets is more volatile as interest rates change, and futures may be used to hedge against that volatility. Also, insurers often agree to purchase corporate bonds under **forward commitments.** In a forward commitment, the insurer agrees to buy bonds before the actual transaction. If management commits the firm to buying bonds in 3 months but fears that yields will drift downward before then, profits on a long futures position can be used to offset the opportunity loss of investing at the possibly lower rate.

Two surveys of large U.S. life insurers, conducted in 1986 and 1987, revealed that about 20 percent of the approximately 100 responding firms were actually using financial futures and that larger firms were more likely to be active in the futures markets. The respondents indicated that futures were most often used 1) to lock in the current yield for an anticipated cash inflow in the near future and 2) to hedge against a decline in the value of fixed-income assets when interest rates were expected to rise. Protecting the yield on a forward commitment was a motivation identified by just under one-half of the responding firms.

The research also revealed that the greatest challenge faced by both users and nonusers of futures was educating managers about these instruments. Experienced firms also indicated that developing internal control systems to monitor futures positions was a problem frequently encountered. Nonusers were particularly impeded by the lack of qualified personnel to implement a hedging program. Not surprisingly, how-

---

[31] These papers are cited in Weil 1973.

[32] The need for immunization and other new financial management techniques is discussed in Forbes 1987.

ever, all respondents strongly agreed that the nature of the life insurance business now exposed them to significant interest rate risk.

Other risk management opportunities are becoming available to insurers since the introduction of insurance-related futures by the Chicago Board of Trade. As of early 1993, light trading was reported on these contracts. Health insurance contracts, which could offer hedging opportunities to life insurers, were under study for possible introduction as early as 1994.[33]

BALANCE SHEET OF PROPERTY/LIABILITY INSURERS

P/L companies face problems that are similar to yet distinct from those of life insurers. Before a discussion of special problems, an examination of the balance sheet, income, and expenses of P/L companies is appropriate.

STATUTORY VERSUS GAAP ACCOUNTING

Interpreting available financial data on P/L insurers is somewhat more difficult than for other financial institutions. Insurance companies, like thrifts, are subject to two sets of accounting rules: regulatory principles, which insurers call **statutory accounting,** and generally accepted accounting principles (GAAP). Statutory accounting rules are prescribed by laws in each state, but most states have adopted a uniform set recommended by the NAIC.

Statutory accounting is a combination of cash-based and accrual accounting; expenses are recognized when paid, but revenues are not recognized until earned. In general, it is a more conservative way of reporting financial results than GAAP. Statutory accounting affects balance sheets and income statements for all insurers, although differences between statutory

---

[33] See Lamm-Tenant 1989; Mulcahy 1991; David Foppert, "Uncertain Futures," *Best's Review,* March 1993, 20–22, 94–96; Hoyt 1989. For results of an earlier survey, see Rebecca M. Hurtz and Mona J. Gardner, "Surviving in a New Environment," *Best's Review* (Life/Health Edition) 85 (September 1984): 152–153.

accounting and GAAP are greater for P/L insurers than for life insurers. Virtually all data on life insurers presented earlier are consistent with GAAP. However, the same cannot be said for data on the P/L industry; this discussion notes significant differences between statutory and GAAP figures as they are relevant.

ASSETS OF P/L INSURERS

Like life insurers, P/L companies invest heavily in bonds and stock but in different proportions. Table 24.5 presents the balance sheet of P/L insurers at the end of 1991.

BONDS. The bond portfolio of P/L companies are dominated by government securities, especially state and local issues, including special revenue bonds, the largest category of P/L assets. P/L insurers choose these investments because interest earned is exempt from federal taxes.

Unfortunately for P/L insurers, their relatively large investment in state, local, and revenue bonds has been a two-edged sword. If underwriting profits are good, the tax shelter provided by municipal bonds is desirable. If underwriting losses occur, the lower yield on municipals hurts profitability. In the 1980s, the latter situation was common.

PREFERRED AND COMMON STOCK. P/L insurers devote more of their portfolios to stock than life insurers do because of differences in the cash flows of the two types of insurers. More is said later about the premium income and expenses of P/L insurers, but their cash inflows are less stable than those of life insurers, and their cash outflows are more strongly affected by inflation and unpredictable natural disasters. Common stock, with the possibility of substantial price appreciation, is a more suitable investment choice for P/L companies than for life insurers.

Statutory accounting requires unrealized gains or losses on the stock holdings of insurers to be reflected on the balance sheet, directly affecting both reported asset holdings and insurers' net worth. In years in which stock market values increase, asset and net worth accounts are both written up; in bad years, they are written down. This procedure is currently inconsistent with GAAP, which requires the reporting of equity securities holdings as the lower of either cost or market

TABLE 24.5	Assets and Obligations of Property/Liability Companies, Year-End 1991 (Approximately 3,900 Firms)

Insurers invest heavily in debt securities, a large proportion of which are government-issued. P/L insurers are not as highly leveraged as life insurers.

	Millions of $	% of Total
Assets		
Bonds		
U.S. Treasury	$104,072	17.30%
State and local	55,918	9.30
Special revenue	120,409	20.02
Other	88,973	14.79
Total Bonds	$369,371	61.41%
Common stock	83,067	13.81
Preferred stock	11,003	1.83
Mortgages and other loans	12,860	2.14
Other assets	125,145	20.81
Total Assets	$601,445	100.00%
Obligations and Surplus (Net Worth)		
Total loss and unearned premium reserves	$442,787	73.62%
Total surplus and common stock	158,658	26.38
Total Obligations and Surplus (Net Worth)	$601,445	100.00%

Source: Prepared by the authors with data from the Insurance Information Institute, *1993 Property/Casualty Insurance Facts.*

value. Consequently, statutory values for assets and net worth often differ from those reported under GAAP. (As noted in previous chapters, however, the Securities and Exchange Commission [SEC] and the accounting profession are increasingly inclined toward requiring market-value accounting for financial institutions.)

MORTGAGES AND OTHER LOANS. The fully taxable income from mortgage loans and their lower potential price appreciation has made mortgages relatively unattractive to P/L insurers.

OTHER ASSETS. The category "other assets" includes all assets, such as cash, not held as investments. It does not include premises of P/L insurers, however. Statutory accounting rules require P/L insurers to report only **admitted assets,** those that could be liquidated should the insurer face a financial emergency. Premises of insurers are not considered admitted assets. Thus, the reported net worth of P/L insurers is understated by nonadmitted assets not shown on the balance sheet.[34]

LIABILITIES AND POLICYHOLDERS' SURPLUS OF P/L INSURERS

Like life insurers, P/L companies estimate expected future claims on existing policies; these estimates are called **loss reserves.** Loss reserves are the sum of claims made but not yet paid and estimates of claims that will be made; they are the largest portion of the industry's liabilities. Because P/L insurers do not rely on mortality and morbidity tables, estimated losses are often based on past experience, with adjustments to reflect increased costs caused by inflation or other factors. Since the Tax Reform Act of 1986, P/L insurers have been required to report their liabilities as the discounted value of a series of future cash outflows.

For the unexpired terms of outstanding policies, P/L insurers have obligations to policyholders who

---

[34] Statutory accounting rules for life insurers also require that they report only admitted assets. The data in Table 24.1, however, were restated by the American Council of Life Insurance to reflect nonadmitted assets such as premises.

have paid premiums in advance. These **unearned premium reserves** are often calculated under the assumption that services have been rendered for only one-half of the amount of premiums paid during the year. For example, assume that an insurer has $2 million in total premiums during a calendar year, received evenly at a rate of $166,667 per month. Obligations on policies written in January would have almost expired by the end of December; those written in February would have about 1 month's obligation remaining; those written in December would have about 11 months left, and so on. On average, the insurer would have obligations remaining on 6 months' worth of premium payments, and the unearned premium reserve for the year would be valued at $1 million.

P/L insurers must also maintain sufficient net worth to absorb net losses in years in which income is insufficient to meet expenses. The net worth of the industry consists of common stock, a relatively small proportion of industry capital, and **policyholders' surplus,** the P/L term for retained earnings. This total does not reflect the value of nonadmitted assets. As in all financial institutions, net worth is viewed as a measure of financial strength and affects the insurer's capacity to write additional policies. In general, state regulations discourage insurers from writing an annual dollar volume of premiums that exceeds three times the surplus account.

Figure 24.4 compares the balance sheets of life and P/L insurers and highlights the differences between them. Although these insurers select similar assets, the proportions differ noticeably, as highlighted by P/Ls' extensive investment in government securities, mostly municipals. Also, P/L insurers do not lend to policyholders.

The main liabilities of both groups are reserves, but the P/L industry has proportionately much more net worth than life insurers. The additional buffer is required because reserves necessary to meet P/Ls' policy obligations are much less predictable.

INCOME AND EXPENSES OF P/L INSURERS

The statutory practice of reporting income using accrual accounting and expenses using cash accounting prevents meaningful presentation of a complete income statement for the P/L industry. Therefore, major components of P/L income and expenses are discussed separately.

REVENUES

Like life insurers, P/L insurers derive their revenues from two sources—premiums and investments. As the top portion of Table 24.6 indicates, premiums compose the largest proportion of P/L revenues, arising from the sale of risk protection both to businesses and individuals. Many types of property can be protected, although automobile insurance is by far the largest single source of total P/L premium revenues. Other important categories of protection (called **lines** in the industry) include workers' compensation, homeowners' insurance, and general liability insurance for businesses and professionals.

PREMIUM INCOME. The $222.991 billion "total premiums written" in the top panel of Table 24.6 is referred to in the industry as "net premiums written." It is premiums collected before deducting those paid but not yet earned. The $222.151 billion is earned premiums, determined according to statutory accounting rules. Accounting rules for unearned premiums on the income statement differ from the method discussed earlier for determining unearned premium reserves on the balance sheet. As a result, unearned premium reserves on the balance sheet are often overstated and net worth understated for the industry. Some experts estimate the extent of reserve overstatement to be as much as 35 percent.[35]

INVESTMENT INCOME. As with life insurers, investment income is reported net of portfolio management expenses but before taxes. Annual investment income for the industry increased more than eightfold between 1975 and 1991, providing an important source of funds to supplement premiums.[36] As illustrated later, however, this growth has not always been enough to guarantee profitability in the industry.

---

[35] See Vaughan 1982, 109, n. 7. Many observers believe that the overly conservative statutory rules hurt the industry, because they overstate its liabilities relative to its net worth. See Mehr 1983, 470–471.

[36] *1993 Property/Casualty Insurance Facts.*

FIGURE 24.4   **Life Insurers and P/L Insurers: A Comparison of Assets, Obligations, and Net Worth**

A notable difference in the assets of life and P/L insurers is the proportion invested in government securities and policy loans. Both types of insurers have large policy reserve liabilities, but life insurers are more highly leveraged.

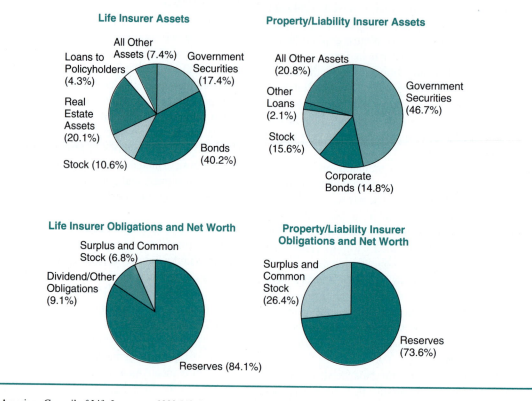

Source: American Council of Life Insurance, *1992 Life Insurance Fact Book;* and Insurance Information Institute, *1993 Property/Casualty Insurance Facts.*

EXPENSES

Expenses of offering insurance protection are the largest category for the industry, totaling almost three-quarters of the total expenses shown in the middle panel of Table 24.6. Refunds, or dividends, to policyholders in profitable lines of business are a small proportion of expenses, and the remainder is normal operating expenses, including salaries and commissions to agents.

The commission structure in the P/L industry differs from that of the life insurance industry. Whereas a life insurance agent might earn up to 100 percent of the first year's premium as commission and relatively little thereafter on the same policy, a P/L

agent might earn only 20 percent of the first year's premium on an automobile policy. Because an automobile policy is usually renewed year after year, however, the agent earns subsequent years' commissions with little effort at resale.

UNDERWRITING GAINS (LOSSES) AND THE IMPACT OF INVESTMENT INCOME

The importance of both income and expenses from underwriting makes it natural to focus on underwriting results. Regulatory accounting rules require insurers to present two levels of underwriting results,

TABLE 24.6	Earnings of Property/Liability Insurers, 1991 (Billions of $)			

P/L insurers have recently faced earnings pressures. In 1991 industry earnings from underwriting were negative. Strong investment income, however, allowed the P/L industry to report a net profit.

Revenues				
Total premiums written		$222.991		
Less unearned premiums		0.840		
Total earned premiums			$222.151	86.64%
Net investment earnings and other income			34.247	13.36
Total Revenues			$256.398	100.00%
Expenses				
Loss expenses		$180.210		74.43%
Policyholder dividends		2.782		1.15
Operating expenses		59.129		24.42
Total Expenses		$242.121		100.00%
Underwriting Results				
Earned premiums		$222.151		
Less:				
Loss expenses		180.210		
Operating expenses		59.129		
Statutory underwriting gain (loss)		($17.188)		
Less dividends to policyholders		2.782		
Net Underwriting Gain (Loss)		($19.970)		

Source: Prepared by the authors with data from the Insurance Information Institute, *1993 Property/Casualty Insurance Facts,* inside cover.

statutory and net underwriting gain (loss). As shown at the bottom of Table 24.6, the difference between the two is that the latter computation includes a deduction for policy dividends. In 1991, the industry reported a net underwriting loss, using statutory accounting rules, in excess of $19 billion. This poor showing was another in a series of underwriting losses dating from the late 1970s. Nonetheless, it represented a slight improvement (although not a consistent one) in underwriting results since 1985, the worst year ever for the P/L industry.

Insurers can and do use investment income to supplement underwriting results. Figure 24.5 shows that investment and underwriting income have usually moved in different directions during the past two decades. Despite the large increase in investment income, combined earnings before taxes declined steadily from 1975 through 1985, as shown in Figure 24.5. Toward the end of the 1980s, combined income again became positive, as underwriting results were somewhat more favorable and investment income continued

to flourish. Reasons for these trends are discussed in more detail in the next section.[37]

CHANGES IN THE P/L INDUSTRY: CAUSES AND RESULTS

The decline in the underwriting fortunes of P/L firms in the 1980s resulted from a coincidence of usual events in the industry and unusual social and economic developments.

---

[37] Ideally, underwriting results reported under GAAP would be the basis of comparison. Unfortunately, there are virtually no data to permit such an analysis because many large P/L firms are mutually owned and report only on a statutory basis. Statutory profits are often lower than they would be if reported on a GAAP basis, so the pattern in Figure 24.5 may exaggerate the financial plight of the industry in the 1980s. Nevertheless, the downward trend would doubtless remain even under GAAP.

FIGURE 24.5   **P/L Income, 1965–1991**

Since the late 1970s, P/L insurers have not earned a profit on underwriting. Investment income has allowed the industry to report positive combined income, however. The cyclical nature of P/L underwriting results is also evident.

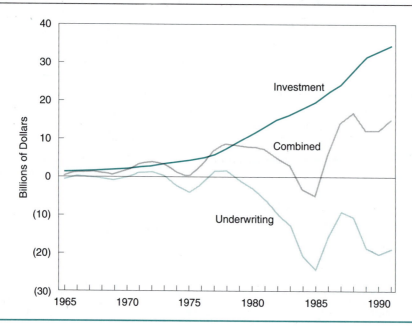

Source: Insurance Information Institute, *1993 Property/Casualty Insurance Facts.*

THE UNDERWRITING CYCLE

The P/L business has always been subject to the **underwriting cycle,** which is characterized by two subperiods known as a soft market and a hard market. In the soft portion of the cycle, premiums are lowered and insurance coverage is amply available. During the hard market, insurers raise premiums and some customers may have difficulty obtaining coverage.

In a soft market, because premiums received are invested in financial assets, increases in the general level of interest rates may give insurers an incentive to write more policies to increase investment income. Frequently, the desire to increase premium income to increase investment income results in price wars in which one company undercuts premiums charged by competitors.[38] If rate wars continue long enough, premium income may be insufficient to cover underwriting expenses and policy claims during the year, resulting in a net underwriting loss.

When insurers raise rates to compensate for the losses, they encounter resistance from customers who like the lower rates, and this resistance postpones insurers' financial recovery. As customers balk against rate increases, insurers say the market turns "hard." If interest rates have fallen, investment income may not make up for continued underwriting losses. Eventually, however, the cycle turns back up as the balance between premium and investment income is restored and the industry regains profitability.

Research examining cycles suggests they occur approximately every 6 years, persist after controlling for changes in interest rates, and differ across lines of insurance.[39] In the mid-1980s, for example, the hard

---

[38] The reduction in premiums as interest rates increase is consistent with the time value of money. As interest rates rise, the higher discount rate reduces the present value of future claims.

[39] See Fields and Venezian 1989.

portion of the cycle was particularly severe for commercial liability coverages—a period that has come to be known as the liability coverage crisis.

Some observers argue that regulators also play a role in perpetuating the underwriting cycle. When insurers are reporting adequate profits, regulators tend to resist approving insurers' requests for rate increases. As costs rise, insurers respond by reducing the quantity of insurance offered at the regulated prices. Eventually, the scarcity of insurance coverage convinces regulators to ease their rate restrictions, policy premiums and underwriting income rise, and the cycle begins anew.[40]

Other factors have also been examined for their role in the underwriting cycle, such as an unanticipated decline in interest rates, which increases the present value of expected future claims, or an unanticipated increase in claims costs. When insurers raise premiums to compensate for these higher costs, they may encounter regulatory scrutiny or extensive public pressure, such as that discussed in the following sections.[41]

The cyclical nature of underwriting losses is seen in Figure 24.5. Underwriting profits turned to losses in the late 1960s, the mid-1970s, and again in the 1980s, all periods of historically high interest rates. In the 1980s, however, the underwriting cycle was accompanied by unprecedented social, economic, and regulatory forces, making recovery from the down part of the cycle more difficult than before.

SOCIAL AND ECONOMIC FORCES

Since the 1960s, Americans have been increasingly prone to sue one another, and courts have awarded large amounts to successful plaintiffs. Escalating malpractice awards against physicians and the growing volume of product liability suits against manufacturers have received considerable publicity as examples of these social trends.[42]

Not only did defendants in these cases feel the effects, so did insurance companies. Premiums collected for insurance protection grossly understated required cash outflows when claims were made. To protect itself, the P/L industry often turns to **reinsurers**—insurance companies for insurance companies. Reinsurers agree, in exchange for a share of premium income, to assume responsibility for claims on policies written by other companies.

Figure 24.6 clarifies the role of reinsurance in the insurance markets. When customers transfer risk to an insurance company, they are participating in the primary market for insurance. This transaction usually takes place with the help of an agent or a broker but may be direct with the company. The company can then pass part of the risk assumed to another insurer through reinsurance.

Figure 24.6 also demonstrates that reinsurance can be used by the **captive insurer market.** A captive insurer is one formed by a business firm to provide its own insurance coverage.

In the 1980s, damage awards resulting from products such as Agent Orange and asbestos took a toll on even reinsurers' capacity to function profitably.[43] At the same time, accelerating inflation affected claims on many lines of insurance. Escalating costs of claims required insurers to increase premium income, investment income, or both. Difficulties were compounded by cost increases occurring during the downside of an underwriting cycle, a circumstance facing the industry in the mid-1980s. Adding to the challenge were increases in competition, such as that from depositories, which further inhibited premium increases to compensate for losses.

INSURERS RESPOND. In 1985 and 1986, P/L companies and reinsurers responded to severe losses in key lines of insurance either by raising premiums so high that many customers could no longer afford them or by declining to sell some lines of insurance altogether. The industry changed major features of some liability

[40] See Sean Mooney, "How Insurance Cycles Work," *Insurance Review* 51 (January 1990): 31–32.

[41] Cummins, Harrington, and Klein 1991 examine cycles and crises in P/L insurance markets, reviewing two possible explanations for market volatility: excessive price cutting by insurers, and external pressures to industry capital.

[42] Statistics on the number of lawsuits, and the damages awarded as a result, are found in *1993 Property/Casualty Insurance Facts.* Other discussion is provided in Marlys Harris, "Crisis in the

Courts," *Insurance Review* 47 (April 1986): 52–57; and Thomas S. Healey, "Insurers under Siege," *Insurance Review* 47 (May 1986): 50–57.

[43] Now Even Insurers Have a Hard Time Getting Coverage," *Business Week,* December 2, 1985, 128–129; and David B. Hilder, "Uncollectable Reinsurance Hurts Firms," *The Wall Street Journal,* April 1, 1986, 6.

FIGURE 24.6   **Reinsurance and the Insurance Markets**

After customers transfer risk to insurance firms, insurers may pass along part of that risk to other insurance firms, known as reinsurers.

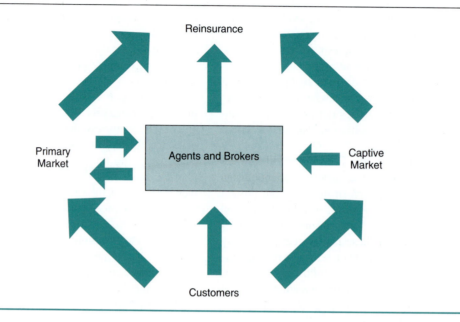

---

policies to protect itself against the so-called **long tail of liability,** under which insurers were forced to pay millions of dollars for claims arising from injuries that occurred decades earlier.

As a result of these developments, many public school systems, charitable organizations, and municipal governments with stable or declining revenue bases found liability insurance unaffordable. Some physicians in high-risk specialties, such as obstetrics, were forced to discontinue practice. Emergency rooms in some communities closed because hospitals could no longer pay for liability insurance. Several companies, unable to get product liability insurance, declined to bring new products to market. Many observers argued that insurers' actions were not in the public interest, because risk protection at affordable prices seemed to be a vanishing commodity.[44] As discussed in more

detail in the next section, insurers argued that higher premiums and more restrictive policies were necessary in view of the unprecedented cost of claims in the 1980s. Not surprisingly, however, customers and regulators were outraged, leading to major calls for reforms of the P/L industry and, in some instances, to outright customer revolt.

P/L INSURERS AND THE REGULATORY DIALECTIC

Few industries can succeed when on a collision course with their customers. When an industry is also regulated, politicians inevitably become involved, and it is even more unlikely that the industry can control its own destiny. As the regulatory dialectic predicts, anti-

---

[44]Because these developments affected so many individuals and businesses, many reports of them are found in the popular and industry press throughout the mid- to late 1980s. Representative accounts include "Business Struggles to Adapt as Insurance Crisis

Spreads," *The Wall Street Journal,* January 21, 1986, 37; Harry Bacas, "Liability: Trying Times," *Nation's Business* 74 (February 1986): 22–27; Welles and Farrell 1989; and articles in most issues of *Best's Review* (Property/Casualty Edition).

thetical actions eventually lead to new regulations. Such appeared to be the fate of P/L insurers as the last decade of the twentieth century began.

McCARRAN-FERGUSON REVISITED: TIME FOR A CHANGE?

Although the McCarran-Ferguson Act of 1945 permitted insurance supervision to be housed at the state level and exempted the insurance industry from federal antitrust laws, Congress left open the possibility of federal regulation. Under the law, federal regulation becomes appropriate 1) when states fail to exercise their regulatory authority diligently or 2) when the industry itself engages in "boycott, coercion, or intimidation." Amidst the so-called insurance crisis of the 1980s, advocates of federal regulation of the insurance industry believed both circumstances prevailed.

According to some observers, including many consumer-advocate groups, skyrocketing insurance premiums and reduced or eliminated coverage are *prima facie* evidence that state regulators were not doing their jobs properly in the 1980s. Because these developments were clearly not in the public interest, these observers argue that the federal government has a right—indeed, an obligation—to assume regulatory control of an industry run amuck. Furthermore, some industry opponents believe that the industry itself colluded to refuse to offer certain types of coverage. For example, according to officials in the Colorado Attorney General's Office, when that state attempted to purchase liability insurance in 1987, not one of 26 major firms was willing to offer a policy at any price—viewed by some as a clear example of industry boycott, an activity prohibited under McCarran-Ferguson.[45]

Events and arguments such as these have led to several as-yet unsuccessful attempts in the U.S. Congress to repeal or substantially modify McCarran-Ferguson to restore regulatory power to federal authorities and to bring the industry under antitrust rules. The latter change, in particular, would have major ramifications for the industry. McCarran-Ferguson's antitrust protection permits insurers to share information about losses so that actuaries can better estimate future costs. Industry opponents believe that the antitrust exemption simply makes it easy for insurers to collude to fix prices; insurers argue, however, that without access to shared data, small insurers could not survive, because they could not afford to collect the necessary information on their own. Thus, the industry is adamantly opposed to federal regulation and has pointed to the thrift crisis as evidence that federally regulated institutions do not always succeed.[46] State regulators, who would also stand to lose under the proposed changes in McCarran-Ferguson, have become proponents of stronger self-regulation and more effective state oversight as a better alternative to another federal bureaucracy.

CUSTOMERS REVOLT: CALIFORNIA'S PROPOSITION 103

By late 1988, voters in California were becoming increasingly impatient with the pace of insurance reform at the federal level. Accordingly, they took matters into their own hands, passing Proposition 103, a citizen referendum mandating sweeping changes in the state's P/L insurance rules. Among its most important provisions were 1) a 20 percent rate cut in automobile insurance for all drivers, with an additional 20 percent cut for "good" drivers; 2) permission for banks domiciled in California to sell insurance; 3) prohibition against insurers' charging automobile premiums based on the residence of the driver; 4) repeal of insurers' protection against state antitrust laws; and

---

[45] Several studies have examined these allegations of collusion and have not found support for that explanation of the crisis. See Clark et al. 1988. Still, a suit filed against four large insurers by the Attorneys General of 19 states was cleared by the U.S. Supreme Court in June 1993, paving the way for a heated court battle on whether "boycott, coercion, or intimidation" occurred during the late 1980s. See Paul M. Barrett, "Antitrust Suit Against Big U.S. Insurers Wins Clearance from Supreme Court," *The Wall Street Journal,* June 29, 1993, A3.

[46] These issues are discussed in Peter Waldman, "Insurers, Long Free of Antitrust Curbs, Face Rising Challenges," *The Wall Street Journal,* July 8, 1988, 1, 6; and "Open Season on an Old Law," 1987. The Colorado example was reported by Charles Howe, Deputy Attorney General, in a speech at the annual meeting of the American Risk and Insurance Association, Denver, Colorado, August 21, 1989.

5) popular election of the state's insurance commissioner.[47]

Proposition 103's passage stunned the P/L industry, which had spent *$70 million* in pre-election advertising to defeat it. Similar voter initiatives soon arose in other states. Although several large insurers challenged the constitutionality of the referendum, the California Supreme Court upheld it in the spring of 1989, and its provisions began to take effect toward the end of that year. Although it is too early to ascertain long-term effects, many experts note that California drivers may be surprised at some of Proposition 103's outcomes. For example, some P/L insurers have announced that they will no longer operate in California—the ultimate regulatory avoidance behavior. If residence is not a factor in automobile insurance prices, rural drivers may find their premiums increasing substantially as they subsidize drivers in Los Angeles, San Francisco, and San Diego. If insurers are not allowed to share data, premiums may not adequately reflect the risk exposure of insurers or their customers.

Nonetheless, Proposition 103 dramatically illustrated the depth of public feeling against P/L insurers. Although the industry's reputation had been deteriorating for years, Proposition 103 demonstrated that insurers could no longer ignore public perceptions. As a result, by 1990, industry leaders and professional organizations began to respond to critics.

IS THE INDUSTRY ALWAYS THE VILLAIN?

Even before Proposition 103 caused P/L insurers to rethink approaches to the problems of the 1980s, the industry started to address factors that it argued had led to the insurance crisis. In particular, insurers began to actively promote key changes in the way liability suits are handled. Taking advantage of the fact that opinion polls showed trial lawyers to be the only group more despised by the public than insurers, the industry embarked on a campaign of **tort reform** across the na-

tion.[48] Tort laws are those defining how incidents of negligence and legal liability between citizens or between citizens and organizations are to be handled. Tort laws are established in each state; they govern the bases on which tort suits can be brought and the methods by which damages may be awarded, including what factors can be considered by juries in making awards. Since 1986, dozens of states have enacted changes in their tort laws, some more sweeping than others. Insurers also promoted other ways of reducing the costs of legal liability, including binding arbitration between plaintiff and defendant outside of court and reduction of the percentage of damages a plaintiff's attorney may receive in a successful suit.

In addition, P/L insurers have begun to publicize the skill and sensitivity with which many companies perform their services in times of trouble. In 1989, for example, insurers played a major role in assisting citizens after both Hurricane Hugo in South Carolina and a major earthquake in the San Francisco-Oakland area. Insurers were also praised for their handling of three major disasters in 1992—the Los Angeles riots and Hurricanes Andrew and Iniki.

Insurers have also developed new coverage and purchasing techniques, including **risk retention groups** and **purchasing groups.** Risk retention groups are entities with similar exposures who agree to pool and share each other's losses. Purchasing groups transfer risk to commercial insurers but negotiate coverage as a group to gain bargaining power.[49] Insurers have also begun offering a **claims-made** form of liability insurance to escape the long tail of liabilities. A claims-made policy covers only loss claims *filed* during the policy period but does not cover all loss occurrences during the period if claims are delayed. Claims-made policies make it more difficult for a policyholder insured in, say, 1995, to file a claim in 1999 for an injury that occurred in 1995. Presumably, insurers are then better able to predict cash obligations they may incur at the time they decide to issue a policy.

Some insurers have also begun to win praise for the skill and sophistication of their financial manage-

---

[47] Steve Waldman, Jennifer Foote, and Elisa Williams, "The Prop 103 'Prairie Fire,'" *Business Week,* May 15, 1989, 50–51; and "Proposition 103" and "Antitrust Issues," *1990 Property/Casualty Insurance Facts,* 7–9.

[48] "Battle for the Cellar," *The Wall Street Journal,* August 28, 1988; and Peter Brimelow and Leslie Spencer, "The Plaintiff Attorneys' Great Honey Rush," *Forbes,* October 16, 1989, 197–203.

[49] Purchasing groups and risk retention groups were permitted by the Risk Retention Act of 1986.

ment, instilling public confidence in the industry again. In 1992, Hurricane Andrew left insurers with claims of more than $10 billion, making it the costliest tropical storm in history. The Florida hurricane, however, did not appear to detract substantially from the financial stability of the industry as a whole. Several insurers have even considered suing home builders in the region, alleging that losses were higher because the insured homes did not meet building code standards.[50]

The industry's troubles are far from over. However, there is some hope that the wounds between the industry and its customers can be healed as the antithesis and synthesis stages of the regulatory dialectic move through the 1990s.

P/L INSURERS: TECHNIQUES FOR INTEGRATED ASSET/ LIABILITY MANAGEMENT

Increasingly, the use of asset/liability management tools such as duration, futures, and options are mentioned as the keys to effective financial management in the new environment.

For example, industry publications stress the importance of estimating a firm's anticipated cash outflows resulting from policy claims, many of which may not actually occur until months or even years after a policy is written. If estimates are carefully made, asset portfolios can be selected with cash inflows to match the anticipated series of outflows. Thus, insurers can attempt to immunize at least portions of the balance sheet.[51] This strategy is quite a contrast to traditional management approaches, which use a lump sum estimate of claims based on past experience and then select asset portfolios to maximize investment income as a supplement to premium income.

Interest rate or stock index futures and options are potential hedges against changes in the value of bond or stock portfolios. Also, the risk associated with unexpected losses may become more manageable as a result of the introduction of catastrophe futures contracts by the Chicago Board of Trade in 1992.[52] The usual cautions involved in futures and options trading apply to insurers. In addition, the NAIC requires that gains and losses on futures positions be directly reflected in additions or reductions of net worth, rather than being amortized over time. Still, in an environment of rising rates, profitable hedges can protect insurers against the shrinkage of net worth caused by a decline in portfolio values, which also must be directly written off against net worth. The emphasis on duration, interest rate futures, and options underscores the similarity of the principles of interest rate risk management and asset/liability management among financial institutions.

PERFORMANCE EVALUATION OF INSURANCE COMPANIES

Never has there been greater interest in evaluating the financial performance of individual life and P/L insurance companies. Managers, financial analysts, regulators, investors, and even policyholders are concerned with underwriting margins, operating costs, and investment portfolio earnings. This increased attention to the performance of insurance firms has arisen for several reasons. One, mentioned earlier, is the new trend in consumer groups who watch insurers' performance to determine whether premiums charged are excessive.

Equally important motivations for more closely scrutinizing insurers are the narrowing profit margins in many sectors of the industry and an alarming rise in

---

[50] An insurer's right to sue a third party is the right of **subrogation.** Subrogation rights accrue to the insurer as part of the insurance contract. For discussion of claims costs and other results of Hurricane Andrew, see Brian Cox, "Florida Insurers May File Andrew Suits," *National Underwriter, Property/Casualty,* October 26, 1992, 1; and Sara Marley and Michael Bradford, "Andrew Losses Estimated at $10.7 Billion," *Business Insurance,* October 26, 1992, 1.

[51] See Jeffrey B. Pantages, "Negating the Interest Rate Risk," *Best's Review* (Property/Casualty Edition) 85 (May 1984): 24–28, 120.

[52] See Niehaus and Mann 1992; Charles P. Edmonds, John S. Jahera, Jr., and Terry Rose, "Hedging the Future," *Best's Review* (Property/ Casualty Edition) 84 (September 1983): 30–32, 118; and Nye and Kolb 1986. For further descriptions of the catastrophe futures contracts, see Cox and Schwebach 1992; D'Arcy and France 1992; Judy Greenwald, "Alternatives to Traditional Cat Coverage," *Business Insurance,* November 7, 1992, 1; and Jonathan F. Lewis, "Trading in Disaster: Catastrophe Contracts Are Slated for CBOE," *Barron's,* November 30, 1992, 19–22.

insolvencies among insurance firms beginning in the late 1980s. Among life insurers, the average number of insolvencies between 1969 and 1983 was one per year. Since 1987, however, an average of 25 companies have failed each year. Historically, most of the failed firms were rather small, but in 1991, six of the failing companies had combined assets of more than $40 billion. In the P/L industry, an average of 33 firms failed each year between 1985 and 1990, up from an average of ten per year in the 1970s. The record for number of failures in a single year was set in 1985, when 52 P/L insolvencies were reported, and that number was matched again in 1989. The failures have led to demands for more effective monitoring of financial performance of life/health and P/L companies by state insurance departments, as well as for more uniform examination and regulation across states.[53]

THE COMBINED RATIO

Because of the unique nature of insurer liabilities, no accurate measure of underwriting profits or losses exists. Nevertheless, P/L analysts have developed measures approximating the separate aspects of underwriting operations: claims losses and ordinary operating expenses. One widely used measure examines claims losses relative to earned premiums:

$$\text{Loss Ratio} = \frac{\text{Loss Expenses}}{\text{Total Earned Premiums}} \qquad [24.5]$$

Another widely used measure is the expense ratio, calculated as

$$\text{Expense Ratio} = \frac{\text{Operating Expenses}}{\text{Total Premiums Written}} \qquad [24.6]$$

A third ratio closely followed for the P/L industry is the **combined ratio,** which is the *sum* of the loss and expense ratios and which is intended to measure

the total relationship between premium income and premium expenses:

$$\text{Combined Ratio} = \text{Loss Ratio} + \text{Expense Ratio} \qquad [24.7]$$

Managers and analysts must be familiar with this performance measure because it is so widely cited. However, it is subject to interpretation problems because, as shown in Equations 24.5 and 24.6, the premiums used in the denominators of the loss ratio and the expense ratio are different. This difficulty increases as the difference between premiums written and premiums earned becomes greater, a difference magnified during times of rapidly increasing policy sales. The use of the combined ratio is justified, though, by the fact that losses incurred are related to premiums earned during the period, whereas operating expenses, most of which are agents' commissions, are related to premiums written during the same period.

COMBINED RATIO ILLUSTRATED. Data in Table 24.6 are used in the following illustration of the combined ratio for the industry in 1991:

$$\text{Loss Ratio} = \frac{\text{Loss Expenses}}{\text{Total Earned Premiums}}$$

$$= \frac{\$180.210}{\$222.151} = 0.811$$

$$\text{Expense Ratio} = \frac{\text{Operating Expenses}}{\text{Total Premiums Written}}$$

$$= \frac{\$59.129}{\$222.991} = 0.265$$

$$\text{Combined Ratio} = 0.811 + 0.265 = 1.076$$

$$= 107.6\%$$

This figure is usually interpreted to mean that underwriting expenses exceeded underwriting income by more than 7 percent. A combined ratio of less than 1 indicates an underwriting profit. Although this illustration uses industry-wide data, it is important for analysts to remember that the combined ratio differs across various lines of insurance. To evaluate the performance of an individual firm, its combined ratio

---

[53] Brewer, Mondschean, and Strahan 1993; Harrington 1992; John H. Snyder, "The Year of the Cats," *Best's Review,* February 1993, 14–20, 84–89; Washburn and Schacht 1989; and Welles and Farrell 1989.

must be compared with those of firms writing similar lines of insurance.

NET UNDERWRITING MARGIN AS A PERFORMANCE MEASURE

The net underwriting margin (Equation 24.3) examines both premium and expense data as a percentage of assets. It is a different way of measuring underwriting results. Because P/L insurers report expenses on a cash basis, the use of total premiums written may be the best choice in the ratio if it is available.

The net underwriting margin indicates the extent to which underwriting gains or losses contribute to overall profitability, and it can be used for both life insurers and P/L insurers, although only a calculation for P/L insurers is shown here. Using data from Tables 24.5 and 24.6, the net underwriting margin for the P/L industry as a whole in 1991 was

$$\text{Net Underwriting Margin} = \frac{\text{Premium Income} - \text{Policy Expenses}}{\text{Total Assets}}$$

$$\frac{\$222.991 - \$242.121}{\$601.445} = -0.032 = -3.2\%$$

In the P/L industry in 1991, for each dollar of admitted assets, 3 cents were lost. Net investment income of $34.247 billion was available to offset some of the shortfall. Because underwriting accounts for the vast majority of insurers' cash inflows and outflows, individual firms are unlikely to meet targets for ROA and RONW unless they carefully watch the margin between premium income and policy expenses. In recent years, this has meant reducing operating expenses, especially commissions, and pricing insurance to better reflect the financial risk the insurer assumes rather than engaging in rate wars to increase market share. Insurers will continue to emphasize cost management and proper pricing of risks.

INSURANCE REGULATORY INFORMATION SYSTEM RATIOS

Measures for evaluating the financial performance of life and P/L insurers have been developed by the NAIC in the Insurance Regulatory Information System, better known as IRIS. The system was designed to detect firms in financial difficulty, and it uses a number of ratio tests to identify problem firms.[54]

Representative examples of the IRIS measures for the P/L industry are shown in the top panel of Table 24.7, and those for life insurers are shown in the bottom panel. Note that the ratios focus not only on the financial position reported for a given year but also on changes from previous years in such variables as surplus, premiums written, or product mix. These ratios provide another set of guidelines for analysts evaluating the performance of insurance firms.

SOURCES OF INDUSTRY INFORMATION

A problem faced by insurance industry analysts is the shortage of performance standards against which to compare individual firms. Aggregate industry data are available in the annual *Fact Books* for both life and P/L insurers, cited throughout this chapter, but the information sheds little light on the performance of individual companies or subgroups. Because conditions in different lines of insurance may differ markedly, aggregate comparison information may mislead the analyst of a particular insurer.

A. M. BEST PUBLICATIONS. The A. M. Best Company of Oldwick, New Jersey, publishes *Best's Aggregates and Averages,* a compilation of statistical information on P/L insurers, with breakdowns by line of insurance. Emphasis in these reports, and in periodic issues of *Best's Review* (a monthly trade publication with editions for both life and P/L insurers), is on larger insurers.

Best also publishes *Best's Insurance Reports* annually for both life and P/L companies. These large volumes present condensed balance sheets and income statements for all active insurers, along with Best's own rating of a firm's financial condition. Best's ratings are based on analysis of liquidity, profitability,

---

[54] A recent study concluded that IRIS ratios are accurate predictors of life insurance company insolvency when used in multivariate models. The ratios were not especially good predictors when used individually. See BarNiv and Hershbarger 1990.

TABLE 24.7   Selected Insurance Regulatory Information System Ratios

The National Association of Insurance Commissioners developed the IRIS system for evaluating the performance of life and P/L insurers. These measures provide useful guidelines for industry analysts.

Property/Liability Insurers
1. Total Earned Premiums/Surplus
2. Change in Total Premiums Written/Total Earned Premiums in Prior Year
3. Net Investment Income/Average Invested Assets
4. Change in Surplus/Surplus
5. Liabilities/Liquid Assets

Life Insurers
1. Additions to Surplus
2. Net Income/Total Revenues
3. Commissions/Premium Payments
4. Real Estate Investments/Total Assets
5. Change in Premium Payments
6. Change in Asset Mix
7. Change in Product Mix

Source: Adapted from C. Arthur Williams and Richard M. Heins, *Risk Management and Insurance* (New York: McGraw-Hill, 1989), 617–618.

---

and leverage ratios and on information such as policy volume and cancellations. These ratings have been considered authoritative by investors and industry observers for many years. Rating methods were revised in 1986 in the wake of increasing criticism that they were not sufficiently sensitive to changing financial conditions in a firm. Studies comparing the effectiveness of Best's ratings and financial ratios for predicting insolvency of P/L insurers concluded that Best's evaluations were valid indicators of the financial status of insurers.[55]

Because of the difficulty in obtaining averages reflecting comparable groups of firms, it is helpful to prepare comparative analyses for several similar insurers rather than to rely solely on available sources of industry information. The data required for such analyses are available in Best publications.

SUMMARY

Insurance companies are founded on probability estimation, better known to insurers as actuarial science. Premiums and reported obligations are based on esti-

mates of the amount and timing of claims a firm will pay in the future. Successful financial management involves balancing premium income and investment income against benefits paid to policyholders. Life and P/L insurers have different financial characteristics, arising from the types of policies they write. They have structural characteristics in common, however, and all experienced earnings pressures in the past decade.

Life insurers have traditionally enjoyed predictable cash flows, thanks to the popularity of whole life insurance. Higher interest rates and changing consumer preferences, however, have forced insurers to develop alternative products, making premium income and obligations to policyholders subject to market conditions and policyholder preferences. Changes in operating conditions have made asset/liability management strategies increasingly important for life insurers.

P/L insurers have faced a similar need to adapt management strategies to changing market and economic conditions, although incentives for change are different. In recent years, the main influences on earnings of P/L insurers have been inflation, larger litigation awards, and consumer pressure for lower premiums. These factors, along with the traditional underwriting cycle, depressed underwriting income so strongly in the 1980s that even rapidly rising investment income could not protect earnings. As with life

---

[55] See Ambrose and Seward 1988; Snyder 1986; and Dannen 1985.

insurers, these operating changes require P/L insurers to adjust asset/liability management strategies.

QUESTIONS

1. Review Figure 24.1. Explain how the individual, by purchasing insurance, can actually achieve a higher level of utility despite the fact that wealth initially declines by P, the amount of the insurance premium. If the individual were not risk averse, would this model of utility be appropriate? Why?

2. Why does a corporation's purchase of insurance potentially reduce shareholder wealth? Why do firms carry insurance despite this effect?

3. Explain in your own words the law of large numbers.

4. Compare and contrast the characteristics of insurance coverage offered by life and P/L insurers. Explain how these characteristics are reflected in the asset and liability choices of the two types of insurers.

5. Compare the assets and liabilities of both life insurers and P/L insurers to those of depository institutions. How do services offered and funds sources result in balance sheet differences across the three industries?

6. How is the insurance industry regulated? How does the structure of insurance regulation compare to that of depository institution regulation? Which approach do you consider more efficient and effective? Why?

7. What are policy reserves? How is the amount of policy reserves on a life insurer's balance sheet related to the law of large numbers? To the estimates of actuaries? To the estimates of premium and investment income?

8. What are the two major revenue sources for life insurers? Explain how actuarial estimates and anticipated investment income affect the level of premiums insurers set.

9. Explain how the net underwriting margin differs from the net interest margin. How similar a role do the two ratios play in financial management decisions? Explain.

10. Compare and contrast the major types of life insurance policies. If you were managing a life insurance firm, which type would you prefer to offer? If you were the customer, what policy characteristics would you prefer to purchase? Why? How have new types of policies changed insurers' focus on asset/liability management?

11. What factors influence life insurance policy premiums? What major assumptions must insurers make to establish

premiums? As expected future rates of return on insurers' investments increase, what is the effect on life insurance premiums?

12. What are separate asset accounts? Why do some insurance managers view these assets as good candidates for immunization? What are the advantages and disadvantages of immunizing these accounts?

13. Using your library resources, find current information on the status of risk-based capital regulations for the life insurance industry. Are they being adopted by the states? If so, explain how similar they are to the NAIC's proposed standards. Compare and contrast the risks assessed for life insurance firms to those evaluated in bank capital standards.

14. In what situations might it be appropriate for life insurers to use financial futures and options? Are these situations similar to or different from those in which depositories would be likely to use futures and options? Explain.

Explain the basic differences between statutory accounting and generally accepted accounting principles. Are the purposes of statutory accounting the same as, or different from, the regulatory accounting principles used in the thrift industry in the 1980s? Do you agree that regulators' and professional accountants' reporting standards should differ? Why or why not?

16. What is the underwriting cycle in the property/liability insurance industry? How do interest rates and regulatory policies influence the cycle? Explain the forces since the mid-1980s that have joined with the underwriting cycle to cause severe problems for P/L insurers.

17. Find recent articles about interest rates and policy premiums for P/L insurance, and identify whether the industry is currently in the up or down phase of the underwriting cycle.

18. What is the function of reinsurers? Do organizations 'th similar functions exist for depositories? Explain.

19. Summarize the views of those who favor a repeal or modification of McCarran-Ferguson. What arguments do those who favor the current regulatory system offer in return? What is your opinion on this issue? What is the current status of the collusion charges filed by several states' Attorneys General?

20. Do you believe that it is appropriate for insurance premiums to be influenced by popular vote, as in the case of California's Proposition 103? Explain. Should demographic data such as age, sex, and place of residence influence insurance premiums? Why or why not?

21. What is the long tail of liability? How has it affected the

financial performance of P/L insurers? Explain how a claims-made form of liability insurance affects insurers' loss exposure.

22. Using recent publications, describe the current status of the catastrophe futures contracts introduced in Chicago in 1992. Explain the characteristics of these contracts and the potential benefit to financial management of P/L firms.

23. What problems do analysts encounter in assessing the performance of insurers through trend analysis and comparison to industry standards? How are these problems different from those encountered in performance analysis of other financial institutions? Of nonfinancial firms?

24. What types of data, other than those from the balance sheet and income statement, do the IRIS ratios employ?

25. As noted in the chapter, to solve the insurance "crisis,"

laws in some states place limits on damage awards to which plaintiffs are entitled in civil suits. From recent publications, find information on the current status of tort reform, particularly in your state. Do you agree that awards should be limited? Why or why not?

26. What are the potential problems with placing regulatory ceilings on liability insurance premiums? The potential benefits? What types of solutions to the problem might you offer to your legislative representatives? Do you believe that everyone has a right to be insured at an affordable cost? Why or why not?

27. As noted in Chapter 16, some proponents of reform favor transferring the deposit insurance system to the private sector. Do you think the P/L industry is equipped to serve as the primary insurer of deposits? Why or why not?

PROBLEMS

1. Suppose an actuary wishes to estimate the mean number and variability of losses that will occur among a group of 1,000 policyholders, each of whom faces a 4 percent probability of loss. Assume a binomial distribution: There are only two possibilities for each person (loss or no loss) and the probability of loss is the same for each person.
- **a.** Calculate the mean number of losses, the standard deviation of losses, and the coefficient of variation of losses for the group.
- **b.** Using the "what-if" feature of your spreadsheet program, show how the law of large numbers works as the number of group members varies from 1,000 to 20,000 in 1,000-person increments. That is, calculate the mean number, standard deviation, and coefficient of variation of losses for groups ranging in size from 1,000 to 20,000, given that each person faces a 4 percent probability of loss. Interpret your results.
- **c.** Does a given individual in a group of 20,000 have a better idea of whether *she personally* will experience a loss than a given individual in a group of 1,000? Explain.

2. Use information from the Commissioners Standard Ordinary Table abbreviated in Table 24.4, as well as an assumed rate of return on invested premiums of 6 percent, to answer the following questions.
- **a.** What is the probability that a policyholder who is 39 years old will live to be 40?
- **b.** What is the pure premium on a $75,000, 1-year term policy for a 39-year-old man? Show two ways to calculate it.
- **c.** If the assumed rate of return on invested premiums were 9 percent, what would the pure premium be for the policy described in part b?
- **d.** Using "what if" analysis, show how the pure premium would vary as the assumed investment rate varied between 0 percent and 20 percent. Based on this analysis, explain how life insurers' use of conservative investment estimates affects their premium income.
- **e.** If, instead, the policyholder wished to take out a *whole life* policy with a face amount of $75,000, identify the additional steps taken to calculate the premium. (No calculations are necessary, but consult the appendix to this chapter for information.) Would the first year's premium on the whole life policy be higher or lower than the premium you calculated in part b? Why?

3. **a.** Using information from the Commissioners Standard Ordinary Table abbreviated in Table 24.4 and an assumed rate of return on invested premiums of 8 percent, calculate the pure premium on a $1 million, 1-year term policy for a 4-year-old boy. If you were the parent of a 4-year-old boy, what factors might influence you to take out a life insurance policy on him? What type of policy would you prefer? Why?
- **b.** Calculate the premium on a $1 million, 1-year term policy for a 70-year-old man. If you were 70 and had no life insurance, what type of policy, if any, would you choose? Why?

4. Based on the data given on Granite Life Insurance Company, answer the following questions.

   a. Using common-size statements, compare Granite's financial condition in 19X4 and 19X5 to that of the industry as a whole, shown in Table 24.1. What similarities and differences in asset/liability structure do you find between Granite and the industry? What effects are these differences likely to have on profitability and solvency?

   b. What trends, if any, appear in Granite's profitability over the two years? In your analysis, be sure to consider the net underwriting margin, ROA, and RONW. (Hint: Use the Dupont ratios, explained in Chapter 22, to assess trends in ROA and RONW.) Compare Granite to industry data in Table 24.2, commenting on similarities and differences.

   c. What additional data on Granite might you wish to have to better assess the company's financial condition? Why?

PROBLEM 24.4   **Granite Life Insurance Company Assets and Obligations, Year-End 19X4 and 19X5 (Millions)**

	19X4		19X5	
Assets				
Government securities		$ 1,677		$ 3,741
Corporate securities		12,510		17,051
Bonds	$11,216		$13,836	
Stock	1,294		3,215	
Real estate loans		10,989		12,411
Real estate investments		971		1,678
Loans to policyholders		1,322		1,953
Other assets		1,665		2,475
Total assets		$29,134		$39,309
Obligations and Net Worth				
Policy reserves	$24,622		$33,534	
Policy dividend obligations	595		781	
Other obligations	1,898		2,907	
Total obligations		$27,115		$37,222
Total net worth (surplus and common stock)		2,019		2,087
Total obligations and net worth		$29,134		$39,309

PROBLEM 24.4   **Granite Life Insurance Company Income and Expenses for 19X4 and 19X5 (Millions)**

	19X4		19X5	
Revenues				
Premium payments	$3,930		$5,760	
Net investment earnings and other income	1,693		2,924	
Total revenues		$5,623		$8,684
Expenses				
Benefit payments	$3,091		$4,666	
Additions to policy reserves	1,258		2,109	
Operating expenses	703		1,443	
Total expenses		5,052		8,218
Net operating income		$ 541		$ 466
Taxes		126		189
Net income		$ 445		$ 277

5. Based on the data for Town and Country Mutual Automobile Insurance Company, answer the following questions:

a. Using common-size analysis, compare Town and Country's financial condition in 19X4 and 19X5 to that of the industry as a whole, shown in Table 24.5. What similarities and differences in asset/liability structure do you find between Town and Country and the industry?

b. What major differences do you find between Town and Country's 19X4 and 19X5 operating results? To what do you believe the differences can be attributed? In your analysis, be sure to consider the net underwriting margin, ROA, RONW, and the combined ratio. (Suggestion: Calculate ROA and RONW on a pretax basis.)

c. How does the firm's combined ratio in 19X5 compare to that for the industry as calculated in the chapter? What could account for any difference you find?

d. What additional information on Town and Country would you like to have to complete your analysis? Why?

PROBLEM 24.5 **Town and Country Mutual Automobile Insurance Company, Assets and Obligations, Year-End 19X4 and 19X5 (Millions)**

	19X4		19X5	
Assets				
Bonds		$ 8,109		$ 9,165
U.S. Treasury	$1,169		$1,106	
State and local	2,779		3,505	
Special revenue	4,097		4,497	
Other	64		57	
Common and preferred stock		3,192		3,260
Mortgages and other loans		2,422		2,501
Other assets		1,652		1,745
Total assets		$15,375		$16,671
Liabilities and Net Worth				
Total loss and unearned premium reserves		$ 7,185		$ 7,879
Total surplus (net worth)		8,190		8,792
Total liabilities and net worth		$15,375		$16,671

PROBLEM 24.5 **Town and Country Mutual Automobile Insurance Company, Income and Expenses for 19X4 and 19X5 (Millions)**

	19X4		19X5	
Revenues				
Total premiums written	$8,011		$8,975	
Less unearned premiums	375		473	
Total earned premiums		$7,636		$8,502
Net investment earnings and other income		682		1,022
Total revenues		$8,318		$9,524
Expenses				
Loss expenses	$6,077		$7,276	
Policyholder dividends	136		4	
Operating expenses	1,355		1,511	
Total expenses		$7,568		$8,791

PROBLEM 24.5 *CONTINUED*	Town and Country Mutual Automobile Insurance Company, Income and Expenses for 19X4 and 19X5 (Millions)	
	19X4	**19X5**
Underwriting Results		
Earned premiums	$7,636	$8,502
Less:		
Loss expenses	6,077	7,276
Operating expenses	1,355	1,511
Statutory underwriting gain (loss)	$ 204	($ 285)
Less dividends to policyholders	136	4
Net underwriting gain (loss)	$ 68	$ 289

SELECTED REFERENCES

Ambrose, Jan Mills, and J. Allen Seward. "Best's Ratings, Financial Ratios and Prior Probabilities." *Journal of Risk and Insurance* 55 (June 1988): 229–244.

American Council of Life Insurance. *Life Insurance Fact Book.* Various issues.

American Insurance Association. "Competition in the Property and Casualty Insurance Industry: An Analysis of Seven Major Lines." Prepared by the American Insurance Association Policy Development and Research, April 1988.

BarNiv, Ran, and Robert A. Hershbarger, "Classifying Financial Distress in the Life Insurance Industry," *Journal of Risk and Insurance* 57 (March 1990): 110–136.

Brewer, Elijah, III, Thomas H. Mondschean, and Philip E. Strahan, "Why the Life Insurance Industry Did Not Face an S&L-type Crisis." *Eonomic Perspectives* (Federal Reserve Bank of Chicago) 17 (September/October 1993): 12–24.

Clarke, Richard N., Fredrick Warren-Boulton, David D. Smith, and Marilyn J. Simon. "Sources of the Crisis in Liability Insurance: An Economic Analysis." *Yale Journal of Regulation* (1988): 367–395.

Cox, Samuel H., and Robert G. Schwebach. "Insurance Futures and Hedging Insurance Price Risk." *Journal of Risk and Insurance* 59 (December 1992): 628–644.

Crosson, Cynthia. "Risk-Based Capital Formula May Force Major Changes." *National Underwriter, Life/Health* (May 4, 1992): 3.

Cummins, J. David, Scott E. Harrington, and Robert W. Klein. "Cycles and Crisis in Property/Casualty Insurance: Causes and Implications for Public Policy." *Journal of Insurance Regulation* (Fall 1991): 50–93.

Cummins, J. David, and Jack Vanderhei. "A Note on the Relative Efficiency of Property-Liability Insurance Distribution Systems." *The Bell Journal of Economics* (1979): 709–719.

Curry, Timothy, and Mark Warshawsky. "Life Insurance Companies in a Changing Environment." *Federal Reserve Bulletin* 72 (July 1986): 449–460.

Dannen, Fredric. "How Good Are A.M. Best's Ratings?" *Institutional Investor* 19 (December 1985).

D'Arcy, Stephen P., and Virginia Grace France. "Catastrophe Futures: A Better Hedge for Insurers." *Journal of Risk and Insurance* 59 (December 1992): 575–601.

Dennon, A. R. "The Facts about Unisex Insurance." *Consumers' Research* 71 (February 1988): 25–27.

Fields, Joseph A., and Emilio C. Venezian. "Interest Rates and Profit Cycles: A Disaggregated Approach." *Journal of Risk and Insurance* 56 (June 1989): 312–319.

Forbes, Stephen W. "The Revolution in the Life Insurance Financial Management." *Journal of the American Society of CLU and ChFC* 41 (January 1987): 70–73.

Grabowski, Henry, W. Kip Viscusi, and William N. Evans. "Price and Availability Tradeoffs of Automobile Insurance Regulation." *Journal of Risk and Insurance* 56 (June 1989): 275–299.

Hank, Leon E. "Can We Make the System Better?" *Best's Review* 43 (October 1989): 20–25, 113–114.

Harrington, Scott E. "The Relationship Between Voluntary and Involuntary Market Rates and Rate Regulation in Automobile Insurance Markets." *Journal of Risk and Insurance* 57 (March 1990): 9–27.

————. "The Solvency of the Insurance Industry." In *Proceedings of a Conference on Bank Structure and Competition,* 779–797. Chicago: Federal Reserve Bank of Chicago, 1992.

Hoyt, Robert E. "Use of Financial Futures by Life Insurers." *Journal of Risk and Insurance* 56 (December 1989): 740–748.

Insurance Information Institute. *Property/Casualty Insurance Facts.* Various issues.

Joskow, Paul L. "Cartels, Competition, and Regulation in the Property-Liability Insurance Industry." *The Bell Journal of Economics* (Autumn 1973): 375–427.

Kopcke, Richard W. "The Federal Income Taxation of Life Insurance Companies." *New England Economic Review* (Federal Reserve Bank of Boston) (March/April 1985): 5–19.

————. "The Capitalization and Portfolio Risk of Insurance Companies." *New England Economic Review* (Federal Reserve Bank of Boston) (July/August 1992): 43–57.

Lamm-Tenant, Joan. "Asset/Liability Management for the Life Insurer: Situation Analysis and Strategy Formulation." *Journal of Risk and Insurance* 56 (September 1989): 501–517.

Lauranzann, Vincent. "Balancing Capital with Risks." *Best's Review* (June 1992): 46–50.

Mayers, David, and Clifford W. Smith, Jr. "On the Corporate Demand for Insurance." *Journal of Business* 55 (1982): 281–296.

McGee, Robert T. "The Cycle in Property/Casualty Insurance." *Quarterly Review* (Federal Reserve Bank of New York) 11 (Autumn 1986): 22–30.

Mehr, Robert I. *Fundamentals of Insurance.* Homewood, IL: Richard D. Irwin, 1983.

Mehr, Robert I., and Sandra G. Gustavson. *Life Insurance: Theory and Practice.* Plano, TX: Business Publications, Inc., 1984.

Mossin, Jan. "Aspects of Rational Insurance Purchasing." *Journal of Political Economy* (1968): 553–568.

Mulcahy, Colleen. "Hedging Health Care Financial Risk Through Futures." *National Underwriter, Life & Health* (April 1, 1991): 47–48.

Niehaus, Greg, and Steven V. Mann. "The Trading of Underwriting Risk: An Analysis of Insurance Futures Contracts and Reinsurance." *Journal of Risk and Insurance* 59 (December 1992): 601–627.

Nye, David J., and Robert W. Kolb. "Inflation, Interest Rates, and Property-Liability Insurer Risk." *Journal of Risk and Insurance* 53 (March 1986): 144–154.

"Open Season on an Old Law." *Journal of American Insurance* (First Quarter 1987): 8–12.

Pesando, James E. "The Interest Sensitivity of the Flow of Funds through Life Insurance Companies: An Econometric Analysis." *Journal of Finance* 29 (September 1974): 1105–1121.

Saunders, Anthony. "The Effect of Changing Regulation on Investment Policy of Life Insurance Companies." In *The Emerging Financial Industry,* edited by Arnold W. Sametz, 85–94. Lexington, MA: Lexington Books, 1984.

Smith, Michael L. "The Life Insurance Policy as an Options Package." *Journal of Risk and Insurance* 49 (December 1982): 583–601.

Snyder, Arthur. "Best's Ratings: A New Look." *Best's Review* (Property/Casualty Edition) 87 (April 1986): 14–16, 122–128.

Stowe, John D., and Collin J. Watson. "A Multivariate Analysis of the Composition of Life Insurer Balance Sheets." *Journal of Risk and Insurance* 52 (June 1985): 222–240.

"Upheaval in Life Insurance." *Business Week,* June 24, 1984, 58–66.

Vaughan, Emmett J. *Fundamentals of Risk and Insurance.* New York: John Wiley and Sons, 1982.

Walden, Michael L. "The Whole Life Insurance Policy as an Options Package: An Empirical Investigation." *Journal of Risk and Insurance* 52 (March 1985): 44–58.

Washburn, John E., and James W. Schacht. "A Bold Step for Regulation." *Best's Review* 43 (October 1989).

Webb, James R. "Real Estate Investment Acquisition Rules for Life Insurance Companies and Pension Funds: A Survey." *AREUEA Journal* 21 (Winter 1984): 495–520.

Weil, Roman. "Macaulay's Duration." *Journal of Business* 46 (October 1973): 589–592.

Welles, Chris, and Christopher Farrell. "Insurers under Siege," *Business Week,* August 21, 1989, 72–79.

APPENDIX 24A

CALCULATION OF THE PREMIUM ON A WHOLE LIFE POLICY

If a 35-year-old man seeks a $100,000 whole life policy, the insurer estimates the expected cash outflow, based on the odds of the purchaser's dying, for each year up to age 100. (Most mortality tables assume a 100 percent probability of death between the ages of 99 and 100.) Table 24A.1 shows the calculation for selected years for men between ages 35 and 100 years, using data from the Commissioners Standard Ordinary Mortality Table (Table 24.4) and a 4 percent discount rate for present value calculations.

PROBABILITY OF CLAIMS

Because a man taking out a policy at age 35 is expected to be one of 9,491,617 who have survived to that point, that number becomes the base against which the probability of claims in subsequent years is measured. For example, of those men living until age 36, 21,216 are expected to die before age 37; that is, of 9,491,617 men insured as of age 35, 21,216 ÷ 9,491,617 = 0.002235 = 0.2235% are expected to die between the ages of 36 and 37. There is, consequently, a 0.002235 probability that this man's beneficiaries under a policy originated at age 35 will make a claim during the second year of the policy. Several of these probabilities are shown in Column 5 of Table 24A.1.

If the insurer does not pay until the *end* of the year, the present value of each year's expected claims is calculated as of the time the policy is sold, as shown in Column 7. For example, the present value of $223.53, the expected cash outflow to the insurer at the *end* of the policy year 2, is $206.66 as of the origination date of the policy (*beginning* of policy year 1):

$$\$223.53 \div (1.04)^2 = \$206.66$$

LUMP SUM PREMIUM REQUIRED

Because insurance protection will be provided until age 100, the total present value of the insurer's cash outflows is the sum over 65 years, or $24,682.38. The total includes some yearly amounts not shown in the table. It is possible for a 35-year-old man to buy a $100,000 whole life policy at age 35 by paying this single sum plus loading, but few people choose this option. Not only does it require considerable cash at one time, but some premiums may never be needed. If the insured dies at age 40 and has prepaid protection until age 100, the prepayment would be nothing but lost money to the individual's beneficiaries, who would receive $100,000 in death benefits regardless of when he dies.

CONVERTING THE LUMP SUM INTO A LEVEL PREMIUM

Most whole life customers elect to pay a level premium. Table 24A.1 assumes the payment of premiums as long as the insured lives. The level premium is based on data in Columns 8 and 9. Insurers count on receiving premiums from some policyholders at the beginning of each policy year to meet the claims of others. But customers who die during a year will not be there to pay the next year's premium, so not only will the insurance company not get their premium payments, it will not earn interest on them either. Insurers would be ignoring the facts if they simply divided the total lump sum premium required to insure a 35 year old (as previously calculated) by the number of years until age 100 and charged that amount each year.

To take these factors into account, the insurer calculates the probability of this customer's surviving to pay his premium at the beginning of each policy year. Shown in Column 8, the number of policyholders expected to reach a given age is divided by the number who reached 35, the base year in the example. For

TABLE 24A.1 Calculation of Level Annual Premium on $100,000 Whole Life Policy for a 35-Year-Old Man

The level annual premium on a whole life policy is a function of the policyholder's age when the policy is first purchased, the face value of the policy, the insurer's assumption about the annual yield to be earned on premiums, and the time value of money.

(1) Policy Year	(2) Age (Years)	(3) Number Living	(4) Number Dying	(5) Probability of Claims by Those Living at Age 35 (4) ÷ 9,491,617	(6) Insurer's Annual Expected Cash Outflow at End of Year (5) × $100,000	(7) Present Value of Cash Outflow as of the Beginning of Year 1 (6) discounted at 4%	(8) Of Those Alive at Age 35 Proportion that Will Pay Premium at Beginning of Year (3) ÷ 9,491,617	(9) Discounted Value of Column 8 as of Beginning of Year 1
1	35	9,491,617	20,027	.002110	$211.00	$202.88	1.000000	1.000000
2	36	9,471,590	21,216	.002235	223.53	206.66	0.997890	0.959510
3	37	9,450,374	22,681	.002390	238.96	212.43	0.995655	0.920539
4	38	9,427,693	24,323	.002563	256.26	219.05	0.993265	0.883009
5	39	9,403,369	26,235	.002764	276.41	227.19	0.990703	0.846857
6	40	9,377,134	28,319	.002984	298.36	235.80	0.987938	0.812013
.	.	.	.	.	.	.	.	.
.	.	.	.	.	.	.	.	.
61	95	146,720	48,412	.005100	510.05	46.62	0.0154578273	0.001469
62	96	98,308	37,804	.003983	398.29	35.01	0.0103573626	0.000947
63	97	60,504	29,054	.003061	306.10	25.87	0.0063744388	0.000560
64	98	31,450	20,693	.002180	218.02	17.72	0.0033134333	0.000280
65	99	10,756	10,756	.001133	113.33	8.85	0.0011332605	0.000092

Total premium due: $24,682.38   Column (9) Total: 19.582582

Annual premium due: $24,682.38 ÷ 19.582582 = $1,260.43

instance, the 9,471,590 men expected to be alive at age 36 are 9,471,590 ÷ 9,491,617 = 0.99789 = 99.789% of those who lived until age 35. Thus, there is a probability in excess of 99 percent that someone taking out a policy at age 35 will be around to pay the premium at age 36, but there is only a 0.11 percent probability that the same policyholder will be around to pay his premium when he is 99 years old.

Column 9 further reduces the probability that a premium payment will actually be received by considering the interest lost by the insurer from not receiving the lump-sum premium in advance, or from not receiving the interest on lost premium payments from those who die. Because premium payments are assumed to be received at the *beginning* of a year for which protection is purchased, the probability that someone will

pay the initial premium is 100 percent—life insurance policies are not issued to dead people. The probability that the second year's policy premium will be made is discounted back only one period, because it is assumed to be made at the beginning of that year—in other words, the end of the first policy year:

$$0.99789 \div 1.04 = 0.95951$$

The sum of the values in Column 9 is the weighted number of premium payments expected, considering the probability of death and the impact of lost interest. When divided into the expected cost of insuring a 35-year-old man for life, the level annual pure premium is $1,260.43, without considering operating costs.

The mutual fund families are competing with the banks and the banks are competing with the brokers. There is going to be an awful lot of competition in this market.

Eric Kobren,

Editor, *Fidelity Insight* (1992)

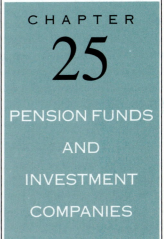

Portfolio managers have used computers to aid investment decision making for decades. But Bradford Lewis of Fidelity Investments, a large mutual fund company, has taken computerized investing one step farther. As the head of Fidelity's Disciplined Equity fund, Mr. Lewis has gained attention for his reliance on "neural network" investing. His personal computer is programmed to mimic the activity of the human brain so well that it not only tells him *when* to buy or sell large blocks of stock (like the typical program trading strategy described in Chapter 11) but it actually decides *what* to buy or sell. Mr. Lewis's goal is for his computer's picks to beat market averages consistently, and he argues that his neural network can exercise judgment and "learn" from its mistakes, as can the human brain, without being subject to human emotions. Colleagues at Fidelity confess to being bewildered at the complexity of Mr. Lewis's approach, but his motivation is a simple one: He wants to keep his job. "I'm flipping burgers if I don't beat the Vanguard index fund," he says, citing a major rival known for its passive investment strategies.[1]

Statistics in Chapter 1 indicate the importance of pension funds and investment companies, the institutions discussed in this chapter. Private pension funds held assets in excess of $1 *trillion* by year-end 1991. Money market and other mutual funds, only one segment of the investment company industry, also controlled well over $1 trillion in financial assets.[2]

Not only does their size make these institutions important, their role in the flow of funds across economic sectors also is significant. Pension funds are intended to offer financial security for the retired population. Investment companies provide professional investment management and diversified portfolios to small savers at reasonable costs.

The managers of these institutions face just as many challenges as do those of depositories, finance companies, and insurance firms in the current economic environment. Management techniques in these two types of nondepositories are examined in the pages that follow.

---

[1] Robert McGough, "Fidelity's Bradford Lewis Takes Aim at Indexes with His 'Neural Network' Computer Program," *The Wall Street Journal,* October 27, 1992, C1, C19.

[2] Board of Governors of the Federal Reserve System, *Flow of Funds Accounts, Sector Statements of Financial Assets and Liabilities,* First Quarter 1992.

TYPES AND GROWTH OF PENSION FUNDS

A pension plan is a program established by an employer to provide retirement and disability benefits to employees. An organization called a pension fund administers the program and manages assets purchased with the contributions of employers and employees.[3] Pension funds obtain resources through contributions in varying proportions from employees and their employers. The fund managers are responsible for managing risk and expected return to assure that assets will be adequate to meet future liabilities, which are the pension benefits promised to employees participating in the plan. As first noted in Chapter 2, like many other financial institutions, pension managers must comply with regulatory requirements in addition to meeting the expectations of employees and their employing firms.

TYPES OF PENSION FUNDS

There are three broad categories of pension funds: federal government, state and local government, and private. Only private funds are covered in this chapter. Federal plans, the largest of which is the Old Age, Survivors, and Disability Insurance System (Social Security), have historically not relied as heavily on asset accumulation to fund benefits. Instead, they collect from those currently employed to pay retirement benefits, and assets under management are quite small in comparison with the number of workers covered. The Social Security system, for example, which in 1991 paid benefits of more than $200 billion to millions of recipients had year-end assets of only $280 billion.[4] Although state and local retirement systems accumulate a larger volume of assets, they also differ in many ways from private funds. Most important, they are not regulated by the same federal laws that govern private plans. Management differs from state to state, depending on regulations and objectives.

There are even two categories of private pension funds, insured and noninsured. An insured plan operates under a service arrangement with a life insurance company, giving the insurer responsibility for collecting receipts, paying benefits, and/or administering the fund's assets. Noninsured plans are twice as large as insured plans. Because of their size and importance, the discussion that follows is confined to managerial issues affecting noninsured private pension plans.

PENSION FUND GROWTH

The lifespan of Americans increased in the twentieth century from an average of about 47 years in 1900 to about 75 years in the early 1990s. The extended lifespan means that employees must plan for retirement income, and pension fund contributions and asset accumulation have grown accordingly. Support from labor unions also contributed to the growth of pensions. In 1949, the Supreme Court ruled that pension benefits could be included in collective bargaining agreements, and the nation's largest unions took advantage of the ruling. The period 1950–1960 was one of strong growth for pension funds; the number of private plan participants more than doubled, and fund assets grew at a similar rate. Private pension fund growth continued at an average annual rate of more than 13 percent between 1970 and 1991.[5] As shown in Figure 25.1, the growth in pension fund assets accelerated in 1974, the year Congress enacted sweeping regulatory legislation for pension plans.

INFLUENCE OF ERISA

As pension plans grew, so did the possibility that some of the funds or sponsoring corporations would fail to meet obligations to participants. Probably the most widely publicized failure occurred when the Studebaker automobile company in South Bend, Indiana, went out of business in 1964. Inadequacies in the Studeba-

---

[3] The pension plan is technically considered to be the formal arrangement under which benefits will be accumulated and distributed, and the fund is the organization for administering the plan. The Employee Retirement Income Security Act of 1974, however, did not distinguish the two, so for accounting purposes the Financial Accounting Standards Board considers the *plan* to be the reporting entity. See Steinberg and Dankner 1983. (References are listed in full at the end of this chapter.) In this chapter, the terms are used interchangeably.

[4] American Council of Life Insurance, *1992 Life Insurance Fact Book.* Because of Congressional pressure, Social Security System assets increased more than ninefold between 1984 and 1991. It is still viewed as a "pay-as-you-go" system, however.

[5] See Steinberg and Dankner 1983, 4; and *1992 Life Insurance Fact Book.*

FIGURE 25.1 **Growth of Private Pension Funds**

The growth of private pension funds has been phenomenal in recent decades, especially since the passage of ERISA in 1974.

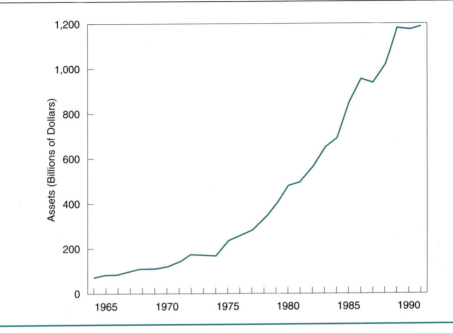

Source: Board of Governors of the Federal Reserve System, *Flow of Funds,* various issues.

ker pension fund left most of the firm's employees with fewer benefits than promised or none at all. Ten years later, Congress passed the Employee Retirement Income Security Act (ERISA), with the intention of preventing pension fund insolvencies. ERISA, introduced in Chapter 2, affected many aspects of the management of privately sponsored pension plans.[6]

BENEFIT VESTING AND FULL FUNDING

As noted in Chapter 2, ERISA set standards for 100 percent vesting of benefits for most employees after 15 or fewer years of service; employees are entitled to vested benefits even if they leave the employer before retirement. The law also attempted to ensure that employers work toward **full funding,** or the equal-

ity of pension assets and accrued liabilities. A pension plan's funding level—that is, the relative levels of assets and current and future liabilities—is a very important measure of its financial stability. The definition and measurement of a pension plan's funding are explained in more detail in subsequent sections.

DEFINED CONTRIBUTIONS VERSUS DEFINED BENEFITS. The funding obligations of the employer are affected by whether the plan is a **defined benefit** program or a **defined contribution** program. A defined benefit plan promises in advance to pay employees a specified level of benefits. The total amount of the fund's liabilities and the date incurred are not known with certainty and depend on the characteristics (such as age and gender) of the company's work force. The fund's liabilities are estimated using actuarial methods, and the employer's contributions are based on those calculations. A major question in the management and regulation of defined benefit plans is whether an employer's contribution to the fund is sufficient to meet future pension liabilities.

---

[6] Besides ERISA, the Multiemployer Pension Plan Amendments Act of 1980 affects plans jointly sponsored by more than one employer.

In a defined contribution plan, the per-employee contributions made by the employer are specified, but benefits paid during retirement are not promised in advance. Instead, they depend on contributions and earnings accumulated over time. Because employees are not promised specific benefits, the question of funding adequacy does not arise.

PENSION BENEFIT GUARANTY CORPORATION

ERISA established the Pension Benefit Guaranty Corporation (PBGC) to assure, within limits, the payment of up to 85 percent of vested benefits if a defined benefit pension fund fails. The PBGC is supported by annual premiums based on the number of participants covered. If a plan is terminated, the PBGC becomes the trustee, taking control of the fund's assets and using them to pay as large a portion of the basic vested benefits as possible. The sponsoring company of a terminated plan may be held liable for unfunded benefits based on a formula established by Congress in the Single Employer Pension Plan Amendment Act of 1986.

The financial condition of the PBGC has generated some concern since the late 1980s. Like the Federal Deposit Insurance Corporation (FDIC), the pension insurance fund must provide coverage to all organizations paying the prescribed premiums, but unlike the FDIC, the PBGC has no regulatory powers and thus no ability to influence the financial position or to control the riskiness of an insured pension plan. In addition, firms with financial problems and unfunded liabilities in excess of a specified percentage of net worth can, under certain circumstances, voluntarily turn their obligations over to the PBGC. Also unlike the FDIC, the PBGC has a very limited line of credit with the Treasury.

The termination of several underfunded plans in the 1980s led to a 1986 year-end deficit of almost $4 billion for the PBGC. After Congress raised insurance premiums, the deficit fell to about $1.5 billion by the end of 1987, when Congress again acted to assist the PBGC. Beginning in 1988, the premium structure was strengthened by another increase in the base rate, plus the ability to charge a risk-adjusted premium related to a plan's unfunded vested benefit obligations. The PBGC has also gained more power to recover costs from firms terminating pension plans, even if the corporations are in bankruptcy proceedings. For example, the Supreme Court ruled in 1990 that a firm could not transfer its existing pension liabilities to the PBGC, only to replace it with a new plan assuming future, but not past, obligations.

ANOTHER FSLIC? Although in recent years, the PBGC has enjoyed increased authority to charge risk-adjusted premiums and to require financially troubled employers to take their pension obligations more seriously, the PBGC's potential liability for plans terminated when firms fail continues to worry many experts. Reasons for their concern are quite similar to those leading to the Federal Savings and Loan Insurance Corporation's (FSLIC) disastrous collapse.

Some analysts believe that the risk-adjusted premiums the PBGC has charged in recent years are not high enough in total to protect the insurer against possible future cash obligations should one or more large employers with inadequately funded pension plans fail. Each year, the PBGC publishes a list of the 50 biggest pension offenders—those most likely to cost the PBGC in the future. The list is often dominated by steel companies, automakers, and airlines, industries that have been rife with financial problems for years but that employ huge numbers of people. In 1991, the PBGC estimated that its future obligations to employees of just a few shaky plans could reach up to $14 billion. Because more than 85,000 pension plans are insured by the PBGC, some experts warn that total future obligations could go much higher—to $40 billion or more.

Yet, it is difficult for the PBGC to raise premiums from healthy firms to pay for the likely costs incurred from insuring weak firms. Private firms are not required to offer pension plans to their workers, and in recent years, several profitable companies have discontinued their company-sponsored retirement funds to avoid the escalating cost of PBGC insurance. (Instead, these employers may contribute to employees' *individual* retirement savings accounts. Employees then become responsible for managing their own money for retirement.) The PBCG, therefore, is increasingly protecting relatively weaker plans and facing exposure to the same moral hazard problem that plagued the FSLIC in its later years: Firms whose pension plans are insured can continue to engage in financially risky activities, yet surrender their obligations to the PBGC should they fail. To avert a crisis later this decade, many analysts believe Congress must act to provide sufficient funding to the PBGC, primarily by making it virtually impossible for private corporations to continue to fund their employees' pension plans inadequately and by giving the PBGC a priority on assets if a firm goes bankrupt.[7]

FIDUCIARY RESPONSIBILITIES

ERISA also addressed the fiduciary responsibilities of pension fund managers. Investment decisions are generally based on the **prudent man rule,** which requires a manager to make decisions with the same care and judgment that a prudent individual (man *or* woman) would use in handling personal investments.

The ERISA guidelines modified this traditional interpretation. ERISA stated that the pension fund fiduciary should emulate investment principles that a person "acting in like capacity and familiar with such matters would use in the conduct of an enterprise of like character with like aims."[8] Some observers therefore believe that ERISA applies a "prudent expert" rule to pension fund management, opening the door to more sophisticated investment techniques. In particular, earlier trust law focuses on individual securities rather than a portfolio and does not recognize the importance of diversification in risk management.

ERISA's impact on strategies for managing pension funds has been a subject of great interest. Evidence on that relationship is examined later in the chapter. At this point, however, two provisions that ERISA did *not* include should be emphasized. No requirements are placed on the level of benefits promised by an employer or on the dollar amount of employer contributions. Nor, as noted earlier, does ERISA require employers to establish pension plans. Rather, the intent is to protect employee interests once a plan has been established and benefits defined.

---

[7] See Abken 1992; Estrella and Hirtle 1988; Warshawsky 1988; Buynak 1987; Munnell 1982; Ellen E. Schultz, "In New Pension Plans, Companies Are Putting the Onus on Workers," *The Wall Street Journal,* July 7, 1992, A1, A7; and Michael Schroeder, "The Crying Game Over Pensions," *Business Week,* April 5, 1993, 70, 71.

[8] Interpretation of ERISA's fiduciary requirements is discussed in Pozen 1977.

PENSION FUNDS: DESCRIPTIVE DATA

ASSET STRUCTURE

Noninsured private pension funds invest the largest proportion of their assets in corporate stock. Under ERISA's encouragement to diversify portfolios, however, other assets are now a bit more important than in 1975, when equities were more than 54 percent of total assets. By 1991, as shown in Table 25.1, equity investments were just under 47½ percent of total assets of private pension funds. U.S. government securities and corporate and foreign bonds are the two other large asset categories. Smaller holdings include deposits, mortgages, commercial (open market) paper, mutual fund shares, and miscellaneous assets.

SOURCES OF FUNDS

Pension funds, unlike some institutions, have no liabilities with face amounts or maturity dates in the traditional sense. They have obligations to covered employees, but most obligations are difficult to quantify and must be estimated by actuaries. Instead of considering pension fund obligations in the traditional balance sheet sense, the ensuing focus is on sources of funds to private pension plans.

Corporations with employees covered by pension plans provide the majority of funds with which assets are purchased. Although employees may also contribute, in many cases they do not. Thus, corporate decisions determine whether the plan is adequately funded, **overfunded,** or **underfunded.** If a plan is overfunded, the value of its assets exceeds that of its estimated obligations, and the fund accumulates net worth, or an excess of assets over liabilities. When a fund is underfunded, it has negative net worth because assets are less than the value of estimated obligations. (It is the possibility of underfunding that is of such concern to observers of the PBGC, which must make good on obligations of underfunded plans should their corporate sponsors fail.) Adequately funded plans have no net worth, and asset values equal the present value of estimated future obligations.

Because corporate contributions to pension funds reduce the corporation's after-tax profits, firms face conflicting influences on the contribution

TABLE 25.1 **Assets of Private Noninsured Pension Funds, 1991 (Millions of $)**

Private pension funds invest primarily in common stock, Treasury securities, and bonds. Although asset proportions vary from year to year, the 1991 data are representative of pension holdings during the past decade.

	Amount	Percentage
Demand deposits, currency, and money market mutual funds	$ 25,500	1.53%
Time deposits	125,100	7.51
Mutual fund shares	73,100	4.39
Corporate equities	790,000	47.42
U.S. government securities	243,000	14.58
Corporate and foreign bonds	178,000	10.68
Mortgages	28,200	1.69
Open market paper	17,500	1.05
Miscellaneous assets	185,700	11.15
Total assets	$1,666,100	100.00%

Source: Board of Governors of the Federal Reserve System, *Flow of Funds Accounts,* 1992, Q1.

decision. On the one hand, ERISA guidelines require eventual full funding; on the other, reductions in pension contributions improve profitability. The problem is further complicated by the fact that asset and obligation values for pension funds change with market conditions.

ACTUARIAL ASSUMPTIONS. The adequacy of contributions also depends on actuarial assumptions. Most obligations depend on future occurrences, such as the retirement age of covered employees and how long they live after retirement. To be **fully funded,** a pension fund's assets must equal the *present value* of future obligations minus the *present value* of future contributions, an amount known as the **funding target.** The funding target is influenced by actuarial assumptions about future obligations and the yield on the fund's assets over time. These assumptions resemble those used to establish reserves in the life insurance industry, illustrated in the previous chapter. Like life insurance actuaries, pension actuaries are cautious, preferring to err by overestimating future obligations rather than by underestimating them.

EFFECTS OF CHANGING ACTUARIAL ASSUMPTIONS. The impact on pension plans of changing even one actuarial assumption has been the subject of research. The assumptions affect new funds that the employer contributes, and thus funds available for investment each year, as well as the plan's standing with regulatory authorities.

Because each pension plan operates under its own set of actuarial assumptions, it is impossible to assess the funding adequacy and net worth, if any, of the pension system as a whole. One study of large Canadian pension funds concluded, however, that under uniform, reasonable actuarial assumptions, most plans were overfunded and that managers would benefit from public, explicit, and uniform actuarial assumptions.[9]

When pension fund actuaries notify the corporate sponsor that a plan is overfunded, contributions may decrease, subsequently affecting pension fund management. For example, the stock market surge and falling interest rates between 1982 and 1986 increased the value of pension fund assets. Actuarial assumptions in some plans were changed, increasing the expected rate of return on assets in the future. Because this rate is used to discount future obligations, estimates of the present value of obligations decreased, and some corporations reduced contributions. As discussed in more detail later, some firms even terminated their pension plans to capture the excess assets. Beginning with the Tax Reform Act of 1986, Congress discouraged terminations by imposing a surtax on recaptured excess pension fund assets, now set at 15 percent.

The risks to corporate sponsors of changing actuarial assumptions to lower their contributions is

_____

[9] See Ezra and Ambachtsheer 1985.

clearly illustrated by General Motors' (GM) 1992 announcement that the assumptions it had recently adopted were not working and that its unfunded pension obligations were therefore almost $2 billion higher than the firm had reported only 2 years earlier. In 1990, GM changed its assumed future rate of return on existing pension assets to 11 percent annually (from the 10 percent its actuaries had previously used). GM also said it was now assuming that retirees would die 2 years earlier than they had in the past (even though most mortality tables at the time were showing increased lifespans for both men and women). After less than 2 years, it was clear these new assumptions were quite unrealistic and that GM would have to start making larger contributions to compensate for the shortfall. Critics noted that, although the poor assumptions did, in fact, result in lower contributions for a brief period, they ultimately resulted in a setback for GM in its effort to strengthen its overall financial position.[10]

MANAGING PENSION FUND ASSETS

The assets and sources of funds for private pension funds suggest that their management is more like that of insurance firms than management of other financial institutions.

LIQUIDITY

Pensions need not consider explicit reserve requirements, but as insurers must protect cash flows to ensure payments to policyholders, pension funds must have cash for benefit payments. Outflows for pension funds and life insurers are much more predictable than for depositories. Furthermore, for new or growing plans, corporate contributions usually exceed payments to covered employees in the same period, so liquidity considerations are not managers' foremost concern.

TAXABILITY

Taxation is an important influence. Earnings on pension fund assets are not taxable at the fund level. For all practical purposes, this removes tax-exempt securities from investment consideration because of their inferior yields.[11]

CORPORATE SPONSOR PREFERENCES

One of the unusual aspects of pension fund management is the potential division of control among several parties. The pension fund itself must operate in the best interests of covered employees but depends on the sponsoring firm for its sources of funds. The plan's administrators may make investment decisions themselves, or they may entrust the responsibility for investing all or a portion of fund assets to professional portfolio managers. The sponsoring firm, the administrators, and the managers may at times have conflicting interests.

EARNINGS LEVEL AND SPONSOR CONTRIBUTIONS. As noted, the better the earnings performance of the fund's assets, the more likely that corporate contributions will be reduced. That possibility introduces a potential conflict between investment performance and access to new funds, because corporate sponsors may choose to meet funding targets by substituting the fund's current earnings for some of their pension fund expenses. The large capital gains earned on pension fund assets in the 1980s sharply reduced the growth in corporate contributions but allowed continued growth in total assets.

FINANCIAL POSITION OF THE CORPORATE SPONSOR. The financial strength of the sponsor also affects asset management. For example, in 1982, U.S. Steel

---

[10] Light 1989; Warshawsky 1988; Neal Templin, "GM Says Pension Liabilities to Exceed Estimates and Will Hurt Balance Sheet," *The Wall Street Journal,* September 25, 1992, A2; and Susan Pulliam, "Hopeful Assumptions Let Firms Minimize Pension Contributions," *The Wall Street Journal,* September 2, 1993, A1, A6.

[11] The tax-free status of pension funds could very well change in the 1990s. In 1989, both Republican and Democratic senators began discussing a proposal to tax short-term capital gains earned by pension funds. The preliminary proposals suggested a tax of 10–15 percent, designed to generate more federal revenues and at the same time encourage pension funds to concentrate on long-term investments rather than short-term trades. This and other ideas have been under serious consideration in the 1990s. See Susan B. Garland, "Congress Has that Lean and Hungry Look," *Business Week,* November 6, 1989, 160, 162; and Munnell 1992.

(now USX) decided not to make its pension contribution in cash. Instead, the firm printed a new issue of preferred stock, assigned it a value of $100 per share, and contributed it to the pension plan. The market value of the securities was unknown at the time, because the stock had never been publicly traded. Through this paper transaction, U.S. Steel added more than $300 million to the equity portion of its own balance sheet and avoided borrowing to meet its pension obligation. That same year, a difficult one for many industrial firms, several companies used the same approach to financing pension obligations.

The sponsor's decision to contribute stock is out of the control of pension fund managers, yet it may strongly affect their discretion. If the securities are publicly traded, as was the case for GM's contribution of almost 20 million shares of preferred stock in 1987, and Chrysler's contribution of $300 million in common stock to its pension fund in 1991, the fund can choose to sell or hold. But in cases like the U.S. Steel preferred stock, financial problems of corporate sponsors may make it difficult for the fund to sell the securities at a price similar to the assigned value.[12] Of course, if the corporate sponsor's financial performance is strong, rising stock prices will increase the value of the pension fund's assets.

The corporate sponsor's financial strength may further affect pension fund management. A study of more than 500 private pension funds argued that corporations tend to view management of the pension fund they sponsor as an extended part of corporate financial policy. Any plan surplus or deficit accrues to the firm's shareholders because it affects the firm's payment obligations. If a firm is financially sound and its pension fund invests in taxable bonds, the tax benefits of the fund are passed to the firm's shareholders in the form of lower future contributions. Likewise, if a pension fund does not perform well, the firm is affected. A recent Financial Accounting Standards Board (FASB) rule requires corporations to record a

pension plan's unfunded liabilities on the balance sheet as a liability of the firm.[13]

A firm in poor financial condition may prefer to have its pension fund invested in risky assets like common stock. If successful, the pension plan earns a high rate of return; if unsuccessful, the fund's liabilities can perhaps be shifted to the PBGC, exposing the PBGC to the moral hazard discussed earlier. Research has not confirmed or denied these potential influences, but underfunded plans are indeed more heavily invested in common stocks.

The company's attractiveness as a takeover target may also influence pension fund management. A strong incentive for underfunding is to avoid acquisition by individuals or firms who wish to gain access to excess pension fund assets and use them for purposes unrelated to providing retirement income to employees. The effect of corporate sponsor preferences on the management of fund assets in an area of continuing study.

FUND PERFORMANCE AND REVERSIONS. During the mid-1980s, the relationship between fund performance and corporate sponsors achieved a new dimension. As the economy strengthened and financial assets rose in value, a larger number of pension funds became overfunded. Some corporate executives took the position that any fund value in excess of the obligations to employees should accrue to the firm's shareholders in a more direct fashion than any considered thus far. These executives reasoned that, by terminating an overfunded plan, the corporate sponsor could immediately capture the after-tax value of the excess assets. The terminated plan could be replaced by an identical plan, by a different type of plan (such as substituting a defined contribution plan for a defined benefit plan), or by no plan at all.

Interestingly enough, such a procedure, which has come to be called a **reversion,** violates no policies of the PBGC or of the Labor and Treasury departments. Some reversions have occurred during corporate acquisitions; for example, after Carl Icahn and TWA acquired Ozark Airlines in 1986, two pension

[12] Amal K. Naj, "GM Contributes $1.04 Billion in Stock to Pension Plans, Citing Tax Benefits," *The Wall Street Journal,* September 16, 1987, 12; William Harris, "Let Them Eat Stock," *Forbes,* November 22, 1982, 41–42; and Bradley A. Stertz, "Chrysler to Issue $720 Million in New Equity," *The Wall Street Journal,* August 8, 1991, A3.

[13] See Reiter 1992; Bodie et al. 1985; and Evan Sturza, "Owning Up to Pensions," *Forbes,* December 26, 1988, 143–144.

plans were terminated and TWA benefited by more than $26 million. The largest volume of assets captured was Exxon's $1.6 billion reversion in mid-1986. Although the number of reversions has declined recently, the opportunity continues to be available to corporate sponsors and will be attractive during upswings in the equity markets. The response of employees covered by plans terminated in this fashion has been quite negative; but legal challenges have been unsuccessful.[14]

INVESTMENT POLICY AND CHOICE OF INVESTMENT MANAGERS

A pension fund's trustees set investment policies for the fund's assets, including standards for risk and return and selection of the investment manager. As noted, many pension funds are not managed by in-house managers. Instead, plan trustees designate external professional managers to make investment decisions. Often, trust departments of commercial banks are selected, but securities firms or other investment advisers also may be used.

Some pension funds spread the management of assets among several external investment advisers. Surveys indicate that the majority of plans use outside management for at least part of the asset portfolio. ERISA has influenced pension plan trustees to develop written statements of investment objectives and to establish formal guidelines for investment managers.[15]

INFLATION

Two obvious effects of inflation on pension funds are its impact on benefit payments and on the return on fund assets.

EFFECT ON RETIREE BENEFITS. Two methods are commonly used to determine a retiree's benefit payments. One, the **career-average plan,** bases retirement income on an employee's average salary over his or her entire career. The other, called a **final-average plan,** weighs income just before retirement more heavily in computing benefits. Under the latter method, inflation strongly affects pension obligations, because employees' cost-of-living raises are directly translated into higher pension fund obligations. Under a career-average plan, even several years of high inflation toward the end of an employee's career may not increase retirement benefits significantly. Between 1950 and 1975, there was a shift toward the final-average method. In 1950, 72 percent of pension plans used the career-average method, but by 1975, 52 percent were using the final-average approach.[16]

EFFECT ON INVESTMENT INCOME. Inflation's impact on interest rates was explored in Chapter 6. That discussion indicated that nominal yields do not always keep up with the rate of inflation. Similar conclusions have been drawn about equity returns. Although traditional wisdom views stocks as good inflation hedges, research shows that stock returns during the 1970s were *negatively* correlated with inflation. One would expect, then, that pension fund managers would have had difficulty protecting returns on their funds' assets from inflation.

A study of pension funds in the mid-1970s showed that few kept up with inflation. Even after adjusting for risk, most funds performed worse than the markets in general, and actively managed funds performed worst.[17] Strategies for avoiding inflation's negative impact are explored in later sections.

INTERNATIONAL DIVERSIFICATION

ERISA has increased the availability of modern portfolio management techniques, including diversification. Recently, pension funds have turned aggressively to international diversification. One motive is a desire to reduce variability in total returns by holding assets with low correlation in expected returns. A second is a desire to improve the risk-adjusted return on

[14] Michael Tackett and Christopher Drew, "Pension Funds Become Bonanza for Companies," *Chicago Tribune,* December 4, 1989, Section 1, 1, 8; and Roger Thompson, "The Battle Over Pension Surpluses," *Nation's Business,* August 1989, 66–67. Some state governments have raided their employees' pension funds, too, to balance operating budgets. See Alan Deutschman, "The Great Pension Robbery," *Fortune,* January 13, 1992, 76–78.

[15] See Cummins et al. 1980. A model of optimal pension fund portfolios is developed in McKenna and Kim 1986.

[16] See Logue and Rogalski 1984, 7.

[17] An overview of these findings is provided in Logue and Rogalski 1984, 15–30.

the portfolio by investing in rapidly growing foreign firms with abundant raw materials and lower labor costs. Of course, managers must be aware of additional risks, such as exchange rate uncertainty, transfer risk, and limited access to market information.[18]

INFLUENCE OF BENEFIT STRUCTURE

The nature of a pension fund's obligations to employees (that is, whether it is a defined benefit or a defined contribution plan) also has an effect on investment policies. Experts say that the difference in investment strategy is primarily because employees in defined contribution plans have considerable influence over the way their funds are invested, and these contributors tend to be rather conservative. Thus, in contrast to defined benefit plans, which invest almost one-half of their funds' assets in common stock, defined contribution plans have just over 40 percent of assets in equities, with larger proportions in fixed-income investments.[19]

Observers note that the more conservative investment choices of defined contribution plans are accompanied by lower rates of return. They warn that these investment policies may not bode well for the future economic well-being of the employees involved, who may need higher returns to ensure that coverage during retirement years will be sufficient.

EMERGING ISSUES IN ASSET MANAGEMENT

Although the issues discussed so far are likely to remain the most important ones for pension fund managers, additional concerns have arisen in recent years.

INFLUENCING THE EQUITY MARKETS AND CORPORATE MANAGEMENT. One of the more interesting issues to evolve as a result of the growth in assets controlled by pension funds is the power that accrues to the managers of these large funds. Pension funds are now viewed as having the potential to influence the

equity markets and even to become involved in internal management decisions of firms whose shares are held in the equity portfolios.

As of early 1988, researchers at the Board of Governors estimated that pension funds owned almost 25 percent of all corporate stocks outstanding in the U.S. equity markets, compared with about 5 percent in 1965. Because of changes in the brokerage industry, pension funds are able to negotiate very low commission rates and face few penalties from frequent trading; the result has been an increase in the turnover rate in the stock market. The need to buy and sell large quantities of stock has brought changes in trading methods; pension fund managers have developed some innovative ways to avoid the cumbersome trading methods of the organized stock exchanges.

Pension fund managers' ability to influence internal management decisions for corporations in which they are heavily invested became a controversial issue in the late 1980s. The power of fund managers to shape corporate destinies is not a new idea, but the concept has been more formally recognized since the organization of the Council of Institutional Investors in the mid-1980s. Corporate responses to takeover attempts, such as poison pills and greenmail, further attracted the attention of pension funds. By gathering the managers of even a few large public and private pension funds, the council could conceivably use proxy votes to influence huge corporations. Whether it would be appropriate for the council to do so is debatable, however.

Proponents of fund-manager involvement in corporate decision making argue that fund managers have an obligation to their employee contributors to assure the strength of the equities they hold in their portfolios. Thus proxy voting—or even demanding a seat on a firm's board of directors—to influence internal managerial decisions are appropriate pension fund activities. On the other side of the argument are those who emphasize that pension fund managers are, by definition, focused on short-term profits rather than on long-term results, and thus they may unduly interfere with the ability of corporate management to protect the long-term interests of shareholders.

Few would disagree that the influence of pension fund managers will continue to be felt in corporate board rooms. In the early 1990s, for example, several firms announced they were changing their

---

[18] For further discussion, see Rosenberg 1989; Ehrlich 1981; and Susan Pulliam, "U.S. Pension Funds Pour Money into International Stock Marts," *The Wall Street Journal,* January 29, 1993, C1.

[19] Leah J. Nathans, "The New Breed of Pensions that May Leave Retirees Poorer," *Business Week,* November 6, 1989, 164–167.

corporate governing structure in response to complaints from large pension fund-owners. The sheer volume of shares under their control and their growing interest in using their power to accomplish certain purposes suggest that CEOs will increasingly be exposed to the views of pension fund managers.[20]

REAL ESTATE INVESTMENTS. As emphasis on portfolio diversification grew after ERISA, a new category of assets for pension funds received considerable attention: real estate–related investments. Table 25.1 showed that less than 2 percent of private pension fund assets has been invested in mortgages recently. Some observers attribute pension funds' tardiness in tapping real estate markets to their managers' lack of expertise. For example, because bank trust departments are familiar with bonds and stocks, they may not give mortgages extensive consideration. Others point to declining yields and widely publicized problems in real estate–related investments in the 1970s and 1980s that may have deterred fund managers. Indeed, some pension funds that did take a plunge into real estate investment in the 1980s have regretted it in the 1990s. Figure 25.2 illustrates why. Attracted by rates of return available in the first half of the 1980s and required to invest billions of dollars of new funds each year (recall the pension growth shown in Figure 25.1), some fund managers purchased real estate without always giving it the rigorous financial scrutiny that would have been appropriate. As many banks and thrifts learned, too, real estate—especially commercial real estate—was one of the worst-performing assets after 1985. Fortunately for employees whose retirement income was dependent on these plans, even those with the greatest concentration had less than 10 percent of their assets invested in mortgages or property. Still, this downturn

in real estate will surely deter other pension funds from investing in it in the near future. Although such a result may seem unequivocally beneficial, many observers believe that greater pension fund investment in the mortgage and real estate markets is socially desirable because housing could become more affordable. Thus, the issue is likely to continue to attract the attention of managers and public policymakers alike.[21]

SOCIAL RESPONSIBILITY. As suggested at the end of the previous paragraph, at times, pension funds receive pressure to adapt investment decisions to societal goals. For example, investment managers have been pressured to avoid investing in certain companies or countries, such as the protests against investing in firms doing business in the Republic of South Africa that were widespread in the 1980s. On other occasions, influence is exerted to encourage managers to make positive investment decisions, including providing equity capital to firms addressing certain economic or social needs. Managers argue that with this "interference," the most efficient portfolio for the pension fund may be unobtainable. Some observers question whether ERISA's prudence rule prohibits social investing, but as yet there is no direct answer. According to ERISA, however, decisions must clearly be in the best interests of the covered employees, must not interfere with diversification, and must coincide with the fund's investment objectives.[22]

MANAGED FUTURES. Joining the growing list of issues facing pension fund managers is whether to add **managed futures** to fund assets. Managed futures are baskets of commodity and financial futures held by an institution *not* for hedging purposes, as have been discussed and illustrated at several points earlier in the book, but for investment purposes. In other words, managed futures are assets held for their own return-risk contribution to a fund's performance, not to offset the risk associated with other assets in the portfolio.

---

[20] For more discussion of these issues, see Brett Duval Fromson, "The Big Owners Roar," *Fortune,* July 30, 1990, 66–78; Terence P. Paré, "Two Cheers for Pushy Investors," *Fortune,* July 30, 1990, 95–98; James A. White, "Giant Pension Funds' Explosive Growth Concentrates Economic Assets and Power," *The Wall Street Journal,* June 28, 1990, C1; Nancy J. Perry, "Who Runs Your Company Anyway?" *Fortune,* September 12, 1988, 140–146; Rosenberg 1988; Munnell 1987; and Warshawsky 1988. The biggest player in the move to influence corporate management is a public pension fund, the California Public Employees' Retirement System. See George Anders, "While Head of Calpers Lectures Other Firms, His Own Board Frets," *The Wall Street Journal,* January 23, 1993, A1, A6.

---

[21] See Richard D. Hylton, "How Real Estate Hit Pension Funds," *Fortune,* December 14, 1992, 123–131; and Rosen 1982. For additional evidence on pension managers' lack of expertise in evaluating and managing real estate assets, see Louargand 1992.

[22] These issues are discussed more fully in *Investment Policy Guidebook for Corporate Pension Plan Trustees* 1984, 121–129. See also Light 1989, 157.

FIGURE 25.2 Rates of Return on Real Estate Investments, 1981–1992

Some pension managers began to invest a greater proportion of fund assets into real estate in the mid-1980s, just at the point when rates of return on real estate began to plunge. The overall performance of some funds was adversely affected.

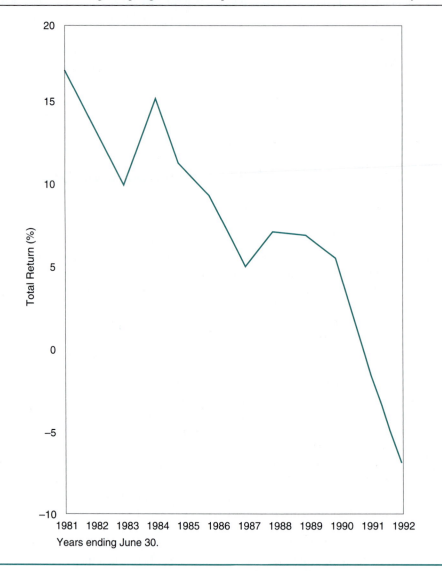

Years ending June 30.

Source: Richard D. Hylton, "How Real Estate Hit Pension Funds," *Fortune,* December 14, 1992, 123.

The managed futures portion of a fund may consist of a wide variety of short and long positions in a wide variety of derivatives, without regard to the remaining composition of the fund's assets. Although managed futures strategies have been around for more than a decade, they have begun to attract substantial attention from pension fund managers only in the past few years. A particular catalyst was the Virginia Retirement System's 1991 announcement that it was committing at least $100 million of its assets to managed futures. That a usually conservative public fund would adopt such a nontraditional approach to fund manage-

| **TABLE 25.2** | **Correlation of Selected Asset Classes, 1980–1990** |

One of the attractions of managed futures is managers' hope that their returns' historical negative correlations with returns on traditional pension fund assets will continue, offering opportunities to reduce overall portfolio risk.

	Standard & Poor's 500	**Bonds**	**International Stocks**	**Managed Futures**
Standard & Poor's 500	1.00			
Bonds	0.29	1.00		
International Stocks	0.47	0.21	1.00	
Managed Futures	−0.02	−0.02	−0.11	1.00

Source: Chicago Board of Trade, *Managed Futures: An Investment Opportunity for Institutional Investors,* 1992.

ment spurred many private pension funds to consider managed futures as well.

The move to managed futures is based in part on fund managers' desire to diversify beyond traditional securities without incurring the liquidity risk and other risks associated with assets such as real estate. Table 25.2 shows correlations between returns on a managed futures index (including commodity and financial futures) and returns on typical pension fund asset categories from 1980 to 1990. Note that the managed futures index had a negative correlation with all other assets in the table, suggesting the potential for reducing overall portfolio risk (as measured by the standard deviation of a portfolio's return, discussed and illustrated in Chapter 13).

Figure 25.3 adds further explanation for the attraction of managed futures. The figure plots annual returns on the same set of asset categories shown in Table 25.2. Notice that, as the correlations in the table suggest, managed futures often moved against returns on stocks and bonds. Note also that average annual returns for the decade are shown in parentheses in the figure. Because the average annual rate of return on managed futures portfolios exceeded the average on other asset classes, some pension fund managers believe they can improve their performance record considerably in this decade, without adding risk, by participating in managed futures programs.

Despite these attractions, not all observers are eager for pension funds to take large positions in managed futures. Critics point to the complexity of managing futures in multiple markets and to the additional costs, either in fees to hire new futures managers or in training for existing management. They also worry that the higher return on managed futures does not adequately compensate for the volatility in futures posi-

tions. Managed futures are sure to be one of the most controversial pension fund activities of this decade.[23]

INTEGRATED MANAGEMENT STRATEGIES

Because pension funds as a whole lack identifiable net worth, it may seem unusual to discuss integrated asset/liability models. At any one time, however, an individual fund has assets and obligations with present values that may or may not be equal. When they are not equal, the fund has either positive or negative net worth that can be affected by changes in market yields. Thus, risk management techniques introduced in previous chapters can be applied to pension fund management. Because of the long-term nature of pension fund assets and liabilities, particular attention has been given to duration-based techniques.

IMMUNIZATION

A pension fund is immunized if its net worth at the end of a holding period is at least equal to its net worth at the beginning of the holding period. The value of a pension fund's assets is affected by changing market yields. Because a pension fund's future obligations are estimated using present-value techniques, their value is also affected by market conditions

---

[23] Stanley W. Angrist, "Virginia's Pension Plan Earmarks $100 Million for Futures Trading," *The Wall Street Journal,* April 26, 1991, C1, C5; "Futures Shock," *The Economist,* August 8, 1992, 69; Chicago Mercantile Exchange, "Roundtable for Pension Plan Sponsors on the Use of Managed Futures," 1991; and Chicago Board of Trade 1992.

FIGURE 25.3   **Managed Futures Versus Other Assets**

The graph shows annual returns on managed futures and several traditional asset categories during a recent decade. (Average returns for each asset class are in parentheses.) Managed futures provided the highest average return during the period and often moved in an opposite direction from returns on traditional assets.

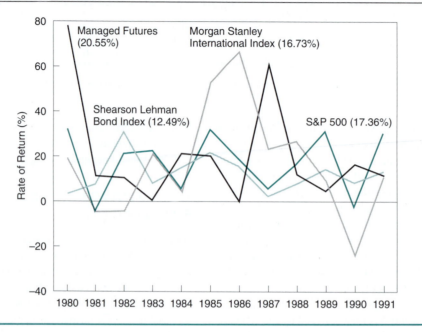

reflected in the discount rate. The net worth of a fund will change if, for a given change in market yields, changes in asset values differ from changes in the present value of future obligations. As illustrated in Table 25.3, to be immunized, a fund must hold assets whose duration multiplied by their beginning market value equals the duration of obligations times their total present value.[24]

The top panel shows the market values of assets and obligations, assuming that the beginning market yield is 5 percent. Obligations of the fund are assumed to be $34.74 per year for 20 years, with a total present value at 5 percent of $432.95. The duration of the obligations, calculated from Equation 9.2, is 8.903 years.

To immunize the fund against changes in market yields, the manager needs to adjust the asset portfolio to reach a duration GAP (DUR_{GAP}) equal to 0. In this example, the manager selects assets with a total present value of $580.88; the bonds selected are pass-through securities with stable cash flows for 16 years. The weighted average duration of the assets is 6.636 years. The excess of asset values over obligations (the fund's net worth) is $147.93. Using Equation 19.1, it is apparent that the fund is immunized:

$$DUR_{GAP} = DUR_A - w_L \, DUR_L$$
$$= 6.636 - [(\$432.95/\$580.88) \times 8.903]$$
$$= 0$$

Another way of visualizing the fund's immunization is to use Equation 25.1 from Table 25.3 and recognize that a fund is immunized if the value of assets times their duration is equal to the product of the value of

---

[24] This discussion and example rely on the work of Kientz and Stickney 1980. Bodie 1990 argues that pension funds' need to immunize was the catalyst for most financial innovations during the past 15 years.

TABLE 25.3	**Immunizing the Net Worth of a Pension Fund**

Because, under ERISA, it is essential that the accumulated assets of a pension fund be sufficient to discharge the fund's obligations, portfolio immunization is a useful asset/liability technique.

Beginning Balance Sheet (Market Rate = 5%)

Cash	$ 65.65	Obligations	$432.95
Bonds	515.23	Net worth	147.93
Total assets	$580.88	Total obligations and net worth	$580.88

Duration of assets = 6.636 years
Duration of obligations = 8.903 years

$$D_A \times V_A = D_L \times V_L = \$3,855 \qquad\qquad [25.1]$$

$DUR_{GAP} = 0$

Revised Balance Sheet (Market Rate = 6%)

Cash	$ 65.65	Obligations	$398.47
Bonds	480.71	Net worth	147.89
Total assets	$546.36	Total obligations and net worth	$546.36

liabilities and their duration. In this case, both of those products equal $3,855.

If market rates increase, for example, to 6 percent, the present value of both assets and liabilities will decrease, as shown in the bottom panel of the table. Because the fund is immunized, however, the decline in value is equal, and net worth is $147.89. If interest rates had fallen, the increase in asset and liability values would also be equal, and net worth would also be unchanged. Recall that even an immunized fund is fully protected for only a one-time, parallel shift in the yield curve.

SPECIAL PROBLEMS IN CALCULATING DURATION FOR PENSION FUNDS. The nature of pension fund liabilities introduces some unusual problems in immunizing a fund's net worth. First, the present value of liabilities is sensitive to actuarial assumptions about mortality. Also, whether liabilities should include only those to employees with vested benefits or should consider potential obligations for all employees is another point of controversy. The assumptions affect the estimates of future cash flows, which are prerequisites to the duration calculation.

A third problem arises from the ongoing nature of pension fund liabilities. The lack of a maturity date for liabilities and the fact that new employees may be joining the sponsoring firm regularly mean that the fund's obligations may stretch far into the future. As a result, the duration of a fund's liabilities will be long.

If plans are underfunded, asset values are smaller than the present value of liabilities, and the duration of assets must be quite large to achieve immunization. Because it is often difficult to find securities with extremely long durations, full immunization may be unattainable. Financial innovations such as futures and options are available, however, as hedges to help pension funds manage the duration GAP when the portfolio cannot be immunized. Using futures and options to manage the GAP would, of course, be different from using managed futures as investments.

PERFORMANCE EVALUATION OF PENSION FUNDS

Because of the nature of the funds sources and obligations of pension funds, performance measures discussed in earlier chapters have little meaning for them. Although pension funds are subject to interest rate and other risks, they cannot be said to have an interest or underwriting "margin," nor are typical leverage or liquidity measures significant. Instead, performance appraisals focus on the yields on a fund's assets.

Even then, evaluating the performance of pension fund managers is difficult, because appropriate comparative data are scarce and because responsibility for managing the assets of a fund may be divided among several management groups. Some data on funds administered by the trust departments of major commercial banks are available through surveys and from Wilshire Associates, a California-based financial information firm. Fund performance is usually compared with overall market indexes for the same period, such as the Standard & Poor's (S&P) 500 or a bond market index. (Conceptual similarities exist between performance measurement of pension funds and mutual funds. Consequently, discussions in later sections about evaluating performance of mutual fund managers have some applicability to pension funds.)

INTERNAL VERSUS EXTERNAL MANAGEMENT

A survey of pension funds in the 1980s reported in *Institutional Investor* revealed that about 36 percent of the responding funds managed assets internally, and just over half of those that did retained management of 20 percent or less of their assets. Those funds managing a sizable portion of assets internally reported that the performance of internal managers, both in equities and in bonds, generally exceeded the returns achieved by external professional managers. They also reported that internal management was accompanied by substantial cost savings. Despite these findings, reliance on external management continues. Almost no pension funds are 100 percent internally managed in the 1990s, in fact, although most funds now choose to retain at least some internally managed assets, reversing the 1970s and 1980s trend toward 100 percent external management.[25]

ACTIVE MANAGEMENT: DESIRABLE OR UNDESIRABLE?

Regardless of whether a pension fund chooses internal or external managers, an important performance issue is whether active portfolio management can achieve greater returns than a simple buy-and-hold strategy. Wilshire Associates data on more than 1,000

funds are reported periodically in *Forbes* magazine. During 1980–1986, the Wilshire data show that the median return on pension funds' equity portfolios was slightly lower than the return on the S&P 500. The median return on fixed-income investments was slightly lower than the Shearson-Lehman bond index over most of the same period. A Brookings Institution study published in 1992 drew extremely unfavorable conclusions about pension fund performance, finding that most underperformed the S&P 500 by an average of 1.3 percent, with large funds doing even worse. The authors concluded that professional managers seem to subtract, rather than add, value to their funds' assets.[26]

A study commissioned by the U.S. Department of Labor and completed in 1986 reported that as pension funds become larger, their portfolios inevitably mirror the market portfolio. Even so, annual turnover in fund portfolios continues to increase. As pension funds continue to grow under the funding provisions of ERISA, many observers believe that their sheer size may make general market conditions, not individual management decisions, the main determinant of performance.

The implication of these findings is that active management of pension funds is not worthwhile and that investment in a portfolio that approximates a market index could offer results as good as, if not superior to, those achieved by active managers. Some funds have used an active management strategy known as **tactical asset allocation,** in which money managers try to make timely movements among stocks, bonds, and cash based on complex quantitative models. These techniques were successful in shielding some funds from the 1987 crash but did not perform well during subsequent periods. In fact, comprehensive studies of pension fund performance indicate that high turnover and frequent reallocation of assets significantly hurt performance. (They are, however, better at selecting individual stocks than at timing the market.) The explanation offered by many observers is that pension

---

[25] "Internal Management Gains Ground," *Institutional Investor* 23 (February 1989): 115–116; and Terry Williams, "The Dawn of a New Age for Internal Portfolios," *Pensions and Investments,* June 10, 1991, 21.

[26] Robert A. G. Monks, "How to Earn More on $1 Trillion," *Fortune,* September 1985, 98–99; "The Forbes/TUCS Institutional Portfolio Report," *Forbes,* February 23, 1987, 156–157; and Lakonishok, Schleifer, and Vishny 1992.

funds cannot beat the market because they *are* the market. In the late 1980s, the proportion of pension fund assets invested in stock and bond **index funds**—so named because the portfolios are deliberately selected to mirror the market as a whole—increased dramatically.[27]

An alternative to active management is the use of **guaranteed investment contracts (GICs),** by which a pension fund contracts with a life insurer to earn a fixed rate of return over a specified period. The fund pays a lump sum to the insurer and receives annuity payments in return. The insurer provides the payments from earnings on its own bond portfolio. Although GICs are designed to reduce uncertainty in pension fund earnings, they are not risk-free. The guarantee is only as sound as the financial condition of the life insurer. This point was brought home dramatically in 1991 when two large insurers, Executive Life and Mutual Benefit Life, became insolvent as the value of their asset portfolios, laden with junk bonds, fell below the value of their obligations to policyholders. Many of those obligations were GICs purchased by pension plans. Some corporations stepped in to make annuity payments to their retired employees after the insurers failed. But other corporate sponsors did not, leaving pensioners without the income they believed was "guaranteed." Even when default risk on GICs is not high, interest rate risk can be a problem. If interest rates rise after a GIC contract is negotiated with an insurer, pension funds with a large volume of GIC investments would be unable to profit from higher market yields.[28]

A similar and increasingly controversial choice for pension fund managers is to purchase **bank investment contracts (BICs),** which are time deposits with guaranteed principal and interest for a specified period. Because BICs are purchased by pension funds on behalf of individuals, each covered employee's vested interest in a plan, up to $100,000, is insured by the FDIC. Observers who believe deposit insurance coverage is already too high claim that the continued growth of BICs is an unwarranted extension of the "safety net." Private insurers selling GICs protest that FDIC insurance for BICs gives banks an unfair advantage in competing for pension fund dollars. Banks, in turn, argue that BICs are a stable source of funds that lower, rather than increase, the risk exposure of the FDIC, and that greater competition between banks and insurers improves the financial system. BICs are sure to remain the subject of lively debate in the next several years.

THE FUND MANAGERS' ANTHEM: "I WANNA HOLD YOUR HAND"

The performance record of pension fund managers continues to suggest that few are successful at achieving superior rates of return and that many clients could do as well, if not better, by passively managing their own assets. So why do pension fund managers continue to be in demand and to command high salaries? Although a definitive answer is elusive, recent research suggests that fund managers may be paid more for the psychological comfort they provide than for their financial expertise. A particularly interesting study by two anthropologists concluded that managers of institutional portfolios tend to focus more on maintaining smooth client relationships and navigating corporate politics than on economic and financial analyses of investment options. Regardless of fund performance, few managers lost their jobs if they could avoid making their corporate clients look bad. The Brookings study mentioned earlier drew a similar conclusion. The authors noted that it seemed to be more important for fund managers to have good reasons for doing poorly than for the funds they managed actually to perform well and that client "handholding" is a key fund management function. These curious findings will undoubtedly spur further research into

---

[27] See Coggin, Fabozzi, and Rahman 1993; Berkowitz, Finney, and Logue 1988; James A. White, "Asset Allocators Long for Glory Days of 1987," *The Wall Street Journal,* May 16, 1989, C1, C23; and Gary Weiss, "Index Funds: Getting More Bonds for the Buck," *Business Week,* September 21, 1987, 104. Despite growing support for indexing, surveys report that 89.9 percent of pension fund managers believe they can beat the market, regardless of evidence to the contrary. See "The Abiding Faith in Active Management," *Institutional Investor* 20 (May 1986): 97, 100.

[28] See Nathans, "The New Breed of Pensions that May Leave Retirees Poorer," 1989; Robert L. Rose, "GICs: Popular, Safe—but Are They Smart?" *The Wall Street Journal,* March 5, 1986, 33; and Larry Light et al., "Are You Really Insured?" *Business Week,* August 5, 1991, 42–48.

the "whys and wherefores" of pension fund performance in the future.[29]

INVESTMENT COMPANIES: AN OVERVIEW

Investment companies raise funds by selling ownership shares to investors, many of whom are small savers. The money is then invested in a variety of assets under the direction of professional managers. Investment companies perform the intermediation functions outlined in Chapter 1, but in a manner different from other institutions.

HOW INVESTMENT COMPANIES OPERATE

Investment company shareholders obtain benefits unavailable from direct investment or other financial intermediaries. They get greater diversification, lower transactions costs, and expert investment opinion at a lower cost than if they invested directly in the financial markets. Most investment companies rely on the sale of shares and do not use financial leverage, so the investor avoids the added risk of owning stock in an intermediary with large liabilities. In contrast to depository institutions, however, investment companies promise no guaranteed return to savers. Returns depend on managers' investment decisions and market conditions, and there is no insurance to protect the saver against loss of principal.

MANAGEMENT COMPANIES. Investment companies are separate from management companies hired to make investment decisions and to market new shares of the investment company. Management companies earn fees for their services, usually a percentage of investment company assets. Along with transactions costs, fees are subtracted from returns on investment company assets before benefits are distributed to shareholders. Because management companies also have shareholders, investment managers must earn profits for them and for the investment company. Thus,

a conflict may arise between the two groups of shareholders as fees and transactions costs increase. Management fees must be disclosed in the prospectus, and investment companies' annual reports give information about expenses. Public disclosure is intended to ensure that fund managers price their services competitively.

Evidence during a recent 10-year period suggests that investors should pay attention to these disclosures in choosing investment companies. Between 1981 and 1991, average annual rates of return to investors in both stock and bond mutual funds were negatively correlated with management expenses as a percentage of fund assets.[30]

OPEN-END COMPANIES: MUTUAL FUNDS

The investment company industry is divided into two broad categories: **open-end** and **closed-end** companies. An open-end fund sells new shares to prospective investors, or redeems shares held by investors, at the fund's current **net asset value.** The net asset value is the difference between the value of the investment company's assets and its liabilities, stated on a per-share basis. Although the phrase *net asset value* is customary in the investment company industry and is used in this discussion, it is conceptually identical to a fund's net worth per share.

Open-end companies are better known as mutual funds; they are the most popular type of investment company and, as noted, control the vast majority of industry assets.

LOAD AND NO-LOAD COMPANIES. An important distinction exists between load and no-load mutual funds. A **load** is a sales charge assessed to the investor when mutual fund shares are purchased or sold. A **front-end load** is charged when shares are purchased; a **back-end load** (a newer feature) is a charge assessed when the investor redeems shares.

When a front-end load is charged, it is added to the price at purchase. Loads usually range from 4 to 8.5 percent, although they can be as low as ½ of 1

---

[29] O'Barr and Conley 1992; and Lakonishok, Schleifer, and Vishny 1992.

[30] Jonathan Clements, "Selecting a Fund? Expenses Can Be Crucial," *The Wall Street Journal,* July 24, 1991, C1, C10.

percent. Often, load funds are marketed to investors through securities brokers or by the management company's sales force, who receive the load as a sales commission. The choice between a load and a no-load fund is an important one for investors. With a front-end load, as little as 91.5 cents of every dollar saved could actually be invested by the fund. Back-end loads, usually in the 5 percent range, also reduce returns. In recent years, sales of no-load funds have increased, although most mutual fund sales are for load funds. In 1991, for example, no-load funds, exclusive of money market funds, accounted for only 35 percent of total mutual fund sales.[31] This percentage has grown slowly in recent years.

12B-1 PLANS. A 1980 ruling by the Securities and Exchange Commission (SEC) allowed mutual funds to cover sales charges differently. The SEC's **Rule 12b-1** now permits mutual funds to charge advertising and selling expenses, including sales commissions to brokers, as an annual operating cost against the fund's assets instead of assessing new purchasers. Brokers who sell shares for the mutual fund still earn a commission, but it is charged against the fund's total assets so that all shareholders in the fund bear the burden, not just new investors. Funds that use the 12b-1 plans can call themselves no-load, but many industry observers view the annual 12b-1 charge as just a load by another name. Some funds use 12b-1 plans and also charge front-end loads to new investors.

At the time the SEC approved 12b-1 plans, it required mutual funds to disclose the way they handled advertising and selling expenses in their prospectuses. Bowing to criticism that such disclosures were insufficient to inform investors of the true cost of selling and advertising, in 1988 the SEC began requiring all funds to provide a hypothetical example of the dollar fees that would be charged on a $1,000 investment earning a 5 percent return over periods of 1, 5, and 10 years. Critics immediately noted that the new SEC disclosure rules ignore the time value of money. This means that, for example, a front-end load fund, charging a 5 percent sales fee at the time of an initial invest-

ment, could appear to be less costly than a fund charging a 5 percent back-end load on accumulations after 5 years, and also less costly than a fund assessing 1 percent 12b-1 fees each year for 5 years—even if the *present value* of the sales charges for the three funds is the same. It is likely, therefore, that disclosure rules will be the subject of continuing scrutiny.[32]

COMPARISON TO CLOSED-END FUNDS. A closed-end investment company will not automatically redeem shares when a current investor wants to liquidate them. The shareholder usually must find another investor willing to buy out the position. Because the price of shares is affected by supply and demand as well as by fund performance, the seller has no guarantee of receiving the net asset value. New closed-end shares are not necessarily issued at net asset value but at market value. If market value is less than net asset value, new shares cannot be issued without diluting the current investors' position, and the company is essentially closed to new investments.

INVESTMENT COMPANIES: REGULATORY INFLUENCES

Investment companies in the United States have gone through several boom-and-bust periods in their relatively short history. They were introduced in the United States by British investors who pooled funds to finance economic development after the Civil War. Closed-end firms were established domestically late in the nineteenth century, and the first mutual fund was founded in the mid-1920s. The performance of many investment companies suffered after the 1929 stock market crash, and the industry lost popularity. Investment losses led to regulatory scrutiny, and new legislation addressed some of the problems encountered by shareholders. By the end of 1940, the year the

---

[31] Unless otherwise noted, statistics cited in this section are drawn from the Investment Company Institute, *1992 Mutual Fund Fact Book.*

[32] For more details on the disclosure controversy, see Catherine Yang, "Fund Shopping Gets Easier," *Business Week,* February 15, 1988, 87; Laura R. Walbert, "Better Late than Never," *Forbes,* September 5, 1988, 126–127; and Jonathan Clements, "Faulty Arithmetic," *Forbes,* May 15, 1989, 112. As noted in a later section, at the time of this writing in 1993, the SEC had proposed additional rule changes for several mutual fund practices, including sales charges and their disclosures.

Investment Company Act was passed, mutual funds had total assets of only about $400 million.

THE INVESTMENT COMPANY ACT OF 1940

The Investment Company Act of 1940, first introduced in Chapter 2, has exerted more direct influence on the industry than any other single law. It regulates the composition and selection of an investment company's board of directors, as well as the agreement between the company and its investment managers. The act requires company managers to clarify investment objectives and makes the objectives subject to the approval of shareholders. For example, some mutual funds concentrate on income-producing investments, some seek long-term capital gains, and others offer a balance between the two.

The act set standards for capital structure, severely limiting mutual funds' use of financial leverage. It also imposed diversification requirements on investment company portfolios. In addition, managers have a fiduciary duty with respect to compensation. Because the language of the law is interpreted broadly, even when fees are disclosed shareholders may argue that they are excessive. Although lawsuits have been filed against investment companies, seeking reduced management compensation, the courts have never ruled against the industry. Still, the possibility of further legal action always exists. Finally, the Investment Advisors Act, also passed in 1940, sets standards for the activities of investment managers.

Although regulated for decades, investment companies express little desire to modify the current structure. As competition with depositories increases, many industry leaders believe that regulation gives shareholders confidence in the absence of federal deposit insurance.

In 1992, however, the SEC decided on its own that it was time to reexamine investment company legislation to see if it continued to meet desired public policy purposes. As a result of a staff study, the agency issued a lengthy document outlining several proposed changes in the Investment Company Act of 1940. Recommendations were primarily directed toward increased competition and better disclosure for investors. Among its many recommendations, the SEC proposed to make it easier for foreign mutual fund companies to sell shares in the United States. It also advocated rule changes that would make load sales charges more competitive, would allow investment companies greater freedom to advertise, and would alter the information contained in fund prospectuses. Finally, the agency proposed a hybrid between a closed- and open-end fund, a so-called **interval fund**—one that would allow investors to redeem their shares only at specified times, such as once a month. Industry leaders especially welcomed the latter proposal because it would permit fund managers to consider investments, such as foreign securities or shares in small businesses, that are less liquid than those typically held by open-end investment companies. As this book went to press, Congress had taken no action on the SEC's recommendations.[33]

TAXATION AND OTHER REGULATIONS

Federal tax laws applying to the public sale of securities have important effects on the operations of investment companies. Federal tax policy for investment companies is based on the conduit theory, introduced in Chapter 2. As long as an investment company distributes at least 97 percent of dividend or interest income and 90 percent of capital gains to shareholders, the fund itself is not taxed. Earnings are taxed at the individual investor's personal tax rate. To qualify for tax benefits, the firm must meet the Internal Revenue Service's minimum standards for diversification.

Because investment companies sell ownership shares publicly, they must adhere to the securities laws passed in 1933 and 1934. They also must regularly disclose their financial position and other managerial and investment policies and must meet the SEC requirements imposed on all publicly traded firms. Some states impose requirements on investment companies selling shares within the state.

GROWTH OF INVESTMENT COMPANIES SINCE 1970

Although regulation promotes the viability of the industry, it does not assure stability. Since 1970, the assets of mutual funds have fluctuated significantly. By

---

[33] SEC Staff Report 1992.

1969, mutual fund assets had reached almost $50 billion, but poor returns and investors' loss of confidence eroded that growth; by 1974, asset holdings had declined to $34 billion. The problems of investment companies were so widespread during this period that many viewed the industry as moribund.

Such reports were premature, however, because the industry revived in the years preceding the phase-out of Regulation (Reg) Q at depository institutions. Savers turned to money market mutual funds (MMMFs) because they offered market rates and desirable liquidity features. Money market fund assets grew from $3.9 billion at year-end 1978 to more than $200 billion only 4 years later. In the early 1990s, money poured into stock and bond funds at the rate of $1 billion *per day!*

Mutual fund managers recognized that investor trust was returning and developed the **family of funds** concept, making it easy for investors to switch from a stock fund to a bond fund, for example, under the management of the same parent organization. Research has indicated that marketing effectiveness influences mutual fund growth considerably, as reflected in the sale of new shares. Some in the industry share the belief that the financial performance of funds is not nearly as important to shareholders as the convenience and service they provide.[34]

These factors are reflected in Figure 25.4. The industry's renewed popularity is also evident in the number of mutual funds, which rose from 564 in 1980 to 3,423 by the end of 1991.

INVESTMENT COMPANIES: DESCRIPTIVE DATA

Most investment companies use minimal financial leverage. Consequently, only asset composition is of interest to most analysts.

ASSETS OF MUTUAL FUNDS

The assets of a mutual fund reflect the fund's stated investment objectives. Broad fund categories for the industry include equity, bond-income, short-term tax-exempt, and taxable money market funds. Note that the words taxable and tax-exempt in this context refer to the tax effects of the funds' income on their shareholders. As explained at several points in the text, investment companies themselves do not pay taxes.[35] The distribution of assets across these four types of funds at the end of 1975 and again in 1991 is shown in Figure 25.5. The phenomenal growth of taxable money market funds during this period is clear; along with bond funds, they were the largest type of mutual fund in 1991.

Although the category title into which an individual fund falls might seem to be a trivial matter, it has proved to be somewhat controversial in recent years. Investment companies placing themselves into relatively low-risk categories such as "balanced" funds or "income" funds have actually been shown to use higher-risk management approaches than funds calling themselves "growth" or even "aggressive growth" types. To the extent that the market uses category names as indicators of risk, many observers fear that investors are being misled. Some experts believe, in fact, that quantitative indexes of risk, such as beta, should be routinely disclosed and used in funds' published materials to prevent potential investor deception.[36]

ASSETS OF MONEY MARKET FUNDS. Money market funds hold only short-term assets. At year-end 1991, over 40 percent of taxable MMMF assets was invested in commercial paper; other large categories were repurchase agreements and Treasury bills (T-bills). The portfolio composition of money market funds is provided in Table 25.4, as is the average maturity of the funds' assets. The average maturity of MMMFs is particularly sensitive to current economic conditions. Because interest rates were quite low by historical standards at the end of 1991 and because the yield

---

[34] See Woerheide 1982; Jeffrey M. Laderman et al., "The People's Choice: Mutual Funds," *Business Week,* February 24, 1986, 54–57; and Laderman and Smith 1993.

[35] There are many ways to categorize the objectives of the nearly 3,500 mutual funds. These four were chosen because they are highlighted by the Investment Company Institute, the industry's most important trade organization. Within these groupings are subgroups with names such as "balanced," "growth," "high-yield," and so forth.

[36] Barbara Donnelly, "What's in a Name? Some Mutual Funds Make It Difficult for Investors to Judge," *The Wall Street Journal,* May 5, 1992, C1, C11.

FIGURE 25.4 **Assets of Mutual Funds, 1940–1991**

Mutual funds have enjoyed great popularity in recent years, spurred by the development of MMMFs in the mid-1970s. Stock and bond funds have also grown rapidly in the same period.

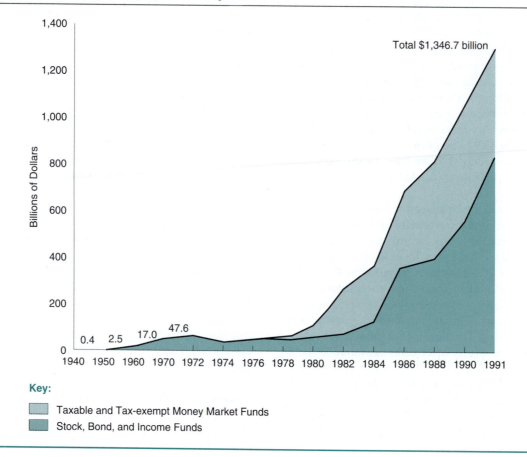

Key:

Taxable and Tax-exempt Money Market Funds

Stock, Bond, and Income Funds

Source: Investment Company Institute, *1992 Mutual Fund Fact Book,* 21. Reprinted with permission.

curve was upward-sloping, average portfolio maturity was the longest since MMMFs' inception. Fund managers were not free to consider long-term investments, but they were attempting at the end of 1991 to capture the highest yields within the narrow spectrum of maturities available to them. In contrast, in the early 1980s, when short-term interest rates were at record-breaking highs and the yield curve was sharply downward-sloping, MMMFs' average portfolio maturity was well under 1 month, as managers again sought to earn the highest returns within their operating constraints.

ASSETS OF EQUITY AND BOND-INCOME FUNDS. The largest category of assets of nonmoney market

mutual funds is common stock. The next largest categories include long-term Treasury securities, municipal bonds, and corporate bonds. Aggregate holdings of equity, bond, and income funds by asset category are shown in Table 25.5.

MANAGING MUTUAL FUND ASSETS

The management of mutual fund assets is very much influenced by the fund's investment objectives. Factors discussed under pension fund management, such as taxability, inflation, and diversification, are important influences in the investment company industry

FIGURE 25.5   **Percentage Distribution of Mutual Fund Assets**

The proportion of industry assets held by stock funds has declined since the late 1970s, and the percentages held by bond and money market funds have risen. Short-term tax-exempt funds have also become attractive to investors seeking tax-exempt income.

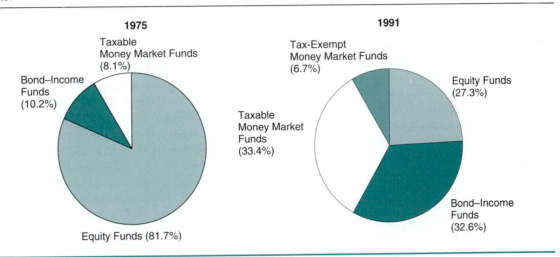

Source: Investment Company Institute, *1986* and *1992 Mutual Fund Fact Books.* Reprinted with permission.

TABLE 25.4   **Assets of Taxable Money Market Mutual Funds, Year-End 1991 (Millions of \$)[a]**

Taxable MMMFs, the largest single category of investment companies, invest heavily in commercial paper, repos, and T-bills. Returns on MMMFs change frequently, reflecting current short-term interest rates.

Commercial paper	\$187,617.2	41.72%
Repurchase agreements	68,205.8	15.17
Eurodollar certificates of deposit	21,641.5	4.81
Treasury bills	47,615.7	10.59
Bankers' acceptances	4,323.4	0.96
Commercial bank certificates of deposit	6,128.6	1.36
Federal agency securities	41,282.6	9.18
Other domestic certificates of deposit	26,898.6	5.98
Other Treasury securities	32,057.0	7.13
Other	13,961.2	3.10
Total assets	\$449,731.6	100.00%
Average asset maturity (days)	50	

[a]Totals reflect rounding.
Source: Investment Company Institute, *1992 Mutual Fund Fact Book,* 114.

TABLE 25.5   **Assets of Equity and Bond-Income Mutual Funds, Year-End 1991 (Millions of \$)[a]**

Equity and bond-income mutual funds invest in stocks, Treasury securities, and bonds. Returns on these funds fluctuate with conditions in the capital markets.

Common stock	\$328,138	40.65%
Municipal bonds	147,714	18.30
Corporate bonds	84,536	10.47
Liquid assets	25,500	3.16
Long-term Treasury securities	170,118	21.08
Short-term government securities	34,900	4.32
Preferred stock	7,991	0.99
Other	8,289	1.03
Total assets	\$807,186	100.00%

[a]Totals reflect rounding.
Source: Investment Company Institute, *1992 Mutual Fund Fact Book,* 32, 93.

and are not repeated here. Additional influences and recent evidence about the ways mutual fund managers fulfill their responsibilities are reviewed in the following sections.

TIMING AND SECURITY SELECTION

Timing refers to the coordination of investment decisions with anticipated market movements. Industry observers have debated the ability of mutual fund managers to time their decisions to achieve superior investment returns. Recent evidence indicates that fund managers' most common approach to timing is to shift cash or other liquid assets into bonds or stocks, or vice versa. For example, when an upswing in the equity market is anticipated, managers use liquid assets to purchase stocks. When a downturn is forecast, they sell stock and hold the proceeds in cash in anticipation of another market movement. Few managers report that they are likely to shift assets from bonds to stocks, or vice versa, based on their expectations.[37]

Fund managers report that the identification of over- or undervalued securities has a more important effect on fund performance than attempts to anticipate market changes and make portfolio adjustments. This belief was confirmed by studies of mutual funds during the period 1973 to 1983. Most researchers have found that few managers correctly anticipate market movements but are better at identifying undervalued securities. Some recent work suggests, however, that mutual fund managers may have better success at timing market movements than has previously been thought, a finding that will undoubtedly spur future research.[38] As exemplified by the opening story for this chapter, many observers also predict that in the 1990s mutual fund security selections will be increasingly computer-driven. This development, which parallels use of expert systems in depository institutions, may signal even less reliance on human judgment as a factor in fund performance than in the past.

Managers of money market funds place more emphasis on timing. In contrast to other mutual funds, research indicates that, during 1975–1980, MMMF managers had a fairly consistent record of timing yield changes accurately. They succeeded in shortening portfolio maturities before rates increased, giving them the ability to invest maturing assets at higher yields, and also succeeded in lengthening portfolio maturities before a decline in yields.[39]

DIVERSIFICATION

Many mutual fund managers set diversification standards for funds beyond those required by the Investment Company Act of 1940 or other regulations. The measures of diversification reported are quite different from those advocated in portfolio theory, such as correlation between individual assets or portfolio variance. Instead, many managers use guidelines such as limiting the amount invested in a single industry or limiting the proportion of the portfolio invested in certain securities.

FUND SIZE

Researchers have also examined the effects of asset growth in the mutual fund industry. They agree that a large fund cannot use the same investment strategy as a small fund, but not that one is better than the other. For example, a large fund has less flexibility to make portfolio adjustments, because trades must necessarily be in large volume. Some mutual fund managers, including those with excellent performance records, have recently decided to control asset growth by closing the funds to new investors after reaching a certain size. However, large funds may provide more safety and diversification than those with fewer assets. They may also be able to afford a larger and better-trained investment staff and may command volume discounts to reduce transactions costs. In the opinion of some observers, the appropriate fund size is based on investment objectives, and no general guidelines govern growth.[40]

---

[37] See Veit and Cheney 1984.

[38] Chen and Stockum 1986; Chua and Woodward 1986; Lee and Rahman 1991; and Shukla and Trzcinka 1992.

[39] See Ferri and Oberhelman 1981.

[40] The opinions of many industry experts are summarized in Laura Walbert, "Bigness and Badness," *Forbes,* July 29, 1985, 70–71. More discussion of fund size and success is found in "Fidelity Changes Tack," *The Economist,* August 8, 1992, 67–68.

SPECIALIZATION

The degree to which a mutual fund should specialize is also subject to debate. Some funds choose goals more specific than growth or income. For example, some choose securities of the health care industry, service industries, Ginnie Mae certificates, junk bonds, socially concerned companies, or new firms. These funds are known as **sector funds.** Many large mutual fund families offer at least one sector fund.

The decision to invest in a sector fund is a decision to forgo the potential benefits of diversification. Yet sector funds attracted many new investors in the 1980s. International investments have been especially popular, and the top-performing mutual funds in the late 1980s included several exclusively international portfolios. Some more highly specialized firms invest in the securities of a single foreign country, such as France or Germany. Such specialization carries added risks from inadequate diversification, as illustrated by the extent to which returns on European sector funds have varied in the 1990s as a result of wide currency fluctuations in those countries.

Some investors have shown interest in a type of mutual fund at the opposite end of the spectrum. Known as a "fund of funds," such a fund affords the maximum degree of diversification by investing in the shares of other mutual funds! A potential problem is excessive diversification, which increases management costs with little reduction in portfolio risk. Most experts argue that any large mutual fund provides sufficient diversification, and little benefit is received from paying managers to select shares of other mutual funds.

PERFORMANCE EVALUATION OF INVESTMENT COMPANIES

Traditional ratio analysis is inappropriate for evaluating most investment companies, but there is considerable interest in other measures of the industry's performance, especially that of mutual funds. Over the past two decades, many academic studies have attempted to establish guidelines for managing fund assets. The four asset management issues discussed earlier have been addressed: 1) timing and security selection; 2) diversification and risk management; 3) fund size;

and 4) specialization. Generally, the research questions whether managers successfully evaluate securities and time portfolio adjustments, whether they achieve appropriate portfolio diversification, and whether they can earn rates of return commensurate with the risk assumed.[41]

EVALUATING RATES OF RETURN

A key question in evaluating investment companies is whether they offer shareholders a rate of return higher than could be obtained through direct investment. For mutual funds, research has attempted to ascertain whether an investor could adopt a simple buy-and-hold strategy and earn a better return than is achieved by the typically active investment style of a mutual fund's professional managers—and the associated costs. Two approaches are used for evaluating rates of return.

COMPARING RISK-ADJUSTED RETURNS. The academic literature generally advocates rating funds by paying close attention to the riskiness of the fund's assets. One method compares *ex post* risk-adjusted rates of return with those that would be expected *ex ante,* using performance measures based on capital market theory and the efficient-markets hypothesis. Many studies have concluded that the efforts of professional managers do not achieve results superior to buy-and-hold strategies.

The findings are consistent with the efficient-markets hypothesis in that even professional investment managers seem unable to outperform the market. Many experts have recommended an approach to mutual fund management similar to that for large pension funds: Invest in a market or index portfolio, and attempt to earn a return equal to the market as a whole. In the 1980s, in fact, bond index funds grew in popularity, as investors seemed to recognize that interest rate forecasting is, at best, an inexact science. The trend may prove to be profitable. One study indicated that between 1982 and 1987, few managers of fixed-income portfolios earned a return as high as the

---

[41] There is a large body of research on this topic. Some representative studies include Friend, Blume, and Crockett 1970, 50–68; Jensen 1968; Sharpe 1966; and Kon and Jen 1979. For a review of this research over the last 25 years, see Shukla and Trzcinka 1992.

Shearson-Lehman bond index. In 1985 and 1986, for example, not even half did as well as the index. A more recent analysis and review of research on aggregate mutual fund performance, however, concludes that mutual fund managers have been able to match market performance. The implication is that mutual funds earn a gross return higher than the market, before adjusting for risk and deducting expenses. Net of managerial expenses and after risk adjustments, performance is still competitive with market indexes.

Despite these results, stock index funds have greatly increased in popularity since 1989. Although the S&P 500 is the most widely used market benchmark among stock index funds, some investment companies offer funds mirroring broader "baskets" of stocks, such as the Wilshire 5000.[42]

A second method of evaluating risk-adjusted performance is to compute one or more statistics for portfolio ranking developed in the academic literature in the mid-1960s and still widely advocated. To calculate the **Sharpe Index,** one divides the average risk premium earned on a portfolio during the rating period by the standard deviation of returns over the period:

$$[25.2]$$

$$SI_p = \frac{(r_p - r_f)}{\sigma_p}$$

This statistic compares the average risk premium on the portfolio $(r_p - r_f)$ to the portfolio's total risk (σ_p) during the same period; the higher the resulting index, the greater the risk premium for the risk of the portfolio and the better the performance. This measure is especially useful for investors who invest all assets in a single mutual fund so that the risk of the fund represents their total risk exposure.

Another portfolio-ranking measure, the **Treynor Index,** divides the average risk premium by the beta (β) of the portfolio:

$$[25.3]$$

$$TI_p = \frac{(r_p - r_f)}{\beta_p}$$

In contrast to the Sharpe Index, the Treynor Index compares the average risk premium with the portfolio's systematic, or market, risk. Like the Sharpe Index, the higher the Treynor Index, the better the performance. The Treynor Index is a useful ranking measure for investors with well-diversified investment holdings, including, perhaps, several mutual funds. Because its beta, by definition, is equal to one, the market portfolio (and, presumably, an index fund managed to mirror the market) will have a Treynor Index equal to the market risk premium $(r_m - r_f)$ for the evaluation period. If a manager is responsible for a portfolio of greater or lesser risk than the market (that is, a portfolio with a beta greater than or less than one), the Treynor Index will allow an analyst to determine whether a fund manager outperformed the market, considering the risk of the fund's assets.[43]

Table 25.6 illustrates the calculation of these two statistics for a hypothetical fund during a 12-month period. In both cases, the hypothetical fund performed worse than the market as a whole. Because the fund's beta was less than 1, an average return less than the average market return would be expected. The indexes show, however, that even taking its relatively low risk into account, the fund performed worse than the market. Investors who held the market portfolio (or an index fund) during this period would have fared better for bearing only a small amount of additional risk (beta of 1 compared with a beta of 0.97).

---

[42] Ippolito 1993; Jonathan Clements, "Mutual Funds: Much Ado About Indexes," *The Wall Street Journal,* May 18, 1990, C1; Jonathan Clements, "Many Funds Don't Track Whole Market," *The Wall Street Journal,* June 6, 1990, C1, C9; George Anders, "Returns Seesaw for Managers Seeking to Top Index on Bonds," *The Wall Street Journal,* April 21, 1986, 33; George Anders, "Managers Fail to Equal Rise of Benchmarks in Stocks, Bonds," *The Wall Street Journal,* January 2, 1987, 24B; and Weiss, "Index Funds Getting More Bond for the Buck," 1987.

---

[43] These indexes were introduced in Sharpe 1966 and Treynor 1965. Because working with rate-of-return data always poses statistical problems, use of the indexes is controversial. See, for example, French and Henderson 1985. Also, rankings according to performance indexes can vary considerably, depending on the measure of market performance used and other model assumptions. See Lehmann and Modest 1987.

TABLE 25.6	**Sharpe and Treynor Indexes for a Hypothetical Portfolio**

The Sharpe and Treynor indexes enable analysts to rank portfolio performance on a risk-adjusted basis. In this example, the fund earned an insufficient return compared to its risk, and it ranks lower on both indexes than does the market portfolio over the same period.

Month	Monthly Risk-Free Rate	Monthly Return on Fund	Monthly Return on Market
1	1.2%	5.6%	6.0%
2	0.6	4.1	3.5
3	1.0	−2.0	−1.0
4	0.7	7.7	7.3
5	1.2	4.1	5.6
6	1.3	3.7	4.0
7	0.6	−3.4	0.5
8	1.1	0.5	−2.3
9	1.0	3.5	5.5
10	0.4	1.0	4.3
11	1.3	5.6	3.6
12	0.8	−2.3	−0.2
Monthly Average:	0.93% (r_f)	2.34% (r_p)	3.07 (r_m)
Monthly Standard Deviation:		3.39% (σ_p)	2.95% (σ_m)
Beta:		0.97 (β_p)	1 (β_m)
Risk Premium:		1.41% ($r_p - r_f$)	2.13% ($r_m - r_f$)

Sharpe Index (25.2):

Fund:

$$\frac{(2.34\% - 0.93\%)}{3.39\%} = 0.42$$

Market Portfolio:

$$\frac{(3.07\% - 0.93\%)}{2.95\%} = 0.72$$

Treynor Index (25.3):

Fund:

$$\frac{(2.34\% - 0.93\%)}{0.97} = 1.45\%$$

Market Portfolio:

$$\frac{(3.07\% - 0.93\%)}{1} = 2.13\%$$

RELATIVE PERFORMANCE EVALUATION. Practitioners tend to evaluate performance by comparing an individual fund to funds with similar investment objectives or to some market index. Surveys of mutual fund managers reveal that they do not consider risk-adjusted performance measures useful and that they tend to use simple comparative techniques instead.[44]

A recent evaluation of relative performance identified a phenomenon sure to be a topic of further study: Mutual funds ranked among the top performers in a given year also tend to earn high returns in the following quarter, while poor performers earn poor returns in the subsequent quarter. In other words, researchers have drawn preliminary conclusions that mutual fund returns are temporally correlated, so investors are wise to react quickly to relative performance evaluations. The researchers did not, however, find funds that sustained superior performance (that is, earned risk-adjusted returns greater than the market indexes) for an extended period of time.[45]

Performance comparison for managers and investors is facilitated by several regularly published reports on the industry. Arthur Weisenberger Services publishes an annual volume entitled *Investment Companies,* including not only performance information but also a fund's history, management, and other pertinent data. Quarterly and monthly reports of performance are also available from Weisenberger.

---

[44] Veit and Cheney 1984.

[45] For further discussion, see Hendricks, Patel, and Zeckhauser 1993.

Barron's publishes a quarterly report on mutual funds prepared by Lipper Analytical Services. *Forbes* and *Business Week* prepare annual reports on mutual funds, including short- and long-term records. Updates on selected funds are provided more frequently. All sources categorize funds by objective and identify load fees and management expenses. They often include a qualitative risk rating and indicate a fund's performance in both up and down markets.

SIZE AND PERFORMANCE

Some comparative studies have concluded that small funds have outperformed large mutual funds in recent years. These results should not be interpreted as blanket support for small funds, however, because smaller funds have less diversification potential and may expose investors to higher risk. Furthermore, other studies fail to detect performance differences based on size. Unless risk-adjusted returns are considered, one cannot conclude that size is instrumental to fund performance.

SUMMARY

This chapter considered asset/liability management in two nondepository intermediaries: pension funds and investment companies. Each industry faces unique regulations and problems in the management of interest rate and other financial market risks. Each also shares the challenges of increasing competition in the financial markets.

Private pension funds are responsible for investing monies to be used later to pay retirement benefits. ERISA established the fiduciary responsibilities of managers, funding standards, methods for guaranteeing benefits, and other important aspects of pension fund management. Most pension fund assets are invested in common stock and corporate bonds, and the funds' obligations are determined actuarially. The main sources of funds to pension plans are employer contributions and earnings on assets. Issues especially important to pension funds are taxation, inflation, diversification, and the financial condition of the corporate sponsor. In recent years, pension funds have applied new techniques for managing portfolio and interest rate risk. Because of the large size of many pension funds, however, active portfolio management is not always advisable. For this reason, index funds, which attempt to mirror the performance of the market as a whole, are increasingly common.

Investment companies are financial intermediaries that sell shares to the public and reinvest proceeds in the financial markets. Open-end companies, called mutual funds, are by far the largest type. Investment companies are regulated by the SEC according to the Investment Company and Investment Advisors Acts of 1940. The industry has grown rapidly in the past two decades. The majority of investment companies' assets are in money market instruments, followed by common stock, Treasury securities, and bonds. International funds are gaining favor as the financial markets become more global.

Most of the portfolio management issues facing pension funds also apply to investment companies. Many experts advocate using risk-adjusted performance measures to determine the success of mutual fund managers. Research on investment company performance, when compared with returns on simple buy-and-hold strategies, has not favored the industry, although there is not universal agreement with this conclusion.

QUESTIONS

1. Explain the difference between defined benefit and defined contribution pension funds. Which types of plans do you think most employees would prefer? Why? How is a fund's asset management affected by its status as a defined benefit or defined contribution plan?

2. Discuss the effects of ERISA on the fiduciary responsibilities of pension fund managers.

3. What is the PBGC? Briefly explain the reasons for its recent financial problems. Compare and contrast these problems with those experienced by the deposit insurance funds. From recent publications, determine what steps have been taken to address the PBGC's difficulties. Do you believe these steps are adequate or inadequate? Why?

4. Why does ERISA place emphasis on full funding of pension liabilities? What are the difficulties in measuring whether or not a plan is fully funded? Explain the influence of actuarial assumptions on the funding status of a plan.

5. In comparison to banks and property/liability insurers, do pension funds have more or less complexity in liquidity management? Explain.

6. Discuss the impact of the corporate sponsor's financial position on the financial management of pension funds. If you had been employed by U.S. Steel (now USX) in 1982 or Chrysler in 1991, would you have been disturbed by the companies' contributions of stock instead of cash? Why or why not?

7. What are reversions? How do they affect a firm's employees? Stockholders? Do you believe that they should be completely unregulated, somewhat regulated, or prohibited altogether? Explain your reasons.

8. Consult recent periodicals and other financial publications for a feature on the involvement of pension fund managers in the internal decisions of corporations in which they hold stock. (CALPERS—the California Public Employees' Retirement System—might be a prime subject.) What are the financial implications of this strategy, both for the fund and the corporation? Do you think it is appropriate? Why or why not?

9. Activists have placed increasing pressure on pension fund managers to address social initiatives in addition to traditional financial objectives. What are the potential problems with managing a portfolio according to social criteria? The potential benefits? What balance between the two types of objectives do you favor? Why?

10. Briefly discuss the recent financial performance of pension funds that invested in real estate in the 1980s. What nontraditional risks and rewards do these assets present?

11. What are managed futures? Do pension funds use them for hedging or for other risk/return purposes? Evaluate the advantages and disadvantages of adding managed futures to a pension fund portfolio.

12. Explain the unique problems faced when applying immunization to pension funds.

13. Do you think active portfolio management is feasible and desirable for pension funds? Explain. Would your answer depend on the size of the fund? What are the risks in replacing active management with guaranteed investment contracts?

14. Using library references, find further details about the failures of Executive Life and Mutual Benefit Life in 1991. How were holders of their GICs affected? What was the impact on the pension fund industry, and how has the industry reassessed these contracts as investment alternatives?

15. If you were a pension fund official and had to choose between tactical asset allocation or managing the portfolio as an index fund, which would you favor? Why? Which management style would you prefer if you were an employee covered by the plan? Why?

16. Should pension funds remain free of taxation? Do you believe that pension funds' tax status should be affected by how often they trade assets or how long they hold them? Explain.

17. What benefits do investment companies offer to shareholders that are not provided by other indirect investment alternatives? By direct investment? Distinguish between open-end and closed-end investment companies. What advantages and disadvantages do each offer shareholders? What is the function of management companies in the investment company industry?

18. What is a load mutual fund? How do loads affect returns to shareholders? Explain the distinction between a front-end load and a back-end load. How has SEC rule 12b-1 changed the way mutual funds charge shareholders for advertising, selling, and brokerage expenses? Would you categorize a 12b-1 plan as a load or a no-load fund?

19. What are the major regulations governing investment companies, and how do they affect the financial management of investment companies? Why do you think investment companies have not pressed Congress for deregulation in recent years?

20. Review recent financial publications to determine whether Congress has taken action on the proposed revisions in the Investment Company Act of 1940. What is their current status? Has the SEC implemented any policy changes for marketing mutual funds? What types of fee disclosures, if any, do you believe mutual funds should make?

21. Investment companies have grown at an exceptionally rapid rate in recent years, despite volatility in the stock and bond markets. Do you expect this growth to continue? What important factors influence your answer?

22. MMMFs are both formidable competitors to and important customers of depositories. Explain.

23. Explain how managers' decisions about timing and security selection affect the performance of mutual funds. Are the effects the same for money market and other mutual funds?

24. What are sector funds? What are the advantages and disadvantages of investing in these funds versus other types of investment companies?

25. Why do you think index funds have grown in popularity in recent years? Do you expect the trend to continue? Why or why not?

26. Compare the Sharpe and Treynor Indexes. Under what circumstances would an investor choose one over the other for evaluating a mutual fund's performance? Why do you think professional fund managers prefer relative performance measures to risk-adjusted measures?

PROBLEMS

1. The Earth Movers Manufacturing Company has hired a consulting firm to provide advice on asset/liability management. The following information has been collected:

Financial Data (Millions)	
Cash	$101.50
Obligations	$885.75
Duration of obligations	23 years
Obligations/total assets	86%

a. Calculate the dollar amounts of total assets and earning assets on the balance sheet.
b. Based on your calculations and these data, is the fund overfunded or underfunded? Explain.
c. Determine the asset duration needed to immunize the net worth position of the pension fund.

2. A pension fund has obligations of $100,000 per year for 50 years and no cash assets. Its only assets are guaranteed investment contracts that promise to pay $125,000 per year for 35 years. The current market rate for both assets and liabilities is 9 percent.
a. What is the present value of the funds' assets? What is their duration?
b. What is the present value of the funds' obligations? What is their duration?
c. Is the fund immunized? Explain. If not, what is its duration GAP?
d. Show how the balance sheet of the fund would change if market rates rose to 9.25 percent and if they fell to 8.75 percent.

3. A pension fund currently has earning assets of $36,750,000 and obligations of $32,000,000. The cash balance is $3,250,000. The current market rate for both assets and liabilities is 6.5 percent, and the fund currently has a duration GAP of 2.3 years. If market rates increase by 1.5 percent, what will be the resulting change in the fund's net worth? (Hint: Formulas in Chapter 19 are useful for answering this question.)

4. Winston Manufacturers estimates the future cash-flow obligations of its pension fund to be $450,000 per year for the next 10 years. The discount rate is 6 percent. The fund's net worth currently stands at $400,000, and the cash balance is $180,000. If management wants to immunize net worth from an unexpected shift in market yields, what average duration must it achieve for its portfolio of earning assets?

5. During a recent 2-year period, the monthly returns on the stock of Running Bear Mutual Fund and on the S&P 500 were as follows:

Month	Return on Running Bear, Percent	Return on S&P 500, Percent
1	2%	1%
2	3	2
3	-3	-1
4	-1	1
5	3	1
6	2	2
7	1	0
8	1	1
9	-2	-1
10	-1	0
11	0	1
12	3	2

Month	Return on Running Bear, Percent	Return on S&P 500, Percent
13	2	2
14	3	2
15	0	1
16	−1	0
17	1	0
18	2	2
19	−1	0
20	1	1
21	4	2
22	3	3
23	2	1
24	3	2

You are interested in evaluating Running Bear's performance over the 2 years on a risk-adjusted basis. The average monthly return on T-bills during the period was 0.86 percent.

a. Calculate the average monthly return and the standard deviation of monthly returns for Running Bear and for the S&P 500.

b. Using the regression program in your spreadsheet package and the 24 monthly returns on Running Bear and the S&P 500, estimate Running Bear's beta coefficient. (Hint: Review the procedure in Chapter 5.)

c. Plot a scattergram showing Running Bear's returns against those on the market. Using your results from part b, sketch the regression line between Running Bear and the market.

d. Calculate the Sharpe and Treynor Indexes for Running Bear and for the S&P 500. How does Running Bear compare to the market?

SELECTED REFERENCES

Abken, Peter J. "Corporate Pensions and Government Insurance." *Economic Review* (Federal Reserve Bank of Atlanta) 77 (March/April 1992): 1–16.

Arnott, Robert D. "The Pension Sponsor's View of Asset Allocation." *Financial Analysts Journal* 41 (September/October 1985): 17–23.

Berkowitz, Stephen A., Louis D. Finney, and Dennis E. Logue. *The Investment Performance of Corporate Pension Plans.* New York: Quorum Books, 1988.

Bodie, Zvi. "Pension Funds and Financial Innovation." *Financial Management* 19 (Autumn 1990): 11–22.

Bodie, Zvi, et al. "Corporation Pension Policy: An Empirical Investigation." *Financial Analysts Journal* 41 (September/October 1985): 10–16.

Buynak, Thomas M. "Is the U.S. Pension-Insurance System Going Broke?" *Economic Commentary* (Federal Reserve Bank of Cleveland), January 15, 1987.

Chen, Carl R., and Steve Stockum. "Selectivity, Market Timing, and Random Beta Behavior of Mutual Funds: A Generalized Model." *Journal of Financial Research* 9 (Spring 1986): 87–96.

Chicago Board of Trade. *Managed Futures: An Investment Opportunity for Institutional Investors.* Chicago, 1992.

Chua, Jess H., and Richard S. Woodward. *Gains from Stock Market Timing.* New York: Salomon Brothers Center for the Study of Financial Institutions, 1986.

Coggin, T. Daniel, Frank J. Fabozzi, and Shafiqur Rahman. "The Investment Performance of U.S. Equity Fund Managers: An Empirical Investigation." *Journal of Finance* 48 (July 1993): 1039–1055.

Cummins, J. David, et al. "Effects of ERISA on the Investment Policies of Private Pension Plans: Survey Evidence." *Journal of Risk and Insurance* 47 (September 1980): 447–476.

Erhlich, Edna E. "International Diversification by United States Pension Funds." *Quarterly Review* (Federal Reserve Bank of New York) 6 (Autumn 1981): 1–14.

Estrella, Arturo, and Beverly Hirtle. "Estimating the Funding Gap of the Pension Benefit Guaranty Corporation." *Quarterly Review* (Federal Reserve Bank New York) (Autumn 1988): 45–59.

Ezra, D. Don, and Keith P. Ambachtsheer. "Pension Funds:

Rich or Poor?" *Financial Analysis Journal* 41 (March/April 1985): 43–56.

Ferri, Michael G., and H. Dennis Oberhelman. "A Study of the Management of Money Market Mutual Funds: 1975–1980." *Financial Management* 10 (August 1981): 24–29.

French, Dan W., and Glenn V. Henderson, Jr. "How Well Does Performance Evaluation Perform?" *Journal of Portfolio Management* (Winter 1985): 15–18.

Friend, Irwin, Marshall Blume, and Jean Crockett. *Mutual Funds and Other Institutional Investors.* New York: McGraw-Hill, 1970.

Hendricks, Darryll, Jayendu Patel, and Richard Zeckhauser, "Hot Hands in Mutual Funds: Short-Run Persistance of Relative Performance, 1974–1988." *Journal of Finance* 48 (March 1993): 93–130.

Investment Company Institute. *Mutual Fund Fact Book.* Various issues.

Investment Policy Guidebook for Corporate Pension Plan Trustees. Brookfield, WI: International Foundation of Employee Benefit Plans, 1984.

Ippolito, Richard A. "On Studies of Mutual Fund Performance, 1962–1991." *Financial Analysts Journal* 49 (January/February 1993): 42–50.

Jensen, Michael D. "The Performance of Mutual Funds in the Period 1945–1964." *Journal of Finance* 23 (May 1968): 389–416.

Kientz, Richard J., and Clyde P. Stickney. "Immunization of Pension Funds and Sensitivity to Actuarial Assumptions." *Journal of Risk and Insurance* 47 (June 1980): 223–239.

Kon, Stanley, and Frank C. Jen. "The Investment Performance of Mutual Funds: An Empirical Investigation of Timing, Selectivity, and Market Efficiency." *Journal of Business* 42 (April 1979): 263–289.

Laderman, Jeffrey M., and Geoffrey Smith. "The Power of Mutual Funds." *Business Week,* January 18, 1993, 62–68.

Lakonishok, Josef, Andrei Schleifer, and Robert Vishny. "The Structure and Performance of the Money Management Industry." *Brookings Papers on Economic Activity: Microeconomics.* Washington, DC: Brookings Institution, 1992.

Lee, Cheng-few, and Shafiqur Rahman. "Market Timing, Selectivity, and Mutual Fund Performance." *Journal of Business* 63 (1991): 261–278.

Lehmann, Bruce N., and David M. Modest. "Mutual Fund Performance Evaluation: A Comparison of Benchmarks and Benchmark Comparisons." *Journal of Finance* 42 (June 1987): 233–265.

Light, Larry. "The Power of Pension Funds." *Business Week,* November 6, 1989, 154–158.

Logue, Dennis E., and Richard J. Rogalski. *Managing Corporate Pension Plans: The Impact of Inflation.* Washington, DC: American Enterprise Institute, 1984.

Louargand, Marc A. "A Survey of Pension Fund Real Estate Portfolio Risk Management Practices." *Journal of Real Estate Research* 7 (Fall 1992): 361–374.

McKenna, Fred W., and Yong H. Kim. "Managerial Risk Preferences, Real Pension Costs, and Long-Run Corporate Pension Fund Investment Policy." *Journal of Risk and Insurance* 53 (March 1986): 29–48.

Munnell, Alicia H. "Current Taxation of Qualified Pension Plans: Has the Time Come?" *New England Economic Review* (Federal Reserve Bank of Boston) (March/April 1992): 12–25.

———. "Guaranteeing Private Pension Benefits: A Potentially Expensive Business." *New England Economic Review* (Federal Reserve Bank of Boston) (March/April 1982): 24–47.

———. "Pension Contribution and the Stock Market." *New England Economic Review* (Federal Reserve Bank of Boston) (November/December 1987): 3–14.

———. "Public versus Private Provision of Retirement Income." *New England Economic Review* (Federal Reserve Bank of Boston) (May/June 1988): 51–57.

O'Barr, William M., and John M. Conley. "Managing Relationships: The Culture of Institutional Investing." *Financial Analysts Journal* 48 (September/October 1992): 21–27.

Pozen, Robert C. "The Prudent Person Rule and ERISA: A Legal Perspective." *Financial Analysts Journal* 33 (March/April 1977): 30–35.

Reiter, Sara Ann. "Economic Measures of Unfunded Pension Obligations." *Quarterly Review of Economics and Finance* 32 (Summer 1992): 110–128.

Rosen, Kenneth T. "The Role of Pension Funds in Housing Finance." *Housing Finance Review* 1 (April 1982): 147–177.

Rosenberg, Hilary. "What Price Turnover?" *Institutional Investor* 22 (October 1988): 211–223.

———. "Will U.S. Pension Funds Go Global?" *Institutional Investor* 23 (March 1989): 121–126.

SEC Staff Report. *Protecting Investors: A Half-Century of Investment Company Regulation.* Chicago, IL: Commerce Clearing House, 1992.

Sharpe, William F. "Mutual Fund Performance." *Journal of Business* 39 (January 1966): 119–138.

Shukla, Ravi, and Charles Trzcinka. "Performance Measurement of Managed Portfolios." *Financial Markets, Institutions and Instruments* 1 (Number 4, 1992).

Steinberg, Richard M., and Harold Dankner. *Pensions: An ERISA Accounting and Management Guide.* New York: John Wiley and Sons, 1983.

Treynor, Jack L. "How to Rate Management of Investment Funds." *Harvard Business Review* (January/February 1965): 131–136.

Veit, E. Theodore, and John M. Cheney. "Managing Investment Portfolios: A Survey of Mutual Funds." *Financial Review* 19 (November 1984): 321–338.

Warshawsky, Mark J. "Pension Plans: Funding, Assets, and Regulatory Environment." *Federal Reserve Bulletin* 74 (November 1988): 717–730.

Woerheide, Walt. "Investor Response to Suggested Criteria for the Selection of Mutual Funds." *Journal of Financial and Quantitative Analysis* 17 (March 1982): 129–137.

It's getting harder to make money on Wall Street these days.

Michael Siconolfi,

Reporter, *The Wall Street Journal* (1992)

In 1990, the headlines declared "For Wall Street's Investment Bankers, Forecast Is for a Blizzard of Pink Slips," and the next year the picture was just as bleak: "Brokerage Firms Scale Back at Fast Pace." But do not jump to premature conclusions that the securities industry is on an irreversible downhill slide! By spring 1992, *The Wall Street Journal* was reporting "Underwriting Fees Headed for a Record."[1]

Obviously, anyone seeking a career in a stable and secure industry should not consider investment banking or brokerage services. Rocked by the crash of 1987 and the sudden reversal in fortunes of the stars of the merger and acquisition era, the securities industry has seen its share of failures, layoffs, and scandals. But, as is true of firms in other segments of the financial services industry, innovation and adaptation are distinguishing characteristics of the surviving securities firms. Some of them are familiar and traditional names, such as Merrill Lynch and Goldman Sachs. Others are struggling to become household names, such as the discount brokerages of Charles Schwab and Quick & Reilly. The past and future challenges for asset/liability managers in securities firms are the subjects of this chapter.

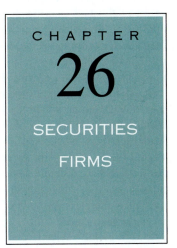

C H A P T E R

26

SECURITIES

FIRMS

---

[1] Michael Siconolfi and William Power, "Underwriting Fees Headed for a Record," *The Wall Street Journal,* March 24, 1992, C1, C11; William Power, "Brokerage Firms Scale Back at Fast Pace," *The Wall Street Journal,* June 21, 1991, C1, C13; and William Power, "For Wall Street's Investment Bankers, Forecast Is for a Blizzard of Pink Slips," *The Wall Street Journal,* December 7, 1990.

SECURITIES FIRMS: AN OVERVIEW

Securities firms perform several different but related financial functions in an industry that has changed greatly in recent decades. Some of the changes date back to 1975, when two separate regulatory rulings introduced new competitors and procedures. Another landmark occurrence was the precipitous drop in the equity markets in October 1987. The results have challenged even the largest securities firms and their most capable managers; changes include failures and mergers of established securities firms, acquisitions of securities firms by companies outside the industry, heightened competition, the development of innovative financial services and instruments, the rise and fall of the junk bond market, and ever more elusive profits.

The services offered by securities firms include investment banking; brokerage services and securities trading; merchant banking; and services such as asset management accounts, financial advisory services, and mutual fund sponsorship. As noted in Chapter 1, securities firms are different from other financial institutions in that they frequently do not perform the intermediation function. This list of securities firms' services suggests, in fact, that firms are more often involved in giving advice to customers and in assisting in funds transfers than in transforming secondary securities to primary securities. However, securities firms are so important to the financial markets and to the process of financial innovation that this book would be incomplete without examining their financial management problems.

INVESTMENT BANKING

Experts once defined investment banking as a "business which has as its function the flotation of new securities, both debt and equity, to the general public . . . for the purpose of raising funds for clients. . . ." Reflecting the radical developments in the securities industry since the mid-1970s, a more recent analysis described the business of investment banking as "financing change itself."[2] Investment bankers'

role in the issuance of securities makes them dominant in the primary securities markets.

FINANCIAL INNOVATIONS: CREATING NEW SECURITIES. Investment bankers assist both private firms and public entities in selecting securities to issue and determining their characteristics (coupon rates, maturities, offering prices, and so on). In recent years, investment bankers have been influential in adding new twists to financial instruments. In 1982, Salomon Brothers created stripped zero-coupon issues from existing Treasury securities, a development first discussed in Chapter 9. In the uncertain interest rate environment of 1984, Merrill Lynch and Company and other investment bankers advised clients to issue bonds with put options, giving the holder the right to redeem the bond at par before maturity. The investor is protected against interest rate risk because the bonds can be liquidated without a loss even if interest rates have risen. Salomon Brothers, in late 1984, introduced securities backed by automobile loans [Certificates for Automobile Receivables (CARs)], discussed in earlier chapters. Investment bankers led the development of mortgage-backed securities. And it was aggressive investment bankers who fueled the huge volume of leveraged buyouts with junk bonds and other innovative financing techniques. Securities firms also spurred growth in the interest rate swaps market by matching suitable counterparties and sometimes even by serving as counterparties themselves. More recently, investment bankers have facilitated the markets for interest rate caps and floors by writing many of these instruments.

Securities firms have economic incentives to innovate. The traditional products about which they have advised clients—stocks and bonds—have commodity-like characteristics; that is, one stock or bond issue is often very similar to another. These securities are traded in large, highly competitive markets; no single investment banking firm can "corner the market" on new stock issues, for example, in an attempt to earn above-average profits consistently. Yet by creating new and unique securities for clients, an investment banking firm may be able—at least temporarily—to dominate that market niche and thus to capture superior profits.

As with any financial activity, however, financial innovation poses risks as well as offers rewards. For

---

[2] These definitions appear in the comprehensive study of the investment banking industry by Friend et al. 1967, 80; and in Bloch 1989. (References are listed in full at the end of this chapter.)

example, a securities firm may direct large amounts of resources to develop a particular product, only to find that it fails to meet market needs, or that the market is too small to be profitable. Alternatively, sophisticated clients may initially embrace innovations developed with the assistance of investment bankers, but then may quickly "outgrow" the need for a securities firm's advice. In other instances, the market for an innovation developed by a single firm may prove to be unexpectedly large, attracting so many competing products that high profit margins are rapidly reduced and the innovator's initial investment takes much longer to recoup than expected.

An observer who understands depository institutions but has not studied securities firms might conclude that these risks pose unacceptable dangers to the financial system. Yet, securities firms are exposed to market discipline to a much greater extent than are depositories. Furthermore, market value accounting rules have applied to the securities industry to a much greater extent than they have, historically, to depositories. An investment banking firm that, in the view of the financial markets, takes on more risk than it can manage should have more difficulty attracting capital, and its cost of capital should increase. Therefore, its pace of innovation should be slowed. If its managers fail to heed the markets' warnings, the firm indeed may fail. But because securities firms cannot abandon their liabilities to the deposit insurance system, their shareholders and creditors should bear the major burden of the failure.

The 1990 failure of Drexel Burnham Lambert is a good example of this form of market discipline at work in the securities industry. Drexel had gained prominence in the 1980s as a result of its innovations in the junk bond and leveraged buyout markets. The aggressiveness of its dealmakers in these markets was legendary, and Drexel grew at a torrid pace for most of the decade. When it became clear in late 1988 that part of the firm's spectacular success was the result of fraud and mismanagement, and not of exceptional skill, the firm began to have difficulty getting financing to meet its liquidity needs. Ultimately, all market sources of cash dried up and Drexel's CEO appealed to the Federal Reserve (Fed) and the Securities and Exchange Commission (SEC) to bail the firm out of its troubles. Both agencies refused, and Drexel declared bankruptcy in February 1990. The financial markets ab-

sorbed news of the firm's end without panic, in considerable contrast to their reaction when Continental Illinois Bank almost collapsed, except for intervention from the Fed, in 1984.[3]

UNDERWRITING. Also important is the underwriting function, in which investment bankers assume the risk of adverse price movements immediately after the issuance of new securities. An underwriter purchases new securities from a client for a price negotiated in advance and then resells them. The difference between the price paid by the underwriter and the price at which the securities are sold to the public (the spread) is a source of profit in the underwriting business—and a source of risk as well. Capital advanced to the issuer may be provided by a group of investment bankers, known as a **syndicate.**[4]

Despite its traditional importance to investment banking, underwriting declined in prominence in the industry during the 1980s—losing out to the more glamorous merger and acquisition specialists. After the crash of 1987, some wondered if the stock market and underwriting would ever return to their former glory. But the skeptics learned a lesson in 1991 and 1992. As shown in Figure 26.1, the volume of stock and bond underwriting reached almost $600 billion in 1991. By October of the following year, underwriting volume had topped the $660 billion mark, with accompanying underwriting fees of more than $5 billion. Low interest rates and surging stock market values served as strong incentives for firms to issue new debt and equity securities, and the investment bankers were there to underwrite those new issues.

ALTERNATIVES TO TRADITIONAL UNDERWRITING. The relationship between investment bankers and their clients depends on the financial position of the client and the breadth of the market for its securities. Sometimes investment bankers, unwilling to bear the risk of

---

[3] For further discussion of financial innovations and the securities industry, see Bloch 1989; Anthony Bianco, "The King of Wall Street," *Business Week,* December 9, 1985, 98–104; Norton 1987; Stigum 1990; Brett Duval Fromson, "Did Drexel Get What It Deserved?" *Fortune.* March 12, 1990, 81–88; and Brett Duval Fromson, "The Last Days of Drexel Burnham," *Fortune,* May 21, 1990, 90–96.

[4] The role of the syndicate in the issuance of new securities is diminishing. For details, see Selby 1985.

| FIGURE 26.1 | Underwriting Volume of U.S. Securities Firms: 1981–1991 |

After years of stagnant underwriting volume in the 1980s, securities firms enjoyed a surge in new securities issues in the early 1990s. This "boom" and "bust" pattern is typical of conditions the securities industry faces.

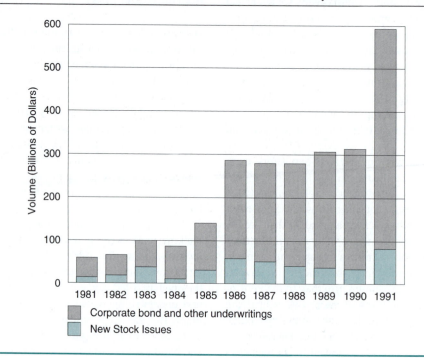

■ Corporate bond and other underwritings
■ New Stock Issues

Source: Michael Siconolfi and William Power, "Underwriting Boom Puts Tortoises Ahead of Wall Street's Hares," *The Wall Street Journal,* March 26, 1992, A1.

underwriting a new issue, sell it on a **best efforts** basis. In best efforts deals, the investment banker does not buy the securities from the issuing firm but merely assists in distribution, profiting from fees for services. An alternative that clients sometimes choose is private placement, for which investment bankers earn fees for bringing buyers and sellers together.

Not surprisingly, technological innovations in recent years have also spurred alternatives to traditional underwriting. In 1990, CapitaLink, a system through which blue chip corporations can issue bonds directly to institutional investors, became available. A company may request bids by computer for bonds it plans to issue; bids are received electronically and issuing costs are less than half the fees usually paid to underwriters. Such changes, while inevitable, further

diminish the potential profitability of services traditionally provided by investment bankers.[5]

MERCHANT BANKING

Merchant banking is the name given to a group of activities such as investing in real estate, taking an equity position in new firms (extending venture capital), or providing financing for mergers and acquisitions. In the late 1980s, as the volume of corporate mergers and acquisitions expanded, many securities firms put their own capital at risk by providing **bridge**

_____

[5] These direct private placements constituted only a few offerings by 1992, however. See Carey et al. 1993.

financing to firms involved in takeover battles. These bridge agreements are, in effect, short-term loans to firms to provide the cash needed to compete in takeovers, leveraged buyouts, or a corporate restructuring. Presumably, if a takeover is successful, the securities firm is repaid in full. If problems arise, however, bridge agreements expose the firm to a high degree of risk. Despite this uncertainty, securities firms have considered the interest and fee income from such arrangements to be potentially quite lucrative. Merchant banking activities can also assist in smoothing out the income variability inherent in the more traditional aspects of investment banking and brokerage. Merchant banking is estimated to have provided about 40 percent of larger securities firms' total income in the latter part of the 1980s.[6] As explained in detail later, these new sources of revenue are welcome additions that have assisted securities firms in combating the loss of brokerage income as a result of regulatory changes.

BROKERAGE AND TRADING

Brokerage and trading services involve handling securities transactions for individual or institutional customers and managing the firm's own securities inventory. Securities firms also act as investment advisers for mutual and pension funds. Full-service brokerage firms conduct security analysis and provide investment advice to clients, and both full-service and discount brokers complete securities transactions.

OTHER FINANCIAL SERVICES

As competition has heightened, securities firms have introduced a variety of financial services to meet the needs of individual and institutional customers. Some firms, such as First Boston, serve only institutional clients, selling their expertise at securitizing assets or at arranging interest rate swaps and other hedging techniques. In recent years, in fact, securities firms

have become huge players in the swaps, caps, collars, and floors markets, enjoying considerable fee income from negotiating these transactions for customers.

Other industry members emphasize services to retail clients. Merrill Lynch's trademarked Cash Management Account (CMA) represented a pioneering effort in the marketing of personal financial services. Merrill Lynch, through the CMA introduced in 1977, offered customers financial services that compete directly with depository institutions. Other firms introduced similar **asset management accounts** shortly thereafter, enabling brokers to attract additional funds from their clients. In turn, they provide investment advice and counsel, regular statements of account, easy access to cash through check-writing privileges in cooperation with participating banks, and the ability to borrow against securities holdings. Any funds "deposited" by an investor earn market rates while under the securities firms' management. Asset management accounts provided depositories with one of the strongest arguments for more rapid deregulation. In March 1980, Walter Wriston, then Chairman of Citicorp, argued that his "dream bank" already existed. He said, "Don Regan runs it, and it's called Merrill Lynch Pierce Fenner and Smith."[7]

In subsequent years, money management has become an increasingly important part of securities firms' activities. These services have taken several forms. Some securities firms have specialized in bringing large pools of private assets under management. A particularly successful product in this regard is the **wrap account,** through which a securities firm offers financial planning, investment management, and brokerage services for high-balance customers (minimum $100,000) for a single, comprehensive ("wrapped") fee established as a percentage of account value, normally 3 percent per year. The securities firm sometimes provides investment management services for its

---

[6]Christopher Farrell, "Investment Banking Takes a New—and Risky—Turn," *Business Week,* June 15, 1987, 92–93; and Sarah Bartlett, "The Splintering of Wall Street," *Business Week,* March 21, 1989, 128–134.

[7]This story is related in Martin Mayer, "Merrill Lynch Quacks Like a Bank," *Fortune,* October 20, 1980, 135. Donald Regan, who was chairman of Merrill Lynch in 1980, left shortly thereafter to become Secretary of the Treasury and later Chief of Staff to President Ronald Reagan, until he was forced to resign in February 1987. More on the head-to-head confrontations between Citicorp and Merrill Lynch is presented in Chapter 27.

wrap accounts in-house, but more often it hires external portfolio managers to whom it pays part of the wrapped fee the customer is charged. The securities firm then executes buy or sell transactions on the account according to instructions from the investment manager. This approach is a considerable contrast to past broker/customer relationships, in which the securities firm has incentives to encourage customers to make a large number of transactions so as to increase its commission income. With wrap accounts, brokers and investment managers instead have incentives to increase customers' wealth, not to trade excessively and unnecessarily (sometimes called **"churning"** by industry observers).

Using their existing in-house research staff, necessary to conduct full-service brokerage business, other securities firms have moved into mutual funds on a large scale, distributing and managing the portfolios of open-end investment companies. As a variation, some securities firms now offer a **mutual fund wrap account,** under which, for a fixed annual fee, they recommend mutual funds to their customers, then pay the funds' management fees out of the wrapped charge on the account. Mutual fund wraps are intended to attract lower-balance customers (minimum $25,000) than are traditional wraps. They have proved exceptionally popular since their introduction in late 1991. These new products and marketing strategies have made securities firms strong competitors with other financial institutions in the 1990s.[8]

SECURITIES FIRMS: REGULATORY INFLUENCES

As indicated in Chapter 2, the securities industry is regulated, primarily by the SEC. In contrast to depository institutions, securities firms have faced no restrictions on geographical expansion. However, their involvement in issuing and trading securities is closely monitored. Several important SEC rulings and Congressional actions since 1975 have exerted strong influence on the industry.

END OF FIXED BROKERAGE COMMISSIONS

On May 1, 1975, an SEC ruling ended the New York Stock Exchange's (NYSE) system of fixed brokerage commissions. NYSE rules had established the same fee structure for all member firms, effectively eliminating price competition among securities firms. Industry members predicted that the **May Day ruling,** as it came to be called, would wreak havoc in the industry.

IMPACT ON FEE STRUCTURES. Although some firms did fail in the aftermath of May Day, their numbers were relatively small, and the securities industry adjusted. But things have never been the same. Once customers recognized their ability to negotiate fees, institutional traders managed to reduce transactions costs on large-volume trades. For the industry as a whole, May Day permanently changed the relative importance of brokerage commission fees as a source of revenues. As Figure 26.2 shows, commission fees declined from more than 50 percent of total broker-dealer revenues in 1975 to about 20 percent in 1991. Revenues from gains on trading securities and investing rose dramatically.

RISE OF DISCOUNT BROKERS. While large-volume institutional investors were enjoying the ability to negotiate lower commission fees, individual investors, whose average trades are much smaller, began to find brokerage services more expensive. The pattern of commission fees for individual and institutional investors in the decade after May Day is shown in Figure 26.3. This disparity opened the door to an industry development that can also be traced directly to the May Day ruling—the entry of discount brokers.

First defined in Chapter 1, discount brokers offer limited investment advice and services and charge lower fees than firms offering a full line of services. By 1985, more than 600 discount brokerage firms were in operation, handling about 20 percent of individuals' stock trades, and many reported strong financial performance. But the stock market crash of 1987

---

[8]For further discussion of the range of activities in contemporary securities firms, see Hayes and Hubbard 1990; "Wall Street's Windfall in Wraps," *Business Week,* July 27, 1992, 67–68; Ellen E. Schultz, "Why Wall Street Is Cooling to Commissions," *The Wall Street Journal,* January 6, 1993, C1, C13; Ellen E. Schultz, "Uncovering the New 'Mutual Fund Wrap' Packages," *The Wall Street Journal,* January 6, 1993, C1.

| FIGURE 26.2 | **Brokerage Commissions as a Source of Revenue After 1975** |

The prohibition of fixed brokerage commission fees as of May 1, 1975, changed the pattern of revenues for securities firms. Commission fees are a much smaller percentage of revenues, because of institutional investors' ability to negotiate volume discounts.

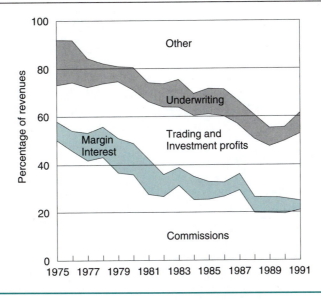

Source: Robert N. McCauley and Steven A. Zimmer, "The Cost of Capital for Securities Firms in the United States and Japan," *Quarterly Review* (Federal Reserve Bank of New York) 16 (Autumn 1991): 22.

dealt a heavy blow to the discount industry, primarily because it turned many small investors away from the equity markets. For example, the average trading volume at Charles Schwab, the largest and perhaps best known of the discount firms, declined 40 percent between October 1987 and May 1989.[9]

But the decline did not last long. Schwab and other discounters reassessed the market and broadened the services offered while continuing to underprice the full-service brokerage firms. By 1991, discount brokers captured more than 11 percent of retail commissions generated, and approximately one in five noninstitutional trades was handled by a discounter.

Within the discount brokerage industry itself, firms have begun to differentiate. Schwab is known for its state-of-the-art technology, attention to customer service, and provision of investment information (half-full service?). At the other end of the industry spectrum are Olde Discount and Waterhouse, which focus on cheap trades and fast execution. As of 1992, all discounters continued to underprice the full-service brokers, however, as is shown in Figure 26.4.[10] Even the fees charged by the most expensive discount broker (Schwab) are less than one-half those charged on similar transactions by full-service firms. Thus, the success of the discounters has given investors an option to

[9] John J. Curran, "Does Deregulation Make Sense?" *Fortune,* June 5, 1989, 181–195; John Heins, "After Cost Cuts, What?" *Forbes,* May 1, 1989, 46; and Gary Weiss, "For Discount Brokers, the Crash Still Isn't Over," *Business Week,* December 5, 1988, 154–155.

[10] See Richard Phalon, "We'll Come Out All Right," *Forbes,* November 19, 1992, 162–163; and Terence P. Paré, "How Schwab Wins Investors," *Fortune,* June 1, 1992, 52–64.

Brokerage Commission Rates, May 1, 1975–December 31, 1984

Although institutional investors were able to negotiate lower commission fees through volume discounts, commission fees for individual investors increased after May 1, 1975.

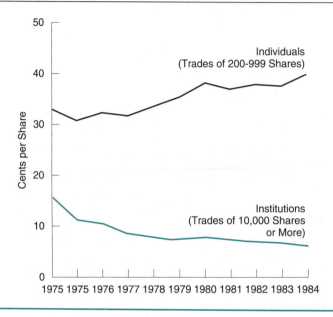

escape the higher fees—shown in Figure 26.3—that initially followed the end of the fixed commission structure.

DIVERSIFICATION AND GLOBALIZATION. An additional change in the industry commonly traced to the May Day ruling is the trend toward diversification. Because brokers anticipated declining revenues from traditional services, they began experimenting with other opportunities to replace or even enhance profits. Asset management accounts, merchant banking endeavors, and mutual fund sponsorship are examples of these efforts to diversify. Many large securities firms began to concentrate on serving U.S. customers in international markets and on attracting a clientele base outside the United States. By the early 1990s, diversification was proving to be an effective strategy. As investor confidence in the domestic equity markets fluctuated, the

diversified firms stabilized earnings through income from fees and foreign exchange trading.

RULE 415: SHELF REGISTRATION

In March 1982, the SEC approved another policy change that has significantly affected the securities industry. The policy, known as Rule 415 and first discussed in Chapter 21, changed the procedures by which firms can issue new securities. Before Rule 415, firms had to seek SEC approval for each new issue. Under the new rule, a procedure known as **shelf registration** was approved. Shelf registration allows a firm to file its intention to issue new securities with the SEC up to 2 years in advance. Once the SEC approves, the firm has the flexibility to choose how many securities to sell and when to sell them "off the shelf." The new policy was intended to eliminate barriers to firms seeking new capital and to lower regulatory costs.

FIGURE 26.4   ## Commission on a Trade of 100 Shares at $30/Share

Full-service brokers' commission fees are substantially higher than those charged by discount brokers on trades of comparable size.

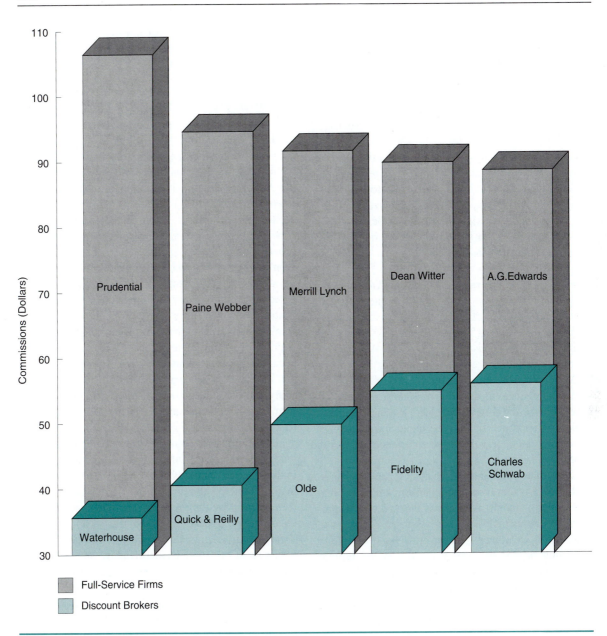

Source: Prepared by the authors with data from Terence P. Paré, "How Schwab Wins Investors," *Fortune,* June 1, 1992, 62.

Opponents of the rule made dire predictions for the new issues markets. Concerns were raised that competition and reduced profits would drive smaller, regional investment banking houses out of business, causing the industry to consolidate and become dominated by a few large firms. Critics also feared that investors would lack access to sufficient current information under the advance registration procedures.

UNDERWRITING SPREADS. The effect on underwriters' spreads on new issues is still inconclusive. A study of new bond issues during the first months of Rule 415 found lower underwriter fees with shelf registrations. Yet a longer-term analysis of the period January 1981– October 1983 found no significant change in underwriter spreads on new bond issues with Rule 415. A study sponsored by the SEC, which analyzed new equity issues between March and December of 1983, found that, on average, firms reduced issuing costs by using shelf registrations.[11]

COMPETITIVE EFFECTS. It is also difficult to conclude how Rule 415 affected concentration in the securities industry. The number of regional firms was already declining before Rule 415. Whether the new policy exacerbated the decline is unclear, but Rule 415 has undoubtedly heightened competition among investment bankers. When a company files a registration statement, it announces its intention to issue new securities. Often, before the firm has decided which investment banker to approach, it may be contacted by one or more potential underwriters, an occurrence practically unheard of before 1982.

Another result that can be at least partially traced to Rule 415 is that investment bankers are more creative in the financing alternatives they present to prospective clients and more aggressive in seeking and maintaining customer relationships. For example, a technique originated since Rule 415 is the **bought deal.** Under this strategy, the underwriter purchases an entire issue using only its own capital instead of including other underwriters in a syndicate. Risk exposure is greater, but profits are not shared. Because bought deals can be negotiated and completed more quickly than syndications, they are a useful competitive tool.[12]

Investment bankers must now be marketers. They contact prospective clients and propose creative financing tailored to individual needs. Swaps, futures, options, and other hedging techniques are often included in these alternatives.

PROHIBITIONS ON INSIDER TRADING

Attempts by brokers, corporate employees, investment bankers, or others with access to privileged data to profit from inside information have been illegal for many years. Beginning in 1986, however, a series of revelations about insider trading provoked renewed interest in the issue. In the spring of 1986, the SEC accused Dennis Levine, an employee of Drexel Burnham Lambert, of accumulating almost $12 million in profits through illegal insider trading. Later that year, Ivan Boesky, who gained prominence on Wall Street through his involvement in mergers and acquisitions, agreed to a civil penalty totaling $100 million and admitted guilt on felony charges. In the mid-1980s, Boesky had been hailed for his uncanny ability to identify firms that were takeover targets before they became apparent to other investors. His arrest revealed that Boesky's knack was not a result of his superior analytical skills but, rather, of his access to inside information. His cooperation with the SEC led to later charges of wrongdoing against Drexel, particularly against its most famous employee, Michael Milken, who was indicted in 1988 on 98 counts of wrongdoing in the securities markets and who, in 1990, pled guilty to six felonies. The ethics of the financial community were viewed by the press and the public with an increasingly skeptical eye.

Equally skeptical, Congress began considering revisions in the 1984 Insider Trading Sanctions Act. After considerable debate, Congress passed the Insider Trading and Securities Fraud Enforcement Act of 1988. Introduced in Chapter 2, this legislation had as its objective further deterring insider trading and reducing difficulties encountered by government agencies when attempting to prosecute illegal securities ac-

---

[11] See Kidwell et al. 1984; Rogowski and Sorenson 1985; and Leon E. Wynter, "SEC Study Reports Shelf Registration Is Boon for Issuers," *The Wall Street Journal,* September 17, 1984.

[12] See Hayes and Hubbard 1990 for further explanation.

tivities. In the law, Congress introduced a revised definition of insider trading, clarifying that it is "the purchase or sale of securities while in possession of 'material' information that is not available to the general public." Material information is anything that would be important to an investor when deciding to buy or sell a security.

The Insider Trading Act amended the 1984 Sanctions Act by stiffening the civil and criminal penalties for those convicted of insider trading. Anyone convicted of profiting from illegal insider trading can be required to pay up to three times the amount gained through the unlawful activity, and the maximum prison term for criminal penalties was increased to 10 years. The SEC was also given greater authority to pursue offenders and is now allowed to pay to obtain information about potential violations.

The 1988 act also placed a responsibility on securities firms to strengthen written policies and procedures designed to prevent the misuse of privileged, material information. A firm failing to do so may itself face civil penalties if employees are found guilty of insider trading. This provision in the Insider Trading Act placed renewed emphasis on the long-standing tradition in the securities industry of maintaining a so-called **Chinese Wall,** an imaginary barrier between the investment banking activities of a securities firm and its brokerage and trading arm. Under the law, a firm may not profit on trades for its own inventory or that of its customers by using information obtained through investment bankers' privileged contacts with clients.

EMERGING ISSUES

The pace of financial and technological innovation in the securities industry suggests that new questions will continue to be raised about the need for regulations and restrictions on firms' activities. Observers also point to changes in the international markets as major influences on U.S. securities firms in the 1990s.

REGULATORY QUESTIONS. One concern that has already arisen is whether growth in merchant banking activities sometimes undermines the motivation of investment bankers to act in the best interests of their clients. For example, in a traditional underwriting arrangement, investment bankers attempt to sell a cor-

poration's newly issued securities at the highest possible price. As a merchant banker, however, the securities firm might be buying those bonds or stocks for its own portfolio and would be seeking a lower, rather than a higher, price. The potential conflict of interest will attract continuing scrutiny.

Another source of potential regulatory change lies in the ongoing debate about the future of the Glass-Steagall Act (G-S). The banking industry has for many years called for the act's repeal, although, as explained in Chapter 21, the largest commercial banks have succeeded in gaining entry into most securities activities despite the survival of Glass-Steagall. The securities industry has been the strongest opponent of lowering the barriers between commercial and investment banking. The Securities Industry Association (SIA), an influential trade organization, has opposed the repeal of Glass-Steagall unless several restrictions are placed on banks seeking entry into its markets.

INVESTMENT BANKING AND INTERNATIONAL MARKETS. As internal barriers to the flow of capital and commerce fall in Europe during this decade, many experts believe that unprecedented opportunities will follow for enterprising securities firms. Freed from the more restrictive business climate of the past, many European industrial firms are likely to restructure as a result of the need to modernize, bringing about a rapid increase in merger, takeover, and buyout activities. U.S. securities firms, with their extensive experience in advising clients during the domestic buyout wave of the 1980s, stand to gain handsomely if they position themselves to compete in the European market.

U.S. securities firms are also hopeful that Japanese financial regulators will be more welcoming to foreign securities firms in the coming years, although progress in opening Japanese markets is slow. Securities firms also have their eyes increasingly on emerging financial markets in Latin America, Southeast Asia, and even formerly Communist countries.

To capture international business, however, U.S. securities firms must go head-to-head against their counterparts from Europe and Japan. Some observers predict that this clash of international interests will result in agreements among securities regulators similar to the coordinated capital rules developed by bank regulators in the late 1980s.

SECURITIES FIRMS: DESCRIPTIVE DATA

Many securities firms are not publicly held but function as partnerships. Consequently, financial data are limited to reports required by the SEC, with aggregate figures published in SEC annual reports. Recent data reveal that assets for the industry as a whole (more than 9,000 firms) exceed $500 billion.[13] The SIA periodically publishes *Securities Industry Trends.* But because not all securities firms participate in all activities, aggregate data do not reflect individual managerial choices, even those for firms of similar type and size.

A SAMPLE BALANCE SHEET

For illustrative purposes, Table 26.1 presents a recent balance sheet for Merrill Lynch (ML), one of the leading firms in the industry. The table shows that ML's largest asset category is receivables, reflecting the fact that securities firms often loan both cash and securities to customers to assist them in making desired transactions. For example, when customers borrow from their securities firms to buy stock, they are said to be **buying on margin.** In 1934, in an effort to curb what it believed was excessive speculation leading to the 1929 stock market "crash," Congress gave the Fed the authority to regulate the proportion of a security's price a purchaser may borrow. Current rules specify that investors must provide at least 50 percent of the initial purchase price of securities and may borrow the remaining 50 percent. (The margin is the percentage of the customer's own money that he or she must provide, and the borrowed portion is the **debit balance.**) Thus, some of the receivables on ML's 1991 balance sheet are customers' debit balances.

Securities firms also enter into repurchase agreements with customers. When customers sell securities to ML with an agreement to repurchase them later, such transactions appear as receivables on the firm's balance sheet. Because securities firms charge market interest rates on both margin loans and repurchase agreements, it is clear they are exposed to interest rate

risk in much the same way as other financial institutions. Naturally, these transactions also expose securities firms to default risk.

ML's second largest asset category is its inventory of securities. To provide customers liquidity, especially when they trade corporate and municipal bonds or unlisted stock, a securities firm usually fills orders from its own inventories rather than waiting until it is possible to match orders with those of other customers. When buying or selling from their inventories, securities firms are permitted to make profits on the transactions, which are then used to offset the cost of financing large inventories of securities. Table 26.1 also shows an "other asset" category. For ML, this designation includes premises, investment in a subsidiary insurance company, and securities held for investment (rather than trading) purposes.

As is true of most firms in the industry, the liabilities and net worth side of the balance sheet shows how highly leveraged Merrill Lynch is. The company obtains most of its funds from short-term borrowings, especially repurchase agreements in which it has sold securities while obligating itself to buy them back later. The table further shows that ML incurs obligations against its securities inventory when it commits itself to sell securities to customers who have not yet paid for them. ML also has a significant quantity of other liabilities, including those to customers who have, for example, opened depositlike cash management accounts. Like other financial institutions, the firm must pay interest or dividends on most of these liabilities, increasing its exposure to interest rate risk should its borrowing costs rise faster than returns on its assets.

As noted, because an aggregate balance sheet for the securities industry as a whole is unavailable, it is important to remember that data on Merrill Lynch are not definitive for the array of firms in the industry. Nonetheless, the data help to show that managers of securities firms, like other financial institutions, face interest rate and default risk and, therefore, are prime users of many of the asset/liability management techniques presented throughout the book.

INCOME AND EXPENSE DATA

Fortunately, aggregate information on income and expenses of the securities industry is published by

---

[13] *Annual Report of the Securities and Exchange Commission,* 1987, Appendix.

TABLE 26.1   Merrill Lynch Consolidated Balance Sheet, Year-end 1991 (Millions of $)

A recent balance sheet from this leading firm in the securities industry shows that assets are dominated by receivables (primarily loans to customers) and securities inventories. Merrill Lynch, like most securities firms, is highly leveraged, raising only a small proportion of total funds from equity capital.

			% of Total
Assets			
Cash and equivalents		$ 4,429	5.1%
Receivables		43,075	49.9
Inventories			
Corporate securities	$9,794		
Government and agency securities	7,108		
Mortgages and mortgage-related securities	4,579		
Money market securities	2,680		
Municipal securities	748		
Total securities inventories		24,908	28.9
Other assets		13,848	16.1
Total Assets		$86,259	100.0%
Liabilities and Net Worth			
Liabilities			
Short-term borrowings	$38,698		
Commitments of securities	9,595		
Other liabilities	26,184		
Long-term borrowings	7,964		
Total liabilities		$82,441	95.6%
Preferred stock		0	0.0
Common equity		3,818	4.4
Total Liabilities and Net Worth		$86,259	100.0%

Source: Prepared by the authors with data from Merrill Lynch, *1991 Annual Report,* 38–39.

industry trade associations. Table 26.2 provides income and expense data for the largest securities firms for selected years between 1981 and 1991. In 1981, just a few years after fixed brokerage commission rates were deregulated, the largest source of revenue was securities commissions. Later in the 1980s, however, firms earned larger proportions of revenues from 1) gains and losses on trading and investing for the firms' own portfolios and 2) other securities-related revenue. The latter category includes fees from mergers and acquisitions, private placements, and dealings in government securities. By the early 1990s, securities commissions had fallen to a distant third.

Fees from underwriting and selling vary over time, indicating the volatility of the new issues market; still, they are consistently the fourth largest source of revenue. They also bear an interesting relationship to margin interest as a source of revenue, which varies in importance, depending on the general level of interest

rates. As noted earlier, securities firms earn margin interest on loans to customers. In 1981, when short-term interest rates were at historic highs, margin interest was nearly 15 percent of total securities firm revenue, and underwriting income was just over half that amount. By 1991, as short-term interest rates plunged, margin interest contributed only a small amount to total revenue; yet underwriting income was three times as large, as corporations hired investment bankers to help them issue new securities at what were, for them, highly desirable low rates.

As in other financial institutions, both fee and interest income are important to the securities industry. The firms' exposure to interest rate and market risk is shown by the importance of trading, underwriting, and margin interest as sources of income. The sensitivity of operations to economic conditions is revealed by differences in the relative importance of income categories from year to year.

TABLE 26.2 Selected Financial Data, Securities Brokers and Dealers, Selected Years (Millions of $)

The relative importance of various sources of revenues and expenses for securities brokers and dealers has changed since the early 1980s. Increased competition and market uncertainties have caused fluctuations in pretax income.

	1981		1985		1988		1989		1990		1991	
Revenues												
Securities commissions	$ 5,340	27.0%	$ 8,238	21.3%	$ 8,791	17.0%	$10,152	17.1%	$ 8,878	16.4%	$10,589	17.4%
Gains/losses in trading and investment accounts	4,811	24.3	11,034	28.6	12,693	24.5	12,831	21.6	12,892	23.9	17,087	28.1
Gains/losses from underwriting and selling	1,690	8.5	5,893	15.3	6,572	12.7	5,700	9.6	4,912	9.1	8,197	13.5
Other securities-related revenue	3,837	19.4	9,125	23.6	17,983	34.7	23,998	40.3	21,335	39.5	19,329	31.8
Margin interest	2,890	14.6	2,578	6.7	3,029	5.8	3,723	6.3	3,075	5.7	2,632	4.3
Other revenue	1,229	6.2	1,758	4.6	2,762	5.3	3,134	5.3	2,942	5.4	2,884	4.7
Total revenues	$19,797	100.0%	$38,625	100.0%	$51,830	100.0%	$59,538	100.0%	$54,034	100.0%	$60,718	100.0%
Expenses												
Registered representatives compensation	$ 3,334	18.9%	$ 6,903	20.0%	$ 7,581	15.4%	$ 7,539	13.1%	$ 6,868	12.7%	$ 8,362	15.2%
Other employee compensation	3,925	22.2	7,670	22.2	11,159	22.6	11,287	19.6	10,848	20.0	12,463	22.7
Floor expenses	725	4.1	1,310	3.8	1,756	3.6	1,855	3.2	1,731	3.2	1,760	3.2
Interest expense	5,685	32.2	10,128	29.4	16,308	33.1	24,070	41.7	22,717	41.9	18,871	34.4
Other expenses	3,986	22.6	8,479	24.6	12,533	25.4	12,944	22.4	12,032	22.2	13,414	24.4
Total expenses	$17,655	100.0%	$34,490	100.0%	$49,337	100.0%	$57,695	100.0%	$54,196	100.0%	$54,869	100.0%
Pretax Income	$ 2,142		$ 4,135		$ 2,493		$ 1,843		($162)		$ 5,849	
Pretax Return on Net Worth	35.9%		29.4%		9.6%		6.9%		−0.7%		23.7%	

Source: Securities Industry Association, *Securities Industry Trends*, various issues.

FIGURE 26.5   **Securities Firms: RONW and Profit Margin**

Pretax RONW and profit margins for securities firms were quite variable in the 1980s and declined substantially after 1982 because of greater competition and changing market conditions. A flood of new securities issues helped the industry rebound in the early 1990s.

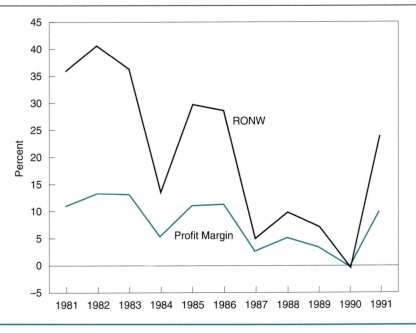

Source: Securities Industry Association, *Securities Industry Trends,* various issues.

Interest expense, incurred on borrowings to purchase securities inventories, is a major expense category, and profitability is greatly affected by changes in interest rates. The industry is labor-intensive, reflected by compensation for "registered representatives" (brokers) and other personnel. Because interest costs are determined by the financial markets and not by an individual firm, management of personnel expenses is extremely important.

Note that the industry reduced the proportionate level of compensation to brokers in the mid-1980s. This was accomplished through drastic personnel cuts totaling almost 20,000 terminations in 1988 alone and by reducing or eliminating generous bonuses often paid to employees in the past. As industry performance improved in the early 1990s, brokerage firms began rehiring, and the personnel reductions came to a temporary halt. Experienced brokers were in such demand, in fact, that some firms introduced incentive compensation plans designed to retain brokers and to

discourage them from accepting positions with rival firms.[14]

Although earnings for the industry survived the changes introduced by May Day and Rule 415, they did not fare so well after the crash of 1987. As shown in Figure 26.5, pretax return on net worth (RONW) and profit margins declined significantly in 1987 and rebounded only slightly in 1988. The 1990 figure, −0.7 percent, is a notable change from the 50 percent pretax RONW reported for the industry in 1980. Fortunately for the industry, the 1991 numbers were stellar compared to recent years, marking a period in the early 1990s of considerable success. But the volatility in earnings is clear: The securities business is not for the fainthearted.

---

[14] Michael Siconolfi, "Big Wall Street Houses Devise Pay Plans to Keep Brokers from Going to Rivals," *The Wall Street Journal,* November 11, 1992, C1, C11.

SECURITIES FIRMS: MANAGING ASSETS AND LIABILITIES

Important aspects of asset/liability management in the securities industry have already been introduced.

DIVERSIFICATION TO PROTECT INCOME

Securities firms have diversified not only to respond to competition but also to protect against swings in commission income resulting from changes in market conditions. Diversification is prominently discussed in the annual reports of many leading securities firms. It has contributed substantially to revenues in recent years.

USE OF RISK MANAGEMENT TOOLS

Securities firms are not only developing hedging techniques for their clients, they are themselves relying on hedging strategies to manage interest rate risk. One of the earliest and most widely publicized examples of hedging in the industry came in 1979, when Salomon Brothers underwrote an IBM bond issue. Just after the underwriting agreement was completed and the coupon rate was established, interest rates jumped sharply. The increase in market rates caused the bonds' market value to drop below Salomon's original estimates, wiping out expected profits. Industry observers assumed that Salomon had taken a big loss but soon learned that the deal had been hedged in the futures market, so the firm's losses were limited. In the increasingly competitive environment facing securities firms, where underwriting spreads and commission fees have been pared, hedges are commonplace. In 1986, the SEC recognized the importance of integrated asset/liability management in the industry by permitting lower capital requirements for securities firms whose corporate bond holdings were hedged, although the agency began placing pressure on securities firms later in the decade to strengthen their capital positions.[15]

PERFORMANCE EVALUATION OF SECURITIES FIRMS

Because many securities firms are privately owned, available financial data are limited. Limited aggregate data are available from several sources, such as Dun and Bradstreet financial ratios; SEC annual reports; SIA publications, with information on industry subgroups; annual rankings of large brokers by *Institutional Investor;* and industry outlooks in *Forbes* and *Fortune.* These sources of data must be used carefully when drawing conclusions about individual firms.

In the absence of good comparative data, a trend analysis of expense and income ratios sheds light on a firm's efficiency and productivity. As with other institutions, a clear result of deregulation in the industry is the need for managers to control operating costs carefully.

A measure sometimes used to evaluate performance of the investment banking function is the volume of securities for which the firm served as the sole underwriter or the leader in a syndicate. The quantity of issues is viewed as a sign of a firm's competence and creativity.

An important performance guideline for the securities industry is RONW. A great deal of variability in this measure is evident in Figure 26.5. In fact, studies at the Federal Reserve Bank of New York indicate that RONWs in the securities industry were much more variable than those of commercial banks in the early to mid-1980s. Interestingly, RONWs for the more diversified firms were lower than for firms specializing in brokerage services—either full-service or discount—or in investment banking. (Later in the decade, however, the response to stock market volatility damaged the performance of the brokerage lines.) The poorer performance of diversified firms found by the Fed researchers could have been attributable to higher operating costs.[16]

A recently published study of economies of scale and scope in the securities industry provides additional insight. The researchers concluded that scale economies do exist but that the optimal firm size is relatively small. Also, the study revealed no significant economies or diseconomies of scope for firms of any

---

[15] How Salomon Brothers Hedged the IBM Deal," *Business Week,* October 29, 1979, 50; and Cynthia S. Grisdella, "Capital Rules Eased for Securities Firms that Hedge Corporate Bond Holdings," *The Wall Street Journal,* November 5, 1986, 4.

[16] Federal Reserve Bank of New York 1986, 286–294.

size. Consequently, the choice between operating as a diversified firm or a specialty firm would not seem to be related to performance. The implication is that the poorer performance reported by some large securities firms may instead be traced to diseconomies of scale.[17]

SUMMARY

This chapter presented asset/liability management issues in the securities industry. Securities firms are financial institutions that provide brokerage, trading, underwriting, merchant banking, and other financial services to wholesale and retail customers. Like many other depository and nondepository financial institutions, securities firms operate under unique regulatory guidelines in an increasingly competitive environment in which risk management is a necessary key to survival. The industry has been at the forefront of financial innovation in recent decades.

The securities industry has met particular pressures since the introduction of competitive commission fees in 1975 and the subsequent imposition of Rule 415. Narrowing profit margins for traditional lines of business provided an incentive for securities firms to seek fee income by serving merger and acquisition clients and engaging in merchant banking activities. These new sources of revenues have been accompanied by higher risks, however.

Some of the problems faced today by the securities industry were internally generated by the unethical and illegal insider trading activities of some industry participants. Congress responded to the growing number of violations by passing the Insider Trading Act of 1988, strengthening the regulatory authority of the SEC. The securities industry also has faced greater competition from commercial banks, who may pose even stronger challenges if the repeal of Glass-Steagall becomes a reality.

QUESTIONS

1.   What economic incentives encourage securities firms to introduce creative financial instruments? How does market discipline influence financial innovation?

2.   Explain the risk transferred to investment bankers when they underwrite new securities issued by corporations. How does formation of a syndicate limit the risk exposure? What is best efforts selling, and why is it sometimes chosen as an alternative to underwriting?

3.   A 1988 study defined the function of investment banking as "financial change itself." Consult recent financial publications or the financial sections of major periodicals to review announcements and reports of investment bankers' activities. Find an example of a recent financial innovation developed by investment bankers to help firms obtain the funding they need. Comment on the potential risk exposure of the investment banker and the issuing corporation.

4.   Explain how merchant banking and bridge financing differ from the more traditional activities of investment banking firms. From an economic viewpoint, explain whether you consider it to be more or less appropriate for securities firms to finance highly leveraged acquisitions than for commercial banks to provide debt capital to finance them. Do you believe inherent conflicts between merchant and investment banking exist? If so, what are they?

5.   Review recent data on the volume of stock and bond underwriting. What economic and competitive factors are influencing this record? What is the relative influence of financial innovation on corporations' decisions to issue new securities?

6.   How do the financial services that securities firms offer individual clients compare to those offered by commercial banks? Does either industry have a clear advantage over the other in attracting customers? If the playing field is not level, which industry currently benefits? Explain any regulatory changes you would recommend.

7.   One recently introduced financial service in securities firms is the wrap account. Compare and contrast a wrap account to more traditional brokerage services. Explain the effect on sources of and potential variability in income of a securities firm as it replaces brokerage with wrap accounts.

8.   What did the 1975 May Day ruling require of the securities industry? What has been the effect on competition in the industry, especially through the introduction of discount brokerage services? How do these changes help to explain securities firms' need to expand beyond traditional lines of service?

9.   Describe the patterns in brokerage commission fees charged after 1975 by full-service firms to individual and institutional clients. What explanations can you offer for these trends, and how did they contribute to the creation of the discount brokerage industry?

10.   Briefly explain Rule 415 and shelf registration. What potential benefits was Rule 415 intended to provide to firms

---

[17] See Goldberg et al. 1991.

raising new capital? What has been the effect on competition among investment banking firms? On the services provided to corporate customers?

11. What is a Chinese wall in a securities firm? In what ways did the 1984 and 1988 Insider Trading Acts "thicken" the wall? In your opinion, what are the most serious detriments to economic and social well-being caused by insider trading? Do you agree with the Congressional view that criminal penalties for insider trading should be severe? Why or why not?

12. Assuming that Congress decides to repeal the Glass-Steagall Act, evaluate the potential for moral hazard if securities firms are allowed to own commercial banks. Do you think securities firms should be allowed access to the discount window or to the payments system, whether or not they own a bank? Why or why not?

13. Refer to Table 3.3 in Chapter 3. What countries allow overlapping ownership of securities firms and commercial banks? What arguments can you offer for the economic efficiency of such relationships? Find a recent article discussing trends in the financial markets of one of these countries and explain any apparent hazards or benefits.

14. Review recent coverage of developments in international financial markets. What inroads have U.S. investment bankers made in the unified European market? in Japan? Has there been any progress toward the development of uniform capital or other regulations under which international securities firms must operate? If so, what are they, and what has provided the incentive for their enactment?

15. As is true of many securities firms, the balance sheet of Merrill Lynch shows a large proportion of assets held as receivables. What is the origin of these accounts? How do they produce revenues for firms in the industry?

16. What are the primary sources of revenue for securities firms? How do changes in the relative proportions of these sources reflect competitive and regulatory changes in the industry?

17. What is margin interest? What federal regulator monitors and controls margin lending? Explain the role played by the margin in generating revenues and returns for securities firms.

18. Explain the risk-management tools adopted by securities firms in recent years to hedge increased risk exposure resulting from expanded financial services and variable economic conditions.

19. Consult current financial publications to evaluate the recent financial performance of the securities industry. How have securities firms been affected by changes in economic activity and interest rate volatility?

SELECTED REFERENCES

Block, Ernest. *Inside Investment Banking.* 2d ed. Homewood, IL: Dow Jones-Irwin, 1989.

Carey, Mark S., et al. "Recent Developments in the Market for Privately Placed Debt." *Federal Reserve Bulletin* 79 (February 1993): 77–92.

Federal Reserve Bank of New York. *Recent Trends in Commercial Bank Profitability.* New York: Federal Reserve Bank of New York, 1986.

Friend, Irwin, et al. *Investment Banking and the New Issues Market.* Cleveland: World Publishing Co., 1967.

Goldberg, Lawrence G., et al. "Economies of Scale and Scope in the Securities Industry." *Journal of Banking and Finance* (February 1991): 91–107.

Hayes, Samuel L., III. "The Transformation of Investment Banking." *Harvard Business Review* 57 (January/February 1979): 153–170.

Hayes, Samuel L., III, and Philip M. Hubbard. *Investment Banking: A Tale of Three Cities.* Boston: Harvard Business School Press, 1990.

Kidwell, David S., et al. "SEC Rule 415: The Ultimate Competitive Bid." *Journal of Financial and Quantitative Analysis* 19 (June 1984): 183–196.

Langevoort, Donald C. *Securities Law Series: Insider Trading Legislation.* (New York: Clark Boardman Co., 1988).

Norton, Robert E. "Upheaval Ahead on Wall Street," *Fortune,* September 14, 1987, 68–77.

Rogowski, Robert J., and Eric H. Sorenson, "Deregulation in Investment Banking: Shelf Registrations, Structure and Performance." *Financial Management* 14 (Spring 1985): 5–15.

Securities Industry Association. *Securities Industries Trends.* Various issues.

Selby, Beth. "The Twilight of the Syndicate." *Institutional Investor* 19 (August 1985): 205–209.

Stigum, Marcia. *The Money Market.* 3d ed. Homewood, IL: Dow Jones-Irwin, 1990.

Walter, Ingo, and Roy C. Smith. "Investment Banking in Europe after 1992." In *Proceedings of a Conference on Bank Structure and Competition,* 312–317. Chicago: Federal Reserve Bank of Chicago, 1989.

It doesn't make sense for AmEx to be in Shearson's business. There are no synergies between the card and the brokerage business.
Anonymous Rating Agency Analyst (1992)

You can point to any number of inefficiencies that could have contributed to it falling apart.
Michael Flanagan,
Brokerage Industry Analyst
referring to the dissolution of the marriage of Shearson and AmEx (1993)

"It's bizarre," "It's peculiar," and "It's sad" are but three observations about a 1993 management shakeup at American Express, at one time considered the quintessential diversified financial services company. The comments refer to the unusual reporting relationships that resulted from the resignation of long-time CEO James Robinson. Robinson was indeed replaced as president and CEO by Harvey Golub, formerly head of the firm's travel and related services division. Then, in an unexpected retention of influence, Robinson won the title of chairman of the board, to whom Golub would report. But wait—at the same time, Robinson also became CEO of Shearson Lehman Brothers brokerage firm, a *subsidiary* of American Express. Thus, he was to report to Golub. So who's in charge here? Said a bewildered financial analyst, "It's as if President Clinton became Secretary of Defense in the middle of a war and reported to the Vice President."

But by mid-March 1993, the speculation about these contorted reporting lines was overshadowed by the announcement that AmEx was selling Shearson Lehman Brokerage to Primerica for approximately $1 billion. AmEx's new CEO confirmed that the resource requirements of Shearson Lehman were interfering with the firm's efforts to rebuild its credit card empire. He also would not rule out the possibility that the Lehman Brothers investment banking operation might be sold in the near future. Fortunately for both Mr. Golub and AmEx, positions of leadership were clarified by mid-1993. Mr. Golub was named chairman and CEO, and demonstrated his authority by selecting a president of his choice. Mr. Robinson no longer played an influential role.[1]

The confusion that seemed to reign at American Express during these personnel changes and divestitures is symbolic of difficulties that

---

[1] Leah Nathans Spiro, "Curiouser and Curiouser at AmEx," *Business Week,* February 8, 1993, 109; "Primerica Creates Broker Powerhouse with Shearson Deal," *Chicago Tribune,* March 13, 1993, Section 2, 11; and Steven Lipin, "Golub Solidifies Hold at American Express, Begins to Change Firm," *The Wall Street Journal,* June 30, 1993, A1, A9.

have plagued the five firms profiled in this chapter. Each was at the crest of the wave of changes that swept the U.S. financial system beginning in 1980. Each has at times savored success and at other times been brought almost to its financial knees by the changing economic and regulatory environment. Their stories are instructive to financial institution managers seeking to navigate the future's unknown waters.

FINANCIAL SERVICES FIRMS: WHAT ARE THEY?

Financial services is a term encompassing all the deposit, credit, investment, insurance, and risk management operations discussed in this book. Traditionally, subgroups of financial services were the focus (voluntarily or involuntarily) of specific institutions. Because of that specialization, earlier chapters emphasized identifying the risk/expected return factors that make each service a unique problem in asset/liability management, with implications for the net interest margin (NIM) and return on net worth (RONW). In the 1980s, however, individual firms increasingly expanded their range of services, becoming providers of financial services in the broad sense.

Some experts believe that eventually, all businesses now grouped together as "financial institutions" will offer the entire range of financial services. If so, the need to emphasize historical and regulatory differences among firms will disappear, and asset/liability management will no longer be partially segmented by type of institution. To this point, however, the move to provide virtually all financial services has been confined to large firms with origins in a variety of industries, including retailing, manufacturing, banking, insurance, securities, and consumer finance.

This chapter explores diversified financial services firms and examines the implications for asset/liability management in the future. Included are profiles of five companies (originally from different industries) that adopted a strategy of offering a similar range of diversified financial services: They are American Express (travel and entertainment services), Citicorp (commercial banking), Merrill Lynch (securities), Prudential (insurance), and Sears (retailing).

DEVELOPMENT OF FINANCIAL SERVICES FIRMS: WHEN AND WHY

Although the rise of financial services firms occurred in the 1980s, their roots extend to an earlier time. Sears offered consumer credit to promote the sale of goods as early as 1911. By 1931, the firm was selling car insurance in its stores through its Allstate Insurance subsidiary. In 1960, Sears acquired a savings and loan association (S&L) in California and entered the field of real estate finance. General Electric, a manufacturer of industrial and consumer goods, became involved in commercial finance through its captive finance company in 1932; it began making personal loans in the 1960s and entered the insurance field in the 1970s.[2]

Still, the extent to which financial services firms now exist is a function of factors identified in this book as recent phenomena: deregulation, a changing economy, and new customer preferences. Table 27.1 shows how depositories, nondepositories, and nonfinancial firms have moved into financial services. In 1960, for example, insurance firms, retailers, and securities dealers offered a small group of financial products and only those not offered by banks and S&Ls. By 1993, nearly all financial products were offered by firms in each industry.[3]

Financial institutions are not the only firms to be affected by deregulation, a changing economy, and changing customer attitudes. The trucking industry, for example, also faced similar phenomena. Yet the rush in the 1980s was to financial services, not to trucking. Why? There are four main reasons.

EASE OF ENTRY

It is expensive to purchase a fleet of trucks and to train long-haul drivers. The cost of entering the financial services industry *de novo* (starting a new firm) is lower because the required investment in real assets is small. Although start-up costs, such as chartering or registration fees, arise with financial services, they are usually smaller than the investment required to enter other industries. In the 1980s, some nonfinancial firms, such as retailers already offering credit cards, found it

---

[2] These developments are identified in Eisenbeis 1981. (References are listed in full at the end of this chapter.) Eisenbeis's data are drawn from Christophe 1974.

[3] Of course, not all products offered in 1993 were perfect substitutes for one another. For example, the term *checking account* could be interpreted to mean a demand deposit at a bank, a universal life insurance policy at an insurer, and a cash management account at a securities firm. Nonetheless, the "checking" row of Table 27.1 illustrates the much wider availability of some form of transactions account in 1993 than in 1960. The same interpretation can be offered for other rows in the table.

TABLE 27.1 Financial Services Offered, 1960 and 1993

During recent decades, the extent to which different types of firms can engage in a diversified range of activities has changed dramatically. Today, firms from many industries can offer financial services.

	Banks		Savings Institutions		Insurance Companies		Retailers		Securities Dealers	
	1960	1993	1960	1993	1960	1993	1960	1993	1960	1993
Checking accounts	★	★		★		★		★		
Savings accounts	★	★	★	★		★		★		★
Time deposits	★	★	★	★		★		★		★
Installment loans	★	★		★		★		★		★
Business loans	★	★	★	★		★		★		★
Mortgage loans	★	★	★	★		★		★		★
Credit cards		★		★		★		★		★
Insurance underwriting		★		★	★	★	★	★		★
Stocks, bonds, brokerage, underwriting		★		★		★		★		
Mutual funds		★		★		★		★	★	★
Real estate		★		★		★		★	★	★
Interstate facilities		★		★		★		★		★

Source: Adapted from Donald L. Koch, "The Emerging Financial Services Industry: Challenge and Innovation," *Economic Review*, Federal Reserve Bank of Atlanta 69 (April 1984): 26. Updated by the authors.

particularly easy to expand their financial services. Financial institutions specializing in one service found it possible to move relatively quickly into others.

SUBSTITUTABILITY OF PRODUCTS

A second reason the move to financial services occurred quickly is that financial products have commodity-like characteristics. It is hard to tell one ear of corn from another, and one savings account is similar to another, as is one whole life policy to another, and so on. A single provider rarely can corner a market at the expense of competitors, and all firms offering a service have an equal opportunity to succeed—or fail.

PERCEIVED PROFITABILITY

Some firms entered the financial services business because they perceived it to be more profitable than their primary lines of business. An executive with J. C. Penney Company, a leading retailer with insurance and thrift subsidiaries, noted, "In general, financial services are more profitable than retailing."[4]

Although executives of many thrifts, banks, and insurance companies might quarrel with this thought, it has led several nonfinancial firms into finance.

SYNERGY

A final motivation for the move toward diversified financial services, espoused by firms that diversified by purchasing other firms, is a belief that the earnings of a diversified firm will exceed those of two or more firms operating separately. As a reporter for *The Wall Street Journal* put it in an article on diversified financial services firms in the 1980s: "With each acquisition, the word 'synergy' was used to the point of exhaustion."[5] Without synergy, of course, firm growth through diversification will not be valued by shareholders who can diversify their personal equity portfolios more cheaply and who recognize the high trans-

---

[4] Steve Weiner and Hank Gilman, "Debate Grows on Retailers' Bank Services," *The Wall Street Journal*, May 18, 1984.

[5] David B. Hilder and Steve Weiner, "Big Brokerage Houses Are Problem Children for Their New Parents," *The Wall Street Journal*, September 13, 1985, 1. (Synergy is first discussed in Chapter 20.) Emphasis on synergy in public statements may also be attributed to the fact that, according to finance theory, shareholders are not well served by nonsynergistic mergers.

TABLE 27.2	Selected Data on Five Diversified Financial Services Firms, Year-End 1991 (Millions $)

The table provides basic financial data on the five diversified financial services firms profiled in this chapter. Their size and financial structures vary, depending on the industry in which they originated.

	Revenues	Rank	Net Income	Rank	Total Assets	Rank	Return on Assets	Rank	Common Equity	Rank	Return on Equity	Rank
American Express	$24,763	3	$789	3	$146,441	3	0.54%	4	$7,465	2	10.57%	2
Citicorp	20,440	4	(457)	5	216,922	1	−0.21%	5	7,349	3	−6.22%	4
Merrill Lynch	12,363	5	696	4	86,259	5	0.81%	3	3,818	5	18.23%	1
Prudential	29,716	2	2,280	1	189,148	2	1.21%	1	6,527[a]	4	NA	—
Sears	57,242	1	1,279	2	106,435	4	1.20%	2	14,188	1	9.01%	3

[a] 1991 policyholders' surplus was $6,527. Prudential is mutually owned and has no common equity.
Source: 1991 annual reports.

actions costs incurred by diversifying corporations. As will be evident in the discussion that follows, synergy has eluded some financial services firms. Nevertheless one cannot dismiss synergy as a motivation for offering a broad range of financial services.

PROFILES OF MAJOR DIVERSIFIED FINANCIAL SERVICES FIRMS

Table 27.2 summarizes data from five major diversified financial services firms as of year-end 1991 and ranks them according to different financial measures. Because Prudential is a mutually owned company, data on net income and total net worth, including all the firm's subsidiaries, are difficult to interpret. It is possible to infer from what is available, however, that Prudential's total net income places it in the higher part of the rankings for 1991.

No firm ranked at the top or bottom on all data items. The reason lies partly in the fact that these firms came to financial services from different origins, and thus have different combinations of assets, business lines, and financial structures. For example, Sears's emphasis on retailing makes it less leveraged than firms that are totally financially oriented; its common equity—whether measured alone or as a percentage of total assets—is largest. Citicorp, with origins in the banking industry concentrating on financial assets, has by far the largest volume of total assets and the lowest ratio of common equity to total assets.

The return on assets (ROA) and return on equity (ROE) performance measures also reflect differing degrees of success as diversified financial services firms entered their second decade. Citicorp reported negative net income, thus failing to take advantage of its highly leveraged position. Merrill Lynch, however, also relying on financial leverage and the smallest of the firms profiled in this chapter, reported a return on common equity of almost 20 percent.

Much of the remainder of the chapter is devoted to case histories of these firms. Although they have chosen different strategies and have met varying degrees of success, they have one thing in common: They have changed their own industries and other financial institutions forever.

MERRILL LYNCH AND COMPANY

Although Sears entered financial services long ago, many observers attribute the recent race to become the prototype diversified financial services firm not to Sears but to Merrill Lynch (ML). In the early 1970s, its chairman, Donald Regan, who later was Chief of Staff to President Ronald Reagan, announced a plan to transform ML into, as *Business Week* termed it, a "womb to tomb" financial services firm.[6] The first

---

[6] "How They Manage the New Financial Conglomerates," *Business Week,* December 20, 1982, 50.

step was to create a publicly owned holding company, Merrill Lynch and Company, to acquire the assets of a privately held securities firm, Merrill Lynch Pierce Fenner and Smith. The latter firm, founded in 1820, is still the holding company's largest subsidiary, despite the holding company's diversification beyond securities.

EXPANSION OF CONSUMER FINANCIAL SERVICES

One of the company's first major forays into product diversification was the Cash Management Account (CMA), offered through its brokerage subsidiary and described in the previous chapter. Introduced in 1977, the CMA held a majority share of the market for that deposit-like service throughout the 1980s, despite the entry of other major competitors. By the end of 1991, ML managed CMA accounts with assets of almost $270 billion. CMA holders have access to cash-dispensing machines in thousands of locations nationwide.

For individuals who do not wish to make stock and bond selections but do want to participate in the securities markets, ML's brokerage arm has stressed mutual funds in recent years. All types are available, from money market to foreign currency funds. By the early 1990s, ML had a range of mutual funds with assets managed by its subsidiaries. More than half the shares sold in 1991 were for funds managed by ML.[7]

ML, THE REAL ESTATE COMPANY. Besides expansion of securities products, ML sought to make progress toward its womb-to-tomb goal by establishing Merrill Lynch Realty, Inc. This holding company was formed in 1979 to acquire local real estate agencies, especially in fast-growing Sun Belt states. By 1981, 13 agencies with 250 offices had been acquired, and by the end of 1986, additional acquisitions had increased ML Realty's total residential real estate offices to 500. Also, Merrill Lynch Realty operated a relocation subsidiary, through which it assisted newcomers to communities in which it had offices, and a mortgage sub-

sidiary, offering homebuyers alternatives to borrowing from a local depository.

In late 1986, however, ML officials admitted that the synergy expected from adding real estate to its product offerings had not materialized. Management initially announced plans to sell the entire real estate unit but later decided to sell shares to the public and retain majority ownership. Analysts noted at the time that the unit (renamed Fine Homes, International) was the least profitable of all ML subsidiaries; by 1989 ML had sold all its remaining interests in real estate–related subsidiaries.[8]

ML, THE INSURANCE COMPANY. Merrill Lynch offers insurance products, often designed to appeal to customers with ML broker relationships. ML introduced insurance to its range of services in the mid-1970s with the acquisition of Family Life Insurance Company. Subsequently, two other life insurance firms were added. In 1991, ML sold the Family Life company; the activities of the other firms were consolidated under its Merrill Lynch Life Insurance Company, which had been founded in 1986 to develop life and annuity products to be marketed exclusively to ML clients.

DEVELOPMENT OF THE RETAIL FINANCIAL CENTER. In 1985, Merrill Lynch unveiled the first of its retail "financial centers" in downtown Manhattan. The largest in ML's nationwide chain, the center was a consolidation of five offices in the same area, reducing operating costs considerably. Cost reduction, however, was not the main strategic rationale for the center. Staffed with financial consultants (no longer called brokers) and on-site specialists in taxation, insurance, and other aspects of personal finance, the objective was to convince clients that ML employees were no longer salespeople but professionals trained in a range of financial services that could be purchased from ML and Company. To serve customers while controlling personnel costs, ML also hired sales assistants, who lacked the stature of financial consultants and were intended to serve small-account customers.

---

[7] Friedman 1989; and Merrill Lynch, *1991 Annual Report* and *1991 Form 10-K*.

[8] Merrill Lynch, *Annual Report 1988,* 37; Steve Swartz, "Merrill Lynch Real Estate Line Will Go Public," *The Wall Street Journal,* December 23, 1986, 2; and Merrill Lynch, *1991 Form 10-K.*

By the early 1990s, ML's 500 offices located throughout the world were staffed by financial consultants. They hold an influential role in enabling the firm to offer a wide range of services to individuals, including brokerage, mutual funds, insurance, and cash management, among others. Customer response has been quite positive; in 1991 alone, assets in individual client accounts rose almost 20 percent and represented at year-end about 2.5 percent of total household financial assets in the United States.[9]

ML, THE BANKER. ML's retail services are enhanced by two nonbank banks: Merrill Lynch Bank and Trust in New Jersey, and Merrill Lynch National Financial in Utah. Both are insured by the Federal Deposit Insurance Corporation (FDIC), and sell certificates of deposit (CDs), issue Visa cards, and offer consumer loans. Through Merrill Lynch Trust Company, a variety of personal trust services are offered in 26 states.

CULTIVATION OF THE COMMERCIAL CUSTOMER

ML has not neglected commercial and governmental customers in its pursuit of the retail dollar, having been a leader in investment banking for decades. In 1984, it acquired the firm of Becker Paribus, an investment banking house but, more importantly, a major commercial paper dealer, thereby becoming the leading participant in that market. ML was also among the largest underwriters of municipal and corporate bonds throughout the 1980s.

ML's investment banking operations have emphasized several specialty areas in recent years: assisting in mergers and acquisitions, expanding internationally, and arranging currency and interest rate swaps. As would be expected, difficulties in the junk bond market in the late 1980s temporarily dampened growth in the previously lucrative domestic merger and acquisition market. Also, several large bridge loans the firm had extended to customers during takeovers soured. ML's management recognized, however, that simultaneous developments abroad offer the possibility of transferring these activities from the United States to Europe and Asia. Furthermore, ML is involved in international banking through its Merrill Lynch International Banks located in London, Geneva, Singapore, and other main financial centers. Management indicates that global banking and other international activities will continue to expand in the 1990s.

On the domestic front, ML has launched another effort to attract commercial customers from its bank competitors. In the late 1980s, ML began an aggressive campaign to attract more small business borrowers. By 1992, ML had loaned more than $500 million to small businesses and was attracting their deposits to its working capital management accounts. As other lines of business promised higher returns in 1993, however, services to small business customers moved to a lower priority.[10]

ML: "FROM WALL STREET TO MAIN STREET"

ML has many strengths. Its worldwide offices give it a major geographic presence, and its potential retail customer base is huge. Its CMA strongly resembles a transaction account, it owns nonbank banks, and its international banking operations are already full-service.

Also, the role of ML in investment banking strengthens its image in wholesale financial services. If and when unrestricted investment banking and commercial banking coexist in a single organization, ML's relationships with corporate customers will make it a fierce competitor for their banking business.

Although the firm is far from being home free, ML substantively improved its performance and efficiency during the early 1990s. While refocusing its brokers to adopt the financial consultant role was initially challenging, the ML training programs and incentive compensation schemes have developed an effective and skilled work force. The firm succeeded in lowering its consultant turnover rate (that is, the proportion of consultants leaving the firm each year) from 19 percent in 1988 to 13 percent in 1991.

---

[9]Merrill Lynch, *1991 Annual Report,* 8.

[10]Lynn W. Adams, "Merrill Lynch Beckoning Bank Customers," *American Banker,* September 9, 1992, 10; and Randall Smith and Michael Siconolfi, "Merrill Quietly Folds a Big Lending Operation," *The Wall Street Journal,* March 31, 1993, C1, C13.

Analysts have criticized ML for its continuing high level of operating costs, but by late 1991, the views were softening. Substantial reductions in managerial and support staff, coupled with increases in financial consultants, set the firm on a productive path. The divestiture of its real estate operations and the narrowed focus of the insurance subsidiary were hailed as positive changes for ML.

The firm's initial goal of serving everyone in every way made it difficult to structure the organization to achieve superior levels of profitability. Although ML's top management said the firm did not want to be a "financial supermarket," where customers "grab their products and services from a shelf," the objective at one time was described as being a "department store." Later, however, the firm's CEO stated its strategy differently, saying, "The idea is that we aren't going to be all things to all people. We're going to be some things to some people."[11]

By early 1993, it appeared that the time and energy spent to refocus and restructure ML were proving to be helpful. Although the firm had not realized the full benefits it sought when the diversification effort was launched more than a decade earlier, ML was prospering with more modest goals and no longer aspiring to be the first fully diversified financial services firm.

PRUDENTIAL INSURANCE COMPANY OF AMERICA

A second major player to enter the financial services scene was Prudential Insurance (Pru), the nation's largest life insurer, operating since 1875. In 1981, Pru sent shock waves through the financial community with its purchase of Bache Group, Inc., the nation's sixth largest securities firm. Negotiations lasted only 13 days, astonishing observers of the usually conservative insurer. One noted that it was a case of "a 900-pound gorilla going after a banana."[12]

THE BACHE ACQUISITION: *THIS* IS SYNERGY?

For several years, Pru's chairman was interested in taking the firm beyond insurance. Although the plan did not initially include commercial banking, securities activities had been high on the list since 1974. When Bache became available, Pru's management agreed to pay $385 million for it. At the time, Bache was in turmoil, because it was involved in a controversial 1980 incident in which two wealthy Texans were accused of trying to corner the silver market.[13] Nonetheless, Pru's management was optimistic that Bache's problems were past and believed the acquisition was an ideal way to enter the brokerage, mutual fund, and underwriting businesses with one giant step.

THE BEST-LAID PLANS OFTEN GO AWRY. Unfortunately, as late as 1992, the Bache acquisition had failed to live up to the expectations of Pru's management. One of Bache's major problems was its low productivity. In 1982, for example, commissions and fees per employee were nearly $15,000 less at Bache than at other leading brokers. Initially, the new management Pru brought in to turn Bache around increased salaries even more and made costly cosmetic changes to the firm's offices. In 1984, Prudential-Bache, the renamed securities firm, posted the largest loss ever for a brokerage house, exceeding $110 million; this was at least partly attributed to high overhead costs. Wall Street analysts estimated that from 1981 through 1984, Pru's average annual return on the Bache deal was −12.5 percent. Although Prudential-Bache was marginally profitable in the mid-1980s, the crash of 1987 was no more kind to Bache than to other securities firms. Undaunted, however, Pru's management decided to expand its securities business in 1989 by purchasing the brokerage segment of Thomson McKinnon, acquiring an additional 158 retail offices and 2,000 brokers. Almost unbelievably, Bache had not reduced its total work force as late as January 1990, although most securities firms (including, as noted, Merrill Lynch) had

---

[11] See Taub 1986; and Steve Swartz and Laurie P. Cohen, "Merrill Lynch Will Sell Units in Real Estate," *The Wall Street Journal,* September 30, 1986, 3–4.

[12] See Carol J. Loomis, "The Fight for Financial Turf," *Fortune* 104 (December 28, 1981): 55.

[13] See Moore 1983. The New York Stock Exchange imposed a $400,000 fine on Bache for the incident, the largest fine ever for a member firm. See "New Bache Chief Pushes a Host of Changes, Including New Name, to Lift Firm's Image," *The Wall Street Journal,* October 29, 1982.

taken draconian reductions by that time. By March of that year, however, layoffs had been announced, since it was revealed that Bache lost about $50 million in 1989.

During the 1980s, life insurers had their own problems from which the insurance division of Pru was not exempt. To address changing customer preferences, Pru introduced the industry's first combination variable/universal life policy in 1985. Although popular with customers, this and other nontraditional products were less profitable than whole life policies, squeezing the firm's overall margin. Also, problems plagued Pru's P/L subsidiary, PRUPAC, and the firm's reinsurance subsidiary, Pru Re, had significant losses through the mid-1980s.

The original strategic plan at the time of the Bache acquisition called for brokers and insurance agents to work side by side, sharing client lists to increase sales. By the early 1990s, however, that desired synergy continued to be elusive. Although the insurance company manages almost $40 billion for customers, insurance agents in 1991 referred only enough brokerage activity to the securities firm to generate $25 million in commissions.

Rocked by lawsuits resulting from sales of limited partnerships and a failed entry into investment banking, in 1991 Bache's CEO was replaced and its name was changed to Prudential Securities. Although performance improved in 1992, it was not attributed to the desired synergy and cross-selling.[14]

MOVE TO BUSINESS LENDING

On another front, like Merrill Lynch, Pru has declared its intention to become active in serving business customers. It serves institutional clients through the Prudential Asset Management Group and the Prudential Asset Management Company. Through these subsidiaries, Pru offers investment operations, products, and services. Services range from asset management to loan originations to the purchase and management of private placements. By 1991, these operations were serving more than 800 institutional clients.

As noted earlier, Pru's entry into investment banking through Pru-Bache was not a successful venture. By 1990, losses had mounted to the point that Pru was forced to support the securities subsidiary with an additional capital injection (that is, a transfer of resources from the parent to increase Bache's net worth). Finally, most of the investment banking activities were discontinued; Pru absorbed a few of the services into its Asset Management Group. And although Pru owns a limited-service bank called Prudential Bank and Trust Company, its services are focused on individuals rather than business customers.

PRUDENTIAL: A "ROCKY" ROAD?

Because the insurance industry, which remains Pru's primary line of business, had especially difficult times in the 1980s and early 1990s, Pru's road to becoming a preeminent financial services provider has been rough. Also, Pru's securities subsidiary has been among the worst performers in a sometimes glittering industry. Fundamental improvements in each of these basic lines of business are necessary before the future envisioned at the time of the merger becomes reality. As at Merrill Lynch before 1986, the firm's initial strategic focus was fuzzy, having been vaguely articulated as being "Number One in each of our chosen major business lines."[15]

Since the move to diversification began, Pru has experienced frequent restructuring. A varied group of subsidiaries has been acquired, including a farm management organization, investment management firms, a home mortgage subsidiary, and real estate brokerage.

In 1989, Pru became one of the first in line to buy a "sick" thrift after the Financial Institutions Reform, Recovery, and Enforcement Act (FIRREA) made it possible for the FDIC to put the depository up

---

[14] See Michael Siconolfi and William Power, "Prudential Securities Seeks New Identity But Seems to be Revisiting '80s Pitfalls," *The Wall Street Journal,* January 28, 1992, C1, C14; Chuck Hawkins, "The Mess at Pru-Bache," *Business Week,* March 4, 1991, 66–72; Matthew Winkler and William Power. "Gap Between Rich and Poor Brokerage Firms Widens," *The Wall Street Journal,* January 24, 1990, C1, C17; Hilder and Weiner, "Big Brokerage Houses Are Problem Children for Their Parents"; William Power, "Wall Street Wields Ax Again as Woes Deepen," *The Wall Street Journal,* January 29, 1990, C1, C17; and Michael Siconolfi, "Prudential-Bache Plans to Eliminate Hundreds of Jobs," *The Wall Street Journal,* March 29, 1990, A4.

[15] Prudential, *Annual Report 1985,* 3.

for sale. Just 25 miles from Prudential Bank and Trust, the S&L—renamed Prudential Savings Bank—permits Pru to become more involved in depository and other retail financial services.[16] Given the recent difficulties in achieving profitability in the S&L industry, the acquisition does not promise immediate relief from the problems that Pru has encountered in its insurance and securities businesses.

Still, Pru has features that make it a major force in the financial markets. Because of the insurance subsidiary's huge asset portfolio, the firm has substantial expertise in portfolio management, including real estate development. Pru has established relationships with many major corporations whose bonds it holds in private placements. The firm also enjoys relative freedom from geographic restrictions.

In addition, Pru's CEO, while emphasizing the "prudence" in the firm's name, continues to look for growth while "digesting the changes of the past." In contrast to other diversified financial services firms profiled in this chapter, Pru has made the commitment to stick with and try to build even its most troubled acquisitions. One explanation for this commitment may rest in management's belief that the mutual form of organization gives it an edge over its competitors. Pru is clearly in the financial services business for the long haul.[17]

AMERICAN EXPRESS

When Prudential bought Bache, Sanford Weill, Chairman of Shearson Loeb Rhoades, the third largest brokerage firm, saw the handwriting on the wall. To avoid being captured by a giant not of his own choosing, Weill approached the leading travel services firm, American Express (AmEx), and asked it to buy Shearson. In April 1981, within a month after the Pru-Bache deal, AmEx paid $930 million for Shearson, renaming it Shearson/American Express.

Like Merrill Lynch and Prudential, AmEx was hardly a newcomer to financial products. Founded in 1850 to transport packages and money across the American frontier, the firm invented the traveler's check in 1891. By the 1960s, AmEx's famous green credit card and its best-selling traveler's checks made the company a household word. The 1981 Shearson acquisition was the first of several billion spent to turn AmEx into a contender for the title of financial services leader.

SHEARSON/AMEX: MAYBE *THIS* IS SYNERGY (NOT)

Weill's goal was to obtain the AmEx cardholder list for Shearson brokers, a seemingly natural marketing tool to increase the company's ability to serve wealthy customers. AmEx executives did not agree to share, however, fearing that cardholders might become disenchanted if their Shearson-managed stock accounts went sour. Weill also hoped to capitalize on the acknowledged strength of AmEx's marketing department to enable Shearson to develop a distinctive image, like that of rival Merrill Lynch. But AmEx continued to place more emphasis on credit card marketing than on the image of the brokerage firm.

Not that the Shearson/AmEx deal was initially unprofitable: Analysts estimated that AmEx's annual return on the Shearson investment from 1981 to 1984 averaged 10.9 percent.[18] As in the Pru organization, however, problems emerged in the attempt to combine corporate cultures. By 1985, Weill and others had quit the company, unable to merge their management styles with that of AmEx's chairman and CEO, James Robinson.

Happily for AmEx, the managers who Robinson brought in to replace Weill at first succeeded in increasing cooperation among personnel. Although by 1986, the firm was touted as a "state of the art financial services conglomerate," AmEx sought to reduce its exposure to cyclical swings in the securities business by selling partial ownership of Shearson to other investors in 1987. AmEx retained controlling interest.[19]

---

[16] Paulette Thomas, "Prudential Cleared to Buy Sick Thrift, among First to Benefit from S&L Bill," *The Wall Street Journal,* August 8, 1989, A3.

[17] See *The Prudential 1991 Annual Report;* Larry Light, "How Much Prudence Is Good for Prudential?" *Business Week,* July 13, 1992, 124–126; "How They Manage the New Financial Conglomerates," 1982.

[18] See Hilder and Weiner, "Big Brokerage Houses Are Problem Children for Their Parents," 1985.

[19] Anthony Bianco, "American Express: A Financial Supermarket That Works," *Business Week,* June 2, 1986, 78–79; Steve Swartz,

Subsequent events made AmEx's decision to retain a major stake in Shearson a fateful one. In late 1987, the cumulative effect of allegations that rival brokerage firm E. F. Hutton had defrauded its customers brought that firm down. Shearson's management decided to acquire many of Hutton's retail offices and employees, unaware of the impending doom in the securities industry that was to follow the crash of 1987. The newly renamed and personnel-heavy Shearson Lehman Hutton was thus poorly positioned to withstand the fallout from the crash. In 1990, the *first quarter* loss at Shearson was so large that AmEx was forced to invest more than $1 billion to keep the brokerage firm from becoming insolvent.

AmEx optimistically announced a major restructuring when, in 1990, it divided Shearson's brokerage and investment banking functions into two firms with different names. Emphasizing a revered name in the securities industry, the investment bank began operating as Lehman Brothers, while brokerage services were subsequently provided by Shearson Lehman Brothers. All reference to E. F. Hutton was eliminated. Many observers were skeptical that the firm could return to its previous heights.

By 1993, Lehman Brothers had proved at least the worst skeptics wrong, because its investment banking operations were enjoying renewed growth as part of the overall boom in the securities business. Still, AmEx was plagued by the relatively poor, though improving, results from Shearson's brokerage division.

In March 1993, as noted earlier in the chapter, AmEx's management announced the sale of Shearson Lehman to Primerica for about $1 billion. Observers greeted this announcement as convincing evidence that the financial supermarket concept, so widely touted in the 1980s, was a dead issue. Comments of the CEO about the sale fueled speculation that the Lehman Brothers investment banking subsidiary would also be on the auction block soon.[20]

AMEX AND THE MIDDLE-INCOME CUSTOMER

In 1983, the upper-income marketing strategy that AmEx had initially pursued took an abrupt turn when AmEx acquired Investors Diversified Services (IDS), a mutual fund and financial planning group headquartered in Minneapolis. At a cost of nearly $800 million, IDS gave AmEx access to millions of middle-income consumers who were either ineligible for or uninterested in AmEx cards and Shearson brokerage accounts.

The IDS purchase had features of strategic importance to AmEx. Unlike many investment companies, IDS had a nationwide sales force. Most personnel were in small or medium-sized communities, unlike Shearson brokers, who were concentrated in large cities. Also, IDS had a life insurance subsidiary, adding a previously unavailable product to the AmEx line. The IDS acquisition permitted the company to simultaneously diversify along customer, geographic, and product lines.

Initially, operating costs for the new sales force were higher than AmEx anticipated, and reorganization was necessary. Soon, however, cross-selling efforts between Shearson and IDS products were successful. Also, increased and very profitable emphasis was placed on financial planning services available through IDS. In the early 1990s, in contrast to the Shearson debacle, observers were praising the success of the IDS acquisition as the "best deal" AmEx had ever made. At that time, earnings growth had averaged 23 percent per year, and assets under IDS's management had doubled. Perhaps more importantly, prospects were bright, and IDS's conservative Midwestern management was viewed as a source of inspiration for other AmEx executives. Indeed, Robinson's successor as AmEx CEO was none other than the former head of IDS, Harvey Golub, who had been credited with building its lucrative financial planning business and on whose more open and approachable management style the entire firm's hopes are now pinned.[21]

"American Express Co. Sets Shearson Issue," *The Wall Street Journal,* March 24, 1987, 3.

[20] Steve Swartz, "Shearson's Bold Move to Purchase Hutton Puts It Near Top Spot," *The Wall Street Journal,* December 3, 1987, 1, 20; William Power, "Shearson Faces Huge Price Tag to Reduce Costs," *The Wall Street Journal,* March 3, 1990, C1, C8; William Power and Michael Siconolfi, "Shearson Split Revives Lehman Name," *The Wall Street Journal,* June 17, 1990, C1, C6; and "Primerica Creates Broker Powerhouse."

[21] See Russell Mitchell, "IDS: Sparkling Jewel in a Tarnished Crown," *Business Week,* March 19, 1990, 113. Events leading to Robinson's ouster and his successor's selection were widely covered in the financial press. Among many sources are Bill Saporito, "The Toppling of King James III," *Fortune,* January 11, 1993, 42–43; and Julie Solomon et al., "Jimmy Leaves Home," *Newsweek,* December 21, 1992, 50–51.

AMEX AND CONSUMER CREDIT

In 1986, AmEx expanded consumer lending operations by opening banks in Delaware and Minnesota. Using the customer base of its credit card and IDS account holders, the banks provide personal and mortgage loans. AmEx is also positioned to enter consumer banking through its network of more than 17,500 point-of-sale authorization terminals and cash-dispensing machines.

In 1987, AmEx announced a new credit card called Optima, designed to compete by charging a lower interest rate on outstanding balances than bank cards. Unlike holders of the famous AmEx travel and entertainment card, who must pay bills in full on receipt, Optima customers may carry over a balance from month to month. Optima was initially viewed as a winner; after only 1 year, it ranked sixth in share of credit card loans outstanding, and it rose to fifth in 1989. But, as with the Shearson acquisition, prospects quickly soured when it was revealed that Optima's increasing market share had been achieved through the use of less-than-prudent credit standards and policies. Delinquencies skyrocketed during the recession of the early 1990s, and the parent company announced huge losses on its credit card division as a result of Optima's difficulties. Although AmEx has indicated that it will continue to market the card and has announced a new pricing system, analysts note that its future is indeed murky.[22]

AMEX AND INTERNATIONAL BANKING

AmEx is not a newcomer to banking. In 1919, to facilitate the traveler's check business, AmEx formed American Express International Banking Corporation (AEIBC), which by 1991 had 83 offices in 40 countries and had been renamed simply American Express Bank (AEB). For much of its recent history, the unit stressed international investment banking through its London office, but AmEx had so little enthusiasm for

this endeavor that AEB was put up for sale in early 1981. There were no takers.

After the Shearson acquisition, AmEx again turned its attention to developing commercial and retail banking products, and AEB received renewed emphasis. In 1983, AmEx added the Trade Development Bank of Switzerland to its international banking group, acquiring an institution with more than $4.5 billion in deposits. At first, AEB was the "crown jewel" of AmEx. It stressed three main banking strategies: services for wealthy individuals (private banking), arrangement of international loan agreements, and international correspondent banking. All three services were fee-based, which was consistent with AmEx's historical emphasis on fee income from traveler's checks and credit cards, as well as with Shearson's fee-based securities operations.

Unfortunately, however, the Trade Development Bank acquisition—with its emphasis on private banking—soon went sour, and AmEx announced its sale in late 1989. Management learned that private banking customers were not interested in AmEx's other services and that fierce competition in the Swiss banking market limited its growth potential. However, AEB continues its involvement in other aspects of global banking, including foreign exchange and international trade financing. It was an early entrant into formerly closed Eastern European markets. AmEx also operates an Edge Corporation in several U.S. cities to serve visiting international customers.[23]

AMEX AND P/L INSURANCE

In 1968, for tax reasons, AmEx acquired Fireman's Fund, one of the nation's ten largest property/liability (P/L) insurers. By the early 1980s, the acquisition seemed to fit conveniently into AmEx's plan to become a diversified financial services firm. The outlook for insurance changed rapidly in the early 1980s, however, and in 1983, AmEx posted its first earnings downturn in 36 years, attributed to severe underwriting losses at Fireman's.

[22] Stephen Kleege, "AmEx Turns to Incentives in a Bid to Revive Optima," *American Banker,* February 25, 1993, 1, 6; Peter Pae, "Optima Backfires on American Express," *The Wall Street Journal,* October 3, 1991, B1–B2; Leah Nathans Spiro, "Behind the Bombshell from AmEx," *Business Week,* October 21, 1991, 124–126.

[23] See John Meehan, "AmEx Cancels Its Membership in a Ritzy Club," *Business Week,* January 15, 1990, 68; and American Express Company, *1991 Annual Report,* 12–13.

Although Fireman's is a stock company, it had been privately held by AmEx since 1968. In 1984, with no quick access to external capital for Fireman's, AmEx was forced to inject $200 million into the insurer to meet the requirements of California regulators. Later, AmEx distanced itself from Fireman's considerably by selling 85 percent of its stock to the public. AmEx's management noted that Fireman's mostly commercial customers did not mesh with the strong retail financial services unit resulting from the Shearson and IDS acquisitions. Before the public sale, however, AmEx transferred Fireman's life insurance operations to IDS, a move that was consistent with the conglomerate's retail focus.

AMEX: HOPING AGAINST HOPE THAT NO ONE LEAVES HOME WITHOUT IT

When it began its quest for financial dominance, AmEx had many competitive strengths. Its image among consumers was unsurpassed: According to a 1984 survey, 75 percent of all Americans knew of AmEx financial products, versus 66 percent for Merrill Lynch, 54 percent for Sears, and 53 percent for Citicorp. Interestingly, AmEx's closest rival for recognition was Prudential, with 72 percent. More recently, a survey showed that among U.S. consumer businesses, only Coca-Cola and McDonald's were better known.[24] AmEx's retail product offerings are designed to appeal to virtually every middle- or upper-income household. It is still perhaps possible that someday few Americans in these income categories will leave home without an AmEx connection.

Although difficulties plagued almost all its acquisitions, for a time AmEx was the most successful of the major financial services firms. Its strategic markets were clearer and narrower than those of ML or Pru, enabling management to focus the firm's resources to achieve synergy among product lines. In addition, AmEx was also willing to divest itself of operations that did not seem to work.

Saying that AmEx was more successful than some of its diversified rivals is not saying a lot, how-

ever. In 1990, *Business Week* profiled the firm in a cover story entitled "The Failed Vision" and quoted then-CEO Robinson as saying, "Now we will stop trying to be all things to all people all over the world." Except for the specific choice of words, Robinson's conclusions are remarkably similar to those attributed earlier in this chapter to managers at Merrill Lynch and Prudential.

And 1990's negative headlines were only the beginning. Well into 1993, lengthy accounts of the downfall of the once-mighty AmEx and its executives were commonplace, with such titles as "The Bill Is Due at American Express" and "Less-than-Fantastic Plastic." Most observers conclude that AmEx simply forgot to serve its customers in its haste to grab market share. Many note that management relied on the firm's past reputation and assumed blind loyalty from those from whom they sought business. Until almost too late, managers failed to acknowledge that AmEx's products and services must be perceived as of equal or better value compared with those offered by competitors. With the focus returning to the original credit card business and with leadership authority firmly in the control of new chairman and CEO Golub, the future looked brighter for this weakened giant by mid-1993. But there is little doubt that the 1980s' vision of AmEx as the nation's financial supermarket will not become reality.[25]

SEARS, ROEBUCK AND COMPANY

If any year can be identified as the year that diversified financial services firms emerged, it is 1981. Not only did the Pru-Bache, and Shearson-AmEx deals occur, but in 1981, the world's largest retailer declared its intention to become the world's largest financial services firm. Sears, founded as a mail-order watch company in 1886, laid the groundwork for this move in 1980 by reorganizing as a holding company, of which only one

[24] For more information on AmEx's reputation and financial performance, see American Express Company, *Annual Report 1984,* 4; Williams 1987; and Friedman and Meehan 1989.

[25] Meehan and Friedman 1990; Saporito 1991; Leah Nathans Spiro and Mark Landler, "Less-than-Fantastic Plastic," *Business Week,* November 9, 1992, 100–101; and Steven Lipin, "Golub Solidifies Hold at American Express, Begins to Change Firm," *The Wall Street Journal,* June 30, 1993, A1, A9. Articles cited in earlier footnotes also provide insight into the firm's decline.

subsidiary was department store and catalog operations. The firm acted on its new intentions swiftly, acquiring two major financial subsidiaries within 1 month.

EMERGENCE OF THE SEARS FINANCIAL NETWORK

The first of these purchases, in October 1981, was Dean Witter Reynolds, then the fifth largest brokerage firm. Only a few days later, Sears startled the financial community by announcing the purchase of Coldwell Banker, the nation's largest commercial real estate agency, with a residential division as well. Total price tag for the two firms: $812 million. With its existing Allstate Insurance subsidiary and its Allstate S&L in California (later renamed the Sears Savings Bank), the new acquisitions formed the Sears Financial Network.

Adding to the existing offices of Dean Witter and Coldwell Banker, Sears announced plans to open one-stop financial centers in at least half of its 800-plus retail outlets. By mid-1982, the first eight prototype centers were in operation, and 308 were open by 1985. The firm then announced that no major expansion of these centers was anticipated, perhaps a prelude of things to come.

SEARS, THE BROKER

Initial reaction to the Dean Witter acquisition was skepticism. Unlike Pru and AmEx, which were parent companies accustomed to wealthy individuals and corporations, Sears's retail customers were thought to be primarily middle- or lower-income families. *Institutional Investor,* a leading Wall Street trade publication, published a cartoon depicting the unlikely sight of a Rolls Royce parked in front of a Sears store. Critics forgot that selling financial products in department stores was nothing new for Sears. The Allstate Insurance Company had been selling policies in stores since 1933 and, in fact, was originally named after a best-selling brand of Sears tires. With the addition of Dean Witter and Coldwell Banker, the in-store list of available financial products was simply expanded.

Sears's management did not seem worried about the alleged incongruity of "stocks and socks." In fact, Sears had no real intention of pursuing the high-

income customer as a main target market. Still, market research indicated that 45 percent of young affluent households shopped at Sears monthly and that 65 percent had Sears credit cards, compared with only 36 percent who had American Express cards.[26]

EVIDENCE ON STOCKS AND SOCKS ACCUMULATES. Early evidence from Dean Witter brokers assigned to Sears stores seemed to confirm that the untapped savings of Sears customers were limitless. Stories of thousands—and, in some cases, millions—of dollars pouring into Dean Witter offices were common. Also, the company's profits were up 130 percent in the first quarter of 1983, prompting many to think that the synergy that seemed to elude other financial service giants had been realized at Sears.

Despite this optimistic beginning, by 1985 it was clear that integrating Dean Witter had been rockier than had first been claimed. Part of the reason is familiar from Pru-Bache's problems: Employee characteristics and management styles differ among industries and cannot be combined easily. To staff its in-store financial centers, Sears trained more than 4,000 new salespeople between 1983 and 1985. But because of defections by experienced Dean Witter brokers during the period, total brokerage employment increased by only 1,700. Investment bankers at Dean Witter were dissatisfied with the more conservative philosophy of Sears executives and left the company, and Dean Witter's position in investment banking slipped considerably during the mid-1980s. Remaining managers were regarded lightly by others on Wall Street.[27]

UNPROFITABLE ACCOUNTS. In addition, brokerage accounts generated by the Dean Witter-Sears relationship were not initially profitable. When the firm did a mass mailing to 19 million credit card holders, encouraging them to open individual retirement accounts (IRAs) through Dean Witter, only a few thousand people responded. Not only was the expense of the campaign considerable, but the company later determined

---

[26] Alfred G. Haggerty, "Financial Centers a Big Success for Sears," *National Underwriter,* November 23, 1984, 56.

[27] See Hilder and Weiner, "Big Brokerage Houses Are Problem Children for Their Parents," 1985; Williams 1985; and Glynn 1985.

that IRAs are not especially profitable, because they rarely involve commission-generating trades.

Sears customers were initially very interested in Dean Witter's mutual funds, but these, too, are low-profit relationships. The lucrative aspects of brokering, such as lending through margin accounts, did not materialize. By 1985, the productivity of Dean Witter brokers, measured by average commissions generated, had fallen to only 70 percent of the industry average and was almost $30,000 lower than in 1983. These problems resulted in an estimated annual return on the Dean Witter acquisition of just 3.3 percent, not considering the additional $300 million Sears lent Dean Witter in 1984 to shore up its capital.[28]

Throughout the 1980s, Dean Witter failed to make a meaningful contribution to Sears's net income. It did virtually no business in the then-lucrative corporate takeover and merger markets, choosing instead a retail strategy. It entered the securities industry's troubled times in a weakened condition, and the lack of support from Sears personnel prevented Dean Witter brokers from obtaining access to potential new customers until Sears's CEO Edward Brennan finally ordered the sharing of customer information toward the end of the decade. Contemporaneous troubles in Sears's retailing operations prevented the firm from investing significant additional amounts in its securities subsidiaries.

Then, almost unexpectedly, beginning in 1990, Dean Witter's fortunes turned around. Analysts attributed the performance improvement to its low-cost approach to the brokerage business at a time when rivals were still bloated from the excesses of the 1980s. Its focus on the retail customer finally began to pay off. Ironically, however, Dean Witter's success did not mean that Sears was at last poised to become the most successful diversified financial services firm after all. Instead, in 1992, Sears announced that it was divesting itself of Dean Witter to concentrate on its seriously weakened core business—merchandising. Observers noted that, although financial services did contribute substantially to the firm's overall profitability in the 1990s, after having drained funds from the corporation

in the previous decade, they did not generate enough cash to finance both their own expansion and the badly needed restructuring of Sears's retailing division. Stockholders were angry at the continued deterioration in Sears's share price, and managers determined that only by focusing on the company's origins would it be likely to survive. So the marriage of stocks and socks is over.[29]

SEARS, THE REAL ESTATE COMPANY

The second 1981 acquisition, Coldwell Banker, initially seemed to fare better. Coldwell Banker did not break totally new ground because of Sears's historic involvement in real estate. The company actually sold houses through the mail from 1908 to 1937, and some towns today boast entire neighborhoods in which homes were purchased from a Sears catalog.[30] Less unusual were the firm's California S&L and PMI Mortgage Insurance Corporation, one of the nation's largest, which Sears had owned since 1973. Starting in 1983, however, Sears added a new twist to real estate brokerage by offering discounts on home furnishings and appliances to homebuyers using Coldwell Banker's services. Although competitors objected, the practice was upheld in most states.

Coldwell's profits increased steadily from 1981 through 1985. Its position in the residential real estate market was especially impressive as the volume of houses sold increased to 10 percent of the national market in 1988, up from only 1.3 percent at the time of acquisition. In 1986, it was second in residential real estate sales and the leader in commercial real estate. However, the firm's involvement in commercial real estate came to an end in 1989, when it sold Coldwell's commercial division for $300 million. By that time, Sears's retail stores were struggling to such an extent that management feared a potential takeover. Thus, the cash inflow from the sale was welcome, as was the divestiture of a subsidiary that was potentially attractive to corporate raiders.

---

[28] Williams 1985; and Hilder and Weiner, "Big Brokerage Houses Are Problem Children for Their Parents," 1985.

[29] Michael Siconolfi, "Dean Witter Proves an Asset to Sears, Confounding Pundits," *The Wall Street Journal,* March 15, 1991, A1, A4; Julia Flynn et al., "Smaller but Wiser," *Business Week,* October 12, 1992, 28–29; Gregory A. Patterson and Francine Schwadel, "Sears Suddenly Undoes Years of Diversifying Beyond Retailing Field," *The Wall Street Journal,* September 30, 1992, A1, A6.

[30] For more information, see Schwartz 1985.

Still, Sears's plans for the residential mortgage market remained grand, at least for a time. It announced that its objective by the mid-1990s was to be involved in more than one-quarter of all home sales in the country and for mortgages on those homes to be originated at financial institutions owned by Sears, insured by PMI, Inc., and packaged for resale by Dean Witter. But real estate and mortgage markets became troubled in the late 1980s and early 1990s, and it became clear these plans could not be realized anytime soon. Furthermore, as noted earlier, Sears's core merchandising business continued to deteriorate badly throughout this period. Thus, when it announced the sale of Dean Witter, management said it was also selling Coldwell Banker, continuing the dismantling of the financial network begun to such fanfare a decade before.

SEARS, THE BANKER

Sears's ownership of an S&L since 1960 made it no stranger to deposit taking as it began its campaign to become the world's leading financial services company. Although Sears sold most of its interest in this thrift subsidiary (to Citicorp, a diversified rival) in 1987, the firm had moved more deeply into consumer banking 2 years earlier by purchasing a small Delaware bank, the Greenwood Trust Company, and selling the commercial loan portfolio to avoid violating bank holding company (BHC) regulations. The purpose of owning tiny Greenwood ($11 million total assets) was to facilitate Sears's most ambitious effort to become the dominant retail financial services company: the Discover card.

DISCOVER WHAT? The Discover card, issued through Greenwood Trust to customers drawn mostly from Sears's credit card holders, was the world's first general-purpose financial services card.[31] Test-marketed in five states in 1985 and offered nationally in 1986, the card was intended to give a holder instant access to virtually any financial service—from making a deposit to buying stock to charging merchandise at a store to taking out a home equity loan. Launching the Discover card was a massive effort, viewed by analysts as Sears's riskiest venture ever.

Sears had to obtain agreement from merchants everywhere to accept the card as readily as they accept Visa, MasterCard, or American Express. Although some merchants agreed immediately (Holiday Inns, American Airlines, and Denny's Restaurants, for example), many were reluctant. Why should J. C. Penney, Macy's, or Marshall Field help the Sears Financial Network earn additional interest income? To entice merchants into accepting the card, Sears charged lower processing fees than rivals Visa, MasterCard, and American Express. Even so, acceptance was not instantaneous. As of mid-1986, 380,000 accepting merchants were estimated, compared with more than 2.5 million accepting Visa cards. By 1990, however, Discover was accepted by more merchants (1,200,000) than the AmEx card (850,000), although it still ranked far behind MasterCard's and Visa's 3 million client merchants.[32]

Sears also had to build a base of customers willing to use the card not only as a credit card but also to take advantage of features Sears believes distinguish Discover from rival cards. Holding a Discover card permits someone to tap a savings account at Greenwood Trust and, in some states, to make deposits into a Greenwood account through an ATM. Sears hoped that by 1990, cardholders would buy CDs, take out loans, or trade securities, all through a member of the Sears Financial Network. There is little evidence that this ever occurred.

To entice potential cardholders, most of whom already carried bank cards, AmEx cards, or both, no annual fees were charged for the first 2 years of Discover's existence, discounts on Sears merchandise were provided for using the card, and a prearranged line of credit was awarded to the 28 million Sears cardholders active in 1985. Yet evidence continued to suggest that Discover cardholders viewed the card more as a substitute for a Sears credit card than as a financial services card. Not one of the respondents to a 1986

---

[31] For information on Discover at the time it was announced, see Williams 1985; "Mighty Sears Tests Its Clout in Credit Cards," *Business Week,* September 2, 1985, 62–63; and Janet Key, "New Card Chief Focus for Sears," *Chicago Tribune,* October 3, 1985, Section 3, 1, 6. Much of the information in this section is drawn from these articles.

[32] James E. Ellis, "Sears' Discover Card Finds Its Way," *Business Week,* September 15, 1986, 166–167; David Greising, "The Discover Card Is No Longer a Joker," *Business Week,* October 9, 1989, 138; and "Discover Card Has Best Performance Ever," *American Banker,* April 25, 1990, 2.

survey had used the card to open a savings account at Greenwood, and only 8 percent had used it at a cash-dispensing machine. Also, no respondent considered Discover to be a substitute for a bank card or other national credit card. One unique feature of Discover, however, appeared to make it particularly attractive to early users. A "cash back" program allowed cardholders who charged $3,000 or more annually to receive a 1 percent rebate on their purchases. (Smaller rebates were established for lower cumulative charges.) Ironically, research shows that few credit card users charge more than half that much in a year; furthermore, the rebate was worth a paltry $30, even to someone who charged the full $3,000.[33]

Sears's losses on the Discover card in 1985 were more than $15 million after taxes and were $106 million in 1986. Losses in 1987 were $124 million, but by 1992, a healthy $239 million profit was earned. Many believed that Sears's image as the premier provider of financial services to middle-income families rested with the success of Discover. As the 1992 profit figures suggest, success did indeed finally seem to be at hand. By the end of that year, Discover boasted more than 40 million cardholders, making Sears the second largest (behind Visa) among bank credit card issuers. It is no wonder that many observers were taken aback when Sears announced that it would sell its Discover operations as part of the Dean Witter sale. But again, executives stated they had no choice but to raise the cash needed to focus on the core business. The investment community initially seemed to agree, for Sears's stock price improved on announcement of the divestiture.[34]

SEARS: THE END OF AN ERA?

Integrating the merchandising subsidiary and the Sears Financial Network proved to be more difficult than anticipated, and management's attention continued to be divided for more than 10 years. Changing consumer preferences presented major problems for both merchandising and financial services. The merchandising group hit perhaps its darkest days in the late 1980s, as competition from both discounters (such as Wal-Mart) and full-service stores (such as J. C. Penney) became relentless. In a dramatic switch from its previous strategy of emphasizing Sears brands and advertising frequent "sale" prices, the firm embarked on a program of so-called everyday low pricing on a full line of name-brand merchandise. Public reaction was lukewarm, and Moody's lowered the firm's bond ratings in anticipation of difficult times. These developments drained funds and energy from the Sears Financial Network. Clearly, the course no longer seemed sustainable after 1992 as evidenced by the firm's announcement that it was discontinuing its catalog sales operations and closing more than 100 retail stores.

The Sears of the mid-1990s is a far different firm from the financial/retailing conglomerate of a decade before, but it still retains ties to the financial services industry. When it announced the sale of Dean Witter and Coldwell Banker, management decided to take 20 percent of Allstate public through the sale of approximately 80 million shares with an expected value of about $2 billion. Allstate has consistently been one of the lowest-cost producers in the P/L industry, managing to escape the severe profit downturn suffered by most firms in the 1980s. Although it, like most other P/L insurers, sustained huge losses in 1992 as a result of Hurricane Andrew, Allstate is still considered one of the industry's most successful companies. While Sears will maintain majority ownership, the reduced control of Allstate signals another step away from even its oldest involvement in financial services.

One of Sears's recent moves even suggests that it is still willing to make new, if more limited, forays into financial services. After a sustained court battle, Sears won the right to issue Visa cards through its existing bank and thrift subsidiaries. (Visa had sought to forbid nonbanking businesses with bank subsidiaries from becoming its affiliates.) But the era of the Sears Financial Network is clearly now financial history.[35]

[33] "Sears Discover Card Use Studied," *ABA Banking Journal* 78 (June 1986): 115; and Greising, "The Discover Card Is No Longer a Joker."

[34] Sears, Roebuck and Company, *1988 Annual Report,* 52; John Schmeitzer, "$3.9 Billion Loss Sears's Worst Ever," *Chicago Tribune,* February 10, 1993, Section 3, 1, 3; and Phil Roosevelt "Sears to Pull Out of Banking," *American Banker,* September 30, 1992, 1, 7.

[35] "An Open Book: Can America Count on the New-Look Sears?" *Chicago Tribune,* January 31, 1993, Special Report; Yvette D. Kantrow, "Sears Wins Court Battle to Start Issuing Visa Cards," *American Banker,* November 6, 1992, 1; and Greg Steinmetz, "Sears's Allstate Unit Expects to Raise More than $2 Billion in Initial Offering," *The Wall Street Journal,* March 19, 1993, A3.

CITICORP

The role of Citicorp as a trend setter in commercial banking is noted at different points in this book. The giant bank's relentless push against regulatory barriers is legendary. This strategic posture allowed Citicorp to develop into a nationwide diversified financial services firm in an era when many commercial banks felt bound both geographically and by product line. Founded in 1812, and the oldest of the contenders for financial services leader, Citicorp epitomizes a firm whose management engaged in "deregulated thinking" long before deregulation was a reality.

CITICORP THE INNOVATOR

Citicorp's recent history as an innovator dates at least to 1961, when First National City Bank developed the negotiable CD, an event discussed in Chapter 5. Thereafter, the bank pioneered liability management through its aggressive use of large CDs, Eurodollar deposits, and repos to evade the shackles of Reg Q.

Until 1968, First National City was not organized as a holding company, and almost all its business was in commercial banking. With the formation of Citicorp, the holding company that now owns the renamed Citibank, a new corporate strategy emerged, including aggressive pursuit of retail banking and product diversification to the full extent allowed. Management decided to attach the "Citi" prefix to virtually every product and service. To a large extent, these strategies remain in place today.

EVERY CITY SHOULD HAVE A CITI. At the time the move to retail banking was initiated, the cost of retail funds was lower and the deposit base more stable than that of wholesale depositors. Competition for corporate business was fierce, not only from other commercial banks but also from finance companies and the commercial paper market. Soon, Citibank had opened hundreds of banking offices and automated teller machines (ATMs) in New York City, later expanding (but less successfully than management had hoped) into upstate New York as branching restrictions were loosened in that state.

By the mid-1970s, the central means of accomplishing Citicorp's strategy was well established: geographic expansion at home and abroad to spread the

"Citi" trademark. Branches, ATMs, loan production offices, Edge Act offices, International Banking Facilities, and every other means of obtaining a physical presence as an interstate and international institution were used. Citicorp also used mass mailings to garner new credit card applicants for Citibank's own Diners' Club and for Visa and MasterCard. Some reports state that the research alone required to direct Citicorp's retail strategy cost $200 million, a marketing expenditure unprecedented at that time among financial institutions.[36]

TEMPORARY SETBACK. In 1980, the outlook for the retail strategy took a dismal turn. The advent of the money market certificate had driven up the cost of retail funds, the 1978 bankruptcy law revision produced skyrocketing losses on credit cards and consumer loans, usury ceilings held down profits on good loans, and the market value of Citicorp's large residential mortgage portfolio dropped precipitously as rates rose.

Furthermore, Citicorp's GAP managers in the international division engaged in deliberate asset/liability mismatching that year to compensate for poor results in the consumer segment; when their rate forecasts were wrong, the result was a loss of more than $35 million. Although the commercial side of the firm had a good year, and the firm had an overall net profit, critics of the institution charged that the retail strategy had backfired. Net losses on consumer banking exceeded $79 million in 1980 and improved only slightly to $42 million the following year.

CITICORP, THE LAWMAKER

Undeterred, Citicorp's management set out to change laws it believed had prevented the retail strategy from being profitable, beginning aggressively and successfully with usury laws. Unable to persuade New York legislators, it looked to other states. Aware of Citicorp's dissatisfaction with New York laws, South Dakota lifted its usury ceiling in late 1980. Citicorp moved its credit card operations there in 1981, instituting an annual fee for cardholders at the same time. The

---

[36] "The New Banking Forces New Strategies," *Business Week,* July 13, 1981, 57.

credit card division grew to be among the firm's most profitable, and renewed efforts at expanding its customer base continued throughout the 1980s. In 1990, Citicorp had a reported 35 million credit card customers—more than any lender in the world. Net income from card operations had grown at an incredible rate of *40 percent per year* since 1983, and a manager in the credit card division was quoted as saying, "We do a thousand things right every day."[37]

CITICORP, RESCUER OF THRIFTS (AND REGULATORS?)

In 1982, Citicorp removed itself from two regulations that large banks complained were the most restrictive they faced: prohibitions against interstate deposit taking and against BHCs having thrift subsidiaries. Early in the year, the Federal Savings and Loan Insurance Corporation (FSLIC) was seeking merger partners for hundreds of thrifts to avoid running out of cash. When the nation's twentieth largest thrift, Fidelity Savings and Loan of Oakland, became insolvent, the Federal Home Loan Bank Board (FHLBB) made an emergency rule permitting out-of-state institutions, including commercial banks, to bid for it. Although two rounds of bids were taken, the second at the insistence of Citicorp's opponents, the New York giant prevailed in August 1982.

The FSLIC stated that Citicorp's bid for Fidelity, immediately renamed Citicorp Savings, would save the insurance fund $143 million, a sum it could ill afford to lose in the worst year for thrift industry failures up to that point. The regulators argued that no S&L anywhere, and no California-based bank, had the financial strength to assume Fidelity, considering the severe losses the institution was experiencing. In return for an $80 million capital injection by Citicorp, the FSLIC agreed to subsidize negative spreads on the thrift for up to 12 years.[38]

Shortly thereafter, the Garn-St Germain bill was passed, clarifying Congress's view that interindustry,

interstate mergers such as the Citicorp–Fidelity combination were the least desirable of all. Citicorp's size and aggressiveness, however, allowed it to expand to Illinois and Florida in 1984, when it made offers the FSLIC could not refuse for two failing thrifts, acquiring 104 deposit-taking facilities in those populous states. (Among the most disappointed of the losing bidders for First Federal of Chicago was Sears.) Later, regulators also accepted a Citicorp offer for a failing Washington, D.C., thrift.

In 1990, Citicorp again changed the name of its thrift subsidiary to Citibank, Federal Savings Bank. Surprisingly, the firm had learned that few customers realized that Citicorp Savings and Citibank were part of the same organization. Further, Citicorp found (probably *not* surprisingly) that the name *bank* had a "distinctively stronger appeal" to customers than *savings and loan*. At that time, the firm announced its increased commitment to retail banking throughout the nation, striking fear into the hearts of managers of small commercial banks across the country.[39]

CITICORP, THE SECURITIES FIRM

Glass-Steagall prohibitions against underwriting domestic corporate securities did not prevent Citicorp from establishing a large investment banking division in the late 1970s, through which it underwrites government and international corporate securities. The firm is well-positioned to increase domestic investment banking, although management has indicated that retail banking will remain the highest priority. Meanwhile, Citicorp's securities division is active in interest rate swaps, private placements, foreign currency markets, and securitization.

On the retail side, Citicorp was among the first commercial banks (but, for once, not *the* first) to offer discount brokerage services to its banking customers. It actively pursues full-line brokerage services abroad and was one of a handful of non-Japanese firms to win a seat on the Tokyo Stock Exchange in 1986, a move viewed as a major step forward for its retail securities

---

[37] Yvette D. Kantrow, "Citicorp Makes King of the Hill as Card Issuer," *American Banker,* March 30, 1990, 1, 7.

[38] More details on this controversial decision can be found in Christopher Conte, "Citicorp Wins Bank Board Nod to Acquire S&L," *The Wall Street Journal,* August 17, 1982; and John Andrew, "Fidelity Federal Says Bid for Fidelity S&L Should Have Won over Citicorp's Proposal," *The Wall Street Journal,* August 23, 1982.

[39] Jed Horowitz, "Citicorp Finds That Citibank Smells Sweeter," *American Banker,* March 22, 1990, 1, 14; and William Gruber, "Citicorp Savings Changes Name, Plans Expansion," *Chicago Tribune,* March 21, 1990, Sec. 3, 3.

activities. (ML and Shearson-AmEx were two other winners.)

CITICORP, THE INSURER

Prohibited from entering insurance on a large scale at home, Citicorp began its insurance activities overseas and, over the years, has increased the products offered and locales served. In 1984, buoyed by its success at influencing state laws or evading the letter of existing regulations, Citicorp planned an experimental life insurance operation in the United States. The experiment was based on a change in South Dakota law permitting out-of-state banks with South Dakota subsidiaries to offer all types of insurance products. In 1985, the Federal Reserve System (Fed) refused to approve Citicorp's application to acquire a South Dakota bank from which to conduct insurance operations. In 1990, however, Delaware agreed to allow Delaware-chartered banks to sell insurance nationwide. Citicorp, proud parent of a Delaware bank, thus was poised to enter this previously forbidden market.

In the Federal Deposit Insurance Corporation Improvement Act (FDICIA), Congress included a provision prohibiting state-chartered banks from underwriting insurance. The legislators provided an exception, however, for any bank previously authorized to engage in insurance activities, of which Citicorp was one. Citicorp's ability to move into insurance at an opportune time was further solidified in 1992, when the Supreme Court refused to hear an appeal of earlier rulings in Citicorp's favor.[40]

WHERE WILL CITI GO?
EVERYWHERE (ALMOST)
WHAT WILL IT DO?
EVERYTHING (ALMOST)

The previous discussion shows that Citicorp has some disadvantages in comparison with its rivals. Chief among them is that it consistently faces greater federal regulation. Especially onerous are increased capital requirements, remaining restrictions on the mingling of investment and commercial banking, and regulations governing the underwriting and sale of most types of insurance. As if external factors were not enough, the investment and commercial banking divisions of Citicorp were fierce internal rivals in the 1980s. Personnel in the two divisions were reluctant to refer customers to one another and engaged in aggressive price competition for the same customers. The situation eased somewhat when one of the main players left to head the reborn Continental Bank.

Citicorp has faced unprecedented challenges in the early 1990s. As were Sears and Prudential, it has been affected by weaknesses in its original lines of business. During the early 1990s, billions of dollars in loans to developing countries and commercial real estate loans were charged off, introducing extreme problems because these losses coincided with regulators' determination to strengthen banks' capital ratios. To meet the revised capital regulations, Citicorp divested itself of some assets considered nonstrategic and sought operating efficiencies. As late as 1993, however, Citicorp's capital remained lower than most of its large commercial bank competitors, not to mention its diversified financial services rivals. In fact, Citi's capital position was so low it was in danger of violating regulators' minimum capital adequacy standards.

Still, it is difficult to ignore this BHC's great strengths. Citicorp's commitment to retail financial services became firmly entrenched with the appointment of John Reed, the strategy's chief architect, as chairman of the board in 1984, succeeding long-time chairman Walter Wriston, who spearheaded the formation of the holding company. Thus, Citicorp has a head start on many of its bank and nonbank rivals, having formulated its retail strategy relatively early. With more than 1,100 domestic banking offices and ownership or sharing of more than 35,000 ATMs worldwide, its geographic presence exceeds that of its competitors by a wide margin. In its 1991 *Annual Report*, Citicorp noted that one in four U.S. households had a banking relationship with Citibank. Adding its 2,000-plus international offices, the totals are indeed impressive, and sure to grow as Citicorp pursues its announced expansions in Europe and Japan.[41]

---

[40] Paul M. Barrett, "Justices Clear Sale of Insurance by Citicorp Unit," *The Wall Street Journal,* January 14, 1992, A4.

[41] Citicorp, *Annual Report 1991,* 7; *Citicorp Reports 1988,* 18; Hector 1990; John Evans, "Citicorp Driving to Open Network of 1,100 Branches across Europe," *American Banker,* May 30, 1990, 1, 10; and Steven Lipin, "Citicorp Chief Reed, Once a Big Thinker, Gets Down to Basics," *The Wall Street Journal,* June 25, 1993, A1, A4.

The firm's asset base, about 15 percent larger than Pru's, its nearest diversified rival, has been an advantage on several occasions, exemplified by the bidding wars for failing thrifts. Size also enhances the firm's ability to raise funds of all types. Further, most of Citicorp's liabilities enjoy the protection of federal deposit insurance, an opportunity unavailable on a large scale to the other firms profiled here.

But perhaps Citicorp's greatest advantage is its rich tradition of creativity and leadership in finance. Year after year, corporate executives and analysts recognize it as among the most innovative firms in any industry. Citicorp has elevated evading regulation to an art. Its very existence guarantees that the regulatory dialectic will continue.

MANAGERIAL IMPLICATIONS OF DIVERSIFIED FINANCIAL SERVICES FIRMS

In 1982, William F. Ford, then-president of the Federal Reserve Bank of Atlanta, assessed emerging financial services firms such as Pru, AmEx, and Sears.[42] His remarks challenged the common wisdom of that time, but he has since been proved to have had remarkable insight. Ford cautioned depository institutions, especially commercial banks, against concluding that these emerging firms would be the major providers of financial services. Instead, he noted that they were entering banking's traditional territory from positions of weakness in their basic businesses. Thus, said Ford, the success of diversified financial firms should not be taken for granted, and bankers should not necessarily enter nonbanking fields to compete.

Four years later, having earlier trumpeted the rise of diversified financial services firms, *Business Week* flatly stated, ". . . the financial supermarket has been a conspicuous bust. . . . the supermarket's advent was catalyzed not by the arguments of think-tank strategists but by such basic human emotions as insecurity, fear, and greed."[43] Although it is too early to abandon

thoughts of diversified financial services firms as viable, and perhaps even formidable, players in the financial markets in the future, one can identify at least some lessons from their first decade.[44]

THE NATIONAL DELIVERY FIRM IS ONLY ONE OF SEVERAL MODELS

A phenomenon observed in other recently deregulated industries has occurred in financial services: More than one delivery system is successful. A study of deregulation in the trucking, airlines, and communications industries noted that three types of organizations are best at surviving the increased competition that comes from lowering barriers to entry in a product or service market: the national distribution firm; the low-cost, cut-rate producer; and the specialty firm.[45]

In financial services, these delivery systems can readily be seen. The national delivery firm is exemplified by the five firms discussed in this chapter. The low-cost producer is embodied in the numerous money market mutual funds that prosper by conducting business through 800-numbers and the U.S. Postal Service, despite fierce competition from money market deposit accounts (MMDAs) at local depository institutions. The continuing existence of specialty firms is seen among the thousands of successful credit unions. None of these institutions is likely to drive the others out of business.

SYNERGY IS NOT AUTOMATIC

The case histories in this chapter indicate that synergy in financial services is easier to promise than to achieve. Managing diversified firms profitably is challenging, especially when the business cultures of the combined firms are not compatible. Thus far, none of the five firms profiled has been the most profitable among financial institutions, and, in fact, all have

[42] See Ford 1982.

[43] Anthony Bianco, "How a Financial Supermarket Was Born," *Business Week,* December 23, 1985, 10.

[44] Two discussions of some of the early lessons of deregulation in financial services are Harvey Rosenblum and Christine Pavel, "Financial Services in Transition: The Effects of Nonbank Competitors," Federal Reserve Bank of Chicago, Staff Memorandum 84–1, 1984; and Poppen 1985. Further discussion is provided in Friedman 1986.

[45] A summary of this study was published in Waite 1982.

suffered serious financial and managerial setbacks on the path to diversification. Integrating and cross-selling services have been elusive. As long as integration is not achieved, synergy, which depends on a unified operating plan, will not be realized. And because diversification without synergy is not valued by shareholders, the equity markets reacted positively to some announced divestitures, such as the sale of Dean Witter by Sears.[46]

AND NEITHER ARE ECONOMIES OF SCALE AND SCOPE

Another lesson from diversified financial services firms is the necessity of superior cost control. Narrow net interest margins are a way of life, and financial goals can be met only through careful attention to noninterest revenues and expenses. Initially, the sheer size of financial conglomerates provoked great concern from smaller competitors, who worried that size would be synonymous with efficiency. Time has proved that this is definitely not the case. In fact, each of the five firms profiled here has been forced to engage in cost-cutting programs, including the streamlining of staffs and offices and even the divestiture of entire subsidiaries.

FINANCIAL SERVICES ARE CUSTOMER-DRIVEN

Perhaps the most important lesson from the study of diversified financial services firms is that the customer is in the driver's seat. This was not always so, when price and service competition were limited and one firm seldom encroached on another. A decade into deregulation, however, customers are sending messages to diversified and nondiversified firms alike.

PEOPLE MAY NOT WANT ONE-STOP FINANCIAL SHOPPING. An analogy can be drawn between financial supermarkets and traditional supermarkets. Despite predictions to the contrary, Kroger, Safeway, and other large food chains have not put ethnic grocery

stores or corner bakeries out of business. In fact, the popularity of specialty food stores has increased in recent years, even though grocery chains have tried to become all things to all people. Many consumers simply enjoy shopping around, seeing firsthand what products and services are available before they buy.

BUT THEY DO WANT CONTROL OVER THEIR FINANCES. In the case of financial supermarkets, an added dimension of consumer behavior is important. Information on an individual's financial status and money management habits is intensely personal. Most people want to control the sharing of that information. Even people willing to buy all their groceries at Kroger may be reluctant to place all their money in a single financial institution. To the extent that this attitude toward personal finance persists, financial supermarkets may not only fail to supplant traditional delivery systems, they may become dinosaurs.

PRICE AND QUALITY ARE IMPORTANT. Commercial relationships between financial institutions and other businesses work similarly. Large corporations have many financial connections, around the country and around the world. They conduct transactions through the institution providing the best service at the best price. The fact that one company can do everything is immaterial unless it offers competitive prices and quality.

Consumers respond to price and quality, too. Although most are less price-sensitive than business customers—for example, consumer deposits are less volatile than commercial deposits, even without Reg Q—they will also sever relationships with institutions whose prices and services are unsatisfactory. Citibank's short-lived effort to force low-balance depositors to use ATMs by charging them to see a human teller is a case in point. Massive exodus to competing depositories quickly caused a reversal in the policy. If diversified financial services firms succeed, it will be because the marketplace desires it, not because their managers or owners do.

FUNDAMENTAL DETERMINANTS OF VALUE ARE UNCHANGED

These lessons, and those throughout the book, point to a final conclusion. Institutional value is not

---

[46]Economists at the Federal Reserve Bank of New York examined other diversified financial services firms over the period 1980–1984 and drew similar conclusions. See Federal Reserve Bank of New York 1986, 297–302.

created with words, intentions, or publicity. Value emerges from careful identification of market opportunities; thorough analysis of these opportunities, including assessment of risk and the expected impact on financial targets; and skillful execution, including the use of available risk-management tools. These principles hold regardless of the type, size, and location of an institution or of its historical origins. In fact, financial deregulation has not changed the determinants of value at all; it has merely broadened the range of opportunities available to individual firms.

SUMMARY

This chapter focused on five prominent diversified financial services firms. Several factors have attracted companies to financial services, including the low cost of entry, the similarity of products offered, the expected profitability, and hopes for synergy. Yet even the leading providers of diversified financial services have so far not achieved the expected level of profitability and synergy.

Several conclusions can be drawn about the experience of diversified financial services firms. First, more than one type of firm will thrive in a deregulated environment. Another lesson is that synergy is elusive. Integration of established operations is difficult at best, and cooperation among former competitors does not develop quickly. Economies of scale and scope are also elusive. Perhaps the most important lesson is that meeting the needs of customers is the key to success. Unless diversified financial services firms respond to the marketplace, they will not achieve their promise— nor, for that matter, will any financial institution.

QUESTIONS

1. Explain the economic and competitive factors affecting firms' decisions to enter financial services in the 1980s. Have any of these influences changed? Discuss current and expected future developments and their potential effects on the viability of the diversified structure for the delivery of financial services.

2. Compare and contrast the strategies used by Prudential and Sears to diversify financial services products during the

1980s and 1990s. Explain similarities and differences in the responses of the two firms to any problems they have encountered in implementing their diversified strategies.

3. Review the summaries of Merrill Lynch, American Express, and Citicorp, and identify the strategies that each used to enter diversified financial services areas. What problems has each company encountered in its bid to reach the top of the financial services industry?

4. Synergy has been identified as the primary motivation for the diversification strategies of the five firms profiled in this chapter. Explain what is meant by synergy, and how it might be measured. Why is diversification without synergy of little or no value to shareholders?

5. As the year 2000 approaches, will you expect to see a larger or smaller proportion of financial services delivered by diversified firms? Explain economic and regulatory developments and customer preferences influencing your expectations.

6. Research has identified three types of organizations that seem to be well suited for coping with deregulation. Describe these three types of organizations, and identify a successful example of each from the financial services industry.

7. What roadblocks to synergy were encountered by the five companies discussed in the chapter following their acquisition of other firms?

8. Of the five firms profiled in this chapter, identify the ones you would describe as successfully achieving synergy. What factors contributed to this success?

9. Do you agree with Paul Volcker's statement, "We don't want Sears in the banking business"? Do you agree with *Business Week's* 1985 conclusion that "the financial supermarket has been a conspicuous bust"? Why or why not?

10. Although many differences exist in the histories and product lines of the firms described in this chapter, numerous similarities are also evident. Review the experiences of the five firms on the road to diversification, and discuss the common "themes" or lessons that can be drawn from their experiences.

11. Interview several friends and acquaintances in their forties and several in their early twenties. Compare and contrast the preferences of the two groups for one-stop financial shopping. How do your survey results influence your views on the future of diversified financial services firms such as Merrill Lynch or Prudential?

12. Choose one of the five firms described in the chapter. Review recent periodicals and the financial press for discussions of current performance. Explain whether this new information indicates positive or negative progress in the firm's quest for synergy, and why.

13. Some experts believe General Electric is actually a more successful diversified financial services firm than Merrill Lynch or American Express. Find descriptive information, and GE's annual report if possible, and evaluate the firm's progress in the financial services markets.

SELECTED REFERENCES

Andrews, Suzanna. "John Reed Builds His Dream House." *Institutional Investor* 21 (March 1987): 107–118.

Chakravarty, Subrata N. "A Credit Card Is Not a Commodity." *Forbes,* October 16, 1989, 128–130.

Christophe, Cleveland A. *Competition in Financial Services.* New York: First National City Corporation, March 1974.

Eisenbeis, Robert A. "Regulation and Financial Innovation: Implications for Financial Structure and Competition among Depository and Non-Depository Institutions." *Issues in Bank Regulation* 4 (Winter 1981): 15–23.

Federal Reserve Bank of New York. *Recent Trends in Commercial Bank Profitability.* New York: Federal Reserve Bank of New York, 1986.

Ford, William F. "Banking's New Competition: Myths and Realities." *Economic Review* (Federal Reserve Bank of Atlanta) 67 (January/February 1982): 4–11.

Friedman, Joel C. "Who Won the Great Financial Services War?" *Magazine of Bank Administration* 62 (May 1986): 82–88.

Friedman, Jon. "The Remaking of Merrill Lynch." *Business Week,* July 17, 1989, 122–125.

Friedman, Jon, and John Meehan. "Can AmEx Win the Masses—and Keep Its Class?" *Business Week,* October 9, 1989, 134–138.

Fromson, Brett Duval. "Merrill Lynch—The Stumbling Herd." *Fortune,* June 20, 1988, 43–50.

Gardner, Robert M. "Sears' Role in Consumer Banking." *Bankers Magazine* 168 (January/February 1985): 6–10.

Glynn, Lenny. "The Dismantling of Dean Witter." *Institutional Investor* 19 (August 1985): 80–92.

Hector, Gary. "Why U.S. Banks Are In Retreat." *Fortune,* May 7, 1990, 95–102.

Johnson, Eugene. "Non-Bank Challengers Are Changing Faces Too." *Credit Union Magazine* 52 (February 1986): 50–54.

Meehan, John, and Jon Friedman. "The Failed Vision." *Business Week,* March 19, 1990, 108–113.

Moore, Thomas, "Ball Takes Bache and Runs with It." *Fortune,* January 24, 1983, 97–100.

Norton, Robert E. "Citibank Wows the Consumer." *Fortune,* June 8, 1987, 47–54.

Pavel, Christine, and Harvey Rosenblum. "Banks and Nonbanks: The Horserace Continues." *Economic Perspectives* (Federal Reserve Bank of Chicago) 9 (May/June 1985): 3–17.

Poppen, Jon C. "Demystifying the Nonbank Financial Supermarket." *Magazine of Bank Administration* 61 (April 1985): 58–64.

Saporito, Bill. "The Bill Is Due at American Express." *Fortune,* November 18, 1991, 99–104, 108, 112.

Schwartz, David M. "When Home Sweet Home Was Just a Mailbox Away." *Smithsonian* 16 (November 1985): 91–100.

Sellers, Patricia. "Why Bigger Is Badder At Sears." *Fortune,* December 5, 1988, 79–84.

Taub, Stephen. "Sizing Up the Brokers." *Financial World,* January 8–21, 1986, 1–4.

Tichy, Noel, and Ron Charan. "Citicorp Faces the World: An Interview with John Reed." *Harvard Business Review* (November/December 1990): 135–144.

Waite, Donald C., III. "Deregulation and the Banking Industry." *The Bankers Magazine* 165 (January/February 1982): 26–35.

Weiner, Steve. "They Buy Their Stocks Where They Buy Their Socks." *Forbes,* March 7, 1988, 60–67.

Williams, Monci Jo. "Sears Roebuck's Struggling Financial Empire." *Fortune,* October 14, 1985, 40–44.

———. "Synergy Works at American Express." *Fortune,* February 16, 1987, 79–80.

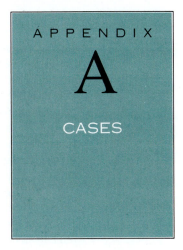

CASE ONE
First National Bank of Rindville

David McDonald, CEO, had been hired by the board of directors of First National Bank of Rindville in early 1985. As he reflected upon his experiences during the past two years, McDonald felt as though he had made much progress in turning around a problem bank.

His basic strategy had been, and continued to be, to purge the loan portfolio of nonperforming loans. The loan portfolio, net of unearned discounts and allowances, had been reduced by almost 50 percent in the latest two years, from approximately $27 million to approximately $14 million. At the same time, deposits were to approach the core level by reducing deposit interest rates to significantly below market rates. The average rate paid on average interest-bearing deposits was reduced from 8.5 percent in 1985 to 7.0 percent in 1986. The bank, under the strategy, was to become a smaller bank—"lean and mean."

Accompanying this basic asset/liability tactical move was an effort to tightly control costs. As the bank became smaller, the total number of employees would be allowed to decline through normal attrition. It had been the experience of the bank that one or two employees would leave the bank each year. Advertising expenses had been slashed by 50 percent in 1985 and 80 percent in 1986 as compared with 1984. Other expenses were tightly controlled as well. In fact, the only expenses that had risen appreciably in the last two years were the legal expenses associated with pursuing recovery of bad loans.

Challenges remained for the young but experienced CEO. He knew that his recommended policy changes over the two years had been implemented by the board without major alteration. Many of these changes were painful to the bank's personnel and to many of the bank's long-time customers—both borrowers and depositors. But McDonald felt that the worst was over and if he could convince the board to "stay the course," the bank soon would return to profitability.

As a part of his preparation for the annual meeting scheduled for March 10, 1987, he thought he should try to anticipate what questions he would probably be asked by stockholders. He would then develop responses. Using his personal computer and spreadsheet software, he built several financial scenarios and pro forma balance sheets. His "most likely" March 31, 1987, summary balance sheet showed the bank beginning to stabilize. The scenario even included small additions to undivided profits resulting from the first quarterly profits since he had taken the helm of the bank (see Exhibit 1.1).

It was with mixed emotions that David McDonald began to prepare his defense of current strategy for the meeting. He knew that he had made some enemies among current stockholders and the board. He also knew his technical banking expertise, hard-nosed business-like approach, and tremendous energy had

Source: John K. Litvan, Associate Professor of Finance, Southwest Missouri State University at Springfield. Used with permission.

EXHIBIT 1.1	**Pro Forma Balance Sheet March 31, 1987**

Assets

Cash and balances due from banks	$ 1,248,202
Interest-bearing deposits	4,600,000
Securities	19,402,461
Federal funds sold	7,800,000
Loans—net	14,309,632
Bank premises and fixtures	885,195
Other real estate owned	251,900
Other assets	1,718,453
Total	$50,215,843

Liabilities

Deposits	$45,721,539
Other liabilites	809,147
Common stock	375,000
Surplus	1,000,000
Undivided profits and capital reserve	2,310,157
Total	$50,215,843

won the respect of others. Sometimes he wondered if he had been too aggressive in pursuing collection of past-due loans and in taking legal action to recover on loan losses. He had heard from some of his fellow CEOs at a recent Illinois Bankers Association meeting that within CEO circles he was building a reputation as a turn-around specialist. "Mack the Knife," he thought to himself.

THE NEXT MORNING AT THE BLUEBIRD CAFE

Jack Harder drove into the parking lot of the Bluebird Cafe at 9:30 A.M., as he had done each business day for the last ten years or more. He was a regular member of the local agricultural coffee club that met there each morning to "shoot the bull." Actually, as a significant stockholder in First National Bank of Rindville, a graduate of the University of Illinois in agricultural economics, and a successful livestock farmer, he considered his morning coffee and chat with other farmers an essential part of his routine. He always felt it was good to keep a close ear to the ground and learn what others were experiencing with respect to current agricultural conditions and the commodities markets.

What he heard around the table this morning did not please him. Several of those in attendance had expressed displeasure with the treatment they had been receiving at First National Bank. The complaints centered around the new agricultural loan officer and his

new "credit standards" and documentation required as part of any new loan agreement. In fact, one of the members of the coffee round table suggested that the bank had lost touch with the local community since "that new hot-shot" from Springfield had been hired as CEO. He said that he was going to move his spring crop production loan at First National to Farmers and Merchants Bank and take his deposit account with him.

Jack did not know quite how to respond to his friends. While they were not directing their comments about First National at him personally, he knew it was well known that he was a shareholder in First National, and Jack got the message. For this reason and because of the contents of a recent letter he had received from CEO David McDonald (see Exhibit 1.2), he decided to attend next month's annual meeting of stockholders and ask some penetrating questions. Among the questions he intended to pursue were the following:

1. Is the bank's balance sheet strong? Is its capital adequate to sustain the bank during the current crisis?

2. Is the bank taking excessive risks with respect to liquidity, interest rate exposures, and financial leverage?

3. How much smaller must the bank become in order to be made profitable? When will the bank become profitable once again?

4. If we lose most of our agricultural loan customers, who will replace them as borrowing clients? What are alternative earning assets that the bank could acquire?

5. Should I try to sell my shares in the bank, and, if so, how much are they worth?

DESCRIPTION OF THE BANK

The bank had been chartered in 1865 under the authority of the National Banking Act of 1865. The employees and officers had taken pride in the fact that the institution was the oldest bank in the county. The bank had established a reputation as a highly stable, strong institution. While strained, the bank came through the Great Depression in good shape. During World War II, the bank sold more war bonds to the public than any other bank in its size category in the state of Illinois. Over the years the bank enjoyed steady growth in assets and earnings. Until the current crisis, dividends

EXHIBIT 1.2   **Letter to Shareholders**

THE FIRST NATIONAL BANK OF RINDVILLE
The County's Oldest Bank
Member FDIC

January 9, 1987

Dear Shareholder:

The Board of Directors has asked that I communicate the following information to you.

Recently, a major shareholder of this bank, Mr. Benjamin Rock of Benton Harbor, Michigan, sold all of his shares to Mr. William Burns of St. Louis, Missouri. The amount of stock involved represents approximately 15 percent of this bank's outstanding shares. It has been expressed to us that Mr. Rock's considerations for selling his stock did not involve concerns of this bank's financial condition. Mr. Rock has been very supportive of current management. Mr. Burns has significant bank holdings, both in Illinois and Missouri, approximating one billion dollars in total banking assets. In addition to Mr. Burns, Farmers and Merchants Bank of Carbondale, Illinois, has recently expressed an interest in the possible acquisition of this bank subject to certain financial determinations.

As of this date, apart from the private sales, the Board of Directors has not received knowledge of any formal tender offers for purchase of the stock of this bank; however, it is conceivable that such a tender offer could be made at some time in the future by any of the aforementioned parties or by another party who may become interested in acquiring this bank.

Certain duties and responsibilities are imposed on the Board of Directors whenever a tender offer is received. Any such offer must be carefully evaluated by the Board of Directors using sound business judgment before any response or recommendations to the shareholders are made by the Board. An important consideration given to any tender offer would be the reasonableness of the offered price. In order to better determine the reasonableness of any such offer, the Board has engaged Big Eight Accounting to audit and certify the bank's December 31, 1986, statement of condition. Also, the Board intends to have the bank's stock professionally valued. With a professionally developed appraisal, the Board could make a more informed decision as to the reasonableness of any tender offers.

The Board believes that the interest shown by the aforementioned investors to acquire the stock of the First National Bank of Rindville demonstrates their belief that this bank has current and expected future value. The Board firmly believes that this bank is about to return to profitability and should begin to enjoy favorable earnings.

Should you have questions, please do not hesitate to contact me or one of the other directors. We would be pleased to hear from you.

Sincerely,

David McDonald, President

DM:sl

had been paid in each year for as long as any current employee, officer, or stockholder could remember.

The headquarters for the bank was located in the downtown area across the street from the county courthouse. A drive-in window and convenient parking lot had been added during a major renovation project in the middle 1960s. The appearance of the bank building was considered to be favorable. During the late 1970s a free-standing drive-in facility had been built on the edge of town, where considerable commercial development was taking place. Across the street from the drive-in was a major grocery store, and in 1983, Wal-Mart Stores opened a 30,000-square-foot discount store. There was significant traffic generated by the retail area, and the bank's drive-in was convenient and served well the needs of many of the bank's deposit customers.

While the bank targeted its lending efforts towards the agricultural community, in recent years there had been efforts to do additional consumer installment and real estate lending. The bank issued no credit cards, but it did receive and process locally generated retail credit card paper of the two major nationally known credit card sponsors. The bank did a limited amount of business lending to retail merchants and to several farm supply and automobile dealers. The bank's primary correspondent bank was located in St. Louis, Missouri, which was several hours away by automobile.

Two other commercial banks, one savings and loan branch office, and a small securities brokerage office were located in Rindville. Several insurance agencies were aggressively marketing mutual funds, annuities, and newer types of life insurance policies. There

 **Yields on Selected Securities**

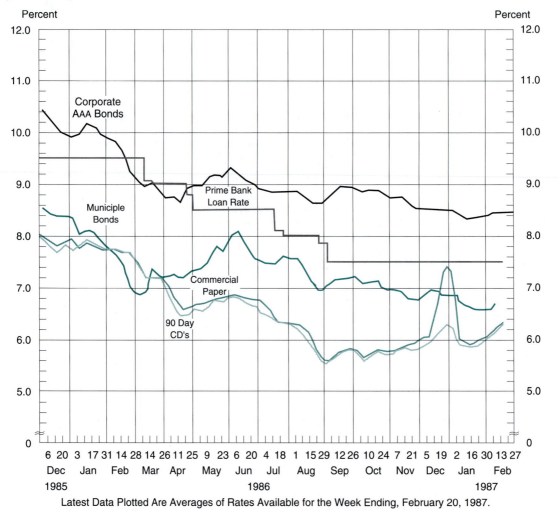

Latest Data Plotted Are Averages of Rates Available for the Week Ending, February 20, 1987.

1987	90 Day CD'S	30–Day Commercial Paper	90–Day Bankers* Acceptances	Corporate AAA Bonds	Corporate BAA Bonds	Municipal Bonds ✳8✳
Dec. 5	5.83	6.02	5.75	8.52	9.98	6.77
12	5.88	6.03	5.84	8.48	9.97	6.94
19	6.08	6.59	6.04	8.51	9.97	6.92
26	6.27	7.39	6.24	8.47	9.98	6.83
Jan. 2	6.22	7.31	6.10	8.49	9.97	6.85
9	5.90	6.01	5.74	8.40	9.82	6.70
16	5.85	5.90	5.73	8.33	9.70	6.65
23	5.82	5.87	5.70	8.31	9.65	6.54
30	5.88	5.94	5.83	8.37	9.68	6.56
Feb. 6	5.97	6.01	5.88	8.38	9.65	6.57
13	6.13	6.20	6.07	8.40	9.67	6.67
20 ✳	6.28	6.29	6.16	8.42	9.68	N.A.
27						

EXHIBIT 1.4 **First National Bank of Rindville Year-end Statements of Financial Condition**

	1986	1985	1984	1983	1982	1981
Assets						
Cash and due from banks	$ 1,947,566	$ 2,495,788	$ 3,059,425	$ 2,765,986	$ 4,189,423	$ 2,685,249
Interest-bearing deposits in other banks	4,700,000	4,200,000	500,000	500,000	N.A.	N.A.
Investment securities, at cost (note 2)	15,497,331	23,085,596	27,884,966	25,949,746	25,511,712	20,098,793
Federal funds sold	12,350,000	3,350,000	4,700,000	3,350,000	5,350,000	5,150,000
Loans (note 3)	15,189,341	20,556,279	28,150,883	29,841,649	24,894,074	24,278,964
Less:						
Unearned discount	261,215	264,089	250,939	268,595	301,742	378,250
Allowance for possible loan losses	440,000	420,000	621,067	124,460	268,901	296,940
Loans, net	14,488,126	19,872,190	27,278,877	29,448,594	24,323,431	23,603,774
Bank premises and equipment, net (note 4)	898,995	927,756	927,237	956,280	857,383	796,071
Accrued interest receivable	708,023	1,160,035	1,458,970	1,591,357	1,616,971	N.A.
Other assets (note 6)	1,072,750	530,234	752,121	350,709	11,137	1,274,100
Other real estate owned	251,900	724,312	N.A.*	N.A.	N.A.	N.A.
Total assets	$51,914,691	$56,345,911	$66,561,596	$64,912,672	$61,860,057	$53,607,987
Liabilities and Stockholders' Equity						
Deposits:						
Noninterest-bearing	5,237,982	6,005,790	7,081,165	7,134,580	9,004,779	9,028,572
Interest-bearing (note 5)	42,222,062	44,903,583	53,472,330	51,365,806	46,729,013	38,961,033
Total deposits	47,460,044	50,909,373	60,553,495	58,500,386	55,733,792	47,989,605
Accrued interest payable	531,576	668,108	N.A.	N.A.	N.A.	N.A.
Other liabilities (note 6)	329,577	100,283	1,016,400	1,231,364	1,157,569	1,307,356
Total liabilities	48,321,197	51,677,764	61,569,895	59,731,750	56,891,361	49,296,961
Stockholders' equity (note 8):						
Common stock—$100 par value, 3,750 shares authorized and issued	375,000	375,000	375,000	375,000	375,000	375,000
Surplus	1,000,000	1,000,000	1,000,000	1,000,000	1,000,000	1,000,000
Undivided profits	2,218,494	3,293,147	3,616,701	3,805,922	3,593,696	2,936,026
Total stockholders' equity	3,593,494	4,668,147	4,991,701	5,180,922	4,968,696	4,311,026
Commitments and contingencies (note 7)						
Total liabilities and stockholders' equity	$51,914,691	$56,345,911	$66,561,596	$64,912,672	$61,860,057	$53,607,987

*N.A. = not available.

were few other providers of financial services in the county of 20,000 population. Total bank assets in the county approached $200 million and deposits totaled approximately $150 million.

The economic environment during 1986 had been somewhat promising in the local area. According to government statistics, the prices of swine (pigs and hogs) had increased 12 percent during 1986 and were higher than they had been at any time since 1982. Since the county was a major producer of swine, this development was predicted to have a positive ripple effect throughout the local economy. Personal income was expected to go up significantly in 1987.

The First National Bank of Rindville
Notes to Balance Sheet
December 31, 1986

1. *Summary of Significant Accounting Policies*
   The accounting and reporting policies of The First National Bank of Rindville (the Bank) conform in all material respects to generally accepted accounting principles within the banking industry. Following is a description of the more significant of these policies:
   a. *Investment Securities*
      Investment securities are stated at cost, adjusted for amortization of premiums and accretion of discounts over the period to maturity of the respective security. Gains and losses upon sales prior to maturity are recorded, as realized, on a specific identification basis.
   b. *Bank Premises and Equipment*
      Bank premises and equipment are stated at cost less accumulated depreciation. Depreciation is computed over the expected lives of the assets, using the straight-line basis. The estimated useful lives of the buildings range from five to fifty years and of equipment from five to fifteen years.
      Expenditures for major renewals and betterments of Bank premises are capitalized, and those for maintenance and repairs are expensed as incurred.
   c. *Loans*
      Interest on installment loans is recognized using the sum-of-the-digits method, which approximates a level yield over the life of the loan. Interest on other loans is computed daily based on the principal amount outstanding using the simple-

interest method. It is the policy of the bank to discontinue the accrual of interest when the account becomes 90 days delinquent or when full collectibility of principal and interest are in doubt. Income on such loans is recognized in subsequent periods only when cash is received.

The allowance for possible loan losses is available to absorb loan charge-offs. The allowance is increased by provisions charged to expense and reduced by loan charge-offs less recoveries. The provision charged to expense each period is that which management believes is sufficient to bring the balance of the allowance to a level adequate to absorb potential loan losses, based on management's knowledge and evaluation of the current loan portfolio.
   d. *Other Real Estate Owned*
      Other real estate owned represents property acquired through foreclosure or deeded to the Bank in lieu of foreclosure on real estate mortgage loans on which the borrowers have defaulted as to payment of principal and interest. Other real estate owned is carried at the lower of the Bank's cost of acquisition or the asset's fair market value.

2. *Investment Securities*
   Book and market values of investment securities at December 31, 1986, are summarized as follows:

	Book Value	Market Value
United States government issues:		
Treasury	$ 9,161,367	$ 9,352,000
Agencies and corporations	5,909,714	5,984,000
Total	15,071,081	15,336,000
Obligations of state and political subdivisions	385,000	454,000
Other securities	41,250	41,000
Total	$15,497,331	$15,831,000

Book values of securities pledged to secure certain deposit accounts and for other purposes at December 31, 1986, amounted to $2,549,096.

3. *Loans*
   The following is a summary of loan categories at December 31, 1986:

Commercial, financial, and agricultural	$ 6,374,162
Industrial revenue bonds	300,000

Municipal warrants	108,200
Real estate mortgage	5,923,136
Installment	2,483,843
Total	$15,189,341

Transactions in balance for possible loan losses for the year ended December 31, 1986, were as follows:

Balance, December 31, 1985	$ 420,000
Provision charged to expense	2,431,972
Loans charged off	(2,776,127)
Recoveries of loans previously charged off	364,155
Balance, December 31, 1986	$ 440,000

The aggregate amount of loans to officers and directors of the Bank and loans to corporations in which officers or directors had substantial beneficial interest was approximately $284,000 at December 31, 1986. These loans were granted under the same general terms and conditions as to the interest rate, collateral, and repayment as loans made to nonaffiliated persons.

4. *Bank Premises and Equipment*
Following is a summary of Bank premises and equipment, net, at December 31, 1986:

Building and land	$ 576,874
Furniture, fixtures, and equipment	833,432
	1,410,306
Less accumulated depreciation	511,311
	$ 898,995

5. *Interest-Bearing Deposits*
Interest-bearing deposits consist of the following at December 31, 1986:

NOW, super NOW, and money market demand accounts	$11,048,050
Savings deposits	2,264,051
Other time deposits	28,909,961
	$42,222,062

Included in other time deposits are certificates of deposit in amounts of $100,000 or more totaling $1,494,758.

6. *Income Taxes*
Income taxes receivable amounting to $1,041,035 are included in other assets in the balance sheet at December 31, 1986. The Bank has no current income tax liability: however, accumulated deferred income taxes of $297,489 are included in other liabilities in the balance sheet at December 31, 1986.

7. *Commitments and Contingencies*
In the normal course of business, there are various commitments outstanding, such as commitments to extend lines of credit and letters of credit, which are not reflected in the Bank's balance sheet. The Bank has standby letters of credit at December 31, 1986, of $30,000.

The Bank is a defendant in a lawsuit filed by a loan customer alleging that the Bank unlawfully demanded payment on certain loans made to the customer and unlawfully utilized the setoff of deposits of the customer against the loans in question. The complaint claims that the actions of the Bank caused damages in excess of $700,000 to the plaintiff. The Bank is vigorously contesting this litigation. In the opinion of management, the lawsuit ultimately will be disposed of in a manner that will not have a material adverse effect upon the financial position of the Bank.

In addition to the matters described above, various legal claims have arisen in the normal course of business that, in the opinion of Bank management after discussion with legal counsel, will not result in any material liability to the Bank.

8. *Regulatory Matters*
On September 27, 1984, the Bank entered into a formal agreement (the Agreement) with the Office of the Comptroller of the Currency. The Agreement was reached as a result of an examination of the Bank in 1984. The Bank continues to operate under the Agreement at December 31, 1986. The Agreement requires the Bank to take certain affirmative actions within a specified period of time. These requirements include, among other things: implementation of a written collection program; establishing formal loan review policies; maintaining an allowance for possible loan losses at a level that is acceptable to the Bank's regulatory authorities; maintaining the Bank's capital at a level acceptable to the Bank's regulatory authorities; establishing asset/liability management policies; and developing a profit plan to improve and sustain earnings. Bank management believes it has taken action necessary to remain in compliance with the Agreement.

EXHIBIT 1.5 **Income Statements**
Statement of Profit (Loss) and Undivided Profits

	1986	1985	1984	1983	1982	1981
Interest income:						
Interest and fees on loans	$1,910,721	$2,883,606	$3,581,404	$3,355,602	$3,631,312	$3,266,412
Interest on investment securities:						
U.S. Treasury securities	1,474,842	2,140,358				
Obligations of other U.S. government agencies and corporations	488,885	845,804				
Obligations of states and political subdivisions	44,353	50,789	388,008	440,468	324,412	170,047
Other securities	2,475	2,475				
Interest on Federal funds sold	440,900	155,420				
Interest on deposits in banks	323,510	225,142				
Interest on taxable securities prior to 1985			2,853,483	2,837,919	2,789,744	2,270,949
Total interest income	4,685,686	6,303,594	6,822,895	6,633,989	6,745,468	5,707,408
Interest expense:						
Interest on deposits greater than $100,000	137,582	171,564	215,901	137,415	112,359	66,768
Interest on other deposits	2,938,149	4,008,402	4,976,284	4,836,508	4,787,661	3,827,287
Interest on Federal funds purchased	0	1,244	0	0	0	0
Total interest expense	3,075,731	4,181,210	5,192,185	4,973,923	4,900,020	3,894,055
Net interest income	1,609,955	2,122,384	1,630,710	1,660,066	1,845,448	1,813,353
Provision for loan losses	2,431,972	1,794,421	1,081,083	370,000	125,000	275,000
Net interest income (loss) after provision for loan losses	(822,017)	327,963	549,627	1,290,066	1,720,448	1,538,353
Other income:						
Service charges on deposit accounts	56,164	75,056	40,339	32,395	15,751	10,424
Income from trust department	39,006	100,636	36,763	36,809	40,716	23,372
Net securities gains	0	32,781	(27,186)	0	0	90,640
Other income	97,756	216,090	62,936	62,911	156,658	16,685
Total other income	192,926	424,563	112,852	132,115	213,125	141,121
Other expenses:						
Salaries and employee benefits	626,599	661,182	609,213	559,701	502,784	428,921
Occupancy and equipment expense, net	155,926	131,008	145,941	132,901	127,180	113,583
Other expense	496,037	567,678	463,944	419,617	331,614	294,385
Total other expense	1,278,562	1,359,868	1,219,098	1,112,219	961,578	836,889
Profit (loss) before income taxes	(1,907,653)	(607,342)	(556,619)	309,962	971,995	842,585
Applicable income tax (benefit)	(833,000)	(283,788)	(442,398)	(52,264)	164,325	407,681
Net profit (loss)	(1,074,653)	(323,554)	(114,221)	362,226	807,670	434,904
Undivided profits, beginning of year	3,293,147	3,616,701	3,805,922	3,593,696	2,936,026	2,614,718
Undivided profits, end of year	$2,218,494	$3,293,147	$3,616,701	$3,805,922	$3,593,696	$2,936,026
Profit (loss) per common share (based on 3,750 shares outstanding)	($286.57)	($86.28)	($30.46)	$96.59	$215.38	$115.97

CASE TWO
First National Corporation

In 1986, Robert Huenephy, senior vice president in charge of the Special Lending Division at First National Corporation advocated establishing an asset-based lending department at the BHC's lead bank. He had periodically discussed the idea with other loan officers and with senior management. Loan officers were generally enthusiastic; senior management was generally cautious. Neither response surprised Bob. Loan officers wanted new loan products to offer their customers and more ways to meet loan goals. Senior management, while aware of the importance of meeting customer loan needs, as well as the competition in the marketplace, was concerned about the potential for higher loan losses.

First National, a conservative bank in a conservative Ohio city, was the anchor bank and the largest subsidiary by far of the parent First National Corporation. Founded in the mid-1800s, the bank had the distinction of holding one of the first 25 national charters. Acquisitions, mergers, or other changes had moved it to fifth-oldest on the national roster. Its favorite historical reflection came from 1933 when, during the Depression, the Clearing House authorized banks to limit withdrawals to 5 percent of the customer's account. First National was the only bank in town to honor deposits in full to all comers.

During its first century, First National concentrated on doing business with corporations and other banks rather than on services to individuals. This strategy was consistent with its long history of fiscal soundness, solid capitalization, customer service, and community involvement. While in recent decades the bank had moved extensively into all aspects of retail banking, it had not abandoned its heritage.

First National was fortunate to be located in a market with a strong and diverse economic base. That market had helped the bank to generate a quality loan portfolio. It had also provided a stable deposit base and assisted in maintaining the bank's strong capital position. In 1986, the city's economy, like that of so many other cities, was moving from manufacturing to service-related jobs, but both manufacturing and services were expected to be important to the city's future. The city's business profile ranged from some of the nation's largest corporations to successful start-up enterprises. While the city's economic diversity did not make it recession-proof, it certainly helped it withstand economic downturns.

At the same time, more rapid growth in southern and western states challenged the city's economic future. It was not a part of the Sun Belt. Further, regulatory changes and a constant stream of new competitors continued to threaten the bank's loan growth and overall market share. In 1980, the Depository Institutions Deregulation and Monetary Control Act permitted savings associations and credit unions to offer their customers additional services in direct competition with banks. In 1982, the Garn-St Germain Depository Institutions Act permitted banks to pay interest without rate limitations on certain types of deposit accounts. In Ohio, legislation permitting statewide banking by 1989 had been passed in the 1970s. By 1985, Ohio law also allowed interstate banking on a reciprocal basis with 14 adjacent or nearby states. By then, First National was already competing for loans with numerous other Ohio commercial banking organizations, savings and loan associations, credit unions, securities firms, insurance companies, retail firms, commercial finance companies, and loan production offices of many out-of-state banks.

The continually growing competition, along with the bank's desire for continued loan growth and improved margins, concerned senior management. Consequently, Fred Yehger, executive vice president of lending, and George Kassidy, president, requested an analysis and development of a business plan for an asset-based lending department.

FIRST NATIONAL'S FINANCIAL POSITION

Bob and a newly formed task force felt that their first job was to review the BHC's financial information to analyze ways asset-based lending might affect the balance sheet and profit position. This review would also provide a basis for comparison when they developed a projected balance sheet and income statement for the proposed product. From the information in Exhibits 2.1 and 2.2, plus other information, they developed

Text continues on page 866

EXHIBIT 2.1 First National Corporation and Subsidiaries, Consolidated Statements of Condition as of December 31, 1983–1985 (Thousands)

	1985		1984		1983	
Assets						
Cash and due from banks	$ 244,079	7.14%	$ 215,830	7.76%	$ 209,700	7.97%
Investment securities:						
U.S. Treasury and agencies	$ 437,225		$ 334,429		$ 378,095	
States and political subdivisions	121,191		122,759		134,128	
Other securities	4,069		3,903		3,907	
Total investment securities	562,485	16.45	461,091	16.59	516,130	19.60
Federal funds sold and reverse repos	452,475	13.23	545,305	19.61	521,530	19.81
Loans:						
Commercial and agricultural	$ 740,798		$ 452,258		$ 488,960	
Real estate—construction	68,583		39,408		27,924	
Real estate—mortgage	368,242		324,203		275,493	
Installment and credit card	622,935		453,502		325,455	
Other	214,358		181,910		149,763	
Total loans	$2,014,916		$1,451,281		$1,267,595	
Less unearned interest	(47,001)		(37,841)		(39,776)	
Less allowance for possible loan losses	(23,325)		(16,734)		(13,440)	
Net loans	1,944,590	56.88	1,396,706	50.24	1,214,379	46.13
Premises and equipment	63,697	1.86	56,589	2.04	57,565	2.19
Acceptances, customers' liability	49,297	1.44	36,797	1.32	43,111	1.64
Other assets	102,232	2.99	67,813	2.44	70,332	2.67
Total assets	$3,418,855	100.00%	$2,780,131	100.00%	$2,632,747	100.00%

EXHIBIT 2.1 CONTINUED

Liabilities and Net Worth

Deposits						
Noninterest-bearing deposits	$ 692,392		$ 557,159		$ 540,736	
Interest-bearing deposits:						
Savings	804,788		585,056		555,157	
Time	1,085,157		810,641		659,151	
Total deposits	$2,582,337	75.53%	$1,952,856	70.24%	$1,755,044	66.66%
Short-term borrowings (primarily fed funds purchased and repos)	405,693	11.87	476,595	17.14	533,783	20.27
Long-term debt	54,807	1.60	45,166	1.62	52,242	1.98
Acceptances executed	49,297	1.44	36,797	1.32	43,111	1.64
Other liabilities	66,836	1.95	47,962	1.73	44,924	1.71
Total liabilities	$3,158,970		$2,559,376		$2,429,104	
Preferred stock	$ 0	0.00	$ 0	0.00	$ 0	0.00
Common stock	52,824	1.55	24,750	0.89	22,500	0.85
Surplus	54,349	1.59	66,625	2.40	52,000	1.98
Undivided profits	152,712	4.47	129,380	4.65	129,143	4.91
Total net worth	$ 259,885		$ 220,755		$ 203,643	
Total liabilities and net worth	$3,418,855	100.00%	$2,780,131	100.00%	$2,632,747	100.00%
Market value of securities at year-end	$ 568,208		$ 458,777		$ 508,723	

EXHIBIT 2.2 **First National Corporation and Subsidiaries, Consolidated Statements of Earnings for Years Ending December 31, 1983–1985 (Thousands)**

	1985	% of Total Operating Income[a]	1984	% of Total Operating Income	1983	% of Total Operating Income
Interest income:						
Interest and fees on loans	$187,405	60.05%	$162,417	54.81%	$128,255	50.57%
Interest on federal funds sold	33,307	10.67	51,032	17.22	46,142	18.19
Interest on investment securities:						
Taxable	43,614	13.98	39,511	13.33	37,462	14.77
Nontaxable	7,045	2.26	7,220	2.44	7,754	3.06
Other interest income	629	0.20	1,033	0.35	2,897	1.14
Total interest income	$272,000		$261,213		$222,510	
Noninterest income:						
Trust income	$ 13,064	4.19	$ 11,460	3.87	$ 9,855	3.89
Service charges and fees	22,390	7.17	17,802	6.01	16,173	6.38
Other operating income	4,612	1.48	5,866	1.98	5,088	2.01
Total noninterest income	40,066		35,128		31,116	
Interest expense:						
Interest on savings deposits	$ 19,086	6.12	$ 16,035	5.41	$ 13,120	5.17
Interest on time deposits	113,524	36.38	100,476	33.91	82,213	32.42
Interest on short-term borrowings	28,740	9.21	50,420	17.01	43,632	17.20
Interest on long-term debt	5,531	1.77	5,023	1.70	4,846	1.91
Total interest expense	166,881		171,954		143,811	
Provision for possible loan losses	9,083	2.91	6,543	2.21	5,915	2.33

EXHIBIT 2.2 CONTINUED

	1985	% of Total Operating Income[a]	1984	% of Total Operating Income	1983	% of Total Operating Income
Noninterest expense:						
Salaries	$ 38,419	12.31	$ 32,966	11.12	$ 30,264	11.93
Pension and other employee benefits	6,612	2.12	5,951	2.01	5,142	2.03
Equipment expense	9,693	3.11	8,160	2.75	7,603	3.00
Occupancy expense	5,692	1.82	4,609	1.56	4,550	1.79
State taxes	4,102	1.31	3,887	1.31	3,719	1.47
Other operating expense	30,516	9.78	25,144	8.48	21,380	8.43
Total noninterest expense	95,034		80,717		72,658	
Net operating income before tax	$ 41,068	13.16	$ 37,127	12.53	$ 31,242	12.32
Taxes	9,843	3.15	7,539	2.54	5,712	2.25
Income before securities gains or losses (IBSGL)	$ 31,225	10.01	$ 29,588	9.98	$ 25,530	10.07
Other income (primarily security gains and losses)	2,906	0.93	101	0.03	102	0.04
Net income	$ 34,131	10.94	$ 29,689	10.02	$ 25,632	10.11
Per share:						
Net income	$3.31		$3.00		$2.59	
Dividends	$1.40		$1.27		$1.18	

[a]Total Operating Income = Total Interest Income + Total Noninterest Income

EXHIBIT 2.3   Selected Financial Information, First National Corporation
(Thousands Except Per-Share Data)

	1985	1984	1983
Results of Operations			
Net interest income	$ 105,119	$ 89,259	$ 78,699
Provision for possible loan losses	9,083	6,543	5,915
Net income	34,131	29,689	25,632
Net income per share[a]	$3.31	$3.00	$2.59
Cash dividends per share[a]	$1.40	$1.27	$1.18
Selected Average Balances			
Total assets	$ 3,043,513	$2,704,906	$2,448,121
Investment securities	540,719	487,980	480,870
Loans—net of unearned interest	1,699,148	1,341,416	1,086,585
Total deposits	2,254,461	1,835,720	1,624,227
Long-term debt	49,627	45,976	46,880
Stockholders' equity	240,508	211,952	196,197
Average number of outstanding shares[a]	10,316,961	9,900,000	9,900,000
Performance Ratios			
Return on average total assets	1.12%	1.10%	1.05%
Return on average interest-earning assets	1.28	1.27	1.22
Return on average equity	14.19	14.01	13.06
Average equity to average total assets	7.90	7.84	8.01
Average equity to average total deposits	10.67	11.55	12.08
Average total loans—net of unearned interest to average total deposits	75.37	73.07	66.90
Dividend payout	42.31	42.36	45.65
Book value per share at year-end[a]	$24.60	$22.30	$20.57

[a]Prior years' amounts are restated to reflect a 2-for-1 stock split in 1985 and a 10% stock dividend in 1984.

Exhibit 2.3. Bob knew that the ways asset-based lending affected RONW or return on assets would be important to senior management and the board of directors.

Fiscal 1985 had been another successful year, with net income increasing by 15 percent to $34.1 million. Return on assets of 1.12 percent and RONW of 14.19 percent were both improvements over 1984. Assets had grown 23 percent and were expected to be nearly $4 billion by December 31, 1986. Deposits had risen 32 percent, and total loans by 39 percent. Bob wondered how much an asset-based lending department could add to that performance.

LOANS AND CREDIT RISK

Based on an existing loan-to-deposit ratio of under 80 percent and low reliance on volatile deposits, Bob felt senior management would not be concerned about whether the bank could handle the potential loan growth that asset-based lending might produce. At the same time, he knew of the bank's traditional sensitivity to credit risk, and asset-based loans certainly carried a higher degree of risk. His analysis would need to demonstrate that the risk was reasonable and that it would provide commensurate return. Bob would need to convince senior management that years of experience by commercial finance companies and other banks had resulted in improved techniques of monitoring and auditing collateral, greatly reducing the traditional risks of asset-based lending. Besides, some loans already in the bank's portfolio could benefit from the closer control that an asset-based department could provide. Risk assumptions would be important in gaining a total commitment from senior management, and since first National had historically followed a more conventional lending practice and structure, a new department could not succeed without that commitment.

EFFICIENCY, PRODUCTIVITY, AND PROFITABILITY

Bob knew higher costs were involved in asset-based lending than in conventional short-term or long-term commercial lending. More people were needed to conduct field audits of collateral and to monitor the loans internally. At the same time, he thought that existing loan officers could provide a more than adequate sales force, as long as a department head with experience in asset-based lending was hired to monitor loan quality and servicing. Costs might also be lowered by engaging a nationally recognized accounting firm to handle the field audits. Perhaps the accounting firm's fees could be passed on to the borrower, if competition would allow it.

Bob and his committee talked with a number of other banks that already had asset-based lending departments. They were frequently discouraged by reports of the lower loan rates now charged because of increased competition. Formerly, a loan priced at 3 percent to 5 percent over prime, not including other fees, was common. Now 1 percent to 2.5 percent over prime was the norm, and sometimes rates were lower. Bob knew that senior management increasingly emphasized higher margins and larger fees. He would need to substantiate that asset-based lending could contribute to those goals.

THE MARKET

A major reason asset-based lending had grown more popular in recent years was that financial institutions were emphasizing the middle market. Asset-based lending offers access to a wider range of companies, enabling increased market share and profitability. First National knew the growing importance of the middle-market companies to its profitability, and Bob was convinced that to effectively serve the middle market, the bank needed to offer asset-based lending.

He no longer viewed asset-based lending as a unique industry, but as a product that could fit comfortably into the larger product line of the bank. First National would also have marketing advantages over commercial finance companies or loan production offices from out-of-town financial institutions. These advantages included knowledge of local companies, a network of contacts, cost savings from market proximity, and cultural similarities with borrowers. First National would need all these advantages to effectively sell against the list of 23 asset-based lending competitors the committee had compiled.

On the other hand, Bob knew that some members of senior management would argue that a "bandwagon" effect was occurring, setting the stage for future problems in the asset-based lending industry. Major concerns included too many lenders chasing too few loans, a shortage of qualified people, and an erosion of margins due to increased competition. Bob had already begun preparing for that argument. Asset-based lending should be handled by experts in the field who know the industries and techniques and insist on spending the time and money to do the job right. The institution would have to offer more than a good job done by professionals skilled in more conventional bank lending. The keys were proper margin evaluation, collateral valuation, and ongoing monitoring. Bob needed to convince senior management that an experienced staff that knew how to appraise and monitor collateral and to conduct financial analysis would provide the assurances they sought, as well as the higher yields.

Bob's committee prepared a product description (Exhibit 2.4), an executive summary (Exhibit 2.5), and supporting documentation on the financial implications to the BHC of establishing an asset-based lending product (Exhibits 2.6–2.10). A member of the committee from the bank's investment department prepared Exhibits 2.11–2.13 to enable further competitive analysis of all the major banks in First National's region. Finally, committee members knew they should be prepared to defend their analysis and recommendations to senior management and, subsequently, to the board of directors.

EXHIBIT 2.4   **The Business Product Description**

Loans from $500,000 to $10,000,000

Primary collateral	Accounts receivable
	Inventory (raw materials and finished goods)
Secondary collateral	Plant and equipment
	Land and buildings

Pricing

Rates from prime + 1.0% to prime + 4.0% (average: prime + 1.75%)
1-time fees to average 0.5% of committed lines

Selling

Department head
Commercial lending staff and sales group
Branch offices

Staffing

Department head at vice president level
Assistant department head (credit and monitoring)
National accounting firm for auditing (at least initially)
Addition of clerical personnel as volume grows
Secretarial assistance

Processing

Lockbox account required for processing accounts receivable
Demand deposit cash collateral control account required for processing accounts receivable
Loans located in commercial loan portfolio
IBM PC-based asset-based lending system for monitoring the status of the account (sales, gross collections, aging, trends) and establishing the current credit availability

Appraisals (Equipment, Land, Buildings)

Situation will dictate the appraiser

Participations

Participate in loans that exceed our size guidelines or our willingness to accept the credit risk as the sole lender

Liquidations

Type of loan and location of business will dictate liquidator

| EXHIBIT 2.5 | **Executive Summary of Assumptions** |

- Have identified the market for an asset-based lending product to:
  1. Fill a gap in our product line to the middle market
  2. Properly monitor the asset-based loans currently booked
- Asset-based lending has become a mainstream product for banks. Currently 70% of the members of the National Commercial Finance Association, a trade group of asset-based lenders, are banks, versus only 27% in 1982.
- Currently have 50% participation in credit lines of $23.8 million with commercial finance companies.
- Currently have 374 loans for $85 million secured by accounts receivable and/or inventory. Of these loans, 14 totaling $45 million would benefit from the discipline of asset-based lending.
- Pro forma financial statements for the asset-based lending function indicate the following (from Exhibits 2.9 and 2.10):
  1. Marginal earnings per share (EPS) of $0.055 at the end of 1990, averaging $0.025 over the next 5 years
  2. Marginal RONW of 16.0% by 1990, averaging 12.9% over the next 5 years
  3. Operating expenses/net revenue to average 32% over the next 5 years
  4. Net interest margin on asset-based loans to average 4.1% over the next 5 years
  5. Accumulated cash flow to reach $1.3 million by the end of 1990
- Product launch date to be June 1, 1986.

| EXHIBIT 2.6 | **Financial Analysis: Cost/Benefit Assumptions** |

Startup	June 1, 1986
Average loan size	$1,250,000
Interest income, interest expense, and loan losses	
Average loan rate	1.75% over prime
Average cost of funds	8.12% 90-day CD rate adjusted for reserves and FDIC insurance premium
Average deposit yield	8.12% 90-day CD rate
Net chargeoffs	1.25%
Commitment fees	0.50% of committed line (one-time)
All lockbox processing fees charged to operating account	
Startup expense	
Product development	$ 5,000
Computerized information system development	5,000
Operations	3,000
Marketing	16,000
Recruiting	19,500
Legal	5,000
Initial setup	5,000
Ongoing operating expense	
Salaries	
Department head	65,000
Assistant department head	30,000
Verification clerk	22,000 (as required by growth)
Secretary (1/3)	6,500
Performance bonus	
Department head	0% (up to 30%)
Assistant department head	0% (up to 20%)
Monitoring expense	
Cost bundled into loan rate and fee structure	
Loans per individual monitor	25
Average field audits	4
Average field audit cost	$ 1,390

EXHIBIT 2.7	**Financial Analysis: Capital Expenditure Schedule (May 1986)**

IBM PC/AT	$10,000
Asset-based software	20,000
Department workstation	7,500
Assistant workstation	6,000
	$43,500

EXHIBIT 2.8	**Asset-Based Lending, Product Balance Sheet (December 31) (Thousands)**

	1986	1987	1988	1989	1990
Assets					
Cash and due from banks					
Float	$ 41	$ 229	$ 351	$ 445	$ 565
Reserve requirements	10	55	84	106	134
Net loans	4,711	24,083	36,346	46,095	58,460
Premises and equipment	39	31	23	15	7
Total Assets	$4,801	$24,398	$36,803	$46,661	$59,166
Liabilities and Net Worth					
Liabilities					
Demand deposits	$ 62	$ 342	$ 524	$ 664	$ 843
Funding requirement	4,408	22,373	33,741	42,779	54,243
Total Liabilities	$4,470	$22,715	$34,265	$43,443	$55,086
Net Worth Accounts					
Undivided profits					
Beginning balance	$ 0	$ (124)	$ (53)	$ 114	$ 363
Plus net income	(124)	123	288	430	585
Less cash dividends (@ 42%)	0	52	121	181	246
Ending balance	(124)	(53)	114	363	703
Capital requirement	456	1,736	2,424	2,855	3,377
Total Net Worth	$ 331	$ 1,683	$ 2,538	$ 3,218	$ 4,080
Total Liabilities and Net Worth	$4,801	$24,398	$36,803	$46,661	$59,166

EXHIBIT 2.9	**Asset-Based Lending Product Income Statement and Cash Flow[b] (Thousands)**

	1986	1987	1988	1989	1990
Projections					
Average number of accounts	2	13	26	34	43
Average outstandings	$2,691	$16,418	$32,023	$41,938	$53,188
Average lines	$4,486	$27,363	$53,371	$69,897	$88,647
Average funding requirement	$2,488	$15,082	$29,377	$38,459	$48,764
Average investable demand deposits	$ 40	$ 263	$ 530	$ 699	$ 887
Ending number of accounts	4	20	29	37	47
Capital expenditures	$ 43.5	0	0	0	0

EXHIBIT 2.9 *CONTINUED*

	1986	1987	1988	1989	1990
Income and Expenses					
Interest income:					
Interest on loans	$ 177	$ 1,847	$ 3,603	$ 4,718	$ 5,984
Commitment fees	40	163	103	82	104
Interest on deposits	4	28	57	76	96
Field audit income	0	0	0	0	0
Total interest income	$ 221	$ 2,038	$ 3,763	$ 4,876	$ 6,184
Interest expense:					
Funding cost	$ 205	$ 1,243	$ 2,422	$ 3,170	$ 4,020
Total Interest Expense	205	1,243	2,422	3,170	4,020
Net interest income	$ 16	$ 795	$ 1,341	$ 1,706	$ 2,164
Loan loss expense	52	286	422	448	534
Net interest income after Loan					
Loss Expense	$ (37)	$ 509	$ 919	$ 1,258	$ 1,630
Other Income:					
Lockbox fees	$ 1	$ 9	$ 17	$ 23	$ 29
Total Other Income	$ 1	$ 9	$ 17	$ 23	$ 29
Operating expense:					
1-time startup expense					
Product development	$ 5				
Computerized information system					
development	5				
Operations	3				
Marketing	16				
Recruiting/legal/setup	30				
Ongoing expense					
Product management	$ 3	$ 3	$ 3	$ 3	$ 3
Computer systems	0	1	1	1	1
Lockbox cost	1	6	11	14	18
Marketing	1	1	1	1	1
User department					
Salaries and benefits	70	121	122	130	139
Other	3	20	35	45	56
Field audit expense	12	74	144	189	240
Depreciation/amortization	5	8	8	8	8
Occupancy	6	6	6	6	6
Overhead allocation (@ 22%)	35	52	73	87	104
Total Operating Expense	$ 195	$ 291	$ 404	$ 483	$ 575
Marginal Analysis					
Net income before tax	$(231)	$ 228	$ 553	$ 797	$ 1,084
Tax (@ 46%)[a]	(107)	105	245	367	498
Net income after tax	$(124)	$ 123	$ 288	$ 430	$ 585

[a]Negative tax figure in 1986 reflects the bank's ability to save taxes on profits from other operations because of the loss on asset-based lending.
[b]Cash flow = Net Income after Tax + Depreciation.

EXHIBIT 2.10	Asset-Based Lending, Product Profitability Analysis					
Product-to-Date Analysis		**1986**	**1987**	**1988**	**1989**	**1990**
Earnings per Share (EPS)						
Net income	Marginal	$ (124)	$ 123	$ 288	$ 430	$ 585
	Average	(124)	(1)	95	179	260
Number of shares		10,565	10,565	10,565	10,565	10,565
EPS	Marginal	$ (0.012)	$ 0.012	$ 0.027	$ 0.041	$ 0.055
	Average	(0.012)	(.000)	0.009	0.017	0.025
Return on Equity (ROE)						
Net income	Marginal	$ (124)	$ 123	$ 288	$ 430	$ 585
	Average	(124)	(1)	95	179	260
Equity	Marginal	187	1,134	2,210	2,893	3,668
	Average	187	661	1,177	1,606	2,018
ROE	Marginal	−66.5%	10.8%	13.0%	14.9%	16.0%
	Average	−66.5%	−0.1%	8.1%	11.2%	12.9%
Operating Expense/Net Revenue (OE/NR)						
Operating expense	Marginal	$ 195	$ 291	$ 404	$ 483	$ 575
	Average	195	243	297	343	390
Net revenue	Marginal	17	804	1,359	1,728	2,193
	Average	17	411	727	977	1,220
OE/NR	Marginal	1,148%	36%	30%	28%	26%
	Average	1,148%	59%	41%	35%	32%
Net Interest Margin (NIM)						
Interest income	Marginal	$ 221	$ 2,039	$ 3,763	$ 4,876	$ 6,184
	Average	221	1,130	2,008	2,725	3,416
Interest expense	Marginal	205	1,243	2,422	3,170	4,020
	Average	205	724	1,290	1,760	2,212
Average investment in earning assets	Marginal	2,691	16,418	32,023	41,938	53,188
	Average	2,691	9,555	17,044	23,268	29,252
NIM	Marginal	0.6%	4.8%	4.2%	4.1%	4.1%
	Average	0.6%	4.2%	4.2%	4.1%	4.1%

EXHIBIT 2.11   Loan Analysis (December 1985 Data)

Name of Bank	Loans to Deposits	Rank	Loan Percentage Change	Rank	Allowance for Loan Losses to Total Loans	Rank	Net Chargeoffs to Average Loans	Rank	Nonperforming[a] Loans to Primary Capital	Rank
City A:										
Bank One	91.4%	17	18.9%	5	1.43%	15	0.34%	9	15.9%	12
Bank Two	90.2	13	28.9	2	1.61	20	0.46	12	3.3	1
First National Bank	83.6	7	24.4	3	1.25	7	0.28	5	3.8	2
Bank Three	80.5	3	20.2	4	0.86	1	0.47	14	16.1	13
Average for City A	86.4		23.1		1.29		0.39		9.8	
City B:										
Bank One	87.5	11	7.3	16	1.18	6	0.74	19	24.2	20
Bank Two	85.4	9	(3.9)	21	1.33	12	0.29	7	18.4	15
Bank Three	73.2	1	33.2	1	1.06	2	0.18	2	8.9	5
Average for City B	82.0		12.2		1.19		0.40		17.2	
City C:										
Bank One	81.4	4	4.6	19	1.90	21	1.22	20	38.3	21
Bank Two	93.0	18	7.6	15	1.52	17	2.28	21	21.9	18
Bank Three	90.5	15	14.5	11	1.14	5	0.43	11	21.0	17
Average for City C	88.3		8.9		1.52		1.31		27.1	
City D:										
Bank One	99.6	21	17.8	6	1.29	9	0.24	3	23.3	19
Bank Two	83.4	6	15.2	9	1.30	10	0.72	18	11.1	6
Bank Three	90.4	14	2.9	20	1.60	19	0.39	10	15.3	10
Bank Four	97.4	20	10.8	13	1.09	3	0.01	1	7.4	3
Bank Five	74.9	2	6.3	18	1.43	14	0.27	4	7.9	4
Average for City D	89.1		10.6		1.34		0.33		13.0	
City E:										
Bank One	94.1	19	16.0	8	1.50	16	0.47	13	18.4	14
Bank Two	87.4	10	14.6	10	1.33	13	0.29	6	13.8	9
Bank Three	84.6	8	11.7	12	1.58	18	0.33	8	13.3	7
Average for City E	88.7		14.1		1.47		0.36		15.2	
City F:										
Bank One	83.0	5	16.5	7	1.12	4	0.60	17	13.7	8
Bank Two	91.2	16	7.3	17	1.26	8	0.52	15	15.6	11
Bank Three	89.6	12	8.7	14	1.31	11	0.56	16	19.9	16
Average for City F	87.9		10.8		1.23		0.56		16.4	
Average for all banks	87.3		13.5		1.34		0.53		15.8	

[a]Nonperforming loans are those on which interest payments, principal payments, or both are not being received but which have not yet been written off.

EXHIBIT 2.12	Margin Analysis (December 1985 Data)				

	% of Average Earning Assets				
Name of Bank	Interest Revenues	Rank	Interest Cost	Rank	Net Interest	Rank
City A						
Bank One	10.62%	19	6.46%	10	4.16%	16
Bank Two	11.88	4	5.94	2	5.94	2
First National Bank	10.75	17	5.93	1	4.82	8
Bank Three	11.05	13	6.74	15	4.31	15
Average for City A	11.08		6.27		4.81	
City B						
Bank One	12.77	2	6.57	13	6.20	1
Bank Two	12.20	3	6.43	9	5.77	3
Bank Three	11.49	7	6.08	3	5.41	5
Average for City B	12.15		6.36		5.79	
City C						
Bank One	11.12	12	6.42	7	4.70	11
Bank Two	13.59	1	7.93	21	5.66	4
Bank Three	11.39	10	6.61	14	4.78	9
Average for City C	12.03		6.99		5.05	
City D						
Bank One	10.12	21	6.28	4	3.84	21
Bank Two	11.72	5	6.40	5	5.32	6
Bank Three	10.95	14	6.41	6	4.54	13
Bank Four	10.61	20	6.50	12	4.11	18
Bank Five	11.50	6	6.79	18	4.71	10
Average for City D	10.98		6.48		4.50	
City E						
Bank One	10.89	15	6.91	19	3.98	19
Bank Two	10.79	16	6.46	11	4.33	14
Bank Three	11.43	9	6.75	16	4.68	12
Average for City E	11.04		6.71		4.33	
City F						
Bank One	10.68	18	6.78	17	3.90	20
Bank Two	11.43	8	6.43	8	5.00	7
Bank Three	11.30	11	7.16	20	4.14	17
Average for City F	11.14		6.79		4.35	
Average for all banks	11.35		6.57		4.78	

| EXHIBIT 2.13 | **Deposit Analysis (December 1985 Data)** |

% of Total Domestic Deposits

Name of Bank	Demand IPC	Rank	Bearing a Regulated Rate	Rank	Bearing a Market Rate	Rank	Deposit Percentage Change from Last Year	Rank
City A								
Bank One	20.5%	12	12.0%	12	64.4%	4	9.6%	11
Bank Two	22.3	9	11.3	15	61.5	8	12.8	6
First National Bank	29.2	2	11.6	14	52.5	21	19.9	2
Bank Three	24.9	4	16.9	4	56.6	16	19.0	3
Average for City A	24.2		13.0		58.8		15.3	
City B								
Bank One	19.8	13	18.5	2	59.5	13	4.3	18
Bank Two	21.7	10	15.3	11	60.1	11	10.7	9
Bank Three	24.7	6	16.1	6	56.8	15	23.7	1
Average for City B	22.1		16.6		58.8		12.9	
City C								
Bank One	22.5	8	17.2	3	56.4	17	(3.6)	20
Bank Two	16.2	21	8.5	17	68.0	1	5.6	15
Bank Three	17.7	20	16.0	8	63.1	5	15.4	5
Average for City C	18.8		13.9		62.5		5.8	
City D								
Bank One	19.0	16	15.4	10	61.8	7	4.5	17
Bank Two	18.3	17	19.3	1	60.1	10	6.0	14
Bank Three	24.8	5	16.4	5	54.1	19	(14.2)	21
Bank Four	25.2	3	15.8	9	53.3	20	6.4	13
Bank Five	19.5	15	16.1	7	60.3	9	4.9	16
Average for City D	21.4		16.6		57.9		1.5	
City E								
Bank One	17.7	19	5.8	20	66.4	2	9.3	12
Bank Two	29.9	1	8.5	18	54.6	18	3.3	19
Bank Three	17.9	18	11.7	13	58.3	14	10.2	10
Average for City E	21.8		8.7		59.8		7.6	
City F								
Bank One	21.0	11	6.6	19	65.9	3	12.6	7
Bank Two	19.7	14	4.2	21	59.6	12	16.5	4
Bank Three	22.8	7	9.5	16	62.5	6	12.0	8
Average for City F	21.2		6.8		62.7		13.7	
Average for all banks	21.7		13.0		59.8		9.0	

CASE THREE
Merit Marine Corporation

January 1985 started with an opportunity for Ginny Shields, a relationship manager for Omni Bank, N.A., and Jeff Finch, a member of the bank's corporate finance department, to expand the bank's reputation for providing financial advisory services to existing credit customers. Ginny, who had moved to Omni Bank's regional office in Miami two months earlier, had identified the need to restructure the balance sheet (shown in Exhibit 3.1, with debt components in Exhibit 3.2) of Merit Marine Corporation, the Florida distributor of Olympus brand marine products. Omni Bank was a large money center financial institution.

Prior to phoning Jeff Finch in New York, Ginny had concluded that Merit was in need of long-term, fixed-rate financing to reduce the firm's interest-rate sensitivity and to better match its funding sources with its level of fixed assets. Merit's inability to obtain reasonably priced fixed-rate debt for $27 million in capital expenditures incurred between 1980 and 1983 had

This case was written by Peter R. Hennessy under the direction of Robert F. Bruner, as a basis for class discussion rather than to illustrate either effective or ineffective handling of an administrative situation. Copyright (c) 1985 by the Darden Graduate Business School Sponsors, Charlottesville, VA. WP2508a

EXHIBIT 3.1 **Merit Marine Corp., Consolidated Balance Sheet for the Years Ended December 31 (Thousands)**

	1980	1981	1982	1983	1984
Assets					
Cash	$ 8,385	$ 3,997	$ 3,635	$ 3,692	$ 4,127
Net receivables	27,068	27,414	16,175	22,100	26,435
Inventories	33,877	27,059	22,094	25,201	21,347
Net rental equipment	25,335	21,672	16,510	27,604	28,976
Prepaid expenses	64	88	17	85	108
Total current assets	$ 94,729	$80,230	$58,431	$ 78,682	$ 80,993
Investments	$ 117	$ 0	$ 0	$ 0	$ 0
Net property, plant, and equipment	6,125	7,503	20,969	24,565	23,204
Other assets	406	301	132	867	579
Total assets	$101,377	$88,034	$79,532	$104,114	$104,776
Liabilities					
Notes payable	$ 66,143	$27,738	$36,877	$ 35,879	$ 31,122
Current portion of long-term debt	691	20,107	195	97	101
Accounts payable	3,847	2,918	4,973	4,480	4,558
Accrued expenses	3,491	3,116	2,160	3,027	2,824
Dividends payable	0	78	77	77	77
Deferred income	0	0	0	0	170
Taxes payable	495	834	964	698	2,788
Total current liabilities	$ 74,667	$54,791	$45,246	$ 44,258	$ 41,640
Long term debt	2,158	3,665	3,503	28,398	28,083
Deferred income taxes	0	0	477	981	1,994
Total liabilities	$ 76,825	$58,456	$49,226	$ 73,637	$ 71,717
Stockholders' equity					
Preferred stock	$ 0	$ 1,290	$ 1,290	$ 1,290	$ 1,290
Common stock	1,000	1,000	1,000	1,000	1,000
Additional paid in capital	8,178	12,487	12,487	12,487	12,487
Treasury stock	0	(1,367)	(1,367)	(1,367)	(1,367)
Retained earnings	15,374	16,168	16,896	17,067	19,649
Total stockholders' equity	$ 24,552	$29,578	$30,306	$ 30,477	$ 33,059
Total liabilities and equity	$101,377	$88,034	$79,532	$104,114	$104,776

left the company relying on two-year, variable-rate financing.

Ginny's conversation with Jeff concentrated on the prospects for restructuring Merit's balance sheet through the use of a private placement and/or an interest-rate swap. Jeff was initially skeptical of the market's receptiveness to an offering of Merit securities based on the firm's size and recent performance (see earnings statements in Exhibit 3.3), yet he agreed to meet with Ginny on his upcoming trip to Miami.

COMPANY BACKGROUND

Located in Tampa, Florida, Merit Marine Corporation had been the exclusive Florida distributor of Olympus brand commercial and recreational marine products

EXHIBIT 3.2	Merit Marine Corp., Debt Components								
	(1)	(2)	(3)	(4)	(5)	(6)	(7)	(8)	(9)
Year	Total Short Term Debt (Col. 2+3)	Floating Rate	Non-interest Bearing	Total Long Term Debt (Col 5+6 or Col. 7+8)	Floating Rate	Fixed Rate	CPLTD[2]	Long Term Portion	Total Debt (Col. 1+4)
1984	$31,122	$22,589[1]	$ 8,533	$28,184	$27,263	$ 921	$ 101	$28,083	$59,306[1]
1983	35,879	15,200	20,679	28,495	26,468	2,027	97	28,398	64,374
1982	36,877	30,706	6,171	3,698	2,196	1,502	195	3,503	40,575
1981	27,738	27,221	517	23,772	22,713	1,385	20,107	3,665	51,510
1980	66,143	64,859	1,284	2,849	1,693	1,156	691	2,158	68,992

[1]Includes $9,866,000 in commercial paper-based debt from Olympus Credit Corp.
[2]Current portion of long-term debt.

Maturing portion of long term debt and notes payable are as follows:

Year	Amount
1985	31,223
1986	25,595
1987	195
1988	317
1989	308

EXHIBIT 3.3	Merit Marine Corp., Consolidated Statement of Earnings for the Years Ended December 31 (Thousands)				
	1980	1981	1982	1983	1984
Net sales	$129,891	$130,012	$89,112	$85,492	$120,472
Cost of sales	$101,869	101,292[1]	66,748[1]	64,590[1]	94,999[1]
Gross profit	28,022	28,720	22,364	20,902	25,473
Selling, general and administration	19,353	22,662	19,630	19,505	18,860
Operating profit	8,669	6,058	2,734	1,397	6,613
Interest income & earned discount	5,158	6,712	4,537	3,144	5,007
Interest (expense)	(9,102)	(11,042)	(5,413)	(4,066)	(6,493)
Other, net (expense)	(361)	(723)	(403)	(874)	(92)
Profit before taxes	4,364	1,005	1,455	(399)	5,035
Income taxes	2,280	114	650	(647)	2,376
Net earnings	$ 2,084	$ 891	$ 805	$ 248	$ 2,659

[1]Liquidation of LIFO layers caused cost of goods sold to be lower by the following amounts: '81, $474,000; '82, $417,000; '83, $344,000; '84, $358,000.

since January 1976, when John Merit, the company's president, had acquired the assets of the Olympus Florida franchise. In 1985, the company was closely held by John Merit and some relatives. John Merit himself held a majority of the common shares. Merit distributed Olympus products to independent marinas across the state and, in addition to the distribution function, ran one of the state's largest marinas at its headquarters in Tampa.

Since 1948, Olympus had been considered the premier manufacturer of engines and steering mechanisms for boats ranging from pleasure crafts to large cabin cruisers. Olympus products accounted for 90 percent of Merit's sales in 1984, with remaining revenues generated from sales and service provided at the firm's Sunshine Marina. (Exhibit 3.4 gives the distribution of Merit's sales.)

Merit's sales of Olympus products to marinas across the state were concentrated in three product lines: drive trains, which included engines and steering mechanisms, Olympia recreational boats, and Olympus replacement parts. Olympus differentiated itself by stressing quality throughout the manufacturing process and by providing the highest level of service in the industry. Through its unique distribution network, Olympus guaranteed marinas one-day delivery of replacement parts. The formula had been successful: Olympus controlled over one-quarter of the $5 billion marine products market in the U.S.

The previous owner of the Florida franchise, Alex Stalworth, had operated the franchise since Olympus' inception in 1948. Prior to selling the franchise, Stalworth had been hesitant to make the sub-stantial investment necessary to serve the booming recreational and commercial boating market in Florida. As a result, beginning in 1977, Merit found it necessary to make substantial investments in new fixed assets for the company, climaxing in 1982 with a $14 million addition to the warehouse and the service center. While the investment had been substantial, the new capacity would allow Merit to more than double sales. With the new facility in place, Merit anticipated that capital expenditures over the next several years would be approximately $3 million a year.

Sales for Merit Marine, which had increased at an annual rate of 16 percent between 1977 and 1981, dropped sharply in 1982 and 1983, as shown in Exhibit 3.3. The decline was a function of a severe recession, high interest rates and oil prices. The subsequent economic recovery and the decline in oil prices brought a stronger market for Olympus' products in Florida, which allowed Merit's 1984 sales to increase 30 percent to $120 million.

INDUSTRY INFORMATION

Total marine product sales were expected to decline by as much as five percent in 1985. However, the Florida market was expected to increase by 5 percent annually for the next several years. The recreational market, which accounted for most sales of Olympus outboard engines and Olympia boats, was highly seasonal and cyclical. Sales of stern drive and sea drive engines, which were used primarily for larger recreational and commercial boats, were less seasonal and slightly less cyclical.

EXHIBIT 3.4	Merit Marine Corp., Distribution of Sales for the Years Ended December 31 (Thousands)				
	1980	**1981**	**1982**	**1983**	**1984**
Total Sales	$129,891	$130,012	$89,112	$85,492	$120,472
Olympus Products	118,201	119,611	75,745	74,378	108,425
Drive Train	52,008	56,217	32,570	30,495	45,538
Olympia Boats	28,368	27,511	16,664	17,107	29,275
Replacement Parts	37,824	35,883	26,511	26,776	33,612
Merit Marina	11,690	10,401	13,367	11,114	12,047
Sales					
Boats & Accessories	3,858	3,224	3,876	3,223	3,614
Gas	4,676	4,265	5,079	4,112	4,698
Service	3,156	2,912	4,411	3,779	3,735

The outboard engine market was concentrated among three major manufacturers—Outboard Marine Corporation (Johnson and Evinrude), Brunswick (Mercury), and Olympus. Japanese manufacturers, such as Yamaha, were just beginning to market outboard engines in the U.S. Olympus competed against Volvo, Mercury, and Chrysler in the stern drive and sea drive markets. Olympia boats, on the other hand, faced a much more fragmented market; over 20 national and regional manufacturers competed for the recreational boat dollar.

BANKING RELATIONSHIP

John Merit's relationship with Omni Bank began in 1967 when he joined Olympus' Treasury Office at the firm's headquarters in Zion, Illinois. When the distributorship became available in Florida in 1976, Merit, with the help of some family financial support, purchased the franchise from Stalworth. Omni Bank, along with Sun Coast bank in Orlando and Ybor National Bank in Tampa, had met Merit Marine's credit

needs since the company was purchased in 1976. Merit had remained loyal to the bank group over the years, but he insisted on the most attractive rates possible.

While both Omni Bank and Sun Coast had $25 million credit commitments to Merit Marine as of January 1985, neither considered themselves Merit's lead bank. (Merit's credit relationships are detailed in Exhibit 3.5.) At year-end 1984, Merit was fully utilizing the $25 million revolver and had $12.7 million of the $40 million line of credit outstanding. John Merit had intimated that lead bank status would go to the bank that offered the most attractive rates. Being the lead bank in the credit group would become more significant as Merit planned to displace current bank debt with below market-rate financing offered by Olympus Credit Corporation to qualified dealers.

SOURCES OF FUNDING

Beginning in the spring of 1984, Olympus Credit Corporation had made available to Olympus distributors $10 million in guaranteed, short-term, floating-rate

---

EXHIBIT 3.5 **Merit Marine Corp., Banking Relationships**

Total available short-term and long-term notes payable to banks and Olympus Credit Corp. aggregated $75,000,000 at December 31, 1985. Compensating balance agreement on bank lines amounts to 5%.

Revolving Credit Agreement

Total:		$25,000,000
Consisting of		
Sun Coast Bank, N.A.	$10,000,000	
Omni Bank	$10,000,000	
Ybor National Bank	$ 5,000,000	

Rate: Prime

Average Usage: 90%

Borrowing Base: 75% of qualified current assets plus $15.0 million for headquarters until mortgaged.

Maturity: December 31, 1986 or 13 months from demand

Covenants:	Working capital	$28.0 million
	Current Ratio	1.5:1.0
	Total liabilities to net worth	3.0:1.0
	Tangible Net Worth	$27.0 million

Unsecured Lines of Credit

Total:		$40,000,000
Consisting of:		
Sun Coast Bank, N.A.	$15,000,000	
Omni Bank	$15,000,000	
Ybor National Bank	$10,000,000	

Rate: Prime

Purpose: Finance inventory and receivables

debt at the A1–P1 commercial paper rate plus 50 basis points. Olympus then announced in December that qualified distributors would be eligible for up to $20 million in commercial paper-based financing, beginning in April of 1985. The prospect of having an additional $10 million in outstandings displaced concerned Ginny Shields and heightened her determination to gain lead bank status.

Omni Bank had priced the $25 million commitment to Merit to achieve a target spread of 110 basis points over the bank's cost of funds. The Merit relationship produced a net contribution of $279,000 in 1983 and $305,000 in the first eleven months of 1984. The contribution for 1984 included earned interest on average deposits of $1.37 million and interest income on average outstanding debt of $14.5 million.

Omni Bank's loan agreement called for Merit Marine to keep compensating balances with the bank based on the total amount of credit committed to the company. To attempt to gain lead bank status, Ginny

Shields, in December 1984, lowered the compensating balance agreement from 5 percent to 2.5 percent of the total credit commitment. Next Ginny positioned Omni Bank to act as Merit's financial advisor with the help of the bank's corporate finance department. It was apparent that Merit needed long-term, fixed-rate funding; accomplishment of this task, however, was easier said than done. Ginny had recalled a memo (shown as Exhibit 3.6) that had recently been distributed to relationship managers describing the profile of a private placement candidate. She realized that Merit would be a borderline case. Merit had been unsuccessful in arranging a reasonably priced mortgage in 1982. Since then, the bank had been unable to provide long-term, fixed-rate financing at an acceptable rate because of Merit's questionable creditworthiness and the prevailing interest rate environment. (Exhibits 3.7 and 3.8 show historic rates and spreads.)

Ginny thought that while Merit did not need additional debt, the firm did need to limit its exposure to

---

EXHIBIT 3.6   Merit Marine Corp.

TO: Relationship Managers
FROM: Capital Markets Division
SUBJECT: *Private Placement* Candidate Profile

The purpose of this profile is to provide the Relationship Managers with a brief description of the conditions under which a given company may or may not be a likely candidate for a private placement.

A. *Is there a need?*
  1. The need to restructure the balance sheet in some way
     a. Interest-rate risk management
     b. Match funding
  2. The identification of a significant cash need in the future
     a. Impending refinancing
     b. Capital expenditures
     c. Merger or acquisition financing
     d. Improving quality of financing

B. *Can a private placement be done—Minimum Financial Criteria*
  1. Sales greater than $75 million
  2. Tangible equity greater than $25 million
  3. Long-term debt/capital less than 50%
  4. No losses in last three years
  5. Pretax interest coverage greater than 1.2 ×

C. *Can the bank get the deal?*
  1. What is the bank's relationship with the client?
  2. Is there a competing party trying to get the same business?

EXHIBIT 3.7   Merit Marine Corp., Rate Structure (as of January 23, 1985)

Maturity (years)	Treasuries	LIBOR[1] Swaps	A-Rated[1] Private Placements	Baa-Rated[2] Private Placements	Ba-Rated[2] Private Placements
3	10.10	T + 108	T + 70	T + 95	T + 120
5	10.61	T + 80	T + 75	T + 100	T + 125
7	10.88	T + 65	T + 80	T + 105	T + 130
10	11.00	T + 60	T + 90	T + 115	T + 140

31-day Commercial Paper (A1–P1)	6-Month LIBOR	Prime Rate (CBR)[3]
8.01	8.75	10.50

10 year average prime rate = 11.71% (std. dev. = 4.32%)

Average spreads:
  LIBOR over A1–P1 commercial paper = 1.02%[4]
  Prime Rate over LIBOR = 1.465%[4]
  Prime Rate over 91-day Treasury Bills = 3.849% (std. dev. = 1.681%)[5]

[1]Spreads are disguised from actual quoted rate. Relative differences between options are valid.
[2]Non-quoted rate. Reflects average premium paid for less than A-rated private placements. Actual rates would be on negotiated basis.
[3]Corporate borrowing rate—approximates prime rate
[4]Average spread between (1/79–11/84)
[5]Average spread between (1/80–12/84)

fluctuations in interest rates by fixing the interest rate on $10 to $15 million in debt. After discussions with John Merit, it was evident that a rate in excess of 12 percent would be unacceptable.

ALTERNATIVES

On January 8, 1985, Jeff Finch and Ginny Shields visited with John Merit in Tampa. The three discussed Merit Marine's funding needs and the possibility of fixing interest payments through an interest rate swap and/or a private placement.

Jeff was uncertain whether institutional investors would be interested in privately placed debt of Merit's quality; however, he suggested the alternative and pointed out that under present market conditions the shorter the maturity, the lower the interest rate. Jeff then introduced the concept of an interest rate swap as a means of effectively fixing interest payments on existing floating-rate debt. Merit was initially unreceptive to the swap alternative due mainly to a lack of understanding of the offer. Upon returning to New York, Jeff requested the right to approach a small num-ber of private investors to see how receptive the market might be to Merit's debt. After speaking with institutional investors, Finch concluded that three alternatives existed to help restructure Merit's capital base.

The first proposal was to fix for three years the interest payments on $10 million in existing debt using an interest rate swap funded with the commercial paper-based debt supplied by Olympus Credit Corporation. If additional interest payments needed to be fixed in the future, a subsequent swap could be arranged since additional commercial paper-based debt would be available to Merit in April 1985. Omni Bank would arrange with Merit to swap interest payments on $10 million of the commercial paper-based, floating-rate debt, which cost Merit the A1–P1 paper rate plus 50 basis points. The bank would pay Merit the six month LIBOR and, in return, Merit would pay a fixed rate equal to the current three-year Treasury note rate plus 108 basis points. Historical six-month LIBOR was 102 basis points higher than the 30-day, A1–P1 commercial paper rate. Merit's effective interest rate under this proposal would vary to the extent that the

| EXHIBIT 3.8 | Merit Marine Corp., Interest Rates (Percent) | | | | |

	Prime[1]	91-Day T-bills	1 Month Commercial Paper	10-Year T-Notes	30-Year T-Notes
1985					
January 23rd	10.5	7.69	8.01	11.0	11.45
1984					
January	11.0	8.93	9.23	11.67	11.75
February	11.0	9.03	9.35	11.84	11.95
March	11.5	9.44	9.81	12.32	12.38
April	12.0	9.69	10.17	12.63	12.65
May	12.5	9.90	10.38	13.41	13.43
June	13.0	9.94	10.82	13.56	13.44
July	13.0	10.13	11.06	13.36	13.21
August	13.0	10.49	11.19	12.72	12.54
September	13.0	10.41	11.11	12.52	12.29
October	12.75	9.97	10.05	12.16	11.98
November	12.0	8.79	9.01	11.57	11.56
December	11.25	8.16	8.39	11.50	11.52
1983					
July	10.50	9.12	9.15	11.38	11.40
August	11.0	9.39	9.41	11.85	11.82
September	11.0	9.05	9.19	11.65	11.63
October	11.0	8.71	9.03	11.54	11.58
November	11.0	8.71	9.10	11.69	11.75
December	11.0	8.96	9.56	11.83	11.88

[1]Average for 10 money center banks; weekly close in 1985; monthly average in 1984 and 1983.
Source: *Federal Reserve Bulletin* (Vol. 69–71).

spread between LIBOR and the commercial paper rate was different than the historical spread of 102 basis points. A larger spread would lower Merit's effective interest rate, while a smaller spread would increase the overall rate. Omni Bank's compensation in the transaction would amount to approximately 25 basis points per year. The bank's compensation, which was included in the 108 basis point spread, was higher than normal since the rate Omni Bank could offer Merit through an interest-rate swap was at least 3 percent lower than bank-funded, fixed-rate debt.

The second alternative considered was a $10 million, three-year private placement at a fixed rate of 12 percent. The debt would be placed with an insurance company that had an appetite for high-yielding, non-investment grade bonds. The 12 percent coupon represented a 125 basis point premium over an A-rated private placement and a 75 basis point premium over a BBB placement. Interest would be paid quarterly and the principal would be repaid at the end of three years.

Since the institutional investor would be matching the transaction with similar term liabilities, there would be no option for Merit to prepay the commitment. This option would leave the commercial paper debt available to support working capital needs and would allow Merit to enter into an interest rate swap if additional interest payments needed to be fixed.

The final alternative combined the same private placement as in the second alternative with a ten-year, $15 million adjustable-rate private placement with a three-year option to fix for a term of three years. If the option to fix were exercised, the remaining term of the loan would be three years from the date of exercise. The principal on the second placement would also be repaid in full upon maturity. The variable-rate note would be set at the 91-day Treasury rate plus 200 basis points, while the rate if Merit chose to fix would be 122 percent of three-year Treasuries. The variable-rate note could not be repaid prior to June 30, 1986. Between June 30, 1986 and March 31, 1988 there would be no prepayment penalty, while prepayment after March 31, 1988 would incur a 5 percent penalty. If Merit exercised the fixed-rate option, no prepayment would be allowed during the three year period. Omni Bank's compensation on the private placement package would be 1 percent of the first $10 million and .5 percent of any additional debt placed.

In making a recommendation to Merit, Jeff had to consider a number of issues. First, Merit Marine could look forward to the possibility of very strong cash flow over the next several years due to a low level of planned capital expenditures and a likelihood of increased sales. In addition, Merit had been concentrating on speeding receivables and reducing the level of inventory carried. Jeff knew that if too much of Merit's debt was fixed for too long a period, the firm would incur a prepayment penalty if cash flow was sufficient to reduce outstanding long-term debt.

A second issue that concerned Jeff involved the permanence of the commercial paper-based, floating-rate debt. If those funds became unavailable during the life of the swap, Merit would have to fund the swap with prime-based debt and would incur the additional interest expense between the prime rate and the commercial paper rate plus 50 basis points.

While the rate structure at three years met the 12 percent level that Merit set as his threshold, Jeff was concerned whether the three-year term was appropriate for the company or whether a longer maturity was needed.

While Jeff considered these alternatives, Ginny was faced with a dilemma regarding the profitability of the relationship. Ginny wondered whether her initiative to position Omni Bank as Merit's financial advisor might move the bank into the lead position in a credit group that had no outstandings. If Jeff were to place the $10 to $25 million in institutional debt, Merit would reduce its bank debt by a like amount; as a result, Omni Bank would stand to lose $10 million in outstandings. The decision to pursue the private placement option would be a function of whether Ginny felt that Merit's condition was evident enough that if Omni Bank did not fix the firm's interest payments, another institution would. In such a case, Omni Bank would not only lose the interest income from the debt that would be assumed by another lender, but would also lose the fees that would have been generated from a swap or private placement. One incentive for Ginny to provide corporate finance services in this situation was the fact that her division would be credited with a shadow profit equal to 60 percent of the fee generated by the corporate finance department.

EXHIBIT 3.9	Merit Marine Corp., External Funds Requirements (Thousands)	
	1983	**1984**
Net Sales	$85,492	$120,472
Sources of funds		
Net income	248	2,659
Depreciation	1,388	1,650
Deferred Taxes	504	672
Total	2,140	4,981
Uses of funds		
Net capital expenditures	4,984	289
Cash dividends (preferred stock)	77	77
Reduction in long-term debt	105	315
Increase in net working capital	21,239	4,929
Increase in other assets	735	(289)
Total	27,140	5,321
External funds required	$25,000	$ 340
Capitalization		
Short-term debt	$35,879	$ 31,122
Long-term debt	28,495	28,184
Total debt	64,374	59,306
Shareholders' equity	30,477	33,059
Total	$94,851	$ 92,365
Short-term debt/Capitalization	37.8%	33.7%
Total debt/Capitalization	67.9%	64.2%
Net working capital/Sales	40.3%	32.4%

EXHIBIT 3.10	Merit Marine Corp., Proforma Assumptions			
	1985	**1986**	**1987**	**1988**
Change in Net Sales	5%	5%	5%	5%
Net income/sales	2.4%	2.4%	2.4%	2.4%
Depreciation expense (000)	$1,700	$1,734	$1,847	$1,755
Increase in Deferred Taxes (000)	$1,022	$ 805	$ 704	$ 592
Dividends (000)	$ 77	$ 77	$ 77	$ 77
Increase in other assets (000)	$ 300	$ 300	$ 300	$ 300
Capital expenditures (000)	$3,000	$3,000	$3,000	$3,000
Net working capital/sales	.31	.30	.29	.28

EXHIBIT 3.11 Merit Marine Corp., Account Profitability

Type	Amount (Millions)	Usage	Rate	Ginny Shields' Division				Omni Bank			
				Income 1985 (Thousands)	1985 ROA	Income 1986 (Thousands)	1986 ROA	Income 1985 (Thousands)	1985 ROA	Income 1986 (Thousands)	1986 ROA
Scenario 1: No change in revolver; 2½% compensating balance; $2.0 million line of credit											
Revolver	$10.0	$10.0	1.1%	$110		$110					
Line of credit (LOC)	$12.0	$2.0	1.1%	22		22					
Compensating balance	$22.0	2.5%	10.0%	55		55					
TOTAL				$187	1.56%	$187	1.56%	$187	1.56%	$187	1.56%
Scenario 2: $25 million private placement, 2½% compensating balance, $2.0 million line of credit											
Revolver											
Fees-Private Placement	0.175	60.0%		105							
Line of credit (LOC)	$12.0	$2.0	1.1%	22		22					
Compensating balance	$12.00	2.5%	10.0%	30		30					
TOTAL				$157	7.85%	$52	2.6%	$227	11.35%	$52	2.6%
Scenario 3: $10 million private placement, 2½% compensating balance, $2.0 million line of credit											
Revolver	$6.0	$6.0	1.1%	66		66					
Fees-Private placement	0.1	60.0%		60							
Line of credit (LOC)	$12.0	$2.0	1.1%	22		22					
Compensating balance	$18.00	2.5%	10.0%	45		45					
TOTAL				$193	2.41%	$133	1.66%	$233	2.91%	$133	1.66%
Scenario 4: $10 million swap, 2½% compensating balance, $2.0 million line of credit											
Revolver	$10.0	$10.0	1.1%	110		110					
Fees-Swap	10.0		.250%	25		25					
Line of credit (LOC)	$12.0	$2.0	1.1%	22		22					
Compensating balance	$22.00	2.5%	10.0%	55		55					
TOTAL				$212	1.77%	$212	1.77%	$212	1.77%	$212	1.77%
Scenario 5: No change and revolver is displaced by private mortgage.											
Revolver											
Line of credit (LOC)	$12.0	$2.0	1.1%	22		22					
Compensating balance	$12.0	2.5%	10.0%	30		30					
TOTAL				$52	2.6%	$52	2.6%	$52	2.6%	$52	2.6%

CASE FOUR
First Wachovia Corporation

Wayne Williams, a vice-president at First Wachovia Corporation, was part of the company's First Wachovia Corporate Services subsidiary, which managed the loan portfolio of lesser developed countries (LDCs) for both Wachovia and its recent merger partner, First Atlanta Corporation. As shown in the financial information in Exhibits 4.1 and 4.2, First Wachovia was an $18.7 billion financial institution headquartered in both Winston-Salem, N.C., and Atlanta, Ga. The holding company was formed in December 1985, following the merger of The Wachovia Corporation and First Atlanta.

Williams' particular concern in October 1987 was the international portfolio's Mexican exposure. First Wachovia held over $200 million in LDC debt in mid-1987, about half of which was in Mexican public-sector instruments. Although the bank had established loss reserves that more than matched the potential LDC exposure, Williams' goal was to recoup as much of the face value of the debt as possible. In his review of alternatives, Williams had run across a prospectus for the IDI Fund, a limited partnership formed to convert sovereign debt to equity in the Mexican private sector. He needed to determine the feasibility and desirability of participating in the IDI Fund.

This case was written by Laura M. Connelly under the supervision of Professor Mark R. Eaker. Copyright (c) 1988 by the Darden Graduate Business School Sponsors, Charlottesville, VA. WP3803L

EXHIBIT 4.1   **First Wachovia Corporation, Balance Sheet (Millions)**

	12/31/86	12/31/85
Assets		
Cash and due from banks	$ 2,100.6	$ 1,914.2
Investment securities	4,288.8	4,214.3
Loans and leases	$11,747.1	$10,702.0
Less allowance for loan losses	163.8	144.5
Net loans and leases	$11,583.3	$10,557.5
Net property and equipment	277.6	253.8
Other assets	439.2	766.7
Total assets	$18,689.6	$17,706.5
Liabilities		
Deposits in domestic offices	$13,185.7	$11,805.3
Deposits in foreign offices	594.9	869.7
Total deposits	$13,780.6	$12,674.9
Federal funds under repo agreements	2,605.4	2,736.9
Borrowed funds: short-term	492.7	299.5
long-term	286.8	295.5
Other liabilities	346.6	666.0
Total liabilities	$17,512.1	$16,672.8
Shareholders' Equity		
Common stock, par value $5 a share	268.4	266.7
Capital surplus	119.1	114.1
Retained earnings	789.9	652.9
Total shareholders' equity	$ 1,177.4	$ 1,033.7
Total liabilities and shareholders' equity	$18,689.6	$17,706.5

| EXHIBIT 4.2 | First Wachovia Corporation, Consolidated Income Statement (Millions) |

	12/31/86	12/31/85
Interest income		
Loans	$1,117.4	$1,124.8
Other	317.9	362.3
Total interest income	$1,435.3	$1,487.0
Interest expense		
Interest on deposits	626.1	692.2
Short-term borrowed funds	177.8	198.4
Long-term borrowed funds	26.4	27.9
Total interest expense	$ 830.3	$ 918.5
Net interest income	605.0	568.5
Provision for loan losses	95.4	80.7
Net interest income after provision	$ 509.6	$ 487.8
Other income		
Other operating revenue	282.7	255.1
Gain on sale of subsidiary	8.9	17.0
Investment securities gains (losses)	12.3	11.3
Total other income	$ 303.8	$ 283.4
Other expense		
Staff	309.0	285.5
Other	278.1	251.8
Total other expense	$ 587.1	$ 537.3
Income before income taxes	226.3	233.9
Applicable income taxes	32.6	46.2
Net income	$ 193.8	$ 187.7

LATIN AMERICAN MARKET

The Latin American debt situation had its roots in the flawed lending theory of the 1970s: governments could not go broke. Ever since Mexico had first suspended debt service in 1982, government officials and financial institutions had searched for innovative ways to relieve countries of debt-service burdens. The U.S. government supported the restructuring of Latin American debt-service schedules. U.S. Treasury Secretary James Baker pushed Latin American governments to formulate growth-oriented strategies emphasizing privatization of state-owned enterprises, direct foreign investment opportunities, and a general loos-ening of government's grasp on the private sector. He also strongly encouraged commercial banks to resume lending to countries that showed a willingness to redirect their economies. Banks with the largest LDC exposures were willing to work with the foreign governments in order to keep the lapsed sovereign debt current on their books (Exhibit 4.3).

In 1982, a secondary market developed for restructured LDC sovereign debt. The market allowed holders of this debt to buy, sell, and trade restructured instruments at amounts less than the face value of the original notes. Discounts in the secondary market ranged from as high as 92 percent for Bolivia to 40 percent for Mexico, as shown in Exhibit 4.4. Institutions trading in the market preferred to swap sovereign debt rather than sell it outright for a number of reasons. Many had not built sufficient reserves to absorb the losses realized when debt was taken off the books at less than face value. There had been a concern that officials would require an LDC debt-holder to write down all of its LDC exposure to realizable market value if a portion was sold outright. The swapping allowed banks to restructure their portfolios without exposing their entire position to a write-off. Bank regulators had indicated that write-offs would not be required.

Debt swaps in the secondary market took a number of forms. Debt-for-debt swaps were completed

| EXHIBIT 4.3 | First Wachovia Corporation, Largest Domestic Latin American Debt-Holders, as of June 1, 1987 |

	Exposure[a] (in billions)	Percent of Holding Company's Capital
Bank		
Citicorp	$10.4	149%
Bank of America	7.5	186
Manufacturers Hanover	7.5	199
Chase	7.0	143
JP Morgan	4.6	89

[a]Includes debt exposure from Mexico, Brazil, Argentina, Peru, and Venezuela.
Source: "A Stunner from The Citi," *Business Week,* June 1, 1987, p. 43, data from IBCA Inc.

EXHIBIT 4.4   **First Wachovia Corporation, Secondary-Market LDC Sovereign Debt Prices (May 1987)**

Country	Cents for Each Dollar of Debt
Rumania	86–89
Colombia	86–88
Ivory Coast	76–78
Yugoslavia	74–77
Venezuela	72–74
Philippines	70–71
Chile	67–69
Morocco	66–68
Panama	66–68
Brazil	64–65
South Africa	60–65
Argentina	59–60
Mexico	58–59
Ecuador	53–56
Egypt	49–51
Poland	43–45
Nigeria	37–39
Zaire	24–26
Peru	13–15

Source: "Swapping Debt—Just Hot Air?" *Euromoney,* Shearson Lehman Bros., International (London), May 1987, p. 118.

with either a trade of sovereign debt or a conversion of restructured debt into another instrument, such as a bond, which was exempt from further restructuring. So long as the market value of the swapped debt was equal, no loss was recorded.

The debt/equity swap was an offshoot of the debt-for-debt swap. Chile instituted the first program in 1985, and since then Mexico, Costa Rica, Ecuador, Brazil, Argentina, and the Philippines had followed suit. *Institutional Investor* estimated that these programs alone would have completed a total of $6 billion in debt/equity conversions by the end of 1987.[1] Because of this success, 15 more countries were investigating ways to institute similar programs by 1988.

[1] "A Guide to Debt-Equity Conversions," A Special Sponsored Section, Shearson Lehman Bros., *Institutional Investor,* September 1987, p. 2.

In a typical debt/equity conversion program, public sector debt that had been part of a restructuring was eligible to be swapped. A multi-national corporation purchased LDC debt in the secondary market at appropriate market discounts on face value. The debt was changed into local currency in cash or negotiable securities at a conversion discount charged by the host government. Each government established conversion discount schedules that were favorable for projects which fueled exports and created jobs and unfavorable for projects that did not fund economically important areas. The conversion fee ranged from 25 percent of the face value of the debt for projects in low-priority industries to a zero discount for certain export-generating projects. After funds were converted to local currency, they were invested in approved local projects as equity. Rules varied about repatriation of funds, but most programs did not allow capital repayment before the scheduled amortization of principal on the restructured debt.

Swaps offered advantages to both LDCs and debt-holders. LDC governments were relieved of a portion of their debt-payment burdens and at the same time were able to attract investment to boost exports and create jobs. The conversion of debt through LDCs' financial networks also promoted the development of local capital markets. For banks, the debt/equity swap offered a tool to cut LDC debt exposure and, in the best case, would result in viable long-term investments at bargain prices for the purchaser.

Financial institutions were active in the swap market as intermediaries in swap transactions. Institutions with Latin American divisions were positioning themselves to be both brokers of LDC debt and managers of equity funds. Specific country knowledge was important because the mechanics of the swap process involved complex regulatory systems in each country. Intermediaries needed experience with documentation and trading skills as well as large networks of local government and business contacts to create viable equity deals. Financial institutions expected eventually to underwrite, resell, and syndicate LDC exposure for debt-holders who did not have the capacity or inclination to originate opportunities themselves in foreign countries.

In 1986, secondary-market trading in Latin American and other country debt totaled close to $5 billion, up $3 billion from 1985. *The Banker* estimated that the total debt swapped in 1987 would approach $7 billion.[2] Although growing, this market represented only a fraction of the total Latin American debt exposure of approximately $380 billion. Through early 1987, financial institutions with large Latin American exposure avoided swapping their own loans in the debt/equity program. They were reluctant to report losses from the government conversion fees related to the swapped portfolios. Also, they feared being required to apply the discounts of the swap transactions to the LDC debt that remained on their books.

Recently, however, there had been signs that the participation of the large debt-holders in the swap market would increase. In May 1987, Citicorp announced that it was setting up a $3 billion reserve against its Latin American exposure. Chairman John Reed stated that he hoped to get rid of $5 billion in LDC debt over the next three years through the secondary market. The financial community expected that a large part of the amount would be converted through debt/equity swaps. American Express and Bankers Trust tested the accounting treatment of LDC debt left on their books after a swap transaction. Their auditor, Arthur Young, stated that no losses would be realized when the swaps were made, if it were possible to establish the fair value of the investment. And, the remaining debt portfolio would stay on the books at full value. Finally, in August the Federal Reserve Board ruled that banks could own up to 100 percent of the equity of companies being denationalized in LDCs, a significant boost from the previous rule of 20 percent.

MEXICO

Facing a slowdown in economic activity in the mid-1970s, Mexico turned to public-sector spending to stimulate local demand. The government depended on foreign lenders and debt to fund a substantial part of this spending. When oil prices shot up in the late 1970s, the government's spending programs grew unchecked, and foreign investors flocked to support the oil-rich country. By 1982 public-sector spending was at an all-time high, and inflation was growing at an alarming rate. Foreign and local investors lost confidence in the government's ability to cut spending, and the country experienced massive capital outflows. These factors set the stage for the foreign-debt crisis of 1982.

The Mexican government enacted a well-planned but ineffective stabilization program over the next three years. Heavy public-sector borrowing crowded private companies out of the local debt markets. Continued growth of government deficits left no room for private investors to stimulate economic resurgence. Under the theory that present hardships would lead to a higher stan-dard of living in the future, President Miguel de la Madrid responded to the debt crisis with a harsh austerity program. De la Madrid's basic policy was to hold down wages while severely devaluing the peso to stimulate exports and meet payments on the country's $100 billion in foreign debt. One result was the depreciation in the free-market peso exchange rate shown in Exhibit 4.5.

MEXICAN SWAP PROGRAM

De la Madrid was faced with finding a way to gain some liquidity in the Mexican capital markets at a time when the local prime lending rate was over 90 percent. In 1986, the government turned to the debt/equity swap market to attract foreign investment and to reduce the foreign debt load. Section 5:11 of the New Restructure Agreement dated August 29, 1985, declared all public-sector debt eligible for swapping. Qualified stocks had the following restrictions:

EXHIBIT 4.5	First Wachovia Corporation, Mexican Peso/Dollar Exchange Rate	
Year	Quarter	Peso/Dollar
1985	I	226.31
	II	239.12
	III	370.50
	IV	447.50
1986	I	486.50
	II	644.50
	III	770.50
	IV	922.00

Source: U.S. Department of Commerce, *Foreign Economic Trends,* May 1987.

---

[2] "Trading Debt for Equity," *The Banker,* February 1987.

EXHIBIT 4.6	First Wachovia Corporation, Mexican Government Discount Schedule for Debt/Equity Swaps

% Discount[a]	Qualifying Projects
0	Acquisition of state-owned firms
5	Investment in firm that exports 80% of production
	New investment in firm that creates jobs and brings in high technology
14	Investment that reduces debt to local banks
15	Investment geared toward partial FICORCA prepayment[b]
16	Investment for total prepayment for FICORCA[b]
25	All other approved investments

[a]The Mexican government would convert the sovereign debt into pesos at the free-market exchange rate prevailing on the closing date after taking the listed discount.
[b]See Exhibit 4.7.

1. They could be issued only to offshore entities and could not be transferred to a Mexican entity before January 1, 1998;

2. no conversion was allowed into other types of securities;

3. no redemption could be made on a basis more favorable than the repayment schedule of the underlying debt.

Dividends could not be guaranteed, but were unrestricted. Swaps had to be approved by the Ministry of Finance and Public Credit and the National Commission on Foreign Relations, and in some circumstances, the Ministry of Foreign Relations. Following approval, the Mexican government would convert debt at the free-market exchange rate. Discounts were applied to the swapped debt, and funds were directed to private investment projects. The conversion discounts shown in Exhibit 4.6 were based on the government's view of the priority of the project to be funded. The Mexican authorities monitored the program closely, and in early 1987 began to impose a .25 percent application fee to ensure sincerity on the part of foreign investors.

Because of the potentially inflationary effects of pumping more pesos into the economy, the annual size of the debt/equity program was limited to 7 percent of the budget deficit.[3] In addition, directing pesos toward investments that generated new production lessened the potential inflationary impact. *Euromoney* estimated that $685 million of debt-swap transactions had been completed and $375 million in additional projects were nearing conversion.[4] The average discount rate on the 250 projects approved was 12 percent.

Although the government was applauded for its success in attracting new investment, the swap program was not without its critics. Some large bank debtholders hesitated to enter the Mexican program. Twice after its inception, the program shut down because of political and economic concerns as well as disputes within the government.

Major participants in the program were multinational corporations that bought Mexican sovereign debt in the secondary market. These companies capitalized new entities and existing subsidiaries by buying debt from banks at the free-market discount of 40 percent and then converting into pesos at the government discount rate of 5-25 percent. *Institutional Investor* projected that the automobile sector absorbed nearly $500 million, and tourism over $300 million of the new investment.[5] The largest conversion projects were Chrysler de Mexico, S.A., $100 million; Nissan Mexicana, $54.4 million; Ford Motor, $21.8 million; Renault Ind. Mex., $14.1 million; GEM, S.A., $9.1 million; and Tramsider, $5.0 million.

Because large bank-led swap funds had not been strong participants in the Mexican swap program, groups of private individuals established smaller

---

[3]The 1986 deficit allowed $1.5 billion in swaps.

[4]"Swapping Debt—Just Hot Air?" *Euromoney,* May 1987, p. 117.
[5]"A Guide to Debt-Equity Conversions," p. 10.

investment portfolios. Their mutual funds were made up of the sovereign debt pledged by institutions that were reluctant to manage their own Mexican equity portfolios. The groups had contacts with Mexican entrepreneurs, who supplied management expertise and crucial government connections. The major challenge faced by these private groups was gaining credibility with investors, who had to commit to equity projects that would not unwind for ten years or longer.

IDI ASSOCIATES

IDI Associates (the Fund) was a limited partnership formed in March 1987 to organize, sponsor, and manage one or more debt/equity swap funds. IDI solicited regional banks willing to pledge their Mexican public-sector debt to be swapped for equity in investments deemed appropriate by the Fund. IDI set a minimum Fund size at $50 million and maximum at $75 million. Minimum participation in the Fund was $5 million, and no one bank could contribute more than 24.9 percent of the total Fund. An organization fee equaling 3 percent of the pledged debt was due up front in cash, and management fees of 1.5 percent annually would be deducted from the cash flow paid to the subscribing banks. IDI was also to receive a fee of 1 percent of the amount of any equity investments it sold after conversion, as well as incentive payments when the return on investment exceeded predetermined levels.

IDI's portfolio strategy was based on its belief that the best investment prospects were established Mexican companies. IDI would concentrate on companies in the top 100 of the Mexican economy with revenues from $25–$200 million and equity from $15–$100 million. The Fund targeted companies that used domestic raw materials and planned to increase export business. Likely investment industries included electronics, machinery, auto parts, chemicals, plastics, and cement. Descriptions of opportunities are presented in Exhibit 4.7.

IDI wished to round out the Fund portfolio with up to 15 percent of debt-for-debt swaps and planned to target potential foreign investors in Mexico willing to swap dollar-denominated debt for Mexican sovereign debt. Management would also consider swapping a portion of its sovereign debt for the dollar-denominated debt of one of its equity investment companies if the company demonstrated the ability to generate cash flow to cover debt service. Exhibit 4.8 shows the structure of the Fund based on a total subscription of $50 million.

After identifying investment opportunities, IDI would direct swap transactions through the government system and monitor the resulting portfolio. Although a passive investor, IDI wanted to be actively involved through attending periodic management meetings and conducting continuous financial analyses of all the Fund's investments. IDI's goal was to be fully invested within two years of the Fund's closing. When this was achieved, IDI would begin the search for innovative ways to recoup dollar investments by structuring equity sales to other offshore entities. Ex-

---

EXHIBIT 4.7   **First Wachovia Corporation, Sample Investments of IDI Fund**

1. *Government-company buyout:* A major group in Mexico was preparing to bid for a government-owned producer of proprietary drugs. The government planned to sell the assets at their book value, using the proceeds to retire outstanding liabilities. The total cash price would be $60 million.

2. *FICORCA pre-payment:* The FICORCA program involved a series of dollar-denominated debt restructurings at favorable interest and exchange rates which were arranged in the early 1980s. An established soft-drink bottler wanted to lock in an advantage resulting from FICORCA borrowing. The company carried loans from foreign banks of $12 million, which were restructured in 1983 under the FICORCA program. Because the peso devaluation rate had exceeded the interest rate charged by FICORCA, peso debt carried on the books of the company was priced at a 30% discount below the value had the obligation remained dollar denominated. The company had an opportunity to purchase a smaller bottler but did not want to eliminate any portion of the sinking fund designed to meet upcoming FICORCA repayment requirements. The company was therefore requesting an equity investment of up to $5 million to pre-pay FICORCA.

3. *Mining project:* A mining company operated by one of the most reputable groups in Mexico needed funds to expand one of its principal mines. Total cost of the expansion program was estimated to be $20 million.

Source: IDI Information Memorandum.

EXHIBIT 4.8 **First Wachovia Corporation, IDI Fund Allocation of Pledged Debt (Thousands)**

Assuming a $50 million fund:	
Total subscription amount	$50,000
Organization fee	1,500
Available for investment	$48,500
Swapped for debt (15%)	7,270
Available for equity investment	$41,230
Conversion discount (8%)	3,300
Invested in equities	$37,930

Source: IDI Mexico Fund I Information Memorandum.

hibit 4.9 shows projected rates of return in optimistic, pessimistic, and base case scenarios.

J. Hallam Dawson and Amsterdam Pacific Corporation were general managers of the Fund. Dawson, chairman of IDI, was managing director of Dawson and Company, a West Coast venture capital firm. Amsterdam Pacific was a California-based investment bank. An advisory board would be formed to counsel the general managers on initial investments and ongoing portfolio analyses, and one or more of the three to five people on the board would be from banks pledging LDC debt.

IDI maintained offices in San Francisco and Mexico. Luis M. de la Fuente, executive vice-president of IDI, directed foreign operations. De la Fuente had joined IDI in February 1987 from Salinas y Rocha, the largest department and furniture store chain in Mexico and one of the country's 20 largest companies. He was known as a creative financial manager with extensive experience in operating finances. IDI was counting on his business, political, and financial connections to be instrumental in the success of the Fund. Exhibit 4.10 offers further background on the Fund's management.

RISKS OF DEBT/EQUITY SWAP MARKET

Although the IDI Fund was attractive to First Wachovia, Williams did not want to lose sight of the risks

involved. There were questions about the viability of the swap market. As larger banks rushed into the LDC debt-management business, sound equity investments might become difficult to find. Even if attractive investments were found, investors in this mutual fund would still be carrying assets in currencies other than those the banks were using as fund sources. Moreover, further devaluations could be harmful to returns if the appreciation in the portfolio did not keep pace. Williams wondered what precedents would be established for the write-down of swapped debt. IDI accountants stated that, in their opinion, no write-down should be required on the pledge of sovereign debt to the Fund. Required write-downs on conversion of debt to equity would equal the government-mandated discount rate.

In addition to the business concerns, risks were associated with the political system in Mexico. Upcoming elections brought the chance of renewed social unrest, which had accompanied de la Madrid's election in 1982. The mechanics of the political system insured that de la Madrid's candidate would win the July 1988 election, but a smooth transition was important. Political pressure during the transition period could force de la Madrid to relax the country's austerity program and give in to other demands, such as letting wages outpace inflation. Williams discovered that the effect of political changes had already been felt: Carlos Salinas Gotari, Minister of Finance, Budgets and Planning and de la Madrid's chosen candidate, closed down the swap market at the beginning of October 1987 to review its impact on the Mexican economy. A determination that the swap program was fueling inflation could cause a breakdown of the entire system.

Williams weighed these issues against the possible results of pursuing other alternatives. Doing nothing would allow time for Mexico's political situation to become more stable, but with Treasury Secretary Baker advocating further renegotiation, First Wachovia would probably be pressured to step up its participation. On the other hand, selling the Mexican exposure in the secondary market would bring immediate cash flow that could be reloaned to more stable ventures. A final option would be swapping Mexican debt for the debt of another, less risky LDC. Williams wondered, however, if making a bet on the viability of one country would be more efficient than spreading the risk over the entire LDC arena. He now had to set about the task of evaluating which method would be right for First Wachovia.

EXHIBIT 4.9   First Wachovia Corporation, Scenario IRR Calculations

BASE CASE

Line	Item (Millions)	Year 1	Year 2	Year 3	Year 4	Year 5	Year 6	Year 7	Year 8	Year 9	Year 10
1	Equity Investments	$37.93	$40.85	$43.99	$47.38	$51.03	$54.96	$47.35	$38.25	$27.46	$14.79
2	Earnings from Equity	4.17	4.49	4.84	5.21	5.61	6.05	5.21	4.21	3.02	1.63
3	Dividends	1.25	1.35	1.45	1.56	1.68	1.81	1.56	1.26	0.91	0.49
4	Withholdings on Dividends	0.69	0.74	0.80	0.86	0.93	1.00	0.86	0.69	0.50	0.27
5	Net Dividends	0.56	0.61	0.65	0.70	0.76	0.82	0.70	0.57	0.41	0.22
6	Loans	7.28	7.28	7.28	7.28	7.28	7.28	5.82	4.36	2.91	1.46
7	Interest	0.65	0.65	0.65	0.65	0.65	0.65	0.52	0.39	0.26	0.13
8	Withholding on Interest	0.10	0.10	0.10	0.10	0.10	0.10	0.08	0.06	0.06	0.02
9	Net Interest	0.56	0.56	0.56	0.56	0.56	0.56	0.45	0.33	0.22	0.11
10	Tax Credits	0.39	0.42	0.45	0.48	0.51	0.55	0.47	0.38	0.27	0.14
11	Management and Other Fees	0.70	0.75	0.79	0.84	0.90	0.96	0.82	0.66	0.48	0.27
12	Current Income	0.81	0.84	0.86	0.89	0.93	0.96	0.79	0.61	0.42	0.21
13	Loan Repayments						1.46	1.46	1.46	1.46	1.46
14	Divestitures						11.84	12.75	13.73	14.79	15.93
15	Divestiture Fees						0.24	0.25	0.27	0.30	0.32
16	Net Cash Flows	0.81	0.84	0.86	0.89	0.93	14.02	14.74	15.53	16.37	17.27
17	Internal Rate of Return—100% = 6.7%										
18	— 60% = 14.2%										

Source: IDI Mexico Fund I Information Memorandum.

EXHIBIT 4.9 CONTINUED

OPTIMISTIC CASE

Line	Item (Millions)	Year 1	Year 2	Year 3	Year 4	Year 5	Year 6	Year 7	Year 8	Year 9	Year 10
1	Equity Investments	$37.93	$42.21	$46.97	$52.27	$58.16	$64.73	$57.62	$48.09	$35.68	$19.85
2	Earnings from Equity	4.93	5.49	6.11	6.79	7.56	8.41	7.49	6.25	4.64	2.58
3	Dividends	1.48	1.65	1.83	2.04	2.27	2.52	2.25	1.88	1.39	0.77
4	Withholdings on Dividends	0.81	0.91	1.01	1.12	1.25	1.39	1.24	1.03	0.77	0.43
5	Net Dividends	0.67	0.74	0.82	0.92	1.02	1.14	1.01	0.84	0.63	0.35
6	Loans	8.37	8.37	8.37	8.37	8.37	8.37	6.69	5.02	3.35	1.67
7	Interest	0.75	0.75	0.75	0.75	0.75	0.75	0.60	0.45	0.30	0.15
8	Withholding on Interest	0.11	0.11	0.11	0.11	0.11	0.11	0.09	0.07	0.05	0.02
9	Net Interest	0.64	0.64	0.64	0.64	0.64	0.64	0.51	0.38	0.26	0.13
10	Tax Credits	0.93	1.02	1.12	1.23	1.36	1.50	1.33	1.10	0.81	0.45
11	Management and Other Fees	0.72	0.78	0.86	0.93	1.02	1.12	0.99	0.82	0.61	0.35
12	Current Income	1.51	1.62	1.73	1.86	2.00	2.16	1.86	1.51	1.08	0.58
13	Loan Repayments						1.67	1.67	1.67	1.67	1.67
14	Divestitures						14.41	16.03	17.84	19.85	22.09
15	Divestiture Fees						0.43	0.48	0.54	0.60	0.66
16	Net Cash Flows	1.51	1.62	1.73	1.86	2.00	17.80	19.08	20.48	22.01	23.68
17	Internal Rate of Return —100% = 11.3%										
18	— 60% = 19.5%										

EXHIBIT 4.9 CONTINUED

PESSIMISTIC CASE

Line	Item (Millions)	Year 1	Year 2	Year 3	Year 4	Year 5	Year 6	Year 7	Year 8	Year 9	Year 10
1	Equity Investments	$37.93	$39.25	$40.62	$42.04	$43.50	$45.02	$37.27	$28.93	$19.96	$10.33
2	Earnings from Equity	3.03	3.14	3.25	3.36	3.48	3.60	2.98	2.31	1.60	0.83
3	Dividends	0.91	0.94	0.97	1.01	1.04	1.08	0.89	0.69	0.48	0.25
4	Withholdings on Dividends	0.50	0.52	0.54	0.55	0.57	0.59	0.49	0.38	0.26	0.14
5	Net Dividends	0.41	0.42	0.44	0.45	0.47	0.49	0.40	0.31	0.22	0.11
6	Loans	7.28	7.28	7.28	7.28	7.28	7.28	5.82	4.36	2.91	1.46
7	Interest	0.58	0.58	0.58	0.58	0.58	0.58	0.47	0.35	0.23	0.12
8	Withholding on Interest	0.09	0.09	0.09	0.09	0.09	0.09	0.07	0.05	0.03	0.02
9	Net Interest	0.49	0.49	0.49	0.49	0.49	0.49	0.40	0.30	0.20	0.10
10	Tax Credits	0.00	0.00	0.00	0.00	0.00	0.00	0.00	0.00	0.00	0.00
11	Management and Other Fees	0.70	0.72	0.74	0.76	0.79	0.81	0.67	0.52	0.37	0.20
12	Current Income	0.20	0.20	0.19	0.18	0.18	0.17	0.13	0.08	0.05	0.01
13	Loan Repayments						1.46	1.46	1.46	1.46	1.46
14	Divestitures						9.32	9.64	9.98	10.33	10.69
15	Divestiture Fees						0.09	0.10	0.10	0.10	0.11
16	Net Cash Flows	0.20	0.20	0.19	0.18	0.18	10.85	11.13	11.42	11.72	12.04
17	Internal Rate of Return—100% = 1.9%										
18	60% = 8.8%										

EXHIBIT 4.9 *CONTINUED*

NOTES TO INTERNAL RATE OF RETURN CASES

(Abbreviations: B = Base Case, P = Pessimistic Case, O = Optimistic Case)

Line	Item	Note
1	Equity Investments	Equals the face value of the debt swapped less an average discount of 8%, plus retained earnings, and adjusted by changes in the real peso/dollar exchange rate of B = 0% per annum, P = −2%, O = +2%.
2	Earnings from Equity	Assumes earnings on Equity Investments in real peso terms (net of Mexican inflation) of: B = 11%, P = 8%, O = 13%.
3	Dividends	A 30% payout ratio is assumed.
4	Withholding on Dividends	Currently the Mexican withholding on dividends paid abroad is 55%.
5	Net Dividends	Dividends less the withholding on those dividends.
6	Loans	Debt is swapped for these loans on the following terms: B & P at face value, O at a 15% premium.
7	Interest	B & O = 9%, P = 8%.
8	Withholding on Interest	Currently 15% for registered lenders.
9	Net Interest	Interest less the withholding.
10	Tax Credits	Assumes current, carried back, or discounted carried forward benefit of the amounts withheld of: B = 50%, P = 0%, O = 100%.
11	Management and Other Fees	The Management Fee is 1.5% of the Equity Investments plus the Loans at the beginning of the year, and Other Fees are $25,000 per annum.
12	Current Income	Net Dividends plus Net Interest plus Tax Credits Less Management and Other Fees.
13	Loan Repayments	The principal portion of the Loans is assumed to be repaid in equal annual installments at the end of years 6–10.
14	Divestitures	Equity Investments are assumed to be sold at their carrying values as defined in Line 1 as follows: ⅕ at the end of year 6, ¼ at year 7, ⅓ at year 8, ½ at year 9, and the balance at year 10.
15	Divestiture Fees	1% of the sales price plus an incentive fee of: B = 1%, P = 0%, O = 2%.
16	Net Cash Flows	Current Income plus Loan Repayments plus Divestitures Less Divestiture Fees.
17	Internal Rate of Return—100%	The Internal Rate of Return on the full face value of the UNS debt and cash contributed to the Fund.
18	— 60%	The Internal Rate of Return on the approximate secondary market value of the contributed debt.

CASE FIVE
Turner Federal Savings and Loan

Ellen Adams, assistant vice president at Turner Federal Savings and Loan, was facing a difficult assignment in July 1983. She had been asked by her manager, the senior vice president of finance, to recommend whether to continue or to abandon the S&L's pilot program for futures hedging. Turner Federal was under increasing regulatory scrutiny because of its low net worth, and Ellen knew that her professional advancement at Turner depended upon this analysis.

Turner Federal was a large, mutually owned urban institution with assets in excess of $6 billion. Like many S&Ls, Turner was founded as a neighborhood home financing association in the 1920s. As the city had grown, particularly after World War II, so had Turner. By 1983, it was the second-largest S&L in the city, and one of the 30 largest in the United States. Unlike other institutions, however, when interest rates had risen dramatically in 1980 and 1981, Turner had continued to make fixed-rate mortgages at lower rates than those offered by competitors. Its long-time CEO, affiliated with Turner Federal since shortly after its founding, continually stressed the institution's community responsibility.

By April 1982, the combination of high deposit interest rates and continued fixed-rate lending had led the District Federal Home Loan Bank to become concerned about Turner's extremely low net worth position. Observers from the bank frequently attended meetings of Turner's Asset/Liability and Investment committees. Management knew that it must formulate specific plans for improving the deteriorating capital position. In the summer of 1982, an out-of-state consulting firm was hired to analyze Turner's rate-sensitivity GAP position. Because of Turner's size and its lack of a system for coordinated data collection, the consulting firm's first report, submitted in September 1982, was based on the balance sheet as of April 30, 1982. Ellen planned to review a copy of this GAP analysis (Exhibit 5.1), as well as the most recent analysis (Exhibit 5.2), based on data from April 30, 1983.

After several weeks of meetings and discussions with the consultants, a hedging policy was developed and submitted to the board of directors for approval. Ellen had outlined the key features of the policy in preparation for her analysis (Exhibit 5.3). After ap-

proving the policy, Turner's management had decided to institute a pilot program, based on the sale of one GNMA contract and one T-bill contract. The plan was simply to watch the behavior of the two contracts over time, including the impact of margin calls on Turner's cash flow.

The incident that had prompted Ellen's current assignment was the recent price behavior of the GNMA futures contract. Although GNMA cash prices and futures prices normally were highly correlated, the basis had been much larger and more erratic than usual. The consultants had interpreted this price behavior as the result of what they called a "short squeeze." GNMA futures contracts were based on a standardized $100,000 par value, with an 8 percent coupon rate. In 1981 and 1982, however, extraordinarily high interest rates had caused new GNMAs to be issued with 16 percent and 17 percent coupons. Although interest rates had fallen since then, for technical reasons related to the nature of GNMA futures contracts and associated delivery procedures, holders of short contracts who were forced to deliver securities at the September 1983 contract expiration date would find it cheaper to deliver GNMAs with 16 percent and 17 percent coupons than those with other coupons. The consultants believed that with $2.5 billion in September futures contracts outstanding in the market, but only $1.4 billion total in GNMAs with 16 percent or 17 percent coupons, some holders of short contracts who could not obtain the high-coupon GNMAs to fulfill their delivery obligations would be at a disadvantage. The phrase *short squeeze* referred to the potential shortage of 16 percent and 17 percent GNMAs.

Because the price of the single GNMA contract Turner had sold had increased during the last week, the association had experienced several margin calls. As a result, some of the S&L's managers had concluded that hedging was too risky to be used as a serious financial management tool. In addition, some managers argued that the S&L was too large to use the futures markets. They believed that the volume of transactions Turner would require in order to significantly incorporate futures into the overall asset/liability management plan was larger than the futures markets could handle successfully. To support their argument, they pointed to

EXHIBIT 5.1   Turner Federal Savings and Loan GAP Analysis as of April 30, 1982 (Thousands)

	Month 1	Month 2	Month 3	Month 4	Month 5	Month 6	Quarter 3	Quarter 4	Quarters 5 and 6	Quarters 7 and 8	Years 3 and 4	Years 5+	Nonearning/ Noninterest-Bearing	Total
Assets														
Cash													$ 5,581	$ 5,581
Fed funds sold	$ 600													600
Investments	13,500	$ 18,045	$ 7,000	$ 8,000	$ 2,500	$ 6,560	$ 10,000	$ 24,100	$ 12,090	$ 114,001	$ 198,363	$ 118,704		532,863
Mortgages	22,420	23,420	23,620	24,620	24,920	25,120	72,460	72,460	144,920	144,920	579,680	3,219,705		4,378,265
Mortgage-backed securities	1,550	1,550	1,550	1,550	1,550	1,550	4,650	4,650	9,300	9,300	37,200	760,816		835,216
Other loans	2,175	2,175	2,175	2,175	2,175	2,175	6,525	6,525	13,050	13,050	52,200	19,368		123,768
Fixed assets													67,185	67,185
Other assets	1,400	1,400	1,400	1,400	1,400	1,400	4,200	3,000	6,000	6,210	22,509	50,749	205,219	306,287
Total assets	$ 41,645	$ 46,590	$ 35,745	$ 37,745	$ 32,545	$ 36,805	$ 97,835	$ 110,735	$ 185,360	$ 287,481	$ 889,952	$4,169,342	$277,985	$6,249,765
Average rate (%)	10.56%	10.09%	10.35%	11.08%	9.92%	10.13%	10.05%	10.44%	9.84%	10.80%	10.46%	9.82%		10.00%
Liabilities and Net Worth														
NOWs	$ 125	$ 125	$ 125	$ 125	$ 125	$ 125	$ 375	$ 375	$ 750	$ 750	$ 4,022	$ 63,200		$ 70,222
Passbooks	2,000	2,000	2,000	2,000	2,000	2,000	6,000	6,000	12,000	12,000	52,473	904,258		1,004,731
Fixed-term CDs	313,890	275,430	521,453	318,841	366,330	606,833	201,195	146,271	157,349	323,119	272,010	38,320		3,541,041
IRAs									27,036					27,036
Jumbo CDs	63,166	41,779	39,768	30,867	16,534	20,316	3,750	561	1,100	200	941			218,982
Reverse repos	522,050	20,312												542,362
Other borrowings	93,500	66,760	60,500	59,100	46,125	40,500	62,300	74,125	68,405	50,000	47,000	13,659		681,974
Net worth													$163,417	163,417
Total liabilities and net worth	$994,731	$ 406,406	$ 623,846	$ 410,933	$ 431,114	$ 669,774	$ 273,620	$ 227,332	$ 266,640	$ 386,069	$ 376,446	$1,019,437	$163,417	$6,249,765
Average rate (%)	13.93%	12.05%	12.99%	14.25%	12.96%	12.75%	10.40%	10.71%	11.31%	13.72%	11.82%	5.50%		11.58%
GAP	($953,086)	($ 359,816)	($ 588,101)	($ 373,188)	($ 398,569)	($ 632,969)	($ 175,785)	($ 116,597)	($ 81,280)	($ 98,588)	$ 513,506	$3,149,905	$114,568	
Cumulative GAP	($953,086)	($1,312,902)	($1,901,003)	($2,274,191)	($2,672,760)	($3,305,729)	($3,481,514)	($3,598,111)	($3,679,391)	($3,777,979)	($3,264,473)	($ 114,568)		
Rate differential	-3.37%	-1.96%	-2.64%	-3.17%	-3.04%	-2.62%	-0.35%	-0.27%	-1.47%	-2.92%	-1.36%	4.32%		-1.58%

EXHIBIT 5.2

Turner Federal Savings and Loan GAP Analysis as of April 30, 1983 (Thousands)

	Month 1	Month 2	Month 3	Month 4	Month 5	Month 6	Quarter 3	Quarter 4	Quarters 5 and 6	Quarters 7 and 8	Years 3 and 4	Years 5+	Nonearning/Noninterest-Bearing	Total
Assets														
Cash													$ 73,123	$ 73,123
Fed funds sold	$ 181,400													181,400
Investments	1,500	$ 595			$ 50		$ 1		$ 8,000	$ 36,032	$ 131,429	$ 83,680		261,287
Mortgages	17,474	17,747	17,747	$ 17,747	18,137	18,927	62,112	$ 114,600	201,067	176,734	582,133	2,262,818		3,507,516
Mortgage-backed securities	3,340	3,340	3,340	3,340	3,340	3,340	10,025	10,250	20,050	20,050	80,210	1,135,888		1,296,288
Other loans	214	214	214	214	214	214	636	636	1,066	1,281	135,442			140,345
Fixed assets													76,857	76,857
Other assets	73,063	1,184	1,184	1,184	1,184	1,184	3,553	2,513	5,025	5,244	18,839	53,791	717,899	885,847
Total assets	$ 277,264	$ 23,080	$ 22,485	$ 22,485	$ 22,925	$ 23,665	$ 76,327	$ 127,774	$ 235,208	$ 239,341	$ 948,053	$3,536,177	$867,879	$6,422,663
Average rate (%)	9.87%	9.70%	9.76%	9.76%	9.76%	9.77%	9.95%	10.56%	10.73%	10.52%	10.54%	10.45%		10.43%
Liabilities and Net Worth														
MMDAs	$ 756,000													$ 756,000
NOWs	262	$ 262	$ 262	$ 262	$ 262	$ 262	$ 786	$ 786	$ 1,575	$ 1,575	$ 8,521	$ 133,185		148,000
Passbooks	9,200	9,200	18,400	46,000	46,000	46,000	73,600	36,800	55,200	55,200	110,400	414,000		920,000
Fixed-term CDs	336,114	188,727	285,541	231,698	284,308	359,464	60,432	333,600	330,148	315,018	247,049	21,601		2,993,700
IRAs		10,500	21,500	2,364	2,129	2,799	3,880	5,532	59,969					108,673
Jumbo CDs	22,169	49,867	33,662	14,356	12,006	10,048	4,251	1,771	100		2,343			150,573
Reverse repos	346,688	28,666										805		376,159
Other borrowings	88,650	110,959	14,500	10,000	36,000	45,300	119,900	99,625	84,300	17,000	7,991	11,086		645,301
Net worth													$324,257	324,257
Total liabilities and net worth	$1,559,083	$ 398,171	$ 373,865	$ 304,680	$ 380,705	$ 463,873	$ 262,849	$ 478,114	$ 531,292	$ 388,793	$ 376,304	$ 580,677	$324,257	$6,422,663
Average rate (%)	8.90%	9.48%	8.90%	8.59%	8.77%	8.86%	8.60%	13.40%	11.70%	10.83%	8.12%	5.00%		9.20%
GAP	($1,281,819)	($ 375,091)	($ 351,380)	($ 282,195)	($ 357,780)	($ 440,208)	($ 186,522)	($ 350,340)	($ 296,084)	($ 149,452)	$ 571,749	$2,955,500	$543,622	
Cumulative GAP	($1,281,819)	($1,656,910)	($2,008,290)	($2,290,485)	($2,648,265)	($3,088,473)	($3,274,995)	($3,625,335)	($3,921,419)	($4,070,871)	($3,499,122)	($ 543,622)		
Rate differential	0.97%	0.22%	0.86%	1.17%	0.99%	0.91%	1.35%	−2.84%	−0.97%	−0.31%	2.42%	5.45%		1.23%

EXHIBIT 5.3   **Key Features of Turner Federal's Financial Futures Hedging Policy**

I.   The objectives of using interest rate futures to manage interest rate risk include:
   A.   To protect the value of mortgage loans, securities, and other rate-sensitive assets
   B.   To fix liability costs
   C.   To protect against other risks resulting from an imbalance between rate-sensitive assets and liabilities
[The policy then went on to specify what futures instruments would be considered; virtually all then available were named.]

II. The size of position limits will be determined by the amount of unmatched rate-sensitive assets and liabilities. Initially, positions less than or equal to 25 percent of mismatched rate-sensitive assets or liabilities are authorized.
III. Each hedge shall be accompanied by a statement providing the following information:
   A.   Purpose of the hedge (for example: "to protect asset value in the securities portfolio")
   B.   Contract to be used (the one with the highest price correlation to the cash instrument)
   C.   Number of contracts (determined by the cash position being hedged)

---

data on the volume of open-interest GNMA and T-bill futures contracts at selected points during the past year (Exhibit 5.4).

Before deciding whether to continue the program, the chief financial officer wanted one more close look at the current policy and pilot program, and Ellen had been selected for the assignment. She realized that, although her ultimate task was to recommend whether or not the pilot program should be continued, she would have to consider many important issues before coming to her decision. In particular, she believed she must analyze the following issues:

■ What types of hedges were appropriate
■ Whether concern about the size of Turner's hedging needs relative to the market were well-founded
■ Whether Turner's current policy statement (on which the pilot hedging program was based) adequately covered all the important decisions involved in a typical hedging transaction

■ Whether hedging, if maintained as a part of asset/liability management, should be internally managed or should continue to be externally managed by consultants and brokerage firms

---

EXHIBIT 5.4   **Open Interest in Selected Futures Contracts**

Date	Type of Contract	Open Interest (Number of Contracts)
7/14/82	September GNMA	18,871
	September T-bill	29,403
10/14/82	December GNMA	18,796
	December T-bill	26,410
1/14/83	March GNMA	15,569
	March T-bill	33,101
4/14/83	June GNMA	20,886
	June T-bill	26,042
7/14/83	September GNMA	29,020
	September T-bill	26,730

CASE SIX
Pricing Strips and the Term Structure

In the early 1980s, investment banks such as Merrill Lynch and Salomon Brothers began offering what are effectively zero-coupon bonds by "stripping" U.S. Treasury issues—that is, separating the coupons from the principal payments. Once separated, each coupon and each principal payment became separate zero-coupon bonds. Known as receipt products, these bonds have been created by a number of investment banks and are recognized by such feline names as CATS, TIGRS, COUGARS, and LIONS.[1] Such default-free financial products provide ideal vehicles for investors who may not want to deal with the problems of reinvesting coupon payments that accompany U.S. Treasury bonds.

Spurred by the innovations of Merrill and others, the U.S. Treasury, in 1985, introduced its own coupon-strippable product by designating some of its notes and bonds as eligible for stripping. Known as STRIPS (Separate Trading of Registered Interest and Principal of Securities), these products have become the dominant zero-coupon instrument. With prices quoted daily in the financial press, a U.S. Treasury strip is a claim to cash flow at a single maturity date. The cash flow for the strip is from either the coupon or principal payment of existing Treasury securities.

Transforming coupon bonds into "zero coupon" instruments like TIGRS or strips requires a thorough understanding of the valuation of debt claims. For there to be a profit in stripping bonds, the sum of the parts must be worth more than the whole bond. To determine this, each coupon and principal payment should be discounted at the appropriate discount rate for a pure discount instrument. After the present values of all the coupon and principal payments are summed, this total is then compared with the market price of the coupon bond. If the sum of the present values exceeds the coupon bond's value, stripping the coupon would be profitable. If the sum of the present values of coupon and principal payments is less than the coupon bond's value, one would want to reconstitute the bond.

As an example, consider a major institutional, investor who owned a large amount of 10-year maturity, 8 percent, default-free coupon bonds selling, given current market conditions, for 92.21 percent of face value (see Table 6.1). The investor was considering lengthening the average maturity of its bond portfolio. One alternative under consideration was to strip the 10-year bond and sell off the shorter maturity portions (1 to 2 years). The investor wondered what price might be obtained for cash flows of various maturities. Of further interest was what the current market revealed about the future course of interest rates.

---

[1] CATS, Certificates of Accrual on Treasury Securities, which are proprietary to Salomon Brothers, Inc., represent ownership interest in future interest and principal payments on selected U.S. government securities. CATS are listed on the New York Stock Exchange and have an active secondary market. In effect, CATS are zero-coupon bonds and are taxed accordingly. TIGRS, Treasury Investment Growth Receipts, are a Merrill Lynch product arising from stripping a Treasury bond of its coupons. They are similar in concept and operation to CATS and COUGARS, Certificates on Government Receipts. COUGARS is a trade name for A. G. Becker Paribas's U.S. treasury strips. LIONS, Lehman Investment Opportunity Notes, are a Treasury strip product marketed by Shearson Lehman Brothers.

Source: Darden Graduate School of Business Administration, University of Virginia.

Parts of this case were adapted from James C. Van Horne, *Financial Market Rates and Flows,* 3rd ed. (Englewood Cliffs, N.J.: Prentice-Hall, 1990). Copyright © 1990 by the Darden Graduate Business School Foundation, Charlottesville, VA.

TABLE 6.1	Prices of 8 Percent Coupon Bonds of Various Maturities
Maturity (in Years)	**Price as Percentage of Face Value**
1	100.00
2	100.00
3	99.21
4	98.49
5	97.18
6	95.99
7	94.90
8	93.92
9	93.02
10	92.21

Note: All bonds are default free and pay *annual* coupons of 8 percent of face value. (Annual coupons are assumed for simplicity.)

CASE SEVEN
Marine Corporation, 1991

Over the weekend of March 23–24, 1991, Willard Bunn III, chairman and chief executive officer of Marine Corporation of Springfield, Illinois, was preparing his recommendation on an important issue to come before the board of directors on the following Monday. The outcome of the issue would determine the 140-year-old company's future as an independent entity.

In front of Bunn was a proposed affiliation agreement from Banc One Corporation of Columbus, Ohio. In it, Banc One expressed its willingness to exchange .849 shares of its stock for each share of Marine. With the exception of a small office it had acquired in the Chicago Loop as part of the acquisition of a Wisconsin bank holding company in 1988, Banc One would in this way be making its initial entry into Illinois. Banc One intended to work through Marine's current management in expanding its presence in Illinois and to use Marine's holding company for further acquisitions under the new name of Banc One Illinois.

INDUSTRY BACKGROUND

The year 1990 was a disastrous one for commercial banking. Earnings plunged, and problem loans hit a post-World War II high. Exclusive of nonrecurring provisions for loans to less developed countries, profits of all U.S. commercial banks averaged .54% of assets in 1990, down from .80% a year earlier. Nonperforming loans as a percentage of assets jumped to 3.03% from 2.24% at year-end 1989. Credit problems were pervasive, as creditors and debtors worried about the effects of recession and the outcome of the war in the Persian Gulf. Large problems surfaced at some of the leading banks in the United States—the Bank of Boston, Midlantic, and the Bank of New England. Well over half of the 50 largest banks reported earnings declines, and 18 had reduced or omitted their dividends in the past two years. Few analysts questioned the survival of the banking system, because the industry was still profitable and most banks had reasonable levels of profitability. Nonetheless, industry analysts worried about the persistent problems in commercial real estate, highly leveraged transactions, Federal Deposit Insurance Corporation (FDIC) funding, and, with their stocks selling at discount to book value, banks' limited access to the capital markets.

Most analysts believed that, beyond 1991, industry consolidation would be the major theme for the decade and that nationwide interstate banking in one form or another was a certainty. Most also believed that mega-regionals, companies with over $100 billion in assets, would surface in different areas of the country, with Banc One, Norwest, and NCNB (formerly North Carolina National Bank and now NationsBank) figuring as likely players. Super-regionals, those banks with $20–$30 billion in assets, were expected to operate in one region of the country, such as the Midwest, and might include NBD (formerly National Bank of Detroit) and National City. Independent banks were thought to have bright futures if they were not an awkward size—too large to offer personal service but too small to offer nationwide services.

MARINE CORPORATION

Against this troubled backdrop, Marine Corporation closed its books on December 31, 1990, with the most successful year in its history. It reported record earnings for the 6th consecutive year, and for the first time, its equity capital exceeded $100 million. The company reported a return on assets of 1.12%—its highest return since 1935—and for the first time in at least 55 years, reported an ROA of more than 1.00% for 2 consecutive years. Marine ended 1990 with an equity-to-asset ration of 8.70%, robust by any standard. Nonperforming loans as a percentage of total loans dropped to .80% in 1990 from 1.22% at the end of 1989, and charge-offs for the entire year were a scant .28% of loans. The bank also had a relatively liquid investment portfolio with an average maturity of 1 year, 8 months. (See Exhibits 7.1 and 7.2 for Marine's income statements and balance sheets.)

This case has been prepared under the supervision of Professors Charles Meiburg of the Darden school and James Gentry of the University of Illinois as a basis for class discussion rather than an illustration of either an effective or ineffective handling of an administrative situation. Copyright © 1991 by the Darden Graduate Business School, Charlottesville, VA.

EXHIBIT 7.1	**Marine Corporation, 1991**

Marine Income Statements, December 31, 1988–90 (in thousands, except earnings per share)

	1990	1989	1988
Interest Income:			
Interest and fees on loans	$75,398	$69,055	$56,522
Interest on federal funds sold	6,156	3,191	3,743
Interest on investment securities			
U.S. government and agency securities	14,785	10,380	11,445
State and political subdivisions	1,378	1,556	1,848
Money market investments	176	196	203
Other	1,087	1,405	830
Total Interest Income	98,980	85,783	74,591
Interest Expense:			
Interest on deposits	53,127	45,181	38,288
Interest on short-term borrowings	2,054	2,091	1,573
Interest on long-term debt	263	311	576
Total Interest Expense	55,444	47,583	40,437
Net Interest Income	43,536	38,200	34,154
Provision for loan losses	2,978	2,916	2,823
Net Interest Income After Provision	40,558	35,284	31,331
Other Income:			
Trust Department revenues	6,588	5,398	4,663
Investment advisory revenues	1,110	1,255	1,278
Service fees	6,315	5,189	4,769
Data processing fees	702	665	671
Security gains	462	26	130
Other	4,083	3,540	2,945
Total Other Income	19,260	16,073	14,456
Other Expenses:			
Salaries	17,840	16,084	14,586
Pensions and other employee benefits	3,729	3,275	2,577
Equipment expenses	3,757	3,454	3,347
Occupancy expense	2,947	2,748	2,712
Fee expense	4,999	4,577	4,250
Other	9,322	8,053	8,210
Total Other Expenses	42,594	38,191	35,682
Income Before Income Taxes	17,224	13,166	10,105
Provision for income taxes	5,056	3,743	2,356
Net Income	$12,168	$ 9,423	$ 7,749
Earnings per Share	$1.90	$1.55	$1.29
Sharing Outstanding (000)	6,396	6,396	6,027

Marine had a lion's share of the commercial banking market in Springfield with 38 percent of the deposits and had meaningful presences in the other three markets where it had banks. Marine also had a young management team; the average age for the senior management group at the holding company was 44 years.

The company's flagship bank was organized in 1851, making Marine the oldest bank in Illinois. Jacob Bunn, one of its organizers, had arrived in Illinois from New Jersey in 1836. When Springfield was selected as Illinois's capital, he recognized the business potential in the area and opened a grocery store in the tiny prairie community that at the time was dotted with log cab-

EXHIBIT 7.2   **Marine Corporation, 1991**

Marine Balance Sheets, December 31, 1989–90
(in thousands)

	1990	1989
Assets:		
Cash and due from banks	$ 115,210	$ 88,729
Federal funds sold	67,330	83,110
Investment securities*	249,034	185,871
Loans:		
Commercial, financial, and agricultural	339,391	338,582
Real estate, construction	13,007	10,681
Real estate, mortgage	199,233	183,361
Installment	161,389	148,672
Total loans	713,020	681,296
Unearned discount	(12,892)	(12,110)
Reserve for possible loan losses	(10,274)	(9,202)
Net loans	689,854	659,984
Premises and equipment, net	23,129	22,827
Other Assets	29,622	29,544
Total Assets	$1,174,179	$1,070,065
Liabilities:		
Deposits:		
Non-interest-bearing demand	$ 207,488	$ 190,434
Savings and NOW accounts	337,545	312,459
Time	478,242	427,578
Total deposits	1,023,275	930,471
Short-term borrowings	34,177	30,810
Other liabilities	11,828	12,222
Long-term debt	2,709	3,214
Total Liabilities	$1,071,989	$ 976,717
Equity:		
Common stock, $.78125 par value	5,124	5,124
Surplus	27,529	27,529
Retained earnings	70,150	61,308
Less treasury stock, at cost	(613)	(613)
Total Stockholders' Equity	$ 102,190	$ 93,348
Total Liabilities and Stockholders' Equity	$1,174,179	$1,070,065

*Estimated market value $251,536 in 1990 and $187,334 in 1989.

ins. Finding no other bank in the community, Bunn and other investors founded the Springfield Marine and Fire Insurance Company, which contained a bank charter. The "Marine" name derived from its early business of financing barge traffic on the Illinois River in a time when waterways, more than the nascent road system, provided transportation for the nation's commerce. Among the bank's early depositors was a lawyer named Abraham Lincoln, who opened his second bank account with the Riggs Bank in Washington when he left Springfield to become the nation's 16th President. After Lincoln's assassination, Jacob Bunn was executor of his estate.

The Bunn family stayed active in the management of the company through the next four generations. Jacob's brother John had run the bank from 1902 to 1920, when Jacob Bunn, Jr., took over, to be succeeded by his brother, George W. Bunn, then by George's son, George W. Bunn, Jr., then by his nephew, Willard Bunn, Jr., and then in 1986 by Willard Bunn III, aged 47 in 1991.

Subsequent generations of the Bunn family had developed other Springfield-based businessess, including a large institutional grocery-supply business that grew from the original grocery store and that currently had for its chief operating officer Willard Bunn III's brother Robert. In the early 1960s, George R. Bunn had invented a new style of coffee maker that by 1991 was sold worldwide through the Bunn-O-Matic Corporation, whose chief executive officer was George R. Bunn's son and Willard's first cousin, Arthur H. Bunn.

The bank also prospered over the next century to become, by the late 1960s, the largest single bank in Illinois outside Chicago. This growth came despite Illinois's restrictive unit-banking laws. The Illinois legislature long resisted branch banking and only tardily passed progressive bank-holding-company laws. (One result of this foot dragging was that Illinois contained 1,200 individual banks, 10% of the nation's total.) When the legislature finally passed a holding-company law in 1981, Marine, which had long been prepared for this opportunity and which favored service-oriented economies such as the state capital it already served, quickly moved to the town housing the state university. Soon afterward, it acquired a bank in the town where State Farm Insurance Company had its headquarters. Marine had decided against joining a consortium of banks and, instead, pursued an independent course.

In its first two acquisitions, it used cash and notes as the mediums of exchange. By 1986, however, the company was considering using stock as a purchase vehicle and knew that it therefore had to add liquidity to its shares. Accordingly, with The Chicago Corporation as the lead underwriter, Marine had an initial public offering at a price, adjusted for stock splits, of $11.50. The company raised nearly $11 million, but its interest was more in raising the number of its shareholders than in raising capital. Adding the new shareholders reduced the Bunn family's interest in the company from 75 percent to 60 percent. This interest was spread among 51 family members living in states scattered from New York to California and from Illinois to Florida.

In the late 1980s, Marine's pace of acquisitions began to slow. It did acquire another bank in the university town of Champaign-Urbana and added another bank and a savings and loan branch in Monticello, a town 20 miles west of Champaign-Urbana, but it was stalled in its effort to make meaningful entries into a number of other attractive central Illinois banking markets.

Although the pace of Marine's geographical expansion slowed, the pace of its functional expansion did not. During the last half of the decade, Marine made meaningful strides in developing an electronic debiting service for insurance companies, first for those companies in its opening area and later for companies located anywhere in the country. In 1990 Marine originated 39 million transactions through the system, second only to Chase Manhattan. [See Exhibit 7.3 for a complete listing of the top originators of payments through automated clearing houses (ACH).] For competitive reasons, Marine did not disclose the actual earnings of this product line but did tell industry analysts that the product made a solid contribution to pretax earnings. Those earnings were derived from both fees and demand-deposit balances.

By the decade's end, Marine also operated the fourth largest bank Farm-Management Department in the country overseeing 145,000 acres of some of the world's most fecund farmland. In addition, its Trust Department had been successful in developing a widely used custodian service.

In the midst of these developments, Marine continued its tradition of community involvement. It supported civic undertakings through both staff time and cash contributions in all the markets it served. In 1986 the City of Springfield awarded Marine Bank the first Mayor's Award for the Arts ever given to a local corporation. Marine was one of a handful of Springfield companies that could be counted on in almost every civic drive; indeed, "Marine" was a household word for both customers and noncustomers.

Also in the midst of these developments, potential suitors from the surrounding states were calling on Marine's management from time to time to talk about possible affiliations. For various reasons, none of these discussions turned serious. Marine's response to all the parties had consistently been that the company was not for sale, was not soliciting offers, but did have a fiduciary responsibility to consider serious offers if they arose. Marine gave that exact response to Banc One's management at an informal meeting in early May of 1990, but Marine continued to talk to Banc One, along with several other companies, over the following months.

Over those months, the company counseled regularly with its traditional investment bankers at The Chicago Corporation. When the discussions turned more serious, the company took the added step of retaining the services of one of the country's top bank analysts, William Weiant, to counsel the Board not on the particulars of any proposed transaction, but rather on the banking industry overall and the intrinsic value of Banc One paper in particular.

Most analysts predicted another good year for Marine in 1991. Earnings-per-share projections for 1992 hovered around $2.05 to $2.25. In January the board of directors had voted to raise the annual dividend rate by 40% to 72¢ per share, more in line with the industry's standard payout ratio. Marine's stock currently traded around $23.00, with a 52-week trading range of $15.25 to $23.75. During 1990, an average of 80,000 shares were traded each month.

BANC ONE CORPORATION

Banc One also had the best year in its history in 1990. Net income rose 16.7% over 1989 to $426 million, 6th among the nation's 50 largest banks. Earnings per share of $2.76 were 9.75% above 1989 and marked the 22nd consecutive year the company had achieved increased earnings for its owners. This record of consistent growth was unsurpassed among the country's 50 largest banking organizations. In fact, the next closest bank to Banc One's record had only 13 years of

EXHIBIT 7.3	**Marine Corporation, 1991**

Top Originators of ACH Payments

Rank 1990	Rank 1989		Debit Transactions	Credit Transactions	Total Transactions	Annual Growth
1	1	Chase Manhattan Bank NA, New York	89,377,645	15,933,045	105,310,690	4%
2	2	Marine Bank of Springfield Ill.	38,090,666	1,374,527	39,465,193	26
3	4	Norwest Bank of Minnesota NA, Minneapolis	30,015,049	7,852,415	37,867,464	31
4	3	Bank of America NT&SA, San Francisco	16,905,607	18,876,597	35,782,204	18
5	5	Northern Trust Co., Chicago	7,891,557	14,105,772	21,997,329	14
6	6	Mellon Bank NA, Pittsburgh	7,207,905	12,672,853	19,880,758	22
7	7	First National Bank of Atlanta	3,372,273	14,807,227	18,179,500	25
8	8	Bank One Columbus NA, Ohio	11,055,511	4,812,580	15,868,091	21
9	29	First National Bank of Chicago	8,308,565	4,479,223	12,787,788	110
10	12	Harris Trust & Savings Bank, Chicago	8,189,531	4,482,701	12,672,232	28
11	11	First Bank NA, Minneapolis	5,649,847	6,302,886	11,952,733	21
12	9	First National Bank of Boston	3,041,842	8,904,167	11,946,009	10
13	70	Citibank Delaware, New Castle	8,651,646	2,838,010	11,489,656	378
14	16	Connecticut National Bank, Hartford	3,251,757	7,879,330	11,131,087	39
15	14	Security Pacific National Bank, Los Angeles	4,626,105	6,330,383	10,956,488	25
16	23	Wells Fargo Bank NA, San Francisco	2,721,038	7,674,839	10,395,877	59
17	15	Chemical Bank, New York	3,670,668	6,721,939	10,392,607	28
18	26	First National Bank of Omaha	8,265,587	2,035,868	10,301,455	60
19	13	Wachovia Bank & Trust Co. NA, Winston-Salem	6,631,588	3,641,905	10,273,493	11
20	10	NCNB Texas National Bank, Dallas	NA	NA	9,381,129	(7)
21	24	CoreStates Financial Corp., Philadelphia	2,642,236	6,195,178	8,837,414	35
22	21	Citizens & Southern National Bank, Atlanta	2,190,177	6,329,785	8,519,962	29
23	25	Manufacturers Hanover Trust Co., New York	2,695,146	5,613,915	8,309,061	29
24	18	Citibank NA, New York	NA	NA	8,136,491	10
25	20	NBD Bank NA, Detroit	2,744,120	5,298,880	8,043,000	15
26	39	United Bank of Denver NA	3,997,376	3,831,147	7,828,523	63
27	19	Texas Commerce Bank NA, Houston	NA	NA	7,516,504	4
28	30	Trust Company Bank, Atlanta	4,749,242	2,726,848	7,476,090	25
29	33	First National Bank of Maryland, Baltimore	2,548,000	4,921,000	7,469,000	29
30	32	AmSouth Bank NA, Birmingham	5,943,521	732,494	6,676,015	15
31	31	Boatmen's First National Bank, Kansas City	6,066,752	560,248	6,627,000	11
32		First Union National Bank of Fla., Jacksonville	3,082,641	3,380,998	6,463,639	*
33	35	National City Bank, Cleveland	4,051,456	2,335,993	6,387,449	21
34	38	Continental Bank NA, Chicago	3,017,710	3,194,081	6,211,791	28
35	37	Norwest Bank of Iowa NA, Des Moines	3,896,468	2,287,862	6,184,330	25
36	22	First City, Texas-Houston NA	NA	NA	6,089,213	(8)
37	27	First Union National Bank, Charlotte	3,063,978	3,022,939	6,086,917	(5)
38	34	First Interstate Bank of California, Los Angeles	1,669,586	3,967,857	5,637,443	1
39	36	Valley National Bank, Phoenix	3,024,737	2,600,335	5,625,072	9
40	28	Shawmut Bank NA, Boston	1,259,472	4,225,415	5,484,887	(12)
41	40	Boatmen's National Bank, St. Louis	3,275,497	2,086,068	5,361,565	14
42	47	Fifth Third Bank, Cincinnati	851,851	4,001,051	4,852,902	29
43	52	First Wisconsin National Bank, Milwaukee	2,150,759	2,672,144	4,822,903	46
44	43	Connecticut Bank & Trust Co. NA, Hartford	1,588,721	3,117,070	4,705,791	11
45	45	NCNB National Bank of N. Carolina, Charlotte	1,969,764	2,493,816	4,463,580	14
46	46	First Interstate Bank of Denver NA	2,952,953	1,466,678	4,419,631	14
47	50	United Jersey Bank, Hackensack	1,880,139	2,485,632	4,365,771	24
48	42	Ameritrust Co. NA, Cleveland	2,538,367	1,815,492	4,353,859	1
49	17	M&I Marshall & Ilsley Bank, Milwaukee	NA	NA	4,133,874	(44)
50	58	Pittsburgh National Bank	1,027,773	3,030,512	4,058,285	45

Source: *American Banker,* reproduced by permission.

increased earnings, and only 4 of the top 50 banks had as many as 5 consecutive years of increases. Banc One's ROA of 1.54% made it #1 in its size category in the country.

The strength of Banc One's balance sheet was unassailable. Management sought consumer and commercial middle-market loan business and shunned large concentrations, foreign loans, speculative real-estate ventures, and highly leveraged transactions. Adhering to a past chairman's decision of making loans no farther away than "where you can ride your bicycle on a Sunday afternoon," Banc One tended to make loans only in its operating areas. Moreover, its equity-to-asset ratio was 9.5% at the end of 1990, the 5th consecutive year Banc One recorded the highest capital ratio among the 50 largest banks in the nation. (See Exhibits 7.4 and 7.5 for financial information on Banc One.)

Banc One's acquisition program had begun earlier than Marine's—in 1967, when it bought its first bank in Mansfield, Ohio. Over the next 24 years, it continued to be an aggressive acquirer, considering acquisitions almost a separate line of business. If the Marine transaction went through, Marine would become Banc One's 99th acquisition.

The core of Banc One's acquisition program was referred to as "The Uncommon Partnership." A central tenet of that partnership was that Banc One would not dilute its shareholders' interest for an acquisition, but it could, for that reason, warrant to the acquiree that, once the acquiree was a shareholder, Banc One would not dilute its holdings in subsequent acquisitions. Another tenet was the consistent approach of "decentralizing the people and centralizing the paper." This approach, although it did lead to some employees taking different jobs within the overall company after an acquisition, did not result in wholesale layoffs. (In fact, the holding company Banc One acquired in Wisconsin had 8% more people on its payroll one year after the acquisition than at the beginning.) Banc One personnel generally did not sit on the affiliates' boards, although in the case of Marine, Executive Vice President William P. Boardman, in charge of the mergers and acquisitions program, would be joining the newly formed board of Banc One Illinois.

The Partnership approach seemed to work well. Most new affiliates were able to increase their ROAs to Banc One's target 1.50% level within a few years after joining Banc One. (See Exhibit 7.6 for further information on The Uncommon Partnership.)

Banc One had made numerous acquisitions in Ohio since 1967, but in 1987 it acquired its first large bank outside Ohio, the $4 billion American Fletcher Bank in Indianapolis, Indiana. After this acquisition, a new holding-company structure organized the banks in each state into separate statewide holding companies, as indicated in Exhibit 7.7. In 1990, in what became the basis for a "breakout" strategy, Banc One acquired MCorp in Texas, which, as one analyst put it, combined "Midwestern stability with Texas-sized growth." Banc One's holding-company expansion plans become more opportunistic than previously. Because the company had a robust capital position and a high multiple on its stock, it could look at interesting opportunities in any part of the country, and one area it had long targeted for future expansion was Illinois. Because of Illinois' restrictive banking laws, however, the national trigger for that state was effective only at December 1, 1990.

Like Marine, Banc One had a technological bent and, in fact, was the acknowledged leader in banking innovation. It was Banc One that first made wide use of automatic teller machines, first processed Merrill Lynch's cash-management account, and later pushed hard for home banking. In the early 1980s, Banc One Senior Vice President John Fisher was so towering a figure in banking technology that he was able to charge a "consulting" fee to visiting bankers. During this time, Banc One, unlike most of its competitors, also began to make substantial commitments to financial research and development, somewhere in the range of 3% of pretax profits.

The company traced its origins to the opening of City National Bank in 1868 in Columbus, Ohio. As with Marine, one family had largely dominated Banc One's management, particularly in the last fifty years. In 1935, at the bottom of the Depression, John H. McCoy relinquished the presidency of a small town bank in Marietta, Ohio, to become president of City National Bank, Columbus's third largest bank. Early on, John H. McCoy infused a highly retail orientation into the bank. Upon his father's death in 1958, John G. McCoy was named Chief Executive of the company. John G. McCoy expanded on his father's retail banking beginnings using the tools of research and high technology, concepts somewhat foreign to most banks

| EXHIBIT 7.4 | **Marine Corporation, 1991** |

Banc One Corporation Consolidated Income Statement, December 31, 1988–90 (in thousands)

	1990	1989	1988
Interest Income:			
Interest and fees on loans and leases	$2,302,514	$2,166,533	$1,875,841
Interest and dividends on securities	440,899	446,013	367,831
Other interest income	58,139	38,510	27,806
Total Interest Income	2,801,552	2,651,056	2,271,478
Interest Expense			
Interest on deposits	1,279,415	1,272,739	1,013,102
Other borrowings	281,231	261,982	197,923
Total Interest Expense	1,560,646	1,534,721	1,211,025
Net Interest Income	1,240,906	1,116,335	1,060,453
Provision for losses on loans of leases	300,332	197,496	183,422
Net Interest Income after Provision	940,574	918,839	877,031
Other Income:			
Income from fiduciary activities	88,130	80,247	74,719
Service charges on deposit accounts	105,195	94,493	86,989
Loan processing and service income	280,673	219,886	181,273
Other income	184,206	117,300	120,089
Total Other Income	658,204	511,926	463,070
Other Expenses:			
Salaries and related costs	501,224	441,400	413,907
Net occupancy expense, exclusive of depreciation	68,508	58,756	53,711
Depreciation and amortization	64,951	56,961	54,230
Other expenses	467,987	410,307	371,278
Total Other Expenses	1,102,670	967,424	893,126
Income before income taxes, equity in earnings of Banc One, Texas, NA, and cumulative effect of change in accounting principle	496,108	463,341	446,975
Income tax (provision) benefit	(119,888)	(115,099)	(106,787)
Income before equity in earnings of Banc One, Texas, NA, and cumulative effect of change in accounting principle	376,220	348,242	340,188
Equity in earnings of Banc One, Texas, NA	47,153		
Income before cumulative effect of change in accounting principle	423,373	348,242	340,188
Cumulative effect of changing method of accounting for income taxes		14,626	
Net Income	$ 423,373	$ 362,868	$ 340,188
Net Income per share	$2.76	$2.52	$2.37
Weighted Average Shares Outstanding (000)	152,259	143,130	142,351

at the time. Moreover, John G. McCoy began within Ohio the now familiar pattern of building Banc One through mergers and acquisitions. In 1984, John G. McCoy was named chairman of the Executive Committee, and his son, John B. McCoy was elected chairman and chief executive officer of Banc One. John B. McCoy, age 48 in 1991, has been the steward of the interstate, and potential national, franchise Banc One

has built. Through owning nearby summer homes in Michigan and winter homes in Florida, members of the McCoy and Bunn families had been personal friends for a quarter of a century.

Banc One described its atmosphere as quasi-"family" throughout the company. It fostered open communications at all levels, and its operating style was decentralized and collegial. Continuity was high

EXHIBIT 7.5   Marine Corporation, 1991

Banc One Corporation Consolidated Balance Sheets, December 31, 1988–90 (in thousands)

	1990	1989
Assets:		
Cash and due from banks	$ 1,881,276	$ 1,687,789
Deposits in other banks, interest bearing	22,648	216,524
Short-term investment	605,755	308,809
Securities*	5,271,721	5,133,227
Loans and Leases		
Commercial, financial, and agricultural	7,769,760	7,562,870
Real estate, commercial	1,249,165	1,153,756
Real estate, construction	1,089,900	937,960
Real estate, residential	2,863,333	2,162,314
Installment (net of unearned income)	4,304,185	3,739,793
Credit card	2,326,254	1,631,805
Leases (net of unearned income)	760,660	720,838
Total loans and leases	20,363,257	17,909,336
Reserve for possible losses	320,205	251,065
Net loans and leases	20,043,052	17,658,271
Note receivable from FDIC	416,250	
Investment in Banc One, Texas, NA	352,553	
Bank premises and equipment, net	475,758	437,104
Other	1,266,922	1,110,513
Total Assets	$30,335,995	$26,552,237
Liabilities:		
Deposits:		
Demand, non-interest bearing	$ 3,729,105	$ 3,544,595
Demand, interest bearing	2,331,155	2,129,957
Time and savings	16,255,758	15,277,653
Total Deposits	22,316,018	20,952,205
Short-term borrowings	3,747,891	2,199,162
Long-term borrowings	581,042	371,563
Other liabilities	791,565	750,153
Total Liabilities	$27,436,516	$24,273,083
Equity:		
Preferred stock	23,156	23,909
Common stock	2,876,323	2,255,245
Total Equity	2,899,479	2,279,154
Toal Liabilities and Equity	$30,335,995	$26,552,237

*Estimated market value $5,349,800 in 1990 and $5,177,500 in 1989.

among its officers, and newly acquired management teams tended to stay in place. One research firm calculated that, of the company's 51 presidents of affiliated banks, 24 had headed their banks since the time of their mergers into Banc One, 14 had been promoted from within their own banks, 11 had been promoted from other banks within the company, and 2 were brought in from outside the company. Banc One nurtured its talented individuals, and its managers developed strong working relationships with one another over time.

By the end of 1990, Banc One had assets of $30.3 billion and operated 52 affiliate banking organizations, with 747 offices, in Indiana, Illinois, Ken-

| EXHIBIT 7.6 | **Marine Corporation, 1991** |

Banc One's Uncommon Partnership

EMPHASIZE HIGH MARGIN PRODUCTS	**AFFILIATE AUTONOMY**
Retail Loans	Management Responsive to Local Needs
Special Lending Niches	Pricing Flexibility
MARKET DIVERSITY AND BALANCE	Peer Competition
	Ability to Share Success
	Develop Management Pool
Avoid Economic and Industry Concentration	**CENTRALIZED SUPPORT**
Extensive Branch System for Core Deposits	Increase Efficiency
Balanced Deposit and Loan Generations	Product Standardization
	Concerns Technical Expertise

Source: *Bank Management,* November 1900.

tucky, Michigan, Ohio, Texas, and Wisconsin. It also operated additional affiliates that engaged in travel services, trust services, mortgage banking, consumer finance, equipment leasing, credit-related life insurance, investment management, data processing, discount brokerage, and venture-capital services.

The market obviously endorsed Banc One's strategy: although it ranked only 22nd in asset size of the nation's banks, its market capitalization of $4.4 billion placed it #3 in the country, behind only Bank of America and J. P. Morgan, each of which was over three times Banc One's size. In January the company had raised its annual dividend to $1.16 per share, and its shares were trading around $33.00, with a 52-week trading range of $19.00 to $35.625. Industry analysts had varying projections for the company's earning per share, but the average numbers were about $3.00 for 1991 and $3.36 for 1992. In 1990 Banc One traded an average of 5.2 million shares per month.

REFLECTIONS

As did anyone in his profession, Willard Bunn knew of the commanding presence of Banc One in the banking industry and knew that it possessed all the characteristics of a sound banking enterprise. It had success-

fully avoided bad loans; it had a strong presence in the consumer business, which provided the company a stable source of deposits; it had developed such fee-producing businesses as corporate trust management and trust products; and it had diversified its business by both geography and product.

However strong the company, and however comfortable Bunn was with the unhurried pace of the conversations, he did have some general concerns. He wondered, for instance, if Banc One's credit quality, although still strong, would decline in the face of added financial pressure on consumers during the recession. In the 1980s, borrowing as never before, Americans had increased their debts, including mortgages, to almost a year's income (compared with a couple of months' income in 1950). Second, Banc One's stock had a beta of approximately 1.00 (versus Marine's 0.89), which meant its movement was highly correlated to the overall stock market performance. Accordingly, the stock price could fall drastically in a bear market, even if the company's fundamentals were sound. With a fixed rate governing the exchange of shares, Marine officials were concerned that a sudden drop in Banc One's stock price could dull the luster of an attractive deal.

Bunn thought he would be prudent to determine what Marine's ROA would have to be for the transaction, at the stated exchange offer, to be nondilutive for Banc One. He believed his directors would want to have this information, because they would not want to commit the company to a goal that would be impossible to meet.

He also wanted to think about the implications of the intended reporting line for Marine. To get started, Banc One Illinois, unlike the other State holding companies, would not report directly to Columbus. Rather, its reporting line would run to Bruce Bailey, Vice Chairman of Banc One Indiana, who had responsibility for the ten Indiana banks outside of Indianapolis. Banc One felt that until Banc One Illinois achieved a critical mass of assets in the area of $4–5 billion, it made no sense to report to corporate headquarters. Added to that, Mr. Bailey was drawing on thirty years of experience with the Banc One company in various management roles, and Banc One management thought he would be particularly helpful to Marine officials in acclimating them to both the Banc One system and its culture.

EXHIBIT 7.7 **Marine Corporation, 1991**

Organization of Banc One Corporation

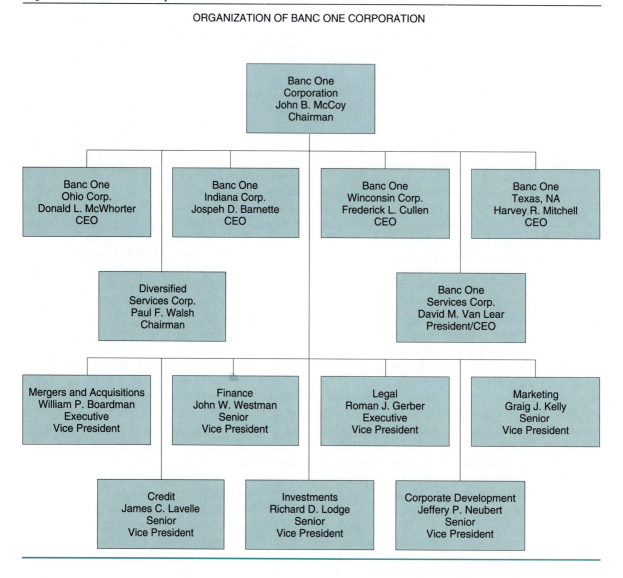

ORGANIZATION OF BANC ONE CORPORATION

RECOMMENDATIONS

As Bunn saw it, his job had two aspects. First, he had to recommend how to proceed with the Banc One overture. Marine could either decline the proposal or elect to take the next step and continue to talk about other aspects of the affiliation. He knew the directors would be concerned with the effects on all four of the company's constituencies—shareholders, employees, customers, and communities—and he had to be prepared to defend his position on each. Second, if he recommended proceeding with negotiations, he had to present his ideas on crafting an agreement that would deal with the concerns he had raised. The board of directors meeting was set for 9:00 a.m. on March 25.

CASE EIGHT
American Express Company and Shearson Lehman Brothers

In January of 1988, Annie Brownell, a senior portfolio manager for Diversified Pension Investments, Inc., began a lengthy review of American Express Company, one of Diversified's key holdings over the past decade. All of Diversified's investments were reviewed periodically and efforts were made to introduce "zero based" thinking as to why a particular stock should continue to be held. The review would take into account not only long term investment values but also how each stock had performed relative to Diversified's expectations and in relation to changing market conditions. Annie was not herself especially familiar with American Express ("AXP") which was why she had been asked to take a good look at it and make recommendations to Diversified's Investment Committee as to what should be done with the stock. She had gathered together annual reports for the past few years, 10K Reports and proxy statements that AXP had sent out to shareholders. She also had copies of prospectuses covering the public offerings by AXP of shares of Fireman's Fund Insurance Co. and Shearson Lehman Brothers, and recent news clippings regarding AXP and Shearson's tie with Nippon Life Insurance Co. of Japan and Shearson's recent acquisition of E.F. Hutton Co.

1986 had been a banner year for AXP. Its net income had passed the $1 billion level for the first time ever to $1.25 billion, up 54% on the previous year, thanks to record performances from each of its four major divisions: American Express Travel Related Services ("TRS"), Shearson Lehman Brothers ("SLB"), American Express Bank ("AEB") and Investors Diversified Services ("IDS"). "To put these achievements in perspective," Annie read in the 1986 AXP Annual Report, "in 1976 the Company reported net income of $194 million and revenues of $2.4 billion [from a business] that was primarily a travel-related services company with a large property-casualty insurance business." The report also commented on

AXP's successes to date and outline its continuing broad strategic objectives.

We have achieved distinction in the financial and travel services industries by drawing on the special attributes of the strong brand names and multiple distribution channels that comprise our family of companies. At the same time, we have targeted only those market segments where we have the ability to be a leader in market share and generate significant financial return. We have not tried to be all things to all people . . .

As we look ahead, the broadest strategic objectives of American Express are:

- *To sustain our position as a quality leader . . .*
- *To increase the precision with which we segment our markets . . .*
- *To expand our presence in growth markets worldwide . . .*
- *To remain a leader in the application of new technologies . . .*
- *To maintain our ability to attract top talent . . .*
- *And, above all, to never lose sight of our principal goal—to increase shareholder value.*

Annie knew that the last several years had been extremely active for AXP, but, nonetheless, years that were profitable for its shareholders. From the beginning of 1980 until the close of 1987, its stock price had risen 229%, as compared with the rise in the S&P index of 500 stocks of 120%. But by the end of 1987 strains were beginning to appear in AXP's banking and investment banking businesses.

She had put together a brief chronology of major events affecting the company (Exhibit 8.1), certain financial and market price information (Exhibits 8.2 through 8.6), and extracts from the Shearson Lehman Brothers prospectus (Exhibit 8.4) and an article from the financial press about the Hutton acquisition (Exhibit 8.5) for further study. A key question seemed to be whether AXP's success was actually the result of a well conceived overall strategy or simply had come about as a result of management's opportunistic

This case was prepared by Prof. Roy C. Smith in February 1988 for use at the New York University Graduate School of Business Administration as a basis for classroom discussion. It is not to be used for any other purpose without the consent of the author. (Revised August 1992).

EXHIBIT 8.1 **American Express Company**

Chronology of Certain Events, 1979–1987

December 1979	AXP acquires 50% interest in Warner Amex Cable Communications Inc., a cable television venture for $175 million.
December 1981	AXP purchases 100% of Shearson Loeb Rhodes, Inc. for 21.3 million shares of stock ($930 million). Shearson Loeb Rhodes is itself a firm made up of seven other securities firms. Sandy Weil, Shearson CEO, becomes Chairman of the AXP Executive Committee, and later President of AXP.
September 1981	Shearson acquires the Boston Company, and other regional securities firms.
December 1983	AXP acquires for $520 million, in cash and stock, five Trade Development Banks from Edmond Safra, a prominent international financier, who becomes Chairman and CEO of American Express International Bank, Ltd. and AXP's largest individual shareholder.
January 1984	AXP acquires Investors Diversified Services, a major distributor and manager of mutual funds for $727 million.
May 1984	Shearson American Express merges with Lehman Brothers Kuhn Loeb, in a colorful transaction valued at $380 million and documented by Ken Auletta's book *Greed and Glory on Wall Street.*
August 1985	AXP sells its 50% interest in Warner Amex Cable Communications venture to Warner for $450 million plus the assumptions of AXP's share of the venture's debt. The net gain to AXP after offsetting charges was $60 million. The 1985 AXP Annual Report noted: ". . . it was probably a mistake for us to invest in cable systems. Their potential as a distribution channel for financial and travel services never panned out . . ."
August 1985	Edmond Safra buys back certain parts of the Trade Development Banks business, resigns as CEO of AEB and as a director of AXP.
October 1985	AXP sells 59% of Fireman's Fund Insurance in an initial public offering for $910 million "because if the cyclicality of the property-casualty insurance business and its direction mainly towards commercial markest . . . which do not match growth and consumer orientations of our other businesses."

October 1985	AXP announces plans to repurchase 10 million shares of its common stocks and in 1986 authorization was secured to repurchase an additional 10 million shares, to offset the issuance of approximately 15.9 million new shares from warrants, stock option plans, dividend reinvestment and for other purposes. By December 1986 over 17 million shares were repurchased for about $1 billion.
October 1985	AXP reacquires the 25% minority interest in First Data Resources Inc. for $38 per share ($250 million), which it had sold in an initial public offering in 1983 for $14 per share.
December 1985	Sandy Weil resigns as President of AXP.
May 1986	AXP sells further shares of Fireman's Fund Insurance for $386 million, further reducing its holdings to 27%. Small gain on sale is offset by other costs and expenses.
December 1986	A further sale of Fireman's Fund Insurance for $215 million (also at no net gain) results in termination of "insurance services" as a line of business for reporting purposes.
March 1987	AXP sells 18% of Shearson Lehman Brothers to Nippon Life Insurance Co., Japan's largest life insurance company, for $508 million in a transaction that involves other relationships between Nippon and both AXP and Shearson.
March 1987	AXP announces a 2 for 1 stock split.
April 1987	AXP announces that it now "owns or manages assets, including assets managed or administered for others, in excess of $200 billion," of which Shearson Lehman Brothers accounted for $158 billion.
May 1987	AXP sells 18% of Shearson Lehman Brothers to the public, and Shearson sells additional new shares at the same time, in an offering of 18 million shares at $34 per share; AXP reports a net gain of $142 million on the transaction which reduces its holdings in Shearson to 60%.
June 1987	AXP announces that its international banking unit added $600 million to its reserves for loan losses, resulting in AXP's reporting an after-tax charge against its second quarter earnings of $520 million.

EXHIBIT 8.1 *CONTINUED*

July 1987	AXP announces a continuation of the 1985/86 stock repurchase program, authorizing a further repurchase of 40 million shares over the next 2–3 years.
October 1987	The stock market crashes. Shearson Lehman Brothers experiences losses, especially as a result of co-managing the U.S. tranche of the ill-fated British petroleum stock underwriting.
December 1987	Shearson Lehman reports fourth quarter loss of $95 million and announces layoff of 1,500 employees. Moody's down-

grades Shearson Lehman Brothers Senior Subordinated debt to A-3, from A-2; S&P retains AA-rating on this debt.

January 1988   AXP reports that AEB is adding a further $350 million to loan loss reserves and that AXP has itself experienced losses of $104 million for the 4th quarter of 1987; net income for 1987, before extraordinary and discontinued items, appears to be $533 million, down from $1.1 billion for 1986.

EXHIBIT 8.2   **American Express Company Summary Operating Results**

(Millions, except per share and percentage amounts)	1986	1985	1984	1983	1982
Operating Results					
Revenues	$14,652	$11,849	$9,655	$6,648	$5,400
Percent increase in revenues	24	23	45	23	13
Expenses	13,039	10,600	8,707	5,794	4,585
Income Taxes	503	437	314	286	206
Income from continuing operations	1,110	812	634	568	609
Percent increase	37	28	11	(7)	13
Net Income	1,250	810	610	515	581
Percent increase	54	33	18	(11)	11
Per Common Share					
Income from continuing operations	4.92	3.56	2.90	2.79	3.17
Net Income	5.55	3.55	2.79	2.53	3.02
Dividends	1.38	1.32	1.28	1.26	1.23
Number of shares outstanding	215	222	217	213	191

EXHIBIT 8.3   **American Express Company Summary Balance Sheet Data**

($ Millions)	1986	1985	1984	1983	1982
Assets					
Time deposits	$ 4,989	$ 6,299	$ 5,223	$ 3,997	$ 2,063
Investment Securities					
Carried at Cost:	18,484	12,615	9,468	8,896	3,585
Carried at lower of cost or market:	1,396	627	315	211	81
Carried at market:	16,561	11,158	8,506	1,420	698
Securities purchased under agreements to sell	12,626	7,745	4,915	534	278
Accounts receivable	22,685	18,140	13,233	10,383	8,143
Loans and discounts, net	11,634	9,152	6,941	6,486	4,217
Other assets	11,101	9,041	8,113	6,980	4,618
Total Assets	99,476	74,777	56,714	38,907	23,683
Liabilities					
Deposits and credit balances	$22,446	$16,203	$13,262	$12,511	$ 6,810
Travelers checks outstanding	2,990	2,679	2,454	2,362	2,177

($ Millions)	1986	1985	1984	1983	1982
Liabilities					
Securities sold under agreements to purchase	18,573	9,960	7,797	730	436
Insurance and annuity reserves	6,403	5,405	4,801	3,194	376
Short-term debt	14,620	10,401	7,941	4,585	3,269
Long-term debt	8,400	5,399	3,856	2,642	1,795
Other liabilities	20,318	19,361	11,996	8,840	5,781
Shareholders' Equity	5,726	5,369	4,607	4,043	3,039

EXHIBIT 8.4   **American Express Company Industry Segment Data**

($ Millions)	1986	1985	1984
TRS			
Revenues	$ 5,951	$ 4,934	$ 4,358
Pretax income	924	843	703
Income from continuing operations	599	515	436
Assets	18,830	16,116	13,645
Shearson Lehman Brothers			
Revenues	4,600	3,246	2,280
Pretax income	488	350	168
Income from continuing operations	316	291	103
Assets	53,978	34,927	22,735
American Express Bank			
Revenues	1,685	1,568	1,548
Pretax income	175	181	193
Income from continuing operations	175	161	156
Assets	17,730	15,657	13,768
IDS Financial Services			
Revenues	2,395	2,201	1,576
Pretax income	140	108	95
Income from continuing operations	96	76	62
Assets	10,206	8,601	6,411
Consolidated			
Revenues	14,652	11,849	9,655
Pretax income	1,613	1,249	948
Income from continuing operations	1,110	812	634
Assets	99,476	74,777	56,714

EXHIBIT 8.5   **American Express Company Consolidated Balance Sheet**

($ Millions)	9/30/87	12/31/86
Assets		
Cash	$ 3,165	$ 2,650
Time Deposits	4,150	4,989
Investment securities at cost	21,494	18,484
Investment securities, lower of cost or market	1,983	1,396
Investment securities at market	17,377	16,561
Securities purchased, agreements to resell	18,422	12,626
Accounts receivable	27,942	22,685
Loans and discounts	12,493	11,634
Land, buildings and equipment	2,343	2,172
Assets held in segregated accounts	1,915	1,304
Other assets	5,410	4,975
Total Assets	116,694	99,476
Liabilities		
Deposits and credit balances	25,751	22,446
Travelers checks outstanding	4,192	2,990
Accounts payable	12,098	8,414
Securities sold repurchase agreements	20,215	18,573
Securities sold, short positions	8,794	4,835
Insurance reserves	8,898	7,910
Short-term debt	14,116	14,620
Long-term debt	9,596	7,723
Collateralized mortgage obligations	162	677
Liabilities in segregated accounts	1,890	1,280
Other liabilities	5,285	4,282
Total Liabilities	110,997	93,750
Shareholders' Equity	5,697	5,726
Total Liabilities and Equity	116,694	99,476

EXHIBIT 8.6   **American Express Company**

Certain Market Price Data

1. AXB Stock Price History, 1980–1987
2. AXP Indexed Stock Price History relative to the S&P 500
3. AXP Indexed Stock Price History relative to a Composite of Selected Companies
4. AXP Indexed Price/Earnings History
5. AXP Indexed Price/Earnings Ratios relative to the S&P 500
6. AXP Indexed Price/Earnings Ratios relative to a Composite of Selected Companies
7. Shearson Lehman Brothers Indexed Stock Price History relative to a composite of Selected Companies

behavior during a fantastic bull market. Why, in particular, after investing so much in Shearson, which AXP clearly believed had strong potential for leadership in the investment banking industry, did it reduce its holdings to 60%? Had AXP's strategy changed? If so, why? The crash certainly had its effect; if AXP was getting out of investment banking, should Diversified follow suit? AXP was a key holding in the financial services sector of Diversified's portfolios; it would have to be replaced if sold. But with what?

Question: In about two pages, summarize the conclusions and recommendations you would make if you were in Annie's position.

American Express Closing Stock Price History

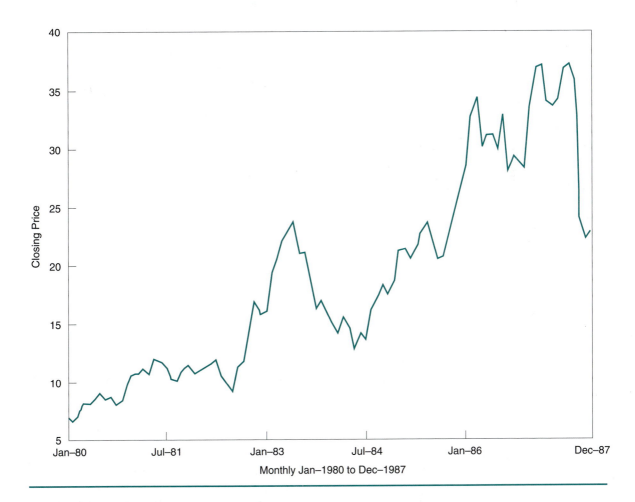

Monthly Jan–1980 to Dec–1987

American Express Indexed Stock Price History Versus the S&P 500

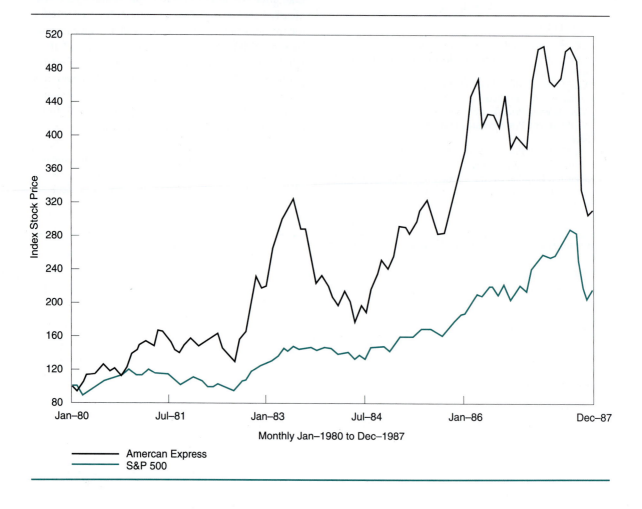

American Express Indexed Stock Price History Versus a Composite of Selected Companies

Composite: Merrill, Lynch & Co. and Citicorp.

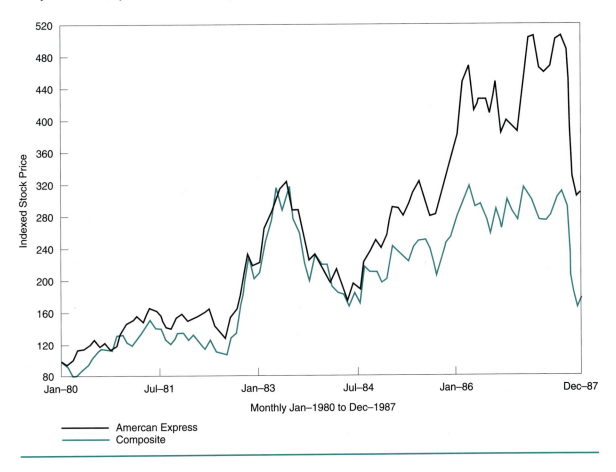

American Express Price/Earnings Ratio History

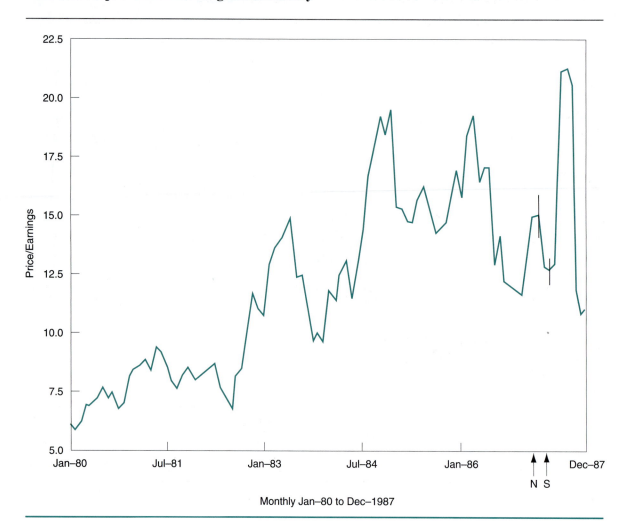

Monthly Jan–80 to Dec–1987

American Express Price/Earnings Ratio History Versus the S&P 500

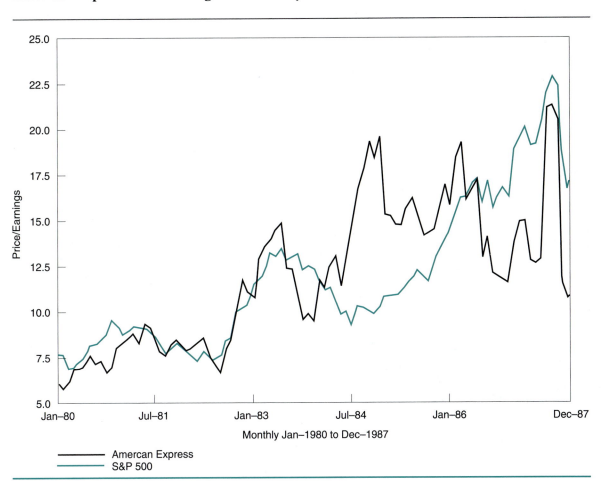

American Express Price/Earnings Ratio History Versus a Composite of Selected Companies

Composite: Merrill, Lynch & Co. and Citicorp.

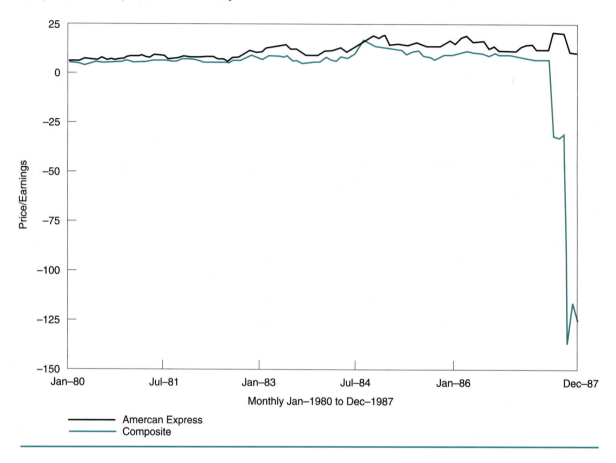

Shearson Lehman Bros. Indexed Stock Price History Versus a Composite of Selected Companies

Composite: Merrill, Lynch & Co. and Citicorp.

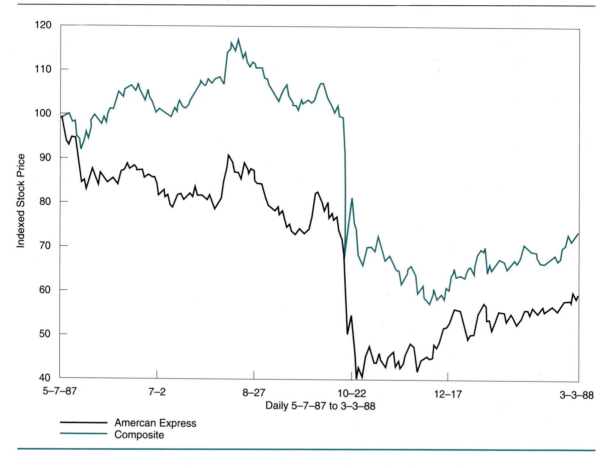

| EXHIBIT 8.7 | **American Express Company** |

Selected data from the May 7, 1987 Prospectus for the initial public offering of 18 million shares of Common Stock of Shearson Lehman Brothers Holdings Inc. offered by American Express Company.

PROSPECTUS

18,000,000 SHARES

SHEARSON LEHMAN BROTHERS HOLDINGS INC.

COMMON STOCK

All of the 18,000,000 shares of Common Stock of Shearson Lehman Brothers Holdings Inc. ("Holdings") offered hereby are being sold by American Express Company ("American Express"). Of these shares, 14,000,000 shares are being offered in the United States by the U.S. Underwriters and 4,000,000 shares are being offered outside the United States in a concurrent offering by the International Underwriters (collectively, the "Offerings"). See "Underwriting."

On April 15,1987, Holdings sold 13,000,000 shares of its Cumulative Convertible Voting Preferred Stock, Series A (the "Series A Preferred Stock") to Nippon Life Insurance Company ("Nippon Life"). In addition, at or about the closing of the Offerings, Holdings will sell or reserve for issuance a maximum of 7,500,000 shares of its restricted Common Stock to certain employees of Holdings and its subsidiaries and 1,000,000 shares of Common Stock to the Shearson Lehman Brothers Holdings Inc. Employee Stock Ownership Plan (the "ESOP"). See "Related Offerings."

Prior to the Offerings and the related transactions described above, American Express owned all of the outstanding Common Stock of Holdings. Upon completion of the Offerings and these related transactions, approximately 60.6% of the outstanding Common Stock of Holdings will be owned by American Express (assuming that the over-allotment options granted to the U.S. Underwriters and the International Underwriters in the Offerings are not exercised), approximately 13% will be owned by Nippon Life, up to approximately 7.4% will be owned by employees of Holdings and its subsidiaries and approximately 1% will be owned by the ESOP (in each case assuming conversion of the Series A Preferred Stock into Common Stock).

For information relating to the factors that were considered in determining the initial offering price, see "Underwriting." Although Holdings will not receive any of the proceeds from the shares sold by American Express in the Offerings, the aggregate net increase in Holdings' stockholders' equity resulting from the sale of the Series A Preferred Stock, the sale of Common Stock to employees and the other transactions described under "Capitalization" will be approximately $628.6 million.

The Common Stock has been accepted for listing on the New York Stock Exchange and the Pacific Stock Exchange.

THESE SECURITIES HAVE NOT BEEN APPROVED OR DISAPPROVED BY THE SECURITIES AND EXCHANGE COMMISSION NOR HAS THE COMMISSION PASSED UPON THE ACCURACY OR ADEQUACY OF THIS PROSPECTUS. ANY REPRESENTATION TO THE CONTRARY IS A CRIMINAL OFFENSE.

	Price to Public	Underwriting Discounts and Commissions (1)	Proceeds to Selling Stockholder (2)
Per Share	$34.00	$1.80	$32.20
Total (3)	$612,000,000	$32,400,000	$579,600,000

EXHIBIT 8.7 *CONTINUED*

(1) Holdings and American Express have agreed to indemnify the U.S. Underwriters and the International Underwriters against certain liabilities, including liabilities under the Securities Act of 1933. See "Underwriting."
(2) Before deducting expenses payable by American Express estimated at $2,416,550.
(3) American Express has granted the U.S. Underwriters a 30-day option to purchase up to 1,550,000 additional shares on the same terms and conditions as set forth above solely to cover over-allotments, if any. The International Underwriters have been granted a similar option to purchase up to 450,000 additional shares. If the options are exercised in full, the total Price to Public, Underwriting Discounts and Commissions and Proceeds to Selling Stockholder will be $680,000,000, $36,000,000 and $644,000,000, respectively. See "Underwriting."

The shares of Common Stock offered by this Prospectus are offered by the U.S. Underwriters subject to prior sale, to withdrawal, cancellation or modification of the offer without notice, to delivery to and acceptance by the U.S. Underwriters and to certain further conditions. It is expected that delivery of the certificates for the shares will be made at the office of Shearson Lehman Brothers Inc., New York, New York, on or about May 14, 1987.

SHEARSON LEHMAN BROTHERS INC.

BEAR, STEARNS & CO. INC.	**THE FIRST BOSTON CORPORATION**
GOLDMAN, SACHS & CO.	**MERRILL LYNCH CAPITAL MARKETS**
MORGAN STANLEY & CO.	**SALOMON BROTHERS INC.**
INCORPORATED	

May 7, 1987

PROSPECTUS SUMMARY

The following summary is qualified in its entirety by the more detailed information and financial statements appearing elsewhere in this Prospectus. Except as otherwise indicated herein, all share and per share data retroactively reflect a recapitalization of Holdings effected in April 1987 and all references in this Prospectus to ownership percentages of Common Stock are calculated assuming full conversion of the Series A Preferred Stock into Common Stock.

THE COMPANY

Holdings is a holding company which, through Shearson Lehman and other subsidiaries, is one of the leading full-line securities firms serving the United States and foreign securities and commodities markets. The Company's principal activities include securities and commodities trading as principal and agent; securities underwriting and investment banking and financial advisory services; private client services, and asset management (including fiduciary and administrative services) and real estate services. Based on total capital for regulatory purposes (including subordinated debt) of $2.973 billion at March 31, 1987, Shearson Lehman is the third largest member firm of the New York Stock Exchange, Inc. (the "NYSE"). The Company conducts its business from its principal headquarters in New York City and, as of December 31, 1986, from 310 other offices located in the United States and from 22 international offices. Prior to the completion of the Offerings and the other transactions described herein, Holdings has been a wholly owned subsidiary of American Express.

EXHIBIT 8.7 *CONTINUED*

Common Stock Outstanding after the Offerings and Related Transactions

	Number of Shares Outstanding
Owned by American Express	60,500,000(1)
Owned by public	18,000,000(1)
Owned by Nippon Life (assuming conversion of the Series A Preferred Stock)	13,000,000(2)
Owned by employees of the Company (restricted shares)	7,368,417(3)
Owned by the ESOP	1,000,000(4)
Total	99,868,417

(1) Assumes that the over-allotment options granted to the U.S. Underwriters and the International Underwriters are not exercised. If the options are exercised in full, American Express will sell a total of 20,000,000 shares of Common Stock to the public and will continue to own a total of 58,500,000 shares.

(2) On April 15, 1987, Holdings sold 13,000,000 shares of Series A Preferred Stock to Nippon Life. See "Related Offerings—Sale of Series A Preferred Stock to Nippon Life."

(3) Contingent upon the closing of the Offerings, Holdings will issue up to 4,868,417 shares of its restricted Common Stock to participants in the Shearson Lehman Brothers Deferred Profit-Sharing Program (the "Program") in exchange for their relinquishment of all present and future rights under the Program, and will reserve for possible future issuance to Program participants outside the United States an additional 131,583 shares, for a total of 5,000,000 shares issued or reserved for issuance. Holdings will also sell a maximum of 2,500,000 shares of its restricted Common Stock to certain employees of the Company (including the Program participants) and grant such employees options to purchase up to 2,500,000 shares of Common Stock (the "Senior Executive Options"). The shares of Common Stock to be sold to certain employees and to be issued to participants in the Program (collectively, the "Restricted Employee Shares") will be subject to certain restrictions on transfer and other conditions, including the continuation of employment with the Company or its affiliates for up to five years. Holdings will also grant options to purchase 1,007,000 shares of Common Stock to certain key employees of the Company not acquiring Restricted Employee Shares (the "Key Employee Options"). See "Related Offerings—Offerings to Employees of the Company."

(4) Contingent upon and concurrently with or during the 30 day period following the closing of the Offerings, Holdings will sell 1,000,000 shares of Common Stock to the ESOP at a price per share equal to the per share proceeds to American Express from the sale of Common Stock in the Offerings (if the ESOP sale is concurrent therewith) or not more than the fair market value of the Common Stock (if the ESOP sale occurs thereafter). See "Related Offerings—Shearson Lehman Brothers Holdings Inc. Employee Stock Ownership Plan" and "Management—Compensation Pursuant to Plans—Shearson Lehman Brothers Holdings Inc. Employee Stock Ownership Plan."

INCREASE IN HOLDINGS' STOCKHOLDERS' EQUITY

The sale by Holdings of Series A Preferred Stock to Nippon Life, Common Stock to employees of the Company and the consummation of the other transactions described herein will result in an estimated aggregate net increase in Holdings' stockholders' equity of approximately $628.6 million consisting of: (i) net proceeds of $508.3 million from the sale of 13,000,000 shares of Series A Preferred Stock at a price per share of $39.10, (ii) net proceeds of $51.0 million from the sale of a maximum of 2,500,000 Restricted Employee Shares at a price per share of $20.40, (iii) net proceeds of $32.2 million from the sale of 1,000,000 shares of Common Stock to the

EXHIBIT 8.7 *CONTINUED*

ESOP (assuming the sale occurs concurrently with the closing of the Offerings) and (iv) the reduction of long-term debt by approximately $69.3 million (representing the accrued liability at March 31, 1987 to current participants in the Program) upon the relinquishment of all present and future rights under the Program, *less* (v) a $32.2 million loan by Holdings to the ESOP in connection with the acquisition of 1,000,000 shares of Common Stock by the ESOP. See "Related Offerings" and "Capitalization."

DIVIDENDS

The Board of Directors of Holdings intends to pay quarterly dividends on the outstanding shares of Common Stock beginning with an initial dividend of $.1875 per share payable with respect to the second quarter of 1987. See "Dividends."

LISTING

The Common Stock has been accepted for listing on the NYSE and the Pacific Stock Exchange, with a symbol of SHE.

RELATIONS WITH AMERICAN EXPRESS

Upon completion of the Offerings and the related transactions described under "Related Offerings," American Express will own approximately 60.6% of the outstanding Common Stock of Holdings (Approximately 58.6% if the U.S. Underwriters' and International Underwriters' over-allotment options are exercised in full). American Express has advised Holdings that it has no present plans to reduce its interest in Holdings through sales or other dispositions. For as long as American Express owns more than 50% of Holdings voting stock, it will continue to have the power to approve any action requiring a vote of the majority of the voting stock of Holdings and to nominate and elect any or all of Holdings' directors. American Express is contractually obligated to vote for two directors to be designated by Nippon Life. See "Agreements Among American Express, Holdings and Nippon Life."

Holdings' Board of Directors is divided into three classes. Class III is initially comprised of five members, two of whom are both officers and directors of American Express, two of whom are outside directors of American Express and one of whom is an advisor to the Board of Directors and former chief executive officer of American Express. Until such time as American Express ceases to own 40% or more of Holdings' voting stock during each day of any consecutive seven months, the majority vote of the Class III directors will be required in addition to the vote of the Board of Directors to approve certain significant corporate actions, including certain mergers, consolidations and acquisitions or dispositions of assets, issuances of capital stock, the declaration of dividends, certain capital expenditures, certain amendments to Holdings' Restated Certificate of Incorporation or By-Laws, changes in Holdings' Chief Executive Officer, changes in the number of directors and the filling of vacancies on the Board of Directors, the incurrence or guaranty of certain indebtedness, the liquidation of Holdings and the establishment of committees of the Board of Directors.

THE COMPANY

Holdings is a holding company which, through Shearson Lehman and other subsidiaries, is one of the leading full-line securities firms serving the United States and foreign securities and commodities markets. The Company's principal activities include securities and commodities trading as principal and agent; securities underwriting and investment banking and financial advisory services; private client services; and asset management (including fiduciary and administrative services) and real estate services. Based on total capital for regulatory purposes (including subordinated debt) of $2.973 billion at March 31, 1987, Shearson Lehman is the third largest member firm of the NYSE.

EXHIBIT 8.7 *CONTINUED*

The Company was originally built through internal growth and then expanded in a series of mergers and acquisitions. The Company was incorporated in 1965 under the name Carter, Berlind & Weill, Inc. as the successor to a partnership formed in 1960. Among the Company's predecessor firms, whose origins date back to as early as 1850, were: Hayden Stone & Co.; Shearson Hammill & Co.; Loeb Rhoades & Co.; Hornblower & Weeks; Lehman Brothers; and Kuhn Leob & Co. Many of these acquisitions occurred in the 1970s prior to the acquisition of Shearson Lehman by American Express in June 1981. Even after its acquisition by American Express in June 1981, the Company has been operated largely as an autonomous enterprise and, despite its expansion during the past 15 years, has enjoyed significant continuity in its management personnel.

Over the past decade, the Company has followed a strategy of actively seeking to diversify its activities within the securities and related industries. Since 1977, when it was largely a commission broker, the Company has significantly expanded the scope of its business activities both domestically and worldwide, focusing on investment banking, capital markets, private client services and asset management and real estate, all of which are supported by the Company's Administration and Operations Group. The relative balance of the Company's businesses should act to reduce the effects on the Company of the cyclical fluctuation typical in the securities industry. Financial stability is also provided by the many sources of recurring income, such as interest income and asset management and administration fees.

The Company has established a significant presence in the international securities markets, and has full-service securities operations in London, through Shearson Lehman Brothers International, Inc. ("Shearson Lehman Brothers International") and its affiliates, and in Tokyo. Full-service securities offices also have been opened or are in the process of being established in Switzerland, Hong Kong, Australia, Italy, France, Germany, Spain and other overseas locations. This strategy of international expansion has been highlighted by the Company's recent acquisition of L. Messel & Co. ("Messels"), a member of the London Stock Exchange, and its minority interest in The McLeod Young Weir Corporation, one of Canada's largest full-service securities firms.

At the same time, the Company has developed one of the largest retail distribution networks in the United States securities industry. The Company has over 5,600 Financial Consultants—account executives who manage the financial affairs of a client and offer advice on a wide range of financial products—based in 311 offices nationwide and servicing over 1.7 million active client accounts. The Company also has approximately 326 sales persons serving international retail and institutional clients from its international offices. During the year ended December 31, 1986, approximately 69% of the equity securities underwritten by the Company were purchased by retail investors. This strong retail distribution capability, together with a strong institutional and international placement capacity, enables the Company to achieve a balanced and broad distribution of securities and to underwrite sizable offerings.

In an environment where securities firms that once acted as agent are increasingly assuming the role of principal, the Company's strong capitalization provides it with a significant competitive advantage. The Company's capital base has enabled it to take significant principal trading positions in the securities markets, to make direct equity investments in leveraged buy-out transactions and to facilitate mergers and acquisitions by providing bridge loans and guaranteeing the placement of debt and equity securities.

The Company is committed to the innovation and development of products designed to satisfy specific needs of issuers and investors, and its investment bankers work closely with its institutional and retail sales forces in designing new products to meet these needs. Examples of significant new products developed by the Company include Money Market Preferred™ Stock ("MMP"™), Interest Rate Caps, Floating Interest Rate Short Tranche Securities℠ ("FIRSTS"℠) and, most recently, Convertible Money Market Preferred™ Stock ("CMMP"™).

The Company has supported the growth in its domestic and international securities business through significant commitments to sophisticated data processing and telecommunications technology, including the recent completion of a 740,000 square foot state-of-the-art information services facility, the Faulkner Center, in New

EXHIBIT 8.7 *CONTINUED*

York City at a cost of approximately $209 million. This facility has the capacity to handle significantly in excess of the Company's current processing and settlement requirements.

Holdings was incorporated in Delaware on December 31, 1983. Holdings' principal executive offices are located at American Express Tower, World Financial Center, New York, New York 10285 and its telephone number is (212) 298-2000.

RELATED OFFERINGS

SALE OF SERIES A PREFERRED STOCK TO NIPPON LIFE

On April 15, 1987, Holdings sold 13,000,000 shares of Series A Preferred Stock to Nippon Life for a cash purchase price, as adjusted, of $508.3 million, or $39.10 per share. Holders of the Series A Preferred Stock are entitled to receive preferential dividends at an annual rate equal to 5% of the per share purchase price, payable quarterly on a cumulative basis.

Founded in 1898, Nippon Life is one of the world's largest life insurance companies and the largest insurance company in Japan with assets of $90.2 billion. Nippon Life has sales representatives located throughout Japan and representative offices in New York, London, Sydney, Frankfurt, Toronto and Singapore. Nippon Life has the world's largest life insurance in force with $1.253 trillion at December 31, 1986. In addition, Nippon Life is an institutional investor, lender and real estate developer.

Subject to the receipt of approval by the Federal Deposit Insurance Corporation (the "FDIC"), which is expected to be obtained by October 15, 1987, (a) the holders of Series A Preferred Stock will be entitled to one vote per share and will vote together with the holders of Common Stock on all matters on which the Common Stock is entitled to vote, and (b) the Series A Preferred Stock will be convertible on a share for share basis into Common Stock (subject to adjustment in the event of any stock splits, stock dividends, recapitalizations or similar events). The holders of Series A Preferred Stock will vote separately as a class on any proposed modifications to the terms of the Series A Preferred Stock. For a complete description of the terms of the Series A Preferred Stock, see "Description of Capital Stock."

In connection with the sale of the Series A Preferred Stock, Holdings, American Express and Nippon Life entered into certain agreements relating to, among other things, the following: nomination by Nippon Life of up to two directors to Holdings' Board of Directors; maintenance of American Express' voting interest in Holdings above certain levels; if American Express seeks to reduce such interest below such levels, Nippon Life's right to (i) purchase certain shares of Holdings Common Stock from American Express or (ii) require Holdings to register the Common Stock issuable upon conversion of the Series A Preferred Stock under the Act or sell shares of Series A Preferred Stock to American Express; limitations on the transferability of Nippon Life's interest in Holdings; Nippon Life's agreement not to increase its equity interest in Holdings above 33⅓% for 25 years; certain pre-emptive rights to permit Nippon Life to maintain its equity interest in Holdings; Nippon Life's right to require American Express to purchase its Series A Preferred Stock if FDIC approval is not obtained by October 15, 1987; and the establishment of certain cooperative efforts between Holdings and Nippon Life. See "Agreements Among American Express, Holdings and Nippon Life."

OFFERINGS TO EMPLOYEES OF THE COMPANY

Most aspects of the Company's business are dependent on highly skilled individuals and the Company seeks to encourage these individuals to remain in its employ. On or about the closing of the Offerings, Holdings will sell or reserve for issuance a maximum of 7,500,000 Restricted Employee Shares to employees of the Company, will grant nonqualified stock options to employees of the Company to purchase up to 3,507,000 shares of its Common Stock and will sell 1,000,000 shares of its Common Stock to the ESOP as follows:

EXHIBIT 8.7 *CONTINUED*

SELECTED CONSOLIDATED FINANCIAL DATA

The following table sets forth selected consolidated financial data for the Company for the periods indicated, and is qualified by reference to the more detailed financial statements, including the notes thereto, included elsewhere herein. The selected consolidated data for each of the five years in the period ended December 31, 1986 are derived, except for note 2 below, from consolidated financial statements examined by Coopers & Lybrand, independent certified public accountants. The selected consolidated data for the three months ended March 31, 1986 and 1987 are derived from unaudited consolidated financial statements also appearing herein and which, in the opinion of management, include all adjustments, consisting only of normal recurring adjustments, necessary for a fair statement of the results for the unaudited interim periods. The Income Statement Data for the three months ended March 31, 1987 are not necessarily indicative of the results that may be expected for the entire year ending December 31, 1987.

	Year Ended December 31,					Three Months Ended March 31,	
	1982	1983	1984	1985	1986	1986	1987
	(dollars in millions, except per share data)						
INCOME STATEMENT DATA (1):						(unaudited)	
Revenues:							
Commissions	$ 444	$ 598	$ 536	$ 713	$ 938	$ 238	$ 302
Investment banking	211	386	425	623	890	126	172
Market making and principal trans-							
actions, net	218	304	477	715	983	341	295
Interest and dividends	303	351	584	825	1,193	254	338
Investment advisory fees	89	110	145	230	310	66	95
Mortgage banking	30	41	70	57	71	14	25
Other	23	21	25	83	215	75	33
	1,318	1,811	2,262	3,246	4,600	1,114	1,260
Expenses:							
Compensation and benefits	589	820	992	1,394	1,919	442	546
Interest	162	206	467	658	1,030	227	306
Communications	119	145	193	223	277	61	74
Occupancy and equipment	74	99	151	191	236	54	68
Advertising and market							
development	37	58	99	110	139	27	36
Brokerage, commissions and clear-							
ance fees	31	35	33	40	50	13	17
Professional services	28	23	53	76	112	19	31
Other	50	100	105	204	349	123	62
	1,090	1,486	2,093	2,896	4,112	966	1,140
Income before taxes	228	325	169	350	488	148	120
Provision for income taxes	104	151	64	149	172	58	44
Net income (2)	$ 124	$ 174	$ 105	$ 201	$ 316	$ 90	$ 76
Net income per share (2) (3)					$ 4.03		$ .97

EXHIBIT 8.7 *CONTINUED*

	Year Ended December 31,					Three Months Ended March 31,	
	1982	1983	1984	1985	1986	1986	1987
	(dollars in millions, except per share data)						
BALANCE SHEET DATA (1):						(unaudited)	
Total assets	$6,351	$9,044	$22,720	$34,927	$53,978	$37,821	$56,622
Total liabilities (exluding long-term indebtedness)	5,490	7,969	20,961	32,431	49,284	35,077	51,090
Long-term indebtedness	309	365	810	1,319	3,336	1,519	4,169
Total stockholders' equity	552	710	949	1,177	1,358	1,225	1,363
Book value per share (3)	$ 7.04	$ 9.05	$ 12.09	$ 15.00	$ 17.30	$ 15.61	$ 17.36
Total capital of Shearson Lehman for regulatory purposes (including subordinated debt)	$ 867	$1,081	$ 1,823	$ 2,171	$ 2,823	$ 2,454	$ 2,973

(1) Includes the results of operations of Lehman Brothers since May 11, 1984, the date of its acquisition.

(2) The Company will amortize ratably over the period of the restrictions described under "Management—Restrictions on Restricted Employee Shares, Senior Executive Options and Key Employee Options" the excess of the per share initial public offering price of unrestricted Common Stock in the Offerings over the effective cost to the employees of the Restricted Employee Shares and the excess of such per share initial public offering price over the exercise price per share of the Senior Executive Options and the Key Employee Options. The resulting average annual charge to income before taxes during such period will not exceed $28.3 million ($33.3 million if the period of the restrictions is reduced as described under "Management Restrictions on Restricted Employee Shares, Senior Executive Options and Key Employee Options"). Upon the relinquishment of all present and future rights of participants in the Program, the Company and American Express will, however, be relieved of any further obligations under the Program. See "Related Offerings—Offerings to Employees of the Company." For the year ended December 31, 1986, the first year of the Program's operation, the Company recorded a charge to income before taxes of approximately $50 million for the benefit of participants in the Program.

In addition, the Company will amortize ratably over the period during which the indebtedness related to the ESOP is outstanding an amount equal to the principal plus the cost of funding such indebtedness.

(3) Net income and book value per share are based on 78,500,000 shares of Common Stock outstanding after giving effect to the recapitalization of Holdings effected during April 1987. Prior to the closing of the Offerings. American Express will contribute to Holdings up to 8,500,000 shares of Common Stock, as described under "Related Offerings." Net income per common share is not presented for years other than the most recent year as all shares have been owned by American Express and such presentation would not be meaningful.

CASE NINE
Salomon Brothers and the Treasury Scandals

Most of the major Wall Street firms benefitted from the expansion of securities activity in the eighties, but none more than Salomon Brothers, the quintessential Wall Street trading house. The success of the firm was widely admired in the industry and its market-power was considered second to none. But in 1991, the behavior of senior Salomon officials in connection with bidding in auctions for U.S. Treasury securities almost brought the firm to its end.

EARLY DAYS

The firm was founded in 1910 by Arthur, Herbert and Percy Salomon with $5,000 of capital when the three brothers left their immigrant father's firm to form their own money brokerage. Salomon Brothers began trading in foreign government bonds in 1915, and became the second authorized dealer in U.S. government securities in 1917, when volume was tiny by today's standards. By the early 1920s, the firm had specialized in fixed-income business and money brokerage constituted only a minor part of its activity. The Salomon partners, however, were considered niche players— specialists in a particular sector of the market. They were not included among the great German Jewish banking firms established in the nineteenth century, nor among the investment banks known for their corporate clients, of which the early Salomon had few, if any.

The Salomon partners made a decent living, but were not especially visible until the late 1960s, when they decided to expand into common stocks on the back of their bond trading knowhow by aggressively bidding for large blocks of shares from institutional investors or corporate issuers. In 1967, Salomon ranked fourth among all underwriters of U.S. securities; in 1977, second, and ten years later, first.

SALOMON IN THE EIGHTIES

In 1981 Salomon shocked Wall Street by announcing that it was selling out to Philip Brothers (later Phibro

Inc.), a large publicly-owned commodities trader for $550 million in cash and convertible securities. The deal was thought to have been pushed through by John Gutfreund, the firm's chairman since the retirement in 1978 of William ("Billy") Salomon, Gutfreund's predecessor and mentor. Billy and the other retired partners were only told of the deal after it had been struck. They would not receive any share in the $250 million premium paid by Phibro over Salomon's book value. Gutfreund and David Tendler, CEO of Phibro, were to become co-CEOs of the new firm. The Phibro side, however, fell apart as commodities profits dwindled, Tendler was forced out and Gutfreund, a one-time English major at Oberlin college and the son of a Brooklyn truck company owner who was a golfing friend of Billy Salomon's, became sole CEO in 1984.

The culture at Salomon, traditionally unsophisticated but paternalistic, became rougher and more political under Gutfreund who saw himself as a central delegator of great authority and influence to those who could be competitive and make money. Salomon's internal atmosphere was considered by many of its competitors as substantially more savage than most. Michael Lewis, a former bond salesman at Salomon based his book *Liars Poker* on anecdotes about the firm that portrayed it as a kind of Animal House for delinquent millionaires.

Trading dominated the firm. Those who didn't trade (or at least sit on the trading floor) were considered paper pushers, secondary players. The firm's culture valued boldness, flare, innovation, initiative and perhaps most of all, street-smarts. It disparaged pedigree, affectations, timidity and hesitation. The culture was binding and almost all of the firm's senior people were lifetime employees. They believed that to make a mark you did something dramatic, like offering to buy $1.4 billion of stock from Time-Warner (which Salomon had done successfully in 1991) and worrying about the consequences later. Sometimes you would get it wrong, and lose a bundle, but if you knew what you were doing you would make a bundle more often than not. If you didn't know what you were doing, you'd be out of there fast. If you knew your markets and had the courage to "bite the ass off a bear," as Gutfreund put it, then you would make money. In a

This case was prepared by Professor Roy C. Smith of the Stern School of Business in June 1992 for classroom use only.

marketplace overflowing with new Treasury and corporate securities, Salomon made out very well.

S&Ls, SWAPS, AND CMOs

Salomon had an advantage which it used to propel its position upwards in the early 1980s—its extensive contacts with the S&L industry. As bond market specialists, Salomon had taken the trouble to cultivate hundreds of S&Ls as customers for their government securities business. When the S&Ls got into trouble because of rising interest rates, they asked Salomon to help.

The firm proposed using "interest rate swaps" as a way of converting some of the S&L's below-market fixed-rate mortgage exposure to variable-rate exposure instead. Under such a swap, Salomon would enter into a contract with the S&L in which it would accept a fixed-rate of interest from the S&L for a specified amount, in exchange for paying the S&L a variable-rate of interest for the same amount. Thus the S&L could pass on its fixed-rate income flow from certain mortgages to Salomon, and replace it with a variable-rate income flow instead which could be matched against its variable deposits. Salomon would then lay off the other side of the transaction, by re-swaping it with, say, a Japanese bank which owed fixed-rate payments on a Eurobond issue but wanted instead to make variable-rate payments to match its variable rate income from bank loans. Using its vast network of bond market customers, and its own willingness to position swaps until they could be resold, Salomon was able to capture a large amount of this business. It therefore became more familiar with the S&L and mortgage industry than anyone else.

The next step for the firm was to develop the collateralized mortgage obligation ("CMO"), the second in a series of mortgage securitization products that began with the mortgage "passthrough," in which the cash flow from a segregated pool of mortgages was passed on directly to investors every month. This was an awkward security to own, because you never knew how much you would receive in any month, as principal repayments of mortgages were unpredictable. The CMO, developed with the help of sophisticated computer programs, streamlined and rationalized the passthrough into a real, institutional grade investment vehicle that traded at a modest interest rate premium over U.S. Treasury securities. The CMO soon became a gold mine for Salomon. Mortgage-backed securities grew at a compounded annual rate of 67% from 1978 to 1987, when the total volume of new issues reached nearly $100 billion. Salomon held a dominant share of the market for this business during this period. By 1991 the volume was over $250 billion. Salomon's profits from this new product line alone totaled several hundred million dollars, or more than 25% of Salomon's net income during its most profitable years in the mid-1980s.

The CMO business finally receded in profitability, as competitors piled into this market segment and Salomon seemed to lost interest in it. But it had learned several important lessons from its CMO experience. Aggressive trading together with computer technology was a dynamite combination. Trading skills could bootstrap Salomon into the top of the underwriting league tables, where new issue fees could be added to trading profits from aftermarket dealing. New products could be extremely profitable, but only for a few years until competitors caught on and took the juice out. But to come up with great new products took more than just courage and street smarts. It took real brains too, the sort that PhDs in mathematics from MIT and the University of Chicago have. Salomon hired many of these so-called "rocket scientists," and used them to search out market anomalies and to develop new ways to exploit what they found.

MANAGING GROWTH

During the eighties new products and new markets, especially those serviced from London and Tokyo, proliferated. Like all of the major New York firms, Salomon's headcount soared—from 2,300 in 1981 to nearly 7,000 in 1987. During this period, the firm's pretax earnings from investment banking (as opposed to commodities) rose from $80 million to nearly $800 million in 1986. In that year, as a concession to improving management efficiency, Gutfreund appointed Salomon Brothers' first full-time chief financial officer who began to allocate revenues and expenses to various profit centers around the firm. Gutfreund also formed an "office of the chairman" to share decision making power among a few select officers at the top.

By the early months of 1987, however, well before the stock market crash in October, trading markets became difficult while overhead expenses were still expanding rapidly. The emphasis at the firm shifted to controlling costs and defending the firm's profitability. A "strategic review" of the profitability of all the firm's businesses was undertaken.

During the summer of 1987, Gutfreund learned that Salomon's largest shareholder, Minerals and Resources Corporation of South Africa (a Phibro legacy) wanted to sell its 14% ownership interest in the firm, no doubt sensing an earnings decline. He was surprised to learn in late September, however, that the South Africans were in the final stages of a deal in which its block of shares would be sold to Ronald Perelman, one of the more successful of the takeover artists of the 1980s who had conquered Revlon a few years before. Gutfreund responded quickly, and contacted Warren Buffett, the billionaire chairman of Berkshire Hathaway who was known as one of America's smartest investors. Buffett often acquired large minority positions in companies he liked and stayed with them for years. Buffett quickly offered to acquire $700 million of new Salomon 9% convertible preferred shares, the proceeds from which would be used to buy the Minerals and Resources block. Buffett also received two seats on the Salomon board of directors and expressed long-term confidence in John Gutfreund. Though rescued on this occasion, Gutfreund remarked that "if we don't get our act together over the next year, we'll be threatened again. And we should be."[1]

That said, Gutfreund next turned to the recommendations of the strategic review. This was a dramatic plan to save $150 million annually in costs by eliminating 800 jobs, abolishing the municipal securities department, and all activities in commercial paper and most other money market instruments. The cutbacks had been leaked to the press, and as a result had to be implemented hurriedly, which made it appear awkward and hasty.

The Buffett deal and the strategic plan, however, were not popular with a number of Salomon's senior officers. Many thought the firm had paid too much for Buffett's friendly investment. Others were also bothered by what they perceived as serious compensation inequities and the exclusion from Gutfreund's office of the chairman of some of the firm's key figures. Plotting and discontent followed, as did a stream of senior level resignations including the heads of both government securities, E. Craig Coates, and corporate bond trading, William J. Voute. John Meriwether, formerly head of bond arbitrage, was appointed head of all fixed income trading in late 1988. He designated one of his top lieutenants from bond arbitrage, 36 year old Paul Mozer, as head of the government securities desk.

Meriwether was the now legendary character who supposedly (according to Michael Lewis) countered a 1986 challenge of a hand of liar's poker from John Gutfreund—"one hand, one million dollars, no tears"—with an offer to play for "real money instead, ten million, no tears." Gutfreund apparently thought ten million was too much to bet on the serial numbers on a dollar bill so he backed off. Salomon folklore depends on this event to illustrate the "right stuff" of the trading floor, to show that even powerful, high-placed executives can't really measure up against the cool-hand Lukes of the trading room.

DOMINATING TRADING MARKETS

The large, established trading markets were volatile and extremely competitive and the advantages went to the firm with the best information and the ability to put it to use. The best informed firm was one that saw the whole order flow and saw it early. Sources, speed and global reach were essential. But so was knowing what to do with the information once you had it. There was no money to be made in brokering a trade of government securities between two institutional investors. Money was made by positioning the firm for an expected market shift, say by borrowing $5 or $10 billion to invest in government bonds and taking an informed guess that the prices of the bonds will go up within a few days. Buying on margin, you can control $5 billion of Treasuries with only $50 million of capital. If the price goes up fifty basis points (.50%) and you sell out within a week you've made $2.5 million, before your financing costs. That's equivalent to an annualized return on investment of 260%. Exposure of this type, however, can be very expensive if it goes wrong (what if prices instead go down by 1.0%?), so new ways of managing risk by hedging positions had to be found.

---

[1] *The Wall Street Journal,* October 2, 1987.

The Salomon traders led the way in exposing the firm to huge market risks, developed new hedging techniques, and broadened the range of instruments traded. Meriwether's fixed income group was very successful in the year following his appointment. Revenues from principal transactions rose 28% above those of 1988 to $1.5 billion. Trading profits rose too, in 1990 by 25% and in 1991 by 75%. Success, however, developed frictions within the firm over compensation. The fixed income traders were irritated by weak performances in other highly compensated parts of the firm (investment banking, equities) and by the revelation in late 1990 that Gutfreund had promised the bond arbitrage group at the beginning of the year 15% of the profits they earned. The bond arbitrage group was not part of the fixed income unit. Though Salomon earnings declined by 36% in 1990 (to $303 million) and top officers took pay cuts, the bond arbitrage traders cleaned up: Lawrence Hilibrand, a 31 year old MIT economist who developed a proprietary, black-box program for bond arbitrage, earned $23 million, and several others in the group earned more than $10 million each.[2] "We reward people based on their performance," said John Gutfreund whose own compensation in 1990 was $2.3 million.[3]

By the end of 1990, Salomon had pushed its trading revenues to more than 80% of total, as compared to 57% in 1987. Its nontrading results were quite acceptable, finishing up in fourth place in U.S. underwriting and third in mergers and acquisitions, but trading was driving the firm now more than ever. Exhibit 9.1 shows summary financial information for the firm for 1990 and prior years from its 1990 Annual Report.

GOVERNMENT SECURITIES

The government securities market is the largest in the world. It consists of short-term "Treasury" bills, a variety of intermediate maturity notes (1–10 years) and long-term bonds. These securities are issued by the U.S. Treasury department to fund maturing obligations and the government's financial requirements, the most evident of which is its fiscal budget deficit, which grew from $60 billion in 1980 to $277 billion in 1990. To finance the budget deficit in 1990, the U.S. Treasury borrowed $264 billion from the public. At the end of the year, total public debt outstanding of the U.S. Treasury was $3.36 trillion, exclusive of various forms of "off-books" debt guaranteed by the Federal government.

Because of their volume, credit quality, substitutability, and transferability, Treasury securities are, in effect, commodities. A variety of futures and options securities based on U.S. Treasuries are available, and trade extensively, in the commodities markets in Chicago and other locations. Treasury and Federal Agency securities (which are not required to be registered with the SEC) are not distributed to the public through underwriting procedures common in corporate finance. Over the years, unique procedures have been developed by the Treasury staff for the sales of government securities. In 1990 and 1991, the securities were auctioned by the Treasury to qualified professional dealers ("primary market dealers") through a sealed bid, "modified-Dutch" auction procedure which was thought to provide the lowest possible interest cost to the Treasury.

At the time of an auction, a dealer indicated how much of the security being auctioned it was willing to purchase at a particular interest rate, and how much at other interest rates. Then, the Treasury starts with the lowest rate, and working upward, accepts bids until the total equals the amount of securities to be sold. The rate for each bid accepted is the rate bid by the dealer, not, as in a typical Dutch auction, the rate for the last bid accepted that then becomes the rate applicable to all of the securities sold. In case of same-price bids, bonds are allocated by the Treasury between dealers in the same rate bracket.

The role of the Federal Reserve in the process is less clear and direct. The Fed is the agency of the government that knows the government bond markets best, acting as it does in open market purchases and sales, and in investing in Treasury securities on behalf of foreign governments. Because of its market knowledge, the Fed has responsibility for approving primary market dealers. It consults with the Treasury regarding new issue procedures, but with respect to the issues themselves it is somewhat in the back seat. The SEC has no direct role in the process, presumably because the securities being issued are exempt from its regulatory purview.

---

[2] Peter Grant and Marcia Parker, "Hurtling Toward Scandal," *Crain's New York Business,* June 1, 1992.

[3] "Money Machine," *Business Week,* June 10, 1991.

Only primary market dealers, of which there are about 40, are permitted to bid at auctions, and to trade in government securities with the Federal Reserve. To become primary market dealers, firms have to demonstrate over a period of years trading skills, capital adequacy, responsible behavior as market-makers and be recommended by others in the community. The Fed monitors their activities, but does not supervise them closely. The Treasury, in recent years somewhat apprehensive about being able to finance smoothly the rapidly growing deficit, treated the primary market dealers with respect and some deference. The dealers were the experts that the Treasury had to depend on to market all the paper. The Treasury invited the primary market dealers in for an exchange of views on the market prior to forthcoming issues. The dealers would then bid for the issues at the auctions, distribute the securities to their customers, and maintain ongoing secondary markets in them. The daily turnover in government securities (by primary market dealers only) in December 1990 was $66.7 billion.

GOVERNMENT BONDS AT SALOMON

Driving trading activities at Salomon was its Government Securities department. This group personified Salomon at its best and at its worst. Its brilliant, aggressive, workaholic young professionals were devoted to preserving Salomon's number one position and powerful reputation. They were also said to be arrogant, ruthless and so singularly focused on beating the competition and making money that they lost sight of everything else. As Floyd Norris of *The New York Times* put it, "At Salomon Brothers, trading has always been a form of war in which the opponent is entitled to no pity and rules are viewed as impediments to be side-stepped, if possible."

Before any government auction, the Salomon's traders endeavor to estimate what the winning rate level will be and how much of the paper can be sold. They would aggregate their own bids for bonds with those of their large institutional customers that had authorized them to do so, in order to present the largest possible block of orders to the Treasury. To minimize their position risks related to the auction, Salomon and other dealers would sell (short) the as yet unissued bonds to customers at a price which they hoped was a good bet. To supply these customers with the bonds

they had sold them, the dealers would have to count on being allocated bonds in the auction; any shortfall would have to be covered by purchasing bonds in the market.

Aggressive traders will bid for more bonds than they have orders for, or at a higher price. The more orders for which they have at the highest price, the more bonds they are allocated. The more they are allocated, the more they control. According to one former Salomon trader:

If you build a book of $3 billion, $5 billion, $8 billion, then you really control the situation. Then you use your muscle, your big war chest of dollars, to force the thing with a drop-dead bid.[4]

The idea is, in effect, to control, or "corner," the market—to make other dealers, and those covering short position, buy from you at whatever price you wish to set. However, cornering the market in Treasury securities is not allowed, though in effect it was until July 1990 when the Treasury imposed limits on how much any firm could bid for a single issue. The problem had never come up before then—the Treasury market was just too large, and no single firm was thought to be big enough to be able to purchase a market-cornering position.

In March of 1990, however, Salomon and its customers successfully, and legally, purchased 75% of a two-year issue. A few months later, Paul Mozer astonished Treasury officials by bidding for 240% of an issue of thirty-year bonds. The Treasury rejected the bid and imposed a limit on bidding to 35% of any single issue.

THE SCANDAL

In August 1991, Salomon admitted that its trading activities had become too aggressive, and that it had made several illegal bids in auctions for government securities, auctions between December 1990 and May 1991. A Treasury official had some doubts about the earlier of these auctions and commenced an investigation of Salomon's bidding activities. When Mozer learned of the investigation, he came clean with his boss, John Meriwether, and admitted in April to falsi-

---

[4] "The Big Squeeze," *The Wall Street Journal*, August 12, 1991.

fying a customer order that Salomon had presented at a February auction. This and other phantom orders put more of the notes being auctioned into Salomon's hands than the 35% maximum which the government's rules allowed. Thus Salomon had established a small corner on the market for these notes. With such a large position in the notes, Salomon would be able to control for a few days the prices at which the notes were later sold to customers and other dealers. This way, Salomon could rig the market.

Once Mozer had explained what he had done in February, Meriwether knew that the firm had a big problem and so informed John Gutfreund and Salomon president Thomas Strauss. The top management group decided that the practice had to be discontinued and that the infractions should be reported to the Federal Reserve (not the Treasury, which they thought would be less sympathetic), but no one was assigned to make the report and no one did. Within a month of this meeting Salomon violated the rules again. At the May 22 auction of two-year notes, Salomon and its customers collectively purchased approximately $10.6 billion out of $11.3 billion in notes that were to be available for purchase by competitive bidders.[5] Salomon thus controlled 94% of the notes put out to bidding. In the process, the firm bid $2 billion for at least one customer, and simultaneously repurchased $500 million from the customer at the auction price while "inadvertently" failing to disclose its own position. Dealers charged that Salomon forced up prices of the notes after cornering the market to squeeze competitors. These competitors—other dealers—had sold notes short to customers in the when-issued market with the intention of covering their positions in the auction, as was usual practice. But there were no notes available for them to purchase in the auction, so they had to go to Salomon, who forced them to pay a much higher price. The squeeze was no secret, many dealers were complaining openly and the Treasury's price data showed abnormal patterns, provoking an inquiry.

In June the SEC and the Justice Department issued subpoenas to Salomon and certain clients. One Treasury official, noting the arrogant disregard by Salomon of the bidding rules, said that it was shocking that Salomon "could do it at the February auction, learn about it in April, not tell us, and do it again in May."[6]

The scandal was too much. The Treasury and the Federal Reserve were outraged and suspended Salomon from participation in government auctions. Salomon's board asked for the resignations of Gutfreund, Strauss, Meriwether, and Mozer and some lesser figures on August 16. John Gutfreund, 61 years old and at the peak of his 38-year career, was out. A tough guy to the end, Gutfreund apparently told his top executives at a closed-door meeting: "I'm not apologizing for anything to anybody. Apologies don't mean s___. What happened, happened."[7]

The Salomon stock price dropped 30%. Many of the firm's relationships with government securities customers were said by these customers to be subject to review. The firm was suddenly subject to civil lawsuits, fines and penalties, and possibly criminal charges. Its eighty year reputation for integrity and fair dealing was severely strained. No matter what the firm did to correct the errors, and to prevent their recurrence, it would have to pay a heavy price for them.

Warren Buffett, now a Salomon director and the firm's largest shareholder, took over as "interim" chairman and chief executive of the firm and resolutely began the process of putting it back together. To help him do so, Buffett selected 43-year-old Deryck C. Maughan as chief operating officer in charge of day-to-day activities. Maughan, until a month prior to these events, had been head of the firm's highly successful Tokyo operations. He was not a trader, not an American citizen (an Englishman, he had been an official in the British Treasury for ten years), and had nothing to do with government securities. Maughan was seen as a good choice to look at matters objectively.

Buffett told Salomon employees that the firm would be taking fewer risks in the future and that it would not be operating as close to the edge as it had in the past. Compliance was to be emphasized. He would be "ruthless' in protecting the firm's reputation. He

---

[5] Statement by Warren Buffet, chairman of Salomon Brothers, Inc. to the subcommittee on securities markets of the House Energy and Commerce Committee, Sept. 4, 1991.

[6] Michael Siconolfi and Laurie Cohen, "How Salomon's Hubris and US Trap led to Leader's Downfall," *The Wall Street Journal*, August 19, 1991.

[7] Ibid.

was able to convince the Treasury and the Fed to allow Salomon to participate in auctions for its own account but not for the accounts of customers) and as the year progressed, the scandal settled down. In May 1992 it was over. Salomon agreed to a $290 million fine, but would not have to face criminal charges, and Buffett resigned as CEO of the firm in favor of Maughan.

As the scandal died down, Wall Street asked itself how this could have happened. Salomon was warlike, domineering, and arrogant, but few thought the firm was actually venal or dishonest. Or stupid, which is what you'd have to be to think you could get away with illegal manipulation of Treasury auctions. Part of the answer seemed to lie in the out-of-date auction process itself, which was governed by the Treasury Department, not the Fed or the SEC which had market regulatory powers and experience. The process allowed bidders to submit their own bids together with bids for customers. It allocated all bonds to be sold among same-price bidders. There were a large number of rules related to bidding, and these changed often, complicating compliance. There were generally no penalties imposed for rule violations, which were required to be reported by the firms themselves on a vol-

untary basis, although a firm's status as a primary market dealer could be jeopardized by misconduct. The bidding process and the Treasury market regulatory environment had long pre-dated the surge in market activity during the eighties and badly needed to be re-examined and reformed.

QUESTIONS:

1. Analyze the Treasury bidding process at the time of the scandal. How did the process itself affect the behavior of bidders? How could the process be modified so as to improve it?

2. What exactly did Salomon do that was illegal? How could this have been prevented?

3. How should the improper trading have been detected? Why wasn't it?

4. What impact would a scandal of this type have on a firm like Salomon?

5. How would you evaluate the steps taken by Warren Buffett to repair the damage?

| EXHIBIT 9.2 | Excerpts from Salomon Brothers' 1990 Annual Report |

Summary of Consolidated Operating Results (Dollars in millions, except per share amounts)

Year Ended December 31,	1990	1989	1988
Income (loss) before taxes:			
Salomon Brothers	$ 416	$ 534	$ 513
Phibro Energy	492	375	227
Philipp Brothers	(168)	(116)	48
Philipp Brothers Downsizing	(155)	—	—
Corporate and Other	(79)	(53)	(35)
Total income before taxes	506	740	753
Income taxes	203	270	473
Net income	$ 303	$ 470	$ 280
Per common share:			
Primary earnings	$ 2.08	$ 3.26	$ 1.65
Fully diluted earnings	2.05	3.20	1.63
Cash dividends	0.64	0.64	0.64
Book value at year-end	25.73	24.08	21.82
Return on average common stockholders' equity	8.3%	14.6%	7.6%

Trading activities are integral to the profitability of each of the Company's business segments. By their very nature, trading results tend to be volatile. The Company accounts for open financial and energy positions and contractual commitments on a market value basis. As market values change, earnings of each of the Company's segments are impacted immediately. Consequently, operating results are highly sensitive to movement in market prices and can vary considerably from period to period. This was particularly evident during 1990, a year characterized by unusually high volatility in the world's energy and financial markets. Accordingly, operating results are best viewed in the context of the Company's performance over the longer term. The Company has been profitable in each of the ten calendar years in which its operations included both Salomon Brothers and Phibro.

As more fully discussed in the accompanying Consolidated Financial Statements, results for Salomon Brothers, Phibro Energy, and Philipp Brothers include an allocation of corporate-level expenses, most of which is interest.

As discussed in Note 1 to the Consolidated Financial Statements, the Company recorded a $155 million pretax charge during 1990 in connection with the downsizing of its Philipp Brothers commodities business. Effective October 1, 1990, certain activities of Philipp Brothers were transferred to Salomon Brothers and Phibro Energy. Cocoa trading continues to be conducted by Philipp Brothers; beginning October 1, 1990, its results are included in Corporate and Other. Remaining Philipp Brothers activities have been or are being sold or liquidated. Consequently, Philipp Brothers no longer represents a reportable industry segment; amounts reported for Philipp Brothers in the table above represent operating results prior to October 1, 1990. The increase in net expenses for Corporate and Other in 1990 resulted principally from fourth quarter cocoa trading losses of $20 million and the costs associated with commodities-related manufacturing facilities that were disposed of in the late 1970s and early 1980s.

Results for 1990 and 1988 were impacted by certain special items. Excluding the Philipp Brothers special charge, 1990 consolidated pretax earnings would have been $661 million, net income would have been $397 million, and return on average common stockholders' equity would have been 11.5%. Net Income for 1988 was adversely affected by a special $180 million income tax provision (see Note 12 to the Consolidated Financial Statements). Excluding this charge, 1988 net income would have been $460 million and return on average common stockholders' equity would have been 13.9%.

Summary of Operating Results (Dollars In millions)

Year Ended December 31,	1990	1989	1988	Percentage Change: 1990 From 1989	1989 From 1988
Principal transactions, including net interest and dividends	$1,683	$1,554	$1,212	8%	28%
Investment banking	416	470	564	(11)	(17)
Commissions and other	220	239	217	(8)	10
Revenues, net of interest expense	2,319	2,263	1,993	2	14
Compensation and benefits	1,126	1,082	920	4	18
Other expenses	777	647	560	20	16
Total noninterest expenses	1,903	1,729	1,480	10	17
Income before taxes	$ 416	$ 534	$ 513	(22)%	4%

Condensed Statement of Financial Condition (In millions)

December 31,	1990	1989	Increase (Decrease)
Assets:			
Cash and cash equivalents	$ 728	$ 177	$ 551
Financial instruments	52,846	71,229	(18,383)
Collateralized short-term financing agreements	39,852	32,708	7,144
Receivables	2,870	2,192	678
Assets securing collateralized mortgage obligations	6,831	6,432	399
Other assets	654	521	133
Total assets	$103,781	$113,259	$ (9,478)
Liabilities and Capital:			
Short-term borrowings	$ 44,940	$ 63,658	$(18,718)
Financial instruments sold, not yet purchased	41,675	36,034	5,641
Payables and accrued liabilities	5,221	2,975	2,246
Collateralized mortgage obligations	6,821	6,372	449
Term debt	682	314	368
Capital	4,442	3,906	536
Total liabilities and capital	$103,781	$113,259	$ (9,478)

Salomon Brothers earned $416 million before taxes in 1990, compared with $534 million in 1989 and $513 million in 1988. Trading activities, which comprise a major portion of Salomon Brothers' operations, have continued to strengthen each year since the 1987 stock market crash. However, investment banking revenues have declined in each of the past two years as the environment, characterized by tightening underwriting margins and lower levels of activity, has grown increasingly difficult.

Trading results in 1990 continued to be solid. The past year's growth in principal transactions, including net interest and dividends, was attributable principally to government bond trading, although other trading activities, such as equities and derivative products, continued to perform strongly. The 1989 improvement spanned a broad range of activities, including equities, government bonds, foreign exchange, and derivative products. In addition to demonstrating trading strength across a wide range of products, Salomon Brothers has continued to develop the international scope of its trading activities. Non-U.S. operations, particularly those in Tokyo and London, are integral components of Salomon Brothers' trading operations.

Investment banking revenues are derived principally from capital raising and advisory services. The capital raising component represents revenues earned primarily from debt and equity underwriting services. In recent years, underwriting margins have tightened significantly. Consequently, Salomon Brothers has responded by investing in technology and systems designed to reduce operating costs while targeting underwriting activities to transactions that are more profitable. Investment banking revenues from capital raising services totaled $190 million in 1990, compared with $233 million in 1989 and $290 million in 1988. Salomon Brothers earns fees from providing advisory services for mergers, acquisitions, leveraged buyouts, and financial restructurings. Merger and acquisition activity has slowed over the past two years. This is reflected in lower levels of investment banking advisory revenues, which were $226 million in 1990, compared with $237 million in 1989 and $274 million in 1988.

The Company's largest single merchant banking exposure is with the Grand Union Corp., a supermarket chain that operates principally in the northeast region of the United States. This exposure totaled $194 million at December 31, 1990 and included $107 million of subordinated loans, $48 million of senior loans, $30 million of open commitments, and a $9 million

Principal Transactions
Including Net Interest and
Dividends
(In Billions of Dollars)

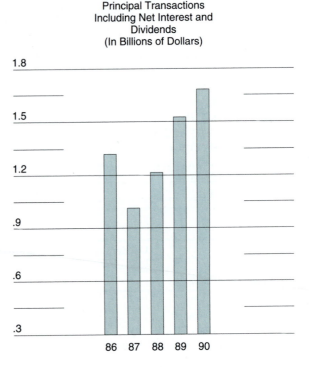

equity investment. The Company's aggregate exposure to Grand Union at December 31, 1989 totaled $179 million. Merchant banking investments and loans, other than Grand Union, totaled $79 million, with sixteen different entities, at December 31, 1990 compared with $137 million at December 31, 1989.

Salomon Brothers' trading activities include high-yield securities that are less than investment grade. These include debt, convertible debt, preferred and convertible preferred equity securities rated lower than "triple B-" by internationally recognized rating agencies, as well as sovereign debt issued by less developed countries. These securities are carried at market value. The aggregate carrying amounts of the high-yield trading portfolio included in Financial Instruments at December 31, 1990 and 1989 were $579 million and $467 million, respectively. These amounts are in addition to the merchant banking investments discussed above, and are not reduced by high-yield securities sold, not yet purchased ($106 million and $149 million at December 31, 1990 and 1989), which are reflected as a liability on the Consolidated Statement of Financial Condition. At December 31, 1990, the largest position with a single counterparty totaled $95

Salomon Brothers
Income Before Taxes
(in millions of dollars)

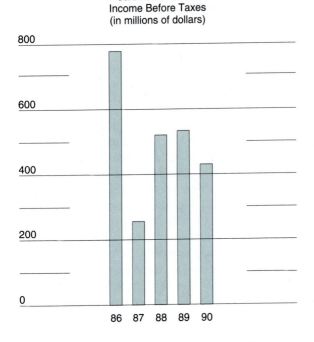

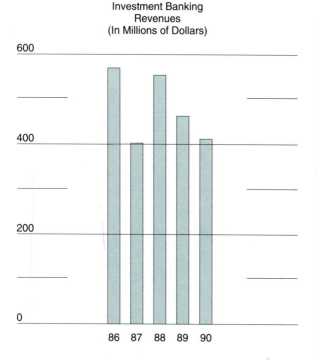

Investment Banking
Revenues
(In Millions of Dollars)

600

400

200

0

86 87 88 89 90

million compared with $94 million at December 31, 1989 with a different counterparty.

Salomon Brothers' noninterest expenses increased by $174 million in 1990. Compensation and benefits expense grew by $44 million or 4% while other expenses grew by $130 million or 20%. Incremental expenses of $86 million, principally in communications and equipment expenses and professional services, were incurred in connection with a multiyear project under which Salomon Brothers will completely replace its existing computer technology and operating and financial systems. Nonrecurring occupancy expenses relating to the relocation of New York and Tokyo operations to new facilities, including moving expenses, lease abandonment costs, and rental expense in connection with duplicate leased facilities, totaled approximately $68 million in 1990. The move to a new headquarters building at Seven World Trade Center in lower Manhattan is expected to be completed by the end of the 1991 first quarter.

In 1989, noninterest expenses grew by $249 million; $162 million of the increase was in compensation and benefits expense; the balance was in other expenses. The increase in compensation expense was, in part, attributable to the implementation of a change in Salomon Brothers' measurement period for compensation from a calendar year to a fiscal year ending September 30. Consequently, 1989 results included an accrual for bonuses paid for the entire fiscal year ended September 30, 1989, as well as an accrual for the first three months of the compensation year ended September 30, 1990. In addition, effective January 1, 1989, Salomon Brothers implemented a new deferred compensation plan for its managing directors. The anticipated plan payout of $100 million plus an amount determined by the Company's return on common stockholders' equity is being accrued over the three-year life of the plan. At December 31, 1990, $76 million had been accrued. The increase in other expenses in 1989 was partly attributable to the acceleration of amortization of leasehold improvements and computer equipment in anticipating of the relocation of certain operations, principally those in New York, and partly attributable to higher systems development expenses.

In a transaction effective at the end of 1989, the Company sold its 20% equity interest in Bond Investors Group Inc to MBIA Inc., a U.S. insurer of municipal bonds. This transaction resulted in a gain of $12 million. During 1989, the Company held a 20% interest in DFC New Zealand Limited ("DFC"), a financially troubled investment bank. In late 1989, the Reserve Bank of New Zealand appointed statutory managers for DFC. As a result of a review by the Company's management, the carrying amount of the investment was reduced to a nominal amount, resulting in a $15 million charge against 1989 earnings. An additional $8 million was charged against earnings during 1990 in connection with the settlement of all outstanding legal matters pertaining to the Company's investment in DFC.

Salomon Brothers' total assets decreased by $9.5 billion in 1990, principally as a result of a lower level of U.S. government and agency securities.

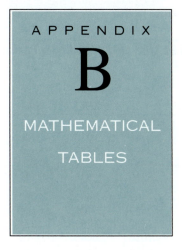

APPENDIX

B

MATHEMATICAL

TABLES

TABLE B.1 Present Value of $1 Due at the End of n Periods

$$PVIF_{k,n} = \frac{1}{(1+k)^n}$$

Period	1%	2%	3%	4%	5%	6%	7%	8%	9%	10%
1	.9901	.9804	.9709	.9615	.9524	.9434	.9346	.9259	.9174	.9091
2	.9803	.9612	.9426	.9246	.9070	.8900	.8734	.8573	.8417	.8264
3	.9706	.9423	.9151	.8890	.8638	.8396	.8163	.7938	.7722	.7513
4	.9610	.9238	.8885	.8548	.8227	.7921	.7629	.7350	.7084	.6830
5	.9515	.9057	.8626	.8219	.7835	.7473	.7130	.6806	.6499	.6209
6	.9420	.8880	.8375	.7903	.7462	.7050	.6663	.6302	.5963	.5645
7	.9327	.8706	.8131	.7599	.7107	.6651	.6227	.5835	.5470	.5132
8	.9235	.8535	.7894	.7307	.6768	.6274	.5820	.5403	.5019	.4665
9	.9143	.8368	.7664	.7026	.6446	.5919	.5439	.5002	.4604	.4241
10	.9053	.8203	.7441	.6756	.6139	.5584	.5083	.4632	.4224	.3855
11	.8963	.8043	.7224	.6496	.5847	.5268	.4751	.4289	.3875	.3505
12	.8874	.7885	.7014	.6246	.5568	.4970	.4440	.3971	.3555	.3186
13	.8787	.7730	.6810	.6006	.5303	.4688	.4150	.3677	.3262	.2897
14	.8700	.7579	.6611	.5775	.5051	.4423	.3878	.3405	.2992	.2633
15	.8613	.7430	.6419	.5553	.4810	.4173	.3624	.3152	.2745	.2394
16	.8528	.7284	.6232	.5339	.4581	.3936	.3387	.2919	.2519	.2176
17	.8444	.7142	.6050	.5134	.4363	.3714	.3166	.2703	.2311	.1978
18	.8360	.7002	.5874	.4936	.4155	.3503	.2959	.2502	.2120	.1799
19	.8277	.6864	.5703	.4746	.3957	.3305	.2765	.2317	.1945	.1635
20	.8195	.6730	.5537	.4564	.3769	.3118	.2584	.2145	.1784	.1486
21	.8114	.6598	.5375	.4388	.3589	.2942	.2415	.1987	.1637	.1351
22	.8034	.6468	.5219	.4220	.3418	.2775	.2257	.1839	.1502	.1228
23	.7954	.6342	.5067	.4057	.3256	.2618	.2109	.1703	.1378	.1117
24	.7876	.6217	.4919	.3901	.3101	.2470	.1971	.1577	.1264	.1015
25	.7798	.6095	.4776	.3751	.2953	.2330	.1842	.1460	.1160	.0923
26	.7720	.5976	.4637	.3604	.2812	.2198	.1722	.1352	.1064	.0839
27	.7644	.5859	.4502	.3468	.2678	.2074	.1609	.1252	.0976	.0763
28	.7568	.5744	.4371	.3335	.2551	.1956	.1504	.1159	.0895	.0693
29	.7493	.5631	.4243	.3207	.2429	.1846	.1406	.1073	.0822	.0630
30	.7419	.5521	.4120	.3083	.2314	.1741	.1314	.0994	.0754	.0573
35	.7059	.5000	.3554	.2534	.1813	.1301	.0937	.0676	.0490	.0356
40	.6717	.4529	.3066	.2083	.1420	.0972	.0668	.0460	.0318	.0221
45	.6391	.4102	.2644	.1712	.1113	.0727	.0476	.0313	.0207	.0137
50	.6080	.3715	.2281	.1407	.0872	.0543	.0339	.0213	.0134	.0085
55	.5785	.3365	.1968	.1157	.0683	.0406	.0242	.0145	.0087	.0053

TABLE B.1 *CONTINUED*

Period	12%	14%	15%	16%	18%	20%	24%	28%	32%	36%
1	.8929	.8772	.8696	.8621	.8475	.8333	.8065	.7813	.7576	.7353
2	.7972	.7695	.7561	.7432	.7182	.6944	.6504	.6104	.5739	.5407
3	.7118	.6750	.6575	.6407	.6086	.5787	.5245	.4768	.4348	.3975
4	.6355	.5921	.5718	.5523	.5158	.4823	.4230	.3725	.3294	.2923
5	.5674	.5194	.4972	.4761	.4371	.4019	.3411	.2910	.2495	.2149
6	.5066	.4556	.4323	.4104	.3704	.3349	.2751	.2274	.1890	.1580
7	.4523	.3996	.3759	.3538	.3139	.2791	.2218	.1776	.1432	.1162
8	.4039	.3506	.3269	.3050	.2660	.2326	.1789	.1388	.1085	.0854
9	.3606	.3075	.2843	.2630	.2255	.1938	.1443	.1084	.0822	.0628
10	.3220	.2697	.2472	.2267	.1911	.1615	.1164	.0847	.0623	.0462
11	.2875	.2366	.2149	.1954	.1619	.1346	.0938	.0662	.0472	.0340
12	.2567	.2076	.1869	.1685	.1372	.1122	.0757	.0517	.0357	.0250
13	.2292	.1821	.1625	.1452	.1163	.0935	.0610	.0404	.0271	.0184
14	.2046	.1597	.1413	.1252	.0985	.0779	.0492	.0316	.0205	.0135
15	.1827	.1401	.1229	.1079	.0835	.0649	.0397	.0247	.0155	.0099
16	.1631	.1229	.1069	.0980	.0708	.0541	.0320	.0193	.0118	.0073
17	.1456	.1078	.0929	.0802	.0600	.0451	.0258	.0150	.0089	.0054
18	.1300	.0946	.0808	.0691	.0508	.0376	.0208	.0118	.0068	.0039
19	.1161	.0829	.0703	.0596	.0431	.0313	.0168	.0092	.0051	.0029
20	.1037	.0728	.0611	.0514	.0365	.0261	.0135	.0072	.0039	.0021
21	.0926	.0638	.0531	.0443	.0309	.0217	.0109	.0056	.0029	.0016
22	.0826	.0560	.0462	.0382	.0262	.0181	.0088	.0044	.0022	.0012
23	.0738	.0491	.0402	.0329	.0222	.0151	.0071	.0034	.0017	.0008
24	.0659	.0431	.0349	.0284	.0188	.0126	.0057	.0027	.0013	.0006
25	.0588	.0378	.0304	.0245	.0160	.0105	.0046	.0021	.0010	.0005
26	.0525	.0331	.0264	.0211	.0135	.0087	.0037	.0016	.0007	.0003
27	.0469	.0291	.0230	.0182	.0115	.0073	.0030	.0013	.0006	.0002
28	.0419	.0255	.0200	.0157	.0097	.0061	.0024	.0010	.0004	.0002
29	.0374	.0224	.0174	.0135	.0082	.0051	.0020	.0008	.0003	.0001
30	.0334	.0196	.0151	.0116	.0070	.0042	.0016	.0006	.0002	.0001
35	.0189	.0102	.0075	.0055	.0030	.0017	.0005	.0002	.0001	*
40	.0107	.0053	.0037	.0026	.0013	.0007	.0002	.0001	*	*
45	.0061	.0027	.0019	.0013	.0006	.0003	.0001	*	*	*
50	.0035	.0014	.0009	.0006	.0003	.0001	*	*	*	*
55	.0020	.0007	.0005	.0003	.0001	*	*	*	*	*

*The factor is zero to four decimal places.

TABLE B.2   Present Value of an Annuity of $1 per Period for n Periods

$$PVIFA_{k,n} = \sum_{t=1}^{n} \frac{1}{(1+k)^t} = \frac{1 - \frac{1}{(1+k)^n}}{k} = \frac{1}{k} - \frac{1}{k(1+k)^n}$$

Number of Periods	1%	2%	3%	4%	5%	6%	7%	8%	9%
1	0.9901	0.9804	0.9709	0.9615	0.9524	0.9434	0.9346	0.9259	0.9174
2	1.9704	1.9416	1.9135	1.8861	1.8594	1.8334	1.8080	1.7833	1.7591
3	2.9410	2.8839	2.8286	2.7751	2.7232	2.6730	2.6243	2.5771	2.5313
4	3.9020	3.8077	3.7171	3.6299	3.5460	3.4651	3.3872	3.3121	3.2397
5	4.8534	4.7135	4.5797	4.4518	4.3295	4.2124	4.1002	3.9927	3.8897
6	5.7955	5.6014	5.4172	5.2421	5.0757	4.9173	4.7665	4.6229	4.4859
7	6.7282	6.4720	6.2303	6.0021	5.7864	5.5824	5.3893	5.2064	5.0330
8	7.6517	7.3255	7.0197	6.7327	6.4632	6.2098	5.9713	5.7466	5.5348
9	8.5660	8.1622	7.7861	7.4353	7.1078	6.8017	6.5152	6.2469	5.9952
10	9.4713	8.9826	8.5302	8.1109	7.7217	7.3601	7.0236	6.7101	6.4177
11	10.3676	9.7868	9.2526	8.7605	8.3064	7.8869	7.4987	7.1390	6.8052
12	11.2551	10.5753	9.9540	9.3851	8.8633	8.3838	7.9427	7.5361	7.1607
13	12.1337	11.3484	10.6350	9.9856	9.3936	8.8527	8.3577	7.9038	7.4869
14	13.0037	12.1062	11.2961	10.5631	9.8986	9.2950	8.7455	8.2442	7.7862
15	13.8651	12.8493	11.9379	11.1184	10.3797	9.7122	9.1079	8.5595	8.0607
16	14.7179	13.5777	12.5611	11.6523	10.8378	10.1059	9.4466	8.8514	8.3126
17	15.5623	14.2919	13.1661	12.1657	11.2741	10.4773	9.7632	9.1216	8.5436
18	16.3983	14.9920	13.7535	12.6593	11.6896	10.8276	10.0591	9.3719	8.7556
19	17.2260	15.6785	14.3238	13.1339	12.0853	11.1581	10.3356	9.6036	8.9501
20	18.0456	16.3514	14.8775	13.5903	12.4622	11.4699	10.5940	9.8181	9.1285
21	18.8570	17.0112	15.4150	14.0292	12.8212	11.7641	10.8355	10.0168	9.2922
22	19.6604	17.6580	15.9369	14.4511	13.1630	12.0416	11.0612	10.2007	9.4424
23	20.4558	18.2922	16.4436	14.8568	13.4886	12.3034	11.2722	10.3711	9.5802
24	21.2434	18.9139	16.9355	15.2470	13.7986	12.5504	11.4693	10.5288	9.7066
25	22.0232	19.5235	17.4131	15.6221	14.0939	12.7834	11.6536	10.6748	9.8226
26	22.7952	20.1210	17.8768	15.9828	14.3752	13.0032	11.8258	10.8100	9.9290
27	23.5596	20.7069	18.3270	16.3296	14.6430	13.2105	11.9867	10.9352	10.0266
28	24.3164	21.2813	18.7641	16.6631	14.8981	13.4062	12.1371	11.0511	10.1161
29	25.0658	21.8444	19.1885	16.9837	15.1411	13.5907	12.2777	11.1584	10.1983
30	25.8077	22.3965	19.6004	17.2920	15.3725	13.7648	12.4090	11.2578	10.2737
35	29.4086	24.9986	21.4872	18.6646	16.3742	14.4982	12.9477	11.6546	10.5668
40	32.8347	27.3555	23.1148	19.7928	17.1591	15.0463	13.3317	11.9246	10.7574
45	36.0945	29.4902	24.5187	20.7200	17.7741	15.4558	13.6055	12.1084	10.8812
50	39.1961	31.4236	25.7298	21.4822	18.2559	15.7619	13.8007	12.2335	10.9617
55	42.1472	33.1748	26.7744	22.1086	18.6335	15.9905	13.9399	12.3186	11.0140

TABLE B.2 *CONTINUED*

Number of Periods	10%	12%	14%	15%	16%	18%	20%	24%	28%	32%
1	0.9091	0.8929	0.8772	0.8696	0.8621	0.8475	0.8333	0.8065	0.7813	0.7576
2	1.7355	1.6901	1.6467	1.6257	1.6052	1.5656	1.5278	1.4568	1.3916	1.3315
3	2.4869	2.4018	2.3216	2.2832	2.2459	2.1743	2.1065	1.9813	1.8684	1.7663
4	3.1699	3.0373	2.9137	2.8550	2.7982	2.6901	2.5887	2.4043	2.2410	2.0957
5	3.7908	3.6048	3.4331	3.3522	3.2743	3.1272	2.9906	2.7454	2.5320	2.3452
6	4.3553	4.1114	3.8887	3.7845	3.6847	3.4976	3.3255	3.0205	2.7594	2.5342
7	4.8684	4.5638	4.2883	4.1604	4.0386	3.8115	3.6046	3.2423	2.9370	2.6775
8	5.3349	4.9676	4.6389	4.4873	4.3436	4.0776	3.8372	3.4212	3.0758	2.7860
9	5.7590	5.3282	4.9464	4.7716	4.6065	4.3030	4.0310	3.5655	3.1842	2.8681
10	6.1446	5.6502	5.2161	5.0188	4.8332	4.4941	4.1925	3.6819	3.2689	2.9304
11	6.4951	5.9377	5.4527	5.2337	5.0286	4.6560	4.3271	3.7757	3.3351	2.9776
12	6.8137	6.1944	5.6603	5.4206	5.1971	4.7932	4.4392	3.8514	3.3868	3.0133
13	7.1034	6.4235	5.8424	5.5831	5.3423	4.9095	4.5327	3.9124	3.4272	3.0404
14	7.3667	6.6282	6.0021	5.7245	5.4675	5.0081	4.6106	3.9616	3.4587	3.0609
15	7.6061	6.8109	6.1422	5.8474	5.5755	5.0916	4.6755	4.0013	3.4834	3.0764
16	7.8237	6.9740	6.2651	5.9542	5.6685	5.1624	4.7296	4.0333	3.5026	3.0882
17	8.0216	7.1196	6.3729	6.0472	5.7487	5.2223	4.7746	4.0591	3.5177	3.0971
18	8.2014	7.2497	6.4674	6.1280	5.8178	5.2732	4.8122	4.0799	3.5294	3.1039
19	8.3649	7.3658	6.5504	6.1982	5.8775	5.3162	4.8435	4.0967	3.5386	3.1090
20	8.5136	7.4694	6.6231	6.2593	5.9288	5.3527	4.8696	4.1103	3.5458	3.1129
21	8.6487	7.5620	6.6870	6.3125	5.9731	5.3837	4.8913	4.1212	3.5514	3.1158
22	8.7715	7.6446	6.7429	6.3587	6.0113	5.4099	4.9094	4.1300	3.5558	3.1180
23	8.8832	7.7184	6.7921	6.3988	6.0442	5.4321	4.9245	4.1371	3.5592	3.1197
24	8.9847	7.7843	6.8351	6.4338	6.0726	5.4509	4.9371	4.1428	3.5619	3.1210
25	9.0770	7.8431	6.8729	6.4641	6.0971	5.4669	4.9476	4.1474	3.5640	3.1220
26	9.1609	7.8957	6.9061	6.4906	6.1182	5.4804	4.9563	4.1511	3.5656	3.1227
27	9.2372	7.9426	6.9352	6.5135	6.1364	5.4919	4.9636	4.1542	3.5669	3.1233
28	9.3066	7.9844	6.9607	6.5335	6.1520	5.5016	4.9697	4.1566	3.5679	3.1237
29	9.3696	8.0218	6.9830	6.5509	6.1656	5.5098	4.9747	4.1585	3.5687	3.1240
30	9.4269	8.0552	7.0027	6.5660	6.1772	5.5168	4.9789	4.1601	3.5693	3.1242
35	9.6442	8.1755	7.0700	6.6166	6.2153	5.5386	4.9915	4.1644	3.5708	3.1248
40	9.7791	8.2438	7.1050	6.6418	6.2335	5.5482	4.9966	4.1659	3.5712	3.1250
45	9.8628	8.2825	7.1232	6.6543	6.2421	5.5523	4.9986	4.1664	3.5714	3.1250
50	9.9148	8.3045	7.1327	6.6605	6.2463	5.5541	4.9995	4.1666	3.5714	3.1250
55	9.9471	8.3170	7.1376	6.6636	6.2482	5.5549	4.9998	4.1666	3.5714	3.1250

TABLE B.3   **Future Value of $1 at the End of n Periods**

$FVIF_{k,n} = (1 + k)^n$

Period	1%	2%	3%	4%	5%	6%	7%	8%	9%	10%
1	1.0100	1.0200	1.0300	1.0400	1.0500	1.0600	1.0700	1.0800	1.0900	1.1000
2	1.0201	1.0404	1.0609	1.0816	1.1025	1.1236	1.1449	1.1664	1.1881	1.2100
3	1.0303	1.0612	1.0927	1.1249	1.1576	1.1910	1.2250	1.2597	1.2950	1.3310
4	1.0406	1.0824	1.1255	1.1699	1.2155	1.2625	1.3108	1.3605	1.4116	1.4641
5	1.0510	1.1041	1.1593	1.2167	1.2763	1.3382	1.4026	1.4693	1.5386	1.6105
6	1.0615	1.1262	1.1941	1.2653	1.3401	1.4185	1.5007	1.5869	1.6771	1.7716
7	1.0721	1.1487	1.2299	1.3159	1.4071	1.5036	1.6058	1.7138	1.8280	1.9487
8	1.0829	1.1717	1.2668	1.3686	1.4775	1.5938	1.7182	1.8509	1.9926	2.1436
9	1.0937	1.1951	1.3048	1.4233	1.5513	1.6895	1.8385	1.9990	2.1719	2.3579
10	1.1046	1.2190	1.3439	1.4802	1.6289	1.7908	1.9672	2.1589	2.3674	2.5937
11	1.1157	1.2434	1.3842	1.5395	1.7103	1.8983	2.1049	2.3316	2.5804	2.8531
12	1.1268	1.2682	1.4258	1.6010	1.7959	2.0122	2.2522	2.5182	2.8127	3.1384
13	1.1381	1.2936	1.4685	1.6651	1.8856	2.1329	2.4098	2.7196	3.0658	3.4523
14	1.1495	1.3195	1.5126	1.7317	1.9799	2.2609	2.5785	2.9372	3.3417	3.7975
15	1.1610	1.3459	1.5580	1.8009	2.0789	2.3966	2.7590	3.1722	3.6425	4.1772
16	1.1726	1.3728	1.6047	1.8730	2.1829	2.5404	2.9522	3.4259	3.9703	4.5950
17	1.1843	1.4002	1.6528	1.9479	2.2920	2.6928	3.1588	3.7000	4.3276	5.0545
18	1.1961	1.4282	1.7024	2.0258	2.4066	2.8543	3.3799	3.9960	4.7171	5.5599
19	1.2081	1.4568	1.7535	2.1068	2.5270	3.0256	3.6165	4.3157	5.1417	6.1159
20	1.2202	1.4859	1.8061	2.1911	2.6533	3.2071	3.8697	4.6610	5.6044	6.7275
21	1.2324	1.5157	1.8603	2.2788	2.7860	3.3996	4.1406	5.0338	6.1088	7.4002
22	1.2447	1.5460	1.9161	2.3699	2.9253	3.6035	4.4304	5.4365	6.6586	8.1403
23	1.2572	1.5769	1.9736	2.4647	3.0715	3.8197	4.7405	5.8715	7.2579	8.9543
24	1.2697	1.6084	2.0328	2.5633	3.2251	4.0489	5.0724	6.3412	7.9111	9.8497
25	1.2824	1.6406	2.0938	2.6658	3.3864	4.2919	5.4274	6.8485	8.6231	10.835
26	1.2953	1.6734	2.1566	2.7725	3.5557	4.5494	5.8074	7.3964	9.3992	11.918
27	1.3082	1.7069	2.2213	2.8834	3.7335	4.8223	6.2139	7.9881	10.245	13.110
28	1.3213	1.7410	2.2879	2.9987	3.9201	5.1117	6.6488	8.6271	11.167	14.421
29	1.3345	1.7758	2.3566	3.1187	4.1161	5.4184	7.1143	9.3173	12.172	15.863
30	1.3478	1.8114	2.4273	3.2434	4.3219	5.7435	7.6123	10.063	13.268	17.449
40	1.4889	2.2080	3.2620	4.8010	7.0400	10.286	14.974	21.725	31.409	45.259
50	1.6446	2.6916	4.3839	7.1067	11.467	18.420	29.457	46.902	74.358	117.39
60	1.8167	3.2810	5.8916	10.520	18.679	32.988	57.946	101.26	176.03	304.48

TABLE B.3 *CONTINUED*

Period	12%	14%	15%	16%	18%	20%	24%	28%	32%	36%
1	1.1200	1.1400	1.1500	1.1600	1.1800	1.2000	1.2400	1.2800	1.3200	1.3600
2	1.2544	1.2996	1.3225	1.3456	1.3924	1.4400	1.5376	1.6384	1.7424	1.8496
3	1.4049	1.4815	1.5209	1.5609	1.6430	1.7280	1.9066	2.0972	2.3000	2.5155
4	1.5735	1.6890	1.7490	1.8106	1.9388	2.0736	2.3642	2.6844	3.0360	3.4210
5	1.7623	1.9254	2.0114	2.1003	2.2878	2.4883	2.9316	3.4360	4.0075	4.6526
6	1.9738	2.1950	2.3131	2.4364	2.6996	2.9860	3.6352	4.3980	5.2899	6.3275
7	2.2107	2.5023	2.6600	2.8262	3.1855	3.5832	4.5077	5.6295	6.9826	8.6054
8	2.4760	2.8526	3.0590	3.2784	3.7589	4.2998	5.5895	7.2058	9.2170	11.703
9	2.7731	3.2519	3.5179	3.8030	4.4355	5.1598	6.9310	9.2234	12.166	15.917
10	3.1058	3.7072	4.0456	4.4114	5.2338	6.1917	8.5944	11.806	16.060	21.647
11	3.4785	4.2262	4.6524	5.1173	6.1759	7.4301	10.657	15.112	21.199	29.439
12	3.8960	4.8179	5.3503	5.9360	7.2876	8.9161	13.215	19.343	27.983	40.037
13	4.3635	5.4924	6.1528	6.8858	8.5994	10.699	16.386	24.759	36.937	54.451
14	4.8871	6.2613	7.0757	7.9875	10.147	12.839	20.319	31.691	48.757	74.053
15	5.4736	7.1379	8.1371	9.2655	11.974	15.407	25.196	40.565	64.359	100.71
16	6.1304	8.1372	9.3576	10.748	14.129	18.488	31.243	51.923	84.954	136.97
17	6.8660	9.2765	10.761	12.468	16.672	22.186	38.741	66.461	112.14	186.28
18	7.6900	10.575	12.375	14.463	19.673	26.623	48.039	85.071	148.02	253.34
19	8.6128	12.056	14.232	16.777	23.214	31.948	59.568	108.89	195.39	344.54
20	9.6463	13.743	16.367	19.461	27.393	38.338	73.864	139.38	257.92	468.57
21	10.804	15.668	18.822	22.574	32.324	46.005	91.592	178.41	340.45	637.26
22	12.100	17.861	21.645	26.186	38.142	55.206	113.57	228.36	449.39	866.67
23	13.552	20.362	24.891	30.376	45.008	66.247	140.83	292.30	593.20	1178.7
24	15.179	23.212	28.625	35.236	53.109	79.497	174.63	374.14	783.02	1603.0
25	17.000	26.462	32.919	40.874	62.669	95.396	216.54	478.90	1033.6	2180.1
26	19.040	30.167	37.857	47.414	73.949	114.48	268.51	613.00	1364.3	2964.9
27	21.325	34.390	43.535	55.000	87.260	137.37	332.95	784.64	1800.9	4032.3
28	23.884	39.204	50.066	63.800	102.97	164.84	412.86	1004.3	2377.2	5483.9
29	26.750	44.693	57.575	74.009	121.50	197.81	511.95	1285.6	3137.9	7458.1
30	29.960	50.950	66.212	85.850	143.37	237.38	634.82	1645.5	4142.1	10143.
40	93.051	188.88	267.86	378.72	750.38	1469.8	5455.9	19427.	66521.	*
50	289.00	700.23	1083.7	1670.7	3927.4	9100.4	46890.	*	*	*
60	897.60	2595.9	4384.0	7370.2	20555.	56348.	*	*	*	*

*FVIF > 99,999.